SELECTED INTELLECTUAL PROPERTY AND UNFAIR COMPETITION

STATUTES, REGULATIONS, AND TREATIES

2019 Edition

Selected and Edited by

ROGER E. SCHECHTER

Professor of Law
George Washington University

WEST ACADEMIC PUBLISHING

COPYRIGHT © 1991, 1993, 1995, WEST PUBLISHING CO.
© West, a Thomson business, 1997, 1999–2001, 2006–2008
© 2009–2012 Thomson Reuters
© 2013, 2014 LEG, Inc. d/b/a West Academic Publishing
© 2015–2018 LEG, Inc. d/b/a West Academic
© 2019 LEG, Inc. d/b/a West Academic
    444 Cedar Street, Suite 700
    St. Paul, MN 55101
    1-877-888-1330

Printed in the United States of America

ISBN: 978-1-68467-231-8

[No claim of copyright is made for official U.S. government statutes, rules or regulations.]

PREFACE

Despite the climate of bitter partisan rancor, the distraction of mid-term Congressional elections, and a news cycle that seems to bring bombshell disclosures daily, since the last edition of this collection the President and Congress accomplished several significant revisions to IP laws.

This new volume makes available that work product.

In keeping with a campaign promise, the President, who characterized the NAFTA Agreement as "the worst trade deal in history" negotiated a new agreement with our trading partners in Mexico and Canada. That treaty, dubbed the "United States, Mexico, Canada Trade Agreement" or USMCA, contains a lengthy chapter dealing with intellectual property issues. While the treaty is yet to be ratified and members of Congress from both parties have expressed serious reservations about some of its terms, I have opted to include it in this volume. That will enable users to contrast the new provisions with those in NAFTA (and in the TRIPS agreement), and will also provide some insight into the domestic law agenda of various industry participants, who often angle for advantageous treaty provisions as a backdoor technique for securing changes to U.S. law.

Not to be outdone by the executive branch, in this past year the Congress completed work on the first major piece of copyright legislation in almost two decades. The Hatch-Goodlatte Music Modernization Act contains three titles. The first, and most significant of those is the actual music modernization portion. Among its many provisions, it provides a new blanket licensing mechanism for firms that want mechanical copyright licenses for musical compositions in order to make digital phonorecord deliveries. This new scheme will eliminate the burdensome requirement of song-by-song licensing under the previous law. This provision also establishes a mechanism to build a comprehensive database of musical compositions and sound recordings, which will be managed by a collecting society. This database will help users determine the ownership of various works and where ownership is divided, the shares owned by all relevant parties. The database may prove to be a great resource for historians and legal academics as well. The other titles of the bill provide protection for pre-1972 sound recordings and formalize a mechanism for copyright owners in sound recordings to share royalties they receive from webcasters with the sound recording producers, mixers, and engineers who worked on those recordings.

As if that substantial piece of legislation was not impressive enough, Congress also ratified the Marrakesh Agreement, and adopted implementing legislation, codified as section 121A of the copyright statute. That treaty and the associated legislation makes it easier for authorized parties to export and import materials in accessible formats for the visually impaired without running afoul of copyright laws.

In a first halting effort to deal with the opioid crisis ravaging the country, Congress also adopted legislation that, among other things, amended the Federal Trade Commission Act to make unfair and deceptive claims concerning products and services for treating substance abuse illegal. By specifying that such conduct was equivalent to the violation of an FTC rule, the statute makes available somewhat more expeditious and powerful enforcement tools for the Commission than are available to it in routine cases of unfair and deceptive advertising.

Remaining on the Congressional agenda are numerous bills sloshing through the legislative pipeline. To take a small sampling of what is pending, in the area of patent law there is a bill that would overturn a recent Supreme Court case regarding claim construction in inter partes review proceedings; another that would require the makers of approved biologics to disclose relevant patents to the FDA for inclusion in the *Purple Book* to enhance transparency; and the latest iteration of legislation that would attempt to rein in threatening letters from the "patent trolls." Two interesting copyright bills pending when the last Congress adjourned have not yet been reintroduced, but are likely to wind up in the hopper in due course. One would establish an administrative "small claims" tribunal within the Copyright Office to allow copyright owners to protect their rights in small stakes cases without incurring the expense of full-blown litigation; and the other would create a resale royalty right giving creators of visual arts an entitlement to a 5% royalty when their work is resold at auction.

One interesting trademark bills would repeal the existing prohibition on the federal registration of flags and coats of arms. With half the members of the Senate running for president in 2020, however, it is unclear how much progress will be made on these initiatives in the year to come.

* * * * *

I was fortunate to convince Michael Sheehan, G.W. '19, to work with me for yet a third time in the compilation of these materials. He continues to astound with his thoroughness, timeliness and good cheer. He now has the audacity to plan to graduate, which will be a great loss to me and to the G.W. community, but a great gain for the bar and for the clients he will serve. I am honored to thank him for his service.

ROGER E. SCHECHTER

Washington, D.C.
April, 2019

TABLE OF CONTENTS

SELECTED INTELLECTUAL PROPERTY AND UNFAIR COMPETITION

STATUTES, REGULATIONS, AND TREATIES

2019 Edition

I. TRADEMARKS AND RELATED MATERIALS

A. TRADEMARK ACT OF 1946

As Amended ("The Lanham Act")
15 U.S.C.A. §§ 1051–1129

Contents

SUBCHAPTER I.   THE PRINCIPAL REGISTER

SUBCHAPTER II.   SUPPLEMENTAL REGISTER

SUBCHAPTER III.   GENERAL PROVISIONS

SUBCHAPTER I.   THE PRINCIPAL REGISTER

§ 1051.   (§ 1) Application for Registration; Verification

(a)   Application for Use of a Trademark

(1)   The owner of a trademark used in commerce may request registration of its trademark on the principal register hereby established by paying the prescribed fee and filing in the Patent and Trademark Office an application and a verified statement, in such form as may be prescribed by the Director, and such number of specimens or facsimiles of the mark as used as may be required by the Director.

(2)   The application shall include specification of the applicant's domicile and citizenship, the date of the applicant's first use of the mark, the date of the applicant's first use of the mark in commerce, the goods in connection with which the mark is used, and a drawing of the mark.

(3)   The statement shall be verified by the applicant and specify that—

(A) the person making the verification believes that he or she, or the juristic person in whose behalf he or she makes the verification, to be the owner of the mark sought to be registered;

(B) to the best of the verifier's knowledge and belief, the facts recited in the application are accurate;

(C) the mark is in use in commerce; and

(D) to the best of the verifier's knowledge and belief, no other person has the right to use such mark in commerce either in the identical form thereof or in such near resemblance thereto as to be likely, when used on or in connection with the goods of such other person, to cause confusion, or to cause mistake, or to deceive, except that, in the case of every application claiming concurrent use, the applicant shall—

(i) state exceptions to the claim of exclusive use—and

(ii) shall specify, to the extent of the verifier's knowledge—

(I) any concurrent use by others;

(II) the goods on or in connection with which and the areas in which each concurrent use exists;

(III) the periods of each use; and

(IV) the goods and area for which the applicant desires registration.

(4) The applicant shall comply with such rules or regulations as may be prescribed by the Director. The Director shall promulgate rules prescribing the requirements for the application and for obtaining a filing date herein.

(b) Application for Bona Fide Intention to Use Trademark

(1) A person who has a bona fide intention, under circumstances showing the good faith of such person, to use a trademark in commerce may request registration of its trademark on the principal register hereby established by paying the prescribed fee and filing in the Patent and Trademark Office an application and a verified statement, in such form as may be prescribed by the Director.

(2) The application shall include specification of the applicant's domicile and citizenship, the goods in connection with which the applicant has a bona fide intention to use the mark, and a drawing of the mark.

(3) The statement shall be verified by the applicant and specify—

(A) that the person making the verification believes that he or she, or the juristic person in whose behalf he or she makes the verification, to be entitled to use the mark in commerce;

(B) the applicant's bona fide intention to use the mark in commerce;

(C) that, to the best of the verifier's knowledge and belief, the facts recited in the application are accurate; and

(D) that, to the best of the verifier's knowledge and belief, no other person has the right to use such mark in commerce either in the identical form thereof or in such near resemblance thereto as to be likely, when used on or in connection with the goods of such other person, to cause confusion, or to cause mistake, or to deceive.

Except for applications filed pursuant to section 1126 of this title, no mark shall be registered until the applicant has met the requirements of subsections (c) and (d) of this section.

(4)   The applicant shall comply with such rules or regulations as may be prescribed by the Director. The Director shall promulgate rules prescribing the requirements for the application and for obtaining a filing date herein.

(c) Amendment of Application Under Subsection (b) to Conform to Requirements of Subsection (a)

At any time during examination of an application filed under subsection (b) of this section, an applicant who has made use of the mark in commerce may claim the benefits of such use for purposes of this chapter, by amending his or her application to bring it into conformity with the requirements of subsection (a) of this section.

(d) Verified Statement That Trademark Is Used in Commerce

(1)   Within six months after the date on which the notice of allowance with respect to a mark is issued under section 1063(b)(2) of this title to an applicant under subsection (b) of this section, the applicant shall file in the Patent and Trademark Office, together with such number of specimens or facsimiles of the mark as used in commerce as may be required by the Director and payment of the prescribed fee, a verified statement that the mark is in use in commerce and specifying the date of the applicant's first use of the mark in commerce and those goods or services specified in the notice of allowance on or in connection with which the mark is used in commerce. Subject to examination and acceptance of the statement of use, the mark shall be registered in the Patent and Trademark Office, a certificate of registration shall be issued for those goods or services recited in the statement of use for which the mark is entitled to registration, and notice of registration shall be published in the Official Gazette of the Patent and Trademark Office. Such examination may include an examination of the factors set forth in subsections (a) through (e) of section 1052 of this title. The notice of registration shall specify the goods or services for which the mark is registered.

(2)   The Director shall extend, for one additional 6-month period, the time for filing the statement of use under paragraph (1), upon written request of the applicant before the expiration of the 6-month period provided in paragraph (1). In addition to an extension under the preceding sentence, the Director may, upon a showing of good cause by the applicant, further extend the time for filing the statement of use under paragraph (1) for periods aggregating not more than 24 months, pursuant to written request of the applicant made before the expiration of the last extension granted under this paragraph. Any request for an extension under this paragraph shall be accompanied by a verified statement that the applicant has a continued bona fide intention to use the mark in commerce and specifying those goods or services identified in the notice of allowance on or in connection with which the applicant has a continued bona fide intention to use the mark in commerce. Any request for an extension under this paragraph shall be accompanied by payment of the prescribed fee. The Director shall issue regulations setting forth guidelines for determining what constitutes good cause for purposes of this paragraph.

(3)   The Director shall notify any applicant who files a statement of use of the acceptance or refusal thereof and, if the statement of use is refused, the reasons for the refusal. An applicant may amend the statement of use.

(4)   The failure to timely file a verified statement of use under paragraph (1) or an extension request under paragraph (2) shall result in abandonment of the application, unless it can be shown to the satisfaction of the Director that the delay in responding was unintentional, in which case the time for filing may be extended, but for a period not to exceed the period specified in paragraphs (1) and (2) for filing a statement of use.

(e) Designation of Resident for Service of Process and Notices

If the applicant is not domiciled in the United States the applicant may designate, by a document filed in the United States Patent and Trademark Office, the name and address of a person resident in the United States on whom may be served notices or process in proceedings affecting the mark. Such notices or process may be served upon the person so designated by leaving with that person or mailing to that person a copy thereof at the address specified in the last designation so filed. If the person so designated cannot be found at the address given in the last designation, or if the registrant does not designate by a document filed in the United States Patent and Trademark Office the name and address of a person resident in the United States on whom may be served notices or process in proceedings affecting the mark, such notices or process may be served on the Director.

§ 1052.   (§ 2) Trademarks Registrable on Principal Register; Concurrent Registration

No trademark by which the goods of the applicant may be distinguished from the goods of others shall be refused registration on the principal register on account of its nature unless it—

(a)   Consists of or comprises immoral, deceptive, or scandalous matter;[1] or matter which may disparage or falsely suggest a connection with persons, living or dead, institutions, beliefs, or national symbols, or bring them into contempt, or disrepute;[2] or a geographical indication which, when used on or in connection with wines or spirits, identifies a place other than the origin of the goods and is first used on or in connection with wines or spirits by the applicant on or after one year after the date on which the WTO Agreement (as defined in section 3501(9) of Title 19) enters into force with respect to the United States.[3]

(b)   Consists of or comprises the flag or coat of arms or other insignia of the United States, or of any State or municipality, or of any foreign nation, or any simulation thereof.

(c)   Consists of or comprises a name, portrait, or signature identifying a particular living individual except by his written consent, or the name, signature, or portrait of a deceased President of the United States during the life of his widow, if any, except by the written consent of the widow.

(d)   Consists of or comprises a mark which so resembles a mark registered in the Patent and Trademark Office, or a mark or trade name previously used in the United States by another and not abandoned, as to be likely, when used on or in connection with the goods of the applicant, to cause confusion, or to cause mistake, or to deceive: Provided, That if the Director determines that confusion, mistake, or deception is not likely to result from the continued use by more than one person of the same or similar marks under conditions and limitations as to the mode or place of use of the marks or the goods on or in connection with which such marks are used, concurrent registrations may be issued to such persons when they have become entitled to use such marks as a result of their concurrent lawful use in commerce prior to (1) the earliest of the filing dates of the applications pending or of any registration issued under this chapter; (2) July 5, 1947, in the case of registrations previously issued under the Act of March 3, 1881, or February 20, 1905, and continuing in full force and effect on that date; or (3) July 5, 1947, in the case of applications filed under the Act of February 20, 1905, and registered after July 5, 1947. Use prior to the filing date of any pending application or a registration shall not be required when the owner of such application or registration consents to the grant of a concurrent registration to the applicant. Concurrent registrations may also be issued by the Director when a court of competent jurisdiction has finally determined that more than one person is entitled to use the same or similar marks in commerce. In issuing concurrent registrations, the Director shall prescribe conditions and limitations as to the mode or place of use of the mark or the goods on or in connection with which such mark is registered to the respective persons.

(e)   Consists of a mark which (1) when used on or in connection with the goods of the applicant is merely descriptive or deceptively misdescriptive of them, (2) when used on or in

---

[1]   The portions of this provision relating to immoral or scandalous marks were declared unconstitutional in *In re Brunetti*, 877 F.3d 1330 (Fed. Cir. 2017). That decision is pending before the Supreme Court as this edition goes to press—*Ed.*

[2]   The portions of this provision relating to disparaging marks were declared unconstitutional in *Matal v. Tam*, ___ U.S., 137 S. Ct. 1744 (2017).—*Ed.*

[3]   The WTO Agreement entered into force with respect to the United States on January 1, 1995.—*Ed.*

connection with the goods of the applicant is primarily geographically descriptive of them, except as indications of regional origin may be registrable under section 1054 of this title, (3) when used on or in connection with the goods of the applicant is primarily geographically deceptively misdescriptive of them, (4) is primarily merely a surname, or (5) comprises any matter that, as a whole, is functional.

(f)   Except as expressly excluded in subsections (a), (b), (c), (d), (e)(3), and (e)(5) of this section, nothing in this chapter shall prevent the registration of a mark used by the applicant which has become distinctive of the applicant's goods in commerce. The Director may accept as prima facie evidence that the mark has become distinctive, as used on or in connection with the applicant's goods in commerce, proof of substantially exclusive and continuous use thereof as a mark by the applicant in commerce for the five years before the date on which the claim of distinctiveness is made. Nothing in this section shall prevent the registration of a mark which, when used on or in connection with the goods of the applicant, is primarily geographically deceptively misdescriptive of them, and which became distinctive of the applicant's goods in commerce before the date of the enactment of the North American Free Trade Agreement Implementation Act.

A mark which would be likely to cause dilution by blurring or dilution by tarnishment under section 1125(c) of this title, may be refused registration only pursuant to a proceeding brought under section 1063 of this title. A registration for a mark which would be likely to cause dilution by blurring or dilution by tarnishment under section 1125(c) of this title, may be canceled pursuant to a proceeding brought under either section 1064 of this title or section 1092 of this title.

§ 1053.   (§ 3) Service Marks Registrable

Subject to the provisions relating to the registration of trademarks, so far as they are applicable, service marks shall be registrable, in the same manner and with the same effect as are trademarks, and when registered they shall be entitled to the protection provided in this chapter in the case of trademarks. Applications and procedure under this section shall conform as nearly as practicable to those prescribed for the registration of trademarks.

§ 1054.   (§ 4) Collective Marks and Certification Marks Registrable

Subject to the provisions relating to the registration of trademarks, so far as they are applicable, collective and certification marks, including indications of regional origin shall be registrable under this chapter, in the same manner and with the same effect as are trademarks, by persons, and nations, States, municipalities, and the like, exercising legitimate control over the use of the marks sought to be registered, even though not possessing an industrial or commercial establishment, and when registered they shall be entitled to the protection provided in this chapter in the case of trademarks, except in the case of certification marks when used so as to represent falsely that the owner or a user thereof makes or sells the goods or performs the services on or in connection with which such mark is used. Applications and procedure under this section shall conform as nearly as practicable to those prescribed for the registration of trademarks.

§ 1055.   (§ 5) Use by Related Companies Affecting Validity and Registration

Where a registered mark or a mark sought to be registered is or may be used legitimately by related companies, such use shall inure to the benefit of the registrant or applicant for registration, and such use shall not affect the validity of such mark or of its registration, provided such mark is not used in such manner as to deceive the public. If first use of a mark by a person is controlled by the registrant or applicant for registration of the mark with respect to the nature and quality of the goods or services, such first use shall inure to the benefit of the registrant or applicant, as the case may be.

§ 1056. (§ 6) Disclaimer of Unregistrable Matter

(a) Compulsory and Voluntary Disclaimers

The Director may require the applicant to disclaim an unregistrable component of a mark otherwise registrable. An applicant may voluntarily disclaim a component of a mark sought to be registered.

(b) Prejudice of Rights

No disclaimer, including those made under subsection (e) of section 1057 of this title shall prejudice or affect the applicant's or registrant's rights then existing or thereafter arising in the disclaimed matter, or his right of registration on another application if the disclaimed matter be or shall have become distinctive of his goods or services.

§ 1057. (§ 7) Certificates of Registration

(a) Issuance and Form

Certificates of registration of marks registered upon the principal register shall be issued in the name of the United States of America, under the seal of the United States Patent and Trademark Office, and shall be signed by the Director or have his signature placed thereon, and a record thereof shall be kept in the United States Patent and Trademark Office. The registration shall reproduce the mark, and state that the mark is registered on the principal register under this chapter, the date of the first use of the mark, the date of the first use of the mark in commerce, the particular goods or services for which it is registered, the number and date of the registration, the term thereof, the date on which the application for registration was received in the United States Patent and Trademark Office, and any conditions and limitations that may be imposed in the registration.

(b) Certificate as Prima Facie Evidence

A certificate of registration of a mark upon the principal register provided by this chapter shall be prima facie evidence of the validity of the registered mark and of the registration of the mark, of the owner's ownership of the mark, and of the owner's exclusive right to use the registered mark in commerce on or in connection with the goods or services specified in the certificate subject to any conditions or limitations stated in the certificate.

(c) Application to Register Mark Considered Constructive Use

Contingent on the registration of a mark on the principal register provided by this chapter, the filing of the application to register such mark shall constitute constructive use of the mark, conferring a right of priority, nationwide in effect, on or in connection with the goods or services specified in the registration against any other person except for a person whose mark has not been abandoned and who, prior to such filing—

(1) has used the mark;

(2) has filed an application to register the mark which is pending or has resulted in registration of the mark; or

(3) has filed a foreign application to register the mark on the basis of which he or she has acquired a right of priority, and timely files an application under section 1126(d) of this title to register the mark which is pending or has resulted in registration of the mark.

(d) Issuance to Assignee

A certificate of registration of a mark may be issued to the assignee of the applicant, but the assignment must first be recorded in the United States Patent and Trademark Office. In case of change of ownership the Director shall, at the request of the owner and upon a proper showing and the payment of the prescribed fee, issue to such assignee a new certificate of registration of the said mark in the name of such assignee, and for the unexpired part of the original period.

(e) Surrender, Cancellation, or Amendment by Registrant

Upon application of the owner the Director may permit any registration to be surrendered for cancelation, and upon cancelation appropriate entry shall be made in the records of the United States Patent and Trademark Office. Upon application of the owner and payment of the prescribed fee, the Director for good cause may permit any registration to be amended or to be disclaimed in part: *Provided,* That the amendment or disclaimer does not alter materially the character of the mark. Appropriate entry shall be made in the records of the United States Patent and Trademark Office and upon the certificate of registration.

(f) Copies of Patent and Trademark Office Records as Evidence

Copies of any records, books, papers, or drawings belonging to the United States Patent and Trademark Office relating to marks, and copies of registrations, when authenticated by the seal of the United States Patent and Trademark Office and certified by the Director, or in his name by an employee of the Office duly designated by the Director, shall be evidence in all cases wherein the originals would be evidence; and any person making application therefor and paying the prescribed fee shall have such copies.

(g) Correction of Patent and Trademark Office Mistake

Whenever a material mistake in a registration, incurred through the fault of the United States Patent and Trademark Office, is clearly disclosed by the records of the Office a certificate stating the fact and nature of such mistake shall be issued without charge and recorded and a printed copy thereof shall be attached to each printed copy of the registration and such corrected registration shall thereafter have the same effect as if the same had been originally issued in such corrected form, or in the discretion of the Director a new certificate of registration may be issued without charge. All certificates of correction heretofore issued in accordance with the rules of the United States Patent and Trademark Office and the registrations to which they are attached shall have the same force and effect as if such certificates and their issue had been specifically authorized by statute.

(h) Correction of Applicant's Mistake

Whenever a mistake has been made in a registration and a showing has been made that such mistake occurred in good faith through the fault of the applicant, the Director is authorized to issue a certificate of correction or, in his discretion, a new certificate upon the payment of the prescribed fee: *Provided,* That the correction does not involve such changes in the registration as to require republication of the mark.

§ 1058.   (§ 8) Duration, Affidavits and Fees

(a) Time Periods for Required Affidavits

Each registration shall remain in force for 10 years, except that the registration of any mark shall be canceled by the Director unless the owner of the registration files in the United States Patent and Trademark Office affidavits that meet the requirements of subsection (b), within the following time periods:

> (1) Within the 1-year period immediately preceding the expiration of 6 years following the date of registration under this Act or the date of the publication under section 12(c).

> (2) Within the 1-year period immediately preceding the expiration of 10 years following the date of registration, and each successive 10-year period following the date of registration.

> (3) The owner may file the affidavit required under this section within the 6-month grace period immediately following the expiration of the periods established in paragraphs (1) and (2), together with the fee described in subsection (b) and the additional grace period surcharge prescribed by the Director.

(b) Requirements for Affidavit

The affidavit referred to in subsection (a) shall—

(1)(A)　state that the mark is in use in commerce;

(B)　set forth the goods and services recited in the registration on or in connection with which the mark is in use in commerce;

(C)　be accompanied by such number of specimens or facsimiles showing current use of the mark in commerce as may be required by the Director; and

(D)　be accompanied by the fee prescribed by the Director; or

(2)(A)　set forth the goods and services recited in the registration on or in connection with which the mark is not in use in commerce;

(B)　include a showing that any nonuse is due to special circumstances which excuse such nonuse and is not due to any intention to abandon the mark; and

(C)　be accompanied by the fee prescribed by the Director.

(c)　Deficient Affidavit

If any submission filed within the period set forth in subsection (a) is deficient, including that the affidavit was not filed in the name of the owner of the registration, the deficiency may be corrected after the statutory time period, within the time prescribed after notification of the deficiency. Such submission shall be accompanied by the additional deficiency surcharge prescribed by the Director.

(d)　Notice of Requirement

Special notice of the requirement for such affidavit shall be attached to each certificate of registration and notice of publication under section 12(c).

(e)　Notification of Acceptance or Refusal

The Director shall notify any owner who files any affidavit required by this section of the Director's acceptance or refusal thereof and, in the case of a refusal, the reasons therefor.

(f)　Designation of Resident for Service of Process and Notices

If the owner is not domiciled in the United States, the owner may designate, by a document filed in the United States Patent and Trademark Office, the name and address of a person resident in the United States on whom may be served notices or process in proceedings affecting the mark. Such notices or process may be served upon the person so designated by leaving with that person or mailing to that person a copy thereof at the address specified in the last designation so filed. If the person so designated cannot be found at the last designated address, or if the owner does not designate by a document filed in the United States Patent and Trademark Office the name and address of a person resident in the United States on whom may be served notices or process in proceedings affecting the mark, such notices or process may be served on the Director.

§ 1059.　(§ 9) Renewal of Registration

(a)　Period of Renewal; Time for Renewal

Subject to the provisions of section 1058 of this title, each registration may be renewed for periods of 10 years at the end of each successive 10-year period following the date of registration upon payment of the prescribed fee and the filing of a written application, in such form as may be prescribed by the Director. Such application may be made at any time within 1 year before the end of each successive 10-year period for which the registration was issued or renewed, or it may be made within a grace period of 6 months after the end of each successive 10-year period, upon payment of a fee and surcharge prescribed therefor. If any application filed under this section is deficient, the deficiency may be corrected within the time prescribed after notification of the deficiency, upon payment of a surcharge prescribed therefor.

(b) Notification of Refusal of Renewal

If the Director refuses to renew the registration, the Director shall notify the registrant of the Director's refusal and the reasons therefor.

(c) Designation of Resident for Service of Process and Notices

If the registrant is not domiciled in the United States the registrant may designate, by a document filed in the United States Patent and Trademark Office, the name and address of a person resident in the United States on whom may be served notices or process in proceedings affecting the mark. Such notices or process may be served upon the person so designated by leaving with that person or mailing to that person a copy thereof at the address specified in the last designation so filed. If the person so designated cannot be found at the address given in the last designation, or if the registrant does not designate by a document filed in the United States Patent and Trademark Office the name and address of a person resident in the United States on whom may be served notices or process in proceedings affecting the mark, such notices or process may be served on the Director.

§ 1060.   (§ 10) Assignment

(a)(1) A registered mark or a mark for which an application to register has been filed shall be assignable with the good will of the business in which the mark is used, or with that part of the good will of the business connected with the use of and symbolized by the mark. Notwithstanding the preceding sentence, no application to register a mark under section 1051(b) of this title shall be assignable prior to the filing of an amendment under section 1051(c) of this title to bring the application into conformity with section 1051(a) of this title or the filing of the verified statement of use under section 1051(d) of this title, except for an assignment to a successor to the business of the applicant, or portion thereof, to which the mark pertains, if that business is ongoing and existing.

(2) In any assignment authorized by this section, it shall not be necessary to include the good will of the business connected with the use of and symbolized by any other mark used in the business or by the name or style under which the business is conducted.

(3) Assignments shall be by instruments in writing duly executed. Acknowledgment shall be prima facie evidence of the execution of an assignment, and when the prescribed information reporting the assignment is recorded in the United States Patent and Trademark Office, the record shall be prima facie evidence of execution.

(4) An assignment shall be void against any subsequent purchaser for valuable consideration without notice, unless the prescribed information reporting the assignment is recorded in the United States Patent and Trademark Office within 3 months after the date of the assignment or prior to the subsequent purchase.

(5) The United States Patent and Trademark Office shall maintain a record of information on assignments, in such form as may be prescribed by the Director.

(b) An assignee not domiciled in the United States may designate by a document filed in the United States Patent and Trademark Office the name and address of a person resident in the United States on whom may be served notices or process in proceedings affecting the mark. Such notices or process may be served upon the person so designated by leaving with that person or mailing to that person a copy thereof at the address specified in the last designation so filed. If the person so designated cannot be found at the address given in the last designation, or if the assignee does not designate by a document filed in the United States Patent and Trademark Office the name and address of a person resident in the United States on whom may be served notices or process in proceedings affecting the mark, such notices or process may be served upon the Director.

§ 1061.   (§ 11) Execution of Acknowledgments and Verifications

Acknowledgments and verifications required under this chapter may be made before any person within the United States authorized by law to administer oaths, or, when made in a foreign country, before any diplomatic or consular officer of the United States or before any official authorized to administer oaths in the foreign country concerned whose authority is proved by a certificate of a diplomatic or consular officer of the United States, or apostille of an official designated by a foreign country which, by treaty or convention, accords like effect to apostilles of designated officials in the United States, and shall be valid if they comply with the laws of the state or country where made.

§ 1062. (§ 12) Publication

(a) Examination and Publication

Upon the filing of an application for registration and payment of the prescribed fee, the Director shall refer the application to the examiner in charge of the registration of marks, who shall cause an examination to be made and, if on such examination it shall appear that the applicant is entitled to registration, or would be entitled to registration upon the acceptance of the statement of use required by section 1051(d) of this title, the Director shall cause the mark to be published in the Official Gazette of the Patent and Trademark Office: *Provided,* That in the case of an applicant claiming concurrent use, or in the case of an application to be placed in an interference as provided for in section 1066 of this title, the mark, if otherwise registrable, may be published subject to the determination of the rights of the parties to such proceedings.

(b) Refusal of Registration; Amendment of Application; Abandonment

If the applicant is found not entitled to registration, the examiner shall advise the applicant thereof and of the reasons therefor. The applicant shall have a period of six months in which to reply or amend his application, which shall then be re-examined. This procedure may be repeated until (1) the examiner finally refuses registration of the mark or (2) the applicant fails for a period of six months to reply or amend or appeal, whereupon the application shall be deemed to have been abandoned, unless it can be shown to the satisfaction of the Director that the delay in responding was unintentional, whereupon such time may be extended.

(c) Republication of Marks Registered Under Prior Acts

A registrant of a mark registered under the provisions of the Act of March 3, 1881, or the Act of February 20, 1905, may, at any time prior to the expiration of the registration thereof, upon the payment of the prescribed fee file with the Director an affidavit setting forth those goods stated in the registration on which said mark is in use in commerce and that the registrant claims the benefits of this chapter for said mark. The Director shall publish notice thereof with a reproduction of said mark in the Official Gazette, and notify the registrant of such publication and of the requirement for the affidavit of use or nonuse as provided for in subsection (b) of section 1058 of this title. Marks published under this subsection shall not be subject to the provisions of section 1063 of this title.

§ 1063. (§ 13) Opposition to Registration

(a) Any person who believes that he would be damaged by the registration of a mark upon the principal register, including the registration of any mark which would be likely to cause dilution by blurring or dilution by tarnishment under section 1125(c) of this title, may, upon payment of the prescribed fee, file an opposition in the Patent and Trademark Office, stating the grounds therefor, within thirty days after the publication under subsection (a) of section 1062 of this title of the mark sought to be registered. Upon written request prior to the expiration of the thirty-day period, the time for filing opposition shall be extended for an additional thirty days, and further extensions of time for filing opposition may be granted by the Director for good cause when requested prior to the expiration of an extension. The Director shall notify the applicant of each extension of the time for filing opposition. An opposition may be amended under such conditions as may be prescribed by the Director.

(b) Unless registration is successfully opposed—

(1) a mark entitled to registration on the principal register based on an application filed under section 1051(a) of this title or pursuant to section 1126 of this title shall be registered in

the Patent and Trademark Office, a certificate of registration shall be issued, and notice of the registration shall be published in the Official Gazette of the Patent and Trademark Office; or

(2) a notice of allowance shall be issued to the applicant if the applicant applied for registration under section 1051(b) of this title.

§ 1064. (§ 14) Cancellation of Registration

A petition to cancel a registration of a mark, stating the grounds relied upon, may, upon payment of the prescribed fee, be filed as follows by any person who believes that he is or will be damaged, including as a result of a likelihood of dilution by blurring or dilution by tarnishment under section 1125(c) of this title, by the registration of a mark on the principal register established by this chapter, or under the Act of March 3, 1881, or the Act of February 20, 1905:

(1) Within five years from the date of the registration of the mark under this chapter.

(2) Within five years from the date of publication under section 1062(c) of this title of a mark registered under the Act of March 3, 1881, or the Act of February 20, 1905.

(3) At any time if the registered mark becomes the generic name for the goods or services, or a portion thereof, for which it is registered, or is functional, or has been abandoned, or its registration was obtained fraudulently or contrary to the provisions of section 1054 of this title or of subsection (a), (b), or (c) of section 1052 of this title for a registration under this chapter, or contrary to similar prohibitory provisions of such prior Acts for a registration under such Acts, or if the registered mark is being used by, or with the permission of, the registrant so as to misrepresent the source of the goods or services on or in connection with which the mark is used. If the registered mark becomes the generic name for less than all of the goods or services for which it is registered, a petition to cancel the registration for only those goods or services may be filed. A registered mark shall not be deemed to be the generic name of goods or services solely because such mark is also used as a name of or to identify a unique product or service. The primary significance of the registered mark to the relevant public rather than purchaser motivation shall be the test for determining whether the registered mark has become the generic name of goods or services on or in connection with which it has been used.

(4) At any time if the mark is registered under the Act of March 3, 1881, or the Act of February 20, 1905, and has not been published under the provisions of subsection (c) of section 1062 of this title.

(5) At any time in the case of a certification mark on the ground that the registrant (A) does not control, or is not able legitimately to exercise control over, the use of such mark, or (B) engages in the production or marketing of any goods or services to which the certification mark is applied, or (C) permits the use of the certification mark for purposes other than to certify, or (D) discriminately refuses to certify or to continue to certify the goods or services of any person who maintains the standards or conditions which such mark certifies:

Provided, That the Federal Trade Commission may apply to cancel on the grounds specified in paragraphs (3) and (5) of this section any mark registered on the principal register established by this chapter, and the prescribed fee shall not be required. Nothing in paragraph (5) shall be deemed to prohibit the registrant from using its certification mark in advertising or promoting recognition of the certification program or of the goods or services meeting the certification standards of the registrant. Such uses of the certification mark shall not be grounds for cancellation under paragraph (5), so long as the registrant does not itself produce, manufacture, or sell any of the certified goods or services to which its identical certification mark is applied.

§ 1065. (§ 15) Incontestability of Right to Use Mark Under Certain Conditions

Except on a ground for which application to cancel may be filed at any time under paragraphs (3) and (5) of section 1064 of this title, and except to the extent, if any, to which the use of a mark registered on the principal register infringes a valid right acquired under the law of any State or Territory by use of a mark or trade name continuing from a date prior to the date of registration under this chapter of such registered mark, the right of the owner to use such registered mark in commerce for the goods or services on or in connection with which such registered mark has been in continuous use for five consecutive years subsequent to the date of such registration and is still in use in commerce, shall be incontestable: *Provided,* That—

(1)   there has been no final decision adverse to the owner's claim of ownership of such mark for such goods or services, or to the owner's right to register the same or to keep the same on the register; and

(2)   there is no proceeding involving said rights pending in the United States Patent and Trademark Office or in a court and not finally disposed of; and

(3)   an affidavit is filed with the Director within one year after the expiration of any such five-year period setting forth those goods or services stated in the registration on or in connection with which such mark has been in continuous use for such five consecutive years and is still in use in commerce, and the other matters specified in paragraphs (1) and (2) of this section; and

(4)   no incontestable right shall be acquired in a mark which is the generic name of the goods or services or a portion thereof, for which it is registered.

Subject to the conditions above specified in this section, the incontestable right with reference to a mark registered under this chapter shall apply to a mark registered under the Act of March 3, 1881, or the Act of February 20, 1905, upon the filing of the required affidavit with the Director within one year after the expiration of any period of five consecutive years after the date of publication of a mark under the provisions of subsection (c) of section 1062 of this title.

The Director shall notify any registrant who files the above-prescribed affidavit of the filing thereof.

§ 1066.   (§ 16) Interference; Declaration by Director

Upon petition showing extraordinary circumstances, the Director may declare than an interference exists when application is made for the registration of a mark which so resembles a mark previously registered by another, or for the registration of which another has previously made application, as to be likely when used on or in connection with the goods or services of the applicant to cause confusion or mistake or to deceive. No interference shall be declared between an application and the registration of a mark the right to the use of which has become incontestable.

§ 1067.   (§ 17) Interference, Opposition, and Proceedings for Concurrent Use Registration or for Cancellation; Notice; Trademark Trial and Appeal Board

(a)   In every case of interference, opposition to registration, application to register as a lawful concurrent user, or application to cancel the registration of a mark, the Director shall give notice to all parties and shall direct a Trademark Trial and Appeal Board to determine and decide the respective rights of registration.

(b)   The Trademark Trial and Appeal Board shall include the Director, Deputy Director* of the United States Patent and Trademark Office, the Commissioner for Patents, the Commissioner for Trademarks, and administrative trademark judges who are appointed by the Secretary of Commerce, in consultation with the Director.

(c)   **Authority of the Secretary**

The Secretary of Commerce may, in his or her discretion, deem the appointment of an administrative trademark judge who, before August 12, 2008, held office pursuant to an appointment

---

*   So in original. The word "the" probably should precede the phrase "Deputy Director."—*Ed.*

by the Director to take effect on the date on which the Director initially appointed the administrative trademark judge.

(d) Defense to Challenge of Appointment

It shall be a defense to a challenge to the appointment of an administrative trademark judge on the basis of the judge's having been originally appointed by the Director that the administrative trademark judge so appointed was acting as a de facto officer.

§ 1068. (§ 18) Action of Director in Interference, Opposition, and Proceedings for Concurrent Use Registration or for Cancellation

In such proceedings the Director may refuse to register the opposed mark, may cancel the registration, in whole or in part, may modify the application or registration by limiting the goods or services specified therein, may otherwise restrict or rectify with respect to the register the registration of a registered mark, may refuse to register any or all of several interfering marks, or may register the mark or marks for the person or persons entitled thereto, as the rights of the parties under this chapter may be established in the proceedings: Provided, That in the case of the registration of any mark based on concurrent use, the Director shall determine and fix the conditions and limitations provided for in subsection (d) of section 1052 of this title. However, no final judgment shall be entered in favor of an applicant under section 1051(b) of this title before the mark is registered, if such applicant cannot prevail without establishing constructive use pursuant to section 1057(c) of this title.

§ 1069. (§ 19) Application of Equitable Principles in Inter Partes Proceedings

In all inter partes proceedings equitable principles of laches, estoppel, and acquiescence, where applicable may be considered and applied.

§ 1070. (§ 20) Appeals to Trademark Trial and Appeal Board From Decisions of Examiners

An appeal may be taken to the Trademark Trial and Appeal Board from any final decision of the examiner in charge of the registration of marks upon the payment of the prescribed fee.

§ 1071. (§ 21) Appeal to Courts

(a) Persons Entitled to Appeal; United States Court of Appeals for the Federal Circuit; Waiver of Civil Action; Election of Civil Action by Adverse Party; Procedure

(1) An applicant for registration of a mark, party to an interference proceeding, party to an opposition proceeding, party to an application to register as a lawful concurrent user, party to a cancellation proceeding, a registrant who has filed an affidavit as provided in section 1058 or section 1141k of this title, or an applicant for renewal, who is dissatisfied with the decision of the Director or Trademark Trial and Appeal Board, may appeal to the United States Court of Appeals for the Federal Circuit thereby waiving his right to proceed under subsection (b) of this section: *Provided,* That such appeal shall be dismissed if any adverse party to the proceeding, other than the Director, shall, within twenty days after the appellant has filed notice of appeal according to paragraph (2) of this subsection, files* notice with the Director that he elects to have all further proceedings conducted as provided in subsection (b) of this section. Thereupon the appellant shall have thirty days thereafter within which to file a civil action under subsection (b) of this section, in default of which the decision appealed from shall govern the further proceedings in the case.

(2) When an appeal is taken to the United States Court of Appeals for the Federal Circuit, the appellant shall file in the United States Patent and Trademark Office a written notice of appeal directed to the Director, within such time after the date of the decision from which the appeal is taken as the Director prescribes, but in no case less than 60 days after that date.

---

   *   Thus in original. Probably should read "file."—*Ed.*

(3) The Director shall transmit to the United States Court of Appeals for the Federal Circuit a certified list of the documents comprising the record in the United States Patent and Trademark Office. The court may request that the Director forward the original or certified copies of such documents during pendency of the appeal. In an ex parte case, the Director shall submit to that court a brief explaining the grounds for the decision of the United States Patent and Trademark Office, addressing all the issues involved in the appeal. The court shall, before hearing an appeal, give notice of the time and place of the hearing to the Director and the parties in the appeal.

(4) The United States Court of Appeals for the Federal Circuit shall review the decision from which the appeal is taken on the record before the United States Patent and Trademark Office. Upon its determination the court shall issue its mandate and opinion to the Director, which shall be entered of record in the United States Patent and Trademark Office and shall govern the further proceedings in the case. However, no final judgment shall be entered in favor of an applicant under section 1051(b) of this title before the mark is registered, if such applicant cannot prevail without establishing constructive use pursuant to section 1057(c) of this title.

(b) Civil Action; Persons Entitled to; Jurisdiction of Court; Status of Director; Procedure

(1) Whenever a person authorized by subsection (a) of this section to appeal to the United States Court of Appeals for the Federal Circuit is dissatisfied with the decision of the Director or Trademark Trial and Appeal Board, said person may, unless appeal has been taken to said United States Court of Appeals for the Federal Circuit, have remedy by a civil action if commenced within such time after such decision, not less than sixty days, as the Director appoints or as provided in subsection (a) of this section. The court may adjudge that an applicant is entitled to a registration upon the application involved, that a registration involved should be canceled, or such other matter as the issues in the proceeding require, as the facts in the case may appear. Such adjudication shall authorize the Director to take any necessary action, upon compliance with the requirements of law. However, no final judgment shall be entered in favor of an applicant under section 1051(b) of this title before the mark is registered, if such applicant cannot prevail without establishing constructive use pursuant to section 1057(c) of this title.

(2) The Director shall not be made a party to an inter partes proceeding under this subsection, but he shall be notified of the filing of the complaint by the clerk of the court in which it is filed and shall have the right to intervene in the action.

(3) In any case where there is no adverse party, a copy of the complaint shall be served on the Director, and, unless the court finds the expenses to be unreasonable, all the expenses of the proceeding shall be paid by the party bringing the case, whether the final decision is in favor of such party or not. In suits brought hereunder, the record in the Patent and Trademark Office shall be admitted on motion of any party, upon such terms and conditions as to costs, expenses, and the further cross-examination of the witnesses as the court imposes, without prejudice to the right of any party to take further testimony. The testimony and exhibits of the record in the Patent and Trademark Office, when admitted, shall have the same effect as if originally taken and produced in the suit.

(4) Where there is an adverse party, such suit may be instituted against the party in interest as shown by the records of the Patent and Trademark Office at the time of the decision complained of, but any party in interest may become a party to the action. If there are adverse parties residing in a plurality of districts not embraced within the same State, or an adverse party residing in a foreign country, the United States District Court for the Eastern District of Virginia shall have jurisdiction and may issue summons against the adverse parties directed to the marshal of any district in which any adverse party resides. Summons against adverse parties residing in foreign countries may be served by publication or otherwise as the court directs.

§ 1072. (§ 22) Registration as Constructive Notice of Claim of Ownership

Registration of a mark on the principal register provided by this chapter or under the Act of March 3, 1881, or the Act of February 20, 1905, shall be constructive notice of the registrant's claim of ownership thereof.

SUBCHAPTER II. THE SUPPLEMENTAL REGISTER

§ 1091. (§ 23) Supplemental Register

(a) Marks Registrable

In addition to the principal register, the Director shall keep a continuation of the register provided in paragraph (b) of section 1 of the Act of March 19, 1920, entitled "An Act to give effect to certain provisions of the convention for the protection of trademarks and commercial names, made and signed in the city of Buenos Aires, in the Argentine Republic, August 20, 1910, and for other purposes", to be called the supplemental register. All marks capable of distinguishing applicant's goods or services and not registrable on the principal register provided in this chapter, except those declared to be unregistrable under subsections (a), (b), (c), (d), and (e)(3) of section 1052 of this title, which are in lawful use in commerce by the owner, thereof, on or in connection with any goods or services may be registered on the supplemental register upon the payment of the prescribed fee and compliance with the provisions of subsections (a) and (e) of section 1051 of this title so far as they are applicable. Nothing in this section shall prevent the registration on the supplemental register of a mark, capable of distinguishing the applicant's goods or services and not registrable on the principal register under this Act, that is declared to be unregistrable under section 1052(e)(3) of this title, if such mark has been in lawful use in commerce by the owner thereof, on or in connection with any goods or services, since before December 8, 1993.

(b) Application and Proceedings for Registration

Upon the filing of an application for registration on the supplemental register and payment of the prescribed fee the Director shall refer the application to the examiner in charge of the registration of marks, who shall cause an examination to be made and if on such examination it shall appear that the applicant is entitled to registration, the registration shall be granted. If the applicant is found not entitled to registration the provisions of subsection (b) of section 1062 of this title shall apply.

(c) Nature of Mark

For the purposes of registration on the supplemental register, a mark may consist of any trademark, symbol, label, package, configuration of goods, name, word, slogan, phrase, surname, geographical name, numeral, device, any matter that as a whole is not functional, or any combination of any of the foregoing, but such mark must be capable of distinguishing the applicant's goods or services.

§ 1092. (§ 24) Publication; Not Subject to Opposition; Cancellation

Marks for the supplemental register shall not be published for or be subject to opposition, but shall be published on registration in the Official Gazette of the Patent and Trademark Office. Whenever any person believes that such person is or will be damaged by the registration of a mark on the supplemental register—

    (1) for which the effective filing date is after the date on which such person's mark became famous and which would be likely to cause dilution by blurring or dilution by tarnishment under section 1125(c) of this title; or

    (2) on grounds other than dilution by blurring or dilution by tarnishment,

such person may at any time, upon payment of the prescribed fee and the filing of a petition stating the ground therefor, apply to the Director to cancel such registration.

The Director shall refer such application to the Trademark Trial and Appeal Board which shall give notice thereof to the registrant. If it is found after a hearing before the Board that the registrant is not entitled to registration, or that the mark has been abandoned, the registration shall be canceled by the Director. However, no final judgment shall be entered in favor of an applicant under section 1051(b) of this title before the mark is registered, if such applicant cannot prevail without establishing constructive use pursuant to section 1057(c) of this title.

§ 1093. (§ 25) Registration Certificates for Marks on Principal and Supplemental Registers to Be Different

The certificates of registration for marks registered on the supplemental register shall be conspicuously different from certificates issued for marks registered on the principal register.

§ 1094. (§ 26) Provisions of Chapter Applicable to Registrations on Supplemental Register

The provisions of this chapter shall govern so far as applicable applications for registration and registrations on the supplemental register as well as those on the principal register, but applications for and registrations on the supplemental register shall not be subject to or receive the advantages of sections 1051(b), 1052(e), 1052(f), 1057(b), 1057(c), 1062(a), 1063 to 1068, inclusive, 1072, 1115 and 1124 of this title.

§ 1095. (§ 27) Registration on Principal Register Not Precluded

Registration of a mark on the supplemental register, or under the Act of March 19, 1920, shall not preclude registration by the registrant on the principal register established by this chapter. Registration of a mark on the supplemental register shall not constitute an admission that the mark has not acquired distinctiveness.

§ 1096. (§ 28) Registration on Supplemental Register Not Used to Stop Importations

Registration on the supplemental register or under the Act of March 19, 1920, shall not be filed in the Department of the Treasury or be used to stop importations.

SUBCHAPTER III.   GENERAL PROVISIONS

§ 1111. (§ 29) Notice of Registration; Display With Mark; Recovery of Profits and Damages in Infringement Suit

Notwithstanding the provisions of section 1072 of this title, a registrant of a mark registered in the Patent and Trademark Office, may give notice that his mark is registered by displaying with the mark the words "Registered in U.S. Patent and Trademark Office" or "Reg. U.S. Pat. & Tm. Off." or the letter R enclosed within a circle, thus ®; and in any suit for infringement under this chapter by such a registrant failing to give such notice of registration, no profits and no damages shall be recovered under the provisions of this chapter unless the defendant had actual notice of the registration.

§ 1112. (§ 30) Classification of Goods and Services; Registration in Plurality of Classes

The Director may establish a classification of goods and services, for convenience of Patent and Trademark Office administration, but not to limit or extend the applicant's or registrant's rights. The applicant may apply to register a mark for any or all of the goods or services on or in connection with which he or she is using or has a bona fide intention to use the mark in commerce: Provided, That if the Director by regulation permits the filing of an application for the registration of a mark for goods or services which fall within a plurality of classes, a fee equaling the sum of the fees for filing an application in each class shall be paid, and the Director may issue a single certificate of registration for such mark.

§ 1113. (§ 31) Fees

(a) Applications; Services; Materials

The Director shall establish fees for the filing and processing of an application for the registration of a trademark or other mark and for all other services performed by and materials furnished by the Patent and Trademark Office related to trademarks and other marks. Fees established under this subsection may be adjusted by the Director once each year to reflect, in the aggregate, any fluctuations during the preceding 12 months in the Consumer Price Index, as determined by the Secretary of Labor. Changes of less than 1 percent may be ignored. No fee established under this section shall take effect until at least 30 days after notice of the fee has been published in the Federal Register and in the Official Gazette of the Patent and Trademark Office.

(b) Waiver; Indian Products

The Director may waive the payment of any fee for any service or material related to trademarks or other marks in connection with an occasional request made by a department or agency of the Government, or any officer thereof. The Indian Arts and Crafts Board will not be charged any fee to register Government trademarks of genuineness and quality for Indian products or for products of particular Indian tribes and groups.

§ 1114. (§ 32) Remedies; Infringement; Innocent Infringement by Printers and Publishers

(1)   Any person who shall, without the consent of the registrant—

     (a)   use in commerce any reproduction, counterfeit, copy, or colorable imitation of a registered mark in connection with the sale, offering for sale, distribution, or advertising of any goods or services on or in connection with which such use is likely to cause confusion, or to cause mistake, or to deceive; or

     (b)   reproduce, counterfeit, copy, or colorably imitate a registered mark and apply such reproduction, counterfeit, copy, or colorable imitation to labels, signs, prints, packages, wrappers, receptacles or advertisements intended to be used in commerce upon or in connection with the sale, offering for sale, distribution, or advertising of goods or services on or in connection with which such use is likely to cause confusion, or to cause mistake, or to deceive;

shall be liable in a civil action by the registrant for the remedies hereinafter provided. Under subsection (b) of this section, the registrant shall not be entitled to recover profits or damages unless the acts have been committed with knowledge that such imitation is intended to be used to cause confusion, or to cause mistake, or to deceive.

As used in this paragraph, the term "any person" includes the United States, all agencies and instrumentalities thereof, and all individuals, firms, corporations, or other persons acting for the United States and with the authorization and consent of the United States, and any State, any instrumentality of a State, and any officer or employee of a State or instrumentality of a State acting in his or her official capacity. The United States, all agencies and instrumentalities thereof, and all individuals, firms, corporations, other persons acting for the United States and with the authorization and consent of the United States, and any State, and any such instrumentality, officer, or employee, shall be subject to the provisions of this Act in the same manner and to the same extent as any nongovernmental entity.

(2)   Notwithstanding any other provision of this chapter, the remedies given to the owner of a right infringed under this chapter or to a person bringing an action under section 1125(a) or (d) of this title shall be limited as follows:

     (A)   Where an infringer or violator is engaged solely in the business of printing the mark or violating matter for others and establishes that he or she was an innocent infringer or innocent violator, the owner of the right infringed or person bringing the action under section 1125(a) of this title shall be entitled as against such infringer or violator only to an injunction against future printing.

(B) Where the infringement or violation complained of is contained in or is part of paid advertising matter in a newspaper, magazine, or other similar periodical or in an electronic communication as defined in section 2510(12) of Title 18, the remedies of the owner of the right infringed or person bringing the action under section 1125(a) of this title as against the publisher or distributor of such newspaper, magazine, or other similar periodical or electronic communication shall be limited to an injunction against the presentation of such advertising matter in future issues of such newspapers, magazines, or other similar periodicals or in future transmissions of such electronic communications. The limitations of this subparagraph shall apply only to innocent infringers and innocent violators.

(C) Injunctive relief shall not be available to the owner of the right infringed or person bringing the action under section 1125(a) of this title with respect to an issue of a newspaper, magazine, or other similar periodical or an electronic communication containing infringing matter or violating matter where restraining the dissemination of such infringing matter or violating matter in any particular issue of such periodical or in an electronic communication would delay the delivery of such issue or transmission of such electronic communication after the regular time for such delivery or transmission, and such delay would be due to the method by which publication and distribution of such periodical or transmission of such electronic communication is customarily conducted in accordance with sound business practice, and not due to any method or device adopted to evade this section or to prevent or delay the issuance of an injunction or restraining order with respect to such infringing matter or violating matter.

(D)(i)(I) A domain name registrar, a domain name registry, or other domain name registration authority that takes any action described under clause (ii) affecting a domain name shall not be liable for monetary relief or, except as provided in subclause (II), for injunctive relief, to any person for such action, regardless of whether the domain name is finally determined to infringe or dilute the mark.

   (II) A domain name registrar, domain name registry, or other domain name registration authority described in subclause (I) may be subject to injunctive relief only if such registrar, registry, or other registration authority has—

      (aa) not expeditiously deposited with a court, in which an action has been filed regarding the disposition of the domain name, documents sufficient for the court to establish the court's control and authority regarding the disposition of the registration and use of the domain name;

      (bb) transferred, suspended, or otherwise modified the domain name during the pendency of the action, except upon order of the court; or

      (cc) willfully failed to comply with any such court order.

(ii) An action referred to under clause (i)(I) is any action of refusing to register, removing from registration, transferring, temporarily disabling, or permanently canceling a domain name—

   (I) in compliance with a court order under section 1125(d) of this title; or

   (II) in the implementation of a reasonable policy by such registrar, registry, or authority prohibiting the registration of a domain name that is identical to, confusingly similar to, or dilutive of another's mark.

(iii) A domain name registrar, a domain name registry, or other domain name registration authority shall not be liable for damages under this section for the registration or maintenance of a domain name for another absent a showing of bad faith intent to profit from such registration or maintenance of the domain name.

(iv) If a registrar, registry, or other registration authority takes an action described under clause (ii) based on a knowing and material misrepresentation by any other person that a domain name is identical to, confusingly similar to, or dilutive of a mark, the person making the knowing and material misrepresentation shall be liable for any damages, including costs and attorney's fees, incurred by the domain name registrant as a result of such action. The court may also grant injunctive relief to the domain name registrant, including the reactivation of the domain name or the transfer of the domain name to the domain name registrant.

(v) A domain name registrant whose domain name has been suspended, disabled, or transferred under a policy described under clause (ii) (II) may, upon notice to the mark owner, file a civil action to establish that the registration or use of the domain name by such registrant is not unlawful under this Act. The court may grant injunctive relief to the domain name registrant, including the reactivation of the domain name or transfer of the domain name to the domain name registrant.

(E) As used in this paragraph—

(i) the term "violator" means a person who violates section 1125(a) of this title; and

(ii) the term "violating matter" means matter that is the subject of a violation under section 1125(a) of this title.

(3)(A) Any person who engages in the conduct described in paragraph (11) of section 110 of title 17, United States Code, and who complies with the requirements set forth in that paragraph is not liable on account of such conduct for a violation of any right under this Act. This subparagraph does not preclude liability, nor shall it be construed to restrict the defenses or limitations on rights granted under this Act, of a person for conduct not described in paragraph (11) of section 110 of title 17, United States Code, even if that person also engages in conduct described in paragraph (11) of section 110 of such title.

(B) A manufacturer, licensee, or licensor of technology that enables the making of limited portions of audio or video content of a motion picture imperceptible as described in subparagraph (A) is not liable on account of such manufacture or license for a violation of any right under this Act, if such manufacturer, licensee, or licensor ensures that the technology provides a clear and conspicuous notice at the beginning of each performance that the performance of the motion picture is altered from the performance intended by the director or copyright holder of the motion picture. The limitations on liability in subparagraph (A) and this subparagraph shall not apply to a manufacturer, licensee, or licensor of technology that fails to comply with this paragraph.

(C) The requirement under subparagraph (B) to provide notice shall apply only with respect to technology manufactured after the end of the 180-day period beginning on April 27, 2005.

(D) Any failure by a manufacturer, licensee, or licensor of technology to qualify for the exemption under subparagraphs (A) and (B) shall not be construed to create an inference that any such party that engages in conduct described in paragraph (11) of section 110 of title 17, United States Code, is liable for trademark infringement by reason of such conduct.

§ 1115. (§ 33) Registration on Principal Register as Evidence of Exclusive Right to Use Mark; Defenses

(a) Evidentiary Value; Defenses

Any registration issued under the Act of March 3, 1881, or the Act of February 20, 1905, or of a mark registered on the principal register provided by this chapter and owned by a party to an action shall be admissible in evidence and shall be prima facie evidence of the validity of the registered mark and of the registration of the mark, of the registrant's ownership of the mark, and of the registrant's exclusive right to use the registered mark in commerce on or in connection with the goods or services specified in the registration subject to any conditions or limitations stated therein, but shall not preclude another person from proving any legal or equitable defense or defect, including those set forth in subsection (b) of this section, which might have been asserted if such mark had not been registered.

(b) Incontestability; Defenses

To the extent that the right to use the registered mark has become incontestable under section 1065 of this title, the registration shall be conclusive evidence of the validity of the registered mark and of the registration of the mark, of the registrant's ownership of the mark, and of the registrant's exclusive right to use the registered mark in commerce. Such conclusive evidence shall relate to the exclusive right to use the mark on or in connection with the goods or services specified in the affidavit filed under the provisions of section 1065 of this title, or in the renewal application filed under the provisions of section 1059 of this title if the goods or services specified in the renewal are fewer in number, subject to any conditions or limitations in the registration or in such affidavit or renewal application. Such conclusive evidence of the right to use the registered mark shall be subject to proof of infringement as defined in section 1114 of this title, and shall be subject to the following defenses or defects:

(1) That the registration or the incontestable right to use the mark was obtained fraudulently; or

(2) That the mark has been abandoned by the registrant; or

(3) That the registered mark is being used, by or with the permission of the registrant or a person in privity with the registrant, so as to misrepresent the source of the goods or services on or in connection with which the mark is used; or

(4) That the use of the name, term, or device charged to be an infringement is a use, otherwise than as a mark, of the party's individual name in his own business, or of the individual name of anyone in privity with such party, or of a term or device which is descriptive of and used fairly and in good faith only to describe the goods or services of such party, or their geographic origin; or

(5) That the mark whose use by a party is charged as an infringement was adopted without knowledge of the registrant's prior use and has been continuously used by such party or those in privity with him from a date prior to (A) the date of constructive use of the mark established pursuant to section 1057(c) of this title, (B) the registration of the mark under this chapter if the application for registration is filed before the effective date of the Trademark Law Revision Act of 1988, or (C) publication of the registered mark under subsection (c) of section 1062 of this title: *Provided, however,* That this defense or defect shall apply only for the area in which such continuous prior use is proved; or

(6) That the mark whose use is charged as an infringement was registered and used prior to the registration under this chapter or publication under subsection (c) of section 1062 of this title of the registered mark of the registrant, and not abandoned: *Provided, however,* That this defense or defect shall apply only for the area in which the mark was used prior to such registration or such publication of the registrant's mark; or

(7) That the mark has been or is being used to violate the antitrust laws of the United States; or

(8) That the mark is functional; or

(9) That equitable principles, including laches, estoppel, and acquiescence, are applicable.

§ 1116. (§ 34) Injunctive Relief

(a) Jurisdiction; Service

The several courts vested with jurisdiction of civil actions arising under this chapter shall have power to grant injunctions, according to the principles of equity and upon such terms as the court may deem reasonable, to prevent the violation of any right of the registrant of a mark registered in the Patent and Trademark Office or to prevent a violation under section 1125(a), (c), or (d) of this title. Any such injunction may include a provision directing the defendant to file with the court and serve on the plaintiff within thirty days after the service on the defendant of such injunction, or such extended period as the court may direct, a report in writing under oath setting forth in detail the manner and form in which the defendant has complied with the injunction. Any such injunction granted upon hearing, after notice to the defendant, by any district court of the United States, may be served on the parties against whom such injunction is granted anywhere in the United States where they may be found, and shall be operative and may be enforced by proceedings to punish for contempt, or otherwise, by the court by which such injunction was granted, or by any other United States district court in whose jurisdiction the defendant may be found.

(b) Transfer of Certified Copies of Court Papers

The said courts shall have jurisdiction to enforce said injunction, as provided in this chapter, as fully as if the injunction had been granted by the district court in which it is sought to be enforced. The clerk of the court or judge granting the injunction shall, when required to do so by the court before which application to enforce said injunction is made, transfer without delay to said court a certified copy of all papers on file in his office upon which said injunction was granted.

(c) Notice to Director

It shall be the duty of the clerks of such courts within one month after the filing of any action, suit, or proceeding involving a mark registered under the provisions of this chapter to give notice thereof in writing to the Director setting forth in order so far as known the names and addresses of the litigants and the designating number or numbers of the registration or registrations upon which the action, suit, or proceeding has been brought, and in the event any other registration be subsequently included in the action, suit, or proceeding by amendment, answer, or other pleading, the clerk shall give like notice thereof to the Director, and within one month after the judgment is entered or an appeal is taken the clerk of the court shall give notice thereof to the Director, and it shall be the duty of the Director on receipt of such notice forthwith to endorse the same upon the file wrapper of the said registration or registrations and to incorporate the same as a part of the contents of said file wrapper.

(d) Civil Actions Arising Out of Use of Counterfeit Marks

(1)(A) In the case of a civil action arising under section 1114(1)(a) of this title or section 220506 of Title 36 with respect to a violation that consists of using a counterfeit mark in connection with the sale, offering for sale, or distribution of goods or services, the court may, upon ex parte application, grant an order under subsection (a) of this section pursuant to this subsection providing for the seizure of goods and counterfeit marks involved in such violation and the means of making such marks, and records documenting the manufacture, sale, or receipt of things involved in such violation.

(B) As used in this subsection the term "counterfeit mark" means—

(i) a counterfeit of a mark that is registered on the principal register in the United States Patent and Trademark Office for such goods or services sold, offered for sale, or distributed and that is in use, whether or not the person against whom relief is sought knew such mark was so registered; or

(ii) a spurious designation that is identical with, or substantially indistinguishable from, a designation as to which the remedies of this chapter are made available by reason of section 220506 of Title 36;

but such term does not include any mark or designation used on or in connection with goods or services of which the manufacture* or producer was, at the time of the manufacture or production in question

---

*   So in original. Probably should read "manufacturer"—*Ed.*

authorized to use the mark or designation for the type of goods or services so manufactured or produced, by the holder of the right to use such mark or designation.

(2)   The court shall not receive an application under this subsection unless the applicant has given such notice of the application as is reasonable under the circumstances to the United States attorney for the judicial district in which such order is sought. Such attorney may participate in the proceedings arising under such application if such proceedings may affect evidence of an offense against the United States. The court may deny such application if the court determines that the public interest in a potential prosecution so requires.

(3)   The application for an order under this subsection shall—

(A)   be based on an affidavit or the verified complaint establishing facts sufficient to support the findings of fact and conclusions of law required for such order; and

(B)   contain the additional information required by paragraph (5) of this subsection to be set forth in such order.

(4)   The court shall not grant such an application unless—

(A)   the person obtaining an order under this subsection provides the security determined adequate by the court for the payment of such damages as any person may be entitled to recover as a result of a wrongful seizure or wrongful attempted seizure under this subsection; and

(B)   the court finds that it clearly appears from specific facts that—

(i)   an order other than an ex parte seizure order is not adequate to achieve the purposes of section 1114 of this title;

(ii)   the applicant has not publicized the requested seizure;

(iii)   the applicant is likely to succeed in showing that the person against whom seizure would be ordered used a counterfeit mark in connection with the sale, offering for sale, or distribution of goods or services;

(iv)   an immediate and irreparable injury will occur if such seizure is not ordered;

(v)   the matter to be seized will be located at the place identified in the application;

(vi)   the harm to the applicant of denying the application outweighs the harm to the legitimate interests of the person against whom seizure would be ordered of granting the application; and

(vii)   the person against whom seizure would be ordered, or persons acting in concert with such person, would destroy, move, hide, or otherwise make such matter inaccessible to the court, if the applicant were to proceed on notice to such person.

(5)   An order under this subsection shall set forth—

(A)   the findings of fact and conclusions of law required for the order;

(B)   a particular description of the matter to be seized, and a description of each place at which such matter is to be seized;

(C)   the time period, which shall end not later than seven days after the date on which such order is issued, during which the seizure is to be made;

(D)   the amount of security required to be provided under this subsection; and

(E)   a date for the hearing required under paragraph (10) of this subsection.

(6)   The court shall take appropriate action to protect the person against whom an order under this subsection is directed from publicity, by or at the behest of the plaintiff, about such order and any seizure under such order.

(7) Any materials seized under this subsection shall be taken into the custody of the court. For seizures made under this section, the court shall enter an appropriate protective order with respect to discovery and use of any records or information that has been seized. The protective order shall provide for appropriate procedures to ensure that confidential, private, proprietary, or privileged information contained in such records is not improperly disclosed or used.

(8) An order under this subsection, together with the supporting documents, shall be sealed until the person against whom the order is directed has an opportunity to contest such order, except that any person against whom such order is issued shall have access to such order and supporting documents after the seizure has been carried out.

(9) The court shall order that service of a copy of the order under this subsection shall be made by a Federal law enforcement officer (such as a United States marshal or an officer or agent of the United States Customs Service, Secret Service, Federal Bureau of Investigation, or Post Office) or may be made by a State or local law enforcement officer, who, upon making service, shall carry out the seizure under the order. The court shall issue orders, when appropriate, to protect the defendant from undue damage from the disclosure of trade secrets or other confidential information during the course of the seizure, including, when appropriate, orders restricting the access of the applicant (or any agent or employee of the applicant) to such secrets or information.

(10)(A) The court shall hold a hearing, unless waived by all the parties, on the date set by the court in the order of seizure. That date shall be not sooner than ten days after the order is issued and not later than fifteen days after the order is issued, unless the applicant for the order shows good cause for another date or unless the party against whom such order is directed consents to another date for such hearing. At such hearing the party obtaining the order shall have the burden to prove that the facts supporting findings of fact and conclusions of law necessary to support such order are still in effect. If that party fails to meet that burden, the seizure order shall be dissolved or modified appropriately.

(B) In connection with a hearing under this paragraph, the court may make such orders modifying the time limits for discovery under the Rules of Civil Procedure as may be necessary to prevent the frustration of the purposes of such hearing.

(11) A person who suffers damage by reason of a wrongful seizure under this subsection has a cause of action against the applicant for the order under which such seizure was made, and shall be entitled to recover such relief as may be appropriate, including damages for lost profits, cost of materials, loss of good will, and punitive damages in instances where the seizure was sought in bad faith, and, unless the court finds extenuating circumstances, to recover a reasonable attorney's fee. The court in its discretion may award prejudgment interest on relief recovered under this paragraph, at an annual interest rate established under section 6621(a)(2) of Title 26, commencing on the date of service of the claimant's pleading setting forth the claim under this paragraph and ending on the date such recovery is granted, or for such shorter time as the court deems appropriate.

§ 1117. (§ 35) Recovery for Violation of Rights

(a) Profits; Damages and Costs; Attorney Fees

When a violation of any right of the registrant of a mark registered in the Patent and Trademark Office, a violation under section 1125(a) or (d) of this title, or a willful violation under section 1125(c) of this title, shall have been established in any civil action arising under this chapter, the plaintiff shall be entitled, subject to the provisions of sections 1111 and 1114 of this title, and subject to the principles of equity, to recover (1) defendant's profits, (2) any damages sustained by the plaintiff, and (3) the costs of the action. The court shall assess such profits and damages or cause the same to be assessed under its direction. In assessing profits the plaintiff shall be required to prove defendant's sales only; defendant must prove all elements of cost or deduction claimed. In assessing damages the court may enter judgment, according to the circumstances of the case, for any sum above the amount found as actual damages, not exceeding three times such amount. If the court shall find that the amount of the recovery based on profits is either inadequate or excessive the court may in its discretion enter judgment for such sum as the court shall find to be just, according to the circumstances of the case. Such sum in either of the above circumstances shall constitute compensation and not a penalty. The court in exceptional cases may award reasonable attorney fees to the prevailing party.

(b) Treble Damages for Use of Counterfeit Mark

In assessing damages under subsection (a) for any violation of section 32(1)(a) of this Act or section 220506 of title 36, United States Code, in a case involving use of a counterfeit mark or designation (as defined in section 34(d) of this Act), the court shall, unless the court finds extenuating circumstances, enter judgment for three times such profits or damages, whichever amount is greater, together with a reasonable attorney's fee, if the violation consists of—

(1) intentionally using a mark or designation, knowing such mark or designation is a counterfeit mark (as defined in section 34(d) of this Act), in connection with the sale, offering for sale, or distribution of goods or services; or

(2) providing goods or services necessary to the commission of a violation specified in paragraph (1), with the intent that the recipient of the goods or services would put the goods or services to use in committing the violation.

In such a case, the court may award prejudgment interest on such amount at an annual interest rate established under section 6621(a)(2) of the Internal Revenue Code of 1986, beginning on the date of the service of the claimant's pleadings setting forth the claim for such entry of judgment and ending on the date such entry is made, or for such shorter time as the court considers appropriate.

(c) Statutory Damages for Use of Counterfeit Marks

In a case involving the use of a counterfeit mark (as defined in section 1116(d) of this title) in connection with the sale, offering for sale, or distribution of goods or services, the plaintiff may elect, at any time before final judgment is rendered by the trial court, to recover, instead of actual damages and profits under subsection (a), an award of statutory damages for any such use in connection with the sale, offering for sale, or distribution of goods or services in the amount of—

(1) not less than $1,000 or more than $200,000 per counterfeit mark per type of goods or services sold, offered for sale, or distributed, as the court considers just; or

(2) if the court finds that the use of the counterfeit mark was willful, not more than $2,000,000 per counterfeit mark per type of goods or services sold, offered for sale, or distributed, as the court considers just.

(d) Statutory Damages for Violation of Section 1125(d)(1)

In a case involving a violation of section 1125(d)(1) of this title, the plaintiff may elect, at any time before final judgment is rendered by the trial court, to recover, instead of actual damages and profits, an award of statutory damages in the amount of not less than $1,000 and not more than $100,000 per domain name, as the court considers just.

(e) In the case of a violation referred to in this section, it shall be a rebuttable presumption that the violation is willful for purposes of determining relief if the violator, or a person acting in concert with the violator, knowingly provided or knowingly caused to be provided materially false contact information to a domain name registrar, domain name registry, or other domain name registration authority in registering, maintaining, or renewing a domain name used in connection with the violation. Nothing in this subsection limits what may be considered a willful violation under this section.

§ 1118. (§ 36) Destruction of Infringing Articles

In any action arising under this chapter, in which a violation of any right of the registrant of a mark registered in the Patent and Trademark Office, a violation under section 1125(a), or a willful violation under section 1125(c) of this title, shall have been established, the court may order that all labels, signs, prints, packages, wrappers, receptacles, and advertisements in the possession of the defendant, bearing the registered mark or, in the case of a violation of section 1125(a), or a willful violation under section 1125(c) of this title, the word, term, name, symbol, device, combination thereof, designation, description, or representation that is the subject of the violation, or any reproduction, counterfeit, copy, or colorable imitation thereof, and all plates, molds, matrices, and other means of making the same, shall be delivered up and destroyed. The party seeking an order under this section for destruction of articles seized under section 1116(d) of this title shall give ten days' notice to the United States attorney for the judicial district in which such order is sought (unless good cause is shown for lesser notice) and such United States attorney may, if such destruction may affect evidence of an offense against the United States, seek a hearing on such destruction or participate in any hearing otherwise to be held with respect to such destruction.

§ 1119.   (§ 37) Power of Court Over Registration

In any action involving a registered mark the court may determine the right to registration, order the cancelation of registrations, in whole or in part, restore canceled registrations, and otherwise rectify the register with respect to the registrations of any party to the action. Decrees and orders shall be certified by the court to the Director, who shall make appropriate entry upon the records of the Patent and Trademark Office, and shall be controlled thereby.

§ 1120.   (§ 38) Civil Liability for False or Fraudulent Registration

Any person who shall procure registration in the Patent and Trademark Office of a mark by a false or fraudulent declaration or representation, oral or in writing, or by any false means, shall be liable in a civil action by any person injured thereby for any damages sustained in consequence thereof.

§ 1121.   (§ 39) Jurisdiction of Federal Courts; State and Local Requirements That Registered Trademarks Be Altered or Displayed Differently; Prohibition

(a)   The district and territorial courts of the United States shall have original jurisdiction and the courts of appeal of the United States (other than the United States Court of Appeals for the Federal Circuit) shall have appellate jurisdiction, of all actions arising under this chapter, without regard to the amount in controversy or to diversity or lack of diversity of the citizenship of the parties.

(b)   No State or other jurisdiction of the United States or any political subdivision or any agency thereof may require alteration of a registered mark, or require that additional trademarks, service marks, trade names, or corporate names that may be associated with or incorporated into the registered mark be displayed in the mark in a manner differing from the display of such additional trademarks, service marks, trade names, or corporate names contemplated by the registered mark as exhibited in the certificate of registration issued by the United States Patent and Trademark Office.

§ 1122.   (§ 40) Liability of States, Instrumentalities of States, and State Officials

(a) Waiver of Sovereign Immunity by the United States

The United States, all agencies and instrumentalities thereof, and all individuals, firms, corporations, other persons acting for the United States and with the authorization and consent of the United States, shall not be immune from suit in Federal or State court by any person, including any governmental or nongovernmental entity, for any violation under this Act.

(b) Waiver of Sovereign Immunity by States

Any State, instrumentality of a State or any officer or employee of a State or instrumentality of a State acting in his or her official capacity, shall not be immune, under the eleventh amendment of the Constitution of the United States or under any other doctrine of sovereign immunity, from suit in

Federal court by any person, including any governmental or non-governmental entity for any violation under this Act.[4]

(c) Remedies

In a suit described in subsection (a) or (b) for a violation described in therein, remedies (including remedies both at law and in equity) are available for the violation to the same extent as such remedies are available for such a violation in a suit against any person other than the United States or any agency or instrumentality thereof, or any individual, firm, corporation, or other person acting for the United States and with authorization and consent of the United States, or a State, instrumentality of a State, or officer or employee of a State or instrumentality of a State acting in his or her official capacity. Such remedies include injunctive relief under section 1116 of this title, actual damages, profits, costs and attorney's fees under section 1117 of this title, destruction of infringing articles under section 1118 of this title, the remedies provided for under sections 1114, 1119, 1120, 1124 and 1125 of this title, and for any other remedies provided under this Act.

§ 1123. (§ 41) Rules and Regulations for Conduct of Proceedings in Patent and Trademark Office

The Director shall make rules and regulations, not inconsistent with law, for the conduct of proceedings in the Patent and Trademark Office under this chapter.

§ 1124. (§ 42) Importation of Goods Bearing Infringing Marks or Names Forbidden

Except as provided in subsection (d) of section 1526 of Title 19, no article of imported merchandise which shall copy or simulate the name of any domestic manufacture, or manufacturer, or trader, or of any manufacturer or trader located in any foreign country which, by treaty, convention, or law affords similar privileges to citizens of the United States, or which shall copy or simulate a trademark registered in accordance with the provisions of this chapter or shall bear a name or mark calculated to induce the public to believe that the article is manufactured in the United States, or that it is manufactured in any foreign country or locality other than the country or locality in which it is in fact manufactured, shall be admitted to entry at any customhouse of the United States; and, in order to aid the officers of the customs in enforcing this prohibition, any domestic manufacturer or trader, and any foreign manufacturer or trader, who is entitled under the provisions of a treaty, convention, declaration, or agreement between the United States and any foreign country to the advantages afforded by law to citizens of the United States in respect to trade-marks and commercial names, may require his name and residence, and the name of the locality in which his goods are manufactured, and a copy of the certificate of registration of his trademark, issued in accordance with the provisions of this chapter, to be recorded in books which shall be kept for this purpose in the Department of the Treasury, under such regulations as the Secretary of the Treasury shall prescribe, and may furnish to the Department facsimiles of his name, the name of the locality in which his goods are manufactured, or of his registered trademark, and thereupon the Secretary of the Treasury shall cause one or more copies of the same to be transmitted to each collector or other proper officer of customs.

§ 1125. (§ 43) False Designations of Origin, False Descriptions, and Dilution Forbidden

(a) Civil Action

(1) Any person who, on or in connection with any goods or services, or any container for goods, uses in commerce any word, term, name, symbol, or device, or any combination thereof, or any false designation of origin, false or misleading description of fact, or false or misleading representation of fact, which—

---

[4] This provision's abrogation of states' sovereign immunity was held to be unconstitutional in *College Savings Bank v. Florida Prepaid Postsecondary Education Expense Board*, 527 U.S. 666, 119 S. Ct. 2219 (1999).—*Ed.*

(A) is likely to cause confusion, or to cause mistake, or to deceive as to the affiliation, connection, or association of such person with another person, or as to the origin, sponsorship, or approval of his or her goods, services, or commercial activities by another person, or

(B) in commercial advertising or promotion, misrepresents the nature, characteristics, qualities, or geographic origin of his or her or another person's goods, services, or commercial activities,

shall be liable in a civil action by any person who believes that he or she is or is likely to be damaged by such act.

(2) As used in this subsection, the term "any person" includes any State, instrumentality of a State or employee of a State or instrumentality of a State acting in his or her official capacity. Any State, and any such instrumentality, officer, or employee, shall be subject to the provisions of this chapter in the same manner and to the same extent as any nongovernmental entity.

(3) In a civil action for trade dress infringement under this Act for trade dress not registered on the principal register, the person who asserts trade dress protection has the burden of proving that the matter sought to be protected is not functional.

(b) Importation

Any goods marked or labeled in contravention of the provisions of this section shall not be imported into the United States or admitted to entry at any customhouse of the United States. The owner, importer, or consignee of goods refused entry at any customhouse under this section may have any recourse by protest or appeal that is given under the customs revenue laws or may have the remedy given by this chapter in cases involving goods refused entry or seized.

(c) Dilution by Blurring; Dilution by Tarnishment

(1) Injunctive Relief.—Subject to the principles of equity, the owner of a famous mark that is distinctive, inherently or through acquired distinctiveness, shall be entitled to an injunction against another person who, at any time after the owner's mark has become famous, commences use of a mark or trade name in commerce that is likely to cause dilution by blurring or dilution by tarnishment of the famous mark, regardless of the presence or absence of actual or likely confusion, of competition, or of actual economic injury.

(2) Definitions.—

(A) For purposes of paragraph (1), a mark is famous if it is widely recognized by the general consuming public of the United States as a designation of source of the goods or services of the mark's owner. In determining whether a mark possesses the requisite degree of recognition, the court may consider all relevant factors, including the following:

(i) The duration, extent, and geographic reach of advertising and publicity of the mark, whether advertised or publicized by the owner or third parties.

(ii) The amount, volume, and geographic extent of sales of goods or services offered under the mark.

(iii) The extent of actual recognition of the mark.

(iv) Whether the mark was registered under the Act of March 3, 1881, or the Act of February 20, 1905, or on the principal register.

(B) For purposes of paragraph (1), 'dilution by blurring' is association arising from the similarity between a mark or trade name and a famous mark that impairs the distinctiveness of the famous mark. In determining whether a mark or trade name is likely to cause dilution by blurring, the court may consider all relevant factors, including the following:

(i) The degree of similarity between the mark or trade name and the famous mark.

(ii) The degree of inherent or acquired distinctiveness of the famous mark.

(iii) The extent to which the owner of the famous mark is engaging in substantially exclusive use of the mark.

(iv) The degree of recognition of the famous mark.

(v) Whether the user of the mark or trade name intended to create an association with the famous mark.

(vi) Any actual association between the mark or trade name and the famous mark.

(C) For purposes of paragraph (1), 'dilution by tarnishment' is association arising from the similarity between a mark or trade name and a famous mark that harms the reputation of the famous mark.

(3) Exclusions.—The following shall not be actionable as dilution by blurring or dilution by tarnishment under this subsection:

(A) Any fair use, including a nominative or descriptive fair use, or facilitation of such fair use, of a famous mark by another person other than as a designation of source for the person's own goods or services, including use in connection with—

(i) advertising or promotion that permits consumers to compare goods or services; or

(ii) identifying and parodying, criticizing, or commenting upon the famous mark owner or the goods or services of the famous mark owner.

(B) All forms of news reporting and news commentary.

(C) Any noncommercial use of a mark.

(4) Burden of Proof.—In a civil action for trade dress dilution under this Act for trade dress not registered on the principal register, the person who asserts trade dress protection has the burden of proving that—

(A) the claimed trade dress, taken as a whole, is not functional and is famous; and

(B) if the claimed trade dress includes any mark or marks registered on the principal register, the unregistered matter, taken as a whole, is famous separate and apart from any fame of such registered marks.

(5) Additional Remedies.—In an action brought under this subsection, the owner of the famous mark shall be entitled to injunctive relief as set forth in section 1116 of this section. The owner of the famous mark shall also be entitled to the remedies set forth in sections 1117(a) and 1118, subject to the discretion of the court and the principles of equity if—

(A) the mark or trade name that is likely to cause dilution by blurring or dilution by tarnishment was first used in commerce by the person against whom the injunction is sought after the date of enactment of the Trademark Dilution Revision Act of 2006; and

(B) in a claim arising under this subsection—

(i) by reason of dilution by blurring, the person against whom the injunction is sought willfully intended to trade on the recognition of the famous mark; or

(ii) by reason of dilution by tarnishment, the person against whom the injunction is sought willfully intended to harm the reputation of the famous mark.

(6)　Ownership of Valid Registration a Complete Bar to Action.—The ownership by a person of a valid registration under the Act of March 3, 1881, or the Act of February 20, 1905, or on the principal register under this Act shall be a complete bar to an action against that person, with respect to that mark, that—

(A)　is brought by another person under the common law or a statute of a State; and

(B)(i)　seeks to prevent dilution by blurring or dilution by tarnishment; or

(ii)　asserts any claim of actual or likely damage or harm to the distinctiveness or reputation of a mark, label, or form of advertisement.

(7)　Savings Clause.—Nothing in this subsection shall be construed to impair, modify, or supersede the applicability of the patent laws of the United States.

(d)　Cyberpiracy Prevention

(1)(A)　A person shall be liable in a civil action by the owner of a mark, including a personal name which is protected as a mark under this section, if, without regard to the goods or services of the parties, that person—

(i)　has a bad faith intent to profit from that mark, including a personal name which is protected as a mark under this section; and

(ii)　registers, traffics in, or uses a domain name that—

(I)　in the case of a mark that is distinctive at the time of registration of the domain name, is identical or confusingly similar to that mark;

(II)　in the case of a famous mark that is famous at the time of registration of the domain name, is identical or confusingly similar to or dilutive of that mark; or

(III)　is a trademark, word, or name protected by reason of section 706 of title 18, United States Code, or section 220506 of title 36, United States Code.

(B)(i)　In determining whether a person has a bad faith intent described under subparagraph (A), a court may consider factors such as, but not limited to—

(I)　the trademark or other intellectual property rights of the person, if any, in the domain name;

(II)　the extent to which the domain name consists of the legal name of the person or a name that is otherwise commonly used to identify that person;

(III)　the person's prior use, if any, of the domain name in connection with the bona fide offering of any goods or services;

(IV)　the person's bona fide noncommercial or fair use of the mark in a site accessible under the domain name;

(V)　the person's intent to divert consumers from the mark owner's online location to a site accessible under the domain name that could harm the goodwill represented by the mark, either for commercial gain or with the intent to tarnish or disparage the mark, by creating a likelihood of confusion as to the source, sponsorship, affiliation, or endorsement of the site;

(VI)　the person's offer to transfer, sell, or otherwise assign the domain name to the mark owner or any third party for financial gain without having used, or having an intent to use, the domain name in the bona fide offering of any goods or services, or the person's prior conduct indicating a pattern of such conduct;

(VII)　the person's provision of material and misleading false contact information when applying for the registration of the domain name, the person's intentional failure to maintain accurate contact information, or the person's prior conduct indicating a pattern of such conduct;

(VIII) the person's registration or acquisition of multiple domain names which the person knows are identical or confusingly similar to marks of others that are distinctive at the time of registration of such domain names, or dilutive of famous marks of others that are famous at the time of registration of such domain names, without regard to the goods or services of the parties; and

(IX) the extent to which the mark incorporated in the person's domain name registration is or is not distinctive and famous within the meaning of subsection (c) of this section.

(ii) Bad faith intent described under subparagraph (A) shall not be found in any case in which the court determines that the person believed and had reasonable grounds to believe that the use of the domain name was a fair use or otherwise lawful.

(C) In any civil action involving the registration, trafficking, or use of a domain name under this paragraph, a court may order the forfeiture or cancellation of the domain name or the transfer of the domain name to the owner of the mark.

(D) A person shall be liable for using a domain name under subparagraph (A) only if that person is the domain name registrant or that registrant's authorized licensee.

(E) As used in this paragraph, the term "traffics in" refers to transactions that include, but are not limited to, sales, purchases, loans, pledges, licenses, exchanges of currency, and any other transfer for consideration or receipt in exchange for consideration.

(2)(A) The owner of a mark may file an in rem civil action against a domain name in the judicial district in which the domain name registrar, domain name registry, or other domain name authority that registered or assigned the domain name is located if—

(i) the domain name violates any right of the owner of a mark registered in the Patent and Trademark Office, or protected under subsection (a) or (c); and

(ii) the court finds that the owner—

(I) is not able to obtain in personam jurisdiction over a person who would have been a defendant in a civil action under paragraph (1); or

(II) through due diligence was not able to find a person who would have been a defendant in a civil action under paragraph (1) by—

(aa) sending a notice of the alleged violation and intent to proceed under this paragraph to the registrant of the domain name at the postal and e-mail address provided by the registrant to the registrar; and

(bb) publishing notice of the action as the court may direct promptly after filing the action.

(B) The actions under subparagraph (A)(ii) shall constitute service of process.

(C) In an in rem action under this paragraph, a domain name shall be deemed to have its situs in the judicial district in which—

(i) the domain name registrar, registry, or other domain name authority that registered or assigned the domain name is located; or

(ii) documents sufficient to establish control and authority regarding the disposition of the registration and use of the domain name are deposited with the court.

(D)(i) The remedies in an in rem action under this paragraph shall be limited to a court order for the forfeiture or cancellation of the domain name or the transfer of the domain name to the owner of the mark. Upon receipt of written notification of a filed, stamped copy of a complaint filed by the owner of a mark in a United States district court under this paragraph, the domain name registrar, domain name registry, or other domain name authority shall—

    (I)   expeditiously deposit with the court documents sufficient to establish the court's control and authority regarding the disposition of the registration and use of the domain name to the court; and

    (II)   not transfer, suspend, or otherwise modify the domain name during the pendency of the action, except upon order of the court.

    (ii)   The domain name registrar or registry or other domain name authority shall not be liable for injunctive or monetary relief under this paragraph except in the case of bad faith or reckless disregard, which includes a willful failure to comply with any such court order.

    (3)   The civil action established under paragraph (1) and the in rem action established under paragraph (2), and any remedy available under either such action, shall be in addition to any other civil action or remedy otherwise applicable.

    (4)   The in rem jurisdiction established under paragraph (2) shall be in addition to any other jurisdiction that otherwise exists, whether in rem or in personam.

§ 1126.   (§ 44) International Conventions

(a) Register of Marks Communicated by International Bureaus

The Director shall keep a register of all marks communicated to him by the international bureaus provided for by the conventions for the protection of industrial property, trade-marks, trade and commercial names, and the repression of unfair competition to which the United States is or may become a party, and upon the payment of the fees required by such conventions and the fees required in this chapter may place the marks so communicated upon such register. This register shall show a facsimile of the mark or trade or commercial name; the name, citizenship, and address of the registrant; the number, date, and place of the first registration of the mark, including the dates on which application for such registration was filed and granted and the term of such registration; a list of goods or services to which the mark is applied as shown by the registration in the country of origin, and such other data as may be useful concerning the mark. This register shall be a continuation of the register provided in section 1(a) of the Act of March 19, 1920.

(b) Benefits of Section to Persons Whose Country of Origin Is Party to Convention or Treaty

Any person whose country of origin is a party to any convention or treaty relating to trademarks, trade or commercial names, or the repression of unfair competition, to which the United States is also a party, or extends reciprocal rights to nationals of the United States by law, shall be entitled to the benefits of this section under the conditions expressed herein to the extent necessary to give effect to any provision of such convention, treaty or reciprocal law, in addition to the rights to which any owner of a mark is otherwise entitled by this chapter.

(c) Prior Registration in Country of Origin; Country of Origin Defined

No registration of a mark in the United States by a person described in subsection (b) of this section shall be granted until such mark has been registered in the country of origin of the applicant, unless the applicant alleges use in commerce.

For the purposes of this section, the country of origin of the applicant is the country in which he has a bona fide and effective industrial or commercial establishment, or if he has not such an establishment the country in which he is domiciled, or if he has not a domicile in any of the countries described in subsection (b) of this section, the country of which he is a national.

(d) Right of Priority

An application for registration of a mark under section 1051, 1053, 1054, or 1091 of this title, or under subsection (e) of this section, filed by a person described in subsection (b) of this section who has previously duly filed an application for registration of the same mark in one of the countries described in subsection (b) of this section shall be accorded the same force and effect as would be accorded to the same application if filed in the United States on the same date on which the application was first filed in such foreign country: *Provided,* That—

(1)   the application in the United States is filed within six months from the date on which the application was first filed in the foreign country;

(2)   the application conforms as nearly as practicable to the requirements of this chapter, including a statement that the applicant has a bona fide intention to use the mark in commerce;

(3)   the rights acquired by third parties before the date of the filing of the first application in the foreign country shall in no way be affected by a registration obtained on an application filed under this subsection;

(4)   nothing in this subsection shall entitle the owner of a registration granted under this section to sue for acts committed prior to the date on which his mark was registered in this country unless the registration is based on use in commerce.

In like manner and subject to the same conditions and requirements, the right provided in this section may be based upon a subsequent regularly filed application in the same foreign country, instead of the first filed foreign application: *Provided,* That any foreign application filed prior to such subsequent application has been withdrawn, abandoned, or otherwise disposed of, without having been laid open to public inspection and without leaving any rights outstanding, and has not served, nor thereafter shall serve, as a basis for claiming a right of priority.

(e)   Registration on Principal or Supplemental Register; Copy of Foreign Registration

A mark duly registered in the country of origin of the foreign applicant may be registered on the principal register if eligible, otherwise on the supplemental register in this chapter provided. Such applicant shall submit, within such time period as may be prescribed by the Director, a true copy, a photocopy, a certification, or a certified copy of the registration in the country of origin of the applicant. The application must state the applicant's bona fide intention to use the mark in commerce, but use in commerce shall not be required prior to registration.

(f)   Domestic Registration Independent of Foreign Registration

The registration of a mark under the provisions of subsections (c), (d), and (e) of this section by a person described in subsection (b) of this section shall be independent of the registration in the country of origin and the duration, validity, or transfer in the United States of such registration shall be governed by the provisions of this chapter.

(g)   Trade or Commercial Names of Foreign Nationals Protected Without Registration

Trade names or commercial names of persons described in subsection (b) of this section shall be protected without the obligation of filing or registration whether or not they form parts of marks.

(h)   Protection of Foreign Nationals Against Unfair Competition

Any person designated in subsection (b) of this section as entitled to the benefits and subject to the provisions of this chapter shall be entitled to effective protection against unfair competition, and the remedies provided in this chapter for infringement of marks shall be available so far as they may be appropriate in repressing acts of unfair competition.

(i)   Citizens or Residents of United States Entitled to Benefits of Section

Citizens or residents of the United States shall have the same benefits as are granted by this section to persons described in subsection (b) of this section.

§ 1127.   (§ 45) Construction and Definitions; Intent of Chapter

In the construction of this chapter, unless the contrary is plainly apparent from the context—

The United States includes and embraces all territory which is under its jurisdiction and control.

The word "commerce" means all commerce which may lawfully be regulated by Congress.

The term "principal register" refers to the register provided for by sections 1051 to 1072 of this title, and the term "supplemental register" refers to the register provided for by sections 1091 to 1096 of this title.

The term "person" and any other word or term used to designate the applicant or other entitled to a benefit or privilege or rendered liable under the provisions of this chapter includes a juristic person as well as a natural person. The term "juristic person" includes a firm, corporation, union, association, or other organization capable of suing and being sued in a court of law.

The term "person" also includes the United States, any agency or instrumentality thereof, or any individual, firm, or corporation acting for the United States and with the authorization and consent of the United States. The United States, any agency or instrumentality thereof, and any individual, firm, or corporation acting for the United States and with the authorization and consent of the United States, shall be subject to the provisions of this Act in the same manner and to the same extent as any nongovernmental entity.

The term "person" also includes any State, any instrumentality of a State, and any officer or employee of a State or instrumentality of a State acting in his or her official capacity. Any State, and any such instrumentality, officer, or employee, shall be subject to the provisions of this Act in the same manner and to the same extent as any nongovernmental entity.

The terms "applicant" and "registrant" embrace the legal representatives, predecessors, successors and assigns of such applicant or registrant.

The term "Director" means the Under Secretary of Commerce for Intellectual Property and Director of the United States Patent and Trademark Office.

The term "related company" means any person whose use of a mark is controlled by the owner of the mark with respect to the nature and quality of the goods or services on or in connection with which the mark is used.

The terms "trade name" and "commercial name" mean any name used by a person to identify his or her business or vocation.

The term "trademark" includes any word, name, symbol, or device, or any combination thereof—

  (1)   used by a person, or

  (2)   which a person has a bona fide intention to use in commerce and applies to register on the principal register established by this chapter,

to identify and distinguish his or her goods, including a unique product, from those manufactured or sold by others and to indicate the source of the goods, even if that source is unknown.

The term "service mark" means any word, name, symbol, or device, or any combination thereof—

  (1)   used by a person, or

  (2)   which a person has a bona fide intention to use in commerce and applies to register on the principal register established by this chapter,

to identify and distinguish the services of one person, including a unique service, from the services of others and to indicate the source of the services, even if that source is unknown. Titles, character names, and other distinctive features of radio or television programs may be registered as service marks notwithstanding that they, or the programs, may advertise the goods of the sponsor.

The term "certification mark" means any word, name, symbol, or device, or any combination thereof—

(1) used by a person other than its owner, or

(2) which its owner has a bona fide intention to permit a person other than the owner to use in commerce and files an application to register on the principal register established by this chapter,

to certify regional or other origin, material, mode of manufacture, quality, accuracy, or other characteristics of such person's goods or services or that the work or labor on the goods or services was performed by members of a union or other organization.

The term "collective mark" means a trademark or service mark—

(1) used by the members of a cooperative, an association, or other collective group or organization, or

(2) which such cooperative, association, or other collective group or organization has a bona fide intention to use in commerce and applies to register on the principal register established by this chapter,

and includes marks indicating membership in a union, an association, or other organization.

The term "mark" includes any trademark, service mark, collective mark, or certification mark.

The term "use in commerce" means the bona fide use of a mark in the ordinary course of trade, and not made merely to reserve a right in a mark. For purposes of this chapter, a mark shall be deemed to be in use in commerce—

(1) on goods when—

(A) it is placed in any manner on the goods or their containers or the displays associated therewith or on the tags or labels affixed thereto, or if the nature of the goods makes such placement impracticable, then on documents associated with the goods or their sale, and

(B) the goods are sold or transported in commerce, and

(2) on services when it is used or displayed in the sale or advertising of services and the services are rendered in commerce, or the services are rendered in more than one State or in the United States and a foreign country and the person rendering the services is engaged in commerce in connection with the services.

A mark shall be deemed to be "abandoned" when either of the following occurs:

(1) When its use has been discontinued with intent not to resume such use. Intent not to resume may be inferred from circumstances. Nonuse for 3 consecutive years shall be prima facie evidence of abandonment. "Use" of a mark means the bona fide use of such mark made in the ordinary course of trade, and not made merely to reserve a right in a mark.

(2) When any course of conduct of the owner, including acts of omission as well as commission, causes the mark to become the generic name for the goods or services on or in connection with which it is used or otherwise to lose its significance as a mark. Purchaser motivation shall not be a test for determining abandonment under this paragraph.

The term "colorable imitation" includes any mark which so resembles a registered mark as to be likely to cause confusion or mistake or to deceive.

The term "registered mark" means a mark registered in the United States Patent and Trademark Office under this chapter or under the Act of March 3, 1881, or the Act of February 20, 1905, or the Act of March 19, 1920. The phrase "marks registered in the Patent and Trademark Office" means registered marks.

The term "Act of March 3, 1881", "Act of February 20, 1905", or "Act of March 19, 1920," means the respective Act as amended.

A "counterfeit" is a spurious mark which is identical with, or substantially indistinguishable from, a registered mark.

The term "domain name" means any alphanumeric designation which is registered with or assigned by any domain name registrar, domain name registry, or other domain name registration authority as part of an electronic address on the Internet.

The term "Internet" has the meaning given that term in section 230(f)(1) of the Communications Act of 1934 (47 U.S.C. 230(f)(1)).

Words used in the singular include the plural and vice versa.

The intent of this chapter is to regulate commerce within the control of Congress by making actionable the deceptive and misleading use of marks in such commerce; to protect registered marks used in such commerce from interference by State, or territorial legislation; to protect persons engaged in such commerce against unfair competition; to prevent fraud and deception in such commerce by the use of reproductions, copies, counterfeits, or colorable imitations of registered marks; and to provide rights and remedies stipulated by treaties and conventions respecting trademarks, trade names, and unfair competition entered into between the United States and foreign nations.

§ 1128.   [REPEALED]

§ 1129.   [TRANSFERRED—Now codified as 15 U.S.C. § 8131, reproduced following the Lanham Act]

SUBCHAPTER IV.   THE MADRID PROTOCOL

§ 1141.   (§ 60) Definitions

In this subchapter:

(1) Basic Application

The term "basic application" means the application for the registration of a mark that has been filed with an Office of a Contracting Party and that constitutes the basis for an application for the international registration of that mark.

(2) Basic Registration

The term "basic registration" means the registration of a mark that has been granted by an Office of a Contracting Party and that constitutes the basis for an application for the international registration of that mark.

(3) Contracting Party

The term "Contracting Party" means any country or inter-governmental organization that is a party to the Madrid Protocol.

(4) Date of Recordal

The term "date of recordal" means the date on which a request for extension of protection, filed after an international registration is granted, is recorded on the International Register.

(5) Declaration of Bona Fide Intention to Use the Mark in Commerce

The term 'declaration of bona fide intention to use the mark in commerce' means a declaration that is signed by the applicant for, or holder of, an international registration who is seeking extension of protection of a mark to the United States and that contains a statement that—

    (A)   the applicant or holder has a bona fide intention to use the mark in commerce;

(B)   the person making the declaration believes himself or herself, or the firm, corporation, or association in whose behalf he or she makes the declaration, to be entitled to use the mark in commerce; and

(C)   no other person, firm, corporation, or association, to the best of his or her knowledge and belief, has the right to use such mark in commerce either in the identical form of the mark or in such near resemblance to the mark as to be likely, when used on or in connection with the goods of such other person, firm, corporation, or association, to cause confusion, mistake, or deception.

(6)   Extension of Protection

The term "extension of protection" means the protection resulting from an international registration that extends to the United States at the request of the holder of the international registration, in accordance with the Madrid Protocol.

(7)   Holder of an International Registration

A "holder" of an international registration is the natural or juristic person in whose name the international registration is recorded on the International Register.

(8)   International Application

The term "international application" means an application for international registration that is filed under the Madrid Protocol.

(9)   International Bureau

The term "International Bureau" means the International Bureau of the World Intellectual Property Organization.

(10) International Register

The term "International Register" means the official collection of data concerning international registrations maintained by the International Bureau that the Madrid Protocol or its implementing regulations require or permit to be recorded.

(11) International Registration

The term "international registration" means the registration of a mark granted under the Madrid Protocol.

(12) International Registration Date

The term "international registration date" means the date assigned to the international registration by the International Bureau.

(13) Madrid Protocol

The term "Madrid Protocol" means the Protocol Relating to the Madrid Agreement Concerning the International Registration of Marks, adopted at Madrid, Spain, on June 27, 1989.

(14) Notification of Refusal

The term "notification of refusal" means the notice sent by the United States Patent and Trademark Office to the International Bureau declaring that an extension of protection cannot be granted.

(15) Office of a Contracting Party

The term "Office of a Contracting Party" means—

(A)   the office, or governmental entity, of a Contracting Party that is responsible for the registration of marks; or

    (B)   the common office, or governmental entity, of more than 1 Contracting Party that is responsible for the registration of marks and is so recognized by the International Bureau.

(16) Office of Origin

The term "office of origin" means the Office of a Contracting Party with which a basic application was filed or by which a basic registration was granted.

(17) Opposition Period

The term "opposition period" means the time allowed for filing an opposition in the United States Patent and Trademark Office, including any extension of time granted under section 1063 of this title.

§ 1141a. (§ 61) International Applications Based on United States Applications or Registrations

(a) In General

The owner of a basic application pending before the United States Patent and Trademark Office, or the owner of a basic registration granted by the United States Patent and Trademark Office may file an international application by submitting to the United States Patent and Trademark Office a written application in such form, together with such fees, as may be prescribed by the Director.

(b) Qualified Owners

A qualified owner, under subsection (a), shall—

    (1)   be a national of the United States;

    (2)   be domiciled in the United States; or

    (3)   have a real and effective industrial or commercial establishment in the United States.

§ 1141b. (§ 62) Certification of the International Application

(a) Certification Procedure

Upon the filing of an application for international registration and payment of the prescribed fees, the Director shall examine the international application for the purpose of certifying that the information contained in the international application corresponds to the information contained in the basic application or basic registration at the time of the certification.

(b) Transmittal

Upon examination and certification of the international application, the Director shall transmit the international application to the International Bureau.

§ 1141c. (§ 63) Restriction, Abandonment, Cancellation, or Expiration of a Basic Application or Basic Registration

With respect to an international application transmitted to the International Bureau under section 1141b of this title, the Director shall notify the International Bureau whenever the basic application or basic registration which is the basis for the international application has been restricted, abandoned, or canceled, or has expired, with respect to some or all of the goods and services listed in the international registration—

    (1)   within 5 years after the international registration date; or

    (2)   more than 5 years after the international registration date if the restriction, abandonment, or cancellation of the basic application or basic registration resulted from an action that began before the end of that 5-year period.

§ 1141d. (§ 64) Request for Extension of Protection Subsequent to International Registration

The holder of an international registration that is based upon a basic application filed with the United States Patent and Trademark Office or a basic registration granted by the Patent and Trademark Office may request an extension of protection of its international registration by filing such a request—

(1) directly with the International Bureau; or

(2) with the United States Patent and Trademark Office for transmittal to the International Bureau, if the request is in such form, and contains such transmittal fee, as may be prescribed by the Director.

§ 1141e. (§ 65) Extension of Protection of an International Registration to the United States Under the Madrid Protocol

(a) In General

Subject to the provisions of section 1141h of this title, the holder of an international registration shall be entitled to the benefits of extension of protection of that international registration to the United States to the extent necessary to give effect to any provision of the Madrid Protocol.

(b) If the United States Is Office of Origin

Where the United States Patent and Trademark Office is the office of origin for a trademark application or registration, any international registration based on such application or registration cannot be used to obtain the benefits of the Madrid Protocol in the United States.

§ 1141f. (§ 66) Effect of Filing a Request for Extension of Protection of an International Registration to the United States

(a) Requirement for Request for Extension of Protection

Request for extension of protection of an international registration to the United States that the International Bureau transmits to the United States Patent and Trademark Office shall be deemed to be properly filed in the United States if such request, when received by the International Bureau, has attached to it a declaration of bona fide intention to use the mark in commerce that is verified by the applicant for, or holder of, the international registration.

(b) Effect of Proper Filing

Unless extension of protection is refused under section 1141h of this title, the proper filing of the request for extension of protection under subsection (a) shall constitute constructive use of the mark, conferring the same rights as those specified in section 1057(c) of this title, as of the earliest of the following:

(1) The international registration date, if the request for extension of protection was filed in the international application.

(2) The date of recordal of the request for extension of protection, if the request for extension of protection was made after the international registration date.

(3) The date of priority claimed pursuant to section 1141g of this title.

§ 1141g. (§ 67) Right of Priority for Request for Extension of Protection to the United States

The holder of an international registration with a request for an extension of protection to the United States shall be entitled to claim a date of priority based on a right of priority within the meaning of Article 4 of the Paris Convention for the Protection of Industrial Property if—

(1) the request for extension of protection contains a claim of priority; and

(2)   the date of international registration or the date of the recordal of the request for extension of protection to the United States is not later than 6 months after the date of the first regular national filing (within the meaning of Article 4(A)(3) of the Paris Convention for the Protection of Industrial Property) or a subsequent application (within the meaning of Article 4(C)(4) of the Paris Convention for the Protection of Industrial Property).

§ 1141h. (§ 68) Examination of and Opposition to Request for Extension of Protection; Notification of Refusal

(a)   Examination and Opposition

(1)   A request for extension of protection described in section 1141f(a) of this title shall be examined as an application for registration on the Principal Register under this Act, and if on such examination it appears that the applicant is entitled to extension of protection under this title, the Director shall cause the mark to be published in the Official Gazette of the United States Patent and Trademark Office.

(2)   Subject to the provisions of subsection (c), a request for extension of protection under this title shall be subject to opposition under section 1063 of this title.

(3)   Extension of protection shall not be refused on the ground that the mark has not been used in commerce.

(4)   Extension of protection shall be refused to any mark not registrable on the Principal Register.

(b)   Notification of Refusal

If,* a request for extension of protection is refused under subsection (a), the Director shall declare in a notification of refusal (as provided in subsection (c)) that the extension of protection cannot be granted, together with a statement of all grounds on which the refusal was based.

(c)   Notice to International Bureau

(1)   Within 18 months after the date on which the International Bureau transmits to the Patent and Trademark Office a notification of a request for extension of protection, the Director shall transmit to the International Bureau any of the following that applies to such request:

(A)   A notification of refusal based on an examination of the request for extension of protection.

(B)   A notification of refusal based on the filing of an opposition to the request.

(C)   A notification of the possibility that an opposition to the request may be filed after the end of that 18-month period.

(2)   If the Director has sent a notification of the possibility of opposition under paragraph (1)(C), the Director shall, if applicable, transmit to the International Bureau a notification of refusal on the basis of the opposition, together with a statement of all the grounds for the opposition, within 7 months after the beginning of the opposition period or within 1 month after the end of the opposition period, whichever is earlier.

(3)   If a notification of refusal of a request for extension of protection is transmitted under paragraph (1) or (2), no grounds for refusal of such request other than those set forth in such notification may be transmitted to the International Bureau by the Director after the expiration of the time periods set forth in paragraph (1) or (2), as the case may be.

(4)   If a notification specified in paragraph (1) or (2) is not sent to the International Bureau within the time period set forth in such paragraph, with respect to a request for extension of

---

*   So in original. The comma probably should not appear.—*Ed.*

protection, the request for extension of protection shall not be refused and the Director shall issue a certificate of extension of protection pursuant to the request.

(d) Designation of Agent for Service of Process

In responding to a notification of refusal with respect to a mark, the holder of the international registration of the mark may designate, by a document filed in the United States Patent and Trademark Office, the name and address of a person residing in the United States on whom notices or process in proceedings affecting the mark may be served. Such notices or process may be served upon the person designated by leaving with that person, or mailing to that person, a copy thereof at the address specified in the last designation filed. If the person designated cannot be found at the address given in the last designation, or if the holder does not designate by a document filed in the United States Patent and Trademark Office the name and address of a person residing in the United States for service of notices or process in proceedings affecting the mark, the notice or process may be served on the Director.

§ 1141i. (§ 69) Effect of Extension of Protection

(a) Issuance of Extension of Protection

Unless a request for extension of protection is refused under section 1141h of this title, the Director shall issue a certificate of extension of protection pursuant to the request and shall cause notice of such certificate of extension of protection to be published in the Official Gazette of the United States Patent and Trademark Office.

(b) Effect of Extension of Protection

From the date on which a certificate of extension of protection is issued under subsection (a)—

(1) such extension of protection shall have the same effect and validity as a registration on the Principal Register; and

(2) the holder of the international registration shall have the same rights and remedies as the owner of a registration on the Principal Register.

§ 1141j. (§ 70) Dependence of Extension of Protection to the United States on the Underlying International Registration

(a) Effect of Cancellation of International Registration

If the International Bureau notifies the United States Patent and Trademark Office of the cancellation of an international registration with respect to some or all of the goods and services listed in the international registration, the Director shall cancel any extension of protection to the United States with respect to such goods and services as of the date on which the international registration was canceled.

(b) Effect of Failure to Renew International Registration

If the International Bureau does not renew an international registration, the corresponding extension of protection to the United States shall cease to be valid as of the date of the expiration of the international registration.

(c) Transformation of an Extension of Protection into a United States Application

The holder of an international registration canceled in whole or in part by the International Bureau at the request of the office of origin, under article 6(4) of the Madrid Protocol, may file an application, under section 1051 or 1126 of this title, for the registration of the same mark for any of the goods and services to which the cancellation applies that were covered by an extension of protection to the United States based on that international registration. Such an application shall be treated as if it had been filed on the international registration date or the date of recordal of the request for extension of protection with the International Bureau, whichever date applies, and, if the extension of protection enjoyed priority under section 1141g of this title, shall enjoy the same priority. Such an application shall be entitled to the benefits conferred by this subsection only if the application is filed not later than 3 months after the date on which the international registration was canceled, in whole or in part, and only if the application complies with all the requirements of this Act which apply to any application filed pursuant to section 1051 or 1126 of this title.

§ 1141k. (§ 71) Duration, Affidavits and Fees

(a) Time Periods for Required Affidavits

Each extension of protection for which a certificate has been issued under section 69 shall remain in force for the term of the international registration upon which it is based, except that the extension of protection of any mark shall be canceled by the Director unless the holder of the international registration files in the United States Patent and Trademark Office affidavits that meet the requirements of subsection (b), within the following time periods:

(1) Within the 1-year period immediately preceding the expiration of 6 years following the date of issuance of the certificate of extension of protection.

(2) Within the 1-year period immediately preceding the expiration of 10 years following the date of issuance of the certificate of extension of protection, and each successive 10-year period following the date of issuance of the certificate of extension of protection.

(3) The holder may file the affidavit required under this section within a grace period of 6 months after the end of the applicable time period established in paragraph (1) or (2), together with the fee described in subsection (b) and the additional grace period surcharge prescribed by the Director.

(b) Requirements for Affidavit

The affidavit referred to in subsection (a) shall—

(1)(A) state that the mark is in use in commerce;

(B) set forth the goods and services recited in the extension of protection on or in connection with which the mark is in use in commerce;

(C) be accompanied by such number of specimens or facsimiles showing current use of the mark in commerce as may be required by the Director; and

(D) be accompanied by the fee prescribed by the Director; or

(2)(A) set forth the goods and services recited in the extension of protection on or in connection with which the mark is not in use in commerce;

(B) include a showing that any nonuse is due to special circumstances which excuse such nonuse and is not due to any intention to abandon the mark; and

(C) be accompanied by the fee prescribed by the Director.

(c) Deficient Affidavit

If any submission filed within the period set forth in subsection (a) is deficient, including that the affidavit was not filed in the name of the holder of the international registration, the deficiency may be corrected after the statutory time period, within the time prescribed after notification of the deficiency. Such submission shall be accompanied by the additional deficiency surcharge prescribed by the Director.

(d) Notice of Requirement

Special notice of the requirement for such affidavit shall be attached to each certificate of extension of protection.

(e) Notification of Acceptance or Refusal

The Director shall notify the holder of the international registration who files any affidavit required by this section of the Director's acceptance or refusal thereof and, in the case of a refusal, the reasons therefor.

(f) Designation of Resident for Service of Process and Notices

If the holder of the international registration of the mark is not domiciled in the United States, the holder may designate, by a document filed in the United States Patent and Trademark Office, the name and address of a person resident in the United States on whom may be served notices or process in proceedings affecting the mark. Such notices or process may be served upon the person so designated by leaving with that person or mailing to that person a copy thereof at the address specified in the last designation so filed. If the person so designated cannot be found at the last designated address, or if the holder does not designate by a document filed in the United States Patent and Trademark Office the name and address of a person resident in the United States on whom may be served notices or process in proceedings affecting the mark, such notices or process may be served on the Director.

§ 1141*l*. (§ 72) Assignment of an Extension of Protection

An extension of protection may be assigned, together with the goodwill associated with the mark, only to a person who is a national of, is domiciled in, or has a bona fide and effective industrial or commercial establishment either in a country that is a Contracting Party or in a country that is a member of an intergovernmental organization that is a Contracting Party.

§ 1141m. (§ 73) Incontestability

The period of continuous use prescribed under section 1065 of this title for a mark covered by an extension of protection issued under this title may begin no earlier than the date on which the Director issues the certificate of the extension of protection under section 1141i of this title, except as provided in section 1141n of this title.

§ 1141n. (§ 74) Rights of Extension of Protection

When a United States registration and a subsequently issued certificate of extension of protection to the United States are owned by the same person, identify the same mark, and list the same goods or services, the extension of protection shall have the same rights that accrued to the registration prior to issuance of the certificate of extension of protection.

* * *

§ 8131. Cyberpiracy Protections for Individuals

(1) In General

(A) CIVIL LIABILITY.—Any person who registers a domain name that consists of the name of another living person, or a name substantially and confusingly similar thereto, without that person's consent, with the specific intent to profit from such name by selling the domain name for financial gain to that person or any third party, shall be liable in a civil action by such person.

(B) EXCEPTION.—A person who in good faith registers a domain name consisting of the name of another living person, or a name substantially and confusingly similar thereto, shall not be liable under this paragraph if such name is used in, affiliated with, or related to a work of authorship protected under title 17, United States Code, including a work made for hire as defined in section 101 of title 17, United States Code, and if the person registering the domain name is the copyright owner or licensee of the work, the person intends to sell the domain name in conjunction with the lawful exploitation of the work, and such registration is not prohibited by a contract between the registrant and the named person. The exception under this subparagraph shall apply only to a civil action brought under paragraph (1) and shall in no manner limit the protections afforded under the Trademark Act of 1946 (15 U.S.C. 1051 et seq.) or other provision of Federal or State law.

(2) Remedies

In any civil action brought under paragraph (1), a court may award injunctive relief, including the forfeiture or cancellation of the domain name or the transfer of the domain name to the plaintiff. The court may also, in its discretion, award costs and attorneys fees to the prevailing party.

(3) Definition

In this subsection, the term "domain name" has the meaning given that term in section 45 of the Trademark Act of 1946 (15 U.S.C. 1127).

(4) Effective Date

This subsection shall apply to domain names registered on or after November 29, 1999.

B. CRIMINAL PROVISIONS OF THE TRADEMARK COUNTERFEITING ACT OF 1984*

18 U.S.C.A. § 2320

§ 2320. Trafficking in Counterfeit Goods or Services

(a) Offenses.—Whoever intentionally—

(1) traffics in goods or services and knowingly uses a counterfeit mark on or in connection with such goods or services,

(2) traffics in labels, patches, stickers, wrappers, badges, emblems, medallions, charms, boxes, containers, cans, cases, hangtags, documentation, or packaging of any type or nature, knowing that a counterfeit mark has been applied thereto, the use of which is likely to cause confusion, to cause mistake, or to deceive,

(3) traffics in goods or services knowing that such good or service is a counterfeit military good or service the use, malfunction, or failure of which is likely to cause serious bodily injury or death, the disclosure of classified information, impairment of combat operations, or other significant harm to a combat operation, a member of the Armed Forces, or to national security, or

(4) traffics in a drug and knowingly uses a counterfeit mark on or in connection with such drug,

or attempts or conspires to violate any of paragraphs (1) through (4) shall be punished as provided in subsection (b).

(b) Penalties.—

(1) In general.—Whoever commits an offense under subsection (a)—

(A) if an individual, shall be fined not more than $2,000,000 or imprisoned not more than 10 years, or both, and, if a person other than an individual, shall be fined not more than $5,000,000; and

(B) for a second or subsequent offense under subsection (a), if an individual, shall be fined not more than $5,000,000 or imprisoned not more than 20 years, or both, and if other than an individual, shall be fined not more than $15,000,000.

(2) Serious bodily injury or death.—

(A) Serious bodily injury.—Whoever knowingly or recklessly causes or attempts to cause serious bodily injury from conduct in violation of subsection (a), if an individual, shall be fined not more than $5,000,000 or imprisoned for not more than 20 years, or both, and if other than an individual, shall be fined not more than $15,000,000.

(B) Death.—Whoever knowingly or recklessly causes or attempts to cause death from conduct in violation of subsection (a), if an individual, shall be fined not more than $5,000,000 or imprisoned for any term of years or for life, or both, and if other than an individual, shall be fined not more than $15,000,000.

(3) Counterfeit military goods or services and counterfeit drugs.—Whoever commits an offense under subsection (a) involving a counterfeit military good or service or drug that uses a counterfeit mark on or in connection with the drug—

---

* Related provisions of this title regarding record piracy and copyright infringement can be found beginning on page 319 of this text.

(A) if an individual, shall be fined not more than $5,000,000, imprisoned not more than 20 years, or both, and if other than an individual, be fined not more than $15,000,000; and

(B) for a second or subsequent offense, if an individual, shall be fined not more than $15,000,000, imprisoned not more than 30 years, or both, and if other than an individual, shall be fined not more than $30,000,000.

(c) Forfeiture and destruction of property; restitution.—Forfeiture, destruction, and restitution relating to this section shall be subject to section 2323, to the extent provided in that section, in addition to any other similar remedies provided by law.

(d) Defenses.—All defenses, affirmative defenses, and limitations on remedies that would be applicable in an action under the Lanham Act shall be applicable in a prosecution under this section. In a prosecution under this section, the defendant shall have the burden of proof, by a preponderance of the evidence, of any such affirmative defense.

(e) Presentence report.—(1) During preparation of the presentence report pursuant to Rule 32(c) of the Federal Rules of Criminal Procedure, victims of the offense shall be permitted to submit, and the probation officer shall receive, a victim impact statement that identifies the victim of the offense and the extent and scope of the injury and loss suffered by the victim, including the estimated economic impact of the offense on that victim.

(2) Persons permitted to submit victim impact statements shall include—

(A) producers and sellers of legitimate goods or services affected by conduct involved in the offense;

(B) holders of intellectual property rights in such goods or services; and

(C) the legal representatives of such producers, sellers, and holders.

(f) Definitions.—For the purposes of this section—

(1) the term "counterfeit mark" means—

(A) a spurious mark—

(i) that is used in connection with trafficking in any goods, services, labels, patches, stickers, wrappers, badges, emblems, medallions, charms, boxes, containers, cans, cases, hangtags, documentation, or packaging of any type or nature;

(ii) that is identical with, or substantially indistinguishable from, a mark registered on the principal register in the United States Patent and Trademark Office and in use, whether or not the defendant knew such mark was so registered;

(iii) that is applied to or used in connection with the goods or services for which the mark is registered with the United States Patent and Trademark Office, or is applied to or consists of a label, patch, sticker, wrapper, badge, emblem, medallion, charm, box, container, can, case, hangtag, documentation, or packaging of any type or nature that is designed, marketed, or otherwise intended to be used on or in connection with the goods or services for which the mark is registered in the United States Patent and Trademark Office; and

(iv) the use of which is likely to cause confusion, to cause mistake, or to deceive; or

(B) a spurious designation that is identical with, or substantially indistinguishable from, a designation as to which the remedies of the Lanham Act are made available by reason of section 220506 of title 36; but such term does not include any mark or designation used in connection with goods or services, or a mark or designation applied to labels, patches, stickers, wrappers, badges, emblems, medallions, charms, boxes, containers, cans, cases, hangtags, documentation, or packaging of any type or nature used in connection with such goods or services, of which the manufacturer or producer was, at the time of the manufacture or production in question, authorized to use the mark or designation for the type of goods or services so manufactured or produced, by the holder of the right to use such mark or designation;

(2)   the term "financial gain" includes the receipt, or expected receipt, of anything of value;

(3)   the term "Lanham Act" means the Act entitled "An Act to provide for the registration and protection of trademarks used in commerce, to carry out the provisions of certain international conventions, and for other purposes", approved July 5, 1946 (15 U.S.C. 1051 et seq.);

(4)   the term "counterfeit military good or service" means a good or service that uses a counterfeit mark on or in connection with such good or service and that—

(A)   is falsely identified or labeled as meeting military specifications, or

(B)   is intended for use in a military or national security application; and

(5)   the term "traffic" means to transport, transfer, or otherwise dispose of, to another, for purposes of commercial advantage or private financial gain, or to make, import, export, obtain control of, or possess, with intent to so transport, transfer, or otherwise dispose of; and

(6)   the term "drug" means a drug, as defined in section 201 of the Federal Food, Drug, and Cosmetic Act (21 U.S.C. 321).

(g)   Limitation on cause of action.—Nothing in this section shall entitle the United States to bring a criminal cause of action under this section for the repackaging of genuine goods or services not intended to deceive or confuse.

(h)   Report to Congress.—(1) Beginning with the first year after the date of enactment of this subsection, the Attorney General shall include in the report of the Attorney General to Congress on the business of the Department of Justice prepared pursuant to section 522 of title 28, an accounting, on a district by district basis, of the following with respect to all actions taken by the Department of Justice that involve trafficking in counterfeit labels for phonorecords, copies of computer programs or computer program documentation or packaging, copies of motion pictures or other audiovisual works (as defined in section 2318 of this title), criminal infringement of copyrights (as defined in section 2319 of this title), unauthorized fixation of and trafficking in sound recordings and music videos of live musical performances (as defined in section 2319A of this title), or trafficking in goods or services bearing counterfeit marks (as defined in section 2320 of this title):

(A)   The number of open investigations.

(B)   The number of cases referred by the United States Customs Service.

(C)   The number of cases referred by other agencies or sources.

(D)   The number and outcome, including settlements, sentences, recoveries, and penalties, of all prosecutions brought under sections 2318, 2319, 2319A, and 2320 of title 18.

(2)(A)   The report under paragraph (1), with respect to criminal infringement of copyright, shall include the following:

(i)   The number of infringement cases in these categories: audiovisual (videos and films); audio (sound recordings); literary works (books and musical compositions); computer programs; video games; and, others.

(ii)   The number of online infringement cases.

(iii)   The number and dollar amounts of fines assessed in specific categories of dollar amounts. These categories shall be: no fines ordered; fines under $500; fines from $500 to $1,000; fines from $1,000 to $5,000; fines from $5,000 to $10,000; and fines over $10,000.

(iv) The total amount of restitution ordered in all copyright infringement cases.

(B) In this paragraph, the term "online infringement cases" as used in paragraph (2) means those cases where the infringer—

(i) advertised or publicized the infringing work on the Internet; or

(ii) made the infringing work available on the Internet for download, reproduction, performance, or distribution by other persons.

(C) The information required under subparagraph (A) shall be submitted in the report required in fiscal year 2005 and thereafter.

(i) **Transshipment and exportation.**—No goods or services, the trafficking in of which is prohibited by this section, shall be transshipped through or exported from the United States. Any such transshipment or exportation shall be deemed a violation of section 42 of an Act to provide for the registration of trademarks used in commerce, to carry out the provisions of certain international conventions, and for other purposes, approved July 5, 1946 (commonly referred to as the "Trademark Act of 1946" or the "Lanham Act").

C. MODEL STATE TRADEMARK BILL*

AN ACT TO PROVIDE FOR THE REGISTRATION AND PROTECTION OF TRADEMARKS

SECTION 1. DEFINITIONS.

(a) The term "trademark" as used herein means any word, name, symbol, or device or any combination thereof used by a person to identify and distinguish the goods of such person, including a unique product, from those manufactured or sold by others, and to indicate the source of the goods, even if that source is unknown.

(b) The term "service mark" as used herein means any word, name, symbol, or device or any combination thereof used by a person, to identify and distinguish the services of one person, including a unique service, from the services of others, and to indicate the source of the services, even if that source is unknown. Titles, character names used by a person, and other distinctive features of radio or television programs may be registered as service marks notwithstanding that they, or the programs, may advertise the goods of the sponsor.

(c) The term "mark" as used herein includes any trademark or service mark, entitled to registration under this Act whether registered or not.

(d) The term "trade name" means any name used by a person to identify a business or vocation of such person.

(e) The term "person" and any other word or term used to designate the applicant or other party entitled to a benefit or privilege or rendered liable under the provisions of this Act includes a juristic person as well as a natural person. The term "juristic person" includes a firm, partnership, corporation, union, association, or other organization capable of suing and being sued in a court of law.

(f) The term "applicant" as used herein embraces the person filing an application for registration of a mark under this Act, and the legal representatives, successors, or assigns of such person.

(g) The term "registrant" as used herein embraces the person to whom the registration of a mark under this Act is issued, and the legal representatives, successors, or assigns of such person.

(h) The term "use" means the bona fide use of a mark in the ordinary course of trade, and not made merely to reserve a right in a mark. For the purposes of this Act, a mark shall be deemed to be in use

(1) on goods when it is placed in any manner on the goods or other containers or the displays associated therewith or on the tags or labels affixed thereto, or if the nature of the goods makes such placement impracticable, then on documents associated with the goods or their sale, and the goods are sold or transported in commerce in this state, and

(2) on services when it is used or displayed in the sale or advertising of services and the services are rendered in this state.

(i) A mark shall be deemed to be "abandoned" when either of the following occurs:

(1) When its use has been discontinued with intent not to resume such use. Intent not to resume may be inferred from circumstances. Nonuse for two consecutive years shall constitute prima facie evidence of abandonment; or

(2) When any course of conduct of the owner, including acts of omission as well as commission, causes the mark to lose its significance as a mark.

---

*   Promulgated by the International Trademark Association (INTA) in 1949. As revised in 1992, 1996, and 2007.— *Ed.*

(j) The term "Secretary" as used herein means the secretary of the state or the designee of the secretary charged with the administration of this Act.

(k) The term "dilution" as used herein means dilution by blurring or dilution by tarnishment, regardless of the presence or absence of

(1) competition between the owner of the famous mark and other parties, or

(2) actual or likely confusion, mistake, or deception, or

(3) actual economic injury.

(l) The term "dilution by blurring" as used herein means association arising from the similarity between a mark or trade name and a famous mark that impairs the distinctiveness of the famous mark.

(m) The term "dilution by tarnishment" as used herein means association arising from the similarity between a mark or trade name and a famous mark that harms the reputation of the famous mark.

SECTION 2.   REGISTRABILITY.

A mark by which the goods or services of any applicant for registration may be distinguished from the goods or services of others shall not be registered if it

(a) consists of or comprises immoral, deceptive or scandalous matter; or

(b) consists of or comprises matter which may disparage or falsely suggest a connection with persons, living or dead, institutions, beliefs, or national symbols, or bring them into contempt, or disrepute; or

(c) consists of or comprises the flag or coat of arms or other insignia of the United States, or of any state or municipality, or of any foreign nation, or any simulation thereof; or

(d) consists of or comprises the name, signature or portrait identifying a particular living individual, except by the individual's written consent; or

(e) consists of a mark which,

(1) when used on or in connection with the goods or services of the applicant, is merely descriptive or deceptively misdescriptive of them, or

(2) when used on or in connection with the goods or services of the applicant is primarily geographically descriptive or deceptively misdescriptive of them, or

(3) is primarily merely a surname;

provided, however, that nothing in this subsection (e) shall prevent the registration of a mark used by the applicant which has become distinctive of the applicant's goods or services. The Secretary may accept as evidence that the mark has become distinctive, as used on or in connection with the applicant's goods or services, proof of continuous use thereof as a mark by the applicant in this state for the five years before the date on which the claim of distinctiveness is made; or

(f) consists of or comprises a mark which so resembles a mark registered in this state or a mark or trade name previously used by another and not abandoned, as to be likely, when used on or in connection with the goods or services of the applicant, to cause confusion or mistake or to deceive.

SECTION 3.   APPLICATION FOR REGISTRATION.

(a) Subject to the limitations set forth in this Act, any person who uses a mark may file in the office of the Secretary, in a manner complying with the requirements of the Secretary, an application for registration of that mark setting forth, but not limited to, the following information:

(1)   the name and business address of the person applying for such registration; and, if a corporation, the state of incorporation, or if a partnership, the state in which the partnership is organized and the names of the general partners, as specified by the Secretary,

(2)   the goods or services on or in connection with which the mark is used and the mode or manner in which the mark is used on or in connection with such goods or services and the class in which such goods or services fall,

(3)   the date when the mark was first used anywhere and the date when it was first used in this state by the applicant or a predecessor in interest, and

(4)   a statement that the applicant is the owner of the mark, that the mark is in use, and that, to the knowledge of the person verifying the application, no other person has registered, either federally or in this state, or has the right to use such mark either in the identical form thereof or in such near resemblance thereto as to be likely, when applied to the goods or services of such other person, to cause confusion, or to cause mistake, or to deceive.

(b)   The Secretary may also require a statement as to whether an application to register the mark, or portions or a composite thereof, has been filed by the applicant or a predecessor in interest in the United States Patent and Trademark Office; and, if so, the applicant shall provide full particulars with respect thereto including the filing date and serial number of each application, the status thereof and, if any application was finally refused registration or has otherwise not resulted in a registration, the reasons therefore.

(c)   The Secretary may also require that a drawing of the mark, complying with such requirements as the Secretary may specify, accompany the application.

(d)   The application shall be signed and verified (by oath, affirmation or declaration subject to perjury laws) by the applicant or by a member of the firm or an officer of the corporation or association applying.

(e)   The application shall be accompanied by three specimens showing the mark as actually used.

(f)   The application shall be accompanied by the application fee payable to the Secretary of state.

SECTION 4.   FILING OF APPLICATIONS.

(a)   Upon the filing of an application for registration and payment of the application fee, the Secretary may cause the application to be examined for conformity with this Act.

(b)   The applicant shall provide any additional pertinent information requested by the Secretary including a description of a design mark and may make, or authorize the Secretary to make, such amendments to the application as may be reasonably requested by the Secretary or deemed by applicant to be advisable to respond to any rejection or objection.

(c)   The Secretary may require the applicant to disclaim an unregisterable component of a mark otherwise registerable, and an applicant may voluntarily disclaim a component of a mark sought to be registered. No disclaimer shall prejudice or affect the applicant's or registrant's rights then existing or thereafter arising in the disclaimed matter, or the applicant's or registrant's rights of registration on another application if the disclaimed matter be or shall have become distinctive of the applicant's or registrant's goods or services.

(d)   Amendments may be made by the Secretary upon the application submitted by the applicant upon applicant's agreement; or a fresh application may be required to be submitted.

(e)   If the applicant is found not to be entitled to registration, the Secretary shall advise the applicant thereof and of the reasons therefor. The applicant shall have a reasonable period of time specified by the Secretary in which to reply or to amend the application, in which event the application shall then be reexamined. This procedure may be repeated until

(1)   the Secretary finally refuses registration of the mark; or

(2) the applicant fails to reply or amend within the specified period, whereupon the application shall be deemed to have been abandoned.

(f) If the Secretary finally refuses registration of the mark, the applicant may seek a writ of mandamus to compel such registration. Such writ may be granted, but without costs to the Secretary, on proof that all the statements in the application are true and that the mark is otherwise entitled to registration.

(g) In the instance of applications concurrently being processed by the Secretary seeking registration of the same or confusingly similar marks for the same or related goods or services, the Secretary shall grant priority to the applications in order of filing. If a prior-filed application is granted a registration, the other application or applications shall then be rejected. Any rejected applicant may bring an action for cancellation of the registration upon grounds of prior or superior rights to the mark, in accordance with the provisions of Section 9 of this Act.

SECTION 5.   CERTIFICATE OF REGISTRATION.

(a) Upon compliance by the applicant with the requirements of this Act, the Secretary shall cause a certificate of registration to be issued and delivered to the applicant. The certificate of registration shall be issued under the signature of the Secretary and the seal of the state, and it shall show the name and business address and, if a corporation, the state of incorporation, or if a partnership, the state in which the partnership is organized and the names of the general partners, as specified by the Secretary, of the person claiming ownership of the mark, the date claimed for the first use of the mark anywhere and the date claimed for the first use of the mark in this state, the class of goods or services and a description of the goods or services on or in connection with which the mark is used, a reproduction of the mark, the registration date and the term of the registration.

(b) Any certificate of registration issued by the Secretary under the provisions hereof or a copy thereof duly certified by the Secretary shall be admissible in evidence as competent and sufficient proof of the registration of such mark in any actions or judicial proceedings in any court of this state.

SECTION 6.   DURATION AND RENEWAL.

(a) A registration of mark hereunder shall be effective for a term of five years from the date of registration and, upon application filed within six months prior to the expiration of such term, in a manner complying with the requirements of the Secretary, the registration may be renewed for a like term from the end of the expiring term. A renewal fee, payable to the Secretary, shall accompany the application for renewal of the registration.

(b) A registration may be renewed for successive periods of five years in like manner.

(c) Any registration in force on the date on which this Act shall become effective shall continue in full force and effect for the unexpired term thereof and may be renewed by filing an application for renewal with the Secretary complying with the requirements of the Secretary and paying the aforementioned renewal fee therefor within six months prior to the expiration of the registration.

(d) All applications for renewal under this Act, whether of registrations made under this Act or of registrations effected under any prior act, shall include a verified statement that the mark has been and is still in use and include a specimen showing actual use of the mark on or in connection with the goods or services.

SECTION 7.   ASSIGNMENTS, CHANGES OF NAME AND OTHER INSTRUMENTS.

(a) Any mark and its registration hereunder shall be assignable with the good will of the business in which the mark is used, or with that part of the good will of the business connected with the use of and symbolized by the mark. Assignment shall be by instruments in writing duly executed and may be recorded with the Secretary upon the payment of the recording fee payable to the Secretary who, upon recording of the assignment, shall issue in the name of the assignee a new certificate for the remainder of the term of the registration or of the last renewal thereof. An assignment of any registration under this Act shall be void as against any subsequent purchaser for valuable consideration without notice, unless it is recorded with the Secretary within three months after the date thereof or prior to such subsequent purchase.

(b) Any registrant or applicant effecting a change of the name of the person to whom the mark was issued or for whom an application was filed may record a certificate of change of name of the registrant or applicant with the Secretary upon the payment of the recording fee. The Secretary may issue in the name of the assignee a certificate of registration of an assigned application. The Secretary may issue in the name of the assignee, a new certificate or registration for the remainder of the term of the registration or last renewal thereof.

(c) Other instruments which relate to a mark registered or application pending pursuant to this Act, such as, by way of example, licenses, security interests or mortgages, may be recorded in the discretion of the Secretary, provided that such instrument is in writing and duly executed.

(d) Acknowledgement shall be prima facie evidence of the execution of an assignment or other instrument and, when recorded by the Secretary, the record shall be prima facie evidence of execution.

(e) A photocopy of any instrument referred to in subsections (a), (b) or (c), above, shall be accepted for recording if it is certified by any of the parties thereto, or their successors, to be a true and correct copy of the original.

SECTION 8.   RECORDS.

The Secretary shall keep for public examination a record of all marks registered or renewed under this Act, as well as a record of all documents recorded pursuant to Section 7.

SECTION 9.   CANCELLATION.

The Secretary shall cancel from the register, in whole or in part:

(a) any registration concerning which the Secretary shall receive a voluntary request for cancellation thereof from the registrant or the assignee of record;

(b) all registrations granted under this Act and not renewed in accordance with the provisions hereof;

(c) any registration concerning which a court of competent jurisdiction shall find

(1) that the registered mark has been abandoned,

(2) that the registrant is not the owner of the mark,

(3) that the registration was granted improperly,

(4) that the registration was obtained fraudulently,

(5) that the mark is or has become the generic name for the goods or services, or a portion thereof, for which it has been registered,

(6) that the registered mark is so similar, as to be likely to cause confusion or mistake or to deceive, to a mark registered by another person in the United States Patent and Trademark Office prior to the date of the filing of the application for registration by the registrant hereunder, and not abandoned; provided, however, that, should the registrant prove that the registrant is the owner of a concurrent registration of a mark in the United States Patent and Trademark Office covering an area including this state, the registration hereunder shall not be cancelled for such area of the state; or

(d) when a court of competent jurisdiction shall order cancellation of a registration on any ground.

SECTION 10.   CLASSIFICATION.

The Secretary shall by regulation establish a classification of goods and services for convenience of administration of this Act, but not to limit or extend the applicant's or registrant's rights, and a single application for registration of a mark may include any or all goods upon which, or services with which, the mark is actually being used indicating the appropriate class or classes of goods or services. When a single application includes goods or services which fall within multiple classes, the Secretary may require payment of a fee for each class. To the extent practical, the classification of goods and services should conform to the classification adopted by the United States Patent and Trademark Office.

SECTION 11.   FRAUDULENT REGISTRATION.

Any person who shall for himself or herself, or on behalf of any other person, procure the filing or registration of any mark in the office of the Secretary under the provisions hereof, by knowingly making any false or fraudulent representation or declaration, orally or in writing, or by any other fraudulent means, shall be liable to pay all damages sustained in consequence of such filing or registration, to be recovered by or on behalf of the party injured thereby in any court of competent jurisdiction.

SECTION 12.   INFRINGEMENT.

Subject to the provisions of Section 16 hereof, any person who shall

(a)   use, without the consent of the registrant, any reproduction, counterfeit, copy, or colorable imitation of a mark registered under this Act in connection with the sale, distribution, offering for sale, or advertising of any goods or services on or in connection with which such use is likely to cause confusion or mistake or to deceive as to the source of origin of such goods or services; or

(b)   reproduce, counterfeit, copy or colorably imitate any such mark and apply such reproduction, counterfeit, copy or colorable imitation to labels, signs, prints, packages, wrappers, receptacles, or advertisements intended to be used upon or in connection with the sale or other distribution in this state of such goods or services;

shall be liable in a civil action by the registrant for any and all of the remedies provided in Section 14 hereof, except that under subsection (b) hereof the registrant shall not be entitled to recover profits or damages unless the acts have been committed with the intent to cause confusion or mistake or to deceive.

SECTION 13.   INJURY TO BUSINESS REPUTATION; DILUTION.

(a)   Subject to the principles of equity, the owner of a mark which is famous and distinctive, inherently or through acquired distinctiveness, in this state shall be entitled to an injunction against another person's commercial use of a mark or trade name, if such use begins after the mark has become famous and is likely to cause dilution of the famous mark, and to obtain such other relief as is provided in this section.

(b)   A mark is famous if it is widely recognized by the general consuming public of this State or a geographic area in this State as a designation of source of the goods or services of the mark's owner. In determining whether a mark is famous, a court may consider factors such as, but not limited to:

(1)   The duration, extent, and geographic reach of advertising and publicity of the mark in this state, whether advertised or publicized by the owner or third parties;

(2)   The amount, volume, and geographic extent of sales of goods or services offered under the mark in this state;

(3)   The extent of actual recognition of the mark in this state; and

(4)   Whether the mark is the subject of a state registration in this state, or a federal registration under the Act of March 3, 1881, or under the Act of February 20, 1905, or on the principal register under the Trademark Act of 1946, as amended.

(c)   In an action brought under this section, the owner of a famous mark shall be entitled to injunctive relief throughout the geographic area in which the mark is found to have become famous prior to commencement of the junior use, but not beyond the borders of this state. If the person against whom the injunctive relief is sought willfully intended to cause dilution of the famous mark, then the owner shall also be entitled to the remedies set forth in this chapter, subject to the discretion of the court and the principles of equity.

(d)   The following shall not be actionable under this section:

(1)   Any fair use, including a nominative or descriptive fair use, or facilitation of such fair use, of a famous mark by another person other than as a designation of source for the person's own goods or services, including use in connection with

(A)   Advertising or promotion that permits consumers to compare goods or services; or

(B)   Identifying and parodying, criticizing, or commenting upon the famous mark owner or the goods or services of the famous mark owner;

(2)   Noncommercial use of the mark; and

(3)   All forms of news reporting and news commentary.

SECTION 14.   REMEDIES.

(a)   Any owner of a mark registered under this Act may proceed by suit to enjoin the manufacture, use, display or sale of any counterfeits or imitations thereof and any court of competent jurisdiction may grant injunctions to restrain such manufacture, use, display or sale as may be by the said court deemed just and reasonable, and may require the defendants to pay to such owner all profits derived from and/or all damages suffered by reason of such wrongful manufacture, use, display or sale; and such court may also order that any such counterfeits or imitations in the possession or under the control of any defendant in such case be delivered to an officer of the court, or to the complainant, to be destroyed. The court, in its discretion, may enter judgment for an amount not to exceed three times such profits and damages and/or reasonable attorneys' fees of the prevailing party in such cases where the court finds the other party committed such wrongful acts with knowledge or in bad faith or otherwise as according to the circumstances of the case.

(b)   The enumeration of any right or remedy herein shall not affect a registrant's right to prosecute under any penal law of this state.

SECTION 15.   FORUM FOR ACTIONS REGARDING REGISTRATION; SERVICE ON OUT OF STATE REGISTRANTS.

(a)   Actions to require cancellation of a mark registered pursuant to this Act or in mandamus to compel registration of a mark pursuant to this Act shall be brought in the [name of court]. In an action in mandamus, the proceeding shall be based solely upon the record before the Secretary. In an action for cancellation, the Secretary shall not be made a party to the proceeding but shall be notified of the filing of the complaint by the clerk of the court in which it is filed and shall be given the right to intervene in the action.

(b)   In any action brought against a non-resident registrant, service may be effected upon the Secretary as agent for service of the registrant in accordance with the procedures established for service upon non-resident corporations and business entities under sections < > of the <general statutes>.

SECTION 16.   COMMON LAW RIGHTS.

Nothing herein shall adversely affect the rights or the enforcement of rights in marks acquired in good faith at any time at common law.

SECTION 17.   FEES.

The Secretary shall by regulation prescribe the fees payable for the various applications and recording fees and for related services. Unless specified by the Secretary, the fees payable herein are not refundable.

SECTION 18.   SEVERABILITY.

If any provision hereof, or the application of such provision to any person or circumstance is held invalid, the remainder of this Act shall not be affected thereby.

SECTION 19.   TIME OF TAKING EFFECT—REPEAL OF PRIOR ACTS; INTENT OF ACT.

(a)   This Act shall be in force and take effect after its enactment but shall not affect any suit, proceeding or appeal then pending. All acts relating to marks and parts of any other acts inconsistent herewith are hereby repealed on the effective date of this Act, provided that as to any application, suit, proceeding or appeal, and for that purpose only, pending at the time this Act takes effect such repeal shall be deemed not to be effective until final determination of said pending application, suit, proceeding or appeal.

(b)   The intent of this Act is to provide a system of state trademark registration and protection substantially consistent with the federal system of trademark registration and protection under the Trademark Act of 1946, as amended. To that end, the construction given the federal Act should be examined as persuasive authority for interpreting and construing the Act.

D. REGULATIONS RELATING TO IMPORTATIONS BEARING REGISTERED AND/OR RECORDED TRADEMARKS OR RECORDED TRADE NAMES

19 CFR §§ 133.1–133.2, 133.21–133.27

§ 133.1   Recordation of Trademarks

(a)   Eligible trademarks. Trademarks registered by the U.S. Patent and Trademark Office under the Trademark Act of March 3, 1881, the Trademark Act of February 20, 1905, or the Trademark Act of 1946 (15 U.S.C. 1051 et seq.) except those registered on the supplemental register under the 1946 Act (15 U.S.C. 1096), may be recorded with the U.S. Customs and Border Protection if the registration is current.

(b)   Notice of recordation and other action. Applicants and recordants will be notified of the approval or denial of an application filed in accordance with §§ 133.2, 133.5, 133.6, and 133.7 of this subpart.

§ 133.2   Application to Record Trademark

An application to record one or more trademarks shall be in writing, addressed to the Intellectual Property Rights (IPR) & Restricted Merchandise Branch, U.S. Customs and Border Protection, 1300 Pennsylvania Avenue, NW., Washington, DC 20229, and shall include the following information:

(a)   The name, complete business address, and citizenship of the trademark owner or owners (if a partnership, the citizenship of each partner; if an association or corporation the State, country, or other political jurisdiction within which it was organized, incorporated, or created);

(b)   The places of manufacture of goods bearing the recorded trademark;

(c)   The name and principal business address of each foreign person or business entity authorized or licensed to use the trademark and a statement as to the use authorized; and

(d)   The identity of any parent or subsidiary company or other foreign company under common ownership or control which uses the trademark abroad. For this purpose:

(1)   Common ownership means individual or aggregate ownership of more than 50 percent of the business entity; and

(2)   Common control means effective control in policy and operations and is not necessarily synonymous with common ownership.

(e)   *Lever-rule protection.* For owners of U.S. trademarks who desire protection against gray market articles on the basis of physical and material differences (see *Lever Bros. Co. v. United States*, 981 F.2d 1330 (D.C. Cir. 1993)), a description of any physical and material difference between the specific articles authorized for importation or sale in the United States and those not so authorized. In each instance, owners who assert that physical and material differences exist must state the basis for such a claim with particularity, and must support such assertions by competent evidence and provide summaries of physical and material differences for publication. CBP determination of physical and material differences may include, but is not limited to, considerations of:

(1)   The specific composition of both the authorized and gray market product(s) (including chemical composition);

(2)   Formulation, product construction, structure, or composite product components, of both the authorized and gray market product;

(3)   Performance and/or operational characteristics of both the authorized and gray market product;

(4)   Differences resulting from legal or regulatory requirements, certification, etc.;

(5)   Other distinguishing and explicitly defined factors that would likely result in consumer deception or confusion as proscribed under applicable law.

(f)   CBP will publish in the Customs Bulletin a notice listing any trademark(s) and the specific products for which gray market protection for physically and materially different products has been requested. CBP will examine the request(s) before issuing a determination whether gray market protection is granted. For parties requesting protection, the application for trademark protection will not take effect until CBP has made and issued this determination. If protection is granted, CBP will publish in the Customs Bulletin a notice that a trademark will receive Lever-rule protection with regard to a specific product.

§ 133.21 Articles Suspected of Bearing Counterfeit Marks

(a)   *Counterfeit mark defined.* A "counterfeit mark" is a spurious mark that is identical with, or substantially indistinguishable from, a mark registered on the Principal Register of the U.S. Patent and Trademark Office.

(b)   *Detention, notice, and disclosure of information—*

(1)   *Detention period.* CBP may detain any article of domestic or foreign manufacture imported into the United States that bears a mark suspected by CBP of being a counterfeit version of a mark that is registered with the U.S. Patent and Trademark Office and is recorded with CBP pursuant to subpart A of this part. The detention will be for a period of up to 30 days from the date on which the merchandise is presented for examination. In accordance with 19 U.S.C. § 1499(c), if, after the detention period, the article is not released, the article will be deemed excluded for the purposes of 19 U.S.C. § 1514(a)(4).

(2)   *Notice of detention to importer and disclosure to owner of the mark—*

(i)   *Notice and seven business day response period.* Within five business days from the date of a decision to detain suspect merchandise, CBP will notify the importer in writing of the detention as set forth in § 151.16(c) of this chapter and 19 U.S.C. § 1499. CBP will also inform the importer that for purposes of assisting CBP in determining whether the detained merchandise bears counterfeit marks:

(A)   CBP may have previously disclosed to the owner of the mark, prior to issuance of the notice of detention, limited importation information concerning the detained merchandise, as described in paragraph (b)(4) of this section, and, in any event, such information will be released to the owner of the mark, if available, no later than the date of issuance of the notice of detention; and

(B)   CBP may disclose to the owner of the mark information that appears on the detained merchandise and/or its retail packaging, including unredacted photographs, images, or samples, as described in paragraph (b)(3) of this section, unless the importer presents information within seven business days of the notification establishing that the detained merchandise does not bear a counterfeit mark.

(ii)   *Failure of importer to respond or insufficient response to notice.* Where the importer does not provide information within the seven business day response period, or the information provided is insufficient for CBP to determine that the merchandise does not bear a counterfeit mark, CBP may proceed with the disclosure of information described in paragraph (b)(3) of this section to the owner of the mark and will so notify the importer.

(3) *Disclosure to owner of the mark of information appearing on detained merchandise and/or its retail packaging, including unredacted photographs, images or samples.* When making a disclosure to the owner of the mark under paragraph (b)(2)(ii) of this section, CBP may disclose information appearing on the merchandise and/or its retail packaging (including labels), images (including photographs) of the merchandise and/or its retail packaging in its condition as presented for examination (i.e., an unredacted condition), or a sample of the merchandise and/or its retail packaging in its condition as presented for examination. The release of a sample will be in accordance with, and subject to, the bond and return requirements of paragraph (c) of this section. The disclosure may include any serial numbers, dates of manufacture, lot codes, batch numbers, universal product codes, or other identifying marks appearing on the merchandise or its retail packaging (including labels), in alphanumeric or other formats.

(4) *Disclosure to owner of the mark of limited importation information.* From the time merchandise is presented for examination, CBP may disclose to the owner of the mark limited importation information in order to obtain assistance in determining whether an imported article bears a counterfeit mark. Where CBP does not disclose this information to the owner of the mark prior to issuance of the notice of detention, it will do so concurrently with the issuance of the notice of detention, unless the information is unavailable, in which case CBP will release the information as soon as possible after issuance of the notice of detention. The limited importation information CBP will disclose to the owner of the mark consists of:

(i) The date of importation;

(ii) The port of entry;

(iii) The description of the merchandise, for merchandise not yet detained, from the paper or electronic equivalent of the entry (as defined in § 142.3(a)(1) or (b) of this chapter), the CBP Form 7512, cargo manifest, advance electronic information or other entry document as appropriate, or, for detained merchandise, from the notice of detention;

(iv) The quantity, for merchandise not yet detained, as declared on the paper or electronic equivalent of the entry (as defined in § 142.3(a)(1) or (b) of this chapter), the CBP Form 7512, cargo manifest, advance electronic information, or other entry document as appropriate, or, for detained merchandise, from the notice of detention; and

(v) The country of origin of the merchandise.

(5) *Disclosure to owner of the mark of redacted photographs, images and samples.* Notwithstanding the notice and seven business day response procedure of paragraph (b)(2) of this section, CBP may, in order to obtain assistance in determining whether an imported article bears a counterfeit mark and at any time after presentation of the merchandise for examination, provide to the owner of the mark photographs, images, or a sample of the suspect merchandise or its retail packaging (including labels), provided that identifying information has been removed, obliterated, or otherwise obscured. Identifying information includes, but is not limited to, serial numbers, dates of manufacture, lot codes, batch numbers, universal product codes, the name or address of the manufacturer, exporter, or importer of the merchandise, or any mark that could reveal the name or address of the manufacturer, exporter, or importer of the merchandise, in alphanumeric or other formats. CBP may release to the owner of the mark a sample under this paragraph when the owner furnishes to CBP a bond in the form and amount specified by CBP, conditioned to indemnify the importer or owner of the imported article against any loss or damage resulting from the furnishing of the sample by CBP to the owner of the mark. CBP may demand the return of the sample at any time. The owner of the mark must return the sample to CBP upon demand or at the conclusion of any examination, testing, or similar procedure performed on the sample. In the event that the sample is damaged, destroyed, or lost while in the possession of the owner of the mark, the owner must, in lieu of return of the sample, certify to CBP that: "The sample described as [insert description] and provided pursuant to 19 CFR 133.21(b)(5) was (damaged/destroyed/lost) during examination, testing, or other use."

(c) *Conditions of disclosure to owner of the mark of information appearing on detained merchandise and / or its retail packaging, including unredacted photographs, images and samples—*

(1) *Disclosure for limited purpose of assisting CBP in counterfeit mark determinations.* In order to obtain assistance in determining whether an imported article bears a counterfeit mark, CBP may disclose to the owner of the mark, prior to seizure, information appearing on the merchandise and/or its retail packaging (including labels), unredacted photographs or images of the merchandise and/or its retail packaging in its condition as presented for examination, or an unredacted sample of the imported merchandise and/or its retail packaging in its condition as presented for examination, in accordance with paragraphs (b)(2)(ii) and (3) of this section. Upon release of such information, photographs, images, or samples, CBP will notify the owner of the mark that some or all of the information being released may be subject to the protections of the Trade Secrets Act, and that CBP is only disclosing the information to the owner of the mark for the purpose of assisting CBP in determining whether the merchandise bears a counterfeit mark.

(2) *Bond.* CBP may release to the owner of the mark a sample under paragraphs (b)(2)(ii) and (3) of this section when the owner furnishes to CBP a bond in the form and amount specified by CBP, conditioned to indemnify the importer or owner of the imported article against any loss or damage resulting from the furnishing of the sample by CBP to the owner of the mark. CBP may demand the return of the sample at any time. The owner of the mark must return the sample to CBP upon demand or at the conclusion of any examination, testing, or similar procedure performed on the sample. In the event that the sample is damaged, destroyed, or lost while in the possession of the owner of the mark, the owner must, in lieu of return of the sample, certify to CBP that: "The sample described as [insert description] and provided pursuant to 19 CFR § 133.21(c) was (damaged/destroyed/lost) during examination, testing, or other use."

(d) *Disclosure to importer of unredacted photographs, images, and samples.* CBP will disclose to the importer unredacted photographs, images, or an unredacted sample of imported merchandise suspected of bearing a counterfeit mark at any time after the merchandise is presented to CBP for examination. CBP may demand the return of the sample at any time. The importer must return the sample to CBP upon demand or at the conclusion of any examination, testing, or similar procedure performed on the sample. In the event that the sample is damaged, destroyed, or lost while in the possession of the importer, the importer must, in lieu of return of the sample, certify to CBP that: "The sample described as [insert description] and provided pursuant to 19 CFR § 133.21(d) was (damaged/destroyed/lost) during examination, testing, or other use."

(e) *Seizure and disclosure to owner of the mark of comprehensive importation information.* Upon a determination by CBP, made any time after the merchandise has been presented for examination, that an article of domestic or foreign manufacture imported into the United States bears a counterfeit mark, CBP will seize such merchandise and, in the absence of the written consent of the owner of the mark, forfeit the seized merchandise in accordance with the customs laws. When merchandise is seized under this section, CBP will disclose to the owner of the mark the following information, if available, within 30 business days from the date of the notice of seizure:

(1)　The date of importation;

(2)　The port of entry;

(3)　The description of the merchandise from the notice of seizure;

(4)　The quantity as set forth in the notice of seizure;

(5)　The country of origin of the merchandise;

(6)　The name and address of the manufacturer;

(7)　The name and address of the exporter; and

(8)　The name and address of the importer.

(f) *Disclosure to owner of the mark, following seizure, of unredacted photographs, images, and samples.* At any time following a seizure of merchandise bearing a counterfeit mark under this section, and upon receipt of a proper request from the owner of the mark, CBP may provide, if available, photographs, images, or a sample of the seized merchandise and its retail packaging, in its condition as presented for examination, to the owner of the mark. To obtain a sample under this paragraph, the owner of the mark must furnish to CBP a bond in the form and amount specified by CBP, conditioned to indemnify the importer or owner of the imported article against any loss or damage resulting from the furnishing of the sample by CBP to the owner of the mark. CBP may demand the return of the sample at any time. The owner of the mark must return the sample to CBP upon demand or at the conclusion of the examination, testing, or other use in pursuit of a related private civil remedy for infringement. In the event that the sample is damaged, destroyed, or lost while in the possession of the owner of the mark, the owner must, in lieu of return of the sample, certify to CBP that: "The sample described as [insert description] and provided pursuant to 19 CFR § 133.21(f) was (damaged/destroyed/lost) during examination, testing, or other use."

(g) *Consent of the mark owner; failure to make appropriate disposition.* The owner of the mark, within thirty days from notification of seizure, may provide written consent to the importer allowing the importation of the seized merchandise in its condition as imported or its exportation, entry after obliteration of the mark, or other appropriate disposition. Otherwise, the merchandise will be disposed of in accordance with § 133.52 of this part, subject to the importer's right to petition for relief from forfeiture under the provisions of part 171 of this chapter.

§ 133.22 Restrictions on Importation of Articles Bearing Copying or Simulating Trademarks

(a) *Copying or simulating trademark or trade name defined.* A "copying or simulating" trademark or trade name is one which may so resemble a recorded mark or name as to be likely to cause the public to associate the copying or simulating mark or name with the recorded mark or name.

(b) *Denial of entry.* Any articles of foreign or domestic manufacture imported into the United States bearing a mark or name copying or simulating a recorded mark or name shall be denied entry and subject to detention as provided in § 133.25.

(c) *Relief from detention of articles bearing copying or simulating trademarks.* Articles subject to the restrictions of this section shall be detained for 30 days from the date on which the goods are presented for Customs examination, to permit the importer to establish that any of the following circumstances are applicable:

(1) The objectionable mark is removed or obliterated as a condition to entry in such a manner as to be illegible and incapable of being reconstituted, for example by:

(i) Grinding off imprinted trademarks wherever they appear;

(ii) Removing and disposing of plates bearing a trademark or trade name;

(2) The merchandise is imported by the recordant of the trademark or trade name or his designate;

(3) The recordant gives written consent to an importation of articles otherwise subject to the restrictions set forth in paragraph (b) of this section or § 133.23(c) of this subpart, and such consent is furnished to appropriate Customs officials;

(4) The articles of foreign manufacture bear a recorded trademark and the one-item personal exemption is claimed and allowed under § 148.55 of this chapter.

(d) *Exceptions for articles bearing counterfeit trademarks.* The provisions of paragraph (c)(1) of this section are not applicable to articles bearing counterfeit trademarks at the time of importation (see § 133.26).

(e) *Release of detained articles.* Articles detained in accordance with § 133.25 may be released to the importer during the 30-day period of detention if any of the circumstances allowing exemption from trademark or trade name restriction set forth in paragraph (c) of this section are established.

(f) *Seizure.* If the importer has not obtained release of detained articles within the period of detention as provided in § 133.25 of this subpart, the merchandise shall be seized and forfeiture proceedings instituted. The importer shall be promptly notified of the seizure and liability to forfeiture and his right to petition for relief in accordance with the provisions of part 171 of this chapter.

§ 133.23 Restrictions on Importation of Gray Market Articles

(a) *Restricted gray market articles defined.* "Restricted gray market articles" are foreign-made articles bearing a genuine trademark or trade name identical with or substantially indistinguishable from one owned and recorded by a citizen of the United States or a corporation or association created or organized within the United States and imported without the authorization of the U.S. owner. "Restricted gray market goods" include goods bearing a genuine trademark or trade name which is:

(1) *Independent licensee.* Applied by a licensee (including a manufacturer) independent of the U.S. owner, or

(2) *Foreign owner.* Applied under the authority of a foreign trademark or trade name owner other than the U.S. owner, a parent or subsidiary of the U.S. owner, or a party otherwise subject to common ownership or control with the U.S. owner (see §§ 133.2(d) and 133.12(d) of this part), from whom the U.S. owner acquired the domestic title, or to whom the U.S. owner sold the foreign title(s); or

(3) *"Lever-rule".* Applied by the U.S. owner, a parent or subsidiary of the U.S. owner, or a party otherwise subject to common ownership or control with the U.S. owner (see §§ 133.2(d) and 133.12(d) of this part), to goods that the Customs Service has determined to be physically and materially different from the articles authorized by the U.S. trademark owner for importation or sale in the U.S. (as defined in § 133.2 of this part).

(b) *Labeling of physically and materially different goods.* Goods determined by the Customs Service to be physically and materially different under the procedures of this part, bearing a genuine mark applied under the authority of the U.S. owner, a parent or subsidiary of the U.S. owner, or a party otherwise subject to common ownership or control with the U.S. owner (see §§ 133.2(d) and 133.12(d) of this part), shall not be detained under the provisions of paragraph (c) of this section where the merchandise or its packaging bears a conspicuous and legible label designed to remain on the product until the first point of sale to a retail consumer in the United States stating that: "This product is not a product authorized by the United States trademark owner for importation and is physically and materially different from the authorized product." The label must be in close proximity to the trademark as it appears in its most prominent location on the article itself or the retail package or container. Other information designed to dispel consumer confusion may also be added.

(c) *Denial of entry.* All restricted gray market goods imported into the United States shall be denied entry and subject to detention as provided in § 133.25, except as provided in paragraph (b) of this section.

(d) *Relief from detention of gray market articles.* Gray market goods subject to the restrictions of this section shall be detained for 30 days from the date on which the goods are presented for Customs examination, to permit the importer to establish that any of the following exceptions, as well as the circumstances described above in § 133.22(c), are applicable:

(1) The trademark or trade name was applied under the authority of a foreign trademark or trade name owner who is the same as the U.S. owner, a parent or subsidiary of the U.S. owner, or a party otherwise subject to common ownership or control with the U.S. owner (in an instance covered by §§ 133.2(d) and 133.12(d) of this part); and/or

(2)   For goods bearing a genuine mark applied under the authority of the U.S. owner, a parent or subsidiary of the U.S. owner, or a party otherwise subject to common ownership or control with the U.S. owner, that the merchandise as imported is not physically and materially different, as described in § 133.2(e), from articles authorized by the U.S. owner for importation or sale in the United States; or

(3)   Where goods are detained for violation of § 133.23(a)(3), as physically and materially different from the articles authorized by the U.S. trademark owner for importation or sale in the U.S., a label in compliance with § 133.23(b) is applied to the goods.

(e)   *Release of detained articles.* Articles detained in accordance with § 133.25 may be released to the importer during the 30-day period of detention if any of the circumstances allowing exemption from trademark restriction set forth in § 133.22(c) of this subpart or in paragraph (d) of this section are established.

(f)   *Seizure.* If the importer has not obtained release of detained articles within the period of detention as provided in § 133.25 of this subpart, the merchandise shall be seized and forfeiture proceedings instituted. The importer shall be notified of the seizure and liability of forfeiture and his right to petition for relief in accordance with the provisions of part 171 of this chapter.

§ 133.24 Restrictions on Articles Accompanying Importer and Mail Importations

(a)   *Detention.* Articles accompanying an importer and mail importations subject to the restrictions of §§ 133.22 and 133.23 shall be detained for 30 days from the date of notice that such restrictions apply, to permit the establishment of whether any of the circumstances described in § 133.22(c) or 133.23(d) are applicable.

(b)   *Notice of detention.* Notice of detention shall be given in the following manner:

(1)   *Articles accompanying importer.* When the articles are carried as accompanying baggage or on the person of persons arriving in the United States, the Customs inspector shall orally advise the importer that the articles are subject to detention.

(2)   *Mail importations.* When the articles arrive by mail in noncommercial shipments, or in commercial shipments valued at $250 or less, notice of the detention shall be given on Customs Form 8.

(c)   *Release of detained articles.*

(1)   *General.* Articles detained in accordance with paragraph (a) of this section may be released to the importer during the 30-day period of detention if any of the circumstances allowing exemption from trademark or trade name restriction(s) set forth in § 133.22(c) or 133.23(d) of this subpart are established.

(2)   *Articles accompanying importer.* Articles arriving as accompanying baggage or on the person of the importer may be exported or destroyed under Customs supervision at the request of the importer, or may be released if:

(i)   The importer removes or obliterates the marks in a manner acceptable to the Customs officer at the time of examination of the articles; or

(ii)   The request of the importer to obtain skillful removal of the marks is granted by the port director under such conditions as he may deem necessary, and upon return of the article to Customs for verification, the marks are found to be satisfactorily removed.

(3)   *Mail importations.* Articles arriving by mail in noncommercial shipments, or in commercial shipments valued at $250 or less, may be exported or destroyed at the request of the addressee or may be released if:

(i)   The addressee appears in person at the appropriate Customs office and at that time removes or obliterates the marks in a manner acceptable to the Customs officer; or

(ii)   The request of the addressee appearing in person to obtain skillful removal of the marks is granted by the port director under such conditions as he may deem necessary, and upon return of the article to Customs for verification, the marks are found to be satisfactorily removed.

(d)   *Seizure.* If the importer has not obtained release of detained articles within the 30-day period of detention, the merchandise shall be seized and forfeiture proceedings instituted. The importer shall be promptly notified of the seizure and liability to forfeiture and his right to petition for relief in accordance with the provisions of part 171 of this chapter.

§ 133.25 Procedure on Detention of Articles Subject to Restriction

(a)   *In general.* Articles subject to the restrictions of §§ 133.22 and 133.23 shall be detained for 30 days from the date on which the merchandise is presented for Customs examination. The importer shall be notified of the decision to detain within 5 days of the decision that such restrictions apply. The importer may, during the 30-day period, establish that any of the circumstances described in § 133.22(c) or § 133.23(d) are applicable. Extensions of the 30-day time period may be freely granted for good cause shown.

(b)   *Notice of detention and disclosure of information.* From the time merchandise is presented for Customs examination until the time a notice of detention is issued, Customs may disclose to the owner of the trademark or trade name any of the following information in order to obtain assistance in determining whether an imported article bears an infringing trademark or trade name. Once a notice of detention is issued, Customs shall disclose to the owner of the trademark or trade name the following information, if available, within 30 days, excluding weekends and holidays, of the date of detention:

(1)   The date of importation;

(2)   The port of entry;

(3)   A description of the merchandise;

(4)   The quantity involved; and

(5)   The country of origin of the merchandise.

(c)   *Disclosure to the trademark or trade name owner.* At any time following presentation of the merchandise for CBP's examination, but prior to seizure, CBP may release a sample of the suspect merchandise to the owner of the trademark or trade name for examination or testing to assist in determining whether the article imported bears an infringing trademark or trade name. To obtain a sample under this paragraph, the owner of the mark must furnish to CBP a bond in the form and amount specified by CBP, conditioned to indemnify the importer or owner of the imported article against any loss or damage resulting from the furnishing of the sample by CBP to the owner of the mark. CBP may demand the return of the sample at any time. The owner must return the sample to CBP upon demand or at the conclusion of the examination or testing, whichever occurs sooner. In the event that the sample is damaged, destroyed, or lost while in the possession of the trademark or trade name owner, the owner must, in lieu of returning the sample, certify to CBP that: "The sample described as [insert description] and provided pursuant to 19 CFR 133.25(c) was (damaged/destroyed/lost) during examination or testing for trademark infringement."

(d)   *Form of notice.* Notice of detention of articles found subject to the restrictions of § 133.22 or § 133.23 shall be given the importer in writing.

§ 133.26 Demand for Redelivery of Released Merchandise

If it is determined that merchandise which has been released from CBP custody is subject to the restrictions of § 133.21, § 133.22 or § 133.23 of this subpart, an authorized CBP official shall promptly make demand for the redelivery of the merchandise under the terms of the bond on CBP Form 301, containing the bond conditions set forth in § 113.62 of this chapter, in accordance with § 141.113 of this chapter. If the merchandise is not redelivered to CBP custody, a claim for liquidated damages shall be made in accordance with § 141.113(h) of this chapter.

§ 133.27 Civil Fines for Those Involved in the Importation of Merchandise Bearing a Counterfeit Mark

In addition to any other penalty or remedy authorized by law, CBP may impose a civil fine under 19 U.S.C. § 1526(f) on any person who directs, assists financially or otherwise, or aids and abets the importation of merchandise for sale or public distribution that bears a counterfeit mark resulting in a seizure of the merchandise under 19 U.S.C. § 1526(e) (see § 133.21 of this subpart), as follows:

(a) First violation. For the first seizure of merchandise under this section, the fine imposed will not be more than the value the merchandise would have had if it were genuine, according to the manufacturer's suggested retail price in the United States at the time of seizure.

(b) Subsequent violations. For the second and each subsequent seizure under this section, the fine imposed will not be more than twice the value the merchandise would have had if it were genuine, according to the manufacturer's suggested retail price in the United States at the time of seizure.

E. PROTOCOL RELATING TO THE MADRID AGREEMENT CONCERNING THE INTERNATIONAL REGISTRATION OF MARKS*

(June 27, 1989)

(As amended at Geneva October 3, 2006 and November 12, 2007)

Contents

Article 1

MEMBERSHIP IN THE MADRID UNION

The States party to this Protocol (hereinafter referred to as "the Contracting States"), even where they are not party to the Madrid Agreement Concerning the International Registration of Marks as revised at Stockholm in 1967 and as amended in 1979 (hereinafter referred to as "the Madrid (Stockholm) Agreement"), and the organizations referred to in Article 14(1)(b) which are party to this

----

* This treaty was transmitted to the Senate on September 5, 2000. The Senate gave its advice and consent to the treaty on October 17, 2002. *See* Treaty No. 106–41.—*Ed.*

Protocol (hereinafter referred to as "the Contracting Organizations") shall be members of the same Union of which countries party to the Madrid (Stockholm) Agreement are members. Any reference in this Protocol to "Contracting Parties" shall be construed as a reference to both Contracting States and Contracting Organizations.

Article 2

SECURING PROTECTION THROUGH INTERNATIONAL REGISTRATION

(1) Where an application for the registration of a mark has been filed with the Office of a Contracting Party, or where a mark has been registered in the register of the Office of a Contracting Party, the person in whose name that application (hereinafter referred to as "the basic application") or that registration (hereinafter referred to as "the basic registration") stands may, subject to the provisions of this Protocol, secure protection for his mark in the territory of the Contracting Parties, by obtaining the registration of that mark in the register of the International Bureau of the World Intellectual Property Organization (hereinafter referred to as "the international registration," "the International Register," "the International Bureau" and "the Organization," respectively), provided that,

(i) where the basic application has been filed with the Office of a Contracting State or where the basic registration has been made by such an Office, the person in whose name that application or registration stands is a national of that Contracting State, or is domiciled, or has a real and effective industrial or commercial establishment, in the said Contracting State,

(ii) where the basic application has been filed with the Office of a Contracting Organization or where the basic registration has been made by such an Office, the person in whose name that application or registration stands is a national of a State member of that Contracting Organization, or is domiciled, or has a real and effective industrial or commercial establishment, in the territory of the said Contracting Organization.

(2) The application for international registration (hereinafter referred to as "the international application") shall be filed with the International Bureau through the intermediary of the Office with which the basic application was filed or by which the basic registration was made (hereinafter referred to as "the Office of origin"), as the case may be.

(3) Any reference in this Protocol to an "Office" or an "Office of a Contracting Party" shall be construed as a reference to the office that is in charge, on behalf of a Contracting Party, of the registration of marks, and any reference in this Protocol to "marks" shall be construed as a reference to trademarks and service marks.

(4) For the purposes of this Protocol, "territory of a Contracting Party" means, where the Contracting Party is a State, the territory of that State and, where the Contracting Party is an intergovernmental organization, the territory in which the constituting treaty of that intergovernmental organization applies.

Article 3

INTERNATIONAL APPLICATION

(1) Every international application under this Protocol shall be presented on the form prescribed by the Regulations. The Office of origin shall certify that the particulars appearing in the international application correspond to the particulars appearing, at the time of the certification, in the basic application or basic registration, as the case may be. Furthermore, the said Office shall indicate,

(i) in the case of a basic application, the date and number of that application,

(ii) in the case of a basic registration, the date and number of that registration as well as the date and number of the application from which the basic registration resulted.

The Office of origin shall also indicate the date of the international application.

(2)   The applicant must indicate the goods and services in respect of which protection of the mark is claimed and also, if possible, the corresponding class or classes according to the classification established by the Nice Agreement Concerning the International Classification of Goods and Services for the Purposes of the Registration of Marks. If the applicant does not give such indication, the International Bureau shall classify the goods and services in the appropriate classes of the said classification. The indication of classes given by the applicant shall be subject to control by the International Bureau, which shall exercise the said control in association with the Office of origin. In the event of disagreement between the said Office and the International Bureau, the opinion of the latter shall prevail.

(3)   If the applicant claims color as a distinctive feature of his mark, he shall be required

(i)   to state the fact, and to file with his international application a notice specifying the color or the combination of colors claimed;

(ii)   to append to his international application copies in color of the said mark, which shall be attached to the notifications given by the International Bureau; the number of such copies shall be fixed by the Regulations.

(4)   The International Bureau shall register immediately the marks filed in accordance with Article 2. The international registration shall bear the date on which the international application was received in the Office of origin, provided that the international application has been received by the International Bureau within a period of two months from that date. If the international application has not been received within that period, the international registration shall bear the date on which the said international application was received by the International Bureau. The International Bureau shall notify the international registration without delay to the Offices concerned. Marks registered in the International Register shall be published in a periodical gazette issued by the International Bureau, on the basis of the particulars contained in the international application.

(5)   With a view to the publicity to be given to marks registered in the International Register, each Office shall receive from the International Bureau a number of copies of the said gazette free of charge and a number of copies at a reduced price, under the conditions fixed by the Assembly referred to in Article 10 (hereinafter referred to as "the Assembly"). Such publicity shall be deemed to be sufficient for the purposes of all the Contracting Parties, and no other publicity may be required of the holder of the international registration.

Article 3*bis*

TERRITORIAL EFFECT

The protection resulting from the international registration shall extend to any Contracting Party only at the request of the person who files the international application or who is the holder of the international registration. However, no such request can be made with respect to the Contracting Party whose Office is the Office of origin.

Article 3*ter*

REQUEST FOR "TERRITORIAL EXTENSION"

(1)   Any request for extension of the protection resulting from the international registration to any Contracting Party shall be specially mentioned in the international application.

(2)   A request for territorial extension may also be made subsequently to the international registration. Any such request shall be presented on the form prescribed by the Regulations. It shall be immediately recorded by the International Bureau, which shall notify such recordal without delay to the Office or Offices concerned. Such recordal shall be published in the periodical gazette of the International Bureau. Such territorial extension shall be effective from the date on which it has been

recorded in the International Register; it shall cease to be valid on the expiry of the international registration to which it relates.

Article 4

EFFECTS OF INTERNATIONAL REGISTRATION

(1)(a) From the date of the registration or recordal effected in accordance with the provisions of Articles 3 and 3*ter,* the protection of the mark in each of the Contracting Parties concerned shall be the same as if the mark had been deposited direct with the Office of that Contracting Party. If no refusal has been notified to the International Bureau in accordance with Article 5(1) and (2) or if a refusal notified in accordance with the said Article has been withdrawn subsequently, the protection of the mark in the Contracting Party concerned shall, as from the said date, be the same as if the mark had been registered by the Office of that Contracting Party.

(b) The indication of classes of goods and services provided for in Article 3 shall not bind the Contracting Parties with regard to the determination of the scope of the protection of the mark.

(2) Every international registration shall enjoy the right of priority provided for by Article 4 of the Paris Convention for the Protection of Industrial Property, without it being necessary to comply with the formalities prescribed in Section D of that Article.

Article 4*bis*

REPLACEMENT OF A NATIONAL OR REGIONAL REGISTRATION BY AN INTERNATIONAL REGISTRATION

(1) Where a mark that is the subject of a national or regional registration in the Office of a Contracting Party is also the subject of an international registration and both registrations stand in the name of the same person, the international registration is deemed to replace the national or regional registration, without prejudice to any rights acquired by virtue of the latter, provided that

(i) the protection resulting from the international registration extends to the said Contracting Party under Article 3*ter*(1) or (2),

(ii) all the goods and services listed in the national or regional registration are also listed in the international registration in respect of the said Contracting Party,

(iii) such extension takes effect after the date of the national or regional registration.

(2) The Office referred to in paragraph (1) shall, upon request, be required to take note in its register of the international registration.

Article 5

REFUSAL AND INVALIDATION OF EFFECTS OF INTERNATIONAL REGISTRATION IN RESPECT OF CERTAIN CONTRACTING PARTIES

(1) Where the applicable legislation so authorizes, any Office of a Contracting Party which has been notified by the International Bureau of an extension to that Contracting Party, under Article 3*ter*(1) or (2), of the protection resulting from the international registration shall have the right to declare in a notification of refusal that protection cannot be granted in the said Contracting Party to the mark which is the subject of such extension. Any such refusal can be based only on the grounds which would apply, under the Paris Convention for the Protection of Industrial Property, in the case of a mark deposited direct with the Office which notifies the refusal. However, protection may not be refused, even partially, by reason only that the applicable legislation would permit registration only in a limited number of classes or for a limited number of goods or services.

(2)(a) Any Office wishing to exercise such right shall notify its refusal to the International Bureau, together with a statement of all grounds, within the period prescribed by the law applicable to that Office and at the latest, subject to subparagraphs (b) and (c), before the expiry of one year from the date on which the notification of the extension referred to in paragraph (1) has been sent to that Office by the International Bureau.

(b)   Notwithstanding subparagraph (a), any Contracting Party may declare that, for international registrations made under this Protocol, the time limit of one year referred to in subparagraph (a) is replaced by 18 months.

(c)   Such declaration may also specify that, when a refusal of protection may result from an opposition to the granting of protection, such refusal may be notified by the Office of the said Contracting Party to the International Bureau after the expiry of the 18-month time limit. Such an Office may, with respect to any given international registration, notify a refusal of protection after the expiry of the 18-month time limit, but only if

(i)   it has, before the expiry of the 18-month time limit, informed the International Bureau of the possibility that oppositions may be filed after the expiry of the 18-month time limit, and

(ii)   the notification of the refusal based on an opposition is made within a time limit of one month from the expiry of the opposition period and, in any case, not later than seven months from the date on which the opposition period begins.

(d)   Any declaration under subparagraph (b) or (c) may be made in the instruments referred to in Article 14(2), and the effective date of the declaration shall be the same as the date of entry into force of this Protocol with respect to the State or intergovernmental organization having made the declaration. Any such declaration may also be made later, in which case the declaration shall have effect three months after its receipt by the Director General of the Organization (hereinafter referred to as "the Director General"), or at any later date indicated in the declaration, in respect of any international registration whose date is the same as or is later than the effective date of the declaration.

(e)   Upon the expiry of a period of ten years from the entry into force of this Protocol, the Assembly shall examine the operation of the system established by subparagraphs (a) to (d). Thereafter, the provisions of the said subparagraphs may be modified by a unanimous decision of the Assembly.*

(3)   The International Bureau shall, without delay, transmit one of the copies of the notification of refusal to the holder of the international registration. The said holder shall have the same remedies as if the mark had been deposited by him direct with the Office which has notified its refusal. Where the International Bureau has received information under paragraph (2)(c)(i), it shall, without delay, transmit the said information to the holder of the international registration.

(4)   The grounds for refusing a mark shall be communicated by the International Bureau to any interested party who may so request.

(5)   Any Office which has not notified, with respect to a given international registration, any provisional or final refusal to the International Bureau in accordance with paragraphs (1) and (2) shall, with respect to that international registration, lose the benefit of the right provided for in paragraph (1).

(6)   Invalidation, by the competent authorities of a Contracting Party, of the effects, in the territory of that Contracting Party, of an international registration may not be pronounced without the holder of such international registration having, in good time, been afforded the opportunity of defending his rights. Invalidation shall be notified to the International Bureau.

---

*   Interpretive statement adopted by the Assembly of the Madrid Union:

"Article 5(2)(e) of the Protocol is understood as allowing the Assembly to keep under review the operation of the system established by subparagraphs (a) to (d), it being also understood that any modification of those provisions shall require a unanimous decision of the Assembly."

Article 5*bis*

DOCUMENTARY EVIDENCE OF LEGITIMACY OF USE
OF CERTAIN ELEMENTS OF THE MARK

Documentary evidence of the legitimacy of the use of certain elements incorporated in a mark, such as armorial bearings, escutcheons, portraits, honorary distinctions, titles, trade names, names of persons other than the name of the applicant, or other like inscriptions, which might be required by the Offices of the Contracting Parties shall be exempt from any legalization as well as from any certification other than that of the Office of origin.

Article 5*ter*

COPIES OF ENTRIES IN INTERNATIONAL REGISTER; SEARCHES FOR
ANTICIPATIONS; EXTRACTS FROM INTERNATIONAL REGISTER

(1)   The International Bureau shall issue to any person applying therefor, upon the payment of a fee fixed by the Regulations, a copy of the entries in the International Register concerning a specific mark.

(2)   The International Bureau may also, upon payment, undertake searches for anticipations among marks that are the subject of international registrations.

(3)   Extracts from the International Register requested with a view to their production in one of the Contracting Parties shall be exempt from any legalization.

Article 6

PERIOD OF VALIDITY OF INTERNATIONAL REGISTRATION; DEPENDENCE
AND INDEPENDENCE OF INTERNATIONAL REGISTRATION

(1)   Registration of a mark at the International Bureau is effected for ten years, with the possibility of renewal under the conditions specified in Article 7.

(2)   Upon expiry of a period of five years from the date of the international registration, such registration shall become independent of the basic application or the registration resulting therefrom, or of the basic registration, as the case may be, subject to the following provisions.

(3)   The protection resulting from the international registration, whether or not it has been the subject of a transfer, may no longer be invoked if, before the expiry of five years from the date of the international registration, the basic application or the registration resulting therefrom, or the basic registration, as the case may be, has been withdrawn, has lapsed, has been renounced or has been the subject of a final decision of rejection, revocation, cancellation or invalidation, in respect of all or some of the goods and services listed in the international registration. The same applies if

(i)   an appeal against a decision refusing the effects of the basic application,

(ii)   an action requesting the withdrawal of the basic application or the revocation, cancellation or invalidation of the registration resulting from the basic application or of the basic registration, or

(iii)   an opposition to the basic application

results, after the expiry of the five-year period, in a final decision of rejection, revocation, cancellation or invalidation, or ordering the withdrawal, of the basic application, or the registration resulting therefrom, or the basic registration, as the case may be, provided that such appeal, action or opposition had begun before the expiry of the said period. The same also applies if the basic application is withdrawn, or the registration resulting from the basic application or the basic registration is renounced, after the expiry of the five-year period, provided that, at the time of the withdrawal or renunciation, the said application or registration was the subject of a proceeding referred to in item (i), (ii) or (iii) and that such proceeding had begun before the expiry of the said period.

(4)   The Office of origin shall, as prescribed in the Regulations, notify the International Bureau of the facts and decisions relevant under paragraph (3), and the International Bureau shall, as prescribed in the Regulations, notify the interested parties and effect any publication accordingly. The Office of origin shall, where applicable, request the International Bureau to cancel, to the extent applicable, the international registration, and the International Bureau shall proceed accordingly.

Article 7

RENEWAL OF INTERNATIONAL REGISTRATION

(1)   Any international registration may be renewed for a period of ten years from the expiry of the preceding period, by the mere payment of the basic fee and, subject to Article 8(7), of the supplementary and complementary fees provided for in Article 8(2).

(2)   Renewal may not bring about any change in the international registration in its latest form.

(3)   Six months before the expiry of the term of protection, the International Bureau shall, by sending an unofficial notice, remind the holder of the international registration and his representative, if any, of the exact date of expiry.

(4)   Subject to the payment of a surcharge fixed by the Regulations, a period of grace of six months shall be allowed for renewal of the international registration.

Article 8

FEES FOR INTERNATIONAL APPLICATION AND REGISTRATION

(1)   The Office of origin may fix, at its own discretion, and collect, for its own benefit, a fee which it may require from the applicant for international registration or from the holder of the international registration in connection with the filing of the international application or the renewal of the international registration.

(2)   Registration of a mark at the International Bureau shall be subject to the advance payment of an international fee which shall, subject to the provisions of paragraph (7)(a), include,

(i)   a basic fee;

(ii)   a supplementary fee for each class of the International Classification, beyond three, into which the goods or services to which the mark is applied will fall;

(iii) a complementary fee for any request for extension of protection under Article 3*ter.*

(3)   However, the supplementary fee specified in paragraph (2)(ii) may, without prejudice to the date of the international registration, be paid within the period fixed by the Regulations if the number of classes of goods or services has been fixed or disputed by the International Bureau. If, upon expiry of the said period, the supplementary fee has not been paid or the list of goods or services has not been reduced to the required extent by the applicant, the international application shall be deemed to have been abandoned.

(4)   The annual product of the various receipts from international registration, with the exception of the receipts derived from the fees mentioned in paragraph (2)(ii) and (iii), shall be divided equally among the Contracting Parties by the International Bureau, after deduction of the expenses and charges necessitated by the implementation of this Protocol.

(5)   The amounts derived from the supplementary fees provided for in paragraph (2)(ii) shall be divided, at the expiry of each year, among the interested Contracting Parties in proportion to the number of marks for which protection has been applied for in each of them during that year, this number being multiplied, in the case of Contracting Parties which make an examination, by a coefficient which shall be determined by the Regulations.

(6)   The amounts derived from the complementary fees provided for in paragraph (2)(iii) shall be divided according to the same rules as those provided for in paragraph (5).

(7)(a) Any Contracting Party may declare that, in connection with each international registration in which it is mentioned under Article 3*ter,* and in connection with the renewal of any such international registration, it wants to receive, instead of a share in the revenue produced by the supplementary and complementary fees, a fee (hereinafter referred to as "the individual fee") whose amount shall be indicated in the declaration, and can be changed in further declarations, but may not be higher than the equivalent of the amount which the said Contracting Party's Office would be entitled to receive from an applicant for a ten-year registration, or from the holder of a registration for a ten-year renewal of that registration, of the mark in the register of the said Office, the said amount being diminished by the savings resulting from the international procedure. Where such an individual fee is payable,

(i) no supplementary fees referred to in paragraph (2)(ii) shall be payable if only Contracting Parties which have made a declaration under this subparagraph are mentioned under Article 3*ter,* and

(ii) no complementary fee referred to in paragraph (2)(iii) shall be payable in respect of any Contracting Party which has made a declaration under this subparagraph.

(b) Any declaration under subparagraph (a) may be made in the instruments referred to in Article 14(2), and the effective date of the declaration shall be the same as the date of entry into force of this Protocol with respect to the State or intergovernmental organization having made the declaration. Any such declaration may also be made later, in which case the declaration shall have effect three months after its receipt by the Director General, or at any later date indicated in the declaration, in respect of any international registration whose date is the same as or is later than the effective date of the declaration.

Article 9

RECORDAL OF CHANGE IN THE OWNERSHIP OF AN INTERNATIONAL REGISTRATION

At the request of the person in whose name the international registration stands, or at the request of an interested Office made ex officio or at the request of an interested person, the International Bureau shall record in the International Register any change in the ownership of that registration, in respect of all or some of the Contracting Parties in whose territories the said registration has effect and in respect of all or some of the goods and services listed in the registration, provided that the new holder is a person who, under Article 2(1), is entitled to file international applications.

Article 9*bis*

RECORDAL OF CERTAIN MATTERS CONCERNING AN INTERNATIONAL REGISTRATION

The International Bureau shall record in the International Register

(i) any change in the name or address of the holder of the international registration,

(ii) the appointment of a representative of the holder of the international registration and any other relevant fact concerning such representative,

(iii) any limitation, in respect of all or some of the Contracting Parties, of the goods and services listed in the international registration,

(iv) any renunciation, cancellation or invalidation of the international registration in respect of all or some of the Contracting Parties,

(v) any other relevant fact, identified in the Regulations, concerning the rights in a mark that is the subject of an international registration.

Article 9*ter*

FEES FOR CERTAIN RECORDALS

Any recordal under Article 9 or under Article 9*bis* may be subject to the payment of a fee.

Article 9*quater*

COMMON OFFICE OF SEVERAL CONTRACTING STATES

(1) If several Contracting States agree to effect the unification of their domestic legislations on marks, they may notify the Director General

(i) that a common Office shall be substituted for the national Office of each of them, and

(ii) that the whole of their respective territories shall be deemed to be a single State for the purposes of the application of all or part of the provisions preceding this Article as well as the provisions of Articles 9*quinquies* and 9*sexies*.

(2) Such notification shall not take effect until three months after the date of the communication thereof by the Director General to the other Contracting Parties.

Article 9*quinquies*

TRANSFORMATION OF AN INTERNATIONAL REGISTRATION INTO NATIONAL OR REGIONAL APPLICATIONS

Where, in the event that the international registration is cancelled at the request of the Office of origin under Article 6(4), in respect of all or some of the goods and services listed in the said registration, the person who was the holder of the international registration files an application for the registration of the same mark with the Office of any of the Contracting Parties in the territory of which the international registration had effect, that application shall be treated as if it had been filed on the date of the international registration according to Article 3(4) or on the date of recordal of the territorial extension according to Article 3*ter* (2) and, if the international registration enjoyed priority, shall enjoy the same priority, provided that

(i) such application is filed within three months from the date on which the international registration was cancelled,

(ii) the goods and services listed in the application are in fact covered by the list of goods and services contained in the international registration in respect of the Contracting Party concerned, and

(iii) such application complies with all the requirements of the applicable law, including the requirements concerning fees.

Article 9*sexies*

RELATIONS BETWEEN STATES PARTY TO BOTH THIS PROTOCOL AND THE MADRID (STOCKHOLM) AGREEMENT

(1)(a) This Protocol alone shall be applicable as regards the mutual relations of States party to both this Protocol and the Madrid (Stockholm) Agreement.

(b) Notwithstanding subparagraph (a), a declaration made under Article 5(2)(b), Article 5(2)(c) or Article 8(7) of this Protocol, by a State party to both this Protocol and the Madrid (Stockholm) Agreement, shall have no effect in the relations with another State party to both this Protocol and the Madrid (Stockholm) Agreement.

(2) The Assembly shall, after the expiry of a period of three years from September 1, 2008, review the application of paragraph (1)(b) and may, at any time thereafter, either repeal it or restrict its scope, by a three-fourths majority. In the vote of the Assembly, only those States which are party to both the Madrid (Stockholm) Agreement and this Protocol shall have the right to participate.

Article 10

ASSEMBLY

(1)(a) The Contracting Parties shall be members of the same Assembly as the countries party to the Madrid (Stockholm) Agreement.

(b)   Each Contracting Party shall be represented in that Assembly by one delegate, who may be assisted by alternate delegates, advisors, and experts.

(c)   The expenses of each delegation shall be borne by the Contracting Party which has appointed it, except for the travel expenses and the subsistence allowance of one delegate for each Contracting Party, which shall be paid from the funds of the Union.

(2)   The Assembly shall, in addition to the functions which it has under the Madrid (Stockholm) Agreement, also

(i)   deal with all matters concerning the implementation of this Protocol;

(ii)   give directions to the International Bureau concerning the preparation for conferences of revision of this Protocol, due account being taken of any comments made by those countries of the Union which are not party to this Protocol;

(iii) adopt and modify the provisions of the Regulations concerning the implementation of this Protocol;

(iv)   perform such other functions as are appropriate under this Protocol.

(3)(a) Each Contracting Party shall have one vote in the Assembly. On matters concerning only countries that are party to the Madrid (Stockholm) Agreement, Contracting Parties that are not party to the said Agreement shall not have the right to vote, whereas, on matters concerning only Contracting Parties, only the latter shall have the right to vote.

(b)   One-half of the members of the Assembly which have the right to vote on a given matter shall constitute the quorum for the purposes of the vote on that matter.

(c)   Notwithstanding the provisions of subparagraph (b), if, in any session, the number of the members of the Assembly having the right to vote on a given matter which are represented is less than one-half but equal to or more than one-third of the members of the Assembly having the right to vote on that matter, the Assembly may make decisions but, with the exception of decisions concerning its own procedure, all such decisions shall take effect only if the conditions set forth hereinafter are fulfilled. The International Bureau shall communicate the said decisions to the members of the Assembly having the right to vote on the said matter which were not represented and shall invite them to express in writing their vote or abstention within a period of three months from the date of the communication. If, at the expiry of this period, the number of such members having thus expressed their vote or abstention attains the number of the members which was lacking for attaining the quorum in the session itself, such decisions shall take effect provided that at the same time the required majority still obtains.

(d)   Subject to the provisions of Articles 5(2)(e), 9*sexies* (2), 12 and 13(2), the decisions of the Assembly shall require two-thirds of the votes cast.

(e)   Abstentions shall not be considered as votes.

(f)   A delegate may represent, and vote in the name of, one member of the Assembly only.

(4)   In addition to meeting in ordinary sessions and extraordinary sessions as provided for by the Madrid (Stockholm) Agreement, the Assembly shall meet in extraordinary session upon convocation by the Director General, at the request of one-fourth of the members of the Assembly having the right to vote on the matters proposed to be included in the agenda of the session. The agenda of such an extraordinary session shall be prepared by the Director General.

Article 11

INTERNATIONAL BUREAU

(1)   International registration and related duties, as well as all other administrative tasks, under or concerning this Protocol, shall be performed by the International Bureau.

(2)(a) The International Bureau shall, in accordance with the directions of the Assembly, make the preparations for the conferences of revision of this Protocol.

(b)   The International Bureau may consult with intergovernmental and international non-governmental organizations concerning preparations for such conferences of revision.

(c)   The Director General and persons designated by him shall take part, without the right to vote, in the discussions at such conferences of revision.

(3)   The International Bureau shall carry out any other tasks assigned to it in relation to this Protocol.

Article 12

FINANCES

As far as Contracting Parties are concerned, the finances of the Union shall be governed by the same provisions as those contained in Article 12 of the Madrid (Stockholm) Agreement, provided that any reference to Article 8 of the said Agreement shall be deemed to be a reference to Article 8 of this Protocol. Furthermore, for the purposes of Article 12(6)(b) of the said Agreement, Contracting Organizations shall, subject to a unanimous decision to the contrary by the Assembly, be considered to belong to contribution class I (one) under the Paris Convention for the Protection of Industrial Property.

Article 13

AMENDMENT OF CERTAIN ARTICLES OF THE PROTOCOL

(1)   Proposals for the amendment of Articles 10, 11, 12, and the present Article, may be initiated by any Contracting Party, or by the Director General. Such proposals shall be communicated by the Director General to the Contracting Parties at least six months in advance of their consideration by the Assembly.

(2)   Amendments to the Articles referred to in paragraph (1) shall be adopted by the Assembly. Adoption shall require three-fourths of the votes cast, provided that any amendment to Article 10, and to the present paragraph, shall require four-fifths of the votes cast.

(3)   Any amendment to the Articles referred to in paragraph (1) shall enter into force one month after written notifications of acceptance, effected in accordance with their respective constitutional processes, have been received by the Director General from three-fourths of those States and intergovernmental organizations which, at the time the amendment was adopted, were members of the Assembly and had the right to vote on the amendment. Any amendment to the said Articles thus accepted shall bind all the States and intergovernmental organizations which are Contracting Parties at the time the amendment enters into force, or which become Contracting Parties at a subsequent date.

Article 14

BECOMING PARTY TO THE PROTOCOL; ENTRY INTO FORCE

(1)(a) Any State that is a party to the Paris Convention for the Protection of Industrial Property may become party to this Protocol.

(b)   Furthermore, any intergovernmental organization may also become party to this Protocol where the following conditions are fulfilled:

(i)   at least one of the member States of that organization is a party to the Paris Convention for the Protection of Industrial Property;

(ii)   that organization has a regional Office for the purposes of registering marks with effect in the territory of the organization, provided that such Office is not the subject of a notification under Article 9*quater.*

(2)   Any State or organization referred to in paragraph (1) may sign this Protocol. Any such State or organization may, if it has signed this Protocol, deposit an instrument of ratification, acceptance or approval of this Protocol or, if it has not signed this Protocol, deposit an instrument of accession to this Protocol.

(3)   The instruments referred to in paragraph (2) shall be deposited with the Director General.

(4)(a) This Protocol shall enter into force three months after four instruments of ratification, acceptance, approval or accession have been deposited, provided that at least one of those instruments has been deposited by a country party to the Madrid (Stockholm) Agreement and at least one other of those instruments has been deposited by a State not party to the Madrid (Stockholm) Agreement or by any of the organizations referred to in paragraph (1)(b).

(b)   With respect to any other State or organization referred to in paragraph (1), this Protocol shall enter into force three months after the date on which its ratification, acceptance, approval or accession has been notified by the Director General.

(5)   Any State or organization referred to in paragraph (1) may, when depositing its instrument of ratification, acceptance or approval of, or accession to, this Protocol, declare that the protection resulting from any international registration effected under this Protocol before the date of entry into force of this Protocol with respect to it cannot be extended to it.

Article 15

DENUNCIATION

(1)   This Protocol shall remain in force without limitation as to time.

(2)   Any Contracting Party may denounce this Protocol by notification addressed to the Director General.

(3)   Denunciation shall take effect one year after the day on which the Director General has received the notification.

(4)   The right of denunciation provided for by this Article shall not be exercised by any Contracting Party before the expiry of five years from the date upon which this Protocol entered into force with respect to that Contracting Party.

(5)(a) Where a mark is the subject of an international registration having effect in the denouncing State or intergovernmental organization at the date on which the denunciation becomes effective, the holder of such registration may file an application for the registration of the same mark with the Office of the denouncing State or intergovernmental organization, which shall be treated as if it had been filed on the date of the international registration according to Article 3(4) or on the date of recordal of the territorial extension according to Article 3ter(2) and, if the international registration enjoyed priority, enjoy the same priority, provided that

(i)   such application is filed within two years from the date on which the denunciation became effective,

(ii)   the goods and services listed in the application are in fact covered by the list of goods and services contained in the international registration in respect of the denouncing State or intergovernmental organization, and

(iii) such application complies with all the requirements of the applicable law, including the requirements concerning fees.

(b) The provisions of subparagraph (a) shall also apply in respect of any mark that is the subject of an international registration having effect in Contracting Parties other than the denouncing State or intergovernmental organization at the date on which denunciation becomes effective and whose holder, because of the denunciation, is no longer entitled to file international applications under Article 2(1).

Article 16

SIGNATURE; LANGUAGES; DEPOSITARY FUNCTIONS

(1)(a) This Protocol shall be signed in a single copy in the English, French and Spanish languages, and shall be deposited with the Director General when it ceases to be open for signature at Madrid. The texts in the three languages shall be equally authentic.

(b) Official texts of this Protocol shall be established by the Director General, after consultation with the interested governments and organizations, in the Arabic, Chinese, German, Italian, Japanese, Portuguese and Russian languages, and in such other languages as the Assembly may designate.

(2) This Protocol shall remain open for signature at Madrid until December 31, 1989.

(3) The Director General shall transmit two copies, certified by the Government of Spain, of the signed texts of this Protocol to all States and intergovernmental organizations that may become party to this Protocol.

(4) The Director General shall register this Protocol with the Secretariat of the United Nations.

(5) The Director General shall notify all States and international organizations that may become or are party to this Protocol of signatures, deposits of instruments of ratification, acceptance, approval or accession, the entry into force of this Protocol and any amendment thereto, any notification of denunciation and any declaration provided for in this Protocol.

F. TRADEMARK LAW TREATY*

(October 27, 1994)

List of Articles

Article 1

Abbreviated Expressions

For the purposes of this Treaty, unless expressly stated otherwise:

(i)   "Office" means the agency entrusted by a Contracting Party with the registration of marks;

(ii)   "registration" means the registration of a mark by an Office;

(iii)   "application" means an application for registration;

(iv)   references to a "person" shall be construed as references to both a natural person and a legal entity;

(v)   "holder" means the person whom the register of marks shows as the holder of the registration;

---

*   The United States became a party to this Treaty on August 12, 2000—*Ed.*

(vi) "register of marks" means the collection of data maintained by an Office, which includes the contents of all registrations and all data recorded in respect of all registrations, irrespective of the medium in which such data are stored;

(vii) "Paris Convention" means the Paris Convention for the Protection of Industrial Property, signed at Paris on March 20, 1883, as revised and amended;

(viii) "Nice Classification" means the classification established by the Nice Agreement Concerning the International Classification of Goods and Services for the Purposes of the Registration of Marks, signed at Nice on June 15, 1957, as revised and amended;

(ix) "Contracting Party" means any State or intergovernmental organization party to this Treaty;

(x) references to an "instrument of ratification" shall be construed as including references to instruments of acceptance and approval;

(xi) "Organization" means the World Intellectual Property Organization;

(xii) "Director General" means the Director General of the Organization;

(xiii) "Regulations" means the Regulations under this Treaty that are referred to in Article 17.

Article 2

Marks to Which the Treaty Applies

(1) [Nature of Marks]

(a) This Treaty shall apply to marks consisting of visible signs, provided that only those Contracting Parties which accept for registration three-dimensional marks shall be obliged to apply this Treaty to such marks.

(b) This Treaty shall not apply to hologram marks and to marks not consisting of visible signs, in particular, sound marks and olfactory marks.

(2) [Kinds of Marks]

(a) This Treaty shall apply to marks relating to goods (trademarks) or services (service marks) or both goods and services.

(b) This Treaty shall not apply to collective marks, certification marks and guarantee marks.

Article 3

Application

(1) [Indications or Elements Contained in or Accompanying an Application; Fee]

(a) Any Contracting Party may require that an application contain some or all of the following indications or elements:

(i) a request for registration;

(ii) the name and address of the applicant;

(iii) the name of a State of which the applicant is a national if he is the national of any State, the name of a State in which the applicant has his domicile, if any, and the name of a State in which the applicant has a real and effective industrial or commercial establishment, if any;

(iv) where the applicant is a legal entity, the legal nature of that legal entity and the State, and, where applicable, the territorial unit within that State, under the law of which the said legal entity has been organized;

(v) where the applicant has a representative, the name and address of that representative;

(vi) where an address for service is required under Article 4(2)(b), such address;

(vii) where the applicant wishes to take advantage of the priority of an earlier application, a declaration claiming the priority of that earlier application, together with indications and evidence in support of the declaration of priority that may be required pursuant to Article 4 of the Paris Convention;

(viii) where the applicant wishes to take advantage of any protection resulting from the display of goods and/or services in an exhibition, a declaration to that effect, together with indications in support of that declaration, as required by the law of the Contracting Party;

(ix) where the Office of the Contracting Party uses characters (letters and numbers) that it considers as being standard and where the applicant wishes that the mark be registered and published in standard characters, a statement to that effect;

(x) where the applicant wishes to claim color as a distinctive feature of the mark, a statement to that effect as well as the name or names of the color or colors claimed and an indication, in respect of each color, of the principal parts of the mark which are in that color;

(xi) where the mark is a three-dimensional mark, a statement to that effect;

(xii) one or more reproductions of the mark;

(xiii) a transliteration of the mark or of certain parts of the mark;

(xiv) a translation of the mark or of certain parts of the mark;

(xv) the names of the goods and/or services for which the registration is sought, grouped according to the classes of the Nice Classification, each group preceded by the number of the class of that Classification to which that group of goods or services belongs and presented in the order of the classes of the said Classification;

(xvi) a signature by the person specified in paragraph (4);

(xvii) a declaration of intention to use the mark, as required by the law of the Contracting Party.

(b) The applicant may file, instead of or in addition to the declaration of intention to use the mark referred to in subparagraph (a)(xvii), a declaration of actual use of the mark and evidence to that effect, as required by the law of the Contracting Party.

(c) Any Contracting Party may require that, in respect of the application, fees be paid to the Office.

(2) [Presentation]

As regards the requirements concerning the presentation of the application, no Contracting Party shall refuse the application,

(i) where the application is presented in writing on paper, if it is presented, subject to paragraph (3), on a form corresponding to the application Form provided for in the Regulations,

(ii) where the Contracting Party allows the transmittal of communications to the Office by telefacsimile and the application is so transmitted, if the paper copy resulting from such transmittal corresponds, subject to paragraph (3), to the application Form referred to in item (i).

(3) [Language]

Any Contracting Party may require that the application be in the language, or in one of the languages, admitted by the Office. Where the Office admits more than one language, the applicant may be required to comply with any other language requirement applicable with respect to the Office, provided that the application may not be required to be in more than one language.

(4) [Signature]

(a) The signature referred to in paragraph (1)(a)(xvi) may be the signature of the applicant or the signature of his representative.

(b) Notwithstanding subparagraph (a), any Contracting Party may require that the declarations referred to in paragraph (1)(a)(xvii) and (b) be signed by the applicant himself even if he has a representative.

(5) [Single Application for Goods and/or Services in Several Classes]

One and the same application may relate to several goods and/or services, irrespective of whether they belong to one class or to several classes of the Nice Classification.

(6) [Actual Use]

Any Contracting Party may require that, where a declaration of intention to use has been filed under paragraph (1)(a)(xvii), the applicant furnish to the Office within a time limit fixed in its law, subject to the minimum time limit prescribed in the Regulations, evidence of the actual use of the mark, as required by the said law.

(7) [Prohibition of Other Requirements]

No Contracting Party may demand that requirements other than those referred to in paragraphs (1) to (4) and (6) be complied with in respect of the application. In particular, the following may not be required in respect of the application throughout its pendency:

(i) the furnishing of any certificate of, or extract from, a register of commerce;

(ii) an indication of the applicant's carrying on of an industrial or commercial activity, as well as the furnishing of evidence to that effect;

(iii) an indication of the applicant's carrying on of an activity corresponding to the goods and/or services listed in the application, as well as the furnishing of evidence to that effect;

(iv) the furnishing of evidence to the effect that the mark has been registered in the register of marks of another Contracting Party or of a State party to the Paris Convention which is not a Contracting Party, except where the applicant claims the application of Article 6*quinquies* of the Paris Convention.

(8) [Evidence]

Any Contracting Party may require that evidence be furnished to the Office in the course of the examination of the application where the Office may reasonably doubt the veracity of any indication or element contained in the application.

Article 4

Representation; Address for Service

(1) [Representatives Admitted to Practice]

Any Contracting Party may require that any person appointed as representative for the purposes of any procedure before the Office be a representative admitted to practice before the Office.

(2) [Mandatory Representation; Address for Service]

(a)   Any Contracting Party may require that, for the purposes of any procedure before the Office, any person who has neither a domicile nor a real and effective industrial or commercial establishment on its territory be represented by a representative.

(b)   Any Contracting Party may, to the extent that it does not require representation in accordance with subparagraph (a), require that, for the purposes of any procedure before the Office, any person who has neither a domicile nor a real and effective industrial or commercial establishment on its territory have an address for service on that territory.

(3)   [Power of Attorney]

(a)   Whenever a Contracting Party allows or requires an applicant, a holder or any other interested person to be represented by a representative before the Office, it may require that the representative be appointed in a separate communication (hereinafter referred to as "power of attorney") indicating the name of, and signed by, the applicant, the holder or the other Person, as the case may be.

(b)   The power of attorney may relate to one or more applications and/or registrations identified in the power of attorney or, subject to any exception indicated by the appointing person, to all existing and future applications and/or registrations of that person.

(c)   The power of attorney may limit the powers of the representative to certain acts. Any Contracting Party may require that any power of attorney under which the representative has the right to withdraw an application or to surrender a registration contain an express indication to that effect.

(d)   Where a communication is submitted to the Office by a person who refers to himself in the communication as a representative but where the Office is, at the time of the receipt of the communication, not in possession of the required power of attorney, the Contracting Party may require that the power of attorney be submitted to the Office within the time limit fixed by the Contracting Party, subject to the minimum time limit prescribed in the Regulations. Any Contracting Party may provide that, where the power of attorney has not been submitted to the Office within the time limit fixed by the Contracting Party, the communication by the said person shall have no effect.

(e)   As regards the requirements concerning the presentation and contents of the power of attorney, no Contracting Party shall refuse the effects of the power of attorney,

(i)   where the power of attorney is presented in writing on paper, if it is presented, subject to paragraph (4), on a form corresponding to the power of attorney Form provided for in the Regulations,

(ii)   where the Contracting Party allows the transmittal of communications to the Office by telefacsimile and the power of attorney is so transmitted, if the paper copy resulting from such transmittal corresponds, subject to paragraph (4), to the power of attorney Form referred to in item (i).

(4)   [Language]

Any Contracting Party may require that the power of attorney be in the language, or in one of the languages, admitted by the Office.

(5)   [Reference to Power of Attorney]

Any Contracting Party may require that any communication made to the Office by a representative for the purposes of a procedure before the Office contain a reference to the power of attorney on the basis of which the representative acts.

(6)   [Prohibition of Other Requirements]

No Contracting Party may demand that requirements other than those referred to in paragraphs (3) to (5) be complied with in respect of the matters dealt with in those paragraphs.

(7)   [Evidence]

Any Contracting Party may require that evidence be furnished to the Office where the Office may reasonably doubt the veracity of any indication contained in any communication referred to in paragraphs (2) to (5).

<h2 style="text-align:center">Article 5</h2>

<h3 style="text-align:center">Filing Date</h3>

(1)   [Permitted Requirements]

(a)   Subject to subparagraph (b) and paragraph (2), a Contracting Party shall accord as the filing date of an application the date on which the Office received the following indications and elements in the language required under Article 3(3):

(i)   an express or implicit indication that the registration of a mark is sought;

(ii)   indications allowing the identity of the applicant to be established;

(iii)   indications sufficient to contact the applicant or his representative, if any, by mail;

(iv)   a sufficiently clear reproduction of the mark whose registration is sought;

(v)   the list of the goods and/or services for which the registration is sought;

(vi)   where Article 3(1)(a)(xvii) or (b) applies, the declaration referred to in Article 3(1)(a)(xvii) or the declaration and evidence referred to in Article 3(1)(b), respectively, as required by the law of the Contracting Party, those declarations being, if so required by the said law, signed by the applicant himself even if he has a representative.

(b)   Any Contracting Party may accord as the filing date of the application the date on which the Office received only some, rather than all, of the indications and elements referred to in subparagraph (a) or received them in a language other than the language required under Article 3(3).

(2)   [Permitted Additional Requirement]

(a)   A Contracting Party may provide that no filing date shall be accorded until the required fees are paid.

(b)   A Contracting Party may apply the requirement referred to in subparagraph (a) only if it applied such requirement at the time of becoming party to this Treaty.

(3)   [Corrections and Time Limits]

The modalities of, and time limits for, corrections under paragraphs (1) and (2) shall be fixed in the Regulations.

(4)   [Prohibition of Other Requirements]

No Contracting Party may demand that requirements other than those referred to in paragraphs (1) and (2) be complied with in respect of the filing date.

<h2 style="text-align:center">Article 6</h2>

<h3 style="text-align:center">Single Registration for Goods and/or Services in Several Classes</h3>

Where goods and/or services belonging to several classes of the Nice Classification have been included in one and the same application, such an application shall result in one and the same registration.

Article 7

Division of Application and Registration

(1) [Division of Application]

(a) Any application listing several goods and/or services (hereinafter referred to as "initial application") may,

(i) at least until the decision by the Office on the registration of the mark,

(ii) during any opposition proceedings against the decision of the Office to register the mark,

(iii) during any appeal proceedings against the decision on the registration of the mark, be divided by the applicant or at his request into two or more applications (hereinafter referred to as "divisional applications") by distributing among the latter the goods and/or services listed in the initial application. The divisional applications shall preserve the filing date of the initial application and the benefit of the right of priority, if any.

(b) Any Contracting Party shall, subject to subparagraph (a), be free to establish requirements for the division of an application, including the payment of fees.

(2) [Division of Registration]

Paragraph (1) shall apply, *mutatis mutandis,* with respect to a division of a registration. Such a division shall be permitted

(i) during any proceedings in which the validity of the registration is challenged before the Office by a third party,

(ii) during any appeal proceedings against a decision taken by the Office during the former proceedings, provided that a Contracting Party may exclude the possibility of the division of registrations if its law allows third parties to oppose the registration of a mark before the mark is registered.

Article 8

Signature

(1) [Communication on Paper]

Where a communication to the Office of a Contracting Party is on paper and a signature is required, that Contracting Party

(i) shall, subject to item (iii), accept a handwritten signature,

(ii) shall be free to allow, instead of a handwritten signature, the use of other forms of signature, such as a printed or stamped signature, or the use of a seal,

(iii) may, where the natural person who signs the communication is its national and such person's address is in its territory, require that a seal be used instead of a handwritten signature,

(iv) may, where a seal is used, require that the seal be accompanied by an indication in letters of the name of the natural person whose seal is used.

(2) [Communication by Telefacsimile]

(a) Where a Contracting Party allows the transmittal of communications to the Office by telefacsimile, it shall consider the communication signed if, on the printout produced by the telefacsimile, the reproduction of the signature, or the reproduction of the seal together with, where required under paragraph (1)(iv), the indication in letters of the name of the natural person whose seal is used, appears.

(b) The Contracting Party referred to in subparagraph (a) may require that the paper whose reproduction was transmitted by telefacsimile be filed with the Office within a certain period, subject to the minimum period prescribed in the Regulations.

(3) [Communication by Electronic Means]

Where a Contracting Party allows the transmittal of communications to the Office by electronic means, it shall consider the communication signed if the latter identifies the sender of the communication by electronic means as prescribed by the Contracting Party.

(4) [Prohibition of Requirement of Certification]

No Contracting Party may require the attestation, notarization, authentication, legalization or other certification of any signature or other means of self-identification referred to in the preceding paragraphs, except, if the law of the Contracting Party so provides, where the signature concerns the surrender of a registration.

Article 9

Classification of Goods and/or Services

(1) [Indications of Goods and/or Services]

Each registration and any publication effected by an Office which concerns an application or registration and which indicates goods and/or services shall indicate the goods and/or services by their names, grouped according to the classes of the Nice Classification, and each group shall be preceded by the number of the class of that Classification to which that group of goods or services belongs and shall be presented in the order of the classes of the said Classification.

(2) [Goods or Services in the Same Class or in Different Classes]

(a) Goods or services may not be considered as being similar to each other on the ground that, in any registration or publication by the Office, they appear in the same class of the Nice Classification.

(b) Goods or services may not be considered as being dissimilar from each other on the ground that, in any registration or publication by the Office, they appear in different classes of the Nice Classification.

Article 10

Changes in Names or Addresses

(1) [Changes in the Name or Address of the Holder]

(a) Where there is no change in the person of the holder but there is a change in his name and/or address, each Contracting Party shall accept that a request for the recordal of the change by the Office in its register of marks be made in a communication signed by the holder or his representative and indicating the registration number of the registration concerned and the change to be recorded. As regards the requirements concerning the presentation of the request, no Contracting Party shall refuse the request,

(i) where the request is presented in writing on paper, if it is presented, subject to subparagraph (c), on a form corresponding to the request Form provided for in the Regulations,

(ii) where the Contracting Party allows the transmittal of communications to the Office by telefacsimile and the request is so transmitted, if the paper copy resulting from such transmittal corresponds, subject to subparagraph (c), to the request Form referred to in item (i).

(b) Any Contracting Party may require that the request indicate

(i) the name and address of the holder;

(ii) where the holder has a representative, the name and address of that representative;

(iii) where the holder has an address for service, such address.

(c) Any Contracting Party may require that the request be in the language, or in one of the languages, admitted by the Office.

(d) Any Contracting Party may require that, in respect of the request, a fee be paid to the Office.

(e) A single request shall be sufficient even where the change relates to more than one registration, provided that the registration numbers of all registrations concerned are indicated in the request.

(2) [Change in the Name or Address of the Applicant]

Paragraph (1) shall apply, *mutatis mutandis,* where the change concerns an application or applications, or both an application or applications and a registration or registrations, provided that, where the application number of any application concerned has not yet been issued or is not known to the applicant or his representative, the request otherwise identifies that application as prescribed in the Regulations.

(3) [Change in the Name or Address of the Representative or in the Address for Service]

Paragraph (1) shall apply, *mutatis mutandis,* to any change in the name or address of the representative, if any, and to any change relating to the address for service, if any.

(4) [Prohibition of Other Requirements]

No Contracting Party may demand that requirements other than those referred to in paragraphs (1) to (3) be complied with in respect of the request referred to in this Article. In particular, the furnishing of any certificate concerning the change may not be required.

(5) [Evidence]

Any Contracting Party may require that evidence be furnished to the Office where the Office may reasonably doubt the veracity of any indication contained in the request.

Article 11

Change in Ownership

(1) [Change in the Ownership of a Registration]

(a) Where there is a change in the person of the holder, each Contracting Party shall accept that a request for the recordal of the change by the Office in its register of marks be made in a communication signed by the holder or his representative, or by the person who acquired the ownership (hereinafter referred to as "new owner") or his representative, and indicating the registration number of the registration concerned and the change to be recorded. As regards the requirements concerning the presentation of the request, no Contracting Party shall refuse the request,

(i) where the request is presented in writing on paper, if it is presented, subject to paragraph (2)(a), on a form corresponding to the request Form provided for in the Regulations,

(ii) where the Contracting Party allows the transmittal of communications to the Office by telefacsimile and the request is so transmitted, if the paper copy resulting from such transmittal corresponds, subject to paragraph (2)(a), to the request Form referred to in item (i).

(b)   Where the change in ownership results from a contract, any Contracting Party may require that the request indicate that fact and be accompanied, at the option of the requesting party, by one of the following:

(i)   a copy of the contract, which copy may be required to be certified, by a notary public or any other competent public authority, as being in conformity with the original contract;

(ii)   an extract of the contract showing the change in ownership, which extract may be required to be certified, by a notary public or any other competent public authority, as being a true extract of the contract;

(iii)   an uncertified certificate of transfer drawn up in the form and with the content as prescribed in the Regulations and signed by both the holder and the new owner;

(iv)   an uncertified transfer document drawn up in the form and with the content as prescribed in the Regulations and signed by both the holder and the new owner.

(c)   Where the change in ownership results from a merger, any Contracting Party may require that the request indicate that fact and be accompanied by a copy of a document, which document originates from the competent authority and evidences the merger, such as a copy of an extract from a register of commerce, and that that copy be certified by the authority which issued the document or by a notary public or any other competent public authority, as being in conformity with the original document.

(d)   Where there is a change in the person of one or more but not all of several co-holders and such change in ownership results from a contract or a merger, any Contracting Party may require that any co-holder in respect of which there is no change in ownership give his express consent to the change in ownership in a document signed by him.

(e)   Where the change in ownership does not result from a contract or a merger but from another ground, for example, from operation of law or a court decision, any Contracting Party may require that the request indicate that fact and be accompanied by a copy of a document evidencing the change and that that copy be certified as being in conformity with the original document by the authority which issued the document or by a notary public or any other competent public authority.

(f)   Any Contracting Party may require that the request indicate

(i)   the name and address of the holder;

(ii)   the name and address of the new owner;

(iii)   the name of a State of which the new owner is a national if he is the national of any State, the name of a State in which the new owner has his domicile, if any, and the name of a State in which the new owner has a real and effective industrial or commercial establishment, if any;

(iv)   where the new owner is a legal entity, the legal nature of that legal entity and the State, and, where applicable, the territorial unit within that State, under the law of which the said legal entity has been organized;

(v)   where the holder has a representative, the name and address of that representative;

(vi)   where the holder has an address for service, such address;

(vii)   where the new owner has a representative, the name and address of that representative;

(viii) where the new owner is required to have an address for service under Article 4(2)(b), such address.

(g)   Any Contracting Party may require that, in respect of the request, a fee be paid to the Office.

(h)   A single request shall be sufficient even where the change relates to more than one registration, provided that the holder and the new owner are the same for each registration and that the registration numbers of all registrations concerned are indicated in the request.

(i)   Where the change of ownership does not affect all the goods and/or services listed in the holder's registration, and the applicable law allows the recording of such change, the Office shall create a separate registration referring to the goods and/or services in respect of which the ownership has changed.

(2)   [Language; Translation]

(a)   Any Contracting Party may require that the request, the certificate of transfer or the transfer document referred to in paragraph (1) be in the language, or in one of the languages, admitted by the Office.

(b)   Any Contracting Party may require that, if the documents referred to in paragraphs (1)(b)(i) and (ii), (c) and (e) are not in the language, or in one of the languages, admitted by the Office, the request be accompanied by a translation or a certified translation of the required document in the language, or in one of the languages, admitted by the Office.

(3)   [Change in the Ownership of an Application]

Paragraphs (1) and (2) shall apply, *mutatis mutandis,* where the change in ownership concerns an application or applications, or both an application or applications and a registration or registrations, provided that, where the application number of any application concerned has not yet been issued or is not known to the applicant or his representative, the request otherwise identifies that application as prescribed in the Regulations.

(4)   [Prohibition of Other Requirements]

No Contracting Party may demand that requirements other than those referred to in paragraphs (1) to (3) be complied with in respect of the request referred to in this Article. In particular, the following may not be required:

(i)   subject to paragraph (1)(c), the furnishing of any certificate of, or extract from, a register of commerce;

(ii)   an indication of the new owner's carrying on of an industrial or commercial activity, as well as the furnishing of evidence to that effect;

(iii)   an indication of the new owner's carrying on of an activity corresponding to the goods and/or services affected by the change in ownership, as well as the furnishing of evidence to either effect;

(iv)   an indication that the holder transferred, entirely or in part, his business or the relevant goodwill to the new owner, as well as the furnishing of evidence to either effect.

(5)   [Evidence]

Any Contracting Party may require that evidence, or further evidence where paragraph (1)(c) or (e) applies, be furnished to the Office where that Office may reasonably doubt the veracity of any indication contained in the request or in any document referred to in the present Article.

Article 12

Correction of a Mistake

(1)   [Correction of a Mistake in Respect of a Registration]

(a)   Each Contracting Party shall accept that the request for the correction of a mistake which was made in the application or other request communicated to the Office and which mistake is reflected in its register of marks and/or any publication by the Office be made in a communication signed by the holder or his representative and indicating the registration number of the registration concerned, the mistake to be corrected and the correction to be entered. As regards the requirements concerning the presentation of the request, no Contracting Party shall refuse the request,

(i)   where the request is presented in writing on paper, if it is presented, subject to subparagraph (c), on a form corresponding to the request Form provided for in the Regulations,

(ii)   where the Contracting Party allows the transmittal of communications to the Office by telefacsimile and the request is so transmitted, if the paper copy resulting from such transmittal corresponds, subject to subparagraph (c), to the request Form referred to in item (i).

(b)   Any Contracting Party may require that the request indicate

(i)   the name and address of the holder;

(ii)   where the holder has a representative, the name and address of that representative;

(iii)   where the holder has an address for service, such address.

(c)   Any Contracting Party may require that the request be in the language, or in one of the languages, admitted by the Office.

(d)   Any Contracting Party may require that, in respect of the request, a fee be paid to the Office.

(e)   A single request shall be sufficient even where the correction relates to more than one registration of the same person, provided that the mistake and the requested correction are the same for each registration and that the registration numbers of all registrations concerned are indicated in the request.

(2)   [Correction of a Mistake in Respect of an Application]

Paragraph (1) shall apply, *mutatis mutandis,* where the mistake concerns an application or applications, or both an application or applications and a registration or registrations, provided that, where the application number of any application concerned has not yet been issued or is not known to the applicant or his representative, the request otherwise identifies that application as prescribed in the Regulations.

(3)   [Prohibition of Other Requirements]

No Contracting Party may demand that requirements other than those referred to in paragraphs (1) and (2) be complied with in respect of the request referred to in this Article.

(4)   [Evidence]

Any Contracting Party may require that evidence be furnished to the Office where the Office may reasonably doubt that the alleged mistake is in fact a mistake.

(5)   [Mistakes Made by the Office]

The Office of a Contracting Party shall correct its own mistakes, *ex officio* or upon request, for no fee.

(6)   [Uncorrectable Mistakes]

No Contracting Party shall be obliged to apply paragraphs (1), (2) and (5) to any mistake which cannot be corrected under its law.

Article 13

Duration and Renewal of Registration

(1)   [Indications or Elements Contained in or Accompanying a Request for Renewal; Fee]

(a)   Any Contracting Party may require that the renewal of a registration be subject to the filing of a request and that such request contain some or all of the following indications:

(i)   an indication that renewal is sought;

(ii)   the name and address of the holder;

(iii)   the registration number of the registration concerned;

(iv)   at the option of the Contracting Party, the filing date of the application which resulted in the registration concerned or the registration date of the registration concerned;

(v)   where the holder has a representative, the name and address of that representative;

(vi)   where the holder has an address for service, such address;

(vii)   where the Contracting Party allows the renewal of a registration to be made for some only of the goods and/or services which are recorded in the register of marks and such a renewal is requested, the names of the recorded goods and/or services for which the renewal is requested or the names of the recorded goods and/or services for which the renewal is not requested, grouped according to the classes of the Nice Classification, each group preceded by the number of the class of that Classification to which that group of goods or services belongs and presented in the order of the classes of the said Classification;

(viii) where a Contracting Party allows a request for renewal to be filed by a person other than the holder or his representative and the request is filed by such a person, the name and address of that person;

(ix)   a signature by the holder or his representative or, where item (viii) applies, a signature by the person referred to in that item.

(b)   Any Contracting Party may require that, in respect of the request for renewal, a fee be paid to the Office. Once the fee has been paid in respect of the initial period of the registration or of any renewal period, no further payment may be required for the maintenance of the registration in respect of that period. Fees associated with the furnishing of a declaration and/or evidence of use shall not be regarded, for the purposes of this subparagraph, as payments required for the maintenance of the registration and shall not be affected by this subparagraph.

(c)   Any Contracting Party may require that the request for renewal be presented, and the corresponding fee referred to in subparagraph (b) be paid, to the Office within the period fixed by the law of the Contracting Party, subject to the minimum periods prescribed in the Regulations.

(2)   [Presentation]

As regards the requirements concerning the presentation of the request for renewal, no Contracting Party shall refuse the request,

(i)   where the request is presented in writing on paper, if it is presented, subject to paragraph (3), on a form corresponding to the request Form provided for in the Regulations,

(ii)   where the Contracting Party allows the transmittal of communications to the Office by telefacsimile and the request is so transmitted, if the paper copy resulting from such transmittal corresponds, subject to paragraph (3), to the request Form referred to in item (i).

(3)   [Language]

Any Contracting Party may require that the request for renewal be in the language, or in one of the languages, admitted by the Office.

(4)   [Prohibition of Other Requirements]

No Contracting Party may demand that requirements other than those referred to in paragraphs (1) to (3) be complied with in respect of the request for renewal. In particular, the following may not be required:

(i)   any reproduction or other identification of the mark;

(ii)   the furnishing of evidence to the effect that the mark has been registered, or that its registration has been renewed, in the register of marks of any other Contracting Party:

(iii)   the furnishing of a declaration and/or evidence concerning use of the mark.

(5)   [Evidence]

Any Contracting Party may require that evidence be furnished to the Office in the course of the examination of the request for renewal where the Office may reasonably doubt the veracity of any indication or element contained in the request for renewal.

(6)   [Prohibition of Substantive Examination]

No Office of a Contracting Party may, for the purposes of effecting the renewal, examine the registration as to substance.

(7)   [Duration]

The duration of the initial period of the registration, and the duration of each renewal period, shall be 10 years.

Article 14

Observations in Case of Intended Refusal

An application or a request under Articles 10 to 13 may not be refused totally or in part by an Office without giving the applicant or the requesting party, as the case may be, an opportunity to make observations on the intended refusal within a reasonable time limit.

Article 15

Obligations to Comply With the Paris Convention

Any Contracting Party shall comply with the provisions of the Paris Convention which concern marks.

Article 16

Service Marks

Any Contracting Party shall register service marks and apply to such marks the provisions of the Paris Convention which concern trademarks.

Article 17

Regulations

(1)   [Content]

(a)   The Regulations annexed to this Treaty provide rules concerning

(i)   matters which this Treaty expressly provides to be "prescribed in the Regulations";

(ii)   any details useful in the implementation of the provisions of this Treaty;

(iii) any administrative requirements, matters or procedures.

(b) The Regulations also contain Model International Forms.

(2) [Conflict Between the Treaty and the Regulations]

In the case of conflict between the provisions of this Treaty and those of the Regulations, the former shall prevail.

Article 18

Revision; Protocols

(1) [Revision]

This Treaty may be revised by a diplomatic conference.

(2) [Protocols]

For the purposes of further developing the harmonization of laws on marks, protocols may be adopted by a diplomatic conference in so far as those protocols do not contravene the provisions of this Treaty.

Article 19

Becoming Party to the Treaty

(1) [Eligibility]

The following entities may sign and, subject to paragraphs (2) and (3) and Article 20(1) and (3), become party to this Treaty:

(i) any State member of the Organization in respect of which marks may be registered with its own Office;

(ii) any intergovernmental organization which maintains an Office in which marks may be registered with effect in the territory in which the constituting treaty of the intergovernmental organization applies, in all its member States or in those of its member States which are designated for such purpose in the relevant application, provided that all the member States of the intergovernmental organization are members of the Organization;

(iii) any State member of the Organization in respect of which marks may be registered only through the Office of another specified State that is member of the Organization;

(iv) any State member of the Organization in respect of which marks may be registered only through the Office maintained by an intergovernmental organization of which that State is a member;

(v) any State member of the Organization in respect of which marks may be registered only through an Office common to a group of States members of the Organization.

(2) [Ratification or Accession]

Any entity referred to in paragraph (1) may deposit

(i) an instrument of ratification, if it has signed this Treaty,

(ii) an instrument of accession, if it has not signed this Treaty.

(3) [Effective Date of Deposit]

(a) Subject to subparagraph (b), the effective date of the deposit of an instrument of ratification or accession shall be,

(i) in the case of a State referred to in paragraph (1)(i), the date on which the instrument of that State is deposited;

(ii) in the case of an intergovernmental organization, the date on which the instrument of that intergovernmental organization is deposited;

(iii) in the case of a State referred to in paragraph (1)(iii), the date on which the following condition is fulfilled: the instrument of that State has been deposited and the instrument of the other, specified State has been deposited;

(iv) in the case of a State referred to in paragraph (1)(iv), the date applicable under (ii), above;

(v) in the case of a State member of a group of States referred to in paragraph (1)(v), the date on which the instruments of all the States members of the group have been deposited.

(b) Any instrument of ratification or accession (referred to in this subparagraph as "instrument") of a State may be accompanied by a declaration making it a condition to its being considered as deposited that the instrument of one other State or one intergovernmental organization, or the instruments of two other States, or the instruments of one other State and one intergovernmental organization, specified by name and eligible to become party to this Treaty, is or are also deposited. The instrument containing such a declaration shall be considered to have been deposited on the day on which the condition indicated in the declaration is fulfilled. However, when the deposit of any instrument specified in the declaration is, itself, accompanied by a declaration of the said kind, that instrument shall be considered as deposited on the day on which the condition specified in the latter declaration is fulfilled.

(c) Any declaration made under paragraph (b) may be withdrawn, in its entirety or in part, at any time. Any such withdrawal shall become effective on the date on which the notification of withdrawal is received by the Director General.

Article 20

Effective Date of Ratifications and Accessions

(1) [Instruments to Be Taken Into Consideration]

For the purposes of this Article, only instruments of ratification or accession that are deposited by entities referred to in Article 19(1) and that have an effective date according to Article 19(3) shall be taken into consideration.

(2) [Entry Into Force of the Treaty]

This Treaty shall enter into force three months after five States have deposited their instruments of ratification or accession.

(3) [Entry Into Force of Ratifications and Accessions Subsequent to the Entry Into Force of the Treaty]

Any entity not covered by paragraph (2) shall become bound by this Treaty three months after the date on which it has deposited its instrument of ratification or accession.

Article 21

Reservations

(1) [Special Kinds of Marks]

Any State or intergovernmental organization may declare through a reservation that, notwithstanding Article 2(1)(a) and (2)(a), any of the provisions of Articles 3(1) and (2), 5, 7, 11 and 13 shall not apply to associated marks, defensive marks or derivative marks. Such reservation shall specify those of the aforementioned provisions to which the reservation relates.

(2) [Modalities]

Any reservation under paragraph (1) shall be made in declaration accompanying the instrument of ratification of, or accession to, this Treaty of the State or intergovernmental organization making the reservation.

(3)   [Withdrawal]

Any reservation under paragraph (1) may be withdrawn at any time.

(4)   [Prohibition of Other Reservations]

No reservation to this Treaty other than the reservation allowed under paragraph (1) shall be permitted.

Article 22

Transitional Provisions

(1)   [Single Application for Goods and Services in Several Classes; Division of Application]

(a)   Any State or intergovernmental organization may declare that, notwithstanding Article 3(5), an application may be filed with the Office only in respect of goods or services which belong to one class of the Nice Classification.

(b)   Any State or intergovernmental organization may declare that, notwithstanding Article 6, where goods and/or services belonging to several classes of the Nice Classification have been included in one and the same application, such application shall result in two or more registrations in the register of marks, provided that each and every such registration shall bear a reference to all other such registrations resulting from the said application.

(c)   Any State or intergovernmental organization that has made a declaration under subparagraph (a) may declare that, notwithstanding Article 7(1), no application may be divided.

(2)   [Single Power of Attorney for More Than One Application and/or Registration]

Any State or intergovernmental organization may declare that, notwithstanding Article 4(3)(b), a power of attorney may only relate to one application or one registration.

(3)   [Prohibition of Requirement of Certification of Signature of Power of Attorney and of Signature of Application]

Any State or intergovernmental organization may declare that, notwithstanding Article 8(4), the signature of a power of attorney or the signature by the applicant of an application may be required to be the subject of an attestation, notarization, authentication, legalization or other certification.

(4)   [Single Request for More Than One Application and/or Registration in Respect of a Change in Name and/or Address, a Change in Ownership or a Correction of a Mistake]

Any State or intergovernmental organization may declare that, notwithstanding Article 10(1)(e), (2) and (3), Article 11(1)(h) and (3) and Article 12(1)(e) and (2), a request for the recordal of a change in name and/or address, a request for the recordal of a change in ownership and a request for the correction of a mistake may only relate to one application or one registration.

(5)   [Furnishing, on the Occasion of Renewal, of Declaration and/or Evidence Concerning Use]

Any State or intergovernmental organization may declare that, notwithstanding Article 13(4)(iii), it will require, on the occasion of renewal, the furnishing of a declaration and/or of evidence concerning use of the mark.

(6)   [Substantive Examination on the Occasion of Renewal]

Any State or intergovernmental organization may declare that, notwithstanding Article 13(6), the Office may, on the occasion of the first renewal of a registration covering services, examine such registration as to substance, provided that such examination shall be limited to the elimination of multiple registrations based on applications filed during a period of six months following the entry into force of the law of such State or organization that introduced, before the entry into force of this Treaty, the possibility of registering service marks.

(7)   [Common Provisions]

(a)   A State or an intergovernmental organization may make a declaration under paragraphs (1) to (6) only if, at the time of depositing its instrument of ratification of, or accession to, this Treaty, the continued application of its law would, without such a declaration, be contrary to the relevant provisions of this Treaty.

(b)   Any declaration under paragraphs (1) to (6) shall accompany the instrument of ratification of, or accession to, this Treaty of the State or intergovernmental organization making the declaration.

(c)   Any declaration made under paragraphs (1) to (6) may be withdrawn at any time.

(8)   [Loss of Effect of Declaration]

(a)   Subject to subparagraph (c), any declaration made under paragraphs (1) to (6) by a State regarded as a developing country in conformity with the established practice of the General Assembly of the United Nations, or by an intergovernmental organization each member of which is such a State, shall lose its effect at the end of a period of eight years from the date of entry into force of this Treaty.

(b)   Subject to subparagraph (c), any declaration made under paragraphs (1) to (6) by a State other than a State referred to in subparagraph (a), or by an intergovernmental organization other than an intergovernmental organization referred to in subparagraph (a), shall lose its effect at the end of a period of six years from the date of entry into force of this Treaty.

(c)   Where a declaration made under paragraphs (1) to (6) has not been withdrawn under paragraph (7)(c), or has not lost its effect under subparagraph (a) or (b), before October 28, 2004, it shall lose its effect on October 28, 2004.

(9)   [Becoming Party to the Treaty]

Until December 31, 1999, any State which, on the date of the adoption of this Treaty, is a member of the International (Paris) Union for the Protection of Industrial Property without being a member of the Organization may, notwithstanding Article 19(1)(i), become a party to this Treaty if marks may be registered with its own Office.

Article 23

Denunciation of the Treaty

(1)   [Notification]

Any Contracting Party may denounce this Treaty by notification addressed to the Director General.

(2)   [Effective Date]

Denunciation shall take effect one year from the date on which the Director General has received the notification. It shall not affect the application of this Treaty to any application pending or any mark registered in respect of the denouncing Contracting Party at the time of the expiration of the said one-year period, provided that the denouncing Contracting Party may, after the expiration of the said one-year period, discontinue applying this Treaty to any registration as from the date on which that registration is due for renewal.

Article 24

Languages of the Treaty; Signature

(1)   [Original Texts; Official Texts]

(a)   This Treaty shall be signed in a single original in the English, Arabic, Chinese, French, Russian and Spanish languages, all texts being equally authentic.

(b)   At the request of a Contracting Party, an official text in a language not referred to in subparagraph (a) that is an official language of that Contracting Party shall be established by the Director General after consultation with the said Contracting Party and any other interested Contracting Party.

(2)   [Time Limit for Signature]

This Treaty shall remain open for signature at the headquarters of the Organization for one year after its adoption.

Article 25

Depositary

The Director General shall be the depositary of this Treaty.

[On March 27, 2006 WIPO adopted a new treaty known as the Singapore Treaty on the Law of Trademarks, the stated purpose of which is to update the Trademark Law Treaty in light of recent technological developments. This treaty has not yet been ratified by the United States and is not yet in force. It will take effect when it is ratified by 15 nations. The text of the treaty can be found on-line at http://www.wipo.int/treaties/en/ip/singapore/singapore_treaty.html]

G. SINGAPORE TREATY ON THE LAW OF TRADEMARKS[1]

List of Articles

Article 1

Abbreviated Expressions

For the purposes of this Treaty, unless expressly stated otherwise:

　　(i)　"Office" means the agency entrusted by a Contracting Party with the registration of marks;

---

[1] This treaty was ratified by the United States on October 1, 2008 and entered into force on March 16, 2009. Forty-eight countries are parties to this treaty as of early 2018.

(ii) "registration" means the registration of a mark by an Office;

(iii) "application" means an application for registration;

(iv) "communication" means any application, or any request, declaration, correspondence or other information relating to an application or a registration, which is filed with the Office;

(v) references to a "person" shall be construed as references to both a natural person and a legal entity;

(vi) "holder" means the person whom the register of marks shows as the holder of the registration;

(vii) "register of marks" means the collection of data maintained by an Office, which includes the contents of all registrations and all data recorded in respect of all registrations, irrespective of the medium in which such data are stored;

(viii) "procedure before the Office" means any procedure in proceedings before the Office with respect to an application or a registration;

(ix) "Paris Convention" means the Paris Convention for the Protection of Industrial Property, signed at Paris on March 20, 1883, as revised and amended;

(x) "Nice Classification" means the classification established by the Nice Agreement Concerning the International Classification of Goods and Services for the Purposes of the Registration of Marks, signed at Nice on June 15, 1957, as revised and amended;

(xi) "license" means a license for the use of a mark under the law of a Contracting Party;

(xii) "licensee" means the person to whom a license has been granted;

(xiii) "Contracting Party" means any State or intergovernmental organization party to this Treaty;

(xiv) "Diplomatic Conference" means the convocation of Contracting Parties for the purpose of revising or amending the Treaty;

(xv) "Assembly" means the Assembly referred to in Article 23;

(xvi) references to an "instrument of ratification" shall be construed as including references to instruments of acceptance and approval;

(xvii) "Organization" means the World Intellectual Property Organization;

(xviii) "International Bureau" means the International Bureau of the Organization;

(xix) "Director General" means the Director General of the Organization;

(xx) "Regulations" means the Regulations under this Treaty that are referred to in Article 22;

(xxi) references to an "Article" or to a "paragraph", "subparagraph" or "item" of an Article shall be construed as including references to the corresponding rule(s) under the Regulations;

(xxii) "TLT 1994" means the Trademark Law Treaty done at Geneva on October 27, 1994.

Article 2

Marks to Which the Treaty Applies

(1) [*Nature of Marks*] Any Contracting Party shall apply this Treaty to marks consisting of signs that can be registered as marks under its law.

(2) [*Kinds of Marks*]

(a)   This Treaty shall apply to marks relating to goods (trademarks) or services (service marks) or both goods and services.

(b)   This Treaty shall not apply to collective marks, certification marks and guarantee marks.

Article 3

Application

(1)   [Indications or Elements Contained in or Accompanying an Application; Fee]

(a)   Any Contracting Party may require that an application contain some or all of the following indications or elements:

(i)   a request for registration;

(ii)   the name and address of the applicant;

(iii)   the name of a State of which the applicant is a national if he/she is the national of any State, the name of a State in which the applicant has his/her domicile, if any, and the name of a State in which the applicant has a real and effective industrial or commercial establishment, if any;

(iv)   where the applicant is a legal entity, the legal nature of that legal entity and the State, and, where applicable, the territorial unit within that State, under the law of which the said legal entity has been organized;

(v)   where the applicant has a representative, the name and address of that representative;

(vi)   where an address for service is required under Article 4(2)(b), such address;

(vii)   where the applicant wishes to take advantage of the priority of an earlier application, a declaration claiming the priority of that earlier application, together with indications and evidence in support of the declaration of priority that may be required pursuant to Article 4 of the Paris Convention;

(viii)   where the applicant wishes to take advantage of any protection resulting from the display of goods and/or services in an exhibition, a declaration to that effect, together with indications in support of that declaration, as required by the law of the Contracting Party;

(ix)   at least one representation of the mark, as prescribed in the Regulations;

(x)   where applicable, a statement, as prescribed in the Regulations, indicating the type of mark as well as any specific requirements applicable to that type of mark;

(xi)   where applicable, a statement, as prescribed in the Regulations, indicating that the applicant wishes that the mark be registered and published in the standard characters used by the Office;

(xii)   where applicable, a statement, as prescribed in the Regulations, indicating that the applicant wishes to claim color as a distinctive feature of the mark;

(xiii)   a transliteration of the mark or of certain parts of the mark;

(xiv)   a translation of the mark or of certain parts of the mark;

(xv)   the names of the goods and/or services for which the registration is sought, grouped according to the classes of the Nice Classification, each group preceded by the number of the class of that Classification to which that group of goods or services belongs and presented in the order of the classes of the said Classification;

(xvi) a declaration of intention to use the mark, as required by the law of the Contracting Party.

(b)   The applicant may file, instead of or in addition to the declaration of intention to use the mark referred to in subparagraph (a)(xvi), a declaration of actual use of the mark and evidence to that effect, as required by the law of the Contracting Party.

(c)   Any Contracting Party may require that, in respect of the application, fees be paid to the Office.

(2)   [*Single Application for Goods and/or Services in Several Classes*] One and the same application may relate to several goods and/or services, irrespective of whether they belong to one class or to several classes of the Nice Classification.

(3)   [*Actual Use*] Any Contracting Party may require that, where a declaration of intention to use has been filed under paragraph (1)(a)(xvi), the applicant furnish to the Office within a time limit fixed in its law, subject to the minimum time limit prescribed in the Regulations, evidence of the actual use of the mark, as required by the said law.

(4)   [*Prohibition of Other Requirements*] No Contracting Party may demand that requirements other than those referred to in paragraphs (1) and (3) and in Article 8 be complied with in respect of the application. In particular, the following may not be required in respect of the application throughout its pendency:

(i)   the furnishing of any certificate of, or extract from, a register of commerce;

(ii)   an indication of the applicant's carrying on of an industrial or commercial activity, as well as the furnishing of evidence to that effect;

(iii)   an indication of the applicant's carrying on of an activity corresponding to the goods and/or services listed in the application, as well as the furnishing of evidence to that effect;

(iv)   the furnishing of evidence to the effect that the mark has been registered in the register of marks of another Contracting Party or of a State party to the Paris Convention which is not a Contracting Party, except where the applicant claims the application of Article 6*quinquies* of the Paris Convention.

(5)   [*Evidence*] Any Contracting Party may require that evidence be furnished to the Office in the course of the examination of the application where the Office may reasonably doubt the veracity of any indication or element contained in the application.

Article 4

Representation; Address for Service

(1)   [*Representatives Admitted to Practice*]

(a)   Any Contracting Party may require that a representative appointed for the purposes of any procedure before the Office

(i)   have the right, under the applicable law, to practice before the Office in respect of applications and registrations and, where applicable, be admitted to practice before the Office;

(ii)   provide, as its address, an address on a territory prescribed by the Contracting Party.

(b)   An act, with respect to any procedure before the Office, by or in relation to a representative who complies with the requirements applied by the Contracting Party under subparagraph (a), shall have the effect of an act by or in relation to the applicant, holder or other interested person who appointed that representative.

(2)   [*Mandatory Representation; Address for Service*]

(a)   Any Contracting Party may require that, for the purposes of any procedure before the Office, an applicant, holder or other interested person who has neither a domicile nor a real and effective industrial or commercial establishment on its territory be represented by a representative.

(b)   Any Contracting Party may, to the extent that it does not require representation in accordance with subparagraph (a), require that, for the purposes of any procedure before the Office, an applicant, holder or other interested person who has neither a domicile nor a real and effective industrial or commercial establishment on its territory have an address for service on that territory.

(3)   [*Power of Attorney*]

(a)   Whenever a Contracting Party allows or requires an applicant, a holder or any other interested person to be represented by a representative before the Office, it may require that the representative be appointed in a separate communication (hereinafter referred to as "power of attorney") indicating the name of the applicant, the holder or the other person, as the case may be.

(b)   The power of attorney may relate to one or more applications and/or registrations identified in the power of attorney or, subject to any exception indicated by the appointing person, to all existing and future applications and/or registrations of that person.

(c)   The power of attorney may limit the powers of the representative to certain acts. Any Contracting Party may require that any power of attorney under which the representative has the right to withdraw an application or to surrender a registration contain an express indication to that effect.

(d)   Where a communication is submitted to the Office by a person who refers to itself in the communication as a representative but where the Office is, at the time of the receipt of the communication, not in possession of the required power of attorney, the Contracting Party may require that the power of attorney be submitted to the Office within the time limit fixed by the Contracting Party, subject to the minimum time limit prescribed in the Regulations. Any Contracting Party may provide that, where the power of attorney has not been submitted to the Office within the time limit fixed by the Contracting Party, the communication by the said person shall have no effect.

(4)   [*Reference to Power of Attorney*] Any Contracting Party may require that any communication made to the Office by a representative for the purposes of a procedure before the Office contain a reference to the power of attorney on the basis of which the representative acts.

(5)   [*Prohibition of Other Requirements*] No Contracting Party may demand that requirements other than those referred to in paragraphs (3) and (4) and in Article 8 be complied with in respect of the matters dealt with in those paragraphs.

(6)   [*Evidence*] Any Contracting Party may require that evidence be furnished to the Office where the Office may reasonably doubt the veracity of any indication contained in any communication referred to in paragraphs (3) and (4).

Article 5

Filing Date

(1)   [*Permitted Requirements*]

(a)   Subject to subparagraph (b) and paragraph (2), a Contracting Party shall accord as the filing date of an application the date on which the Office received the following indications and elements in the language required under Article 8(2):

(i)   an express or implicit indication that the registration of a mark is sought;

(ii)   indications allowing the identity of the applicant to be established;

(iii) indications allowing the applicant or its representative, if any, to be contacted by the Office;

(iv)   a sufficiently clear representation of the mark whose registration is sought;

(v)   the list of the goods and/or services for which the registration is sought;

(vi)   where Article 3(1)(a)(xvi) or (b) applies, the declaration referred to in Article 3(1)(a)(xvi) or the declaration and evidence referred to in Article 3(1)(b), respectively, as required by the law of the Contracting Party.

(b)   Any Contracting Party may accord as the filing date of the application the date on which the Office received only some, rather than all, of the indications and elements referred to in subparagraph (a) or received them in a language other than the language required under Article 8(2).

(2)   [*Permitted Additional Requirement*]

(a)   A Contracting Party may provide that no filing date shall be accorded until the required fees are paid.

(b)   A Contracting Party may apply the requirement referred to in subparagraph (a) only if it applied such requirement at the time of becoming party to this Treaty.

(3)   [*Corrections and Time Limits*] The modalities of, and time limits for, corrections under paragraphs (1) and (2) shall be fixed in the Regulations.

(4)   [*Prohibition of Other Requirements*] No Contracting Party may demand that requirements other than those referred to in paragraphs (1) and (2) be complied with in respect of the filing date.

Article 6

Single Registration for Goods and/or Services in Several Classes

Where goods and/or services belonging to several classes of the Nice Classification have been included in one and the same application, such an application shall result in one and the same registration.

Article 7

Division of Application and Registration

(1)   [*Division of Application*]

(a)   Any application listing several goods and/or services (hereinafter referred to as "initial application") may,

(i)   at least until the decision by the Office on the registration of the mark,

(ii)   during any opposition proceedings against the decision of the Office to register the mark,

(iii) during any appeal proceedings against the decision on the registration of the mark,

be divided by the applicant or at its request into two or more applications (hereinafter referred to as "divisional applications") by distributing among the latter the goods and/or services listed in the initial application. The divisional applications shall preserve the filing date of the initial application and the benefit of the right of priority, if any.

(b)   Any Contracting Party shall, subject to subparagraph (a), be free to establish requirements for the division of an application, including the payment of fees.

(2)   [*Division of Registration*] Paragraph (1) shall apply, mutatis mutandis, with respect to a division of a registration. Such a division shall be permitted

(i)   during any proceedings in which the validity of the registration is challenged before the Office by a third party,

(ii)   during any appeal proceedings against a decision taken by the Office during the former proceedings,

provided that a Contracting Party may exclude the possibility of the division of registrations if its law allows third parties to oppose the registration of a mark before the mark is registered.

Article 8

Communications

(1)   [*Means of Transmittal and Form of Communications*] Any Contracting Party may choose the means of transmittal of communications and whether it accepts communications on paper, communications in electronic form or any other form of communication.

(2)   [*Language of Communications*]

(a)   Any Contracting Party may require that any communication be in a language admitted by the Office. Where the Office admits more than one language, the applicant, holder or other interested person may be required to comply with any other language requirement applicable with respect to the Office, provided that no indication or element of the communication may be required to be in more than one language.

(b)   No Contracting Party may require the attestation, notarization, authentication, legalization or any other certification of any translation of a communication other than as provided under this Treaty.

(c)   Where a Contracting Party does not require a communication to be in a language admitted by its Office, the Office may require that a translation of that communication by an official translator or a representative, into a language admitted by the Office, be supplied within a reasonable time limit.

(3)   [*Signature of Communications on Paper*]

(a)   Any Contracting Party may require that a communication on paper be signed by the applicant, holder or other interested person. Where a Contracting Party requires a communication on paper to be signed, that Contracting Party shall accept any signature that complies with the requirements prescribed in the Regulations.

(b)   No Contracting Party may require the attestation, notarization, authentication, legalization or other certification of any signature except, where the law of the Contracting Party so provides, if the signature concerns the surrender of a registration.

(c)   Notwithstanding subparagraph (b), a Contracting Party may require that evidence be filed with the Office where the Office may reasonably doubt the authenticity of any signature of a communication on paper.

(4)   [*Communications Filed in Electronic Form or by Electronic Means of Transmittal*] Where a Contracting Party permits the filing of communications in electronic form or by electronic means of transmittal, it may require that any such communications comply with the requirements prescribed in the Regulations.

(5)   [*Presentation of a Communication*] Any Contracting Party shall accept the presentation of a communication the content of which corresponds to the relevant Model International Form, if any, provided for in the Regulations.

(6)   [*Prohibition of Other Requirements*] No Contracting Party may demand that, in respect of paragraphs (1) to (5), requirements other than those referred to in this Article be complied with.

(7)   [*Means of Communication with Representative*] Nothing in this Article regulates the means of communication between an applicant, holder or other interested person and its representative.

Article 9

Classification of Goods and/or Services

(1)   [*Indications of Goods and/or Services*] Each registration and any publication effected by an Office which concerns an application or registration and which indicates goods and/or services shall indicate the goods and/or services by their names, grouped according to the classes of the Nice Classification, and each group shall be preceded by the number of the class of that Classification to which that group of goods or services belongs and shall be presented in the order of the classes of the said Classification.

(2)   [*Goods or Services in the Same Class or in Different Classes*]

     (a)   Goods or services may not be considered as being similar to each other on the ground that, in any registration or publication by the Office, they appear in the same class of the Nice Classification.

     (b)   Goods or services may not be considered as being dissimilar from each other on the ground that, in any registration or publication by the Office, they appear in different classes of the Nice Classification.

Article 10

Changes in Names or Addresses

(1)   [*Changes in the Name or Address of the Holder*]

     (a)   Where there is no change in the person of the holder but there is a change in its name and/or address, each Contracting Party shall accept that a request for the recordal of the change by the Office in its register of marks be made by the holder in a communication indicating the registration number of the registration concerned and the change to be recorded.

     (b)   Any Contracting Party may require that the request indicate

         (i)   the name and address of the holder;

         (ii)   where the holder has a representative, the name and address of that representative;

         (iii)   where the holder has an address for service, such address.

     (c)   Any Contracting Party may require that, in respect of the request, a fee be paid to the Office.

     (d)   A single request shall be sufficient even where the change relates to more than one registration, provided that the registration numbers of all registrations concerned are indicated in the request.

(2)   [*Change in the Name or Address of the Applicant*] Paragraph (1) shall apply, *mutatis mutandis*, where the change concerns an application or applications, or both an application or applications and a registration or registrations, provided that, where the application number of any application concerned has not yet been issued or is not known to the applicant or its representative, the request otherwise identifies that application as prescribed in the Regulations.

(3)   [*Change in the Name or Address of the Representative or in the Address for Service*] Paragraph (1) shall apply, *mutatis mutandis*, to any change in the name or address of the representative, if any, and to any change relating to the address for service, if any.

(4)   [*Prohibition of Other Requirements*] No Contracting Party may demand that requirements other than those referred to in paragraphs (1) to (3) and in Article 8 be complied with in respect of the request referred to in this Article. In particular, the furnishing of any certificate concerning the change may not be required.

(5)   [*Evidence*] Any Contracting Party may require that evidence be furnished to the Office where the Office may reasonably doubt the veracity of any indication contained in the request.

Article 11

Change in Ownership

(1)   [*Change in the Ownership of a Registration*]

(a)   Where there is a change in the person of the holder, each Contracting Party shall accept that a request for the recordal of the change by the Office in its register of marks be made by the holder or by the person who acquired the ownership (hereinafter referred to as "new owner") in a communication indicating the registration number of the registration concerned and the change to be recorded.

(b)   Where the change in ownership results from a contract, any Contracting Party may require that the request indicate that fact and be accompanied, at the option of the requesting party, by one of the following:

(i)   a copy of the contract, which copy may be required to be certified, by a notary public or any other competent public authority, as being in conformity with the original contract;

(ii)   an extract of the contract showing the change in ownership, which extract may be required to be certified, by a notary public or any other competent public authority, as being a true extract of the contract;

(iii)   an uncertified certificate of transfer drawn up in the form and with the content as prescribed in the Regulations and signed by both the holder and the new owner;

(iv)   an uncertified transfer document drawn up in the form and with the content as prescribed in the Regulations and signed by both the holder and the new owner.

(c)   Where the change in ownership results from a merger, any Contracting Party may require that the request indicate that fact and be accompanied by a copy of a document, which document originates from the competent authority and evidences the merger, such as a copy of an extract from a register of commerce, and that that copy be certified by the authority which issued the document or by a notary public or any other competent public authority, as being in conformity with the original document.

(d)   Where there is a change in the person of one or more but not all of several co-holders and such change in ownership results from a contract or a merger, any Contracting Party may require that any co-holder in respect of which there is no change in ownership give its express consent to the change in ownership in a document signed by it.

(e)   Where the change in ownership does not result from a contract or a merger but from another ground, for example, from operation of law or a court decision, any Contracting Party may require that the request indicate that fact and be accompanied by a copy of a document evidencing the change and that that copy be certified as being in conformity with the original document by the authority which issued the document or by a notary public or any other competent public authority.

(f)   Any Contracting Party may require that the request indicate

(i)   the name and address of the holder;

(ii)   the name and address of the new owner;

(iii) the name of a State of which the new owner is a national if he/she is the national of any State, the name of a State in which the new owner has his/her domicile, if any, and the name of a State in which the new owner has a real and effective industrial or commercial establishment, if any;

(iv) where the new owner is a legal entity, the legal nature of that legal entity and the State, and, where applicable, the territorial unit within that State, under the law of which the said legal entity has been organized;

(v) where the holder has a representative, the name and address of that representative;

(vi) where the holder has an address for service, such address;

(vii) where the new owner has a representative, the name and address of that representative;

(viii) where the new owner is required to have an address for service under Article 4(2)(b), such address.

(g) Any Contracting Party may require that, in respect of the request, a fee be paid to the Office.

(h) A single request shall be sufficient even where the change relates to more than one registration, provided that the holder and the new owner are the same for each registration and that the registration numbers of all registrations concerned are indicated in the request.

(i) Where the change of ownership does not affect all the goods and/or services listed in the holder's registration, and the applicable law allows the recording of such change, the Office shall create a separate registration referring to the goods and/or services in respect of which the ownership has changed.

(2) [*Change in the Ownership of an Application*] Paragraph (1) shall apply, *mutatis mutandis*, where the change in ownership concerns an application or applications, or both an application or applications and a registration or registrations, provided that, where the application number of any application concerned has not yet been issued or is not known to the applicant or its representative, the request otherwise identifies that application as prescribed in the Regulations.

(3) [*Prohibition of Other Requirements*] No Contracting Party may demand that requirements other than those referred to in paragraphs (1) and (2) and in Article 8 be complied with in respect of the request referred to in this Article. In particular, the following may not be required:

(i) subject to paragraph (1)(c), the furnishing of any certificate of, or extract from, a register of commerce;

(ii) an indication of the new owner's carrying on of an industrial or commercial activity, as well as the furnishing of evidence to that effect;

(iii) an indication of the new owner's carrying on of an activity corresponding to the goods and/or services affected by the change in ownership, as well as the furnishing of evidence to either effect;

(iv) an indication that the holder transferred, entirely or in part, its business or the relevant goodwill to the new owner, as well as the furnishing of evidence to either effect.

(4) [*Evidence*] Any Contracting Party may require that evidence, or further evidence where paragraph (1)(c) or (e) applies, be furnished to the Office where that Office may reasonably doubt the veracity of any indication contained in the request or in any document referred to in the present Article.

Article 12

Correction of a Mistake

(1)   [*Correction of a Mistake in Respect of a Registration*]

(a)   Each Contracting Party shall accept that the request for the correction of a mistake which was made in the application or other request communicated to the Office and which mistake is reflected in its register of marks and/or any publication by the Office be made by the holder in a communication indicating the registration number of the registration concerned, the mistake to be corrected and the correction to be entered.

(b)   Any Contracting Party may require that the request indicate

(i)   the name and address of the holder;

(ii)   where the holder has a representative, the name and address of that representative;

(iii)   where the holder has an address for service, such address.

(c)   Any Contracting Party may require that, in respect of the request, a fee be paid to the Office.

(d)   A single request shall be sufficient even where the correction relates to more than one registration of the same person, provided that the mistake and the requested correction are the same for each registration and that the registration numbers of all registrations concerned are indicated in the request.

(2)   [*Correction of a Mistake in Respect of an Application*] Paragraph (1) shall apply, *mutatis mutandis*, where the mistake concerns an application or applications, or both an application or applications and a registration or registrations, provided that, where the application number of any application concerned has not yet been issued or is not known to the applicant or its representative, the request otherwise identifies that application as prescribed in the Regulations.

(3)   [*Prohibition of Other Requirements*] No Contracting Party may demand that requirements other than those referred to in paragraphs (1) and (2) and in Article 8 be complied with in respect of the request referred to in this Article.

(4)   [*Evidence*] Any Contracting Party may require that evidence be furnished to the Office where the Office may reasonably doubt that the alleged mistake is in fact a mistake.

(5)   [*Mistakes Made by the Office*] The Office of a Contracting Party shall correct its own mistakes, *ex officio* or upon request, for no fee.

(6)   [*Uncorrectable Mistakes*] No Contracting Party shall be obliged to apply paragraphs (1), (2) and (5) to any mistake which cannot be corrected under its law.

Article 13

Duration and Renewal of Registration

(1)   [*Indications or Elements Contained in or Accompanying a Request for Renewal; Fee*]

(a)   Any Contracting Party may require that the renewal of a registration be subject to the filing of a request and that such request contain some or all of the following indications:

(i)   an indication that renewal is sought;

(ii)   the name and address of the holder;

(iii)   the registration number of the registration concerned;

(iv)   at the option of the Contracting Party, the filing date of the application which resulted in the registration concerned or the registration date of the registration concerned;

(v)   where the holder has a representative, the name and address of that representative;

(vi)   where the holder has an address for service, such address;

(vii)   where the Contracting Party allows the renewal of a registration to be made for some only of the goods and/or services which are recorded in the register of marks and such a renewal is requested, the names of the recorded goods and/or services for which the renewal is requested or the names of the recorded goods and/or services for which the renewal is not requested, grouped according to the classes of the Nice Classification, each group preceded by the number of the class of that Classification to which that group of goods or services belongs and presented in the order of the classes of the said Classification;

(viii) where a Contracting Party allows a request for renewal to be filed by a person other than the holder or its representative and the request is filed by such a person, the name and address of that person.

(b)   Any Contracting Party may require that, in respect of the request for renewal, a fee be paid to the Office. Once the fee has been paid in respect of the initial period of the registration or of any renewal period, no further payment may be required for the maintenance of the registration in respect of that period. Fees associated with the furnishing of a declaration and/or evidence of use shall not be regarded, for the purposes of this subparagraph, as payments required for the maintenance of the registration and shall not be affected by this subparagraph.

(c)   Any Contracting Party may require that the request for renewal be presented, and the corresponding fee referred to in subparagraph (b) be paid, to the Office within the period fixed by the law of the Contracting Party, subject to the minimum periods prescribed in the Regulations.

(2)   [*Prohibition of Other Requirements*] No Contracting Party may demand that requirements other than those referred to in paragraph (1) and in Article 8 be complied with in respect of the request for renewal. In particular, the following may not be required:

(i)   any representation or other identification of the mark;

(ii)   the furnishing of evidence to the effect that the mark has been registered, or that its registration has been renewed, in any other register of marks;

(iii)   the furnishing of a declaration and/or evidence concerning use of the mark.

(3)   [*Evidence*] Any Contracting Party may require that evidence be furnished to the Office in the course of the examination of the request for renewal where the Office may reasonably doubt the veracity of any indication or element contained in the request for renewal.

(4)   [*Prohibition of Substantive Examination*] No Office of a Contracting Party may, for the purposes of effecting the renewal, examine the registration as to substance.

(5)   [*Duration*] The duration of the initial period of the registration, and the duration of each renewal period, shall be 10 years.

Article 14

Relief Measures in Case of Failure to Comply with Time Limits

(1)   [*Relief Measure Before the Expiry of a Time Limit*] A Contracting Party may provide for the extension of a time limit for an action in a procedure before the Office in respect of an application or a registration, if a request to that effect is filed with the Office prior to the expiry of the time limit.

(2)   [*Relief Measures After the Expiry of a Time Limit*] Where an applicant, holder or other interested person has failed to comply with a time limit ("the time limit concerned") for an action in a procedure before the Office of a Contracting Party in respect of an application or a registration, the Contracting Party shall provide for one or more of the following relief measures, in accordance with the requirements prescribed in the Regulations, if a request to that effect is filed with the Office:

(i)   extension of the time limit concerned for the period prescribed in the Regulations;

(ii)   continued processing with respect to the application or registration;

(iii)   reinstatement of the rights of the applicant, holder or other interested person with respect to the application or registration if the Office finds that the failure to comply with the time limit concerned occurred in spite of due care required by the circumstances having been taken or, at the option of the Contracting Party, that the failure was unintentional.

(3)   [*Exceptions*] No Contracting Party shall be required to provide for any of the relief measures referred to in paragraph (2) with respect to the exceptions prescribed in the Regulations.

(4)   [*Fee*] Any Contracting Party may require that a fee be paid in respect of any of the relief measures referred to in paragraphs (1) and (2).

(5)   [*Prohibition of Other Requirements*] No Contracting Party may demand that requirements other than those referred to in this Article and in Article 8 be complied with in respect of any of the relief measures referred to in paragraph (2).

Article 15

Obligation to Comply with the Paris Convention

Any Contracting Party shall comply with the provisions of the Paris Convention which concern marks.

Article 16

Service Marks

Any Contracting Party shall register service marks and apply to such marks the provisions of the Paris Convention which concern trademarks.

Article 17

Request for Recordal of a License

(1)   [*Requirements Concerning the Request for Recordal*] Where the law of a Contracting Party provides for the recordal of a license with its Office, that Contracting Party may require that the request for recordal

(i)   be filed in accordance with the requirements prescribed in the Regulations, and

(ii)   be accompanied by the supporting documents prescribed in the Regulations.

(2)   [*Fee*] Any Contracting Party may require that, in respect of the recordal of a license, a fee be paid to the Office.

(3)   [*Single Request Relating to Several Registrations*] A single request shall be sufficient even where the license relates to more than one registration, provided that the registration numbers of all registrations concerned are indicated in the request, the holder and the licensee are the same for all registrations, and the request indicates the scope of the license in accordance with the Regulations with respect to all registrations.

(4)   [*Prohibition of Other Requirements*]

(a)   No Contracting Party may demand that requirements other than those referred to in paragraphs (1) to (3) and in Article 8 be complied with in respect of the recordal of a license with its Office. In particular, the following may not be required:

(i)   the furnishing of the registration certificate of the mark which is the subject of the license;

(ii)   the furnishing of the license contract or a translation of it;

          (iii) an indication of the financial terms of the license contract.

    (b) Subparagraph (a) is without prejudice to any obligations existing under the law of a Contracting Party concerning the disclosure of information for purposes other than the recording of the license in the register of marks.

    (5) *[Evidence]* Any Contracting Party may require that evidence be furnished to the Office where the Office may reasonably doubt the veracity of any indication contained in the request or in any document referred to in the Regulations.

    (6) *[Requests Relating to Applications]* Paragraphs (1) to (5) shall apply, *mutatis mutandis,* to requests for recordal of a license for an application, where the law of a Contracting Party provides for such recordal.

Article 18

Request for Amendment or Cancellation of the Recordal of a License

    (1) *[Requirements Concerning the Request]* Where the law of a Contracting Party provides for the recordal of a license with its Office, that Contracting Party may require that the request for amendment or cancellation of the recordal of a license

          (i) be filed in accordance with the requirements prescribed in the Regulations, and

          (ii) be accompanied by the supporting documents prescribed in the Regulations.

    (2) *[Other Requirements]* Article 17(2) to (6) shall apply, *mutatis mutandis,* to requests for amendment or cancellation of the recordal of a license.

Article 19

Effects of the Non-Recordal of a License

    (1) *[Validity of the Registration and Protection of the Mark]* The non-recordal of a license with the Office or with any other authority of the Contracting Party shall not affect the validity of the registration of the mark which is the subject of the license or the protection of that mark.

    (2) *[Certain Rights of the Licensee]* A Contracting Party may not require the recordal of a license as a condition for any right that the licensee may have under the law of that Contracting Party to join infringement proceedings initiated by the holder or to obtain, by way of such proceedings, damages resulting from an infringement of the mark which is the subject of the license.

    (3) *[Use of a Mark Where License Is Not Recorded]* A Contracting Party may not require the recordal of a license as a condition for the use of a mark by a licensee to be deemed to constitute use by the holder in proceedings relating to the acquisition, maintenance and enforcement of marks.

Article 20

Indication of the License

Where the law of a Contracting Party requires an indication that the mark is used under a license, full or partial non-compliance with that requirement shall not affect the validity of the registration of the mark which is the subject of the license or the protection of that mark, and shall not affect the application of Article 19(3).

Article 21

Observations in Case of Intended Refusal

An application under Article 3 or a request under Articles 7, 10 to 14, 17 and 18 may not be refused totally or in part by an Office without giving the applicant or the requesting party, as the case may be, an opportunity to make observations on the intended refusal within a reasonable time limit.

In respect of Article 14, no Office shall be required to give an opportunity to make observations where the person requesting the relief measure has already had an opportunity to present an observation on the facts on which the decision is to be based.

Article 22

Regulations

(1) [*Content*]

    (a) The Regulations annexed to this Treaty provide rules concerning

        (i) matters which this Treaty expressly provides to be "prescribed in the Regulations";

        (ii) any details useful in the implementation of the provisions of this Treaty;

        (iii) any administrative requirements, matters or procedures.

    (b) The Regulations also contain Model International Forms.

(2) [*Amending the Regulations*] Subject to paragraph (3), any amendment of the Regulations shall require three-fourths of the votes cast.

(3) [*Requirement of Unanimity*]

    (a) The Regulations may specify provisions of the Regulations which may be amended only by unanimity.

    (b) Any amendment of the Regulations resulting in the addition of provisions to, or the deletion of provisions from, the provisions specified in the Regulations pursuant to subparagraph (a) shall require unanimity.

    (c) In determining whether unanimity is attained, only votes actually cast shall be taken into consideration. Abstentions shall not be considered as votes.

(4) [*Conflict Between the Treaty and the Regulations*] In the case of conflict between the provisions of this Treaty and those of the Regulations, the former shall prevail.

Article 23

Assembly

(1) [*Composition*]

    (a) The Contracting Parties shall have an Assembly.

    (b) Each Contracting Party shall be represented in the Assembly by one delegate, who may be assisted by alternate delegates, advisors and experts. Each delegate may represent only one Contracting Party.

(2) [*Tasks*] The Assembly shall

    (i) deal with matters concerning the development of this Treaty;

    (ii) amend the Regulations, including the Model International Forms;

    (iii) determine the conditions for the date of application of each amendment referred to in item (ii);

    (iv) perform such other functions as are appropriate to implementing the provisions of this Treaty.

(3) [*Quorum*]

    (a) One-half of the members of the Assembly which are States shall constitute a quorum.

(b)   Notwithstanding subparagraph (a), if, in any session, the number of the members of the Assembly which are States and are represented is less than one-half but equal to or more than one-third of the members of the Assembly which are States, the Assembly may make decisions but, with the exception of decisions concerning its own procedure, all such decisions shall take effect only if the conditions set forth hereinafter are fulfilled. The International Bureau shall communicate the said decisions to the members of the Assembly which are States and were not represented and shall invite them to express in writing their vote or abstention within a period of three months from the date of the communication. If, at the expiration of this period, the number of such members having thus expressed their vote or abstention attains the number of the members which was lacking for attaining the quorum in the session itself, such decisions shall take effect, provided that at the same time the required majority still obtains.

(4)   [*Taking Decisions in the Assembly*]

(a)   The Assembly shall endeavor to take its decisions by consensus.

(b)   Where a decision cannot be arrived at by consensus, the matter at issue shall be decided by voting. In such a case,

(i)   each Contracting Party that is a State shall have one vote and shall vote only in its own name; and

(ii)   any Contracting Party that is an intergovernmental organization may participate in the vote, in place of its Member States, with a number of votes equal to the number of its Member States which are party to this Treaty. No such intergovernmental organization shall participate in the vote if any one of its Member States exercises its right to vote and vice versa. In addition, no such intergovernmental organization shall participate in the vote if any one of its Member States party to this Treaty is a Member State of another such intergovernmental organization and that other intergovernmental organization participates in that vote.

(5)   [*Majorities*]

(a)   Subject to Articles 22(2) and (3), the decisions of the Assembly shall require two-thirds of the votes cast.

(b)   In determining whether the required majority is attained, only votes actually cast shall be taken into consideration. Abstentions shall not be considered as votes.

(6)   [*Sessions*] The Assembly shall meet upon convocation by the Director General and, in the absence of exceptional circumstances, during the same period and at the same place as the General Assembly of the Organization.

(7)   [*Rules of Procedure*] The Assembly shall establish its own rules of procedure, including rules for the convocation of extraordinary sessions.

Article 24

International Bureau

(1)   [*Administrative Tasks*]

(a)   The International Bureau shall perform the administrative tasks concerning this Treaty.

(b)   In particular, the International Bureau shall prepare the meetings and provide the secretariat of the Assembly and of such committees of experts and working groups as may be established by the Assembly.

(2)   [*Meetings Other than Sessions of the Assembly*] The Director General shall convene any committee and working group established by the Assembly.

(3)   [*Role of the International Bureau in the Assembly and Other Meetings*]

(a)   The Director General and persons designated by the Director General shall participate, without the right to vote, in all meetings of the Assembly, the committees and working groups established by the Assembly.

(b)   The Director General or a staff member designated by the Director General shall be *ex officio* secretary of the Assembly, and of the committees and working groups referred to in subparagraph (a).

(4)   [*Conferences*]

(a)   The International Bureau shall, in accordance with the directions of the Assembly, make the preparations for any revision conferences.

(b)   The International Bureau may consult with Member States of the Organization, intergovernmental organizations and international and national non-governmental organizations concerning the said preparations.

(c)   The Director General and persons designated by the Director General shall take part, without the right to vote, in the discussions at revision conferences.

(5)   [*Other Tasks*] The International Bureau shall carry out any other tasks assigned to it in relation to this Treaty.

Article 25

Revision or Amendment

This Treaty may only be revised or amended by a diplomatic conference. The convocation of any diplomatic conference shall be decided by the Assembly.

Article 26

Becoming Party to the Treaty

(1)   [*Eligibility*] The following entities may sign and, subject to paragraphs (2) and (3) and Article 28(1) and (3), become party to this Treaty:

(i)   any State member of the Organization in respect of which marks may be registered with its own Office;

(ii)   any intergovernmental organization which maintains an Office in which marks may be registered with effect in the territory in which the constituting treaty of the intergovernmental organization applies, in all its Member States or in those of its Member States which are designated for such purpose in the relevant application, provided that all the Member States of the intergovernmental organization are members of the Organization;

(iii)   any State member of the Organization in respect of which marks may be registered only through the Office of another specified State that is a member of the Organization;

(iv)   any State member of the Organization in respect of which marks may be registered only through the Office maintained by an intergovernmental organization of which that State is a member;

(v)   any State member of the Organization in respect of which marks may be registered only through an Office common to a group of States members of the Organization.

(2)   [*Ratification or Accession*] Any entity referred to in paragraph (1) may deposit

(i)   an instrument of ratification, if it has signed this Treaty,

(ii)   an instrument of accession, if it has not signed this Treaty.

(3)   [*Effective Date of Deposit*] The effective date of the deposit of an instrument of ratification or accession shall be,

      (i)   in the case of a State referred to in paragraph (1)(i), the date on which the instrument of that State is deposited;

      (ii)   in the case of an intergovernmental organization, the date on which the instrument of that intergovernmental organization is deposited;

      (iii)   in the case of a State referred to in paragraph (1)(iii), the date on which the following condition is fulfilled: the instrument of that State has been deposited and the instrument of the other, specified State has been deposited;

      (iv)   in the case of a State referred to in paragraph (1)(iv), the date applicable under item (ii), above;

      (v)   in the case of a State member of a group of States referred to in paragraph (1)(v), the date on which the instruments of all the States members of the group have been deposited.

Article 27

Application of the TLT 1994 and This Treaty

(1)   [*Relations Between Contracting Parties to Both This Treaty and the TLT 1994*] This Treaty alone shall be applicable as regards the mutual relations of Contracting Parties to both this Treaty and the TLT 1994.

(2)   [*Relations Between Contracting Parties to This Treaty and Contracting Parties to the TLT 1994 That Are Not Party to This Treaty*] Any Contracting Party to both this Treaty and the TLT 1994 shall continue to apply the TLT 1994 in its relations with Contracting Parties to the TLT 1994 that are not party to this Treaty.

Article 28

Entry into Force; Effective Date of Ratifications and Accessions

(1)   [*Instruments to Be Taken into Consideration*] For the purposes of this Article, only instruments of ratification or accession that are deposited by entities referred to in Article 26(1) and that have an effective date according to Article 26(3) shall be taken into consideration.

(2)   [*Entry into Force of the Treaty*] This Treaty shall enter into force three months after ten States or intergovernmental organizations referred to in Article 26(1)(ii) have deposited their instruments of ratification or accession.

(3)   [*Entry into Force of Ratifications and Accessions Subsequent to the Entry into Force of the Treaty*] Any entity not covered by paragraph (2) shall become bound by this Treaty three months after the date on which it has deposited its instrument of ratification or accession.

Article 29

Reservations

(1)   [*Special Kinds of Marks*] Any State or intergovernmental organization may declare through a reservation that, notwithstanding Article 2(1) and (2)(a), any of the provisions of Articles 3(1), 5, 7, 8(5), 11 and 13 shall not apply to associated marks, defensive marks or derivative marks. Such reservation shall specify those of the aforementioned provisions to which the reservation relates.

(2)   [*Multiple-class Registration*] Any State or intergovernmental organization, whose legislation at the date of adoption of this Treaty provides for a multiple-class registration for goods and for a multiple-class registration for services may, when acceding to this Treaty, declare through a reservation that the provisions of Article 6 shall not apply.

(3) [*Substantive Examination on the Occasion of Renewal*] Any State or intergovernmental organization may declare through a reservation that, notwithstanding Article 13(4), the Office may, on the occasion of the first renewal of a registration covering services, examine such registration as to substance, provided that such examination shall be limited to the elimination of multiple registrations based on applications filed during a period of six months following the entry into force of the law of such State or organization that introduced, before the entry into force of this Treaty, the possibility of registering service marks.

(4) [*Certain Rights of the Licensee*] Any State or intergovernmental organization may declare through a reservation that, notwithstanding Article 19(2), it requires the recordal of a license as a condition for any right that the licensee may have under the law of that State or intergovernmental organization to join infringement proceedings initiated by the holder or to obtain, by way of such proceedings, damages resulting from an infringement of the mark which is the subject of the license.

(5) [*Modalities*] Any reservation under paragraphs (1), (2), (3) or (4) shall be made in a declaration accompanying the instrument of ratification of, or accession to, this Treaty of the State or intergovernmental organization making the reservation.

(6) [*Withdrawal*] Any reservation under paragraphs (1), (2), (3) or (4) may be withdrawn at any time.

(7) [*Prohibition of Other Reservations*] No reservation to this Treaty other than the reservations allowed under paragraphs (1), (2), (3) and (4) shall be permitted.

Article 30

Denunciation of the Treaty

(1) [*Notification*] Any Contracting Party may denounce this Treaty by notification addressed to the Director General.

(2) [*Effective Date*] Denunciation shall take effect one year from the date on which the Director General has received the notification. It shall not affect the application of this Treaty to any application pending or any mark registered in respect of the denouncing Contracting Party at the time of the expiration of the said one-year period, provided that the denouncing Contracting Party may, after the expiration of the said one-year period, discontinue applying this Treaty to any registration as from the date on which that registration is due for renewal.

Article 31

Languages of the Treaty; Signature

(1) [*Original Texts; Official Texts*]

(a) This Treaty shall be signed in a single original in the English, Arabic, Chinese, French, Russian and Spanish languages, all texts being equally authentic.

(b) An official text in a language not referred to in subparagraph (a) that is an official language of a Contracting Party shall be established by the Director General after consultation with the said Contracting Party and any other interested Contracting Party.

(2) [*Time Limit for Signature*] This Treaty shall remain open for signature at the headquarters of the Organization for one year after its adoption.

Article 32

Depositary

The Director General shall be the depositary of this Treaty.

TRADEMARKS & RELATED MATERIALS

RESOLUTION BY THE DIPLOMATIC CONFERENCE SUPPLEMENTARY TO THE SINGAPORE TREATY ON THE LAW OF TRADEMARKS

1.   The Diplomatic Conference for the Adoption of a Revised Trademark Law Treaty, held in Singapore in March 2006, agreed that the Treaty adopted by the Conference would be named "Singapore Treaty on the Law of Trademarks" (hereinafter referred to as "the Treaty").

2.   When adopting the Treaty, the Diplomatic Conference agreed that the words "procedure before the Office" in Article 1(viii) would not cover judicial procedures under the Contracting Parties' legislation.

3.   Acknowledging the fact that the Treaty provides for effective and efficient trademark formality procedures for Contracting Parties, the Diplomatic Conference understood that Articles 2 and 8, respectively, did not impose any obligations on Contracting Parties to:

(i)   register new types of marks, as referred to in Rule 3, paragraphs (4), (5) and (6) of the Regulations; or

(ii)   implement electronic filing systems or other automation systems.

Each Contracting Party shall have the option to decide whether and when to provide for the registration of new types of marks, as referred to above.

4.   With a view to facilitating the implementation of the Treaty in Developing and Least Developed Countries (LDCs), the Diplomatic Conference requested the World Intellectual Property Organization (WIPO) and the Contracting Parties to provide additional and adequate technical assistance comprising technological, legal and other forms of support to strengthen the institutional capacity of those countries to implement the Treaty and enable those countries to take full advantage of the provisions of the Treaty.

5.   Such assistance should take into account the level of technological and economic development of beneficiary countries. Technological support would help improve the information and communication technology infrastructure of those countries, thus contributing to narrowing the technological gap between Contracting Parties. The Diplomatic Conference noted that some countries underlined the importance of the Digital Solidarity Fund (DSF) as being relevant to narrowing the digital divide.

6.   Furthermore, upon entry into force of the Treaty, Contracting Parties will undertake to exchange and share, on a multilateral basis, information and experience on legal, technical and institutional aspects regarding the implementation of the Treaty and how to take full advantage of opportunities and benefits resulting therefrom.

7.   The Diplomatic Conference, acknowledging the special situation and needs of LDCs, agreed that LDCs shall be accorded special and differential treatment for the implementation of the Treaty, as follows:

(a)   LDCs shall be the primary and main beneficiaries of technical assistance by the Contracting Parties and the World Intellectual Property Organization (WIPO);

(b)   such technical assistance includes the following:

(i)   assistance in establishing the legal framework for the implementation of the Treaty,

(ii)   information, education and awareness raising as regards the impact of acceding to the Treaty,

(iii) assistance in revising administrative practices and procedures of national trademark registration authorities,

(iv) assistance in building up the necessary trained manpower and facilities of the IP Offices, including information and communication technology capacity to effectively implement the Treaty and its Regulations.

8. The Diplomatic Conference requested the Assembly to monitor and evaluate, at every ordinary session, the progress of the assistance related to implementation efforts and the benefits resulting from such implementation.

9. The Diplomatic Conference agreed that any dispute that may arise between two or more Contracting Parties with respect to the interpretation or the application of this Treaty should be settled amicably through consultation and mediation under the auspices of the Director General.

H. UNIFORM DOMAIN NAME DISPUTE RESOLUTION POLICY

(As Approved by ICANN on October 24, 1999)

1.   *Purpose.* This Uniform Domain Name Dispute Resolution Policy (the "Policy") has been adopted by the Internet Corporation for Assigned Names and Numbers ("ICANN"), is incorporated by reference into your Registration Agreement, and sets forth the terms and conditions in connection with a dispute between you and any party other than us (the registrar) over the registration and use of an Internet domain name registered by you. Proceedings under Paragraph 4 of this Policy will be conducted according to the Rules for Uniform Domain Name Dispute Resolution Policy (the "Rules of Procedure"), which are available at *www.icann.org/udrp/udrp-rules-24oct99.htm*, and the selected administrative-dispute-resolution service provider's supplemental rules.

2.   *Your Representations.* By applying to register a domain name, or by asking us to maintain or renew a domain name registration, you hereby represent and warrant to us that (a) the statements that you made in your Registration Agreement are complete and accurate; (b) to your knowledge, the registration of the domain name will not infringe upon or otherwise violate the rights of any third party; (c) you are not registering the domain name for an unlawful purpose; and (d) you will not knowingly use the domain name in violation of any applicable laws or regulations. It is your responsibility to determine whether your domain name registration infringes or violates someone else's rights.

3.   *Cancellations, Transfers, and Changes.* We will cancel, transfer or otherwise make changes to domain name registrations under the following circumstances:

   a.   subject to the provisions of Paragraph 8, our receipt of written or appropriate electronic instructions from you or your authorized agent to take such action;

   b.   our receipt of an order from a court or arbitral tribunal, in each case of competent jurisdiction, requiring such action; and/or

   c.   our receipt of a decision of an Administrative Panel requiring such action in any administrative proceeding to which you were a party and which was conducted under this Policy or a later version of this Policy adopted by ICANN. (See Paragraph 4(i) and (k) below.)

We may also cancel, transfer or otherwise make changes to a domain name registration in accordance with the terms of your Registration Agreement or other legal requirements.

4.   *Mandatory Administrative Proceeding.* This Paragraph sets forth the type of disputes for which you are required to submit to a mandatory administrative proceeding. These proceedings will be conducted before one of the administrative-dispute-resolution service providers listed at *www. icann.org/udrp/approved-providers.htm* (each, a "Provider").

   a.   *Applicable Disputes.* You are required to submit to a mandatory administrative proceeding in the event that a third party (a "complainant") asserts to the applicable Provider, in compliance with the Rules of Procedure, that

      (i)   your domain name is identical or confusingly similar to a trademark or service mark in which the complainant has rights; and

      (ii)   you have no rights or legitimate interests in respect of the domain name; and

      (iii) your domain name has been registered and is being used in bad faith.

TRADEMARKS & RELATED MATERIALS

In the administrative proceeding, the complainant must prove that each of these three elements are present.

b. *Evidence of Registration and Use in Bad Faith.* For the purposes of Paragraph 4(a)(iii), the following circumstances, in particular but without limitation, if found by the Panel to be present, shall be evidence of the registration and use of a domain name in bad faith:

(i) circumstances indicating that you have registered or you have acquired the domain name primarily for the purpose of selling, renting, or otherwise transferring the domain name registration to the complainant who is the owner of the trademark or service mark or to a competitor of that complainant, for valuable consideration in excess of your documented out-of-pocket costs directly related to the domain name; or

(ii) you have registered the domain name in order to prevent the owner of the trademark or service mark from reflecting the mark in a corresponding domain name, provided that you have engaged in a pattern of such conduct; or

(iii) you have registered the domain name primarily for the purpose of disrupting the business of a competitor; or

(iv) by using the domain name, you have intentionally attempted to attract, for commercial gain, Internet users to your web site or other on-line location, by creating a likelihood of confusion with the complainant's mark as to the source, sponsorship, affiliation, or endorsement of your web site or location or of a product or service on your web site or location.

c. *How to Demonstrate Your Rights to and Legitimate Interests in the Domain Name in Responding to a Complaint.* When you receive a complaint, you should refer to Paragraph 5 of the Rules of Procedure in determining how your response should be prepared. Any of the following circumstances, in particular but without limitation, if found by the Panel to be proved based on its evaluation of all evidence presented, shall demonstrate your rights or legitimate interests to the domain name for purposes of Paragraph 4(a)(ii):

(i) before any notice to you of the dispute, your use of, or demonstrable preparations to use, the domain name or a name corresponding to the domain name in connection with a bona fide offering of goods or services; or

(ii) you (as an individual, business, or other organization) have been commonly known by the domain name, even if you have acquired no trademark or service mark rights; or

(iii) you are making a legitimate noncommercial or fair use of the domain name, without intent for commercial gain to misleadingly divert consumers or to tarnish the trademark or service mark at issue.

d. *Selection of Provider.* The complainant shall select the Provider from among those approved by ICANN by submitting the complaint to that Provider. The selected Provider will administer the proceeding, except in cases of consolidation as described in Paragraph 4(f).

e. *Initiation of Proceeding and Process and Appointment of Administrative Panel.* The Rules of Procedure state the process for initiating and conducting a proceeding and for appointing the panel that will decide the dispute (the "Administrative Panel").

f. *Consolidation.* In the event of multiple disputes between you and a complainant, either you or the complainant may petition to consolidate the disputes before a single Administrative Panel. This petition shall be made to the first Administrative Panel appointed to hear a pending dispute between the parties. This Administrative Panel may consolidate before it any or all such disputes in its sole discretion, provided that the disputes being consolidated are governed by this Policy or a later version of this Policy adopted by ICANN.

g. *Fees.* All fees charged by a Provider in connection with any dispute before an Administrative Panel pursuant to this Policy shall be paid by the complainant, except in cases where you elect to expand the Administrative Panel from one to three panelists as provided in Paragraph 5(b)(iv) of the Rules of Procedure, in which case all fees will be split evenly by you and the complainant.

h.   *Our Involvement in Administrative Proceedings.* We do not, and will not, participate in the administration or conduct of any proceeding before an Administrative Panel. In addition, we will not be liable as a result of any decisions rendered by the Administrative Panel.

i.   *Remedies.* The remedies available to a complainant pursuant to any proceeding before an Administrative Panel shall be limited to requiring the cancellation of your domain name or the transfer of your domain name registration to the complainant.

j.   *Notification and Publication.* The Provider shall notify us of any decision made by an Administrative Panel with respect to a domain name you have registered with us. All decisions under this Policy will be published in full over the Internet, except when an Administrative Panel determines in an exceptional case to redact portions of its decision.

k.   *Availability of Court Proceedings.* The mandatory administrative proceeding requirements set forth in Paragraph 4 shall not prevent either you or the complainant from submitting the dispute to a court of competent jurisdiction for independent resolution before such mandatory administrative proceeding is commenced or after such proceeding is concluded. If an Administrative Panel decides that your domain name registration should be canceled or transferred, we will wait ten (10) business days (as observed in the location of our principal office) after we are informed by the applicable Provider of the Administrative Panel's decision before implementing that decision. We will then implement the decision unless we have received from you during that ten (10) business day period official documentation (such as a copy of a complaint, file-stamped by the clerk of the court) that you have commenced a lawsuit against the complainant in a jurisdiction to which the complainant has submitted under *Paragraph 3(b)(xiii)* of the Rules of Procedure. (In general, that jurisdiction is either the location of our principal office or of your address as shown in our Who is database. See *Paragraphs 1* and *3(b)(xiii)* of the Rules of Procedure for details.) If we receive such documentation within the ten (10) business day period, we will not implement the Administrative Panel's decision, and we will take no further action, until we receive (i) evidence satisfactory to us of a resolution between the parties; (ii) evidence satisfactory to us that your lawsuit has been dismissed or withdrawn; or (iii) a copy of an order from such court dismissing your lawsuit or ordering that you do not have the right to continue to use your domain name.

5.   *All Other Disputes and Litigation.* All other disputes between you and any party other than us regarding your domain name registration that are not brought pursuant to the mandatory administrative proceeding provisions of *Paragraph 4* shall be resolved between you and such other party through any court, arbitration or other proceeding that may be available.

6.   *Our Involvement in Disputes.* We will not participate in any way in any dispute between you and any party other than us regarding the registration and use of your domain name. You shall not name us as a party or otherwise include us in any such proceeding. In the event that we are named as a party in any such proceeding, we reserve the right to raise any and all defenses deemed appropriate, and to take any other action necessary to defend ourselves.

7.   *Maintaining the Status Quo.* We will not cancel, transfer, activate, deactivate, or otherwise change the status of any domain name registration under this Policy except as provided in Paragraph 3 above.

8.   *Transfers During a Dispute.*

a.   *Transfers of a Domain Name to a New Holder.* You may not transfer your domain name registration to another holder (i) during a pending administrative proceeding brought pursuant to Paragraph 4 or for a period of fifteen (15) business days (as observed in the location of our principal place of business) after such proceeding is concluded; or (ii) during a pending court proceeding or arbitration commenced regarding your domain name unless the party to whom the domain name registration is being transferred agrees, in writing, to be bound by the decision of the court or arbitrator. We reserve the right to cancel any transfer of a domain name registration to another holder that is made in violation of this subparagraph.

b.   *Changing Registrars.* You may not transfer your domain name registration to another registrar during a pending administrative proceeding brought pursuant to Paragraph 4 or for a period of fifteen (15) business days (as observed in the location of our principal place of business) after such proceeding is concluded. You may transfer administration of your domain name registration to another registrar during a pending court action or arbitration, provided that the domain name you have registered with us shall continue to be subject to the proceedings commenced against you in accordance with the terms of this Policy. In the event that you transfer a domain name registration to us during the pendency of a court action or arbitration, such dispute shall remain subject to the domain name dispute policy of the registrar from which the domain name registration was transferred.

9.   *Policy Modifications.* We reserve the right to modify this Policy at any time with the permission of ICANN. We will post our revised Policy at least thirty (30) calendar days before it becomes effective. Unless this Policy has already been invoked by the submission of a complaint to a Provider, in which event the version of the Policy in effect at the time it was invoked will apply to you until the dispute is over, all such changes will be binding upon you with respect to any domain name registration dispute, whether the dispute arose before, on or after the effective date of our change. In the event that you object to a change in this Policy, your sole remedy is to cancel your domain name registration with us, provided that you will not be entitled to a refund of any fees you paid to us. The revised Policy will apply to you until you cancel your domain name registration.

II. COPYRIGHT AND RELATED MATERIALS

A. THE COPYRIGHT ACT OF 1909

Contents

CHAPTER 1. REGISTRATION OF COPYRIGHT

---

§ 1.   Exclusive Rights as to Copyrighted Works

Any person entitled thereto, upon complying with the provisions of this title, shall have the exclusive right:

(a)   To print, reprint, publish, copy, and vend the copyrighted work;

(b)   To translate the copyrighted work into other languages or dialects, or make any other version thereof, if it be a literary work; to dramatize it if it be a nondramatic work; to convert it into a novel or other nondramatic work if it be a drama; to arrange or adapt it if it be a musical work; to complete, execute, and finish it if it be a model or design for a work of art;

(c)[2]   To deliver, authorize the delivery of, read, or present the copyrighted work in public for profit if it be a lecture, sermon, address or similar production, or other nondramatic literary work; to make or procure the making of any transcription or record thereof by or from which, in whole or in part, it may in any manner or by any method be exhibited, delivered, presented, produced, or reproduced; and to play or perform it in public for profit, and to exhibit, represent, produce, or reproduce it in any manner or by any method whatsoever. The damages for the infringement by broadcast of any work referred to in this subsection shall not exceed the sum of $100 where the infringing broadcaster shows that he was not aware that he was infringing and that such infringement could not have been reasonably foreseen; and

(d)   To perform or represent the copyrighted work publicly if it be a drama or, if it be a dramatic work and not reproduced in copies for sale, to vend any manuscript or any record whatsoever thereof; to make or to procure the making of any transcription or record thereof by or from which, in whole or in part, it may in any manner or by any method be exhibited, performed, represented, produced, or reproduced; and to exhibit, perform, represent, produce, or reproduce it in any manner or by any method whatsoever; and

(e)   To perform the copyrighted work publicly for profit if it be a musical composition; and for the purpose of public performance for profit, and for the purposes set forth in subsection (a) hereof, to make any arrangement or setting of it or of the melody of it in any system of notation or any form of record in which the thought of an author may be recorded and from which it may be read or reproduced: *Provided,* That the provisions of this title, so far as they secure copyright controlling the parts of instruments serving to reproduce mechanically the musical work, shall include only compositions published and copyrighted after July 1, 1909, and shall not include the works of a foreign author or composer unless the foreign state or nation of which such author or composer is a citizen or subject grants, either by treaty, convention, agreement, or law, to citizens of the United States similar rights. And as a condition of extending the copyright control to such mechanical reproductions, that whenever the owner of a musical copyright has used or permitted or knowingly acquiesced in the use of the copyrighted work upon the parts of instruments serving to reproduce mechanically the musical work, any other person may make similar use of the copyrighted work upon the payment to the copyright proprietor of a royalty of 2 cents on each such part manufactured, to be paid by the manufacturer thereof; and the copyright proprietor may require, and if so the manufacturer shall furnish, a report under oath on the 20th day of each month on the number of parts of instruments manufactured during the previous month serving to reproduce mechanically said musical work, and royalties shall be due on the parts manufactured during any month upon the 20th of the next succeeding month. The payment of the royalty provided for by this section shall free the articles or devices for which such royalty has been paid from further contribution to the copyright except in case of public performance for profit. It shall be the duty of the copyright owner, if he uses the musical composition himself for the manufacture of parts of instruments serving to reproduce mechanically the musical work, or licenses others to do so, to file notice thereof, accompanied by a recording fee, in the copyright office, and any failure to file such notice shall be a complete defense to any suit, action, or proceeding for any infringement of such copyright.

---

[2]   Section 1(c) as amended by the Act of July 17, 1952 (66 Stat. 752), effective January 1, 1953.

In case of failure of such manufacturer to pay to the copyright proprietor within thirty days after demand in writing the full sum of royalties due at said rate at the date of such demand, the court may award taxable costs to the plaintiff and a reasonable counsel fee, and the court may, in its discretion, enter judgment therein for any sum in addition over the amount found to be due as royalty in accordance with the terms of this title, not exceeding three times such amount.

The reproduction or rendition of a musical composition by or upon coin-operated machines shall not be deemed a public performance for profit unless a fee is charged for admission to the place where such reproduction or rendition occurs.

(f)[3] To produce and distribute to the public by sale or other transfer of ownership, or by rental, lease, or lending, reproductions of the copyrighted work if it be a sound recording: *Provided,* That the exclusive right of the owner of a copyright in a sound recording to reproduce it is limited to the right to duplicate the sound recording in a tangible form that directly or indirectly recaptures the actual sounds fixed in the recording: *Provided further,* That this right does not extend to the making or duplication of another sound recording that is an independent fixation of other sounds, even though such sounds imitate or simulate those in the copyrighted sound recording; or to the reproductions made by transmitting organizations exclusively for their own use.

§ 2. Rights of Author or Proprietor of Unpublished Work

Nothing in this title shall be construed to annul or limit the right of the author or proprietor of an unpublished work, at common law or in equity, to prevent the copying, publication, or use of such unpublished work without his consent, and to obtain damages therefor.

§ 3. Protection of Component Parts of Work Copyrighted; Composite Works or Periodicals

The copyright provided by this title shall protect all the copyrightable component parts of the work copyrighted, and all matter therein in which copyright is already subsisting, but without extending the duration or scope of such copyright. The copyright upon composite works or periodicals shall give to the proprietor thereof all the rights in respect thereto which he would have if each part were individually copyrighted under this title.

§ 4. All Writings of Author Included

The works for which copyright may be secured under this title shall include all the writings of an author.

§ 5. Classification of Works for Registration

The application for registration shall specify to which of the following classes the work in which copyright is claimed belongs:

(a) Books, including composite and cyclopedic works, directories, gazetteers, and other compilations.

(b) Periodicals, including newspapers.

(c) Lectures, sermons, addresses (prepared for oral delivery).

(d) Dramatic or dramatico-musical compositions.

(e) Musical compositions.

(f) Maps.

---

[3] Subsection (f) was added by the Act of October 15, 1971 (85 Stat. 391), effective February 15, 1972. See Sec. 5(n), n1.

(g)   Works of art; models or designs for works of art.

(h)   Reproductions of a work of art.

(i)   Drawings or plastic works of a scientific or technical character.

(j)   Photographs.

(k)   Prints and pictorial illustrations including prints or labels used for articles of merchandise.

(*l*)   Motion-picture photoplays.

(m)   Motion pictures other than photoplays.

(n)   Sound recordings.[4]

The above specifications shall not be held to limit the subject matter of copyright as defined in section 4 of this title, nor shall any error in classification invalidate or impair the copyright protection secured under this title.

§ 6.   Registration of Prints and Labels

Commencing July 1, 1940, the Register of Copyrights is charged with the registration of claims to copyright properly presented, in all prints and labels published in connection with the sale or advertisement of articles of merchandise, including all claims to copyright in prints and labels pending in the Patent Office and uncleared at the close of business June 30, 1940. There shall be paid for registering a claim of copyright in any such print or label not a trade-mark $6, which sum shall cover the expense of furnishing a certificate of such registration, under the seal of the Copyright Office, to the claimant of copyright.

§ 7.   Copyright on Compilations of Works in Public Domain or of Copyrighted Works; Subsisting Copyrights Not Affected

Compilations or abridgments, adaptations, arrangements, dramatizations, translations, or other versions of works in the public domain or of copyrighted works when produced with the consent of the proprietor of the copyright in such works, or works republished with new matter, shall be regarded as new works subject to copyright under the provisions of this title; but the publication of any such new works shall not affect the force or validity of any subsisting copyright upon the matter employed or any part thereof, or be construed to imply an exclusive right to such use of the original works, or to secure or extend copyright in such original works.

§ 8.   Copyright Not to Subsist in Works in Public Domain, or Published Prior to July 1, 1909, and Not Already Copyrighted, or Government Publications; Publication by Government of Copyrighted Material

No copyright shall subsist in the original text of any work which is in the public domain, or in any work which was published in this country or any foreign country prior to July 1, 1909, and has not been already copyrighted in the United States, or in any publication of the United States Government, or any reprint, in whole or in part, thereof: *Provided,* That copyright may be secured by

---

[4]   Subsection (n) was added by the Act of October 15, 1971 (85 Stat. 391). Sec. 3 of said Act reads as follows:

This Act shall take effect four months after its enactment [date of enactment: October 15, 1971] except that section 2 of this Act [amending Sec. 101(e)] shall take effect immediately upon its enactment. The provisions of title 17, United States Code, as amended by section 1 of this Act, shall apply only to sound recordings fixed, published, and copyrighted on and after the effective date of this Act and before January 1, 1975, and nothing in title 17, United States Code, as amended by section 1 of this Act, shall be applied retroactively or be construed as affecting in any way any rights with respect to sound recordings fixed before the effective date of this Act.

Sec. 101 of the Act of December 31, 1974 (88 Stat. 1873) amended Sec. 3 of the Act of October 15, 1971 by striking out the words "and before January 1, 1975". The effect of this amendment was to make Sec. 5(n) of the Copyright Act applicable to all sound recordings fixed, published and copyrighted on and after February 15, 1972.

the Postmaster General on behalf of the United States in the whole or any part of the publications authorized by section 2506 of title 39.

The publication or republication by the Government, either separately or in a public document, of any material in which copyright is subsisting shall not be taken to cause any abridgment or annulment of the copyright or to authorize any use or appropriation of such copyright material without the consent of the copyright proprietor.

§ 9. Authors or Proprietors, Entitled: Aliens[5]

The author or proprietor of any work made the subject of copyright by this title, or his executors, administrators, or assigns, shall have copyright for such work under the conditions and for the terms specified in this title: *Provided, however,* That the copyright secured by this title shall extend to the work of an author or proprietor who is a citizen or subject of a foreign state or nation only under the conditions described in subsections (a), (b), or (c) below:

(a)   When an alien author or proprietor shall be domiciled within the United States at the time of the first publication of his work; or

(b)   When the foreign state or nation of which such author or proprietor is a citizen or subject grants, either by treaty, convention, agreement, or law, to citizens of the United States the benefit of copyright on substantially the same basis as to its own citizens, or copyright protection, substantially equal to the protection secured to such foreign author under this title or by treaty; or when such foreign state or nation is a party to an international agreement which provides for reciprocity in the granting of copyright, by the terms of which agreement the United States may, at its pleasure, become a party thereto.

The existence of the reciprocal conditions aforesaid shall be determined by the President of the United States, by proclamation made from time to time, as the purposes of this title may require: *Provided,* That whenever the President shall find that the authors, copyright owners, or proprietors of works first produced or published abroad and subject to copyright or to renewal of copyright under the laws of the United States, including works subject to ad interim copyright, are or may have been temporarily unable to comply with the conditions and formalities prescribed with respect to such works by the copyright laws of the United States, because of the disruption or suspension of facilities essential for such compliance, he may by proclamation grant such extension of time as he may deem appropriate for the fulfillment of such conditions or formalities by authors, copyright owners, or proprietors who are citizens of the United States or who are nationals of countries which accord substantially equal treatment in this respect to authors, copyright owners, or proprietors who are citizens of the United States: *Provided further,* That no liability shall attach under this title for lawful uses made or acts done prior to the effective date of such proclamation in connection with such works, or in respect to the continuance for one year subsequent to such date of any business undertaking or enterprise lawfully undertaken prior to such date involving expenditure or contractual obligation in connection with the exploitation, production, reproduction, circulation, or performance of any such work.

The President may at any time terminate any proclamation authorized herein or any part thereof or suspend or extend its operation for such period or periods of time as in his judgment the interests of the United States may require.

(c)   When the Universal Copyright Convention, signed at Geneva on September 6, 1952, shall be in force[6] between the United States of America and the foreign state or nation of which such author is a citizen or subject, or in which the work was first published. Any work to which copyright is extended pursuant to this subsection shall be exempt from the following provisions of this title: (1) The requirement in section 1(e) that a foreign state or nation must grant to United States citizens

---

[5]   Section 9 as amended by the Act of August 31, 1954 (68 Stat. 1030), effective September 16, 1955.

[6]   The Universal Copyright Convention came into force on September 16, 1955.

mechanical reproduction rights similar to those specified therein; (2) the obligatory deposit requirements of the first sentence of section 13; (3) the provisions of sections 14, 16, 17, and 18; (4) the import prohibitions of section 107, to the extent that they are related to the manufacturing requirements of section 16; and (5) the requirements of sections 19 and 20: *Provided, however,* That such exemptions shall apply only if from the time of first publication all the copies of the work published with the authority of the author or other copyright proprietor shall bear the symbol © accompanied by the name of the copyright proprietor and the year of first publication placed in such manner and location as to give reasonable notice of claim of copyright.

Upon the coming into force of the Universal Copyright Convention in a foreign state or nation as hereinbefore provided, every book or periodical of a citizen or subject thereof in which ad interim copyright was subsisting on the effective date of said coming into force shall have copyright for twenty-eight years from the date of first publication abroad without the necessity of complying with the further formalities specified in section 23 of this title.

The provisions of this subsection shall not be extended to works of an author who is a citizen of, or domiciled in the United States of America regardless of place of first publication, or to works first published in the United States.

§ 10. Publication of Work With Notice

Any person entitled thereto by this title may secure copyright for his work by publication thereof with the notice of copyright required by this title; and such notice shall be affixed to each copy thereof published or offered for sale in the United States by authority of the copyright proprietor, except in the case of books seeking ad interim protection under section 22 of this title.

§ 11. Registration of Claim and Issuance of Certificate

Such person may obtain registration of his claim to copyright by complying with the provisions of this title, including the deposit of copies, and upon such compliance the Register of Copyrights shall issue to him the certificates provided for in section 209 of this title.

§ 12. Works Not Reproduced for Sale

Copyright may also be had of the works of an author, of which copies are not reproduced for sale, by the deposit, with claim of copyright, of one complete copy of such work if it be a lecture or similar production or a dramatic, musical, or dramatico-musical composition; of a title and description, with one print taken from each scene or act, if the work be a motion-picture photoplay; of a photographic print if the work be a photograph; of a title and description, with not less than two prints taken from different sections of a complete motion picture, if the work be a motion picture other than a photoplay; or of a photograph or other identifying reproduction thereof, if it be a work of art or a plastic work or drawing. But the privilege of registration of copyright secured hereunder shall not exempt the copyright proprietor from the deposit of copies, under sections 13 and 14 of this title, where the work is later reproduced in copies for sale.

§ 13. Deposit of Copies After Publication; Action or Proceeding for Infringement[7]

After copyright has been secured by publication of the work with the notice of copyright as provided in section 10 of this title, there shall be promptly deposited in the Copyright Office or in the mail addressed to the Register of Copyrights, Washington, District of Columbia, two complete copies of the best edition thereof then published, or if the work is by an author who is a citizen or subject of a foreign state or nation and has been published in a foreign country, one complete copy of the best edition then published in such foreign country, which copies or copy, if the work be a book or periodical, shall have been produced in accordance with the manufacturing provisions specified in section 16 of this title; or if such work be a contribution to a periodical, for which contribution special registration

---

[7]   Section 13 as amended by the Act of March 29, 1956 (70 Stat. 63).

is requested, one copy of the issue or issues containing such contribution; or if the work belongs to a class specified in subsections (g), (h), (i) or (k) of section 5 of this title, and if the Register of Copyrights determines that it is impracticable to deposit copies because of their size, weight, fragility, or monetary value he may permit the deposit of photographs or other identifying reproductions in lieu of copies of the work as published under such rules and regulations as he may prescribe with the approval of the Librarian of Congress; or if the work is not reproduced in copies for sale there shall be deposited the copy, print, photograph, or other identifying reproduction provided by section 12 of this title, such copies or copy, print, photograph, or other reproduction to be accompanied in each case by a claim of copyright. No action or proceeding shall be maintained for infringement of copyright in any work until the provisions of this title with respect to the deposit of copies and registration of such work shall have been complied with.

§ 14. Same; Failure to Deposit; Demand; Penalty

Should the copies called for by section 13 of this title not be promptly deposited as provided in this title, the Register of Copyrights may at any time after the publication of the work, upon actual notice, require the proprietor of the copyright to deposit them, and after the said demand shall have been made, in default of the deposit of copies of the work within three months from any part of the United States, except an outlying territorial possession of the United States, or within six months from any outlying territorial possession of the United States, or from any foreign country, the proprietor of the copyright shall be liable to a fine of $100 and to pay to the Library of Congress twice the amount of the retail price of the best edition of the work, and the copyright shall become void.

§ 15. Same; Postmaster's Receipt; Transmission by Mail Without Cost

The postmaster to whom are delivered the articles deposited as provided in sections 12 and 13 of this title shall, if requested, give a receipt therefor and shall mail them to their destination without cost to the copyright claimant.

§ 16. Mechanical Work to Be Done in United States[8]

Of the printed book or periodical specified in section 5, subsections (a) and (b), of this title, except the original text of a book or periodical of foreign origin in a language or languages other than English, the text of all copies accorded protection under this title, except as below provided, shall be printed from type set within the limits of the United States, either by hand or by the aid of any kind of typesetting machine, or from plates made within the limits of the United States from type set therein, or, if the text be produced by lithographic process, or photoengraving process, then by a process wholly performed within the limits of the United States, and the printing of the text and binding of the said book shall be performed within the limits of the United States; which requirements shall extend also to the illustrations within a book consisting of printed text and illustrations produced by lithographic process, or photoengraving process, and also to separate lithographs or photoengravings, except where in either case the subjects represented are located in a foreign country and illustrate a scientific work or reproduce a work of art: *Provided, however,* That said requirements shall not apply to works in raised characters for the use of the blind, or to books or periodicals of foreign origin in a language or languages other than English, or to works printed or produced in the United States by any other process than those above specified in this section, or to copies of books or periodicals, first published abroad in the English language, imported into the United States within five years after first publication in a foreign state or nation up to the number of fifteen hundred copies of each such book or periodical if said copies shall contain notice of copyright in accordance with sections 10, 19, and 20 of this title and if ad interim copyright in said work shall have been obtained pursuant to section 22 of this title prior to the importation into the United States of any copy except those permitted by the provisions of section 107 of this title: *Provided further,* That the provisions of this section shall not affect the right of importation under the provisions of section 107 of this title.

---

[8] Section 16 as amended by the Act of August 31, 1954 (68 Stat. 1030), effective September 16, 1955.

§ 17. Affidavit to Accompany Copies

In the case of the book the copies so deposited shall be accompanied by an affidavit under the official seal of any officer authorized to administer oaths within the United States, duly made by the person claiming copyright or by his duly authorized agent or representative residing in the United States, or by the printer who has printed the book, setting forth that the copies deposited have been printed from type set within the limits of the United States or from plates made within the limits of the United States from type set therein; or, if the text be produced by lithographic process, or photoengraving process, that such process was wholly performed within the limits of the United States and that the printing of the text and binding of the said book have also been performed within the limits of the United States. Such affidavit shall state also the place where and the establishment or establishments in which such type was set or plates were made or lithographic process, or photoengraving process or printing and binding were performed and the date of the completion of the printing of the book or the date of publication.

§ 18. Making False Affidavit

Any person who, for the purpose of obtaining registration of a claim to copyright, shall knowingly make a false affidavit as to his having complied with the above conditions shall be deemed guilty of a misdemeanor, and upon conviction thereof shall be punished by a fine of not more than $1,000, and all of his rights and privileges under said copyright shall thereafter be forfeited.

§ 19. Notice; Form[9]

The notice of copyright required by section 10 of this title shall consist either of the word "Copyright," the abbreviation "Copr.," or the symbol ©, accompanied by the name of the copyright proprietor, and if the work be a printed literary, musical, or dramatic work, the notice shall include also the year in which the copyright was secured by publication. In the case, however, of copies of works specified in subsections (f) to (k), inclusive, of section 5 of this title, the notice may consist of the letter C enclosed within a circle, thus ©, accompanied by the initials, monogram, mark, or symbol of the copyright proprietor: *Provided,* That on some accessible portion of such copies or of the margin, back, permanent base, or pedestal, or of the substance on which such copies shall be mounted, his name shall appear. But in the case of works in which copyright was subsisting on July 1, 1909, the notice of copyright may be either in one of the forms prescribed herein or may consist of the following words: "Entered according to Act of Congress, in the year _____, by A.B., in the office of the Librarian of Congress, at Washington, D.C.," or, at his option, the word "Copyright," together with the year the copyright was entered and the name of the party by whom it was taken out; thus, "Copyright, 19__, by A.B."

In the case of reproductions of works specified in subsection (n) of section 5 of this title, the notice shall consist of the symbol P (the letter P in a circle), the year of first publication of the sound recording, and the name of the owner of copyright in the sound recording, or an abbreviation by which the name can be recognized, or a generally known alternative designation of the owner: *Provided,* That if the producer of the sound recording is named on the labels or containers of the reproduction, and if no other name appears on the labels or containers of the reproduction, and if no other name appears in conjunction with the notice, his name shall be considered a part of the notice.

---

[9] Section 19 as amended by the Act of August 31, 1954 (68 Stat. 1030), effective September 16, 1955, and by the Act of October 15, 1971 (85 Stat. 391), effective February 15, 1972. See Sec. 5(n), n1.

§ 20. Same; Place of Application of; One Notice in Each Volume or Number of Newspaper or Periodical[10]

The notice of copyright shall be applied, in the case of a book or other printed publication, upon its title page or the page immediately following, or if a periodical either upon the title page or upon the first page of text of each separate number or under the title heading, or if a musical work either upon its title page or the first page of music, or if a sound recording on the surface of reproductions thereof or on the label or container in such manner and location as to give reasonable notice to the claim of copyright. One notice of copyright in each volume or in each number of a newspaper or periodical published shall suffice.

§ 21. Same; Effect of Accidental Omission From Copy or Copies

Where the copyright proprietor has sought to comply with the provisions of this title with respect to notice, the omission by accident or mistake of the prescribed notice from a particular copy or copies shall not invalidate the copyright or prevent recovery for infringement against any person who, after actual notice of the copyright, begins an undertaking to infringe it, but shall prevent the recovery of damages against an innocent infringer who has been misled by the omission of the notice; and in a suit for infringement no permanent injunction shall be had unless the copyright proprietor shall reimburse to the innocent infringer his reasonable outlay innocently incurred if the court, in its discretion, shall so direct.

§ 22. Ad Interim Protection of Book or Periodical Published Abroad[11]

In the case of a book or periodical first published abroad in the English language, the deposit in the Copyright Office, not later than six months after its publication abroad, of one complete copy of the foreign edition, with a request for the reservation of the copyright and a statement of the name and nationality of the author and of the copyright proprietor and of the date of publication of the said book or periodical, shall secure to the author or proprietor an ad interim copyright therein, which shall have all the force and effect given to copyright by this title, and shall endure until the expiration of five years after the date of first publication abroad.

§ 23. Same; Extension to Full Term[12]

Whenever within the period of such ad interim protection an authorized edition of such books or periodicals shall be published within the United States, in accordance with the manufacturing provisions specified in section 16 of this title, and whenever the provisions of this title as to deposit of copies, registration, filing of affidavits, and the printing of the copyright notice shall have been duly complied with, the copyright shall be extended to endure in such book or periodical for the term provided in this title.

§ 24. Duration; Renewal and Extension

The copyright secured by this title shall endure for twenty-eight years from the date of first publication, whether the copyrighted work bears the author's true name or is published anonymously or under an assumed name: *Provided,* That in the case of any posthumous work or of any periodical, cyclopedic, or other composite work upon which the copyright was originally secured by the proprietor thereof, or of any work copyrighted by a corporate body (otherwise than as assignee or licensee of the individual author) or by an employer for whom such work is made for hire, the proprietor of such copyright shall be entitled to a renewal and extension of the copyright in such work for the further term of twenty-eight years when application for such renewal and extension shall have been made to

---

[10] Section 20 as amended by the Act of October 15, 1971 (85 Stat. 391), effective February 15, 1972. See Sec. 5(n), n1.

[11] Section 22 as amended by the Act of June 3, 1949 (63 Stat. 153).

[12] Section 23 as amended by the Act of June 3, 1949 (63 Stat. 153).

the copyright office and duly registered therein within one year prior to the expiration of the original term of copyright: *And provided further,* That in the case of any other copyrighted work, including a contribution by an individual author to a periodical or to a cyclopedic or other composite work, the author of such work, if still living, or the widow, widower, or children of the author, if the author be not living, or if such author, widow, widower, or children be not living, then the author's executors, or in the absence of a will, his next of kin shall be entitled to a renewal and extension of the copyright in such work for a further term of twenty-eight years when application for such renewal and extension shall have been made to the copyright office and duly registered therein within one year prior to the expiration of the original term of copyright: *And provided further,* That in default of the registration of such application for renewal and extension, the copyright in any work shall determine at the expiration of twenty-eight years from first publication.

§ 25. Renewal of Copyrights Registered in Patent Office Under Repealed Law

Subsisting copyrights originally registered in the Patent Office prior to July 1, 1940, under section 3 of the act of June 18, 1874, shall be subject to renewal in behalf of the proprietor upon application made to the Register of Copyrights within one year prior to the expiration of the original term of twenty-eight years.

§ 26. Terms Defined[13]

In the interpretation and construction of this title "the date of publication" shall in the case of a work of which copies are reproduced for sale or distribution be held to be the earliest date when copies of the first authorized edition were placed on sale, sold, or publicly distributed by the proprietor of the copyright or under his authority, and the word "author" shall include an employer in the case of works made for hire. For the purposes of this section and sections 10, 11, 13, 14, 21, 101, 106, 109, 209, 215, but not for any other purpose, a reproduction of a work described in subsection 5(n) shall be considered to be a copy thereof. "Sound recordings" are works that result from the fixation of a series of musical, spoken, or other sounds, but not including the sounds accompanying a motion picture. "Reproductions of sound recordings" are material objects in which sounds other than those accompanying a motion picture are fixed by any method now known or later developed, and from which the sounds can be perceived, reproduced, or otherwise communicated, either directly or with the aid of a machine or device, and include the "parts of instruments serving to reproduce mechanically the musical work," "mechanical reproductions," and "interchangeable parts, such as discs or tapes for use in mechanical music-producing machines" referred to in sections 1(e) and 101(e) of this title.

§ 27. Copyright Distinct From Property in Object Copyrighted; Effect of Sale of Object, and of Assignment of Copyright

The copyright is distinct from the property in the material object copyrighted, and the sale or conveyance, by gift or otherwise, of the material object shall not of itself constitute a transfer of the copyright, nor shall the assignment of the copyright constitute a transfer of the title to the material object; but nothing in this title shall be deemed to forbid, prevent, or restrict the transfer of any copy of a copyrighted work the possession of which has been lawfully obtained.

§ 28. Assignments and Bequests

Copyright secured under this title or previous copyright laws of the United States may be assigned, granted, or mortgaged by an instrument in writing signed by the proprietor of the copyright, or may be bequeathed by will.

---

[13] Section 26 as amended by the Act of October 15, 1971 (85 Stat. 391), effective February 15, 1972. See Sec. 5(n), n1.

§ 29. Same; Executed in Foreign Country; Acknowledgment and Certificate

Every assignment of copyright executed in a foreign country shall be acknowledged by the assignor before a consular officer or secretary of legation of the United States authorized by law to administer oaths or perform notarial acts. The certificate of such acknowledgment under the hand and official seal of such consular officer or secretary of legation shall be prima facie evidence of the execution of the instrument.

§ 30. Same; Record

Every assignment of copyright shall be recorded in the copyright office within three calendar months after its execution in the United States or within six calendar months after its execution without the limits of the United States, in default of which it shall be void as against any subsequent purchaser or mortgagee for a valuable consideration, without notice, whose assignment has been duly recorded.

§ 31. Same; Certificate of Record

The Register of Copyrights shall, upon payment of the prescribed fee, record such assignment, and shall return it to the sender with a certificate of record attached under seal of the copyright office, and upon the payment of the fee prescribed by this title he shall furnish to any person requesting the same a certified copy thereof under the said seal.

§ 32. Same; Use of Name of Assignee in Notice

When an assignment of the copyright in a specified book or other work has been recorded the assignee may substitute his name for that of the assignor in the statutory notice of copyright prescribed by this title.

CHAPTER 2. INFRINGEMENT PROCEEDINGS[14]

---

[14] Sections 101(f), 102, 103, 110 and 111 were repealed by the Act of June 25, 1948 (62 Stat. 869), effective September 1, 1948. However, see sections 1338, 1440 and 2072 (Title 28, United States Code), appearing infra and the Federal Rules of Civil Procedure.

---

§ 101. Infringement

If any person shall infringe the copyright in any work protected under the copyright laws of the United States such person shall be liable:

   (a) **Injunction**—To an injunction restraining such infringement:

   (b) **Damages and Profits; Amount; Other Remedies**—To pay to the copyright proprietor such damages as the copyright proprietor may have suffered due to the infringement, as well as all the profits which the infringer shall have made from such infringement, and in proving profits the plaintiff shall be required to prove sales only, and the defendant shall be required to prove every element of cost which he claims, or in lieu of actual damages and profits, such damages as to the court shall appear to be just, and in assessing such damages the court may, in its discretion, allow the amounts as hereinafter stated, but in case of a newspaper reproduction of a copyrighted photograph, such damages shall not exceed the sum of $200 nor be less than the sum of $50, and in the case of the infringement of an undramatized or nondramatic work by means of motion pictures, where the infringer shall show that he was not aware that he was infringing, and that such infringement could not have been reasonably foreseen, such damages shall not exceed the sum of $100; and in the case of an infringement of a copyrighted dramatic or dramatico-musical work by a maker of motion pictures and his agencies for distribution thereof to exhibitors, where such infringer shows that he was not aware that he was infringing a copyrighted work, and that such infringements could not reasonably have been foreseen, the entire sum of such damages recoverable by the copyright proprietor from such infringing maker and his agencies for the distribution to exhibitors of such infringing motion picture shall not exceed the sum of $5,000 nor be less than $250, and such damages shall in no other case exceed the sum of $5,000 nor be less than the sum of $250, and shall not be regarded as a penalty. But the foregoing exceptions shall not deprive the copyright proprietor of any other remedy given him under this law, nor shall the limitation as to the amount of recovery apply to infringements occurring after the actual notice to a defendant, either by service of process in a suit or other written notice served upon him.

   First. In the case of a painting, statue, or sculpture, $10 for every infringing copy made or sold by or found in the possession of the infringer or his agents or employees;

   Second. In the case of any work enumerated in section 5 of this title, except a painting, statue, or sculpture, $1 for every infringing copy made or sold by or found in the possession of the infringer or his agents or employees;

   Third. In the case of a lecture, sermon, or address, $50 for every infringing delivery;

   Fourth. In the case of a dramatic or dramatico-musical or a choral or orchestral composition, $100 for the first and $50 for every subsequent infringing performance; in the case of other musical compositions $10 for every infringing performance;

   (c) **Impounding During Action**—To deliver up on oath, to be impounded during the pendency of the action, upon such terms and conditions as the court may prescribe, all articles alleged to infringe a copyright;

   (d) **Destruction of Infringing Copies and Plates**—To deliver up on oath for destruction all the infringing copies or devices, as well as all plates, molds, matrices, or other means for making such infringing copies as the court may order.

(e) Interchangeable Parts for Use in Mechanical Music—Producing Machines[15]— Interchangeable parts, such as discs or tapes for use in mechanical music-producing machines adapted to reproduce copyrighted musical works, shall be considered copies of the copyrighted musical works which they serve to reproduce mechanically for the purpose of this section 101 and sections 106 and 109 of this title, and the unauthorized manufacture, use, or sale of such interchangeable parts shall constitute an infringement of the copyrighted work rendering the infringer liable in accordance with all provisions of this title dealing with infringements of copyright and, in a case of willful infringement for profit, to criminal prosecution pursuant to section 104 of this title. Whenever any person, in the absence of a license agreement, intends to use a copyrighted musical composition upon the parts of instruments serving to reproduce mechanically the musical work, relying upon the compulsory license provision of this title, he shall serve notice of such intention, by registered mail, upon the copyright proprietor at his last address disclosed by the records of the copyright office, sending to the copyright office a duplicate of such notice.

§ 104. Willful Infringement for Profit[16]

(a) Except as provided in subsection (b), any person who willfully and for profit shall infringe any copyright secured by this title, or who shall knowingly and willfully aid or abet such infringement, shall be deemed guilty of a misdemeanor, and upon conviction thereof shall be punished by imprisonment for not exceeding one year or by a fine of not less than $100 nor more than $1,000, or both, in the discretion of the court: *Provided, however,* That nothing in this title shall be so construed as to prevent the performance of religious or secular works such as oratorios, cantatas, masses, or octavo choruses by public schools, church choirs, or vocal societies, rented, borrowed, or obtained from some public library, public school, church choir, school choir, or vocal society, provided the performance is given for charitable or educational purposes and not for profit.

(b) Any person who willfully and for profit shall infringe any copyright provided by section 1(f) of this title, or who should knowingly and willfully aid or abet such infringement, shall be fined not more than $25,000 or imprisoned not more than one year, or both, for the first offense and shall be fined not more than $50,000 or imprisoned not more than two years, or both, for any subsequent offense.

§ 105. Fraudulent Notice of Copyright, or Removal or Alteration of Notice

Any person who, with fraudulent intent, shall insert or impress any notice of copyright required by this title, or words of the same purport, in or upon any uncopyrighted article, or with fraudulent intent shall remove or alter the copyright notice upon any article duly copyrighted shall be guilty of a misdemeanor, punishable by a fine of not less than $100 and not more than $1,000. Any person who shall knowingly issue or sell any article bearing a notice of United States copyright which has not been copyrighted in this country, or who shall knowingly import any article bearing such notice or words of the same purport, which has not been copyrighted in this country, shall be liable to a fine of $100.

§ 106. Importation of Article Bearing False Notice or Piratical Copies of Copyrighted Work

The importation into the United States of any article bearing a false notice of copyright when there is no existing copyright thereon in the United States, or of any piratical copies of any work copyrighted in the United States, is prohibited.

---

[15] Section 101(e) as amended by the Act of October 15, 1971 (85 Stat. 391).
[16] Section 104 as amended by the Act of December 31, 1974 (88 Stat. 1873).

§ 107. Importation, During Existence of Copyright, of Piratical Copies, or of Copies Not Produced in Accordance With Section 16 of This Title

During the existence of the American copyright in any book the importation into the United States of any piratical copies thereof or of any copies thereof (although authorized by the author or proprietor) which have not been produced in accordance with the manufacturing provisions specified in section 16 of this title, or any plates of the same not made from type set within the limits of the United States, or any copies thereof produced by lithographic or photoengraving process not performed within the limits of the United States, in accordance with the provisions of section 16 of this title, is prohibited: *Provided, however,* That, except as regards piratical copies, such prohibition shall not apply:

(a) To works in raised characters for the use of the blind.

(b) To a foreign newspaper or magazine, although containing matter copyrighted in the United States, printed or reprinted by authority of the copyright proprietor, unless such newspaper or magazine contains also copyright matter printed or reprinted without such authorization.

(c) To the authorized edition of a book in a foreign language or languages of which only a translation into English has been copyrighted in this country.

(d) To any book published abroad with the authorization of the author or copyright proprietor when imported under the circumstances stated in one of the four subdivisions following, that is to say:

First. When imported, not more than one copy at one time, for individual use and not for sale; but such privilege of importation shall not extend to a foreign reprint of a book by an American author copyrighted in the United States.

Second. When imported by the authority or for the use of the United States.

Third. When imported, for use and not for sale, not more than one copy of any such book in any one invoice, in good faith by or for any society or institution incorporated for educational, literary, philosophical, scientific, or religious purposes, or for the encouragement of the fine arts, or for any college, academy, school, or seminary of learning, or for any State, school, college, university, or free public library in the United States.

Fourth. When such books form parts of libraries or collections purchased en bloc for the use of societies, institutions, or libraries designated in the foregoing paragraph, or form parts of the libraries or personal baggage belonging to persons or families arriving from foreign countries and are not intended for sale: *Provided,* That copies imported as above may not lawfully be used in any way to violate the rights of the proprietor of the American copyright or annul or limit the copyright protection secured by this title, and such unlawful use shall be deemed an infringement of copyright.

§ 108. Forfeiture and Destruction of Articles Prohibited Importation

Any and all articles prohibited importation by this title which are brought into the United States from any foreign country (except in the mails) shall be seized and forfeited by like proceedings as those provided by law for the seizure and condemnation of property imported into the United States in violation of the customs revenue laws. Such articles when forfeited shall be destroyed in such manner as the Secretary of the Treasury or the court, as the case may be, shall direct: *Provided, however,* That all copies of authorized editions of copyright books imported in the mails or otherwise in violation of the provisions of this title may be exported and returned to the country of export whenever it is shown to the satisfaction of the Secretary of the Treasury, in a written application, that such importation does not involve willful negligence or fraud.

§ 109. Importation of Prohibited Articles; Regulations; Proof of Deposit of Copies by Complainants

The Secretary of the Treasury and the Postmaster General are hereby empowered and required to make and enforce individually or jointly such rules and regulations as shall prevent the importation into the United States of articles prohibited importation by this title, and may require, as conditions precedent to exclusion of any work in which copyright is claimed, the copyright proprietor or any person claiming actual or potential injury by reason of actual or contemplated importations of copies of such work to file with the Post Office Department or the Treasury Department a certificate of the Register of Copyrights that the provisions of section 13 of this title have been fully complied with, and to give notice of such compliance to postmasters or to customs officers at the ports of entry in the United States in such form and accompanied by such exhibits as may be deemed necessary for the practical and efficient administration and enforcement of the provisions of sections 106 and 107 of this title.

§ 112. Injunctions; Service and Enforcement[17]

Any court mentioned in section 1338 of Title 28 or judge thereof shall have power, upon complaint filed by any party aggrieved, to grant injunctions to prevent and restrain the violation of any right secured by this title, according to the course and principles of courts of equity, on such terms as said court or judge may deem reasonable. Any injunction that may be granted restraining and enjoining the doing of anything forbidden by this title may be served on the parties against whom such injunction may be granted anywhere in the United States, and shall be operative throughout the United States and be enforceable by proceedings in contempt or otherwise by any other court or judge possessing jurisdiction of the defendants.

§ 113. Transmission of Certified Copies of Papers for Enforcement of Injunction by Other Court

The clerk of the court, or judge granting the injunction, shall, when required so to do by the court hearing the application to enforce said injunction, transmit without delay to said court a certified copy of all the papers in said cause that are on file in his office.

§ 114. Review of Orders, Judgments, or Decrees[18]

The orders, judgments, or decrees of any court mentioned in section 1338 of Title 28 arising under the copyright laws of the United States may be reviewed on appeal in the manner and to the extent now provided by law for the review of cases determined in said courts, respectively.

§ 115. Limitations[19]

(a) **Criminal Proceedings**—No criminal proceedings shall be maintained under the provisions of this title unless the same is commenced within three years after the cause of action arose.

(b) **Civil Actions**—No civil action shall be maintained under the provisions of this title unless the same is commenced within three years after the claim accrued.

§ 116. Costs; Attorney's Fees

In all actions, suits, or proceedings under this title, except when brought by or against the United States or any officer thereof, full costs shall be allowed, and the court may award to the prevailing party a reasonable attorney's fee as part of the costs.

---

[17] Sections 112 and 114 as amended by the Act of October 31, 1951 (65 Stat. 710).

[18] Ibid.

[19] Section 115 as amended by the Act of September 7, 1957 (71 Stat. 633), effective September 7, 1958.

CHAPTER 3.　COPYRIGHT OFFICE

---

§ 201.　Copyright Office; Preservation of Records

All records and other things relating to copyrights required by law to be preserved shall be kept and preserved in the copyright office, Library of Congress, District of Columbia, and shall be under the control of the register of copyrights, who shall, under the direction and supervision of the Librarian of Congress, perform all the duties relating to the registration of copyrights.

§ 202.　Register, Assistant Register, and Subordinates

There shall be appointed by the Librarian of Congress a Register of Copyrights, and one Assistant Register of Copyrights, who shall have authority during the absence of the Register of Copyrights to attach the copyright office seal to all papers issued from the said office and to sign such certificates and other papers as may be necessary. There shall also be appointed by the Librarian such subordinate assistants to the register as may from time to time be authorized by law.

§ 203.　Same; Deposit of Moneys Received; Reports

The Register of Copyrights shall make daily deposits in some bank in the District of Columbia, designated for this purpose by the Secretary of the Treasury as a national depository, of all moneys received to be applied as copyright fees, and shall make weekly deposits with the Secretary of the Treasury, in such manner as the latter shall direct, of all copyright fees actually applied under the provisions of this title, and annual deposits of sums received which it has not been possible to apply as copyright fees or to return to the remitters, and shall also make monthly reports to the Secretary of the Treasury and to the Librarian of Congress of the applied copyright fees for each calendar month, together with a statement of all remittances received, trust funds on hand, moneys refunded, and unapplied balances.

§ 204.　Same; Bond

The Register of Copyrights shall give bond to the United States in the sum of $20,000, in form to be approved by the General Counsel for the Department of the Treasury and with sureties satisfactory to the Secretary of the Treasury, for the faithful discharge of his duties.

§ 205. Same; Annual Report

The Register of Copyrights shall make an annual report to the Librarian of Congress, to be printed in the annual report on the Library of Congress, of all copyright business for the previous fiscal year, including the number and kind of works which have been deposited in the copyright office during the fiscal year, under the provisions of this title.

§ 206. Seal of Copyright Office

The seal used in the copyright office on July 1, 1909, shall be the seal of the copyright office, and by it all papers issued from the copyright office requiring authentication shall be authenticated.

§ 207. Rules for Registration of Claims[21]

Subject to the approval of the Librarian of Congress, the Register of Copyrights shall be authorized to make rules and regulations for the registration of claims to copyright as provided by this title.

§ 208. Record Books in Copyright Office

The Register of Copyrights shall provide and keep such record books in the copyright office as are required to carry out the provisions of this title, and whenever deposit has been made in the copyright office of a copy of any work under the provisions of this title he shall make entry thereof.

§ 209. Certificate of Registration; Effect as Evidence; Receipt for Copies Deposited

In the case of each entry the person recorded as the claimant of the copyright shall be entitled to a certificate of registration under seal of the copyright office, to contain the name and address of said claimant, the name of the country of which the author of the work is a citizen or subject, and when an alien author domiciled in the United States at the time of said registration, then a statement of that fact, including his place of domicile, the name of the author (when the records of the copyright office shall show the same), the title of the work which is registered for which copyright is claimed, the date of the deposit of the copies of such work, the date of publication if the work has been reproduced in copies for sale, or publicly distributed, and such marks as to class designation and entry number as shall fully identify the entry. In the case of a book, the certificate shall also state the receipt of the affidavit, as provided by section 17 of this title, and the date of the completion of the printing, or the date of the publication of the book, as stated in the said affidavit. The Register of Copyrights shall prepare a printed form for the said certificate, to be filled out in each case as above provided for in the case of all registrations made after July 1, 1909, and in the case of all previous registrations so far as the copyright office record books shall show such facts, which certificate, sealed with the seal of the copyright office, shall, upon payment of the prescribed fee, be given to any person making application for the same. Said certificate shall be admitted in any court as prima facie evidence of the facts stated therein. In addition to such certificate the register of copyrights shall furnish, upon request, without additional fee, a receipt for the copies of the work deposited to complete the registration.

§ 210. Catalog of Copyright Entries; Effect as Evidence

The Register of Copyrights shall fully index all copyright registrations and assignments and shall print at periodic intervals a catalog of the titles of articles deposited and registered for copyright, together with suitable indexes, and at stated intervals shall print complete and indexed catalog for each class of copyright entries, and may thereupon, if expedient, destroy the original manuscript catalog cards containing the titles included in such printed volumes and representing the entries made during such intervals. The current catalog of copyright entries and the index volumes herein provided

---

[21] Published in the Federal Register and Title 37 of the Code of Federal Regulations. See infra, for the current regulations.

for shall be admitted in any court as prima facie evidence of the facts stated therein as regards any copyright registration.

§ 211. Same; Distribution and Sale; Disposal of Proceeds[22]

The said printed current catalogs as they are issued shall be promptly distributed by the Superintendent of Documents to the collectors of customs of the United States and to the postmasters of all exchange offices of receipt of foreign mails, in accordance with revised list of such collectors of customs and postmasters prepared by the Secretary of the Treasury and the Postmaster General, and they shall also be furnished in whole or in part to all parties desiring them at a price to be determined by the Register of Copyrights for each part of the catalog not exceeding $25 for the complete yearly catalog of copyright entries. The consolidated catalogs and indexes shall also be supplied to all persons ordering them at such prices as may be fixed by the Register of Copyrights, and all subscriptions for the catalogs shall be received by the Superintendent of Documents, who shall forward the said publications; and the moneys thus received shall be paid into the Treasury of the United States and accounted for under such laws and Treasury regulations as shall be in force at the time.

§ 212. Records and Works Deposited in Copyright Office Open to Public Inspection; Taking Copies of Entries

The record books of the copyright office, together with the indexes to such record books, and all works deposited and retained in the copyright office, shall be open to public inspection; and copies may be taken of the copyright entries actually made in such record books, subject to such safeguards and regulations as shall be prescribed by the Register of Copyrights and approved by the Librarian of Congress.

§ 213. Disposition of Articles Deposited in Office

Of the articles deposited in the copyright office under the provisions of the copyright laws of the United States, the Librarian of Congress shall determine what books and other articles shall be transferred to the permanent collections of the Library of Congress, including the law library, and what other books or articles shall be placed in the reserve collections of the Library of Congress for sale or exchange, or be transferred to other governmental libraries in the District of Columbia for use therein.

§ 214. Destruction of Articles Deposited in Office Remaining Undisposed of; Removal of by Author or Proprietor; Manuscripts of Unpublished Works

Of any articles undisposed of as above provided, together with all titles and correspondence relating thereto, the Librarian of Congress and the Register of Copyrights jointly shall, at suitable intervals, determine what of these received during any period of years it is desirable or useful to preserve in the permanent files of the copyright office, and, after due notice as hereinafter provided, may within their discretion cause the remaining articles and other things to be destroyed: *Provided,* That there shall be printed in the Catalog of Copyright Entries from February to November, inclusive, a statement of the years of receipt of such articles and a notice to permit any author, copyright proprietor, or other lawful claimant to claim and remove before the expiration of the month of December of that year anything found which relates to any of his productions deposited or registered for copyright within the period of years stated, not reserved or disposed of as provided for in this title. No manuscript of an unpublished work shall be destroyed during its term of copyright without specific notice to the copyright proprietor of record, permitting him to claim and remove it.

[§§ 215–216 are omitted]

---

22 Section 211 as amended by the Act of April 27, 1948 (62 Stat. 202) effective May 27, 1948.

B. COPYRIGHT ACT OF 1976*

As Amended
17 U.S.C.A. §§ 101–810, 1101

Contents

CHAPTER 1. SUBJECT MATTER AND SCOPE OF COPYRIGHT

---

* Chapter 9, relating to semiconductor chips, Chapter 10, relating to digital audio recording devices, Chapter 12, relating to copyright protection and management systems and Chapter 13, relating to protection for original vessel hull designs are not technically part of the copyright act, although they are codified in Title 17. Consequently, they appear as separate subchapters in this volume following this statute—*Ed.*

(3)   Statutory License Where Retransmissions into Local Market Available.
- (A)   Rules for Subscribers to Signals Under Subsection (e).
- (B)   Rules for Lawful Subscribers as of Date of Enactment of 2010 Act.
- (C)   Future Applicability.
- (D)   Other Provisions Not Affected.
- (E)   Waiver.
- (F)   Available Defined.

(4)   Noncompliance With Reporting and Payment Requirements.

(5)   Willful Alterations.

(6)   Violation of Territorial Restrictions on Statutory License for Network Stations.
- (A)   Individual Violations.
- (B)   Pattern of Violations.
- (C)   Previous Subscribers Excluded.
- (D)   Burden of Proof.
- (E)   Exception.

(7)   Discrimination by a Satellite Carrier.

(8)   Geographic Limitation on Secondary Transmissions.

(9)   Loser Pays for Signal Intensity Measurement; Recovery of Measurement Costs in a Civil Action.

(10) Inability to Conduct Measurement.

(11) Service to Recreational Vehicles and Commercial Trucks.
- (A)   Exemption.
- (B)   Documentation Requirements.
- (C)   Updated Documentation Requirements.

(12) Statutory License Contingent on Compliance with FCC Rules and Remedial Steps.

(13) Waivers.

(14) Restricted Transmission of Out-of-State Distant Network Signals into Certain Markets.
- (A)   Out-of-State Network Affiliates.
- (B)   Exception.

(b)   Deposit of Statements and Fees; Verification Procedures.
- (1)   Deposits With the Register of Copyrights.
- (2)   Verification of Accounts and Fee Payments.
- (3)   Investment of Fees.
- (4)   Persons to Whom Fees Are Distributed.
- (5)   Procedures for Distribution.
  - (A)   Filing of Claims for Fees.
  - (B)   Determination of Controversy; Distributions.
  - (C)   Withholding of Fees During Controversy.

(c)   Adjustment of Royalty Fees.
- (1)   Applicability and Determination of Royalty Fees for Signals.
  - (A)   Initial Fee.
  - (B)   Fee Set by Voluntary Negotiation.
  - (C)   Negotiations.
  - (D)   Agreements Binding on Parties; Filing of Agreements; Public Notice.
  - (E)   Period Agreement Is in Effect.
  - (F)   Fee Set by Copyright Royalty Judges Proceeding.
- (2)   Annual Royalty Fee Adjustment.

(d)   Definitions.
- (1)   Distributor.
- (2)   Network Station.
- (3)   Primary Network Station.
- (4)   Primary Transmission.

---

§ 101. Definitions

Except as otherwise provided in this title, as used in this title, the following terms and their variant forms mean the following:

An "anonymous work" is a work on the copies or phonorecords of which no natural person is identified as author.

An "architectural work" is the design of a building as embodied in any tangible medium of expression, including a building, architectural plans, or drawings. The work includes the overall form as well as the arrangement and composition of spaces and elements in the design, but does not include individual standard features.

"Audiovisual works" are works that consist of a series of related images which are intrinsically intended to be shown by the use of machines or devices such as projectors, viewers, or electronic equipment, together with accompanying sounds, if any, regardless of the nature of the material objects, such as films or tapes, in which the works are embodied.

The "Berne Convention" is the Convention for the Protection of Literary and Artistic Works, signed at Berne, Switzerland, on September 9, 1886, and all acts, protocols, and revisions thereto.

The "best edition" of a work is the edition, published in the United States at any time before the date of deposit, that the Library of Congress determines to be most suitable for its purposes.

A person's "children" are that person's immediate offspring, whether legitimate or not, and any children legally adopted by that person.

A "collective work" is a work, such as a periodical issue, anthology, or encyclopedia, in which a number of contributions, constituting separate and independent works in themselves, are assembled into a collective whole.

A "compilation" is a work formed by the collection and assembling of preexisting materials or of data that are selected, coordinated, or arranged in such a way that the resulting work as a whole constitutes an original work of authorship. The term "compilation" includes collective works.

A "computer program" is a set of statements or instructions to be used directly or indirectly in a computer in order to bring about a certain result.

"Copies" are material objects, other than phonorecords, in which a work is fixed by any method now known or later developed, and from which the work can be perceived, reproduced, or otherwise communicated, either directly or with the aid of a machine or device. The term "copies" includes the material object, other than a phonorecord, in which the work is first fixed.

"Copyright owner", with respect to any one of the exclusive rights comprised in a copyright, refers to the owner of that particular right.

A "Copyright Royalty Judge" is a Copyright Royalty Judge appointed under section 802 of this title, and includes any individual serving as an interim Copyright Royalty Judge under such section.

A work is "created" when it is fixed in a copy or phonorecord for the first time; where a work is prepared over a period of time, the portion of it that has been fixed at any particular time constitutes the work as of that time, and where the work has been prepared in different versions, each version constitutes a separate work.

A "derivative work" is a work based upon one or more preexisting works, such as a translation, musical arrangement, dramatization, fictionalization, motion picture version, sound recording, art reproduction, abridgment, condensation, or any other form in which a work may be recast, transformed, or adapted. A work consisting of editorial revisions, annotations, elaborations, or other modifications which, as a whole, represent an original work of authorship, is a "derivative work".

A "device", "machine", or "process" is one now known or later developed.

A "digital transmission" is a transmission in whole or in part in a digital or other non-analog format.

To "display" a work means to show a copy of it, either directly or by means of a film, slide, television image, or any other device or process or, in the case of a motion picture or other audiovisual work, to show individual images nonsequentially.

An "establishment" is a store, shop, or any similar place of business open to the general public for the primary purpose of selling goods or services in which the majority of the gross square feet of space that is nonresidential is used for that purpose, and in which nondramatic musical works are performed publicly.

The term "financial gain" includes receipt, or expectation of receipt, of anything of value, including the receipt of other copyrighted works.

A work is "fixed" in a tangible medium of expression when its embodiment in a copy or phonorecord, by or under the authority of the author, is sufficiently permanent or stable to permit it to be perceived, reproduced, or otherwise communicated for a period of more than transitory duration. A work consisting of sounds, images, or both, that are being transmitted, is "fixed" for purposes of this title if a fixation of the work is being made simultaneously with its transmission.

A "food service or drinking establishment" is a restaurant, inn, bar, tavern, or any other similar place of business in which the public or patrons assemble for the primary purpose of being served food or drink, in which the majority of the gross square feet of space that is nonresidential is used for that purpose, and in which nondramatic musical works are performed publicly.

The "Geneva Phonograms Convention" is the Convention for the Protection of Producers of Phonograms Against Unauthorized Duplication of Their Phonograms, concluded at Geneva, Switzerland, on October 29, 1971.

The "gross square feet of space" of an establishment means the entire interior space of that establishment, and any adjoining outdoor space used to serve patrons, whether on a seasonal basis or otherwise.

The terms "including" and "such as" are illustrative and not limitative.

An "international agreement" is—

(1)   the Universal Copyright Convention;

(2)   the Geneva Phonograms Convention;

(3)   the Berne Convention;

(4)   the WTO Agreement;

(5)   the WIPO Copyright Treaty;

(6)   the WIPO Performances and Phonograms Treaty; and

(7)   any other copyright treaty to which the United States is a party.

A "joint work" is a work prepared by two or more authors with the intention that their contributions be merged into inseparable or interdependent parts of a unitary whole.

"Literary works" are works, other than audiovisual works, expressed in words, numbers, or other verbal or numerical symbols or indicia, regardless of the nature of the material objects, such as books, periodicals, manuscripts, phonorecords, film, tapes, disks, or cards, in which they are embodied.

The term "motion picture exhibition facility" means a movie theater, screening room, or other venue that is being used primarily for the exhibition of a copyrighted motion picture, if such exhibition is open to the public or is made to an assembled group of viewers outside of a normal circle of a family and its social acquaintances.

"Motion pictures" are audiovisual works consisting of a series of related images which, when shown in succession, impart an impression of motion, together with accompanying sounds, if any.

To "perform" a work means to recite, render, play, dance, or act it, either directly or by means of any device or process or, in the case of a motion picture or other audiovisual work, to show its images in any sequence or to make the sounds accompanying it audible.

A "performing rights society" is an association, corporation, or other entity that licenses the public performance of nondramatic musical works on behalf of copyright owners of such works, such as the American Society of Composers, Authors and Publishers (ASCAP), Broadcast Music, Inc. (BMI), and SESAC, Inc.

"Phonorecords" are material objects in which sounds, other than those accompanying a motion picture or other audiovisual work, are fixed by any method now known or later developed, and from which the sounds can be perceived, reproduced, or otherwise communicated, either directly or with the aid of a machine or device. The term "phonorecords" includes the material object in which the sounds are first fixed.

"Pictorial, graphic, and sculptural works" include two-dimensional and three-dimensional works of fine, graphic, and applied art, photographs, prints and art reproductions, maps, globes, charts, diagrams, models, and technical drawings, including architectural plans. Such works shall include works of artistic craftsmanship insofar as their form but not their mechanical or utilitarian aspects are concerned; the design of a useful article, as defined in this section, shall be considered a pictorial, graphic, or sculptural work only if, and only to the extent that, such design incorporates pictorial, graphic, or sculptural features that can be identified separately from, and are capable of existing independently of, the utilitarian aspects of the article.

For purposes of Section 513, "proprietor" is an individual, corporation, partnership, or other entity, as the case may be, that owns an establishment or a food service or drinking establishment, except that no owner or operator of a radio or television station licensed by the Federal Communications Commission, cable system or satellite carrier, cable or satellite carrier service or programmer, provider of online services or network access or the operator of facilities therefor, telecommunications company, or any other such audio or audiovisual service or programmer now known or as may be developed in the future, commercial subscription music service, or owner or operator of any other transmission service, shall under any circumstances be deemed to be a proprietor.

A "pseudonymous work" is a work on the copies or phonorecords of which the author is identified under a fictitious name.

"Publication" is the distribution of copies or phonorecords of a work to the public by sale or other transfer of ownership, or by rental, lease, or lending. The offering to distribute copies or phonorecords to a group of persons for purposes of further distribution, public performance, or public display, constitutes publication. A public performance or display of a work does not of itself constitute publication.

To perform or display a work "publicly" means—

(1) to perform or display it at a place open to the public or at any place where a substantial number of persons outside of a normal circle of a family and its social acquaintances is gathered; or

(2) to transmit or otherwise communicate a performance or display of the work to a place specified by clause (1) or to the public, by means of any device or process, whether the members of the public capable of receiving the performance or display receive it in the same place or in separate places and at the same time or at different times.

"Registration", for purposes of sections 205(c)(2), 405, 406, 410(d), 411, 412, and 506(e), means a registration of a claim in the original or the renewed and extended term of copyright.

"Sound recordings" are works that result from the fixation of a series of musical, spoken, or other sounds, but not including the sounds accompanying a motion picture or other audiovisual work, regardless of the nature of the material objects, such as disks, tapes, or other phonorecords, in which they are embodied.

"State" includes the District of Columbia and the Commonwealth of Puerto Rico, and any territories to which this title is made applicable by an Act of Congress.

A "transfer of copyright ownership" is an assignment, mortgage, exclusive license, or any other conveyance, alienation, or hypothecation of a copyright or of any of the exclusive rights comprised in a copyright, whether or not it is limited in time or place of effect, but not including a nonexclusive license.

A "transmission program" is a body of material that, as an aggregate, has been produced for the sole purpose of transmission to the public in sequence and as a unit.

To "transmit" a performance or display is to communicate it by any device or process whereby images or sounds are received beyond the place from which they are sent.

A "treaty party" is a country or intergovernmental organization other than the United States that is a party to an international agreement.

The "United States", when used in a geographical sense, comprises the several States, the District of Columbia and the Commonwealth of Puerto Rico, and the organized territories under the jurisdiction of the United States Government.

For purposes of section 411, a work is a "United States work" only if—

(1) in the case of a published work, the work is first published—

(A) in the United States;

(B) simultaneously in the United States and another treaty party or parties, whose law grants a term of copyright protection that is the same as or longer than the term provided in the United States;

(C) simultaneously in the United States and a foreign nation that is not a treaty party; or

(D) in a foreign nation that is not a treaty party, and all of the authors of the work are nationals, domiciliaries, or habitual residents of, or in the case of an audiovisual work legal entities with headquarters in, the United States;

(2) in the case of an unpublished work, all the authors of the work are nationals, domiciliaries, or habitual residents of the United States, or, in the case of an unpublished audiovisual work, all the authors are legal entities with headquarters in the United States; or

(3)   in the case of a pictorial, graphic, or sculptural work incorporated in a building or structure, the building or structure is located in the United States.

A "useful article" is an article having an intrinsic utilitarian function that is not merely to portray the appearance of the article or to convey information. An article that is normally a part of a useful article is considered a "useful article".

The author's "widow" or "widower" is the author's surviving spouse under the law of the author's domicile at the time of his or her death, whether or not the spouse has later remarried.

The "WIPO Copyright Treaty" is the WIPO Copyright Treaty concluded at Geneva, Switzerland, on December 20, 1996.

The "WIPO Performances and Phonograms Treaty" is the WIPO Performances and Phonograms Treaty concluded at Geneva, Switzerland, on December 20, 1996.

A "work of visual art" is—

(1)   a painting, drawing, print, or sculpture, existing in a single copy, in a limited edition of 200 copies or fewer that are signed and consecutively numbered by the author, or, in the case of a sculpture, in multiple cast, carved, or fabricated sculptures of 200 or fewer that are consecutively numbered by the author and bear the signature or other identifying mark of the author; or

(2)   a still photographic image produced for exhibition purposes only, existing in a single copy that is signed by the author, or in a limited edition of 200 copies or fewer that are signed and consecutively numbered by the author.

A work of visual art does not include—

(A)(i)   any poster, map, globe, chart, technical drawing, diagram, model, applied art, motion picture or other audiovisual work, book, magazine, newspaper, periodical, data base, electronic information service, electronic publication, or similar publication;

(ii)   any merchandising item or advertising, promotional, descriptive, covering, or packaging material or container;

(iii)   any portion or part of any item described in clause (i) or (ii);

(B)   any work made for hire; or

(C)   any work not subject to copyright protection under this title.

A "work of the United States Government" is a work prepared by an officer or employee of the United States Government as part of that person's official duties.

A "work made for hire" is—

(1)   a work prepared by an employee within the scope of his or her employment; or

(2)   a work specially ordered or commissioned for use as a contribution to a collective work, as a part of a motion picture or other audiovisual work, as a translation, as a supplementary work, as a compilation, as an instructional text, as a test, as answer material for a test, or as an atlas, if the parties expressly agree in a written instrument signed by them that the work shall be considered a work made for hire. For the purpose of the foregoing sentence, a "supplementary work" is a work prepared for publication as a secondary adjunct to a work by another author for the purpose of introducing, concluding, illustrating, explaining, revising, commenting upon, or assisting in the use of the other work, such as forewords, afterwords, pictorial illustrations, maps, charts, tables, editorial notes, musical arrangements, answer material for tests, bibliographies, appendixes, and indexes, and an "instructional text" is a literary, pictorial, or graphic work prepared for publication and with the purpose of use in systematic instructional activities.

In determining whether any work is eligible to be considered a work made for hire under paragraph (2), neither the amendment contained in section 1011(d) of the Intellectual Property and Communications Omnibus Reform Act of 1999, as enacted by section 1000(a)(9) of Public Law 106–113, nor the deletion of the words added by that amendment—

(A)   shall be considered or otherwise given any legal significance, or

(B)   shall be interpreted to indicate congressional approval or disapproval of, or acquiescence in, any judicial determination, by the courts or the Copyright Office. Paragraph (2) shall be interpreted as if both section 2(a)(1) of the Work Made For Hire and Copyright Corrections Act of 2000 and section 1011(d) of the Intellectual Property and Communications Omnibus Reform Act of 1999, as enacted by section 1000(a)(9) of Public Law 106–113, were never enacted, and without regard to any inaction or awareness by the Congress at any time of any judicial determinations.

The terms "WTO Agreement" and "WTO member country" have the meanings given those terms in paragraphs (9) and (10), respectively, of section 2 of the Uruguay Round Agreements Act.

§ 102.   Subject Matter of Copyright: In General

(a)   Copyright protection subsists, in accordance with this title, in original works of authorship fixed in any tangible medium of expression, now known or later developed, from which they can be perceived, reproduced, or otherwise communicated, either directly or with the aid of a machine or device. Works of authorship include the following categories:

(1)   literary works;

(2)   musical works, including any accompanying words;

(3)   dramatic works, including any accompanying music;

(4)   pantomimes and choreographic works;

(5)   pictorial, graphic, and sculptural works;

(6)   motion pictures and other audiovisual works;

(7)   sound recordings; and

(8)   architectural works.

(b)   In no case does copyright protection for an original work of authorship extend to any idea, procedure, process, system, method of operation, concept, principle, or discovery, regardless of the form in which it is described, explained, illustrated, or embodied in such work.

§ 103.   Subject Matter of Copyright: Compilations and Derivative Works

(a)   The subject matter of copyright as specified by section 102 includes compilations and derivative works, but protection for a work employing preexisting material in which copyright subsists does not extend to any part of the work in which such material has been used unlawfully.

(b)   The copyright in a compilation or derivative work extends only to the material contributed by the author of such work, as distinguished from the preexisting material employed in the work, and does not imply any exclusive right in the preexisting material. The copyright in such work is independent of, and does not affect or enlarge the scope, duration, ownership, or subsistence of, any copyright protection in the preexisting material.

§ 104.   Subject Matter of Copyright: National Origin

(a)   **Unpublished Works.**—The works specified by sections 102 and 103, while unpublished, are subject to protection under this title without regard to the nationality or domicile of the author.

(b) Published Works.—The works specified by sections 102 and 103, when published, are subject to protection under this title if—

(1)   on the date of first publication, one or more of the authors is a national or domiciliary of the United States, or is a national, domiciliary, or sovereign authority of a treaty party, or is a stateless person, wherever that person may be domiciled; or

(2)   the work is first published in the United States or in a foreign nation that, on the date of first publication, is a treaty party; or

(3)   the work is a sound recording that was first fixed in a treaty party; or

(4)   the work is a pictorial, graphic, or sculptural work that is incorporated in a building or other structure, or an architectural work that is embodied in a building and the building or structure is located in the United States or a treaty party; or

(5)   the work is first published by the United Nations or any of its specialized agencies, or by the Organization of American States; or

(6)   the work comes within the scope of a Presidential proclamation. Whenever the President finds that a particular foreign nation extends, to works by authors who are nationals or domiciliaries of the United States or to works that are first published in the United States, copyright protection on substantially the same basis as that on which the foreign nation extends protection to works of its own nationals and domiciliaries and works first published in that nation, the President may by proclamation extend protection under this title to works of which one or more of the authors is, on the date of first publication, a national, domiciliary, or sovereign authority of that nation, or which was first published in that nation. The President may revise, suspend, or revoke any such proclamation or impose any conditions or limitations on protection under a proclamation.

For purposes of paragraph (2), a work that is published in the United States or a treaty party within 30 days after publication in a foreign nation that is not a treaty party shall be considered to be first published in the United States or such treaty party, as the case may be.

(c)   Effect of Berne Convention.—No right or interest in a work eligible for protection under this title may be claimed by virtue of, or in reliance upon, the provisions of the Berne Convention, or the adherence of the United States thereto. Any rights in a work eligible for protection under this title that derive from this title, other Federal or State statutes, or the common law, shall not be expanded or reduced by virtue of, or in reliance upon, the provisions of the Berne Convention, or the adherence of the United States thereto.

(d)   Effect of Phonograms Treaties.—Notwithstanding the provisions of subsection (b), no works other than sound recordings shall be eligible for protection under this title solely by virtue of the adherence of the United States to the Geneva Phonograms Convention or the WIPO Performances and Phonograms Treaty.

§ 104A. Copyright in Restored Works

(a)   Automatic Protection and Term.—

(1)   Term.—

(A)   Copyright subsists, in accordance with this section, in restored works, and vests automatically on the date of restoration.

(B)   Any work in which copyright is restored under this section shall subsist for the remainder of the term of copyright that the work would have otherwise been granted in the United States if the work never entered the public domain in the United States.

(2) **Exception.**—Any work in which the copyright was ever owned or administered by the Alien Property Custodian and in which the restored copyright would be owned by a government or instrumentality thereof, is not a restored work.

(b) **Ownership of Restored Copyright.**—A restored work vests initially in the author or initial rightholder of the work as determined by the law of the source country of the work.

(c) **Filing of Notice of Intent to Enforce Restored Copyright Against Reliance Parties.**—On or after the date of restoration, any person who owns a copyright in a restored work or an exclusive right therein may file with the Copyright Office a notice of intent to enforce that person's copyright or exclusive right or may serve such a notice directly on a reliance party. Acceptance of a notice by the Copyright Office is effective as to any reliance parties but shall not create a presumption of the validity of any of the facts stated therein. Service on a reliance party is effective as to that reliance party and any other reliance parties with actual knowledge of such service and of the contents of that notice.

(d) **Remedies for Infringement of Restored Copyrights.**—

(1) **Enforcement of Copyright in Restored Works in the Absence of a Reliance Party.**—As against any party who is not a reliance party, the remedies provided in chapter 5 of this title shall be available on or after the date of restoration of a restored copyright with respect to an act of infringement of the restored copyright that is commenced on or after the date of restoration.

(2) **Enforcement of Copyright in Restored Works as Against Reliance Parties.**—As against a reliance party, except to the extent provided in paragraphs (3) and (4), the remedies provided in chapter 5 of this title shall be available, with respect to an act of infringement of a restored copyright, on or after the date of restoration of the restored copyright if the requirements of either of the following subparagraphs are met:

(A)(i) The owner of the restored copyright (or such owner's agent) or the owner of an exclusive right therein (or such owner's agent) files with the Copyright Office, during the 24-month period beginning on the date of restoration, a notice of intent to enforce the restored copyright; and

(ii)(I) the act of infringement commenced after the end of the 12-month period beginning on the date of publication of the notice in the Federal Register;

(II) the act of infringement commenced before the end of the 12-month period described in subclause (I) and continued after the end of that 12-month period, in which case remedies shall be available only for infringement occurring after the end of that 12-month period; or

(III) copies or phonorecords of a work in which copyright has been restored under this section are made after publication of the notice of intent in the Federal Register.

(B)(i) The owner of the restored copyright (or such owner's agent) or the owner of an exclusive right therein (or such owner's agent) serves upon a reliance party a notice of intent to enforce a restored copyright; and

(ii)(I) the act of infringement commenced after the end of the 12-month period beginning on the date the notice of intent is received;

(II) the act of infringement commenced before the end of the 12-month period described in subclause (I) and continued after the end of that 12-month period, in which case remedies shall be available only for the infringement occurring after the end of that 12-month period; or

(III) copies or phonorecords of a work in which copyright has been restored under this section are made after receipt of the notice of intent.

In the event that notice is provided under both subparagraphs (A) and (B), the 12-month period referred to in such subparagraphs shall run from the earlier of publication or service of notice.

(3) Existing Derivative Works.—(A) In the case of a derivative work that is based upon a restored work and is created—

(i) before the date of the enactment of the Uruguay Round Agreements Act, if the source country of the derivative work is an eligible country on such date, or

(ii) before the date of adherence or proclamation, if the source country of the derivative work is not an eligible country on such date of enactment,

a reliance party may continue to exploit that work for the duration of the restored copyright if the reliance party pays to the owner of the restored copyright reasonable compensation for conduct which would be subject to a remedy for infringement but for the provisions of this paragraph.

(B) In the absence of an agreement between the parties, the amount of such compensation shall be determined by an action in United States district court, and shall reflect any harm to the actual or potential market for or value of the restored work from the reliance party's continued exploitation of the work, as well as compensation for the relative contributions of expression of the author of the restored work and the reliance party to the derivative work.

(4) Commencement of Infringement for Reliance Parties.—For purposes of section 412, in the case of reliance parties, infringement shall be deemed to have commenced before registration when acts which would have constituted infringement had the restored work been subject to copyright were commenced before the date of restoration.

(e) Notices of Intent to Enforce a Restored Copyright.—

(1) Notices of Intent Filed with the Copyright Office.—(A)(i) A notice of intent filed with the Copyright Office to enforce a restored copyright shall be signed by the owner of the restored copyright or the owner of an exclusive right therein, who files the notice under subsection (d)(2)(A)(i) (hereafter in this paragraph referred to as the "owner"), or by the owner's agent, shall identify the title of the restored work, and shall include an English translation of the title and any other alternative titles known to the owner by which the restored work may be identified, and an address and telephone number at which the owner may be contacted. If the notice is signed by an agent, the agency relationship must have been constituted in a writing signed by the owner before the filing of the notice. The Copyright Office may specifically require in regulations other information to be included in the notice, but failure to provide such other information shall not invalidate the notice or be a basis for refusal to list the restored work in the Federal Register.

(ii) If a work in which copyright is restored has no formal title, it shall be described in the notice of intent in detail sufficient to identify it.

(iii) Minor errors or omissions may be corrected by further notice at any time after the notice of intent is filed. Notices of corrections for such minor errors or omissions shall be accepted after the period established in subsection (d)(2)(A)(i). Notices shall be published in the Federal Register pursuant to subparagraph (B).

(B)(i) The Register of Copyrights shall publish in the Federal Register, commencing not later than 4 months after the date of restoration for a particular nation and every 4 months thereafter for a period of 2 years, lists identifying restored works and the ownership thereof if a notice of intent to enforce a restored copyright has been filed.

(ii) Not less than 1 list containing all notices of intent to enforce shall be maintained in the Public Information Office of the Copyright Office and shall be available for public inspection and copying during regular business hours pursuant to sections 705 and 708.

(C)   The Register of Copyrights is authorized to fix reasonable fees based on the costs of receipt, processing, recording, and publication of notices of intent to enforce a restored copyright and corrections thereto.

(D)(i)   Not later than 90 days before the date the Agreement on Trade-Related Aspects of Intellectual Property referred to in section 101(d)(15) of the Uruguay Round Agreements Act enters into force with respect to the United States, the Copyright Office shall issue and publish in the Federal Register regulations governing the filing under this subsection of notices of intent to enforce a restored copyright.

(ii)   Such regulations shall permit owners of restored copyrights to file simultaneously for registration of the restored copyright.

(2)   **Notices of Intent Served on a Reliance Party.**—(A) Notices of intent to enforce a restored copyright may be served on a reliance party at any time after the date of restoration of the restored copyright.

(B)   Notices of intent to enforce a restored copyright served on a reliance party shall be signed by the owner or the owner's agent, shall identify the restored work and the work in which the restored work is used, if any, in detail sufficient to identify them, and shall include an English translation of the title, any other alternative titles known to the owner by which the work may be identified, the use or uses to which the owner objects, and an address and telephone number at which the reliance party may contact the owner. If the notice is signed by an agent, the agency relationship must have been constituted in writing and signed by the owner before service of the notice.

(3)   **Effect of Material False Statements.**—Any material false statement knowingly made with respect to any restored copyright identified in any notice of intent shall make void all claims and assertions made with respect to such restored copyright.

(f)   **Immunity From Warranty and Related Liability.**—

(1)   **In General.**—Any person who warrants, promises, or guarantees that a work does not violate an exclusive right granted in section 106 shall not be liable for legal, equitable, arbitral, or administrative relief if the warranty, promise, or guarantee is breached by virtue of the restoration of copyright under this section, if such warranty, promise, or guarantee is made before January 1, 1995.

(2)   **Performances.**—No person shall be required to perform any act if such performance is made infringing by virtue of the restoration of copyright under the provisions of this section, if the obligation to perform was undertaken before January 1, 1995.

(g)   **Proclamation of Copyright Restoration.**—Whenever the President finds that a particular foreign nation extends, to works by authors who are nationals or domiciliaries of the United States, restored copyright protection on substantially the same basis as provided under this section, the President may by proclamation extend restored protection provided under this section to any work—

(1)   of which one or more of the authors is, on the date of first publication, a national, domiciliary, or sovereign authority of that nation; or

(2)   which was first published in that nation.

The President may revise, suspend, or revoke any such proclamation or impose any conditions or limitations on protection under such a proclamation.

(h)   **Definitions.**—For purposes of this section and section 109(a):

(1)   The term "date of adherence or proclamation" means the earlier of the date on which a foreign nation which, as of the date the WTO Agreement enters into force with respect to the

United States, is not a nation adhering to the Berne Convention or a WTO member country, becomes—

    (A) a nation adhering to the Berne Convention;

    (B) a WTO member country;

    (C) a nation adhering to the WIPO Copyright Treaty;

    (D) a nation adhering to the WIPO Performances and Phonograms Treaty; or

    (E) subject to a Presidential proclamation under subsection (g).

(2) The "date of restoration" of a restored copyright is

    (A) January 1, 1996, if the source country of the restored work is a nation adhering to the Berne Convention or a WTO member country on such date, or

    (B) the date of adherence or proclamation, in the case of any other source country of the restored work.

(3) The term "eligible country" means a nation, other than the United States, that—

    (A) becomes a WTO member country after the date of the enactment of the Uruguay Round Agreements Act;

    (B) on such date of enactment is, or after such date of enactment becomes, a nation adhering to the Berne Convention;

    (C) adheres to the WIPO Copyright Treaty;

    (D) adheres to the WIPO Performances and Phonograms Treaty; or

    (E) after such date of enactment becomes subject to a proclamation under subsection (g).

(4) The term "reliance party" means any person who—

    (A) with respect to a particular work, engages in acts, before the source country of that work becomes an eligible country, which would have violated section 106 if the restored work had been subject to copyright protection, and who, after the source country becomes an eligible country, continues to engage in such acts;

    (B) before the source country of a particular work becomes an eligible country, makes or acquires 1 or more copies or phonorecords of that work; or

    (C) as the result of the sale or other disposition of a derivative work covered under subsection (d)(3), or significant assets of a person described in subparagraph (A) or (B), is a successor, assignee, or licensee of that person.

(5) The term "restored copyright" means copyright in a restored work under this section.

(6) The term "restored work" means an original work of authorship that—

    (A) is protected under subsection (a);

    (B) is not in the public domain in its source country through expiration of term of protection;

    (C) is in the public domain in the United States due to—

        (i) noncompliance with formalities imposed at any time by United States copyright law, including failure of renewal, lack of proper notice, or failure to comply with any manufacturing requirements;

        (ii) lack of subject matter protection in the case of sound recordings fixed before February 15, 1972; or

(iii) lack of national eligibility;

(D) has at least one author or rightholder who was, at the time the work was created, a national or domiciliary of an eligible country, and if published, was first published in an eligible country and not published in the United States during the 30-day period following publication in such eligible country; and

(E) if the source country for the work is an eligible country solely by virtue of its adherence to the WIPO Performances and Phonograms Treaty, is a sound recording.

(7) The term "rightholder" means the person—

(A) who, with respect to a sound recording, first fixes a sound recording with authorization, or

(B) who has acquired rights from the person described in subparagraph (A) by means of any conveyance or by operation of law.

(8) The "source country" of a restored work is—

(A) a nation other than the United States;

(B) in the case of an unpublished work—

(i) the eligible country in which the author or rightholder is a national or domiciliary, or, if a restored work has more than 1 author or rightholder, of which the majority of foreign authors or rightholders are nationals or domiciliaries; or

(ii) if the majority of authors or rightholders are not foreign, the nation other than the United States which has the most significant contacts with the work; and

(C) in the case of a published work—

(i) the eligible country in which the work is first published, or

(ii) if the restored work is published on the same day in 2 or more eligible countries, the eligible country which has the most significant contacts with the work.

§ 105. Subject Matter of Copyright: United States Government Works

Copyright protection under this title is not available for any work of the United States Government, but the United States Government is not precluded from receiving and holding copyrights transferred to it by assignment, bequest, or otherwise.

§ 106. Exclusive Rights in Copyrighted Works

Subject to sections 107 through 122, the owner of copyright under this title has the exclusive rights to do and to authorize any of the following:

(1) to reproduce the copyrighted work in copies or phonorecords;

(2) to prepare derivative works based upon the copyrighted work;

(3) to distribute copies or phonorecords of the copyrighted work to the public by sale or other transfer of ownership, or by rental, lease, or lending;

(4) in the case of literary, musical, dramatic, and choreographic works, pantomimes, and motion pictures and other audiovisual works, to perform the copyrighted work publicly;

(5) in the case of literary, musical, dramatic, and choreographic works, pantomimes, and pictorial, graphic, or sculptural works, including the individual images of a motion picture or other audiovisual work, to display the copyrighted work publicly and

(6) in the case of sound recordings, to perform the copyrighted work publicly by means of a digital audio transmission.

§ 106A. Rights of Certain Authors to Attribution and Integrity

(a) Rights of Attribution and Integrity.—Subject to section 107 and independent of the exclusive rights provided in section 106, the author of a work of visual art—

(1) shall have the right—

(A) to claim authorship of that work, and

(B) to prevent the use of his or her name as the author of any work of visual art which he or she did not create;

(2) shall have the right to prevent the use of his or her name as the author of the work of visual art in the event of a distortion, mutilation, or other modification of the work which would be prejudicial to his or her honor or reputation; and

(3) subject to the limitations set forth in section 113(d), shall have the right—

(A) to prevent any intentional distortion, mutilation, or other modification of that work which would be prejudicial to his or her honor or reputation, and any intentional distortion, mutilation, or modification of that work is a violation of that right, and

(B) to prevent any destruction of a work of recognized stature, and any intentional or grossly negligent destruction of that work is a violation of that right.

(b) Scope and Exercise of Rights.—Only the author of a work of visual art has the rights conferred by subsection (a) in that work, whether or not the author is the copyright owner. The authors of a joint work of visual art are co-owners of the rights conferred by subsection (a) in that work.

(c) Exceptions.—(1) The modification of a work of visual art which is a result of the passage of time or the inherent nature of the materials is not a distortion, mutilation, or other modification described in subsection (a)(3)(A).

(2) The modification of a work of visual art which is the result of conservation, or of the public presentation, including lighting and placement, of the work is not a destruction, distortion, mutilation, or other modification described in subsection (a)(3) unless the modification is caused by gross negligence.

(3) The rights described in paragraphs (1) and (2) of subsection (a) shall not apply to any reproduction, depiction, portrayal, or other use of a work in, upon, or in any connection with any item described in subparagraph (A) or (B) of the definition of "work of visual art" in section 101, and any such reproduction, depiction, portrayal, or other use of a work is not a destruction, distortion, mutilation, or other modification described in paragraph (3) of subsection (a).

(d) Duration of Rights.—(1) With respect to works of visual art created on or after the effective date set forth in section 610(a) of the Visual Artists Rights Act of 1990,* the rights conferred by subsection (a) shall endure for a term consisting of the life of the author.

(2) With respect to works of visual art created before the effective date set forth in section 610(a) of the Visual Artists Rights Act of 1990,* but title to which has not, as of such effective date, been transferred from the author, the rights conferred by subsection (a) shall be coextensive with, and shall expire at the same time as, the rights conferred by section 106.

(3) In the case of a joint work prepared by two or more authors, the rights conferred by subsection (a) shall endure for a term consisting of the life of the last surviving author.

(4) All terms of the rights conferred by subsection (a) run to the end of the calendar year in which they would otherwise expire.

(e) Transfer and Waiver.—(1) The rights conferred by subsection (a) may not be transferred, but those rights may be waived if the author expressly agrees to such waiver in a written instrument

---

* June 1, 1991—*Ed.*

signed by the author. Such instrument shall specifically identify the work, and uses of that work, to which the waiver applies, and the waiver shall apply only to the work and uses so identified. In the case of a joint work prepared by two or more authors, a waiver of rights under this paragraph made by one such author waives such rights for all such authors.

(2)   Ownership of the rights conferred by subsection (a) with respect to a work of visual art is distinct from ownership of any copy of that work, or of a copyright or any exclusive right under a copyright in that work. Transfer of ownership of any copy of a work of visual art, or of a copyright or any exclusive right under a copyright, shall not constitute a waiver of the rights conferred by subsection (a). Except as may otherwise be agreed by the author in a written instrument signed by the author, a waiver of the rights conferred by subsection (a) with respect to a work of visual art shall not constitute a transfer of ownership of any copy of that work, or of ownership of a copyright or of any exclusive right under a copyright in that work.

§ 107.   Limitations on Exclusive Rights: Fair Use

Notwithstanding the provisions of sections 106 and 106A, the fair use of a copyrighted work, including such use by reproduction in copies or phonorecords or by any other means specified by that section, for purposes such as criticism, comment, news reporting, teaching (including multiple copies for classroom use), scholarship, or research, is not an infringement of copyright. In determining whether the use made of a work in any particular case is a fair use the factors to be considered shall include—

(1)   the purpose and character of the use, including whether such use is of a commercial nature or is for nonprofit educational purposes;

(2)   the nature of the copyrighted work;

(3)   the amount and substantiality of the portion used in relation to the copyrighted work as a whole; and

(4)   the effect of the use upon the potential market for or value of the copyrighted work.

The fact that a work is unpublished shall not itself bar a finding of fair use if such finding is made upon consideration of all the above factors.

§ 108.   Limitations on Exclusive Rights: Reproduction by Libraries and Archives

(a)   Except as otherwise provided in this title and notwithstanding the provisions of section 106, it is not an infringement of copyright for a library or archives, or any of its employees acting within the scope of their employment, to reproduce no more than one copy or phonorecord of a work, except as provided in subsections (b) and (c), or to distribute such copy or phonorecord, under the conditions specified by this section, if—

(1)   the reproduction or distribution is made without any purpose of direct or indirect commercial advantage;

(2)   the collections of the library or archives are (i) open to the public, or (ii) available not only to researchers affiliated with the library or archives or with the institution of which it is a part, but also to other persons doing research in a specialized field; and

(3)   the reproduction or distribution of the work includes a notice of copyright that appears on the copy or phonorecord that is reproduced under the provisions of this section, or includes a legend stating that the work may be protected by copyright if no such notice can be found on the copy or phonorecord that is reproduced under the provisions of this section.

(b)   The rights of reproduction and distribution under this section apply to three copies or phonorecords of an unpublished work duplicated solely for purposes of preservation and security or for deposit for research use in another library or archives of the type described by clause (2) of subsection (a), if—

(1)   the copy or phonorecord reproduced is currently in the collections of the library or archives; and

(2)   any such copy or phonorecord that is reproduced in digital format is not otherwise distributed in that format and is not made available to the public in that format outside the premises of the library or archives.

(c)   The right of reproduction under this section applies to three copies or phonorecords of a published work duplicated solely for the purpose of replacement of a copy or phonorecord that is damaged, deteriorating, lost, or stolen, or if the existing format in which the work is stored has become obsolete, if—

(1)   the library or archives has, after a reasonable effort, determined that an unused replacement cannot be obtained at a fair price; and

(2)   any such copy or phonorecord that is reproduced in digital format is not made available to the public in that format outside the premises of the library or archives in lawful possession of such copy.

For purposes of this subsection, a format shall be considered obsolete if the machine or device necessary to render perceptible a work stored in that format is no longer manufactured or is no longer reasonably available in the commercial marketplace.

(d)   The rights of reproduction and distribution under this section apply to a copy, made from the collection of a library or archives where the user makes his or her request or from that of another library or archives, of no more than one article or other contribution to a copyrighted collection or periodical issue, or to a copy or phonorecord of a small part of any other copyrighted work, if—

(1)   the copy or phonorecord becomes the property of the user, and the library or archives has had no notice that the copy or phonorecord would be used for any purpose other than private study, scholarship, or research; and

(2)   the library or archives displays prominently, at the place where orders are accepted, and includes on its order form, a warning of copyright in accordance with requirements that the Register of Copyrights shall prescribe by regulation.

(e)   The rights of reproduction and distribution under this section apply to the entire work, or to a substantial part of it, made from the collection of a library or archives where the user makes his or her request or from that of another library or archives, if the library or archives has first determined, on the basis of a reasonable investigation, that a copy or phonorecord of the copyrighted work cannot be obtained at a fair price, if—

(1)   the copy or phonorecord becomes the property of the user, and the library or archives has had no notice that the copy or phonorecord would be used for any purpose other than private study, scholarship, or research; and

(2)   the library or archives displays prominently, at the place where orders are accepted, and includes on its order form, a warning of copyright in accordance with requirements that the Register of Copyrights shall prescribe by regulation.

(f)   Nothing in this section—

(1)   shall be construed to impose liability for copyright infringement upon a library or archives or its employees for the unsupervised use of reproducing equipment located on its premises: *Provided,* That such equipment displays a notice that the making of a copy may be subject to the copyright law;

(2)   excuses a person who uses such reproducing equipment or who requests a copy or phonorecord under subsection (d) from liability for copyright infringement for any such act, or for any later use of such copy or phonorecord, if it exceeds fair use as provided by section 107;

(3) shall be construed to limit the reproduction and distribution by lending of a limited number of copies and excerpts by a library or archives of an audiovisual news program, subject to clauses (1), (2), and (3) of subsection (a); or

(4) in any way affects the right of fair use as provided by section 107, or any contractual obligations assumed at any time by the library or archives when it obtained a copy or phonorecord of a work in its collections.

(g) The rights of reproduction and distribution under this section extend to the isolated and unrelated reproduction or distribution of a single copy or phonorecord of the same material on separate occasions, but do not extend to cases where the library or archives, or its employee—

(1) is aware or has substantial reason to believe that it is engaging in the related or concerted reproduction or distribution of multiple copies or phonorecords of the same material, whether made on one occasion or over a period of time, and whether intended for aggregate use by one or more individuals or for separate use by the individual members of a group; or

(2) engages in the systematic reproduction or distribution of single or multiple copies or phonorecords of material described in subsection (d): *Provided,* That nothing in this cause prevents a library or archives from participating in interlibrary arrangements that do not have, as their purpose or effect, that the library or archives receiving such copies or phonorecords for distribution does so in such aggregate quantities as to substitute for a subscription to or purchase of such work.

(h)(1) For purposes of this section, during the last 20 years of any term of copyright of a published work, a library or archives, including a nonprofit educational institution that functions as such, may reproduce, distribute, display, or perform in facsimile or digital form a copy or phonorecord of such work, or portions thereof, for purposes of preservation, scholarship, or research, if such library or archives has first determined, on the basis of a reasonable investigation, that none of the conditions set forth in subparagraphs (A), (B), and (C) of paragraph (2) apply.

(2) No reproduction, distribution, display, or performance is authorized under this subsection if—

(A) the work is subject to normal commercial exploitation;

(B) a copy or phonorecord of the work can be obtained at a reasonable price: or

(C) the copyright owner or its agent provides notice pursuant to regulations promulgated by the Register of Copyrights that either of the conditions set forth in subparagraphs (A) and (B) applies.

(3) The exemption provided in this subsection does not apply to any subsequent uses by users other than such library or archives.

(i) The rights of reproduction and distribution under this section do not apply to a musical work, a pictorial, graphic or sculptural work, or a motion picture or other audiovisual work other than an audiovisual work dealing with news, except that no such limitation shall apply with respect to rights granted by subsections (b), (c), and (h), or with respect to pictorial or graphic works published as illustrations, diagrams, or similar adjuncts to works of which copies are reproduced or distributed in accordance with subsections (d) and (e).

§ 109. Limitations on Exclusive Rights: Effect of Transfer of Particular Copy or Phonorecord

(a) Notwithstanding the provisions of section 106(3), the owner of a particular copy or phonorecord lawfully made under this title, or any person authorized by such owner, is entitled, without the authority of the copyright owner, to sell or otherwise dispose of the possession of that copy or phonorecord. Notwithstanding the preceding sentence, copies or phonorecords of works subject to restored copyright under section 104A that are manufactured before the date of restoration of copyright or, with respect to reliance parties, before publication or service of notice under section 104A(e), may be sold or otherwise disposed of without the authorization of the owner of the restored copyright for purposes of direct or indirect commercial advantage only during the 12-month period beginning on—

(1) the date of the publication in the Federal Register of the notice of intent filed with the Copyright Office under section 104A(d)(2)(A), or

(2) the date of the receipt of actual notice served under section 104A(d)(2)(B), whichever occurs first.

(b)(1)(A) Notwithstanding the provisions of subsection (a), unless authorized by the owners of copyright in the sound recording or the owner of copyright in a computer program (including any tape, disk, or other medium embodying such program), and in the case of a sound recording in the musical works embodied therein, neither the owner of a particular phonorecord nor any person in possession of a particular copy of a computer program (including any tape, disk, or other medium embodying such program), may, for the purposes of direct or indirect commercial advantage, dispose of, or authorize the disposal of, the possession of that phonorecord or computer program (including any tape, disk, or other medium embodying such program) by rental, lease, or lending, or by any other act or practice in the nature of rental, lease, or lending. Nothing in the preceding sentence shall apply to the rental, lease, or lending of a phonorecord for nonprofit purposes by a nonprofit library or nonprofit educational institution. The transfer of possession of a lawfully made copy of a computer program by a nonprofit educational institution to another nonprofit educational institution or to faculty, staff, and students does not constitute rental, lease, or lending for direct or indirect commercial purposes under this subsection.

(B) This subsection does not apply to—

(i) a computer program which is embodied in a machine or product and which cannot be copied during the ordinary operation or use of the machine or product; or

(ii) a computer program embodied in or used in conjunction with a limited purpose computer that is designed for playing video games and may be designed for other purposes.

(C) Nothing in this subsection affects any provision of chapter 9 of this title.

(2)(A) Nothing in this subsection shall apply to the lending of a computer program for nonprofit purposes by a nonprofit library, if each copy of a computer program which is lent by such library has affixed to the packaging containing the program a warning of copyright in accordance with requirements that the Register of Copyrights shall prescribe by regulation.

(B) Not later than three years after the date of the enactment of the Computer Software Rental Amendments Act of 1990, and at such times thereafter as the Register of Copyrights considers appropriate, the Register of Copyrights, after consultation with representatives of copyright owners and librarians, shall submit to the Congress a report stating whether this paragraph has achieved its intended purpose of maintaining the integrity of the copyright system while providing nonprofit libraries the capability to fulfill their function. Such report shall advise the Congress as to any information or recommendations that the Register of Copyrights considers necessary to carry out the purposes of this subsection.

(3) Nothing in this subsection shall affect any provision of the antitrust laws. For purposes of the preceding sentence, "antitrust laws" has the meaning given that term in the first section of the Clayton Act and includes section 5 of the Federal Trade Commission Act to the extent that section relates to unfair methods of competition.

(4) Any person who distributes a phonorecord or a copy of a computer program (including any tape, disk, or other medium embodying such program) in violation of paragraph (1) is an infringer of copyright under section 501 of this title and is subject to the remedies set forth in sections 502, 503,

504, and 505. Such violation shall not be a criminal offense under section 506 or cause such person to be subject to the criminal penalties set forth in section 2319 of title 18.

(c) Notwithstanding the provisions of section 106(5), the owner of a particular copy lawfully made under this title, or any person authorized by such owner, is entitled, without the authority of the copyright owner, to display that copy publicly, either directly or by the projection of no more than one image at a time, to viewers present at the place where the copy is located.

(d) The privileges prescribed by subsections (a) and (c) do not, unless authorized by the copyright owner, extend to any person who has acquired possession of the copy or phonorecord from the copyright owner, by rental, lease, loan, or otherwise, without acquiring ownership of it.

(e) Notwithstanding the provisions of sections 106(4) and 106(5), in the case of an electronic audiovisual game intended for use in coin-operated equipment, the owner of a particular copy of such a game lawfully made under this title, is entitled, without the authority of the copyright owner of the game, to publicly perform or display that game in coin-operated equipment, except that this subsection shall not apply to any work of authorship embodied in the audiovisual game if the copyright owner of the electronic audiovisual game is not also the copyright owner of the work of authorship.

§ 110. Limitations on Exclusive Rights: Exemption of Certain Performances and Displays

Notwithstanding the provisions of section 106, the following are not infringements of copyright:

(1) performance or display of a work by instructors or pupils in the course of face-to-face teaching activities of a nonprofit educational institution, in a classroom or similar place devoted to instruction, unless, in the case of a motion picture or other audiovisual work, the performance, or the display of individual images, is given by means of a copy that was not lawfully made under this title, and that the person responsible for the performance knew or had reason to believe was not lawfully made;

(2) except with respect to a work produced or marketed primarily for performance or display as part of mediated instructional activities transmitted via digital networks, or a performance or display that is given by means of a copy or phonorecord that is not lawfully made and acquired under this title, and the transmitting government body or accredited nonprofit educational institution knew or had reason to believe was not lawfully made and acquired, the performance of a nondramatic literary or musical work or reasonable and limited portions of any other work, or display of a work in an amount comparable to that which is typically displayed in the course of a live classroom session, by or in the course of a transmission, if—

(A) the performance or display is made by, at the direction of, or under the actual supervision of an instructor as an integral part of a class session offered as a regular part of the systematic mediated instructional activities of a governmental body or an accredited nonprofit educational institution;

(B) the performance or display is directly related and of material assistance to the teaching content of the transmission;

(C) the transmission is made solely for, and, to the extent technologically feasible, the reception of such transmission is limited to—

(i) students officially enrolled in the course for which the transmission is made; or

(ii) officers or employees of governmental bodies as a part of their official duties or employment; and

(D) the transmitting body or institution—

(i) institutes policies regarding copyright, provides informational materials to faculty, students, and relevant staff members that accurately describe, and promote compliance with, the laws of the United States relating to copyright, and provides notice to students that materials used in connection with the course may be subject to copyright protection; and

(ii) in the case of digital transmissions—

(I) applies technological measures that reasonably prevent—

(aa) retention of the work in accessible form by recipients of the transmission from the transmitting body or institution for longer than the class session; and

(bb) unauthorized further dissemination of the work in accessible form by such recipients to others; and

(II) does not engage in conduct that could reasonably be expected to interfere with technological measures used by copyright owners to prevent such retention or unauthorized further dissemination.

(3) performance of a nondramatic literary or musical work or of a dramatic-musical work of a religious nature, or display of a work, in the course of services at a place of worship or other religious assembly;

(4) performance of a nondramatic literary or musical work otherwise than in a transmission to the public, without any purpose of direct or indirect commercial advantage and without payment of any fee or other compensation for the performance to any of its performers, promoters, or organizers, if—

(A) there is no direct or indirect admission charge; or

(B) the proceeds, after deducting the reasonable costs of producing the performance, are used exclusively for educational, religious, or charitable purposes and not for private financial gain, except where the copyright owner has served notice of objection to the performance under the following conditions:

(i) the notice shall be in writing and signed by the copyright owner or such owner's duly authorized agent; and

(ii) the notice shall be served on the person responsible for the performance at least seven days before the date of the performance, and shall state the reasons for the objection; and

(iii) the notice shall comply, in form, content, and manner of service, with requirements that the Register of Copyrights shall prescribe by regulation;

(5)(A) except as provided in subparagraph (B), communication of a transmission embodying a performance or display of a work by the public reception of the transmission on a single receiving apparatus of a kind commonly used in private homes, unless—

(i) a direct charge is made to see or hear the transmission; or

(ii) the transmission thus received is further transmitted to the public;

(B) communication by an establishment of a transmission or retransmission embodying a performance or display of a nondramatic musical work intended to be received by the general public, originated by a radio or television broadcast station licensed as such by the Federal Communications Commission, or, if an audiovisual transmission, by a cable system or satellite carrier, if—

(i) in the case of an establishment other than a food service or drinking establishment, either the establishment in which the communication occurs has less than 2,000 gross square feet of space (excluding space used for customer parking and for no other purpose), or the establishment in which the communication occurs has

2,000 or more gross square feet of space (excluding space used for customer parking and for no other purpose) and—

    (I)   if the performance is by audio means only, the performance is communicated by means of a total of not more than 6 loudspeakers, of which not more than 4 loudspeakers are located in any 1 room or adjoining outdoor space; or

    (II)   if the performance or display is by audiovisual means, any visual portion of the performance or display is communicated by means of a total of not more than 4 audiovisual devices, of which not more than 1 audiovisual device is located in any 1 room, and no such audiovisual device has a diagonal screen size greater than 55 inches, and any audio portion of the performance or display is communicated by means of a total of not more than 6 loudspeakers, of which not more than 4 loudspeakers are located in any 1 room or adjoining outdoor space;

  (ii)   in the case of a food service or drinking establishment, either the establishment in which the communication occurs has less than 3,750 gross square feet of space (excluding space used for customer parking and for no other purpose), or the establishment in which the communication occurs has 3,750 gross square feet of space or more (excluding space used for customer parking and for no other purpose) and—

    (I)   if the performance is by audio means only, the performance is communicated by means of a total of not more than 6 loudspeakers, of which not more than 4 loudspeakers are located in any 1 room or adjoining outdoor space; or

    (II)   if the performance or display is by audiovisual means, any visual portion of the performance or display is communicated by means of a total of not more than 4 audiovisual devices, of which not more than one audiovisual device is located in any 1 room, and no such audiovisual device has a diagonal screen size greater than 55 inches, and any audio portion of the performance or display is communicated by means of a total of not more than 6 loudspeakers, of which not more than 4 loudspeakers are located in any 1 room or adjoining outdoor space,

  (iii)   no direct charge is made to see or hear the transmission or retransmission;

  (iv)   the transmission or retransmission is not further transmitted beyond the establishment where it is received; and

  (v)   the transmission or retransmission is licensed by the copyright owner of the work so publicly performed or displayed;

  (6)   performance of a nondramatic musical work by a governmental body or a nonprofit agricultural or horticultural organization, in the course of an annual agricultural or horticultural fair or exhibition conducted by such body or organization; the exemption provided by this clause shall extend to any liability for copyright infringement that would otherwise be imposed on such body or organization, under doctrines of vicarious liability or related infringement, for a performance by a concessionnaire, business establishment, or other person at such fair or exhibition, but shall not excuse any such person from liability for the performance;

  (7)   performance of a nondramatic musical work by a vending establishment open to the public at large without any direct or indirect admission charge, where the sole purpose of the performance is to promote the retail sale of copies or phonorecords of the work or of the audiovisual or other devices utilized in such performance, and the performance is not transmitted beyond the place where the establishment is located and is within the immediate area where the sale is occurring;

  (8)   performance of a nondramatic literary work, by or in the course of a transmission specifically designed for and primarily directed to blind or other handicapped persons who are unable to read normal printed material as a result of their handicap, or deaf or other handicapped

persons who are unable to hear the aural signals accompanying a transmission of visual signals, if the performance is made without any purpose of direct or indirect commercial advantage and its transmission is made through the facilities of: (i) a governmental body; or (ii) a noncommercial educational broadcast station (as defined in section 397 of title 47); or (iii) a radio subcarrier authorization (as defined in 47 CFR 73.293–73.295 and 73.593–73.595); or (iv) a cable system (as defined in section 111(f));

(9) performance on a single occasion of a dramatic literary work published at least ten years before the date of the performance, by or in the course of a transmission specifically designed for and primarily directed to blind or other handicapped persons who are unable to read normal printed material as a result of their handicap, if the performance is made without any purpose of direct or indirect commercial advantage and its transmission is made through the facilities of a radio subcarrier authorization referred to in clause (8)(iii), *Provided,* That the provisions of this clause shall not be applicable to more than one performance of the same work by the same performers or under the auspices of the same organization;

(10) notwithstanding paragraph (4) the following is not an infringement of copyright: performance of a nondramatic literary or musical work in the course of a social function which is organized and promoted by a nonprofit veterans' organization or a nonprofit fraternal organization to which the general public is not invited, but not including the invitees of the organizations, if the proceeds from the performance, after deducting the reasonable costs of producing the performance, are used exclusively for charitable purposes and not for financial gain. For purposes of this section the social functions of any college or university fraternity or sorority shall not be included unless the social function is held solely to raise funds for a specific charitable purpose; and

(11) the making imperceptible, by or at the direction of a member of a private household, of limited portions of audio or video content of a motion picture, during a performance in or transmitted to that household for private home viewing, from an authorized copy of the motion picture, or the creation or provision of a computer program or other technology that enables such making imperceptible and that is designed and marketed to be used, at the direction of a member of a private household, for such making imperceptible, if no fixed copy of the altered version of the motion picture is created by such computer program or other technology.

The exemptions provided under paragraph (5) shall not be taken into account in any administrative, judicial, or other governmental proceeding to set or adjust the royalties payable to copyright owners for the public performance or display of their works. Royalties payable to copyright owners for any public performance or display of their works other than such performances or displays as are exempted under paragraph (5) shall not be diminished in any respect as a result of such exemption.

In paragraph (2), the term 'mediated instructional activities' with respect to the performance or display of a work by digital transmission under this section refers to activities that use such work as an integral part of the class experience, controlled by or under the actual supervision of the instructor and analogous to the type of performance or display that would take place in a live classroom setting. The term does not refer to activities that use, in 1 or more class sessions of a single course, such works as textbooks, course packs, or other material in any media, copies or phonorecords of which are typically purchased or acquired by the students in higher education for their independent use and retention or are typically purchased or acquired for elementary and secondary students for their possession and independent use.

For purposes of paragraph (2), accreditation—

(A) with respect to an institution providing post-secondary education, shall be as determined by a regional or national accrediting agency recognized by the Council on Higher Education Accreditation or the United States Department of Education; and

(B) with respect to an institution providing elementary or secondary education, shall be as recognized by the applicable state certification or licensing procedures.

For purposes of paragraph (2), no governmental body or accredited nonprofit educational institution shall be liable for infringement by reason of the transient or temporary storage of material carried out through the automatic technical process of a digital transmission of the performance or display of that material as authorized under paragraph (2). No such material stored on the system or network controlled or operated by the transmitting body or institution under this paragraph shall be maintained on such system or network in a manner ordinarily accessible to anyone other than anticipated recipients. No such copy shall be maintained on the system or network in a manner ordinarily accessible to such anticipated recipients for a longer period than is reasonably necessary to facilitate the transmissions for which it was made.

For purposes of paragraph (11), the term "making imperceptible" does not include the addition of audio or video content that is performed or displayed over or in place of existing content in a motion picture.

Nothing in paragraph (11) shall be construed to imply further rights under section 106 of this title, or to have any effect on defenses or limitations on rights granted under any other section of this title or under any other paragraph of this section.

§ 111. Limitations on Exclusive Rights: Secondary Transmissions of Broadcast Programming by Cable

(a) Certain Secondary Transmissions Exempted.—The secondary transmission of a performance or display of a work embodied in a primary transmission is not an infringement of copyright if—

(1) the secondary transmission is not made by a cable system, and consists entirely of the relaying, by the management of a hotel, apartment house, or similar establishment, of signals transmitted by a broadcast station licensed by the Federal Communications Commission, within the local service area of such station, to the private lodgings of guests or residents of such establishment, and no direct charge is made to see or hear the secondary transmission; or

(2) the secondary transmission is made solely for the purpose and under the conditions specified by paragraph (2) of section 110; or

(3) the secondary transmission is made by any carrier who has no direct or indirect control over the content or selection of the primary transmission or over the particular recipients of the secondary transmission, and whose activities with respect to the secondary transmission consist solely of providing wires, cables, or other communications channels for the use of others: Provided, That the provisions of this paragraph extend only to the activities of said carrier with respect to secondary transmissions and do not exempt from liability the activities of others with respect to their own primary or secondary transmissions;

(4) the secondary transmission is made by a satellite carrier pursuant to a statutory license under section 119 or section 122;

(5) the secondary transmission is not made by a cable system but is made by a governmental body, or other nonprofit organization, without any purpose of direct or indirect commercial advantage, and without charge to the recipients of the secondary transmission other than assessments necessary to defray the actual and reasonable costs of maintaining and operating the secondary transmission service.

(b) Secondary Transmission of Primary Transmission to Controlled Group.— Notwithstanding the provisions of subsections (a) and (c), the secondary transmission to the public of a performance or display of a work embodied in a primary transmission is actionable as an act of infringement under section 501, and is fully subject to the remedies provided by sections 502 through 506, if the primary transmission is not made for reception by the public at large but is controlled and limited to reception by particular members of the public: Provided, however, That such secondary transmission is not actionable as an act of infringement if—

(1) the primary transmission is made by a broadcast station licensed by the Federal Communications Commission; and

(2) the carriage of the signals comprising the secondary transmission is required under the rules, regulations, or authorizations of the Federal Communications Commission; and

(3) the signal of the primary transmitter is not altered or changed in any way by the secondary transmitter.

(c) Secondary Transmissions by Cable Systems.—

(1) Subject to the provisions of paragraphs (2), (3), and (4) of this subsection and section 114(d), secondary transmissions to the public by a cable system of a performance or display of a work embodied in a primary transmission made by a broadcast station licensed by the Federal Communications Commission or by an appropriate governmental authority of Canada or Mexico shall be subject to statutory licensing upon compliance with the requirements of subsection (d) where the carriage of the signals comprising the secondary transmission is permissible under the rules, regulations, or authorizations of the Federal Communications Commission.

(2) Notwithstanding the provisions of paragraph (1) of this subsection, the willful or repeated secondary transmission to the public by a cable system of a primary transmission made by a broadcast station licensed by the Federal Communications Commission or by an appropriate governmental authority of Canada or Mexico and embodying a performance or display of a work is actionable as an act of infringement under section 501, and is fully subject to the remedies provided by sections 502 through 506, in the following cases:

(A) where the carriage of the signals comprising the secondary transmission is not permissible under the rules, regulations, or authorizations of the Federal Communications Commission; or

(B) where the cable system has not deposited the statement of account and royalty fee required by subsection (d).

(3) Notwithstanding the provisions of paragraph (1) of this subsection and subject to the provisions of subsection (e) of this section, the secondary transmission to the public by a cable system of a performance or display of a work embodied in a primary transmission made by a broadcast station licensed by the Federal Communications Commission or by an appropriate governmental authority of Canada or Mexico is actionable as an act of infringement under section 501, and is fully subject to the remedies provided by sections 502 through 506 and section 510, if the content of the particular program in which the performance or display is embodied, or any commercial advertising or station announcements transmitted by the primary transmitter during, or immediately before or after, the transmission of such program, is in any way willfully altered by the cable system through changes, deletions, or additions, except for the alteration, deletion, or substitution of commercial advertisements performed by those engaged in television commercial advertising market research: Provided, That the research company has obtained the prior consent of the advertiser who has purchased the original commercial advertisement, the television station broadcasting that commercial advertisement, and the cable system performing the secondary transmission: And provided further, That such commercial alteration, deletion, or substitution is not performed for the purpose of deriving income from the sale of that commercial time.

(4) Notwithstanding the provisions of paragraph (1) of this subsection, the secondary transmission to the public by a cable system of a performance or display of a work embodied in a primary transmission made by a broadcast station licensed by an appropriate governmental authority of Canada or Mexico is actionable as an act of infringement under section 501, and is fully subject to the remedies provided by sections 502 through 506, if (A) with respect to Canadian

signals, the community of the cable system is located more than 150 miles from the United States-Canadian border and is also located south of the forty-second parallel of latitude, or (B) with respect to Mexican signals, the secondary transmission is made by a cable system which received the primary transmission by means other than direct interception of a free space radio wave emitted by such broadcast television station, unless prior to April 15, 1976, such cable system was actually carrying, or was specifically authorized to carry, the signal of such foreign station on the system pursuant to the rules, regulations, or authorizations of the Federal Communications Commission.

(d) Statutory License for Secondary Transmissions by Cable Systems.—

    (1) Statement of Account and Royalty Fees.—Subject to paragraph (5), a cable system whose secondary transmissions have been subject to statutory licensing under subsection (c) shall, on a semiannual basis, deposit with the Register of Copyrights, in accordance with requirements that the Register shall prescribe by regulation the following:

        (A) A statement of account, covering the six months next preceding, specifying the number of channels on which the cable system made secondary transmissions to its subscribers, the names and locations of all primary transmitters whose transmissions were further transmitted by the cable system, the total number of subscribers, the gross amounts paid to the cable system for the basic service of providing secondary transmissions of primary broadcast transmitters, and such other data as the Register of Copyrights may from time to time prescribe by regulation. In determining the total number of subscribers and the gross amounts paid to the cable system for the basic service of providing secondary transmissions of primary broadcast transmitters, the system shall not include subscribers and amounts collected from subscribers receiving secondary transmissions pursuant to section 119. Such statement shall also include a special statement of account covering any non-network television programming that was carried by the cable system in whole or in part beyond the local service area of the primary transmitter, under rules, regulations, or authorizations of the Federal Communications Commission permitting the substitution or addition of signals under certain circumstances, together with logs showing the times, dates, stations, and programs involved in such substituted or added carriage.

        (B) Except in the case of a cable system whose royalty fee is specified in subparagraph (E) or (F), a total royalty fee payable to copyright owners pursuant to paragraph (3) for the period covered by the statement, computed on the basis of specified percentages of the gross receipts from subscribers to the cable service during such period for the basic service of providing secondary transmissions of primary broadcast transmitters, as follows:

            (i) 1.064 percent of such gross receipts for the privilege of further transmitting, beyond the local service area of such primary transmitter, any non-network programming of a primary transmitter in whole or in part, such amount to be applied against the fee, if any, payable pursuant to clauses (ii) through (iv);

            (ii) 1.064 percent of such gross receipts for the first distant signal equivalent;

            (iii) 0.701 percent of such gross receipts for each of the second, third, and fourth distant signal equivalents; and

            (iv) 0.330 percent of such gross receipts for the fifth distant signal equivalent and each distant signal equivalent thereafter.

        (C) In computing amounts under clauses (ii) through (iv) of subparagraph (B)—

            (i) any fraction of a distant signal equivalent shall be computed at its fractional value;

            (ii) in the case of any cable system located partly within and partly outside of the local service area of a primary transmitter, gross receipts shall be limited to those gross receipts derived from subscribers located outside of the local service area of such primary transmitter; and

(iii) if a cable system provides a secondary transmission of a primary transmitter to some but not all communities served by that cable system—

(I) the gross receipts and the distant signal equivalent values for such secondary transmission shall be derived solely on the basis of the subscribers in those communities where the cable system provides such secondary transmission; and

(II) the total royalty fee for the period paid by such system shall not be less than the royalty fee calculated under subparagraph (B)(i) multiplied by the gross receipts from all subscribers to the system.

(D) A cable system that, on a statement submitted before the date of the enactment of the Satellite Television Extension and Localism Act of 2010, computed its royalty fee consistent with the methodology under subparagraph (C)(iii), or that amends a statement filed before such date of enactment to compute the royalty fee due using such methodology, shall not be subject to an action for infringement, or eligible for any royalty refund or offset, arising out of its use of such methodology on such statement.

(E) If the actual gross receipts paid by subscribers to a cable system for the period covered by the statement for the basic service of providing secondary transmissions of primary broadcast transmitters are $263,800 or less—

(i) gross receipts of the cable system for the purpose of this paragraph shall be computed by subtracting from such actual gross receipts the amount by which $263,800 exceeds such actual gross receipts, except that in no case shall a cable system's gross receipts be reduced to less than $10,400; and

(ii) the royalty fee payable under this paragraph to copyright owners pursuant to paragraph (3) shall be 0.5 percent, regardless of the number of distant signal equivalents, if any.

(F) If the actual gross receipts paid by subscribers to a cable system for the period covered by the statement for the basic service of providing secondary transmissions of primary broadcast transmitters are more than $263,800 but less than $527,600, the royalty fee payable under this paragraph to copyright owners pursuant to paragraph (3) shall be—

(i) 0.5 percent of any gross receipts up to $263,800, regardless of the number of distant signal equivalents, if any; and

(ii) 1 percent of any gross receipts in excess of $263,800, but less than $527,600, regardless of the number of distant signal equivalents, if any.

(G) A filing fee, as determined by the Register of Copyrights pursuant to section 708(a).

(2) **Handling of Fees.**—The Register of Copyrights shall receive all fees (including the filing fee specified in paragraph (1)(G)) deposited under this section and, after deducting the reasonable costs incurred by the Copyright Office under this section, shall deposit the balance in the Treasury of the United States, in such manner as the Secretary of the Treasury directs. All funds held by the Secretary of the Treasury shall be invested in interest-bearing United States securities for later distribution with interest by the Librarian of Congress upon authorization by the Copyright Royalty Judges.

(3) **Distribution of Royalty Fees to Copyright Owners.**—The royalty fees thus deposited shall, in accordance with the procedures provided by paragraph (4), be distributed to those among the following copyright owners who claim that their works were the subject of secondary transmissions by cable systems during the relevant semiannual period:

(A) Any such owner whose work was included in a secondary transmission made by a cable system of a non-network television program in whole or in part beyond the local service area of the primary transmitter.

(B) Any such owner whose work was included in a secondary transmission identified in a special statement of account deposited under paragraph (1)(A).

(C) Any such owner whose work was included in non-network programming consisting exclusively of aural signals carried by a cable system in whole or in part beyond the local service area of the primary transmitter of such programs.

(4) **Procedures for Royalty Fee Distribution.**—The royalty fees thus deposited shall be distributed in accordance with the following procedures:

(A) During the month of July in each year, every person claiming to be entitled to statutory license fees for secondary transmissions shall file a claim with the Copyright Royalty Judges, in accordance with requirements that the Copyright Royalty Judges shall prescribe by regulation. Notwithstanding any provisions of the antitrust laws, for purposes of this clause any claimants may agree among themselves as to the proportionate division of statutory licensing fees among them, may lump their claims together and file them jointly or as a single claim, or may designate a common agent to receive payment on their behalf.

(B) After the first day of August of each year, the Copyright Royalty Judges shall determine whether there exists a controversy concerning the distribution of royalty fees. If the Copyright Royalty Judges determine that no such controversy exists, the Copyright Royalty Judges shall authorize the Librarian of Congress to proceed to distribute such fees to the copyright owners entitled to receive them, or to their designated agents, subject to the deduction of reasonable administrative costs under this section. If the Copyright Royalty Judges find the existence of a controversy, the Copyright Royalty Judges shall, pursuant to chapter 8 of this title, conduct a proceeding to determine the distribution of royalty fees.

(C) During the pendency of any proceeding under this subsection, the Copyright Royalty Judges shall have the discretion to authorize the Librarian of Congress to proceed to distribute any amounts that are not in controversy.

(5) **3.75 Percent Rate and Syndicated Exclusivity Surcharge Not Applicable to Multicast Streams.**—The royalty rates specified in sections 256.2(c) and 256.2(d) of title 37, Code of Federal Regulations (commonly referred to as the "3.75 percent rate" and the "syndicated exclusivity surcharge", respectively), as in effect on the date of the enactment of the Satellite Television Extension and Localism Act of 2010, as such rates may be adjusted, or such sections redesignated, thereafter by the Copyright Royalty Judges, shall not apply to the secondary transmission of a multicast stream.

(6) **Verification of Accounts and Fee Payments.**—The Register of Copyrights shall issue regulations to provide for the confidential verification by copyright owners whose works were embodied in the secondary transmissions of primary transmissions pursuant to this section of the information reported on the semiannual statements of account filed under this subsection for accounting periods beginning on or after January 1, 2010, in order that the auditor designated under subparagraph (A) is able to confirm the correctness of the calculations and royalty payments reported therein. The regulations shall—

(A) establish procedures for the designation of a qualified independent auditor—

(i) with exclusive authority to request verification of such a statement of account on behalf of all copyright owners whose works were the subject of secondary transmissions of primary transmissions by the cable system (that deposited the statement) during the accounting period covered by the statement; and

(ii) who is not an officer, employee, or agent of any such copyright owner for any purpose other than such audit;

(B) establish procedures for safeguarding all non-public financial and business information provided under this paragraph;

(C)(i) require a consultation period for the independent auditor to review its conclusions with a designee of the cable system;

(ii) establish a mechanism for the cable system to remedy any errors identified in the auditor's report and to cure any underpayment identified; and

(iii) provide an opportunity to remedy any disputed facts or conclusions;

(D) limit the frequency of requests for verification for a particular cable system and the number of audits that a multiple system operator can be required to undergo in a single year; and

(E) permit requests for verification of a statement of account to be made only within 3 years after the last day of the year in which the statement of account is filed.

(7) Acceptance of Additional Deposits.—Any royalty fee payments received by the Copyright Office from cable systems for the secondary transmission of primary transmissions that are in addition to the payments calculated and deposited in accordance with this subsection shall be deemed to have been deposited for the particular accounting period for which they are received and shall be distributed as specified under this subsection.

(e) Nonsimultaneous Secondary Transmissions by Cable Systems.—

(1) Notwithstanding those provisions of the subsection (f)(2) relating to nonsimultaneous secondary transmissions by a cable system, any such transmissions are actionable as an act of infringement under section 501, and are fully subject to the remedies provided by sections 502 through 506 and section 510, unless—

(A) the program on the videotape is transmitted no more than one time to the cable system's subscribers;

(B) the copyrighted program, episode, or motion picture videotape, including the commercials contained within such program, episode, or picture, is transmitted without deletion or editing;

(C) an owner or officer of the cable system (i) prevents the duplication of the videotape while in the possession of the system, (ii) prevents unauthorized duplication while in the possession of the facility making the videotape for the system if the system owns or controls the facility, or takes reasonable precautions to prevent such duplication if it does not own or control the facility, (iii) takes adequate precautions to prevent duplication while the tape is being transported, and (iv) subject to paragraph (2), erases or destroys, or causes the erasure or destruction of, the videotape;

(D) within forty-five days after the end of each calendar quarter, an owner or officer of the cable system executes an affidavit attesting (i) to the steps and precautions taken to prevent duplication of the videotape, and (ii) subject to paragraph (2), to the erasure or destruction of all videotapes made or used during such quarter;

(E) such owner or officer places or causes each such affidavit, and affidavits received pursuant to paragraph (2)(C), to be placed in a file, open to public inspection, at such system's main office in the community where the transmission is made or in the nearest community where such system maintains an office; and

(F) the nonsimultaneous transmission is one that the cable system would be authorized to transmit under the rules, regulations, and authorizations of the Federal Communications Commission in effect at the time of the nonsimultaneous transmission if the transmission had been made simultaneously, except that this subparagraph shall not apply to inadvertent or accidental transmissions.

(2)   If a cable system transfers to any person a videotape of a program nonsimultaneously transmitted by it, such transfer is actionable as an act of infringement under section 501, and is fully subject to the remedies provided by sections 502 through 506, except that, pursuant to a written, nonprofit contract providing for the equitable sharing of the costs of such videotape and its transfer, a videotape nonsimultaneously transmitted by it, in accordance with paragraph (1), may be transferred by one cable system in Alaska to another system in Alaska, by one cable system in Hawaii permitted to make such nonsimultaneous transmissions to another such cable system in Hawaii, or by one cable system in Guam, the Northern Mariana Islands, the Federated States of Micronesia, the Republic of Palau, or the Republic of the Marshall Islands, to another cable system in any of those five entities, if—

(A)   each such contract is available for public inspection in the offices of the cable systems involved, and a copy of such contract is filed, within thirty days after such contract is entered into, with the Copyright Office (which Office shall make each such contract available for public inspection);

(B)   the cable system to which the videotape is transferred complies with paragraph (1)(A), (B), (C)(i), (iii), and (iv), and (D) through (F); and

(C)   such system provides a copy of the affidavit required to be made in accordance with paragraph (1)(D) to each cable system making a previous nonsimultaneous transmission of the same videotape.

(3)   This subsection shall not be construed to supersede the exclusivity protection provisions of any existing agreement, or any such agreement hereafter entered into, between a cable system and a television broadcast station in the area in which the cable system is located, or a network with which such station is affiliated.

(4)   As used in this subsection, the term "videotape" means the reproduction of the images and sounds of a program or programs broadcast by a television broadcast station licensed by the Federal Communications Commission, regardless of the nature of the material objects, such as tapes or films, in which the reproduction is embodied.

(f)   **Definitions.**—As used in this section, the following terms mean the following:

(1)   **Primary Transmission.**—A "primary transmission" is a transmission made to the public by a transmitting facility whose signals are being received and further transmitted by a secondary transmission service, regardless of where or when the performance or display was first transmitted. In the case of a television broadcast station, the primary stream and any multicast streams transmitted by the station constitute primary transmissions.

(2)   **Secondary Transmission.**—A "secondary transmission" is the further transmitting of a primary transmission simultaneously with the primary transmission, or nonsimultaneously with the primary transmission if by a cable system not located in whole or in part within the boundary of the forty-eight contiguous States, Hawaii, or Puerto Rico: Provided, however, That a nonsimultaneous further transmission by a cable system located in Hawaii of a primary transmission shall be deemed to be a secondary transmission if the carriage of the television broadcast signal comprising such further transmission is permissible under the rules, regulations, or authorizations of the Federal Communications Commission.

(3)   **Cable System.**—A "cable system" is a facility, located in any State, territory, trust territory, or possession of the United States, that in whole or in part receives signals transmitted or programs broadcast by one or more television broadcast stations licensed by the Federal Communications Commission, and makes secondary transmissions of such signals or programs by wires, cables, microwave, or other communications channels to subscribing members of the public who pay for such service. For purposes of determining the royalty fee under subsection

(d)(1), two or more cable systems in contiguous communities under common ownership or control or operating from one headend shall be considered as one system.

(4) Local Service Area of a Primary Transmitter.—The "local service area of a primary transmitter", in the case of both the primary stream and any multicast streams transmitted by a primary transmitter that is a television broadcast station, comprises the area where such primary transmitter could have insisted upon its signal being retransmitted by a cable system pursuant to the rules, regulations, and authorizations of the Federal Communications Commission in effect on April 15, 1976, or such station's television market as defined in section 76.55(e) of title 47, Code of Federal Regulations (as in effect on September 18, 1993), or any modifications to such television market made, on or after September 18, 1993, pursuant to section 76.55(e) or 76.59 of title 47, Code of Federal Regulations, or within the noise-limited contour as defined in § 73.622(e)(1) of title 47, Code of Federal Regulations, or in the case of a television broadcast station licensed by an appropriate governmental authority of Canada or Mexico, the area in which it would be entitled to insist upon its signal being retransmitted if it were a television broadcast station subject to such rules, regulations, and authorizations. In the case of a low power television station, as defined by the rules and regulations of the Federal Communications Commission, the "local service area of a primary transmitter" comprises the designated market area, as defined in section 122(j)(2)(C), that encompasses the community of license of such station and any community that is located outside such designated market area that is either wholly or partially within 20 miles of the transmitter site, or in the case of such a station located in a standard metropolitan statistical area which has one of the 50 largest populations of all standard metropolitan statistical areas (based on the 1980 decennial census of population taken by the Secretary of Commerce), wholly or partially within 20 miles of such transmitter site. The "local service area of a primary transmitter", in the case of a radio broadcast station, comprises the primary service area of such station, pursuant to the rules and regulations of the Federal Communications Commission.

(5) Distant Signal Equivalent.—

(A) In General.—Except as provided under subparagraph (B), a "distant signal equivalent"—

(i) is the value assigned to the secondary transmission of any non-network television programming carried by a cable system in whole or in part beyond the local service area of the primary transmitter of such programming; and

(ii) is computed by assigning a value of one to each primary stream and to each multicast stream (other than a simulcast) that is an independent station, and by assigning a value of one-quarter to each primary stream and to each multicast stream (other than a simulcast) that is a network station or a noncommercial educational station.

(B) Exceptions.—The values for independent, network, and noncommercial educational stations specified in subparagraph (A) are subject to the following:

(i) Where the rules and regulations of the Federal Communications Commission require a cable system to omit the further transmission of a particular program and such rules and regulations also permit the substitution of another program embodying a performance or display of a work in place of the omitted transmission, or where such rules and regulations in effect on the date of the enactment of the Copyright Act of 1976 permit a cable system, at its election, to effect such omission and substitution of a nonlive program or to carry additional programs not transmitted by primary transmitters within whose local service area the cable system is located, no value shall be assigned for the substituted or additional program.

(ii) Where the rules, regulations, or authorizations of the Federal Communications Commission in effect on the date of the enactment of the Copyright

Act of 1976 permit a cable system, at its election, to omit the further transmission of a particular program and such rules, regulations, or authorizations also permit the substitution of another program embodying a performance or display of a work in place of the omitted transmission, the value assigned for the substituted or additional program shall be, in the case of a live program, the value of one full distant signal equivalent multiplied by a fraction that has as its numerator the number of days in the year in which such substitution occurs and as its denominator the number of days in the year.

(iii) In the case of the secondary transmission of a primary transmitter that is a television broadcast station pursuant to the late-night or specialty programming rules of the Federal Communications Commission, or the secondary transmission of a primary transmitter that is a television broadcast station on a part-time basis where full-time carriage is not possible because the cable system lacks the activated channel capacity to retransmit on a full-time basis all signals that it is authorized to carry, the values for independent, network, and noncommercial educational stations set forth in subparagraph (A), as the case may be, shall be multiplied by a fraction that is equal to the ratio of the broadcast hours of such primary transmitter retransmitted by the cable system to the total broadcast hours of the primary transmitter.

(iv) No value shall be assigned for the secondary transmission of the primary stream or any multicast streams of a primary transmitter that is a television broadcast station in any community that is within the local service area of the primary transmitter.

(6) Network Station.—

(A) Treatment of Primary Stream.—The term "network station" shall be applied to a primary stream of a television broadcast station that is owned or operated by, or affiliated with, one or more of the television networks in the United States providing nationwide transmissions, and that transmits a substantial part of the programming supplied by such networks for a substantial part of the primary stream's typical broadcast day.

(B) Treatment of Multicast Streams.—The term "network station" shall be applied to a multicast stream on which a television broadcast station transmits all or substantially all of the programming of an interconnected program service that—

(i) is owned or operated by, or affiliated with, one or more of the television networks described in subparagraph (A); and

(ii) offers programming on a regular basis for 15 or more hours per week to at least 25 of the affiliated television licensees of the interconnected program service in 10 or more States.

(7) Independent Station.—The term "independent station" shall be applied to the primary stream or a multicast stream of a television broadcast station that is not a network station or a noncommercial educational station.

(8) Noncommercial Educational Station.—The term "noncommercial educational station" shall be applied to the primary stream or a multicast stream of a television broadcast station that is a noncommercial educational broadcast station as defined in section 397 of the Communications Act of 1934, as in effect on the date of the enactment of the Satellite Television Extension and Localism Act of 2010.

(9) Primary Stream.—A "primary stream" is—

(A) the single digital stream of programming that, before June 12, 2009, was substantially duplicating the programming transmitted by the television broadcast station as an analog signal; or

(B) if there is no stream described in subparagraph (A), then the single digital stream of programming transmitted by the television broadcast station for the longest period of time.

(10) Primary Transmitter.—A "primary transmitter" is a television or radio broadcast station licensed by the Federal Communications Commission, or by an appropriate governmental authority of Canada or Mexico, that makes primary transmissions to the public.

(11) Multicast Stream.—A "multicast stream" is a digital stream of programming that is transmitted by a television broadcast station and is not the station's primary stream.

(12) Simulcast.—A "simulcast" is a multicast stream of a television broadcast station that duplicates the programming transmitted by the primary stream or another multicast stream of such station.

(13) Subscriber; Subscribe.—

(A) Subscriber.—The term "subscriber" means a person or entity that receives a secondary transmission service from a cable system and pays a fee for the service, directly or indirectly, to the cable system.

(B) Subscribe.—The term "subscribe" means to elect to become a subscriber.

§ 112. Limitations on Exclusive Rights: Ephemeral Recordings

(a)(1) Notwithstanding the provisions of section 106, and except in the case of a motion picture or other audiovisual work, it is not an infringement of copyright for a transmitting organization entitled to transmit to the public a performance or display of a work, under a license, including a statutory license under section 114(f), or transfer of the copyright or under the limitations on exclusive rights in sound recordings specified by section 114(a), or for a transmitting organization that is a broadcast radio or television station licensed as such by the Federal Communications Commission and that makes a broadcast transmission of a performance of a sound recording in a digital format on a nonsubscription basis, to make no more than one copy or phonorecord of a particular transmission program embodying the performance or display, if—

(A) the copy or phonorecord is retained and used solely by the transmitting organization that made it, and no further copies or phonorecords are reproduced from it; and

(B) the copy or phonorecord is used solely for the transmitting organization's own transmissions within its local service area, or for purposes of archival preservation or security; and

(C) unless preserved exclusively for archival purposes, the copy or phonorecord is destroyed within six months from the date the transmission program was first transmitted to the public.

(2) In a case in which a transmitting organization entitled to make a copy or phonorecord under paragraph (1) in connection with the transmission to the public of a performance or display of a work is prevented from making such copy or phonorecord by reason of the application by the copyright owner of technical measures that prevent the reproduction of the work, the copyright owner shall make available to the transmitting organization the necessary means for permitting the making of such copy or phonorecord as permitted under that paragraph, if it is technologically feasible and economically reasonable for the copyright owner to do so. If the copyright owner fails to do so in a timely manner in light of the transmitting organization's reasonable business requirements, the transmitting organization shall not be liable for a violation of section 1201(a)(1) of this title for engaging in such activities as are necessary to make such copies or phonorecords as permitted under paragraph (1) of this subsection.

(b)   Notwithstanding the provisions of section 106, it is not an infringement of copyright for a governmental body or other nonprofit organization entitled to transmit a performance or display of a work, under section 110(2) or under the limitations on exclusive rights in sound recordings specified by section 114(a), to make no more than thirty copies or phonorecords of a particular transmission program embodying the performance or display, if—

(1)   no further copies or phonorecords are reproduced from the copies or phonorecords made under this clause; and

(2)   except for one copy or phonorecord that may be preserved exclusively for archival purposes, the copies or phonorecords are destroyed within seven years from the date the transmission program was first transmitted to the public.

(c)   Notwithstanding the provisions of section 106, it is not an infringement of copyright for a governmental body or other nonprofit organization to make for distribution no more than one copy or phonorecord, for each transmitting organization specified in clause (2) of this subsection, of a particular transmission program embodying a performance of a nondramatic musical work of a religious nature, or of a sound recording of such a musical work, if—

(1)   there is no direct or indirect charge for making or distributing any such copies or phonorecords; and

(2)   none of such copies or phonorecords is used for any performance other than a single transmission to the public by a transmitting organization entitled to transmit to the public a performance of the work under a license or transfer of the copyright; and

(3)   except for one copy or phonorecord that may be preserved exclusively for archival purposes, the copies or phonorecords are all destroyed within one year from the date the transmission program was first transmitted to the public.

(d)   Notwithstanding the provisions of section 106, it is not an infringement of copyright for a governmental body or other nonprofit organization entitled to transmit a performance of a work under section 110(8) to make no more than ten copies or phonorecords embodying the performance, or to permit the use of any such copy or phonorecord by any governmental body or nonprofit organization entitled to transmit a performance of a work under section 110(8), if—

(1)   any such copy or phonorecord is retained and used solely by the organization that made it, or by a governmental body or nonprofit organization entitled to transmit a performance of a work under section 110(8), and no further copies or phonorecords are reproduced from it; and

(2)   any such copy or phonorecord is used solely for transmissions authorized under section 110(8), or for purposes of archival preservation or security; and

(3)   the governmental body or nonprofit organization permitting any use of any such copy or phonorecord by any governmental body or nonprofit organization under this subsection does not make any charge for such use.

(e)   Statutory License.—

(1)   A transmitting organization entitled to transmit to the public a performance of a sound recording under the limitation on exclusive rights specified by section 114(d)(1)(C)(iv) or under a statutory license in accordance with section 114(f) is entitled to a statutory license, under the conditions specified by this subsection, to make no more than 1 phonorecord of the sound recording (unless the terms and conditions of the statutory license allow for more), if the following conditions are satisfied:

(A)   The phonorecord is retained and used solely by the transmitting organization that made it, and no further phonorecords are reproduced from it.

(B) The phonorecord is used solely for the transmitting organization's own transmissions originating in the United States under a statutory license in accordance with section 114(f) or the limitation on exclusive rights specified by section 114(d)(1)(C)(iv).

(C) Unless preserved exclusively for purposes of archival preservation, the phonorecord is destroyed within 6 months from the date the sound recording was first transmitted to the public using the phonorecord.

(D) Phonorecords of the sound recording have been distributed to the public under the authority of the copyright owner or the copyright owner authorizes the transmitting entity to transmit the sound recording, and the transmitting entity makes the phonorecord under this subsection from a phonorecord lawfully made and acquired under the authority of the copyright owner.

(2) Notwithstanding any provision of the antitrust laws, any copyright owners of sound recordings and any transmitting organizations entitled to a statutory license under this subsection may negotiate and agree upon royalty rates and license terms and conditions for making phonorecords of such sound recordings under this section and the proportionate division of fees paid among copyright owners, and may designate common agents to negotiate, agree to, pay, or receive such royalty payments.

(3) Proceedings under chapter 8 shall determine reasonable rates and terms of royalty payments for the activities specified by paragraph (1) during the 5-year period beginning on January 1 of the second year following the year in which the proceedings are to be commenced, or such other period as the parties may agree. Such rates shall include a minimum fee for each type of service offered by transmitting organizations. Any copyright owners of sound recordings or any transmitting organizations entitled to a statutory license under this subsection may submit to the Copyright Royalty Judges licenses covering such activities with respect to such sound recordings. The parties to each proceeding shall bear their own costs.

(4) The schedule of reasonable rates and terms determined by the Copyright Royalty Judges shall, subject to paragraph (5), be binding on all copyright owners of sound recordings and transmitting organizations entitled to a statutory license under this subsection during the 5-year period specified in paragraph (3), or such other period as the parties may agree. Such rates shall include a minimum fee for each type of service offered by transmitting organizations. The Copyright Royalty Judges shall establish rates that most clearly represent the fees that would have been negotiated in the marketplace between a willing buyer and a willing seller. In determining such rates and terms, the Copyright Royalty Judges shall base their decision on economic, competitive, and programming information presented by the parties, including—

(A) whether use of the service may substitute for or may promote the sales of phonorecords or otherwise interferes with or enhances the copyright owner's traditional streams of revenue; and

(B) the relative roles of the copyright owner and the transmitting organization in the copyrighted work and the service made available to the public with respect to relative creative contribution, technological contribution, capital investment, cost, and risk.

In establishing such rates and terms, the Copyright Royalty Judges may consider the rates and terms under voluntary license agreements described in paragraphs (3) and (4). The Copyright Royalty Judges shall also establish requirements by which copyright owners may receive reasonable notice of the use of their sound recordings under this section, and under which records of such use shall be kept and made available by transmitting organizations entitled to obtain a statutory license under this subsection.

(5) License agreements voluntarily negotiated at any time between 1 or more copyright owners of sound recordings and 1 or more transmitting organizations entitled to obtain a

statutory license under this subsection shall be given effect in lieu of any decision by the Librarian of Congress or determination by the Copyright Royalty Judges.

(6)(A)   Any person who wishes to make a phonorecord of a sound recording under a statutory license in accordance with this subsection may do so without infringing the exclusive right of the copyright owner of the sound recording under section 106(1)—

(i)   by complying with such notice requirements as the Copyright Royalty Judges shall prescribe by regulation and by paying royalty fees in accordance with this subsection; or

(ii)   if such royalty fees have not been set, by agreeing to pay such royalty fees as shall be determined in accordance with this subsection.

(B)   Any royalty payments in arrears shall be made on or before the 20th day of the month next succeeding the month in which the royalty fees are set.

(7)   If a transmitting organization entitled to make a phonorecord under this subsection is prevented from making such phonorecord by reason of the application by the copyright owner of technical measures that prevent the reproduction of the sound recording, the copyright owner shall make available to the transmitting organization the necessary means for permitting the making of such phonorecord as permitted under this subsection, if it is technologically feasible and economically reasonable for the copyright owner to do so. If the copyright owner fails to do so in a timely manner in light of the transmitting organization's reasonable business requirements, the transmitting organization shall not be liable for a violation of section 1201(a)(1) of this title for engaging in such activities as are necessary to make such phonorecords as permitted under this subsection.

(8)   Nothing in this subsection annuls, limits, impairs, or otherwise affects in any way the existence or value of any of the exclusive rights of the copyright owners in a sound recording, except as otherwise provided in this subsection, or in a musical work, including the exclusive rights to reproduce and distribute a sound recording or musical work, including by means of a digital phonorecord delivery, under sections 106(1), 106(3), and 115, and the right to perform publicly a sound recording or musical work, including by means of a digital audio transmission, under sections 106(4) and 106(6).

(f)(1)   Notwithstanding the provisions of section 106, and without limiting the application of subsection (b), it is not an infringement of copyright for a governmental body or other nonprofit educational institution entitled under section 110(2) to transmit a performance or display to make copies or phonorecords of a work that is in digital form and, solely to the extent permitted in paragraph (2), of a work that is in analog form, embodying the performance or display to be used for making transmissions authorized under section 110(2), if—

(A)   such copies or phonorecords are retained and used solely by the body or institution that made them, and no further copies or phonorecords are reproduced from them, except as authorized under section 110(2); and

(B)   such copies or phonorecords are used solely for transmissions authorized under section 110(2).

(2)   This subsection does not authorize the conversion of print or other analog versions of works into digital formats, except that such conversion is permitted hereunder, only with respect to the amount of such works authorized to be performed or displayed under section 110(2), if—

(A)   no digital version of the work is available to the institution; or

(B)   the digital version of the work that is available to the institution is subject to technological protection measures that prevent its use for section 110(2).

(g)   The transmission program embodied in a copy or phonorecord made under this section is not subject to protection as a derivative work under this title except with the express consent of the owners of copyright in the preexisting works employed in the program.

§ 113. Scope of Exclusive Rights in Pictorial, Graphic, and Sculptural Works

(a) Subject to the provisions of subsections (b) and (c) of this section, the exclusive right to reproduce a copyrighted pictorial, graphic, or sculptural work in copies under section 106 includes the right to reproduce the work in or on any kind of article, whether useful or otherwise.

(b) This title does not afford, to the owner of copyright in a work that portrays a useful article as such, any greater or lesser rights with respect to the making, distribution, or display of the useful article so portrayed than those afforded to such works under the law, whether title 17 or the common law or statutes of a State, in effect on December 31, 1977, as held applicable and construed by a court in an action brought under this title.

(c) In the case of a work lawfully reproduced in useful articles that have been offered for sale or other distribution to the public, copyright does not include any right to prevent the making, distribution, or display of pictures or photographs of such articles in connection with advertisements or commentaries related to the distribution or display of such articles, or in connection with news reports.

(d)(1) In a case in which—

(A) a work of visual art has been incorporated in or made part of a building in such a way that removing the work from the building will cause the destruction, distortion, mutilation, or other modification of the work as described in section 106A(a)(3), and

(B) the author consented to the installation of the work in the building either before the effective date set forth in section 610(a) of the Visual Artists Rights Act of 1990, or in a written instrument executed on or after such effective date that is signed by the owner of the building and the author and that specifies that installation of the work may subject the work to destruction, distortion, mutilation, or other modification, by reason of its removal,

then the rights conferred by paragraphs (2) and (3) of section 106A(a) shall not apply.

(2) If the owner of a building wishes to remove a work of visual art which is a part of such building and which can be removed from the building without the destruction, distortion, mutilation, or other modification of the work as described in section 106A(a)(3), the author's rights under paragraphs (2) and (3) of section 106A(a) shall apply unless—

(A) the owner has made a diligent, good faith attempt without success to notify the author of the owner's intended action affecting the work of visual art, or

(B) the owner did provide such notice in writing and the person so notified failed, within 90 days after receiving such notice, either to remove the work or to pay for its removal.

For purposes of subparagraph (A), an owner shall be presumed to have made a diligent, good faith attempt to send notice if the owner sent such notice by registered mail to the author at the most recent address of the author that was recorded with the Register of Copyrights pursuant to paragraph (3). If the work is removed at the expense of the author, title to that copy of the work shall be deemed to be in the author.

(3) The Register of Copyrights shall establish a system of records whereby any author of a work of visual art that has been incorporated in or made part of a building, may record his or her identity and address with the Copyright Office. The Register shall also establish procedures under which any such author may update the information so recorded, and procedures under which owners of buildings may record with the Copyright Office evidence of their efforts to comply with this subsection.

§ 114. Scope of Exclusive Rights in Sound Recordings

(a) The exclusive rights of the owner of copyright in a sound recording are limited to the rights specified by clauses (1), (2), (3) and (6) of section 106, and do not include any right of performance under section 106(4).

(b)   The exclusive right of the owner of copyright in a sound recording under clause (1) of section 106 is limited to the right to duplicate the sound recording in the form of phonorecords or copies that directly or indirectly recapture the actual sounds fixed in the recording. The exclusive right of the owner of copyright in a sound recording under clause (2) of section 106 is limited to the right to prepare a derivative work in which the actual sounds fixed in the sound recording are rearranged, remixed, or otherwise altered in sequence or quality. The exclusive rights of the owner of copyright in a sound recording under clauses (1) and (2) of section 106 do not extend to the making or duplication of another sound recording that consists entirely of an independent fixation of other sounds, even though such sounds imitate or simulate those in the copyrighted sound recording. The exclusive rights of the owner of copyright in a sound recording under clauses (1), (2), and (3) of section 106 do not apply to sound recordings included in educational television and radio programs (as defined in section 397 of title 47) distributed or transmitted by or through public broadcasting entities (as defined by section 118(f)); *Provided,* That copies or phonorecords of said programs are not commercially distributed by or through public broadcasting entities to the general public.

(c)   This section does not limit or impair the exclusive right to perform publicly, by means of a phonorecord, any of the works specified by section 106(4).

(d)   Limitations on Exclusive Right.—Notwithstanding the provisions of section 106(6)—

(1)   Exempt Transmissions and Retransmissions.—The performance of a sound recording publicly by means of a digital audio transmission, other than as a part of an interactive service, is not an infringement of section 106(6) if the performance is part of—

(A)   a nonsubscription broadcast transmission;

(B)   a retransmission of a nonsubscription broadcast transmission: *Provided,* That, in the case of a retransmission of a radio station's broadcast transmission—

(i)   the radio station's broadcast transmission is not willfully or repeatedly retransmitted more than a radius of 150 miles from the site of the radio broadcast transmitter, however—

(I)   the 150 mile limitation under this clause shall not apply when a nonsubscription broadcast transmission by a radio station licensed by the Federal Communications Commission is retransmitted on a nonsubscription basis by a terrestrial broadcast station, terrestrial translator, or terrestrial repeater licensed by the Federal Communications Commission; and

(II)   in the case of a subscription retransmission of a nonsubscription broadcast retransmission covered by subclause (I), the 150 mile radius shall be measured from the transmitter site of such broadcast retransmitter;

(ii)   the retransmission is of radio station broadcast transmissions that are—

(I)   obtained by the retransmitter over the air;

(II)   not electronically processed by the retransmitter to deliver separate and discrete signals; and

(III) retransmitted only within the local communities served by the retransmitter;

(iii) the radio station's broadcast transmission was being retransmitted to cable systems (as defined in section 111(f)) by a satellite carrier on January 1, 1995, and that retransmission was being retransmitted by cable systems as a separate and discrete signal, and the satellite carrier obtains the radio station's broadcast transmission in an analog format: *Provided,* That the broadcast transmission being retransmitted may embody the programming of no more than one radio station; or

(iv) the radio station's broadcast transmission is made by a noncommercial educational broadcast station funded on or after January 1, 1995, under section 396(k) of the Communications Act of 1934 (47 U.S.C. 396(k)), consists solely of noncommercial educational and cultural radio programs, and the retransmission, whether or not simultaneous, is a nonsubscription terrestrial broadcast retransmission; or

(C) a transmission that comes within any of the following categories—

(i) a prior or simultaneous transmission incidental to an exempt transmission, such as a feed received by and then retransmitted by an exempt transmitter: *Provided*, That such incidental transmissions do not include any subscription transmission directly for reception by members of the public;

(ii) a transmission within a business establishment, confined to its premises or the immediately surrounding vicinity;

(iii) a retransmission by any retransmitter, including a multichannel video programming distributor as defined in section 602(12) of the Communications Act of 1934 (47 U.S.C. 522(12)), of a transmission by a transmitter licensed to publicly perform the sound recording as a part of that transmission, if the retransmission is simultaneous with the licensed transmission and authorized by the transmitter; or

(iv) a transmission to a business establishment for use in the ordinary course of its business: *Provided*, That the business recipient does not retransmit the transmission outside of its premises or the immediately surrounding vicinity, and that the transmission does not exceed the sound recording performance complement. Nothing in this clause shall limit the scope of the exemption in clause (ii).

(2) *Statutory Licensing of Certain Transmissions.*—The performance of a sound recording publicly by means of a subscription digital audio transmission not exempt under paragraph (1), an eligible nonsubscription transmission, or a transmission not exempt under paragraph (1) that is made by a preexisting satellite digital audio radio service shall be subject to statutory licensing, in accordance with subsection (f) if—

(A)(i) the transmission is not part of an interactive service;

(ii) except in the case of a transmission to a business establishment, the transmitting entity does not automatically and intentionally cause any device receiving the transmission to switch from one program channel to another; and

(iii) except as provided in section 1002(e), the transmission of the sound recording is accompanied, if technically feasible, by the information encoded in that sound recording, if any, by or under the authority of the copyright owner of that sound recording, that identifies the title of the sound recording, the featured recording artist who performs on the sound recording, and related information, including information concerning the underlying musical work and its writer;

(B) in the case of a subscription transmission not exempt under paragraph (1) that is made by a preexisting subscription service in the same transmission medium used by such service on July 31, 1998, or in the case of a transmission not exempt under paragraph (1) that is made by a preexisting satellite digital audio radio service—

(i) the transmission does not exceed the sound recording performance complement; and

(ii) the transmitting entity does not cause to be published by means of an advance program schedule or prior announcement the titles of the specific sound recordings or phonorecords embodying such sound recordings to be transmitted; and

(C) in the case of an eligible nonsubscription transmission or a subscription transmission not exempt under paragraph (1) that is made by a new subscription service or by a preexisting subscription service other than in the same transmission medium used by such service on July 31, 1998—

(i) the transmission does not exceed the sound recording performance complement, except that this requirement shall not apply in the case of a retransmission of a broadcast transmission if the retransmission is made by a transmitting entity that does not have the right or ability to control the programming of the broadcast station making the broadcast transmission, unless—

(I) the broadcast station makes broadcast transmissions—

(aa) in digital format that regularly exceed the sound recording performance complement; or

(bb) in analog format, a substantial portion of which, on a weekly basis, exceed the sound recording performance complement; and

(II) the sound recording copyright owner or its representative has notified the transmitting entity in writing that broadcast transmissions of the copyright owner's sound recordings exceed the sound recording performance complement as provided in this clause;

(ii) the transmitting entity does not cause to be published, or induce or facilitate the publication, by means of an advance program schedule or prior announcement, the titles of the specific sound recordings to be transmitted, the phonorecords embodying such sound recordings, or, other than for illustrative purposes, the names of the featured recording artists, except that this clause does not disqualify a transmitting entity that makes a prior announcement that a particular artist will be featured within an unspecified future time period, and in the case of a retransmission of a broadcast transmission by a transmitting entity that does not have the right or ability to control the programming of the broadcast transmission, the requirement of this clause shall not apply to a prior oral announcement by the broadcast station, or to an advance program schedule published, induced, or facilitated by the broadcast station, if the transmitting entity does not have actual knowledge and has not received written notice from the copyright owner or its representative that the broadcast station publishes or induces or facilitates the publication of such advance program schedule, or if such advance program schedule is a schedule of classical music programming published by the broadcast station in the same manner as published by that broadcast station on or before September 30, 1998;

(iii) the transmission—

(I) is not part of an archived program of less than 5 hours duration;

(II) is not part of an archived program of 5 hours or greater in duration that is made available for a period exceeding 2 weeks;

(III) is not part of a continuous program which is of less than 3 hours duration; or

(IV) is not part of an identifiable program in which performances of sound recordings are rendered in a predetermined order, other than an archived or continuous program, that is transmitted at—

(aa) more than 3 times in any 2-week period that have been publicly announced in advance, in the case of a program of less than 1 hour in duration, or

(bb) more than 4 times in any 2-week period that have been publicly announced in advance, in the case of a program of 1 hour or more in duration, except that the requirement of this subclause shall not apply in the case of a retransmission of a broadcast transmission by a transmitting entity that does not have the right or ability to control the programming of the broadcast transmission, unless the transmitting entity is given notice in writing by the copyright owner of the sound recording that the broadcast station makes broadcast transmissions that regularly violate such requirement;

(iv) the transmitting entity does not knowingly perform the sound recording, as part of a service that offers transmissions of visual images contemporaneously with transmissions of sound recordings, in a manner that is likely to cause confusion, to cause mistake, or to deceive, as to the affiliation, connection, or association of the copyright owner or featured recording artist with the transmitting entity or a particular product or service advertised by the transmitting entity, or as to the origin, sponsorship, or approval by the copyright owner or featured recording artist of the activities of the transmitting entity other than the performance of the sound recording itself;

(v) the transmitting entity cooperates to prevent, to the extent feasible without imposing substantial costs or burdens, a transmission recipient or any other person or entity from automatically scanning the transmitting entity's transmissions alone or together with transmissions by other transmitting entities in order to select a particular sound recording to be transmitted to the transmission recipient, except that the requirement of this clause shall not apply to a satellite digital audio service that is in operation, or that is licensed by the Federal Communications Commission, on or before July 31, 1998;

(vi) the transmitting entity takes no affirmative steps to cause or induce the making of a phonorecord by the transmission recipient, and if the technology used by the transmitting entity enables the transmitting entity to limit the making by the transmission recipient of phonorecords of the transmission directly in a digital format, the transmitting entity sets such technology to limit such making of phonorecords to the extent permitted by such technology;

(vii) phonorecords of the sound recording have been distributed to the public under the authority of the copyright owner or the copyright owner authorizes the transmitting entity to transmit the sound recording, and the transmitting entity makes the transmission from a phonorecord lawfully made under the authority of the copyright owner, except that the requirement of this clause shall not apply to a retransmission of a broadcast transmission by a transmitting entity that does not have the right or ability to control the programming of the broadcast transmission, unless the transmitting entity is given notice in writing by the copyright owner of the sound recording that the broadcast station makes broadcast transmissions that regularly violate such requirement;

(viii) the transmitting entity accommodates and does not interfere with the transmission of technical measures that are widely used by sound recording copyright owners to identify or protect copyrighted works, and that are technically feasible of being transmitted by the transmitting entity without imposing substantial costs on the transmitting entity or resulting in perceptible aural or visual degradation of the digital signal, except that the requirement of this clause shall not apply to a satellite digital audio service that is in operation, or that is licensed under the authority of the Federal Communications Commission, on or before July 31, 1998, to the extent that such service has designed, developed, or made commitments to procure equipment or technology that is not compatible with such technical measures before such technical measures are widely adopted by sound recording copyright owners; and

(ix) the transmitting entity identifies in textual data the sound recording during, but not before, the time it is performed, including the title of the sound recording, the title of the phonorecord embodying such sound recording, if any, and the featured recording artist, in a manner to permit it to be displayed to the transmission recipient by the device or technology intended for receiving the service provided by the transmitting entity, except that the obligation in this clause shall not take effect until 1 year after the date of the enactment of the Digital Millennium Copyright Act and shall not apply in the case of a retransmission of a broadcast transmission by a transmitting entity that does not have the right or ability to control the programming of the broadcast transmission, or in the case in which devices or technology intended for receiving the service provided by the transmitting entity that have the capability to display such textual data are not common in the marketplace.

(3) Licenses for Transmissions by Interactive Services.—

(A) No interactive service shall be granted an exclusive license under section 106(6) for the performance of a sound recording publicly by means of digital audio transmission for a period in excess of 12 months, except that with respect to an exclusive license granted to an interactive service by a licensor that holds the copyright to 1,000 or fewer sound recordings, the period of such license shall not exceed 24 months: *Provided, however,* That the grantee of such exclusive license shall be ineligible to receive another exclusive license for the performance of that sound recording for a period of 13 months from the expiration of the prior exclusive license.

(B) The limitation set forth in subparagraph (A) of this paragraph shall not apply if—

(i) the licensor has granted and there remain in effect licenses under section 106(6) for the public performance of sound recordings by means of digital audio transmission by at least 5 different interactive services: *Provided, however,* That each such license must be for a minimum of 10 percent of the copyrighted sound recordings owned by the licensor that have been licensed to interactive services, but in no event less than 50 sound recordings; or

(ii) the exclusive license is granted to perform publicly up to 45 seconds of a sound recording and the sole purpose of the performance is to promote the distribution or performance of that sound recording.

(C) Notwithstanding the grant of an exclusive or nonexclusive license of the right of public performance under section 106(6), an interactive service may not publicly perform a sound recording unless a license has been granted for the public performance of any copyrighted musical work contained in the sound recording: *Provided,* That such license to publicly perform the copyrighted musical work may be granted either by a performing rights society representing the copyright owner or by the copyright owner.

(D) The performance of a sound recording by means of a retransmission of a digital audio transmission is not an infringement of section 106(6) if—

(i) the retransmission is of a transmission by an interactive service licensed to publicly perform the sound recording to a particular member of the public as part of that transmission; and

(ii) the retransmission is simultaneous with the licensed transmission, authorized by the transmitter, and limited to that particular member of the public intended by the interactive service to be the recipient of the transmission.

(E) For the purposes of this paragraph—

(i) a "licensor" shall include the licensing entity and any other entity under any material degree of common ownership, management, or control that owns copyrights in sound recordings; and

(ii) a "performing rights society" is an association or corporation that licenses the public performance of nondramatic musical works on behalf of the copyright owner, such as the American Society of Composers, Authors and Publishers, Broadcast Music, Inc., and SESAC, Inc.

(4) Rights Not Otherwise Limited.—

(A) Except as expressly provided in this section, this section does not limit or impair the exclusive right to perform a sound recording publicly by means of a digital audio transmission under section 106(6).

(B) Nothing in this section annuls or limits in any way—

(i) the exclusive right to publicly perform a musical work, including by means of a digital audio transmission, under section 106(4);

(ii) the exclusive rights in a sound recording or the musical work embodied therein under sections 106(1), 106(2) and 106(3); or

(iii) any other rights under any other clause of section 106, or remedies available under this title, as such rights or remedies exist either before or after the date of enactment of the Digital Performance Right in Sound Recordings Act of 1995.

(C) Any limitations in this section on the exclusive right under section 106(6) apply only to the exclusive right under section 106(6) and not to any other exclusive rights under section 106. Nothing in this section shall be construed to annul, limit, impair or otherwise affect in any way the ability of the owner of a copyright in a sound recording to exercise the rights under sections 106(1), 106(2) and 106(3), or to obtain the remedies available under this title pursuant to such rights, as such rights and remedies exist either before or after the date of enactment of the Digital Performance Right in Sound Recordings Act of 1995.

(e) Authority for Negotiations.—

(1) Notwithstanding any provision of the antitrust laws, in negotiating statutory licenses in accordance with subsection (f), any copyright owners of sound recordings and any entities performing sound recordings affected by this section may negotiate and agree upon the royalty rates and license terms and conditions for the performance of such sound recordings and the proportionate division of fees paid among copyright owners, and may designate common agents on a nonexclusive basis to negotiate, agree to, pay, or receive payments.

(2) For licenses granted under section 106(6), other than statutory licenses, such as for performances by interactive services or performances that exceed the sound recording performance complement—

(A) copyright owners of sound recordings affected by this section may designate common agents to act on their behalf to grant licenses and receive and remit royalty payments: *Provided,* That each copyright owner shall establish the royalty rates and material license terms and conditions unilaterally, that is, not in agreement, combination, or concert with other copyright owners of sound recordings; and

(B) entities performing sound recordings affected by this section may designate common agents to act on their behalf to obtain licenses and collect and pay royalty fees: *Provided,* That each entity performing sound recordings shall determine the royalty rates and material license terms and conditions unilaterally, that is, not in agreement, combination, or concert with other entities performing sound recordings.

(f) Licenses for Certain Nonexempt Transmissions.—

(1)(A) Proceedings under chapter 8 shall determine reasonable rates and terms of royalty payments for transmissions subject to statutory licensing under subsection (d)(2) during the 5-year period beginning on January 1 of the second year following the year in which the proceedings are to be commenced pursuant to subparagraph (A) or (B) of section 804(b)(3), as the case may be, or such other period as the parties may agree. The parties to each proceeding shall bear their own costs.

(B)   The schedule of reasonable rates and terms determined by the Copyright Royalty Judges shall, subject to paragraph (2), be binding on all copyright owners of sound recordings and entities performing sound recordings affected by this paragraph during the 5-year period specified in subparagraph (A), or such other period as the parties may agree. Such rates and terms shall distinguish among the different types of services then in operation and shall include a minimum fee for each such type of service, such differences to be based on criteria including the quantity and nature of the use of sound recordings and the degree to which use of the service may substitute for or may promote the purchase of phonorecords by consumers. The Copyright Royalty Judges shall establish rates and terms that most clearly represent the rates and terms that would have been negotiated in the marketplace between a willing buyer and a willing seller. In determining such rates and terms, the Copyright Royalty Judges—

(i)   shall base their decision on economic, competitive, and programming information presented by the parties, including—

(I)   whether use of the service may substitute for or may promote the sales of phonorecords or otherwise may interfere with or may enhance the sound recording copyright owner's other streams of revenue from the copyright owner's sound recordings; and

(II)   the relative roles of the copyright owner and the transmitting entity in the copyrighted work and the service made available to the public with respect to relative creative contribution, technological contribution, capital investment, cost, and risk; and

(ii)   may consider the rates and terms for comparable types of audio transmission services and comparable circumstances under voluntary license agreements.

(C)   The procedures under subparagraphs (A) and (B) shall also be initiated pursuant to a petition filed by any sound recording copyright owner or any transmitting entity indicating that a new type of service on which sound recordings are performed is or is about to become operational, for the purpose of determining reasonable terms and rates of royalty payments with respect to such new type of service for the period beginning with the inception of such new type of service and ending on the date on which the royalty rates and terms for eligible nonsubscription services and new subscription services, or preexisting subscription services and preexisting satellite digital audio radio services, as the case may be, most recently determined under subparagraph (A) or (B) and chapter 8 expire, or such other period as the parties may agree.

(2)   License agreements voluntarily negotiated at any time between 1 or more copyright owners of sound recordings and 1 or more entities performing sound recordings shall be given effect in lieu of any decision by the Librarian of Congress or determination by the Copyright Royalty Judges.

(3)(A) The Copyright Royalty Judges shall also establish requirements by which copyright owners may receive reasonable notice of the use of their sound recordings under this section, and under which records of such use shall be kept and made available by entities performing sound recordings. The notice and recordkeeping rules in effect on the day before the effective date of the Copyright Royalty and Distribution Reform Act of 2004 shall remain in effect unless and until new regulations are promulgated by the Copyright Royalty Judges. If new regulations are promulgated under this subparagraph, the Copyright Royalty Judges shall take into account the substance and effect of the rules in effect on the day before the effective date of the Copyright Royalty and Distribution Reform Act of 2004 and shall, to the extent practicable, avoid significant disruption of the functions of any designated agent authorized to collect and distribute royalty fees.

(B) Any person who wishes to perform a sound recording publicly by means of a transmission eligible for statutory licensing under this subsection may do so without infringing the exclusive right of the copyright owner of the sound recording—

(i) by complying with such notice requirements as the Copyright Royalty Judges shall prescribe by regulation and by paying royalty fees in accordance with this subsection; or

(ii) if such royalty fees have not been set, by agreeing to pay such royalty fees as shall be determined in accordance with this subsection.

(C) Any royalty payments in arrears shall be made on or before the twentieth day of the month next succeeding the month in which the royalty fees are set.

(4)(A) Notwithstanding section 112(e) and the other provisions of this subsection, the receiving agent may enter into agreements for the reproduction and performance of sound recordings under section 112(e) and this section by any 1 or more commercial webcasters or noncommercial webcasters for a period of not more than 11 years beginning on January 1, 2005, that, once published in the Federal Register pursuant to subparagraph (B), shall be binding on all copyright owners of sound recordings and other persons entitled to payment under this section, in lieu of any determination by the Copyright Royalty Judges. Any such agreement for commercial webcasters may include provisions for payment of royalties on the basis of a percentage of revenue or expenses, or both, and include a minimum fee. Any such agreement may include other terms and conditions, including requirements by which copyright owners may receive notice of the use of their sound recordings and under which records of such use shall be kept and made available by commercial webcasters or noncommercial webcasters. The receiving agent shall be under no obligation to negotiate any such agreement. The receiving agent shall have no obligation to any copyright owner of sound recordings or any other person entitled to payment under this section in negotiating any such agreement, and no liability to any copyright owner of sound recordings or any other person entitled to payment under this section for having entered into such agreement.

(B) The Copyright Office shall cause to be published in the Federal Register any agreement entered into pursuant to subparagraph (A). Such publication shall include a statement containing the substance of subparagraph (C). Such agreements shall not be included in the Code of Federal Regulations. Thereafter, the terms of such agreement shall be available, as an option, to any commercial webcaster or noncommercial webcaster meeting the eligibility conditions of such agreement.

(C) Neither subparagraph (A) nor any provisions of any agreement entered into pursuant to subparagraph (A), including any rate structure, fees, terms, conditions, or notice and recordkeeping requirements set forth therein, shall be admissible as evidence or otherwise taken into account in any administrative, judicial, or other government proceeding involving the setting or adjustment of the royalties payable for the public performance or reproduction in ephemeral phonorecords or copies of sound recordings, the determination of terms or conditions related thereto, or the establishment of notice or recordkeeping requirements by the Copyright Royalty Judges under paragraph (3) or section 112(e)(4). It is the intent of Congress that any royalty rates, rate structure, definitions, terms, conditions, or notice and recordkeeping requirements, included in such agreements shall be considered as a compromise motivated by the unique business, economic and political circumstances of webcasters, copyright owners, and performers rather than as matters that would have been negotiated in the marketplace between a willing buyer and a willing seller, or otherwise meet the objectives set forth in section 801(b). This subparagraph shall not apply to the extent that the receiving agent and a webcaster that is party to an agreement entered into pursuant to subparagraph (A) expressly authorize the submission of the agreement in a proceeding under this subsection.

(D) Nothing in the Webcaster Settlement Act of 2008, the Webcaster Settlement Act of 2009, or any agreement entered into pursuant to subparagraph (A) shall be taken into account by the United States Court of Appeals for the District of Columbia Circuit in its review of the determination by the Copyright Royalty Judges of May 1, 2007, of rates and terms for the digital performance of sound recordings and ephemeral recordings, pursuant to sections 112 and 114.

(E) As used in this paragraph—

(i) the term "noncommercial webcaster" means a webcaster that—

(I) is exempt from taxation under section 501 of the Internal Revenue Code of 1986 (26 U.S.C. 501);

(II) has applied in good faith to the Internal Revenue Service for exemption from taxation under section 501 of the Internal Revenue Code and has a commercially reasonable expectation that such exemption shall be granted; or

(III) is operated by a State or possession or any governmental entity or subordinate thereof, or by the United States or District of Columbia, for exclusively public purposes;

(ii) the term "receiving agent" shall have the meaning given that term in section 261.2 of title 37, Code of Federal Regulations, as published in the Federal Register on July 8, 2002; and

(iii) the term "webcaster" means a person or entity that has obtained a compulsory license under section 112 or 114 and the implementing regulations therefore.

(F) The authority to make settlements pursuant to subparagraph (A) shall expire at 11:59 p.m. Eastern time on the 39th day after the date of the enactment of the Webcaster Settlement Act of 2009.

(g) Proceeds From Licensing of Transmissions.—

(1) Except in the case of a transmission licensed under a statutory license in accordance with subsection (f) of this section—

(A) a featured recording artist who performs on a sound recording that has been licensed for a transmission shall be entitled to receive payments from the copyright owner of the sound recording in accordance with the terms of the artist's contract; and

(B) a nonfeatured recording artist who performs on a sound recording that has been licensed for a transmission shall be entitled to receive payments from the copyright owner of the sound recording in accordance with the terms of the nonfeatured recording artist's applicable contract or other applicable agreement.

(2) An agent designated to distribute receipts from the licensing of transmissions in accordance with subsection (f) shall distribute such receipts as follows:

(A) 50 percent of the receipts shall be paid to the copyright owner of the exclusive right under section 106(6) of this title to publicly perform a sound recording by means of a digital audio transmission.

(B) 2 1/2 percent of the receipts shall be deposited in an escrow account managed by an independent administrator jointly appointed by copyright owners of sound recordings and the American Federation of Musicians (or any successor entity) to be distributed to nonfeatured musicians (whether or not members of the American Federation of Musicians) who have performed on sound recordings.

(C) 2 1/2 percent of the receipts shall be deposited in an escrow account managed by an independent administrator jointly appointed by copyright owners of sound recordings and the American Federation of Television and Radio Artists (or any successor entity) to be distributed to nonfeatured vocalists (whether or not members of the American Federation of Television and Radio Artists) who have performed on sound recordings.

(D) 45 percent of the receipts shall be paid, on a per sound recording basis, to the recording artist or artists featured on such sound recording (or the persons conveying rights in the artists' performance in the sound recordings).

(3) A nonprofit agent designated to distribute receipts from the licensing of transmissions in accordance with subsection (f) may deduct from any of its receipts, prior to the distribution of such receipts to any person or entity entitled thereto other than copyright owners and performers who have elected to receive royalties from another designated agent and have notified such nonprofit agent in writing of such election, the reasonable costs of such agent incurred after November 1, 1995, in—

(A) the administration of the collection, distribution, and calculation of the royalties;

(B) the settlement of disputes relating to the collection and calculation of the royalties; and

(C) the licensing and enforcement of rights with respect to the making of ephemeral recordings and performances subject to licensing under section 112 and this section, including those incurred in participating in negotiations or arbitration proceedings under section 112 and this section, except that all costs incurred relating to the section 112 ephemeral recordings right may only be deducted from the royalties received pursuant to section 112.

(4) Notwithstanding paragraph (3), any designated agent designated to distribute receipts from the licensing of transmissions in accordance with subsection (f) may deduct from any of its receipts, prior to the distribution of such receipts, the reasonable costs identified in paragraph (3) of such agent incurred after November 1, 1995, with respect to such copyright owners and performers who have entered with such agent a contractual relationship that specifies that such costs may be deducted from such royalty receipts.

(5) Letter of Direction.—

(A) In General.—A nonprofit collective designated by the Copyright Royalty Judges to distribute receipts from the licensing of transmissions in accordance with subsection (f) shall adopt and reasonably implement a policy that provides, in circumstances determined by the collective to be appropriate, for acceptance of instructions from a payee identified under subparagraph (A) or (D) of paragraph (2) to distribute, to a producer, mixer, or sound engineer who was part of the creative process that created a sound recording, a portion of the payments to which the payee would otherwise be entitled from the licensing of transmissions of the sound recording. In this section, such instructions shall be referred to as a "letter of direction".

(B) Acceptance of letter.—To the extent that a collective described in subparagraph (A) accepts a letter of direction under that subparagraph, the person entitled to payment pursuant to the letter of direction shall, during the period in which the letter of direction is in effect and carried out by the collective, be treated for all purposes as the owner of the right to receive such payment, and the payee providing the letter of direction to the collective shall be treated as having no interest in such payment.*

---

* This provision is not effective until January 1, 2020.—*Ed.*

(C) Authority of Collective.—This paragraph shall not be construed in such a manner so that the collective is not authorized to accept or act upon payment instructions in circumstances other than those to which this paragraph applies.

(6) Sound Recordings Fixed Before November 1, 1995.—

(A) Payment Absent Letter of Direction.—A nonprofit collective designated by the Copyright Royalty Judges to distribute receipts from the licensing of transmissions in accordance with subsection (f) (in this paragraph referred to as the "collective") shall adopt and reasonably implement a policy that provides, in circumstances determined by the collective to be appropriate, for the deduction of 2 percent of all the receipts that are collected from the licensing of transmissions of a sound recording fixed before November 1, 1995, but which is withdrawn from the amount otherwise payable under paragraph (2)(D) to the recording artist or artists featured on the sound recording (or the persons conveying rights in the artists' performance in the sound recording), and the distribution of such amount to 1 or more persons described in subparagraph (B) of this paragraph, after deduction of costs described in paragraph (3) or (4), as applicable, if each of the following requirements is met:

(i) Certification of Attempt to Obtain a Letter of Direction.—The person described in subparagraph (B) who is to receive the distribution has certified to the collective, under penalty of perjury, that—

(I) for a period of not less than 120 days, that person made reasonable efforts to contact the artist payee for such sound recording to request and obtain a letter of direction instructing the collective to pay to that person a portion of the royalties payable to the featured recording artist or artists; and

(II) during the period beginning on the date on which that person began the reasonable efforts described in subclause (I) and ending on the date of that person's certification to the collective, the artist payee did not affirm or deny in writing the request for a letter of direction.

(ii) Collective Attempt to Contact Artist.—After receipt of the certification described in clause (i) and for a period of not less than 120 days before the first distribution by the collective to the person described in subparagraph (B), the collective attempts, in a reasonable manner as determined by the collective, to notify the artist payee of the certification made by the person described in subparagraph (B).

(iii) No Objection Received.—The artist payee does not, as of the date that was 10 business days before the date on which the first distribution is made, submit to the collective in writing an objection to the distribution.

(B) Eligibility for Payment.—A person shall be eligible for payment under subparagraph (A) if the person—

(i)   is a producer, mixer, or sound engineer of the sound recording;

(ii)   has entered into a written contract with a record company involved in the creation or lawful exploitation of the sound recording, or with the recording artist or artists featured on the sound recording (or the persons conveying rights in the artists' performance in the sound recording), under which the person seeking payment is entitled to participate in royalty payments that are based on the exploitation of the sound recording and are payable from royalties otherwise payable to the recording artist or artists featured on the sound recording (or the persons conveying rights in the artists' performance in the sound recording);

(iii)   made a creative contribution to the creation of the sound recording; and

(iv)   submits to the collective—

(I) a written certification stating, under penalty of perjury, that the person meets the requirements in clauses (i) through (iii); and

(II) a true copy of the contract described in clause (ii).

(C) Multiple Certifications.—Subject to subparagraph (D), in a case in which more than 1 person described in subparagraph (B) has met the requirements for a distribution under subparagraph (A) with respect to a sound recording as of the date that is 10 business days before the date on which the distribution is made, the collective shall divide the 2 percent distribution equally among all such persons.

(D) Objection to Payment.—Not later than 10 business days after the date on which the collective receives from the artist payee a written objection to a distribution made pursuant to subparagraph (A), the collective shall cease making any further payment relating to such distribution. In any case in which the collective has made 1 or more distributions pursuant to subparagraph (A) to a person described in subparagraph (B) before the date that is 10 business days after the date on which the collective receives from the artist payee an objection to such distribution, the objection shall not affect that person's entitlement to any distribution made before the collective ceases such distribution under this subparagraph.

(E) Ownership of the Right to Receive Payments.—To the extent that the collective determines that a distribution will be made under subparagraph (A) to a person described in subparagraph (B), such person shall, during the period covered by such distribution, be treated for all purposes as the owner of the right to receive such payments, and the artist payee to whom such payments would otherwise be payable shall be treated as having no interest in such payments.[*]

(F) Artist Payee Defined.—In this paragraph, the term "artist payee" means a person, other than a person described in subparagraph (B), who owns the right to receive all or part of the receipts payable under paragraph (2)(D) with respect to a sound recording. In a case in which there are multiple artist payees with respect to a sound recording, an objection by 1 such payee shall apply only to that payee's share of the receipts payable under paragraph (2)(D), and shall not preclude payment under subparagraph (A) from the share of an artist payee that does not so object.

(7) Preemption of State Property Laws.—The holding and distribution of receipts under section 112 and this section by a nonprofit collective designated by the Copyright Royalty Judges in accordance with this subsection and regulations adopted by the Copyright Royalty Judges, or by an independent administrator pursuant to subparagraphs (B) and (C) of section 114(g)(2), shall supersede and preempt any State law (including common law) concerning escheatment or abandoned property, or any analogous provision, that might otherwise apply.

(h) Licensing to Affiliates.—

(1) If the copyright owner of a sound recording licenses an affiliated entity the right to publicly perform a sound recording by means of a digital audio transmission under section 106(6), the copyright owner shall make the licensed sound recording available under section 106(6) on no less favorable terms and conditions to all bona fide entities that offer similar services, except that, if there are material differences in the scope of the requested license with respect to the type of service, the particular sound recordings licensed, the frequency of use, the number of subscribers served, or the duration, then the copyright owner may establish different terms and conditions for such other services.

(2) The limitation set forth in paragraph (1) of this subsection shall not apply in the case where the copyright owner of a sound recording licenses—

---

[*] This subsection is not effective until January 1, 2020.—*Ed.*

(A)   an interactive service; or

(B)   an entity to perform publicly up to 45 seconds of the sound recording and the sole purpose of the performance is to promote the distribution or performance of that sound recording.

(i)   [Repealed.]

(j)   Definitions.—As used in this section, the following terms have the following meanings:

(1)   An "affiliated entity" is an entity engaging in digital audio transmissions covered by section 106(6), other than an interactive service, in which the licensor has any direct or indirect partnership or any ownership interest amounting to 5 percent or more of the outstanding voting or non-voting stock.

(2)   An "archived program" is a predetermined program that is available repeatedly on the demand of the transmission recipient and that is performed in the same order from the beginning, except that an archived program shall not include a recorded event or broadcast transmission that makes no more than an incidental use of sound recordings, as long as such recorded event or broadcast transmission does not contain an entire sound recording or feature a particular sound recording.

(3)   A "broadcast" transmission is a transmission made by a terrestrial broadcast station licensed as such by the Federal Communications Commission.

(4)   A "continuous program" is a predetermined program that is continuously performed in the same order and that is accessed at a point in the program that is beyond the control of the transmission recipient.

(5)   A "digital audio transmission" is a digital transmission as defined in section 101, that embodies the transmission of a sound recording. This term does not include the transmission of any audiovisual work.

(6)   An "eligible nonsubscription transmission" is a noninteractive nonsubscription digital audio transmission not exempt under subsection (d)(1) that is made as part of a service that provides audio programming consisting, in whole or in part, of performances of sound recordings, including retransmissions of broadcast transmissions, if the primary purpose of the service is to provide to the public such audio or other entertainment programming, and the primary purpose of the service is not to sell, advertise, or promote particular products or services other than sound recordings, live concerts, or other music-related events.

(7)   An "interactive service" is one that enables a member of the public to receive a transmission of a program specially created for the recipient, or on request, a transmission of a particular sound recording, whether or not as part of a program, which is selected by or on behalf of the recipient. The ability of individuals to request that particular sound recordings be performed for reception by the public at large, or in the case of a subscription service, by all subscribers of the service, does not make a service interactive, if the programming on each channel of the service does not substantially consist of sound recordings that are performed within 1 hour of the request or at a time designated by either the transmitting entity or the individual making such request. If an entity offers both interactive and noninteractive services (either concurrently or at different times), the noninteractive component shall not be treated as part of an interactive service.

(8)   A "new subscription service" is a service that performs sound recordings by means of noninteractive subscription digital audio transmissions and that is not a preexisting subscription service or a preexisting satellite digital audio radio service.

(9)   A "nonsubscription" transmission is any transmission that is not a subscription transmission.

(10) A "preexisting satellite digital audio radio service" is a subscription satellite digital audio radio service provided pursuant to a satellite digital audio radio service license issued by the Federal Communications Commission on or before July 31, 1998, and any renewal of such license to the extent of the scope of the original license, and may include a limited number of sample channels representative of the subscription service that are made available on a nonsubscription basis in order to promote the subscription service.

(11) A "preexisting subscription service" is a service that performs sound recordings by means of noninteractive audio-only subscription digital audio transmissions, which was in existence and was making such transmissions to the public for a fee on or before July 31, 1998, and may include a limited number of sample channels representative of the subscription service that are made available on a nonsubscription basis in order to promote the subscription service.

(12) A "retransmission" is a further transmission of an initial transmission, and includes any further retransmission of the same transmission. Except as provided in this section, a transmission qualifies as a "retransmission" only if it is simultaneous with the initial transmission. Nothing in this definition shall be construed to exempt a transmission that fails to satisfy a separate element required to qualify for an exemption under section 114(d)(1).

(13) The "sound recording performance complement" is the transmission during any 3-hour period, on a particular channel used by a transmitting entity, of no more than—

(A) 3 different selections of sound recordings from any one phonorecord lawfully distributed for public performance or sale in the United States, if no more than 2 such selections are transmitted consecutively; or

(B) 4 different selections of sound recordings—

(i) by the same featured recording artist; or

(ii) from any set or compilation of phonorecords lawfully distributed together as a unit for public performance or sale in the United States,

if no more than three such selections are transmitted consecutively:

Provided, That the transmission of selections in excess of the numerical limits provided for in clauses (A) and (B) from multiple phonorecords shall nonetheless qualify as a sound recording performance complement if the programming of the multiple phonorecords was not willfully intended to avoid the numerical limitations prescribed in such clauses.

(14) A "subscription" transmission is a transmission that is controlled and limited to particular recipients, and for which consideration is required to be paid or otherwise given by or on behalf of the recipient to receive the transmission or a package of transmissions including the transmission.

(15) A "transmission" is either an initial transmission or a retransmission.

§ 115. Scope of Exclusive Rights in Nondramatic Musical Works: Compulsory License for Making and Distributing Phonorecords

In the case of nondramatic musical works, the exclusive rights provided by clauses (1) and (3) of section 106, to make and to distribute phonorecords of such works, are subject to compulsory licensing under the conditions specified by this section.

(a) **Availability and Scope of Compulsory License in General.—**

(1) **Eligibility for Compulsory License.—**

(A) **Conditions for Compulsory License.—**A person may by complying with the provisions of this section obtain a compulsory license to make and distribute phonorecords of a nondramatic musical work, including by means of digital phonorecord delivery. A person may obtain a compulsory license only if the primary purpose in making phonorecords of the musical work is to distribute them to the public for private use, including by means of digital phonorecord delivery, and—

(i) phonorecords of such musical work have previously been distributed to the public in the United States under the authority of the copyright owner of the work, including by means of digital phonorecord delivery; or

(ii) in the case of a digital music provider seeking to make and distribute digital phonorecord deliveries of a sound recording embodying a musical work under a compulsory license for which clause (i) does not apply—

(I) the first fixation of such sound recording was made under the authority of the musical work copyright owner, and the sound recording copyright owner has the authority of the musical work copyright owner to make and distribute digital phonorecord deliveries embodying such work to the public in the United States; and

(II) the sound recording copyright owner, or the authorized distributor of the sound recording copyright owner, has authorized the digital music provider to make and distribute digital phonorecord deliveries of the sound recording to the public in the United States.

(B) **Duplication of Sound Recording.**—A person may not obtain a compulsory license for the use of the work in the making of phonorecords duplicating a sound recording fixed by another, including by means of digital phonorecord delivery, unless—

(i) such sound recording was fixed lawfully; and

(ii) the making of the phonorecords was authorized by the owner of the copyright in the sound recording or, if the sound recording was fixed before February 15, 1972, by any person who fixed the sound recording pursuant to an express license from the owner of the copyright in the musical work or pursuant to a valid compulsory license for use of such work in a sound recording.

(2) **Musical Arrangement.**—A compulsory license includes the privilege of making a musical arrangement of the work to the extent necessary to conform it to the style or manner of interpretation of the performance involved, but the arrangement shall not change the basic melody or fundamental character of the work, and shall not be subject to protection as a derivative work under this title, except with the express consent of the copyright owner.

(b) **Procedures to Obtain Compulsory License.**—

(1) **Phonorecords Other than Digital Phonorecord Deliveries.**—A person who seeks to obtain a compulsory license under subsection (a) to make and distribute phonorecords of a musical work other than by means of digital phonorecord delivery shall, before, or not later than 30 calendar days after, making, and before distributing, any phonorecord of the work, serve notice of intention to do so on the copyright owner. If the registration or other public records of the Copyright Office do not identify the copyright owner and include an address at which notice can be served, it shall be sufficient to file the notice of intention with the Copyright Office. The notice shall comply, in form, content, and manner of service, with requirements that the Register of Copyrights shall prescribe by regulation.

(2) **Digital Phonorecord Deliveries.**—A person who seeks to obtain a compulsory license under subsection (a) to make and distribute phonorecords of a musical work by means of digital phonorecord delivery—

(A) prior to the license availability date, shall, before, or not later than 30 calendar days after, first making any such digital phonorecord delivery, serve a notice of intention to do so on the copyright owner (but may not file the notice with the Copyright Office, even if the public records of the Office do not identify the owner or the owner's address), and such notice shall comply, in form, content, and manner of service, with requirements that the Register of Copyrights shall prescribe by regulation; or

(B) on or after the license availability date, shall, before making any such digital phonorecord delivery, follow the procedure described in subsection (d)(2), except as provided in paragraph (3).

(3) **Record Company Individual Download Licenses.**—Notwithstanding paragraph (2)(B), a record company may, on or after the license availability date, obtain an individual download license in accordance with the notice requirements described in paragraph (2)(A) (except for the requirement that notice occur prior to the license availability date). A record company that obtains an individual download license as permitted under this paragraph shall provide statements of account and pay royalties as provided in subsection (c)(2)(I).

(4) **Failure to Obtain License.**—

(A) **Phonorecords Other than Digital Phonorecord Deliveries.**—In the case of phonorecords made and distributed other than by means of digital phonorecord delivery, the failure to serve or file the notice of intention required by paragraph (1) forecloses the possibility of a compulsory license under paragraph (1). In the absence of a voluntary license, the failure to obtain a compulsory license renders the making and distribution of phonorecords actionable as acts of infringement under section 501 and subject to the remedies provided by sections 502 through 506.

(B) **Digital Phonorecord Deliveries.**—

(i) **In General.**—In the case of phonorecords made and distributed by means of digital phonorecord delivery:

(I) The failure to serve the notice of intention required by paragraph (2)(A) or paragraph (3), as applicable, forecloses the possibility of a compulsory license under such paragraph.

(II) The failure to comply with paragraph (2)(B) forecloses the possibility of a blanket license for a period of 3 years after the last calendar day on which the notice of license was required to be submitted to the mechanical licensing collective under such paragraph.

(ii) **Effect of Failure.**—In either case described in subclause (I) or (II) of clause (i), in the absence of a voluntary license, the failure to obtain a compulsory license renders the making and distribution of phonorecords by means of digital phonorecord delivery actionable as acts of infringement under section 501 and subject to the remedies provided by sections 502 through 506.

(c) **General Conditions Applicable to Compulsory License.**—

(1) **Royalty Payable Under Compulsory License.**—

(A) **Identification Requirement.**—To be entitled to receive royalties under a compulsory license obtained under subsection (b)(1) the copyright owner must be identified in the registration or other public records of the Copyright Office. The owner is entitled to royalties for phonorecords made and distributed after being so identified, but is not entitled to recover for any phonorecords previously made and distributed.

(B) **Royalty for Phonorecords Other than Digital Phonorecord Deliveries.**— Except as provided by subparagraph (A), for every phonorecord made and distributed under a compulsory license under subsection (a) other than by means of digital phonorecord delivery, with respect to each work embodied in the phonorecord, the royalty shall be the royalty prescribed under subparagraphs (D) through (F), paragraph (2)(A), and chapter 8. For purposes of this subparagraph, a phonorecord is considered "distributed" if the person exercising the compulsory license has voluntarily and permanently parted with its possession.

(C) **Royalty for Digital Phonorecord Deliveries.**—For every digital phonorecord delivery of a musical work made under a compulsory license under this section, the royalty payable shall be the royalty prescribed under subparagraphs (D) through (F), paragraph (2)(A), and chapter 8.

(D) **Authority to Negotiate.**—Notwithstanding any provision of the antitrust laws, any copyright owners of nondramatic musical works and any persons entitled to obtain a compulsory license under subsection (a) may negotiate and agree upon the terms and rates of royalty payments under this section and the proportionate division of fees paid among copyright owners, and may designate common agents on a nonexclusive basis to negotiate, agree to, pay or receive such royalty payments. Such authority to negotiate the terms and rates of royalty payments includes, but is not limited to, the authority to negotiate the year during which the royalty rates prescribed under this subparagraph, subparagraphs (E) and (F), paragraph (2)(A), and chapter 8 shall next be determined.

(E) **Determination of Reasonable Rates and Terms.**—Proceedings under chapter 8 shall determine reasonable rates and terms of royalty payments for the activities specified by this section during the period beginning with the effective date of such rates and terms, but not earlier than January 1 of the second year following the year in which the petition requesting the proceeding is filed, and ending on the effective date of successor rates and terms, or such other period as the parties may agree. Any copyright owners of nondramatic musical works and any persons entitled to obtain a compulsory license under subsection (a) may submit to the Copyright Royalty Judges licenses covering such activities. The parties to each proceeding shall bear their own costs.

(F) **Schedule of Reasonable Rates.**—The schedule of reasonable rates and terms determined by the Copyright Royalty Judges shall, subject to paragraph (2)(A), be binding on all copyright owners of nondramatic musical works and persons entitled to obtain a compulsory license under subsection (a) during the period specified in subparagraph (E), such other period as may be determined pursuant to subparagraphs (D) and (E), or such other period as the parties may agree. The Copyright Royalty Judges shall establish rates and terms that most clearly represent the rates and terms that would have been negotiated in the marketplace between a willing buyer and a willing seller. In determining such rates and terms for digital phonorecord deliveries, the Copyright Royalty Judges shall base their decision on economic, competitive, and programming information presented by the parties, including—

(i)   whether use of the compulsory licensee's service may substitute for or may promote the sales of phonorecords or otherwise may interfere with or may enhance the musical work copyright owner's other streams of revenue from its musical works; and

(ii)   the relative roles of the copyright owner and the compulsory licensee in the copyrighted work and the service made available to the public with respect to the relative creative contribution, technological contribution, capital investment, cost, and risk.

(2)   **Additional Terms and Conditions.**—

(A)   **Voluntary Licenses and Contractual Royalty Rates.**—

(i)   **In General.**—License agreements voluntarily negotiated at any time between one or more copyright owners of nondramatic musical works and one or more persons entitled to obtain a compulsory license under subsection (a) shall be given effect in lieu of any determination by the Copyright Royalty Judges. Subject to clause (ii), the royalty rates determined pursuant to subparagraphs (E) and (F) of paragraph (1) shall be given effect as to digital phonorecord deliveries in lieu of any contrary royalty rates specified in a contract pursuant to which a recording artist who is the author of a nondramatic musical work grants a license under that person's exclusive rights in the musical work under paragraphs (1) and (3) of section 106 or commits another person to grant a license in that musical work under paragraphs (1) and (3) of section 106, to a person desiring to fix in a tangible medium of expression a sound recording embodying the musical work.

(ii) **Applicability.**—The second sentence of clause (i) shall not apply to—

(I) a contract entered into on or before June 22, 1995, and not modified thereafter for the purpose of reducing the royalty rates determined pursuant to subparagraphs (E) and (F) of paragraph (1) or of increasing the number of musical works within the scope of the contract covered by the reduced rates, except if a contract entered into on or before June 22, 1995, is modified thereafter for the purpose of increasing the number of musical works within the scope of the contract, any contrary royalty rates specified in the contract shall be given effect in lieu of royalty rates determined pursuant to subparagraphs (E) and (F) of paragraph (1) for the number of musical works within the scope of the contract as of June 22, 1995; and

(II) a contract entered into after the date that the sound recording is fixed in a tangible medium of expression substantially in a form intended for commercial release, if at the time the contract is entered into, the recording artist retains the right to grant licenses as to the musical work under paragraphs (1) and (3) of section 106.

(B) **Sound Recording Information.**—Except as provided in section 1002(e), a digital phonorecord delivery licensed under this paragraph shall be accompanied by the information encoded in the sound recording, if any, by or under the authority of the copyright owner of that sound recording, that identifies the title of the sound recording, the featured recording artist who performs on the sound recording, and related information, including information concerning the underlying musical work and its writer.

(C) **Infringement Remedies.**—

(i) **In General.**—A digital phonorecord delivery of a sound recording is actionable as an act of infringement under section 501, and is fully subject to the remedies provided by sections 502 through 506, unless—

(I) the digital phonorecord delivery has been authorized by the sound recording copyright owner; and

(II) the entity making the digital phonorecord delivery has obtained a compulsory license under subsection (a) or has otherwise been authorized by the musical work copyright owner, or by a record company pursuant to an individual download license, to make and distribute phonorecords of each musical work embodied in the sound recording by means of digital phonorecord delivery.

(ii) **Other Remedies.**—Any cause of action under this subparagraph shall be in addition to those available to the owner of the copyright in the nondramatic musical work under subparagraph (J) and section 106(4) and the owner of the copyright in the sound recording under section 106(6).

(D) **Liability of Sound Recording Owners.**—The liability of the copyright owner of a sound recording for infringement of the copyright in a nondramatic musical work embodied in the sound recording shall be determined in accordance with applicable law, except that the owner of a copyright in a sound recording shall not be liable for a digital phonorecord delivery by a third party if the owner of the copyright in the sound recording does not license the distribution of a phonorecord of the nondramatic musical work.

(E) **Recording Devices and Media.**—Nothing in section 1008 shall be construed to prevent the exercise of the rights and remedies allowed by this paragraph, subparagraph (J), and chapter 5 in the event of a digital phonorecord delivery, except that no action alleging infringement of copyright may be brought under this title against a manufacturer, importer or distributor of a digital audio recording device, a digital audio recording medium, an analog recording device, or an analog recording medium, or against a consumer, based on the actions described in such section.

(F) **Preservation of Rights.**—Nothing in this section annuls or limits—

(i) the exclusive right to publicly perform a sound recording or the musical work embodied therein, including by means of a digital transmission, under paragraphs (4) and (6) of section 106;

(ii) except for compulsory licensing under the conditions specified by this section, the exclusive rights to reproduce and distribute the sound recording and the musical work embodied therein under paragraphs (1) and (3) of section 106, including by means of a digital phonorecord delivery; or

(iii) any other rights under any other provision of section 106, or remedies available under this title, as such rights or remedies exist before, on, or after the date of enactment of the Digital Performance Right in Sound Recordings Act of 1995.

(G) **Exempt Transmissions and Retransmissions.**—The provisions of this section concerning digital phonorecord deliveries shall not apply to any exempt transmissions or retransmissions under section 114(d)(1). The exemptions created in section 114(d)(1) do not expand or reduce the rights of copyright owners under paragraphs (1) through (5) of section 106 with respect to such transmissions and retransmissions.

(H) **Distribution by Rental, Lease, or Lending.**—A compulsory license obtained under subsection (b)(1) to make and distribute phonorecords includes the right of the maker of such a phonorecord to distribute or authorize distribution of such phonorecord, other than by means of a digital phonorecord delivery, by rental, lease, or lending (or by acts or practices in the nature of rental, lease, or lending). With respect to each nondramatic musical work embodied in the phonorecord, the royalty shall be a proportion of the revenue received by the compulsory licensee from every such act of distribution of the phonorecord under this clause equal to the proportion of the revenue received by the compulsory licensee from distribution of the phonorecord under subsection (a)(1)(A)(ii)(II) that is payable by a compulsory licensee under that clause and under chapter 8. The Register of Copyrights shall issue regulations to carry out the purpose of this subparagraph.

(I) **Payment of Royalties and Statements of Account.**—Except as provided in paragraphs (4)(A)(i) and (10)(B) of subsection (d), royalty payments shall be made on or before the twentieth day of each month and shall include all royalties for the month next preceding. Each monthly payment shall be made under oath and shall comply with requirements that the Register of Copyrights shall prescribe by regulation. The Register shall also prescribe regulations under which detailed cumulative annual statements of account, certified by a certified public accountant, shall be filed for every compulsory license under subsection (a). The regulations covering both the monthly and the annual statements of account shall prescribe the form, content, and manner of certification with respect to the number of records made and the number of records distributed.

(J) **Notice of Default and Termination of Compulsory License.**—In the case of a license obtained under paragraph (1), (2)(A), or (3) of subsection (b), if the copyright owner does not receive the monthly payment and the monthly and annual statements of account when due, the owner may give written notice to the licensee that, unless the default is remedied not later than 30 days after the date on which the notice is sent, the compulsory license will be automatically terminated. Such termination renders either the making or the distribution, or both, of all phonorecords for which the royalty has not been paid, actionable as acts of infringement under section 501 and fully subject to the remedies provided by sections 502 through 506. In the case of a license obtained under subsection (b)(2)(B), license authority under the compulsory license may be terminated as provided in subsection (d)(4)(E).

(d) Blanket License for Digital Uses, Mechanical Licensing Collective, and Digital Licensee Coordinator.—

(1) **Blanket License for Digital Uses.—**

(A) **In General.—**A digital music provider that qualifies for a compulsory license under subsection (a) may, by complying with the terms and conditions of this subsection, obtain a blanket license from copyright owners through the mechanical licensing collective to make and distribute digital phonorecord deliveries of musical works through one or more covered activities.

(B) **Included Activities.—**A blanket license—

(i) covers all musical works (or shares of such works) available for compulsory licensing under this section for purposes of engaging in covered activities, except as provided in subparagraph (C);

(ii) includes the making and distribution of server, intermediate, archival, and incidental reproductions of musical works that are reasonable and necessary for the digital music provider to engage in covered activities licensed under this subsection, solely for the purpose of engaging in such covered activities; and

(iii) does not cover or include any rights or uses other than those described in clauses (i) and (ii).

(C) **Other Licenses.—**A voluntary license for covered activities entered into by or under the authority of 1 or more copyright owners and 1 or more digital music providers, or authority to make and distribute permanent downloads of a musical work obtained by a digital music provider from a sound recording copyright owner pursuant to an individual download license, shall be given effect in lieu of a blanket license under this subsection with respect to the musical works (or shares thereof) covered by such voluntary license or individual download authority and the following conditions apply:

(i) Where a voluntary license or individual download license applies, the license authority provided under the blanket license shall exclude any musical works (or shares thereof) subject to the voluntary license or individual download license.

(ii) An entity engaged in covered activities under a voluntary license or authority obtained pursuant to an individual download license that is a significant nonblanket licensee shall comply with paragraph (6)(A).

(iii) The rates and terms of any voluntary license shall be subject to the second sentence of clause (i) and clause (ii) of subsection (c)(2)(A) and paragraph (9)(C), as applicable.

(D) **Protection Against Infringement Actions.—**A digital music provider that obtains and complies with the terms of a valid blanket license under this subsection shall not be subject to an action for infringement of the exclusive rights provided by paragraphs (1) and (3) of section 106 under this title arising from use of a musical work (or share thereof) to engage in covered activities authorized by such license, subject to paragraph (4)(E).

(E) **Other Requirements and Conditions Apply.**—Except as expressly provided in this subsection, each requirement, limitation, condition, privilege, right, and remedy otherwise applicable to compulsory licenses under this section shall apply to compulsory blanket licenses under this subsection.

(2) **Availability of Blanket License.**—

(A) **Procedure for Obtaining License.**—A digital music provider may obtain a blanket license by submitting a notice of license to the mechanical licensing collective that specifies the particular covered activities in which the digital music provider seeks to engage, as follows:

(i)   The notice of license shall comply in form and substance with requirements that the Register of Copyrights shall establish by regulation.

(ii)   Unless rejected in writing by the mechanical licensing collective not later than 30 calendar days after the date on which the mechanical licensing collective receives the notice, the blanket license shall be effective as of the date on which the notice of license was sent by the digital music provider, as shown by a physical or electronic record.

(iii)   A notice of license may only be rejected by the mechanical licensing collective if—

(I)   the digital music provider or notice of license does not meet the requirements of this section or applicable regulations, in which case the requirements at issue shall be specified with reasonable particularity in the notice of rejection; or

(II)   the digital music provider has had a blanket license terminated by the mechanical licensing collective during the 3-year period preceding the date on which the mechanical licensing collective receives the notice pursuant to paragraph (4)(E).

(iv)   If a notice of license is rejected under clause (iii)(I), the digital music provider shall have 30 calendar days after receipt of the notice of rejection to cure any deficiency and submit an amended notice of license to the mechanical licensing collective. If the deficiency has been cured, the mechanical licensing collective shall so confirm in writing, and the license shall be effective as of the date that the original notice of license was provided by the digital music provider.

(v)   A digital music provider that believes a notice of license was improperly rejected by the mechanical licensing collective may seek review of such rejection in an appropriate district court of the United States. The district court shall determine the matter de novo based on the record before the mechanical licensing collective and any additional evidence presented by the parties.

(B) **Blanket License Effective Date.**—Blanket licenses shall be made available by the mechanical licensing collective on and after the license availability date. No such license shall be effective prior to the license availability date.

(3) **Mechanical Licensing Collective.**—

(A) **In General.**—The mechanical licensing collective shall be a single entity that—

(i)   is a nonprofit entity, not owned by any other entity, that is created by copyright owners to carry out responsibilities under this subsection;

(ii)   is endorsed by, and enjoys substantial support from, musical work copyright owners that together represent the greatest percentage of the licensor market for uses of such works in covered activities, as measured over the preceding 3 full calendar years;

(iii) is able to demonstrate to the Register of Copyrights that the entity has, or will have prior to the license availability date, the administrative and technological capabilities to perform the required functions of the mechanical licensing collective under this subsection and that is governed by a board of directors in accordance with subparagraph (D)(i); and

(iv) has been designated by the Register of Copyrights, with the approval of the Librarian of Congress pursuant to section 702, in accordance with subparagraph (B).

(B) **Designation of Mechanical Licensing Collective.—**

(i) **Initial Designation.—**Not later than 270 days after the enactment date, the Register of Copyrights shall initially designate the mechanical licensing collective as follows:

(I) Not later than 90 calendar days after the enactment date, the Register shall publish notice in the Federal Register soliciting information to assist in identifying the appropriate entity to serve as the mechanical licensing collective, including the name and affiliation of each member of the board of directors described under subparagraph (D)(i) and each committee established pursuant to clauses (iii), (iv), and (v) of subparagraph (D).

(II) After reviewing the information requested under subclause (I) and making a designation, the Register shall publish notice in the Federal Register setting forth—

(aa) the identity of and contact information for the mechanical licensing collective; and

(bb) the reasons for the designation.

(ii) **Periodic Review of Designation.—**Following the initial designation of the mechanical licensing collective, the Register shall, every 5 years, beginning with the fifth full calendar year to commence after the initial designation, publish notice in the Federal Register in the month of January soliciting information concerning whether the existing designation should be continued, or a different entity meeting the criteria described in clauses (i) through (iii) of subparagraph (A) shall be designated. Following publication of such notice, the Register shall—

(I) after reviewing the information submitted and conducting additional proceedings as appropriate, publish notice in the Federal Register of a continuing designation or new designation of the mechanical licensing collective, as the case may be, and the reasons for such a designation, with any new designation to be effective as of the first day of a month that is not less than 6 months and not longer than 9 months after the date on which the Register publishes the notice, as specified by the Register; and

(II) if a new entity is designated as the mechanical licensing collective, adopt regulations to govern the transfer of licenses, funds, records, data, and administrative responsibilities from the existing mechanical licensing collective to the new entity.

(iii) **Closest Alternative Designation.—**If the Register is unable to identify an entity that fulfills each of the qualifications set forth in clauses (i) through (iii) of subparagraph (A), the Register shall designate the entity that most nearly fulfills such qualifications for purposes of carrying out the responsibilities of the mechanical licensing collective.

(C) **Authorities and Functions.—**

(i) **In General.—**The mechanical licensing collective is authorized to perform the following functions, subject to more particular requirements as described in this subsection:

(I) Offer and administer blanket licenses, including receipt of notices of license and reports of usage from digital music providers.

(II) Collect and distribute royalties from digital music providers for covered activities.

(III) Engage in efforts to identify musical works (and shares of such works) embodied in particular sound recordings, and to identify and locate the copyright owners of such musical works (and shares of such works).

(IV) Maintain the musical works database and other information relevant to the administration of licensing activities under this section.

(V) Administer a process by which copyright owners can claim ownership of musical works (and shares of such works), and a process by which royalties for works for which the owner is not identified or located are equitably distributed to known copyright owners.

(VI) Administer collections of the administrative assessment from digital music providers and significant nonblanket licensees, including receipt of notices of nonblanket activity.

(VII) Invest in relevant resources, and arrange for services of outside vendors and others, to support the activities of the mechanical licensing collective.

(VIII) Engage in legal and other efforts to enforce rights and obligations under this subsection, including by filing bankruptcy proofs of claims for amounts owed under licenses, and acting in coordination with the digital licensee coordinator.

(IX) Initiate and participate in proceedings before the Copyright Royalty Judges to establish the administrative assessment under this subsection.

(X) Initiate and participate in proceedings before the Copyright Office with respect to activities under this subsection.

(XI) Gather and provide documentation for use in proceedings before the Copyright Royalty Judges to set rates and terms under this section.

(XII) Maintain records of the activities of the mechanical licensing collective and engage in and respond to audits described in this subsection.

(XIII) Engage in such other activities as may be necessary or appropriate to fulfill the responsibilities of the mechanical licensing collective under this subsection.

(ii) **Restrictions Concerning Licensing and Administrative Activities.—** With respect to the administration of licenses, except as provided in clauses (i) and (iii) and subparagraph (E)(v), the mechanical licensing collective may only—

(I) issue blanket licenses pursuant to subsection (d)(1); and

(II) administer blanket licenses for reproduction or distribution rights in musical works for covered activities, including collecting and distributing royalties, pursuant to blanket licenses.

(iii) **Additional Administrative Activities.**—Subject to paragraph (11)(C), the mechanical licensing collective may also administer, including by collecting and distributing royalties, voluntary licenses issued by, or individual download licenses obtained from, copyright owners only for reproduction or distribution rights in musical works for covered activities, for which the mechanical licensing collective shall charge reasonable fees for such services.

(iv) **Restriction on Lobbying.**—The mechanical licensing collective may not engage in government lobbying activities, but may engage in the activities described in subclauses (IX), (X), and (XI) of clause (i).

(D) **Governance.**—

(i) **Board of Directors.**—The mechanical licensing collective shall have a board of directors consisting of 14 voting members and 3 nonvoting members, as follows:

(I) Ten voting members shall be representatives of music publishers—

(aa) to which songwriters have assigned exclusive rights of reproduction and distribution of musical works with respect to covered activities; and

(bb) none of which may be owned by, or under common control with, any other board member.

(II) Four voting members shall be professional songwriters who have retained and exercise exclusive rights of reproduction and distribution with respect to covered activities with respect to musical works they have authored.

(III) One nonvoting member shall be a representative of the nonprofit trade association of music publishers that represents the greatest percentage of the licensor market for uses of musical works in covered activities, as measured for the 3-year period preceding the date on which the member is appointed.

(IV) One nonvoting member shall be a representative of the digital licensee coordinator, provided that a digital licensee coordinator has been designated pursuant to paragraph (5)(B). Otherwise, the nonvoting member shall be the nonprofit trade association of digital licensees that represents the greatest percentage of the licensee market for uses of musical works in covered activities, as measured over the preceding 3 full calendar years.

(V) One nonvoting member shall be a representative of a nationally recognized nonprofit trade association whose primary mission is advocacy on behalf of songwriters in the United States.

(ii) **Bylaws.**—

(I) **Establishment.**—Not later than 1 year after the date on which the mechanical licensing collective is initially designated by the Register of Copyrights under subparagraph (B)(i), the collective shall establish bylaws to determine issues relating to the governance of the collective, including, but not limited to—

(aa) the length of the term for each member of the board of directors;

(bb) the staggering of the terms of the members of the board of directors;

(cc) a process for filling a seat on the board of directors that is vacated before the end of the term with respect to that seat;

(dd) a process for electing a member to the board of directors; and

(ee) a management structure for daily operation of the collective.

(II) **Public Availability.**—The mechanical licensing collective shall make the bylaws established under subclause (I) available to the public.

(iii) **Board Meetings.**—The board of directors shall meet not less frequently than biannually and discuss matters pertinent to the operations of the mechanical licensing collective, including the mechanical licensing collective budget.

(iv) **Operations Advisory Committee.**—The board of directors of the mechanical licensing collective shall establish an operations advisory committee consisting of not fewer than 6 members to make recommendations to the board of directors concerning the operations of the mechanical licensing collective, including the efficient investment in and deployment of information technology and data resources. Such committee shall have an equal number of members of the committee who are—

(I) musical work copyright owners who are appointed by the board of directors of the mechanical licensing collective; and

(II) representatives of digital music providers who are appointed by the digital licensee coordinator.

(v) **Unclaimed Royalties Oversight Committee.**—The board of directors of the mechanical licensing collective shall establish and appoint an unclaimed royalties oversight committee consisting of 10 members, 5 of which shall be musical work copyright owners and 5 of which shall be professional songwriters whose works are used in covered activities.

(vi) **Dispute Resolution Committee.**—The board of directors of the mechanical licensing collective shall establish and appoint a dispute resolution committee that shall—

(I) consist of not fewer than 6 members; and

(II) include an equal number of representatives of musical work copyright owners and professional songwriters.

(vii) **Mechanical Licensing Collective Annual Report.**—

(I) **In General.**—Not later than June 30 of each year commencing after the license availability date, the mechanical licensing collective shall post, and make available online for a period of not less than 3 years, an annual report that sets forth information regarding—

(aa) the operational and licensing practices of the collective;

(bb) how royalties are collected and distributed;

(cc) budgeting and expenditures;

(dd) the collective total costs for the preceding calendar year;

(ee) the projected annual mechanical licensing collective budget;

(ff) aggregated royalty receipts and payments;

(gg) expenses that are more than 10 percent of the annual mechanical licensing collective budget; and

(hh) the efforts of the collective to locate and identify copyright owners of unmatched musical works (and shares of works).

(II) **Submission.**—On the date on which the mechanical licensing collective posts each report required under subclause (I), the collective shall provide a copy of the report to the Register of Copyrights.

(viii) **Independent Officers.**—An individual serving as an officer of the mechanical licensing collective may not, at the same time, also be an employee or agent of any member of the board of directors of the collective or any entity represented by a member of the board of directors, as described in clause (i).

(ix) **Oversight and Accountability.**—

(I) **In General.**—The mechanical licensing collective shall—

(aa) ensure that the policies and practices of the collective are transparent and accountable;

(bb) identify a point of contact for publisher inquiries and complaints with timely redress; and

(cc) establish an anti-comingling policy for funds not collected under this section and royalties collected under this section.

(II) **Audits.**—

(aa) **In General.**—Beginning in the fourth full calendar year that begins after the initial designation of the mechanical licensing collective by the Register of Copyrights under subparagraph (B)(i), and in every fifth calendar year thereafter, the collective shall retain a qualified auditor that shall—

(AA) examine the books, records, and operations of the collective;

(BB) prepare a report for the board of directors of the collective with respect to the matters described in item (bb); and

(CC) not later than December 31 of the year in which the qualified auditor is retained, deliver the report described in subitem (BB) to the board of directors of the collective.

(bb) **Matters Addressed.**—Each report prepared under item (aa) shall address the implementation and efficacy of procedures of the mechanical licensing collective—

(AA) for the receipt, handling, and distribution of royalty funds, including any amounts held as unclaimed royalties;

(BB) to guard against fraud, abuse, waste, and the unreasonable use of funds; and

(CC) to protect the confidentiality of financial, proprietary, and other sensitive information.

(cc) **Public Availability.**—With respect to each report prepared under item (aa), the mechanical licensing collective shall—

(AA) submit the report to the Register of Copyrights; and

(BB) make the report available to the public.

(E) **Musical Works Database.**—

(i) **Establishment and Maintenance of Database.**—The mechanical licensing collective shall establish and maintain a database containing information relating to musical works (and shares of such works) and, to the extent known, the identity and location of the copyright owners of such works (and shares thereof) and the sound recordings in which the musical works are embodied. In furtherance of maintaining such database, the mechanical licensing collective shall engage in efforts to identify the musical works embodied in particular sound recordings, as well as to identify and locate the copyright owners of such works (and shares thereof), and update such data as appropriate.

(ii) **Matched Works.**—With respect to musical works (and shares thereof) that have been matched to copyright owners, the musical works database shall include—

(I) the title of the musical work;

(II) the copyright owner of the work (or share thereof), and the ownership percentage of that owner;

(III) contact information for such copyright owner;

(IV) to the extent reasonably available to the mechanical licensing collective—

(aa) the international standard musical work code for the work; and

(bb) identifying information for sound recordings in which the musical work is embodied, including the name of the sound recording, featured artist, sound recording copyright owner, producer, international standard recording code, and other information commonly used to assist in associating sound recordings with musical works; and

(V) such other information as the Register of Copyrights may prescribe by regulation.

(iii) **Unmatched Works.**—With respect to unmatched musical works (and shares of works) in the database, the musical works database shall include—

(I) to the extent reasonably available to the mechanical licensing collective—

(aa) the title of the musical work;

(bb) the ownership percentage for which an owner has not been identified;

(cc) if a copyright owner has been identified but not located, the identity of such owner and the ownership percentage of that owner;

(dd) identifying information for sound recordings in which the work is embodied, including sound recording name, featured artist, sound recording copyright owner, producer, international standard recording code, and other information commonly used to assist in associating sound recordings with musical works; and

(ee) any additional information reported to the mechanical licensing collective that may assist in identifying the work; and

(II) such other information relating to the identity and ownership of musical works (and shares of such works) as the Register of Copyrights may prescribe by regulation.

(iv) **Sound Recording Information.**—Each musical work copyright owner with any musical work listed in the musical works database shall engage in commercially reasonable efforts to deliver to the mechanical licensing collective, including for use in the musical works database, to the extent such information is not then available in the database, information regarding the names of the sound recordings in which that copyright owner's musical works (or shares thereof) are embodied, to the extent practicable.

(v) **Accessibility of Database.**—The musical works database shall be made available to members of the public in a searchable, online format, free of charge. The mechanical licensing collective shall make such database available in a bulk, machine-readable format, through a widely available software application, to the following entities:

(I)   Digital music providers operating under the authority of valid notices of license, free of charge.

(II)   Significant nonblanket licensees in compliance with their obligations under paragraph (6), free of charge.

(III) Authorized vendors of the entities described in subclauses (I) and (II), free of charge.

(IV)   The Register of Copyrights, free of charge (but the Register shall not treat such database or any information therein as a Government record).

(V)   Any other person or entity for a fee not to exceed the marginal cost to the mechanical licensing collective of providing the database to such person or entity.

(vi) **Additional Requirements.**—The Register of Copyrights shall establish requirements by regulations to ensure the usability, interoperability, and usage restrictions of the musical works database.

(F) **Notices of License and Nonblanket Activity.—**

(i) **Notices of Licenses.**—The mechanical licensing collective shall receive, review, and confirm or reject notices of license from digital music providers, as provided in paragraph (2)(A). The collective shall maintain a current, publicly accessible list of blanket licenses that includes contact information for the licensees and the effective dates of such licenses.

(ii) **Notices of Nonblanket Activity.**—The mechanical licensing collective shall receive notices of nonblanket activity from significant nonblanket licensees, as provided in paragraph (6)(A). The collective shall maintain a current, publicly accessible list of notices of nonblanket activity that includes contact information for significant nonblanket licensees and the dates of receipt of such notices.

(G) **Collection and Distribution of Royalties.—**

(i) **In General.**—Upon receiving reports of usage and payments of royalties from digital music providers for covered activities, the mechanical licensing collective shall—

(I)   engage in efforts to—

(aa) identify the musical works embodied in sound recordings reflected in such reports, and the copyright owners of such musical works (and shares thereof);

(bb) confirm uses of musical works subject to voluntary licenses and individual download licenses, and the corresponding pro rata amounts to be deducted from royalties that would otherwise be due under the blanket license; and

(cc) confirm proper payment of royalties due;

(II)   distribute royalties to copyright owners in accordance with the usage and other information contained in such reports, as well as the ownership and other information contained in the records of the collective; and

        (III) deposit into an interest-bearing account, as provided in subparagraph (H)(ii), royalties that cannot be distributed due to—

           (aa) an inability to identify or locate a copyright owner of a musical work (or share thereof); or

           (bb) a pending dispute before the dispute resolution committee of the mechanical licensing collective.

        (ii) **Other Collection Efforts.**—Any royalties recovered by the mechanical licensing collective as a result of efforts to enforce rights or obligations under a blanket license, including through a bankruptcy proceeding or other legal action, shall be distributed to copyright owners based on available usage information and in accordance with the procedures described in subclauses (I) and (II) of clause (i), on a pro rata basis in proportion to the overall percentage recovery of the total royalties owed, with any pro rata share of royalties that cannot be distributed deposited in an interest-bearing account as provided in subparagraph (H)(ii).

    (H) **Holding of Accrued Royalties.**—

        (i) **Holding Period.**—The mechanical licensing collective shall hold accrued royalties associated with particular musical works (and shares of works) that remain unmatched for a period of not less than 3 years after the date on which the funds were received by the mechanical licensing collective, or not less than 3 years after the date on which the funds were accrued by a digital music provider that subsequently transferred such funds to the mechanical licensing collective pursuant to paragraph (10)(B), whichever period expires sooner.

        (ii) **Interest-bearing Account.**—Accrued royalties for unmatched works (and shares thereof) shall be maintained by the mechanical licensing collective in an interest-bearing account that earns monthly interest—

           (I)   at the Federal, short-term rate; and

           (II) that accrues for the benefit of copyright owners entitled to payment of such accrued royalties.

    (I)   **Musical Works Claiming Process.**—When a copyright owner of an unmatched work (or share of a work) has been identified and located in accordance with the procedures of the mechanical licensing collective, the collective shall—

        (i)   update the musical works database and the other records of the collective accordingly; and

        (ii) provided that accrued royalties for the musical work (or share thereof) have not yet been included in a distribution pursuant to subparagraph (J)(i), pay such accrued royalties and a proportionate amount of accrued interest associated with that work (or share thereof) to the copyright owner, accompanied by a cumulative statement of account reflecting usage of such work and accrued royalties based on information provided by digital music providers to the mechanical licensing collective.

    (J) **Distribution of Unclaimed Accrued Royalties.**—

        (i)   **Distribution Procedures.**—After the expiration of the prescribed holding period for accrued royalties provided in subparagraph (H)(i), the mechanical licensing collective shall distribute such accrued royalties, along with a proportionate share of accrued interest, to copyright owners identified in the records of the collective, subject to the following requirements, and in accordance with the policies and procedures established under clause (ii):

(I) The first such distribution shall occur on or after January 1 of the second full calendar year to commence after the license availability date, with not less than 1 such distribution to take place during each calendar year thereafter.

(II) Copyright owners' payment shares for unclaimed accrued royalties for particular reporting periods shall be determined in a transparent and equitable manner based on data indicating the relative market shares of such copyright owners as reflected in reports of usage provided by digital music providers for covered activities for the periods in question, including, in addition to usage data provided to the mechanical licensing collective, usage data provided to copyright owners under voluntary licenses and individual download licenses for covered activities, to the extent such information is available to the mechanical licensing collective. In furtherance of the determination of equitable market shares under this subparagraph—

(aa) the mechanical licensing collective may require copyright owners seeking distributions of unclaimed accrued royalties to provide, or direct the provision of, information concerning the usage of musical works under voluntary licenses and individual download licenses for covered activities; and

(bb) the mechanical licensing collective shall take appropriate steps to safeguard the confidentiality and security of usage, financial, and other sensitive data used to compute market shares in accordance with the confidentiality provisions prescribed by the Register of Copyrights under paragraph (12)(C).

(ii) **Establishment of Distribution Policies.**—The unclaimed royalties oversight committee established under subparagraph (D)(v) shall establish policies and procedures for the distribution of unclaimed accrued royalties and accrued interest in accordance with this subparagraph, including the provision of usage data to copyright owners to allocate payments and credits to songwriters pursuant to clause (iv), subject to the approval of the board of directors of the mechanical licensing collective.

(iii) **Public Notice of Unclaimed Accrued Royalties.**—The mechanical licensing collective shall—

(I) maintain a publicly accessible online facility with contact information for the collective that lists unmatched musical works (and shares of works), through which a copyright owner may assert an ownership claim with respect to such a work (and a share of such a work);

(II) engage in diligent, good-faith efforts to publicize, throughout the music industry—

(aa) the existence of the collective and the ability to claim unclaimed accrued royalties for unmatched musical works (and shares of such works) held by the collective;

(bb) the procedures by which copyright owners may identify themselves and provide contact, ownership, and other relevant information to the collective in order to receive payments of accrued royalties;

(cc) any transfer of accrued royalties for musical works under paragraph (10)(B), not later than 180 days after the date on which the transfer is received; and (dd) any pending distribution of unclaimed accrued royalties and accrued interest, not less than 90 days before the date on which the distribution is made; and

(III) as appropriate, participate in music industry conferences and events for the purpose of publicizing the matters described in subclause (II).

(iv) **Songwriter Payments.**—Copyright owners that receive a distribution of unclaimed accrued royalties and accrued interest shall pay or credit a portion to songwriters (or the authorized agents of songwriters) on whose behalf the copyright owners license or administer musical works for covered activities, in accordance with applicable contractual terms, but notwithstanding any agreement to the contrary—

(I) such payments and credits to songwriters shall be allocated in proportion to reported usage of individual musical works by digital music providers during the reporting periods covered by the distribution from the mechanical licensing collective; and

(II) in no case shall the payment or credit to an individual songwriter be less than 50 percent of the payment received by the copyright owner attributable to usage of musical works (or shares of works) of that songwriter.

(K) **Dispute Resolution.**—The dispute resolution committee established under subparagraph (D)(vi) shall establish policies and procedures—

(i) for copyright owners to address in a timely and equitable manner disputes relating to ownership interests in musical works licensed under this section and allocation and distribution of royalties by the mechanical licensing collective, subject to the approval of the board of directors of the mechanical licensing collective;

(ii) that shall include a mechanism to hold disputed funds in accordance with the requirements described in subparagraph (H)(ii) pending resolution of the dispute; and

(iii) except as provided in paragraph (11)(D), that shall not affect any legal or equitable rights or remedies available to any copyright owner or songwriter concerning ownership of, and entitlement to royalties for, a musical work.

(L) **Verification of Payments by Mechanical Licensing Collective.**—

(i) **Verification Process.**—A copyright owner entitled to receive payments of royalties for covered activities from the mechanical licensing collective may, individually or with other copyright owners, conduct an audit of the mechanical licensing collective to verify the accuracy of royalty payments by the mechanical licensing collective to such copyright owner, as follows:

(I) A copyright owner may audit the mechanical licensing collective only once in a year for any or all of the 3 calendar years preceding the year in which the audit is commenced, and may not audit records for any calendar year more than once.

(II) The audit shall be conducted by a qualified auditor, who shall perform the audit during the ordinary course of business by examining the books, records, and data of the mechanical licensing collective, according to generally accepted auditing standards and subject to applicable confidentiality requirements prescribed by the Register of Copyrights under paragraph (12)(C).

(III) The mechanical licensing collective shall make such books, records, and data available to the qualified auditor and respond to reasonable requests for relevant information, and shall use commercially reasonable efforts to facilitate access to relevant information maintained by third parties.

(IV) To commence the audit, any copyright owner shall file with the Copyright Office a notice of intent to conduct an audit of the mechanical licensing collective, identifying the period of time to be audited, and shall simultaneously deliver a copy of such notice to the mechanical licensing collective. The Register of Copyrights shall cause the notice of audit to be published in the Federal Register not later than 45 calendar days after the date on which the notice is received.

(V) The qualified auditor shall determine the accuracy of royalty payments, including whether an underpayment or overpayment of royalties was made by the mechanical licensing collective to each auditing copyright owner, except that, before providing a final audit report to any such copyright owner, the qualified auditor shall provide a tentative draft of the report to the mechanical licensing collective and allow the mechanical licensing collective a reasonable opportunity to respond to the findings, including by clarifying issues and correcting factual errors.

(VI) The auditing copyright owner or owners shall bear the cost of the audit. In case of an underpayment to any copyright owner, the mechanical licensing collective shall pay the amounts of any such underpayment to such auditing copyright owner, as appropriate. In case of an overpayment by the mechanical licensing collective, the mechanical licensing collective may debit the account of the auditing copyright owner or owners for such overpaid amounts, or such owner or owners shall refund overpaid amounts to the mechanical licensing collective, as appropriate.

(ii) **Alternative Verification Procedures.**—Nothing in this subparagraph shall preclude a copyright owner and the mechanical licensing collective from agreeing to audit procedures different from those described in this subparagraph, except that a notice of the audit shall be provided to and published by the Copyright Office as described in clause (i)(IV).

(M) **Records of Mechanical Licensing Collective.**—

(i) **Records Maintenance.**—The mechanical licensing collective shall ensure that all material records of the operations of the mechanical licensing collective, including those relating to notices of license, the administration of the claims process of the mechanical licensing collective, reports of usage, royalty payments, receipt and maintenance of accrued royalties, royalty distribution processes, and legal matters, are preserved and maintained in a secure and reliable manner, with appropriate commercially reasonable safeguards against unauthorized access, copying, and disclosure, and subject to the confidentiality requirements prescribed by the Register of Copyrights under paragraph (12)(C) for a period of not less than 7 years after the date of creation or receipt, whichever occurs later.

(ii) **Records Access.**—The mechanical licensing collective shall provide prompt access to electronic and other records pertaining to the administration of a copyright owner's musical works upon reasonable written request of the owner or the authorized representative of the owner.

(4) **Terms and Conditions of Blanket License.**—A blanket license is subject to, and conditioned upon, the following requirements:

(A) **Royalty Reporting and Payments.**—

(i) **Monthly Reports and Payment.**—A digital music provider shall report and pay royalties to the mechanical licensing collective under the blanket license on a monthly basis in accordance with clause (ii) and subsection (c)(2)(I), except that the monthly reporting shall be due on the date that is 45 calendar days, rather than 20 calendar days, after the end of the monthly reporting period.

(ii) **Data to Be Reported.**—In reporting usage of musical works to the mechanical licensing collective, a digital music provider shall provide usage data for musical works used under the blanket license and usage data for musical works used in covered activities under voluntary licenses and individual download licenses. In the report of usage, the digital music provider shall—

(I)   with respect to each sound recording embodying a musical work—

(aa) provide identifying information for the sound recording, including sound recording name, featured artist, and, to the extent acquired by the digital music provider in connection with its use of sound recordings of musical works to engage in covered activities, including pursuant to subparagraph (B), sound recording copyright owner, producer, international standard recording code, and other information commonly used in the industry to identify sound recordings and match them to the musical works the sound recordings embody;

(bb) to the extent acquired by the digital music provider in the metadata provided by sound recording copyright owners or other licensors of sound recordings in connection with the use of sound recordings of musical works to engage in covered activities, including pursuant to subparagraph (B), provide information concerning authorship and ownership of the applicable rights in the musical work embodied in the sound recording (including each songwriter, publisher name, and respective ownership share) and the international standard musical work code; and

(cc) provide the number of digital phonorecord deliveries of the sound recording, including limited downloads and interactive streams;

(II) identify and provide contact information for all musical work copyright owners for works embodied in sound recordings as to which a voluntary license, rather than the blanket license, is in effect with respect to the uses being reported; and

(III) provide such other information as the Register of Copyrights shall require by regulation.

(iii) **Format and Maintenance of Reports.**—Reports of usage provided by digital music providers to the mechanical licensing collective shall be in a machine-readable format that is compatible with the information technology systems of the mechanical licensing collective and meets the requirements of regulations adopted by the Register of Copyrights. The Register shall also adopt regulations setting forth requirements under which records of use shall be maintained and made available to the mechanical licensing collective by digital music providers engaged in covered activities under a blanket license.

(iv) **Adoption of Regulations.**—The Register of Copyrights shall adopt regulations—

(I)   setting forth requirements under which records of use shall be maintained and made available to the mechanical licensing collective by digital music providers engaged in covered activities under a blanket license; and

(II) regarding adjustments to reports of usage by digital music providers, including mechanisms to account for overpayment and underpayment of royalties in prior periods.

(B) **Collection of Sound Recording Information.**—A digital music provider shall engage in good-faith, commercially reasonable efforts to obtain from sound recording copyright owners and other licensors of sound recordings made available through the service of such digital music provider information concerning—

(i) sound recording copyright owners, producers, international standard recording codes, and other information commonly used in the industry to identify sound recordings and match them to the musical works the sound recordings embody; and

(ii) the authorship and ownership of musical works, including songwriters, publisher names, ownership shares, and international standard musical work codes.

(C) **Payment of Administrative Assessment.**—A digital music provider and any significant nonblanket licensee shall pay the administrative assessment established under paragraph (7)(D) in accordance with this subsection and applicable regulations.

(D) **Verification of Payments by Digital Music Providers.**—

(i) **Verification Process.**—The mechanical licensing collective may conduct an audit of a digital music provider operating under the blanket license to verify the accuracy of royalty payments by the digital music provider to the mechanical licensing collective as follows:

(I) The mechanical licensing collective may commence an audit of a digital music provider not more frequently than once in any 3-calendar-year period to cover a verification period of not more than the 3 full calendar years preceding the date of commencement of the audit, and such audit may not audit records for any such 3-year verification period more than once.

(II) The audit shall be conducted by a qualified auditor, who shall perform the audit during the ordinary course of business by examining the books, records, and data of the digital music provider, according to generally accepted auditing standards and subject to applicable confidentiality requirements prescribed by the Register of Copyrights under paragraph (12)(C).

(III) The digital music provider shall make such books, records, and data available to the qualified auditor and respond to reasonable requests for relevant information, and shall use commercially reasonable efforts to provide access to relevant information maintained with respect to a digital music provider by third parties.

(IV) To commence the audit, the mechanical licensing collective shall file with the Copyright Office a notice of intent to conduct an audit of the digital music provider, identifying the period of time to be audited, and shall simultaneously deliver a copy of such notice to the digital music provider. The Register of Copyrights shall cause the notice of audit to be published in the Federal Register not later than 45 calendar days after the date on which notice is received.

(V) The qualified auditor shall determine the accuracy of royalty payments, including whether an underpayment or overpayment of royalties was made by the digital music provider to the mechanical licensing collective, except that, before providing a final audit report to the mechanical licensing collective, the qualified auditor shall provide a tentative draft of the report to the digital music provider and allow the digital music provider a reasonable opportunity to respond to the findings, including by clarifying issues and correcting factual errors.

(VI) The mechanical licensing collective shall pay the cost of the audit, unless the qualified auditor determines that there was an underpayment by the digital music provider of not less than 10 percent, in which case the digital music provider shall bear the reasonable costs of the audit, in addition to paying the amount of any underpayment to the mechanical licensing collective. In case of an overpayment by the digital music provider, the mechanical licensing collective shall provide a credit to the account of the digital music provider.

(VII) A digital music provider may not assert section 507 or any other Federal or State statute of limitations, doctrine of laches or estoppel, or similar provision as a defense to a legal action arising from an audit under this subparagraph if such legal action is commenced not more than 6 years after the commencement of the audit that is the basis for such action.

(ii) **Alternative Verification Procedures.**—Nothing in this subparagraph shall preclude the mechanical licensing collective and a digital music provider from agreeing to audit procedures different from those described in this subparagraph, except that a notice of the audit shall be provided to and published by the Copyright Office as described in clause (i)(IV).

(E) **Default Under Blanket License.**—

(i) **Conditions of Default.**—A digital music provider shall be in default under a blanket license if the digital music provider—

(I) fails to provide 1 or more monthly reports of usage to the mechanical licensing collective when due;

(II) fails to make a monthly royalty or late fee payment to the mechanical licensing collective when due, in all or material part;

(III) provides 1 or more monthly reports of usage to the mechanical licensing collective that, on the whole, is or are materially deficient as a result of inaccurate, missing, or unreadable data, where the correct data was available to the digital music provider and required to be reported under this section and applicable regulations;

(IV) fails to pay the administrative assessment as required under this subsection and applicable regulations; or

(V) after being provided written notice by the mechanical licensing collective, refuses to comply with any other material term or condition of the blanket license under this section for a period of not less than 60 calendar days.

(ii) **Notice of Default and Termination.**—In case of a default by a digital music provider, the mechanical licensing collective may proceed to terminate the blanket license of the digital music provider as follows:

(I) The mechanical licensing collective shall provide written notice to the digital music provider describing with reasonable particularity the default and advising that unless such default is cured not later than 60 calendar days after the date of the notice, the blanket license will automatically terminate at the end of that period.

(II) If the digital music provider fails to remedy the default before the end of the 60-day period described in subclause (I), the license shall terminate without any further action on the part of the mechanical licensing collective. Such termination renders the making of all digital phonorecord deliveries of all musical works (and shares thereof) covered by the blanket license for which the royalty or administrative assessment has not been paid actionable as acts of infringement under section 501 and subject to the remedies provided by sections 502 through 506.

(iii) **Notice to Copyright Owners.**—The mechanical licensing collective shall provide written notice of any termination under this subparagraph to copyright owners of affected works.

(iv) **Review by Federal District Court.**—A digital music provider that believes a blanket license was improperly terminated by the mechanical licensing collective may seek review of such termination in an appropriate district court of the United States. The district court shall determine the matter de novo based on the record before the mechanical licensing collective and any additional supporting evidence presented by the parties.

(5) **Digital Licensee Coordinator.**—

(A) **In General.**—The digital licensee coordinator shall be a single entity that—

(i) is a nonprofit, not owned by any other entity, that is created to carry out responsibilities under this subsection;

(ii) is endorsed by and enjoys substantial support from digital music providers and significant nonblanket licensees that together represent the greatest percentage of the licensee market for uses of musical works in covered activities, as measured over the preceding 3 calendar years;

(iii) is able to demonstrate that it has, or will have prior to the license availability date, the administrative capabilities to perform the required functions of the digital licensee coordinator under this subsection; and

(iv) has been designated by the Register of Copyrights, with the approval of the Librarian of Congress pursuant to section 702, in accordance with subparagraph (B).

(B) **Designation of Digital Licensee Coordinator.**—

(i) **Initial Designation.**—The Register of Copyrights shall initially designate the digital licensee coordinator not later than 270 days after the enactment date, in accordance with the same procedure described for designation of the mechanical licensing collective in paragraph (3)(B)(i).

(ii) **Periodic Review of Designation.**—Following the initial designation of the digital licensee coordinator, the Register of Copyrights shall, every 5 years, beginning with the fifth full calendar year to commence after the initial designation, determine whether the existing designation should be continued, or a different entity meeting the criteria described in clauses (i) through (iii) of subparagraph (A) should be designated, in accordance with the same procedure described for the mechanical licensing collective in paragraph (3)(B)(ii).

(iii) **Inability to Designate.**—If the Register of Copyrights is unable to identify an entity that fulfills each of the qualifications described in clauses (i) through (iii) of subparagraph (A) to serve as the digital licensee coordinator, the Register may decline to designate a digital licensee coordinator. The determination of the Register not to designate a digital licensee coordinator shall not negate or otherwise affect any provision of this subsection except to the limited extent that a provision references the digital licensee coordinator. In such case, the reference to the digital licensee coordinator shall be without effect unless and until a new digital licensee coordinator is designated.

(C) **Authorities and Functions.**—

(i) **In General.**—The digital licensee coordinator is authorized to perform the following functions, subject to more particular requirements as described in this subsection:

(I)   Establish a governance structure, criteria for membership, and any dues to be paid by its members.

(II)   Engage in efforts to enforce notice and payment obligations with respect to the administrative assessment, including by receiving information from and coordinating with the mechanical licensing collective.

(III) Initiate and participate in proceedings before the Copyright Royalty Judges to establish the administrative assessment under this subsection.

(IV) Initiate and participate in proceedings before the Copyright Office with respect to activities under this subsection.

(V)   Gather and provide documentation for use in proceedings before the Copyright Royalty Judges to set rates and terms under this section.

(VI) Maintain records of its activities.

(VII)Assist in publicizing the existence of the mechanical licensing collective and the ability of copyright owners to claim royalties for unmatched musical works (and shares of works) through the collective.

(VIII) Engage in such other activities as may be necessary or appropriate to fulfill its responsibilities under this subsection.

(ii) **Restriction on Lobbying.**—The digital licensee coordinator may not engage in government lobbying activities, but may engage in the activities described in subclauses (III), (IV), and (V) of clause (i).

(iii) **Assistance with Publicity for Unclaimed Royalties.**—The digital licensee coordinator shall make reasonable, good-faith efforts to assist the mechanical licensing collective in the efforts of the collective to locate and identify copyright owners of unmatched musical works (and shares of such works) by encouraging digital music providers to publicize the existence of the collective and the ability of copyright owners to claim unclaimed accrued royalties, including by—

(I)   posting contact information for the collective at reasonably prominent locations on digital music provider websites and applications; and

(II)   conducting in-person outreach activities with songwriters.

(6)   **Requirements for Significant Nonblanket Licensees.—**

(A) **In General.—**

(i)   **Notice of Activity.**—Not later than 45 calendar days after the license availability date, or 45 calendar days after the end of the first full calendar month in which an entity initially qualifies as a significant nonblanket licensee, whichever occurs later, a significant nonblanket licensee shall submit a notice of nonblanket activity to the mechanical licensing collective. The notice of nonblanket activity shall comply in form and substance with requirements that the Register of Copyrights shall establish by regulation, and a copy shall be made available to the digital licensee coordinator.

(ii)   **Reporting and Payment Obligations.**—The notice of nonblanket activity submitted to the mechanical licensing collective shall be accompanied by a report of usage that contains the information described in paragraph (4)(A)(ii), as well as any payment of the administrative assessment required under this subsection and applicable regulations. Thereafter, subject to clause (iii), a significant nonblanket licensee shall continue to provide monthly reports of usage, accompanied by any required payment of the administrative assessment, to the mechanical licensing collective. Such reports and payments shall be submitted not later than 45 calendar days after the end of the calendar month being reported.

(iii) **Discontinuation of Obligations.**—An entity that has submitted a notice of nonblanket activity to the mechanical licensing collective that has ceased to qualify as a significant nonblanket licensee may so notify the collective in writing. In such case, as of the calendar month in which such notice is provided, such entity shall no longer be required to provide reports of usage or pay the administrative assessment, but if such entity later qualifies as a significant nonblanket licensee, such entity shall again be required to comply with clauses (i) and (ii).

(B) **Reporting by Mechanical Licensing Collective to Digital Licensee Coordinator.**—

(i) **Monthly Reports of Noncompliant Licensees.**—The mechanical licensing collective shall provide monthly reports to the digital licensee coordinator setting forth any significant nonblanket licensees of which the collective is aware that have failed to comply with subparagraph (A).

(ii) **Treatment of Confidential Information.**—The mechanical licensing collective and digital licensee coordinator shall take appropriate steps to safeguard the confidentiality and security of financial and other sensitive data shared under this subparagraph, in accordance with the confidentiality requirements prescribed by the Register of Copyrights under paragraph (12)(C).

(C) **Legal Enforcement Efforts.**—

(i) **Federal Court Action.**—Should the mechanical licensing collective or digital licensee coordinator become aware that a significant nonblanket licensee has failed to comply with subparagraph (A), either may commence an action in an appropriate district court of the United States for damages and injunctive relief. If the significant nonblanket licensee is found liable, the court shall, absent a finding of excusable neglect, award damages in an amount equal to three times the total amount of the unpaid administrative assessment and, notwithstanding anything to the contrary in section 505, reasonable attorney's fees and costs, as well as such other relief as the court determines appropriate. In all other cases, the court shall award relief as appropriate. Any recovery of damages shall be payable to the mechanical licensing collective as an offset to the collective total costs.

(ii) **Statute of Limitations for Enforcement Action.**—Any action described in this subparagraph shall be commenced within the time period described in section 507(b).

(iii) **Other Rights and Remedies Preserved.**—The ability of the mechanical licensing collective or digital licensee coordinator to bring an action under this subparagraph shall in no way alter, limit or negate any other right or remedy that may be available to any party at law or in equity.

(7) **Funding of Mechanical Licensing Collective.**—

(A) **In General.**—The collective total costs shall be funded by—

(i) an administrative assessment, as such assessment is established by the Copyright Royalty Judges pursuant to subparagraph (D) from time to time, to be paid by—

(I) digital music providers that are engaged, in all or in part, in covered activities pursuant to a blanket license; and

(II) significant nonblanket licensees; and

(ii) voluntary contributions from digital music providers and significant nonblanket licensees as may be agreed with copyright owners.

(B) **Voluntary Contributions.—**

(i) **Agreements Concerning Contributions.—**Except as provided in clause (ii), voluntary contributions by digital music providers and significant nonblanket licensees shall be determined by private negotiation and agreement, and the following conditions apply:

(I) The date and amount of each voluntary contribution to the mechanical licensing collective shall be documented in a writing signed by an authorized agent of the mechanical licensing collective and the contributing party.

(II) Such agreement shall be made available as required in proceedings before the Copyright Royalty Judges to establish or adjust the administrative assessment in accordance with applicable statutory and regulatory provisions and rulings of the Copyright Royalty Judges.

(ii) **Treatment of Contributions.—**Each voluntary contribution described in clause (i) shall be treated for purposes of an administrative assessment proceeding as an offset to the collective total costs that would otherwise be recovered through the administrative assessment. Any allocation or reallocation of voluntary contributions between or among individual digital music providers or significant nonblanket licensees shall be a matter of private negotiation and agreement among such parties and outside the scope of the administrative assessment proceeding.

(C) **Interim Application of Accrued Royalties.—**In the event that the administrative assessment, together with any funding from voluntary contributions as provided in subparagraphs (A) and (B), is inadequate to cover current collective total costs, the collective, with approval of its board of directors, may apply unclaimed accrued royalties on an interim basis to defray such costs, subject to future reimbursement of such royalties from future collections of the assessment.

(D) **Determination of Administrative Assessment.—**

(i) **Administrative Assessment to Cover Collective Total Costs.—**The administrative assessment shall be used solely and exclusively to fund the collective total costs.

(ii) **Separate Proceeding Before Copyright Royalty Judges.—**The amount and terms of the administrative assessment shall be determined and established in a separate and independent proceeding before the Copyright Royalty Judges, according to the procedures described in clauses (iii) and (iv). The administrative assessment determined in such proceeding shall—

(I) be wholly independent of royalty rates and terms applicable to digital music providers, which shall not be taken into consideration in any manner in establishing the administrative assessment;

(II) be established by the Copyright Royalty Judges in an amount that is calculated to defray the reasonable collective total costs;

(III) be assessed based on usage of musical works by digital music providers and significant nonblanket licensees in covered activities under both compulsory and nonblanket licenses;

(IV) may be in the form of a percentage of royalties payable under this section for usage of musical works in covered activities (regardless of whether a different rate applies under a voluntary license), or any other usage-based metric reasonably calculated to equitably allocate the collective total costs across digital music providers and significant nonblanket licensees engaged in covered activities, and shall include as a component a minimum fee for all digital music providers and significant nonblanket licensees; and

(V) take into consideration anticipated future collective total costs and collections of the administrative assessment, including, as applicable—

(aa) any portion of past actual collective total costs of the mechanical licensing collective not funded by previous collections of the administrative assessment or voluntary contributions because such collections or contributions together were insufficient to fund such costs;

(bb) any past collections of the administrative assessment and voluntary contributions that exceeded past actual collective total costs, resulting in a surplus; and

(cc) the amount of any voluntary contributions by digital music providers or significant nonblanket licensees in relevant periods, described in subparagraphs (A) and (B) of paragraph (7).

(iii) **Initial Administrative Assessment.**—The procedure for establishing the initial administrative assessment shall be as follows:

(I) Not later than 270 days after the enactment date, the Copyright Royalty Judges shall commence a proceeding to establish the initial administrative assessment by publishing a notice in the Federal Register seeking petitions to participate.

(II) The mechanical licensing collective and digital licensee coordinator shall participate in the proceeding described in subclause (I), along with any interested copyright owners, digital music providers or significant nonblanket licensees that have notified the Copyright Royalty Judges of their desire to participate.

(III) The Copyright Royalty Judges shall establish a schedule for submission by the parties of information that may be relevant to establishing the administrative assessment, including actual and anticipated collective total costs of the mechanical licensing collective, actual and anticipated collections from digital music providers and significant nonblanket licensees, and documentation of voluntary contributions, as well as a schedule for further proceedings, which shall include a hearing, as the Copyright Royalty Judges determine appropriate.

(IV) The initial administrative assessment shall be determined, and such determination shall be published in the Federal Register by the Copyright Royalty Judges, not later than 1 year after commencement of the proceeding described in this clause. The determination shall be supported by a written record. The initial administrative assessment shall be effective as of the license availability date, and shall continue in effect unless and until an adjusted administrative assessment is established pursuant to an adjustment proceeding under clause (iv).

(iv) **Adjustment of Administrative Assessment.**—The administrative assessment may be adjusted by the Copyright Royalty Judges periodically, in accordance with the following procedures:

(I) Not earlier than 1 year after the most recent publication of a determination of the administrative assessment by the Copyright Royalty Judges, the mechanical licensing collective, the digital licensee coordinator, or one or more interested copyright owners, digital music providers, or significant nonblanket licensees, may file a petition with the Copyright Royalty Judges in the month of May to commence a proceeding to adjust the administrative assessment.

(II) Notice of the commencement of such proceeding shall be published in the Federal Register in the month of June following the filing of any petition, with a schedule of requested information and additional proceedings, as described in clause (iii)(III). The mechanical licensing collective and digital licensee coordinator shall participate in such proceeding, along with any interested copyright owners, digital music providers, or significant nonblanket licensees that have notified the Copyright Royalty Judges of their desire to participate.

(III) The determination of the adjusted administrative assessment, which shall be supported by a written record, shall be published in the Federal Register during June of the calendar year following the commencement of the proceeding. The adjusted administrative assessment shall take effect January 1 of the year following such publication.

(v) **Adoption of Voluntary Agreements.**—In lieu of reaching their own determination based on evaluation of relevant data, the Copyright Royalty Judges shall approve and adopt a negotiated agreement to establish the amount and terms of the administrative assessment that has been agreed to by the mechanical licensing collective and the digital licensee coordinator (or if none has been designated, interested digital music providers and significant nonblanket licensees representing more than half of the market for uses of musical works in covered activities), except that the Copyright Royalty Judges shall have the discretion to reject any such agreement for good cause shown. An administrative assessment adopted under this clause shall apply to all digital music providers and significant nonblanket licensees engaged in covered activities during the period the administrative assessment is in effect.

(vi) **Continuing Authority to Amend.**—The Copyright Royalty Judges shall retain continuing authority to amend a determination of an administrative assessment to correct technical or clerical errors, or modify the terms of implementation, for good cause, with any such amendment to be published in the Federal Register.

(vii) **Appeal of Administrative Assessment.**—The determination of an administrative assessment by the Copyright Royalty Judges shall be appealable, not later than 30 calendar days after publication in the Federal Register, to the Court of Appeals for the District of Columbia Circuit by any party that fully participated in the proceeding. The administrative assessment as established by the Copyright Royalty Judges shall remain in effect pending the final outcome of any such appeal, and the mechanical licensing collective, digital licensee coordinator, digital music providers, and significant nonblanket licensees shall implement appropriate financial or other measures not later than 90 days after any modification of the assessment to reflect and account for such outcome.

(viii) **Regulations.**—The Copyright Royalty Judges may adopt regulations to govern the conduct of proceedings under this paragraph.

(8) **Establishment of Rates and Terms Under Blanket License.**—

(A) **Restrictions on Ratesetting Participation.**—Neither the mechanical licensing collective nor the digital licensee coordinator shall be a party to a proceeding described in subsection (c)(1)(E), except that the mechanical licensing collective or the digital licensee coordinator may gather and provide financial and other information for the use of a party to such a proceeding and comply with requests for information as required under applicable statutory and regulatory provisions and rulings of the Copyright Royalty Judges.

(B) **Application of Late Fees.**—In any proceeding described in subparagraph (A) in which the Copyright Royalty Judges establish a late fee for late payment of royalties for uses of musical works under this section, such fee shall apply to covered activities under blanket licenses, as follows:

(i) Late fees for past due royalty payments shall accrue from the due date for payment until payment is received by the mechanical licensing collective.

(ii) The availability of late fees shall in no way prevent a copyright owner or the mechanical licensing collective from asserting any other rights or remedies to which such copyright owner or the mechanical licensing collective may be entitled under this title.

(C) **Interim Rate Agreements in General.**—For any covered activity for which no rate or terms have been established by the Copyright Royalty Judges, the mechanical licensing collective and any digital music provider may agree to an interim rate and terms for such activity under the blanket license, and any such rate and terms—

(i) shall be treated as nonprecedential and not cited or relied upon in any ratesetting proceeding before the Copyright Royalty Judges or any other tribunal; and

(ii) shall automatically expire upon the establishment of a rate and terms for such covered activity by the Copyright Royalty Judges, under subsection (c)(1)(E).

(D) **Adjustments for Interim Rates.**—The rate and terms established by the Copyright Royalty Judges for a covered activity to which an interim rate and terms have been agreed under subparagraph (C) shall supersede the interim rate and terms and apply retroactively to the inception of the activity under the blanket license. In such case, not later than 90 days after the effective date of the rate and terms established by the Copyright Royalty Judges—

(i) if the rate established by the Copyright Royalty Judges exceeds the interim rate, the digital music provider shall pay to the mechanical licensing collective the amount of any underpayment of royalties due; or

(ii) if the interim rate exceeds the rate established by the Copyright Royalty Judges, the mechanical licensing collective shall credit the account of the digital music provider for the amount of any overpayment of royalties due.

(9) **Transition to Blanket Licenses.**—

(A) **Substitution of Blanket License.**—On the license availability date, a blanket license shall, without any interruption in license authority enjoyed by such digital music provider, be automatically substituted for and supersede any existing compulsory license previously obtained under this section by the digital music provider from a copyright owner to engage in 1 or more covered activities with respect to a musical work, except that such substitution shall not apply to any authority obtained from a record company pursuant to a compulsory license to make and distribute permanent downloads unless and until such record company terminates such authority in writing to take effect at the end of a monthly reporting period, with a copy to the mechanical licensing collective.

(B) **Expiration of Existing Licenses.**—Except to the extent provided in subparagraph (A), on and after the license availability date, licenses other than individual download licenses obtained under this section for covered activities prior to the license availability date shall no longer continue in effect.

(C) **Treatment of Voluntary Licenses.**—A voluntary license for a covered activity in effect on the license availability date will remain in effect unless and until the voluntary license expires according to the terms of the voluntary license, or the parties agree to amend or terminate the voluntary license. In a case where a voluntary license for a covered activity entered into before the license availability date incorporates the terms of this section by reference, the terms so incorporated (but not the rates) shall be those in effect immediately prior to the license availability date, and those terms shall continue to apply unless and until such voluntary license is terminated or amended, or the parties enter into a new voluntary license.

(D) **Further Acceptance of Notices for Covered Activities by Copyright Office.**—On and after the enactment date—

(i) the Copyright Office shall no longer accept notices of intention with respect to covered activities; and

(ii) notices of intention filed before the enactment date will no longer be effective or provide license authority with respect to covered activities, except that, before the license availability date, there shall be no liability under section 501 for the reproduction or distribution of a musical work (or share thereof) in covered activities if a valid notice of intention was filed for such work (or share) before the enactment date.

(10) **Prior Unlicensed Uses.**—

(A) **Limitation on Liability in General.**—A copyright owner that commences an action under section 501 on or after January 1, 2018, against a digital music provider for the infringement of the exclusive rights provided by paragraph (1) or (3) of section 106 arising from the unauthorized reproduction or distribution of a musical work by such digital music provider in the course of engaging in covered activities prior to the license availability date, shall, as the copyright owner's sole and exclusive remedy against the digital music provider, be eligible to recover the royalty prescribed under subsection (c)(1)(C) and chapter 8, from the digital music provider, provided that such digital music provider can demonstrate compliance with the requirements of subparagraph (B), as applicable. In all other cases the limitation on liability under this subparagraph shall not apply.

(B) **Requirements for Limitation on Liability.**—The following requirements shall apply on the enactment date and through the end of the period that expires 90 days after the license availability date to digital music providers seeking to avail themselves of the limitation on liability described in subparagraph (A):

(i) Not later than 30 calendar days after first making a particular sound recording of a musical work available through its service via one or more covered activities, or 30 calendar days after the enactment date, whichever occurs later, a digital music provider shall engage in good-faith, commercially reasonable efforts to identify and locate each copyright owner of such musical work (or share thereof). Such required matching efforts shall include the following:

(I) Good-faith, commercially reasonable efforts to obtain from the owner of the corresponding sound recording made available through the digital music provider's service the following information:

(aa) Sound recording name, featured artist, sound recording copyright owner, producer, international standard recording code, and other information commonly used in the industry to identify sound recordings and match them to the musical works they embody.

(bb) Any available musical work ownership information, including each songwriter and publisher name, percentage ownership share, and international standard musical work code.

(II) Employment of 1 or more bulk electronic matching processes that are available to the digital music provider through a third-party vendor on commercially reasonable terms, except that a digital music provider may rely on its own bulk electronic matching process if that process has capabilities comparable to or better than those available from a third-party vendor on commercially reasonable terms.

(ii) The required matching efforts shall be repeated by the digital music provider not less than once per month for so long as the copyright owner remains unidentified or has not been located.

(iii) If the required matching efforts are successful in identifying and locating a copyright owner of a musical work (or share thereof) by the end of the calendar month in which the digital music provider first makes use of the work, the digital music provider shall provide statements of account and pay royalties to such copyright owner in accordance with this section and applicable regulations.

(iv) If the copyright owner is not identified or located by the end of the calendar month in which the digital music provider first makes use of the work, the digital music provider shall accrue and hold royalties calculated under the applicable statutory rate in accordance with usage of the work, from initial use of the work until the accrued royalties can be paid to the copyright owner or are required to be transferred to the mechanical licensing collective, as follows:

(I) Accrued royalties shall be maintained by the digital music provider in accordance with generally accepted accounting principles.

(II) If a copyright owner of an unmatched musical work (or share thereof) is identified and located by or to the digital music provider before the license availability date, the digital music provider shall—

(aa) not later than 45 calendar days after the end of the calendar month during which the copyright owner was identified and located, pay the copyright owner all accrued royalties, such payment to be accompanied by a cumulative statement of account that includes all of the information that would have been provided to the copyright owner had the digital music provider been providing monthly statements of account to the copyright owner from initial use of the work in accordance with this section and applicable regulations, including the requisite certification under subsection (c)(2)(I);

(bb) beginning with the accounting period following the calendar month in which the copyright owner was identified and located, and for all other accounting periods prior to the license availability date, provide monthly statements of account and pay royalties to the copyright owner as required under this section and applicable regulations; and

(cc) beginning with the monthly royalty reporting period commencing on the license availability date, report usage and pay royalties for such musical work (or share thereof) for such reporting period and reporting periods thereafter to the mechanical licensing collective, as required under this subsection and applicable regulations.

(III) If a copyright owner of an unmatched musical work (or share thereof) is not identified and located by the license availability date, the digital music provider shall—

(aa) not later than 45 calendar days after the license availability date, transfer all accrued royalties to the mechanical licensing collective, such payment to be accompanied by a cumulative statement of account that includes all of the information that would have been provided to the copyright owner had the digital music provider been serving monthly statements of account on the copyright owner from initial use of the work in accordance with this section and applicable regulations, including the requisite certification under subsection (c)(2)(I), and accompanied by an additional certification by a duly authorized officer of the digital music provider that the digital music provider has fulfilled the requirements of clauses (i) and (ii) of subparagraph (B) but has not been successful in locating or identifying the copyright owner; and

(bb) beginning with the monthly royalty reporting period commencing on the license availability date, report usage and pay royalties for such musical work (or share thereof) for such period and reporting periods thereafter to the mechanical licensing collective, as required under this subsection and applicable regulations.

(v) A digital music provider that complies with the requirements of this subparagraph with respect to unmatched musical works (or shares of works) shall not be liable for or accrue late fees for late payments of royalties for such works until such time as the digital music provider is required to begin paying monthly royalties to the copyright owner or the mechanical licensing collective, as applicable.

(C) **Adjusted Statute of Limitations.**—Notwithstanding anything to the contrary in section 507(b), with respect to any claim of infringement of the exclusive rights provided by paragraphs (1) and (3) of section 106 against a digital music provider arising from the unauthorized reproduction or distribution of a musical work by such digital music provider in the course of engaging in covered activities that accrued not more than 3 years prior to the license availability date, such action may be commenced not later than the later of—

(i) 3 years after the date on which the claim accrued; or

(ii) 2 years after the license availability date.

(D) **Other Rights and Remedies Preserved.**—Except as expressly provided in this paragraph, nothing in this paragraph shall be construed to alter, limit, or negate any right or remedy of a copyright owner with respect to unauthorized use of a musical work.

(11) **Legal Protections for Licensing Activities.**—

(A) **Exemption for Compulsory License Activities.**—The antitrust exemption described in subsection (c)(1)(D) shall apply to negotiations and agreements between and among copyright owners and persons entitled to obtain a compulsory license for covered activities, and common agents acting on behalf of such copyright owners or persons, including with respect to the administrative assessment established under this subsection.

(B) **Limitation on Common Agent Exemption.**—Notwithstanding the antitrust exemption provided in subsection (c)(1)(D) and subparagraph (A) of this paragraph (except for the administrative assessment referenced in such subparagraph (A) and except as provided in paragraph (8)(C)), neither the mechanical licensing collective nor the digital licensee coordinator shall serve as a common agent with respect to the establishment of royalty rates or terms under this section.

(C) **Antitrust Exemption for Administrative Activities.**—Notwithstanding any provision of the antitrust laws, copyright owners and persons entitled to obtain a compulsory license under this section may designate the mechanical licensing collective to administer voluntary licenses for the reproduction or distribution of musical works in covered activities on behalf of such copyright owners and persons, subject to the following conditions:

(i) Each copyright owner shall establish the royalty rates and material terms of any such voluntary license individually and not in agreement, combination, or concert with any other copyright owner.

(ii) Each person entitled to obtain a compulsory license under this section shall establish the royalty rates and material terms of any such voluntary license individually and not in agreement, combination, or concert with any other digital music provider.

(iii) The mechanical licensing collective shall maintain the confidentiality of the voluntary licenses in accordance with the confidentiality provisions prescribed by the Register of Copyrights under paragraph (12)(C).

(D) **Liability for Good-faith Activities.**—The mechanical licensing collective shall not be liable to any person or entity based on a claim arising from its good-faith administration of policies and procedures adopted and implemented to carry out the responsibilities described in subparagraphs (J) and (K) of paragraph (3), except to the extent of correcting an underpayment or overpayment of royalties as provided in paragraph (3)(L)(i)(VI), but the collective may participate in a legal proceeding as a stakeholder party if the collective is holding funds that are the subject of a dispute between copyright owners. For purposes of this subparagraph, the term "good-faith administration" means administration in a manner that is not grossly negligent.

(E) **Preemption of State Property Laws.**—The holding and distribution of funds by the mechanical licensing collective in accordance with this subsection shall supersede and preempt any State law (including common law) concerning escheatment or abandoned property, or any analogous provision, that might otherwise apply.

(F) **Rule of Construction.**—Except as expressly provided in this subsection, nothing in this subsection shall negate or limit the ability of any person to pursue an action in Federal court against the mechanical licensing collective or any other person based upon a claim arising under this title or other applicable law.

(12) **Regulations.**—

(A) **Adoption by Register of Copyrights and Copyright Royalty Judges.**—The Register of Copyrights may conduct such proceedings and adopt such regulations as may be necessary or appropriate to effectuate the provisions of this subsection, except for regulations concerning proceedings before the Copyright Royalty Judges to establish the administrative assessment, which shall be adopted by the Copyright Royalty Judges.

(B) **Judicial Review of Regulations.**—Except as provided in paragraph (7)(D)(vii), regulations adopted under this subsection shall be subject to judicial review pursuant to chapter 7 of title 5.

(C) **Protection of Confidential Information.**—The Register of Copyrights shall adopt regulations to provide for the appropriate procedures to ensure that confidential, private, proprietary, or privileged information contained in the records of the mechanical licensing collective and digital licensee coordinator is not improperly disclosed or used, including through any disclosure or use by the board of directors or personnel of either entity, and specifically including the unclaimed royalties oversight committee and the dispute resolution committee of the mechanical licensing collective.

(13) **Savings Clauses.**—

(A) **Limitation on Activities and Rights Covered.**—This subsection applies solely to uses of musical works subject to licensing under this section. The blanket license shall not be construed to extend or apply to activities other than covered activities or to rights other than the exclusive rights of reproduction and distribution licensed under this section, or serve or act as the basis to extend or expand the compulsory license under this section to activities and rights not covered by this section on the day before the enactment date.

(B) **Rights of Public Performance Not Affected.**—The rights, protections, and immunities granted under this subsection, the data concerning musical works collected and made available under this subsection, and the definitions under subsection (e) shall not extend to, limit, or otherwise affect any right of public performance in a musical work.

(e) Definitions.—As used in this section:

(1) **Accrued Interest.**—The term "accrued interest" means interest accrued on accrued royalties, as described in subsection (d)(3)(H)(ii).

(2) **Accrued Royalties.**—The term "accrued royalties" means royalties accrued for the reproduction or distribution of a musical work (or share thereof) in a covered activity, calculated in accordance with the applicable royalty rate under this section.

(3) **Administrative Assessment.**—The term "administrative assessment" means the fee established pursuant to subsection (d)(7)(D).

(4) **Audit.**—The term "audit" means a royalty compliance examination to verify the accuracy of royalty payments, or the conduct of such an examination, as applicable.

(5) **Blanket License.**—The term "blanket license" means a compulsory license described in subsection (d)(1)(A) to engage in covered activities.

(6) **Collective Total Costs.**—The term "collective total costs"—

(A) means the total costs of establishing, maintaining, and operating the mechanical licensing collective to fulfill its statutory functions, including—

(i) startup costs;

(ii) financing, legal, audit, and insurance costs;

(iii) investments in information technology, infrastructure, and other long-term resources;

(iv) outside vendor costs;

(v) costs of licensing, royalty administration, and enforcement of rights;

(vi) costs of bad debt; and

(vii) costs of automated and manual efforts to identify and locate copyright owners of musical works (and shares of such musical works) and match sound recordings to the musical works the sound recordings embody; and

(B) does not include any added costs incurred by the mechanical licensing collective to provide services under voluntary licenses.

(7) **Covered Activity.**—The term "covered activity" means the activity of making a digital phonorecord delivery of a musical work, including in the form of a permanent download, limited download, or interactive stream, where such activity qualifies for a compulsory license under this section.

(8) **Digital Music Provider.**—The term "digital music provider" means a person (or persons operating under the authority of that person) that, with respect to a service engaged in covered activities—

(A) has a direct contractual, subscription, or other economic relationship with end users of the service, or, if no such relationship with end users exists, exercises direct control over the provision of the service to end users;

(B) is able to fully report on any revenues and consideration generated by the service; and

(C) is able to fully report on usage of sound recordings of musical works by the service (or procure such reporting).

(9) **Digital Licensee Coordinator.**—The term "digital licensee coordinator" means the entity most recently designated pursuant to subsection (d)(5).

(10) **Digital Phonorecord Delivery.**—The term "digital phonorecord delivery" means each individual delivery of a phonorecord by digital transmission of a sound recording that results in a specifically identifiable reproduction by or for any transmission recipient of a phonorecord of that sound recording, regardless of whether the digital transmission is also a public performance of the sound recording or any musical work embodied therein, and includes a permanent download, a limited download, or an interactive stream. A digital phonorecord delivery does not result from a real-time, noninteractive subscription transmission of a sound recording where no reproduction of the sound recording or the musical work embodied therein is made from the inception of the transmission through to its receipt by the transmission recipient in order to make the sound recording audible. A digital phonorecord delivery does not include the digital transmission of sounds accompanying a motion picture or other audiovisual work as defined in section 101.

(11) **Enactment Date.**—The term "enactment date" means the date of the enactment of the Musical Works Modernization Act.

(12) **Individual Download License.**—The term "individual download license" means a compulsory license obtained by a record company to make and distribute, or authorize the making and distribution of, permanent downloads embodying a specific individual musical work.

(13) **Interactive Stream.**—The term "interactive stream" means a digital transmission of a sound recording of a musical work in the form of a stream, where the performance of the sound recording by means of such transmission is not exempt under section 114(d)(1) and does not in itself, or as a result of a program in which it is included, qualify for statutory licensing under section 114(d)(2). An interactive stream is a digital phonorecord delivery.

(14) **Interested.**—The term "interested", as applied to a party seeking to participate in a proceeding under subsection (d)(7)(D), is a party as to which the Copyright Royalty Judges have not determined that the party lacks a significant interest in such proceeding.

(15) **License Availability Date.**—The term "license availability date" means January 1 following the expiration of the 2-year period beginning on the enactment date.

(16) **Limited Download.**—The term "limited download" means a digital transmission of a sound recording of a musical work in the form of a download, where such sound recording is accessible for listening only for a limited amount of time or specified number of times.

(17) **Matched.**—The term "matched", as applied to a musical work (or share thereof), means that the copyright owner of such work (or share thereof) has been identified and located.

(18) **Mechanical Licensing Collective.**—The term "mechanical licensing collective" means the entity most recently designated as such by the Register of Copyrights under subsection (d)(3).

(19) **Mechanical Licensing Collective Budget.**—The term "mechanical licensing collective budget" means a statement of the financial position of the mechanical licensing collective for a fiscal year or quarter thereof based on estimates of expenditures during the period and proposals for financing those expenditures, including a calculation of the collective total costs.

(20) **Musical Works Database.**—The term "musical works database" means the database described in subsection (d)(3)(E).

(21) **Nonprofit.**—The term "nonprofit" means a nonprofit created or organized in a State.

(22) **Notice of License.**—The term "notice of license" means a notice from a digital music provider provided under subsection (d)(2)(A) for purposes of obtaining a blanket license.

(23) **Notice of Nonblanket Activity.**—The term "notice of nonblanket activity" means a notice from a significant nonblanket licensee provided under subsection (d)(6)(A) for purposes of notifying the mechanical licensing collective that the licensee has been engaging in covered activities.

(24) **Permanent Download.**—The term "permanent download" means a digital transmission of a sound recording of a musical work in the form of a download, where such sound recording is accessible for listening without restriction as to the amount of time or number of times it may be accessed.

(25) **Qualified Auditor.**—The term "qualified auditor" means an independent, certified public accountant with experience performing music royalty audits.

(26) **Record Company.**—The term "record company" means an entity that invests in, produces, and markets sound recordings of musical works, and distributes such sound recordings for remuneration through multiple sales channels, including a corporate affiliate of such an entity engaged in distribution of sound recordings.

(27) **Report of Usage.**—The term "report of usage" means a report reflecting an entity's usage of musical works in covered activities described in subsection (d)(4)(A).

(28) **Required Matching Efforts.**—The term "required matching efforts" means efforts to identify and locate copyright owners of musical works as described in subsection (d)(10)(B)(i).

(29) **Service.**—The term "service", as used in relation to covered activities, means any site, facility, or offering by or through which sound recordings of musical works are digitally transmitted to members of the public.

(30) **Share.**—The term "share", as applied to a musical work, means a fractional ownership interest in such work.

(31) **Significant Nonblanket Licensee.**—The term "significant nonblanket licensee"—

(A) means an entity, including a group of entities under common ownership or control that, acting under the authority of one or more voluntary licenses or individual download licenses, offers a service engaged in covered activities, and such entity or group of entities—

(i) is not currently operating under a blanket license and is not obligated to provide reports of usage reflecting covered activities under subsection (d)(4)(A);

(ii) has a direct contractual, subscription, or other economic relationship with end users of the service or, if no such relationship with end users exists, exercises direct control over the provision of the service to end users; and

(iii) either—

(I) on any day in a calendar month, makes more than 5,000 different sound recordings of musical works available through such service; or

(II) derives revenue or other consideration in connection with such covered activities greater than $50,000 in a calendar month, or total revenue or other consideration greater than $500,000 during the preceding 12 calendar months; and

(B) does not include—

(i) an entity whose covered activity consists solely of free-to-the-user streams of segments of sound recordings of musical works that do not exceed 90 seconds in length, are offered only to facilitate a licensed use of musical works that is not a covered activity, and have no revenue directly attributable to such streams constituting the covered activity; or

(ii) a "public broadcasting entity" as defined in section 118(f).

(32) **Songwriter.**—The term "songwriter" means the author of all or part of a musical work, including a composer or lyricist.

(33) **State.**—The term "State" means each State of the United States, the District of Columbia, and each territory or possession of the United States.

(34) **Unclaimed Accrued Royalties.**—The term "unclaimed accrued royalties" means accrued royalties eligible for distribution under subsection (d)(3)(J).

(35) **Unmatched.**—The term "unmatched", as applied to a musical work (or share thereof), means that the copyright owner of such work (or share thereof) has not been identified or located.

(36) **Voluntary License.**—The term "voluntary license" means a license for use of a musical work (or share thereof) other than a compulsory license obtained under this section.

§ 116. Negotiated Licenses for Public Performances by Means of Coin-Operated Phonorecord Players

(a) **Applicability of Section.**—This section applies to any nondramatic musical work embodied in a phonorecord.

(b) **Negotiated Licenses.**—

(1) **Authority for Negotiations.**—Any owners of copyright in works to which this section applies and any operators of coin-operated phonorecord players may negotiate and agree upon the terms and rates of royalty payments for the performance of such works and the proportionate division of fees paid among copyright owners, and may designate common agents to negotiate, agree to, pay, or receive such royalty payments.

(2) **Chapter 8 Proceeding.**—Parties not subject to such a negotiation may have the terms and rates and the division of fees described in paragraph (1) determined in a proceeding in accordance with the provisions of chapter 8.

(c) **License Agreements Superior to Determinations by Copyright Royalty Judges.**— License agreements between one or more copyright owners and one or more operators of coin-operated phonorecord players, which are negotiated in accordance with subsection (b), shall be given effect in lieu of any otherwise applicable determination by the Copyright Royalty Judges.

(d) **Definitions.**—As used in this section, the following terms mean the following:

(1) A "coin-operated phonorecord player" is a machine or device that—

(A) is employed solely for the performance of nondramatic musical works by means of phonorecords upon being activated by the insertion of coins, currency, tokens, or other monetary units or their equivalent;

(B) is located in an establishment making no direct or indirect charge for admission;

(C) is accompanied by a list which is comprised of the titles of all the musical works available for performance on it, and is affixed to the phonorecord player or posted in the establishment in a prominent position where it can be readily examined by the public; and

(D) affords a choice of works available for performance and permits the choice to be made by the patrons of the establishment in which it is located.

(2) An "operator" is any person who, alone or jointly with others—

(A) owns a coin-operated phonorecord player;

(B) has the power to make a coin-operated phonorecord player available for placement in an establishment for purposes of public performance; or

(C) has the power to exercise primary control over the selection of the musical works made available for public performance on a coin-operated phonorecord player.

§ 117. Limitations on Exclusive Rights: Computer Programs

(a) Making of Additional Copy or Adaptation by Owner of Copy.—Notwithstanding the provisions of section 106, it is not an infringement for the owner of a copy of a computer program to make or authorize the making of another copy or adaptation of that computer program provided:

(1) that such a new copy or adaptation is created as an essential step in the utilization of the computer program in conjunction with a machine and that it is used in no other manner, or

(2) that such new copy or adaptation is for archival purposes only and that all archival copies are destroyed in the event that continued possession of the computer program should cease to be rightful.

(b) Lease, Sale, or Other Transfer of Additional Copy or Adaptation.—Any exact copies prepared in accordance with the provisions of this section may be leased, sold, or otherwise transferred, along with the copy from which such copies were prepared, only as part of the lease, sale, or other transfer of all rights in the program. Adaptations so prepared may be transferred only with the authorization of the copyright owner.

(c) Machine Maintenance or Repair.—Notwithstanding the provisions of section 106, it is not an infringement for the owner or lessee of a machine to make or authorize the making of a copy of a computer program if such copy is made solely by virtue of the activation of a machine that lawfully contains an authorized copy of the computer program, for purposes only of maintenance or repair of that machine, if—

(1) such new copy is used in no other manner and is destroyed immediately after the maintenance or repair is completed; and

(2) with respect to any computer program or part thereof that is not necessary for that machine to be activated, such program or part thereof is not accessed or used other than to make such new copy by virtue of the activation of the machine.

(d) Definitions.—For purposes of this section—

(1) the "maintenance" of a machine is the servicing of the machine in order to make it work in accordance with its original specifications and any changes to those specifications authorized for that machine; and

(2) the "repair" of a machine is the restoring of the machine to the state of working in accordance with its original specifications and any changes to those specifications authorized for that machine.

§ 118. Scope of Exclusive Rights: Use of Certain Works in Connection With Noncommercial Broadcasting

(a) The exclusive rights provided by section 106 shall, with respect to the works specified by subsection (b) and the activities specified by subsection (d), be subject to the conditions and limitations prescribed by this section.

(b) Notwithstanding any provision of the antitrust laws, any owners of copyright in published nondramatic musical works and published pictorial, graphic, and sculptural works and any public broadcasting entities, respectively, may negotiate and agree upon the terms and rates of royalty payments and the proportionate division of fees paid among various copyright owners, and may designate common agents to negotiate, agree to, pay, or receive payments.

(1) Any owner of copyright in a work specified in this subsection or any public broadcasting entity may submit to the Copyright Royalty Judges proposed licenses covering such activities with respect to such works.

(2) License agreements voluntarily negotiated at any time between one or more copyright owners and one or more public broadcasting entities shall be given effect in lieu of any

determination by the Librarian of Congress or the Copyright Royalty Judges, if copies of such agreements are filed with the Copyright Royalty Judges within 30 days of execution in accordance with regulations that the Copyright Royalty Judges shall issue.

(3) Voluntary negotiation proceedings initiated pursuant to a petition filed under section 804(a) for the purpose of determining a schedule of terms and rates of royalty payments by public broadcasting entities to owners of copyright in works specified by this subsection and the proportionate division of fees paid among various copyright owners shall cover the 5-year period beginning on January 1 of the second year following the year in which the petition is filed. The parties to each negotiation proceeding shall bear their own costs.

(4) In the absence of license agreements negotiated under paragraph (2) or (3), the Copyright Royalty Judges shall, pursuant to chapter 8, conduct a proceeding to determine and publish in the Federal Register a schedule of rates and terms which, subject to paragraph (2), shall be binding on all owners of copyright in works specified by this subsection and public broadcasting entities, regardless of whether such copyright owners have submitted proposals to the Copyright Royalty Judges. In establishing such rates and terms the Copyright Royalty Judges may consider the rates for comparable circumstances under voluntary license agreements negotiated as provided in paragraph (2) or (3). The Copyright Royalty Judges shall also establish requirements by which copyright owners may receive reasonable notice of the use of their works under this section, and under which records of such use shall be kept by public broadcasting entities.

(c) Subject to the terms of any voluntary license agreements that have been negotiated as provided by subsection (b)(2) or (3), a public broadcasting entity may, upon compliance with the provisions of this section, including the rates and terms established by the Copyright Royalty Judges under subsection (b)(4), engage in the following activities with respect to published nondramatic musical works and published pictorial, graphic, and sculptural works:

(1) performance or display of a work by or in the course of a transmission made by a noncommercial educational broadcast station referred to in subsection (f); and

(2) production of a transmission program, reproduction of copies or phonorecords of such a transmission program, and distribution of such copies or phonorecords, where such production, reproduction, or distribution is made by a nonprofit institution or organization solely for the purpose of transmissions specified in paragraph (1); and

(3) the making of reproductions by a governmental body or a nonprofit institution of a transmission program simultaneously with its transmission as specified in paragraph (1), and the performance or display of the contents of such program under the conditions specified by paragraph (1) of section 110, but only if the reproductions are used for performances or displays for a period of no more than seven days from the date of the transmission specified in paragraph (1), and are destroyed before or at the end of such period. No person supplying, in accordance with paragraph (2), a reproduction of a transmission program to governmental bodies or nonprofit institutions under this paragraph shall have any liability as a result of failure of such body or institution to destroy such reproduction: *Provided,* That it shall have notified such body or institution of the requirement for such destruction pursuant to this paragraph: *And provided further,* That if such body or institution itself fails to destroy such reproduction it shall be deemed to have infringed.

(d) Except as expressly provided in this subsection, this section shall have no applicability to works other than those specified in subsection (b).

Owners of copyright in nondramatic literary works and public broadcasting entities may, during the course of voluntary negotiations, agree among themselves, respectively, as to the terms and rates of royalty payments without liability under the antitrust laws. Any such terms and rates of royalty payments shall be effective upon filing with the Copyright Royalty Judges, in accordance with regulations that the Copyright Royalty Judges shall prescribe as provided in section 803(b)(6).

(e) Nothing in this section shall be construed to permit, beyond the limits of fair use as provided by section 107, the unauthorized dramatization of a nondramatic musical work, the production of a transmission program drawn to any substantial extent from a published compilation of pictorial, graphic, or sculptural works, or the unauthorized use of any portion of an audiovisual work.

(f) As used in this section, the term "public broadcasting entity" means a noncommercial educational broadcast station as defined in section 397 of title 47 and any nonprofit institution or organization engaged in the activities described in paragraph (2) of subsection (c).

§ 119. Limitations on Exclusive Rights: Secondary Transmissions of Distant Television Programming by Satellite

(a) Secondary Transmissions by Satellite Carriers.—

(1) Non-network Stations.—Subject to the provisions of paragraphs (4), (5), and (7) of this subsection and section 114(d), secondary transmissions of a performance or display of a work embodied in a primary transmission made by a non-network station shall be subject to statutory licensing under this section if the secondary transmission is made by a satellite carrier to the public for private home viewing or for viewing in a commercial establishment, with regard to secondary transmissions the satellite carrier is in compliance with the rules, regulations, or authorizations of the Federal Communications Commission governing the carriage of television broadcast station signals, and the carrier makes a direct or indirect charge for each retransmission service to each subscriber receiving the secondary transmission or to a distributor that has contracted with the carrier for direct or indirect delivery of the secondary transmission to the public for private home viewing or for viewing in a commercial establishment.

(2) Network Stations.—

(A) In General.—Subject to the provisions of subparagraph (B) of this paragraph and paragraphs (4), (5), (6), and (7) of this subsection and section 114(d), secondary transmissions of a performance or display of a work embodied in a primary transmission made by a network station shall be subject to statutory licensing under this section if the secondary transmission is made by a satellite carrier to the public for private home viewing, with regard to secondary transmissions the satellite carrier is in compliance with the rules, regulations, or authorizations of the Federal Communications Commission governing the carriage of television broadcast station signals, and the carrier makes a direct or indirect charge for such retransmission service to each subscriber receiving the secondary transmission.

(B) Secondary Transmissions to Unserved Households.—

(i) In General.—The statutory license provided for in subparagraph (A) shall be limited to secondary transmissions of the signals of no more than two network stations in a single day for each television network to persons who reside in unserved households.

(ii) Accurate Determinations of Eligibility.—

(I) Accurate Predictive Model.—In determining presumptively whether a person resides in an unserved household under subsection (d)(10)(A), a court shall rely on the Individual Location Longley-Rice model set forth by the Federal Communications Commission in Docket No. 98–201, as that model may be amended by the Commission over time under section 339(c)(3) of the Communications Act of 1934 to increase the accuracy of that model.

(II) Accurate Measurements.—For purposes of site measurements to determine whether a person resides in an unserved household under subsection (d)(10)(A), a court shall rely on section 339(c)(4) of the Communications Act of 1934.

(III) Accurate Predictive Model With Respect to Digital Signals.—Notwithstanding subclause (I), in determining presumptively whether a person resides in an unserved household under subsection (d)(10)(A) with respect to digital signals, a court shall rely on a predictive model set forth by the Federal Communications Commission pursuant to a rulemaking as provided in section 339(c)(3) of the Communications Act of 1934 (47 U.S.C. 339(c)(3)), as that model may be amended by the Commission over time under such section to increase the accuracy of that model. Until such time as the Commission sets forth such model, a court shall rely on the predictive model as recommended by the Commission with respect to digital signals in its Report to Congress in ET Docket No. 05–182, FCC 05–199 (released December 9, 2005).

(iii) C-band Exemption to Unserved Households.—

(I) In General.—The limitations of clause (i) shall not apply to any secondary transmissions by C-band services of network stations that a subscriber to C-band service received before any termination of such secondary transmissions before October 31, 1999.

(II) Definition.—In this clause, the term "C-band service" means a service that is licensed by the Federal Communications Commission and operates in the Fixed Satellite Service under part 25 of title 47, Code of Federal Regulations.

(C) Submission of Subscriber Lists to Networks.—

(i) Initial Lists.—A satellite carrier that makes secondary transmissions of a primary transmission made by a network station pursuant to subparagraph (A) shall, not later than 90 days after commencing such secondary transmissions, submit to the network that owns or is affiliated with the network station a list identifying (by name and address, including street or rural route number, city, State, and 9-digit zip code) all subscribers to which the satellite carrier makes secondary transmissions of that primary transmission to subscribers in unserved households.

(ii) Monthly Lists.—After the submission of the initial lists under clause (i), the satellite carrier shall, not later than the 15th of each month, submit to the network a list, aggregated by designated market area, identifying (by name and address, including street or rural route number, city, State, and 9-digit zip code) any persons who have been added or dropped as subscribers under clause (i) since the last submission under this subparagraph.

(iii) Use of Subscriber Information.—Subscriber information submitted by a satellite carrier under this subparagraph may be used only for purposes of monitoring compliance by the satellite carrier with this subsection.

(iv) Applicability.—The submission requirements of this subparagraph shall apply to a satellite carrier only if the network to which the submissions are to be made places on file with the Register of Copyrights a document identifying the name and address of the person to whom such submissions are to be made. The Register shall maintain for public inspection a file of all such documents.

(3) Statutory License Where Retransmissions into Local Market Available.—

(A) Rules for Subscribers to Signals Under Subsection (e)—

(i) For Those Receiving Distant Signals.—In the case of a subscriber of a satellite carrier who is eligible to receive the secondary transmission of the primary transmission of a network station solely by reason of subsection (e) (in this subparagraph referred to as a "distant signal"), and who, as of October 1, 2004, is receiving the distant signal of that network station, the following shall apply:

(I) In a case in which the satellite carrier makes available to the subscriber the secondary transmission of the primary transmission of a local network station affiliated with the same television network pursuant to the statutory license under section 122, the statutory license under paragraph (2) shall apply only to secondary transmissions by that satellite carrier to that subscriber of the distant signal of a station affiliated with the same television network—

(aa) if, within 60 days after receiving the notice of the satellite carrier under section 338(h)(1) of the Communications Act of 1934, the subscriber elects to retain the distant signal; but

(bb) only until such time as the subscriber elects to receive such local signal.

(II) Notwithstanding subclause (I), the statutory license under paragraph (2) shall not apply with respect to any subscriber who is eligible to receive the distant signal of a television network station solely by reason of subsection (e), unless the satellite carrier, within 60 days after the date of the enactment of the Satellite Home Viewer Extension and Reauthorization Act of 2004, submits to that television network a list, aggregated by designated market area (as defined in section 122(j)(2)(C)), that—

(aa) identifies that subscriber by name and address (street or rural route number, city, State, and zip code) and specifies the distant signals received by the subscriber; and

(bb) states, to the best of the satellite carrier's knowledge and belief, after having made diligent and good faith inquiries, that the subscriber is eligible under subsection (e) to receive the distant signals.

(ii) For Those Not Receiving Distant Signals.—In the case of any subscriber of a satellite carrier who is eligible to receive the distant signal of a network station solely by reason of subsection (e) and who did not receive a distant signal of a station affiliated with the same network on October 1, 2004, the statutory license under paragraph (2) shall not apply to secondary transmissions by that satellite carrier to that subscriber of the distant signal of a station affiliated with the same network.

(B) Rules for Lawful Subscribers as of Date of Enactment of 2010 Act.—In the case of a subscriber of a satellite carrier who, on the day before the date of the enactment of the Satellite Television Extension and Localism Act of 2010, was lawfully receiving the secondary transmission of the primary transmission of a network station under the statutory license under paragraph (2) (in this subparagraph referred to as the "distant signal"), other than subscribers to whom subparagraph (A) applies, the statutory license under paragraph (2) shall apply to secondary transmissions by that satellite carrier to that subscriber of the distant signal of a station affiliated with the same television network, and the subscriber's household shall continue to be considered to be an unserved household with respect to such network, until such time as the subscriber elects to terminate such secondary transmissions, whether or not the subscriber elects to subscribe to receive the secondary transmission of the primary transmission of a local network station affiliated with the same network pursuant to the statutory license under section 122.

(C) Future Applicability.—

(i) **When Local Signal Available at Time of Subscription.**—The statutory license under paragraph (2) shall not apply to the secondary transmission by a satellite carrier of the primary transmission of a network station to a person who is not a subscriber lawfully receiving such secondary transmission as of the date of the enactment of the Satellite Television Extension and Localism Act of 2010 and, at the time such person seeks to subscribe to receive such secondary transmission, resides in a local market where the satellite carrier makes available to that person the secondary transmission of the primary transmission of a local network station affiliated with the same network pursuant to the statutory license under section 122.

(ii) **When Local Signal Available After Subscription.**—In the case of a subscriber who lawfully subscribes to and receives the secondary transmission by a satellite carrier of the primary transmission of a network station under the statutory license under paragraph (2) (in this clause referred to as the "distant signal") on or after the date of the enactment of the Satellite Television Extension and Localism Act of 2010, the statutory license under paragraph (2) shall apply to secondary transmissions by that satellite carrier to that subscriber of the distant signal of a station affiliated with the same television network, and the subscriber's household shall continue to be considered to be an unserved household with respect to such network, until such time as the subscriber elects to terminate such secondary transmissions, but only if such subscriber subscribes to the secondary transmission of the primary transmission of a local network station affiliated with the same network within 60 days after the satellite carrier makes available to the subscriber such secondary transmission of the primary transmission of such local network station.

(D) **Other Provisions Not Affected.**—This paragraph shall not affect the applicability of the statutory license to secondary transmissions to unserved households included under paragraph (11).

(E) **Waiver.**—A subscriber who is denied the secondary transmission of a network station under subparagraph (B) or (C) may request a waiver from such denial by submitting a request, through the subscriber's satellite carrier, to the network station in the local market affiliated with the same network where the subscriber is located. The network station shall accept or reject the subscriber's request for a waiver within 30 days after receipt of the request. If the network station fails to accept or reject the subscriber's request for a waiver within that 30-day period, that network station shall be deemed to agree to the waiver request. Unless specifically stated by the network station, a waiver that was granted before the date of the enactment of the Satellite Home Viewer Extension and Reauthorization Act of 2004 under section 339(c)(2) of the Communications Act of 1934 shall not constitute a waiver for purposes of this subparagraph.

(F) **Available Defined.**—For purposes of this paragraph, a satellite carrier makes available a secondary transmission of the primary transmission of a local station to a subscriber or person if the satellite carrier offers that secondary transmission to other subscribers who reside in the same 9-digit zip code as that subscriber or person.

(4) **Noncompliance With Reporting and Payment Requirements.**—Notwithstanding the provisions of paragraphs (1) and (2), the willful or repeated secondary transmission to the public by a satellite carrier of a primary transmission made by a non-network station or a network station and embodying a performance or display of a work is actionable as an act of infringement under section 501, and is fully subject to the remedies provided by sections 502 through 506, where the satellite carrier has not deposited the statement of account and royalty fee required by subsection (b), or has failed to make the submissions to networks required by paragraph (2)(C).

(5) **Willful Alterations.**—Notwithstanding the provisions of paragraphs (1) and (2), the secondary transmission to the public by a satellite carrier of a performance or display of a work

embodied in a primary transmission made by a non-network station or a network station is actionable as an act of infringement under section 501, and is fully subject to the remedies provided by sections 502 through 506 and section 510, if the content of the particular program in which the performance or display is embodied, or any commercial advertising or station announcement transmitted by the primary transmitter during, or immediately before or after, the transmission of such program, is in any way willfully altered by the satellite carrier through changes, deletions, or additions, or is combined with programming from any other broadcast signal.

(6) Violation of Territorial Restrictions on Statutory License for Network Stations.—

    (A) Individual Violations.—The willful or repeated secondary transmission by a satellite carrier of a primary transmission made by a network station and embodying a performance or display of a work to a subscriber who is not eligible to receive the transmission under this section is actionable as an act of infringement under section 501 and is fully subject to the remedies provided by sections 502 through 506, except that—

        (i)   no damages shall be awarded for such act of infringement if the satellite carrier took corrective action by promptly withdrawing service from the ineligible subscriber, and

        (ii)   any statutory damages shall not exceed $250 for such subscriber for each month during which the violation occurred.

    (B) Pattern of Violations.—If a satellite carrier engages in a willful or repeated pattern or practice of delivering a primary transmission made by a network station and embodying a performance or display of a work to subscribers who are not eligible to receive the transmission under this section, then in addition to the remedies set forth in subparagraph (A)—

        (i)   if the pattern or practice has been carried out on a substantially nationwide basis, the court shall order a permanent injunction barring the secondary transmission by the satellite carrier, for private home viewing, of the primary transmissions of any primary network station affiliated with the same network, and the court may order statutory damages of not to exceed $2,500,000 for each 3-month period during which the pattern or practice was carried out; and

        (ii)   if the pattern or practice has been carried out on a local or regional basis, the court shall order a permanent injunction barring the secondary transmission, for private home viewing in that locality or region, by the satellite carrier of the primary transmissions of any primary network station affiliated with the same network, and the court may order statutory damages of not to exceed $2,500,000 for each 6-month period during which the pattern or practice was carried out.

    (C) Previous Subscribers Excluded.—Subparagraphs (A) and (B) do not apply to secondary transmissions by a satellite carrier to persons who subscribed to receive such secondary transmissions from the satellite carrier or a distributor before November 16, 1988.

    (D) Burden of Proof.—In any action brought under this paragraph, the satellite carrier shall have the burden of proving that its secondary transmission of a primary transmission by a network station is to a subscriber who is eligible to receive the secondary transmission under this section.

    (E) Exception.—The secondary transmission by a satellite carrier of a performance or display of a work embodied in a primary transmission made by a network station to subscribers who do not reside in unserved households shall not be an act of infringement if—

(i) the station on May 1, 1991, was retransmitted by a satellite carrier and was not on that date owned or operated by or affiliated with a television network that offered interconnected program service on a regular basis for 15 or more hours per week to at least 25 affiliated television licensees in 10 or more States;

(ii) as of July 1, 1998, such station was retransmitted by a satellite carrier under the statutory license of this section; and

(iii) the station is not owned or operated by or affiliated with a television network that, as of January 1, 1995, offered interconnected program service on a regular basis for 15 or more hours per week to at least 25 affiliated television licensees in 10 or more States.

The court shall direct one half of any statutory damages ordered under clause (i) to be deposited with the Register of Copyrights for distribution to copyright owners pursuant to subsection (b). The Copyright Royalty Judges shall issue regulations establishing procedures for distributing such funds, on a proportional basis, to copyright owners whose works were included in the secondary transmissions that were the subject of the statutory damages.

(7) Discrimination by a Satellite Carrier.—Notwithstanding the provisions of paragraph (1), the willful or repeated secondary transmission to the public by a satellite carrier of a performance or display of a work embodied in a primary transmission made by a non-network station or a network station is actionable as an act of infringement under section 501, and is fully subject to the remedies provided by sections 502 through 506, if the satellite carrier unlawfully discriminates against a distributor.

(8) Geographic Limitation on Secondary Transmissions.—The statutory license created by this section shall apply only to secondary transmissions to households located in the United States.

(9) Loser Pays for Signal Intensity Measurement; Recovery of Measurement Costs in a Civil Action.—In any civil action filed relating to the eligibility of subscribing households as unserved households—

(A) a network station challenging such eligibility shall, within 60 days after receipt of the measurement results and a statement of such costs, reimburse the satellite carrier for any signal intensity measurement that is conducted by that carrier in response to a challenge by the network station and that establishes the household is an unserved household; and

(B) a satellite carrier shall, within 60 days after receipt of the measurement results and a statement of such costs, reimburse the network station challenging such eligibility for any signal intensity measurement that is conducted by that station and that establishes the household is not an unserved household.

(10) Inability to Conduct Measurement.—If a network station makes a reasonable attempt to conduct a site measurement of its signal at a subscriber's household and is denied access for the purpose of conducting the measurement, and is otherwise unable to conduct a measurement, the satellite carrier shall within 60 days notice thereof, terminate service of the station's network to that household.

(11) Service to Recreational Vehicles and Commercial Trucks.—

(A) **Exemption.**—

(i) **In General.**—For purposes of this subsection, and subject to clauses (ii) and (iii), the term "unserved household" shall include—

(I) recreational vehicles as defined in regulations of the Secretary of Housing and Urban Development under section 3282.8 of title 24, Code of Federal Regulations; and

(II) commercial trucks that qualify as commercial motor vehicles under regulations of the Secretary of Transportation under section 383.5 of title 49, Code of Federal Regulations.

(ii) **Limitation.**—Clause (i) shall apply only to a recreational vehicle or commercial truck if any satellite carrier that proposes to make a secondary transmission of a network station to the operator of such a recreational vehicle or commercial truck complies with the documentation requirements under subparagraphs (B) and (C).

(iii) **Exclusion.**—For purposes of this subparagraph, the terms "recreational vehicle" and "commercial truck" shall not include any fixed dwelling, whether a mobile home or otherwise.

(B) **Documentation Requirements.**—A recreational vehicle or commercial truck shall be deemed to be an unserved household beginning 10 days after the relevant satellite carrier provides to the network that owns or is affiliated with the network station that will be secondarily transmitted to the recreational vehicle or commercial truck the following documents:

(i) **Declaration.**—A signed declaration by the operator of the recreational vehicle or commercial truck that the satellite dish is permanently attached to the recreational vehicle or commercial truck, and will not be used to receive satellite programming at any fixed dwelling.

(ii) **Registration.**—In the case of a recreational vehicle, a copy of the current State vehicle registration for the recreational vehicle.

(iii) **Registration and License.**—In the case of a commercial truck, a copy of—

(I) the current State vehicle registration for the truck; and

(II) a copy of a valid, current commercial driver's license, as defined in regulations of the Secretary of Transportation under section 383 of title 49, Code of Federal Regulations, issued to the operator.

(C) **Updated Documentation Requirements.**—If a satellite carrier wishes to continue to make secondary transmissions to a recreational vehicle or commercial truck for more than a 2-year period, that carrier shall provide each network, upon request, with updated documentation in the form described under subparagraph (B) during the 90 days before expiration of that 2-year period.

(12) **Statutory License Contingent on Compliance with FCC Rules and Remedial Steps.**—Notwithstanding any other provision of this section, the willful or repeated secondary transmission to the public by a satellite carrier of a primary transmission embodying a performance or display of a work made by a broadcast station licensed by the Federal Communications Commission is actionable as an act of infringement under section 501, and is fully subject to the remedies provided by sections 502 through 506, if, at the time of such transmission, the satellite carrier is not in compliance with the rules, regulations, and authorizations of the Federal Communications Commission concerning the carriage of television broadcast station signals.

(13) **Waivers.**—A subscriber who is denied the secondary transmission of a signal of a network station under subsection (a)(2)(B) may request a waiver from such denial by submitting a request, through the subscriber's satellite carrier, to the network station asserting that the secondary transmission is prohibited. The network station shall accept or reject a subscriber's request for a waiver within 30 days after receipt of the request. If a television network station fails to accept or reject a subscriber's request for a waiver within the 30-day period after receipt of the request, that station shall be deemed to agree to the waiver request and have filed such

written waiver. Unless specifically stated by the network station, a waiver that was granted before the date of the enactment of the Satellite Home Viewer Extension and Reauthorization Act of 2004 under section 339(c)(2) of the Communications Act of 1934, and that was in effect on such date of enactment, shall constitute a waiver for purposes of this paragraph.

(14) Restricted Transmission of Out-of-State Distant Network Signals into Certain Markets.—

(A) Out-of-State Network Affiliates.—Notwithstanding any other provision of this title, the statutory license in this subsection and subsection (b) shall not apply to any secondary transmission of the primary transmission of a network station located outside of the State of Alaska to any subscriber in that State to whom the secondary transmission of the primary transmission of a television station located in that State is made available by the satellite carrier pursuant to section 122.

(B) Exception.—The limitation in subparagraph (A) shall not apply to the secondary transmission of the primary transmission of a digital signal of a network station located outside of the State of Alaska if at the time that the secondary transmission is made, no television station licensed to a community in the State and affiliated with the same network makes primary transmissions of a digital signal.

(b) Deposit of Statements and Fees; Verification Procedures.—

(1) Deposits With the Register of Copyrights.—A satellite carrier whose secondary transmissions are subject to statutory licensing under subsection (a) shall, on a semiannual basis, deposit with the Register of Copyrights, in accordance with requirements that the Register shall prescribe by regulation—

(A) a statement of account, covering the preceding 6-month period, specifying the names and locations of all non-network stations and network stations whose signals were retransmitted, at any time during that period, to subscribers as described in subsections (a)(1) and (a)(2), the total number of subscribers that received such retransmissions, and such other data as the Register of Copyrights may from time to time prescribe by regulation;

(B) a royalty fee payable to copyright owners pursuant to paragraph (4) for that 6-month period, computed by multiplying the total number of subscribers receiving each secondary transmission of a primary stream or multicast stream of each non-network station or network station during each calendar year month by the appropriate rate in effect under this subsection; and

(C) a filing fee, as determined by the Register of Copyrights pursuant to section 708(a).

(2) Verification of Accounts and Fee Payments.—The Register of Copyrights shall issue regulations to permit interested parties to verify and audit the statements of account and royalty fees submitted by satellite carriers under this subsection.

(3) Investment of Fees.—The Register of Copyrights shall receive all fees (including the filing fee specified in paragraph (1)(C)) deposited under this section and, after deducting the reasonable costs incurred by the Copyright Office under this section (other than the costs deducted under paragraph (5)), shall deposit the balance in the Treasury of the United States, in such manner as the Secretary of the Treasury directs. All funds held by the Secretary of the Treasury shall be invested in interest-bearing securities of the United States for later distribution with interest by the Librarian of Congress as provided by this title.

(4) Persons to Whom Fees Are Distributed.—The royalty fees deposited under paragraph (3) shall, in accordance with the procedures provided by paragraph (5), be distributed to those copyright owners whose works were included in a secondary transmission made by a satellite carrier during the applicable 6-month accounting period and who file a claim with the Copyright Royalty Judges under paragraph (5).

(5) Procedures for Distribution.—The royalty fees deposited under paragraph (3) shall be distributed in accordance with the following procedures:

(A) Filing of Claims for Fees.—During the month of July in each year, each person claiming to be entitled to statutory license fees for secondary transmissions shall file a claim with the Copyright Royalty Judges, in accordance with requirements that the Copyright Royalty Judges shall prescribe by regulation. For purposes of this paragraph, any claimants may agree among themselves as to the proportionate division of statutory license fees among them, may lump their claims together and file them jointly or as a single claim, or may designate a common agent to receive payment on their behalf.

(B) Determination of Controversy; Distributions.—After the first day of August of each year, the Copyright Royalty Judges shall determine whether there exists a controversy concerning the distribution of royalty fees. If the Copyright Royalty Judges determine that no such controversy exists, the Copyright Royalty Judges shall authorize the Librarian of Congress to proceed to distribute such fees to the copyright owners entitled to receive them, or to their designated agents, subject to the deduction of reasonable administrative costs under this section. If the Copyright Royalty Judges find the existence of a controversy, the Copyright Royalty Judges shall, pursuant to chapter 8 of this title, conduct a proceeding to determine the distribution of royalty fees.

(C) Withholding of Fees During Controversy.—During the pendency of any proceeding under this subsection, the Copyright Royalty Judges shall have the discretion to authorize the Librarian of Congress to proceed to distribute any amounts that are not in controversy.

(c) Adjustment of Royalty Fees.—

(1) Applicability and Determination of Royalty Fees for Signals.—

(A) Initial Fee.—The appropriate fee for purposes of determining the royalty fee under subsection (b)(1)(B) for the secondary transmission of the primary transmissions of network stations and non-network stations shall be the appropriate fee set forth in part 258 of title 37, Code of Federal Regulations, as in effect on July 1, 2009, as modified under this paragraph.

(B) Fee Set by Voluntary Negotiation.—On or before June 1, 2010, the Copyright Royalty Judges shall cause to be published in the Federal Register of the initiation of voluntary negotiation proceedings for the purpose of determining the royalty fee to be paid by satellite carriers for the secondary transmission of the primary transmissions of network stations and non-network stations under subsection (b)(1)(B).

(C) Negotiations.—Satellite carriers, distributors, and copyright owners entitled to royalty fees under this section shall negotiate in good faith in an effort to reach a voluntary agreement or agreements for the payment of royalty fees. Any such satellite carriers, distributors and copyright owners may at any time negotiate and agree to the royalty fee, and may designate common agents to negotiate, agree to, or pay such fees. If the parties fail to identify common agents, the Copyright Royalty Judges shall do so, after requesting recommendations from the parties to the negotiation proceeding. The parties to each negotiation proceeding shall bear the cost thereof.

(D) Agreements Binding on Parties; Filing of Agreements; Public Notice.—

(i) Voluntary Agreements; Filing.—Voluntary agreements negotiated at any time in accordance with this paragraph shall be binding upon all satellite carriers, distributors, and copyright owners that are parties thereto. Copies of such agreements shall be filed with the Copyright Office within 30 days after execution in accordance with regulations that the Register of Copyrights shall prescribe.

(ii) Procedure for Adoption of Fees.—

(I) Publication of Notice.—Within 10 days after publication in the Federal Register of a notice of the initiation of voluntary negotiation proceedings, parties who have reached a voluntary agreement may request that the royalty fees in that agreement be applied to all satellite carriers, distributors, and copyright owners without convening a proceeding under subparagraph (F).

(II) Public Notice of Fees.—Upon receiving a request under subclause (I), the Copyright Royalty Judges shall immediately provide public notice of the royalty fees from the voluntary agreement and afford parties an opportunity to state that they object to those fees.

(III) Adoption of Fees.—The Copyright Royalty Judges shall adopt the royalty fees from the voluntary agreement for all satellite carriers, distributors, and copyright owners without convening the proceeding under subparagraph (F) unless a party with an intent to participate in that proceeding and a significant interest in the outcome of that proceeding objects under subclause (II).

(E) Period Agreement Is in Effect.—The obligation to pay the royalty fees established under a voluntary agreement which has been filed with the Copyright Royalty Judges in accordance with this paragraph shall become effective on the date specified in the agreement, and shall remain in effect until December 31, 2019, or in accordance with the terms of the agreement, whichever is later.

(F) Fee Set by Copyright Royalty Judges Proceeding.—

(i) Notice of Initiation of the Proceeding.—On or before September 1, 2010, the Copyright Royalty Judges shall cause notice to be published in the Federal Register of the initiation of a proceeding for the purpose of determining the royalty fees to be paid for the secondary transmission of the primary transmissions of network stations and non-network stations under subsection (b)(1)(B) by satellite carriers and distributors—

(I) in the absence of a voluntary agreement filed in accordance with subparagraph (D) that establishes royalty fees to be paid by all satellite carriers and distributors; or

(II) if an objection to the fees from a voluntary agreement submitted for adoption by the Copyright Royalty Judges to apply to all satellite carriers, distributors, and copyright owners is received under subparagraph (D) from a party with an intent to participate in the proceeding and a significant interest in the outcome of that proceeding.

Such proceeding shall be conducted under chapter 8.

(ii) Establishment of Royalty Fees.—In determining royalty fees under this subparagraph, the Copyright Royalty Judges shall establish fees for the secondary transmissions of the primary transmissions of network stations and non-network stations that most clearly represent the fair market value of secondary transmissions, except that the Copyright Royalty Judges shall adjust royalty fees to account for the obligations of the parties under any applicable voluntary agreement filed with the Copyright Royalty Judges in accordance with subparagraph (D). In determining the fair market value, the Judges shall base their decision on economic, competitive, and programming information presented by the parties, including—

(I) the competitive environment in which such programming is distributed, the cost of similar signals in similar private and compulsory license marketplaces, and any special features and conditions of the retransmission marketplace;

(II) the economic impact of such fees on copyright owners and satellite carriers; and

(III) the impact on the continued availability of secondary transmissions to the public.

(iii) Effective Date for Decision of Copyright Royalty Judges.—The obligation to pay the royalty fees established under a determination that is made by the Copyright Royalty Judges in a proceeding under this paragraph shall be effective as of January 1, 2010.

(iv) Persons Subject to Royalty Fees.—The royalty fees referred to in clause (iii) shall be binding on all satellite carriers, distributors and copyright owners, who are not party to a voluntary agreement filed with the Copyright Office under subparagraph (D).

(2) Annual Royalty Fee Adjustment.—Effective January 1 of each year, the royalty fee payable under subsection (b)(1)(B) for the secondary transmission of the primary transmissions of network stations and non-network stations shall be adjusted by the Copyright Royalty Judges to reflect any changes occurring in the cost of living as determined by the most recent Consumer Price Index (for all consumers and for all items) published by the Secretary of Labor before December 1 of the preceding year. Notification of the adjusted fees shall be published in the Federal Register at least 25 days before January 1.

(d) Definitions.—As used in this section—

(1) Distributor.—The term "distributor" means an entity that contracts to distribute secondary transmissions from a satellite carrier and, either as a single channel or in a package with other programming, provides the secondary transmission either directly to individual subscribers or indirectly through other program distribution entities in accordance with the provisions of this section.

(2) Network Station.—The term "network station" means—

(A) a television station licensed by the Federal Communications Commission, including any translator station or terrestrial satellite station that rebroadcasts all or substantially all of the programming broadcast by a network station, that is owned or operated by, or affiliated with, one or more of the television networks in the United States that offer an interconnected program service on a regular basis for 15 or more hours per week to at least 25 of its affiliated television licensees in 10 or more States; or

(B) a noncommercial educational broadcast station (as defined in section 397 of the Communications Act of 1934);

except that the term does not include the signal of the Alaska Rural Communications Service, or any successor entity to that service.

(3) Primary Network Station.—The term "primary network station" means a network station that broadcasts or rebroadcasts the basic programming service of a particular national network.

(4) Primary Transmission.—The term "primary transmission" has the meaning given that term in section 111(f) of this title.

(5) Private Home Viewing.—The term "private home viewing" means the viewing, for private use in a household by means of satellite reception equipment that is operated by an individual in that household and that serves only such household, of a secondary transmission delivered by a satellite carrier of a primary transmission of a television station licensed by the Federal Communications Commission.

(6) Satellite Carrier.—The term "satellite carrier" means an entity that uses the facilities of a satellite or satellite service licensed by the Federal Communications Commission and operates in the Fixed-Satellite Service under part 25 of title 47, Code of Federal Regulations, or the Direct Broadcast Satellite Service under part 100 of title 47, Code of Federal Regulations, to establish and operate a channel of communications for point-to-multipoint distribution of television station signals, and that owns or leases a capacity or service on a satellite in order to provide such point-to-multipoint distribution, except to the extent that such entity provides such distribution pursuant to tariff under the Communications Act of 1934, other than for private home viewing pursuant to this section.

(7) Secondary Transmission.—The term "secondary transmission" has the meaning given that term in section 111(f) of this title.

(8) Subscriber; Subscribe.—

   (A) Subscriber.—The term "subscriber" means a person or entity that receives a secondary transmission service from a satellite carrier and pays a fee for the service, directly or indirectly, to the satellite carrier or to a distributor.

   (B) Subscribe.—The term "subscribe" means to elect to become a subscriber.

(9) Non-network Station.—The term "non-network station" means a television station, other than a network station, licensed by the Federal Communications Commission, that is secondarily transmitted by a satellite carrier.

(10) Unserved Household.—The term "unserved household", with respect to a particular television network, means a household that—

   (A) cannot receive, through the use of an antenna, an over-the-air signal containing the primary stream, or, on or after the qualifying date, the multicast stream, originating in that household's local market and affiliated with that network of—

      (i) if the signal originates as an analog signal, Grade B intensity as defined by the Federal Communications Commission in section 73.683(a) of title 47, Code of Federal Regulations, as in effect on January 1, 1999; or

      (ii) if the signal originates as a digital signal, intensity defined in the values for the digital television noise-limited service contour, as defined in regulations issued by the Federal Communications Commission (section 73.622(e) of title 47, Code of Federal Regulations), as such regulations may be amended from time to time;

   (B) is subject to a waiver that meets the standards of subsection (a) (13), whether or not the waiver was granted before the date of the enactment of the Satellite Television Extension and Localism Act of 2010;

   (C) is a subscriber to whom subsection (e) applies;

   (D) is a subscriber to whom subsection (a)(11) applies; or

   (E) is a subscriber to whom the exemption under subsection (a)(2)(B)(iii) applies.

(11) Local Market.—The term "local market" has the meaning given such term under section 122(j).

(12) Commercial Establishment.—The term "commercial establishment"—

   (A) means an establishment used for commercial purposes, such as a bar, restaurant, private office, fitness club, oil rig, retail store, bank or other financial institution, supermarket, automobile or boat dealership, or any other establishment with a common business area; and

(B) does not include a multi-unit permanent or temporary dwelling where private home viewing occurs, such as a hotel, dormitory, hospital, apartment, condominium, or prison.

(13) Qualifying Date.—The term "qualifying date", for purposes of paragraph (10)(A), means—

(A) October 1, 2010, for multicast streams that exist on March 31, 2010; and

(B) January 1, 2011, for all other multicast streams.

(14) Multicast Stream.—The term "multicast stream" means a digital stream containing programming and program-related material affiliated with a television network, other than the primary stream.

(15) Primary Stream.—The term "primary stream" means—

(A) the single digital stream of programming as to which a television broadcast station has the right to mandatory carriage with a satellite carrier under the rules of the Federal Communications Commission in effect on July 1, 2009; or

(B) if there is no stream described in subparagraph (A), then either—

(i) the single digital stream of programming associated with the network last transmitted by the station as an analog signal; or

(ii) if there is no stream described in clause (i), then the single digital stream of programming affiliated with the network that, as of July 1, 2009, had been offered by the television broadcast station for the longest period of time.

(e) Moratorium on Copyright Liability.—Until December 31, 2019, a subscriber who does not receive a signal of Grade A intensity (as defined in the regulations of the Federal Communications Commission under section 73.683(a) of title 47, Code of Federal Regulations, as in effect on January 1, 1999, or predicted by the Federal Communications Commission using the Individual Location Longley-Rice methodology described by the Federal Communications Commission in Docket No. 98–201) of a local network television broadcast station shall remain eligible to receive signals of network stations affiliated with the same network, if that subscriber had satellite service of such network signal terminated after July 11, 1998, and before October 31, 1999, as required by this section, or received such service on October 31, 1999.

(f) Expedited Consideration by Justice Department of Voluntary Agreements to Provide Satellite Secondary Transmissions to Local Markets.—

(1) In General.—In a case in which no satellite carrier makes available, to subscribers located in a local market, as defined in section 122(j)(2), the secondary transmission into that market of a primary transmission of one or more television broadcast stations licensed by the Federal Communications Commission, and two or more satellite carriers request a business review letter in accordance with section 50.6 of title 28, Code of Federal Regulations (as in effect on July 7, 2004), in order to assess the legality under the antitrust laws of proposed business conduct to make or carry out an agreement to provide such secondary transmission into such local market, the appropriate official of the Department of Justice shall respond to the request no later than 90 days after the date on which the request is received.

(2) Definition.—For purposes of this subsection, the term "antitrust laws"—

(A) has the meaning given that term in subsection (a) of the first section of the Clayton Act (15 U.S.C. 12(a)), except that such term includes section 5 of the Federal Trade Commission Act (15 U.S.C. 45) to the extent such section 5 applies to unfair methods of competition; and

(B) includes any State law similar to the laws referred to in paragraph (1).

(g) Certain Waivers Granted to Providers of Local-into-Local Service to All DMAs.—

(1) Injunction Waiver.—A court that issued an injunction pursuant to subsection (a)(7)(B) before the date of the enactment of this subsection shall waive such injunction if the court recognizes the entity against which the injunction was issued as a qualified carrier.

(2) Limited Temporary Waiver.—

(A) In General.—Upon a request made by a satellite carrier, a court that issued an injunction against such carrier under subsection (a)(7)(B) before the date of the enactment of this subsection shall waive such injunction with respect to the statutory license provided under subsection (a)(2) to the extent necessary to allow such carrier to make secondary transmissions of primary transmissions made by a network station to unserved households located in short markets in which such carrier was not providing local service pursuant to the license under section 122 as of December 31, 2009.

(B) Expiration of Temporary Waiver.—A temporary waiver of an injunction under subparagraph (A) shall expire after the end of the 120-day period beginning on the date such temporary waiver is issued unless extended for good cause by the court making the temporary waiver.

(C) Failure to Provide Local-into-Local Service to All DMAs.—

(i) Failure to Act Reasonably and in Good Faith.—If the court issuing a temporary waiver under subparagraph (A) determines that the satellite carrier that made the request for such waiver has failed to act reasonably or has failed to make a good faith effort to provide local-into-local service to all DMAs, such failure—

(I) is actionable as an act of infringement under section 501 and the court may in its discretion impose the remedies provided for in sections 502 through 506 and subsection (a)(6)(B) of this section; and

(II) shall result in the termination of the waiver issued under subparagraph (A).

(ii) Failure to Provide Local-into-local Service.—If the court issuing a temporary waiver under subparagraph (A) determines that the satellite carrier that made the request for such waiver has failed to provide local-into-local service to all DMAs, but determines that the carrier acted reasonably and in good faith, the court may in its discretion impose financial penalties that reflect—

(I) the degree of control the carrier had over the circumstances that resulted in the failure;

(II) the quality of the carrier's efforts to remedy the failure; and

(III) the severity and duration of any service interruption.

(D) Single Temporary Waiver Available.—An entity may only receive one temporary waiver under this paragraph.

(E) Short Market Defined.—For purposes of this paragraph, the term "short market" means a local market in which programming of one or more of the four most widely viewed television networks nationwide as measured on the date of the enactment of this subsection is not offered on the primary stream transmitted by any local television broadcast station.

(3) Establishment of Qualified Carrier Recognition.—

(A) Statement of Eligibility.—An entity seeking to be recognized as a qualified carrier under this subsection shall file a statement of eligibility with the court that imposed the injunction. A statement of eligibility must include—

(i)   an affidavit that the entity is providing local-into-local service to all DMAs;

(ii)   a motion for a waiver of the injunction;

(iii)   a motion that the court appoint a special master under Rule 53 of the Federal Rules of Civil Procedure;

(iv)   an agreement by the carrier to pay all expenses incurred by the special master under paragraph (4)(B)(ii); and

(v)   a certification issued pursuant to section 342(a) of Communications Act of 1934.

(B) Grant of Recognition as a Qualified Carrier.—Upon receipt of a statement of eligibility, the court shall recognize the entity as a qualified carrier and issue the waiver under paragraph (1). Upon motion pursuant to subparagraph (A)(iii), the court shall appoint a special master to conduct the examination and provide a report to the court as provided in paragraph (4)(B).

(C) Voluntary Termination.—At any time, an entity recognized as a qualified carrier may file a statement of voluntary termination with the court certifying that it no longer wishes to be recognized as a qualified carrier. Upon receipt of such statement, the court shall reinstate the injunction waived under paragraph (1).

(D) Loss of Recognition Prevents Future Recognition.—No entity may be recognized as a qualified carrier if such entity had previously been recognized as a qualified carrier and subsequently lost such recognition or voluntarily terminated such recognition under subparagraph (C).

(4) Qualified Carrier Obligations and Compliance.—

(A) Continuing Obligations.—

(i) In General.—An entity recognized as a qualified carrier shall continue to provide local-into-local service to all DMAs.

(ii) Cooperation With Compliance Examination.—An entity recognized as a qualified carrier shall fully cooperate with the special master appointed by the court under paragraph (3)(B) in an examination set forth in subparagraph (B).

(B) Qualified Carrier Compliance Examination.—

(i) Examination and Report.—A special master appointed by the court under paragraph (3)(B) shall conduct an examination of, and file a report on, the qualified carrier's compliance with the royalty payment and household eligibility requirements of the license under this section. The report shall address the qualified carrier's conduct during the period beginning on the date on which the qualified carrier is recognized as such under paragraph (3)(B) and ending on April 30, 2012.

(ii) Records of Qualified Carrier.—Beginning on the date that is one year after the date on which the qualified carrier is recognized as such under paragraph (3)(B), but not later than December 1, 2011, the qualified carrier shall provide the special master with all records that the special master considers to be directly pertinent to the following requirements under this section:

(I)   Proper calculation and payment of royalties under the statutory license under this section.

(II)   Provision of service under this license to eligible subscribers only.

(iii) Submission of Report.—The special master shall file the report required by clause (i) not later than July 24, 2012, with the court referred to in paragraph (1) that issued the injunction, and the court shall transmit a copy of the report to the

Register of Copyrights, the Committees on the Judiciary and on Energy and Commerce of the House of Representatives, and the Committees on the Judiciary and on Commerce, Science, and Transportation of the Senate.

(iv) Evidence of Infringement.—The special master shall include in the report a statement of whether the examination by the special master indicated that there is substantial evidence that a copyright holder could bring a successful action under this section against the qualified carrier for infringement.

(v) Subsequent Examination.—If the special master's report includes a statement that its examination indicated the existence of substantial evidence that a copyright holder could bring a successful action under this section against the qualified carrier for infringement, the special master shall, not later than 6 months after the report under clause (i) is filed, initiate another examination of the qualified carrier's compliance with the royalty payment and household eligibility requirements of the license under this section since the last report was filed under clause (iii). The special master shall file a report on the results of the examination conducted under this clause with the court referred to in paragraph (1) that issued the injunction, and the court shall transmit a copy to the Register of Copyrights, the Committees on the Judiciary and on Energy and Commerce of the House of Representatives, and the Committees on the Judiciary and on Commerce, Science, and Transportation of the Senate. The report shall include a statement described in clause (iv).

(vi) Compliance.—Upon motion filed by an aggrieved copyright owner, the court recognizing an entity as a qualified carrier shall terminate such designation upon finding that the entity has failed to cooperate with an examination required by this subparagraph.

(vii) Oversight.—During the period of time that the special master is conducting an examination under this subparagraph, the Comptroller General shall monitor the degree to which the entity seeking to be recognized or recognized as a qualified carrier under paragraph (3) is complying with the special master's examination. The qualified carrier shall make available to the Comptroller General all records and individuals that the Comptroller General considers necessary to meet the Comptroller General's obligations under this clause. The Comptroller General shall report the results of the monitoring required by this clause to the Committees on the Judiciary and on Energy and Commerce of the House of Representatives and the Committees on the Judiciary and on Commerce, Science, and Transportation of the Senate at intervals of not less than six months during such period.

(C) Affirmation.—A qualified carrier shall file an affidavit with the district court and the Register of Copyrights 30 months after such status was granted stating that, to the best of the affiant's knowledge, it is in compliance with the requirements for a qualified carrier. The qualified carrier shall attach to its affidavit copies of all reports or orders issued by the court, the special master, and the Comptroller General.

(D) Compliance Determination.—Upon the motion of an aggrieved television broadcast station, the court recognizing an entity as a qualified carrier may make a determination of whether the entity is providing local-into-local service to all DMAs.

(E) Pleading Requirement.—In any motion brought under subparagraph (D), the party making such motion shall specify one or more designated market areas (as such term is defined in section 122(j)(2)(C)) for which the failure to provide service is being alleged, and, for each such designated market area, shall plead with particularity the circumstances of the alleged failure.

(F) Burden of Proof.—In any proceeding to make a determination under subparagraph (D), and with respect to a designated market area for which failure to provide service is alleged, the entity recognized as a qualified carrier shall have the burden of proving that the entity provided local-into-local service with a good quality satellite signal to at least 90 percent of the households in such designated market area (based on the most recent census data released by the United States Census Bureau) at the time and place alleged.

(5) Failure to Provide Service.—

(A) Penalties.—If the court recognizing an entity as a qualified carrier finds that such entity has willfully failed to provide local-into-local service to all DMAs, such finding shall result in the loss of recognition of the entity as a qualified carrier and the termination of the waiver provided under paragraph (1), and the court may, in its discretion—

(i) treat such failure as an act of infringement under section 501, and subject such infringement to the remedies provided for in sections 502 through 506 and subsection (a)(6)(B) of this section; and

(ii) impose a fine of not less than $250,000 and not more than $5,000,000.

(B) Exception for Nonwillful Violation.—If the court determines that the failure to provide local-into-local service to all DMAs is nonwillful, the court may in its discretion impose financial penalties for noncompliance that reflect—

(i) the degree of control the entity had over the circumstances that resulted in the failure;

(ii) the quality of the entity's efforts to remedy the failure and restore service; and

(iii) the severity and duration of any service interruption.

(6) Penalties for Violations of License.—A court that finds, under subsection (a)(6)(A), that an entity recognized as a qualified carrier has willfully made a secondary transmission of a primary transmission made by a network station and embodying a performance or display of a work to a subscriber who is not eligible to receive the transmission under this section shall reinstate the injunction waived under paragraph (1), and the court may order statutory damages of not more than $2,500,000.

(7) Local-into-Local Service to All DMAs Defined.—For purposes of this subsection:

(A) In General.—An entity provides "local-into-local service to all DMAs" if the entity provides local service in all designated market areas (as such term is defined in section 122(j)(2)(C)) pursuant to the license under section 122.

(B) Household Coverage.—For purposes of subparagraph (A), an entity that makes available local-into-local service with a good quality satellite signal to at least 90 percent of the households in a designated market area based on the most recent census data released by the United States Census Bureau shall be considered to be providing local service to such designated market area.

(C) Good Quality Satellite Signal Defined.—The term "good quality satellite signal" has the meaning given such term under section 342(e)(2) of Communications Act of 1934.

(h) Termination of License.—This section shall cease to be effective on December 31, 2019.

§ 120.   Scope of Exclusive Rights in Architectural Works

(a) Pictorial Representations Permitted.—The copyright in an architectural work that has been constructed does not include the right to prevent the making, distributing, or public display of pictures, paintings, photographs, or other pictorial representations of the work, if the building in which the work is embodied is located in or ordinarily visible from a public place.

(b) Alterations to and Destruction of Buildings.—Notwithstanding the provisions of section 106(2), the owners of a building embodying an architectural work may, without the consent of the author or copyright owner of the architectural work, make or authorize the making of alterations to such building, and destroy or authorize the destruction of such building.

§ 121. Limitations on Exclusive Rights: Reproduction for Blind or Other People With Disabilities

(a)   Notwithstanding the provisions of section 106 it is not an infringement of copyright for an authorized entity to reproduce or to distribute copies or phonorecords of a previously published literary work or of a previously published musical work that has been fixed in the form of text or notation if such copies or phonorecords are reproduced or distributed in accessible formats exclusively for use by eligible persons.

(b)(1) Copies or phonorecords to which this section applies shall—

(A)   not be reproduced or distributed in a format other than an accessible format exclusively for use by eligible persons;

(B)   bear a notice that any further reproduction or distribution in a format other than an accessible format is an infringement; and

(C)   include a copyright notice identifying the copyright owner and the date of the original publication.

(2)   The provisions of this subsection shall not apply to standardized, secure, or norm-referenced tests and related testing material, or to computer programs, except the portions thereof that are in conventional human language (including descriptions of pictorial works) and displayed to users in the ordinary course of using the computer programs.

(c)   Notwithstanding the provisions of section 106, it is not an infringement of copyright for a publisher of print instructional materials for use in elementary or secondary schools to create and distribute to the National Instructional Materials Access Center copies of the electronic files described in sections 612(a)(23)(C), 613(a)(6), and section 674(e) of the Individuals with Disabilities Education Act that contain the contents of print instructional materials using the National Instructional Material Accessibility Standard (as defined in section 674(e)(3) of that Act), if—

(1)   the inclusion of the contents of such print instructional materials is required by any State educational agency or local educational agency;

(2)   the publisher had the right to publish such print instructional materials in print formats; and

(3)   such copies are used solely for reproduction or distribution of the contents of such print instructional materials in accessible formats.

(d)   For purposes of this section, the term—

(1)   "accessible format" means an alternative manner or form that gives an eligible person access to the work when the copy or phonorecord in the accessible format is used exclusively by the eligible person to permit him or her to have access as feasibly and comfortably as a person without such disability as described in paragraph (3);

(2)   "authorized entity" means a nonprofit organization or a governmental agency that has a primary mission to provide specialized services relating to training, education, or adaptive reading or information access needs of blind or other persons with disabilities;

(3)   "eligible person" means an individual who, regardless of any other disability—

(A)   is blind;

    (B) has a visual impairment or perceptual or reading disability that cannot be improved to give visual function substantially equivalent to that of a person who has no such impairment or disability and so is unable to read printed works to substantially the same degree as a person without an impairment or disability; or

    (C) is otherwise unable, through physical disability, to hold or manipulate a book or to focus or move the eyes to the extent that would be normally acceptable for reading; and

    (4) "print instructional materials" has the meaning given under section 674(e)(3)(C) of the Individuals with Disabilities Education Act.

§ 121A. Limitations on Exclusive Rights: Reproduction for Blind or Other People with Disabilities in Marrakesh Treaty Countries

    (a) Notwithstanding the provisions of sections 106 and 602, it is not an infringement of copyright for an authorized entity, acting pursuant to this section, to export copies or phonorecords of a previously published literary work or of a previously published musical work that has been fixed in the form of text or notation in accessible formats to another country when the exportation is made either to—

    (1) an authorized entity located in a country that is a Party to the Marrakesh Treaty; or

    (2) an eligible person in a country that is a Party to the Marrakesh Treaty,

if prior to the exportation of such copies or phonorecords, the authorized entity engaged in the exportation did not know or have reasonable grounds to know that the copies or phonorecords would be used other than by eligible persons.

    (b) Notwithstanding the provisions of sections 106 and 602, it is not an infringement of copyright for an authorized entity or an eligible person, or someone acting on behalf of an eligible person, acting pursuant to this section, to import copies or phonorecords of a previously published literary work or of a previously published musical work that has been fixed in the form of text or notation in accessible formats.

    (c) In conducting activities under subsection (a) or (b), an authorized entity shall establish and follow its own practices, in keeping with its particular circumstances, to—

    (1) establish that the persons the authorized entity serves are eligible persons;

    (2) limit to eligible persons and authorized entities the distribution of accessible format copies by the authorized entity;

    (3) discourage the reproduction and distribution of unauthorized copies;

    (4) maintain due care in, and records of, the handling of copies of works by the authorized entity, while respecting the privacy of eligible persons on an equal basis with others; and

    (5) facilitate effective cross-border exchange of accessible format copies by making publicly available—

    (A) the titles of works for which the authorized entity has accessible format copies or phonorecords and the specific accessible formats in which they are available; and

    (B) information on the policies, practices, and authorized entity partners of the authorized entity for the cross-border exchange of accessible format copies.

    (d) Nothing in this section shall be construed to establish—

    (1) a cause of action under this title; or

    (2) a basis for regulation by any Federal agency.

    (e) Nothing in this section shall be construed to limit the ability to engage in any activity otherwise permitted under this title.

(f)   For purposes of this section—

(1)   the terms "accessible format", "authorized entity", and "eligible person" have the meanings given those terms in section 121; and

(2)   the term "Marrakesh Treaty" means the Marrakesh Treaty to Facilitate Access to Published Works by Visually Impaired Persons and Persons with Print Disabilities concluded at Marrakesh, Morocco, on June 28, 2013.

§ 122. Limitations on Exclusive Rights: Secondary Transmissions of Local Television Programming by Satellite

(a)   Secondary Transmissions into Local Markets.—

(1)   Secondary Transmissions of Television Broadcast Stations Within a Local Market.—A secondary transmission of a performance or display of a work embodied in a primary transmission of a television broadcast station into the station's local market shall be subject to statutory licensing under this section if—

(A)   the secondary transmission is made by a satellite carrier to the public;

(B)   with regard to secondary transmissions, the satellite carrier is in compliance with the rules, regulations, or authorizations of the Federal Communications Commission governing the carriage of television broadcast station signals; and

(C)   the satellite carrier makes a direct or indirect charge for the secondary transmission to—

(i)   each subscriber receiving the secondary transmission; or

(ii)   a distributor that has contracted with the satellite carrier for direct or indirect delivery of the secondary transmission to the public.

(2)   Significantly Viewed Stations.—

(A)   In General.—A secondary transmission of a performance or display of a work embodied in a primary transmission of a television broadcast station to subscribers who receive secondary transmissions of primary transmissions under paragraph (1) shall be subject to statutory licensing under this paragraph if the secondary transmission is of the primary transmission of a network station or a non-network station to a subscriber who resides outside the station's local market but within a community in which the signal has been determined by the Federal Communications Commission to be significantly viewed in such community, pursuant to the rules, regulations, and authorizations of the Federal Communications Commission in effect on April 15, 1976, applicable to determining with respect to a cable system whether signals are significantly viewed in a community.

(B)   Waiver.—A subscriber who is denied the secondary transmission of the primary transmission of a network station or a non-network station under subparagraph (A) may request a waiver from such denial by submitting a request, through the subscriber's satellite carrier, to the network station or non-network station in the local market affiliated with the same network or non-network where the subscriber is located. The network station or non-network station shall accept or reject the subscriber's request for a waiver within 30 days after receipt of the request. If the network station or non-network station fails to accept or reject the subscriber's request for a waiver within that 30-day period, that network station or non-network station shall be deemed to agree to the waiver request.

(3)   Secondary Transmission of Low Power Programming.—

(A)   In General.—Subject to subparagraphs (B) and (C), a secondary transmission of a performance or display of a work embodied in a primary transmission of a television broadcast station to subscribers who receive secondary transmissions of primary transmissions under paragraph (1) shall be subject to statutory licensing under this paragraph if the secondary transmission is of the primary transmission of a television broadcast station that is licensed as a low power television station, to a subscriber who resides within the same designated market area as the station that originates the transmission.

(B) No Applicability to Repeaters and Translators.—Secondary transmissions provided for in subparagraph (A) shall not apply to any low power television station that retransmits the programs and signals of another television station for more than 2 hours each day.

(C) No Impact on Other Secondary Transmissions Obligations.—A satellite carrier that makes secondary transmissions of a primary transmission of a low power television station under a statutory license provided under this section is not required, by reason of such secondary transmissions, to make any other secondary transmissions.

(4) Special Exceptions.—A secondary transmission of a performance or display of a work embodied in a primary transmission of a television broadcast station to subscribers who receive secondary transmissions of primary transmissions under paragraph (1) shall, if the secondary transmission is made by a satellite carrier that complies with the requirements of paragraph (1), be subject to statutory licensing under this paragraph as follows:

(A) States With Single Full-power Network Station.—In a State in which there is licensed by the Federal Communications Commission a single full-power station that was a network station on January 1, 1995, the statutory license provided for in this paragraph shall apply to the secondary transmission by a satellite carrier of the primary transmission of that station to any subscriber in a community that is located within that State and that is not within the first 50 television markets as listed in the regulations of the Commission as in effect on such date (47 C.F.R. 76.51).

(B) States With All Network Stations and Non-network Stations in Same Local Market.—In a State in which all network stations and non-network stations licensed by the Federal Communications Commission within that State as of January 1, 1995, are assigned to the same local market and that local market does not encompass all counties of that State, the statutory license provided under this paragraph shall apply to the secondary transmission by a satellite carrier of the primary transmissions of such station to all subscribers in the State who reside in a local market that is within the first 50 major television markets as listed in the regulations of the Commission as in effect on such date (section 76.51 of title 47, Code of Federal Regulations).

(C) Additional Stations.—In the case of that State in which are located 4 counties that—

(i)   on January 1, 2004, were in local markets principally comprised of counties in another State, and

(ii)   had a combined total of 41,340 television households, according to the U.S. Television Household Estimates by Nielsen Media Research for 2004,

the statutory license provided under this paragraph shall apply to secondary transmissions by a satellite carrier to subscribers in any such county of the primary transmissions of any network station located in that State, if the satellite carrier was making such secondary transmissions to any subscribers in that county on January 1, 2004.

(D) Certain Additional Stations.—If 2 adjacent counties in a single State are in a local market comprised principally of counties located in another State, the statutory license provided for in this paragraph shall apply to the secondary transmission by a satellite carrier to subscribers in those 2 counties of the primary transmissions of any network station located in the capital of the State in which such 2 counties are located, if—

(i) the 2 counties are located in a local market that is in the top 100 markets for the year 2003 according to Nielsen Media Research; and

(ii) the total number of television households in the 2 counties combined did not exceed 10,000 for the year 2003 according to Nielsen Media Research.

(E) Networks of Noncommercial Educational Broadcast Stations.—In the case of a system of three or more noncommercial educational broadcast stations licensed to a single State, public agency, or political, educational, or special purpose subdivision of a State, the statutory license provided for in this paragraph shall apply to the secondary transmission of the primary transmission of such system to any subscriber in any county or county equivalent within such State, if such subscriber is located in a designated market area that is not otherwise eligible to receive the secondary transmission of the primary transmission of a noncommercial educational broadcast station located within the State pursuant to paragraph (1).

(5) Applicability of Royalty Rates and Procedures.—The royalty rates and procedures under section 119(b) shall apply to the secondary transmissions to which the statutory license under paragraph (4) applies.

(b) Reporting Requirements.—

(1) Initial Lists.—A satellite carrier that makes secondary transmissions of a primary transmission made by a network station under subsection (a) shall, within 90 days after commencing such secondary transmissions, submit to the network that owns or is affiliated with the network station—

(A) a list identifying (by name in alphabetical order and street address, including county and 9-digit zip code) all subscribers to which the satellite carrier makes secondary transmissions of that primary transmission under subsection (a); and

(B) a separate list, aggregated by designated market area (by name and address, including street or rural route number, city, State, and 9-digit zip code), which shall indicate those subscribers being served pursuant to paragraph (2) of subsection (a).

(2) Subsequent Lists.—After the list is submitted under paragraph (1), the satellite carrier shall, on the 15th of each month, submit to the network—

(A) a list identifying (by name in alphabetical order and street address, including county and 9-digit zip code) any subscribers who have been added or dropped as subscribers since the last submission under this subsection; and

(B) a separate list, aggregated by designated market area (by name and street address, including street or rural route number, city, State, and 9-digit zip code), identifying those subscribers whose service pursuant to paragraph (2) of subsection (a) has been added or dropped since the last submission under this subsection.

(3) Use of Subscriber Information.—Subscriber information submitted by a satellite carrier under this subsection may be used only for the purposes of monitoring compliance by the satellite carrier with this section.

(4) Requirements of Networks.—The submission requirements of this subsection shall apply to a satellite carrier only if the network to which the submissions are to be made places on file with the Register of Copyrights a document identifying the name and address of the person to whom such submissions are to be made. The Register of Copyrights shall maintain for public inspection a file of all such documents.

(c) No Royalty Fee Required for Certain Secondary Transmissions.—A satellite carrier whose secondary transmissions are subject to statutory licensing under paragraphs (1), (2), and (3) of subsection (a) shall have no royalty obligation for such secondary transmissions.

(d) Noncompliance With Reporting and Regulatory Requirements.—Notwithstanding subsection (a), the willful or repeated secondary transmission to the public by a satellite carrier into the local market of a television broadcast station of a primary transmission embodying a performance or display of a work made by that television broadcast station is actionable as an act of infringement under section 501, and is fully subject to the remedies provided under sections 502 through 506, if the satellite carrier has not complied with the reporting requirements of subsection (b) or with the rules, regulations, and authorizations of the Federal Communications Commission concerning the carriage of television broadcast signals.

(e) Willful Alterations.—Notwithstanding subsection (a), the secondary transmission to the public by a satellite carrier into the local market of a television broadcast station of a performance or display of a work embodied in a primary transmission made by that television broadcast station is actionable as an act of infringement under section 501, and is fully subject to the remedies provided by sections 502 through 506 and section 510, if the content of the particular program in which the performance or display is embodied, or any commercial advertising or station announcement transmitted by the primary transmitter during, or immediately before or after, the transmission of such program, is in any way willfully altered by the satellite carrier through changes, deletions, or additions, or is combined with programming from any other broadcast signal.

(f) Violation of Territorial Restrictions on Statutory License for Television Broadcast Stations.—

(1) Individual Violations.—The willful or repeated secondary transmission to the public by a satellite carrier of a primary transmission embodying a performance or display of a work made by a television broadcast station to a subscriber who does not reside in that station's local market, and is not subject to statutory licensing under section 119, subject to statutory licensing by reason of paragraph (2)(A), (3), or (4) of subsection (a), or subject to a private licensing agreement, is actionable as an act of infringement under section 501 and is fully subject to the remedies provided by sections 502 through 506, except that—

(A) no damages shall be awarded for such act of infringement if the satellite carrier took corrective action by promptly withdrawing service from the ineligible subscriber; and

(B) any statutory damages shall not exceed $250 for such subscriber for each month during which the violation occurred.

(2) Pattern of Violations.—If a satellite carrier engages in a willful or repeated pattern or practice of secondarily transmitting to the public a primary transmission embodying a performance or display of a work made by a television broadcast station to subscribers who do not reside in that station's local market, and are not subject to statutory licensing under section 119, subject to statutory licensing by reason of paragraph (2)(A), (3), or (4) of subsection (a), or subject to a private licensing agreement, then in addition to the remedies under paragraph (1)—

(A) if the pattern or practice has been carried out on a substantially nationwide basis, the court—

(i) shall order a permanent injunction barring the secondary transmission by the satellite carrier of the primary transmissions of that television broadcast station (and if such television broadcast station is a network station, all other television broadcast stations affiliated with such network); and

(ii) may order statutory damages not exceeding $2,500,000 for each 6-month period during which the pattern or practice was carried out; and

(B) if the pattern or practice has been carried out on a local or regional basis with respect to more than one television broadcast station, the court—

(i) shall order a permanent injunction barring the secondary transmission in that locality or region by the satellite carrier of the primary transmissions of any television broadcast station; and

(ii) may order statutory damages not exceeding $2,500,000 for each 6-month period during which the pattern or practice was carried out.

(g) Burden of Proof.—In any action brought under subsection (f), the satellite carrier shall have the burden of proving that its secondary transmission of a primary transmission by a television broadcast station is made only to subscribers located within that station's local market or subscribers being served in compliance with section 119, paragraph (2)(A), (3), or (4) of subsection (a), or a private licensing agreement.

(h) Geographic Limitations on Secondary Transmissions.—The statutory license created by this section shall apply to secondary transmissions to locations in the United States.

(i) Exclusivity With Respect to Secondary Transmissions of Broadcast Stations by Satellite to Members of the Public.—No provision of section 111 or any other law (other than this section and section 119) shall be construed to contain any authorization, exemption, or license through which secondary transmissions by satellite carriers of programming contained in a primary transmission made by a television broadcast station may be made without obtaining the consent of the copyright owner.

(j) Definitions.—In this section—

(1) Distributor.—The term "distributor" means an entity that contracts to distribute secondary transmissions from a satellite carrier and, either as a single channel or in a package with other programming, provides the secondary transmission either directly to individual subscribers or indirectly through other program distribution entities.

(2) Local Market.—

(A) In General.—The term "local market", in the case of both commercial and noncommercial television broadcast stations, means the designated market area in which a station is located, and—

(i) in the case of a commercial television broadcast station, all commercial television broadcast stations licensed to a community within the same designated market area are within the same local market; and

(ii) in the case of a noncommercial educational television broadcast station, the market includes any station that is licensed to a community within the same designated market area as the noncommercial educational television broadcast station.

(B) County of License.—In addition to the area described in subparagraph (A), a station's local market includes the county in which the station's community of license is located.

(C) Designated Market Area.—For purposes of subparagraph (A), the term "designated market area" means a designated market area, as determined by Nielsen Media Research and published in the 1999–2000 Nielsen Station Index Directory and Nielsen Station Index United States Television Household Estimates or any successor publication.

(D) Certain Areas Outside of Any Designated Market Area.—Any census area, borough, or other area in the State of Alaska that is outside of a designated market area, as determined by Nielsen Media Research, shall be deemed to be part of one of the local markets in the State of Alaska. A satellite carrier may determine which local market in the State of Alaska will be deemed to be the relevant local market in connection with each subscriber in such census area, borough, or other area.

(E) Market Determination.—The local market of a commercial television broadcast station may be modified by the Federal Communications Commission in accordance with section 338(*l*) of the Communications Act of 1934 (47 U.S.C. 338).

(3) Low Power Television Station.—The term "low power television station" means a low power TV station as defined in section 74.701(f) of title 47, Code of Federal Regulations, as in effect on June 1, 2004. For purposes of this paragraph, the term 'low power television station' includes a low power television station that has been accorded primary status as a Class A television licensee under section 73.6001(a) of title 47, Code of Federal Regulations.

(4) Network Station; Non-network Station; Satellite Carrier; Secondary Transmission.—The terms "network station", "non-network station", "satellite carrier", and "secondary transmission" have the meanings given such terms under section 119(d).

(5) Noncommercial Educational Broadcast Station.—The term "noncommercial educational broadcast station" means a television broadcast station that is a noncommercial educational broadcast station as defined in section 397 of the Communications Act of 1934, as in effect on the date of the enactment of the Satellite Television Extension and Localism Act of 2010.

(6) Subscriber.—The term "subscriber" means a person or entity that receives a secondary transmission service from a satellite carrier and pays a fee for the service, directly or indirectly, to the satellite carrier or to a distributor.

(7) Television Broadcast Station.—The term "television broadcast station"—

(A) means an over-the-air, commercial or noncommercial television broadcast station licensed by the Federal Communications Commission under subpart E of part 73 of title 47, Code of Federal Regulations, except that such term does not include a low-power or translator television station; and

(B) includes a television broadcast station licensed by an appropriate governmental authority of Canada or Mexico if the station broadcasts primarily in the English language and is a network station as defined in section 119(d)(2)(A).

CHAPTER 2. COPYRIGHT OWNERSHIP AND TRANSFER

—————

§ 201. Ownership of Copyright

(a) Initial Ownership.—Copyright in a work protected under this title vests initially in the author or authors of the work. The authors of a joint work are coowners of copyright in the work.

(b) Works Made for Hire.—In the case of a work made for hire, the employer or other person for whom the work was prepared is considered the author for purposes of this title, and, unless the parties have expressly agreed otherwise in a written instrument signed by them, owns all of the rights comprised in the copyright.

(c) Contributions to Collective Works.—Copyright in each separate contribution to a collective work is distinct from copyright in the collective work as a whole, and vests initially in the author of the contribution. In the absence of an express transfer of the copyright or of any rights under it, the owner of copyright in the collective work is presumed to have acquired only the privilege of reproducing and distributing the contribution as part of that particular collective work, any revision of that collective work, and any later collective work in the same series.

(d) Transfer of Ownership.—

(1) The ownership of a copyright may be transferred in whole or in part by any means of conveyance or by operation of law, and may be bequeathed by will or pass as personal property by the applicable laws of intestate succession.

(2) Any of the exclusive rights comprised in a copyright, including any subdivision of any of the rights specified by section 106, may be transferred as provided by clause (1) and owned separately. The owner of any particular exclusive right is entitled, to the extent of that right, to all of the protection and remedies accorded to the copyright owner by this title.

(e) Involuntary Transfer.—When an individual author's ownership of a copyright, or of any of the exclusive rights under a copyright, has not previously been transferred voluntarily by that individual author, no action by any governmental body or other official or organization purporting to seize, expropriate, transfer, or exercise rights of ownership with respect to the copyright, or any of the exclusive rights under a copyright, shall be given effect under this title except as provided under Title 11.

§ 202. Ownership of Copyright as Distinct From Ownership of Material Object

Ownership of a copyright, or of any of the exclusive rights under a copyright, is distinct from ownership of any material object in which the work is embodied. Transfer of ownership of any material object, including the copy or phonorecord in which the work is first fixed, does not of itself convey any rights in the copyrighted work embodied in the object; nor, in the absence of an agreement, does transfer of ownership of a copyright or of any exclusive rights under a copyright convey property rights in any material object.

§ 203. Termination of Transfers and Licenses Granted by the Author

(a) Conditions for Termination.—In the case of any work other than a work made for hire, the exclusive or nonexclusive grant of a transfer or license of copyright or of any right under a copyright, executed by the author on or after January 1, 1978, otherwise than by will, is subject to termination under the following conditions:

(1) In the case of a grant executed by one author, termination of the grant may be effected by that author or, if the author is dead, by the person or persons who, under clause (2) of this subsection, own and are entitled to exercise a total of more than one-half of that author's termination interest. In the case of a grant executed by two or more authors of a joint work, termination of the grant may be effected by a majority of the authors who executed it; if any of such authors is dead, the termination interest of any such author may be exercised as a unit by the person or persons who, under clause (2) of this subsection, own and are entitled to exercise a total of more than one-half of that author's interest.

(2) Where an author is dead, his or her termination interest is owned, and may be exercised, as follows:

(A) The widow or widower owns the author's entire termination interest unless there are any surviving children or grandchildren of the author, in which case the widow or widower owns one-half of the author's interest.

(B)　The author's surviving children, and the surviving children of any dead child of the author, own the author's entire termination interest unless there is a widow or widower, in which case the ownership of one-half of the author's interest is divided among them.

(C)　The rights of the author's children and grandchildren are in all cases divided among them and exercised on a per stirpes basis according to the number of such author's children represented; the share of the children of a dead child in a termination interest can be exercised only by the action of a majority of them.

(D)　In the event that the author's widow or widower, children, and grandchildren are not living, the author's executor, administrator, personal representative, or trustee shall own the author's entire termination interest.

(3)　Termination of the grant may be effected at any time during a period of five years beginning at the end of thirty-five years from the date of execution of the grant; or, if the grant covers the right of publication of the work, the period begins at the end of thirty-five years from the date of publication of the work under the grant or at the end of forty years from the date of execution of the grant, whichever term ends earlier.

(4)　The termination shall be effected by serving an advance notice in writing, signed by the number and proportion of owners of termination interests required under clauses (1) and (2) of this subsection, or by their duly authorized agents, upon the grantee or the grantee's successor in title.

(A)　The notice shall state the effective date of the termination, which shall fall within the five-year period specified by clause (3) of this subsection, and the notice shall be served not less than two or more than ten years before that date. A copy of the notice shall be recorded in the Copyright Office before the effective date of termination, as a condition to its taking effect.

(B)　The notice shall comply, in form, content, and manner of service, with requirements that the Register of Copyrights shall prescribe by regulation.

(5)　Termination of the grant may be effected notwithstanding any agreement to the contrary, including an agreement to make a will or to make any future grant.

(b)　Effect of Termination.—Upon the effective date of termination, all rights under this title that were covered by the terminated grants revert to the author, authors, and other persons owning termination interests under clauses (1) and (2) of subsection (a), including those owners who did not join in signing the notice of termination under clause (4) of subsection (a), but with the following limitations:

(1)　A derivative work prepared under authority of the grant before its termination may continue to be utilized under the terms of the grant after its termination, but this privilege does not extend to the preparation after the termination of other derivative works based upon the copyrighted work covered by the terminated grant.

(2)　The future rights that will revert upon termination of the grant become vested on the date the notice of termination has been served as provided by clause (4) of subsection (a). The rights vest in the author, authors, and other persons named in, and in the proportionate shares provided by, clauses (1) and (2) of subsection (a).

(3)　Subject to the provisions of clause (4) of this subsection, a further grant, or agreement to make a further grant, of any right covered by a terminated grant is valid only if it is signed by the same number and proportion of the owners, in whom the right has vested under clause (2) of this subsection, as are required to terminate the grant under clauses (1) and (2) of subsection (a). Such further grant or agreement is effective with respect to all of the persons in whom the right it covers has vested under clause (2) of this subsection, including those who did not join in signing it. If any person dies after rights under a terminated grant have vested in him or her, that person's legal representatives, legatees, or heirs at law represent him or her for purposes of this clause.

(4)   A further grant, or agreement to make a further grant, of any right covered by a terminated grant is valid only if it is made after the effective date of the termination. As an exception, however, an agreement for such a further grant may be made between the persons provided by clause (3) of this subsection and the original grantee or such grantee's successor in title, after the notice of termination has been served as provided by clause (4) of subsection (a).

(5)   Termination of a grant under this section affects only those rights covered by the grants that arise under this title, and in no way affects rights arising under any other Federal, State, or foreign laws.

(6)   Unless and until termination is effected under this section, the grant, if it does not provide otherwise, continues in effect for the term of copyright provided by this title.

§ 204.   Execution of Transfers of Copyright Ownership

(a)   A transfer of copyright ownership, other than by operation of law, is not valid unless an instrument of conveyance, or a note or memorandum of the transfer, is in writing and signed by the owner of the rights conveyed or such owner's duly authorized agent.

(b)   A certificate of acknowledgement is not required for the validity of a transfer, but is prima facie evidence of the execution of the transfer if—

(1)   in the case of a transfer executed in the United States, the certificate is issued by a person authorized to administer oaths within the United States; or

(2)   in the case of a transfer executed in a foreign country, the certificate is issued by a diplomatic or consular officer of the United States, or by a person authorized to administer oaths whose authority is proved by a certificate of such an officer.

§ 205.   Recordation of Transfers and Other Documents

(a)   **Conditions for Recordation.**—Any transfer of copyright ownership or other document pertaining to a copyright may be recorded in the Copyright Office if the document filed for recordation bears the actual signature of the person who executed it, or if it is accompanied by a sworn or official certification that it is a true copy of the original, signed document. A sworn or official certification may be submitted to the Copyright Office electronically, pursuant to regulations established by the Register of Copyrights.

(b)   **Certificate of Recordation.**—The Register of Copyrights shall, upon receipt of a document as provided by subsection (a) and of the fee provided by section 708, record the document and return it with a certificate of recordation.

(c)   **Recordation as Constructive Notice.**—Recordation of a document in the Copyright Office gives all persons constructive notice of the facts stated in the recorded document, but only if—

(1)   the document, or material attached to it, specifically identifies the work to which it pertains so that, after the document is indexed by the Register of Copyrights, it would be revealed by a reasonable search under the title or registration number of the work; and

(2)   registration has been made for the work.

(d)   **Priority Between Conflicting Transfers.**—As between two conflicting transfers, the one executed first prevails if it is recorded, in the manner required to give constructive notice under subsection (c), within one month after its execution in the United States or within two months after its execution outside the United States, or at any time before recordation in such manner of the later transfer. Otherwise the later transfer prevails if recorded first in such manner, and if taken in good faith, for valuable consideration or on the basis of a binding promise to pay royalties, and without notice of the earlier transfer.

   (e) **Priority Between Conflicting Transfer of Ownership and Nonexclusive License.**— A nonexclusive license, whether recorded or not, prevails over a conflicting transfer of copyright ownership if the license is evidenced by a written instrument signed by the owner of the rights licensed or such owner's duly authorized agent, and if—

   (1)   the license was taken before execution of the transfer; or

   (2)   the license was taken in good faith before recordation of the transfer and without notice of it.

CHAPTER 3. DURATION OF COPYRIGHT

---

§ 301. Preemption With Respect to Other Laws

   (a)   On and after January 1, 1978, all legal or equitable rights that are equivalent to any of the exclusive rights within the general scope of copyright as specified by section 106 in works of authorship that are fixed in a tangible medium of expression and come within the subject matter of copyright as specified by sections 102 and 103, whether created before or after that date and whether published or unpublished, are governed exclusively by this title. Thereafter, no person is entitled to any such right or equivalent right in any such work under the common law or statutes of any State.

   (b)   Nothing in this title annuls or limits any rights or remedies under the common law or statutes of any State with respect to—

   (1)   subject matter that does not come within the subject matter of copyright as specified by sections 102 and 103, including works of authorship not fixed in any tangible medium of expression; or

   (2)   any cause of action arising from undertakings commenced before January 1, 1978;

   (3)   activities violating legal or equitable rights that are not equivalent to any of the exclusive rights within the general scope of copyright as specified by section 106; or

   (4)   State and local landmarks, historic preservation, zoning, or building codes, relating to architectural works protected under section 102(a)(8).

(c)   Notwithstanding the provisions of section 303, and in accordance with chapter 14, no sound recording fixed before February 15, 1972, shall be subject to copyright under this title. With respect to sound recordings fixed before February 15, 1972, the preemptive provisions of subsection (a) shall apply to activities that are commenced on and after the date of enactment of the Classics Protection and Access Act. Nothing in this subsection may be construed to affirm or negate the preemption of rights and remedies pertaining to any cause of action arising from the nonsubscription broadcast transmission of sound recordings under the common law or statutes of any State for activities that do not qualify as covered activities under chapter 14 undertaken during the period between the date of enactment of the Classics Protection and Access Act and the date on which the term of prohibition on unauthorized acts under section 1401(a)(2) expires for such sound recordings. Any potential preemption of rights and remedies related to such activities undertaken during that period shall apply in all respects as it did the day before the date of enactment of the Classics Protection and Access Act.

(d)   Nothing in this title annuls or limits any rights or remedies under any other Federal statute.

(e)   The scope of Federal preemption under this section is not affected by the adherence of the United States to the Berne Convention or the satisfaction of obligations of the United States thereunder.

(f)(1)   On or after the effective date set forth in section 610(a)* of the Visual Artists Rights Act of 1990, all legal or equitable rights that are equivalent to any of the rights conferred by section 106A with respect to works of visual art to which the rights conferred by section 106A apply are governed exclusively by section 106A and section 113(d) and the provisions of this title relating to such sections. Thereafter, no person is entitled to any such right or equivalent right in any work of visual art under the common law or statutes of any State.

(2)   Nothing in paragraph (1) annuls or limits any rights or remedies under the common law or statutes of any State with respect to—

(A)   any cause of action from undertakings commenced before the effective date set forth in section 610(a) of the Visual Artists Rights Act of 1990;

(B)   activities violating legal or equitable rights that are not equivalent to any of the rights conferred by section 106A with respect to works of visual art; or

(C)   activities violating legal or equitable rights which extend beyond the life of the author.

§ 302.   Duration of Copyright: Works Created on or After January 1, 1978

(a)   **In General.**—Copyright in a work created on or after January 1, 1978, subsists from its creation and, except as provided by the following subsections, endures for a term consisting of the life of the author and 70 years after the author's death.

(b)   **Joint Works.**—In the case of a joint work prepared by two or more authors who did not work for hire, the copyright endures for a term consisting of the life of the last surviving author and 70 years after such last surviving author's death.

(c)   **Anonymous Works, Pseudonymous Works, and Works Made for Hire.**—In the case of an anonymous work, a pseudonymous work, or a work made for hire, the copyright endures for a term of 95 years from the year of its first publication, or a term of 120 years from the year of its creation, whichever expires first. If, before the end of such term, the identity of one or more of the authors of an anonymous or pseudonymous work is revealed in the records of a registration made for that work under subsections (a) or (d) of section 408, or in the records provided by this subsection, the copyright in the work endures for the term specified by subsection (a) or (b), based on the life of the author or authors whose identity has been revealed. Any person having an interest in the copyright in an anonymous or pseudonymous work may at any time record, in records to be maintained by the Copyright Office for that purpose, a statement identifying one or more authors of the work; the

---

*   June 1, 1991.—*Ed.*

statement shall also identify the person filing it, the nature of that person's interest, the source of the information recorded, and the particular work affected, and shall comply in form and content with requirements that the Register of Copyrights shall prescribe by regulation.

(d) **Records Relating to Death of Authors.**—Any person having an interest in a copyright may at any time record in the Copyright Office a statement of the date of death of the author of the copyrighted work, or a statement that the author is still living on a particular date. The statement shall identify the person filing it, the nature of that person's interest, and the source of the information recorded, and shall comply in form and content with requirements that the Register of Copyrights shall prescribe by regulation. The Register shall maintain current records of information relating to the death of authors of copyrighted works, based on such recorded statements and, to the extent the Register considers practicable, on data contained in any of the records of the Copyright Office or in other reference sources.

(e) **Presumption as to Author's Death.**—After a period of 95 years from the year of first publication of a work, or a period of 120 years from the year of its creation, whichever expires first, any person who obtains from the Copyright Office a certified report that the records provided by subsection (d) disclose nothing to indicate that the author of the work is living, or died less than 70 years before, is entitled to the benefit of a presumption that the author has been dead for at least 70 years. Reliance in good faith upon this presumption shall be a complete defense to any action for infringement under this title.

§ 303. Duration of Copyright: Works Created but Not Published or Copyrighted Before January 1, 1978

(a) Copyright in a work created before January 1, 1978, but not theretofore in the public domain or copyrighted, subsists from January 1, 1978, and endures for the term provided by section 302. In no case, however, shall the term of copyright in such a work expire before December 31, 2002; and, if the work is published on or before December 31, 2002, the term of copyright shall not expire before December 31, 2047.

(b) The distribution before January 1, 1978, of a phonorecord shall not for any purpose constitute a publication of any musical work, dramatic work, or literary work embodied therein.

§ 304. Duration of Copyright: Subsisting Copyrights

(a) **Copyrights in Their First Term on January 1, 1978.**—

(1)(A) Any copyright, the first term of which is subsisting on January 1, 1978, shall endure for 28 years from the date it was originally secured.

(B) In the case of—

(i) any posthumous work or of any periodical, cyclopedic, or other composite work upon which the copyright was originally secured by the proprietor thereof, or

(ii) any work copyrighted by a corporate body (otherwise than as assignee or licensee of the individual author) or by an employer for whom such work is made for hire,

the proprietor of such copyright shall be entitled to a renewal and extension of the copyright in such work for the further term of 67 years.

(C) In the case of any other copyrighted work, including a contribution by an individual author to a periodical or to a cyclopedic or other composite work—

(i) the author of such work, if the author is still living,

(ii) the widow, widower, or children of the author, if the author is not living,

(iii) the author's executors, if such author, widow, widower, or children are not living, or

(iv) the author's next of kin, in the absence of a will of the author,

shall be entitled to a renewal and extension of the copyright in such work for a further term of 67 years.

(2)(A) At the expiration of the original term of copyright in a work specified in paragraph (1)(B) of this subsection, the copyright shall endure for a renewed and extended further term of 67 years, which—

(i) if an application to register a claim to such further term has been made to the Copyright Office within 1 year before the expiration of the original term of copyright, and the claim is registered, shall vest, upon the beginning of such further term, in the proprietor of the copyright who is entitled to claim the renewal of copyright at the time the application is made; or

(ii) if no such application is made or the claim pursuant to such application is not registered, shall vest, upon the beginning of such further term, in the person or entity that was the proprietor of the copyright as of the last day of the original term of copyright.

(B) At the expiration of the original term of copyright in a work specified in paragraph (1)(C) of this subsection, the copyright shall endure for a renewed and extended further term of 67 years, which—

(i) if an application to register a claim to such further term has been made to the Copyright Office within 1 year before the expiration of the original term of copyright, and the claim is registered, shall vest, upon the beginning of such further term, in any person who is entitled under paragraph (1)(C) to the renewal and extension of the copyright at the time the application is made; or

(ii) if no such application is made or the claim pursuant to such application is not registered, shall vest, upon the beginning of such further term, in any person entitled under paragraph (1)(C), as of the last day of the original term of copyright, to the renewal and extension of the copyright.

(3)(A) An application to register a claim to the renewed and extended term of copyright in a work may be made to the Copyright Office—

(i) within 1 year before the expiration of the original term of copyright by any person entitled under paragraph (1)(B) or (C) to such further term of 67 years; and

(ii) at any time during the renewed and extended term by any person in whom such further term vested, under paragraph (2)(A) or (B), or by any successor or assign of such person, if the application is made in the name of such person.

(B) Such an application is not a condition of the renewal and extension of the copyright in a work for a further term of 67 years.

(4)(A) If an application to register a claim to the renewed and extended term of copyright in a work is not made within 1 year before the expiration of the original term of copyright in a work, or if the claim pursuant to such application is not registered, then a derivative work prepared under authority of a grant of a transfer or license of the copyright that is made before the expiration of the original term of copyright may continue to be used under the terms of the grant during the renewed and extended term of copyright without infringing the copyright, except that such use does not extend to the preparation during such renewed and extended term of other derivative works based upon the copyrighted work covered by such grant.

(B) If an application to register a claim to the renewed and extended term of copyright in a work is made within 1 year before its expiration, and the claim is registered, the certificate of such registration shall constitute prima facie evidence as to the validity of the copyright during its renewed and extended term and of the facts stated in the certificate. The evidentiary weight to be accorded the certificates of a registration of a renewed and extended term of copyright made after the end of that 1-year period shall be within the discretion of the court.

(b) Copyrights in Their Renewal Term at the Time of the Effective Date of the Sonny Bono Copyright Term Extension Act.—Any copyright still in its renewal term at the time that the Sonny Bono Copyright Term Extension Act becomes effective shall have a copyright term of 95 years from the date copyright was originally secured.

(c) Termination of Transfers and Licenses Covering Extended Renewal Term.—In the case of any copyright subsisting in either its first or renewal term on January 1, 1978, other than a copyright in a work made for hire, the exclusive or nonexclusive grant of a transfer or license of the renewal copyright or any right under it, executed before January 1, 1978, by any of the persons designated by subsection (a)(1)(C) of this section, otherwise than by will, is subject to termination under the following conditions:

(1) In the case of a grant executed by a person or persons other than the author, termination of the grant may be effected by the surviving person or persons who executed it. In the case of a grant executed by one or more of the authors of the work, termination of the grant may be effected, to the extent of a particular author's share in the ownership of the renewal copyright, by the author who executed it or, if such author is dead, by the person or persons who, under clause (2) of this subsection, own and are entitled to exercise a total of more than one-half of that author's termination interest.

(2) Where an author is dead, his or her termination interest is owned, and may be exercised, as follows:

(A) The widow or widower owns the author's entire termination interest unless there are any surviving children or grandchildren of the author, in which case the widow or widower owns one-half of the author's interest.

(B) The author's surviving children, and the surviving children of any dead child of the author, own the author's entire termination interest unless there is a widow or widower, in which case the ownership of one-half of the author's interest is divided among them.

(C) The rights of the author's children and grandchildren are in all cases divided among them and exercised on a per stirpes basis according to the number of such author's children represented; the share of the children of a dead child in a termination interest can be exercised only by the action of a majority of them.

(D) In the event that the author's widow or widower, children, and grandchildren are not living, the author's executor, administrator, personal representative, or trustee shall own the author's entire termination interest.

(3) Termination of the grant may be effected at any time during a period of five years beginning at the end of fifty-six years from the date copyright was originally secured, or beginning on January 1, 1978, whichever is later.

(4) The termination shall be effected by serving an advance notice in writing upon the grantee or the grantee's successor in title. In the case of a grant executed by a person or persons other than the author, the notice shall be signed by all of those entitled to terminate the grant under clause (1) of this subsection, or by their duly authorized agents. In the case of a grant executed by one or more of the authors of the work, the notice as to any one author's share shall be signed by that author or his or her duly authorized agent or, if that author is dead, by the

number and proportion of the owners of his or her termination interest required under clauses (1) and (2) of this subsection, or by their duly authorized agents.

(A)   The notice shall state the effective date of the termination, which shall fall within the five-year period specified by clause (3) of this subsection, or, in the case of a termination under subsection (a), within the five-year period specified by subsection (d)(2), and the notice shall be served not less than two or more than ten years before that date. A copy of the notice shall be recorded in the Copyright Office before the effective date of termination, as a condition to its taking effect.

(B)   The notice shall comply, in form, content, and manner of service, with requirements that the Register of Copyrights shall prescribe by regulation.

(5)   Termination of the grant may be effected notwithstanding any agreement to the contrary, including an agreement to make a will or to make any future grant.

(6)   In the case of a grant executed by a person or persons other than the author, all rights under this title that were covered by the terminated grant revert, upon the effective date of termination, to all of those entitled to terminate the grant under clause (1) of this subsection. In the case of a grant executed by one or more of the authors of the work, all of a particular author's rights under this title that were covered by the terminated grant revert, upon the effective date of termination, to that author or, if that author is dead, to the persons owning his or her termination interest under clause (2) of this subsection, including those owners who did not join in signing the notice of termination under clause (4) of this subsection. In all cases the reversion of rights is subject to the following limitations:

(A)   A derivative work prepared under authority of the grant before its termination may continue to be utilized under the terms of the grant after its termination, but this privilege does not extend to the preparation after the termination of other derivative works based upon the copyrighted work covered by the terminated grant.

(B)   The future rights that will revert upon termination of the grant become vested on the date the notice of termination has been served as provided by clause (4) of this subsection.

(C)   Where the author's rights revert to two or more persons under clause (2) of this subsection, they shall vest in those persons in the proportionate shares provided by that clause. In such a case, and subject to the provisions of subclause (D) of this clause, a further grant, or agreement to make a further grant, of a particular author's share with respect to any right covered by a terminated grant is valid only if it is signed by the same number and proportion of the owners, in whom the right has vested under this clause, as are required to terminate the grant under clause (2) of this subsection. Such further grant or agreement is effective with respect to all of the persons in whom the right it covers has vested under this subclause, including those who did not join in signing it. If any person dies after rights under a terminated grant have vested in him or her, that person's legal representatives, legatees, or heirs at law represent him or her for purposes of this subclause.

(D)   A further grant, or agreement to make a further grant, of any right covered by a terminated grant is valid only if it is made after the effective date of the termination. As an exception, however, an agreement for such a further grant may be made between the author or any of the persons provided by the first sentence of clause (6) of this subsection, or between the persons provided by subclause (C) of this clause, and the original grantee or such grantee's successor in title, after the notice of termination has been served as provided by clause (4) of this subsection.

(E)   Termination of a grant under this subsection affects only those rights covered by the grant that arise under this title, and in no way affects rights arising under any other Federal, State, or foreign laws.

(F)   Unless and until termination is effected under this subsection, the grant, if it does not provide otherwise, continues in effect for the remainder of the extended renewal term.

(d) Termination Rights Provided in Subsection (c) Which Have Expired on or Before the Effective Date of the Sonny Bono Copyright Term Extension Act.—In the case of any copyright other than a work made for hire, subsisting in its renewal term on the effective date of the Sonny Bono Copyright Term Extension Act for which the termination right provided in subsection (c) has expired by such date, where the author or owner of the termination right has not previously exercised such termination right, the exclusive or nonexclusive grant of a transfer or license of the renewal copyright or any right under it, executed before January 1, 1978, by any of the persons designated in subsection (a)(1)(C) of this section, other than by will, is subject to termination under the following conditions:

(1)   The conditions specified in subsections (c)(1), (2), (4), (5), and (6) of this section apply to terminations of the last 20 years of copyright term as provided by the amendments made by the Sonny Bono Copyright Term Extension Act.

(2)   Termination of the grant may be effected at any time during a period of 5 years beginning at the end of 75 years from the date copyright was originally secured.

§ 305. Duration of Copyright: Terminal Date

All terms of copyright provided by sections 302 through 304 run to the end of the calendar year in which they would otherwise expire.

CHAPTER 4. COPYRIGHT NOTICE, DEPOSIT, AND REGISTRATION

---

§ 401. Notice of Copyright: Visually Perceptible Copies

(a) General Provisions.—Whenever a work protected under this title is published in the United States or elsewhere by authority of the copyright owner, a notice of copyright as provided by this section may be placed on publicly distributed copies from which the work can be visually perceived, either directly or with the aid of a machine or device.

(b) Form of Notice.—If a notice appears on the copies, it shall consist of the following three elements:

(1) the symbol © (the letter C in a circle), or the word "Copyright", or the abbreviation "Copr."; and

(2) the year of first publication of the work; in the case of compilations or derivative works incorporating previously published material, the year date of first publication of the compilation or derivative work is sufficient. The year date may be omitted where a pictorial, graphic, or sculptural work, with accompanying text matter, if any, is reproduced in or on greeting cards, postcards, stationery, jewelry, dolls, toys, or any useful articles; and

(3) the name of the owner of copyright in the work, or an abbreviation by which the name can be recognized, or a generally known alternative designation of the owner.

(c) Position of Notice.—The notice shall be affixed to the copies in such manner and location as to give reasonable notice of the claim of copyright. The Register of Copyrights shall prescribe by regulation, as examples, specific methods of affixation and positions of the notice on various types of works that will satisfy this requirement, but these specifications shall not be considered exhaustive.

(d) Evidentiary Weight of Notice.—If a notice of copyright in the form and position specified by this section appears on the published copy or copies to which a defendant in a copyright infringement suit had access, then no weight shall be given to such a defendant's interposition of a defense based on innocent infringement in mitigation of actual or statutory damages, except as provided in the last sentence of section 504(c)(2).

§ 402. Notice of Copyright: Phonorecords of Sound Recordings

(a) General Provisions.—Whenever a sound recording protected under this title is published in the United States or elsewhere by authority of the copyright owner, a notice of copyright as provided by this section may be placed on publicly distributed phonorecords of the sound recording.

(b) Form of Notice.—If a notice appears on the phonorecords, it shall consist of the following three elements:

(1) the symbol P (the letter P in a circle); and

(2) the year of first publication of the sound recording; and

(3) the name of the owner of copyright in the sound recording, or an abbreviation by which the name can be recognized, or a generally known alternative designation of the owner; if the producer of the sound recording is named on the phonorecord labels or containers, and if no other name appears in conjunction with the notice, the producer's name shall be considered a part of the notice.

(c) Position of Notice.—The notice shall be placed on the surface of the phonorecord, or on the phonorecord label or container, in such manner and location as to give reasonable notice of the claim of copyright.

(d) Evidentiary Weight of Notice.—If a notice of copyright in the form and position specified by this section appears on the published phonorecord or phonorecords to which a defendant in a copyright infringement suit had access, then no weight shall be given to such a defendant's interposition of a defense based on innocent infringement in mitigation of actual or statutory damages, except as provided in the last sentence of section 504(c)(2).

§ 403. Notice of Copyright: Publications Incorporating United States Government Works

Sections 401(d) and 402(d) shall not apply to a work published in copies or phonorecords consisting predominantly of one or more works of the United States Government unless the notice of copyright appearing on the published copies or phonorecords to which a defendant in the copyright infringement suit had access includes a statement identifying, either affirmatively or negatively, those portions of the copies or phonorecords embodying any work or works protected under this title.

§ 404. Notice of Copyright: Contributions to Collective Works

(a) A separate contribution to a collective work may bear its own notice of copyright, as provided by sections 401 through 403. However, a single notice applicable to the collective work as a whole is sufficient to invoke the provisions of section 401(d) or 402(d) as applicable with respect to the separate contributions it contains (not including advertisements inserted on behalf of persons other than the owner of copyright in the collective work), regardless of the ownership of copyright in the contributions and whether or not they have been previously published.

(b) With respect to copies and phonorecords publicly distributed by authority of the copyright owner before the effective date of the Berne Convention Implementation Act of 1988, where the person named in a single notice applicable to a collective work as a whole is not the owner of copyright in a separate contribution that does not bear its own notice, the case is governed by the provisions of section 406(a).

§ 405. Notice of Copyright: Omission of Notice on Certain Copies and Phonorecords

(a) Effect of Omission on Copyright.—With respect to copies and phonorecords publicly distributed by authority of the copyright owner before the effective date of the Berne Convention Implementation Act of 1988, the omission of the copyright notice described in sections 401 through 403 from copies or phonorecords publicly distributed by authority of the copyright owner does not invalidate the copyright in a work if—

(1) the notice has been omitted from no more than a relatively small number of copies or phonorecords distributed to the public; or

(2) registration for the work has been made before or is made within five years after the publication without notice, and a reasonable effort is made to add notice to all copies or phonorecords that are distributed to the public in the United States after the omission has been discovered; or

(3) the notice has been omitted in violation of an express requirement in writing that, as a condition of the copyright owner's authorization of the public distribution of copies or phonorecords, they bear the prescribed notice.

(b) Effect of Omission on Innocent Infringers.—Any person who innocently infringes a copyright, in reliance upon an authorized copy or phonorecord from which the copyright notice has been omitted and which was publicly distributed by authority of the copyright owner before the effective date of the Berne Convention Implementation Act of 1988, incurs no liability for actual or statutory damages under section 504 for any infringing acts committed before receiving actual notice that registration for the work has been made under section 408, if such person proves that he or she was misled by the omission of notice. In a suit for infringement in such a case the court may allow or disallow recovery of any of the infringer's profits attributable to the infringement, and may enjoin the continuation of the infringing undertaking or may require, as a condition for permitting the continuation of the infringing undertaking, that the infringer pay the copyright owner a reasonable license fee in an amount and on terms fixed by the court.

(c) **Removal of Notice.**—Protection under this title is not affected by the removal, destruction, or obliteration of the notice, without the authorization of the copyright owner, from any publicly distributed copies or phonorecords.

§ 406. Notice of Copyright: Error in Name or Date on Certain Copies and Phonorecords

(a) **Error in Name.**—With respect to copies and phonorecords publicly distributed by authority of the copyright owner before the effective date of the Berne Convention Implementation Act of 1988, where the person named in the copyright notice on copies or phonorecords publicly distributed by authority of the copyright owner is not the owner of copyright, the validity and ownership of the copyright are not affected. In such a case, however, any person who innocently begins an undertaking that infringes the copyright has a complete defense to any action for such infringement if such person proves that he or she was misled by the notice and began the undertaking in good faith under a purported transfer or license from the person named therein, unless before the undertaking was begun—

(1) registration for the work had been made in the name of the owner of copyright; or

(2) a document executed by the person named in the notice and showing the ownership of the copyright had been recorded.

The person named in the notice is liable to account to the copyright owner for all receipts from transfers or licenses purportedly made under the copyright by the person named in the notice.

(b) **Error in Date.**—When the year date in the notice on copies or phonorecords distributed before the effective date of the Berne Convention Implementation Act of 1988, by authority of the copyright owner is earlier than the year in which publication first occurred, any period computed from the year of first publication under section 302 is to be computed from the year in the notice. Where the year date is more than one year later than the year in which publication first occurred, the work is considered to have been published without any notice and is governed by the provisions of section 405.

(c) **Omission of Name or Date.**—Where copies or phonorecords publicly distributed before the effective date of the Berne Convention Implementation Act of 1988 by authority of the copyright owner contain no name or no date that could reasonably be considered a part of the notice, the work is considered to have been published without any notice and is governed by the provisions of section 405 as in effect on the day before the effective date of the Berne Convention Implementation Act of 1988.

§ 407. Deposit of Copies or Phonorecords for Library of Congress

(a) Except as provided by subsection (c), and subject to the provisions of subsection (e), the owner of copyright or of the exclusive right of publication in a work published in the United States shall deposit, within three months after the date of such publication—

(1) two complete copies of the best edition; or

(2) if the work is a sound recording, two complete phonorecords of the best edition, together with any printed or other visually perceptible material published with such phonorecords.

Neither the deposit requirements of this subsection nor the acquisition provisions of subsection (e) are conditions of copyright protection.

(b)   The required copies or phonorecords shall be deposited in the Copyright Office for the use or disposition of the Library of Congress. The Register of Copyrights shall, when requested by the depositor and upon payment of the fee prescribed by section 708, issue a receipt for the deposit.

(c)   The Register of Copyrights may be regulation exempt any categories of material from the deposit requirements of this section, or require deposit of only one copy or phonorecord with respect to any categories. Such regulations shall provide either for complete exemption from the deposit requirements of this section, or for alternative forms of deposit aimed at providing a satisfactory archival record of a work without imposing practical or financial hardships on the depositor, where the individual author is the owner of copyright in a pictorial, graphic, or sculptural work and (i) less than five copies of the work have been published, or (ii) the work has been published in a limited edition consisting of numbered copies, the monetary value of which would make the mandatory deposit of two copies of the best edition of the work burdensome, unfair, or unreasonable.

(d)   At any time after publication of a work as provided by subsection (a), the Register of Copyrights may make written demand for the required deposit on any of the persons obligated to make the deposit under subsection (a). Unless deposit is made within three months after the demand is received, the person or persons on whom the demand was made are liable—

(1)   to a fine of not more than $250 for each work; and

(2)   to pay into a specially designated fund in the Library of Congress the total retail price of the copies or phonorecords demanded, or, if no retail price has been fixed, the reasonable cost to the Library of Congress of acquiring them; and

(3)   to pay a fine of $2,500, in addition to any fine or liability imposed under clauses (1) and (2), if such person willfully or repeatedly fails or refuses to comply with such a demand.

(e)   With respect to transmission programs that have been fixed and transmitted to the public in the United States but have not been published, the Register of Copyrights shall, after consulting with the Librarian of Congress and other interested organizations and officials, establish regulations governing the acquisition, through deposit or otherwise, of copies or phonorecords of such programs for the collections of the Library of Congress.

(1)   The Librarian of Congress shall be permitted, under the standards and conditions set forth in such regulations, to make a fixation of a transmission program directly from a transmission to the public, and to reproduce one copy or phonorecord from such fixation for archival purposes.

(2)   Such regulations shall also provide standards and procedures by which the Register of Copyrights may make written demand, upon the owner of the right of transmission in the United States, for the deposit of a copy or phonorecord of a specific transmission program. Such deposit may, at the option of the owner of the right of transmission in the United States, be accomplished by gift, by loan for purposes of reproduction, or by sale at a price not to exceed the cost of reproducing and supplying the copy or phonorecord. The regulations established under this clause shall provide reasonable periods of not less than three months for compliance with a demand, and shall allow for extensions of such periods and adjustments in the scope of the demand or the methods for fulfilling it, as reasonably warranted by the circumstances. Willful failure or refusal to comply with the conditions prescribed by such regulations shall subject the owner of the right of transmission in the United States to liability for an amount, not to exceed the cost of reproducing and supplying the copy or phonorecord in question, to be paid into a specially designated fund in the Library of Congress.

(3)   Nothing in this subsection shall be construed to require the making or retention, for purposes of deposit, of any copy or phonorecord of an unpublished transmission program, the transmission of which occurs before the receipt of a specific written demand as provided by clause (2).

(4)   No activity undertaken in compliance with regulations prescribed under clauses (1) or (2) of this subsection shall result in liability if intended solely to assist in the acquisition of copies or phonorecords under this subsection.

§ 408.   Copyright Registration in General

(a)   Registration Permissive.—At any time during the subsistence of the first term of copyright in any published or unpublished work in which the copyright was secured before January 1, 1978, and during the subsistence of any copyright secured on or after that date, the owner of copyright or of any exclusive right in the work may obtain registration of the copyright claim by delivering to the Copyright Office the deposit specified by this section, together with the application and fee specified by sections 409 and 708. Such registration is not a condition of copyright protection.

(b)   Deposit for Copyright Registration.—Except as provided by subsection (c), the material deposited for registration shall include—

(1)   in the case of an unpublished work, one complete copy or phonorecord;

(2)   in the case of the published work, two complete copies or phonorecords of the best edition;

(3)   in the case of a work first published outside the United States, one complete copy or phonorecord as so published;

(4)   in the case of a contribution to a collective work, one complete copy or phonorecord of the best edition of the collective work.

Copies or phonorecords deposited for the Library of Congress under section 407 may be used to satisfy the deposit provisions of this section, if they are accompanied by the prescribed application and fee, and by any additional identifying material that the Register may, by regulation, require. The Register shall also prescribe regulations establishing requirements under which copies or phonorecords acquired for the Library of Congress under subsection (e) of section 407, otherwise than by deposit, may be used to satisfy the deposit provisions of this section.

(c)   Administrative Classification and Optional Deposit.—

(1)   The Register of Copyrights is authorized to specify by regulation the administrative classes into which works are to be placed for purposes of deposit and registration, and the nature of the copies or phonorecords to be deposited in the various classes specified. The regulations may require or permit, for particular classes, the deposit of identifying material instead of copies or phonorecords, the deposit of only one copy or phonorecord where two would normally be required, or a single registration for a group of related works. This administrative classification of works has no significance with respect to the subject matter of copyright or the exclusive rights provided by this title.

(2)   Without prejudice to the general authority provided under clause (1), the Register of Copyrights shall establish regulations specifically permitting a single registration for a group of works by the same individual author, all first published as contributions to periodicals, including newspapers, within a twelve-month period, on the basis of a single deposit, application, and registration fee, under the following conditions:

(A)   if the deposit consists of one copy of the entire issue of the periodical, or of the entire section in the case of a newspaper, in which each contribution was first published; and

(B)   if the application identifies each work separately, including the periodical containing it and its date of first publication.

(3)   As an alternative to separate renewal registrations under subsection (a) of section 304, a single renewal registration may be made for a group of works by the same individual author,

all first published as contributions to periodicals, including newspapers, upon the filing of a single application and fee, under all of the following conditions:

  (A) the renewal claimant or claimants, and the basis of claim or claims under section 304(a), is the same for each of the works; and

  (B) the works were all copyrighted upon their first publication, either through separate copyright notice and registration or by virtue of a general copyright notice in the periodical issue as a whole; and

  (C) the renewal application and fee are received not more than twenty-eight or less than twenty-seven years after the thirty-first day of December of the calendar year in which all of the works were first published; and

  (D) the renewal application identifies each work separately, including the periodical containing it and its date of first publication.

 (d) Corrections and Amplifications.—The Register may also establish, by regulation, formal procedures for the filing of an application for supplementary registration, to correct an error in a copyright registration or to amplify the information given in a registration. Such application shall be accompanied by the fee provided by section 708, and shall clearly identify the registration to be corrected or amplified. The information contained in a supplementary registration augments but does not supersede that contained in the earlier registration.

 (e) Published Edition of Previously Registered Work.—Registration for the first published edition of a work previously registered in unpublished form may be made even though the work as published is substantially the same as the unpublished version.

 (f) Preregistration of Works Being Prepared for Commercial Distribution.—

  (1) Rulemaking—Not later than 180 days after the date of enactment of this subsection, the Register of Copyrights shall issue regulations to establish procedures for preregistration of a work that is being prepared for commercial distribution and has not been published.

  (2) Class of Works—The regulations established under paragraph (1) shall permit preregistration for any work that is in a class of works that the Register determines has had a history of infringement prior to authorized commercial distribution.

  (3) Application for Registration—Not later than 3 months after the first publication of a work preregistered under this subsection, the applicant shall submit to the Copyright Office—

  (A) an application for registration of the work;

  (B) a deposit; and

  (C) the applicable fee.

  (4) Effect of Untimely Application—An action under this chapter for infringement of a work preregistered under this subsection, in a case in which the infringement commenced no later than 2 months after the first publication of the work, shall be dismissed if the items described in paragraph (3) are not submitted to the Copyright Office in proper form within the earlier of—

  (A) 3 months after the first publication of the work; or

  (B) 1 month after the copyright owner has learned of the infringement.

§ 409. Application for Copyright Registration

The application for copyright registration shall be made on a form prescribed by the Register of Copyrights and shall include—

  (1) the name and address of the copyright claimant;

(2) in the case of a work other than an anonymous or pseudonymous work, the name and nationality or domicile of the author or authors, and, if one or more of the authors is dead, the dates of their deaths;

(3) if the work is anonymous or pseudonymous, the nationality or domicile of the author or authors;

(4) in the case of a work made for hire, a statement to this effect;

(5) if the copyright claimant is not the author, a brief statement of how the claimant obtained ownership of the copyright;

(6) the title of the work, together with any previous or alternative titles under which the work can be identified;

(7) the year in which creation of the work was completed;

(8) if the work has been published, the date and nation of its first publication;

(9) in the case of a compilation or derivative work, an identification of any preexisting work or works that it is based on or incorporates, and a brief, general statement of the additional material covered by the copyright claim being registered; and

(10) any other information regarded by the Register of Copyrights as bearing upon the preparation or identification of the work or the existence, ownership, or duration of the copyright.

If an application is submitted for the renewed and extended term provided for in section 304(a)(3)(A) and an original term registration has not been made, the Register may request information with respect to the existence, ownership, or duration of the copyright for the original term.

§ 410. Registration of Claim and Issuance of Certificate

(a) When, after examination, the Register of Copyrights determines that, in accordance with the provisions of this title, the material deposited constitutes copyrightable subject matter and that the other legal and formal requirements of this title have been met, the Register shall register the claim and issue to the applicant a certificate of registration under the seal of the Copyright Office. The certificate shall contain the information given in the application, together with the number and effective date of the registration.

(b) In any case in which the Register of Copyrights determines that, in accordance with the provisions of this title, the material deposited does not constitute copyrightable subject matter or that the claim is invalid for any other reason, the Register shall refuse registration and shall notify the applicant in writing of the reasons for such refusal.

(c) In any judicial proceedings the certificate of a registration made before or within five years after first publication of the work shall constitute prima facie evidence of the validity of the copyright and of the facts stated in the certificate. The evidentiary weight to be accorded the certificate of a registration made thereafter shall be within the discretion of the court.

(d) The effective date of a copyright registration is the day on which an application, deposit, and fee, which are later determined by the Register of Copyrights or by a court of competent jurisdiction to be acceptable for registration, have all been received in the Copyright Office.

§ 411. Registration and Civil Infringement Actions

(a) Except for an action brought for a violation of the rights of the author under section 106A(a), and subject to the provisions of subsection (b), no civil action for infringement of the copyright in any United States work shall be instituted until preregistration or registration of the copyright claim has been made in accordance with this title. In any case, however, where the deposit, application, and fee required for registration have been delivered to the Copyright Office in proper form and registration has been refused, the applicant is entitled to institute a civil action for infringement if notice thereof, with a copy of the complaint, is served on the Register of Copyrights. The Register may, at his or her option, become a party to the action with respect to the issue of registrability of the copyright claim by entering an appearance within sixty days after such service, but the Register's failure to become a party shall not deprive the court of jurisdiction to determine that issue.

(b)(1) A certificate of registration satisfies the requirements of this section and section 412, regardless of whether the certificate contains any inaccurate information, unless—

> (A) the inaccurate information was included on the application for copyright registration with knowledge that it was inaccurate; and

> (B) the inaccuracy of the information, if known, would have caused the Register of Copyrights to refuse registration.

> (2) In any case in which inaccurate information described under paragraph (1) is alleged, the court shall request the Register of Copyrights to advise the court whether the inaccurate information, if known, would have caused the Register of Copyrights to refuse registration.

> (3) Nothing in this subsection shall affect any rights, obligations, or requirements of a person related to information contained in a registration certificate, except for the institution of and remedies in infringement actions under this section and section 412.

(c) In the case of a work consisting of sounds, images, or both, the first fixation of which is made simultaneously with its transmission, the copyright owner may, either before or after such fixation takes place, institute an action for infringement under section 501, fully subject to the remedies provided by sections 502 through 505 and section 510, if, in accordance with requirements that the Register of Copyrights shall prescribe by regulation, the copyright owner—

> (1) serves notice upon the infringer, not less than 48 hours before such fixation, identifying the work and the specific time and source of its first transmission, and declaring an intention to secure copyright in the work; and

> (2) makes registration for the work, if required by subsection (a), within three months after its first transmission.

§ 412.   Registration as Prerequisite to Certain Remedies for Infringement

In any action under this title, other than an action brought for a violation of the rights of the author under section 106A(a), an action for infringement of the copyright of a work that has been preregistered under section 408(f) before the commencement of the infringement and that has an effective date of registration not later than the earlier of 3 months after the first publication of the work or 1 month after the copyright owner has learned of the infringement, or an action instituted under section 411(c), no award of statutory damages or of attorney's fees, as provided by sections 504 and 505, shall be made for—

> (1) any infringement of copyright in an unpublished work commenced before the effective date of its registration; or

> (2) any infringement of copyright commenced after first publication of the work and before the effective date of its registration, unless such registration is made within three months after the first publication of the work.

CHAPTER 5. COPYRIGHT INFRINGEMENT AND REMEDIES

§ 501. Infringement of Copyright

(a) Anyone who violates any of the exclusive rights of the copyright owner as provided by sections 106 through 122 or of the author as provided in section 106A(a), or who imports copies or phonorecords into the United States in violation of section 602, is an infringer of the copyright or right of the author, as the case may be. For purposes of this chapter (other than section 506), any reference to copyright shall be deemed to include the rights conferred by section 106A(a). As used in this subsection the term "anyone" includes any State, any instrumentality of a State, and any officer or employee of a State or instrumentality of a State acting in his or her official capacity. Any State, and any such instrumentality, officer, or employee, shall be subject to the provisions of this title in the same manner and to the same extent as any nongovernmental entity.

(b) The legal or beneficial owner of an exclusive right under a copyright is entitled, subject to the requirements of section 411, to institute an action for any infringement of that particular right committed while he or she is the owner of it. The court may require such owner to serve written notice of the action with a copy of the complaint upon any person shown, by the records of the Copyright Office or otherwise, to have or claim an interest in the copyright, and shall require that such notice be served upon any person whose interest is likely to be affected by a decision in the case. The court may require the joinder, and shall permit the intervention, of any person having or claiming an interest in the copyright.

(c) For any secondary transmission by a cable system that embodies a performance or a display of a work which is actionable as an act of infringement under subsection (c) of section 111, a television broadcast station holding a copyright or other license to transmit or perform the same version of that work shall, for purposes of subsection (b) of this section, be treated as a legal or beneficial owner if such secondary transmission occurs within the local service area of that television station.

(d) For any secondary transmission by a cable system that is actionable as an act of infringement pursuant to section 111(c)(3), the following shall also have standing to sue: (i) the primary transmitter whose transmission has been altered by the cable system; and (ii) any broadcast station within whose local service area the secondary transmission occurs.

(e) With respect to any secondary transmission that is made by a satellite carrier of a performance or display of a work embodied in a primary transmission and is actionable as an act of infringement under section 119(a)(5), a network station holding a copyright or other license to transmit or perform the same version of that work shall, for purposes of subsection (b) of this section, be treated as a legal or beneficial owner if such secondary transmission occurs within the local service area of that station.

(f)(1) With respect to any secondary transmission that is made by a satellite carrier of a performance or display of a work embodied in a primary transmission and is actionable as an act of infringement under section 122, a television broadcast station holding a copyright or other license to transmit or perform the same version of that work shall, for purposes of subsection (b) of this section, be treated as a legal or beneficial owner if such secondary transmission occurs within the local market of that station.

(2) A television broadcast station may file a civil action against any satellite carrier that has refused to carry television broadcast signals, as required under section 122(a)(2), to enforce that television broadcast station's rights under section 338(a) of the Communications Act of 1934.

§ 502. Remedies for Infringement: Injunctions

(a) Any court having jurisdiction of a civil action arising under this title may, subject to the provisions of section 1498 of title 28, grant temporary and final injunctions on such terms as it may deem reasonable to prevent or restrain infringement of a copyright.

(b) Any such injunction may be served anywhere in the United States on the person enjoined; it shall be operative throughout the United States and shall be enforceable, by proceedings in contempt or otherwise, by any United States court having jurisdiction of that person. The clerk of the court granting the injunction shall, when requested by any other court in which enforcement of the injunction is sought, transmit promptly to the other court a certified copy of all the papers in the case on file in such clerk's office.

§ 503. Remedies for Infringement: Impounding and Disposition of Infringing Articles

(a)(1) At any time while an action under this title is pending, the court may order the impounding, on such terms as it may deem reasonable—

(A) of all copies or phonorecords claimed to have been made or used in violation of the exclusive right of the copyright owner;

(B) of all plates, molds, matrices, masters, tapes, film negatives, or other articles by means of which such copies or phonorecords may be reproduced; and

(C) of records documenting the manufacture, sale, or receipt of things involved in any such violation, provided that any records seized under this subparagraph shall be taken into the custody of the court.

(2) For impoundments of records ordered under paragraph (1)(C), the court shall enter an appropriate protective order with respect to discovery and use of any records or information that has been impounded. The protective order shall provide for appropriate procedures to ensure that confidential, private, proprietary, or privileged information contained in such records is not improperly disclosed or used.

(3) The relevant provisions of paragraphs (2) through (11) of section 34(d) of the Trademark Act (15 U.S.C. § 1116(d)(2) through (11)) shall extend to any impoundment of records ordered

under paragraph (1)(C) that is based upon an ex parte application, notwithstanding the provisions of rule 65 of the Federal Rules of Civil Procedure. Any references in paragraphs (2) through (11) of section 34(d) of the Trademark Act to section 32 of such Act shall be read as references to section 501 of this title, and references to use of a counterfeit mark in connection with the sale, offering for sale, or distribution of goods or services shall be read as references to infringement of a copyright.

(b)   As part of a final judgment or decree, the court may order the destruction or other reasonable disposition of all copies or phonorecords found to have been made or used in violation of the copyright owner's exclusive rights, and of all plates, molds, matrices, masters, tapes, film negatives, or other articles by means of which such copies or phonorecords may be reproduced.

§ 504.   Remedies for Infringement: Damages and Profits

(a)   In General.—Except as otherwise provided by this title, an infringer of copyright is liable for either—

(1)   the copyright owner's actual damages and any additional profits of the infringer, as provided by subsection (b); or

(2)   statutory damages, as provided by subsection (c).

(b)   Actual Damages and Profits.—The copyright owner is entitled to recover the actual damages suffered by him or her as a result of the infringement, and any profits of the infringer that are attributable to the infringement and are not taken into account in computing the actual damages. In establishing the infringer's profits, the copyright owner is required to present proof only of the infringer's gross revenue, and the infringer is required to prove his or her deductible expenses and the elements of profit attributable to factors other than the copyrighted work.

(c)   Statutory Damages.—

(1)   Except as provided by clause (2) of this subsection, the copyright owner may elect, at any time before final judgment is rendered, to recover, instead of actual damages and profits, an award of statutory damages for all infringements involved in the action, with respect to any one work, for which any one infringer is liable individually, or for which any two or more infringers are liable jointly and severally, in a sum of not less than $750 or more than $30,000 as the court considers just. For the purposes of this subsection, all the parts of a compilation or derivative work constitute one work.

(2)   In a case where the copyright owner sustains the burden of proving, and the court finds, that infringement was committed willfully, the court in its discretion may increase the award of statutory damages to a sum of not more than $150,000. In a case where the infringer sustains the burden of proving, and the court finds, that such infringer was not aware and had no reason to believe that his or her acts constituted an infringement of copyright, the court in its discretion may reduce the award of statutory damages to a sum of not less than $200. The court shall remit statutory damages in any case where an infringer believed and had reasonable grounds for believing that his or her use of the copyrighted work was a fair use under section 107, if the infringer was: (i) an employee or agent of a nonprofit educational institution, library, or archives acting within the scope of his or her employment who, or such institution, library, or archives itself, which infringed by reproducing the work in copies or phonorecords; or (ii) a public broadcasting entity which or a person who, as a regular part of the nonprofit activities of a public broadcasting entity (as defined in section 118(f)) infringed by performing a published nondramatic literary work or by reproducing a transmission program embodying a performance of such a work.

(3)(A)   In a case of infringement, it shall be a rebuttable presumption that the infringement was committed willfully for purposes of determining relief if the violator, or a person acting in concert with the violator, knowingly provided or knowingly caused to be provided materially false contact information to a domain name registrar, domain name registry, or other domain name registration authority in registering, maintaining, or renewing a domain name used in connection with the infringement.

(B) Nothing in this paragraph limits what may be considered willful infringement under this subsection.

(C) For purposes of this paragraph, the term "domain name" has the meaning given that term in section 45 of the Act entitled "An Act to provide for the registration and protection of trademarks used in commerce, to carry out the provisions of certain international conventions, and for other purposes" approved July 5, 1946 (commonly referred to as the "Trademark Act of 1946"; 15 U.S.C. 1127).

(d) **Additional Damages in Certain Cases.**—In any case in which the court finds that a defendant proprietor of an establishment who claims as a defense that its activities were exempt under section 110(5) did not have reasonable grounds to believe that its use of a copyrighted work was exempt under such section, the plaintiff shall be entitled to, in addition to any award of damages under this section, an additional award of two times the amount of the license fee that the proprietor of the establishment concerned should have paid the plaintiff for such use during the preceding period of up to 3 years.

§ 505. Remedies for Infringement: Costs and Attorney's Fees

In any civil action under this title, the court in its discretion may allow the recovery of full costs by or against any party other than the United States or an officer thereof. Except as otherwise provided by this title, the court may also award a reasonable attorney's fee to the prevailing party as part of the costs.

§ 506. Criminal Offenses

(a) Criminal Infringement.—

(1) In General—Any person who willfully infringes a copyright shall be punished as provided under section 2319 of title 18, if the infringement was committed—

(A) for purposes of commercial advantage or private financial gain;

(B) by the reproduction or distribution, including by electronic means, during any 180-day period, of 1 or more copies or phonorecords of 1 or more copyrighted works, which have a total retail value of more than $1,000; or

(C) by the distribution of a work being prepared for commercial distribution, by making it available on a computer network accessible to members of the public, if such person knew or should have known that the work was intended for commercial distribution.

(2) Evidence—For purposes of this subsection, evidence of reproduction or distribution of a copyrighted work, by itself, shall not be sufficient to establish willful infringement of a copyright.

(3) Definition—In this subsection, the term "work being prepared for commercial distribution" means—

(A) a computer program, a musical work, a motion picture or other audiovisual work, or a sound recording, if, at the time of unauthorized distribution—

(i) the copyright owner has a reasonable expectation of commercial distribution; and

(ii) the copies or phonorecords of the work have not been commercially distributed; or

(B) a motion picture, if, at the time of unauthorized distribution, the motion picture—

(i) has been made available for viewing in a motion picture exhibition facility; and

(ii) has not been made available in copies for sale to the general public in the United States in a format intended to permit viewing outside a motion picture exhibition facility.

(b) Forfeiture, Destruction, and Restitution.—Forfeiture, destruction, and restitution relating to this section shall be subject to section 2323 of title 18, to the extent provided in that section, in addition to any other similar remedies provided by law.

(c) Fraudulent Copyright Notice.—Any person who, with fraudulent intent, places on any article a notice of copyright or words of the same purport that such person knows to be false, or who, with fraudulent intent, publicly distributes or imports for public distribution any article bearing such notice or words that such person knows to be false, shall be fined not more than $2,500.

(d) Fraudulent Removal of Copyright Notice.—Any person who, with fraudulent intent, removes or alters any notice of copyright appearing on a copy of a copyrighted work shall be fined not more than $2,500.

(e) False Representation.—Any person who knowingly makes a false representation of a material fact in the application for copyright registration provided for by section 409, or in any written statement filed in connection with the application, shall be fined not more than $2,500.

(f) Rights of Attribution and Integrity.—Nothing in this section applies to infringement of the rights conferred by section 106A(a).

§ 507. Limitations on Actions

(a) Criminal Proceedings.—Except as expressly provided otherwise in this title, no criminal proceeding shall be maintained under the provisions of this title unless it is commenced within 5 years after the cause of action arose.

(b) Civil Actions.—No civil action shall be maintained under the provisions of this title unless it is commenced within three years after the claim accrued.

§ 508. Notification of Filing and Determination of Actions

(a) Within one month after the filing of any action under this title, the clerks of the courts of the United States shall send written notification to the Register of Copyrights setting forth, as far as is shown by the papers filed in the court, the names and addresses of the parties and the title, author, and registration number of each work involved in the action. If any other copyrighted work is later included in the action by amendment, answer, or other pleading, the clerk shall also send a notification concerning it to the Register within one month after the pleading is filed.

(b) Within one month after any final order or judgment is issued in the case, the clerk of the court shall notify the Register of it, sending with the notification a copy of the order or judgment together with the written opinion, if any, of the court.

(c) Upon receiving the notifications specified in this section, the Register shall make them a part of the public records of the Copyright Office.

§ 509. [Repealed]

§ 510. Remedies for Alteration of Programing by Cable Systems

(a) In any action filed pursuant to section 111(c)(3), the following remedies shall be available:

(1) Where an action is brought by a party identified in subsections (b) or (c) of section 501, the remedies provided by sections 502 through 505, and the remedy provided by subsection (b) of this section; and

(2) When an action is brought by a party identified in subsection (d) of section 501, the remedies provided by sections 502 and 505, together with any actual damages suffered by such party as a result of the infringement, and the remedy provided by subsection (b) of this section.

(b) In any action filed pursuant to section 111(c)(3), the court may decree that, for a period not to exceed thirty days, the cable system shall be deprived of the benefit of a statutory license for one or more distant signals carried by such cable system.

§ 511. Liability of States, Instrumentalities of States, and State Officials for Infringement of Copyright

(a) In General.—Any State, any instrumentality of a State, and any officer or employee of a State or instrumentality of a State acting in his or her official capacity, shall not be immune, under the Eleventh Amendment of the Constitution of the United States or under any other doctrine of sovereign immunity, from suit in Federal court by any person, including any governmental or nongovernmental entity, for a violation of any of the exclusive rights of a copyright owner provided by sections 106 through 122, for importing copies of phonorecords in violation of section 602, or for any other violation under this title.[1]

(b) Remedies.—In a suit described in subsection (a) for a violation described in that subsection, remedies (including remedies both at law and in equity) are available for the violation to the same extent as such remedies are available for such a violation in a suit against any public or private entity other than a State, instrumentality of a State, or officer or employee of a State acting in his or her official capacity. Such remedies include impounding and disposition of infringing articles under section 503, actual damages and profits and statutory damages under section 504, costs and attorney's fees under section 505, and the remedies provided in section 510.

§ 512. Limitations on Liability Relating to Material Online

(a) Transitory Digital Network Communications.—A service provider shall not be liable for monetary relief, or, except as provided in subsection (j), for injunctive or other equitable relief, for infringement of copyright by reason of the provider's transmitting, routing, or providing connections for, material through a system or network controlled or operated by or for the service provider, or by reason of the intermediate and transient storage of that material in the course of such transmitting, routing, or providing connections, if—

(1) the transmission of the material was initiated by or at the direction of a person other than the service provider;

(2) the transmission, routing, provision of connections, or storage is carried out through an automatic technical process without selection of the material by the service provider;

(3) the service provider does not select the recipients of the material except as an automatic response to the request of another person;

(4) no copy of the material made by the service provider in the course of such intermediate or transient storage is maintained on the system or network in a manner ordinarily accessible to anyone other than anticipated recipients, and no such copy is maintained on the system or

---

[1] This provision's abrogation of states' sovereign immunity was held to be unconstitutional in *National Association of Boards of Pharmacy v. Board of Regents of the University System of Georgia*, 633 F.3d 1297 (11th Cir. 2011).—*Ed.*

network in a manner ordinarily accessible to such anticipated recipients for a longer period than is reasonably necessary for the transmission, routing, or provision of connections; and

(5) the material is transmitted through the system or network without modification of its content.

(b) System Caching.—

(1) Limitation on Liability.—A service provider shall not be liable for monetary relief, or, except as provided in subsection (j), for injunctive or other equitable relief, for infringement of copyright by reason of the intermediate and temporary storage of material on a system or network controlled or operated by or for the service provider in a case in which—

(A) the material is made available online by a person other than the service provider;

(B) the material is transmitted from the person described in subparagraph (A) through the system or network to a person other than the person described in subparagraph (A) at the direction of that other person; and

(C) the storage is carried out through an automatic technical process for the purpose of making the material available to users of the system or network who, after the material is transmitted as described in subparagraph (B), request access to the material from the person described in subparagraph (A),

if the conditions set forth in paragraph (2) are met.

(2) Conditions.—The conditions referred to in paragraph (1) are that—

(A) the material described in paragraph (1) is transmitted to the subsequent users described in paragraph (1)(C) without modification to its content from the manner in which the material was transmitted from the person described in paragraph (1)(A);

(B) the service provider described in paragraph (1) complies with rules concerning the refreshing, reloading, or other updating of the material when specified by the person making the material available online in accordance with a generally accepted industry standard data communications protocol for the system or network through which that person makes the material available, except that this subparagraph applies only if those rules are not used by the person described in paragraph (1)(A) to prevent or unreasonably impair the intermediate storage to which this subsection applies;

(C) the service provider does not interfere with the ability of technology associated with the material to return to the person described in paragraph (1)(A) the information that would have been available to that person if the material had been obtained by the subsequent users described in paragraph (1)(C) directly from that person, except that this subparagraph applies only if that technology—

(i) does not significantly interfere with the performance of the provider's system or network or with the intermediate storage of the material;

(ii) is consistent with generally accepted industry standard communications protocols; and

(iii) does not extract information from the provider's system or network other than the information that would have been available to the person described in paragraph (1)(A) if the subsequent users had gained access to the material directly from that person;

(D) if the person described in paragraph (1)(A) has in effect a condition that a person must meet prior to having access to the material, such as a condition based on payment of a fee or provision of a password or other information, the service provider permits access to the stored material in significant part only to users of its system or network that have met those conditions and only in accordance with those conditions; and

(E) if the person described in paragraph (1)(A) makes that material available online without the authorization of the copyright owner of the material, the service provider responds expeditiously to remove, or disable access to, the material that is claimed to be infringing upon notification of claimed infringement as described in subsection (c)(3), except that this subparagraph applies only if—

(i) the material has previously been removed from the originating site or access to it has been disabled, or a court has ordered that the material be removed from the originating site or that access to the material on the originating site be disabled; and

(ii) the party giving the notification includes in the notification a statement confirming that the material has been removed from the originating site or access to it has been disabled or that a court has ordered that the material be removed from the originating site or that access to the material on the originating site be disabled.

(c) Information Residing on Systems or Networks at Direction of Users.—

(1) In General.—A service provider shall not be liable for monetary relief, or, except as provided in subsection (j), for injunctive or other equitable relief, for infringement of copyright by reason of the storage at the direction of a user of material that resides on a system or network controlled or operated by or for the service provider, if the service provider—

(A)(i) does not have actual knowledge that the material or an activity using the material on the system or network is infringing;

(ii) in the absence of such actual knowledge, is not aware of facts or circumstances from which infringing activity is apparent; or

(iii) upon obtaining such knowledge or awareness, acts expeditiously to remove, or disable access to, the material;

(B) does not receive a financial benefit directly attributable to the infringing activity, in a case in which the service provider has the right and ability to control such activity; and

(C) upon notification of claimed infringement as described in paragraph (3), responds expeditiously to remove, or disable access to, the material that is claimed to be infringing or to be the subject of infringing activity.

(2) Designated Agent.—The limitations on liability established in this subsection apply to a service provider only if the service provider has designated an agent to receive notifications of claimed infringement described in paragraph (3), by making available through its service, including on its website in a location accessible to the public, and by providing to the Copyright Office, substantially the following information:

(A) the name, address, phone number, and electronic mail address of the agent.

(B) other contact information which the Register of Copyrights may deem appropriate.

The Register of Copyrights shall maintain a current directory of agents available to the public for inspection, including through the Internet, and may require payment of a fee by service providers to cover the costs of maintaining the directory.

(3) Elements of Notification.—

(A) To be effective under this subsection, a notification of claimed infringement must be a written communication provided to the designated agent of a service provider that includes substantially the following:

(i) A physical or electronic signature of a person authorized to act on behalf of the owner of an exclusive right that is allegedly infringed.

(ii)   Identification of the copyrighted work claimed to have been infringed, or, if multiple copyrighted works at a single online site are covered by a single notification, a representative list of such works at that site.

(iii) Identification of the material that is claimed to be infringing or to be the subject of infringing activity and that is to be removed or access to which is to be disabled, and information reasonably sufficient to permit the service provider to locate the material.

(iv)   Information reasonably sufficient to permit the service provider to contact the complaining party, such as an address, telephone number, and, if available, an electronic mail address at which the complaining party may be contacted.

(v)   A statement that the complaining party has a good faith belief that use of the material in the manner complained of is not authorized by the copyright owner, its agent, or the law.

(vi)   A statement that the information in the notification is accurate, and under penalty of perjury, that the complaining party is authorized to act on behalf of the owner of an exclusive right that is allegedly infringed.

(B)(i)   Subject to clause (ii), a notification from a copyright owner or from a person authorized to act on behalf of the copyright owner that fails to comply substantially with the provisions of subparagraph (A) shall not be considered under paragraph (1)(A) in determining whether a service provider has actual knowledge or is aware of facts or circumstances from which infringing activity is apparent.

(ii) In a case in which the notification that is provided to the service provider's designated agent fails to comply substantially with all the provisions of subparagraph (A) but substantially complies with clauses (ii), (iii), and (iv) of subparagraph (A), clause (i) of this subparagraph applies only if the service provider promptly attempts to contact the person making the notification or takes other reasonable steps to assist in the receipt of notification that substantially complies with all the provisions of subparagraph (A).

(d) **Information Location Tools.**—A service provider shall not be liable for monetary relief, or, except as provided in subsection (j), for injunctive or other equitable relief, for infringement of copyright by reason of the provider referring or linking users to an online location containing infringing material or infringing activity, by using information location tools, including a directory, index, reference, pointer, or hypertext link, if the service provider—

(1)(A) does not have actual knowledge that the material or activity is infringing;

(B) in the absence of such actual knowledge, is not aware of facts or circumstances from which infringing activity is apparent; or

(C) upon obtaining such knowledge or awareness, acts expeditiously to remove, or disable access to, the material;

(2) does not receive a financial benefit directly attributable to the infringing activity, in a case in which the service provider has the right and ability to control such activity; and

(3) upon notification of claimed infringement as described in subsection (c)(3), responds expeditiously to remove, or disable access to, the material that is claimed to be infringing or to be the subject of infringing activity, except that, for purposes of this paragraph, the information described in subsection (c)(3)(A)(iii) shall be identification of the reference or link, to material or activity claimed to be infringing, that is to be removed or access to which is to be disabled, and information reasonably sufficient to permit the service provider to locate that reference or link.

(e) **Limitation on Liability of Nonprofit Educational Institutions.**—

(1)   When a public or other nonprofit institution of higher education is a service provider, and when a faculty member or graduate student who is an employee of such institution is performing a teaching or research function, for the purposes of subsections (a) and (b) such faculty member or graduate student shall be considered to be a person other than the institution, and for the purposes of subsections (c) and (d) such faculty member's or graduate student's knowledge or awareness of his or her infringing activities shall not be attributed to the institution, if—

(A)   such faculty member's or graduate student's infringing activities do not involve the provision of online access to instructional materials that are or were required or recommended, within the preceding 3-year period, for a course taught at the institution by such faculty member or graduate student;

(B)   the institution has not, within the preceding 3-year period, received more than two notifications described in subsection (c)(3) of claimed infringement by such faculty member or graduate student, and such notifications of claimed infringement were not actionable under subsection (f); and

(C)   the institution provides to all users of its system or network informational materials that accurately describe, and promote compliance with, the laws of the United States relating to copyright.

(2)   For the purposes of this subsection, the limitations on injunctive relief contained in subsections (j)(2) and (j)(3), but not those in (j)(1), shall apply.

(f)   Misrepresentations.—Any person who knowingly materially misrepresents under this section—

(1)   that material or activity is infringing, or

(2)   that material or activity was removed or disabled by mistake or misidentification,

shall be liable for any damages, including costs and attorneys' fees, incurred by the alleged infringer, by any copyright owner or copyright owner's authorized licensee, or by a service provider, who is injured by such misrepresentation, as the result of the service provider relying upon such misrepresentation in removing or disabling access to the material or activity claimed to be infringing, or in replacing the removed material or ceasing to disable access to it.

(g)   Replacement of Removed or Disabled Material and Limitation on Other Liability.—

(1)   No Liability for Taking Down Generally.—Subject to paragraph (2), a service provider shall not be liable to any person for any claim based on the service provider's good faith disabling of access to, or removal of, material or activity claimed to be infringing or based on facts or circumstances from which infringing activity is apparent, regardless of whether the material or activity is ultimately determined to be infringing.

(2)   Exception.—Paragraph (1) shall not apply with respect to material residing at the direction of a subscriber of the service provider on a system or network controlled or operated by or for the service provider that is removed, or to which access is disabled by the service provider, pursuant to a notice provided under subsection (c)(1)(C), unless the service provider—

(A)   takes reasonable steps promptly to notify the subscriber that it has removed or disabled access to the material;

(B)   upon receipt of a counter notification described in paragraph (3), promptly provides the person who provided the notification under subsection (c)(1)(C) with a copy of the counter notification, and informs that person that it will replace the removed material or cease disabling access to it in 10 business days; and

(C)   replaces the removed material and ceases disabling access to it not less than 10, nor more than 14, business days following receipt of the counter notice, unless its designated agent first receives notice from the person who submitted the notification under subsection (c)(1)(C) that such person has filed an action seeking a court order to restrain the subscriber from engaging in infringing activity relating to the material on the service provider's system or network.

(3) Contents of Counter Notification.—To be effective under this subsection, a counter notification must be a written communication provided to the service provider's designated agent that includes substantially the following:

(A) A physical or electronic signature of the subscriber.

(B) Identification of the material that has been removed or to which access has been disabled and the location at which the material appeared before it was removed or access to it was disabled.

(C) A statement under penalty of perjury that the subscriber has a good faith belief that the material was removed or disabled as a result of mistake or misidentification of the material to be removed or disabled.

(D) The subscriber's name, address, and telephone number, and a statement that the subscriber consents to the jurisdiction of Federal District Court for the judicial district in which the address is located, or if the subscriber's address is outside of the United States, for any judicial district in which the service provider may be found, and that the subscriber will accept service of process from the person who provided notification under subsection (c)(1)(C) or an agent of such person.

(4) Limitation on Other Liability.—A service provider's compliance with paragraph (2) shall not subject the service provider to liability for copyright infringement with respect to the material identified in the notice provided under subsection (c)(1)(C).

(h) Subpoena to Identify Infringer.—

(1) Request.—A copyright owner or a person authorized to act on the owner's behalf may request the clerk of any United States district court to issue a subpoena to a service provider for identification of an alleged infringer in accordance with this subsection.

(2) Contents of Request.—The request may be made by filing with the clerk—

(A) a copy of a notification described in subsection (c)(3)(A);

(B) a proposed subpoena; and

(C) a sworn declaration to the effect that the purpose for which the subpoena is sought is to obtain the identity of an alleged infringer and that such information will only be used for the purpose of protecting rights under this title.

(3) Contents of Subpoena.—The subpoena shall authorize and order the service provider receiving the notification and the subpoena to expeditiously disclose to the copyright owner or person authorized by the copyright owner information sufficient to identify the alleged infringer of the material described in the notification to the extent such information is available to the service provider.

(4) Basis for Granting Subpoena.—If the notification filed satisfies the provisions of subsection (c)(3)(A), the proposed subpoena is in proper form, and the accompanying declaration is properly executed, the clerk shall expeditiously issue and sign the proposed subpoena and return it to the requester for delivery to the service provider.

(5) Actions of Service Provider Receiving Subpoena.—Upon receipt of the issued subpoena, either accompanying or subsequent to the receipt of a notification described in subsection (c)(3)(A), the service provider shall expeditiously disclose to the copyright owner or person authorized by the copyright owner the information required by the subpoena, notwithstanding any other provision of law and regardless of whether the service provider responds to the notification.

(6) Rules Applicable to Subpoena.—Unless otherwise provided by this section or by applicable rules of the court, the procedure for issuance and delivery of the subpoena, and the remedies for noncompliance with the subpoena, shall be governed to the greatest extent practicable by those provisions of the Federal Rules of Civil Procedure governing the issuance, service, and enforcement of a subpoena duces tecum.

(i) Conditions for Eligibility.—

(1) Accommodation of Technology.—The limitations on liability established by this section shall apply to a service provider only if the service provider—

    (A) has adopted and reasonably implemented, and informs subscribers and account holders of the service provider's system or network of, a policy that provides for the termination in appropriate circumstances of subscribers and account holders of the service provider's system or network who are repeat infringers; and

    (B) accommodates and does not interfere with standard technical measures.

(2) Definition.—As used in this subsection, the term "standard technical measures" means technical measures that are used by copyright owners to identify or protect copyrighted works and—

    (A) have been developed pursuant to a broad consensus of copyright owners and service providers in an open, fair, voluntary, multi-industry standards process;

    (B) are available to any person on reasonable and nondiscriminatory terms; and

    (C) do not impose substantial costs on service providers or substantial burdens on their systems or networks.

(j) Injunctions.—The following rules shall apply in the case of any application for an injunction under section 502 against a service provider that is not subject to monetary remedies under this section:

(1) Scope of Relief.—

    (A) With respect to conduct other than that which qualifies for the limitation on remedies set forth in subsection (a), the court may grant injunctive relief with respect to a service provider only in one or more of the following forms:

        (i) An order restraining the service provider from providing access to infringing material or activity residing at a particular online site on the provider's system or network.

        (ii) An order restraining the service provider from providing access to a subscriber or account holder of the service provider's system or network who is engaging in infringing activity and is identified in the order, by terminating the accounts of the subscriber or account holder that are specified in the order.

        (iii) Such other injunctive relief as the court may consider necessary to prevent or restrain infringement of copyrighted material specified in the order of the court at a particular online location, if such relief is the least burdensome to the service provider among the forms of relief comparably effective for that purpose.

    (B) If the service provider qualifies for the limitation on remedies described in subsection (a), the court may only grant injunctive relief in one or both of the following forms:

        (i) An order restraining the service provider from providing access to a subscriber or account holder of the service provider's system or network who is using the provider's service to engage in infringing activity and is identified in the order, by terminating the accounts of the subscriber or account holder that are specified in the order.

(ii)   An order restraining the service provider from providing access, by taking reasonable steps specified in the order to block access, to a specific, identified, online location outside the United States.

(2)   Considerations.—The court, in considering the relevant criteria for injunctive relief under applicable law, shall consider—

(A)   whether such an injunction, either alone or in combination with other such injunctions issued against the same service provider under this subsection, would significantly burden either the provider or the operation of the provider's system or network;

(B)   the magnitude of the harm likely to be suffered by the copyright owner in the digital network environment if steps are not taken to prevent or restrain the infringement;

(C)   whether implementation of such an injunction would be technically feasible and effective, and would not interfere with access to noninfringing material at other online locations; and

(D)   whether other less burdensome and comparably effective means of preventing or restraining access to the infringing material are available.

(3)   Notice and Ex Parte Orders.—Injunctive relief under this subsection shall be available only after notice to the service provider and an opportunity for the service provider to appear are provided, except for orders ensuring the preservation of evidence or other orders having no material adverse effect on the operation of the service provider's communications network.

(k)   Definitions.—

(1)   Service Provider.—

(A)   As used in subsection (a), the term "service provider" means an entity offering the transmission, routing, or providing of connections for digital online communications, between or among points specified by a user, of material of the user's choosing, without modification to the content of the material as sent or received.

(B)   As used in this section, other than subsection (a), the term "service provider" means a provider of online services or network access, or the operator of facilities therefor, and includes an entity described in subparagraph (A).

(2)   Monetary Relief.—As used in this section, the term "monetary relief means damages, costs, attorneys" fees, and any other form of monetary payment.

(*l*)   Other Defenses Not Affected.—The failure of a service provider's conduct to qualify for limitation of liability under this section shall not bear adversely upon the consideration of a defense by the service provider that the service provider's conduct is not infringing under this title or any other defense.

(m)   Protection of Privacy.—Nothing in this section shall be construed to condition the applicability of subsections (a) through (d) on—

(1)   a service provider monitoring its service or affirmatively seeking facts indicating infringing activity, except to the extent consistent with a standard technical measure complying with the provisions of subsection (i); or

(2)   a service provider gaining access to, removing, or disabling access to material in cases in which such conduct is prohibited by law.

(n)   Construction.—Subsections (a), (b), (c), and (d) describe separate and distinct functions for purposes of applying this section. Whether a service provider qualifies for the limitation on liability in any one of those subsections shall be based solely on the criteria in that subsection, and shall not affect a determination of whether that service provider qualifies for the limitations on liability under any other such subsection.

§ 513. Determination of Reasonable License Fees for Individual Proprietors

In the case of any performing rights society subject to a consent decree which provides for the determination of reasonable license rates or fees to be charged by the performing rights society, notwithstanding the provisions of that consent decree, an individual proprietor who owns or operates fewer than 7 non-publicly traded establishments in which nondramatic musical works are performed publicly and who claims that any license agreement offered by that performing rights society is unreasonable in its license rate or fee as to that individual proprietor, shall be entitled to determination of a reasonable license rate or fee as follows:

(1) The individual proprietor may commence such proceeding for determination of a reasonable license rate or fee by filing an application in the applicable district court under paragraph (2) that a rate disagreement exists and by serving a copy of the application on the performing rights society. Such proceeding shall commence in the applicable district court within 90 days after the service of such copy, except that such 90-day requirement shall be subject to the administrative requirements of the court.

(2) The proceeding under paragraph (1) shall be held, at the individual proprietor's election, in the judicial district of the district court with jurisdiction over the applicable consent decree or in that place of holding court of a district court that is the seat of the Federal circuit (other than the Court of Appeals for the Federal Circuit) in which the proprietor's establishment is located.

(3) Such proceeding shall be held before the judge of the court with jurisdiction over the consent decree governing the performing rights society. At the discretion of the court, the proceeding shall be held before a special master or magistrate judge appointed by such judge. Should that consent decree provide for the appointment of an advisor or advisors to the court for any purpose, any such advisor shall be the special master so named by the court.

(4) In any such proceeding, the industry rate shall be presumed to have been reasonable at the time it was agreed to or determined by the court. Such presumption shall in no way affect a determination of whether the rate is being correctly applied to the individual proprietor.

(5) Pending the completion of such proceeding, the individual proprietor shall have the right to perform publicly the copyrighted musical compositions in the repertoire of the performing rights society by paying an interim license rate or fee into an interest bearing escrow account with the clerk of the court, subject to retroactive adjustment when a final rate or fee has been determined, in an amount equal to the industry rate, or, in the absence of an industry rate, the amount of the most recent license rate or fee agreed to by the parties.

(6) Any decision rendered in such proceeding by a special master or magistrate judge named under paragraph (3) shall be reviewed by the judge of the court with jurisdiction over the consent decree governing the performing rights society. Such proceeding, including such review, shall be concluded within 6 months after its commencement.

(7) Any such final determination shall be binding only as to the individual proprietor commencing the proceeding, and shall not be applicable to any other proprietor or any other performing rights society, and the performing rights society shall be relieved of any obligation of nondiscrimination among similarly situated music users that may be imposed by the consent decree governing its operations.

(8) An individual proprietor may not bring more than one proceeding provided for in this section for the determination of a reasonable license rate or fee under any license agreement with respect to any one performing rights society.

(9)   For purposes of this section, the term "industry rate" means the license fee a performing rights society has agreed to with, or which has been determined by the court for, a significant segment of the music user industry to which the individual proprietor belongs.

CHAPTER 6.   IMPORTATION AND EXPORTATION

§ 601.   [Repealed*]

§ 602.   Infringing Importation or Exportation of Copies or Phonorecords

(a)   Infringing Importation or Exportation.—

(1)   Importation. Importation into the United States, without the authority of the owner of copyright under this title, of copies or phonorecords of a work that have been acquired outside the United States is an infringement of the exclusive right to distribute copies or phonorecords under section 106, actionable under section 501.

(2)   Importation or Exportation of Infringing Items. Importation into the United States or exportation from the United States, without the authority of the owner of copyright under this title, of copies or phonorecords, the making of which either constituted an infringement of copyright, or which would have constituted an infringement of copyright if this title had been applicable, is an infringement of the exclusive right to distribute copies or phonorecords under section 106, actionable under sections 501 and 506.

(3)   Exceptions. This subsection does not apply to—

(A)   importation or exportation of copies or phonorecords under the authority or for the use of the Government of the United States or of any State or political subdivision of a State, but not including copies or phonorecords for use in schools, or copies of any audiovisual work imported for purposes other than archival use;

(B)   importation or exportation, for the private use of the importer or exporter and not for distribution, by any person with respect to no more than one copy or phonorecord of any one work at any one time, or by any person arriving from outside the United States or departing from the United States with respect to copies or phonorecords forming part of such person's personal baggage; or

(C)   importation by or for an organization operated for scholarly, education, or religious purposes and not for private gain, with respect to no more than one copy of an audiovisual work solely for its archival purposes, and no more than five copies or phonorecords of any other work for its library lending or archival purposes, unless the importation of such copies or phonorecords is part of an activity consisting of systematic reproduction or distribution, engaged in by such organization in violation of the provisions of section 108(g)(2).

(b)   Import Prohibition.—In a case where the making of the copies or phonorecords would have constituted an infringement of copyright if this title had been applicable, their importation is prohibited. In a case where the copies or phonorecords were lawfully made, United States Customs and Border Protection has no authority to prevent their importation. In either case, the Secretary of the Treasury is authorized to prescribe, by regulation, a procedure under which any person claiming

---

*   This section was repealed by the Copyright Cleanup, Clarification, and Corrections Act of 2010, Pub.L. 111–295 (Dec. 9, 2010).

an interest in the copyright in a particular work may, upon payment of a specified fee, be entitled to notification by United States Customs and Border Protection of the importation of articles that appear to be copies or phonorecords of the work.

§ 603.   Importation Prohibitions: Enforcement and Disposition of Excluded Articles

(a)   The Secretary of the Treasury and the United States Postal Service shall separately or jointly make regulations for the enforcement of the provisions of this title prohibiting importation.

(b)   These regulations may require, as a condition for the exclusion of articles under section 602—

(1)   that the person seeking exclusion obtain a court order enjoining importation of the articles; or

(2)   that the person seeking exclusion furnish proof, of a specified nature and in accordance with prescribed procedures, that the copyright in which such person claims an interest is valid and that the importation would violate the prohibition in section 602; the person seeking exclusion may also be required to post a surety bond for any injury that may result if the detention or exclusion of the articles proves to be unjustified.

(c)   Articles imported in violation of the importation prohibitions of this title are subject to seizure and forfeiture in the same manner as property imported in violation of the customs revenue laws. Forfeited articles shall be destroyed as directed by the Secretary of the Treasury or the court, as the case may be.

CHAPTER 7. COPYRIGHT OFFICE

§ 701.   The Copyright Office: General Responsibilities and Organization

(a)   All administrative functions and duties under this title, except as otherwise specified, are the responsibility of the Register of Copyrights as director of the Copyright Office of the Library of Congress. The Register of Copyrights, together with the subordinate officers and employees of the Copyright Office, shall be appointed by the Librarian of Congress, and shall act under the Librarian's general direction and supervision.

(b)   In addition to the functions and duties set out elsewhere in this chapter, the Register of Copyrights shall perform the following functions:

(1)   Advise Congress on national and international issues relating to copyright, other matters arising under this title, and related matters.

(2)   Provide information and assistance to Federal departments and agencies and the Judiciary on national and international issues relating to copyright, other matters arising under this title, and related matters.

(3)   Participate in meetings of international intergovernmental organizations and meetings with foreign government officials relating to copyright, other matters arising under this title, and related matters, including as a member of United States delegations as authorized by the appropriate Executive branch authority.

(4)   Conduct studies and programs regarding copyright, other matters arising under this title, and related matters, the administration of the Copyright Office, or any function vested in the Copyright Office by law, including educational programs conducted cooperatively with foreign intellectual property offices and international intergovernmental organizations.

(5)   Perform such other functions as Congress may direct, or as may be appropriate in furtherance of the functions and duties specifically set forth in this title.

(c)   The Register of Copyrights shall adopt a seal to be used on and after January 1, 1978, to authenticate all certified documents issued by the Copyright Office.

(d)   The Register of Copyrights shall make an annual report to the Librarian of Congress of the work and accomplishments of the Copyright Office during the previous fiscal year. The annual report of the Register of Copyrights shall be published separately and as a part of the annual report of the Librarian of Congress.

(e)   Except as provided by section 706(b) and the regulations issued thereunder, all actions taken by the Register of Copyrights under this title are subject to the provisions of the Administrative Procedure Act of June 11, 1946, as amended (c. 324, 60 Stat. 237, title 5, United States Code, Chapter 5, Subchapter II and Chapter 7).

(f)   The Register of Copyrights shall be compensated at the rate of pay in effect for level III of the Executive Schedule under section 5314 of title 5. The Librarian of Congress shall establish not more than four positions for Associate Registers of Copyrights, in accordance with the recommendations of the Register of Copyrights. The Librarian shall make appointments to such positions after consultation with the Register of Copyrights. Each Associate Register of Copyrights shall be paid at a rate not to exceed the maximum annual rate of basic pay payable for GS-18 of the General Schedule under section 5332 of title 5.*

---

*   On April 26, 2017, the House of Representatives, by a vote of 378 to 48 passed H.R. 1695, which would amend section 701 to change how the Register of Copyrights is selected. As this book goes to press, the bill is awaiting action in the Senate. For the convenience of readers this footnotes sets out the text of how section 701 will read if the House bill become law:

§ 701.   The Copyright Office: General responsibilities and organization

(a)   REGISTER AND DIRECTOR.—

(1)   IN GENERAL.—All administrative functions and duties under this title, except as otherwise specified, are the responsibility of the Register of Copyrights as Director of the Copyright Office of the Library of Congress. The Register of Copyrights shall be a citizen of the United States with a professional background and experience in copyright law, shall be capable of identifying and supervising a Chief Information Officer or other similar official responsible for managing modern information technology systems, and shall be appointed by the President from the individuals recommended under paragraph (6), by and with the advice and consent of the Senate. The Register of Copyrights, together with the subordinate officers and employees of the Copyright Office, shall act under the Librarian's general direction and supervision.

(2)   DUTIES.—In addition to the functions and duties set out elsewhere in this chapter, the Register of Copyrights shall perform the following functions:

(A)   Advise Congress on national and international issues relating to copyright, other matters arising under this title, and related matters.

(B)   Provide information and assistance to Federal departments and agencies and the Judiciary on national and international issues relating to copyright, other matters arising under this title, and related matters.

§ 702. Copyright Office Regulations

The Register of Copyrights is authorized to establish regulations not inconsistent with law for the administration of the functions and duties made the responsibility of the Register under this title. All regulations established by the Register under this title are subject to the approval of the Librarian of Congress.

§ 703. Effective Date of Actions in Copyright Office

In any case in which time limits are prescribed under this title for the performance of an action in the Copyright Office, and in which the last day of the prescribed period falls on a Saturday, Sunday, holiday, or other nonbusiness day within the District of Columbia or the Federal Government, the

---

(C) Participate in meetings of international intergovernmental organizations and meetings with foreign government officials relating to copyright, other matters arising under this title, and related matters, including as a member of United States delegations as authorized by the appropriate Executive branch authority.

(D) Conduct studies and programs regarding copyright, other matters arising under this title, and related matters, the administration of the Copyright Office, or any function vested in the Copyright Office by law, including educational programs conducted cooperatively with foreign intellectual property offices and international intergovernmental organizations.

(E) Perform such other functions as Congress may direct, or as may be appropriate in furtherance of the functions and duties specifically set forth in this title.

(3) OATH.—The Register of Copyrights shall, before taking office, take an oath to discharge faithfully the duties of the Copyright Office described in paragraph (2).

(4) REMOVAL.—

(A) IN GENERAL.—The Register of Copyrights may be removed from office by the President.

(B) NOTIFICATION.—The President shall provide notification to both Houses of Congress of a removal under subparagraph (A).

(5) TERM OF OFFICE.—

(A) IN GENERAL.—Subject to subparagraph (B), the Register of Copyrights—

(i) shall be appointed for a term of 10 years; and

(ii) may serve until a successor is appointed, confirmed, and taken the oath of office.

(B) LIMITATION.—The Register of Copyrights may not continue to serve after the date on which Congress adjourns sine die after the date on which the 10-year period described in subparagraph (A)(i) ends.

(C) REAPPOINTMENT.—An individual appointed to the position of Register of Copyrights, by and with the advice and consent of the Senate, may be reappointed to that position in accordance with the requirements of this section.

(6) PANEL FOR REGISTER OF COPYRIGHTS RECOMMENDATIONS.—There is established a panel to recommend a list of at least 3 individuals to the President for appointment as the Register of Copyrights. The panel shall be composed of the following:

(A) The Speaker of the House of Representatives.

(B) The President pro tempore of the Senate.

(C) The majority and minority leaders of the House of Representatives and the Senate.

(D) The Librarian of Congress."

(b) SEAL.—The Register of Copyrights shall adopt a seal to be used on and after January 1, 1978, to authenticate all certified documents issued by the Copyright Office.

(c) ANNUAL REPORT.—The Register of Copyrights shall make an annual report to the Librarian of Congress of the work and accomplishments of the Copyright Office during the previous fiscal year. The annual report of the Register of Copyrights shall be published separately and as a part of the annual report of the Librarian of Congress.

(d) APPLICABILITY OF TITLE 5.—Except as provided by section 706(b) and the regulations issued thereunder, all actions taken by the Register of Copyrights under this title are subject to the provisions of the Administrative Procedure Act of June 11, 1946, as amended (c. 324, 60 Stat. 237, title 5, United States Code, Chapter 5, Subchapter II and Chapter 7).

(e) COMPENSATION.—The Register of Copyrights shall be compensated at the rate of pay in effect for level III of the Executive Schedule under section 5314 of title 5. The Librarian of Congress shall establish not more than four positions for Associate Registers of Copyrights, in accordance with the recommendations of the Register of Copyrights. The Librarian shall make appointments to such positions after consultation with the Register of Copyrights. Each Associate Register of Copyrights shall be paid at a rate not to exceed the maximum annual rate of basic pay payable for GS-18 of the General Schedule under section 5332 of title 5.

action may be taken on the next succeeding business day, and is effective as of the date when the period expired.

§ 704. Retention and Disposition of Articles Deposited in Copyright Office

(a) Upon their deposit in the Copyright Office under sections 407 and 408, all copies, phonorecords, and identifying material, including those deposited in connection with claims that have been refused registration, are the property of the United States Government.

(b) In the case of published works, all copies, phonorecords, and identifying material deposited are available to the Library of Congress for its collections, or for exchange or transfer to any other library. In the case of unpublished works, the Library is entitled, under regulations that the Register of Copyrights shall prescribe, to select any deposits for its collections or for transfer to the National Archives of the United States or to a Federal records center, as defined in section 2901 of title 44.

(c) The Register of Copyrights is authorized, for specific or general categories of works, to make a facsimile reproduction of all or any part of the material deposited under section 408, and to make such reproduction a part of the Copyright Office records of the registration, before transferring such material to the Library of Congress as provided by subsection (b), or before destroying or otherwise disposing of such material as provided by subsection (d).

(d) Deposits not selected by the Library under subsection (b), or identifying portions or reproductions of them, shall be retained under the control of the Copyright Office, including retention in Government storage facilities, for the longest period considered practicable and desirable by the Register of Copyrights and the Librarian of Congress. After that period it is within the joint discretion of the Register and the Librarian to order their destruction or other disposition; but, in the case of unpublished works, no deposit shall be knowingly or intentionally destroyed or otherwise disposed of during its term of copyright unless a facsimile reproduction of the entire deposit has been made a part of the Copyright Office records as provided by subsection (c).

(e) The depositor of copies, phonorecords, or identifying material under section 408, or the copyright owner of record, may request retention, under the control of the Copyright Office, of one or more of such articles for the full term of copyright in the work. The Register of Copyrights shall prescribe, by regulation, the conditions under which such requests are to be made and granted, and shall fix the fee to be charged under section 708(a) if the request is granted.

§ 705. Copyright Office Records: Preparation, Maintenance, Public Inspection, and Searching

(a) The Register of Copyrights shall ensure that records of deposits, registrations, recordations, and other actions taken under this title are maintained, and that indexes of such records are prepared.

(b) Such records and indexes, as well as the articles deposited in connection with completed copyright registrations and retained under the control of the Copyright Office, shall be open to public inspection.

(c) Upon request and payment of the fee specified by section 708, the Copyright Office shall make a search of its public records, indexes, and deposits, and shall furnish a report of the information they disclose with respect to any particular deposits, registrations, or recorded documents.

§ 706. Copies of Copyright Office Records

(a) Copies may be made of any public records or indexes of the Copyright Office; additional certificates of copyright registration and copies of any public records or indexes may be furnished upon request and payment of the fees specified by section 708.

(b) Copies or reproductions of deposited articles retained under the control of the Copyright Office shall be authorized or furnished only under the conditions specified by the Copyright Office regulations.

§ 707. Copyright Office Forms and Publications

(a) Catalog of Copyright Entries.—The Register of Copyrights shall compile and publish at periodic intervals catalogs of all copyright registrations. These catalogs shall be divided into parts in accordance with the various classes of works, and the Register has discretion to determine, on the basis of practicability and usefulness, the form and frequency of publication of each particular part.

(b) Other Publications.—The Register shall furnish, free of charge upon request, application forms for copyright registration and general informational material in connection with the functions of the Copyright Office. The Register also has the authority to publish compilations of information, bibliographies, and other material he or she considers to be of value to the public.

(c) Distribution of Publications.—All publications of the Copyright Office shall be furnished to depository libraries as specified under section 1905 of title 44, and, aside from those furnished free of charge, shall be offered for sale to the public at prices based on the cost of reproduction and distribution.

§ 708. Copyright Office Fees

(a) *Fees.* Fees shall be paid to the Register of Copyrights—

(1) on filing each application under section 408 for registration of a copyright claim or for a supplementary registration, including the issuance of a certificate of registration if registration is made;

(2) on filing each application for registration of a claim for renewal of a subsisting copyright under section 304(a), including the issuance of a certificate of registration if registration is made;

(3) for the issuance of a receipt for a deposit under section 407;

(4) for the recordation, as provided by section 205, of a transfer of copyright ownership or other document;

(5) for the filing, under section 115(b), of a notice of intention to obtain a compulsory license;

(6) for the recordation, under section 302(c), of a statement revealing the identity of an author of an anonymous or pseudonymous work, or for the recordation, under section 302(d), of a statement relating to the death of an author;

(7) for the issuance, under section 706, of an additional certificate of registration;

(8) for the issuance of any other certification;

(9) for the making and reporting of a search as provided by section 705, and for any related services;

(10) on filing a statement of account based on secondary transmissions of primary transmissions pursuant to section 119 or 122; and

(11) on filing a statement of account based on secondary transmissions of primary transmissions pursuant to section 111.

The Register is authorized to fix fees for other services, including the cost of preparing copies of Copyright Office records, whether or not such copies are certified, based on the cost of providing the service. Fees established under paragraphs (10) and (11) shall be reasonable and may not exceed one-half of the cost necessary to cover reasonable expenses incurred by the Copyright Office for the collection and administration of the statements of account and any royalty fees deposited with such statements

(b) *Adjustment of Fees.* The Register of Copyrights may, by regulation, adjust the fees for the services specified in subsection (a) in the following manner:

(1)   The Register shall conduct a study of the costs incurred by the Copyright Office for the registration of claims, the recordation of documents, and the provision of services. The study shall also consider the timing of any adjustment in fees and the authority to use such fees consistent with the budget.

(2)   The Register may, on the basis of the study under paragraph (1), and subject to paragraph (5), adjust fees to not more than that necessary to cover the reasonable costs incurred by the Copyright Office for the services described in paragraph (1), plus a reasonable inflation adjustment to account for any estimated increase in costs.

(3)   Any fee established under paragraph (2) shall be rounded off to the nearest dollar, or for a fee less than $12, rounded off to the nearest 50 cents.

(4)   Fees established under this subsection shall be fair and equitable and give due consideration to the objectives of the copyright system.

(5)   If the Register determines under paragraph (2) that fees should be adjusted, the Register shall prepare a proposed fee schedule and submit the schedule with the accompanying economic analysis to the Congress. The fees proposed by the Register may be instituted after the end of 120 days after the schedule is submitted to the Congress unless, within that 120-day period, a law is enacted stating in substance that the Congress does not approve the schedule.

(c)   The fees prescribed by or under this section are applicable to the United States Government and any of its agencies, employees, or officers but the Register of Copyrights has discretion to waive the requirement of this subsection in occasional or isolated cases involving relatively small amounts.

(d)(1)   Except as provided in paragraph (2), all fees received under this section shall be deposited by the Register of Copyrights in the Treasury of the United States and shall be credited to the appropriations for necessary expenses of the Copyright Office. Such fees that are collected shall remain available until expended. The Register may, in accordance with regulations that he or she shall prescribe, refund any sum paid by mistake or in excess of the fee required by this section.

(2)   In the case of fees deposited against future services, the Register of Copyrights shall request the Secretary of the Treasury to invest in interest-bearing securities in the United States Treasury any portion of the fees that, as determined by the Register, is not required to meet current deposit account demands. Funds from such portion of fees shall be invested in securities that permit funds to be available to the Copyright Office at all times if they are determined to be necessary to meet current deposit account demands. Such investments shall be in public debt securities with maturities suitable to the needs of the Copyright Office, as determined by the Register of Copyrights, and bearing interest at rates determined by the Secretary of the Treasury, taking into consideration current market yields on outstanding marketable obligations of the United States of comparable maturities.

(3)   The income on such investments shall be deposited in the Treasury of the United States and shall be credited to the appropriations for necessary expenses of the Copyright Office.

§ 709.   Delay in Delivery Caused by Disruption of Postal or Other Services

In any case in which the Register of Copyrights determines, on the basis of such evidence as the Register may by regulation require, that a deposit, application, fee, or any other material to be delivered to the Copyright Office by a particular date, would have been received in the Copyright Office in due time except for a general disruption or suspension of postal or other transportation or communications services, the actual receipt of such material in the Copyright Office within one month after the date on which the Register determines that the disruption or suspension of such services has terminated, shall be considered timely.

§ 710.   [Repealed]

CHAPTER 8. PROCEEDINGS BY COPYRIGHT ROYALTY JUDGES

---

§ 801. Copyright Royalty Judges; Appointment and Functions

(a) Appointment.—The Librarian of Congress shall appoint 3 full-time Copyright Royalty Judges, and shall appoint 1 of the 3 as the Chief Copyright Royalty Judge. The Librarian shall make appointments to such positions after consultation with the Register of Copyrights.

(b) Functions.—Subject to the provisions of this chapter, the functions of the Copyright Royalty Judges shall be as follows:

(1) To make determinations and adjustments of reasonable terms and rates of royalty payments as provided in sections 112(e), 114, 115, 116, 118, 119, and 1004. The rates applicable under sections 114(f)(1)(B), 115, and 116 shall be calculated to achieve the following objectives:

(A) To maximize the availability of creative works to the public.

(B) To afford the copyright owner a fair return for his or her creative work and the copyright user a fair income under existing economic conditions.

(C) To reflect the relative roles of the copyright owner and the copyright user in the product made available to the public with respect to relative creative contribution, technological contribution, capital investment, cost, risk, and contribution to the opening of new markets for creative expression and media for their communication.

(D) To minimize any disruptive impact on the structure of the industries involved and on generally prevailing industry practices.

(2) To make determinations concerning the adjustment of the copyright royalty rates under section 111 solely in accordance with the following provisions:

(A) The rates established by section 111(d)(1)(B) may be adjusted to reflect—

(i) national monetary inflation or deflation; or

(ii) changes in the average rates charged cable subscribers for the basic service of providing secondary transmissions to maintain the real constant dollar level of the royalty fee per subscriber which existed as of the date of October 19, 1976, except that—

(I) if the average rates charged cable system subscribers for the basic service of providing secondary transmissions are changed so that the average rates exceed national monetary inflation, no change in the rates established by section 111(d)(1)(B) shall be permitted; and

(II) no increase in the royalty fee shall be permitted based on any reduction in the average number of distant signal equivalents per subscriber.

The Copyright Royalty Judges may consider all factors relating to the maintenance of such level of payments, including, as an extenuating factor, whether the industry has been restrained by subscriber rate regulating authorities from increasing the rates for the basic service of providing secondary transmissions.

(B) In the event that the rules and regulations of the Federal Communications Commission are amended at any time after April 15, 1976, to permit the carriage by cable systems of additional television broadcast signals beyond the local service area of the primary transmitters of such signals, the royalty rates established by section 111(d)(1)(B) may be adjusted to ensure that the rates for the additional distant signal equivalents resulting from such carriage are reasonable in the light of the changes effected by the amendment to such rules and regulations. In determining the reasonableness of rates proposed following an amendment of Federal Communications Commission rules and regulations, the Copyright Royalty Judges shall consider, among other factors, the economic impact on copyright owners and users; except that no adjustment in royalty rates shall be made under this subparagraph with respect to any distant signal equivalent or fraction thereof represented by—

(i) carriage of any signal permitted under the rules and regulations of the Federal Communications Commission in effect on April 15, 1976, or the carriage of a signal of the same type (that is, independent, network, or noncommercial educational) substituted for such permitted signal; or

(ii) a television broadcast signal first carried after April 15, 1976, pursuant to an individual waiver of the rules and regulations of the Federal Communications Commission, as such rules and regulations were in effect on April 15, 1976.

(C) In the event of any change in the rules and regulations of the Federal Communications Commission with respect to syndicated and sports program exclusivity after April 15, 1976, the rates established by section 111(d)(1)(B) may be adjusted to assure that such rates are reasonable in light of the changes to such rules and regulations, but any such adjustment shall apply only to the affected television broadcast signals carried on those systems affected by the change.

(D) The gross receipts limitations established by section 111(d)(1) (C) and (D) shall be adjusted to reflect national monetary inflation or deflation or changes in the average rates charged cable system subscribers for the basic service of providing secondary transmissions to maintain the real constant dollar value of the exemption provided by such section, and the royalty rate specified therein shall not be subject to adjustment.

(3)(A) To authorize the distribution, under sections 111, 119, and 1007, of those royalty fees collected under sections 111, 119, and 1005, as the case may be, to the extent that the Copyright Royalty Judges have found that the distribution of such fees is not subject to controversy.

(B) In cases where the Copyright Royalty Judges determine that controversy exists, the Copyright Royalty Judges shall determine the distribution of such fees, including partial distributions, in accordance with section 111, 119, or 1007, as the case may be.

(C) Notwithstanding section 804(b)(8), the Copyright Royalty Judges, at any time after the filing of claims under section 111, 119, or 1007, may, upon motion of one or more of the claimants and after publication in the Federal Register of a request for responses to the motion from interested claimants, make a partial distribution of such fees, if, based upon all responses received during the 30-day period beginning on the date of such publication, the Copyright Royalty Judges conclude that no claimant entitled to receive such fees has stated a reasonable objection to the partial distribution, and all such claimants—

(i) agree to the partial distribution;

(ii) sign an agreement obligating them to return any excess amounts to the extent necessary to comply with the final determination on the distribution of the fees made under subparagraph (B);

(iii) file the agreement with the Copyright Royalty Judges; and

(iv)   agree that such funds are available for distribution.

(D)   The Copyright Royalty Judges and any other officer or employee acting in good faith in distributing funds under subparagraph (C) shall not be held liable for the payment of any excess fees under subparagraph (C). The Copyright Royalty Judges shall, at the time the final determination is made, calculate any such excess amounts.

(4)   To accept or reject royalty claims filed under sections 111, 119, and 1007, on the basis of timeliness or the failure to establish the basis for a claim.

(5)   To accept or reject rate adjustment petitions as provided in section 804 and petitions to participate as provided in section 803(b) (1) and (2).

(6)   To determine the status of a digital audio recording device or a digital audio interface device under sections 1002 and 1003, as provided in section 1010.

(7)(A)   To adopt as a basis for statutory terms and rates or as a basis for the distribution of statutory royalty payments, an agreement concerning such matters reached among some or all of the participants in a proceeding at any time during the proceeding, except that—

(i)   the Copyright Royalty Judges shall provide to those that would be bound by the terms, rates, or other determination set by any agreement in a proceeding to determine royalty rates an opportunity to comment on the agreement and shall provide to participants in the proceeding under section 803(b)(2) that would be bound by the terms, rates, or other determination set by the agreement an opportunity to comment on the agreement and object to its adoption as a basis for statutory terms and rates; and

(ii)   the Copyright Royalty Judges may decline to adopt the agreement as a basis for statutory terms and rates for participants that are not parties to the agreement, if any participant described in clause (i) objects to the agreement and the Copyright Royalty Judges conclude, based on the record before them if one exists, that the agreement does not provide a reasonable basis for setting statutory terms or rates.

(B)   License agreements voluntarily negotiated pursuant to section 112(e)(5), 114(f)(3), 115(c)(3)(E)(i), 116(c), or 118(b)(2) that do not result in statutory terms and rates shall not be subject to clauses (i) and (ii) of subparagraph (A).

(C)   Interested parties may negotiate and agree to, and the Copyright Royalty Judges may adopt, an agreement that specifies as terms notice and recordkeeping requirements that apply in lieu of those that would otherwise apply under regulations.

(8)   To determine the administrative assessment to be paid by digital music providers under section 115(d). The provisions of section 115(d) shall apply to the conduct of proceedings by the Copyright Royalty Judges under section 115(d) and not the procedures described in this section, or section 803, 804, or 805.

(9)   To perform other duties, as assigned by the Register of Copyrights within the Library of Congress, except as provided in section 802(g), at times when Copyright Royalty Judges are not engaged in performing the other duties set forth in this section.

(c)   Rulings.—The Copyright Royalty Judges may make any necessary procedural or evidentiary rulings in any proceeding under this chapter and may, before commencing a proceeding under this chapter, make any such rulings that would apply to the proceedings conducted by the Copyright Royalty Judges.

(d)   Administrative Support.—The Librarian of Congress shall provide the Copyright Royalty Judges with the necessary administrative services related to proceedings under this chapter.

(e)   Location in Library of Congress.—The offices of the Copyright Royalty Judges and staff shall be in the Library of Congress.

(f) Effective Date of Actions.—On and after the date of the enactment of the Copyright Royalty and Distribution Reform Act of 2004, in any case in which time limits are prescribed under this title for performance of an action with or by the Copyright Royalty Judges, and in which the last day of the prescribed period falls on a Saturday, Sunday, holiday, or other nonbusiness day within the District of Columbia or the Federal Government, the action may be taken on the next succeeding business day, and is effective as of the date when the period expired.

§ 802. Copyright Royalty Judgeships; Staff

(a) Qualifications of Copyright Royalty Judges.—

    (1) In General.—Each Copyright Royalty Judge shall be an attorney who has at least 7 years of legal experience. The Chief Copyright Royalty Judge shall have at least 5 years of experience in adjudications, arbitrations, or court trials. Of the other 2 Copyright Royalty Judges, 1 shall have significant knowledge of copyright law, and the other shall have significant knowledge of economics. An individual may serve as a Copyright Royalty Judge only if the individual is free of any financial conflict of interest under subsection (h).

    (2) Definition.—In this subsection, the term 'adjudication' has the meaning given that term in section 551 of title 5, but does not include mediation.

(b) Staff.—The Chief Copyright Royalty Judge shall hire 3 full-time staff members to assist the Copyright Royalty Judges in performing their functions.

(c) Terms.—The individual first appointed as the Chief Copyright Royalty Judge shall be appointed to a term of 6 years, and of the remaining individuals first appointed as Copyright Royalty Judges, 1 shall be appointed to a term of 4 years, and the other shall be appointed to a term of 2 years. Thereafter, the terms of succeeding Copyright Royalty Judges shall each be 6 years. An individual serving as a Copyright Royalty Judge may be reappointed to subsequent terms. The term of a Copyright Royalty Judge shall begin when the term of the predecessor of that Copyright Royalty Judge ends. When the term of office of a Copyright Royalty Judge ends, the individual serving that term may continue to serve until a successor is selected.

(d) Vacancies or Incapacity.—

    (1) Vacancies.—If a vacancy should occur in the position of Copyright Royalty Judge, the Librarian of Congress shall act expeditiously to fill the vacancy, and may appoint an interim Copyright Royalty Judge to serve until another Copyright Royalty Judge is appointed under this section. An individual appointed to fill the vacancy occurring before the expiration of the term for which the predecessor of that individual was appointed shall be appointed for the remainder of that term.

    (2) Incapacity.—In the case in which a Copyright Royalty Judge is temporarily unable to perform his or her duties, the Librarian of Congress may appoint an interim Copyright Royalty Judge to perform such duties during the period of such incapacity.

(e) Compensation.—

    (1) Judges.—The Chief Copyright Royalty Judge shall receive compensation at the rate of basic pay payable for level AL-1 for administrative law judges pursuant to section 5372(b) of title 5, and each of the other two Copyright Royalty Judges shall receive compensation at the rate of basic pay payable for level AL-2 for administrative law judges pursuant to such section. The compensation of the Copyright Royalty Judges shall not be subject to any regulations adopted by the Office of Personnel Management pursuant to its authority under section 5376(b)(1) of title 5.

    (2) Staff Members.—Of the staff members appointed under subsection (b)—

        (A) the rate of pay of 1 staff member shall be not more than the basic rate of pay payable for level 10 of GS-15 of the General Schedule;

(B)   the rate of pay of 1 staff member shall be not less than the basic rate of pay payable for GS-13 of the General Schedule and not more than the basic rate of pay payable for level 10 of GS-14 of such Schedule; and

(C)   the rate of pay for the third staff member shall be not less than the basic rate of pay payable for GS-8 of the General Schedule and not more than the basic rate of pay payable for level 10 of GS-11 of such Schedule.

(3)   **Locality Pay.**—All rates of pay referred to under this subsection shall include locality pay.

(f)   **Independence of Copyright Royalty Judge.—**

(1)   **In Making Determinations.—**

(A)   **In General.—**

(i)   Subject to subparagraph (B) and clause (ii) of this subparagraph, the Copyright Royalty Judges shall have full independence in making determinations concerning adjustments and determinations of copyright royalty rates and terms, the distribution of copyright royalties, the acceptance or rejection of royalty claims, rate adjustment petitions, and petitions to participate, and in issuing other rulings under this title, except that the Copyright Royalty Judges may consult with the Register of Copyrights on any matter other than a question of fact.

(ii)   One or more Copyright Royalty Judges may, or by motion to the Copyright Royalty Judges, any participant in a proceeding may, request from the Register of Copyrights an interpretation of any material questions of substantive law that relate to the construction of provisions of this title and arise in the course of the proceeding. Any request for a written interpretation shall be in writing and on the record, and reasonable provision shall be made to permit participants in the proceeding to comment on the material questions of substantive law in a manner that minimizes duplication and delay. Except as provided in subparagraph (B), the Register of Copyrights shall deliver to the Copyright Royalty Judges a written response within 14 days after the receipt of all briefs and comments from the participants. The Copyright Royalty Judges shall apply the legal interpretation embodied in the response of the Register of Copyrights if it is timely delivered, and the response shall be included in the record that accompanies the final determination. The authority under this clause shall not be construed to authorize the Register of Copyrights to provide an interpretation of questions of procedure before the Copyright Royalty Judges, the ultimate adjustments and determinations of copyright royalty rates and terms, the ultimate distribution of copyright royalties, or the acceptance or rejection of royalty claims, rate adjustment petitions, or petitions to participate in a proceeding.

(B)   **Novel Questions.—**

(i)   In any case in which a novel material question of substantive law concerning an interpretation of those provisions of this title that are the subject of the proceeding is presented, the Copyright Royalty Judges shall request a decision of the Register of Copyrights, in writing, to resolve such novel question. Reasonable provision shall be made for comment on such request by the participants in the proceeding, in such a way as to minimize duplication and delay. The Register of Copyrights shall transmit his or her decision to the Copyright Royalty Judges within 30 days after the Register of Copyrights receives all of the briefs or comments of the participants. Such decision shall be in writing and included by the Copyright Royalty Judges in the record that accompanies their final determination. If such a decision is timely delivered to the Copyright Royalty Judges, the Copyright Royalty Judges shall apply the legal determinations embodied in the decision of the Register of Copyrights in resolving material questions of substantive law.

(ii) In clause (i), a "novel question of law" is a question of law that has not been determined in prior decisions, determinations, and rulings described in section 803(a).

(C) Consultation.—Notwithstanding the provisions of subparagraph (A), the Copyright Royalty Judges shall consult with the Register of Copyrights with respect to any determination or ruling that would require that any act be performed by the Copyright Office, and any such determination or ruling shall not be binding upon the Register of Copyrights.

(D) Review of Legal Conclusions by the Register of Copyrights.—The Register of Copyrights may review for legal error the resolution by the Copyright Royalty Judges of a material question of substantive law under this title that underlies or is contained in a final determination of the Copyright Royalty Judges. If the Register of Copyrights concludes, after taking into consideration the views of the participants in the proceeding, that any resolution reached by the Copyright Royalty Judges was in material error, the Register of Copyrights shall issue a written decision correcting such legal error, which shall be made part of the record of the proceeding. The Register of Copyrights shall issue such written decision not later than 60 days after the date on which the final determination by the Copyright Royalty Judges is issued. Additionally, the Register of Copyrights shall cause to be published in the Federal Register such written decision, together with a specific identification of the legal conclusion of the Copyright Royalty Judges that is determined to be erroneous. As to conclusions of substantive law involving an interpretation of the statutory provisions of this title, the decision of the Register of Copyrights shall be binding as precedent upon the Copyright Royalty Judges in subsequent proceedings under this chapter. When a decision has been rendered pursuant to this subparagraph, the Register of Copyrights may, on the basis of and in accordance with such decision, intervene as of right in any appeal of a final determination of the Copyright Royalty Judges pursuant to section 803(d) in the United States Court of Appeals for the District of Columbia Circuit. If, prior to intervening in such an appeal, the Register of Copyrights gives notification to, and undertakes to consult with, the Attorney General with respect to such intervention, and the Attorney General fails, within a reasonable period after receiving such notification, to intervene in such appeal, the Register of Copyrights may intervene in such appeal in his or her own name by any attorney designated by the Register of Copyrights for such purpose. Intervention by the Register of Copyrights in his or her own name shall not preclude the Attorney General from intervening on behalf of the United States in such an appeal as may be otherwise provided or required by law.

(E) Effect on Judicial Review.—Nothing in this section shall be interpreted to alter the standard applied by a court in reviewing legal determinations involving an interpretation or construction of the provisions of this title or to affect the extent to which any construction or interpretation of the provisions of this title shall be accorded deference by a reviewing court.

(2) Performance Appraisals.—

(A) In General.—Notwithstanding any other provision of law or any regulation of the Library of Congress, and subject to subparagraph (B), the Copyright Royalty Judges shall not receive performance appraisals.

(B) Relating to Sanction or Removal.—To the extent that the Librarian of Congress adopts regulations under subsection (h) relating to the sanction or removal of a Copyright Royalty Judge and such regulations require documentation to establish the cause of such sanction or removal, the Copyright Royalty Judge may receive an appraisal related specifically to the cause of the sanction or removal.

(g) Inconsistent Duties Barred.—No Copyright Royalty Judge may undertake duties that conflict with his or her duties and responsibilities as a Copyright Royalty Judge.

(h) Standards of Conduct.—The Librarian of Congress shall adopt regulations regarding the standards of conduct, including financial conflict of interest and restrictions against ex parte communications, which shall govern the Copyright Royalty Judges and the proceedings under this chapter.

(i) Removal or Sanction.—The Librarian of Congress may sanction or remove a Copyright Royalty Judge for violation of the standards of conduct adopted under subsection (h), misconduct, neglect of duty, or any disqualifying physical or mental disability. Any such sanction or removal may be made only after notice and opportunity for a hearing, but the Librarian of Congress may suspend the Copyright Royalty Judge during the pendency of such hearing. The Librarian shall appoint an interim Copyright Royalty Judge during the period of any such suspension.[2]

§ 803. Proceedings of Copyright Royalty Judges

(a) Proceedings.—

(1) In General.—The Copyright Royalty Judges shall act in accordance with this title, and to the extent not inconsistent with this title, in accordance with subchapter II of chapter 5 of title 5, in carrying out the purposes set forth in section 801. The Copyright Royalty Judges shall act in accordance with regulations issued by the Copyright Royalty Judges and the Librarian of Congress, and on the basis of a written record, prior determinations and interpretations of the Copyright Royalty Tribunal, Librarian of Congress, the Register of Copyrights, copyright arbitration royalty panels (to the extent those determinations are not inconsistent with a decision of the Librarian of Congress or the Register of Copyrights), and the Copyright Royalty Judges (to the extent those determinations are not inconsistent with a decision of the Register of Copyrights that was timely delivered to the Copyright Royalty Judges pursuant to section 802(f)(1) (A) or (B), or with a decision of the Register of Copyrights pursuant to section 802(f)(1)(D)), under this chapter, and decisions of the court of appeals under this chapter before, on, or after the effective date of the Copyright Royalty and Distribution Reform Act of 2004.

(2) Judges Acting as Panel and Individually.—The Copyright Royalty Judges shall preside over hearings in proceedings under this chapter en banc. The Chief Copyright Royalty Judge may designate a Copyright Royalty Judge to preside individually over such collateral and administrative proceedings, and over such proceedings under paragraphs (1) through (5) of subsection (b), as the Chief Judge considers appropriate.

(3) Determinations.—Final determinations of the Copyright Royalty Judges in proceedings under this chapter shall be made by majority vote. A Copyright Royalty Judge dissenting from the majority on any determination under this chapter may issue his or her dissenting opinion, which shall be included with the determination.

(b) Procedures.—

(1) Initiation.—

(A) Call for Petitions to Participate.—

(i) The Copyright Royalty Judges shall cause to be published in the Federal Register notice of commencement of proceedings under this chapter, calling for the filing of petitions to participate in a proceeding under this chapter for the purpose of making the relevant determination under section 111, 112, 114, 115, 116, 118, 119, 1004, or 1007, as the case may be—

---

[2] This provision's restrictions on the Librarian of Congress's authority to remove Copyright Royalty Judges were found to be unconstitutional in *Intercollegiate Broadcasting System, Inc. v. Copyright Royalty Board*, 684 F.3d 1332 (D.C. Cir. 2012).—*Ed.*

(I) promptly upon a determination made under section 804(a);

(II) by no later than January 5 of a year specified in paragraph (2) of section 804(b) for the commencement of proceedings;

(III) by no later than January 5 of a year specified in subparagraph (A) or (B) of paragraph (3) of section 804(b) for the commencement of proceedings, or as otherwise provided in subparagraph (A) or (C) of such paragraph for the commencement of proceedings;

(IV) as provided under section 804(b)(8); or

(V) by no later than January 5 of a year specified in any other provision of section 804(b) for the filing of petitions for the commencement of proceedings, if a petition has not been filed by that date, except that the publication of notice requirement shall not apply in the case of proceedings under section 111 that are scheduled to commence in 2005.

(ii) Petitions to participate shall be filed by no later than 30 days after publication of notice of commencement of a proceeding under clause (i), except that the Copyright Royalty Judges may, for substantial good cause shown and if there is no prejudice to the participants that have already filed petitions, accept late petitions to participate at any time up to the date that is 90 days before the date on which participants in the proceeding are to file their written direct statements. Notwithstanding the preceding sentence, petitioners whose petitions are filed more than 30 days after publication of notice of commencement of a proceeding are not eligible to object to a settlement reached during the voluntary negotiation period under paragraph (3), and any objection filed by such a petitioner shall not be taken into account by the Copyright Royalty Judges.

(B) Petitions to Participate.—Each petition to participate in a proceeding shall describe the petitioner's interest in the subject matter of the proceeding. Parties with similar interests may file a single petition to participate.

(2) Participation in General.—Subject to paragraph (4), a person may participate in a proceeding under this chapter, including through the submission of briefs or other information, only if—

(A) that person has filed a petition to participate in accordance with paragraph (1) (either individually or as a group under paragraph (1)(B));

(B) the Copyright Royalty Judges have not determined that the petition to participate is facially invalid;

(C) the Copyright Royalty Judges have not determined, sua sponte or on the motion of another participant in the proceeding, that the person lacks a significant interest in the proceeding; and

(D) the petition to participate is accompanied by either—

(i) in a proceeding to determine royalty rates, a filing fee of $150; or

(ii) in a proceeding to determine distribution of royalty fees—

(I) a filing fee of $150; or

(II) a statement that the petitioner (individually or as a group) will not seek a distribution of more than $1000, in which case the amount distributed to the petitioner shall not exceed $1000.

(3) Voluntary Negotiation Period.—

(A) Commencement of Proceedings.—

(i) Rate Adjustment Proceeding.—Promptly after the date for filing of petitions to participate in a proceeding, the Copyright Royalty Judges shall make available to all participants in the proceeding a list of such participants and shall initiate a voluntary negotiation period among the participants.

(ii) Distribution Proceeding.—Promptly after the date for filing of petitions to participate in a proceeding to determine the distribution of royalties, the Copyright Royalty Judges shall make available to all participants in the proceeding a list of such participants. The initiation of a voluntary negotiation period among the participants shall be set at a time determined by the Copyright Royalty Judges.

(B) Length of Proceedings.—The voluntary negotiation period initiated under subparagraph (A) shall be 3 months.

(C) Determination of Subsequent Proceedings.—At the close of the voluntary negotiation proceedings, the Copyright Royalty Judges shall, if further proceedings under this chapter are necessary, determine whether and to what extent paragraphs (4) and (5) will apply to the parties.

(4) Small Claims Procedure in Distribution Proceedings.—

(A) In General.—If, in a proceeding under this chapter to determine the distribution of royalties, the contested amount of a claim is $10,000 or less, the Copyright Royalty Judges shall decide the controversy on the basis of the filing of the written direct statement by the participant, the response by any opposing participant, and 1 additional response by each such party.

(B) Bad Faith Inflation of Claim.—If the Copyright Royalty Judges determine that a participant asserts in bad faith an amount in controversy in excess of $10,000 for the purpose of avoiding a determination under the procedure set forth in subparagraph (A), the Copyright Royalty Judges shall impose a fine on that participant in an amount not to exceed the difference between the actual amount distributed and the amount asserted by the participant.

(5) Paper Proceedings.—The Copyright Royalty Judges in proceedings under this chapter may decide, sua sponte or upon motion of a participant, to determine issues on the basis of the filing of the written direct statement by the participant, the response by any opposing participant, and one additional response by each such participant. Prior to making such decision to proceed on such a paper record only, the Copyright Royalty Judges shall offer to all parties to the proceeding the opportunity to comment on the decision. The procedure under this paragraph—

(A) shall be applied in cases in which there is no genuine issue of material fact, there is no need for evidentiary hearings, and all participants in the proceeding agree in writing to the procedure; and

(B) may be applied under such other circumstances as the Copyright Royalty Judges consider appropriate.

(6) Regulations.—

(A) In General.—The Copyright Royalty Judges may issue regulations to carry out their functions under this title. All regulations issued by the Copyright Royalty Judges are subject to the approval of the Librarian of Congress and are subject to judicial review pursuant to chapter 7 of title 5, except as set forth in subsection (d). Not later than 120 days after Copyright Royalty Judges or interim Copyright Royalty Judges, as the case may be, are first appointed after the enactment of the Copyright Royalty and Distribution Reform Act of 2004, such judges shall issue regulations to govern proceedings under this chapter.

(B) Interim Regulations.—Until regulations are adopted under subparagraph (A), the Copyright Royalty Judges shall apply the regulations in effect under this chapter on the day before the effective date of the Copyright Royalty and Distribution Reform Act of 2004, to the extent such regulations are not inconsistent with this chapter, except that functions carried out under such regulations by the Librarian of Congress, the Register of Copyrights, or copyright arbitration royalty panels that, as of such date of enactment, are to be carried out by the Copyright Royalty Judges under this chapter, shall be carried out by the Copyright Royalty Judges under such regulations.

(C) Requirements.—Regulations issued under subparagraph (A) shall include the following:

(i) The written direct statements and written rebuttal statements of all participants in a proceeding under paragraph (2) shall be filed by a date specified by the Copyright Royalty Judges, which, in the case of written direct statements, may be not earlier than 4 months, and not later than 5 months, after the end of the voluntary negotiation period under paragraph (3). Notwithstanding the preceding sentence, the Copyright Royalty Judges may allow a participant in a proceeding to file an amended written direct statement based on new information received during the discovery process, within 15 days after the end of the discovery period specified in clause (iv).

(ii)(I) Following the submission to the Copyright Royalty Judges of written direct statements and written rebuttal statements by the participants in a proceeding under paragraph (2), the Copyright Royalty Judges, after taking into consideration the views of the participants in the proceeding, shall determine a schedule for conducting and completing discovery.

(II) In this chapter, the term "written direct statements" means witness statements, testimony, and exhibits to be presented in the proceedings, and such other information that is necessary to establish terms and rates, or the distribution of royalty payments, as the case may be, as set forth in regulations issued by the Copyright Royalty Judges.

(iii) Hearsay may be admitted in proceedings under this chapter to the extent deemed appropriate by the Copyright Royalty Judges.

(iv) Discovery in connection with written direct statements shall be permitted for a period of 60 days, except for discovery ordered by the Copyright Royalty Judges in connection with the resolution of motions, orders, and disputes pending at the end of such period. The Copyright Royalty Judges may order a discovery schedule in connection with written rebuttal statements.

(v) Any participant under paragraph (2) in a proceeding under this chapter to determine royalty rates may request of an opposing participant nonprivileged documents directly related to the written direct statement or written rebuttal statement of that participant. Any objection to such a request shall be resolved by a motion or request to compel production made to the Copyright Royalty Judges in accordance with regulations adopted by the Copyright Royalty Judges. Each motion or request to compel discovery shall be determined by the Copyright Royalty Judges, or by a Copyright Royalty Judge when permitted under subsection (a)(2). Upon such motion, the Copyright Royalty Judges may order discovery pursuant to regulations established under this paragraph.

(vi)(I) Any participant under paragraph (2) in a proceeding under this chapter to determine royalty rates may, by means of written motion or on the record, request of an opposing participant or witness other relevant information and materials if, absent the discovery sought, the Copyright Royalty Judges' resolution of the proceeding would be substantially impaired. In determining whether discovery will be granted under this clause, the Copyright Royalty Judges may consider—

(aa) whether the burden or expense of producing the requested information or materials outweighs the likely benefit, taking into account the needs and resources of the participants, the importance of the issues at stake, and the probative value of the requested information or materials in resolving such issues;

(bb) whether the requested information or materials would be unreasonably cumulative or duplicative, or are obtainable from another source that is more convenient, less burdensome, or less expensive; and

(cc) whether the participant seeking discovery has had ample opportunity by discovery in the proceeding or by other means to obtain the information sought.

(II) This clause shall not apply to any proceeding scheduled to commence after December 31, 2010.

(vii) In a proceeding under this chapter to determine royalty rates, the participants entitled to receive royalties shall collectively be permitted to take no more than 10 depositions and secure responses to no more than 25 interrogatories, and the participants obligated to pay royalties shall collectively be permitted to take no more than 10 depositions and secure responses to no more than 25 interrogatories. The Copyright Royalty Judges shall resolve any disputes among similarly aligned participants to allocate the number of depositions or interrogatories permitted under this clause.

(viii) The rules and practices in effect on the day before the effective date of the Copyright Royalty and Distribution Reform Act of 2004, relating to discovery in proceedings under this chapter to determine the distribution of royalty fees, shall continue to apply to such proceedings on and after such effective date.

(ix) In proceedings to determine royalty rates, the Copyright Royalty Judges may issue a subpoena commanding a participant or witness to appear and give testimony, or to produce and permit inspection of documents or tangible things, if the Copyright Royalty Judges' resolution of the proceeding would be substantially impaired by the absence of such testimony or production of documents or tangible things. Such subpoena shall specify with reasonable particularity the materials to be produced or the scope and nature of the required testimony. Nothing in this clause shall preclude the Copyright Royalty Judges from requesting the production by a nonparticipant of information or materials relevant to the resolution by the Copyright Royalty Judges of a material issue of fact.

(x) The Copyright Royalty Judges shall order a settlement conference among the participants in the proceeding to facilitate the presentation of offers of settlement among the participants. The settlement conference shall be held during a 21-day period following the 60-day discovery period specified in clause (iv) and shall take place outside the presence of the Copyright Royalty Judges.

(xi) No evidence, including exhibits, may be submitted in the written direct statement or written rebuttal statement of a participant without a sponsoring witness, except where the Copyright Royalty Judges have taken official notice, or in the case of incorporation by reference of past records, or for good cause shown.

(c) Determination of Copyright Royalty Judges.—

(1) Timing.—The Copyright Royalty Judges shall issue their determination in a proceeding not later than 11 months after the conclusion of the 21-day settlement conference period under subsection (b)(6)(C)(x), but, in the case of a proceeding to determine successors to rates or terms that expire on a specified date, in no event later than 15 days before the expiration of the then current statutory rates and terms.

(2) Rehearings.—

(A) In General.—The Copyright Royalty Judges may, in exceptional cases, upon motion of a participant in a proceeding under subsection (b)(2), order a rehearing, after the determination in the proceeding is issued under paragraph (1), on such matters as the Copyright Royalty Judges determine to be appropriate.

(B) Timing for Filing Motion.—Any motion for a rehearing under subparagraph (A) may only be filed within 15 days after the date on which the Copyright Royalty Judges deliver to the participants in the proceeding their initial determination.

(C) Participation by Opposing Party Not Required.—In any case in which a rehearing is ordered, any opposing party shall not be required to participate in the rehearing, except that nonparticipation may give rise to the limitations with respect to judicial review provided for in subsection (d)(1).

(D) No Negative Inference.—No negative inference shall be drawn from lack of participation in a rehearing.

(E) Continuity of Rates and Terms.—

(i) If the decision of the Copyright Royalty Judges on any motion for a rehearing is not rendered before the expiration of the statutory rates and terms that were previously in effect, in the case of a proceeding to determine successors to rates and terms that expire on a specified date, then—

(I) the initial determination of the Copyright Royalty Judges that is the subject of the rehearing motion shall be effective as of the day following the date on which the rates and terms that were previously in effect expire; and

(II) in the case of a proceeding under section 114(f)(1)(C), royalty rates and terms shall, for purposes of section 114(f)(3)(B), be deemed to have been set at those rates and terms contained in the initial determination of the Copyright Royalty Judges that is the subject of the rehearing motion, as of the date of that determination.

(ii) The pendency of a motion for a rehearing under this paragraph shall not relieve persons obligated to make royalty payments who would be affected by the determination on that motion from providing the statements of account and any reports of use, to the extent required, and paying the royalties required under the relevant determination or regulations.

(iii) Notwithstanding clause (ii), whenever royalties described in clause (ii) are paid to a person other than the Copyright Office, the entity designated by the Copyright Royalty Judges to which such royalties are paid by the copyright user (and any successor thereto) shall, within 60 days after the motion for rehearing is resolved or, if the motion is granted, within 60 days after the rehearing is concluded, return any excess amounts previously paid to the extent necessary to comply with the final determination of royalty rates by the Copyright Royalty Judges. Any underpayment of royalties resulting from a rehearing shall be paid within the same period.

(3) Contents of Determination.—A determination of the Copyright Royalty Judges shall be supported by the written record and shall set forth the findings of fact relied on by the

Copyright Royalty Judges. Among other terms adopted in a determination, the Copyright Royalty Judges may specify notice and recordkeeping requirements of users of the copyrights at issue that apply in lieu of those that would otherwise apply under regulations.

(4) Continuing Jurisdiction.—The Copyright Royalty Judges may issue an amendment to a written determination to correct any technical or clerical errors in the determination or to modify the terms, but not the rates, of royalty payments in response to unforeseen circumstances that would frustrate the proper implementation of such determination. Such amendment shall be set forth in a written addendum to the determination that shall be distributed to the participants of the proceeding and shall be published in the Federal Register.

(5) Protective Order.—The Copyright Royalty Judges may issue such orders as may be appropriate to protect confidential information, including orders excluding confidential information from the record of the determination that is published or made available to the public, except that any terms or rates of royalty payments or distributions may not be excluded.

(6) Publication of Determination.—By no later than the end of the 60-day period provided in section 802(f)(1)(D), the Librarian of Congress shall cause the determination, and any corrections thereto, to be published in the Federal Register. The Librarian of Congress shall also publicize the determination and corrections in such other manner as the Librarian considers appropriate, including, but not limited to, publication on the Internet. The Librarian of Congress shall also make the determination, corrections, and the accompanying record available for public inspection and copying.

(7) Late Payment.—A determination of the Copyright Royalty Judges may include terms with respect to late payment, but in no way shall such terms prevent the copyright holder from asserting other rights or remedies provided under this title.

(d) Judicial Review.—

(1) Appeal.—Any determination of the Copyright Royalty Judges under subsection (c) may, within 30 days after the publication of the determination in the Federal Register, be appealed, to the United States Court of Appeals for the District of Columbia Circuit, by any aggrieved participant in the proceeding under subsection (b)(2) who fully participated in the proceeding and who would be bound by the determination. Any participant that did not participate in a rehearing may not raise any issue that was the subject of that rehearing at any stage of judicial review of the hearing determination. If no appeal is brought within that 30-day period, the determination of the Copyright Royalty Judges shall be final, and the royalty fee or determination with respect to the distribution of fees, as the case may be, shall take effect as set forth in paragraph (2).

(2) Effect of Rates.—

(A) Expiration on Specified Date.—When this title provides that the royalty rates and terms that were previously in effect are to expire on a specified date, any adjustment or determination by the Copyright Royalty Judges of successor rates and terms for an ensuing statutory license period shall be effective as of the day following the date of expiration of the rates and terms that were previously in effect, even if the determination of the Copyright Royalty Judges is rendered on a later date. A licensee shall be obligated to continue making payments under the rates and terms previously in effect until such time as rates and terms for the successor period are established. Whenever royalties pursuant to this section are paid to a person other than the Copyright Office, the entity designated by the Copyright Royalty Judges to which such royalties are paid by the copyright user (and any successor thereto) shall, within 60 days after the final determination of the Copyright Royalty Judges establishing rates and terms for a successor period or the exhaustion of all rehearings or appeals of such determination, if any, return any excess amounts previously paid to the extent necessary to comply with the final determination of royalty rates. Any underpayment of royalties by a copyright user shall be paid to the entity designated by the Copyright Royalty Judges within the same period.

(B) Other Cases.—In cases where rates and terms have not, prior to the inception of an activity, been established for that particular activity under the relevant license, such rates and terms shall be retroactive to the inception of activity under the relevant license covered by such rates and terms. In other cases where rates and terms do not expire on a specified date, successor rates and terms shall take effect on the first day of the second month that begins after the publication of the determination of the Copyright Royalty Judges in the Federal Register, except as otherwise provided in this title, or by the Copyright Royalty Judges, or as agreed by the participants in a proceeding that would be bound by the rates and terms. Except as otherwise provided in this title, the rates and terms, to the extent applicable, shall remain in effect until such successor rates and terms become effective.

(C) Obligation to Make Payments.—

(i) The pendency of an appeal under this subsection shall not relieve persons obligated to make royalty payments under section 111, 112, 114, 115, 116, 118, 119, or 1003, who would be affected by the determination on appeal, from—

(I) providing the applicable statements of account and reports of use; and

(II) paying the royalties required under the relevant determination or regulations.

(ii) Notwithstanding clause (i), whenever royalties described in clause (i) are paid to a person other than the Copyright Office, the entity designated by the Copyright Royalty Judges to which such royalties are paid by the copyright user (and any successor thereto) shall, within 60 days after the final resolution of the appeal, return any excess amounts previously paid (and interest thereon, if ordered pursuant to paragraph (3)) to the extent necessary to comply with the final determination of royalty rates on appeal. Any underpayment of royalties resulting from an appeal (and interest thereon, if ordered pursuant to paragraph (3)) shall be paid within the same period.

(3) Jurisdiction of Court.—Section 706 of title 5 shall apply with respect to review by the court of appeals under this subsection. If the court modifies or vacates a determination of the Copyright Royalty Judges, the court may enter its own determination with respect to the amount or distribution of royalty fees and costs, and order the repayment of any excess fees, the payment of any underpaid fees, and the payment of interest pertaining respectively thereto, in accordance with its final judgment. The court may also vacate the determination of the Copyright Royalty Judges and remand the case to the Copyright Royalty Judges for further proceedings in accordance with subsection (a).

(e) Administrative Matters.—

(1) Deduction of Costs of Library of Congress and Copyright Office From Filing Fees.—

(A) Deduction From Filing Fees.—The Librarian of Congress may, to the extent not otherwise provided under this title, deduct from the filing fees collected under subsection (b) for a particular proceeding under this chapter the reasonable costs incurred by the Librarian of Congress, the Copyright Office, and the Copyright Royalty Judges in conducting that proceeding, other than the salaries of the Copyright Royalty Judges and the 3 staff members appointed under section 802(b).

(B) Authorization of Appropriations.—There are authorized to be appropriated such sums as may be necessary to pay the costs incurred under this chapter not covered by the filing fees collected under subsection (b). All funds made available pursuant to this subparagraph shall remain available until expended.

(2) **Positions Required for Administration of Compulsory Licensing.**—Section 307 of the Legislative Branch Appropriations Act, 1994, shall not apply to employee positions in the Library of Congress that are required to be filled in order to carry out section 111, 112, 114, 115, 116, 118, or 119 or chapter 10.

§ 804. Institution of Proceedings

(a) **Filing of Petition.**—With respect to proceedings referred to in paragraphs (1) and (2) of section 801(b) concerning the determination or adjustment of royalty rates as provided in sections 111, 112, 114, 115, 116, 118, 119, and 1004, during the calendar years specified in the schedule set forth in subsection (b), any owner or user of a copyrighted work whose royalty rates are specified by this title, or are established under this chapter before or after the enactment of the Copyright Royalty and Distribution Reform Act of 2004, may file a petition with the Copyright Royalty Judges declaring that the petitioner requests a determination or adjustment of the rate. The Copyright Royalty Judges shall make a determination as to whether the petitioner has such a significant interest in the royalty rate in which a determination or adjustment is requested. If the Copyright Royalty Judges determine that the petitioner has such a significant interest, the Copyright Royalty Judges shall cause notice of this determination, with the reasons for such determination, to be published in the Federal Register, together with the notice of commencement of proceedings under this chapter. With respect to proceedings under paragraph (1) of section 801(b) concerning the determination or adjustment of royalty rates as provided in sections 112 and 114, during the calendar years specified in the schedule set forth in subsection (b), the Copyright Royalty Judges shall cause notice of commencement of proceedings under this chapter to be published in the Federal Register as provided in section 803(b)(1)(A).

(b) **Timing of Proceedings.**—

(1) **Section 111 Proceedings.**—

(A) A petition described in subsection (a) to initiate proceedings under section 801(b)(2) concerning the adjustment of royalty rates under section 111 to which subparagraph (A) or (D) of section 801(b)(2) applies may be filed during the year 2015 and in each subsequent fifth calendar year.

(B) In order to initiate proceedings under section 801(b)(2) concerning the adjustment of royalty rates under section 111 to which subparagraph (B) or (C) of section 801(b)(2) applies, within 12 months after an event described in either of those subsections, any owner or user of a copyrighted work whose royalty rates are specified by section 111, or by a rate established under this chapter before or after the enactment of the Copyright Royalty and Distribution Reform Act of 2004, may file a petition with the Copyright Royalty Judges declaring that the petitioner requests an adjustment of the rate. The Copyright Royalty Judges shall then proceed as set forth in subsection (a) of this section. Any change in royalty rates made under this chapter pursuant to this subparagraph may be reconsidered in the year 2015, and each fifth calendar year thereafter, in accordance with the provisions in section 801(b)(2)(B) or (C), as the case may be. A petition for adjustment of rates established by section 111(d)(1)(B) as a result of a change in the rules and regulations of the Federal Communications Commission shall set forth the change on which the petition is based.

(C) Any adjustment of royalty rates under section 111 shall take effect as of the first accounting period commencing after the publication of the determination of the Copyright Royalty Judges in the Federal Register, or on such other date as is specified in that determination.

(2) **Certain Section 112 Proceedings.**—Proceedings under this chapter shall be commenced in the year 2007 to determine reasonable terms and rates of royalty payments for the activities described in section 112(e)(1) relating to the limitation on exclusive rights specified by

section 114(d)(1)(C)(iv), to become effective on January 1, 2009. Such proceedings shall be repeated in each subsequent fifth calendar year.

(3) Section 114 and Corresponding 112 Proceedings.—

(A) For Eligible Nonsubscription Services and New Subscription Services.— Proceedings under this chapter shall be commenced as soon as practicable after the date of enactment of the Copyright Royalty and Distribution Reform Act of 2004 to determine reasonable terms and rates of royalty payments under sections 114 and 112 for the activities of eligible nonsubscription transmission services and new subscription services, to be effective for the period beginning on January 1, 2006, and ending on December 31, 2010. Such proceedings shall next be commenced in January 2009 to determine reasonable terms and rates of royalty payments, to become effective on January 1, 2011. Thereafter, such proceedings shall be repeated in each subsequent fifth calendar year.

(B) For Preexisting Subscription and Satellite Digital Audio Radio Services.—Proceedings under this chapter shall be commenced in January 2006 to determine reasonable terms and rates of royalty payments under sections 114 and 112 for the activities of preexisting subscription services, to be effective during the period beginning on January 1, 2008, and ending on December 31, 2012, and preexisting satellite digital audio radio services, to be effective during the period beginning on January 1, 2007, and ending on December 31, 2012. Such proceedings shall next be commenced in 2011 to determine reasonable terms and rates of royalty payments, to become effective on January 1, 2013. Thereafter, such proceedings shall be repeated in each subsequent fifth calendar year except that—

(i) with respect to preexisting subscription services, the terms and rates finally determined for the rate period ending on December 31, 2022, shall remain in effect through December 31, 2027, and there shall be no proceeding to determine terms and rates for preexisting subscription services for the period beginning on January 1, 2023, and ending on December 31, 2027; and" "*

(ii) with respect to pre-existing satellite digital audio radio services, the terms and rates set forth by the Copyright Royalty Judges on December 14, 2017, in their initial determination for the rate period ending on December 31, 2022, shall be in effect through December 31, 2027, without any change based on a rehearing under section 803(c)(2) and without the possibility of appeal under section 803(d), and there shall be no proceeding to determine terms and rates for preexisting satellite digital audio radio services for the period beginning on January 1, 2023, and ending on December 31, 2027.

(C)(i) Notwithstanding any other provision of this chapter, this subparagraph shall govern proceedings commenced pursuant to section 114(f)(1)(C) concerning new types of services.

(ii) Not later than 30 days after a petition to determine rates and terms for a new type of service is filed by any copyright owner of sound recordings, or such new type of service, indicating that such new type of service is or is about to become operational, the Copyright Royalty Judges shall issue a notice for a proceeding to determine rates and terms for such service.

(iii) The proceeding shall follow the schedule set forth in subsections (b), (c), and (d) of section 803, except that—

(I) the determination shall be issued by not later than 24 months after the publication of the notice under clause (ii); and

---

* So in original.—*Ed.*

           (II) the decision shall take effect as provided in subsections (c)(2) and (d)(2) of section 803 and section 114(f)(3)(B)(ii) and (C).

        (iv) The rates and terms shall remain in effect for the period set forth in section 114(f)(1)(C) or 114(f)(2)(C), as the case may be.

    (4) Section 115 Proceedings.—A petition described in subsection (a) to initiate proceedings under section 801(b)(1) concerning the adjustment or determination of royalty rates as provided in section 115 may be filed in the year 2006 and in each subsequent fifth calendar year, or at such other times as the parties have agreed under section 115(c)(3) (B) and (C).

    (5) Section 116 Proceedings.—

      (A) A petition described in subsection (a) to initiate proceedings under section 801(b) concerning the determination of royalty rates and terms as provided in section 116 may be filed at any time within 1 year after negotiated licenses authorized by section 116 are terminated or expire and are not replaced by subsequent agreements.

      (B) If a negotiated license authorized by section 116 is terminated or expires and is not replaced by another such license agreement which provides permission to use a quantity of musical works not substantially smaller than the quantity of such works performed on coin-operated phonorecord players during the 1-year period ending March 1, 1989, the Copyright Royalty Judges shall, upon petition filed under paragraph (1) within 1 year after such termination or expiration, commence a proceeding to promptly establish an interim royalty rate or rates for the public performance by means of a coin-operated phonorecord player of nondramatic musical works embodied in phonorecords which had been subject to the terminated or expired negotiated license agreement. Such rate or rates shall be the same as the last such rate or rates and shall remain in force until the conclusion of proceedings by the Copyright Royalty Judges, in accordance with section 803, to adjust the royalty rates applicable to such works, or until superseded by a new negotiated license agreement, as provided in section 116(b).

    (6) Section 118 Proceedings.—A petition described in subsection (a) to initiate proceedings under section 801(b)(1) concerning the determination of reasonable terms and rates of royalty payments as provided in section 118 may be filed in the year 2006 and in each subsequent fifth calendar year.

    (7) Section 1004 Proceedings.—A petition described in subsection (a) to initiate proceedings under section 801(b)(1) concerning the adjustment of reasonable royalty rates under section 1004 may be filed as provided in section 1004(a)(3).

    (8) Proceedings Concerning Distribution of Royalty Fees.—With respect to proceedings under section 801(b)(3) concerning the distribution of royalty fees in certain circumstances under section 111, 119, or 1007, the Copyright Royalty Judges shall, upon a determination that a controversy exists concerning such distribution, cause to be published in the Federal Register notice of commencement of proceedings under this chapter.

§ 805. General Rule for Voluntarily Negotiated Agreements

    Any rates or terms under this title that—(1) are agreed to by participants to a proceeding under section 803(b)(3), (2) are adopted by the Copyright Royalty Judges as part of a determination under this chapter, and (3) are in effect for a period shorter than would otherwise apply under a determination pursuant to this chapter, shall remain in effect for such period of time as would otherwise apply under such determination, except that the Copyright Royalty Judges shall adjust the rates pursuant to the voluntary negotiations to reflect national monetary inflation during the additional period the rates remain in effect.

CHAPTER 11. SOUND RECORDINGS AND MUSIC VIDEOS

Sec.
1101. Unauthorized Fixation and Trafficking in Sound Recordings and Music Videos.

---

§ 1101. Unauthorized Fixation and Trafficking in Sound Recordings and Music Videos

(a) **Unauthorized Acts.**—Anyone who, without the consent of the performer or performers involved—

(1) fixes the sound or sounds and images of a live musical performance in a copy or phonorecord, or reproduces copies or phonorecords of such a performance from an unauthorized fixation,

(2) transmits or otherwise communicates to the public the sounds or sounds and images of a live musical performance, or

(3) distributes or offers to distribute, sells or offers to sell, rents or offers to rent, or traffics in any copy or phonorecord fixed as described in paragraph (1), regardless of whether the fixations occurred in the United States,

shall be subject to the remedies provided in sections 502 through 505, to the same extent as an infringer of copyright.

(b) **Definitions.**—In this section, the term "traffic" has the same meaning as in section 2320(e) of title 18.

(c) **Applicability.**—This section shall apply to any act or acts that occur on or after the date of the enactment of the Uruguay Round Agreements Act.

(d) **State Law Not Preempted.**—Nothing in this section may be construed to annul or limit any rights or remedies under the common law or statutes of any State.

C. CRIMINAL PROVISIONS RELATING TO RECORD PIRACY AND COPYRIGHT INFRINGEMENT*

18 U.S.C.A. §§ 2318–19B, 2323

§ 2318. Trafficking in Counterfeit Labels, Illicit Labels, or Counterfeit Documentation or Packaging

(a)(1) Whoever, in any of the circumstances described in subsection (c), knowingly traffics in—

(A) a counterfeit label or illicit label affixed to, enclosing, or accompanying, or designed to be affixed to, enclose, or accompany—

(i) a phonorecord;

(ii) a copy of a computer program;

(iii) a copy of a motion picture or other audiovisual work;

(iv) a copy of a literary work;

(v) a copy of a pictorial, graphic, or sculptural work;

(vi) a work of visual art; or

(vii) documentation or packaging; or

(B) counterfeit documentation or packaging,

shall be fined under this title or imprisoned for not more than 5 years, or both.

(b) As used in this section—

(1) the term "counterfeit label" means an identifying label or container that appears to be genuine, but is not;

(2) the term "traffic" has the same meaning as in section 2320(f) of this title**;

(3) the terms "copy", "phonorecord", "motion picture", "computer program", "audiovisual work", "literary work", "pictorial, graphic, or sculptural work", "sound recording", "work of visual art", and "copyright owner" have, respectively, the meanings given those terms in section 101 (relating to definitions) of title 17;

(4) the term "illicit label" means a genuine certificate, licensing document, registration card, or similar labeling component—

(A) that is used by the copyright owner to verify that a phonorecord, a copy of a computer program, a copy of a motion picture or other audiovisual work, a copy of a literary work, a copy of a pictorial, graphic, or sculptural work, a work of visual art, or documentation or packaging is not counterfeit or infringing of any copyright; and

(B) that is, without the authorization of the copyright owner—

(i) distributed or intended for distribution not in connection with the copy, phonorecord, or work of visual art to which such labeling component was intended to be affixed by the respective copyright owner; or

---

* Related provisions of this title regarding the Trademark Counterfeiting Act of 1984 can be found in section I(B) of this text.

** According to section 2320(f)(5), the term "traffic" means "to transport, transfer, or otherwise dispose of, to another, for purposes of commercial advantage or private financial gain, or to make, import, export, obtain control of, or possess, with intent to so transport, transfer, or otherwise dispose of."

(ii)   in connection with a genuine certificate or licensing document, knowingly falsified in order to designate a higher number of licensed users or copies than authorized by the copyright owner, unless that certificate or document is used by the copyright owner solely for the purpose of monitoring or tracking the copyright owner's distribution channel and not for the purpose of verifying that a copy or phonorecord is noninfringing;

(5)   the term "documentation or packaging" means documentation or packaging, in physical form, for a phonorecord, copy of a computer program, copy of a motion picture or other audiovisual work, copy of a literary work, copy of a pictorial, graphic, or sculptural work, or work of visual art; and

(6)   the term "counterfeit documentation or packaging" means documentation or packaging that appears to be genuine, but is not.

(c)   The circumstances referred to in subsection (a) of this section are—

(1)   the offense is committed within the special maritime and territorial jurisdiction of the United States; or within the special aircraft jurisdiction of the United States (as defined in section 46501 of title 49);

(2)   the mail or a facility of interstate or foreign commerce is used or intended to be used in the commission of the offense;

(3)   the counterfeit label or illicit label is affixed to, encloses, or accompanies, or is designed to be affixed to, enclose, or accompany—

(A)   a phonorecord of a copyrighted sound recording or copyrighted musical work;

(B)   a copy of a copyrighted computer program;

(C)   a copy of a copyrighted motion picture or other audiovisual work;

(D)   a copy of a literary work;

(E)   a copy of a pictorial, graphic, or sculptural work;

(F)   a work of visual art; or

(G)   copyrighted documentation or packaging; or

(4)   the counterfeited documentation or packaging is copyrighted.

(d)   Forfeiture and Destruction of Property; Restitution.—Forfeiture, destruction, and restitution relating to this section shall be subject to section 2323, to the extent provided in that section, in addition to any other similar remedies provided by law.

(e)   Civil Remedies.—

(1)   In General.—Any copyright owner who is injured, or is threatened with injury, by a violation of subsection (a) may bring a civil action in an appropriate United States district court.

(2)   Discretion of Court.—In any action brought under paragraph (1), the court—

(A)   may grant 1 or more temporary or permanent injunctions on such terms as the court determines to be reasonable to prevent or restrain a violation of subsection (a);

(B)   at any time while the action is pending, may order the impounding, on such terms as the court determines to be reasonable, of any article that is in the custody or control of the alleged violator and that the court has reasonable cause to believe was involved in a violation of subsection (a); and

(C)   may award to the injured party—

(i)   reasonable attorney fees and costs; and

(ii)(I) actual damages and any additional profits of the violator, as provided in paragraph (3); or

(II) statutory damages, as provided in paragraph (4).

(3) Actual Damages and Profits.—

(A) In General.—The injured party is entitled to recover—

(i) the actual damages suffered by the injured party as a result of a violation of subsection (a), as provided in subparagraph (B) of this paragraph; and

(ii) any profits of the violator that are attributable to a violation of subsection (a) and are not taken into account in computing the actual damages.

(B) Calculation of Damages.—The court shall calculate actual damages by multiplying—

(i) the value of the phonorecords, copies, or works of visual art which are, or are intended to be, affixed with, enclosed in, or accompanied by any counterfeit labels, illicit labels, or counterfeit documentation or packaging, by

(ii) the number of phonorecords, copies, or works of visual art which are, or are intended to be, affixed with, enclosed in, or accompanied by any counterfeit labels, illicit labels, or counterfeit documentation or packaging.

(C) Definition.—For purposes of this paragraph, the "value" of a phonorecord, copy, or work of visual art is—

(i) in the case of a copyrighted sound recording or copyrighted musical work, the retail value of an authorized phonorecord of that sound recording or musical work;

(ii) in the case of a copyrighted computer program, the retail value of an authorized copy of that computer program;

(iii) in the case of a copyrighted motion picture or other audiovisual work, the retail value of an authorized copy of that motion picture or audiovisual work;

(iv) in the case of a copyrighted literary work, the retail value of an authorized copy of that literary work;

(v) in the case of a pictorial, graphic, or sculptural work, the retail value of an authorized copy of that work; and

(vi) in the case of a work of visual art, the retail value of that work.

(4) Statutory Damages.—The injured party may elect, at any time before final judgment is rendered, to recover, instead of actual damages and profits, an award of statutory damages for each violation of subsection (a) in a sum of not less than $2,500 or more than $25,000, as the court considers appropriate.

(5) Subsequent Violation.—The court may increase an award of damages under this subsection by 3 times the amount that would otherwise be awarded, as the court considers appropriate, if the court finds that a person has subsequently violated subsection (a) within 3 years after a final judgment was entered against that person for a violation of that subsection.

(6) Limitation on Actions.—A civil action may not be commenced under this subsection unless it is commenced within 3 years after the date on which the claimant discovers the violation of subsection (a).

§ 2319.   Criminal Infringement of a Copyright

(a)   Any person who violates section 506(a) (relating to criminal offenses) of title 17 shall be punished as provided in subsections (b), (c) and (d) of this section and such penalties shall be in addition to any other provisions of title 17 or any other law.

(b)   Any person who commits an offense under section 506(a)(1)(A) of title 17—

(1)   shall be imprisoned not more than 5 years, or fined in the amount set forth in this title, or both, if the offense consists of the reproduction or distribution, including by electronic means, during any 180-day period, of at least 10 copies or phonorecords, of 1 or more copyrighted works, which have a total retail value of more than $2,500;

(2)   shall be imprisoned not more than 10 years, or fined in the amount set forth in this title, or both, if the offense is a felony and is a second or subsequent offense under subsection (a); and

(3)   shall be imprisoned not more than 1 year, or fined in the amount set forth in this title, or both, in any other case.

(c)   Any person who commits an offense under section 506(a)(1)(B) of title 17, United States Code—

(1)   shall be imprisoned not more than 3 years, or fined in the amount set forth in this title, or both, if the offense consists of the reproduction or distribution of 10 or more copies or phonorecords of 1 or more copyrighted works, which have a total retail value of $2,500 or more;

(2)   shall be imprisoned not more than 6 years, or fined in the amount set forth in this title, or both, if the offense is a felony and is a second or subsequent offense under subsection (a); and

(3)   shall be imprisoned not more than 1 year, or fined in the amount set forth in this title, or both, if the offense consists of the reproduction or distribution of 1 or more copies or phonorecords of 1 or more copyrighted works, which have a total retail value of more than $1,000.

(d)   Any person who commits an offense under section 506(a)(1)(C) of title 17—

(1)   shall be imprisoned not more than 3 years, fined under this title, or both;

(2)   shall be imprisoned not more than 5 years, fined under this title, or both, if the offense was committed for purposes of commercial advantage or private financial gain;

(3)   shall be imprisoned not more than 6 years, fined under this title, or both, if the offense is a felony and is a second or subsequent offense under subsection (a); and

(4)   shall be imprisoned not more than 10 years, fined under this title, or both, if the offense is a felony and is a second or subsequent offense under paragraph (2).

(e)(1)   During preparation of the presentence report pursuant to Rule 32(c) of the Federal Rules of Criminal Procedure, victims of the offense shall be permitted to submit, and the probation officer shall receive, a victim impact statement that identifies the victim of the offense and the extent and scope of the injury and loss suffered by the victim, including the estimated economic impact of the offense on that victim.

(2)   Persons permitted to submit victim impact statements shall include—

(A)   producers and sellers of legitimate works affected by conduct involved in the offense;

(B)   holders of intellectual property rights in such works; and

(C)   the legal representatives of such producers, sellers, and holders.

(f)   As used in this section—

(1)   the terms "phonorecord" and "copies" have, respectively, the meanings set forth in section 101 (relating to definitions) of title 17;

(2)   the terms "reproduction" and "distribution" refer to the exclusive rights of a copyright owner under clauses (1) and (3) respectively of section 106 (relating to exclusive rights in copyrighted works), as limited by sections 107 through 122, of title 17;

(3)   the term "financial gain" has the meaning given the term in section 101 of title 17; and

(4)   the term "work being prepared for commercial distribution" has the meaning given the term in section 506(a) of title 17.

§ 2319A. Unauthorized Fixation of and Trafficking in Sound Recordings and Music Videos of Live Musical Performances

(a) Offense.—Whoever, without the consent of the performer or performers involved, knowingly and for purposes of commercial advantage or private financial gain—

(1)   fixes the sounds or sounds and images of a live musical performance in a copy or phonorecord, or reproduces copies or phonorecords of such a performance from an unauthorized fixation;

(2)   transmits or otherwise communicates to the public the sounds or sounds and images of a live musical performance; or

(3)   distributes or offers to distribute, sells or offers to sell, rents or offers to rent, or traffics in any copy or phonorecord fixed as described in paragraph (1), regardless of whether the fixations occurred in the United States;

shall be imprisoned for not more than 5 years or fined in the amount set forth in this title, or both, or if the offense is a second or subsequent offense, shall be imprisoned for not more than 10 years or fined in the amount set forth in this title, or both.

(b) Forfeiture and Destruction of Property; Restitution.—Forfeiture, destruction, and restitution relating to this section shall be subject to section 2323, to the extent provided in that section, in addition to any other similar remedies provided by law.

(c) Seizure and Forfeiture.—If copies or phonorecords of sounds or sounds and images of a live musical performance are fixed outside of the United States without the consent of the performer or performers involved, such copies or phonorecords are subject to seizure and forfeiture in the United States in the same manner as property imported in violation of the customs laws. The Secretary of Homeland Security shall issue regulations by which any performer may, upon payment of a specified fee, be entitled to notification by United States Customs and Border Protection of the importation of copies or phonorecords that appear to consist of unauthorized fixations of the sounds or sounds and images of a live musical performance.

(d) Victim Impact Statement.—(1) During preparation of the presentence report pursuant to Rule 32(c) of the Federal Rules of Criminal Procedure, victims of the offense shall be permitted to submit, and the probation officer shall receive, a victim impact statement that identifies the victim of the offense and the extent and scope of the injury and loss suffered by the victim, including the estimated economic impact of the offense on that victim.

(2)   Persons permitted to submit victim impact statements shall include—

(A)   producers and sellers of legitimate works affected by conduct involved in the offense;

(B)   holders of intellectual property rights in such works; and

(C)   the legal representatives of such producers, sellers, and holders.

(e) Definitions.—As used in this section—

(1) the terms "copy", "fixed", "musical work", "phonorecord", "reproduce", "sound recordings", and "transmit" mean those terms within the meaning of title 17; and

(2) the term "traffic" has the same meaning as in section 2320(e) of this title.

(f) Applicability.—This section shall apply to any Act or Acts that occur on or after the date of the enactment of the Uruguay Round Agreements Act.

§ 2319B. Unauthorized Recording of Motion Pictures in a Motion Picture Exhibition Facility

(a) Offense.—Any person who, without the authorization of the copyright owner, knowingly uses or attempts to use an audiovisual recording device to transmit or make a copy of a motion picture or other audiovisual work protected under title 17, or any part thereof, from a performance of such work in a motion picture exhibition facility, shall—

(1) be imprisoned for not more than 3 years, fined under this title, or both; or

(2) if the offense is a second or subsequent offense, be imprisoned for no more than 6 years, fined under this title, or both.

The possession by a person of an audiovisual recording device in a motion picture exhibition facility may be considered as evidence in any proceeding to determine whether that person committed an offense under this subsection, but shall not, by itself, be sufficient to support a conviction of that person for such offense.

(b) Forfeiture and Destruction of Property; Restitution.—Forfeiture, destruction, and restitution relating to this section shall be subject to section 2323, to the extent provided in that section, in addition to any other similar remedies provided by law.

(c) Authorized Activities.—This section does not prevent any lawfully authorized investigative, protective, or intelligence activity by an officer, agent, or employee of the United States, a State, or a political subdivision of a State, or by a person acting under a contract with the United States, a State, or a political subdivision of a State.

(d) Immunity for Theaters.—With reasonable cause, the owner or lessee of a motion picture exhibition facility where a motion picture or other audiovisual work is being exhibited, the authorized agent or employee of such owner or lessee, the licensor of the motion picture or other audiovisual work being exhibited, or the agent or employee of such licensor—

(1) may detain, in a reasonable manner and for a reasonable time, any person suspected of a violation of this section with respect to that motion picture or audiovisual work for the purpose of questioning or summoning a law enforcement officer; and

(2) shall not be held liable in any civil or criminal action arising out of a detention under paragraph (1).

(e) Victim Impact Statement.—

(1) In General—During the preparation of the presentence report under rule 32(c) of the Federal Rules of Criminal Procedure, victims of an offense under this section shall be permitted to submit to the probation officer a victim impact statement that identifies the victim of the offense and the extent and scope of the injury and loss suffered by the victim, including the estimated economic impact of the offense on that victim.

(2) Contents—A victim impact statement submitted under this subsection shall include—

(A) producers and sellers of legitimate works affected by conduct involved in the offense;

(B)   holders of intellectual property rights in the works described in subparagraph (A); and

(C)   the legal representatives of such producers, sellers, and holders.

(f)   State Law Not Preempted.—Nothing in this section may be construed to annul or limit any rights or remedies under the laws of any State.

(g)   Definitions.—In this section, the following definitions shall apply:

(1)   Title 17 Definitions—The terms "audiovisual work", "copy", "copyright owner", "motion picture", "motion picture exhibition facility", and "transmit" have, respectively, the meanings given those terms in section 101 of title 17.

(2)   Audiovisual Recording Device—The term 'audiovisual recording device' means a digital or analog photographic or video camera, or any other technology or device capable of enabling the recording or transmission of a copyrighted motion picture or other audiovisual work, or any part thereof, regardless of whether audiovisual recording is the sole or primary purpose of the device.

§ 2323.   Forfeiture, Destruction, and Restitution

(a)   Civil Forfeiture.—

(1)   Property subject to forfeiture.—The following property is subject to forfeiture to the United States Government:

(A)   Any article, the making or trafficking of which is, prohibited under section 506 of title 17, or section 2318, 2319, 2319A, 2319B, or 2320, or chapter 90, of this title.

(B)   Any property used, or intended to be used, in any manner or part to commit or facilitate the commission of an offense referred to in subparagraph (A).

(C)   Any property constituting or derived from any proceeds obtained directly or indirectly as a result of the commission of an offense referred to in subparagraph (A).

(2)   Procedures.—The provisions of chapter 46 relating to civil forfeitures shall extend to any seizure or civil forfeiture under this section. For seizures made under this section, the court shall enter an appropriate protective order with respect to discovery and use of any records or information that has been seized. The protective order shall provide for appropriate procedures to ensure that confidential, private, proprietary, or privileged information contained in such records is not improperly disclosed or used. At the conclusion of the forfeiture proceedings, unless otherwise requested by an agency of the United States, the court shall order that any property forfeited under paragraph (1) be destroyed, or otherwise disposed of according to law.

(b)   Criminal Forfeiture.—

(1)   Property subject to forfeiture.—The court, in imposing sentence on a person convicted of an offense under section 506 of title 17, or section 2318, 2319, 2319A, 2319B, or 2320, or chapter 90, of this title, shall order, in addition to any other sentence imposed, that the person forfeit to the United States Government any property subject to forfeiture under subsection (a) for that offense.

(2)   Procedures.—

(A)   In general.—The forfeiture of property under paragraph (1), including any seizure and disposition of the property and any related judicial or administrative proceeding, shall be governed by the procedures set forth in section 413 of the Comprehensive Drug Abuse Prevention and Control Act of 1970 (21 U.S.C. 853), other than subsection (d) of that section.

(B)   Destruction.—At the conclusion of the forfeiture proceedings, the court, unless otherwise requested by an agency of the United States shall order that any—

(i) forfeited article or component of an article bearing or consisting of a counterfeit mark be destroyed or otherwise disposed of according to law; and

(ii) infringing items or other property described in subsection (a)(1)(A) and forfeited under paragraph (1) of this subsection be destroyed or otherwise disposed of according to law.

(c) **Restitution.**—When a person is convicted of an offense under section 506 of title 17 or section 2318, 2319, 2319A, 2319B, or 2320, or chapter 90, of this title, the court, pursuant to sections 3556, 3663A, and 3664 of this title, shall order the person to pay restitution to any victim of the offense as an offense against property referred to in section 3663A(c)(1)(A)(ii) of this title.

D. THE SEMICONDUCTOR CHIP PROTECTION ACT OF 1984

17 U.S.C.A. §§ 901–914

Contents

---

§ 901. Definitions

(a) As used in this chapter—

(1) a "semiconductor chip product" is the final or intermediate form of any product—

(A) having two or more layers of metallic, insulating, or semiconductor material, deposited or otherwise placed on, or etched away or otherwise removed from, a piece of semiconductor material in accordance with a predetermined pattern; and

(B) intended to perform electronic circuitry functions;

(2) a "mask work" is a series of related images, however fixed or encoded—

(A) having or representing the predetermined, three-dimensional pattern of metallic, insulating, or semiconductor material present or removed from the layers of a semiconductor chip product; and

(B) in which series the relation of the images to one another is that each image has the pattern of the surface of one form of the semiconductor chip product;

(3) a mask work is "fixed" in a semiconductor chip product when its embodiment in the product is sufficiently permanent or stable to permit the mask work to be perceived or reproduced from the product for a period of more than transitory duration;

(4) to "distribute" means to sell, or to lease, bail, or otherwise transfer, or to offer to sell, lease, bail, or otherwise transfer;

(5) to "commercially exploit" a mask work is to distribute to the public for commercial purposes a semiconductor chip product embodying the mask work; except that such term includes an offer to sell or transfer a semiconductor chip product only when the offer is in writing and occurs after the mask work is fixed in the semiconductor chip product;

327

(6) the "owner" of a mask work is the person who created the mask work, the legal representative of that person if that person is deceased or under a legal incapacity, or a party to whom all the rights under this chapter of such person or representative are transferred in accordance with section 903(b); except that, in the case of a work made within the scope of a person's employment, the owner is the employer for whom the person created the mask work or a party to whom all the rights under this chapter of the employer are transferred in accordance with section 903(b);

(7) an "innocent purchaser" is a person who purchases a semiconductor chip product in good faith and without having notice of protection with respect to the semiconductor chip product;

(8) having "notice of protection" means having actual knowledge that, or reasonable grounds to believe that, a mask work is protected under this chapter; and

(9) an "infringing semiconductor chip product" is a semiconductor chip product which is made, imported, or distributed in violation of the exclusive rights of the owner of a mask work under this chapter.

(b) For purposes of this chapter, the distribution or importation of a product incorporating a semiconductor chip product as a part thereof is a distribution or importation of that semiconductor chip product.

§ 902. Subject Matter of Protection

(a)(1) Subject to the provisions of subsection (b), a mask work fixed in a semiconductor chip product, by or under the authority of the owner of the mask work, is eligible for protection under this chapter if—

(A) on the date on which the mask work is registered under section 908, or is first commercially exploited anywhere in the world, whichever occurs first, the owner of the mask work is (i) a national or domiciliary of the United States, (ii) a national, domiciliary, or sovereign authority of a foreign nation that is a party to a treaty affording protection to mask works to which the United States is also a party, or (iii) a stateless person, wherever that person may be domiciled;

(B) the mask work is first commercially exploited in the United States; or

(C) the mask work comes within the scope of a Presidential proclamation issued under paragraph (2).

(2) Whenever the President finds that a foreign nation extends, to mask works of owners who are nationals or domiciliaries of the United States protection (A) on substantially the same basis as that on which the foreign nation extends protection to mask works of its own nationals and domiciliaries and mask works first commercially exploited in that nation, or (B) on substantially the same basis as provided in this chapter, the President may by proclamation extend protection under this chapter to mask works (i) of owners who are, on the date on which the mask works are registered under section 908, or the date on which the mask works are first commercially exploited anywhere in the world, whichever occurs first, nationals, domiciliaries, or sovereign authorities of that nation, or (ii) which are first commercially exploited in that nation. The President may revise, suspend, or revoke any such proclamation or impose any conditions or limitations on protection extended under any such proclamation.

(b) Protection under this chapter shall not be available for a mask work that—

(1) is not original; or

(2) consists of designs that are staple, commonplace, or familiar in the semiconductor industry, or variations of such designs, combined in a way that, considered as a whole, is not original.

(c)   In no case does protection under this chapter for a mask work extend to any idea, procedure, process, system, method of operation, concept, principle, or discovery, regardless of the form in which it is described, explained, illustrated, or embodied in such work.

§ 903.   Ownership, Transfer, Licensing, and Recordation

(a)   The exclusive rights in a mask work subject to protection under this chapter belong to the owner of the mask work.

(b)   The owner of the exclusive rights in a mask work may transfer all of those rights, or license all or less than all of those rights, by any written instrument signed by such owner or a duly authorized agent of the owner. Such rights may be transferred or licensed by operation of law, may be bequeathed by will, and may pass as personal property by the applicable laws of intestate succession.

(c)(1)   Any document pertaining to a mask work may be recorded in the Copyright Office if the document filed for recordation bears the actual signature of the person who executed it, or if it is accompanied by a sworn or official certification that it is a true copy of the original, signed document. The Register of Copyrights shall, upon receipt of the document and the fee specified pursuant to section 908(d), record the document and return it with a certificate of recordation. The recordation of any transfer or license under this paragraph gives all persons constructive notice of the facts stated in the recorded document concerning the transfer or license.

(2)   In any case in which conflicting transfers of the exclusive rights in a mask work are made, the transfer first executed shall be void as against a subsequent transfer which is made for a valuable consideration and without notice of the first transfer, unless the first transfer is recorded in accordance with paragraph (1) within three months after the date on which it is executed, but in no case later than the day before the date of such subsequent transfer.

(d)   Mask works prepared by an officer or employee of the United States Government as part of that person's official duties are not protected under this chapter, but the United States Government is not precluded from receiving and holding exclusive rights in mask works transferred to the Government under subsection (b).

§ 904.   Duration of Protection

(a)   The protection provided for a mask work under this chapter shall commence on the date on which the mask work is registered under section 908, or the date on which the mask work is first commercially exploited anywhere in the world, whichever occurs first.

(b)   Subject to subsection (c) and the provisions of this chapter, the protection provided under this chapter to a mask work shall end ten years after the date on which such protection commences under subsection (a).

(c)   All terms of protection provided in this section shall run to the end of the calendar year in which they would otherwise expire.

§ 905.   Exclusive Rights in Mask Works

The owner of a mask work provided protection under this chapter has the exclusive rights to do and to authorize any of the following:

(1)   to reproduce the mask work by optical, electronic, or any other means;

(2)   to import or distribute a semiconductor chip product in which the mask work is embodied; and

(3)   to induce or knowingly to cause another person to do any of the acts described in paragraphs (1) and (2).

§ 906. Limitation on Exclusive Rights: Reverse Engineering; First Sale

(a)   Notwithstanding the provisions of section 905, it is not an infringement of the exclusive rights of the owner of a mask work for—

(1)   a person to reproduce the mask work solely for the purpose of teaching, analyzing, or evaluating the concepts or techniques embodied in the mask work or the circuitry, logic flow, or organization of components used in the mask work; or

(2)   a person who performs the analysis or evaluation described in paragraph (1) to incorporate the results of such conduct in an original mask work which is made to be distributed.

(b)   Notwithstanding the provisions of section 905(2), the owner of a particular semiconductor chip product made by the owner of the mask work, or by any person authorized by the owner of the mask work, may import, distribute, or otherwise dispose of or use, but not reproduce, that particular semiconductor chip product without the authority of the owner of the mask work.

§ 907. Limitation on Exclusive Rights: Innocent Infringement

(a)   Notwithstanding any other provision of this chapter, an innocent purchaser of an infringing semiconductor chip product—

(1)   shall incur no liability under this chapter with respect to the importation or distribution of units of the infringing semiconductor chip product that occurs before the innocent purchaser has notice of protection with respect to the mask work embodied in the semiconductor chip product; and

(2)   shall be liable only for a reasonable royalty on each unit of the infringing semiconductor chip product that the innocent purchaser imports or distributes after having notice of protection with respect to the mask work embodied in the semiconductor chip product.

(b)   The amount of the royalty referred to in subsection (a)(2) shall be determined by the court in a civil action for infringement unless the parties resolve the issue by voluntary negotiation, mediation, or binding arbitration.

(c)   The immunity of an innocent purchaser from liability referred to in subsection (a)(1) and the limitation of remedies with respect to an innocent purchaser referred to in subsection (a)(2) shall extend to any person who directly or indirectly purchases an infringing semiconductor chip product from an innocent purchaser.

(d)   The provisions of subsections (a), (b), and (c) apply only with respect to those units of an infringing semiconductor chip product that an innocent purchaser purchased before having notice of protection with respect to the mask work embodied in the semiconductor chip product.

§ 908. Registration of Claims of Protection

(a)   The owner of a mask work may apply to the Register of Copyrights for registration of a claim of protection in a mask work. Protection of a mask work under this chapter shall terminate if application for registration of a claim of protection in the mask work is not made as provided in this chapter within two years after the date on which the mask work is first commercially exploited anywhere in the world.

(b)   The Register of Copyrights shall be responsible for all administrative functions and duties under this chapter. Except for section 708, the provisions of chapter 7 of this title relating to the general responsibilities, organization, regulatory authority, actions, records, and publications of the Copyright Office shall apply to this chapter, except that the Register of Copyrights may make such changes as may be necessary in applying those provisions to this chapter.

(c)   The application for registration of a mask work shall be made on a form prescribed by the Register of Copyrights. Such form may require any information regarded by the Register as bearing upon the preparation or identification of the mask work, the existence or duration of protection of the mask work under this chapter, or ownership of the mask work. The application shall be accompanied by the fee set pursuant to subsection (d) and the identifying material specified pursuant to such subsection.

(d)   The Register of Copyrights shall by regulation set reasonable fees for the filing of applications to register claims of protection in mask works under this chapter, and for other services relating to the administration of this chapter or the rights under this chapter, taking into consideration the cost of providing those services, the benefits of a public record, and statutory fee schedules under this title. The Register shall also specify the identifying material to be deposited in connection with the claim for registration.

(e)   If the Register of Copyrights, after examining an application for registration, determines, in accordance with the provisions of this chapter, that the application relates to a mask work which is entitled to protection under this chapter, then the Register shall register the claim of protection and issue to the applicant a certificate of registration of the claim of protection under the seal of the Copyright Office. The effective date of registration of a claim of protection shall be the date on which an application, deposit of identifying material, and fee, which are determined by the Register of Copyrights or by a court of competent jurisdiction to be acceptable for registration of the claim, have all been received in the Copyright Office.

(f)   In any action for infringement under this chapter, the certificate of registration of a mask work shall constitute prima facie evidence (1) of the facts stated in the certificate, and (2) that the applicant issued the certificate has met the requirements of this chapter, and the regulations issued under this chapter, with respect to the registration of claims.

(g)   Any applicant for registration under this section who is dissatisfied with the refusal of the Register of Copyrights to issue a certificate of registration under this section may seek judicial review of that refusal by bringing an action for such review in an appropriate United States district court not later than sixty days after the refusal. The provisions of chapter 7 of title 5 shall apply to such judicial review. The failure of the Register of Copyrights to issue a certificate of registration within four months after an application for registration is filed shall be deemed to be a refusal to issue a certificate of registration for purposes of this subsection and section 910(b)(2), except that, upon a showing of good cause, the district court may shorten such four-month period.

§ 909.   Mask Work Notice

(a)   The owner of a mask work provided protection under this chapter may affix notice to the mask work, and to masks and semiconductor chip products embodying the mask work, in such manner and location as to give reasonable notice of such protection. The Register of Copyrights shall prescribe by regulation, as examples, specific methods of affixation and positions of notice for purposes of this section, but these specifications shall not be considered exhaustive. The affixation of such notice is not a condition of protection under this chapter, but shall constitute prima facie evidence of notice of protection.

(b)   The notice referred to in subsection (a) shall consist of—

(1)   the words "mask work", the symbol *M*, or the symbol ®M (the letter M in a circle); and

(2)   the name of the owner or owners of the mask work or an abbreviation by which the name is recognized or is generally known.

§ 910.   Enforcement of Exclusive Rights

(a)   Except as otherwise provided in this chapter, any person who violates any of the exclusive rights of the owner of a mask work under this chapter, by conduct in or affecting commerce, shall be liable as an infringer of such rights. As used in this subsection, the term "any person" includes any

State, any instrumentality of a State, and any officer or employee of a State or instrumentality of a State acting in his or her official capacity. Any State, and any such instrumentality, officer, or employee, shall be subject to the provisions of this chapter in the same manner and to the same extent as any nongovernmental entity.

(b)(1) The owner of a mask work protected under this chapter, or the exclusive licensee of all rights under this chapter with respect to the mask work, shall, after a certificate of registration of a claim of protection in that mask work has been issued under section 908, be entitled to institute a civil action for any infringement with respect to the mask work which is committed after the commencement of protection of the mask work under section 904(a).

(2) In any case in which an application for registration of a claim of protection in a mask work and the required deposit of identifying material and fee have been received in the Copyright Office in proper form and registration of the mask work has been refused, the applicant is entitled to institute a civil action for infringement under this chapter with respect to the mask work if notice of the action, together with a copy of the complaint, is served on the Register of Copyrights, in accordance with the Federal Rules of Civil Procedure. The Register may, at his or her option, become a party to the action with respect to the issue of whether the claim of protection is eligible for registration by entering an appearance within sixty days after such service, but the failure of the Register to become a party to the action shall not deprive the court of jurisdiction to determine that issue.

(c)(1) The Secretary of the Treasury and the United States Postal Service shall separately or jointly issue regulations for the enforcement of the rights set forth in section 905 with respect to importation. These regulations may require, as a condition for the exclusion of articles from the United States, that the person seeking exclusion take any one or more of the following actions:

(A) Obtain a court order enjoining, or an order of the International Trade Commission under section 337 of the Tariff Act of 1930 excluding, importation of the articles.

(B) Furnish proof that the mask work involved is protected under this chapter and that the importation of the articles would infringe the rights in the mask work under this chapter.

(C) Post a surety bond for any injury that may result if the detention or exclusion of the articles proves to be unjustified.

(2) Articles imported in violation of the rights set forth in section 905 are subject to seizure and forfeiture in the same manner as property imported in violation of the customs laws. Any such forfeited articles shall be destroyed as directed by the Secretary of the Treasury or the court, as the case may be, except that the articles may be returned to the country of export whenever it is shown to the satisfaction of the Secretary of the Treasury that the importer had no reasonable grounds for believing that his or her acts constituted a violation of the law.

§ 911. Civil Actions

(a) Any court having jurisdiction of a civil action arising under this chapter may grant temporary restraining orders, preliminary injunctions, and permanent injunctions on such terms as the court may deem reasonable to prevent or restrain infringement of the exclusive rights in a mask work under this chapter.

(b) Upon finding an infringer liable, to a person entitled under section 910(b)(1) to institute a civil action, for an infringement of any exclusive right under this chapter, the court shall award such person actual damages suffered by the person as a result of the infringement. The court shall also award such person the infringer's profits that are attributable to the infringement and are not taken into account in computing the award of actual damages. In establishing the infringer's profits, such person is required to present proof only of the infringer's gross revenue, and the infringer is required to prove his or her deductible expenses and the elements of profit attributable to factors other than the mask work.

(c)   At any time before final judgment is rendered, a person entitled to institute a civil action for infringement may elect, instead of actual damages and profits as provided by subsection (b), an award of statutory damages for all infringements involved in the action, with respect to any one mask work for which any one infringer is liable individually, or for which any two or more infringers are liable jointly and severally, in an amount not more than $250,000 as the court considers just.

(d)   An action for infringement under this chapter shall be barred unless the action is commenced within three years after the claim accrues.

(e)(1) At any time while an action for infringement of the exclusive rights in a mask work under this chapter is pending, the court may order the impounding, on such terms as it may deem reasonable, of all semiconductor chip products, and any drawings, tapes, masks, or other products by means of which such products may be reproduced, that are claimed to have been made, imported, or used in violation of those exclusive rights. Insofar as practicable, applications for orders under this paragraph shall be heard and determined in the same manner as an application for a temporary restraining order or preliminary injunction.

(2)   As part of a final judgment or decree, the court may order the destruction or other disposition of any infringing semiconductor chip products, and any masks, tapes, or other articles by means of which such products may be reproduced.

(f)   In any civil action arising under this chapter, the court in its discretion may allow the recovery of full costs, including reasonable attorneys' fees, to the prevailing party.

(g)(1) Any State, any instrumentality of a State, and any officer or employee of a State or instrumentality of a State acting in his or her official capacity, shall not be immune, under the Eleventh Amendment of the Constitution of the United States or under any other doctrine of sovereign immunity, from suit in Federal court by any person, including any governmental or nongovernmental entity, for a violation of any of the exclusive rights of the owner of a mask work under this chapter [17 USCA §§ 901 et seq.], or for any other violation under this chapter [17 USCA §§ 901 et seq.].

(2)   In a suit described in paragraph (1) for a violation described in that paragraph, remedies (including remedies both at law and in equity) are available for the violation to the same extent as such remedies are available for such a violation in a suit against any public or private entity other than a State, instrumentality of a State, or officer or employee of a State acting in his or her official capacity. Such remedies include actual damages and profits under subsection (b), statutory damages under subsection (c), impounding and disposition of infringing articles under subsection (e), and costs and attorney's fees under subsection (f).

§ 912. Relation to Other Laws

(a)   Nothing in this chapter shall affect any right or remedy held by any person under chapters 1 through 8 or 10 of this title, or under title 35.

(b)   Except as provided in section 908(b) of this title, references to "this title" or "title 17" in chapters 1 through 8 or 10 of this title shall be deemed not to apply to this chapter.

(c)   The provisions of this chapter shall preempt the laws of any State to the extent those laws provide any rights or remedies with respect to a mask work which are equivalent to those rights or remedies provided by this chapter, except that such preemption shall be effective only with respect to actions filed on or after January 1, 1986.

(d)   Notwithstanding subsection (c), nothing in this chapter shall detract from any rights of a mask work owner, whether under Federal law (exclusive of this chapter) or under the common law or the statutes of a State, heretofore or hereafter declared or enacted, with respect to any mask work first commercially exploited before July 1, 1983.

§ 913. Transitional Provisions

(a) No application for registration under section 908 may be filed, and no civil action under section 910 or other enforcement proceeding under this chapter may be instituted, until sixty days after the date of the enactment of this chapter.

(b) No monetary relief under section 911 may be granted with respect to any conduct that occurred before the date of the enactment of this chapter, except as provided in subsection (d).

(c) Subject to subsection (a), the provisions of this chapter apply to all mask works that are first commercially exploited or are registered under this chapter, or both, on or after the date of the enactment of this chapter.

(d)(1) Subject to subsection (a), protection is available under this chapter to any mask work that was first commercially exploited on or after July 1, 1983, and before the date of the enactment of this chapter, if a claim of protection in the mask work is registered in the Copyright Office before July 1, 1985, under section 908.

(2) In the case of any mask work described in paragraph (1) that is provided protection under this chapter, infringing semiconductor chip product units manufactured before the date of the enactment of this chapter may, without liability under sections 910 and 911, be imported into or distributed in the United States, or both, until two years after the date of registration of the mask work under section 908, but only if the importer or distributor, as the case may be, first pays or offers to pay the reasonable royalty referred to in section 907(a)(2) to the mask work owner, on all such units imported or distributed, or both, after the date of the enactment of this chapter.

(3) In the event that a person imports or distributes infringing semiconductor chip product units described in paragraph (2) of this subsection without first paying or offering to pay the reasonable royalty specified in such paragraph, or if the person refuses or fails to make such payment, the mask work owner shall be entitled to the relief provided in sections 910 and 911.

§ 914. International Transitional Provisions

(a) Notwithstanding the conditions set forth in subparagraphs (A) and (C) of section 902(a)(1) with respect to the availability of protection under this chapter to nationals, domiciliaries, and sovereign authorities of a foreign nation, the Secretary of Commerce may, upon the petition of any person, or upon the Secretary's own motion, issue an order extending protection under this chapter to such foreign nationals, domiciliaries, and sovereign authorities if the Secretary finds—

(1) that the foreign nation is making good faith efforts and reasonable progress toward—

(A) entering into a treaty described in section 902(a)(1)(A); or

(B) enacting legislation that would be in compliance with subparagraph (A) or (B) of section 902(a)(2); and

(2) that the nationals, domiciliaries, and sovereign authorities of the foreign nation, and persons controlled by them, are not engaged in the misappropriation, or unauthorized distribution or commercial exploitation, of mask works; and

(3) that issuing the order would promote the purposes of this chapter and international comity with respect to the protection of mask works.

(b) While an order under subsection (a) is in effect with respect to a foreign nation, no application for registration of a claim for protection in a mask work under this chapter may be denied solely because the owner of the mask work is a national, domiciliary, or sovereign authority of that foreign nation, or solely because the mask work was first commercially exploited in that foreign nation.

(c) Any order issued by the Secretary of Commerce under subsection (a) shall be effective for such period as the Secretary designates in the order, except that no such order may be effective after the date on which the authority of the Secretary of Commerce terminates under subsection (e). The effective date of any such order shall also be designated in the order. In the case of an order issued upon the petition of a person, such effective date may be no earlier than the date on which the Secretary receives such petition.

(d)(1) Any order issued under this section shall terminate if—

(A) the Secretary of Commerce finds that any of the conditions set forth in paragraphs (1), (2), and (3) of subsection (a) no longer exist; or

(B) mask works of nationals, domiciliaries, and sovereign authorities of that foreign nation or mask works first commercially exploited in that foreign nation become eligible for protection under subparagraph (A) or (C) of section 902(a)(1).

(2) Upon the termination or expiration of an order issued under this section, registrations of claims of protection in mask works made pursuant to that order shall remain valid for the period specified in section 904.

(e) The authority of the Secretary of Commerce under this section shall commence on the date of the enactment of this chapter, and shall terminate on July 1, 1991.

(f)(1) The Secretary of Commerce shall promptly notify the Register of Copyrights and the Committees on the Judiciary of the Senate and the House of Representatives of the issuance or termination of any order under this section, together with a statement of the reasons for such action. The Secretary shall also publish such notification and statement of reasons in the Federal Register.

(2) Two years after the date of the enactment of this chapter, the Secretary of Commerce, in consultation with the Register of Copyrights, shall transmit to the Committees on the Judiciary of the Senate and the House of Representatives a report on the actions taken under this section and on the current status of international recognition of mask work protection. The report shall include such recommendations for modifications of the protection accorded under this chapter to mask works owned by nationals, domiciliaries, or sovereign authorities of foreign nations as the Secretary, in consultation with the Register of Copyrights, considers would promote the purposes of this chapter and international comity with respect to mask work protection. Not later than July 1, 1990, the Secretary of Commerce, in consultation with the Register of Copyrights, shall transmit to the Committees on the Judiciary of the Senate and the House of Representatives a report updating the matters contained in the report transmitted under the preceding sentence.

E. AUDIO HOME RECORDING ACT OF 1992

CHAPTER 10—DIGITAL AUDIO RECORDING DEVICES AND MEDIA

17 U.S.C.A. §§ 1001–1010

SUBCHAPTER A—DEFINITIONS

SUBCHAPTER A—DEFINITIONS

§ 1001. Definitions

As used in this chapter, the following terms have the following meanings:

(1) A "digital audio copied recording" is a reproduction in a digital recording format of a digital musical recording, whether that reproduction is made directly from another digital musical recording or indirectly from a transmission.

(2) A "digital audio interface device" is any machine or device that is designed specifically to communicate digital audio information and related interface data to a digital audio recording device through a nonprofessional interface.

(3) A "digital audio recording device" is any machine or device of a type commonly distributed to individuals for use by individuals, whether or not included with or as part of some other machine or device, the digital recording function of which is designed or marketed for the primary purpose of, and that is capable of, making a digital audio copied recording for private use, except for—

(A) professional model products, and

(B) dictation machines, answering machines, and other audio recording equipment that is designed and marketed primarily for the creation of sound recordings resulting from the fixation of nonmusical sounds.

(4)(A) A "digital audio recording medium" is any material object in a form commonly distributed for use by individuals, that is primarily marketed or most commonly used by consumers for the purpose of making digital audio copied recordings by use of a digital audio recording device.

(B) Such term does not include any material object—

(i) that embodies a sound recording at the time it is first distributed by the importer or manufacturer; or

(ii) that is primarily marketed and most commonly used by consumers either for the purpose of making copies of motion pictures or other audiovisual works or for the purpose of making copies of nonmusical literary works, including computer programs or data bases.

(5)(A) A "digital musical recording" is a material object—

(i) in which are fixed, in a digital recording format, only sounds, and material, statements, or instructions incidental to those fixed sounds, if any, and

(ii) from which the sounds and material can be perceived, reproduced, or otherwise communicated, either directly or with the aid of a machine or device.

(B) A "digital musical recording" does not include a material object—

(i) in which the fixed sounds consist entirely of spoken word recordings, or

(ii) in which one or more computer programs are fixed, except that a digital musical recording may contain statements or instructions constituting the fixed sounds and incidental material, and statements or instructions to be used directly or indirectly in order to bring about the perception, reproduction, or communication of the fixed sounds and incidental material.

(C) For purposes of this paragraph—

(i) a "spoken word recording" is a sound recording in which are fixed only a series of spoken words, except that the spoken words may be accompanied by incidental musical or other sounds, and

(ii) the term "incidental" means related to and relatively minor by comparison.

(6) "Distribute" means to sell, lease, or assign a product to consumers in the United States, or to sell, lease, or assign a product in the United States for ultimate transfer to consumers in the United States.

(7) An "interested copyright party" is—

(A) the owner of the exclusive right under section 106(1) of this title to reproduce a sound recording of a musical work that has been embodied in a digital musical recording or analog musical recording lawfully made under this title that has been distributed;

(B) the legal or beneficial owner of, or the person that controls, the right to reproduce in a digital musical recording or analog musical recording a musical work that has been embodied in a digital musical recording or analog musical recording lawfully made under this title that has been distributed;

(C) a featured recording artist who performs on a sound recording that has been distributed; or

(D) any association or other organization—

(i) representing persons specified in subparagraph (A), (B), or (C), or

(ii) engaged in licensing rights in musical works to music users on behalf of writers and publishers.

(8) To "manufacture" means to produce or assemble a product in the United States. A "manufacturer" is a person who manufactures.

(9) A "music publisher" is a person that is authorized to license the reproduction of a particular musical work in a sound recording.

(10) A "professional model product" is an audio recording device that is designed, manufactured, marketed, and intended for use by recording professionals in the ordinary course of a lawful business, in accordance with such requirements as the Secretary of Commerce shall establish by regulation.

(11) The term "serial copying" means the duplication in a digital format of a copyrighted musical work or sound recording from a digital reproduction of a digital musical recording. The term "digital reproduction of a digital musical recording" does not include a digital musical recording as distributed, by authority of the copyright owner, for ultimate sale to consumers.

(12) The "transfer price" of a digital audio recording device or a digital audio recording medium—

(A)   is, subject to subparagraph (B)—

(i)   in the case of an imported product, the actual entered value at United States Customs (exclusive of any freight, insurance, and applicable duty), and

(ii)   in the case of a domestic product, the manufacturer's transfer price (FOB the manufacturer, and exclusive of any direct sales taxes or excise taxes incurred in connection with the sale); and

(B)   shall, in a case in which the transferor and transferee are related entities or within a single entity, not be less than a reasonable arms-length price under the principles of the regulations adopted pursuant to section 482 of the Internal Revenue Code of 1986, or any successor provision to such section.

(13) A "writer" is the composer or lyricist of a particular musical work.

SUBCHAPTER B—COPYING CONTROLS

§ 1002.   Incorporation of Copying Controls

(a) Prohibition on Importation, Manufacture, and Distribution.—No person shall import, manufacture, or distribute any digital audio recording device or digital audio interface device that does not conform to—

(1)   the Serial Copy Management System;

(2)   a system that has the same functional characteristics as the Serial Copy Management System and requires that copyright and generation status information be accurately sent, received, and acted upon between devices using the system's method of serial copying regulation and devices using the Serial Copy Management System; or

(3)   any other system certified by the Secretary of Commerce as prohibiting unauthorized serial copying.

(b) Development of Verification Procedure.—The Secretary of Commerce shall establish a procedure to verify, upon the petition of an interested party, that a system meets the standards set forth in subsection (a)(2).

(c) Prohibition on Circumvention of the System.—No person shall import, manufacture, or distribute any device, or offer or perform any service, the primary purpose or effect of which is to avoid, bypass, remove, deactivate, or otherwise circumvent any program or circuit which implements, in whole or in part, a system described in subsection (a).

(d) Encoding of Information on Digital Musical Recordings.—

(1) Prohibition on Encoding Inaccurate Information.—No person shall encode a digital musical recording of a sound recording with inaccurate information relating to the category code, copyright status, or generation status of the source material for the recording.

(2) Encoding of Copyright Status Not Required.—Nothing in this chapter requires any person engaged in the importation or manufacture of digital musical recordings to encode any such digital musical recording with respect to its copyright status.

(e) Information Accompanying Transmissions in Digital Format.—Any person who transmits or otherwise communicates to the public any sound recording in digital format is not required under this chapter to transmit or otherwise communicate the information relating to the copyright status of the sound recording. Any such person who does transmit or otherwise communicate such copyright status information shall transmit or communicate such information accurately.

SUBCHAPTER C—ROYALTY PAYMENTS

§ 1003. Obligation to Make Royalty Payments

(a) Prohibition on Importation and Manufacture.—No person shall import into and distribute, or manufacture and distribute, any digital audio recording device or digital audio recording medium unless such person records the notice specified by this section and subsequently deposits the statements of account and applicable royalty payments for such device or medium specified in section 1004.

(b) Filing of Notice.—The importer or manufacturer of any digital audio recording device or digital audio recording medium, within a product category or utilizing a technology with respect to which such manufacturer or importer has not previously filed a notice under this subsection, shall file with the Register of Copyrights a notice with respect to such device or medium, in such form and content as the Register shall prescribe by regulation.

(c) Filing of Quarterly and Annual Statements of Account.—

(1) Generally.—Any importer or manufacturer that distributes any digital audio recording device or digital audio recording medium that it manufactured or imported shall file with the Register of Copyrights, in such form and content as the Register shall prescribe by regulation, such quarterly and annual statements of account with respect to such distribution as the Register shall prescribe by regulation.

(2) Certification, Verification, and Confidentiality.—Each such statement shall be certified as accurate by an authorized officer or principal of the importer or manufacturer. The Register shall issue regulations to provide for the verification and audit of such statements and to protect the confidentiality of the information contained in such statements. Such regulations shall provide for the disclosure, in confidence, of such statements to interested copyright parties.

(3) Royalty Payments.—Each such statement shall be accompanied by the royalty payments specified in section 1004.

§ 1004. Royalty Payments

(a) Digital Audio Recording Devices.—

(1) Amount of Payment.—The royalty payment due under section 1003 for each digital audio recording device imported into and distributed in the United States, or manufactured and distributed in the United States, shall be 2 percent of the transfer price. Only the first person to manufacture and distribute or import and distribute such device shall be required to pay the royalty with respect to such device.

(2) Calculation for Devices Distributed With Other Devices.—With respect to a digital audio recording device first distributed in combination with one or more devices, either as a physically integrated unit or as separate components, the royalty payment shall be calculated as follows:

(A) If the digital audio recording device and such other devices are part of a physically integrated unit, the royalty payment shall be based on the transfer price of the unit, but shall be reduced by any royalty payment made on any digital audio recording device included within the unit that was not first distributed in combination with the unit.

(B) If the digital audio recording device is not part of a physically integrated unit and substantially similar devices have been distributed separately at any time during the preceding 4 calendar quarters, the royalty payment shall be based on the average transfer price of such devices during those 4 quarters.

(C) If the digital audio recording device is not part of a physically integrated unit and substantially similar devices have not been distributed separately at any time during the preceding 4 calendar quarters, the royalty payment shall be based on a constructed price reflecting the proportional value of such device to the combination as a whole.

(3) Limits on Royalties.—Notwithstanding paragraph (1) or (2), the amount of the royalty payment for each digital audio recording device shall not be less than $1 nor more than the royalty maximum. The royalty maximum shall be $8 per device, except that in the case of a physically integrated unit containing more than 1 digital audio recording device, the royalty maximum for such unit shall be $12. During the 6th year after the effective date of this chapter, and not more than once each year thereafter, any interested copyright party may petition the Copyright Royalty Judges to increase the royalty maximum and, if more than 20 percent of the royalty payments are at the relevant royalty maximum, the Copyright Royalty Judges shall prospectively increase such royalty maximum with the goal of having no more than 10 percent of such payments at the new royalty maximum; however the amount of any such increase as a percentage of the royalty maximum shall in no event exceed the percentage increase in the Consumer Price Index during the period under review.

(b) Digital Audio Recording Media.—The royalty payment due under section 1003 for each digital audio recording medium imported into and distributed in the United States, or manufactured and distributed in the United States, shall be 3 percent of the transfer price. Only the first person to manufacture and distribute or import and distribute such medium shall be required to pay the royalty with respect to such medium.

§ 1005. Deposit of Royalty Payments and Deduction of Expenses

The Register of Copyrights shall receive all royalty payments deposited under this chapter and, after deducting the reasonable costs incurred by the Copyright Office under this chapter, shall deposit the balance in the Treasury of the United States as offsetting receipts, in such manner as the Secretary of the Treasury directs. All funds held by the Secretary of the Treasury shall be invested in interest-bearing United States securities for later distribution with interest under section 1007. The Register may, in the Register's discretion, 4 years after the close of any calendar year, close out the royalty payments account for that calendar year, and may treat any funds remaining in such account and any subsequent deposits that would otherwise be attributable to that calendar year as attributable to the succeeding calendar year.

§ 1006. Entitlement to Royalty Payments

(a) Interested Copyright Parties.—The royalty payments deposited pursuant to section 1005 shall, in accordance with the procedures specified in section 1007, be distributed to any interested copyright party—

(1) whose musical work or sound recording has been—

(A) embodied in a digital musical recording or an analog musical recording lawfully made under this title that has been distributed, and

(B) distributed in the form of digital musical recordings or analog musical recordings or disseminated to the public in transmissions, during the period to which such payments pertain; and

(2) who has filed a claim under section 1007.

(b) Allocation of Royalty Payments to Groups.—The royalty payments shall be divided into 2 funds as follows:

(1) The Sound Recordings Fund.—66⅔ percent of the royalty payments shall be allocated to the Sound Recordings Fund. 2⅝ percent of the royalty payments allocated to the Sound Recordings Fund shall be placed in an escrow account managed by an independent administrator jointly appointed by the interested copyright parties described in section 1001(7)(A) and the American Federation of Musicians (or any successor entity) to be distributed to nonfeatured musicians (whether or not members of the American Federation of Musicians or any successor entity) who have performed on sound recordings distributed in the United States. 1⅜ percent of the royalty payments allocated to the Sound Recordings Fund shall be placed in an escrow account managed by an independent administrator jointly appointed by the interested copyright parties described in section 1001(7)(A) and the American Federation of Television and Radio Artists (or any successor entity) to be distributed to nonfeatured vocalists (whether or not members of the American Federation of Television and Radio Artists or any successor entity) who have performed on sound recordings distributed in the United States. 40 percent of the remaining royalty payments in the Sound Recordings Fund shall be distributed to the interested copyright parties described in section 1001(7)(C), and 60 percent of such remaining royalty payments shall be distributed to the interested copyright parties described in section 1001(7)(A).

(2) The Musical Works Fund.—

(A) 33⅓ percent of the royalty payments shall be allocated to the Musical Works Fund for distribution to interested copyright parties described in section 1001(7)(B).

(B)(i) Music publishers shall be entitled to 50 percent of the royalty payments allocated to the Musical Works Fund.

(ii) Writers shall be entitled to the other 50 percent of the royalty payments allocated to the Musical Works Fund.

(c) Allocation of Royalty Payments Within Groups.—If all interested copyright parties within a group specified in subsection (b) do not agree on a voluntary proposal for the distribution of the royalty payments within each group, the Copyright Royalty Judges shall, pursuant to the procedures specified under section 1007(c), allocate royalty payments under this section based on the extent to which, during the relevant period—

(1) for the Sound Recordings Fund, each sound recording was distributed in the form of digital musical recordings or analog musical recordings; and

(2) for the Musical Works Fund, each musical work was distributed in the form of digital musical recordings or analog musical recordings or disseminated to the public in transmissions.

§ 1007. Procedures for Distributing Royalty Payments

(a) Filing of Claims and Negotiations.—

(1) Filing of Claims.—During the first 2 months of each calendar year, every interested copyright party seeking to receive royalty payments to which such party is entitled under section 1006 shall file with the Copyright Royalty Judges a claim for payments collected during the preceding year in such form and manner as the Copyright Royalty Judges shall prescribe by regulation.

(2) **Negotiations.**—Notwithstanding any provision of the antitrust laws, for purposes of this section interested copyright parties within each group specified in section 1006(b) may agree among themselves to the proportionate division of royalty payments, may lump their claims together and file them jointly or as a single claim, or may designate a common agent, including any organization described in section 1001(7)(D), to negotiate or receive payment on their behalf; except that no agreement under this subsection may modify the allocation of royalties specified in section 1006(b).

(b) Distribution of Payments in the Absence of a Dispute.—After the period established for the filing of claims under subsection (a), in each year, the Copyright Royalty Judges shall determine whether there exists a controversy concerning the distribution of royalty payments under section 1006(c). If the Copyright Royalty Judges determine that no such controversy exists, the Copyright Royalty Judges shall, within 30 days after such determination, authorize the distribution of the royalty payments as set forth in the agreements regarding the distribution of royalty payments entered into pursuant to subsection (a). The Librarian of Congress shall, before such royalty payments are distributed, deduct the reasonable administrative costs incurred under this section.

(c) Resolution of Disputes.—If the Copyright Royalty Judges find the existence of a controversy, the Copyright Royalty Judges shall, pursuant to chapter 8 of this title, conduct a proceeding to determine the distribution of royalty payments. During the pendency of such a proceeding, the Copyright Royalty Judges shall withhold from distribution an amount sufficient to satisfy all claims with respect to which a controversy exists, but shall, to the extent feasible, authorize the distribution of any amounts that are not in controversy. The Librarian of Congress shall, before such royalty payments are distributed, deduct the reasonable administrative costs incurred under this section.

SUBCHAPTER D—PROHIBITION ON CERTAIN INFRINGEMENT ACTIONS, REMEDIES, AND ARBITRATION

§ 1008. Prohibition on Certain Infringement Actions

No action may be brought under this title alleging infringement of copyright based on the manufacture, importation, or distribution of a digital audio recording device, a digital audio recording medium, an analog recording device, or an analog recording medium, or based on the noncommercial use by a consumer of such a device or medium for making digital musical recordings or analog musical recordings.

§ 1009. Civil Remedies

(a) Civil Actions.—Any interested copyright party injured by a violation of section 1002 or 1003 may bring a civil action in an appropriate United States district court against any person for such violation.

(b) Other Civil Actions.—Any person injured by a violation of this chapter may bring a civil action in an appropriate United States district court for actual damages incurred as a result of such violation.

(c) Powers of the Court.—In an action brought under subsection (a), the court—

(1) may grant temporary and permanent injunctions on such terms as it deems reasonable to prevent or restrain such violation;

(2) in the case of a violation of section 1002, or in the case of an injury resulting from a failure to make royalty payments required by section 1003, shall award damages under subsection (d);

(3)   in its discretion may allow the recovery of costs by or against any party other than the United States or an officer thereof; and

(4)   in its discretion may award a reasonable attorney's fee to the prevailing party.

(d) Award of Damages.—

(1) Damages for Section 1002 or 1003 Violations.—

(A) Actual Damages.—(i) In an action brought under subsection (a), if the court finds that a violation of section 1002 or 1003 has occurred, the court shall award to the complaining party its actual damages if the complaining party elects such damages at any time before final judgment is entered.

(ii)   In the case of section 1003, actual damages shall constitute the royalty payments that should have been paid under section 1004 and deposited under section 1005. In such a case, the court, in its discretion, may award an additional amount of not to exceed 50 percent of the actual damages.

(B) Statutory Damages for Section 1002 Violations.—

(i)   Device.—A complaining party may recover an award of statutory damages for each violation of section 1002(a) or (c) in the sum of not more than $2,500 per device involved in such violation or per device on which a service prohibited by section 1002(c) has been performed, as the court considers just.

(ii)   Digital Musical Recording.—A complaining party may recover an award of statutory damages for each violation of section 1002(d) in the sum of not more than $25 per digital musical recording involved in such violation, as the court considers just.

(iii) Transmission.—A complaining party may recover an award of damages for each transmission or communication that violates section 1002(e) in the sum of not more than $10,000, as the court considers just.

(2)   Repeated Violations.—In any case in which the court finds that a person has violated section 1002 or 1003 within 3 years after a final judgment against that person for another such violation was entered, the court may increase the award of damages to not more than double the amounts that would otherwise be awarded under paragraph (1), as the court considers just.

(3)   Innocent Violations of Section 1002.—The court in its discretion may reduce the total award of damages against a person violating section 1002 to a sum of not less than $250 in any case in which the court finds that the violator was not aware and had no reason to believe that its acts constituted a violation of section 1002.

(e)   Payment of Damages.—Any award of damages under subsection (d) shall be deposited with the Register pursuant to section 1005 for distribution to interested copyright parties as though such funds were royalty payments made pursuant to section 1003.

(f)   Impounding of Articles.—At any time while an action under subsection (a) is pending, the court may order the impounding, on such terms as it deems reasonable, of any digital audio recording device, digital musical recording, or device specified in section 1002(c) that is in the custody or control of the alleged violator and that the court has reasonable cause to believe does not comply with, or was involved in a violation of, section 1002.

(g)   Remedial Modification and Destruction of Articles.—In an action brought under subsection (a), the court may, as part of a final judgment or decree finding a violation of section 1002, order the remedial modification or the destruction of any digital audio recording device, digital musical recording, or device specified in section 1002(c) that—

(1)   does not comply with, or was involved in a violation of, section 1002, and

(2)   is in the custody or control of the violator or has been impounded under subsection (f).

§ 1010. Determination of Certain Disputes

(a) Scope of Determination.—Before the date of first distribution in the United States of a digital audio recording device or a digital audio interface device, any party manufacturing, importing, or distributing such device, and any interested copyright party may mutually agree to petition the Copyright Royalty Judges to determine whether such device is subject to section 1002, or the basis on which royalty payments for such device are to be made under section 1003.

(b) Initiation of Proceedings.—The parties under subsection (a) shall file the petition with the Copyright Royalty Judges requesting the commencement of a proceeding. Within 2 weeks after receiving such a petition, the Chief Copyright Royalty Judge shall cause notice to be published in the Federal Register of the initiation of the proceeding.

(c) Stay of Judicial Proceedings.—Any civil action brought under section 1009 against a party to a proceeding under this section shall, on application of one of the parties to the proceeding, be stayed until completion of the proceeding.

(d) Proceeding.—The Copyright Royalty Judges shall conduct a proceeding with respect to the matter concerned, in accordance with such procedures as the Copyright Royalty Judges may adopt. The Copyright Royalty Judges shall act on the basis of a fully documented written record. Any party to the proceeding may submit relevant information and proposals to the Copyright Royalty Judges. The parties to the proceeding shall each bear their respective costs of participation.

(e) Judicial Review.—Any determination of the Copyright Royalty Judges under subsection (d) may be appealed, by a party to the proceeding, in accordance with section 803(d) of this title. The pendency of an appeal under this subsection shall not stay the determination of the Copyright Royalty Judges. If the court modifies the determination of the Copyright Royalty Judges, the court shall have jurisdiction to enter its own decision in accordance with its final judgment. The court may further vacate the determination of the Copyright Royalty Judges and remand the case for proceedings as provided in this section.

F. COPYRIGHT PROTECTION AND MANAGEMENT SYSTEMS

CHAPTER 12—COPYRIGHT PROTECTION AND MANAGEMENT SYSTEMS

17 U.S.C.A. §§ 1201–1205

---

§ 1201. Circumvention of Copyright Protection Systems

(a) Violations Regarding Circumvention of Technological Measures.—

(1)(A) No person shall circumvent a technological measure that effectively controls access to a work protected under this title. The prohibition contained in the preceding sentence shall take effect at the end of the 2-year period beginning on the date of the enactment of this chapter.

(B) The prohibition contained in subparagraph (A) shall not apply to persons who are users of a copyrighted work which is in a particular class of works, if such persons are, or are likely to be in the succeeding 3-year period, adversely affected by virtue of such prohibition in their ability to make noninfringing uses of that particular class of works under this title, as determined under subparagraph (C).

(C) During the 2-year period described in subparagraph (A), and during each succeeding 3-year period, the Librarian of Congress, upon the recommendation of the Register of Copyrights, who shall consult with the Assistant Secretary for Communications and Information of the Department of Commerce and report and comment on his or her views in making such recommendation, shall make the determination in a rulemaking proceeding for purposes of subparagraph (B) of whether persons who are users of a copyrighted work are, or are likely to be in the succeeding 3-year period, adversely affected by the prohibition under subparagraph (A) in their ability to make noninfringing uses under this title of a particular class of copyrighted works. In conducting such rulemaking, the Librarian shall examine—

(i) the availability for use of copyrighted works;

(ii) the availability for use of works for nonprofit archival, preservation, and educational purposes;

(iii) the impact that the prohibition on the circumvention of technological measures applied to copyrighted works has on criticism, comment, news reporting, teaching, scholarship, or research;

(iv) the effect of circumvention of technological measures on the market for or value of copyrighted works; and

(v) such other factors as the Librarian considers appropriate.

(D) The Librarian shall publish any class of copyrighted works for which the Librarian has determined, pursuant to the rulemaking conducted under subparagraph (C), that noninfringing uses by persons who are users of a copyrighted work are, or are likely to be, adversely affected, and the prohibition contained in subparagraph (A) shall not apply to such users with respect to such class of works for the ensuing 3-year period.[*]

---

[*] Pursuant to this provision, the Librarian promulgated the following regulation, effective for the three-year period beginning on October 28, 2018. It is codified in Title 37 of the Code of Federal Regulations. (Certain key phrases in the subsection (b) have been italicized for clarity.)

§ 201.40 Exemptions to prohibition against circumvention.

(a) **General.** This section prescribes the classes of copyrighted works for which the Librarian of Congress has determined, pursuant to 17 U.S.C. 1201(a)(1)(C) and (D), that noninfringing uses by persons who are users of such works are, or are likely to be, adversely affected. The prohibition against circumvention of technological measures that control access to copyrighted works set forth in 17 U.S.C. 1201(a)(1)(A) shall not apply to such users of the prescribed classes of copyrighted works.

(b) **Classes of copyrighted works.** Pursuant to the authority set forth in 17 U.S.C. 1201(a)(1)(C) and (D), and upon the recommendation of the Register of Copyrights, the Librarian has determined that the prohibition against circumvention of technological measures that effectively control access to copyrighted works set forth in 17 U.S.C. 1201(a)(1)(A) shall not apply to persons who engage in noninfringing uses of the following classes of copyrighted works:

(1) *Motion pictures* (including television shows and videos), as defined in 17 U.S.C. 101, where the motion picture is lawfully made and acquired on a DVD protected by the Content Scramble System, on a Blu-ray disc protected by the Advanced Access Content System, or via a digital transmission protected by a technological measure, and the person engaging in circumvention under paragraph (b)(1)(i) and (b)(1)(ii)(A) and (B) of this section reasonably believes that non-circumventing alternatives are unable to produce the required level of high-quality content, or the circumvention is undertaken using screen-capture technology that appears to be offered to the public as enabling the reproduction of motion pictures after content has been lawfully acquired and decrypted, where circumvention is undertaken solely in order to make use of short portions of the motion pictures in the following instances:

    (i) For the purpose of criticism or comment:

        (A) For use in documentary filmmaking, or other films where the motion picture clip is used in parody or for its biographical or historically significant nature;

        (B) For use in noncommercial videos (including videos produced for a paid commission if the commissioning entity's use is noncommercial); or

        (C) For use in nonfiction multimedia e-books.

    (ii) For educational purposes:

        (A) By college and university faculty and students or kindergarten through twelfth-grade (K–12) educators and students (where the K–12 student is circumventing under the direct supervision of an educator), including of accredited general educational development (GED) programs, for the purpose of criticism, comment, teaching, or scholarship;

        (B) By faculty of massive open online courses (MOOCs) offered by accredited nonprofit educational institutions to officially enrolled students through online platforms (which platforms themselves may be operated for profit), in film studies or other courses requiring close analysis of film and media excerpts, for the purpose of criticism or comment, where the MOOC provider through the online platform limits transmissions to the extent technologically feasible to such officially enrolled students, institutes copyright policies and provides copyright informational materials to faculty, students, and relevant staff members, and applies technological measures that reasonably prevent unauthorized further dissemination of a work in accessible form to others or retention of the work for longer than the course session by recipients of a transmission through the platform, as contemplated by 17 U.S.C. 110(2); or

        (C) By educators and participants in nonprofit digital and media literacy programs offered by libraries, museums, and other nonprofit entities with an educational mission, in the course of face-to-face instructional activities, for the purpose of criticism or comment, except that such users may only circumvent using screen-capture technology that appears to be offered to the public as enabling the reproduction of motion pictures after content has been lawfully acquired and decrypted.

(2)(i) *Motion pictures* (including television shows and videos), as defined in 17 U.S.C. 101, where the motion picture is lawfully acquired on a DVD protected by the Content Scramble System, on a Blu-ray disc protected by the Advanced Access Content System, or via a digital transmission protected by a technological measure, where:

    (A) Circumvention is undertaken by a disability services office or other unit of a kindergarten through twelfth-grade educational institution, college, or university engaged in and/or responsible for the provision of accessibility services to students, for the purpose of adding captions and/or audio description to a motion picture to create an accessible version as a necessary accommodation for a student or students with disabilities under an applicable disability law, such as the Americans With Disabilities Act, the Individuals with Disabilities Education Act, or Section 504 of the Rehabilitation Act;

    (B) The educational institution unit in paragraph (b)(2)(i)(A) of this section has, after a reasonable effort, determined that an accessible version cannot be obtained at a fair price or in a timely manner; and

(C) The accessible versions are provided to students or educators and stored by the educational institution in a manner intended to reasonably prevent unauthorized further dissemination of a work.

(ii) For purposes of this paragraph (b)(2), "audio description" means an oral narration that provides an accurate rendering of the motion picture.

(3) *Literary works, distributed electronically*, that are protected by technological measures that either prevent the enabling of read-aloud functionality or interfere with screen readers or other applications or assistive technologies:

(i) When a copy of such a work is lawfully obtained by a blind or other person with a disability, as such a person is defined in 17 U.S.C. 121; provided, however, that the rights owner is remunerated, as appropriate, for the price of the mainstream copy of the work as made available to the general public through customary channels; or

(ii) When such work is a nondramatic literary work, lawfully obtained and used by an authorized entity pursuant to 17 U.S.C. 121.

(4) *Literary works consisting of compilations of data generated by medical devices* that are wholly or partially implanted in the body or by their corresponding personal monitoring systems, where such circumvention is undertaken by a patient for the sole purpose of lawfully accessing the data generated by his or her own device or monitoring system and does not constitute a violation of applicable law, including without limitation the Health Insurance Portability and Accountability Act of 1996, the Computer Fraud and Abuse Act of 1986 or regulations of the Food and Drug Administration, and is accomplished through the passive monitoring of wireless transmissions that are already being produced by such device or monitoring system.

(5) *Computer programs* that enable the following types of lawfully acquired wireless devices to connect to a wireless telecommunications network, when circumvention is undertaken solely in order to connect to a wireless telecommunications network and such connection is authorized by the operator of such network:

(i) Wireless telephone handsets (i.e., cellphones);

(ii) All-purpose tablet computers;

(iii) Portable mobile connectivity devices, such as mobile hotspots, removable wireless broadband modems, and similar devices; and

(iv) Wearable wireless devices designed to be worn on the body, such as smartwatches or fitness devices.

(6) *Computer programs that enable smartphones and portable all-purpose mobile computing devices to execute lawfully obtained software applications*, where circumvention is accomplished for the sole purpose of enabling interoperability of such applications with computer programs on the smartphone or device, or to permit removal of software from the smartphone or device. For purposes of this paragraph (b)(6), a "portable all-purpose mobile computing device" is a device that is primarily designed to run a wide variety of programs rather than for consumption of a particular type of media content, is equipped with an operating system primarily designed for mobile use, and is intended to be carried or worn by an individual.

(7) *Computer programs that enable smart televisions to execute lawfully obtained software applications*, where circumvention is accomplished for the sole purpose of enabling interoperability of such applications with computer programs on the smart television.

(8) *Computer programs that enable voice assistant devices to execute lawfully obtained software applications*, where circumvention is accomplished for the sole purpose of enabling interoperability of such applications with computer programs on the device, or to permit removal of software from the device, and is not accomplished for the purpose of gaining unauthorized access to other copyrighted works. For purposes of this paragraph (b)(8), a "voice assistant device" is a device that is primarily designed to run a wide variety of programs rather than for consumption of a particular type of media content, is designed to take user input primarily by voice, and is designed to be installed in a home or office.

(9) *Computer programs that are contained in and control the functioning of a lawfully acquired motorized land vehicle* such as a personal automobile, commercial vehicle, or mechanized agricultural vehicle, except for programs accessed through a separate subscription service, when circumvention is a necessary step to allow the diagnosis, repair, or lawful modification of a vehicle function, where such circumvention does not constitute a violation of applicable law, including without limitation regulations promulgated by the Department of Transportation or the Environmental Protection Agency, and is not accomplished for the purpose of gaining unauthorized access to other copyrighted works.

(10) *Computer programs that are contained in and control the functioning of a lawfully acquired smartphone or home appliance or home system*, such as a refrigerator, thermostat, HVAC, or electrical system, when circumvention is a necessary step to allow the diagnosis, maintenance, or repair of such a device or system, and is not accomplished for the purpose of gaining access to other copyrighted works. For purposes of this paragraph (b)(10):

(i) The "maintenance" of a device or system is the servicing of the device or system in order to make it work in accordance with its original specifications and any changes to those specifications authorized for that device or system; and

(ii) The "repair" of a device or system is the restoring of the device or system to the state of working in accordance with its original specifications and any changes to those specifications authorized for that device or system.

(11)(i) *Computer programs*, where the circumvention is undertaken on a lawfully acquired device or machine on which the computer program operates, or is undertaken on a computer, computer system, or computer network on which the computer program operates with the authorization of the owner or operator of such computer, computer system, or computer network, solely for the purpose of good-faith security research and does not violate any applicable law, including without limitation the Computer Fraud and Abuse Act of 1986.

(ii) For purposes of this paragraph (b)(11), "good-faith security research" means accessing a computer program solely for purposes of good-faith testing, investigation, and/or correction of a security flaw or vulnerability, where such activity is carried out in an environment designed to avoid any harm to individuals or the public, and where the information derived from the activity is used primarily to promote the security or safety of the class of devices or machines on which the computer program operates, or those who use such devices or machines, and is not used or maintained in a manner that facilitates copyright infringement.

(12)(i) *Video games* in the form of computer programs embodied in physical or downloaded formats that have been lawfully acquired as complete games, when the copyright owner or its authorized representative has ceased to provide access to an external computer server necessary to facilitate an authentication process to enable gameplay, solely for the purpose of:

(A) Permitting access to the video game to allow copying and modification of the computer program to restore access to the game for personal, local gameplay on a personal computer or video game console; or

(B) Permitting access to the video game to allow copying and modification of the computer program to restore access to the game on a personal computer or video game console when necessary to allow preservation of the game in a playable form by an eligible library, archives, or museum, where such activities are carried out without any purpose of direct or indirect commercial advantage and the video game is not distributed or made available outside of the physical premises of the eligible library, archives, or museum.

(ii) Video games in the form of computer programs embodied in physical or downloaded formats that have been lawfully acquired as complete games, that do not require access to an external computer server for gameplay, and that are no longer reasonably available in the commercial marketplace, solely for the purpose of preservation of the game in a playable form by an eligible library, archives, or museum, where such activities are carried out without any purpose of direct or indirect commercial advantage and the video game is not distributed or made available outside of the physical premises of the eligible library, archives, or museum.

(iii) Computer programs used to operate video game consoles solely to the extent necessary for an eligible library, archives, or museum to engage in the preservation activities described in paragraph (b)(12)(i)(B) or (b)(12)(ii) of this section.

(iv) For purposes of this paragraph (b)(12), the following definitions shall apply:

(A) For purposes of paragraph (b)(12)(i)(A) and (b)(12)(ii) of this section, "complete games" means video games that can be played by users without accessing or reproducing copyrightable content stored or previously stored on an external computer server.

(B) For purposes of paragraph (b)(12)(i)(B) of this section, "complete games" means video games that meet the definition in paragraph (b)(12)(iv)(A) of this section, or that consist of both a copy of a game intended for a personal computer or video game console and a copy of the game's code that was stored or previously stored on an external computer server.

(C) "Ceased to provide access" means that the copyright owner or its authorized representative has either issued an affirmative statement indicating that external server support for the video game has ended and such support is in fact no longer available or, alternatively, server support has been discontinued for a period of at least six months; provided, however, that server support has not since been restored.

(D) "Local gameplay" means gameplay conducted on a personal computer or video game console, or locally connected personal computers or consoles, and not through an online service or facility.

(E) A library, archives, or museum is considered "eligible" when the collections of the library, archives, or museum are open to the public and/or are routinely made available to researchers who are not affiliated with the library, archives, or museum.

(13)(i) Computer programs, except video games, that have been lawfully acquired and that are no longer reasonably available in the commercial marketplace, solely for the purpose of lawful preservation of a computer program, or of digital materials dependent upon a computer program as a condition of access, by an eligible library, archives, or museum, where such activities are carried out without any purpose of direct or indirect commercial advantage and the program is not distributed or made available outside of the physical premises of the eligible library, archives, or museum.

(ii) For purposes of the exemption in paragraph (b)(13)(i) of this section, a library, archives, or museum is considered "eligible" if—

(E)   Neither the exception under subparagraph (B) from the applicability of the prohibition contained in subparagraph (A), nor any determination made in a rulemaking conducted under subparagraph (C), may be used as a defense in any action to enforce any provision of this title other than this paragraph.

(2)   No person shall manufacture, import, offer to the public, provide, or otherwise traffic in any technology, product, service, device, component, or part thereof, that—

(A)   is primarily designed or produced for the purpose of circumventing a technological measure that effectively controls access to a work protected under this title;

(B)   has only limited commercially significant purpose or use other than to circumvent a technological measure that effectively controls access to a work protected under this title; or

(C)   is marketed by that person or another acting in concert with that person with that person's knowledge for use in circumventing a technological measure that effectively controls access to a work protected under this title.

(3)   As used in this subsection—

(A)   to "circumvent a technological measure" means to descramble a scrambled work, to decrypt an encrypted work, or otherwise to avoid, bypass, remove, deactivate, or impair a technological measure, without the authority of the copyright owner; and

(B)   a technological measure "effectively controls access to a work" if the measure, in the ordinary course of its operation, requires the application of information, or a process or a treatment, with the authority of the copyright owner, to gain access to the work.

(b)   Additional Violations.—

(1)   No person shall manufacture, import, offer to the public, provide, or otherwise traffic in any technology, product, service, device, component, or part thereof, that—

(A)   is primarily designed or produced for the purpose of circumventing protection afforded by a technological measure that effectively protects a right of a copyright owner under this title in a work or a portion thereof;

(A)   The collections of the library, archives, or museum are open to the public and/or are routinely made available to researchers who are not affiliated with the library, archives, or museum;

(B)   The library, archives, or museum has a public service mission;

(C)   The library, archives, or museum's trained staff or volunteers provide professional services normally associated with libraries, archives, or museums;

(D)   The collections of the library, archives, or museum are composed of lawfully acquired and/or licensed materials; and

(E)   The library, archives, or museum implements reasonable digital security measures as appropriate for the activities permitted by this paragraph (b)(13).

(14) Computer programs that operate 3D printers that employ microchip-reliant technological measures to limit the use of feedstock, when circumvention is accomplished solely for the purpose of using alternative feedstock and not for the purpose of accessing design software, design files, or proprietary data.

(c)   Persons who may initiate circumvention. To the extent authorized under paragraph (b) of this section, the circumvention of a technological measure that restricts wireless telephone handsets or other wireless devices from connecting to a wireless telecommunications network may be initiated by the owner of any such handset or other device, by another person at the direction of the owner, or by a provider of a commercial mobile radio service or a commercial mobile data service at the direction of such owner or other person, solely in order to enable such owner or a family member of such owner to connect to a wireless telecommunications network, when such connection is authorized by the operator of such network.

(d)   [Reserved by 80 FR 65961]

(B) has only limited commercially significant purpose or use other than to circumvent protection afforded by a technological measure that effectively protects a right of a copyright owner under this title in a work or a portion thereof; or

(C) is marketed by that person or another acting in concert with that person with that person's knowledge for use in circumventing protection afforded by a technological measure that effectively protects a right of a copyright owner under this title in a work or a portion thereof.

(2) As used in this subsection—

(A) to "circumvent protection afforded by a technological measure" means avoiding, bypassing, removing, deactivating, or otherwise impairing a technological measure; and

(B) a technological measure "effectively protects a right of a copyright owner under this title" if the measure, in the ordinary course of its operation, prevents, restricts, or otherwise limits the exercise of a right of a copyright owner under this title.

(c) Other Rights, Etc., Not Affected.—

(1) Nothing in this section shall affect rights, remedies, limitations, or defenses to copyright infringement, including fair use, under this title.

(2) Nothing in this section shall enlarge or diminish vicarious or contributory liability for copyright infringement in connection with any technology, product, service, component, or part thereof.

(3) Nothing in this section shall require that the design of, or design and selection of parts and components for, a consumer electronics, telecommunications, or computing product provide for a response to any particular technological measure, so long as such part or component, or the product in which such part or component is integrated, does not otherwise fall within the prohibitions of subsection (a)(2) or (b)(1).

(4) Nothing in this section shall enlarge or diminish any rights of free speech or the press for activities using consumer electronics, telecommunications, or computing products.

(d) Exemption for Nonprofit Libraries, Archives, and Educational Institutions.—

(1) A nonprofit library, archives, or educational institution which gains access to a commercially exploited copyrighted work solely in order to make a good faith determination of whether to acquire a copy of that work for the sole purpose of engaging in conduct permitted under this title shall not be in violation of subsection (a)(1)(A). A copy of a work to which access has been gained under this paragraph—

(A) may not be retained longer than necessary to make such good faith determination; and

(B) may not be used for any other purpose.

(2) The exemption made available under paragraph (1) shall only apply with respect to a work when an identical copy of that work is not reasonably available in another form.

(3) A nonprofit library, archives, or educational institution that willfully for the purpose of commercial advantage or financial gain violates paragraph (1)—

(A) shall, for the first offense, be subject to the civil remedies under section 1203; and

(B) shall, for repeated or subsequent offenses, in addition to the civil remedies under section 1203, forfeit the exemption provided under paragraph (1).

(4) This subsection may not be used as a defense to a claim under subsection (a)(2) or (b), nor may this subsection permit a nonprofit library, archives, or educational institution to

manufacture, import, offer to the public, provide, or otherwise traffic in any technology, product, service, component, or part thereof, which circumvents a technological measure.

(5)   In order for a library or archives to qualify for the exemption under this subsection, the collections of that library or archives shall be—

(A)   open to the public; or

(B)   available not only to researchers affiliated with the library or archives or with the institution of which it is a part, but also to other persons doing research in a specialized field.

(e)   Law Enforcement, Intelligence, and Other Government Activities.—This section does not prohibit any lawfully authorized investigative, protective, information security, or intelligence activity of an officer, agent, or employee of the United States, a State, or a political subdivision of a State, or a person acting pursuant to a contract with the United States, a State, or a political subdivision of a State. For purposes of this subsection, the term "information security" means activities carried out in order to identify and address the vulnerabilities of a government computer, computer system, or computer network.

(f)   Reverse Engineering.—

(1)   Notwithstanding the provisions of subsection (a)(1)(A), a person who has lawfully obtained the right to use a copy of a computer program may circumvent a technological measure that effectively controls access to a particular portion of that program for the sole purpose of identifying and analyzing those elements of the program that are necessary to achieve interoperability of an independently created computer program with other programs, and that have not previously been readily available to the person engaging in the circumvention, to the extent any such acts of identification and analysis do not constitute infringement under this title.

(2)   Notwithstanding the provisions of subsections (a)(2) and (b), a person may develop and employ technological means to circumvent a technological measure, or to circumvent protection afforded by a technological measure, in order to enable the identification and analysis under paragraph (1), or for the purpose of enabling interoperability of an independently created computer program with other programs, if such means are necessary to achieve such interoperability, to the extent that doing so does not constitute infringement under this title.

(3)   The information acquired through the acts permitted under paragraph (1), and the means permitted under paragraph (2), may be made available to others if the person referred to in paragraph (1) or (2), as the case may be, provides such information or means solely for the purpose of enabling interoperability of an independently created computer program with other programs, and to the extent that doing so does not constitute infringement under this title or violate applicable law other than this section.

(4)   For purposes of this subsection, the term "interoperability" means the ability of computer programs to exchange information, and of such programs mutually to use the information which has been exchanged.

(g)   Encryption Research.—

(1)   Definitions.—For purposes of this subsection—

(A)   the term "encryption research" means activities necessary to identify and analyze flaws and vulnerabilities of encryption technologies applied to copyrighted works, if these activities are conducted to advance the state of knowledge in the field of encryption technology or to assist in the development of encryption products; and

(B)   the term "encryption technology" means the scrambling and descrambling of information using mathematical formulas or algorithms.

(2)   Permissible Acts of Encryption Research.—Notwithstanding the provisions of subsection (a)(1)(A), it is not a violation of that subsection for a person to circumvent a technological measure as applied to a copy, phonorecord, performance, or display of a published work in the course of an act of good faith encryption research if—

(A) the person lawfully obtained the encrypted copy, phonorecord, performance, or display of the published work;

(B) such act is necessary to conduct such encryption research;

(C) the person made a good faith effort to obtain authorization before the circumvention; and

(D) such act does not constitute infringement under this title or a violation of applicable law other than this section, including section 1030 of title 18 and those provisions of title 18 amended by the Computer Fraud and Abuse Act of 1986.

(3) **Factors in Determining Exemption.**—In determining whether a person qualifies for the exemption under paragraph (2), the factors to be considered shall include—

(A) whether the information derived from the encryption research was disseminated, and if so, whether it was disseminated in a manner reasonably calculated to advance the state of knowledge or development of encryption technology, versus whether it was disseminated in a manner that facilitates infringement under this title or a violation of applicable law other than this section, including a violation of privacy or breach of security;

(B) whether the person is engaged in a legitimate course of study, is employed, or is appropriately trained or experienced, in the field of encryption technology; and

(C) whether the person provides the copyright owner of the work to which the technological measure is applied with notice of the findings and documentation of the research, and the time when such notice is provided.

(4) **Use of Technological Means for Research Activities.**—Notwithstanding the provisions of subsection (a)(2), it is not a violation of that subsection for a person to—

(A) develop and employ technological means to circumvent a technological measure for the sole purpose of that person performing the acts of good faith encryption research described in paragraph (2); and

(B) provide the technological means to another person with whom he or she is working collaboratively for the purpose of conducting the acts of good faith encryption research described in paragraph (2) or for the purpose of having that other person verify his or her acts of good faith encryption research described in paragraph (2).

(5) **Report to Congress.**—Not later than 1 year after the date of the enactment of this chapter, the Register of Copyrights and the Assistant Secretary for Communications and Information of the Department of Commerce shall jointly report to the Congress on the effect this subsection has had on—

(A) encryption research and the development of encryption technology;

(B) the adequacy and effectiveness of technological measures designed to protect copyrighted works; and

(C) protection of copyright owners against the unauthorized access to their encrypted copyrighted works.

The report shall include legislative recommendations, if any.

(h) **Exceptions Regarding Minors.**—In applying subsection (a) to a component or part, the court may consider the necessity for its intended and actual incorporation in a technology, product, service, or device, which—

(1) does not itself violate the provisions of this title; and

(2)   has the sole purpose to prevent the access of minors to material on the Internet.

(i)   Protection of Personally Identifying Information.—

(1)   Circumvention Permitted.—Notwithstanding the provisions of subsection (a)(1)(A), it is not a violation of that subsection for a person to circumvent a technological measure that effectively controls access to a work protected under this title, if—

(A)   the technological measure, or the work it protects, contains the capability of collecting or disseminating personally identifying information reflecting the online activities of a natural person who seeks to gain access to the work protected;

(B)   in the normal course of its operation, the technological measure, or the work it protects, collects or disseminates personally identifying information about the person who seeks to gain access to the work protected, without providing conspicuous notice of such collection or dissemination to such person, and without providing such person with the capability to prevent or restrict such collection or dissemination;

(C)   the act of circumvention has the sole effect of identifying and disabling the capability described in subparagraph (A), and has no other effect on the ability of any person to gain access to any work; and (D) the act of circumvention is carried out solely for the purpose of preventing the collection or dissemination of personally identifying information about a natural person who seeks to gain access to the work protected, and is not in violation of any other law.

(2)   Inapplicability to Certain Technological Measures.—This subsection does not apply to a technological measure, or a work it protects, that does not collect or disseminate personally identifying information and that is disclosed to a user as not having or using such capability.

(j)   Security Testing.—

(1)   Definition.—For purposes of this subsection, the term "security testing" means accessing a computer, computer system, or computer network, solely for the purpose of good faith testing, investigating, or correcting, a security flaw or vulnerability. with the authorization of the owner or operator of such computer, computer system, or computer network.

(2)   Permissible Acts of Security Testing.—Notwithstanding the provisions of subsection (a)(1)(A), it is not a violation of that subsection for a person to engage in an act of security testing, if such act does not constitute infringement under this title or a violation of applicable law other than this section, including section 1030 of title 18 and those provisions of title 18 amended by the Computer Fraud and Abuse Act of 1986.

(3)   Factors in Determining Exemption.—In determining whether a person qualifies for the exemption under paragraph (2), the factors to be considered shall include—

(A)   whether the information derived from the security testing was used solely to promote the security of the owner or operator of such computer, computer system or computer network, or shared directly with the developer of such computer, computer system, or computer network; and

(B)   whether the information derived from the security testing was used or maintained in a manner that does not facilitate infringement under this title or a violation of applicable law other than this section, including a violation of privacy or breach of security.

(4)   Use of Technological Means for Security Testing.—Notwithstanding the provisions of subsection (a)(2), it is not a violation of that subsection for a person to develop, produce, distribute or employ technological means for the sole purpose of performing the acts of security testing described in subsection (2), provided such technological means does not otherwise violate section (a)(2).

(k) Certain Analog Devices and Certain Technological Measures.—

(1) Certain Analog Devices.—

(A) Effective 18 months after the date of the enactment of this chapter, no person shall manufacture, import, offer to the public, provide or otherwise traffic in any—

(i) VHS format analog video cassette recorder unless such recorder conforms to the automatic gain control copy control technology;

(ii) 8mm format analog video cassette camcorder unless such camcorder conforms to the automatic gain control technology;

(iii) Beta format analog video cassette recorder, unless such recorder conforms to the automatic gain control copy control technology, except that this requirement shall not apply until there are 1,000 Beta format analog video cassette recorders sold in the United States in any one calendar year after the date of the enactment of this chapter;

(iv) 8mm format analog video cassette recorder that is not an analog video cassette camcorder, unless such recorder conforms to the automatic gain control copy control technology, except that this requirement shall not apply until there are 20,000 such recorders sold in the United States in any one calendar year after the date of the enactment of this chapter; or

(v) analog video cassette recorder that records using an NTSC format video input and that is not otherwise covered under clauses (i) through (iv), unless such device conforms to the automatic gain control copy control technology.

(B) Effective on the date of the enactment of this chapter, no person shall manufacture, import, offer to the public, provide or otherwise traffic in—

(i) any VHS format analog video cassette recorder or any 8mm format analog video cassette recorder if the design of the model of such recorder has been modified after such date of enactment so that a model of recorder that previously conformed to the automatic gain control copy control technology no longer conforms to such technology; or

(ii) any VHS format analog video cassette recorder, or any 8mm format analog video cassette recorder that is not an 8mm analog video cassette camcorder, if the design of the model of such recorder has been modified after such date of enactment so that a model of recorder that previously conformed to the four-line colorstripe copy control technology no longer conforms to such technology.

Manufacturers that have not previously manufactured or sold a VHS format analog video cassette recorder, or an 8mm format analog cassette recorder, shall be required to conform to the four-line colorstripe copy control technology in the initial model of any such recorder manufactured after the date of the enactment of this chapter, and thereafter to continue conforming to the four-line colorstripe copy control technology. For purposes of this subparagraph, an analog video cassette recorder "conforms to" the four-line colorstripe copy control technology if it records a signal that, when played back by the playback function of that recorder in the normal viewing mode, exhibits, on a reference display device, a display containing distracting visible lines through portions of the viewable picture.

(2) Certain Encoding Restrictions.—No person shall apply the automatic gain control copy control technology or colorstripe copy control technology to prevent or limit consumer copying except such copying—

(A) of a single transmission, or specified group of transmissions, of live events or of audiovisual works for which a member of the public has exercised choice in selecting the transmissions, including the content of the transmissions or the time of receipt of such transmissions, or both, and as to which such member is charged a separate fee for each such transmission or specified group of transmissions;

(B) from a copy of a transmission of a live event or an audiovisual work if such transmission is provided by a channel or service where payment is made by a member of the public for such channel or service in the form of a subscription fee that entitles the member of the public to receive all of the programming contained in such channel or service;

(C) from a physical medium containing one or more prerecorded audiovisual works; or

(D) from a copy of a transmission described in subparagraph (A) or from a copy made from a physical medium described in subparagraph (C).

In the event that a transmission meets both the conditions set forth in subparagraph (A) and those set forth in subparagraph (B), the transmission shall be treated as a transmission described in subparagraph (A).

(3) **Inapplicability.**—This subsection shall not—

(A) require any analog video cassette camcorder to conform to the automatic gain control copy control technology with respect to any video signal received through a camera lens;

(B) apply to the manufacture, importation, offer for sale, provision of, or other trafficking in, any professional analog video cassette recorder; or

(C) apply to the offer for sale or provision of, or other trafficking in, any previously owned analog video cassette recorder, if such recorder was legally manufactured and sold when new and not subsequently modified in violation of paragraph (1)(B).

(4) **Definitions.**—For purposes of this subsection:

(A) An "analog video cassette recorder" means a device that records, or a device that includes a function that records, on electromagnetic tape in an analog format the electronic impulses produced by the video and audio portions of a television program, motion picture, or other form of audiovisual work.

(B) An "analog video cassette camcorder" means an analog video cassette recorder that contains a recording function that operates through a camera lens and through a video input that may be connected with a television or other video playback device.

(C) An analog video cassette recorder "conforms" to the automatic gain control copy control technology if it—

(i) detects one or more of the elements of such technology and does not record the motion picture or transmission protected by such technology; or

(ii) records a signal that, when played back, exhibits a meaningfully distorted or degraded display.

(D) The term "professional analog video cassette recorder" means an analog video cassette recorder that is designed, manufactured, marketed, and intended for use by a person who regularly employs such a device for a lawful business or industrial use, including making, performing, displaying, distributing, or transmitting copies of motion pictures on a commercial scale.

(E) The terms "VHS format", "8mm format", "Beta format", "automatic gain control copy control technology", "colorstripe copy control technology", "four-line version of the colorstripe copy control technology", and "NTSC" have the meanings that are commonly understood in the consumer electronics and motion picture industries as of the date of the enactment of this chapter.

(5) **Violations.**—Any violation of paragraph (1) of this subsection shall be treated as a violation of subsection (b)(1) of this section. Any violation of paragraph (2) of this subsection shall be deemed an "act of circumvention" for the purposes of section 1203(c)(3)(A) of this chapter.

§ 1202. Integrity of Copyright Management Information

(a) **False Copyright Management Information.**—No person shall knowingly and with the intent to induce, enable, facilitate, or conceal infringement—

(1) provide copyright management information that is false, or

(2) distribute or import for distribution copyright management information that is false.

(b) **Removal or Alteration of Copyright Management Information.**—No person shall, without the authority of the copyright owner or the law—

(1) intentionally remove or alter any copyright management information,

(2) distribute or import for distribution copyright management information knowing that the copyright management information has been removed or altered without authority of the copyright owner or the law, or

(3) distribute, import for distribution, or publicly perform works, copies of works, or phonorecords, knowing that copyright management information has been removed or altered without authority of the copyright owner or the law,

knowing, or, with respect to civil remedies under section 1203, having reasonable grounds to know, that it will induce, enable, facilitate, or conceal an infringement of any right under this title.

(c) **Definition.**—As used in this section, the term "copyright management information" means any of the following information conveyed in connection with copies or phonorecords of a work or performances or displays of a work, including in digital form, except that such term does not include any personally identifying information about a user of a work or of a copy, phonorecord, performance, or display of a work:

(1) The title and other information identifying the work, including the information set forth on a notice of copyright.

(2) The name of, and other identifying information about, the author of a work.

(3) The name of, and other identifying information about, the copyright owner of the work, including the information set forth in a notice of copyright.

(4) With the exception of public performances of works by radio and television broadcast stations, the name of, and other identifying information about, a performer whose performance is fixed in a work other than an audiovisual work.

(5) With the exception of public performances of works by radio and television broadcast stations, in the case of an audiovisual work, the name of, and other identifying information about, a writer, performer, or director who is credited in the audiovisual work.

(6) Terms and conditions for use of the work.

(7) Identifying numbers or symbols referring to such information or links to such information.

(8) Such other information as the Register of Copyrights may prescribe by regulation, except that the Register of Copyrights may not require the provision of any information concerning the user of a copyrighted work.

(d) **Law Enforcement, Intelligence, and Other Government Activities.**—This section does not prohibit any lawfully authorized investigative, protective, information security, or intelligence activity of an officer, agent, or employee of the United States, a State, or a political subdivision of a State, or a person acting pursuant to a contract with the United States, a State, or a political subdivision of a State. For purposes of this subsection, the term "information security" means activities carried out in order to identify and address the vulnerabilities of a government computer, computer system, or computer network.

(e) Limitations on Liability.—

(1) Analog Transmissions.—In the case of an analog transmission, a person who is making transmissions in its capacity as a broadcast station, or as a cable system, or someone who provides programming to such station or system, shall not be liable for a violation of subsection (b) if—

(A) avoiding the activity that constitutes such violation is not technically feasible or would create an undue financial hardship on such person; and

(B) such person did not intend, by engaging in such activity, to induce, enable, facilitate, or conceal infringement of a right under this title.

(2) Digital Transmissions.—

(A) If a digital transmission standard for the placement of copyright management information for a category of works is set in a voluntary, consensus standard-setting process involving a representative cross-section of broadcast stations or cable systems and copyright owners of a category of works that are intended for public performance by such stations or systems, a person identified in paragraph (1) shall not be liable for a violation of subsection (b) with respect to the particular copyright management information addressed by such standard if—

(i) the placement of such information by someone other than such person is not in accordance with such standard; and

(ii) the activity that constitutes such violation is not intended to induce, enable, facilitate, or conceal infringement of a right under this title.

(B) Until a digital transmission standard has been set pursuant to subparagraph (A) with respect to the placement of copyright management information for a category of works, a person identified in paragraph (1) shall not be liable for a violation of subsection (b) with respect to such copyright management information, if the activity that constitutes such violation is not intended to induce, enable, facilitate, or conceal infringement of a right under this title, and if—

(i) the transmission of such information by such person would result in a perceptible visual or aural degradation of the digital signal; or

(ii) the transmission of such information by such person would conflict with—

(I) an applicable government regulation relating to transmission of information in a digital signal;

(II) an applicable industry-wide standard relating to the transmission of information in a digital signal that was adopted by a voluntary consensus standards body prior to the effective date of this chapter; or

(III) an applicable industry-wide standard relating to the transmission of information in a digital signal that was adopted in a voluntary, consensus standards-setting process open to participation by a representative cross-section of broadcast stations or cable systems and copyright owners of a category of works that are intended for public performance by such stations or systems.

(3) Definitions.—As used in this subsection—

(A)   the term "broadcast station" has the meaning given that term in section 3 of the Communications Act of 1934 (47 U.S.C. 53); and

(B)   the term "cable system" has the meaning given that term in section 602 of the Communications Act of 1934 (47 U.S.C. 522).

§ 1203.   Civil Remedies

(a)   **Civil Actions.**—Any person injured by a violation of section 1201 or 1202 may bring a civil action in an appropriate United States district court for such violation.

(b)   **Powers of the Court.**—In an action brought under subsection (a), the court—

(1)   may grant temporary and permanent injunctions on such terms as it deems reasonable to prevent or restrain a violation, but in no event shall impose a prior restraint on free speech or the press protected under the 1st amendment to the Constitution;

(2)   at any time while an action is pending, may order the impounding, on such terms as it deems reasonable, of any device or product that is in the custody or control of the alleged violator and that the court has reasonable cause to believe was involved in a violation;

(3)   may award damages under subsection (c);

(4)   in its discretion may allow the recovery of costs by or against any party other than the United States or an officer thereof;

(5)   in its discretion may award reasonable attorney's fees to the prevailing party; and

(6)   may, as part of a final judgment or decree finding a violation, order the remedial modification or the destruction of any device or product involved in the violation that is in the custody or control of the violator or has been impounded under paragraph (2).

(c)   **Award of Damages.**—

(1)   **In General.**—Except as otherwise provided in this title, a person committing a violation of section 1201 or 1202 is liable for either—

(A)   the actual damages and any additional profits of the violator, as provided in paragraph (2), or

(B)   statutory damages, as provided in paragraph (3).

(2)   **Actual Damages.**—The court shall award to the complaining party the actual damages suffered by the party as a result of the violation, and any profits of the violator that are attributable to the violation and are not taken into account in computing the actual damages, if the complaining party elects such damages at any time before final judgment is entered.

(3)   **Statutory Damages.**—

(A)   At any time before final judgment is entered, a complaining party may elect to recover an award of statutory damages for each violation of section 1201 in the sum of not less than $200 or more than $2,500 per act of circumvention, device, product, component, offer, or performance of service, as the court considers just.

(B)   At any time before final judgment is entered, a complaining party may elect to recover an award of statutory damages for each violation of section 1202 in the sum of not less than $2,500 or more than $25,000.

(4)   **Repeated Violations.**—In any case in which the injured party sustains the burden of proving, and the court finds, that a person has violated section 1201 or 1202 within 3 years after a final judgment was entered against the person for another such violation, the court may increase the award of damages up to triple the amount that would otherwise be awarded, as the court considers just.

(5) Innocent Violations.—

(A) In General.—The court in its discretion may reduce or remit the total award of damages in any case in which the violator sustains the burden of proving, and the court finds, that the violator was not aware and had no reason to believe that its acts constituted a violation.

(B) Nonprofit Library, Archives, Educational Institutions, or Public Broadcasting Entities.—

(i)   Definition.—In this subparagraph, the term "public broadcasting entity" has the meaning given such term under section 118(f).

(ii)   In General.—In the case of a nonprofit library, archives, educational institution, or public broadcasting entity, the court shall remit damages in any case in which the library, archives, educational institution, or public broadcasting entity sustains the burden of proving, and the court finds, that the library, archives, educational institution, or public broadcasting entity was not aware and had no reason to believe that its acts constituted a violation.

§ 1204.   Criminal Offenses and Penalties

(a)   In General.—Any person who violates section 1201 or 1202 willfully and for purposes of commercial advantage or private financial gain—

(1)   shall be fined not more than $500,000 or imprisoned for not more than 5 years, or both, for the first offense; and

(2)   shall be fined not more than $1,000,000 or imprisoned for not more than 10 years, or both, for any subsequent offense.

(b)   Limitation for Nonprofit Library, Archives, Educational Institution, or Public Broadcasting Entity.—Subsection (a) shall not apply to a nonprofit library, archives, educational institution, or public broadcasting entity (as defined under section 118(f)).

(c)   Statute of Limitations.—No criminal proceeding shall be brought under this section unless such proceeding is commenced within 5 years after the cause of action arose.

§ 1205.   Savings Clause

Nothing in this chapter abrogates, diminishes, or weakens the provisions of, nor provides any defense or element of mitigation in a criminal prosecution or civil action under, any Federal or State law that prevents the violation of the privacy of an individual in connection with the individual's use of the Internet.

G. VESSEL HULL DESIGN PROTECTION ACT

CHAPTER 13—PROTECTION OF ORIGINAL DESIGNS

17 U.S.C.A. §§ 1301–1332

-----

§ 1301. Designs Protected

(a) Designs Protected.—

(1) In General.—The designer or other owner of an original design of a useful article which makes the article attractive or distinctive in appearance to the purchasing or using public may secure the protection provided by this chapter upon complying with and subject to this chapter.

(2) Vessel Features.—The design of a vessel hull, deck, or combination of a hull and deck, including a plug or mold, is subject to protection under this chapter, notwithstanding section 1302(4).

(3) Exceptions.—Department of Defense rights in a registered design under this chapter, including the right to build to such registered design, shall be determined solely by operation of section 2320 of title 10 or by the instrument under which the design was developed for the United States Government.

(b) Definitions.—For the purpose of this chapter, the following terms have the following meanings:

(1) A design is "original" if it is the result of the designer's creative endeavor that provides a distinguishable variation over prior work pertaining to similar articles which is more than merely trivial and has not been copied from another source.

(2) A "useful article" is a vessel hull or deck, including a plug or mold, which in normal use has an intrinsic utilitarian function that is not merely to portray the appearance of the article or to convey information. An article which normally is part of a useful article shall be deemed to be a useful article.

(3) A "vessel" is a craft

(A) that is designed and capable of independently steering a course on or through water through its own means of propulsion; and

(B) that is designed and capable of carrying and transporting one or more passengers.

(4) A "hull" is the exterior frame or body of a vessel, exclusive of the deck, superstructure, masts, sails, yards, rigging, hardware, fixtures, and other attachments.

(5) A "plug" means a device or model used to make a mold for the purpose of exact duplication, regardless of whether the device or model has an intrinsic utilitarian function that is not only to portray the appearance of the product or to convey information.

(6) A "mold" means a matrix or form in which a substance for material is used, regardless of whether the matrix or form has an intrinsic utilitarian function that is not only to portray the appearance of the product or to convey information.

(7) A "deck" is the horizontal surface of a vessel that covers the hull, including exterior cabin and cockpit surfaces, and exclusive of masts, sails, yards, rigging, hardware, fixtures, and other attachments.

§ 1302. Designs Not Subject to Protection

Protection under this chapter shall not be available for a design that is—

(1) not original;

(2) staple or commonplace, such as a standard geometric figure, a familiar symbol, an emblem, or a motif, or another shape, pattern, or configuration which has become standard, common, prevalent, or ordinary;

(3) different from a design excluded by paragraph (2) only in insignificant details or in elements which are variants commonly used in the relevant trades;

(4) dictated solely by a utilitarian function of the article that embodies it; or

(5) embodied in a useful article that was made public by the designer or owner in the United States or a foreign country more than 2 years before the date of the application for registration under this chapter.

§ 1303. Revisions, Adaptations, and Rearrangements

Protection for a design under this chapter shall be available notwithstanding the employment in the design of subject matter excluded from protection under section 1302 if the design is a substantial revision, adaptation, or rearrangement of such subject matter. Such protection shall be independent of any subsisting protection in subject matter employed in the design, and shall not be construed as securing any right to subject matter excluded from protection under this chapter or as extending any subsisting protection under this chapter.

§1304. Commencement of Protection

The protection provided for a design under this chapter shall commence upon the earlier of the date of publication of the registration under section 1313(a) or the date the design is first made public as defined by section 1310(b).

§1305. Term of Protection

(a) In General.—Subject to subsection (b), the protection provided under this chapter for a design shall continue for a term of 10 years beginning on the date of the commencement of protection under section 1304.

(b) Expiration.—All terms of protection provided in this section shall run to the end of the calendar year in which they would otherwise expire.

(c) Termination of Rights.—Upon expiration or termination of protection in a particular design under this chapter, all rights under this chapter in the design shall terminate, regardless of the number of different articles in which the design may have been used during the term of its protection.

§1306. Design Notice

(a) Contents of Design Notice.—

(1) Whenever any design for which protection is sought under this chapter is made public under section 1310(b), the owner of the design shall, subject to the provisions of section 1307, mark it or have it marked legibly with a design notice consisting of—

(A) the words "Protected Design", the abbreviation "Prot'd Des.", or the letter "D" with a circle, or the symbol *D*;

(B) the year of the date on which protection for the design commenced; and

(C) the name of the owner, an abbreviation by which the name can be recognized, or a generally accepted alternative designation of the owner.

Any distinctive identification of the owner may be used for purposes of subparagraph (C) if it has been recorded by the Administrator before the design marked with such identification is registered.

(2) After registration, the registration number may be used instead of the elements specified in subparagraphs (B) and (C) of paragraph (1).

(b) Location of Notice.—The design notice shall be so located and applied as to give reasonable notice of design protection while the useful article embodying the design is passing through its normal channels of commerce.

(c) Subsequent Removal of Notice.—When the owner of a design has complied with the provisions of this section, protection under this chapter shall not be affected by the removal, destruction, or obliteration by others of the design notice on an article.

§1307. Effect of Omission of Notice

(a) Actions With Notice.—Except as provided in subsection (b), the omission of the notice prescribed in section 1306 shall not cause loss of the protection under this chapter or prevent recovery for infringement under this chapter against any person who, after receiving written notice of the design protection, begins an undertaking leading to infringement under this chapter.

(b) Actions Without Notice.—The omission of the notice prescribed in section 1306 shall prevent any recovery under section 1323 against a person who began an undertaking leading to infringement under this chapter before receiving written notice of the design protection. No injunction shall be issued under this chapter with respect to such undertaking unless the owner of the design reimburses that person for any reasonable expenditure or contractual obligation in connection with such undertaking that was incurred before receiving written notice of the design protection, as the court in its discretion directs. The burden of providing written notice of design protection shall be on the owner of the design.

§ 1308. Exclusive Rights

The owner of a design protected under this chapter has the exclusive right to—

(1) make, have made, or import, for sale or for use in trade, any useful article embodying that design; and

(2) sell or distribute for sale or for use in trade any useful article embodying that design.

§ 1309. Infringement

(a) Acts of Infringement.—Except as provided in subsection (b), it shall be infringement of the exclusive rights in a design protected under this chapter for any person, without the consent of the owner of the design, within the United States and during the term of such protection, to—

(1) make, have made, or import, for sale or for use in trade, any infringing article as defined in subsection (e); or

(2) sell or distribute for sale or for use in trade any such infringing article.

(b) Acts of Sellers and Distributors.—A seller or distributor of an infringing article who did not make or import the article shall be deemed to have infringed on a design protected under this chapter only if that person—

(1) induced or acted in collusion with a manufacturer to make, or an importer to import such article, except that merely purchasing or giving an order to purchase such article in the ordinary course of business shall not of itself constitute such inducement or collusion; or

(2) refused or failed, upon the request of the owner of the design, to make a prompt and full disclosure of that person's source of such article, and that person orders or reorders such article after receiving notice by registered or certified mail of the protection subsisting in the design.

(c) Acts Without Knowledge.—It shall not be infringement under this section to make, have made, import, sell, or distribute, any article embodying a design which was created without knowledge that a design was protected under this chapter and was copied from such protected design.

(d) Acts in Ordinary Course of Business.—A person who incorporates into that person's product of manufacture an infringing article acquired from others in the ordinary course of business, or who, without knowledge of the protected design embodied in an infringing article, makes or processes the infringing article for the account of another person in the ordinary course of business, shall not be deemed to have infringed the rights in that design under this chapter except under a condition contained in paragraph (1) or (2) of subsection (b). Accepting an order or reorder from the source of the infringing article shall be deemed ordering or reordering within the meaning of subsection (b)(2).

(e) Infringing Article Defined.—As used in this section, an "infringing article" is any article the design of which has been copied from a design protected under this chapter, without the consent of the owner of the protected design. An infringing article is not an illustration or picture of a protected design in an advertisement, book, periodical, newspaper, photograph, broadcast, motion picture, or similar medium. A design shall not be deemed to have been copied from a protected design if it is original and not substantially similar in appearance to a protected design.

(f) Establishing Originality.—The party to any action or proceeding under this chapter who alleges rights under this chapter in a design shall have the burden of establishing the design's originality whenever the opposing party introduces an earlier work which is identical to such design, or so similar as to make prima facie showing that such design was copied from such work.

(g) Reproduction for Teaching or Analysis.—It is not an infringement of the exclusive rights of a design owner for a person to reproduce the design in a useful article or in any other form solely for the purpose of teaching, analyzing, or evaluating the appearance, concepts, or techniques embodied in the design, or the function of the useful article embodying the design.

§ 1310. Application for Registration

(a) Time Limit for Application for Registration.—Protection under this chapter shall be lost if application for registration of the design is not made within 2 years after the date on which the design is first made public.

(b) When Design is Made Public.—A design is made public when an existing useful article embodying the design is anywhere publicly exhibited, publicly distributed, or offered for sale or sold to the public by the owner of the design or with the owner's consent.

(c) Application by Owner of Design.—Application for registration may be made by the owner of the design.

(d) Contents of Application.—The application for registration shall be made to the Administrator and shall state—

    (1)   the name and address of the designer or designers of the design;

    (2)   the name and address of the owner if different from the designer;

    (3)   the specific name of the useful article embodying the design;

    (4)   the date, if any, that the design was first made public, if such date was earlier than the date of the application;

    (5)   affirmation that the design has been fixed in a useful article; and

    (6)   such other information as may be required by the Administrator.

The application for registration may include a description setting forth the salient features of the design, but the absence of such a description shall not prevent registration under this chapter.

(e) Sworn Statement.—The application for registration shall be accompanied by a statement under oath by the applicant or the applicant's duly authorized agent or representative, setting forth, to the best of the applicant's knowledge and belief—

    (1)   that the design is original and was created by the designer or designers named in the application;

    (2)   that the design has not previously been registered on behalf of the applicant or the applicant's predecessor in title; and

    (3)   that the applicant is the person entitled to protection and to registration under this chapter.

If the design has been made public with the design notice prescribed in section 1306, the statement shall also describe the exact form and position of the design notice.

(f) Effect of Errors.—

(1)   Error in any statement or assertion as to the utility of the useful article named in the application under this section, the design of which is sought to be registered, shall not affect the protection secured under this chapter.

(2)   Errors in omitting a joint designer or in naming an alleged joint designer shall not affect the validity of the registration, or the actual ownership or the protection of the design, unless it is shown that the error occurred with deceptive intent.

(g) Design Made in Scope of Employment.—In a case in which the design was made within the regular scope of the designer's employment and individual authorship of the design is difficult or impossible to ascribe and the application so states, the name and address of the employer for whom the design was made may be stated instead of that of the individual designer.

(h) Pictorial Representation of Design.—The application for registration shall be accompanied by two copies of a drawing or other pictorial representation of the useful article embodying the design, having one or more views, adequate to show the design, in a form and style suitable for reproduction, which shall be deemed a part of the application.

(i) Design in More Than One Useful Article.—If the distinguishing elements of a design are in substantially the same form in different useful articles, the design shall be protected as to all such useful articles when protected as to one of them, but not more than one registration shall be required for the design.

(j) Application for More Than One Design.—More than one design may be included in the same application under such conditions as may be prescribed by the Administrator. For each design included in an application the fee prescribed for a single design shall be paid.

§ 1311. Benefit of Earlier Filing Date in Foreign Country

An application for registration of a design filed in the United States by any person who has, or whose legal representative or predecessor or successor in title has, previously filed an application for registration of the same design in a foreign country which extends to designs of owners who are citizens of the United States, or to applications filed under this chapter, similar protection to that provided under this chapter shall have that same effect as if filed in the United States on the date on which the application was first filed in such foreign country, if the application in the United States is filed within 6 months after the earliest date on which any such foreign application was filed.

§ 1312. Oaths and Acknowledgments

(a) In General.—Oaths and acknowledgments required by this chapter—

(1)   may be made—

(A)   before any person in the United States authorized by law to administer oaths; or

(B)   when made in a foreign country, before any diplomatic or consular officer of the United States authorized to administer oaths, or before any official authorized to administer oaths in the foreign country concerned, whose authority shall be proved by a certificate of a diplomatic or consular officer of the United States; and

(2)   shall be valid if they comply with the laws of the State or country where made.

(b) Written Declaration in Lieu of Oath.—

(1)   The Administrator may by rule prescribe that any document which is to be filed under this chapter in the Office of the Administrator and which is required by any law, rule, or other regulation to be under oath, may be subscribed to by a written declaration in such form as the Administrator may prescribe, and such declaration shall be in lieu of the oath otherwise required.

(2)   Whenever a written declaration under paragraph (1) is used, the document containing the declaration shall state that willful false statements are punishable by fine or imprisonment,

or both, pursuant to section 1001 of title 18, and may jeopardize the validity of the application or document or a registration resulting therefrom.

§ 1313. Examination of Application and Issue or Refusal of Registration

(a) Determination of Registrability of Design; Registration.—Upon the filing of an application for registration in proper form under section 1310, and upon payment of the fee prescribed under section 1316, the Administrator shall determine whether or not the application relates to a design which on its face appears to be subject to protection under this chapter, and, if so, the Register shall register the design. Registration under this subsection shall be announced by publication. The date of registration shall be the date of publication.

(b) Refusal to Register; Reconsideration.—If, in the judgment of the Administrator, the application for registration relates to a design which on its face is not subject to protection under this chapter, the Administrator shall send to the applicant a notice of refusal to register and the grounds for the refusal. Within 3 months after the date on which the notice of refusal is sent, the applicant may, by written request, seek reconsideration of the application. After consideration of such a request, the Administrator shall either register the design or send to the applicant a notice of final refusal to register.

(c) Application to Cancel Registration.—Any person who believes he or she is or will be damaged by a registration under this chapter may, upon payment of the prescribed fee, apply to the Administrator at any time to cancel the registration on the ground that the design is not subject to protection under this chapter, stating the reasons for the request. Upon receipt of an application for cancellation, the Administrator shall send to the owner of the design, as shown in the records of the Office of the Administrator, a notice of the application, and the owner shall have a period of 3 months after the date on which such notice is mailed in which to present arguments to the Administrator for support of the validity of the registration. The Administrator shall also have the authority to establish, by regulation, conditions under which the opposing parties may appear and be heard in support of their arguments. If, after the periods provided for the presentation of arguments have expired, the Administrator determines that the applicant for cancellation has established that the design is not subject to protection under this chapter, the Administrator shall order the registration stricken from the record. Cancellation under this subsection shall be announced by publication, and notice of the Administrator's final determination with respect to any application for cancellation shall be sent to the applicant and to the owner of record. Costs of the cancellation procedure under this subsection shall be borne by the nonprevailing party or parties, and the Administrator shall have the authority to assess and collect such costs.

§ 1314. Certification of Registration

Certificates of registration shall be issued in the name of the United States under the seal of the Office of the Administrator and shall be recorded in the official records of the Office. The certificate shall state the name of the useful article, the date of filing of the application, the date of registration, and the date the design was made public, if earlier than the date of filing of the application, and shall contain a reproduction of the drawing or other pictorial representation of the design. If a description of the salient features of the design appears in the application, the description shall also appear in the certificate. A certificate of registration shall be admitted in any court as prima facie evidence of the facts stated in the certificate.

§ 1315. Publication of Announcements and Indexes

(a) Publications of the Administrator.—The Administrator shall publish lists and indexes of registered designs and cancellations of designs and may also publish the drawings or other pictorial representations of registered designs for sale or other distribution.

(b) File of Representatives of Registered Designs.—The Administrator shall establish and maintain a file of the drawings or other pictorial representations of registered designs. The file shall be available for use by the public under such conditions as the Administrator may prescribe.

§ 1316. Fees

The Administrator shall by regulation set reasonable fees for the filing of applications to register designs under this chapter and for other services relating to the administration of this chapter, taking into consideration the cost of providing these services and the benefit of a public record.

§ 1317. Regulations

The Administrator may establish regulations for the administration of this chapter.

§ 1318. Copies of Records

Upon payment of the prescribed fee, any person may obtain a certified copy of any official record of the Office of the Administrator that relates to this chapter. That copy shall be admissible in evidence with the same effect as the original.

§ 1319. Correction of Errors in Certificates

The Administrator may, by a certificate of correction under seal, correct any error in a registration incurred through the fault of the Office, or, upon payment of the required fee, any error of a clerical or typographical nature occurring in good faith but not through the fault of the Office. Such registration, together with the certificate, shall thereafter have the same effect as if it had been originally issued in such corrected form.

§ 1320. Ownership and Transfer

(a) Property Right in Design.—The property right in a design subject to protection under this chapter shall vest in the designer, the legal representatives of a deceased designer or of one under legal incapacity, the employer for whom the designer created the design in the case of a design made within the regular scope of the designer's employment, or a person to whom the rights of the designer or of such employer have been transferred. The person in whom the property right is vested shall be considered the owner of the design.

(b) Transfer of Property Right.—The property right in a registered design, or a design for which an application for registration has been or may be filed, may be assigned, granted, conveyed, or mortgaged by an instrument in writing, signed by the owner, or may be bequeathed by will.

(c) Oath or Acknowledgment of Transfer.—An oath or acknowledgment under section 1312 shall be prima facie evidence of the execution of an assignment, grant, conveyance, or mortgage under subsection (b).

(d) Recordation of Transfer.—An assignment, grant, conveyance, or mortgage under subsection (b) shall be void as against any subsequent purchaser or mortgagee for a valuable consideration, unless it is recorded in the Office of the Administrator within 3 months after its date of execution or before the date of such subsequent purchase or mortgage.

§ 1321. Remedy for Infringement

(a) In General.—The owner of a design is entitled, after issuance of a certificate of registration of the design under this chapter, to institute an action for any infringement of the design.

(b) Review of Refusal to Register.—

(1) Subject to paragraph (2), the owner of a design may seek judicial review of a final refusal of the Administrator to register the design under this chapter by bringing a civil action,

and may in the same action, if the court adjudges the design subject to protection under this chapter, enforce the rights in that design under this chapter.

(2) The owner of a design may seek judicial review under this section if—

(A) the owner has previously duly filed and prosecuted to final refusal an application in proper form for registration of the design;

(B) the owner causes a copy of the complaint in the action to be delivered to the Administrator within 10 days after the commencement of the action; and

(C) the defendant has committed acts in respect to the design which would constitute infringement with respect to a design protected under this chapter.

(c) Administrator as Party to Action.—The Administrator may, at the Administrator's option, become a party to the action with respect to the issue of registrability of the design claim by entering an appearance within 60 days after being served with the complaint, but the failure of the Administrator to become a party shall not deprive the court of jurisdiction to determine that issue.

(d) Use of Arbitration to Resolve Dispute.—The parties to an infringement dispute under this chapter, within such time as may be specified by the Administrator by regulation, may determine the dispute, or any aspect of the dispute, by arbitration. Arbitration shall be governed by title 9. The parties shall give notice of any arbitration award to the Administrator, and such award shall, as between the parties to the arbitration, be dispositive of the issues to which it relates. The arbitration award shall be unenforceable until such notice is given. Nothing in this subsection shall preclude the Administrator from determining whether a design is subject to registration in a cancellation proceeding under section 1313(c).

§ 1322. Injunctions

(a) In General.—A court having jurisdiction over actions under this chapter may grant injunctions in accordance with the principles of equity to prevent infringement of a design under this chapter, including, in its discretion, prompt relief by temporary restraining orders and preliminary injunctions.

(b) Damages for Injunctive Relief Wrongfully Obtained.—A seller or distributor who suffers damage by reason of injunctive relief wrongfully obtained under this section has a cause of action against the applicant for such injunctive relief and may recover such relief as may be appropriate, including damages for lost profits, cost of materials, loss of good will, and punitive damages in instances where the injunctive relief was sought in bad faith, and, unless the court finds extenuating circumstances, reasonable attorney's fees.

§ 1323. Recovery for Infringement

(a) Damages.—Upon a finding for the claimant in an action for infringement under this chapter, the court shall award the claimant damages adequate to compensate for the infringement. In addition, the court may increase the damages to such amount, not exceeding $50,000 or $1 per copy, whichever is greater, as the court determines to be just. The damages awarded shall constitute compensation and not a penalty. The court may receive expert testimony as an aid to the determination of damages.

(b) Infringer's Profits.—As an alternative to the remedies provided in subsection (a), the court may award the claimant the infringer's profits resulting from the sale of the copies if the court finds that the infringer's sales are reasonably related to the use of the claimant's design. In such a case, the claimant shall be required to prove only the amount of the infringer's sales and the infringer shall be required to prove its expenses against such sales.

(c) Statute of Limitations.—No recovery under subsection (a) or (b) shall be had for any infringement committed more than 3 years before the date on which the complaint is filed.

(d) Attorney's Fees.—In an action for infringement under this chapter, the court may award reasonable attorney's fees to the prevailing party.

(e) Disposition of Infringing and Other Articles.—The court may order that all infringing articles, and any plates, molds, patterns, models, or other means specifically adapted for making the articles, be delivered up for destruction or other disposition as the court may direct.

§ 1324. Power of Court Over Registration

In any action involving the protection of a design under this chapter, the court, when appropriate, may order registration of a design under this chapter or the cancellation of such a registration. Any such order shall be certified by the court to the Administrator, who shall make an appropriate entry upon the record.

§ 1325. Liability for Action on Registration Fraudulently Obtained

Any person who brings an action for infringement knowing that registration of the design was obtained by a false or fraudulent representation materially affecting the rights under this chapter, shall be liable in the sum of $10,000, or such part of that amount as the court may determine. That amount shall be to compensate the defendant and shall be charged against the plaintiff and paid to the defendant, in addition to such costs and attorney's fees of the defendant as may be assessed by the court.

§ 1326. Penalty for False Marking

(a) In General.—Whoever, for the purpose of deceiving the public, marks upon, applies to, or uses in advertising in connection with an article made, used, distributed, or sold, a design which is not protected under this chapter, a design notice specified in section 1306, or any other words or symbols importing that the design is protected under this chapter, knowing that the design is not so protected, shall pay a civil fine of not more than $500 for each such offense.

(b) Suit by Private Persons.—Any person may sue for the penalty established by subsection (a), in which event one-half of the penalty shall be awarded to the person suing and the remainder shall be awarded to the United States.

§ 1327. Penalty for False Representation

Whoever knowingly makes a false representation materially affecting the rights obtainable under this chapter for the purpose of obtaining registration of a design under this chapter shall pay a penalty of not less than $500 and not more than $1,000, and any rights or privileges that individual may have in the design under this chapter shall be forfeited.

§ 1328. Enforcement by Treasury and Postal Service

(a) Regulations.—The Secretary of the Treasury and the United States Postal Service shall separately or jointly issue regulations for the enforcement of the rights set forth in section 1308 with respect to importation. Such regulations may require, as a condition for the exclusion of articles from the United States, that the person seeking exclusion take any one or more of the following actions:

(1) Obtain a court order enjoining, or an order of the International Trade Commission under section 337 of the Tariff Act of 1930 excluding, importation of the articles.

(2) Furnish proof that the design involved is protected under this chapter and that the importation of the articles would infringe the rights in the design under this chapter.

(3) Post a surety bond for any injury that may result if the detention or exclusion of the articles proves to be unjustified.

(b) Seizure and Forfeiture.—Articles imported in violation of the rights set forth in section 1308 are subject to seizure and forfeiture in the same manner as property imported in violation of the customs laws. Any such forfeited articles shall be destroyed as directed by the Secretary of the Treasury or the court, as the case may be, except that the articles may be returned to the country of export whenever it is shown to the satisfaction of the Secretary of the Treasury that the importer had no reasonable grounds for believing that his or her acts constituted a violation of the law.

§ 1329. Relation to Design Patent Law

The issuance of a design patent under title 35, United States Code, for an original design for an article of manufacture shall terminate any protection of the original design under this chapter.

§ 1330. Common Law and Other Rights Unaffected

Nothing in this chapter shall annual or limit—

(1)   common law or other rights or remedies, if any, available to or held by any person with respect to a design which has not been registered under this chapter; or

(2)   any right under the trademark laws or any right protected against unfair competition.

§ 1331. Administrator; Office of the Administrator

In this chapter, the "Administrator" is the Register of Copyrights, and the "Office of the Administrator" and the "Office" refer to the Copyright Office of the Library of Congress.

§ 1332. No Retroactive Effect

Protection under this chapter shall not be available for any design that has been made public under section 1310(b) before the effective date of this chapter.

H. UNAUTHORIZED USE OF PRE-1972 SOUND RECORDINGS

17 U.S.C.A. § 1401

§ 1401. Unauthorized use of pre-1972 sound recordings

(a) In general.—

(1) Unauthorized acts.—Anyone who, on or before the last day of the applicable transition period under paragraph (2), and without the consent of the rights owner, engages in covered activity with respect to a sound recording fixed before February 15, 1972, shall be subject to the remedies provided in sections 502 through 505 and 1203 to the same extent as an infringer of copyright or a person that engages in unauthorized activity under chapter 12.

(2) Term of prohibition.—

(A) In general.—The prohibition under paragraph (1)—

(i) subject to clause (ii), shall apply to a sound recording described in that paragraph—

(I) through December 31 of the year that is 95 years after the year of first publication; and

(II) for a further transition period as prescribed under subparagraph (B) of this paragraph; and

(ii) shall not apply to any sound recording after February 15, 2067.

(B) Transition periods.—

(i) Pre-1923 recordings.—In the case of a sound recording first published before January 1, 1923, the transition period described in subparagraph (A)(i)(II) shall end on December 31 of the year that is 3 years after the date of enactment of this section.

(ii) 1923–1946 recordings.—In the case of a sound recording first published during the period beginning on January 1, 1923, and ending on December 31, 1946, the transition period described in subparagraph (A)(i)(II) shall end on the date that is 5 years after the last day of the period described in subparagraph (A)(i)(I).

(iii) 1947–1956 recordings.—In the case of a sound recording first published during the period beginning on January 1, 1947, and ending on December 31, 1956, the transition period described in subparagraph (A)(i)(II) shall end on the date that is 15 years after the last day of the period described in subparagraph (A)(i)(I).

(iv) Post-1956 recordings.—In the case of a sound recording fixed before February 15, 1972, that is not described in clause (i), (ii), or (iii), the transition period described in subparagraph (A)(i)(II) shall end on February 15, 2067.

(3) Rule of construction.—For the purposes of this subsection, the term "anyone" includes any State, any instrumentality of a State, and any officer or employee of a State or instrumentality of a State acting in the official capacity of the officer or employee, as applicable.

(b) Certain authorized transmissions and reproductions.—A public performance by means of a digital audio transmission of a sound recording fixed before February 15, 1972, or a reproduction in an ephemeral phonorecord or copy of a sound recording fixed before February 15, 1972, shall, for purposes of subsection (a), be considered to be authorized and made with the consent of the rights owner if—

(1) the transmission or reproduction would satisfy the requirements for statutory licensing under section 112(e)(1) or section 114(d)(2), or would be exempt under section 114(d)(1), as the case may be, if the sound recording were fixed on or after February 15, 1972; and

(2) the transmitting entity pays the statutory royalty for the transmission or reproduction pursuant to the rates and terms adopted under sections 112(e)and 114(f), and complies with other obligations, in the same manner as required by regulations adopted by the Copyright Royalty Judges under sections 112(e) and 114(f) for sound recordings that are fixed on or after February 15, 1972, except in the case of a transmission that would be exempt under section 114(d)(1).

(c) **Certain noncommercial uses of sound recordings that are not being commercially exploited.—**

(1) **In general.—**Noncommercial use of a sound recording fixed before February 15, 1972, that is not being commercially exploited by or under the authority of the rights owner shall not violate subsection (a) if—

(A) the person engaging in the noncommercial use, in order to determine whether the sound recording is being commercially exploited by or under the authority of the rights owner, makes a good faith, reasonable search for, but does not find, the sound recording—

(i) in the records of schedules filed in the Copyright Office as described in subsection (f)(5)(A); and

(ii) on services offering a comprehensive set of sound recordings for sale or streaming;

(B) the person engaging in the noncommercial use files a notice identifying the sound recording and the nature of the use in the Copyright Office in accordance with the regulations issued under paragraph (3)(B); and

(C) during the 90-day period beginning on the date on which the notice described in subparagraph (B) is indexed into the public records of the Copyright Office, the rights owner of the sound recording does not, in its discretion, opt out of the noncommercial use by filing notice thereof in the Copyright Office in accordance with the regulations issued under paragraph (5).

(2) **Rules of construction.—**For purposes of this subsection—

(A) merely recovering costs of production and distribution of a sound recording resulting from a use otherwise permitted under this subsection does not itself necessarily constitute a commercial use of the sound recording;

(B) the fact that a person engaging in the use of a sound recording also engages in commercial activities does not itself necessarily render the use commercial; and

(C) the fact that a person files notice of a noncommercial use of a sound recording in accordance with the regulations issued under paragraph (3)(B) does not itself affect any limitation on the exclusive rights of a copyright owner described in section 107, 108, 109, 110, or 112(f) as applied to a claim under subsection (a) of this section pursuant to subsection (f)(1)(A) of this section.

(3) **Notice of covered activity.—**Not later than 180 days after the date of enactment of this section, the Register of Copyrights shall issue regulations that—

(A) provide specific, reasonable steps that, if taken by a filer, are sufficient to constitute a good faith, reasonable search under paragraph (1)(A) to determine whether a recording is being commercially exploited, including the services that satisfy the good faith, reasonable search requirement under paragraph (1)(A) for purposes of the safe harbor described in paragraph (4)(A); and

(B) establish the form, content, and procedures for the filing of notices under paragraph (1)(B).

(4) Safe harbor.—

(A) In general.—A person engaging in a noncommercial use of a sound recording otherwise permitted under this subsection who establishes that the person made a good faith, reasonable search under paragraph (1)(A) without finding commercial exploitation of the sound recording by or under the authority of the rights owner shall not be found to be in violation of subsection (a).

(B) Steps sufficient but not necessary.—Taking the specific, reasonable steps identified by the Register of Copyrights in the regulations issued under paragraph (3)(A) shall be sufficient, but not necessary, for a filer to satisfy the requirement to conduct a good faith, reasonable search under paragraph (1)(A) for purposes of subparagraph (A) of this paragraph.

(5) Opting out of covered activity.—

(A) In general.—Not later than 180 days after the date of enactment of this section, the Register of Copyrights shall issue regulations establishing the form, content, and procedures for the rights owner of a sound recording that is the subject of a notice under paragraph (1)(B) to, in its discretion, file notice opting out of the covered activity described in the notice under paragraph (1)(B) during the 90-day period beginning on the date on which the notice under paragraph (1)(B) is indexed into the public records of the Copyright Office.

(B) Rule of construction.—The fact that a rights holder opts out of a noncommercial use of a sound recording by filing notice thereof in the Copyright Office in accordance with the regulations issued under subparagraph (A) does not itself enlarge or diminish any limitation on the exclusive rights of a copyright owner described in section 107, 108, 109, 110, or 112(f) as applied to a claim under subsection (a) of this section pursuant to subsection (f)(1)(A) of this section.

(6) Civil penalties for certain acts.—

(A) Filing of notices of noncommercial use.—Any person who willfully engages in a pattern or practice of filing a notice of noncommercial use of a sound recording as described in paragraph (1)(B) fraudulently describing the use proposed, or knowing that the use proposed is not permitted under this subsection, shall be assessed a civil penalty in an amount that is not less than $250, and not more than $1000, for each such notice, in addition to any other remedies that may be available under this title based on the actual use made.

(B) Filing of opt-out notices.—

(i) In general.—Any person who files an opt-out notice as described in paragraph (1)(C), knowing that the person is not the rights owner or authorized to act on behalf of the rights owner of the sound recording to which the notice pertains, shall be assessed a civil penalty in an amount not less than $250, and not more than $1,000, for each such notice.

(ii) Pattern or practice.—Any person who engages in a pattern or practice of making filings as described in clause (i) shall be assessed a civil penalty in an amount not less than $10,000 for each such filing.

(C) Definition.—For purposes of this paragraph, the term "knowing"—

(i) does not require specific intent to defraud; and

(ii) with respect to information about ownership of the sound recording in question, means that the person—

(I) has actual knowledge of the information;

(II) acts in deliberate ignorance of the truth or falsity of the information; or

(III) acts in grossly negligent disregard of the truth or falsity of the information.

(d) Payment of royalties for transmissions of performances by direct licensing of statutory services.—

(1) In general.—A public performance by means of a digital audio transmission of a sound recording fixed before February 15, 1972, shall, for purposes of subsection (a), be considered to be authorized and made with the consent of the rights owner if the transmission is made pursuant to a license agreement voluntarily negotiated at any time between the rights owner and the entity performing the sound recording.

(2) Payment of royalties to nonprofit collective under certain license agreements.—

(A) Licenses entered into on or after date of enactment.—To the extent that a license agreement described in paragraph (1) entered into on or after the date of enactment of this section extends to a public performance by means of a digital audio transmission of a sound recording fixed before February 15, 1972, that meets the conditions of subsection (b)—

(i) the licensee shall, with respect to such transmission, pay to the collective designated to distribute receipts from the licensing of transmissions in accordance with section 114(f), 50 percent of the performance royalties for that transmission due under the license; and

(ii) the royalties paid under clause (i) shall be fully credited as payments due under the license.

(B) Certain agreements entered into before enactment.—To the extent that a license agreement described in paragraph (1), entered into during the period beginning on January 1 of the year in which this section is enacted and ending on the day before the date of enactment of this section, or a settlement agreement with a preexisting satellite digital audio radio service (as defined in section 114(j)) entered into during the period beginning on January 1, 2015, and ending on the day before the date of enactment of this section, extends to a public performance by means of a digital audio transmission of a sound recording fixed before February 15, 1972, that meets the conditions of subsection (b)—

(i) the rights owner shall, with respect to such transmission, pay to the collective designated to distribute receipts from the licensing of transmissions in accordance with section 114(f) an amount that is equal to the difference between—

(I) 50 percent of the difference between—

(aa) the rights owner's total gross performance royalty fee receipts or settlement monies received for all such transmissions covered under the license or settlement agreement, as applicable; and

(bb) the rights owner's total payments for outside legal expenses, including any payments of third-party claims, that are directly attributable to the license or settlement agreement, as applicable; and

(II) the amount of any royalty receipts or settlement monies under the agreement that are distributed by the rights owner to featured and nonfeatured artists before the date of enactment of this section; and

(ii) the royalties paid under clause (i) shall be fully credited as payments due under the license or settlement agreement, as applicable.

(3) Distribution of royalties and settlement monies by collective.—The collective described in paragraph (2) shall, in accordance with subparagraphs (B) through (D) of section 114(g)(2), and paragraphs (5) and (6) of section 114(g), distribute the royalties or settlement monies received under paragraph (2) under a license or settlement described in paragraph (2), which shall be the only payments to which featured and nonfeatured artists are entitled by virtue of the transmissions described in paragraph (2), except for settlement monies described in paragraph (2) that are distributed by the rights owner to featured and nonfeatured artists before the date of enactment of this section.

(4) Payment of royalties under license agreements entered before enactment or not otherwise described in paragraph (2).—

(A) In general.—To the extent that a license agreement described in paragraph (1) entered into before the date of enactment of this section, or any other license agreement not as described in paragraph (2), extends to a public performance by means of a digital audio transmission of a sound recording fixed before February 15, 1972, that meets the conditions of subsection (b), the payments made by the licensee pursuant to the license shall be made in accordance with the agreement.

(B) Additional payments not required.—To the extent that a licensee has made, or will make in the future, payments pursuant to a license as described in subparagraph (A), the provisions of paragraphs (2) and (3) shall not require any additional payments from, or additional financial obligations on the part of, the licensee.

(C) Rule of construction.—Nothing in this subsection may be construed to prohibit the collective designated to distribute receipts from the licensing of transmissions in accordance with section 114(f) from administering royalty payments under any license not described in paragraph (2).

(e) Preemption with respect to certain past acts.—

(1) In general.—This section preempts any claim of common law copyright or equivalent right under the laws of any State arising from a digital audio transmission or reproduction that is made before the date of enactment of this section of a sound recording fixed before February 15, 1972, if—

(A) the digital audio transmission would have satisfied the requirements for statutory licensing under section 114(d)(2) or been exempt under section 114(d)(1), or the reproduction would have satisfied the requirements of section 112(e)(1), as the case may be, if the sound recording were fixed on or after February 15, 1972; and

(B) either—

(i) except in the case of a transmission that would have been exempt under section 114(d)(1), not later than 270 days after the date of enactment of this section, the transmitting entity pays statutory royalties and provides notice of the use of the relevant sound recordings in the same manner as required by regulations adopted by the Copyright Royalty Judges for sound recordings that are fixed on or after February 15, 1972, for all the digital audio transmissions and reproductions satisfying the requirements for statutory licensing under sections 112(e)(1) and 114(d)(2) during the 3 years before that date of enactment; or

(ii) an agreement voluntarily negotiated between the rights owner and the entity performing the sound recording (including a litigation settlement agreement entered into before the date of enactment of this section) authorizes or waives liability for any such transmission or reproduction and the transmitting entity has paid for and reported such digital audio transmission under that agreement.

(2) Rule of construction for common law copyright.—For purposes of paragraph (1), a claim of common law copyright or equivalent right under the laws of any State includes a claim that characterizes conduct subject to that paragraph as an unlawful distribution, act of record piracy, or similar violation.

(3) Rule of construction for public performance rights.—Nothing in this section may be construed to recognize or negate the existence of public performance rights in sound recordings under the laws of any State.

(f) Limitations on remedies.—

(1) Fair use; uses by libraries, archives, and educational institutions.—

(A) In general.—The limitations on the exclusive rights of a copyright owner described in sections 107, 108, 109, 110, and 112(f) shall apply to a claim under subsection (a) with respect to a sound recording fixed before February 15, 1972.

(B) Rule of construction for section 108(h).—With respect to the application of section 108(h) to a claim under subsection (a) with respect to a sound recording fixed before February 15, 1972, the phrase "during the last 20 years of any term of copyright of a published work" in such section 108(h)shall be construed to mean at any time after the date of enactment of this section.

(2) Actions.—The limitations on actions described in section 507 shall apply to a claim under subsection (a) with respect to a sound recording fixed before February 15, 1972.

(3) Material online.—Section 512 shall apply to a claim under subsection (a) with respect to a sound recording fixed before February 15, 1972.

(4) Principles of equity.—Principles of equity apply to remedies for a violation of this section to the same extent as such principles apply to remedies for infringement of copyright.

(5) Filing requirement for statutory damages and attorneys' fees.—

(A) Filing of information on sound recordings.—

(i) Filing requirement.—Except in the case of a transmitting entity that has filed contact information for that transmitting entity under subparagraph (B), in any action under this section, an award of statutory damages or of attorneys' fees under section 504 or 505 may be made with respect to an unauthorized use of a sound recording under subsection (a) only if—

(I) the rights owner has filed with the Copyright Office a schedule that specifies the title, artist, and rights owner of the sound recording and contains such other information, as practicable, as the Register of Copyrights prescribes by regulation; and

(II) the use occurs after the end of the 90-day period beginning on the date on which the information described in subclause (I) is indexed into the public records of the Copyright Office.

(ii) Regulations.—Not later than 180 days after the date of enactment of this section, the Register of Copyrights shall issue regulations that—

(I) establish the form, content, and procedures for the filing of schedules under clause (i);

(II) provide that a person may request that the person receive timely notification of a filing described in subclause (I); and

(III) set forth the manner in which a person may make a request under subclause (II).

(B) Filing of contact information for transmitting entities.—

(i) Filing requirement.—Not later than 30 days after the date of enactment of this section, the Register of Copyrights shall issue regulations establishing the form, content, and procedures for the filing of contact information by any entity that, as of the date of enactment of this section, performs a sound recording fixed before February 15, 1972, by means of a digital audio transmission.

(ii) Time limit on filings.—The Register of Copyrights may accept filings under clause (i) only until the 180th day after the date of enactment of this section.

(iii) Limitation on statutory damages and attorneys' fees.—

(I) Limitation.—An award of statutory damages or of attorneys' fees under section 504 or 505 may not be made against an entity that has filed contact information for that entity under clause (i) with respect to an unauthorized use by that entity of a sound recording under subsection (a) if the use occurs before the end of the 90-day period beginning on the date on which the entity receives a notice that—

(aa) is sent by or on behalf of the rights owner of the sound recording;

(bb) states that the entity is not legally authorized to use that sound recording under subsection (a); and

(cc) identifies the sound recording in a schedule conforming to the requirements prescribed by the regulations issued under subparagraph (A)(ii).

(II) Undeliverable notices.—In any case in which a notice under subclause (I) is sent to an entity by mail or courier service and the notice is returned to the sender because the entity either is no longer located at the address provided in the contact information filed under clause (i) or has refused to accept delivery, or the notice is sent by electronic mail and is undeliverable, the 90-day period under subclause (I) shall begin on the date of the attempted delivery.

(C) Section 412.—Section 412 shall not limit an award of statutory damages under section 504(c) or attorneys' fees under section 505 with respect to a covered activity in violation of subsection (a).

(6) Applicability of other provisions.—

(A) In general.—Subject to subparagraph (B), no provision of this title shall apply to or limit the remedies available under this section except as otherwise provided in this section.

(B) Applicability of definitions.—Any term used in this section that is defined in section 101 shall have the meaning given that term in section 101.

(g) Application of section 230 safe harbor.—For purposes of section 230 of the Communications Act of 1934 (47 U.S.C. 230), subsection (a) shall be considered to be a "law pertaining to intellectual property" under subsection (e)(2) of such section 230.

(h) Application to rights owners.—

(1) Transfers.—With respect to a rights owner described in subsection (*l*)(2)(B)—

(A) subsections (d) and (e) of section 201 and section 204 shall apply to a transfer described in subsection (*l*)(2)(B) to the same extent as with respect to a transfer of copyright ownership; and

(B) notwithstanding section 411, that rights owner may institute an action with respect to a violation of this section to the same extent as the owner of an exclusive right under a copyright may institute an action under section 501(b).

(2) Application of other provisions.—The following provisions shall apply to a rights owner under this section to the same extent as any copyright owner:

(A) Section 112(e)(2).

    (B) Section 112(e)(7).

    (C) Section 114(e).

    (D) Section 114(h).

(i) **Ephemeral recordings.**—An authorized reproduction made under this section shall be subject to section 112(g) to the same extent as a reproduction of a sound recording fixed on or after February 15, 1972.

(j) **Rule of construction.**—A rights owner of, or featured recording artist who performs on, a sound recording under this chapter shall be deemed to be an interested copyright party, as defined in section 1001, to the same extent as a copyright owner or featured recording artist under chapter 10.

(k) **Treatment of States and State instrumentalities, officers, and employees.**—Any State, and any instrumentality, officer, or employee described in subsection (a)(3), shall be subject to the provisions of this section in the same manner and to the same extent as any nongovernmental entity.

(l) **Definitions.**—In this section:

    (1) **Covered activity.**—The term "covered activity" means any activity that the copyright owner of a sound recording would have the exclusive right to do or authorize under section 106 or 602, or that would violate section 1201 or 1202, if the sound recording were fixed on or after February 15, 1972.

    (2) **Rights owner.**—The term "rights owner" means—

        (A) the person that has the exclusive right to reproduce a sound recording under the laws of any State, as of the day before the date of enactment of this section; or

        (B) any person to which a right to enforce a violation of this section may be transferred, in whole or in part, after the date of enactment of this section, under—

            (i) subsections (d) and (e) of section 201; and

            (ii) section 204.

I. BERNE CONVENTION FOR THE PROTECTION OF LITERARY AND ARTISTIC WORKS

(Paris Act of July 24, 1971, as amended on September 28, 1979)

Article 1

[Establishment of a Union][1]

The countries to which this Convention applies constitute a Union for the protection of the rights of authors in their literary and artistic works.

Article 2

[Protected Works: 1. "Literary and artistic works"; 2. Possible requirement of fixation; 3. Derivative works; 4. Official texts; 5. Collections; 6. Obligation to protect; beneficiaries of protection; 7. Works of applied art and industrial designs; 8. News]

(1)   The expression "literary and artistic works" shall include every production in the literary, scientific and artistic domain, whatever may be the mode or form of its expression, such as books, pamphlets and other writings; lectures, addresses, sermons and other works of the same nature; dramatic or dramatico-musical works; choreographic works and entertainments in dumb show; musical compositions with or without words; cinematographic works to which are assimilated works expressed by a process analogous to cinematography; works of drawing, painting, architecture, sculpture, engraving and lithography; photographic works to which are assimilated works expressed by a process analogous to photography; works of applied art; illustrations, maps, plans, sketches and three-dimensional works relative to geography, topography, architecture or science.

(2)   It shall, however, be a matter for legislation in the countries of the Union to prescribe that works in general or any specified categories of works shall not be protected unless they have been fixed in some material form.

(3)   Translations, adaptations, arrangements of music and other alterations of a literary or artistic work shall be protected as original works without prejudice to the copyright in the original work.

(4)   It shall be a matter for legislation in the countries of the Union to determine the protection to be granted to official texts of a legislative, administrative and legal nature, and to official translations of such texts.

(5)   Collections of literary or artistic works such as encyclopaedias and anthologies which, by reason of the selection and arrangement of their contents, constitute intellectual creations shall be protected as such, without prejudice to the copyright in each of the works forming part of such collections.

(6)   The works mentioned in this Article shall enjoy protection in all countries of the Union. This protection shall operate for the benefit of the author and his successors in title.

(7)   Subject to the provisions of Article 7(4) of this Convention, it shall be a matter for legislation in the countries of the Union to determine the extent of the application of their laws to works of applied art and industrial designs and models, as well as the conditions under which such works, designs and models shall be protected. Works protected in the country of origin solely as designs and models shall be entitled in another country of the Union only to such special protection as is granted in that country to designs and models; however, if no such special protection is granted in that country, such works shall be protected as artistic works.

---

[1]   Each Article and the Appendix have been given titles to facilitate their identification. There are no titles in the signed (English) text.

(8)   The protection of this Convention shall not apply to news of the day or to miscellaneous facts having the character of mere items of press information.

Article 2bis

[Possible Limitation of Protection of Certain Works: 1. Certain speeches; 2. Certain uses of lectures and addresses; 3. Right to make collections of such works]

(1)   It shall be a matter for legislation in the countries of the Union to exclude, wholly or in part, from the protection provided by the preceding Article political speeches and speeches delivered in the course of legal proceedings.

(2)   It shall also be a matter for legislation in the countries of the Union to determine the conditions under which lectures, addresses and other works of the same nature which are delivered in public may be reproduced by the press, broadcast, communicated to the public by wire and made the subject of public communication as envisaged in Article IIbis(I) of this Convention, when such use is justified by the informatory purpose.

(3)   Nevertheless, the author shall enjoy the exclusive right of making a collection of his works mentioned in the preceding paragraphs.

Article 3

[Criteria of Eligibility for Protection: 1. Nationality of author; place of publication of work; 2. Residence of author; 3. "Published" works; 4. "Simultaneously published" works]

(1)   The protection of this Convention shall apply to:

(a)   authors who are nationals of one of the countries of the Union, for their works, whether published or not;

(b)   authors who are not nationals of one of the countries of the Union, for their works first published in one of those countries, or simultaneously in a country outside the Union and in a country of the Union.

(2)   Authors who are not nationals of one of the countries of the Union but who have their habitual residence in one of them shall, for the purposes of this Convention, be assimilated to nationals of that country.

(3)   The expression "published works" means works published with the consent of their authors, whatever may be the means of manufacture of the copies, provided that the availability of such copies has been such as to satisfy the reasonable requirements of the public, having regard to the nature of the work. The performance of a dramatic, dramatico-musical, cinematographic or musical work, the public recitation of a literary work, the communication by wire or the broadcasting of literary or artistic works, the exhibition of a work of art and the construction of a work of architecture shall not constitute publication.

(4)   A work shall be considered as having been published simultaneously in several countries if it has been published in two or more countries within thirty days of its first publication.

Article 4

[Criteria of Eligibility for Protection of Cinematographic Works, Works of Architecture and Certain Artistic Works]

The protection of this Convention shall apply, even if the conditions of Article 3 are not fulfilled, to:

(a)   authors of cinematographic works the maker of which has his headquarters or habitual residence in one of the countries of the Union;

(b)   authors of works of architecture erected in a country of the Union or of other artistic works incorporated in a building or other structure located in a country of the Union.

Article 5

[Rights Guaranteed: 1. and 2. Outside the country of origin; 3. In the country of origin; 4. "Country of origin"]

(1)   Authors shall enjoy, in respect of works for which they are protected under this Convention, in countries of the Union other than the country of origin, the rights which their respective laws do now or may hereafter grant to their nationals, as well as the rights specially granted by this Convention.

(2)   The enjoyment and the exercise of these rights shall not be subject to any formality; such enjoyment and such exercise shall be independent of the existence of protection in the country of origin of the work. Consequently, apart from the provisions of this Convention, the extent of protection, as well as the means of redress afforded to the author to protect his rights, shall be governed exclusively by the laws of the country where protection is claimed.

(3)   Protection in the country of origin is governed by domestic law. However, when the author is not a national of the country of origin of the work for which he is protected under this Convention, he shall enjoy in that country the same rights as national authors.

(4)   The country of origin shall be considered to be:

(a)   in the case of works first published in a country of the Union, that country; in the case of works published simultaneously in several countries of the Union which grant different terms of protection, the country whose legislation grants the shortest term of protection;

(b)   in the case of works published simultaneously in a country outside the Union and in a country of the Union, the latter country;

(c)   in the case of unpublished works or of works first published in a country outside the Union, without simultaneous publication in a country of the Union, the country of the Union of which the author is a national, provided that:

(i)   when these are cinematographic works the maker of which has his headquarters or his habitual residence in a country of the Union, the country of origin shall be that country, and

(ii)   when these are works of architecture erected in a country of the Union or other artistic works incorporated in a building or other structure located in a country of the Union, the country of origin shall be that country.

Article 6

[Possible Restriction of Protection In Respect of Certain Works of Nationals of Certain Countries Outside the Union: 1. In the country of the first publication and in other countries; 2. No retroactivity; 3. Notice]

(1)   Where any country outside the Union fails to protect in an adequate manner the works of authors who are nationals of one of the countries of the Union, the latter country may restrict the protection given to the works of authors who are, at the date of the first publication thereof, nationals of the other country and are not habitually resident in one of the countries of the Union. If the country of first publication avails itself of this right, the other countries of the Union shall not be required to grant to works thus subjected to special treatment a wider protection than that granted to them in the country of first publication.

(2)   No restrictions introduced by virtue of the preceding paragraph shall affect the rights which an author may have acquired in respect of a work published in a country of the Union before such restrictions were put into force.

(3)   The countries of the Union which restrict the grant of copyright in accordance with this Article shall give notice thereof to the Director General of the World Intellectual Property

Organisation (hereinafter designated as "the Director General") by a written declaration specifying the countries in regard to which protection is restricted, and the restrictions to which rights of authors who are nationals of those countries are subjected. The Director General shall immediately communicate this declaration to all the countries of the Union.

Article 6*bis*

[*Moral Rights:* 1. To claim authorship; to object to certain modifications and other derogatory actions; 2. After the author's death; 3. Means of redress]

(1)   Independently of the author's economic rights, and even after the transfer of the said rights, the author shall have the right to claim authorship of the work and to object to any distortion, mutilation or other modification of, or other derogatory action in relation to, the said work, which would be prejudicial to his honour or reputation.

(2)   The rights granted to the author in accordance with the preceding paragraph shall, after his death, be maintained, at least until the expiry of the economic rights, and shall be exercisable by the persons or institutions authorised by the legislation of the country where protection is claimed. However, those countries whose legislation, at the moment of their ratification of or accession to this Act, does not provide for the protection after the death of the author of all the rights set out in the preceding paragraph may provide that some of these rights may, after his death, cease to be maintained.

(3)   The means of redress for safeguarding the rights granted by this Article shall be governed by the legislation of the country where protection is claimed.

Article 7

[*Term of Protection:* 1. Generally; 2. For cinematographic works; 3. For anonymous and pseudonymous works; 4. For photographic works and works of applied art; 5. Starting date of computation; 6. Longer terms; 7. Shorter terms; 8. Applicable law; "comparison" of terms]

(1)   The term of protection granted by this Convention shall be the life of the author and fifty years after his death.

(2)   However, in the case of cinematographic works, the countries of the Union may provide that the term of protection shall expire fifty years after the work has been made available to the public with the consent of the author, or, failing such an event within fifty years from the making of such a work, fifty years after the making.

(3)   In the case of anonymous or pseudonymous works, the term of protection granted by this Convention shall expire fifty years after the work has been lawfully made available to the public. However, when the pseudonym adopted by the author leaves no doubt as to his identity, the term of protection shall be that provided in paragraph (1). If the author of an anonymous or pseudonymous work discloses his identity during the above-mentioned period, the term of protection applicable shall be that provided in paragraph (1). The countries of the Union shall not be required to protect anonymous or pseudonymous works in respect of which it is reasonable to presume that their author has been dead for fifty years.

(4)   It shall be a matter for legislation in the countries of the Union to determine the term of protection of photographic works and that of works of applied art in so far as they are protected as artistic works; however, this term shall last at least until the end of a period of twenty-five years from the making of such a work.

(5)   The term of protection subsequent to the death of the author and the terms provided by paragraphs (2), (3) and (4) shall run from the date of death or of the event referred to in those paragraphs, but such terms shall always be deemed to begin on the first of January of the year following the death or such event.

(6)   The countries of the Union may grant a term of protection in excess of those provided by the preceding paragraphs.

(7)   Those countries of the Union bound by the Rome Act of this Convention which grant, in their national legislation in force at the time of signature of the present Act, shorter terms of protection than those provided for in the preceding paragraphs shall have the right to maintain such terms when ratifying or acceding to the present Act.

(8)   In any case, the term shall be governed by the legislation of the country where protection is claimed; however, unless the legislation of that country otherwise provides, the term shall not exceed the term fixed in the country of origin of the work.

Article 7*bis*

[Term of Protection for Works of Joint Authorship]

The provisions of the preceding Article shall also apply in the case of a work of joint authorship, provided that the terms measured from the death of the author shall be calculated from the death of the last surviving author.

Article 8

[Right of Translation]

Authors of literary and artistic works protected by this Convention shall enjoy the exclusive right of making and of authorising the translation of their works throughout the term of protection of their rights in the original works.

Article 9

[Right of Reproduction: 1. Generally; 2. Possible exceptions; 3. Sound and visual recordings]

(1)   Authors of literary and artistic works protected by this Convention shall have the exclusive right of authorising the reproduction of these works, in any manner or form.

(2)   It shall be a matter for legislation in the countries of the Union to permit the reproduction of such works in certain special cases, provided that such reproduction does not conflict with a normal exploitation of the work and does not unreasonably prejudice the legitimate interests of the author.

(3)   Any sound or visual recording shall be considered as a reproduction for the purposes of this Convention.

Article 10

[Certain Free Uses of Works: 1. Quotations; 2. Illustrations for teaching; 3. Indication of source and author]

(1)   It shall be permissible to make quotations from a work which has already been lawfully made available to the public, provided that their making is compatible with fair practice, and their extent does not exceed that justified by the purpose, including quotations from newspaper articles and periodicals in the form of press summaries.

(2)   It shall be a matter for legislation in the countries of the Union, and for special agreements existing or to be concluded between them, to permit the utilisation, to the extent justified by the purpose, of literary or artistic works by way of illustration in publications, broadcasts or sound or visual recordings for teaching, provided such utilisation is compatible with fair practice.

(3)   Where use is made of works in accordance with the preceding paragraphs of this Article, mention shall be made of the source, and of the name of the author if it appears thereon.

Article 10bis

[Further Possible Free Uses of Works: 1. Of certain articles and broadcast works; 2. Of works seen or heard in connection with current events]

(1)   It shall be a matter for legislation in the countries of the Union to permit the reproduction by the press, the broadcasting or the communication to the public by wire of articles published in newspapers or periodicals on current economic, political or religious topics, and of broadcast works of the same character, in cases in which the reproduction, broadcasting or such communication thereof is not expressly reserved. Nevertheless, the source must always be clearly indicated; the legal consequences of a breach of this obligation shall be determined by the legislation of the country where protection is claimed.

(2)   It shall also be a matter for legislation in the countries of the Union to determine the conditions under which, for the purpose of reporting current events by means of photography, cinematography, broadcasting or communication to the public by wire, literary or artistic works seen or heard in the course of the event may, to the extent justified by the informatory purpose, be reproduced and made available to the public.

Article 11

[Certain Rights in Dramatic and Musical Works: 1. Right of public performance and of communication to the public of a performance; 2. In respect of translations]

(1)   Authors of dramatic, dramatico-musical and musical works shall enjoy the exclusive right of authorising:

(i)   the public performance of their works, including such public performance by any means or process;

(ii)   any communication to the public of the performance of their works.

(2)   Authors of dramatic or dramatico-musical works shall enjoy, during the full term of their rights in the original works, the same rights with respect to translations thereof.

Article 11bis

[Broadcasting and Related Rights: 1. Broadcasting and other wireless communications, public communication of broadcast by wire or rebroadcast, public communication of broadcast by loudspeaker or analogous instruments; 2. Compulsory licenses; 3. Recording; ephemeral recordings]

(1)   Authors of literary and artistic works shall enjoy the exclusive right of authorising:

(i)   the broadcasting of their works or the communication thereof to the public by any other means of wireless diffusion of signs, sounds or images;

(ii)   any communication to the public by wire or by rebroadcasting of the broadcast of the work, when this communication is made by an organisation other than the original one;

(iii)   the public communication by loudspeaker or any other analogous instrument transmitting, by signs, sounds or images, the broadcast of the work.

(2)   It shall be a matter for legislation in the countries of the Union to determine the conditions under which the rights mentioned in the preceding paragraph may be exercised, but these conditions shall apply only in the countries where they have been prescribed. They shall not in any circumstances be prejudicial to the moral rights of the author, nor to his right to obtain equitable remuneration which, in the absence of agreement, shall be fixed by competent authority.

(3)   In the absence of any contrary stipulation, permission granted in accordance with paragraph (1) of this Article shall not imply permission to record, by means of instruments recording sounds or images, the work broadcast. It shall, however, be a matter for legislation in the countries of the Union

to determine the regulations for ephemeral recordings made by a broadcasting organisation by means of its own facilities and used for its own broadcasts. The preservation of these recordings in official archives may, on the ground of their exceptional documentary character, be authorised by such legislation.

Article 11ter

[Certain Rights in Literary Works: 1. Right of public recitation and of communication to the public of a recitation; 2. In respect of translations]

(1)   Authors of literary works shall enjoy the exclusive right of authorising:

(i)   the public recitation of their works, including such public recitation by any means or process;

(ii)   any communication to the public of the recitation of their works.

(2)   Authors of literary works shall enjoy, during the full term of their rights in the original works, the same rights with respect to translations thereof.

Article 12

[Right of Adaptation, Arrangement and Other Alteration]

· Authors of literary or artistic works shall enjoy the exclusive right of authorising adaptations, arrangements and other alterations of their works.

Article 13

[Possible Limitation of the Right of Recording of Musical Works and Any Words Pertaining Thereto: 1. Compulsory licenses; 2. Transitory measures; 3. Seizure on importation of copies made without the author's permission]

(1)   Each country of the Union may impose for itself reservations and conditions on the exclusive right granted to the author of a musical work and to the author of any words, the recording of which together with the musical work has already been authorised by the latter, to authorise the sound recording of that musical work, together with such words, if any; but all such reservations and conditions shall apply only in the countries which have imposed them and shall not, in any circumstances, be prejudicial to the rights of these authors to obtain equitable remuneration which, in the absence of agreement, shall be fixed by competent authority.

(2)   Recordings of musical works made in a country of the Union in accordance with Article 13(3) of the Conventions signed at Rome on June 2, 1928, and at Brussels on June 26, 1948, may be reproduced in that country without the permission of the author of the musical work until a date two years after that country becomes bound by this Act.

(3)   Recordings made in accordance with paragraphs (1) and (2) of this Article and imported without permission from the parties concerned into a country where they are treated as infringing recordings shall be liable to seizure.

Article 14

[Cinematographic and Related Rights: 1. Cinematographic adaptation and reproduction; distribution; public performance and public communication by wire of works thus adapted or reproduced; 2. Adaptation of cinematographic productions; 3. No compulsory licenses]

(1)   Authors of literary or artistic works shall have the exclusive right of authorising:

(i)   the cinematographic adaptation and reproduction of these works, and the distribution of the works thus adapted or reproduced;

(ii)   the public performance and communication to the public by wire of the works thus adapted or reproduced.

(2)   The adaptation into any other artistic form of a cinematographic production derived from literary or artistic works shall, without prejudice to the authorisation of the author of the cinematographic production, remain subject to the authorisation of the authors of the original works.

(3)   The provisions of Article 13(1) shall not apply.

Article 14*bis*

[*Special Provisions Concerning Cinematographic Works:* 1. Assimilation to "original" works; 2. Ownership; limitation of certain rights of certain contributors; 3. Certain other contributors]

(1)   Without prejudice to the copyright in any work which may have been adapted or reproduced, a cinematographic work shall be protected as an original work. The owner of copyright in a cinematographic work shall enjoy the same rights as the author of an original work, including the rights referred to in the preceding Article.

(2)(a) Ownership of copyright in a cinematographic work shall be a matter for legislation in the country where protection is claimed.

(b)   However, in the countries of the Union which, by legislation, include among the owners of copyright in a cinematographic work authors who have brought contributions to the making of the work, such authors, if they have undertaken to bring such contributions, may not, in the absence of any contrary or special stipulation, object to the reproduction, distribution, public performance, communication to the public by wire, broadcasting or any other communication to the public, or to the subtitling or dubbing of texts, of the work.

(c)   The question whether or not the form of the undertaking referred to above should, for the application of the preceding subparagraph (b), be in a written agreement or a written act of the same effect shall be a matter for the legislation of the country where the maker of the cinematographic work has his headquarters or habitual residence. However, it shall be a matter for the legislation of the country of the Union where protection is claimed to provide that the said undertaking shall be in a written agreement or a written act of the same effect. The countries whose legislation so provides shall notify the Director General by means of a written declaration, which will be immediately communicated by him to all the other countries of the Union.

(d)   By "contrary or special stipulation" is meant any restrictive condition which is relevant to the aforesaid undertaking.

(3)   Unless the national legislation provides to the contrary, the provisions of paragraph (2)(b) above shall not be applicable to authors of scenarios, dialogues and musical works created for the making of the cinematographic work, or to the principal director thereof. However, those countries of the Union whose legislation does not contain rules providing for the application of the said paragraph (2)(b) to such director shall notify the Director General by means of a written declaration, which will be immediately communicated by him to all the other countries of the Union.

Article 14*ter*

[*"Droit de suite" in Works of Art and Manuscripts:* 1. Right to an interest in resales; 2. Applicable law; 3. Procedure]

(1)   The author, or after his death the persons or institutions authorised by national legislation, shall, with respect to original works of art and original manuscripts of writers and composers, enjoy the inalienable right to an interest in any sale of the work subsequent to the first transfer by the author of the work.

(2)   The protection provided by the preceding paragraph may be claimed in a country of the Union only if legislation in the country to which the author belongs so permits, and to the extent permitted by the country where this protection is claimed.

(3)   The procedure for collection and the amounts shall be matters for determination by national legislation.

Article 15

[*Right to Enforce Protected Rights:* 1. Where author's name is indicated or where pseudonym leaves no doubt as to author's identity; 2. In the case of cinematographic works; 3. In the case of anonymous and pseudonymous works; 4. In the case of certain unpublished works of unknown authorship]

(1)   In order that the author of a literary or artistic work protected by this Convention shall, in the absence of proof to the contrary, be regarded as such, and consequently be entitled to institute infringement proceedings in the countries of the Union, it shall be sufficient for his name to appear on the work in the usual manner. This paragraph shall be applicable even if this name is a pseudonym, where the pseudonym adopted by the author leaves no doubt as to his identity.

(2)   The person or body corporate whose name appears on a cinematographic work in the usual manner shall, in the absence of proof to the contrary, be presumed to be the maker of the said work.

(3)   In the case of anonymous and pseudonymous works, other than those referred to in paragraph (1) above, the publisher whose name appears on the work shall, in the absence of proof to the contrary, be deemed to represent the author, and in this capacity he shall be entitled to protect and enforce the author's rights. The provisions of this paragraph shall cease to apply when the author reveals his identity and establishes his claim to authorship of the work.

(4)(a) In the case of unpublished works where the identity of the author is unknown, but where there is every ground to presume that he is a national of a country of the Union, it shall be a matter for legislation in that country to designate the competent authority which shall represent the author and shall be entitled to protect and enforce his rights in the countries of the Union.

(b)   Countries of the Union which make such designation under the terms of this provision shall notify the Director General by means of a written declaration giving full information concerning the authority thus designated. The Director General shall at once communicate this declaration to all other countries of the Union.

Article 16

[*Infringing Copies:* 1. Seizure; 2. Seizure on importation; 3. Applicable law]

(1)   Infringing copies of a work shall be liable to seizure in any country of the Union where the work enjoys legal protection.

(2)   The provisions of the preceding paragraph shall also apply to reproductions coming from a country where the work is not protected, or has ceased to be protected.

(3)   The seizure shall take place in accordance with the legislation of each country.

Article 17

[*Possibility of Control of Circulation, Presentation and Exhibition of Works*]

The provisions of this Convention cannot in any way affect the right of the Government of each country of the Union to permit, to control, or to prohibit, by legislation or regulation, the circulation, presentation, or exhibition of any work or production in regard to which the competent authority may find it necessary to exercise that right.

Article 18

[Works Existing on Convention's Entry Into Force: 1. Protectable where protection not yet expired in country of origin; 2. Non-protectable where protection already expired in country where it is claimed; 3. Application of these principles; 4. Special cases]

(1)   This Convention shall apply to all works which, at the moment of its coming into force, have not yet fallen into the public domain in the country of origin through the expiry of the term of protection.

(2)   If, however, through the expiry of the term of protection which was previously granted, a work has fallen into the public domain of the country where protection is claimed, that work shall not be protected anew.

(3)   The application of this principle shall be subject to any provisions contained in special conventions to that effect existing or to be concluded between countries of the Union. In the absence of such provisions, the respective countries shall determine, each in so far as it is concerned, the conditions of application of this principle.

(4)   The preceding provisions shall also apply in the case of new accessions to the Union and to cases in which protection is extended by the application of Article 7 or by the abandonment of reservations.

Article 19

[Protection Greater Than Resulting From Convention]

The provisions of this Convention shall not preclude the making of a claim to the benefit of any greater protection which may be granted by legislation in a country of the Union.

Article 20

[Special Agreements Among Countries of the Union]

The Governments of the countries of the Union reserve the right to enter into special agreements among themselves, in so far as such agreements grant to authors more extensive rights than those granted by the Convention, or contain other provisions not contrary to this Convention. The provisions of existing agreements which satisfy these conditions shall remain applicable.

Article 21

[Special Provisions Regarding Developing Countries: 1. Reference to Appendix; 2. Appendix part of Act]

(1)   Special provisions regarding developing countries are included in the Appendix.

(2)   Subject to the provisions of Article 28(1)(b), the Appendix forms an integral part of this Act.

[Articles 22–32 are omitted]

Article 33

[Disputes: 1. Jurisdiction of the International Court of Justice; 2. Reservation as to such jurisdiction; 3. Withdrawal of reservation]

(1)   Any dispute between two or more countries of the Union concerning the interpretation or application of this Convention, not settled by negotiation, may, by any one of the countries concerned, be brought before the International Court of Justice by application in conformity with the Statute of the Court, unless the countries concerned agree on some other method of settlement. The country bringing the dispute before the Court shall inform the International Bureau; the International Bureau shall bring the matter to the attention of the other countries of the Union.

(2)   Each country may, at the time it signs this Act or deposits its instrument of ratification or accession, declare that it does not consider itself bound by the provisions of paragraph (1). With regard to any dispute between such country and any other country of the Union, the provisions of paragraph (1) shall not apply.

(3)   Any country having made a declaration in accordance with the provisions of paragraph (2) may, at any time, withdraw its declaration by notification addressed to the Director General.

[Articles 34–38 are omitted]

APPENDIX

SPECIAL PROVISIONS REGARDING DEVELOPING COUNTRIES

Article I

[*Faculties Open to Developing Countries:* 1. Availability of certain faculties; declaration; 2. Duration of effect of declaration; 3. Cessation of developing country status; 4. Existing stocks of copies; 5. Declarations concerning certain territories; 6. Limits of reciprocity]

(1)   Any country regarded as a developing country in conformity with the established practice of the General Assembly of the United Nations which ratifies or accedes to this Act, of which this Appendix forms an integral part, and which, having regard to its economic situation and its social or cultural needs, does not consider itself immediately in a position to make provision for the protection of all the rights as provided for in this Act, may, by a notification deposited with the Director General at the time of depositing its instrument of ratification or accession or, subject to Article V(1)(c), at any time thereafter, declare that it will avail itself of the faculty provided for in Article II, or of the faculty provided for in Article III, or of both of those faculties. It may, instead of availing itself of the faculty provided for in Article II, make a declaration according to Article V(1)(a).

(2)(a) Any declaration under paragraph (1) notified before the expiration of the period of ten years from the entry into force of Articles 1 to 21 and this Appendix according to Article 28(2) shall be effective until the expiration of the said period. Any such declaration may be renewed in whole or in part for periods of ten years each by a notification deposited with the Director General not more than fifteen months and not less than three months before the expiration of the ten-year period then running.

(b)   Any declaration under paragraph (1) notified after the expiration of the period of ten years from the entry into force of Articles 1 to 21 and this Appendix according to Article 28(2) shall be effective until the expiration of the ten-year period then running. Any such declaration may be renewed as provided for in the second sentence of subparagraph (a).

(3)   Any country of the Union which has ceased to be regarded as a developing country as referred to in paragraph (1) shall no longer be entitled to renew its declaration as provided in paragraph (2), and, whether or not it formally withdraws its declaration, such country shall be precluded from availing itself of the faculties referred to in paragraph (1) from the expiration of the ten-year period then running or from the expiration of a period of three years after it has ceased to be regarded as a developing country, whichever period expires later.

(4)   Where, at the time when the declaration made under paragraph (1) or (2) ceases to be effective, there are copies in stock which were made under a licence granted by virtue of this Appendix, such copies may continue to be distributed until their stock is exhausted.

(5)   Any country which is bound by the provisions of this Act and which has deposited a declaration or a notification in accordance with Article 31(1) with respect to the application of this Act to a particular territory, the situation of which can be regarded as analogous to that of the countries

referred to in paragraph (1), may, in respect of such territory, make the declaration referred to in paragraph (1) and the notification of renewal referred to in paragraph (2). As long as such declaration or notification remains in effect, the provisions of this Appendix shall be applicable to the territory in respect of which it was made.

(6)(a) The fact that a country avails itself of any of the faculties referred to in paragraph (1) does not permit another country to give less protection to works of which the country of origin is the former country than it is obliged to grant under Articles 1 to 20.

(b) The right to apply reciprocal treatment provided for in Article 30(2)(b), second sentence, shall not, until the date on which the period applicable under Article I(3) expires, be exercised in respect of works the country of origin of which is a country which has made a declaration according to Article V(1)(a).

Article II

[*Limitations on the Right of Translation:* 1. Licenses grantable by competent authority; 2. to 4. Conditions allowing the grant of such licenses; 5. Purposes for which licenses may be granted; 6. Termination of licenses; 7. Works composed mainly of illustrations; 8. Works withdrawn from circulation; 9. Licenses for broadcasting organisations]

(1) Any country which has declared that it will avail itself of the faculty provided for in this Article shall be entitled, so far as works published in printed or analogous forms of reproduction are concerned, to substitute for the exclusive right of translation provided for in Article 8 a system of non-exclusive and non-transferable licenses, granted by the competent authority under the following conditions and subject to Article IV.

(2)(a) Subject to paragraph (3), if, after the expiration of a period of three years, or of any longer period determined by the national legislation of the said country, commencing on the date of the first publication of the work, a translation of such work has not been published in a language in general use in that country by the owner of the right of translation, or with his authorisation, any national of such country may obtain a licence to make a translation of the work in the said language and publish the translation in printed or analogous forms of reproduction.

(b) A licence under the conditions provided for in this Article may also be granted if all the editions of the translation published in the language concerned are out of print.

(3)(a) In the case of translations into a language which is not in general use in one or more developed countries which are members of the Union, a period of one year shall be substituted for the period of three years referred to in paragraph (2)(a).

(b) Any country referred to in paragraph (1) may, with the unanimous agreement of the developed countries which are members of the Union and in which the same language is in general use, substitute, in the case of translations into that language, for the period of three years referred to in paragraph (2)(a) a shorter period as determined by such agreement but not less than one year. However, the provisions of the foregoing sentence shall not apply where the language in question is English, French or Spanish. The Director General shall be notified of any such agreement by the Governments which have concluded it.

(4)(a) No licence obtainable after three years shall be granted under this Article until a further period of six months has elapsed, and no licence obtainable after one year shall be granted under this Article until a further period of nine months has elapsed

(i) from the date on which the applicant complies with the requirements mentioned in Article IV(1), or

(ii) where the identity or the address of the owner of the right of translation is unknown, from the date on which the applicant sends, as provided for in Article IV(2), copies of his application submitted to the authority competent to grant the licence.

(b)   If, during the said period of six or nine months, a translation in the language in respect of which the application was made is published by the owner of the right of translation or with his authorisation, no licence under this Article shall be granted.

(5)   Any licence under this Article shall be granted only for the purpose of teaching, scholarship or research.

(6)   If a translation of a work is published by the owner of the right of translation or with his authorisation at a price reasonably related to that normally charged in the country for comparable works, any licence granted under this Article shall terminate if such translation is in the same language and with substantially the same content as the translation published under the licence. Any copies already made before the licence terminates may continue to be distributed until their stock is exhausted.

(7)   For works which are composed mainly of illustrations, a licence to make and publish a translation of the text and to reproduce and publish the illustrations may be granted only if the conditions of Article III are also fulfilled.

(8)   No licence shall be granted under this Article when the author has withdrawn from circulation all copies of his work.

(9)(a) A licence to make a translation of a work which has been published in printed or analogous forms of reproduction may also be granted to any broadcasting organisation having its headquarters in a country referred to in paragraph (1), upon an application made to the competent authority of that country by the said organisation, provided that all of the following conditions are met:

   (i)   the translation is made from a copy made and acquired in accordance with the laws of the said country;

   (ii)   the translation is only for use in broadcasts intended exclusively for teaching or for the dissemination of the results of specialised technical or scientific research to experts in a particular profession;

   (iii) the translation is used exclusively for the purposes referred to in condition (ii) through broadcasts made lawfully and intended for recipients on the territory of the said country, including broadcasts made through the medium of sound or visual recordings lawfully and exclusively made for the purpose of such broadcasts;

   (iv)   all uses made of the translation are without any commercial purpose.

(b)   Sound or visual recordings of a translation which was made by a broadcasting organisation under a licence granted by virtue of this paragraph may, for the purposes and subject to the conditions referred to in subparagraph (a) and with the agreement of that organisation, also be used by any other broadcasting organisation having its headquarters in the country whose competent authority granted the licence in question.

(c)   Provided that all of the criteria and conditions set out in subparagraph (a) are met, a licence may also be granted to a broadcasting organisation to translate any text incorporated in an audio-visual fixation where such fixation was itself prepared and published for the sole purpose of being used in connection with systematic instructional activities.

(d)   Subject to subparagraphs (a) to (c), the provisions of the preceding paragraphs shall apply to the grant and exercise of any licence granted under this paragraph.

Article III

[*Limitation on the Right of Reproduction:* 1. Licences grantable by competent authority; 2. to 5. Conditions allowing the grant of such licences; 6. Termination of licences. 7. Works to which this Article applies]

(1)   Any country which has declared that it will avail itself of the faculty provided for in this Article shall be entitled to substitute for the exclusive right of reproduction provided for in Article 9 a

system of non-exclusive and non-transferable licences, granted by the competent authority under the following conditions and subject to Article IV.

(2)(a) If, in relation to a work to which this Article applies by virtue of paragraph (7), after the expiration of

(i) the relevant period specified in paragraph (3), commencing on the date of first publication of a particular edition of the work, or

(ii) any longer period determined by national legislation of the country referred to in paragraph (1), commencing on the same date,

copies of such edition have not been distributed in that country to the general public or in connection with systematic instructional activities, by the owner of the right of reproduction or with his authorisation, at a price reasonably related to that normally charged in the country for comparable works, any national of such country may obtain a licence to reproduce and publish such edition at that or a lower price for use in connection with systematic instructional activities.

(b) A licence to reproduce and publish an edition which has been distributed as described in subparagraph (a) may also be granted under the conditions provided for in this Article if, after the expiration of the applicable period, no authorised copies of that edition have been on sale for a period of six months in the country concerned to the general public or in connection with systematic instructional activities at a price reasonably related to that normally charged in the country for comparable works.

(3) The period referred to in paragraph (2)(a)(i) shall be five years, except that

(i) for works of the natural and physical sciences, including mathematics, and of technology, the period shall be three years;

(ii) for works of fiction, poetry, drama and music, and for art books, the period shall be seven years.

(4)(a) No licence obtainable after three years shall be granted under this Article until a period of six months has elapsed

(i) from the date on which the applicant complies with the requirements mentioned in Article IV(1), or

(ii) where the identity or the address of the owner of the right of reproduction is unknown, from the date on which the applicant sends, as provided for in Article IV(2), copies of his application submitted to the authority competent to grant the licence.

(b) Where licences are obtainable after other periods and Article IV(2) is applicable, no licence shall be granted until a period of three months has elapsed from the date of the dispatch of the copies of the application.

(c) If, during the period of six or three months referred to in subparagraphs (a) and (b), a distribution as described in paragraph 2(a) has taken place, no licence shall be granted under this Article.

(d) No licence shall be granted if the author has withdrawn from circulation all copies of the edition for the reproduction and publication of which the licence has been applied for.

(5) A licence to reproduce and publish a translation of a work shall not be granted under this Article in the following cases:

(i) where the translation was not published by the owner of the right of translation or with his authorisation, or

(ii) where the translation is not in a language in general use in the country in which the licence is applied for.

(6)   If copies of an edition of a work are distributed in the country referred to in paragraph (1) to the general public or in connection with systematic instructional activities, by the owner of the right of reproduction or with his authorisation, at a price reasonably related to that normally charged in the country for comparable works, any licence granted under this Article shall terminate if such edition is in the same language and with substantially the same content as the edition which was published under the said licence. Any copies already made before the licence terminates may continue to be distributed until their stock is exhausted.

(7)(a) Subject to subparagraph (b), the works to which this Article applies shall be limited to works published in printed or analogous forms of reproduction.

(b)   This Article shall also apply to the reproduction in audio-visual form of lawfully made audio-visual fixations including any protected works incorporated therein and to the translation of any incorporated text into a language in general use in the country in which the licence is applied for, always provided that the audio-visual fixations in question were prepared and published for the sole purpose of being used in connection with systematic instructional activities.

Article IV

[Provisions Common to Licences Under Articles II and III: 1. and 2. Procedure. 3. Indication of author and title of work; 4. Exportation of copies; 5. Notice; 6. Compensation]

(1)   A licence under Article II or Article III may be granted only if the applicant, in accordance with the procedure of the country concerned, establishes either that he has requested, and has been denied, authorisation by the owner of the right to make and publish the translation or to reproduce and publish the edition, as the case may be, or that, after due diligence on his part, he was unable to find the owner of the right. At the same time as making the request, the applicant shall inform any national or international information center referred to in paragraph (2).

(2)   If the owner of the right cannot be found, the applicant for a licence shall send, by registered airmail, copies of his application, submitted to the authority competent to grant the licence, to the publisher whose name appears on the work and to any national or international information centre which may have been designated, in a notification to that effect deposited with the Director General, by the Government of the country in which the publisher is believed to have his principal place of business.

(3)   The name of the author shall be indicated on all copies of the translation or reproduction published under a licence granted under Article II or Article III. The title of the work shall appear on all such copies. In the case of a translation, the original title of the work shall appear in any case on all the said copies.

(4)(a) No licence granted under Article II or Article III shall extend to the export of copies, and any such licence shall be valid only for publication of the translation or of the reproduction, as the case may be, in the territory of the country in which it has been applied for.

(b)   For the purposes of subparagraph (a), the notion of export shall include the sending of copies from any territory to the country which, in respect of that territory, has made a declaration under Article I(5).

(c)   Where a governmental or other public entity of a country which has granted a licence to make a translation under Article II into a language other than English, French or Spanish sends copies of a translation published under such licence to another country, such sending of copies shall not, for the purposes of subparagraph (a), be considered to constitute export if all of the following conditions are met:

(i)   the recipients are individuals who are nationals of the country whose competent authority has granted the licence, or organisations grouping such individuals;

(ii)   the copies are to be used only for the purpose of teaching, scholarship or research;

(iii) the sending of the copies and their subsequent distribution to recipients is without any commercial purpose; and

(iv) the country to which the copies have been sent has agreed with the country whose competent authority has granted the licence to allow the receipt, or distribution, or both, and the Director General has been notified of the agreement by the Government of the country in which the licence has been granted.

(5) All copies published under a licence granted by virtue of Article II or Article III shall bear a notice in the appropriate language stating that the copies are available for distribution only in the country or territory to which the said licence applies.

(6)(a) Due provision shall be made at the national level to ensure

(i) that the licence provides, in favour of the owner of the right of translation or of reproduction, as the case may be, for just compensation that is consistent with standards of royalties normally operating on licences freely negotiated between persons in the two countries concerned, and

(ii) payment and transmittal of the compensation: should national currency regulations intervene, the competent authority shall make all efforts, by the use of international machinery, to ensure transmittal in internationally convertible currency or its equivalent.

(b) Due provision shall be made by national legislation to ensure a correct translation of the work, or an accurate reproduction of the particular edition, as the case may be.

Article V

[*Alternative Possibility for Limitation of the Right of Translation:* 1. Regime provided for under the 1886 and 1896 Acts; 2. No possibility of change to regime under Article II; 3. Time limit for choosing the alternative possibility]

(1)(a) Any country entitled to make a declaration that it will avail itself of the faculty provided for in Article II may, instead, at the time of ratifying or acceding to this Act:

(i) if it is a country to which Article 30(2)(a) applies, make a declaration under that provision as far as the right of translation is concerned;

(ii) if it is a country to which Article 30(2)(a) does not apply, and even if it is not a country outside the Union, make a declaration as provided for in Article 30(2)(b), first sentence.

(b) In the case of a country which ceases to be regarded as a developing country as referred to in Article I(1), a declaration made according to this paragraph shall be effective until the date on which the period applicable under Article I(3) expires.

(c) Any country which has made a declaration according to this paragraph may not subsequently avail itself of the faculty provided for in Article II even if it withdraws the said declaration.

(2) Subject to paragraph (3), any country which has availed itself of the faculty provided for in Article II may not subsequently make a declaration according to paragraph (1).

(3) Any country which has ceased to be regarded as a developing country as referred to in Article I(1) may, not later than two years prior to the expiration of the period applicable under Article I(3), make a declaration to the effect provided for in Article 30(2)(b), first sentence, notwithstanding the fact that it is not a country outside the Union. Such declaration shall take effect at the date on which the period applicable under Article I(3) expires.

Article VI

[*Possibilities of Applying, or Admitting the Application of, Certain Provisions of the Appendix Before Becoming Bound by It:* 1. Declaration; 2. Depository and effective date of declaration]

BERNE CONVENTION

(1) Any country of the Union may declare, as from the date of this Act, and at any time before becoming bound by Articles 1 to 21 and this Appendix:

(i) if it is a country which, were it bound by Articles 1 to 21 and this Appendix, would be entitled to avail itself of the faculties referred to in Article I(1), that it will apply the provisions of Article II or of Article III or of both to works whose country of origin is a country which, pursuant to (ii) below, admits the application of those Articles to such works, or which is bound by Articles 1 to 21 and this Appendix; such declaration may, instead of referring to Article II, refer to Article V;

(ii) that it admits the application of this Appendix to works of which it is the country of origin by countries which have made a declaration under (i) above or a notification under Article I.

(2) Any declaration made under paragraph (1) shall be in writing and shall be deposited with the Director General. The declaration shall become effective from the date of its deposit.

J. WIPO COPYRIGHT TREATY

Adopted by the Diplomatic Conference on December 20, 1996

Contents

Preamble

The Contracting Parties,

Desiring to develop and maintain the protection of the rights of authors in their literary and artistic works in a manner as effective and uniform as possible,

Recognizing the need to introduce new international rules and clarify the interpretation of certain existing rules in order to provide adequate solutions to the questions raised by new economic, social, cultural and technological developments,

Recognizing the profound impact of the development and convergence of information and communication technologies on the creation and use of literary and artistic works,

Emphasizing the outstanding significance of copyright protection as an incentive for literary and artistic creation,

Recognizing the need to maintain a balance between the rights of authors and the larger public interest, particularly education, research and access to information, as reflected in the Berne Convention,

Have agreed as follows:

Article 1

Relation to the Berne Convention

(1)   This Treaty is a special agreement within the meaning of Article 20 of the Berne Convention for the Protection of Literary and Artistic Works, as regards Contracting Parties that are countries of the Union established by that Convention. This Treaty shall not have any connection with treaties other than the Berne Convention, nor shall it prejudice any rights and obligations under any other treaties.

(2)   Nothing in this Treaty shall derogate from existing obligations that Contracting Parties have to each other under the Berne Convention for the Protection of Literary and Artistic Works.

(3)   Hereinafter, "Berne Convention" shall refer to the Paris Act of July 24, 1971 of the Berne Convention for the Protection of Literary and Artistic Works.

(4)   Contracting Parties shall comply with Articles 1 to 21 and the Appendix of the Berne Convention.

Article 2

Scope of Copyright Protection

Copyright protection extends to expressions and not to ideas, procedures, methods of operation or mathematical concepts as such.

Article 3

Application of Articles 2 to 6 of the Berne Convention

Contracting Parties shall apply *mutatis mutandis* the provisions of Articles 2 to 6 of the Berne Convention in respect of the protection provided for in this Treaty.

Article 4

Computer Programs

Computer programs are protected as literary works within the meaning of Article 2 of the Berne Convention. Such protection applies to computer programs, whatever may be the mode or form of their expression.

Article 5

Compilations of Data (Databases)

Compilations of data or other material, in any form, which by reason of the selection or arrangement of their contents constitute intellectual creations, are protected as such. This protection does not extend to the data or the material itself and is without prejudice to any copyright subsisting in the data or material contained in the compilation.

Article 6

Right of Distribution

(1)   Authors of literary and artistic works shall enjoy the exclusive right of authorizing the making available to the public of the original and copies of their works through sale or other transfer of ownership.

(2)   Nothing in this Treaty shall affect the freedom of Contracting Parties to determine the conditions, if any, under which the exhaustion of the right in paragraph (1) applies after the first sale or other transfer of ownership of the original or a copy of the work with the authorization of the author.

Article 7

Right of Rental

(1)   Authors of:

    (i)   computer programs;

    (ii)   cinematographic works; and

    (iii)   works embodied in phonograms as determined in the national law of Contracting Parties,

shall enjoy the exclusive right of authorizing commercial rental to the public of the originals or copies of their works.

(2)   Paragraph (1) shall not apply:

    (i)   in the case of computer programs where the program itself is not the essential object of the rental; and

    (ii)   in the case of cinematographic works, unless such commercial rental has led to widespread copying of such works materially impairing the exclusive right of reproduction.

(3)   Notwithstanding the provisions of paragraph (1), a Contracting Party that, on April 15, 1994, had and continues to have in force a system of equitable remuneration of authors for the rental of copies of their works embodied in phonograms may maintain that system provided that the commercial rental of works embodied in phonograms is not giving rise to the material impairment of the exclusive rights of reproduction of authors.

Article 8

Right of Communication to the Public

Without prejudice to the provisions of Articles 11(1)(ii), 11*bis*(1)(i) and (ii), 11*ter*(1)(ii), 14(1)(ii) and 14*bis*(1) of the Berne Convention, authors of literary and artistic works shall enjoy the exclusive right of authorizing any communication to the public of their works, by wire or wireless means, including the making available to the public of their works in such a way that members of the public may access these works from a place and at a time individually chosen by them.

Article 9

Duration of the Protection of Photographic Works

In respect of photographic works, the Contracting Parties shall not apply the provisions of Article 7(4) of the Berne Convention.

Article 10

Limitations and Exceptions

(1)   Contracting Parties may, in their national legislation, provide for limitations of or exceptions to the rights granted to authors of literary and artistic works under this Treaty in certain special cases that do not conflict with a normal exploitation of the work and do not unreasonably prejudice the legitimate interests of the author.

(2)   Contracting Parties shall, when applying the Berne Convention, confine any limitations of or exceptions to rights provided for therein to certain special cases that do not conflict with a normal exploitation of the work and do not unreasonably prejudice the legitimate interests of the author.

Article 11

Obligations Concerning Technological Measures

Contracting Parties shall provide adequate legal protection and effective legal remedies against the circumvention of effective technological measures that are used by authors in connection with the exercise of their rights under this Treaty or the Berne Convention and that restrict acts, in respect of their works, which are not authorized by the authors concerned or permitted by law.

Article 12

Obligations Concerning Rights Management Information

(1)   Contracting Parties shall provide adequate and effective legal remedies against any person knowingly performing any of the following acts knowing or, with respect to civil remedies having reasonable grounds to know, that it will induce, enable, facilitate or conceal an infringement of any right covered by this Treaty or the Berne Convention:

(i)   to remove or alter any electronic rights management information without authority;

(ii)   to distribute, import for distribution, broadcast or communicate to the public, without authority, works or copies of works knowing that electronic rights management information has been removed or altered without authority.

(2)   As used in this Article, "rights management information" means information which identifies the work, the author of the work, the owner of any right in the work, or information about the terms and conditions of use of the work, and any numbers or codes that represent such information, when any of these items of information is attached to a copy of a work or appears in connection with the communication of a work to the public.

Article 13

Application in Time

Contracting Parties shall apply the provisions of Article 18 of the Berne Convention to all protection provided for in this Treaty.

Article 14

Provisions on Enforcement of Rights

(1)   Contracting Parties undertake to adopt, in accordance with their legal systems, the measures necessary to ensure the application of this Treaty.

(2)   Contracting Parties shall ensure that enforcement procedures are available under their law so as to permit effective action against any act of infringement of rights covered by this Treaty, including expeditious remedies to prevent infringements and remedies which constitute a deterrent to further infringements.

Article 15

Assembly

(1)(a) The Contracting Parties shall have an Assembly.

(b)   Each Contracting Party shall be represented by one delegate who may be assisted by alternate delegates, advisors and experts.

(c)   The expenses of each delegation shall be borne by the Contracting Party that has appointed the delegation. The Assembly may ask the World Intellectual Property Organization (hereinafter referred to as "WIPO") to grant financial assistance to facilitate the participation of delegations of Contracting Parties that are regarded as developing countries in conformity with the established practice of the General Assembly of the United Nations or that are countries in transition to a market economy.

(2)(a) The Assembly shall deal with matters concerning the maintenance and development of this Treaty and the application and operation of this Treaty.

(b)   The Assembly shall perform the function allocated to it under Article 17(2) in respect of the admission of certain intergovernmental organizations to become party to this Treaty.

(c)   The Assembly shall decide the convocation of any diplomatic conference for the revision of this Treaty and give the necessary instructions to the Director General of WIPO for the preparation of such diplomatic conference.

(3)(a) Each Contracting Party that is a State shall have one vote and shall vote only in its own name.

(b)   Any Contracting Party that is an intergovernmental organization may participate in the vote, in place of its Member States, with a number of votes equal to the number of its Member States which are party to this Treaty. No such intergovernmental organization shall participate in the vote if any one of its Member States exercises its right to vote and vice versa.

(4)   The Assembly shall meet in ordinary session once every two years upon convocation by the Director General of WIPO.

(5)   The Assembly shall establish its own rules of procedure, including the convocation of extraordinary sessions, the requirements of a quorum and, subject to the provisions of this Treaty, the required majority for various kinds of decisions.

Article 16

International Bureau

The International Bureau of WIPO shall perform the administrative tasks concerning the Treaty.

Article 17

Eligibility for Becoming Party to the Treaty

(1)   Any Member State of WIPO may become party to this Treaty.

(2)   The Assembly may decide to admit any intergovernmental organization to become party to this Treaty which declares that it is competent in respect of, and has its own legislation binding on all its Member States on, matters covered by this Treaty and that it has been duly authorized, in accordance with its internal procedures, to become party to this Treaty.

(3)   The European Community, having made the declaration referred to in the preceding paragraph in the Diplomatic Conference that has adopted this Treaty, may become party to this Treaty.

Article 18

Rights and Obligations under the Treaty

Subject to any specific provisions to the contrary in this Treaty, each Contracting Party shall enjoy all of the rights and assume all of the obligations under this Treaty.

Article 19

Signature of the Treaty

This Treaty shall be open for signature until December 31, 1997, by any Member State of WIPO and by the European Community.

Article 20

Entry into Force of the Treaty

This Treaty shall enter into force three months after 30 instruments of ratification or accession by States have been deposited with the Director General of WIPO.

Article 21

Effective Date of Becoming Party to the Treaty

This Treaty shall bind

(i)   the 30 States referred to in Article 20, from the date on which this Treaty has entered into force;

(ii)   each other State from the expiration of three months from the date on which the State has deposited its instrument with the Director General of WIPO;

(iii)   the European Community, from the expiration of three months after the deposit of its instrument of ratification or accession if such instrument has been deposited after the entry into force of this Treaty according to Article 20, or, three months after the entry into force of this Treaty if such instrument has been deposited before the entry into force of this Treaty;

(iv)   any other intergovernmental organization that is admitted to become party to this Treaty, from the expiration of three months after the deposit of its instrument of accession.

Article 22

No Reservations to the Treaty

No reservation to this Treaty shall be admitted.

Article 23

Denunciation of the Treaty

This Treaty may be denounced by any Contracting Party by notification addressed to the Director General of WIPO. Any denunciation shall take effect one year from the date on which the Director General of WIPO received the notification.

Article 24

Languages of the Treaty

(1)   This Treaty is signed in a single original in English, Arabic, Chinese, French, Russian and Spanish languages, the versions in all these languages being equally authentic.

(2)   An official text in any language other than those referred to in paragraph (1) shall be established by the Director General of WIPO on the request of an interested party, after consultation with all the interested parties. For the purposes of this paragraph, "interested party" means any Member State of WIPO whose official language, or one of whose official languages, is involved and the European Community, and any other intergovernmental organization that may become party to this Treaty, if one of its official languages is involved.

Article 25

Depositary

The Director General of WIPO is the depositary of this Treaty.

K. WIPO PERFORMANCES AND PHONOGRAMS TREATY

Adopted by the Diplomatic Conference on December 20, 1996

Contents

Preamble

CHAPTER I.   GENERAL PROVISIONS

CHAPTER II.   RIGHTS OF PERFORMERS

CHAPTER III.   RIGHTS OF PRODUCERS OF PHONOGRAMS

CHAPTER IV.   COMMON PROVISIONS

CHAPTER V.   ADMINISTRATIVE AND FINAL CLAUSES

Preamble

The Contracting Parties,

Desiring to develop and maintain the protection of the rights of performers and producers of phonograms in a manner as effective and uniform as possible,

Recognizing the need to introduce new international rules in order to provide adequate solutions to the questions raised by economic, social, cultural and technological developments,

Recognizing the profound impact of the development and convergence of information and communication technologies on the production and use of performances and phonograms,

Recognizing the need to maintain a balance between the rights of the performers and producers of phonograms and the larger public interest, particularly education, research and access to information,

Have agreed as follows:

CHAPTER I.   GENERAL PROVISIONS

Article 1

Relation to Other Conventions

(1)   Nothing in this Treaty shall derogate from existing obligations that Contracting Parties have to each other under the International Convention for the Protection of Performers, Producers of Phonograms and Broadcasting Organizations done in Rome, October 26, 1961 (hereinafter the "Rome Convention").

(2)   Protection granted under this Treaty shall leave intact and shall in no way affect the protection of copyright in literary and artistic works. Consequently, no provision of this Treaty may be interpreted as prejudicing such protection.

(3)   This Treaty shall not have any connection with, nor shall it prejudice any rights and obligations under, any other treaties.

Article 2

Definitions

For the purposes of this Treaty:

(a)   "performers" are actors, singers, musicians, dancers, and other persons who act, sing, deliver, declaim, play in, interpret, or otherwise perform literary or artistic works or expressions of folklore;

(b)   "phonogram" means the fixation of the sounds of a performance or of other sounds, or of a representation of sounds other than in the form of a fixation incorporated in a cinematographic or other audiovisual work;

(c)   "fixation" means the embodiment of sounds, or of the representations thereof, from which they can be perceived, reproduced or communicated through a device;

(d)   "producer of a phonogram" means the person, or the legal entity, who or which takes the initiative and has the responsibility for the first fixation of the sounds of a performance or other sounds, or the representations of sounds;

(e)   "publication" of a fixed performance or a phonogram means the offering of copies of the fixed performance or the phonogram to the public, with the consent of the rightholder, and provided that copies are offered to the public in reasonable quantity;

(f)   "broadcasting" means the transmission by wireless means for public reception of sounds or of images and sounds or of the representations thereof; such transmission by satellite is also "broadcasting"; transmission of encrypted signals is "broadcasting" where the means for decrypting are provided to the public by the broadcasting organization or with its consent;

(g)   "communication to the public" of a performance or a phonogram means the transmission to the public by any medium, otherwise than by broadcasting, of sounds of a performance or the sounds or the representations of sounds fixed in a phonogram. For the purposes of Article 15, "communication to the public" includes making the sounds or representations of sounds fixed in a phonogram audible to the public.

Article 3

Beneficiaries of Protection Under This Treaty

(1)   Contracting Parties shall accord the protection provided under this Treaty to the performers and producers of phonograms who are nationals of other Contracting Parties.

(2)   The nationals of other Contracting Parties shall be understood to be those performers or producers of phonograms who would meet the criteria for eligibility for protection provided under the Rome Convention, were all the Contracting Parties to this Treaty Contracting States of that Convention. In respect of these criteria of eligibility, Contracting Parties shall apply the relevant definitions in Article 2 of this Treaty.

(3)   Any Contracting Party availing itself of the possibilities provided in Article 5(3) of the Rome Conventions or, for the purposes of Article 5 of the same Convention, Article thereof 17 shall make a notification as foreseen in those provisions to the Director General of the World Intellectual Property Organization (WIPO).

Article 4

National Treatment

(1)   Each Contracting Party shall accord to nationals of other Contracting Parties, as defined in Article 3(2), the treatment it accords to its own nationals with regard to the exclusive rights specifically granted in this Treaty and to the right to equitable remuneration provided for in Article 15 of this Treaty.

(2)   The obligation provided for in paragraph (1) does not apply to the extent that another Contracting Party makes use of the reservations permitted by Article 15(3) of this Treaty.

CHAPTER II.   RIGHTS OF PERFORMERS

Article 5

Moral Rights of Performers

(1)   Independently of a performer's economic rights, and even after the transfer of those rights, the performer shall, as regards his live aural performances or performances fixed in phonograms have the right to claim to be identified as the performer of his performances, except where omission is dictated by the manner of the use of the performance, and to object to any distortion, mutilation or other modification of his performances that would be prejudicial to his reputation.

(2)   The rights granted to a performer in accordance with paragraph (1) shall, after his death, be maintained, at least until the expiry of the economic rights, and shall be exercisable by the persons or institutions authorized by the legislation of the Contracting Party where protection is claimed.

However, those Contracting Parties whose legislation, at the moment of their ratification of or accession to this Treaty, does not provide for protection after the death of the performer of all rights set out in the preceding paragraph may provide that some of these rights will, after his death, cease to be maintained.

(3) The means of redress for safeguarding the rights granted under this Article shall be governed by the legislation of the Contracting Party where protection is claimed.

Article 6

Economic Rights of Performers in Their Unfixed Performances

Performers shall enjoy the exclusive right of authorizing, as regards their performances:

(i) the broadcasting and communication to the public of their unfixed performances except where the performance is already a broadcast performance; and

(ii) the fixation of their unfixed performances.

Article 7

Right of Reproduction

Performers shall enjoy the exclusive right of authorizing the direct or indirect reproduction of their performances fixed in phonograms, in any manner or form.

Article 8

Right of Distribution

(1) Performers shall enjoy the exclusive right of authorizing the making available to the public of the original and copies of their performances fixed in phonograms through sale or other transfer of ownership.

(2) Nothing in this Treaty shall affect the freedom of Contracting Parties to determine the conditions, if any, under which the exhaustion of the right in paragraph (1) applies after the first sale or other transfer of ownership of the original or a copy of the fixed performance with the authorization of the performer.

Article 9

Right of Rental

(1) Performers shall enjoy the exclusive right of authorizing the commercial rental to the public of the original and copies of their performances fixed in phonograms as determined in the national law of Contracting Parties, even after distribution of them by, or pursuant to, authorization by the performer.

(2) Notwithstanding the provisions of paragraph (1), a Contracting Party that, on April 15, 1994, had and continues to have in force a system of equitable remuneration of performers for the rental of copies of their performances fixed in phonograms, may maintain that system provided that the commercial rental of phonograms is not giving rise to the material impairment of the exclusive rights of reproduction of performers.

Article 10

Right of Making Available of Fixed Performances

Performers shall enjoy the exclusive right of authorizing the making available to the public of their performances fixed in phonograms, by wire or wireless means, in such a way that members of the public may access them from a place and at a time individually chosen by them.

CHAPTER III.   RIGHTS OF PRODUCERS OF PHONOGRAMS

Article 11

Right of Reproduction

Producers of phonograms shall enjoy the exclusive right of authorizing the direct or indirect reproduction of their phonograms, in any manner or form.

Article 12

Right of Distribution

(1)   Producers of phonograms shall enjoy the exclusive right of authorizing the making available to the public of the original and copies of their phonograms through sale or other transfer of ownership.

(2)   Nothing in this Treaty shall affect the freedom of Contracting Parties to determine the conditions, if any, under which the exhaustion of the right in paragraph (1) applies after the first sale or transfer of ownership of the original or a copy of the phonogram with the authorization of the producer of phonograms.

Article 13

Right of Rental

(1)   Producers of phonograms shall enjoy the exclusive right of authorizing the commercial rental to the public of the original and copies of their phonograms, even after distribution of them by or pursuant to authorization by the producer.

(2)   Notwithstanding the provisions of paragraph (1), a Contracting Party that, on April 15, 1994, had and continues to have in force a system of equitable remuneration of producers of phonograms for the rental of copies of their phonograms, may maintain that system provided that the commercial rental of phonograms is not giving rise to the material impairment of the exclusive rights of reproduction of producers of phonograms.

Article 14

Right of Making Available of Phonograms

Producers of phonograms shall enjoy the exclusive right of authorizing the making available to the public of their phonograms, by wire or wireless means, in such a way that members of the public may access them from a place and at a time individually chosen by them.

CHAPTER IV.   COMMON PROVISIONS

Article 15

Right to Remuneration for Broadcasting and Communication to the Public

(1)   Performers and producers of phonograms shall enjoy the right to a single equitable remuneration for the direct or indirect use of phonograms published for commercial purposes for broadcasting or for any communication to the public.

(2)   Contracting Parties may establish in their national legislation that the single equitable remuneration shall be claimed from the user by the performer or by the producer of a phonogram or by both. Contracting Parties may enact national legislation that, in the absence of an agreement between the performer and the producer of a phonogram, sets the terms according to which performers and producers of phonograms shall share the single equitable remuneration.

(3)   Any Contracting Party may in a notification deposited with the Director General of WIPO, declare that it will apply the provisions of paragraph (1) only in respect of certain uses, or that it will limit their application in some other way, or that it will not apply these provisions at all.

(4)   For the purposes of this Article, phonograms made available to the public by wire or wireless means in such a way that members of the public may access them from a place and at a time individually chosen by them shall be considered as if they had been published for commercial purposes.

Article 16

Limitations and Exceptions

(1)   Contracting Parties may, in their national legislation, provide for the same kinds of limitations or exceptions with regard to the protection of performers and producers of phonograms as they provide for, in their national legislation, in connection with the protection of copyright in literary and artistic works.

(2)   Contracting Parties shall confine any limitations of or exceptions to rights provided for in this Treaty to certain special cases which do not conflict with a normal exploitation of the performance or phonogram and do not unreasonably prejudice the legitimate interests of the performer or of the producer of phonograms.

Article 17

Term of Protection

(1)   The term of protection to be granted to performers under this Treaty shall last, at least, until the end of a period of 50 years computed from the end of the year in which the performance was fixed in a phonogram.

(2)   The term of protection to be granted to producers of phonograms under this Treaty shall last, at least, until the end of a period of 50 years computed from the end of the year in which the phonogram was published, or failing such publication within 50 years from fixation of the phonogram, 50 years from the end of the year in which the fixation was made.

Article 18

Obligations Concerning Technological Measures

Contracting Parties shall provide adequate legal protection and effective legal remedies against the circumvention of effective technological measures that are used by performers or producers of phonograms in connection with the exercise of their rights under this Treaty and that restrict acts, in respect of their performances or phonograms, which are not authorized by the performers or the producers of phonograms concerned or permitted by law.

Article 19

Obligations Concerning Rights Management Information

(1)   Contracting Parties shall provide adequate and effective legal remedies against any person knowingly performing any of the following acts knowing or, with respect to civil remedies, having reasonable grounds to know that it will induce, enable, facilitate or conceal an infringement of any right covered by this Treaty:

    (i)   to remove or alter any electronic rights management information without authority;

    (ii)   to distribute, import for distribution, broadcast, communicate or make available to the public, without authority, performances, copies of fixed performances or phonograms knowing that electronic rights management information has been removed or altered without authority.

(2) As used in this Article, "rights management information" means information which identifies the performer, the performance of the performer, the producer of the phonogram, the phonogram, the owner of any right in the performance or phonogram, or information about the terms and conditions of use of the performance or phonogram, and any numbers or codes that represent such information, when any of these items of information is attached to a copy of a fixed performance or a phonogram or appears in connection with the communication or making available of a fixed performance or a phonogram to the public.

Article 20

Formalities

The enjoyment and exercise of the rights provided for in this Treaty shall not be subject to any formality.

Article 21

Reservations

Subject to the provisions of Article 15(3), no reservations to this Treaty shall be permitted.

Article 22

Application in Time

(1) Contracting Parties shall apply the provisions of Article 18 of the Berne Convention, *mutatis mutandis,* to the rights of performers and producers of phonograms provided for in this Treaty.

(2) Notwithstanding paragraph (1), a Contracting Party may limit the application of Article 5 of this Treaty to performances which occurred after the entry into force of this Treaty for that Party.

Article 23

Provisions on Enforcement of Rights

(1) Contracting Parties undertake to adopt, in accordance with their legal systems, the measures necessary to ensure the application of this Treaty.

(2) Contracting Parties shall ensure that enforcement procedures are available under their law so as to permit effective action against any act of infringement of rights covered by this Treaty, including expeditious remedies to prevent infringements and remedies which constitute a deterrent to further infringements.

CHAPTER V. ADMINISTRATIVE AND FINAL CLAUSES

Article 24

Assembly

(1)(a) The Contracting Parties shall have an Assembly.

(b) Each Contracting Party shall be represented by one delegate who may be assisted by alternate delegates, advisors and experts.

(c) The expenses of each delegation shall be borne by the Contracting Party that has appointed the delegation. The Assembly may ask WIPO to grant financial assistance to facilitate the participation of delegations of Contracting Parties that are regarded as developing countries in conformity with the established practice of the General Assembly of the United Nations or that are countries in transition to a market economy.

(2)(a) The Assembly shall deal with matters concerning the maintenance and development of this Treaty and the application and operation of this Treaty.

(b) The Assembly shall perform the function allocated to it under Article 26(2) in respect of the admission of certain intergovernmental organizations to become party to this Treaty.

(c) The Assembly shall decide the convocation of any diplomatic conference for the revision of this Treaty and give the necessary instructions to the Director General of WIPO for the preparation of such diplomatic conference.

(3)(a) Each Contracting Party that is a State shall have one vote and shall vote only in its own name.

(b) Any Contracting Party that is an intergovernmental organization may participate in the vote, in place of its Member States, with a number of votes equal to the number of its Member States which are party to this Treaty. No such intergovernmental organization shall participate in the vote if any one of its Member States exercises its right to vote and vice versa.

(4) The Assembly shall meet in ordinary session once every two years upon convocation by the Director General of WIPO.

(5) The Assembly shall establish its own rules of procedure, including the convocation of extraordinary sessions, the requirements of a quorum and, subject to the provisions of this Treaty, the required majority for various kinds of decisions.

Article 25

International Bureau

The International Bureau of WIPO shall perform the administrative tasks concerning the Treaty.

Article 26

Eligibility for Becoming Party to the Treaty

(1) Any Member State of WIPO may become party to this Treaty.

(2) The Assembly may decide to admit any intergovernmental organization to become party to this Treaty which declares that it is competent in respect of, and has its own legislation binding on all its Member States on, matters covered by this Treaty and that it has been duly authorized, in accordance with its internal procedures, to become party to this Treaty.

(3) The European Community, having made the declaration referred to in the preceding paragraph in the Diplomatic Conference that has adopted this Treaty, may become party to this Treaty.

Article 27

Rights and Obligations Under the Treaty

Subject to any specific provisions to the contrary in this Treaty, each Contracting Party shall enjoy all of the rights and assume all of the obligations under this Treaty.

Article 28

Signature of the Treaty

This Treaty shall be open for signature until December 31, 1997, by any Member State of WIPO and by the European Community.

Article 29

Entry Into Force of the Treaty

This Treaty shall enter into force three months after 30 instruments of ratification or accession by States have been deposited with the Director General of WIPO.

Article 30

Effective Date of Becoming Party to the Treaty

This Treaty shall bind

(i)   the 30 States referred to in Article 29, from the date on which this Treaty has entered into force;

(ii)   each other State from the expiration of three months from the date on which the State has deposited its instrument with the Director General of WIPO;

(iii) the European Community, from the expiration of three months after the deposit of its instrument of ratification or accession if such instrument has been deposited after the entry into force of this Treaty according to Article 29, or, three months after the entry into force of this Treaty if such instrument has been deposited before the entry into force of this Treaty;

(iv)   any other intergovernmental organization that is admitted to become party to this Treaty, from the expiration of three months after the deposit of its instrument of accession.

Article 31

Denunciation of the Treaty

This Treaty may be denounced by any Contracting Party by notification addressed to the Director General of WIPO. Any denunciation shall take effect one year from the date on which the Director General of WIPO received the notification.

Article 32

Languages of the Treaty

(1)   This Treaty is signed in a single original in English, Arabic, Chinese, French, Russian and Spanish languages, the versions in all these languages being equally authentic.

(2)   An official text in any language other than those referred to in paragraph (1) shall be established by the Director General of WIPO on the request of an interested party, after consultation with all the interested parties. For the purposes of this paragraph, "interested party" means any Member State of WIPO whose official language, or one of whose official languages, is involved and the European Community, and any other intergovernmental organization that may become party to this Treaty, if one of its official languages is involved.

Article 33

Depositary

The Director General of WIPO is the depositary of this Treaty.

L. BEIJING TREATY ON AUDIOVISUAL PERFORMANCES*

Contents

Preamble

The Contracting Parties,

Desiring to develop and maintain the protection of the rights of performers in their audiovisual performances in a manner as effective and uniform as possible,

Recalling the importance of the Development Agenda recommendations, adopted in 2007 by the General Assembly of the Convention Establishing the World Intellectual Property Organization (WIPO), which aim to ensure that development considerations form an integral part of the Organization's work,

---

*   This treaty was approved by a Diplomatic Conference of the World Intellectual Property Organization on June 24, 2012 and signed by the U.S. two days later. Thus far it has been ratified or acceded to by 24 nations, but not by the United States. It will enter into force by its own terms once it has been ratified or acceded to by 30 nations.—*Ed.*

Recognizing the need to introduce new international rules in order to provide adequate solutions to the questions raised by economic, social, cultural and technological developments,

Recognizing the profound impact of the development and convergence of information and communication technologies on the production and use of audiovisual performances,

Recognizing the need to maintain a balance between the rights of performers in their audiovisual performances and the larger public interest, particularly education, research and access to information,

Recognizing that the WIPO Performances and Phonograms Treaty (WPPT) done in Geneva on December 20, 1996, does not extend protection to performers in respect of their performances fixed in audiovisual fixations,

Referring to the Resolution concerning Audiovisual Performances adopted by the Diplomatic Conference on Certain Copyright and Neighboring Rights Questions on December 20, 1996,

Have agreed as follows:

Article 1

Relation to Other Conventions and Treaties

(1)   Nothing in this Treaty shall derogate from existing obligations that Contracting Parties have to each other under the WPPT or the International Convention for the Protection of Performers, Producers of Phonograms and Broadcasting Organizations done in Rome on October 26, 1961.

(2)   Protection granted under this Treaty shall leave intact and shall in no way affect the protection of copyright in literary and artistic works. Consequently, no provision of this Treaty may be interpreted as prejudicing such protection.

(3)   This Treaty shall not have any connection with treaties other than the WPPT, nor shall it prejudice any rights and obligations under any other treaties[1,2].

Article 2

Definitions

For the purposes of this Treaty:

(a)   "performers" are actors, singers, musicians, dancers, and other persons who act, sing, deliver, declaim, play in, interpret, or otherwise perform literary or artistic works or expressions of folklore[3];

(b)   "audiovisual fixation" means the embodiment of moving images, whether or not accompanied by sounds or by the representations thereof, from which they can be perceived, reproduced or communicated through a device[4];

(c)   "broadcasting" means the transmission by wireless means for public reception of sounds or of images or of images and sounds or of the representations thereof; such transmission by satellite is also

---

[1]   Agreed statement concerning Article 1: It is understood that nothing in this Treaty affects any rights or obligations under the WIPO Performances and Phonograms Treaty (WPPT) or their interpretation and it is further understood that paragraph 3 does not create any obligations for a Contracting Party to this Treaty to ratify or accede to the WPPT or to comply with any of its provisions.

[2]   Agreed statement concerning Article 1(3): It is understood that Contracting Parties who are members of the World Trade Organization (WTO) acknowledge all the principles and objectives of the Agreement on Trade-Related Aspects of Intellectual Property Rights (TRIPS Agreement) and understand that nothing in this Treaty affects the provisions of the TRIPS Agreement, including, but not limited to, the provisions relating to anti-competitive practices.

[3]   Agreed statement concerning Article 2(a): It is understood that the definition of "performers" includes those who perform a literary or artistic work that is created or first fixed in the course of a performance.

[4]   Agreed statement concerning Article 2(b): It is hereby confirmed that the definition of "audiovisual fixation" contained in Article 2(b) is without prejudice to Article 2(c) of the WPPT.

"broadcasting"; transmission of encrypted signals is "broadcasting" where the means for decrypting are provided to the public by the broadcasting organization or with its consent;

(d) "communication to the public" of a performance means the transmission to the public by any medium, otherwise than by broadcasting, of an unfixed performance, or of a performance fixed in an audiovisual fixation. For the purposes of Article 11, "communication to the public" includes making a performance fixed in an audiovisual fixation audible or visible or audible and visible to the public.

Article 3

Beneficiaries of Protection

(1) Contracting Parties shall accord the protection granted under this Treaty to performers who are nationals of other Contracting Parties.

(2) Performers who are not nationals of one of the Contracting Parties but who have their habitual residence in one of them shall, for the purposes of this Treaty, be assimilated to nationals of that Contracting Party.

Article 4

National Treatment

(1) Each Contracting Party shall accord to nationals of other Contracting Parties the treatment it accords to its own nationals with regard to the exclusive rights specifically granted in this Treaty and the right to equitable remuneration provided for in Article 11 of this Treaty.

(2) A Contracting Party shall be entitled to limit the extent and term of the protection accorded to nationals of another Contracting Party under paragraph (1), with respect to the rights granted in Article 11(1) and 11(2) of this Treaty, to those rights that its own nationals enjoy in that other Contracting Party.

(3) The obligation provided for in paragraph (1) does not apply to a Contracting Party to the extent that another Contracting Party makes use of the reservations permitted by Article 11(3) of this Treaty, nor does it apply to a Contracting Party, to the extent that it has made such reservation.

Article 5

Moral Rights

(1) Independently of a performer's economic rights, and even after the transfer of those rights, the performer shall, as regards his live performances or performances fixed in audiovisual fixations, have the right:

(i) to claim to be identified as the performer of his performances, except where omission is dictated by the manner of the use of the performance; and

(ii) to object to any distortion, mutilation or other modification of his performances that would be prejudicial to his reputation, taking due account of the nature of audiovisual fixations.

(2) The rights granted to a performer in accordance with paragraph (1) shall, after his death, be maintained, at least until the expiry of the economic rights, and shall be exercisable by the persons or institutions authorized by the legislation of the Contracting Party where protection is claimed. However, those Contracting Parties whose legislation, at the moment of their ratification of or accession to this Treaty, does not provide for protection after the death of the performer of all rights set out in the preceding paragraph may provide that some of these rights will, after his death, cease to be maintained.

(3)   The means of redress for safeguarding the rights granted under this Article shall be governed by the legislation of the Contracting Party where protection is claimed⁵.

Article 6

Economic Rights of Performers in their Unfixed Performances

Performers shall enjoy the exclusive right of authorizing, as regards their performances:

(i)   the broadcasting and communication to the public of their unfixed performances except where the performance is already a broadcast performance; and

(ii)   the fixation of their unfixed performances.

Article 7

Right of Reproduction

Performers shall enjoy the exclusive right of authorizing the direct or indirect reproduction of their performances fixed in audiovisual fixations, in any manner or form⁶.

Article 8

Right of Distribution

(1)   Performers shall enjoy the exclusive right of authorizing the making available to the public of the original and copies of their performances fixed in audiovisual fixations through sale or other transfer of ownership.

(2)   Nothing in this Treaty shall affect the freedom of Contracting Parties to determine the conditions, if any, under which the exhaustion of the right in paragraph (1) applies after the first sale or other transfer of ownership of the original or a copy of the fixed performance with the authorization of the performer⁷.

Article 9

Right of Rental

(1)   Performers shall enjoy the exclusive right of authorizing the commercial rental to the public of the original and copies of their performances fixed in audiovisual fixations as determined in the national law of Contracting Parties, even after distribution of them by, or pursuant to, authorization by the performer.

---

⁵   Agreed statement concerning Article 5: For the purposes of this Treaty and without prejudice to any other treaty, it is understood that, considering the nature of audiovisual fixations and their production and distribution, modifications of a performance that are made in the normal course of exploitation of the performance, such as editing, compression, dubbing, or formatting, in existing or new media or formats, and that are made in the course of a use authorized by the performer, would not in themselves amount to modifications within the meaning of Article 5(1)(ii). Rights under Article 5(1)(ii) are concerned only with changes that are objectively prejudicial to the performer's reputation in a substantial way. It is also understood that the mere use of new or changed technology or media, as such, does not amount to modification within the meaning of Article 5(1)(ii).

⁶   Agreed statement concerning Article 7: The reproduction right, as set out in Article 7, and the exceptions permitted thereunder through Article 13, fully apply in the digital environment, in particular to the use of performances in digital form. It is understood that the storage of a protected performance in digital form in an electronic medium constitutes a reproduction within the meaning of this Article.

⁷   Agreed statement concerning Articles 8 and 9: As used in these Articles, the expression "original and copies," being subject to the right of distribution and the right of rental under the said Articles, refers exclusively to fixed copies that can be put into circulation as tangible objects.

(2)   Contracting Parties are exempt from the obligation of paragraph (1) unless the commercial rental has led to widespread copying of such fixations materially impairing the exclusive right of reproduction of performers[8].

Article 10

Right of Making Available of Fixed Performances

Performers shall enjoy the exclusive right of authorizing the making available to the public of their performances fixed in audiovisual fixations, by wire or wireless means, in such a way that members of the public may access them from a place and at a time individually chosen by them.

Article 11

Right of Broadcasting and Communication to the Public

(1)   Performers shall enjoy the exclusive right of authorizing the broadcasting and communication to the public of their performances fixed in audiovisual fixations.

(2)   Contracting Parties may in a notification deposited with the Director General of WIPO declare that, instead of the right of authorization provided for in paragraph (1), they will establish a right to equitable remuneration for the direct or indirect use of performances fixed in audiovisual fixations for broadcasting or for communication to the public. Contracting Parties may also declare that they will set conditions in their legislation for the exercise of the right to equitable remuneration.

(3)   Any Contracting Party may declare that it will apply the provisions of paragraphs (1) or (2) only in respect of certain uses, or that it will limit their application in some other way, or that it will not apply the provisions of paragraphs (1) and (2) at all.

Article 12

Transfer of Rights

(1)   A Contracting Party may provide in its national law that once a performer has consented to fixation of his or her performance in an audiovisual fixation, the exclusive rights of authorization provided for in Articles 7 to 11 of this Treaty shall be owned or exercised by or transferred to the producer of such audiovisual fixation subject to any contract to the contrary between the performer and the producer of the audiovisual fixation as determined by the national law.

(2)   A Contracting Party may require with respect to audiovisual fixations produced under its national law that such consent or contract be in writing and signed by both parties to the contract or by their duly authorized representatives.

(3)   Independent of the transfer of exclusive rights described above, national laws or individual, collective or other agreements may provide the performer with the right to receive royalties or equitable remuneration for any use of the performance, as provided for under this Treaty including as regards Articles 10 and 11.

Article 13

Limitations and Exceptions

(1)   Contracting Parties may, in their national legislation, provide for the same kinds of limitations or exceptions with regard to the protection of performers as they provide for, in their national legislation, in connection with the protection of copyright in literary and artistic works.

---

[8]   Agreed statement concerning Articles 8 and 9: As used in these Articles, the expression "original and copies," being subject to the right of distribution and the right of rental under the said Articles, refers exclusively to fixed copies that can be put into circulation as tangible objects.

(2)   Contracting Parties shall confine any limitations of or exceptions to rights provided for in this Treaty to certain special cases which do not conflict with a normal exploitation of the performance and do not unreasonably prejudice the legitimate interests of the performer[9].

Article 14

Term of Protection

The term of protection to be granted to performers under this Treaty shall last, at least, until the end of a period of 50 years computed from the end of the year in which the performance was fixed.

Article 15

Obligations concerning Technological Measures

Contracting Parties shall provide adequate legal protection and effective legal remedies against the circumvention of effective technological measures that are used by performers in connection with the exercise of their rights under this Treaty and that restrict acts, in respect of their performances, which are not authorized by the performers concerned or permitted by law[10,11].

Article 16

Obligations concerning Rights Management Information

(1)   Contracting Parties shall provide adequate and effective legal remedies against any person knowingly performing any of the following acts knowing, or with respect to civil remedies having reasonable grounds to know, that it will induce, enable, facilitate, or conceal an infringement of any right covered by this Treaty:

(i)   to remove or alter any electronic rights management information without authority;

(ii)   to distribute, import for distribution, broadcast, communicate or make available to the public, without authority, performances or copies of performances fixed in audiovisual fixations knowing that electronic rights management information has been removed or altered without authority.

(2)   As used in this Article, "rights management information" means information which identifies the performer, the performance of the performer, or the owner of any right in the performance, or information about the terms and conditions of use of the performance, and any numbers or codes that represent such information, when any of these items of information is attached to a performance fixed in an audiovisual fixation[12].

---

[9]   Agreed statement concerning Article 13: The Agreed statement concerning Article 10 (on Limitations and Exceptions) of the WIPO Copyright Treaty (WCT) is applicable *mutatis mutandis* also to Article 13 (on Limitations and Exceptions) of the Treaty.

[10]   Agreed statement concerning Article 15 as it relates to Article 13: It is understood that nothing in this Article prevents a Contracting Party from adopting effective and necessary measures to ensure that a beneficiary may enjoy limitations and exceptions provided in that Contracting Party's national law, in accordance with Article 13, where technological measures have been applied to an audiovisual performance and the beneficiary has legal access to that performance, in circumstances such as where appropriate and effective measures have not been taken by rights holders in relation to that performance to enable the beneficiary to enjoy the limitations and exceptions under that Contracting Party's national law. Without prejudice to the legal protection of an audiovisual work in which a performance is fixed, it is further understood that the obligations under Article 15 are not applicable to performances unprotected or no longer protected under the national law giving effect to this Treaty.

[11]   Agreed statement concerning Article 15: The expression "technological measures used by performers" should, as this is the case regarding the WPPT, be construed broadly, referring also to those acting on behalf of performers, including their representatives, licensees or assignees, including producers, service providers, and persons engaged in communication or broadcasting using performances on the basis of due authorization.

[12]   Agreed statement concerning Article 16: The Agreed statement concerning Article 12 (on Obligations concerning Rights Management Information) of the WCT is applicable *mutatis mutandis* also to Article 16 (on Obligations concerning Rights Management Information) of the Treaty.

Article 17

Formalities

The enjoyment and exercise of the rights provided for in this Treaty shall not be subject to any formality.

Article 18

Reservations and Notifications

(1)   Subject to provisions of Article 11(3), no reservations to this Treaty shall be permitted.

(2)   Any notification under Article 11(2) or 19(2) may be made in instruments of ratification or accession, and the effective date of the notification shall be the same as the date of entry into force of this Treaty with respect to the Contracting Party having made the notification. Any such notification may also be made later, in which case the notification shall have effect three months after its receipt by the Director General of WIPO or at any later date indicated in the notification.

Article 19

Application in Time

(1)   Contracting Parties shall accord the protection granted under this Treaty to fixed performances that exist at the moment of the entry into force of this Treaty and to all performances that occur after the entry into force of this Treaty for each Contracting Party.

(2)   Notwithstanding the provisions of paragraph (1), a Contracting Party may declare in a notification deposited with the Director General of WIPO that it will not apply the provisions of Articles 7 to 11 of this Treaty, or any one or more of those, to fixed performances that existed at the moment of the entry into force of this Treaty for each Contracting Party. In respect of such Contracting Party, other Contracting Parties may limit the application of the said Articles to performances that occurred after the entry into force of this Treaty for that Contracting Party.

(3)   The protection provided for in this Treaty shall be without prejudice to any acts committed, agreements concluded or rights acquired before the entry into force of this Treaty for each Contracting Party.

(4)   Contracting Parties may in their legislation establish transitional provisions under which any person who, prior to the entry into force of this Treaty, engaged in lawful acts with respect to a performance, may undertake with respect to the same performance acts within the scope of the rights provided for in Articles 5 and 7 to 11 after the entry into force of this Treaty for the respective Contracting Parties.

Article 20

Provisions on Enforcement of Rights

(1)   Contracting Parties undertake to adopt, in accordance with their legal systems, the measures necessary to ensure the application of this Treaty.

(2)   Contracting Parties shall ensure that enforcement procedures are available under their law so as to permit effective action against any act of infringement of rights covered by this Treaty, including expeditious remedies to prevent infringements and remedies which constitute a deterrent to further infringements.

Article 21

Assembly

(1) (a) The Contracting Parties shall have an Assembly.

(b) Each Contracting Party shall be represented in the Assembly by one delegate who may be assisted by alternate delegates, advisors and experts.

(c) The expenses of each delegation shall be borne by the Contracting Party that has appointed the delegation. The Assembly may ask WIPO to grant financial assistance to facilitate the participation of delegations of Contracting Parties that are regarded as developing countries in conformity with the established practice of the General Assembly of the United Nations or that are countries in transition to a market economy.

(2) (a) The Assembly shall deal with matters concerning the maintenance and development of this Treaty and the application and operation of this Treaty.

(b) The Assembly shall perform the function allocated to it under Article 23(2) in respect of the admission of certain intergovernmental organizations to become party to this Treaty.

(c) The Assembly shall decide the convocation of any diplomatic conference for the revision of this Treaty and give the necessary instructions to the Director General of WIPO for the preparation of such diplomatic conference.

(3) (a) Each Contracting Party that is a State shall have one vote and shall vote only in its own name.

(b) Any Contracting Party that is an intergovernmental organization may participate in the vote, in place of its Member States, with a number of votes equal to the number of its Member States which are party to this Treaty. No such intergovernmental organization shall participate in the vote if any one of its Member States exercises its right to vote and vice versa.

(4) The Assembly shall meet upon convocation by the Director General and, in the absence of exceptional circumstances, during the same period and at the same place as the General Assembly of WIPO.

(5) The Assembly shall endeavor to take its decisions by consensus and shall establish its own rules of procedure, including the convocation of extraordinary sessions, the requirements of a quorum and, subject to the provisions of this Treaty, the required majority for various kinds of decisions.

Article 22

International Bureau

The International Bureau of WIPO shall perform the administrative tasks concerning the Treaty.

Article 23

Eligibility for Becoming Party to the Treaty

(1) Any Member State of WIPO may become party to this Treaty.

(2) The Assembly may decide to admit any intergovernmental organization to become party to this Treaty which declares that it is competent in respect of, and has its own legislation binding on all its Member States on, matters covered by this Treaty and that it has been duly authorized, in accordance with its internal procedures, to become party to this Treaty.

(3) The European Union, having made the declaration referred to in the preceding paragraph in the Diplomatic Conference that has adopted this Treaty, may become party to this Treaty.

Article 24

Rights and Obligations under the Treaty

Subject to any specific provisions to the contrary in this Treaty, each Contracting Party shall enjoy all of the rights and assume all of the obligations under this Treaty.

Article 25

Signature of the Treaty

This Treaty shall be open for signature at the headquarters of WIPO by any eligible party for one year after its adoption.

Article 26

Entry into Force of the Treaty

This Treaty shall enter into force three months after 30 eligible parties referred to in Article 23 have deposited their instruments of ratification or accession.

Article 27

Effective Date of Becoming Party to the Treaty

This Treaty shall bind:

(i)   the 30 eligible parties referred to in Article 26, from the date on which this Treaty has entered into force;

(ii)   each other eligible party referred to in Article 23, from the expiration of three months from the date on which it has deposited its instrument of ratification or accession with the Director General of WIPO.

Article 28

Denunciation of the Treaty

This Treaty may be denounced by any Contracting Party by notification addressed to the Director General of WIPO. Any denunciation shall take effect one year from the date on which the Director General of WIPO received the notification.

Article 29

Languages of the Treaty

(1)   This Treaty is signed in a single original in English, Arabic, Chinese, French, Russian and Spanish languages, the versions in all these languages being equally authentic.

(2)   An official text in any language other than those referred to in paragraph (1) shall be established by the Director General of WIPO on the request of an interested party, after consultation with all the interested parties. For the purposes of this paragraph, "interested party" means any Member State of WIPO whose official language, or one of whose official languages, is involved and the European Union, and any other intergovernmental organization that may become party to this Treaty, if one of its official languages is involved.

Article 30

Depositary

The Director General of WIPO is the depositary of this Treaty.

M. MARRAKESH TREATY TO FACILITATE ACCESS TO PUBLISHED WORKS FOR PERSONS WHO ARE BLIND, VISUALLY IMPAIRED OR OTHERWISE PRINT DISABLED*

Contents**

Preamble

The Contracting Parties,

Recalling the principles of non-discrimination, equal opportunity, accessibility and full and effective participation and inclusion in society, proclaimed in the Universal Declaration of Human Rights and the United Nations Convention on the Rights of Persons with Disabilities,

Mindful of the challenges that are prejudicial to the complete development of persons with visual impairments or with other print disabilities, which limit their freedom of expression, including the freedom to seek, receive and impart information and ideas of all kinds on an equal basis with others, including through all forms of communication of their choice, their enjoyment of the right to education, and the opportunity to conduct research,

Emphasizing the importance of copyright protection as an incentive and reward for literary and artistic creations and of enhancing opportunities for everyone, including persons with visual

---

*   This Treaty was adopted by the Diplomatic Conference to Conclude a Treaty to Facilitate Access to Published Works by Visually Impaired Persons and Persons with Print Disabilities on June 27, 2013.

**   Following Senate ratification on February 8, 2019, this treaty entered into force with respect to the United States on May 8, 2019. So far, 54 countries have ratified this treaty.

impairments or with other print disabilities, to participate in the cultural life of the community, to enjoy the arts and to share scientific progress and its benefits,

Aware of the barriers of persons with visual impairments or with other print disabilities to access published works in achieving equal opportunities in society, and the need to both expand the number of works in accessible formats and to improve the circulation of such works,

Taking into account that the majority of persons with visual impairments or with other print disabilities live in developing and least-developed countries,

Recognizing that, despite the differences in national copyright laws, the positive impact of new information and communication technologies on the lives of persons with visual impairments or with other print disabilities may be reinforced by an enhanced legal framework at the international level,

Recognizing that many Member States have established limitations and exceptions in their national copyright laws for persons with visual impairments or with other print disabilities, yet there is a continuing shortage of available works in accessible format copies for such persons, and that considerable resources are required for their effort of making works accessible to these persons, and that the lack of possibilities of cross-border exchange of accessible format copies has necessitated duplication of these efforts,

Recognizing both the importance of rightholders' role in making their works accessible to persons with visual impairments or with other print disabilities and the importance of appropriate limitations and exceptions to make works accessible to these persons, particularly when the market is unable to provide such access,

Recognizing the need to maintain a balance between the effective protection of the rights of authors and the larger public interest, particularly education, research and access to information, and that such a balance must facilitate effective and timely access to works for the benefit of persons with visual impairments or with other print disabilities,

Reaffirming the obligations of Contracting Parties under the existing international treaties on the protection of copyright and the importance and flexibility of the three-step test for limitations and exceptions established in Article 9(2) of the Berne Convention for the Protection of Literary and Artistic Works and other international instruments,

Recalling the importance of the Development Agenda recommendations, adopted in 2007 by the General Assembly of the World Intellectual Property Organization (WIPO), which aim to ensure that development considerations form an integral part of the Organization's work,

Recognizing the importance of the international copyright system and desiring to harmonize limitations and exceptions with a view to facilitating access to and use of works by persons with visual impairments or with other print disabilities,

Have agreed as follows:

Article 1

Relation to Other Conventions and Treaties

Nothing in this Treaty shall derogate from any obligations that Contracting Parties have to each other under any other treaties, nor shall it prejudice any rights that a Contracting Party has under any other treaties.

Article 2

Definitions

For the purposes of this Treaty:

(a)   "works" means literary and artistic works within the meaning of Article 2(1) of the Berne Convention for the Protection of Literary and Artistic Works, in the form of text, notation and/or related illustrations, whether published or otherwise made publicly available in any media[2];

(b)   "accessible format copy" means a copy of a work in an alternative manner or form which gives a beneficiary person access to the work, including to permit the person to have access as feasibly and comfortably as a person without visual impairment or other print disability. The accessible format copy is used exclusively by beneficiary persons and it must respect the integrity of the original work, taking due consideration of the changes needed to make the work accessible in the alternative format and of the accessibility needs of the beneficiary persons;

(c)   "authorized entity" means an entity that is authorized or recognized by the government to provide education, instructional training, adaptive reading or information access to beneficiary persons on a non-profit basis. It also includes a government institution or non-profit organization that provides the same services to beneficiary persons as one of its primary activities or institutional obligations[3].

An authorized entity establishes and follows its own practices:

(i)   to establish that the persons it serves are beneficiary persons;

(ii)   to limit to beneficiary persons and/or authorized entities its distribution and making available of accessible format copies;

(iii) to discourage the reproduction, distribution and making available of unauthorized copies; and

(iv)   to maintain due care in, and records of, its handling of copies of works, while respecting the privacy of beneficiary persons in accordance with Article 8.

Article 3

Beneficiary Persons

A beneficiary person is a person who:

(a)   is blind;

(b)   has a visual impairment or a perceptual or reading disability which cannot be improved to give visual function substantially equivalent to that of a person who has no such impairment or disability and so is unable to read printed works to substantially the same degree as a person without an impairment or disability; or[4]

(c)   is otherwise unable, through physical disability, to hold or manipulate a book or to focus or move the eyes to the extent that would be normally acceptable for reading;

regardless of any other disabilities.

---

[2]   Agreed statement concerning Article 2(a): For the purposes of this Treaty, it is understood that this definition includes such works in audio form, such as audiobooks.

[3]   Agreed statement concerning Article 2(c): For the purposes of this Treaty, it is understood that "entities recognized by the government" may include entities receiving financial support from the government to provide education, instructional training, adaptive reading or information access to beneficiary persons on a non-profit basis.

[4]   Agreed statement concerning Article 3(b): Nothing in this language implies that "cannot be improved" requires the use of all possible medical diagnostic procedures and treatments.

Article 4

National Law Limitations and Exceptions Regarding Accessible Format Copies

1.   (a)   Contracting Parties shall provide in their national copyright laws for a limitation or exception to the right of reproduction, the right of distribution, and the right of making available to the public as provided by the WIPO Copyright Treaty (WCT), to facilitate the availability of works in accessible format copies for beneficiary persons. The limitation or exception provided in national law should permit changes needed to make the work accessible in the alternative format.

(b)   Contracting Parties may also provide a limitation or exception to the right of public performance to facilitate access to works for beneficiary persons.

2.   A Contracting Party may fulfill Article 4(1) for all rights identified therein by providing a limitation or exception in its national copyright law such that:

(a)   Authorized entities shall be permitted, without the authorization of the copyright rightholder, to make an accessible format copy of a work, obtain from another authorized entity an accessible format copy, and supply those copies to beneficiary persons by any means, including by non-commercial lending or by electronic communication by wire or wireless means, and undertake any intermediate steps to achieve those objectives, when all of the following conditions are met:

(i)   the authorized entity wishing to undertake said activity has lawful access to that work or a copy of that work;

(ii)   the work is converted to an accessible format copy, which may include any means needed to navigate information in the accessible format, but does not introduce changes other than those needed to make the work accessible to the beneficiary person;

(iii) such accessible format copies are supplied exclusively to be used by beneficiary persons; and

(iv) the activity is undertaken on a non-profit basis;

and

(b)   A beneficiary person, or someone acting on his or her behalf including a primary caretaker or caregiver, may make an accessible format copy of a work for the personal use of the beneficiary person or otherwise may assist the beneficiary person to make and use accessible format copies where the beneficiary person has lawful access to that work or a copy of that work.

3.   A Contracting Party may fulfill Article 4(1) by providing other limitations or exceptions in its national copyright law pursuant to Articles 10 and 11[5].

4.   A Contracting Party may confine limitations or exceptions under this Article to works which, in the particular accessible format, cannot be obtained commercially under reasonable terms for beneficiary persons in that market. Any Contracting Party availing itself of this possibility shall so declare in a notification deposited with the Director General of WIPO at the time of ratification of, acceptance of or accession to this Treaty or at any time thereafter[6].

5.   It shall be a matter for national law to determine whether limitations or exceptions under this Article are subject to remuneration.

---

[5]   Agreed statement concerning Article 4(3): It is understood that this paragraph neither reduces nor extends the scope of applicability of limitations and exceptions permitted under the Berne Convention, as regards the right of translation, with respect to persons with visual impairments or with other print disabilities.

[6]   Agreed statement concerning Article 4(4): It is understood that a commercial availability requirement does not prejudge whether or not a limitation or exception under this Article is consistent with the three-step test.

Article 5

Cross-Border Exchange of Accessible Format Copies

1.   Contracting Parties shall provide that if an accessible format copy is made under a limitation or exception or pursuant to operation of law, that accessible format copy may be distributed or made available by an authorized entity to a beneficiary person or an authorized entity in another Contracting Party[7].

2.   A Contracting Party may fulfill Article 5(1) by providing a limitation or exception in its national copyright law such that:

(a)   authorized entities shall be permitted, without the authorization of the rightholder, to distribute or make available for the exclusive use of beneficiary persons accessible format copies to an authorized entity in another Contracting Party; and

(b)   authorized entities shall be permitted, without the authorization of the rightholder and pursuant to Article 2(c), to distribute or make available accessible format copies to a beneficiary person in another Contracting Party;

provided that prior to the distribution or making available the originating authorized entity did not know or have reasonable grounds to know that the accessible format copy would be used for other than beneficiary persons[8].

3.   A Contracting Party may fulfill Article 5(1) by providing other limitations or exceptions in its national copyright law pursuant to Articles 5(4), 10 and 11.

4.   (a)   When an authorized entity in a Contracting Party receives accessible format copies pursuant to Article 5(1) and that Contracting Party does not have obligations under Article 9 of the Berne Convention, it will ensure, consistent with its own legal system and practices, that the accessible format copies are only reproduced, distributed or made available for the benefit of beneficiary persons in that Contracting Party's jurisdiction.

(b)   The distribution and making available of accessible format copies by an authorized entity pursuant to Article 5(1) shall be limited to that jurisdiction unless the Contracting Party is a Party to the WIPO Copyright Treaty or otherwise limits limitations and exceptions implementing this Treaty to the right of distribution and the right of making available to the public to certain special cases which do not conflict with a normal exploitation of the work and do not unreasonably prejudice the legitimate interests of the rightholder[9, 10].

(c)   Nothing in this Article affects the determination of what constitutes an act of distribution or an act of making available to the public.

5.   Nothing in this Treaty shall be used to address the issue of exhaustion of rights.

---

[7]   Agreed statement concerning Article 5(1): It is further understood that nothing in this Treaty reduces or extends the scope of exclusive rights under any other treaty.

[8]   Agreed statement concerning Article 5(2): It is understood that, to distribute or make available accessible format copies directly to a beneficiary person in another Contracting Party, it may be appropriate for an authorized entity to apply further measures to confirm that the person it is serving is a beneficiary person and to follow its own practices as described in Article 2(c).

[9]   Agreed statement concerning Article 5(4)(b): It is understood that nothing in this Treaty requires or implies that a Contracting Party adopt or apply the three-step test beyond its obligations under this instrument or under other international treaties.

[10]   Agreed statement concerning Article 5(4)(b): It is understood that nothing in this Treaty creates any obligations for a Contracting Party to ratify or accede to the WCT or to comply with any of its provisions and nothing in this Treaty prejudices any rights, limitations and exceptions contained in the WCT.

COPYRIGHT AND RELATED MATERIALS

Article 6

Importation of Accessible Format Copies

To the extent that the national law of a Contracting Party would permit a beneficiary person, someone acting on his or her behalf, or an authorized entity, to make an accessible format copy of a work, the national law of that Contracting Party shall also permit them to import an accessible format copy for the benefit of beneficiary persons, without the authorization of the rightholder[11].

Article 7

Obligations Concerning Technological Measures

Contracting Parties shall take appropriate measures, as necessary, to ensure that when they provide adequate legal protection and effective legal remedies against the circumvention of effective technological measures, this legal protection does not prevent beneficiary persons from enjoying the limitations and exceptions provided for in this Treaty[12].

Article 8

Respect for Privacy

In the implementation of the limitations and exceptions provided for in this Treaty, Contracting Parties shall endeavor to protect the privacy of beneficiary persons on an equal basis with others.

Article 9

Cooperation to Facilitate Cross-Border Exchange

1.   Contracting Parties shall endeavor to foster the cross-border exchange of accessible format copies by encouraging the voluntary sharing of information to assist authorized entities in identifying one another. The International Bureau of WIPO shall establish an information access point for this purpose.

2.   Contracting Parties undertake to assist their authorized entities engaged in activities under Article 5 to make information available regarding their practices pursuant to Article 2(c), both through the sharing of information among authorized entities, and through making available information on their policies and practices, including related to cross-border exchange of accessible format copies, to interested parties and members of the public as appropriate.

3.   The International Bureau of WIPO is invited to share information, where available, about the functioning of this Treaty.

4.   Contracting Parties recognize the importance of international cooperation and its promotion, in support of national efforts for realization of the purpose and objectives of this Treaty[13].

---

[11] Agreed statement concerning Article 6: It is understood that the Contracting Parties have the same flexibilities set out in Article 4 when implementing their obligations under Article 6.

[12] Agreed statement concerning Article 7: It is understood that authorized entities, in various circumstances, choose to apply technological measures in the making, distribution and making available of accessible format copies and nothing herein disturbs such practices when in accordance with national law.

[13] Agreed statement concerning Article 9: It is understood that Article 9 does not imply mandatory registration for authorized entities nor does it constitute a precondition for authorized entities to engage in activities recognized under this Treaty; but it provides for a possibility for sharing information to facilitate the cross-border exchange of accessible format copies.

Article 10

General Principles on Implementation

1.   Contracting Parties undertake to adopt the measures necessary to ensure the application of this Treaty.

2.   Nothing shall prevent Contracting Parties from determining the appropriate method of implementing the provisions of this Treaty within their own legal system and practice[14].

3.   Contracting Parties may fulfill their rights and obligations under this Treaty through limitations or exceptions specifically for the benefit of beneficiary persons, other limitations or exceptions, or a combination thereof, within their national legal system and practice. These may include judicial, administrative or regulatory determinations for the benefit of beneficiary persons as to fair practices, dealings or uses to meet their needs consistent with the Contracting Parties' rights and obligations under the Berne Convention, other international treaties, and Article 11.

Article 11

General Obligations on Limitations and Exceptions

In adopting measures necessary to ensure the application of this Treaty, a Contracting Party may exercise the rights and shall comply with the obligations that that Contracting Party has under the Berne Convention, the Agreement on Trade-Related Aspects of Intellectual Property Rights and the WIPO Copyright Treaty, including their interpretative agreements so that:

(a)   in accordance with Article 9(2) of the Berne Convention, a Contracting Party may permit the reproduction of works in certain special cases provided that such reproduction does not conflict with a normal exploitation of the work and does not unreasonably prejudice the legitimate interests of the author;

(b)   in accordance with Article 13 of the Agreement on Trade-Related Aspects of Intellectual Property Rights, a Contracting Party shall confine limitations or exceptions to exclusive rights to certain special cases which do not conflict with a normal exploitation of the work and do not unreasonably prejudice the legitimate interests of the rightholder;

(c)   in accordance with Article 10(1) of the WIPO Copyright Treaty, a Contracting Party may provide for limitations of or exceptions to the rights granted to authors under the WCT in certain special cases, that do not conflict with a normal exploitation of the work and do not unreasonably prejudice the legitimate interests of the author;

(d)   in accordance with Article 10(2) of the WIPO Copyright Treaty, a Contracting Party shall confine, when applying the Berne Convention, any limitations of or exceptions to rights to certain special cases that do not conflict with a normal exploitation of the work and do not unreasonably prejudice the legitimate interests of the author.

Article 12

Other Limitations and Exceptions

1.   Contracting Parties recognize that a Contracting Party may implement in its national law other copyright limitations and exceptions for the benefit of beneficiary persons than are provided by this Treaty having regard to that Contracting Party's economic situation, and its social and cultural needs, in conformity with that Contracting Party's international rights and obligations, and in the case of a

---

[14] Agreed statement concerning Article 10(2): It is understood that when a work qualifies as a work under Article 2(a), including such works in audio form, the limitations and exceptions provided for by this Treaty apply *mutatis mutandis* to related rights as necessary to make the accessible format copy, to distribute it and to make it available to beneficiary persons.

least-developed country taking into account its special needs and its particular international rights and obligations and flexibilities thereof.

2.   This Treaty is without prejudice to other limitations and exceptions for persons with disabilities provided by national law.

Article 13

Assembly

1.   (a)   The Contracting Parties shall have an Assembly.

(b)   Each Contracting Party shall be represented in the Assembly by one delegate who may be assisted by alternate delegates, advisors and experts.

(c)   The expenses of each delegation shall be borne by the Contracting Party that has appointed the delegation. The Assembly may ask WIPO to grant financial assistance to facilitate the participation of delegations of Contracting Parties that are regarded as developing countries in conformity with the established practice of the General Assembly of the United Nations or that are countries in transition to a market economy.

2.   (a)   The Assembly shall deal with matters concerning the maintenance and development of this Treaty and the application and operation of this Treaty.

(b)   The Assembly shall perform the function allocated to it under Article 15 in respect of the admission of certain intergovernmental organizations to become party to this Treaty.

(c)   The Assembly shall decide the convocation of any diplomatic conference for the revision of this Treaty and give the necessary instructions to the Director General of WIPO for the preparation of such diplomatic conference.

3.   (a)   Each Contracting Party that is a State shall have one vote and shall vote only in its own name.

(b)   Any Contracting Party that is an intergovernmental organization may participate in the vote, in place of its Member States, with a number of votes equal to the number of its Member States which are party to this Treaty. No such intergovernmental organization shall participate in the vote if any one of its Member States exercises its right to vote and vice versa.

4.   The Assembly shall meet upon convocation by the Director General and, in the absence of exceptional circumstances, during the same period and at the same place as the General Assembly of WIPO.

5.   The Assembly shall endeavor to take its decisions by consensus and shall establish its own rules of procedure, including the convocation of extraordinary sessions, the requirements of a quorum and, subject to the provisions of this Treaty, the required majority for various kinds of decisions.

Article 14

International Bureau

The International Bureau of WIPO shall perform the administrative tasks concerning this Treaty.

Article 15

Eligibility for Becoming Party to the Treaty

1.   Any Member State of WIPO may become party to this Treaty.

2.   The Assembly may decide to admit any intergovernmental organization to become party to this Treaty which declares that it is competent in respect of, and has its own legislation binding on all its

Member States on, matters covered by this Treaty and that it has been duly authorized, in accordance with its internal procedures, to become party to this Treaty.

3.   The European Union, having made the declaration referred to in the preceding paragraph at the Diplomatic Conference that has adopted this Treaty, may become party to this Treaty.

Article 16

Rights and Obligations Under the Treaty

Subject to any specific provisions to the contrary in this Treaty, each Contracting Party shall enjoy all of the rights and assume all of the obligations under this Treaty.

Article 17

Signature of the Treaty

This Treaty shall be open for signature at the Diplomatic Conference in Marrakesh, and thereafter at the headquarters of WIPO by any eligible party for one year after its adoption.

Article 18

Entry into Force of the Treaty

This Treaty shall enter into force three months after 20 eligible parties referred to in Article 15 have deposited their instruments of ratification or accession.

Article 19

Effective Date of Becoming Party to the Treaty

This Treaty shall bind:

(a)   the 20 eligible parties referred to in Article 18, from the date on which this Treaty has entered into force;

(b)   each other eligible party referred to in Article 15, from the expiration of three months from the date on which it has deposited its instrument of ratification or accession with the Director General of WIPO.

Article 20

Denunciation of the Treaty

This Treaty may be denounced by any Contracting Party by notification addressed to the Director General of WIPO. Any denunciation shall take effect one year from the date on which the Director General of WIPO received the notification.

Article 21

Languages of the Treaty

1.   This Treaty is signed in a single original in English, Arabic, Chinese, French, Russian and Spanish languages, the versions in all these languages being equally authentic.

2.   An official text in any language other than those referred to in Article 21(1) shall be established by the Director General of WIPO on the request of an interested party, after consultation with all the interested parties. For the purposes of this paragraph, "interested party" means any Member State of WIPO whose official language, or one of whose official languages, is involved and the European Union, and any other intergovernmental organization that may become party to this Treaty, if one of its official languages is involved.

Article 22

Depositary

The Director General of WIPO is the depositary of this Treaty.

Done in Marrakesh on the 27th day of June, 2013.

III. PATENTS AND RELATED MATERIALS

A. PATENT ACT

35 U.S.C.A. §§ 1–390

Contents

Part

PART I.   UNITED STATES PATENT AND TRADEMARK OFFICE

Chap.

CHAPTER 1. ESTABLISHMENT, OFFICERS AND EMPLOYEES FUNCTIONS

Sec.

-----

§ 1.   Establishment

(a) **Establishment.** The United States Patent and Trademark office is established as an agency of the United States, within the Department of Commerce. In carrying out its functions, the United States Patent and Trademark Office shall be subject to the policy direction of the Secretary of

-----

* Part V of the Patent Act was added by Pub. L. 112–211, also known as the Patent Law Treaties Implementation Act of 2012. These amendments did not take effect immediately. The provisions set out in the body of the text reflect all amendments made by the Patent Law Treaties Implementation Act of 2012. For relevant sections, the effective date is indicated in a footnote that also provides the text of the statute that governs prior to that effective date.

Commerce, but otherwise shall retain responsibility for decisions regarding the management and administration of its operations and shall exercise independent control of its budget allocations and expenditures, personnel decisions and processes, procurements, and other administrative and management functions in accordance with this title and applicable provisions of law. Those operations designed to grant and issue patents and those operations which are designed to facilitate the registration of trademarks shall be treated as separate operating units within the Office.

(b) **Offices.** The United States Patent and Trademark Office shall maintain its principal office in the metropolitan Washington, D.C., area, for the service of process and papers and for the purpose of carrying out its functions. The United States Patent and Trademark Office shall be deemed, for purposes of venue in civil actions, to be a resident of the district in which its principal office is located, except where jurisdiction is otherwise provided by law. The United States Patent and Trademark Office may establish satellite offices in such other places in the United States as it considers necessary and appropriate in the conduct of its business.

(c) **Reference.** For purposes of this title, the United States Patent and Trademark Office shall also be referred to as the "Office" and the "Patent and Trademark Office".

§ 2.   Powers and Duties

(a) **In General.** The United States Patent and Trademark Office, subject to the policy direction of the Secretary of Commerce—

(1) shall be responsible for the granting and issuing of patents and the registration of trademarks; and

(2) shall be responsible for disseminating to the public information with respect to patents and trademarks.

(b) **Specific Powers.** The Office—

(1) shall adopt and use a seal of the Office, which shall be judicially noticed and with which letters patent, certificates of trademark registrations, and papers issued by the Office shall be authenticated;

(2) may establish regulations, not inconsistent with law, which—

(A) shall govern the conduct of proceedings in the Office;

(B) shall be made in accordance with section 553 of title 5;

(C) shall facilitate and expedite the processing of patent applications, particularly those which can be filed, stored, processed, searched, and retrieved electronically, subject to the provisions of section 122 relating to the confidential status of applications;

(D) may govern the recognition and conduct of agents, attorneys, or other persons representing applicants or other parties before the Office, and may require them, before being recognized as representatives of applicants or other persons, to show that they are of good moral character and reputation and are possessed of the necessary qualifications to render to applicants or other persons valuable service, advice, and assistance in the presentation or prosecution of their applications or other business before the Office;

(E) shall recognize the public interest in continuing to safeguard broad access to the United States patent system through the reduced fee structure for small entities under section 41(h)(1);

(F) provide for the development of a performance-based process that includes quantitative and qualitative measures and standards for evaluating cost-effectiveness and is consistent with the principles of impartiality and competitiveness; and

(G) may, subject to any conditions prescribed by the Director and at the request of the patent applicant, provide for prioritization of examination of applications for products, processes, or technologies that are important to the national economy or national competitiveness without recovering the aggregate extra cost of providing such prioritization, notwithstanding section 41 or any other provision of law;

(3)   may acquire, construct, purchase, lease, hold, manage, operate, improve, alter, and renovate any real, personal, or mixed property, or any interest therein, as it considers necessary to carry out its functions;

(4)(A)   may make such purchases, contracts for the construction, maintenance, or management and operation of facilities, and contracts for supplies or services, without regard to the provisions of subtitle I and chapter 33 of title 40, division C (except sections 3302, 3501(b), 3509, 3906, 4710, and 4711) of subtitle I of title 41, and the McKinney-Vento Homeless Assistance Act (42 U.S.C. 11301 et seq.); and

(B)   may enter into and perform such purchases and contracts for printing services, including the process of composition, platemaking, presswork, silk screen processes, binding, microform, and the products of such processes, as it considers necessary to carry out the functions of the Office, without regard to sections 501 through 517 and 1101 through 1123 of title 44;

(5)   may use, with their consent, services, equipment, personnel, and facilities of other departments, agencies, and instrumentalities of the Federal Government, on a reimbursable basis, and cooperate with such other departments, agencies, and instrumentalities in the establishment and use of services, equipment, and facilities of the Office;

(6)   may, when the Director determines that it is practicable, efficient, and cost-effective to do so, use, with the consent of the United States and the agency, instrumentality, Patent and Trademark Office, or international organization concerned, the services, records, facilities, or personnel of any State or local government agency or instrumentality or foreign patent and trademark office or international organization to perform functions on its behalf;

(7)   may retain and use all of its revenues and receipts, including revenues from the sale, lease, or disposal of any real, personal, or mixed property, or any interest therein, of the Office;

(8)   shall advise the President, through the Secretary of Commerce, on national and certain international intellectual property policy issues;

(9)   shall advise Federal departments and agencies on matters of intellectual property policy in the United States and intellectual property protection in other countries;

(10) shall provide guidance, as appropriate, with respect to proposals by agencies to assist foreign governments and international intergovernmental organizations on matters of intellectual property protection;

(11) may conduct programs, studies, or exchanges of items or services regarding domestic and international intellectual property law and the effectiveness of intellectual property protection domestically and throughout the world, and the Office is authorized to expend funds to cover the subsistence expenses and travel-related expenses, including per diem, lodging costs, and transportation costs, of persons attending such programs who are not Federal employees;

(12)(A)   shall advise the Secretary of Commerce on programs and studies relating to intellectual property policy that are conducted, or authorized to be conducted, cooperatively with foreign intellectual property offices and international intergovernmental organizations; and

(B)   may conduct programs and studies described in subparagraph (A); and

(13)(A)   in coordination with the Department of State, may conduct programs and studies cooperatively with foreign intellectual property offices and international intergovernmental organizations; and

(B) with the concurrence of the Secretary of State, may authorize the transfer of not to exceed $100,000 in any year to the Department of State for the purpose of making special payments to international intergovernmental organizations for studies and programs for advancing international cooperation concerning patents, trademarks, and other matters.

(c) Clarification of Specific Powers.

(1) The special payments under subsection (b)(13)(B) shall be in addition to any other payments or contributions to international organizations described in subsection (b)(13)(B) and shall not be subject to any limitations imposed by law on the amounts of such other payments or contributions by the United States Government.

(2) Nothing in subsection (b) shall derogate from the duties of the Secretary of State or from the duties of the United States Trade Representative as set forth in section 141 of the Trade Act of 1974 (19 U.S.C. 2171).

(3) Nothing in subsection (b) shall derogate from the duties and functions of the Register of Copyrights or otherwise alter current authorities relating to copyright matters.

(4) In exercising the Director's powers under paragraphs (3) and (4)(A) of subsection (b), the Director shall consult with the Administrator of General Services.

(5) In exercising the Director's powers and duties under this section, the Director shall consult with the Register of Copyrights on all copyright and related matters.

(d) Construction. Nothing in this section shall be construed to nullify, void, cancel, or interrupt any pending request-for-proposal let or contract issued by the General Services Administration for the specific purpose of relocating or leasing space to the United States Patent and Trademark Office.

§ 3.   Officers and Employees

(a) Under Secretary and Director.

(1) *In general.* The powers and duties of the United States Patent and Trademark Office shall be vested in an Under Secretary of Commerce for Intellectual Property and Director of the United States Patent and Trademark Office (in this title referred to as the "Director"), who shall be a citizen of the United States and who shall be appointed by the President, by and with the advice and consent of the Senate. The Director shall be a person who has a professional background and experience in patent or trademark law.

(2) *Duties.*

(A) In general. The Director shall be responsible for providing policy direction and management supervision for the Office and for the issuance of patents and the registration of trademarks. The Director shall perform these duties in a fair, impartial, and equitable manner.

(B) Consulting with the Public Advisory Committees. The Director shall consult with the Patent Public Advisory Committee established in section 5 on a regular basis on matters relating to the patent operations of the Office, shall consult with the Trademark Public Advisory Committee established in section 5 on a regular basis on matters relating to the trademark operations of the Office, and shall consult with the respective Public Advisory Committee before submitting budgetary proposals to the Office of Management and Budget or changing or proposing to change patent or trademark user fees or patent or trademark regulations which are subject to the requirement to provide notice and opportunity for public comment under section 553 of title 5, as the case may be.

(3) *Oath.* The Director shall, before taking office, take an oath to discharge faithfully the duties of the Office.

(4) *Removal.* The Director may be removed from office by the President. The President shall provide notification of any such removal to both Houses of Congress.

(b) Officers and Employees of the Office.

(1) *Deputy Under Secretary and Deputy Director.* The Secretary of Commerce, upon nomination by the Director, shall appoint a Deputy Under Secretary of Commerce for Intellectual Property and Deputy Director of the United States Patent and Trademark Office who shall be vested with the authority to act in the capacity of the Director in the event of the absence or incapacity of the Director. The Deputy Director shall be a citizen of the United States who has a professional background and experience in patent or trademark law.

(2) *Commissioners.*

(A) Appointment and duties. The Secretary of Commerce shall appoint a Commissioner for Patents and a Commissioner for Trademarks, without regard to chapter 33, 51, or 53 of title 5. The Commissioner for Patents shall be a citizen of the United States with demonstrated management ability and professional background and experience in patent law and serve for a term of 5 years. The Commissioner for Trademarks shall be a citizen of the United States with demonstrated management ability and professional background and experience in trademark law and serve for a term of 5 years. The Commissioner for Patents and the Commissioner for Trademarks shall serve as the chief operating officers for the operations of the Office relating to patents and trademarks, respectively, and shall be responsible for the management and direction of all aspects of the activities of the Office that affect the administration of patent and trademark operations, respectively. The Secretary may reappoint a Commissioner to subsequent terms of 5 years as long as the performance of the Commissioner as set forth in the performance agreement in subparagraph (B) is satisfactory.

(B) Salary and performance agreement. The Commissioners shall be paid an annual rate of basic pay not to exceed the maximum rate of basic pay for the Senior Executive Service established under section 5382 of title 5, including any applicable locality-based comparability payment that may be authorized under section 5304(h)(2)(C) of title 5. The compensation of the Commissioners shall be considered, for purposes of section 207(c)(2)(A) of title 18, United States Code, to be the equivalent of that described under clause (ii) of section 207(c)(2)(A) of title 18. In addition, the Commissioners may receive a bonus in an amount of up to, but not in excess of, 50 percent of the Commissioners' annual rate of basic pay, based upon an evaluation by the Secretary of Commerce, acting through the Director, of the Commissioners' performance as defined in an annual performance agreement between the Commissioners and the Secretary. The annual performance agreements shall incorporate measurable organization and individual goals in key operational areas as delineated in an annual performance plan agreed to by the Commissioners and the Secretary. Payment of a bonus under this subparagraph may be made to the Commissioners only to the extent that such payment does not cause the Commissioners' total aggregate compensation in a calendar year to equal or exceed the amount of the salary of the Vice President under section 104 of title 3.

(C) Removal. The Commissioners may be removed from office by the Secretary for misconduct or nonsatisfactory performance under the performance agreement described in subparagraph (B), without regard to the provisions of title 5. The Secretary shall provide notification of any such removal to both Houses of Congress.

(3) *Other officers and employees.* The Director shall—

(A) appoint such officers, employees (including attorneys), and agents of the Office as the Director considers necessary to carry out the functions of the Office; and

(B) define the title, authority, and duties of such officers and employees and delegate to them such of the powers vested in the Office as the Director may determine.

The Office shall not be subject to any administratively or statutorily imposed limitation on positions or personnel, and no positions or personnel of the Office shall be taken into account for purposes of applying any such limitation.

(4) *Training of examiners.* The Office shall submit to the Congress a proposal to provide an incentive program to retain as employees patent and trademark examiners of the primary examiner grade or higher who are eligible for retirement, for the sole purpose of training patent and trademark examiners.

(5) *National security positions.* The Director, in consultation with the Director of the Office of Personnel Management, shall maintain a program for identifying national security positions and providing for appropriate security clearances, in order to maintain the secrecy of certain inventions, as described in section 181, and to prevent disclosure of sensitive and strategic information in the interest of national security.

(6) *Administrative patent judges and administrative trademark judges.* The Director may fix the rate of basic pay for the administrative patent judges appointed pursuant to section 6 and the administrative trademark judges appointed pursuant to section 17 of the Trademark Act of 1946 (15 U.S.C. 1067) at not greater than the rate of basic pay payable for level III of the Executive Schedule under section 5314 of title 5. The payment of a rate of basic pay under this paragraph shall not be subject to the pay limitation under section 5306(e) or 5373 of title 5.

(c) **Continued Applicability of Title 5.** Officers and employees of the Office shall be subject to the provisions of title 5, relating to Federal employees.

(d) **Adoption of Existing Labor Agreements.** The Office shall adopt all labor agreements which are in effect, as of the day before the effective date of the Patent and Trademark Office Efficiency Act, with respect to such Office (as then in effect).

(e) **Carryover of Personnel.**

(1) From PTO. Effective as of the effective date of the Patent and Trademark Office Efficiency Act, all officers and employees of the Patent and Trademark Office on the day before such effective date shall become officers and employees of the Office, without a break in service.

(2) Other personnel. Any individual who, on the day before the effective date of the Patent and Trademark Office Efficiency Act, is an officer or employee of the Department of Commerce (other than an officer or employee under paragraph (1)) shall be transferred to the Office, as necessary to carry out the purposes of that Act, if—

(A) such individual serves in a position for which a major function is the performance of work reimbursed by the Patent and Trademark Office, as determined by the Secretary of Commerce;

(B) such individual serves in a position that performed work in support of the Patent and Trademark Office during at least half of the incumbent's work time, as determined by the Secretary of Commerce; or

(C) such transfer would be in the interest of the Office, as determined by the Secretary of Commerce in consultation with the Director.

Any transfer under this paragraph shall be effective as of the same effective date as referred to in paragraph (1), and shall be made without a break in service.

(f) **Transition provisions.**

(1) *Interim appointment of Director.* On or after the effective date of the Patent and Trademark Office Efficiency Act, the President shall appoint an individual to serve as the

Director until the date on which a Director qualifies under subsection (a). The President shall not make more than one such appointment under this subsection.

(2) *Continuation in office of certain officers.*

(A) The individual serving as the Assistant Commissioner for Patents on the day before the effective date of the Patent and Trademark Office Efficiency Act may serve as the Commissioner for Patents until the date on which a Commissioner for Patents is appointed under subsection (b).

(B) The individual serving as the Assistant Commissioner for Trademarks on the day before the effective date of the Patent and Trademark Office Efficiency Act may serve as the Commissioner for Trademarks until the date on which a Commissioner for Trademarks is appointed under subsection (b).

§ 4.   Restrictions on Officers and Employees as to Interest in Patents

Officers and employees of the Patent and Trademark Office shall be incapable, during the period of their appointments and for one year thereafter, of applying for a patent and of acquiring, directly or indirectly, except by inheritance or bequest, any patent or any right or interest in any patent, issued or to be issued by the Office. In patents applied for thereafter they shall not be entitled to any priority date earlier than one year after the termination of their appointment.

§ 5.   Patent and Trademark Office Advisory Committees

(a)   Establishment of Public Advisory Committees.

(1) *Appointment.* The United States Patent and Trademark Office shall have a Patent Public Advisory Committee and a Trademark Public Advisory Committee, each of which shall have nine voting members who shall be appointed by the Secretary of Commerce and serve at the pleasure of the Secretary of Commerce. In each year, 3 members shall be appointed to each Advisory Committee for 3-year terms that shall begin on December 1 of that year. Any vacancy on an Advisory Committee shall be filled within 90 days after it occurs. A new member who is appointed to fill a vacancy shall be appointed to serve for the remainder of the predecessor's term.

(2) *Chair.* The Secretary of Commerce, in consultation with the Director, shall designate a Chair and Vice Chair of each Advisory Committee from among the members appointed under paragraph (1). If the Chair resigns before the completion of his or her term, or is otherwise unable to exercise the functions of the Chair, the Vice Chair shall exercise the functions of the Chair.

(b)   Basis for Appointments. Members of each Advisory Committee—

(1) shall be citizens of the United States who shall be chosen so as to represent the interests of diverse users of the United States Patent and Trademark Office with respect to patents, in the case of the Patent Public Advisory Committee, and with respect to trademarks, in the case of the Trademark Public Advisory Committee;

(2) shall include members who represent small and large entity applicants located in the United States in proportion to the number of applications filed by such applicants, but in no case shall members who represent small entity patent applicants, including small business concerns, independent inventors, and nonprofit organizations, constitute less than 25 percent of the members of the Patent Public Advisory Committee, and such members shall include at least one independent inventor; and

(3) shall include individuals with substantial background and achievement in finance, management, labor relations, science, technology, and office automation.

In addition to the voting members, each Advisory Committee shall include a representative of each labor organization recognized by the United States Patent and Trademark Office. Such representatives shall be nonvoting members of the Advisory Committee to which they are appointed.

(c) Meetings. Each Advisory Committee shall meet at the call of the chair to consider an agenda set by the chair.

(d) Duties. Each Advisory Committee shall—

(1) review the policies, goals, performance, budget, and user fees of the United States Patent and Trademark Office with respect to patents, in the case of the Patent Public Advisory Committee, and with respect to Trademarks, in the case of the Trademark Public Advisory Committee, and advise the Director on these matters;

(2) within 60 days after the end of each fiscal year—

(A) prepare an annual report on the matters referred to in paragraph (1);

(B) transmit the report to the Secretary of Commerce, the President, and the Committees on the Judiciary of the Senate and the House of Representatives; and

(C) publish the report in the Official Gazette of the United States Patent and Trademark Office.

(e) Compensation. Each member of each Advisory Committee shall be compensated for each day (including travel time) during which such member is attending meetings or conferences of that Advisory Committee or otherwise engaged in the business of that Advisory Committee, at the rate which is the daily equivalent of the annual rate of basic pay in effect for level III of the Executive Schedule under section 5314 of title 5. While away from such member's home or regular place of business such member shall be allowed travel expenses, including per diem in lieu of subsistence, as authorized by section 5703 of title 5.

(f) Access to Information. Members of each Advisory Committee shall be provided access to records and information in the United States Patent and Trademark Office, except for personnel or other privileged information and information concerning patent applications required to be kept in confidence by section 122.

(g) Applicability of Certain Ethics Laws. Members of each Advisory Committee shall be special Government employees within the meaning of section 202 of title 18.

(h) Inapplicability of Federal Advisory Committee Act. The Federal Advisory Committee Act (5 U.S.C. App.) shall not apply to each Advisory Committee.

(i) Open Meetings. The meetings of each Advisory Committee shall be open to the public, except that each Advisory Committee may by majority vote meet in executive session when considering personnel, privileged, or other confidential information.

(j) Inapplicability of Patent Prohibition. Section 4 shall not apply to voting members of the Advisory Committees.

§ 6. Patent Trial and Appeal Board

(a) In General.—There shall be in the Office a Patent Trial and Appeal Board. The Director, the Deputy Director, the Commissioner for Patents, the Commissioner for Trademarks, and the administrative patent judges shall constitute the Patent Trial and Appeal Board. The administrative patent judges shall be persons of competent legal knowledge and scientific ability who are appointed by the Secretary, in consultation with the Director. Any reference in any Federal law, Executive order, rule, regulation, or delegation of authority, or any document of or pertaining to the Board of Patent Appeals and Interferences is deemed to refer to the Patent Trial and Appeal Board.

(b) Duties.—The Patent Trial and Appeal Board shall—

(1) on written appeal of an applicant, review adverse decisions of examiners upon applications for patents pursuant to section 134(a);

(2) review appeals of reexaminations pursuant to section 134(b);

(3)   conduct derivation proceedings pursuant to section 135; and

(4)   conduct inter partes reviews and post-grant reviews pursuant to chapters 31 and 32.

(c) 3-Member Panels.—Each appeal, derivation proceeding, post-grant review, and inter partes review shall be heard by at least 3 members of the Patent Trial and Appeal Board, who shall be designated by the Director. Only the Patent Trial and Appeal Board may grant rehearings.

(d) Treatment of Prior Appointments.—The Secretary of Commerce may, in the Secretary's discretion, deem the appointment of an administrative patent judge who, before the date of the enactment of this subsection, held office pursuant to an appointment by the Director to take effect on the date on which the Director initially appointed the administrative patent judge. It shall be a defense to a challenge to the appointment of an administrative patent judge on the basis of the judge's having been originally appointed by the Director that the administrative patent judge so appointed was acting as a de facto officer.

§ 7.   Library

The Director shall maintain a library of scientific and other works and periodicals, both foreign and domestic, in the Patent and Trademark Office to aid the officers in the discharge of their duties.

§ 8.   Classification of Patents

The Director may revise and maintain the classification by subject matter of United States letters patent, and such other patents and printed publications as may be necessary or practicable, for the purpose of determining with readiness and accuracy the novelty of inventions for which applications for patent are filed.

§ 9.   Certified Copies of Records

The Director may furnish certified copies of specifications and drawings of patents issued by the Patent and Trademark Office, and of other records available either to the public or to the person applying therefor.

§ 10.   Publications

(a)   The Director may print, or cause to be printed, the following:

1.   Patents, including specifications and drawings, together with copies of the same. The Patent and Trademark Office may print the headings of the drawings for patents for the purpose of photolithography.

2.   Certificates of trade-mark registrations, including statements and drawings, together with copies of the same.

3.   The Official Gazette of the United States Patent and Trademark Office.

4.   Annual indexes of patents and patentees, and of trade-marks and registrants.

5.   Annual volumes of decisions in patent and trade-mark cases.

6.   Pamphlet copies of the patent laws and rules of practice, laws and rules relating to trade-marks, and circulars or other publications relating to the business of the Office.

(b)   The Director may exchange any of the publications specified in items 3, 4, 5, and 6 of subsection (a) of this section for publications desirable for the use of the Patent and Trademark Office.

§ 11.   Exchange of Copies of Patents and Applications With Foreign Countries

The Director may exchange copies of specifications and drawings of United States patents for those of foreign countries. The Director shall not enter into an agreement to provide such copies of specifications and drawings of United States patents and applications to a foreign country, other than a NAFTA country or a WTO member country, without the express authorization of the Secretary of Commerce. For purposes of this section, the terms "NAFTA country" and "WTO member country" have the meanings given those terms in section 104(b).

§ 12.   Copies of Patents and Applications for Public Libraries

The Director may supply copies of specifications and drawings of patents in printed or electronic form to public libraries in the United States which shall maintain such copies for the use of the public, at the rate for each year's issue established for this purpose in section 41(d).

§ 13.   Annual Report to Congress

The Director shall report to the Congress, not later than 180 days after the end of each fiscal year, the moneys received and expended by the Office, the purposes for which the moneys were spent, the quality and quantity of the work of the Office, the nature of training provided to examiners, the evaluation of the Commissioner of Patents and the Commissioner of Trademarks by the Secretary of Commerce, the compensation of the Commissioners, and other information relating to the Office.

CHAPTER 2. PROCEEDINGS IN THE PATENT AND TRADEMARK OFFICE

Sec.

---

§ 21.   Filing Date and Day for Taking Action

(a)   The Director may by rule prescribe that any paper or fee required to be filed in the Patent and Trademark Office will be considered filed in the Office on the date on which it was deposited with the United States Postal Service or would have been deposited with the United States Postal Service but for postal service interruptions or emergencies designated by the Director.

(b)   When the day, or the last day, for taking any action or paying any fee in the United States Patent and Trademark Office falls on Saturday, Sunday, or a federal holiday within the District of Columbia, the action may be taken, or the fee paid, on the next succeeding secular or business day.

§ 22.   Printing of Papers Filed

The Director may require papers filed in the Patent and Trademark Office to be printed or typewritten, or an electronic medium.

§ 23.   Testimony in Patent and Trademark Office Cases

The Director may establish rules for taking affidavits and depositions required in cases in the Patent and Trademark Office. Any officer authorized by law to take depositions to be used in the courts of the United States, or of the State where he resides, may take such affidavits and depositions.

§ 24.   Subpoenas, Witnesses

The clerk of any United States court for the district wherein testimony is to be taken for use in any contested case in the Patent and Trademark Office, shall, upon the application of any party thereto, issue a subpoena for any witness residing or being within such district, commanding him to appear and testify before an officer in such district authorized to take depositions and affidavits, at the time and place stated in the subpoena. The provisions of the Federal Rules of Civil Procedure relating to the attendance of witnesses and to the production of documents and things shall apply to contested cases in the Patent and Trademark Office.

Every witness subpoenaed and in attendance shall be allowed the fees and traveling expenses allowed to witnesses attending the United States district courts.

A judge of a court whose clerk issued a subpoena may enforce obedience to the process or punish disobedience as in other like cases, on proof that a witness, served with such subpoena, neglected or refused to appear or to testify. No witness shall be deemed guilty of contempt for disobeying such subpoena unless his fees and traveling expenses in going to, and returning from, and one day's attendance at the place of examination, are paid or tendered him at the time of the service of the subpoena; nor for refusing to disclose any secret matter except upon appropriate order of the court which issued the subpoena.

§ 25. Declaration in Lieu of Oath

(a) The Director may by rule prescribe that any document to be filed in the Patent and Trademark Office and which is required by any law, rule, or other regulation to be under oath may be subscribed to by a written declaration in such form as the Director may prescribe, such declaration to be in lieu of the oath otherwise required.

(b) Whenever such written declaration is used, the document must warn the declarant that willful false statements and the like are punishable by fine or imprisonment, or both (18 U.S.C. 1001).

§ 26. Effect of Defective Execution

Any document to be filed in the Patent and Trademark Office and which is required by any law, rule, or other regulation to be executed in a specified manner may be provisionally accepted by the Director despite a defective execution, provided a properly executed document is submitted within such time as may be prescribed.

§ 27. Revival of Applications; Reinstatement of Reexamination Proceedings

The Director may establish procedures, including the requirement for payment of the fee specified in section 41(a)(7), to revive an unintentionally abandoned application for patent, accept an unintentionally delayed payment of the fee for issuing each patent, or accept an unintentionally delayed response by the patent owner in a reexamination proceeding, upon petition by the applicant for patent or patent owner.

CHAPTER 3. PRACTICE BEFORE PATENT AND TRADEMARK OFFICE

Sec.
31. [Repealed].
32. Suspension or Exclusion From Practice.
33. Unauthorized Representation as Practitioner.

––––––––––

§ 31. [Repealed]

§ 32. Suspension or Exclusion From Practice

The Director may, after notice and opportunity for a hearing suspend or exclude, either generally or in any particular case, from further practice before the Patent and Trademark Office, any person, agent, or attorney shown to be incompetent or disreputable, or guilty of gross misconduct, or who does not comply with the regulations established under section 2(b)(2)(D), or who shall, by word, circular, letter, or advertising, with intent to defraud in any manner, deceive, mislead, or threaten any applicant or prospective applicant, or other person having immediate or prospective business before the Office. The reasons for any such suspension or exclusion shall be duly recorded. The Director shall have the discretion to designate any attorney who is an officer or employee of the United States Patent and Trademark Office to conduct the hearing required by this section. A proceeding under this section shall be commenced not later than the earlier of either the date that is 10 years after the date on which the misconduct forming the basis for the proceeding occurred, or 1 year after the date on which the misconduct forming the basis for the proceeding is made known to an officer or employee of the Office as prescribed in the regulations established under section 2(b)(2)(D). The United States District Court for the Eastern District of Virginia, under such conditions and upon such proceedings as it by its rules determines, may review the action of the Director upon the petition of the person so refused recognition or so suspended or excluded.

§ 33. Unauthorized Representation as Practitioner

Whoever, not being recognized to practice before the Patent and Trademark Office, holds himself out or permits himself to be held out as so recognized, or as being qualified to prepare or prosecute applications for patent, shall be fined not more than $1,000 for each offense.

CHAPTER 4. PATENT FEES; FUNDING; SEARCH SYSTEMS

Sec.
41. Patent Fees; Patent and Trademark Search System.
42. Patent and Trademark Office Funding.

---

§ 41. Patent Fees; Patent and Trademark Search System

(a) **General Fees.**—The Director shall charge the following fees:

(1) **Filing and Basic National Fees.**—

(A) On filing each application for an original patent, except for design, plant, or provisional applications, $330.

(B) On filing each application for an original design patent, $220.

(C) On filing each application for an original plant patent, $220.

(D) On filing each provisional application for an original patent, $220.

(E) On filing each application for the reissue of a patent, $330.

(F) The basic national fee for each international application filed under the treaty defined in section 351(a) entering the national stage under section 371, $330.

(G) In addition, excluding any sequence listing or computer program listing filed in an electronic medium as prescribed by the Director, for any application the specification and drawings of which exceed 100 sheets of paper (or equivalent as prescribed by the Director if filed in an electronic medium), $270 for each additional 50 sheets of paper (or equivalent as prescribed by the Director if filed in an electronic medium) or fraction thereof.

(2) **Excess Claims Fees.**—

(A) In general.—In addition to the fee specified in paragraph (1)—

(i) on filing or on presentation at any other time, $220 for each claim in independent form in excess of 3;

    (ii) on filing or on presentation at any other time, $52 for each claim (whether dependent or independent) in excess of 20; and

    (iii) for each application containing a multiple dependent claim, $390.

    (B) Multiple dependent claims.—For the purpose of computing fees under subparagraph (A), a multiple dependent claim referred to in section 112 or any claim depending therefrom shall be considered as separate dependent claims in accordance with the number of claims to which reference is made.

    (C) Refunds; errors in payment.—The Director may by regulation provide for a refund of any part of the fee specified in subparagraph (A) for any claim that is canceled before an examination on the merits, as prescribed by the Director, has been made of the application under section 131. Errors in payment of the additional fees under this paragraph may be rectified in accordance with regulations prescribed by the Director.

(3) Examination Fees.—

    (A) In general.—

    (i) For examination of each application for an original patent, except for design, plant, provisional, or international applications, $220.

    (ii) For examination of each application for an original design patent, $140.

    (iii) For examination of each application for an original plant patent, $170.

    (iv) For examination of the national stage of each international application, $220.

    (v) For examination of each application for the reissue of a patent, $650.

    (B) Applicability of other fee provisions.—The provisions of paragraphs (3) and (4) of section 111(a) relating to the payment of the fee for filing the application shall apply to the payment of the fee specified in subparagraph (A) with respect to an application filed under section 111(a). The provisions of section 371(d) relating to the payment of the national fee shall apply to the payment of the fee specified in subparagraph (A) with respect to an international application.

(4) Issue Fees.—

    (A) For issuing each original patent, except for design or plant patents, $1,510.

    (B) For issuing each original design patent, $860.

    (C) For issuing each original plant patent, $1,190.

    (D) For issuing each reissue patent, $1,510.

(5) Disclaimer Fee.—On filing each disclaimer, $140.

(6) Appeal Fees.—

    (A) On filing an appeal from the examiner to the Patent Trial and Appeal Board, $540.

    (B) In addition, on filing a brief in support of the appeal, $540, and on requesting an oral hearing in the appeal before the Patent Trial and Appeal Board, $1,080.

(7) Revival Fees.—On filing each petition for the revival of an abandoned application for a patent, for the delayed payment of the fee for issuing each patent, for the delayed response by the patent owner in any reexamination proceeding, for the delayed payment of the fee for maintaining a patent in force, for the delayed submission of a priority or benefit claim, or for the extension of the 12-month period for filing a subsequent application, $1,700.00. The Director may refund any part of the fee specified in this paragraph, in exceptional circumstances as determined by the Director.

(8) Extension Fees.—For petitions for 1-month extensions of time to take actions required by the Director in an application—

(A) on filing a first petition, $130;

(B) on filing a second petition, $360; and

(C) on filing a third or subsequent petition, $620.

(b) Maintenance Fees.—

(1) In General.—The Director shall charge the following fees for maintaining in force all patents based on applications filed on or after December 12, 1980:

(A) Three years and 6 months after grant, $980.

(B) Seven years and 6 months after grant, $2,480.

(C) Eleven years and 6 months after grant, $4,110.

(2) Grace Period; Surcharge.—Unless payment of the applicable maintenance fee under paragraph (1) is received in the Office on or before the date the fee is due or within a grace period of 6 months thereafter, the patent shall expire as of the end of such grace period. The Director may require the payment of a surcharge as a condition of accepting within such 6-month grace period the payment of an applicable maintenance fee.

(3) No Maintenance Fee for Design or Plant Patent.—No fee may be established for maintaining a design or plant patent in force.

(c) Delays in Payment of Maintenance Fees.—

(1) Acceptance.—The Director may accept the payment of any maintenance fee required by subsection (b) after the 6-month grace period if the delay is shown to the satisfaction of the Director to have been unintentional. The Director may require the payment of the fee specified in subsection (a)(7) as a condition of accepting payment of any maintenance fee after the 6-month grace period. If the Director accepts payment of a maintenance fee after the 6-month grace period, the patent shall be considered as not having expired at the end of the grace period.

(2) Effect on Rights of Others.—A patent, the term of which has been maintained as a result of the acceptance of a payment of a maintenance fee under this subsection, shall not abridge or affect the right of any person or that person's successors in business who made, purchased, offered to sell, or used anything protected by the patent within the United States, or imported anything protected by the patent into the United States after the 6-month grace period but prior to the acceptance of a maintenance fee under this subsection, to continue the use of, to offer for sale, or to sell to others to be used, offered for sale, or sold, the specific thing so made, purchased, offered for sale, used, or imported. The court before which such matter is in question may provide for the continued manufacture, use, offer for sale, or sale of the thing made, purchased, offered for sale, or used within the United States, or imported into the United States, as specified, or for the manufacture, use, offer for sale, or sale in the United States of which substantial preparation was made after the 6-month grace period but before the acceptance of a maintenance fee under this subsection, and the court may also provide for the continued practice of any process that is practiced, or for the practice of which substantial preparation was made, after the 6-month grace period but before the acceptance of a maintenance fee under this subsection, to the extent and under such terms as the court deems equitable for the protection of investments made or business commenced after the 6-month grace period but before the acceptance of a maintenance fee under this subsection.

(d) Patent Search and Other Fees.—

(1) Patent Search Fees.—

(A) In General.—The Director shall charge the fees specified under subparagraph (B) for the search of each application for a patent, except for provisional applications. The

Director shall adjust the fees charged under this paragraph to ensure that the fees recover an amount not to exceed the estimated average cost to the Office of searching applications for patent by Office personnel.

(B) Specific fees.—The fees referred to in subparagraph (A) are—

(i) $540 for each application for an original patent, except for design, plant, provisional, or international applications;

(ii) $100 for each application for an original design patent;

(iii) $330 for each application for an original plant patent;

(iv) $540 for the national stage of each international application; and

(v) $540 for each application for the reissue of a patent.

(C) Applicability of Other Provisions.—The provisions of paragraphs (3) and (4) of section 111(a) relating to the payment of the fee for filing the application shall apply to the payment of the fee specified in this paragraph with respect to an application filed under section 111(a). The provisions of section 371(d) relating to the payment of the national fee shall apply to the payment of the fee specified in this paragraph with respect to an international application.

(D) Refunds.—The Director may by regulation provide for a refund of any part of the fee specified in this paragraph for any applicant who files a written declaration of express abandonment as prescribed by the Director before an examination has been made of the application under section 131.

(2) Other Fees.—

(A) In General.—The Director shall establish fees for all other processing, services, or materials relating to patents not specified in this section to recover the estimated average cost to the Office of such processing, services, or materials, except that the Director shall charge the following fees for the following services:

(i) For recording a document affecting title, $40 per property.

(ii) For each photocopy, $.25 per page.

(iii) For each black and white copy of a patent, $3.

(B) Copies for Libraries.—The yearly fee for providing a library specified in section 12 with uncertified printed copies of the specifications and drawings for all patents in that year shall be $50.

(e) Waiver of Fees; Copies Regarding Notice.—The Director may waive the payment of any fee for any service or material related to patents in connection with an occasional or incidental request made by a department or agency of the Government, or any officer thereof. The Director may provide any applicant issued a notice under section 132 with a copy of the specifications and drawings for all patents referred to in that notice without charge.

(f) Adjustment of Fees.—The fees established in subsections (a) and (b) of this section may be adjusted by the Director on October 1, 1992, and every year thereafter, to reflect any fluctuations occurring during the previous 12 months in the Consumer Price Index, as determined by the Secretary of Labor. Changes of less than 1 per centum may be ignored.

(g) [Repealed.]

(h) Fees for Small Entities.—

(1) Reductions in Fees.—Subject to paragraph (3), fees charged under subsections (a), (b), and (d)(1) shall be reduced by 50 percent with respect to their application to any small business concern as defined under section 3 of the Small Business Act, and to any independent inventor or nonprofit organization as defined in regulations issued by the Director.

(2) Surcharges and Other Fees.—With respect to its application to any entity described in paragraph (1), any surcharge or fee charged under subsection (c) or (d) shall not be higher than the surcharge or fee required of any other entity under the same or substantially similar circumstances.

(3) Reduction for Electronic Filing.—The fee charged under subsection (a)(1)(A) shall be reduced by 75 percent with respect to its application to any entity to which paragraph (1) applies, if the application is filed by electronic means as prescribed by the Director.

(i) Electronic Patent and Trademark Data.—

(1) Maintenance of Collections.—The Director shall maintain, for use by the public, paper, microform, or electronic collections, collections of United States patents, foreign patent documents, and United States trademark registrations arranged to permit search for and retrieval of information. The Director may not impose fees directly for the use of such collections, or for the use of the public patent or trademark search rooms or libraries.

(2) Availability of Automated Search Systems.—The Director shall provide for the full deployment of the automated search systems of the Patent and Trademark Office so that such systems are available for use by the public, and shall assure full access by the public to, and dissemination of, patent and trademark information, using a variety of automated methods, including electronic bulletin boards and remote access by users to mass storage and retrieval systems.

(3) Access Fees.—The Director may establish reasonable fees for access by the public to the automated search systems of the Patent and Trademark Office. If such fees are established, a limited amount of free access shall be made available to users of the systems for purposes of education and training. The Director may waive the payment by an individual of fees authorized by this subsection upon a showing of need or hardship, and if such a waiver is in the public interest.

(4) Annual Report to Congress.—The Director shall submit to the Congress an annual report on the automated search systems of the Patent and Trademark Office and the access by the public to such systems. The Director shall also publish such report in the Federal Register. The Director shall provide an opportunity for the submission of comments by interested persons on each such report.

§ 42. Patent and Trademark Office Funding

(a) All fees for services performed by or materials furnished by the Patent and Trademark Office will be payable to the Director.

(b) All fees paid to the Director and all appropriations for defraying the costs of the activities of the Patent and Trademark Office will be credited to the Patent and Trademark Office Appropriation Account in the Treasury of the United States.

(c)(1)   To the extent and in the amounts provided in advance in appropriations Acts, fees authorized in this title or any other Act to be charged or established by the Director shall be collected by and shall, subject to paragraph (3), be available to the Director to carry out the activities of the Patent and Trademark Office.

(2)   There is established in the Treasury a Patent and Trademark Fee Reserve Fund. If fee collections by the Patent and Trademark Office for a fiscal year exceed the amount appropriated to the Office for that fiscal year, fees collected in excess of the appropriated amount shall be deposited in the Patent and Trademark Fee Reserve Fund. To the extent and in the amounts

provided in appropriations Acts, amounts in the Fund shall be made available until expended only for obligation and expenditure by the Office in accordance with paragraph (3).

(3)(A) Any fees that are collected under this title, and any surcharges on such fees, may only be used for expenses of the Office relating to the processing of patent applications and for other activities, services, and materials relating to patents and to cover a proportionate share of the administrative costs of the Office.

(B) Any fees that are collected under section 31 of the Trademark Act of 1946, and any surcharges on such fees, may only be used for expenses of the Office relating to the processing of trademark registrations and for other activities, services, and materials relating to trademarks and to cover a proportionate share of the administrative costs of the Office.

(d) The Director may refund any fee paid by mistake or any amount paid in excess of that required.

(e) The Secretary of Commerce shall, on the day each year on which the President submits the annual budget to the Congress, provide to the Committees on the Judiciary of the Senate and the House of Representatives—

(1) a list of patent and trademark fee collections by the Patent and Trademark Office during the preceding fiscal year;

(2) a list of activities of the Patent and Trademark Office during the preceding fiscal year which were supported by patent fee expenditures, trademark fee expenditures, and appropriations;

(3) budget plans for significant programs, projects, and activities of the Office, including out-year funding estimates;

(4) any proposed disposition of surplus fees by the Office; and

(5) such other information as the committees consider necessary.

PART II.   PATENTABILITY OF INVENTIONS AND GRANT OF PATENTS

CHAPTER 10.   PATENTABILITY OF INVENTIONS

§ 100.   Definitions

When used in this title unless the context otherwise indicates—

(a)   The term "invention" means invention or discovery.

(b)   The term "process" means process, art or method, and includes a new use of a known process, machine, manufacture, composition of matter, or material.

(c)   The terms "United States" and "this country" mean the United States of America, its territories and possessions.

(d)   The word "patentee" includes not only the patentee to whom the patent was issued but also the successors in title to the patentee.

(e)   The term "third-party requester" means a person requesting ex parte reexamination under section 302.

(f)   The term "inventor" means the individual or, if a joint invention, the individuals collectively who invented or discovered the subject matter of the invention.

(g)   The terms "joint inventor" and "coinventor" mean any 1 of the individuals who invented or discovered the subject matter of a joint invention.

(h)   The term "joint research agreement" means a written contract, grant, or cooperative agreement entered into by 2 or more persons or entities for the performance of experimental, developmental, or research work in the field of the claimed invention.

(i)(1)   The term "effective filing date" for a claimed invention in a patent or application for patent means—

(A)   if subparagraph (B) does not apply, the actual filing date of the patent or the application for the patent containing a claim to the invention; or

(B)   the filing date of the earliest application for which the patent or application is entitled, as to such invention, to a right of priority under section 119, 365(a), 365(b), 386(a), or 386(b) or to the benefit of an earlier filing date under section 120, 121, 365(c), or 386(c).

(2)   The effective filing date for a claimed invention in an application for reissue or reissued patent shall be determined by deeming the claim to the invention to have been contained in the patent for which reissue was sought.

(j)   The term "claimed invention" means the subject matter defined by a claim in a patent or an application for a patent.

§ 101.   Inventions Patentable

Whoever invents or discovers any new and useful process, machine, manufacture, or composition of matter, or any new and useful improvement thereof, may obtain a patent therefor, subject to the conditions and requirements of this title.

§ 102.   Conditions for Patentability; Novelty

(a)   Novelty; Prior Art.—A person shall be entitled to a patent unless—

(1)   the claimed invention was patented, described in a printed publication, or in public use, on sale, or otherwise available to the public before the effective filing date of the claimed invention; or

(2)   the claimed invention was described in a patent issued under section 151, or in an application for patent published or deemed published under section 122(b), in which the patent or application, as the case may be, names another inventor and was effectively filed before the effective filing date of the claimed invention.

(b) Exceptions.—

(1) Disclosures Made 1 Year or Less Before the Effective Filing Date of the Claimed Invention.—A disclosure made 1 year or less before the effective filing date of a claimed invention shall not be prior art to the claimed invention under subsection (a)(1) if—

(A) the disclosure was made by the inventor or joint inventor or by another who obtained the subject matter disclosed directly or indirectly from the inventor or a joint inventor; or

(B) the subject matter disclosed had, before such disclosure, been publicly disclosed by the inventor or a joint inventor or another who obtained the subject matter disclosed directly or indirectly from the inventor or a joint inventor.

(2) Disclosures Appearing in Applications and Patents.—A disclosure shall not be prior art to a claimed invention under subsection (a)(2) if—

(A) the subject matter disclosed was obtained directly or indirectly from the inventor or a joint inventor;

(B) the subject matter disclosed had, before such subject matter was effectively filed under subsection (a)(2), been publicly disclosed by the inventor or a joint inventor or another who obtained the subject matter disclosed directly or indirectly from the inventor or a joint inventor; or

(C) the subject matter disclosed and the claimed invention, not later than the effective filing date of the claimed invention, were owned by the same person or subject to an obligation of assignment to the same person.

(c) Common Ownership Under Joint Research Agreements.—Subject matter disclosed and a claimed invention shall be deemed to have been owned by the same person or subject to an obligation of assignment to the same person in applying the provisions of subsection (b)(2)(C) if—

(1) the subject matter disclosed was developed and the claimed invention was made by, or on behalf of, 1 or more parties to a joint research agreement that was in effect on or before the effective filing date of the claimed invention;

(2) the claimed invention was made as a result of activities undertaken within the scope of the joint research agreement; and

(3) the application for patent for the claimed invention discloses or is amended to disclose the names of the parties to the joint research agreement.

(d) Patents and Published Applications Effective as Prior Art.—For purposes of determining whether a patent or application for patent is prior art to a claimed invention under subsection (a)(2), such patent or application shall be considered to have been effectively filed, with respect to any subject matter described in the patent or application—

(1) if paragraph (2) does not apply, as of the actual filing date of the patent or the application for patent; or

(2) if the patent or application for patent is entitled to claim a right of priority under section 119, 365(a), 365(b), 386(a), or 386(b), or to claim the benefit of an earlier filing date under section 120, 121, 365(c), or 386(b), based upon 1 or more prior filed applications for patent, as of the filing date of the earliest such application that describes the subject matter.

§ 103. Conditions for Patentability; Non-Obvious Subject Matter

A patent for a claimed invention may not be obtained, notwithstanding that the claimed invention is not identically disclosed as set forth in section 102, if the differences between the claimed invention and the prior art are such that the claimed invention as a whole would have been obvious before the effective filing date of the claimed invention to a person having ordinary skill in the art to which the claimed invention pertains. Patentability shall not be negated by the manner in which the invention was made.

§ 104.   [Repealed]

§ 105.   Inventions in Outer Space

(a)   Any invention made, used or sold in outer space on a space object or component thereof under the jurisdiction or control of the United States shall be considered to be made, used or sold within the United States for the purposes of this title, except with respect to any space object or component thereof that is specifically identified and otherwise provided for by an international agreement to which the United States is a party, or with respect to any space object or component thereof that is carried on the registry of a foreign state in accordance with the Convention on Registration of Objects Launched into Outer Space.

(b)   Any invention made, used or sold in outer space on a space object or component thereof that is carried on the registry of a foreign state in accordance with the Convention on Registration of Objects Launched into Outer Space, shall be considered to be made, used or sold within the United States for the purposes of this title if specifically so agreed in an international agreement between the United States and the state of registry.

CHAPTER 11.   APPLICATION FOR PATENT

§ 111.   Application

(a) In General.—

(1) **Written Application.**—An application for patent shall be made, or authorized to be made, by the inventor, except as otherwise provided in this title, in writing to the Director.

(2) **Contents.**—Such application shall include—

(A) a specification as prescribed by section 112;

(B) a drawing as prescribed by section 113; and

(C) an oath or declaration as prescribed by section 115.

(3) **Fee, Oath or Declaration, and Claims.**—The application shall be accompanied by the fee required by law. The fee, oath or declaration, and 1 or more claims may be submitted after the filing date of the application, within such period and under such conditions, including the payment of a surcharge, as may be prescribed by the Director. Upon failure to submit the fee,

oath or declaration, and 1 or more claims within such prescribed period, the application shall be regarded as abandoned.

(4) **Filing Date.**—The filing date of an application shall be the date on which a specification, with or without claims, is received in the United States Patent and Trademark Office.

(b) Provisional Application.—

(1) **Authorization.**—A provisional application for patent shall be made or authorized to be made by the inventor, except as otherwise provided in this title, in writing to the Director. Such application shall include—

(A) a specification as prescribed by section 112(a); and

(B) a drawing as prescribed by section 113.

(2) **Claim.**—A claim, as required by subsections (b) through (e) of section 112, shall not be required in a provisional application.

(3) **Fee.**—The application shall be accompanied by the fee required by law. The fee may be submitted after the filing date of the application, within such period and under such conditions, including the payment of a surcharge, as may be prescribed by the Director. Upon failure to submit the fee within such prescribed period, the application shall be regarded as abandoned.

(4) **Filing Date.**—The filing date of a provisional application shall be the date on which a specification, with or without claims, is received in the United States Patent and Trademark Office.

(5) **Abandonment.**—Notwithstanding the absence of a claim, upon timely request and as prescribed by the Director, a provisional application may be treated as an application filed under subsection (a). Subject to section 119(e)(3), if no such request is made, the provisional application shall be regarded as abandoned 12 months after the filing date of such application and shall not be subject to revival after such 12-month period.

(6) **Other Basis for Provisional Application.**—Subject to all the conditions in this subsection and section 119(e), and as prescribed by the Director, an application for patent filed under subsection (a) may be treated as a provisional application for patent.

(7) **No Right of Priority or Benefit of Earliest Filing Date.**—A provisional application shall not be entitled to the right of priority of any other application under section 119, 365(a), or 386(a) or to the benefit of an earlier filing date in the United States under section, 120, 121, 365(c), or 386(c).

(8) **Applicable Provisions.**—The provisions of this title relating to applications for patent shall apply to provisional applications for patent, except as otherwise provided, and except that provisional applications for patent shall not be subject to sections 131 and 135.

(c) Prior Filed Application.—Notwithstanding the provisions of subsection (a), the Director may prescribe the conditions, including the payment of a surcharge, under which a reference made upon the filing of an application under subsection (a) to a previously filed application, specifying the previously filed application by application number and the intellectual property authority or country in which the application was filed, shall constitute the specification and any drawings of the subsequent application for purposes of a filing date. A copy of the specification and any drawings of the previously filed application shall be submitted within such period and under such conditions as may be prescribed by the Director. A failure to submit the copy of the specification and any drawings of the previously filed application within the prescribed period shall result in the application being regarded as abandoned. Such application shall be treated as having never been filed, unless—

(1) the application is revived under section 27; and

(2)   a copy of the specification and any drawings of the previously filed application are submitted to the Director.

§ 112.   Specification

(a)   In General.—The specification shall contain a written description of the invention, and of the manner and process of making and using it, in such full, clear, concise, and exact terms as to enable any person skilled in the art to which it pertains, or with which it is most nearly connected, to make and use the same, and shall set forth the best mode contemplated by the inventor or joint inventor of carrying out the invention.

(b)   Conclusion.—The specification shall conclude with one or more claims particularly pointing out and distinctly claiming the subject matter which the inventor or a joint inventor regards as the invention.

(c)   Form.—A claim may be written in independent or, if the nature of the case admits, in dependent or multiple dependent form.

(d)   Reference in Dependent Forms.—Subject to subsection (e), a claim in dependent form shall contain a reference to a claim previously set forth and then specify a further limitation of the subject matter claimed. A claim in dependent form shall be construed to incorporate by reference all the limitations of the claim to which it refers.

(e)   Reference in Multiple Dependent Form.—A claim in multiple dependent form shall contain a reference, in the alternative only, to more than one claim previously set forth and then specify a further limitation of the subject matter claimed. A multiple dependent claim shall not serve as a basis for any other multiple dependent claim. A multiple dependent claim shall be construed to incorporate by reference all the limitations of the particular claim in relation to which it is being considered.

(f)   Element in Claim for a Combination.—An element in a claim for a combination may be expressed as a means or step for performing a specified function without the recital of structure, material, or acts in support thereof, and such claim shall be construed to cover the corresponding structure, material, or acts described in the specification and equivalents thereof.

§ 113.   Drawings

The applicant shall furnish a drawing where necessary for the understanding of the subject matter sought to be patented. When the nature of such subject matter admits of illustration by a drawing and the applicant has not furnished such a drawing, the Director may require its submission within a time period of not less than two months from the sending of a notice thereof. Drawings submitted after the filing date of the application may not be used (i) to overcome any insufficiency of the specification due to lack of an enabling disclosure or otherwise inadequate disclosure therein, or (ii) to supplement the original disclosure thereof for the purpose of interpretation of the scope of any claim.

§ 114.   Models, Specimens

The Director may require the applicant to furnish a model of convenient size to exhibit advantageously the several parts of his invention.

When the invention relates to a composition of matter, the Director may require the applicant to furnish specimens or ingredients for the purpose of inspection or experiment.

§ 115.   Inventor's Oath or Declaration

(a)   Naming the Inventor; Inventor's Oath or Declaration.—An application for patent that is filed under section 111(a) or commences the national stage under section 371 shall include, or be amended to include, the name of the inventor for any invention claimed in the application. Except as otherwise provided in this section, each individual who is the inventor or a joint inventor of a claimed invention in an application for patent shall execute an oath or declaration in connection with the application.

(b) Required Statements.—An oath or declaration under subsection (a) shall contain statements that—

(1) the application was made or was authorized to be made by the affiant or declarant; and

(2) such individual believes himself or herself to be the original inventor or an original joint inventor of a claimed invention in the application.

(c) Additional Requirements.—The Director may specify additional information relating to the inventor and the invention that is required to be included in an oath or declaration under subsection (a).

(d) Substitute Statement.—

(1) In general.—In lieu of executing an oath or declaration under subsection (a), the applicant for patent may provide a substitute statement under the circumstances described in paragraph (2) and such additional circumstances that the Director may specify by regulation.

(2) Permitted circumstances.—A substitute statement under paragraph (1) is permitted with respect to any individual who—

(A) is unable to file the oath or declaration under subsection (a) because the individual—

(i) is deceased;

(ii) is under legal incapacity; or

(iii) cannot be found or reached after diligent effort; or

(B) is under an obligation to assign the invention but has refused to make the oath or declaration required under subsection (a).

(3) Contents.—A substitute statement under this subsection shall—

(A) identify the individual with respect to whom the statement applies;

(B) set forth the circumstances representing the permitted basis for the filing of the substitute statement in lieu of the oath or declaration under subsection (a); and

(C) contain any additional information, including any showing, required by the Director.

(e) Making Required Statements in Assignment of Record.—An individual who is under an obligation of assignment of an application for patent may include the required statements under subsections (b) and (c) in the assignment executed by the individual, in lieu of filing such statements separately.

(f) Time for Filing.—The applicant for patent shall provide each required oath or declaration under subsection (a), substitute statement under subsection (d), or recorded assignment meeting the requirements of subsection (e) no later than the date on which the issue fee for the patent is paid.

(g) Earlier-Filed Application Containing Required Statements or Substitute Statement.—

(1) Exception.—The requirements under this section shall not apply to an individual with respect to an application for patent in which the individual is named as the inventor or a joint inventor and that claims the benefit under section 120, 121, 365(c), or 386(c) of the filing of an earlier-filed application, if—

(A) an oath or declaration meeting the requirements of subsection (a) was executed by the individual and was filed in connection with the earlier-filed application;

(B) a substitute statement meeting the requirements of subsection (d) was filed in connection with the earlier filed application with respect to the individual; or

(C) an assignment meeting the requirements of subsection (e) was executed with respect to the earlier-filed application by the individual and was recorded in connection with the earlier-filed application.

(2) Copies of oaths, declarations, statements, or assignments.—Notwithstanding paragraph (1), the Director may require that a copy of the executed oath or declaration, the substitute statement, or the assignment filed in connection with the earlier-filed application be included in the later-filed application.

(h) **Supplemental and Corrected Statements; Filing Additional Statements.**—

(1) **In general.**—Any person making a statement required under this section may withdraw, replace, or otherwise correct the statement at any time. If a change is made in the naming of the inventor requiring the filing of 1 or more additional statements under this section, the Director shall establish regulations under which such additional statements may be filed.

(2) **Supplemental statements not required.**—If an individual has executed an oath or declaration meeting the requirements of subsection (a) or an assignment meeting the requirements of subsection (e) with respect to an application for patent, the Director may not thereafter require that individual to make any additional oath, declaration, or other statement equivalent to those required by this section in connection with the application for patent or any patent issuing thereon.

(3) **Savings clause.**—A patent shall not be invalid or unenforceable based upon the failure to comply with a requirement under this section if the failure is remedied as provided under paragraph (1).

(i) **Acknowledgment of Penalties.**—Any declaration or statement filed pursuant to this section shall contain an acknowledgment that any willful false statement made in such declaration or statement is punishable under section 1001 of title 18 by fine or imprisonment of not more than 5 years, or both.

§ 116. Inventors

(a) **Joint Inventions.**—When an invention is made by two or more persons jointly, they shall apply for patent jointly and each make the required oath, except as otherwise provided in this title. Inventors may apply for a patent jointly even though (1) they did not physically work together or at the same time, (2) each did not make the same type or amount of contribution, or (3) each did not make a contribution to the subject matter of every claim of the patent.

(b) **Omitted Inventor.**—If a joint inventor refuses to join in an application for patent or cannot be found or reached after diligent effort, the application may be made by the other inventor on behalf of himself and the omitted inventor. The Director, on proof of the pertinent facts and after such notice to the omitted inventor as he prescribes, may grant a patent to the inventor making the application, subject to the same rights which the omitted inventor would have had if he had been joined. The omitted inventor may subsequently join in the application.

(c) **Correction of Errors in Application.**—Whenever through error a person is named in an application for patent as the inventor, or through error an inventor is not named in an application, the Director may permit the application to be amended accordingly, under such terms as he prescribes.

§ 117. Death or Incapacity of Inventor

Legal representatives of deceased inventors and of those under legal incapacity may make application for patent upon compliance with the requirements and on the same terms and conditions applicable to the inventor.

§ 118. Filing by Other Than Inventor

A person to whom the inventor has assigned or is under an obligation to assign the invention may make an application for patent. A person who otherwise shows sufficient proprietary interest in the matter may make an application for patent on behalf of and as agent for the inventor on proof of the pertinent facts and a showing that such action is appropriate to preserve the rights of the parties. If the Director grants a patent on an application filed under this section by a person other than the inventor, the patent shall be granted to the real party in interest and upon such notice to the inventor as the Director considers to be sufficient.

§ 119. Benefit of Earlier Filing Date; Right of Priority

(a) An application for patent for an invention filed in this country by any person who has, or whose legal representatives or assigns have, previously regularly filed an application for a patent for the same invention in a foreign country which affords similar privileges in the case of applications filed in the United States or to citizens of the United States or in a WTO member country, shall have the same effect as the same application would have if filed in this country on the date on which the application for patent for the same invention was first filed in such foreign country, if the application in this country is filed within 12 months from the earliest date on which such foreign application was filed. The Director may prescribe regulations, including the requirement for payment of the fee specified in section 41(a)(7), pursuant to which the 12-month period set forth in this subsection may be extended by an additional 2 months if the delay in filing the application in this country within the 12-month period was unintentional.

(b)(1) No application for patent shall be entitled to this right of priority unless a claim is filed in the Patent and Trademark Office, identifying the foreign application by specifying the application number on that foreign application, the intellectual property authority or country in or for which the application was filed, and the date of filing the application, at such time during the pendency of the application as required by the Director.

(2) The Director may consider the failure of the applicant to file a timely claim for priority as a waiver of any such claim. The Director may establish procedures, including the requirement for payment of the fee specified in section 41(a)(7), to accept an unintentionally delayed claim under this section.

(3) The Director may require a certified copy of the original foreign application, specification, and drawings upon which it is based, a translation if not in the English language, and such other information as the Director considers necessary. Any such certification shall be made by the foreign intellectual property authority in which the foreign application was filed and show the date of the application and of the filing of the specification and other papers.

(c) In like manner and subject to the same conditions and requirements, the right provided in this section may be based upon a subsequent regularly filed application in the same foreign country instead of the first filed foreign application, provided that any foreign application filed prior to such subsequent application has been withdrawn, abandoned, or otherwise disposed of, without having been laid open to public inspection and without leaving any rights outstanding, and has not served, nor thereafter shall serve, as a basis for claiming a right of priority.

(d) Applications for inventors' certificates filed in a foreign country in which applicants have a right to apply, at their discretion, either for a patent or for an inventor's certificate shall be treated in this country in the same manner and have the same effect for purpose of the right of priority under this section as applications for patents, subject to the same conditions and requirements of this section as apply to applications for patents, provided such applicants are entitled to the benefits of the Stockholm Revision of the Paris Convention at the time of such filing.

(e)(1)   An application for patent filed under section 111(a) or section 363 for an invention disclosed in the manner provided by section 112(a) (other than the requirement to disclose the best mode) in a provisional application filed under section 111(b), by an inventor or inventors named in the provisional application, shall have the same effect, as to such invention, as though filed on the date of the provisional application filed under section 111(b), if the application for patent filed under section 111(a) or section 363 is filed not later than 12 months after the date on which the provisional application was filed and if it contains or is amended to contain a specific reference to the provisional application. The Director may prescribe regulations, including the requirement for payment of the fee specified in section 41(a)(7), pursuant to which the 12-month period set forth in this subsection may be extended by an additional 2 months if the delay in filing the application under section 111(a) or section 363 within the 12-month period was unintentional. No application shall be entitled to the benefit of an earlier filed provisional application under this subsection unless an amendment containing the specific reference to the earlier filed provisional application is submitted at such time during the pendency of the application as required by the Director. The Director may consider the failure to submit such an amendment within that time period as a waiver of any benefit under this subsection. The Director may establish procedures, including the payment of the fee specified in section 41(a)(7), to accept an unintentionally delayed submission of an amendment under this subsection.

(2)   A provisional application filed under section 111(b) may not be relied upon in any proceeding in the Patent and Trademark Office unless the fee set forth in subparagraph (A) or (C) of section 41(a)(1) has been paid.

(3)   If the day that is 12 months after the filing date of a provisional application falls on a Saturday, Sunday, or Federal holiday within the District of Columbia, the period of pendency of the provisional application shall be extended to the next succeeding secular or business day. For an application for patent filed under section 363 in a Receiving Office other than the Patent and Trademark Office, the 12-month and additional 2-month period set forth in this subsection shall be extended as provided under the treaty and Regulations as defined in section 351.

(f)   Applications for plant breeder's rights filed in a WTO member country (or in a foreign UPOV Contracting Party) shall have the same effect for the purpose of the right of priority under subsections (a) through (c) of this section as applications for patents, subject to the same conditions and requirements of this section as apply to applications for patents.

(g)   As used in this section—

(1)   the term "WTO member country" has the same meaning as the term is defined in section 104(b)(2); and

(2)   the term "UPOV Contracting Party" means a member of the International Convention for the Protection of New Varieties of Plants.

§ 120.   Benefit of Earlier Filing Date in the United States

An application for patent for an invention disclosed in the manner provided by section 112(a) (other than the requirement to disclose the best mode) in an application previously filed in the United States, or as provided by section 363 or 385 which names an inventor or joint inventor in the previously filed application shall have the same effect, as to such invention, as though filed on the date of the prior application, if filed before the patenting or abandonment of or termination of proceedings on the first application or on an application similarly entitled to the benefit of the filing date of the first application and if it contains or is amended to contain a specific reference to the earlier filed application. No application shall be entitled to the benefit of an earlier filed application under this section unless an amendment containing the specific reference to the earlier filed application is submitted at such time during the pendency of the application as required by the Director. The Director may consider the failure to submit such an amendment within that time period as a waiver of any benefit under this section. The Director may establish procedures, including the requirement for payment of the fee specified in section 41(a)(7), to accept an unintentionally delayed submission of an amendment under this section.

§ 121. Divisional Applications

If two or more independent and distinct inventions are claimed in one application, the Director may require the application to be restricted to one of the inventions. If the other invention is made the subject of a divisional application which complies with the requirements of section 120 it shall be entitled to the benefit of the filing date of the original application. A patent issuing on an application with respect to which a requirement for restriction under this section has been made, or on an application filed as a result of such a requirement, shall not be used as a reference either in the Patent and Trademark Office or in the courts against a divisional application or against the original application or any patent issued on either of them, if the divisional application is filed before the issuance of the patent on the other application. The validity of a patent shall not be questioned for failure of the Director to require the application to be restricted to one invention.

§ 122. Confidential Status of Applications; Publication of Patent Applications

(a) Confidentiality. Except as provided in subsection (b), applications for patents shall be kept in confidence by the Patent and Trademark Office and no information concerning the same given without authority of the applicant or owner unless necessary to carry out the provisions of an Act of Congress or in such special circumstances as may be determined by the Director.

(b) Publication.

(1) In general.

(A) Subject to paragraph (2), each application for a patent shall be published, in accordance with procedures determined by the Director, promptly after the expiration of a period of 18 months from the earliest filing date for which a benefit is sought under this title. At the request of the applicant, an application may be published earlier than the end of such 18-month period.

(B) No information concerning published patent applications shall be made available to the public except as the Director determines.

(C) Notwithstanding any other provision of law, a determination by the Director to release or not to release information concerning a published patent application shall be final and nonreviewable.

(2) Exceptions.

(A) An application shall not be published if that application is—

(i) no longer pending;

(ii) subject to a secrecy order under section 181;

(iii) a provisional application filed under section 111(b); or

(iv) an application for a design patent filed under chapter 16.

(B)(i) If an applicant makes a request upon filing, certifying that the invention disclosed in the application has not and will not be the subject of an application filed in another country, or under a multilateral international agreement, that requires publication of applications 18 months after filing, the application shall not be published as provided in paragraph (1).

(ii)   An applicant may rescind a request made under clause (i) at any time.

(iii)   An applicant who has made a request under clause (i) but who subsequently files, in a foreign country or under a multilateral international agreement specified in clause (i), an application directed to the invention disclosed in the application filed in the Patent and Trademark Office, shall notify the Director of such filing not later than 45 days after the date of the filing of such foreign or international application. A failure of the applicant to provide such notice within the prescribed period shall result in the application being regarded as abandoned.

(iv)   If an applicant rescinds a request made under clause (i) or notifies the Director that an application was filed in a foreign country or under a multilateral international agreement specified in clause (i), the application shall be published in accordance with the provisions of paragraph (1) on or as soon as is practical after the date that is specified in clause (i).

(v)   If an applicant has filed applications in one or more foreign countries, directly or through a multilateral international agreement, and such foreign filed applications corresponding to an application filed in the Patent and Trademark Office or the description of the invention in such foreign filed applications is less extensive than the application or description of the invention in the application filed in the Patent and Trademark Office, the applicant may submit a redacted copy of the application filed in the Patent and Trademark Office eliminating any part or description of the invention in such application that is not also contained in any of the corresponding applications filed in a foreign country. The Director may only publish the redacted copy of the application unless the redacted copy of the application is not received within 16 months after the earliest effective filing date for which a benefit is sought under this title. The provisions of section 154(d) shall not apply to a claim if the description of the invention published in the redacted application filed under this clause with respect to the claim does not enable a person skilled in the art to make and use the subject matter of the claim.

(c)   Protest and Pre-issuance Opposition. The Director shall establish appropriate procedures to ensure that no protest or other form of pre-issuance opposition to the grant of a patent on an application may be initiated after publication of the application without the express written consent of the applicant.

(d)   National Security. No application for patent shall be published under subsection (b)(1) if the publication or disclosure of such invention would be detrimental to the national security. The Director shall establish appropriate procedures to ensure that such applications are promptly identified and the secrecy of such inventions is maintained in accordance with chapter 17.

(e)   Preissuance Submissions by Third Parties.—

(1)   In General.—Any third party may submit for consideration and inclusion in the record of a patent application, any patent, published patent application, or other printed publication of potential relevance to the examination of the application, if such submission is made in writing before the earlier of—

(A)   the date a notice of allowance under section 151 is given or mailed in the application for patent; or

(B)   the later of—

(i)   6 months after the date on which the application for patent is first published under section 122 by the Office, or

(ii)   the date of the first rejection under section 132 of any claim by the examiner during the examination of the application for patent.

(2) Other Requirements.—Any submission under paragraph (1) shall—

(A) set forth a concise description of the asserted relevance of each submitted document;

(B) be accompanied by such fee as the Director may prescribe; and

(C) include a statement by the person making such submission affirming that the submission was made in compliance with this section.

§ 123. Micro Entity Defined

(a) In General.—For purposes of this title, the term "micro entity" means an applicant who makes a certification that the applicant—

(1) qualifies as a small entity, as defined in regulations issued by the Director;

(2) has not been named as an inventor on more than 4 previously filed patent applications, other than applications filed in another country, provisional applications under section 111(b), or international applications filed under the treaty defined in section 351(a) for which the basic national fee under section 41(a) was not paid;

(3) did not, in the calendar year preceding the calendar year in which the applicable fee is being paid, have a gross income, as defined in section 61(a) of the Internal Revenue Code of 1986, exceeding 3 times the median household income for that preceding calendar year, as most recently reported by the Bureau of the Census; and

(4) has not assigned, granted, or conveyed, and is not under an obligation by contract or law to assign, grant, or convey, a license or other ownership interest in the application concerned to an entity that, in the calendar year preceding the calendar year in which the applicable fee is being paid, had a gross income, as defined in section 61(a) of the Internal Revenue Code of 1986, exceeding 3 times the median household income for that preceding calendar year, as most recently reported by the Bureau of the Census.

(b) Applications Resulting From Prior Employment.—An applicant is not considered to be named on a previously filed application for purposes of subsection (a)(2) if the applicant has assigned, or is under an obligation by contract or law to assign, all ownership rights in the application as the result of the applicant's previous employment.

(c) Foreign Currency Exchange Rate.—If an applicant's or entity's gross income in the preceding calendar year is not in United States dollars, the average currency exchange rate, as reported by the Internal Revenue Service, during that calendar year shall be used to determine whether the applicant's or entity's gross income exceeds the threshold specified in paragraphs (3) or (4) of subsection (a).

(d) Institutions of Higher Education.—For purposes of this section, a micro entity shall include an applicant who certifies that—

(1) the applicant's employer, from which the applicant obtains the majority of the applicant's income, is an institution of higher education as defined in section 101(a) of the Higher Education Act of 1965 (20 U.S.C. 1001(a)); or

(2) the applicant has assigned, granted, conveyed, or is under an obligation by contract or law, to assign, grant, or convey, a license or other ownership interest in the particular applications to such an institution of higher education.

(e) Director's Authority.—In addition to the limits imposed by this section, the Director may, in the Director's discretion, impose income limits, annual filing limits, or other limits on who may qualify as a micro entity pursuant to this section if the Director determines that such additional limits are reasonably necessary to avoid an undue impact on other patent applicants or owners or are otherwise reasonably necessary and appropriate. At least 3 months before any limits proposed to be imposed pursuant to this subsection take effect, the Director shall inform the Committee on the Judiciary of the House of Representatives and the Committee on the Judiciary of the Senate of any such proposed limits.

CHAPTER 12.   EXAMINATION OF APPLICATION

----

§ 131.   Examination of Application

The Director shall cause an examination to be made of the application and the alleged new invention; and if on such examination it appears that the applicant is entitled to a patent under the law, the Director shall issue a patent therefor.

§ 132.   Notice of Rejection; Reexamination

(a) Whenever, on examination, any claim for a patent is rejected, or any objection or requirement made, the Director shall notify the applicant thereof, stating the reasons for such rejection, or objection or requirement, together with such information and references as may be useful in judging of the propriety of continuing the prosecution of his application; and if after receiving such notice, the applicant persists in his claim for a patent, with or without amendment, the application shall be reexamined. No amendment shall introduce new matter into the disclosure of the invention.

(b) The Director shall prescribe regulations to provide for the continued examination of applications for patent at the request of the applicant. The Director may establish appropriate fees for such continued examination and shall provide a 50 percent reduction in such fees for small entities that qualify for reduced fees under section 41(h)(1).

§ 133.   Time for Prosecuting Application

Upon failure of the applicant to prosecute the application within six months after any action therein, of which notice has been given or mailed to the applicant, or within such shorter time, not less than thirty days, as fixed by the Director in such action, the application shall be regarded as abandoned by the parties thereto.

§ 134.   Appeal to the Patent Trial and Appeal Board

(a) **Patent Applicant.** An applicant for a patent, any of whose claims has been twice rejected, may appeal from the decision of the primary examiner to the Patent Trial and Appeal Board, having once paid the fee for such appeal.

(b) **Patent Owner.** A patent owner in a reexamination may appeal from the final rejection of any claim by the primary examiner to the Patent Trial and Appeal Board, having once paid the fee for such appeal.

§ 135.   Derivation Proceedings

(a) **Institution of Proceeding.—**

(1) **In General.—**An applicant for patent may file a petition with respect to an invention to institute a derivation proceeding in the Office. The petition shall set forth with particularity

the basis for finding that an individual named in an earlier application as the inventor or a joint inventor derived such invention from an individual named in the petitioner's application as the inventor or a joint inventor and, without authorization, the earlier application claiming such invention was filed. Whenever the Director determines that a petition filed under this subsection demonstrates that the standards for instituting a derivation proceeding are met, the Director may institute a derivation proceeding.

(2) **Time for Filing.**—A petition under this section with respect to an invention that is the same or substantially the same invention as a claim contained in a patent issued on an earlier application, or contained in an earlier application when published or deemed published under section 122(b), may not be filed unless such petition is filed during the 1-year period following the date on which the patent containing such claim was granted or the earlier application containing such claim was published, whichever is earlier.

(3) **Earlier Application.**—For purposes of this section, an application shall not be deemed to be an earlier application with respect to an invention, relative to another application, unless a claim to the invention was or could have been made in such application having an effective filing date that is earlier than the effective filing date of any claim to the invention that was or could have been made in such other application.

(4) **No Appeal.**—A determination by the Director whether to institute a derivation proceeding under paragraph (1) shall be final and not appealable.

(b) **Determination by Patent Trial and Appeal Board.**—In a derivation proceeding instituted under subsection (a), the Patent Trial and Appeal Board shall determine whether an inventor named in the earlier application derived the claimed invention from an inventor named in the petitioner's application and, without authorization, the earlier application claiming such invention was filed. In appropriate circumstances, the Patent Trial and Appeal Board may correct the naming of the inventor in any application or patent at issue. The Director shall prescribe regulations setting forth standards for the conduct of derivation proceedings, including requiring parties to provide sufficient evidence to prove and rebut a claim of derivation.

(c) **Deferral of Decision.**—The Patent Trial and Appeal Board may defer action on a petition for a derivation proceeding until the expiration of the 3-month period beginning on the date on which the Director issues a patent that includes the claimed invention that is the subject of the petition. The Patent Trial and Appeal Board also may defer action on a petition for a derivation proceeding, or stay the proceeding after it has been instituted, until the termination of a proceeding under chapter 30, 31, or 32 involving the patent of the earlier applicant.

(d) **Effect of Final Decision.**—The final decision of the Patent Trial and Appeal Board, if adverse to claims in an application for patent, shall constitute the final refusal by the Office on those claims. The final decision of the Patent Trial and Appeal Board, if adverse to claims in a patent, shall, if no appeal or other review of the decision has been or can be taken or had, constitute cancellation of those claims, and notice of such cancellation shall be endorsed on copies of the patent distributed after such cancellation.

(e) **Settlement.**—Parties to a proceeding instituted under subsection (a) may terminate the proceeding by filing a written statement reflecting the agreement of the parties as to the correct inventor of the claimed invention in dispute. Unless the Patent Trial and Appeal Board finds the agreement to be inconsistent with the evidence of record, if any, it shall take action consistent with the agreement. Any written settlement or understanding of the parties shall be filed with the Director. At the request of a party to the proceeding, the agreement or understanding shall be treated as business confidential information, shall be kept separate from the file of the involved patents or applications, and shall be made available only to Government agencies on written request, or to any person on a showing of good cause.

(f) **Arbitration.**—Parties to a proceeding instituted under subsection (a) may, within such time as may be specified by the Director by regulation, determine such contest or any aspect thereof by arbitration. Such arbitration shall be governed by the provisions of title 9, to the extent such title is not inconsistent with this section. The parties shall give notice of any arbitration award to the Director, and such award shall, as between the parties to the arbitration, be dispositive of the issues to which it relates. The arbitration award shall be unenforceable until such notice is given. Nothing in this subsection shall preclude the Director from determining the patentability of the claimed inventions involved in the proceeding.

CHAPTER 13.   REVIEW OF PATENT AND TRADEMARK OFFICE DECISIONS

---

§ 141.   Appeal to Court of Appeals for the Federal Circuit

(a)   Examinations.—An applicant who is dissatisfied with the final decision in an appeal to the Patent Trial and Appeal Board under section 134(a) may appeal the Board's decision to the United States Court of Appeals for the Federal Circuit. By filing such an appeal, the applicant waives his or her right to proceed under section 145.

(b)   Reexaminations.—A patent owner who is dissatisfied with the final decision in an appeal of a reexamination to the Patent Trial and Appeal Board under section 134(b) may appeal the Board's decision only to the United States Court of Appeals for the Federal Circuit.

(c)   Post-Grant and Inter Partes Reviews.—A party to an inter partes review or a post-grant review who is dissatisfied with the final written decision of the Patent Trial and Appeal Board under section 318(a) or 328(a) (as the case may be) may appeal the Board's decision only to the United States Court of Appeals for the Federal Circuit.

(d)   Derivation Proceedings.—A party to a derivation proceeding who is dissatisfied with the final decision of the Patent Trial and Appeal Board in the proceeding may appeal the decision to the United States Court of Appeals for the Federal Circuit, but such appeal shall be dismissed if any adverse party to such derivation proceeding, within 20 days after the appellant has filed notice of appeal in accordance with section 142, files notice with the Director that the party elects to have all further proceedings conducted as provided in section 146. If the appellant does not, within 30 days after the filing of such notice by the adverse party, file a civil action under section 146, the Board's decision shall govern the further proceedings in the case.

§ 142.   Notice of Appeal

When an appeal is taken to the United States Court of Appeals for the Federal Circuit, the appellant shall file in the Patent and Trademark Office a written notice of appeal directed to the Director, within such time after the date of the decision from which the appeal is taken as the Director prescribes, but in no case less than 60 days after that date.

§ 143.   Proceedings on Appeal

With respect to an appeal described in section 142, the Director shall transmit to the United States Court of Appeals for the Federal Circuit a certified list of the documents comprising the record in the Patent and Trademark Office. The court may request that the Director forward the original or certified copies of such documents during pendency of the appeal. In an ex parte case, the Director shall submit to the court in writing the grounds for the decision of the Patent and Trademark Office, addressing all of the issues raised in the appeal. The Director shall have the right to intervene in an appeal from a decision entered by the Patent Trial and Appeal Board in a derivation proceeding under section 135 or in an inter partes or postgrant review under chapter 31 or 32.

§ 144. Decision on Appeal

The United States Court of Appeals for the Federal Circuit shall review the decision from which an appeal is taken on the record before the Patent and Trademark Office. Upon its determination the court shall issue to the Director its mandate and opinion, which shall be entered of record in the Patent and Trademark Office and shall govern the further proceedings in the case.

§ 145. Civil Action to Obtain Patent

An applicant dissatisfied with the decision of the Patent Trial and Appeal Board in an appeal under section 134(a) may unless appeal has been taken to the United States Court of Appeals for the Federal Circuit, have remedy by civil action against the Director in the United States District Court for the Eastern District of Virginia if commenced within such time after such decision, not less than sixty days, as the Director appoints. The court may adjudge that such applicant is entitled to receive a patent for his invention, as specified in any of his claims involved in the decision of the Patent Trial and Appeal Board, as the facts in the case may appear and such adjudication shall authorize the Director to issue such patent on compliance with the requirements of law. All the expenses of the proceedings shall be paid by the applicant.

§ 146. Civil Action in Case of Derivation Proceeding

Any party to a derivation proceeding dissatisfied with the decision of the Patent Trial and Appeal Board on the derivation proceeding, may have remedy by civil action, if commenced within such time after such decision, not less than sixty days, as the Director appoints or as provided in section 141, unless he has appealed to the United States Court of Appeals for the Federal Circuit, and such appeal is pending or has been decided. In such suits the record in the Patent and Trademark Office shall be admitted on motion of either party upon the terms and conditions as to costs, expenses, and the further cross-examination of the witnesses as the court imposes, without prejudice to the right of the parties to take further testimony. The testimony and exhibits of the record in the Patent and Trademark Office when admitted shall have the same effect as if originally taken and produced in the suit.

Such suit may be instituted against the party in interest as shown by the records of the Patent and Trademark Office at the time of the decision complained of, but any party in interest may become a party to the action. If there be adverse parties residing in a plurality of districts not embraced within the same state, or an adverse party residing in a foreign country, the United States District Court for the Eastern District of Virginia shall have jurisdiction and may issue summons against the adverse parties directed to the marshal of any district in which any adverse party resides. Summons against adverse parties residing in foreign countries may be served by publication or otherwise as the court directs. The Director shall not be a necessary party but he shall be notified of the filing of the suit by the clerk of the court in which it is filed and shall have the right to intervene. Judgment of the court in favor of the right of an applicant to a patent shall authorize the Director to issue such patent on the filing in the Patent and Trademark Office of a certified copy of the judgment and on compliance with the requirements of law.

CHAPTER 14. ISSUE OF PATENT

§ 151.   Issue of Patent

(a) **In General.**—If it appears that an applicant is entitled to a patent under the law, a written notice of allowance of the application shall be given or mailed to the applicant. The notice shall specify a sum, constituting the issue fee and any required publication fee, which shall be paid within 3 months thereafter.

(b) **Effect of Payment.**—Upon payment of this sum the patent may issue, but if payment is not timely made, the application shall be regarded as abandoned.

§ 152.   Issue of Patent to Assignee

Patents may be granted to the assignee of the inventor of record in the Patent and Trademark Office, upon the application made and the specification sworn to by the inventor, except as otherwise provided in this title.

§ 153.   How Issued

Patents shall be issued in the name of the United States of America, under the seal of the Patent and Trademark Office, and shall be signed by the Director or have his signature placed thereon and shall be recorded in the Patent and Trademark Office.

§ 154.   Contents and Term of Patent; Provisional Rights

(a) **In General.**—

(1) **Contents.**—Every patent shall contain a short title of the invention and a grant to the patentee, his heirs or assigns, of the right to exclude others from making, using, offering for sale, or selling the invention throughout the United States or importing the invention into the United States, and, if the invention is a process, of the right to exclude others from using, offering for sale or selling throughout the United States, or importing into the United States, products made by that process, referring to the specification for the particulars thereof.

(2) **Term.**—Subject to the payment of fees under this title, such grant shall be for a term beginning on the date on which the patent issues and ending 20 years from the date on which the application for the patent was filed in the United States or, if the application contains a specific reference to an earlier filed application or applications under section 120, 121, 365(c), 386(a), or 386(b) from the date on which the earliest such application was filed.

(3) **Priority.**—Priority under section 119, 365(a), 365(b), 386(a), or 386(b) shall not be taken into account in determining the term of a patent.

(4) **Specification and Drawing.**—A copy of the specification and drawing shall be annexed to the patent and be a part of such patent.

(b) **Adjustment of Patent Term.**

(1) **Patent Term Guarantees.**

(A) Guarantee of prompt Patent and Trademark Office responses. Subject to the limitations under paragraph (2), if the issue of an original patent is delayed due to the failure of the Patent and Trademark Office to—

(i)   provide at least one of the notifications under section 132 or a notice of allowance under section 151 not later than 14 months after—

(I)   the date on which an application was filed under section 111(a); or

(II)   the date of commencement of the national stage under section 371 in an international application;

(ii)   respond to a reply under section 132, or to an appeal taken under section 134, within 4 months after the date on which the reply was filed or the appeal was taken;

(iii) act on an application within 4 months after the date of a decision by the Patent Trial and Appeal Board under section 134 or 135 or a decision by a Federal court under section 141, 145, or 146 in a case in which allowable claims remain in the application; or

(iv)   issue a patent within 4 months after the date on which the issue fee was paid under section 151 and all outstanding requirements were satisfied,

the term of the patent shall be extended 1 day for each day after the end of the period specified in clause (i), (ii), (iii), or (iv), as the case may be, until the action described in such clause is taken.

(B)   Guarantee of no more than 3-year application pendency. Subject to the limitations under paragraph (2), if the issue of an original patent is delayed due to the failure of the United States Patent and Trademark Office to issue a patent within 3 years after the actual filing date of the application under section 111(a) in the United States or, in the case of an international application, the date of commencement of the national stage under section 371 in the international application, not including—

(i)   any time consumed by continued examination of the application requested by the applicant under section 132(b);

(ii)   any time consumed by a proceeding under section 135(a), any time consumed by the imposition of an order under section 181, or any time consumed by appellate review by the Patent Trial and Appeal Board or by a Federal court; or

(iii) any delay in the processing of the application by the United States Patent and Trademark Office requested by the applicant except as permitted by paragraph (3)(C),

the term of the patent shall be extended 1 day for each day after the end of that 3-year period until the patent is issued.

(C)   Guarantee or adjustments for delays due to derivation proceedings, secrecy orders, and appeals. Subject to the limitations under paragraph (2), if the issue of an original patent is delayed due to—

(i)   a proceeding under section 135(a);

(ii)   the imposition of an order under section 181; or

(iii) appellate review by the Patent Trial and Appeal Board or by a Federal court in a case in which the patent was issued under a decision in the review reversing an adverse determination of patentability,

the term of the patent shall be extended 1 day for each day of the pendency of the proceeding, order, or review, as the case may be.

(2) **Limitations.**

(A) **In General.** To the extent that periods of delay attributable to grounds specified in paragraph (1) overlap, the period of any adjustment granted under this subsection shall not exceed the actual number of days the issuance of the patent was delayed.

(B) Disclaimed Term. No patent the term of which has been disclaimed beyond a specified date may be adjusted under this section beyond the expiration date specified in the disclaimer.

(C) Reduction of Period of Adjustment.

(i)   The period of adjustment of the term of a patent under paragraph (1) shall be reduced by a period equal to the period of time during which the applicant failed to engage in reasonable efforts to conclude prosecution of the application.

(ii) With respect to adjustments to patent term made under the authority of paragraph (1)(B), an applicant shall be deemed to have failed to engage in reasonable efforts to conclude processing or examination of an application for the cumulative total of any periods of time in excess of 3 months that are taken to respond to a notice from the Office making any rejection, objection, argument, or other request, measuring such 3-month period from the date the notice was given or mailed to the applicant.

(iii) The Director shall prescribe regulations establishing the circumstances that constitute a failure of an applicant to engage in reasonable efforts to conclude processing or examination of an application.

(3) Procedures for Patent Term Adjustment Determination.

(A) The Director shall prescribe regulations establishing procedures for the application for and determination of patent term adjustments under this subsection.

(B) Under the procedures established under subparagraph (A), the Director shall—

(i)   make a determination of the period of any patent term adjustment under this subsection, and shall transmit a notice of that determination no later than the date of issuance of the patent; and

(ii) provide the applicant one opportunity to request reconsideration of any patent term adjustment determination made by the Director.

(C) The Director shall reinstate all or part of the cumulative period of time of an adjustment under paragraph (2)(C) if the applicant, prior to the issuance of the patent, makes a showing that, in spite of all due care, the applicant was unable to respond within the 3-month period, but in no case shall more than three additional months for each such response beyond the original 3-month period be reinstated.

(D) The Director shall proceed to grant the patent after completion of the Director's determination of a patent term adjustment under the procedures established under this subsection, notwithstanding any appeal taken by the applicant of such determination.

(4) Appeal of Patent Term Adjustment Determination.

(A) An applicant dissatisfied with the Director's decision on the applicant's request for reconsideration under paragraph (3)(B)(ii) shall have exclusive remedy by a civil action against the Director filed in the United States District Court for the Eastern District of Virginia within 180 days after the date of the Director's decision on the applicant's request for reconsideration. Chapter 7 of title 5, shall apply to such action. Any final judgment resulting in a change to the period of adjustment of the patent term shall be served on the Director, and the Director shall thereafter alter the term of the patent to reflect such change.

(B) The determination of a patent term adjustment under this subsection shall not be subject to appeal or challenge by a third party prior to the grant of the patent.

(c) Continuation.—

(1) **Determination.**—The term of a patent that is in force on or that results from an application filed before the date that is 6 months after the date of the enactment of the Uruguay

Round Agreements Act shall be the greater of the 20-year term as provided in subsection (a), or 17 years from grant, subject to any terminal disclaimers.

(2) **Remedies.**—The remedies of sections 283, 284, and 285 shall not apply to Acts which—

(A) were commenced or for which substantial investment was made before the date that is 6 months after the date of the enactment of the Uruguay Round Agreements Act; and

(B) became infringing by reason of paragraph (1).

(3) **Remuneration.**—The acts referred to in paragraph (2) may be continued only upon the payment of an equitable remuneration to the patentee that is determined in an action brought under chapter 28 and chapter 29 (other than those provisions excluded by paragraph (2)).

(d) **Provisional Rights.**—

(1) **In General.** In addition to other rights provided by this section, a patent shall include the right to obtain a reasonable royalty from any person who, during the period beginning on the date of publication of the application for such patent under section 122(b), or in the case of an international application filed under the treaty defined in section 351(a) designating the United States under Article 21(2)(a) of such treaty, or an international design application filed under the treaty defined in section 381(a)(1) designating the United States under Article 5 of such treaty the date of publication of the application, and ending on the date the patent is issued—

(A)(i) makes, uses, offers for sale, or sells in the United States the invention as claimed in the published patent application or imports such an invention into the United States; or

(ii) if the invention as claimed in the published patent application is a process, uses, offers for sale, or sells in the United States or imports into the United States products made by that process as claimed in the published patent application; and

(B) had actual notice of the published patent application and, in a case in which the right arising under this paragraph is based upon an international application designating the United States that is published in a language other than English, had a translation of the international application into the English language.

(2) **Right Based on Substantially Identical Inventions.** The right under paragraph (1) to obtain a reasonable royalty shall not be available under this subsection unless the invention as claimed in the patent is substantially identical to the invention as claimed in the published patent application.

(3) **Time Limitation on Obtaining a Reasonable Royalty.** The right under paragraph (1) to obtain a reasonable royalty shall be available only in an action brought not later than 6 years after the patent is issued. The right under paragraph (1) to obtain a reasonable royalty shall not be affected by the duration of the period described in paragraph (1).

(4) **Requirements for International Applications.**—

(A) **Effective Date.** The right under paragraph (1) to obtain a reasonable royalty based upon the publication under the treaty defined in section 351(a) of an international application designating the United States shall commence on the date of publication under the treaty of the international application, or, if the publication under the treaty of the international application is in a language other than English, on the date on which the Patent and Trademark Office receives a translation of the publication in the English language.

(B) **Copies.** The Director may require the applicant to provide a copy of the international application and a translation thereof.

§ 155. **[Repealed]**

§ 155A. [Repealed]

§ 156. Extension of Patent Term

(a) The term of a patent which claims a product, a method of using a product, or a method of manufacturing a product shall be extended in accordance with this section from the original expiration date of the patent if—

 (1) the term of the patent has not expired before an application is submitted under subsection (d)(1) for its extension;

 (2) the term of the patent has never been extended under subsection (e)(1) of this section;

 (3) an application for extension is submitted by the owner of record of the patent or its agent and in accordance with the requirements of paragraphs (1) through (4) of subsection (d);

 (4) the product has been subject to a regulatory review period before its commercial marketing or use;

 (5)(A) except as provided in subparagraph (B) or (C), the permission for the commercial marketing or use of the product after such regulatory review period is the first permitted commercial marketing or use of the product under the provision of law under which such regulatory review period occurred;

 (B) in the case of a patent which claims a method of manufacturing the product which primarily uses recombinant DNA technology in the manufacture of the product, the permission for the commercial marketing or use of the product after such regulatory review period is the first permitted commercial marketing or use of a product manufactured under the process claimed in the patent; or

 (C) for purposes of subparagraph (A), in the case of a patent which—

  (i) claims a new animal drug or a veterinary biological product which (I) is not covered by the claims in any other patent which has been extended, and (II) has received permission for the commercial marketing or use in non-food-producing animals and in food-producing animals, and

  (ii) was not extended on the basis of the regulatory review period for use in non-food-producing animals,

the permission for the commercial marketing or use of the drug or product after the regulatory review period for use in food-producing animals is the first permitted commercial marketing or use of the drug or product for administration to a food-producing animal.

The product referred to in paragraphs (4) and (5) is hereinafter in this section referred to as the "approved product".

(b) Except as provided in subsection (d)(5)(F), the rights derived from any patent the term of which is extended under this section shall during the period during which the term of the patent is extended—

 (1) in the case of a patent which claims a product, be limited to any use approved for the product—

  (A) before the expiration of the term of the patent—

   (i) under the provision of law under which the applicable regulatory review occurred, or

   (ii) under the provision of law under which any regulatory review described in paragraph (1), (4), or (5) of subsection (g) occurred, and

(B) on or after the expiration of the regulatory review period upon which the extension of the patent was based;

(2) in the case of a patent which claims a method of using a product, be limited to any use claimed by the patent and approved for the product—

(A) before the expiration of the term of the patent—

(i) under any provision of law under which an applicable regulatory review occurred, and

(ii) under the provision of law under which any regulatory review described in paragraph (1), (4), or (5) of subsection (g) occurred, and

(B) on or after the expiration of the regulatory review period upon which the extension of the patent was based; and

(3) in the case of a patent which claims a method of manufacturing a product, be limited to the method of manufacturing as used to make—

(A) the approved product, or

(B) the product if it has been subject to a regulatory review period described in paragraph (1), (4), or (5) of subsection (g).

As used in this subsection, the term "product" includes an approved product.

(c) The term of a patent eligible for extension under subsection (a) shall be extended by the time equal to the regulatory review period for the approved product which period occurs after the date the patent is issued, except that—

(1) each period of the regulatory review period shall be reduced by any period determined under subsection (d)(2)(B) during which the applicant for the patent extension did not act with due diligence during such period of the regulatory review period;

(2) after any reduction required by paragraph (1), the period of extension shall include only one-half of the time remaining in the periods described in paragraphs (1)(B)(i), (2)(B)(i), (3)(B)(i), (4)(B)(i), and (5)(B)(i) of subsection (g);

(3) if the period remaining in the term of a patent after the date of the approval of the approved product under the provision of law under which such regulatory review occurred when added to the regulatory review period as revised under paragraphs (1) and (2) exceeds fourteen years, the period of extension shall be reduced so that the total of both such periods does not exceed fourteen years; and

(4) in no event shall more than one patent be extended under subsection (e)(1) for the same regulatory review period for any product.

(d)(1) To obtain an extension of the term of a patent under this section, the owner of record of the patent or its agent shall submit an application to the Director. Except as provided in paragraph (5), such an application may only be submitted within the sixty-day period beginning on the date the product received permission under the provision of law under which the applicable regulatory review period occurred for commercial marketing or use, or in the case of a drug product described in subsection (i), within the sixty-day period beginning on the covered date (as defined in subsection (i)). The application shall contain—

(A) the identity of the approved product and the Federal statute under which regulatory review occurred;

(B) the identity of the patent for which an extension is being sought and the identity of each claim of such patent which claims the approved product or a method of using or manufacturing the approved product;

(C) information to enable the Director to determine under subsections (a) and (b) the eligibility of a patent for extension and the rights that will be derived from the extension and information to enable the Director and the Secretary of Health and Human Services or the Secretary of Agriculture to determine the period of the extension under subsection (g);

(D) a brief description of the activities undertaken by the applicant during the applicable regulatory review period with respect to the approved product and the significant dates applicable to such activities; and

(E) such patent or other information as the Director may require.

For purposes of determining the date on which a product receives permission under the second sentence of this paragraph, if such permission is transmitted after 4:30 P.M., Eastern Time, on a business day, or is transmitted on a day that is not a business day, the product shall be deemed to receive such permission on the next business day. For purposes of the preceding sentence, the term "business day" means any Monday, Tuesday, Wednesday, Thursday, or Friday, excluding any legal holiday under section 6103 of title 5.

(2)(A) Within 60 days of the submittal of an application for extension of the term of a patent under paragraph (1), the Director shall notify—

(i) the Secretary of Agriculture if the patent claims a drug product or a method of using or manufacturing a drug product and the drug product is subject to the Virus-Serum-Toxin Act, and

(ii) the Secretary of Health and Human Services if the patent claims any other drug product, a medical device, or a food additive or color additive or a method of using or manufacturing such a product, device, or additive and if the product, device, and additive are subject to the Federal Food, Drug, and Cosmetic Act,

of the extension application and shall submit to the Secretary who is so notified a copy of the application. Not later than 30 days after the receipt of an application from the Director, the Secretary receiving the application shall review the dates contained in the application pursuant to paragraph (1)(C) and determine the applicable regulatory review period, shall notify the Director of the determination, and shall publish in the Federal Register a notice of such determination.

(B)(i) If a petition is submitted to the Secretary making the determination under subparagraph (A), not later than 180 days after the publication of the determination under subparagraph (A), upon which it may reasonably be determined that the applicant did not act with due diligence during the applicable regulatory review period, the Secretary making the determination shall, in accordance with regulations promulgated by such Secretary, determine if the applicant acted with due diligence during the applicable regulatory review period. The Secretary making the determination shall make such determination not later than 90 days after the receipt of such a petition. For a drug product, device, or additive subject to the Federal Food, Drug, and Cosmetic Act or the Public Health Service Act, the Secretary may not delegate the authority to make the determination prescribed by this clause to an office below the Office of the Director of Food and Drugs. For a product subject to the Virus-Serum-Toxin Act, the Secretary of Agriculture may not delegate the authority to make the determination prescribed by this clause to an office below the Office of the Assistant Secretary for Marketing and Inspection Services.

(ii) The Secretary making a determination under clause (i) shall notify the Director of the determination and shall publish in the Federal Register a notice of such determination together with the factual and legal basis for such determination. Any interested person may request, within the 60-day period beginning on the publication of a determination, the Secretary making the determination to hold an informal hearing on the determination. If such a request is made within such period, such Secretary shall hold such hearing not later than 30 days after the date of the request, or at the request of the person making the request, not later than 60 days after such date. The Secretary who is holding the hearing shall provide notice of the hearing to the owner of the patent involved and to any interested person and provide the owner and any interested person an opportunity to participate in the hearing.

Within 30 days after the completion of the hearing, such Secretary shall affirm or revise the determination which was the subject of the hearing and shall notify the Director of any revision of the determination and shall publish any such revision in the Federal Register.

(3)   For the purposes of paragraph (2)(B), the term "due diligence" means that degree of attention, continuous directed effort, and timeliness as may reasonably be expected from, and are ordinarily exercised by, a person during a regulatory review period.

(4)   An application for the extension of the term of a patent is subject to the disclosure requirements prescribed by the Director.

(5)(A)   If the owner of record of the patent or its agent reasonably expects that the applicable regulatory review period described in paragraph (1)(B)(ii), (2)(B)(ii), (3)(B)(ii), (4)(B)(ii), or (5)(B)(ii) of subsection (g) that began for a product that is the subject of such patent may extend beyond the expiration of the patent term in effect, the owner or its agent may submit an application to the Director for an interim extension during the period beginning 6 months, and ending 15 days, before such term is due to expire. The application shall contain—

(i)   the identity of the product subject to regulatory review and the Federal statute under which such review is occurring;

(ii)   the identity of the patent for which interim extension is being sought and the identity of each claim of such patent which claims the product under regulatory review or a method of using or manufacturing the product;

(iii)   information to enable the Director to determine under subsection (a)(1), (2), and (3) the eligibility of a patent for extension;

(iv)   a brief description of the activities undertaken by the applicant during the applicable regulatory review period to date with respect to the product under review and the significant dates applicable to such activities; and

(v)   such patent or other information as the Director may require.

(B)   If the Director determines that, except for permission to market or use the product commercially, the patent would be eligible for an extension of the patent term under this section, the Director shall publish in the Federal Register a notice of such determination, including the identity of the product under regulatory review, and shall issue to the applicant a certificate of interim extension for a period of not more than 1 year.

(C)   The owner of record of a patent, or its agent, for which an interim extension has been granted under subparagraph (B), may apply for not more than 4 subsequent interim extensions under this paragraph, except that, in the case of a patent subject to subsection (g)(6)(C), the owner of record of the patent, or its agent, may apply for only 1 subsequent interim extension under this paragraph. Each such subsequent application shall be made during the period beginning 60 days before, and ending 30 days before, the expiration of the preceding interim extension.

(D)   Each certificate of interim extension under this paragraph shall be recorded in the official file of the patent and shall be considered part of the original patent.

(E)   Any interim extension granted under this paragraph shall terminate at the end of the 60-day period beginning on the date on which the product involved receives permission for commercial marketing or use, except that, if within that 60-day period the applicant notifies the Director of such permission and submits any additional information under paragraph (1) of this subsection not previously contained in the application for interim extension, the patent shall be further extended, in accordance with the provisions of this section—

(i)   for not to exceed 5 years from the date of expiration of the original patent term; or

(ii)   if the patent is subject to subsection (g)(6)(C), from the date on which the product involved receives approval for commercial marketing or use.

(F)   The rights derived from any patent the term of which is extended under this paragraph shall, during the period of interim extension—

(i)   in the case of a patent which claims a product, be limited to any use then under regulatory review;

(ii)   in the case of a patent which claims a method of using a product, be limited to any use claimed by the patent then under regulatory review; and

(iii)   in the case of a patent which claims a method of manufacturing a product, be limited to the method of manufacturing as used to make the product then under regulatory review.

(e)(1)   A determination that a patent is eligible for extension may be made by the Director solely on the basis of the representations contained in the application for the extension. If the Director determines that a patent is eligible for extension under subsection (a) and that the requirements of paragraphs (1) through (4) of subsection (d) have been complied with, the Director shall issue to the applicant for the extension of the term of the patent a certificate of extension, under seal, for the period prescribed by subsection (c). Such certificate shall be recorded in the official file of the patent and shall be considered as part of the original patent.

(2)   If the term of a patent for which an application has been submitted under subsection (d)(1) would expire before a certificate of extension is issued or denied under paragraph (1) respecting the application, the Director shall extend, until such determination is made, the term of the patent for periods of up to one year if he determines that the patent is eligible for extension.

(f)   For purposes of this section:

(1)   The term "product" means:

(A)   A drug product.

(B)   Any medical device, food additive, or color additive subject to regulation under the Federal Food, Drug, and Cosmetic Act.

(2)   The term "drug product" means the active ingredient of—

(A)   a new drug, antibiotic drug, or human biological product (as those terms are used in the Federal Food, Drug, and Cosmetic Act and the Public Health Service Act), or

(B)   a new animal drug or veterinary biological product (as those terms are used in the Federal Food, Drug, and Cosmetic Act and the Virus-Serum-Toxin Act) which is not primarily manufactured using recombinant DNA, recombinant RNA, hybridoma technology, or other processes involving site specific genetic manipulation techniques,

including any salt or ester of the active ingredient, as a single entity or in combination with another active ingredient.

(3)   The term "major health or environmental effects test" means a test which is reasonably related to the evaluation of the health or environmental effects of a product, which requires at least six months to conduct, and the data from which is submitted to receive permission for commercial marketing or use. Periods of analysis or evaluation of test results are not to be included in determining if the conduct of a test required at least six months.

(4)(A)   Any reference to section 351 is a reference to section 351 of the Public Health Service Act.

(B)   Any reference to section 503, 505, 507, 512, or 515 is a reference to section 503, 505, 507, 512, or 515 of the Federal Food, Drug, and Cosmetic Act.

(C)   Any reference to the Virus-Serum-Toxin Act is a reference to the Act of March 4, 1913 (21 U.S.C. 151–158).

(5)   The term "informal hearing" has the meaning prescribed for such term by section 201(y) of the Federal Food, Drug, and Cosmetic Act.

(6)   The term "patent" means a patent issued by the United States Patent and Trademark Office.

(7)   The term "date of enactment" as used in this section means September 24, 1984, for a human drug product, a medical device, food additive, or color additive.

(8)   The term "date of enactment" as used in this section means the date of enactment of the Generic Animal Drug and Patent Term Restoration Act for an animal drug or a veterinary biological product.

(g)   For purposes of this section, the term "regulatory review period" has the following meanings:

(1)(A)   In the case of a product which is a new drug, antibiotic drug, or human biological product, the term means the period described in subparagraph (B) to which the limitation described in paragraph (6) applies.

(B)   The regulatory review period for a new drug, antibiotic drug, or human biological product is the sum of—

(i)   the period beginning on the date an exemption under subsection (i) of section 505 or subsection (d) of section 507 became effective for the approved product and ending on the date an application was initially submitted for such drug product under section 351, 505, or 507, and

(ii)   the period beginning on the date the application was initially submitted for the approved product under section 351, subsection (b) of section 505, or section 507 and ending on the date such application was approved under such section.

(2)(A)   In the case of a product which is a food additive or color additive, the term means the period described in subparagraph (B) to which the limitation described in paragraph (6) applies.

(B)   The regulatory review period for a food or color additive is the sum of—

(i)   the period beginning on the date a major health or environmental effects test on the additive was initiated and ending on the date a petition was initially submitted with respect to the product under the Federal Food, Drug, and Cosmetic Act requesting the issuance of a regulation for use of the product, and

(ii)   the period beginning on the date a petition was initially submitted with respect to the product under the Federal Food, Drug, and Cosmetic Act requesting the issuance of a regulation for use of the product, and ending on the date such regulation became effective or, if objections were filed to such regulation, ending on the date such objections were resolved and commercial marketing was permitted or, if commercial marketing was permitted and later revoked pending further proceedings as a result of such objections, ending on the date such proceedings were finally resolved and commercial marketing was permitted.

(3)(A)   In the case of a product which is a medical device, the term means the period described in subparagraph (B) to which the limitation described in paragraph (6) applies.

(B)   The regulatory review period for a medical device is the sum of—

(i)   the period beginning on the date a clinical investigation on humans involving the device was begun and ending on the date an application was initially submitted with respect to the device under section 515, and

(ii)   the period beginning on the date an application was initially submitted with respect to the device under section 515 and ending on the date such application was approved under such Act or the period beginning on the date a notice of completion of a product development protocol was initially submitted under section 515(f)(5) and ending on the date the protocol was declared completed under section 515(f)(6).

(4)(A)   In the case of a product which is a new animal drug, the term means the period described in subparagraph (B) to which the limitation described in paragraph (6) applies.

(B)   The regulatory review period for a new animal drug product is the sum of—

(i)   the period beginning on the earlier of the date a major health or environmental effects test on the drug was initiated or the date an exemption under subsection (j) of section 512 became effective for the approved new animal drug product and ending on the date an application was initially submitted for such animal drug product under section 512, and

(ii)   the period beginning on the date the application was initially submitted for the approved animal drug product under subsection (b) of section 512 and ending on the date such application was approved under such section.

(5)(A)   In the case of a product which is a veterinary biological product, the term means the period described in subparagraph (B) to which the limitation described in paragraph (6) applies.

(B)   The regulatory period for a veterinary biological product is the sum of—

(i)   the period beginning on the date the authority to prepare an experimental biological product under the Virus-Serum-Toxin Act became effective and ending on the date an application for a license was submitted under the Virus-Serum-Toxin Act, and

(ii)   the period beginning on the date an application for a license was initially submitted for approval under the Virus-Serum-Toxin Act and ending on the date such license was issued.

(6)   A period determined under any of the preceding paragraphs is subject to the following limitations:

(A)   If the patent involved was issued after the date of the enactment of this section, the period of extension determined on the basis of the regulatory review period determined under any such paragraph may not exceed five years.

(B)   If the patent involved was issued before the date of the enactment of this section and—

(i)   no request for an exemption described in paragraph (1)(B) or (4)(B) was submitted and no request for the authority, described in paragraph (5)(B) was submitted,

(ii)   no major health or environmental effects test described in paragraph (2)(B) or (4)(B) was initiated and no petition for a regulation or application for registration described in such paragraph was submitted, or

(iii)   no clinical investigation described in paragraph (3) was begun or product development protocol described in such paragraph was submitted,

before such date for the approved product the period of extension determined on the basis of the regulatory review period determined under any such paragraph may not exceed five years.

(C)   If the patent involved was issued before the date of the enactment of this section and if an action described in subparagraph (B) was taken before the date of the enactment of this section with respect to the approved product and the commercial marketing or use of the product has not been approved before such date, the period of extension determined on the basis of the regulatory review period determined under such paragraph may not exceed two years or in the case of an approved product which is a new animal drug or veterinary biological product (as those terms are used in the Federal Food, Drug, and Cosmetic Act or the Virus-Serum-Toxin Act), three years.

(h)   The Director may establish such fees as the Director determines appropriate to cover the costs to the Office of receiving and acting upon applications under this section.

(i)(1)   For purposes of this section, if the Secretary of Health and Human Services provides notice to the sponsor of an application or request for approval, conditional approval, or indexing of a drug product for which the Secretary intends to recommend controls under the Controlled Substances Act, beginning on the covered date, the drug product shall be considered to—

(A)   have been approved or indexed under the relevant provision of the Public Health Service Act or Federal Food, Drug, and Cosmetic Act; and

(B)   have permission for commercial marketing or use.

(2)   In this subsection, the term 'covered date' means the later of—

(A)   the date an application is approved—

(i)   under section 351(a)(2)(C) of the Public Health Service Act; or

(ii)   under section 505(b) or 512(c) of the Federal Food, Drug, and Cosmetic Act;

(B)   the date an application is conditionally approved under section 571(b) of the Federal Food, Drug, and Cosmetic Act;

(C)   the date a request for indexing is granted under section 572(d) of the Federal Food, Drug, and Cosmetic Act; or

(D)   the date of issuance of the interim final rule controlling the drug under section 201(j) of the Controlled Substances Act.

§ 157.   [Repealed]

CHAPTER 15. PLANT PATENTS

---

§ 161.   Patents for Plants

Whoever invents or discovers and asexually reproduces any distinct and new variety of plant, including cultivated sports, mutants, hybrids, and newly found seedlings, other than a tuberpropagated plant or a plant found in an uncultivated state, may obtain a patent therefor, subject to the conditions and requirements of this title.

The provisions of this title relating to patents for inventions shall apply to patents for plants, except as otherwise provided.

§ 162.   Description, Claim

No plant patent shall be declared invalid for noncompliance with section 112 if the description is as complete as is reasonably possible.

The claim in the specification shall be in formal terms to the plant shown and described.

§ 163. Grant

In the case of a plant patent the grant shall include the right to exclude others from asexually reproducing the plant, and from using, offering for sale, or selling the plant so reproduced, or any of its parts, throughout the United States, or from importing the plant so reproduced, or any parts thereof, into the United States.

§ 164. Assistance of Department of Agriculture

The President may by Executive order direct the Secretary of Agriculture, in accordance with the requests of the Director, for the purpose of carrying into effect the provisions of this title with respect to plants (1) to furnish available information of the Department of Agriculture, (2) to conduct through the appropriate bureau or division of the Department research upon special problems, or (3) to detail to the Director officers and employees of the Department.

CHAPTER 16. DESIGNS

---

§ 171. Patents for Designs

(a) In General.—Whoever invents any new, original and ornamental design for an article of manufacture may obtain a patent therefor, subject to the conditions and requirements of this title.

(b) Applicability of this Title.—The provisions of this title relating to patents for inventions shall apply to patents for designs, except as otherwise provided.

(c) Filing Date.—The filing date of an application for patent for design shall be the date on which the specification as prescribed by section 112 and any required drawings are filed.

§ 172. Right of Priority

The right of priority provided for by subsections (a) through (d) of section 119 shall be six months in the case of designs. The right of priority provided for by section 119(e) shall not apply to designs.

§ 173. Term of Design Patent

Patents for designs shall be granted for the term of 15 years from the date of grant.

CHAPTER 17. SECRECY OF CERTAIN INVENTIONS AND FILING APPLICATIONS IN FOREIGN COUNTRY

---

§ 181. Secrecy of Certain Inventions and Withholding of Patent

Whenever publication or disclosure by the publication of an application or by the grant of a patent on an invention in which the Government has a property interest might, in the opinion of the head of the interested Government agency, be detrimental to the national security, the Commissioner upon being so notified shall order that the invention be kept secret and shall withhold the publication of the application or the grant of a patent therefor under the conditions set forth hereinafter.

Whenever the publication or disclosure of an invention by the publication of an application or by the granting of a patent, in which the Government does not have a property interest, might, in the opinion of the Commissioner, be detrimental to the national security, he shall make the application for patent in which such invention is disclosed available for inspection to the Atomic Energy Commission, the Secretary of Defense, and the chief officer of any other department or agency of the Government designated by the President as a defense agency of the United States.

Each individual to whom the application is disclosed shall sign a dated acknowledgment thereof, which acknowledgment shall be entered in the file of the application. If, in the opinion of the Atomic Energy Commission, the Secretary of a Defense Department, or the chief officer of another department or agency so designated, the publication or disclosure of the invention by the publication of an application or by the granting of a patent therefor would be detrimental to the national security, the Atomic Energy Commission, the Secretary of a Defense Department, or such other chief officer shall notify the Commissioner of Patents and the Commissioner of Patents shall order that the invention be kept secret and shall withhold the publication of the application or the grant of a patent for such period as the national interest requires, and notify the applicant thereof. Upon proper showing by the head of the department or agency who caused the secrecy order to be issued that the examination of the application might jeopardize the national interest, the Commissioner of Patents shall thereupon maintain the application in a sealed condition and notify the applicant thereof. The owner of an application which has been placed under a secrecy order shall have a right to appeal from the order to the Secretary of Commerce under rules prescribed by him.

An invention shall not be ordered kept secret and the publication of an application or the grant of a patent withheld for a period of more than one year. The Commissioner of Patents shall renew the order at the end thereof, or at the end of any renewal period, for additional periods of one year upon notification by the head of the department or the chief officer of the agency who caused the order to be issued that an affirmative determination has been made that the national interest continues so to require. An order in effect, or issued, during a time when the United States is at war, shall remain in effect for the duration of hostilities and one year following cessation of hostilities. An order in effect, or issued, during a national emergency declared by the President shall remain in effect for the duration of the national emergency and six months thereafter. The Commissioner of Patents may rescind any order upon notification by the heads of the departments and the chief officers of the agencies who caused the order to be issued that the publication or disclosure of the invention is no longer deemed detrimental to the national security.

§ 182. Abandonment of Invention for Unauthorized Disclosure

The invention disclosed in an application for patent subject to an order made pursuant to section 181 may be held abandoned upon its being established by the Commissioner of Patents that in violation of said order the invention has been published or disclosed or that an application for a patent therefor has been filed in a foreign country by the inventor, his successors, assigns, or legal representatives, or anyone in privity with him or them, without the consent of the Commissioner of Patents. The abandonment shall be held to have occurred as of the time of violation. The consent of the Commissioner of Patents shall not be given without the concurrence of the heads of the departments and the chief officers of the agencies who caused the order to be issued. A holding of abandonment shall constitute forfeiture by the applicant, his successors, assigns, or legal representatives, or anyone in privity with him or them, of all claims against the United States based upon such invention.

§ 183.   **Right to Compensation**

An applicant, his successors, assigns, or legal representatives, whose patent is withheld as herein provided, shall have the right, beginning at the date the applicant is notified that, except for such order, his application is otherwise in condition for allowance, or February 1, 1952, whichever is later, and ending six years after a patent is issued thereon, to apply to the head of any department or agency who caused the order to be issued for compensation for the damage caused by the order of secrecy and/or for the use of the invention by the Government, resulting from his disclosure. The right to compensation for use shall begin on the date of the first use of the invention by the Government. The head of the department or agency is authorized, upon the presentation of a claim, to enter into an agreement with the applicant, his successors, assigns, or legal representatives, in full settlement for the damage and/or use. This settlement agreement shall be conclusive for all purposes notwithstanding any other provision of law to the contrary. If full settlement of the claim cannot be effected, the head of the department or agency may award and pay to such applicant, his successors, assigns, or legal representatives, a sum not exceeding 75 per centum of the sum which the head of the department or agency considers just compensation for the damage and/or use. A claimant may bring suit against the United States in the United States Court of Federal Claims or in the District Court of the United States for the district in which such claimant is a resident for an amount which when added to the award shall constitute just compensation for the damage and/or use of the invention by the Government. The owner of any patent issued upon an application that was subject to a secrecy order issued pursuant to section 181, who did not apply for compensation as above provided, shall have the right, after the date of issuance of such patent, to bring suit in the United States Court of Federal Claims for just compensation for the damage caused by reason of the order of secrecy and/or use by the Government of the invention resulting from his disclosure. The right to compensation for use shall begin on the date of the first use of the invention by the Government. In a suit under the provisions of this section the United States may avail itself of all defenses it may plead in an action under section 1498 of title 28. This section shall not confer a right of action on anyone or his successors, assigns, or legal representatives who, while in the full-time employment or service of the United States, discovered, invented, or developed the invention on which the claim is based.

§ 184.   **Filing of Application in Foreign Country**

(a)   **Filing in a Foreign Country.**—Except when authorized by a license obtained from the Commissioner of Patents a person shall not file or cause or authorize to be filed in any foreign country prior to six months after filing in the United States an application for patent or for the registration of a utility model, industrial design, or model in respect of an invention made in this country. A license shall not be granted with respect to an invention subject to an order issued by the Commissioner of Patents pursuant to section 181 without the concurrence of the head of the departments and the chief officers of the agencies who caused the order to be issued. The license may be granted retroactively where an application has been filed abroad through error and the application does not disclose an invention within the scope of section 181.

(b)   **Application.**—The term "application" when used in this chapter includes applications and any modifications, amendments, or supplements thereto, or divisions thereof.

(c)   **Subsequent Modifications, Amendments, and Supplements.**—The scope of a license shall permit subsequent modifications, amendments, and supplements containing additional subject matter if the application upon which the request for the license is based is not, or was not, required to be made available for inspection under section 181 of this title and if such modifications, amendments, and supplements do not change the general nature of the invention in a manner which would require such application to be made available for inspection under such section 181. In any case in which a license is not, or was not, required in order to file an application in any foreign country, such subsequent modifications, amendments, and supplements may be made, without a license, to the application filed in the foreign country if the United States application was not required to be made available for inspection under section 181 and if such modifications, amendments, and supplements do not, or did not, change the general nature of the invention in a manner which would require the United States application to have been made available for inspection under such section 181.

§ 185. Patent Barred for Filing Without License

Notwithstanding any other provisions of law any person, and his successors, assigns, or legal representatives, shall not receive a United States patent for an invention if that person, or his successors, assigns, or legal representatives shall, without procuring the license prescribed in section 184, have made, or consented to or assisted another's making, application in a foreign country for a patent or for the registration of a utility model, industrial design, or model in respect of the invention. A United States patent issued to such person, his successors, assigns, or legal representatives shall be invalid, unless the failure to procure such license was through error, and the patent does not disclose subject matter within the scope of section 181.

§ 186. Penalty

Whoever, during the period or periods of time an invention has been ordered to be kept secret and the grant of a patent thereon withheld pursuant to section 181, shall, with knowledge of such order and without due authorization, willfully publish or disclose or authorize or cause to be published or disclosed the invention, or material information with respect thereto, or whoever willfully, in violation of the provisions of section 184, shall file or cause or authorize to be filed in any foreign country an application for patent or for the registration of a utility model, industrial design, or model in respect of any invention made in the United States, shall, upon conviction, be fined not more than $10,000 or imprisoned for not more than two years, or both.

§ 187. Nonapplicability to Certain Persons

The prohibitions and penalties of this chapter shall not apply to any officer or agent of the United States acting within the scope of his authority, nor to any person acting upon his written instructions or permission.

§ 188. Rules and Regulations, Delegation of Power

The Atomic Energy Commission, the Secretary of a defense department, the chief officer of any other department or agency of the Government designated by the President as a defense agency of the United States, and the Secretary of Commerce, may separately issue rules and regulations to enable the respective department or agency to carry out the provisions of this chapter, and may delegate any power conferred by this chapter.

CHAPTER 18. PATENT RIGHTS IN INVENTIONS MADE WITH FEDERAL ASSISTANCE

---

§ 200.   Policy and Objective

It is the policy and objective of the Congress to use the patent system to promote the utilization of inventions arising from federally supported research or development; to encourage maximum participation of small business firms in federally supported research and development efforts; to promote collaboration between commercial concerns and nonprofit organizations, including universities; to ensure that inventions made by nonprofit organizations and small business firms are used in a manner to promote free competition and enterprise without unduly encumbering future research and discovery; to promote the commercialization and public availability of inventions made in the United States by United States industry and labor; to ensure that the Government obtains sufficient rights in federally supported inventions to meet the needs of the Government and protect the public against nonuse or unreasonable use of inventions; and to minimize the costs of administering policies in this area.

§ 201.   Definitions

As used in this chapter—

(a)   The term "Federal agency" means any executive agency as defined in section 105 of title 5, and the military departments as defined by section 102 of title 5.

(b)   The term "funding agreement" means any contract, grant, or cooperative agreement entered into between any Federal agency, other than the Tennessee Valley Authority, and any contractor for the performance of experimental, developmental, or research work funded in whole or in part by the Federal Government. Such term includes any assignment, substitution of parties, or subcontract of any type entered into for the performance of experimental developmental, or research work under a funding agreement as herein defined.

(c)   The term "contractor" means any person, small business firm, or nonprofit organization that is a party to a funding agreement.

(d)   The term "invention" means any invention or discovery which is or may be patentable or otherwise protectable under this title or any novel variety of plant which is or may be protectable under the Plant Variety Protection Act (7 U.S.C. 2321 et seq.).

(e)   The term "subject invention" means any invention of the contractor conceived or first actually reduced to practice in the performance of work under a funding agreement: *Provided,* That in the case of a variety of plant, the date of determination (as defined in section 41(d) of the Plant Variety Protection Act (7 U.S.C. 2401(d))) must also occur during the period of contract performance.

(f)   The term "practical application" means to manufacture in the case of a composition or product, to practice in the case of a process or method, or to operate in the case of a machine or system; and, in each case, under such conditions as to establish that the invention is being utilized and that its benefits are to the extent permitted by law or Government regulations available to the public on reasonable terms.

(g)   The term "made" when used in relation to any invention means the conception or first actual reduction to practice of such invention.

(h)   The term "small business firm" means a small business concern as defined at section 2 of Public Law 85–536 (15 U.S.C. 632) and implementing regulations of the Administrator of the Small Business Administration.

(i)   The term "nonprofit organization" means universities and other institutions of higher education or an organization of the type described in section 501(c)(3) of the Internal Revenue

Code of 1986 (26 U.S.C. 501(c)) and exempt from taxation under section 501(a) of the Internal Revenue Code (26 U.S.C. 501(a)) or any nonprofit scientific or educational organization qualified under a State nonprofit organization statute.

§ 202. Disposition of Rights

(a) Each nonprofit organization or small business firm may, within a reasonable time after disclosure as required by paragraph (c)(1) of this section, elect to retain title to any subject invention: *Provided, however,* That a funding agreement may provide otherwise (i) when the contractor is not located in the United States or does not have a place of business located in the United States or is subject to the control of a foreign government, (ii) in exceptional circumstances when it is determined by the agency that restriction or elimination of the right to retain title to any subject invention will better promote the policy and objectives of this chapter, (iii) when it is determined by a Government authority which is authorized by statute or Executive order to conduct foreign intelligence or counter-intelligence activities that the restriction or elimination of the right to retain title to any subject invention is necessary to protect the security of such activities or, (iv) when the funding agreement includes the operation of a Government-owned, contractor-operated facility of the Department of Energy primarily dedicated to that Department's naval nuclear propulsion or weapons related programs and all funding agreement limitations under this subparagraph on the contractor's right to elect title to a subject invention are limited to inventions occurring under the above two programs of the Department of Energy. The rights of the nonprofit organization or small business firm shall be subject to the provisions of paragraph (c) of this section and the other provisions of this chapter.

(b)(1) The rights of the Government under subsection (a) shall not be exercised by a Federal agency unless it first determines that at least one of the conditions identified in clauses (i) through (iii) of subsection (a) exists. Except in the case of subsection (a)(iii), the agency shall file with the Secretary of Commerce, within thirty days after the award of the applicable funding agreement, a copy of such determination. In the case of a determination under subsection (a)(ii), the statement shall include an analysis justifying the determination. In the case of determinations applicable to funding agreements with small business firms, copies shall also be sent to the Chief Counsel for Advocacy of the Small Business Administration. If the Secretary of Commerce believes that any individual determination or pattern of determinations is contrary to the policies and objectives of this chapter or otherwise not in conformance with this chapter, the Secretary shall so advise the head of the agency concerned and the Administrator of the Office of Federal Procurement Policy, and recommend corrective actions.

(2) Whenever the Administrator of the Office of Federal Procurement Policy has determined that one or more Federal agencies are utilizing the authority of clause (i) or (ii) of subsection (a) of this section in a manner that is contrary to the policies and objectives of this chapter, the Administrator is authorized to issue regulations describing classes of situations in which agencies may not exercise the authorities of those clauses;

(3) If the contractor believes that a determination is contrary to the policies and objectives of this chapter or constitutes an abuse of discretion by the agency, the determination shall be subject to the last paragraph of section 203(b).

(c) Each funding agreement with a small business firm or nonprofit organization shall contain appropriate provisions to effectuate the following:

(1) That the contractor disclose each subject invention to the Federal agency within a reasonable time after it becomes known to contractor personnel responsible for the administration of patent matters, and that the Federal Government may receive title to any subject invention not disclosed to it within such time.

(2) That the contractor make a written election within two years after disclosure to the Federal agency (or such additional time as may be approved by the Federal agency) whether the contractor will retain title to a subject invention: *Provided,* That in any case where the 1-year

period referred to in section 102(b) would end before the end of that 2-year period, the period for election may be shortened by the Federal agency to a date that is not more than sixty days before the end of that 1-year period: *And provided further,* That the Federal Government may receive title to any subject invention in which the contractor does not elect to retain rights or fails to elect rights within such times.

(3)   That a contractor electing rights in a subject invention agrees to file a patent application prior to the expiration of the 1-year period referred to in section 102(b), and shall thereafter file corresponding patent applications in other countries in which it wishes to retain title within reasonable times, and that the Federal Government may receive title to any subject inventions in the United States or other countries in which the contractor has not filed patent applications on the subject invention within such times.

(4)   With respect to any invention in which the contractor elects rights, the Federal agency shall have a nonexclusive, nontransferable, irrevocable, paid-up license to practice or have practiced for or on behalf of the United States any subject invention throughout the world: *Provided,* That the funding agreement may provide for such additional rights, including the right to assign or have assigned foreign patent rights in the subject invention, as are determined by the agency as necessary for meeting the obligations of the United States under any treaty, international agreement, arrangement of cooperation, memorandum of understanding, or similar arrangement, including military agreement relating to weapons development and production.

(5)   The right of the Federal agency to require periodic reporting on the utilization or efforts at obtaining utilization that are being made by the contractor or his licensees or assignees: *Provided,* That any such information as well as any information on utilization or efforts at obtaining utilization obtained as part of a proceeding under section 203 of this chapter shall be treated by the Federal agency as commercial and financial information obtained from a person and privileged and confidential and not subject to disclosure under section 552 of title 5.

(6)   An obligation on the part of the contractor, in the event a United States patent application is filed by or on its behalf or by any assignee of the contractor, to include within the specification of such application and any patent issuing thereon, a statement specifying that the invention was made with Government support and that the Government has certain rights in the invention.

(7)   In the case of a nonprofit organization, (A) a prohibition upon the assignment of rights to a subject invention in the United States without the approval of the Federal agency, except where such assignment is made to an organization which has as one of its primary functions the management of inventions (provided that such assignee shall be subject to the same provisions as the contractor); (B) a requirement that the contractor share royalties with the inventor; (C) except with respect to a funding agreement for the operation of a Government-owned-contractor-operated facility, a requirement that the balance of any royalties or income earned by the contractor with respect to subject inventions, after payment of expenses (including payments to inventors) incidental to the administration of subject inventions, be utilized for the support of scientific research or education; (D) a requirement that, except where it is determined to be infeasible following a reasonable inquiry, a preference in the licensing of subject inventions shall be given to small business firms; and (E) with respect to a funding agreement for the operation of a Government-owned-contractor-operated facility, requirements (i) that after payment of patenting costs, licensing costs, payments to inventors, and other expenses incidental to the administration of subject inventions, 100 percent of the balance of any royalties or income earned and retained by the contractor during any fiscal year up to an amount equal to 5 percent of the annual budget of the facility, shall be used by the contractor for scientific research, development, and education consistent with the research and development mission and objectives of the facility, including activities that increase the licensing potential of other inventions of the facility; provided that if said balance exceeds 5 percent of the annual budget of the facility, that 15 percent of such excess shall be paid to the Treasury of the United States and the remaining 85 percent

shall be used for the same purposes described above in this clause; and (ii) that, to the extent it provides the most effective technology transfer, the licensing of subject inventions shall be administered by contractor employees on location at the facility.

(8)   The requirements of sections 203 and 204 of this chapter.

(d)   If a contractor does not elect to retain title to a subject invention in cases subject to this section, the Federal agency may consider and after consultation with the contractor grant requests for retention of rights by the inventor subject to the provisions of this Act and regulations promulgated hereunder.

(e)   In any case when a Federal employee is a coinventor of any invention made with a nonprofit organization, small business firm, or a non-Federal inventor, the Federal agency employing such coinventor may, for the purpose of consolidating rights in the invention and if it finds that it would expedite the development of the invention—

(1)   license or assign whatever rights it may acquire in the subject invention to the nonprofit organization, small business firm, or non-Federal inventor in accordance with the provisions of this chapter; or

(2)   acquire any rights in the subject invention from the nonprofit organization, small business firm, or non-Federal inventor, but only to the extent the party from whom the rights are acquired voluntarily enters into the transaction and no other transaction under this chapter is conditioned on such acquisition.

(f)(1)   No funding agreement with a small business firm or nonprofit organization shall contain a provision allowing a Federal agency to require the licensing to third parties of inventions owned by the contractor that are not subject inventions unless such provision has been approved by the head of the agency and a written justification has been signed by the head of the agency. Any such provision shall clearly state whether the licensing may be required in connection with the practice of a subject invention, a specifically identified work object, or both. The head of the agency may not delegate the authority to approve provisions or sign justifications required by this paragraph.

(2)   A Federal agency shall not require the licensing of third parties under any such provision unless the head of the agency determines that the use of the invention by others is necessary for the practice of a subject invention or for the use of a work object of the funding agreement and that such action is necessary to achieve the practical application of the subject invention or work object. Any such determination shall be on the record after an opportunity for an agency hearing. Any action commenced for judicial review of such determination shall be brought within sixty days after notification of such determination.

§ 203.   March-In Rights

(a)   With respect to any subject invention in which a small business firm or nonprofit organization has acquired title under this chapter, the Federal agency under whose funding agreement the subject invention was made shall have the right, in accordance with such procedures as are provided in regulations promulgated hereunder to require the contractor, an assignee or exclusive licensee of a subject invention to grant a nonexclusive, partially exclusive, or exclusive license in any field of use to a responsible applicant or applicants, upon terms that are reasonable under the circumstances, and if the contractor, assignee, or exclusive licensee refuses such request, to grant such a license itself, if the Federal agency determines that such—

(1)   action is necessary because the contractor or assignee has not taken, or is not expected to take within a reasonable time, effective steps to achieve practical application of the subject invention in such field of use;

(2)   action is necessary to alleviate health or safety needs which are not reasonably satisfied by the contractor, assignee, or their licensees;

(3)　action is necessary to meet requirements for public use specified by Federal regulations and such requirements are not reasonably satisfied by the contractor, assignee, or licensees; or

(4)　action is not necessary because the agreement required by section 204 has not been obtained or waived or because a licensee of the exclusive right to use or sell any subject invention in the United States is in breach of its agreement obtained pursuant to section 204.

(b)　A determination pursuant to this section or section 202(b)(4) shall not be subject to chapter 71 of title 41. An administrative appeals procedure shall be established by regulations promulgated in accordance with section 206. Additionally, any contractor, inventor, assignee, or exclusive licensee adversely affected by a determination under this section may, at any time within sixty days after the determination is issued, file a petition in the United States Claims Court, which shall have jurisdiction to determine the appeal on the record and to affirm, reverse, remand or modify, as appropriate, the determination of the Federal agency. In cases described in paragraphs (1) and (3) of subsection (a), the agency's determination shall be held in abeyance pending the exhaustion of appeals or petitions filed under the preceding sentence.

§ 204.　Preference for United States Industry

Notwithstanding any other provision of this chapter, no small business firm or nonprofit organization which receives title to any subject invention and no assignee of any such small business firm or nonprofit organization shall grant to any person the exclusive right to use or sell any subject invention in the United States unless such person agrees that any products embodying the subject invention or produced through the use of the subject invention will be manufactured substantially in the United States. However, in individual cases, the requirement for such an agreement may be waived by the Federal agency under whose funding agreement the invention was made upon a showing by the small business firm, nonprofit organization, or assignee that reasonable but unsuccessful efforts have been made to grant licenses on similar terms to potential licensees that would be likely to manufacture substantially in the United States or that under the circumstances domestic manufacture is not commercially feasible.

§ 205.　Confidentiality

Federal agencies are authorized to withhold from disclosure to the public information disclosing any invention in which the Federal Government owns or may own a right, title, or interest (including a nonexclusive license) for a reasonable time in order for a patent application to be filed. Furthermore, Federal agencies shall not be required to release copies of any document which is part of an application for patent filed with the United States Patent and Trademark Office or with any foreign patent office.

§ 206.　Uniform Clauses and Regulations

The Secretary of Commerce may issue regulations which may be made applicable to Federal agencies implementing the provisions of sections 202 through 204 of this chapter and shall establish standard funding agreement provisions required under this chapter. The regulations and the standard funding agreement shall be subject to public comment before their issuance.

§ 207.　Domestic and Foreign Protection of Federally Owned Inventions

(a)　Each Federal agency is authorized to—

(1)　apply for, obtain, and maintain patents or other forms of protection in the United States and in foreign countries on inventions in which the Federal Government owns a right, title, or interest;

(2)　grant nonexclusive, exclusive, or partially exclusive licenses under federally owned inventions, royalty-free or for royalties or other consideration, and on such terms and conditions, including the grant to the licensee of the right of enforcement pursuant to the provisions of chapter 29 as determined appropriate in the public interest;

(3) undertake all other suitable and necessary steps to protect and administer rights to federally owned inventions on behalf of the Federal Government either directly or through contract, including acquiring rights for and administering royalties to the Federal Government in any invention, but only to the extent the party from whom the rights are acquired voluntarily enters into the transaction, to facilitate the licensing of a federally owned invention; and

(4) transfer custody and administration, in whole or in part, to another Federal agency, of the right, title, or interest in any federally owned invention.

(b) For the purpose of assuring the effective management of Government-owned inventions, the Secretary of Commerce is authorized to—

(1) assist Federal agency efforts to promote the licensing and utilization of Government-owned inventions;

(2) assist Federal agencies in seeking protection and maintaining inventions in foreign countries, including the payment of fees and costs connected therewith; and

(3) consult with and advise Federal agencies as to areas of science and technology research and development with potential for commercial utilization.

§ 208.   Regulations Governing Federal Licensing

The Secretary of Commerce is authorized to promulgate regulations specifying the terms and conditions upon which any federally owned invention, other than inventions owned by the Tennessee Valley Authority, may be licensed on a nonexclusive, partially exclusive, or exclusive basis.

§ 209.   Licensing Federally Owned Inventions

(a) **Authority.**—A Federal agency may grant an exclusive or partially exclusive license on a federally owned invention under section 207(a)(2) only if—

(1) granting the license is a reasonable and necessary incentive to—

(A) call forth the investment capital and expenditures needed to bring the invention to practical application; or

(B) otherwise promote the invention's utilization by the public;

(2) the Federal agency finds that the public will be served by the granting of the license, as indicated by the applicant's intentions, plans, and ability to bring the invention to practical application or otherwise promote the invention's utilization by the public, and that the proposed scope of exclusivity is not greater than reasonably necessary to provide the incentive for bringing the invention to practical application, as proposed by the applicant, or otherwise to promote the invention's utilization by the public;

(3) the applicant makes a commitment to achieve practical application of the invention within a reasonable time, which time may be extended by the agency upon the applicant's request and the applicant's demonstration that the refusal of such extension would be unreasonable;

(4) granting the license will not tend to substantially lessen competition or create or maintain a violation of the Federal antitrust laws; and

(5) in the case of an invention covered by a foreign patent application or patent, the interests of the Federal Government or United States industry in foreign commerce will be enhanced.

(b) **Manufacture in United States.**—A Federal agency shall normally grant a license under section 207(a)(2) to use or sell any federally owned invention in the United States only to a licensee who agrees that any products embodying the invention or produced through the use of the invention will be manufactured substantially in the United States.

(c) **Small Business.**—First preference for the granting of any exclusive or partially exclusive licenses under section 207(a)(2) shall be given to small business firms having equal or greater likelihood as other applicants to bring the invention to practical application within a reasonable time.

(d) **Terms and Conditions.**—Any licenses granted under section 207(a)(2) shall contain such terms and conditions as the granting agency considers appropriate, and shall include provisions—

(1) retaining a nontransferable, irrevocable, paid-up license for any Federal agency to practice the invention or have the invention practiced throughout the world by or on behalf of the Government of the United States;

(2) requiring periodic reporting on utilization of the invention, and utilization efforts, by the licensee, but only to the extent necessary to enable the Federal agency to determine whether the terms of the license are being complied with, except that any such report shall be treated by the Federal agency as commercial and financial information obtained from a person and privileged and confidential and not subject to disclosure under section 552 of title 5; and

(3) Empowering the Federal agency to terminate the license in whole or in part if the agency determines that—

(A) the licensee is not executing its commitment to achieve practical application of the invention, including commitments contained in any plan submitted in support of its request for a license, and the licensee cannot otherwise demonstrate to the satisfaction of the Federal agency that it has taken, or can be expected to take within a reasonable time, effective steps to achieve practical application of the invention;

(B) the licensee is in breach of an agreement described in subsection (b);

(C) termination is necessary to meet requirements for public use specified by Federal regulations issued after the date of the license, and such requirements are not reasonably satisfied by the licensee; or

(D) the licensee has been found by a court of competent jurisdiction to have violated the Federal antitrust laws in connection with its performance under the license agreement.

(e) **Public Notice.**—No exclusive or partially exclusive license may be granted under section 207(a)(2) unless public notice of the intention to grant an exclusive or partially exclusive license on a federally owned invention has been provided in an appropriate manner at least 15 days before the license is granted, and the Federal agency has considered all comments received before the end of the comment period in response to that public notice. This subsection shall not apply to the licensing of inventions made under a cooperative research and development agreement entered into under section 12 of the Stevenson-Wydler Technology Innovation Act of 1980 (15 U.S.C. 3710a).

(f) **Plan.**—No Federal agency shall grant any license under a patent or patent application on a federally owned invention unless the person requesting the license has supplied the agency with a plan for development or marketing of the invention, except that any such plan shall be treated by the Federal agency as commercial and financial information obtained from a person and privileged and confidential and not subject to disclosure under section 552 of title 5.

§ 210. Precedence of Chapter

(a) This chapter shall take precedence over any other Act which would require a disposition of rights in subject inventions of small business firms or nonprofit organizations contractors in a manner that is inconsistent with this chapter, including but not necessarily limited to the following:

(1) section 10(a) of the Act of June 29, 1935, as added by title I of the Act of August 14, 1946 (7 U.S.C. 427i(a); 60 Stat. 1085);

(2)   section 205(a) of the Act of August 14, 1946 U.S.C. 1624(a); (60 Stat. 1090);

(3)   section 501(c) of the Federal Mine Safety and Health Act of 1977 (30 U.S.C. 951(c); 83 Stat. 742);

(4)   section 106(c) of the National Traffic and Motor Vehicle Safety Act of 1966 (15 U.S.C. 1395(c); 80 Stat. 721);

(5)   section 12 of the National Science Foundation Act of 1950 (42 U.S.C. 1871(a); 82 Stat. 360);

(6)   section 152 of the Atomic Energy Act of 1954 (42 U.S.C. 2182; 68 Stat. 943);

(7)   section 20135 of title 51;

(8)   section 6 of the Coal Research and Development Act of 1960 (30 U.S.C. 666; 74 Stat. 337);

(9)   section 4 of the Helium Act Amendments of 1960 (50 U.S.C. 167b; 74 Stat. 920);

(10)   section 32 of the Arms Control and Disarmament Act of 1961 (22 U.S.C. 2572; 75 Stat. 634);

(11)   section 9 of the Federal Nonnuclear Energy Research and Development Act of 1974 (42 U.S.C. 5908; 88 Stat. 1878);

(12)   section 5(d) of the Consumer Product Safety Act (15 U.S.C. 2054(d); 86 Stat. 1211);

(13)   section 3 of the Act of April 5, 1944 (30 U.S.C. 323; 58 Stat. 191);

(14)   section 8001(c)(3) of the Solid Waste Disposal Act (42 U.S.C. 6981(c); 90 Stat. 2829);

(15)   section 219 of the Foreign Assistance Act of 1961 (22 U.S.C. 2179; 83 Stat. 806);

(16)   section 427(b) of the Federal Mine Health and Safety Act of 1977 (30 U.S.C. 937(b); 86 Stat. 155);

(17)   section 306(d) of the Surface Mining and Reclamation Act of 1977 (30 U.S.C. 1226(d); 91 Stat. 455);

(18)   section 21(d) of the Federal Fire Prevention and Control Act of 1974 (15 U.S.C. 2218(d); 88 Stat. 1548);

(19) section 6(b) of the Solar Photovoltaic Energy Research Development and Demonstration Act of 1978 (42 U.S.C. 5585(b); 92 Stat. 2516);

(20) section 12 of the Native Latex Commercialization and Economic Development Act of 1978 (7 U.S.C. 178j, 92 Stat. 2533); and

(21) section 408 of the Water Resources and Development Act of 1978 (42 U.S.C. 7879; 92 Stat. 1360).

The Act creating this chapter shall be construed to take precedence over any future Act unless that Act specifically cites this Act and provides that it shall take precedence over this Act.

(b)   Nothing in this chapter is intended to alter the effect of the laws cited in paragraph (a) of this section or any other laws with respect to the disposition of rights in inventions made in the performance of funding agreements with persons other than nonprofit organizations or small business firms.

(c)   Nothing in this chapter is intended to limit the authority of agencies to agree to the disposition of rights in inventions made in the performance of work under funding agreements with persons other than nonprofit organizations or small business firms in accordance with the Statement of Government Patent Policy issued on February 18, 1983 [36 Fed.Reg. 16887], agency regulations, or other applicable regulations or to otherwise limit the authority of agencies to allow such persons to retain ownership of inventions except that all funding agreements, including those with other than small business firms and nonprofit organizations, shall include the requirements established in section 202(c)(4) and section 203. Any disposition of rights in inventions made in accordance with the Statement or implementing regulations, including any disposition occurring before enactment of this section, are hereby authorized.

(d) Nothing in this chapter shall be construed to require the disclosure of intelligence sources or methods or to otherwise affect the authority granted to the Director of Central Intelligence by statute or Executive order for the protection of intelligence sources or methods.

(e) The provisions of the Stevenson-Wydler Technology Innovation Act of 1980, shall take precedence over the provisions of this chapter to the extent that they permit or require a disposition of rights in subject inventions which is inconsistent with this chapter.

§ 211.   Relationship to Antitrust Laws

Nothing in this chapter shall be deemed to convey to any person immunity from civil or criminal liability, or to create any defenses to actions, under any antitrust law.

§ 212.   Disposition of Rights in Educational Awards

No scholarship, fellowship, training grant, or other funding agreement made by a Federal agency primarily to an awardee for educational purposes will contain any provision giving the Federal agency any rights to inventions made by the awardee.

PART III. PATENTS AND PROTECTION
OF PATENT RIGHTS

CHAPTER 25. AMENDMENT AND CORRECTION OF PATENTS

§ 251.   Reissue of Defective Patents

(a) **In General.**—Whenever any patent is, through error deemed wholly or partly inoperative or invalid, by reason of a defective specification or drawing, or by reason of the patentee claiming more or less than he had a right to claim in the patent, the Director shall, on the surrender of such patent and the payment of the fee required by law, reissue the patent for the invention disclosed in the original patent, and in accordance with a new and amended application, for the unexpired part of the term of the original patent. No new matter shall be introduced into the application for reissue.

(b) Multiple Reissued Patents.—The Director may issue several reissued patents for distinct and separate parts of the thing patented, upon demand of the applicant, and upon payment of the required fee for a reissue for each of such reissued patents.

(c) Applicability of this Title.—The provisions of this title relating to applications for patent shall be applicable to applications for reissue of a patent, except that application for reissue may be made and sworn to by the assignee of the entire interest if the application does not seek to enlarge the scope of the claims of the original patent or the application for the original patent was filed by the assignee of the entire interest.

(d) Reissue Patent Enlarging Scope of Claims.—No reissued patent shall be granted enlarging the scope of the claims of the original patent unless applied for within two years from the grant of the original patent.

§ 252. Effect of Reissue

The surrender of the original patent shall take effect upon the issue of the reissued patent, and every reissued patent shall have the same effect and operation in law, on the trial of actions for causes thereafter arising, as if the same had been originally granted in such amended form, but in so far as the claims of the original and reissued patents are substantially identical, such surrender shall not affect any action then pending nor abate any cause of action then existing, and the reissued patent, to the extent that its claims are substantially identical with the original patent, shall constitute a continuation thereof and have effect continuously from the date of the original patent.

A reissued patent shall not abridge or affect the right of any person or that person's successors in business who, prior to the grant of a reissue, made, purchased, offered to sell, or used within the United States, or imported into the United States, anything patented by the reissued patent, to continue the use of, to offer to sell, or to sell to others to be used, offered for sale, or sold, the specific thing so made, purchased, offered for sale, used, or imported unless the making, using, offering for sale, or selling of such thing infringes a valid claim of the reissued patent which was in the original patent. The court before which such matter is in question may provide for the continued manufacture, use, offer for sale, or sale of the thing made, purchased, offered for sale, used, or imported as specified, or for the manufacture, use, offer for sale, or sale in the United States of which substantial preparation was made before the grant of the reissue, and the court may also provide for the continued practice of any process patented by the reissue that is practiced, or for the practice of which substantial preparation was made, before the grant of the reissue, to the extent and under such terms as the court deems equitable for the protection of investments made or business commenced before the grant of the reissue.

§ 253. Disclaimer

(a) In General.—Whenever a claim of a patent is invalid the remaining claims shall not thereby be rendered invalid. A patentee, whether of the whole or any sectional interest therein, may, on payment of the fee required by law, make disclaimer of any complete claim, stating therein the extent of his interest in such patent. Such disclaimer shall be in writing, and recorded in the Patent and Trademark Office; and it shall thereafter be considered as part of the original patent to the extent of the interest possessed by the disclaimant and by those claiming under him.

(b) Additional Disclaimer or Dedication.—In the manner set forth in subsection (a), any patentee or applicant may disclaim or dedicate to the public the entire term, or any terminal part of the term, of the patent granted or to be granted.

§ 254.　　Certificate of Correction of Patent and Trademark Office Mistake

Whenever a mistake in a patent, incurred through the fault of the Patent and Trademark Office, is clearly disclosed by the records of the Office, the Director may issue a certificate of correction stating the fact and nature of such mistake, under seal, without charge, to be recorded in the records of patents. A printed copy thereof shall be attached to each printed copy of the patent, and such certificate shall be considered as part of the original patent. Every such patent, together with such certificate, shall have the same effect and operation in law on the trial of actions for causes thereafter arising as if the same had been originally issued in such corrected form. The Director may issue a corrected patent without charge in lieu of and with like effect as a certificate of correction.

§ 255.　　Certificate of Correction of Applicant's Mistake

Whenever a mistake of a clerical or typographical nature, or of minor character, which was not the fault of the Patent and Trademark Office, appears in a patent and a showing has been made that such mistake occurred in good faith, the Director may, upon payment of the required fee, issue a certificate of correction, if the correction does not involve such changes in the patent as would constitute new matter or would require re-examination. Such patent, together with the certificate, shall have same effect and operation in law on the trial of actions for causes thereafter arising as if the same had been originally issued in such corrected form.

§ 256.　　Correction of Named Inventor

(a)　Correction.—Whenever through error a person is named in an issued patent as the inventor, or through error an inventor is not named in an issued patent, the Director may, on application of all the parties and assignees, with proof of the facts and such other requirements as may be imposed, issue a certificate correcting such error.

(b)　Patent Valid if Error Corrected.—The error of omitting inventors or naming persons who are not inventors shall not invalidate the patent in which such error occurred if it can be corrected as provided in this section. The court before which such matter is called in question may order correction of the patent on notice and hearing of all parties concerned and the Director shall issue a certificate accordingly.

§ 257.　　Supplemental Examinations to Consider, Reconsider, or Correct Information

(a)　Request for Supplemental Examination.—A patent owner may request supplemental examination of a patent in the Office to consider, reconsider, or correct information believed to be relevant to the patent, in accordance with such requirements as the Director may establish. Within 3 months after the date a request for supplemental examination meeting the requirements of this section is received, the Director shall conduct the supplemental examination and shall conclude such examination by issuing a certificate indicating whether the information presented in the request raises a substantial new question of patentability.

(b)　Reexamination Ordered.—If the certificate issued under subsection (a) indicates that a substantial new question of patentability is raised by 1 or more items of information in the request, the Director shall order reexamination of the patent. The reexamination shall be conducted according to procedures established by chapter 30, except that the patent owner shall not have the right to file a statement pursuant to section 304. During the reexamination, the Director shall address each substantial new question of patentability identified during the supplemental examination, notwithstanding the limitations in chapter 30 relating to patents and printed publication or any other provision of such chapter.

(c)　Effect.—

(1)　In General.—A patent shall not be held unenforceable on the basis of conduct relating to information that had not been considered, was inadequately considered, or was incorrect in a prior examination of the patent if the information was considered, reconsidered, or corrected during a supplemental examination of the patent. The making of a request under subsection (a), or the absence thereof, shall not be relevant to enforceability of the patent under section 282.

　　(2)　Exceptions.—

　　　　(A)　Prior Allegations.—Paragraph (1) shall not apply to an allegation pled with particularity in a civil action, or set forth with particularity in a notice received by the patent owner under section 505(j)(2)(B)(iv)(II) of the Federal Food, Drug, and Cosmetic Act (21 U.S.C. 355(j)(2)(B)(iv)(II)), before the date of a supplemental examination request under subsection (a) to consider, reconsider, or correct information forming the basis for the allegation.

　　　　(B)　Patent Enforcement Actions.—In an action brought under section 337(a) of the Tariff Act of 1930 (19 U.S.C. 1337(a)), or section 281 of this title, paragraph (1) shall not apply to any defense raised in the action that is based upon information that was considered, reconsidered, or corrected pursuant to a supplemental examination request under subsection (a), unless the supplemental examination, and any reexamination ordered pursuant to the request, are concluded before the date on which the action is brought.

(d)　Fees and Regulations.—

　　(1)　Fees.—The Director shall, by regulation, establish fees for the submission of a request for supplemental examination of a patent, and to consider each item of information submitted in the request. If reexamination is ordered under subsection (b), fees established and applicable to ex parte reexamination proceedings under chapter 30 shall be paid, in addition to fees applicable to supplemental examination.

　　(2)　Regulations.—The Director shall issue regulations governing the form, content, and other requirements of requests for supplemental examination, and establishing procedures for reviewing information submitted in such requests.

(e)　Fraud.—If the Director becomes aware, during the course of a supplemental examination or reexamination proceeding ordered under this section, that a material fraud on the Office may have been committed in connection with the patent that is the subject of the supplemental examination, then in addition to any other actions the Director is authorized to take, including the cancellation of any claims found to be invalid under section 307 as a result of a reexamination ordered under this section, the Director shall also refer the matter to the Attorney General for such further action as the Attorney General may deem appropriate. Any such referral shall be treated as confidential, shall not be included in the file of the patent, and shall not be disclosed to the public unless the United States charges a person with a criminal offense in connection with such referral.

(f)　Rule of Construction.—Nothing in this section shall be construed—

　　(1)　to preclude the imposition of sanctions based upon criminal or antitrust laws (including section 1001(a) of title 18, the first section of the Clayton Act, and section 5 of the Federal Trade Commission Act to the extent that section relates to unfair methods of competition);

　　(2)　to limit the authority of the Director to investigate issues of possible misconduct and impose sanctions for misconduct in connection with matters or proceedings before the Office; or

　　(3)　to limit the authority of the Director to issue regulations under chapter 3 relating to sanctions for misconduct by representatives practicing before the Office.

CHAPTER 26.　OWNERSHIP AND ASSIGNMENT

§ 261.   Ownership; Assignment

Subject to the provisions of this title, patents shall have the attributes of personal property. The Patent and Trademark Office shall maintain a register of interests in patents and applications for patents and shall record any document related thereto upon request, and may require a fee therefor.

Applications for patent, patents, or any interest therein, shall be assignable in law by an instrument in writing. The applicant, patentee, or his assigns or legal representatives may in like manner grant and convey an exclusive right under his application for patent, or patents, to the whole or any specified part of the United States.

A certificate of acknowledgment under the hand and official seal of a person authorized to administer oaths within the United States, or, in a foreign country, of a diplomatic or consular officer of the United States or an officer authorized to administer oaths whose authority is proved by a certificate of a diplomatic or consular officer of the United States, or apostille of an official designated by a foreign country which, by treaty or convention, accords like effect to apostilles of designated officials in the United States, shall be prima facie evidence of the execution of an assignment, grant or conveyance of a patent or application for patent.

An interest that constitutes an assignment, grant or conveyance shall be void as against any subsequent purchaser or mortgagee for a valuable consideration, without notice, unless it is recorded in the Patent and Trademark Office within three months from its date or prior to the date of such subsequent purchase or mortgage.

§ 262.   Joint Owners

In the absence of any agreement to the contrary, each of the joint owners of a patent may make, use, offer to sell, or sell the patented invention within the United States, or import the patented invention into the United States without the consent of and without accounting to the other owners.

CHAPTER 27. GOVERNMENT INTERESTS IN PATENTS

Sec.
267.   Time for Taking Action in Government Applications.

---

§ 267.   Time for Taking Action in Government Applications

Notwithstanding the provisions of sections 133 and 151, the Director may extend the time for taking any action to three years, when an application has become the property of the United States and the head of the appropriate department or agency of the Government has certified to the Director that the invention disclosed therein is important to the armament or defense of the United States.

CHAPTER 28. INFRINGEMENT OF PATENTS

Sec.
271.   Infringement of Patent.
272.   Temporary Presence in the United States.
273.   Defense to Infringement Based on Prior Commercial Use.

---

§ 271.   Infringement of Patent

(a)   Except as otherwise provided in this title, whoever without authority makes, uses, offers to sell, or sells any patented invention, within the United States or imports into the United States any patented invention during the term of the patent therefor, infringes the patent.

(b)   Whoever actively induces infringement of a patent shall be liable as an infringer.

(c)   Whoever offers to sell or sells within the United States or imports into the United States a component of a patented machine, manufacture, combination or composition, or a material or apparatus for use in practicing a patented process, constituting a material part of the invention, knowing the same to be especially made or especially adapted for use in an infringement of such patent, and not a staple article or commodity of commerce suitable for substantial noninfringing use, shall be liable as a contributory infringer.

(d)   No patent owner otherwise entitled to relief for infringement or contributory infringement of a patent shall be denied relief or deemed guilty of misuse or illegal extension of the patent right by reason of his having done one or more of the following: (1) derived revenue from acts which if performed by another without his consent would constitute contributory infringement of the patent; (2) licensed or authorized another to perform acts which if performed without his consent would constitute contributory infringement of the patent; (3) sought to enforce his patent rights against infringement or contributory infringement; (4) refused to license or use any rights to the patent; or (5) conditioned the license of any rights to the patent or the sale of the patented product on the acquisition of a license to rights in another patent or purchase of a separate product, unless, in view of the circumstances, the patent owner has market power in the relevant market for the patent or patented product on which the license or sale is conditioned.

(e)(1)   It shall not be an act of infringement to make, use, offer to sell, or sell within the United States or import into the United States a patented invention (other than a new animal drug or veterinary biological product (as those terms are used in the Federal Food, Drug, and Cosmetic Act and the Act of March 4, 1913) which is primarily manufactured using recombinant DNA, recombinant RNA, hybridoma technology, or other processes involving site specific genetic manipulation techniques) solely for uses reasonably related to the development and submission of information under a Federal law which regulates the manufacture, use, or sale of drugs or veterinary biological products.

(2)   It shall be an act of infringement to submit—

(A)   an application under section 505(j) of the Federal Food, Drug, and Cosmetic Act or described in section 505(b)(2) of such Act for a drug claimed in a patent or the use of which is claimed in a patent,

(B)   an application under section 512 of such Act or under the Act of March 4, 1913 (21 U.S.C. 151–158) for a drug or veterinary biological product which is not primarily manufactured using recombinant DNA, recombinant RNA, hybridoma technology, or other processes involving site specific genetic manipulation techniques and which is claimed in a patent or the use of which is claimed in a patent, or

(C)(i)   with respect to a patent that is identified in the list of patents described in section 351(*l*)(3) of the Public Health Service Act (including as provided under section 351(*l*)(7) of such Act), an application seeking approval of a biological product, or

(ii)   if the applicant for the application fails to provide the application and information required under section 351(*l*)(2)(A) of such Act, an application seeking approval of a biological product for a patent that could be identified pursuant to section 351(*l*)(3)(A)(i) of such Act,

if the purpose of such submission is to obtain approval under such Act to engage in the commercial manufacture, use, or sale of a drug, veterinary biological product, or biological product claimed in a patent or the use of which is claimed in a patent before the expiration of such patent.

(3)   In any action for patent infringement brought under this section, no injunctive or other relief may be granted which would prohibit the making, using, offering to sell, or selling within the United States or importing into the United States of a patented invention under paragraph (1).

(4)   For an act of infringement described in paragraph (2)—

(A) the court shall order the effective date of any approval of the drug or veterinary biological product involved in the infringement to be a date which is not earlier than the date of the expiration of the patent which has been infringed,

(B) injunctive relief may be granted against an infringer to prevent the commercial manufacture, use, offer to sell, or sale within the United States or importation into the United States of an approved drug, veterinary biological product, or biological product,

(C) damages or other monetary relief may be awarded against an infringer only if there has been commercial manufacture, use, offer to sell, or sale within the United States or importation into the United States of an approved drug, veterinary biological product, or biological product, and

(D) the court shall order a permanent injunction prohibiting any infringement of the patent by the biological product involved in the infringement until a date which is not earlier than the date of the expiration of the patent that has been infringed under paragraph (2)(C), provided the patent is the subject of a final court decision, as defined in section 351(k)(6) of the Public Health Service Act, in an action for infringement of the patent under section 351(*l*)(6) of such Act, and the biological product has not yet been approved because of section 351(k)(7) of such Act.

The remedies prescribed by subparagraphs (A), (B), (C), and (D) are the only remedies which may be granted by a court for an act of infringement described in paragraph (2), except that a court may award attorney fees under section 285.

(5) Where a person has filed an application described in paragraph (2) that includes a certification under subsection (b)(2)(A)(iv) or (j)(2)(A)(vii)(IV) of section 505 of the Federal Food, Drug, and Cosmetic Act (21 U.S.C. 355), and neither the owner of the patent that is the subject of the certification nor the holder of the approved application under subsection (b) of such section for the drug that is claimed by the patent or a use of which is claimed by the patent brought an action for infringement of such patent before the expiration of 45 days after the date on which the notice given under subsection (b)(3) or (j)(2)(B) of such section was received, the courts of the United States shall, to the extent consistent with the Constitution, have subject matter jurisdiction in any action brought by such person under section 2201 of title 28 for a declaratory judgment that such patent is invalid or not infringed.

(6)(A) Subparagraph (B) Applies, in lieu of paragraph (4), in the case of a patent—

(i) that is identified, as applicable, in the list of patents described in section 351(*l*)(4) of the Public Health Service Act or the lists of patents described in section 351(*l*)(5)(B) of such Act with respect to a biological product; and

(ii) for which an action for infringement of the patent with respect to the biological product—

(I) was brought after the expiration of the 30-day period described in subparagraph (A) or (B), as applicable, of section 351(*l*)(6) of such Act; or

(II) was brought before the expiration of the 30-day period described in subclause (I), but which was dismissed without prejudice or was not prosecuted to judgment in good faith.

(B) In an action for infringement of a patent described in subparagraph (A), the sole and exclusive remedy that may be granted by a court, upon a finding that the making, using, offering to sell, selling, or importation into the United States of the biological product that is the subject of the action infringed the patent, shall be a reasonable royalty.

(C) The owner of a patent that should have been included in the list described in section 351(*l*)(3)(A) of the Public Health Service Act, including as provided under section 351(*l*)(7) of such Act for a biological product, but was not timely included in such list, may not bring an action under this section for infringement of the patent with respect to the biological product.

(f)(1)   Whoever without authority supplies or causes to be supplied in or from the United States all or a substantial portion of the components of a patented invention, where such components are uncombined in whole or in part, in such manner as to actively induce the combination of such components outside of the United States in a manner that would infringe the patent if such combination occurred within the United States, shall be liable as an infringer.

(2)   Whoever without authority supplies or causes to be supplied in or from the United States any component of a patented invention that is especially made or especially adapted for use in the invention and not a staple article or commodity of commerce suitable for substantial noninfringing use, where such component is uncombined in whole or in part, knowing that such component is so made or adapted and intending that such component will be combined outside of the United States in a manner that would infringe the patent if such combination occurred within the United States, shall be liable as an infringer.

(g)   Whoever without authority imports into the United States or offers to sell, sells, or uses within the United States a product which is made by a process patented in the United States shall be liable as an infringer, if the importation, offer to sell, sale, or use of the product occurs during the term of such process patent. In an action for infringement of a process patent, no remedy may be granted for infringement on account of the noncommercial use or retail sale of a product unless there is no adequate remedy under this title for infringement on account of the importation or other use, offer to sell, or sale of that product. A product which is made by a patented process will, for purposes of this title, not be considered to be so made after—

(1)   it is materially changed by subsequent processes; or

(2)   it becomes a trivial and nonessential component of another product.

(h)   As used in this section, the term "whoever" includes any State, any instrumentality of a State, and any officer or employee of a State or instrumentality of a State acting in his official capacity. Any State, and any such instrumentality, officer, or employee, shall be subject to the provisions of this title in the same manner and to the same extent as any nongovernmental entity.

(i)   As used in this section, an "offer for sale" or an "offer to sell" by a person other than the patentee, or any designee of the patentee, is that in which the sale will occur before the expiration of the term of the patent.

§ 272.   Temporary Presence in the United States

The use of any invention in any vessel, aircraft or vehicle of any country which affords similar privileges to vessels, aircraft or vehicles of the United States, entering the United States temporarily or accidentally, shall not constitute infringement of any patent, if the invention is used exclusively for the needs of the vessel, aircraft or vehicle and is not offered for sale or sold in or used for the manufacture of anything to be sold in or exported from the United States.

§ 273.   Defense to Infringement Based on Prior Commercial Use

(a)   **In General.**—A person shall be entitled to a defense under section 282(b) with respect to subject matter consisting of a process, or consisting of a machine, manufacture, or composition of matter used in a manufacturing or other commercial process, that would otherwise infringe a claimed invention being asserted against the person if—

(1)   such person, acting in good faith, commercially used the subject matter in the United States, either in connection with an internal commercial use or an actual arm's length sale or other arm's length commercial transfer of a useful end result of such commercial use; and

(2)   such commercial use occurred at least 1 year before the earlier of either—

(A)   the effective filing date of the claimed invention; or

(B) the date on which the claimed invention was disclosed to the public in a manner that qualified for the exception from prior art under section 102(b).

(b) Burden of Proof.—A person asserting a defense under this section shall have the burden of establishing the defense by clear and convincing evidence.

(c) Additional Commercial Uses.—

(1) Premarketing Regulatory Review.—Subject matter for which commercial marketing or use is subject to a premarketing regulatory review period during which the safety or efficacy of the subject matter is established, including any period specified in section 156(g), shall be deemed to be commercially used for purposes of subsection (a)(1) during such regulatory review period.

(2) Nonprofit Laboratory Use.—A use of subject matter by a nonprofit research laboratory or other nonprofit entity, such as a university or hospital, for which the public is the intended beneficiary, shall be deemed to be a commercial use for purposes of subsection (a)(1), except that a defense under this section may be asserted pursuant to this paragraph only for continued and noncommercial use by and in the laboratory or other nonprofit entity.

(d) Exhaustion of Rights.—Notwithstanding subsection (e)(1), the sale or other disposition of a useful end result by a person entitled to assert a defense under this section in connection with a patent with respect to that useful end result shall exhaust the patent owner's rights under the patent to the extent that such rights would have been exhausted had such sale or other disposition been made by the patent owner.

(e) Limitations and Exceptions.—

(1) Personal Defense.—

(A) In General.—A defense under this section may be asserted only by the person who performed or directed the performance of the commercial use described in subsection (a), or by an entity that controls, is controlled by, or is under common control with such person.

(B) Transfer of Right.—Except for any transfer to the patent owner, the right to assert a defense under this section shall not be licensed or assigned or transferred to another person except as an ancillary and subordinate part of a good-faith assignment or transfer for other reasons of the entire enterprise or line of business to which the defense relates.

(C) Restriction on Sites.—A defense under this section, when acquired by a person as part of an assignment or transfer described in subparagraph (B), may only be asserted for uses at sites where the subject matter that would otherwise infringe a claimed invention is in use before the later of the effective filing date of the claimed invention or the date of the assignment or transfer of such enterprise or line of business.

(2) Derivation.—A person may not assert a defense under this section if the subject matter on which the defense is based was derived from the patentee or persons in privity with the patentee.

(3) Not a General License.—The defense asserted by a person under this section is not a general license under all claims of the patent at issue, but extends only to the specific subject matter for which it has been established that a commercial use that qualifies under this section occurred, except that the defense shall also extend to variations in the quantity or volume of use of the claimed subject matter, and to improvements in the claimed subject matter that do not infringe additional specifically claimed subject matter of the patent.

(4) Abandonment of Use.—A person who has abandoned commercial use (that qualifies under this section) of subject matter may not rely on activities performed before the date of such abandonment in establishing a defense under this section with respect to actions taken on or after the date of such abandonment.

(5) University Exception.—

(A) In General.—A person commercially using subject matter to which subsection (a) applies may not assert a defense under this section if the claimed invention with respect to which the defense is asserted was, at the time the invention was made, owned or subject to an obligation of assignment to either an institution of higher education (as defined in section 101(a) of the Higher Education Act of 1965 (20 U.S.C. 1001(a)), or a technology transfer organization whose primary purpose is to facilitate the commercialization of technologies developed by one or more such institutions of higher education.

(B) Exception.—Subparagraph (A) shall not apply if any of the activities required to reduce to practice the subject matter of the claimed invention could not have been undertaken using funds provided by the Federal Government.

(f) Unreasonable Assertion of Defense.—If the defense under this section is pleaded by a person who is found to infringe the patent and who subsequently fails to demonstrate a reasonable basis for asserting the defense, the court shall find the case exceptional for the purpose of awarding attorney fees under section 285.

(g) Invalidity.—A patent shall not be deemed to be invalid under section 102 or 103 solely because a defense is raised or established under this section.

CHAPTER 29.   REMEDIES FOR INFRINGEMENT OF PATENT, AND OTHER ACTIONS

---

§ 281.   Remedy for Infringement of Patent

A patentee shall have remedy by civil action for infringement of his patent.

§ 282.   Presumption of Validity; Defenses

(a) In General.—A patent shall be presumed valid. Each claim of a patent (whether in independent, dependent, or multiple dependent form) shall be presumed valid independently of the validity of other claims; dependent or multiple dependent claims shall be presumed valid even though dependent upon an invalid claim. The burden of establishing invalidity of a patent or any claim thereof shall rest on the party asserting such invalidity.

(b) Defenses.—The following shall be defenses in any action involving the validity or infringement of a patent and shall be pleaded:

(1) Noninfringement, absence of liability for infringement or unenforceability.

(2) Invalidity of the patent or any claim in suit on any ground specified in part II of this title as a condition for patentability.

(3) Invalidity of the patent or any claim in suit for failure to comply with—

(A) any requirement of section 112, except that the failure to disclose the best mode shall not be a basis on which any claim of a patent may be canceled or held invalid or otherwise unenforceable; or

(B) any requirement of section 251.

(4) Any other fact or act made a defense by this title.

(c) Notice of Actions; Actions During Extension of Patent Term.—In an action involving the validity or infringement of a patent the party asserting invalidity or noninfringement shall give notice in the pleadings or otherwise in writing to the adverse party at least thirty days before the trial, of the country, number, date, and name of the patentee of any patent, the title, date, and page numbers of any publication to be relied upon as anticipation of the patent in suit or, except in actions in the United States Court of Federal Claims, as showing the state of the art, and the name and address of any person who may be relied upon as the prior inventor or as having prior knowledge of or as having previously used or offered for sale the invention of the patent in suit. In the absence of such notice proof of the said matters may not be made at the trial except on such terms as the court requires. Invalidity of the extension of a patent term or any portion thereof under section 154(b) or 156 because of the material failure—

(1) by the applicant for the extension, or

(2) by the Director,

to comply with the requirements of such section shall be a defense in any action involving the infringement of a patent during the period of the extension of its term and shall be pleaded. A due diligence determination under section 156(d)(2) is not subject to review in such an action.

§ 283. Injunction

The several courts having jurisdiction of cases under this title may grant injunctions in accordance with the principles of equity to prevent the violation of any right secured by patent, on such terms as the court deems reasonable.

§ 284. Damages

Upon finding for the claimant the court shall award the claimant damages adequate to compensate for the infringement, but in no event less than a reasonable royalty for the use made of the invention by the infringer, together with interest and costs as fixed by the court.

When the damages are not found by a jury, the court shall assess them. In either event the court may increase the damages up to three times the amount found or assessed. Increased damages under this paragraph shall not apply to provisional rights under section 154(d).

The court may receive expert testimony as an aid to the determination of damages or of what royalty would be reasonable under the circumstances.

§ 285.   Attorney Fees

The court in exceptional cases may award reasonable attorney fees to the prevailing party.

§ 286.   Time Limitation on Damages

Except as otherwise provided by law, no recovery shall be had for any infringement committed more than six years prior to the filing of the complaint or counterclaim for infringement in the action.

In the case of claims against the United States Government for use of a patented invention, the period before bringing suit, up to six years, between the date of receipt of a written claim for compensation by the department or agency of the Government having authority to settle such claim, and the date of mailing by the Government of a notice to the claimant that his claim has been denied shall not be counted as part of the period referred to in the preceding paragraph. Increased damages under this paragraph shall not apply to provisional rights under section 154(d).

§ 287.   Limitation on Damages and Other Remedies; Marking and Notice

(a)   Patentees, and persons making, offering for sale, or selling within the United States any patented article for or under them, or importing any patented article into the United States, may give notice to the public that the same is patented, either by fixing thereon the word "patent" or the abbreviation "pat.", together with the number of the patent, or by fixing thereon the word "patent" or the abbreviation "pat." together with an address of a posting on the Internet, accessible to the public without charge for accessing the address, that associates the patented article with the number of the patent, or when, from the character of the article, this can not be done, by fixing to it, or to the package wherein one or more of them is contained, a label containing a like notice. In the event of failure so to mark, no damages shall be recovered by the patentee in any action for infringement, except on proof that the infringer was notified of the infringement and continued to infringe thereafter, in which event damages may be recovered only for infringement occurring after such notice. Filing of an action for infringement shall constitute such notice.

(b)(1)   An infringer under section 271(g) shall be subject to all the provisions of this title relating to damages and injunctions except to the extent those remedies are modified by this subsection or section 9006 of the Process Patent Amendments Act of 1988. The modifications of remedies provided in this subsection shall not be available to any person who—

(A)   practiced the patented process;

(B)   owns or controls, or is owned or controlled by, the person who practiced the patented process; or

(C)   had knowledge before the infringement that a patented process was used to make the product the importation, use, offer for sale, or sale of which constitutes the infringement.

(2)   No remedies for infringement under section 271(g) shall be available with respect to any product in the possession of, or in transit to, the person subject to liability under such section before that person had notice of infringement with respect to that product. The person subject to liability shall bear the burden of proving any such possession or transit.

(3)(A)   In making a determination with respect to the remedy in an action brought for infringement under section 271(g), the court shall consider—

(i)   the good faith demonstrated by the defendant with respect to a request for disclosure,

(ii)   the good faith demonstrated by the plaintiff with respect to a request for disclosure, and

(iii)   the need to restore the exclusive rights secured by the patent.

(B)   For purposes of subparagraph (A), the following are evidence of good faith:

(i)   a request for disclosure made by the defendant;

    (ii)   a response within a reasonable time by the person receiving the request for disclosure; and

    (iii)   the submission of the response by the defendant to the manufacturer, or if the manufacturer is not known, to the supplier, of the product to be purchased by the defendant, together with a request for a written statement that the process claimed in any patent disclosed in the response is not used to produce such product.

The failure to perform any acts described in the preceding sentence is evidence of absence of good faith unless there are mitigating circumstances. Mitigating circumstances include the case in which, due to the nature of the product, the number of sources for the product, or like commercial circumstances, a request for disclosure is not necessary or practicable to avoid infringement.

    (4)(A)   For purposes of this subsection, a "request for disclosure" means a written request made to a person then engaged in the manufacture of a product to identify all process patents owned by or licensed to that person, as of the time of the request, that the person then reasonably believes could be asserted to be infringed under section 271(g) if that product were imported into, or sold, offered for sale, or used in, the United States by an unauthorized person. A request for disclosure is further limited to a request—

    (i)   which is made by a person regularly engaged in the United States in the sale of the same type of products as those manufactured by the person to whom the request is directed, or which includes facts showing that the person making the request plans to engage in the sale of such products in the United States;

    (ii)   which is made by such person before the person's first importation, use, offer for sale, or sale of units of the product produced by an infringing process and before the person had notice of infringement with respect to the product; and

    (iii)   which includes a representation by the person making the request that such person will promptly submit the patents identified pursuant to the request to the manufacturer, or if the manufacturer is not known, to the supplier, of the product to be purchased by the person making the request, and will request from that manufacturer or supplier a written statement that none of the processes claimed in those patents is used in the manufacture of the product.

    (B)   In the case of a request for disclosure received by a person to whom a patent is licensed, that person shall either identify the patent or promptly notify the licensor of the request for disclosure.

    (C)   A person who has marked, in the manner prescribed by subsection (a), the number of the process patent on all products made by the patented process which have been offered for sale or sold by that person in the United States, or imported by the person into the United States, before a request for disclosure is received is not required to respond to the request for disclosure. For purposes of the preceding sentence, the term "all products" does not include products made before the effective date of the Process Patent Amendments Act of 1988.

    (5)(A)   For purposes of this subsection, notice of infringement means actual knowledge, or receipt by a person of a written notification, or a combination thereof, of information sufficient to persuade a reasonable person that it is likely that a product was made by a process patented in the United States.

    (B)   A written notification from the patent holder charging a person with infringement shall specify the patented process alleged to have been used and the reasons for a good faith belief that such process was used. The patent holder shall include in the notification such information as is reasonably necessary to explain fairly the patent holder's belief, except that the patent holder is not required to disclose any trade secret information.

    (C)   A person who receives a written notification described in subparagraph (B) or a written response to a request for disclosure described in paragraph (4) shall be deemed to have notice of infringement with respect to any patent referred to in such written notification or response unless that person, absent mitigating circumstances—

(i)   promptly transmits the written notification or response to the manufacturer or, if the manufacturer is not known, to the supplier, of the product purchased or to be purchased by that person; and

(ii)   receives a written statement from the manufacturer or supplier which on its face sets forth a well grounded factual basis for a belief that the identified patents are not infringed.

(D)   For purposes of this subsection, a person who obtains a product made by a process patented in the United States in a quantity which is abnormally large in relation to the volume of business of such person or an efficient inventory level shall be rebuttably presumed to have actual knowledge that the product was made by such patented process.

(6)   A person who receives a response to a request for disclosure under this subsection shall pay to the person to whom the request was made a reasonable fee to cover actual costs incurred in complying with the request, which may not exceed the cost of a commercially available automated patent search of the matter involved, but in no case more than $500.

(c)(1)   With respect to a medical practitioner's performance of a medical activity that constitutes an infringement under section 271(a) or (b), the provisions of sections 281, 283, 284, and 285 shall not apply against the medical practitioner or against a related health care entity with respect to such medical activity.

(2)   For the purposes of this subsection:

(A)   the term "medical activity" means the performance of a medical or surgical procedure on a body, but shall not include (i) the use of a patented machine, manufacture, or composition of matter in violation of such patent, (ii) the practice of a patented use of a composition of matter in violation of such patent, or (iii) the practice of a process in violation of a biotechnology patent.

(B)   the term "medical practitioner" means any natural person who is licensed by a State to provide the medical activity described in subsection (c)(1) or who is acting under the direction of such person in the performance of the medical activity.

(C)   the term "related health care entity" shall mean an entity with which a medical practitioner has a professional affiliation under which the medical practitioner performs the medical activity, including but not limited to a nursing home, hospital, university, medical school, health maintenance organization, group medical practice, or a medical clinic.

(D)   the term "professional affiliation" shall mean staff privileges, medical staff membership, employment or contractual relationship, partnership or ownership interest, academic appointment, or other affiliation under which a medical practitioner provides the medical activity on behalf of, or in association with, the health care entity.

(E)   the term "body" shall mean a human body, organ or cadaver, or a nonhuman animal used in medical research or instruction directly relating to the treatment of humans.

(F)   the term "patented use of a composition of matter" does not include a claim for a method of performing a medical or surgical procedure on a body that recites the use of a composition of matter where the use of that composition of matter does not directly contribute to achievement of the objective of the claimed method.

(G)   the term "State" shall mean any State or territory of the United States, the District of Columbia, and the Commonwealth of Puerto Rico.

(3)   This subsection does not apply to the activities of any person, or employee or agent of such person (regardless of whether such person is a tax exempt organization under section 501(c) of the Internal Revenue Code), who is engaged in the commercial development, manufacture, sale, importation, or distribution of a machine, manufacture, or composition of matter or the provision of

pharmacy or clinical laboratory services (other than clinical laboratory services provided in a physician's office), where such activities are:

(A) directly related to the commercial development, manufacture, sale, importation, or distribution of a machine, manufacture, or composition of matter or the provision of pharmacy or clinical laboratory services (other than clinical laboratory services provided in a physician's office), and

(B) regulated under the Federal Food, Drug, and Cosmetic Act, the Public Health Service Act, or the Clinical Laboratories Improvement Act.

(4) This subsection shall not apply to any patent issued based on an application which has an effective filing date before September 30, 1996.

§ 288. Action for Infringement of a Patent Containing an Invalid Claim

Whenever a claim of a patent is invalid, an action may be maintained for the infringement of a claim of the patent which may be valid. The patentee shall recover no costs unless a disclaimer of the invalid claim has been entered at the Patent and Trademark Office before the commencement of the suit.

§ 289. Additional Remedy for Infringement of Design Patent

Whoever during the term of a patent for a design, without license of the owner, (1) applies the patented design, or any colorable imitation thereof, to any article of manufacture for the purpose of sale, or (2) sells or exposes for sale any article of manufacture to which such design or colorable imitation has been applied shall be liable to the owner to the extent of his total profit, but not less than $250, recoverable in any United States district court having jurisdiction of the parties.

Nothing in this section shall prevent, lessen, or impeach any other remedy which an owner of an infringed patent has under the provisions of this title, but he shall not twice recover the profit made from the infringement.

§ 290. Notice of Patent Suits

The clerks of the courts of the United States, within one month after the filing of an action under this title shall give notice thereof in writing to the Director, setting forth so far as known the names and addresses of the parties, name of the inventor, and the designating number of the patent upon which the action has been brought. If any other patent is subsequently included in the action he shall give like notice thereof. Within one month after the decision is rendered or a judgment issued the clerk of the court shall give notice thereof to the Director. The Director shall, on receipt of such notices, enter the same in the file of such patent.

§ 291. Derived Patents

(a) **In General.**—The owner of a patent may have relief by civil action against the owner of another patent that claims the same invention and has an earlier effective filing date, if the invention claimed in such other patent was derived from the inventor of the invention claimed in the patent owned by the person seeking relief under this section.

(b) **Filing Limitation.**—An action under this section may be filed only before the end of the 1-year period beginning on the date of the issuance of the first patent containing a claim to the allegedly derived invention and naming an individual alleged to have derived such invention as the inventor or joint inventor.

§ 292. False Marking

(a) Whoever, without the consent of the patentee, marks upon, or affixes to, or uses in advertising in connection with anything made, used, offered for sale, or sold by such person within the United States, or imported by the person into the United States, the name or any imitation of the name of the patentee, the patent number, or the words "patent," "patentee," or the like, with the intent of counterfeiting or imitating the mark of the patentee, or of deceiving the public and inducing them to believe that the thing was made, offered for sale, sold, or imported into the United States by or with the consent of the patentee; or

Whoever marks upon, or affixes to, or uses in advertising in connection with any unpatented article, the word "patent" or any word or number importing that the same is patented, for the purpose of deceiving the public; or

Whoever marks upon, or affixes to, or uses in advertising in connection with any article, the words "patent applied for," "patent pending," or any word importing that an application for patent has been made, when no application for patent has been made, or if made, is not pending, for the purpose of deceiving the public—

Shall be fined not more than $500 for every such offense.

Only the United States may sue for the penalty authorized by this subsection.

(b) A person who has suffered a competitive injury as a result of a violation of this section may file a civil action in a district court of the United States for recovery of damages adequate to compensate for the injury.

(c) The marking of a product, in a manner described in subsection (a), with matter relating to a patent that covered that product but has expired is not a violation of this section.

§ 293. Nonresident Patentee; Service and Notice

Every patentee not residing in the United States may file in the Patent and Trademark Office a written designation stating the name and address of a person residing within the United States on whom may be served process or notice of proceedings affecting the patent or rights thereunder. If the person designated cannot be found at the address given in the last designation, or if no person has been designated, the United States District Court for the Eastern District of Virginia shall have jurisdiction and summons shall be served by publication or otherwise as the court directs. The court shall have the same jurisdiction to take any action respecting the patent or rights thereunder that it would have if the patentee were personally within the jurisdiction of the court.

§ 294. Voluntary Arbitration

(a) A contract involving a patent or any right under a patent may contain a provision requiring arbitration of any dispute relating to patent validity or infringement arising under the contract. In the absence of such a provision, the parties to an existing patent validity or infringement dispute may agree in writing to settle such dispute by arbitration. Any such provision or agreement shall be valid, irrevocable, and enforceable, except for any grounds that exist at law or in equity for revocation of a contract.

(b) Arbitration of such disputes, awards by arbitrators and confirmation of awards shall be governed by title 9, to the extent such title is not inconsistent with this section. In any such arbitration proceeding, the defenses provided for under section 282 shall be considered by the arbitrator if raised by any party to the proceeding.

(c) An award by an arbitrator shall be final and binding between the parties to the arbitration but shall have no force or effect on any other person. The parties to an arbitration may agree that in the event a patent which is the subject matter of an award is subsequently determined to be invalid or unenforceable in a judgment rendered by a court of competent jurisdiction from which no appeal can or has been taken, such award may be modified by any court of competent jurisdiction upon application by any party to the arbitration. Any such modification shall govern the rights and obligations between such parties from the date of such modification.

(d) When an award is made by an arbitrator, the patentee, his assignee or licensee shall give notice thereof in writing to the Director. There shall be a separate notice prepared for each patent involved in such proceeding. Such notice shall set forth the names and addresses of the parties, the name of the inventor, and the name of the patent owner, shall designate the number of the patent, and shall contain a copy of the award. If an award is modified by a court, the party requesting such modification shall give notice of such modification to the Director. The Director shall, upon receipt of either notice, enter the same in the record of the prosecution of such patent. If the required notice is not filed with the Director, any party to the proceeding may provide such notice to the Director.

(e) The award shall be unenforceable until the notice required by subsection (d) is received by the Director.

§ 295. Presumption: Product Made by Patented Process

In actions alleging infringement of a process patent based on the importation, sale, offer for sale, or use of a product which is made from a process patented in the United States, if the court finds—

    (1) that a substantial likelihood exists that the product was made by the patented process, and

    (2) that the plaintiff has made a reasonable effort to determine the process actually used in the production of the product and was unable to so determine,

the product shall be presumed to have been so made, and the burden of establishing that the product was not made by the process shall be on the party asserting that it was not so made.

§ 296. Liability of States, Instrumentalities of States, and State Officials for Infringement of Patents

(a) **In General.**—Any State, any instrumentality of a State, and any officer or employee of a State or instrumentality of a State acting in his official capacity, shall not be immune, under the eleventh amendment of the Constitution of the United States or under any other doctrine of sovereign immunity, from suit in Federal court by any person, including any governmental or nongovernmental entity, for infringement of a patent under section 271, or for any other violation under this title.[1]

(b) **Remedies.**—In a suit described in subsection (a) for a violation described in that subsection, remedies (including remedies both at law and in equity) are available for the violation to the same extent as such remedies are available for such a violation in a suit against any private entity. Such remedies include damages, interest, costs, and treble damages under section 284, attorney fees under section 285, and the additional remedy for infringement of design patents under section 289.

§ 297. Improper and Deceptive Invention Promotion

(a) **In General.** An invention promoter shall have a duty to disclose the following information to a customer in writing, prior to entering into a contract for invention promotion services:

    (1) the total number of inventions evaluated by the invention promoter for commercial potential in the past 5 years, as well as the number of those inventions that received positive evaluations, and the number of those inventions that received negative evaluations;

    (2) the total number of customers who have contracted with the invention promoter in the past 5 years, not including customers who have purchased trade show services, research,

---

[1] This provision's abrogation of states' sovereign immunity was held to be unconstitutional in *Florida Prepaid Postsecondary Education Expense Board v. College Savings Bank*, 527 U.S. 627, 119 S. Ct. 2199 (1999).—*Ed.*

advertising, or other nonmarketing services from the invention promoter, or who have defaulted in their payment to the invention promoter;

(3) the total number of customers known by the invention promoter to have received a net financial profit as a direct result of the invention promotion services provided by such invention promoter;

(4) the total number of customers known by the invention promoter to have received license agreements for their inventions as a direct result of the invention promotion services provided by such invention promoter; and

(5) the names and addresses of all previous invention promotion companies with which the invention promoter or its officers have collectively or individually been affiliated in the previous 10 years.

(b) Civil Action.

(1) Any customer who enters into a contract with an invention promoter and who is found by a court to have been injured by any material false or fraudulent statement or representation, or any omission of material fact, by that invention promoter (or any agent, employee, director, officer, partner, or independent contractor of such invention promoter), or by the failure of that invention promoter to disclose such information as required under subsection (a), may recover in a civil action against the invention promoter (or the officers, directors, or partners of such invention promoter), in addition to reasonable costs and attorneys' fees—

(A) the amount of actual damages incurred by the customer; or

(B) at the election of the customer at any time before final judgment is rendered, statutory damages in a sum of not more than $5,000, as the court considers just.

(2) Notwithstanding paragraph (1), in a case where the customer sustains the burden of proof, and the court finds, that the invention promoter intentionally misrepresented or omitted a material fact to such customer, or willfully failed to disclose such information as required under subsection (a), with the purpose of deceiving that customer, the court may increase damages to not more than three times the amount awarded, taking into account past complaints made against the invention promoter that resulted in regulatory sanctions or other corrective actions based on those records compiled by the Commissioner of Patents under subsection (d).

(c) Definitions. For purposes of this section—

(1) a "contract for invention promotion services" means a contract by which an invention promoter undertakes invention promotion services for a customer;

(2) a "customer" is any individual who enters into a contract with an invention promoter for invention promotion services;

(3) the term "invention promoter" means any person, firm, partnership, corporation, or other entity who offers to perform or performs invention promotion services for, or on behalf of, a customer, and who holds itself out through advertising in any mass media as providing such services, but does not include—

(A) any department or agency of the Federal Government or of a State or local government;

(B) any nonprofit, charitable, scientific, or educational organization, qualified under applicable State law or described under section 170(b)(1)(A) of the Internal Revenue Code of 1986;

(C) any person or entity involved in the evaluation to determine commercial potential of, or offering to license or sell, a utility patent or a previously filed nonprovisional utility patent application;

(D) any party participating in a transaction involving the sale of the stock or assets of a business; or

(E) any party who directly engages in the business of retail sales of products or the distribution of products; and

(4) the term "invention promotion services" means the procurement or attempted procurement for a customer of a firm, corporation, or other entity to develop and market products or services that include the invention of the customer.

(d) Records of Complaints.

(1) Release of Complaints. The Commissioner of Patents shall make all complaints received by the Patent and Trademark Office involving invention promoters publicly available, together with any response of the invention promoters. The Commissioner of Patents shall notify the invention promoter of a complaint and provide a reasonable opportunity to reply prior to making such complaint publicly available.

(2) Request for Complaints. The Commissioner of Patents may request complaints relating to invention promotion services from any Federal or State agency and include such complaints in the records maintained under paragraph (1), together with any response of the invention promoters.

§ 298.   Advice of Counsel

The failure of an infringer to obtain the advice of counsel with respect to any allegedly infringed patent, or the failure of the infringer to present such advice to the court or jury, may not be used to prove that the accused infringer willfully infringed the patent or that the infringer intended to induce infringement of the patent.

§ 299.   Joinder of Parties

(a) Joinder of Accused Infringers.—With respect to any civil action arising under any Act of Congress relating to patents, other than an action or trial in which an act of infringement under section 271(e)(2) has been pled, parties that are accused infringers may be joined in one action as defendants or counterclaim defendants, or have their actions consolidated for trial, only if—

(1) any right to relief is asserted against the parties jointly, severally, or in the alternative with respect to or arising out of the same transaction, occurrence, or series of transactions or occurrences relating to the making, using, importing into the United States, offering for sale, or selling of the same accused product or process; and

(2) questions of fact common to all defendants or counterclaim defendants will arise in the action.

(b) Allegations Insufficient For Joinder.—For purposes of this subsection, accused infringers may not be joined in one action as defendants or counterclaim defendants, or have their actions consolidated for trial, based solely on allegations that they each have infringed the patent or patents in suit.

(c) Waiver.—A party that is an accused infringer may waive the limitations set forth in this section with respect to that party.

CHAPTER 30. PRIOR ART CITATIONS TO OFFICE AND EX PARTE REEXAMINATION OF PATENTS

---

§ 301.   Citation of Prior Art and Written Statements

(a)   **In General.**—Any person at any time may cite to the Office in writing—

(1)   prior art consisting of patents or printed publications which that person believes to have a bearing on the patentability of any claim of a particular patent; or

(2)   statements of the patent owner filed in a proceeding before a Federal court or the Office in which the patent owner took a position on the scope of any claim of a particular patent.

(b)   **Official File.**—If the person citing prior art or written statements pursuant to subsection (a) explains in writing the pertinence and manner of applying the prior art or written statements to at least 1 claim of the patent, the citation of the prior art or written statements and the explanation thereof shall become a part of the official file of the patent.

(c)   **Additional Information.**—A party that submits a written statement pursuant to subsection (a)(2) shall include any other documents, pleadings, or evidence from the proceeding in which the statement was filed that addresses the written statement.

(d)   **Limitations.**—A written statement submitted pursuant to subsection (a)(2), and additional information submitted pursuant to subsection (c), shall not be considered by the Office for any purpose other than to determine the proper meaning of a patent claim in a proceeding that is ordered or instituted pursuant to section 304, 314, or 324. If any such written statement or additional information is subject to an applicable protective order, such statement or information shall be redacted to exclude information that is subject to that order.

(e)   **Confidentiality.**—Upon the written request of the person citing prior art or written statements pursuant to subsection (a), that person's identity shall be excluded from the patent file and kept confidential.

§ 302.   Request for Reexamination

Any person at any time may file a request for reexamination by the Office of any claim of a patent on the basis of any prior art cited under the provisions of section 301. The request must be in writing and must be accompanied by payment of a reexamination fee established by the Director pursuant to the provisions of section 41. The request must set forth the pertinency and manner applying cited prior art to every claim for which reexamination is requested. Unless the requesting person is the owner of the patent, the Director promptly will send a copy of the request to the owner of record of the patent.

§ 303.   Determination of Issue by Director

(a)   Within three months following the filing of a request for reexamination under the provisions of section 302, the Director will determine whether a substantial new question of patentability affecting any claim of the patent concerned is raised by the request, with or without consideration of other patents or printed publications. On his own initiative, and any time, the Director may determine whether a substantial new question of patentability is raised by patents and publications discovered by him or cited under the provisions of section 301 or 302. The existence of a substantial new question of patentability is not precluded by the fact that a patent or printed publication was previously cited by or to the Office or considered by the Office.

(b)   A record of the Director's determination under subsection (a) of this section will be placed in the official file of the patent, and a copy promptly will be given or mailed to the owner of record of the patent and to the person requesting reexamination, if any.

(c)   A determination by the Director pursuant to subsection (a) of this section that no substantial new question of patentability has been raised will be final and nonappealable. Upon such a determination, the Director may refund a portion of the reexamination fee required under section 302.

§ 304.   Reexamination Order by Director

If, in a determination made under the provisions of subsection 303(a), the Director finds that a substantial new question of patentability affecting any claim of a patent is raised, the determination will include an order for reexamination of the patent for resolution of the question. The patent owner will be given a reasonable period, not less than two months from the date a copy of the determination is given or mailed to him, within which he may file a statement on such question, including any amendment to his patent and new claim or claims he may wish to propose, for consideration in the reexamination. If the patent owner files such a statement, he promptly will serve a copy of it on the person who has requested reexamination under the provisions of section 302. Within a period of two months from the date of service, that person may file and have considered in the reexamination a reply to any statement filed by the patent owner. That person promptly will serve on the patent owner a copy of any reply filed.

§ 305.   Conduct of Reexamination Proceedings

After the times for filing the statement and reply provided for by section 304 have expired, reexamination will be conducted according to the procedures established for initial examination under the provisions of sections 132 and 133. In any reexamination proceeding under this chapter, the patent owner will be permitted to propose any amendment to his patent and a new claim or claims thereto, in order to distinguish the invention as claimed from the prior art cited under the provisions of section 301, or in response to a decision adverse to the patentability of a claim of a patent. No proposed amended or new claim enlarging the scope of a claim of the patent will be permitted in a reexamination proceeding under this chapter. All reexamination proceedings under this section, including any appeal to the Patent Trial and Appeal Board, will be conducted with special dispatch within the Office.

§ 306.   Appeal

The patent owner involved in a reexamination proceeding under this chapter may appeal under the provisions of section 134, and may seek court review under the provisions of sections 141 to 144, with respect to any decision adverse to the patentability of any original or proposed amended or new claim of the patent.

§ 307.   Certificate of Patentability, Unpatentability, and Claim Cancellation

(a)   In a reexamination proceeding under this chapter, when the time for appeal has expired or any appeal proceeding has terminated, the Director will issue and publish a certificate canceling any claim of the patent finally determined to be unpatentable, confirming any claim of the patent determined to be patentable, and incorporating in the patent any proposed amended or new claim determined to be patentable.

(b)   Any proposed amended or new claim determined to be patentable and incorporated into a patent following a reexamination proceeding will have the same effect as that specified in section 252 for reissued patents on the right of any person who made, purchased, or used within the United States, or imported into the United States, anything patented by such proposed amended or new claim, or who made substantial preparation for the same, prior to issuance of a certificate under the provisions of subsection (a) of this section.

CHAPTER 31. INTER PARTES REVIEW

---

§ 311.   Inter Partes Review

(a) In General.—Subject to the provisions of this chapter, a person who is not the owner of a patent may file with the Office a petition to institute an inter partes review of the patent. The Director shall establish, by regulation, fees to be paid by the person requesting the review, in such amounts as the Director determines to be reasonable, considering the aggregate costs of the review.

(b) Scope.—A petitioner in an inter partes review may request to cancel as unpatentable 1 or more claims of a patent only on a ground that could be raised under section 102 or 103 and only on the basis of prior art consisting of patents or printed publications.

(c) Filing Deadline.—A petition for inter partes review shall be filed after the later of either—

(1)   the date that is 9 months after the grant of a patent; or

(2)   if a post-grant review is instituted under chapter 32, the date of the termination of such post-grant review.

§ 312.   Petitions

(a) Requirements of Petition. A petition filed under section 311 may be considered only if—

(1)   the petition is accompanied by payment of the fee established by the Director under section 311;

(2)   the petition identifies all real parties in interest;

(3)   the petition identifies, in writing and with particularity, each claim challenged, the grounds on which the challenge to each claim is based, and the evidence that supports the grounds for the challenge to each claim, including—

(A) copies of patents and printed publications that the petitioner relies upon in support of the petition; and

(B) affidavits or declarations of supporting evidence and opinions, if the petitioner relies on expert opinions;

(4)   the petition provides such other information as the Director may require by regulation; and

(5)   the petitioner provides copies of any of the documents required under paragraphs (2), (3), and (4) to the patent owner or, if applicable, the designated representative of the patent owner.

(b) Public Availability.—As soon as practicable after the receipt of a petition under section 311, the Director shall make the petition available to the public.

§ 313. Preliminary Response to Petition

If an inter partes review petition is filed under section 311, the patent owner shall have the right to file a preliminary response to the petition, within a time period set by the Director, that sets forth reasons why no inter partes review should be instituted based upon the failure of the petition to meet any requirement of this chapter.

§ 314. Institution of Inter Partes Review

(a) Threshold.—The Director may not authorize an inter partes review to be instituted unless the Director determines that the information presented in the petition filed under section 311 and any response filed under section 313 shows that there is a reasonable likelihood that the petitioner would prevail with respect to at least 1 of the claims challenged in the petition.

(b) Timing.—The Director shall determine whether to institute an inter partes review under this chapter pursuant to a petition filed under section 311 within 3 months after—

(1) receiving a preliminary response to the petition under section 313; or

(2) if no such preliminary response is filed, the last date on which such response may be filed.

(c) Notice.—The Director shall notify the petitioner and patent owner, in writing, of the Director's determination under subsection (a), and shall make such notice available to the public as soon as is practicable. Such notice shall include the date on which the review shall commence.

(d) No Appeal.—The determination by the Director whether to institute an inter partes review under this section shall be final and nonappealable.

§ 315. Relation to Other Proceedings or Actions

(a) Infringer's Civil Action.—

(1) Inter Partes Review Barred by Civil Action.—An inter partes review may not be instituted if, before the date on which the petition for such a review is filed, the petitioner or real party in interest filed a civil action challenging the validity of a claim of the patent.

(2) Stay of Civil Action.—If the petitioner or real party in interest files a civil action challenging the validity of a claim of the patent on or after the date on which the petitioner files a petition for inter partes review of the patent, that civil action shall be automatically stayed until either—

(A) the patent owner moves the court to lift the stay;

(B) the patent owner files a civil action or counterclaim alleging that the petitioner or real party in interest has infringed the patent; or

(C) the petitioner or real party in interest moves the court to dismiss the civil action.

(3) Treatment of Counterclaim.—A counterclaim challenging the validity of a claim of a patent does not constitute a civil action challenging the validity of a claim of a patent for purposes of this subsection.

(b) Patent Owner's Action.—An inter partes review may not be instituted if the petition requesting the proceeding is filed more than 1 year after the date on which the petitioner, real party in interest, or privy of the petitioner is served with a complaint alleging infringement of the patent. The time limitation set forth in the preceding sentence shall not apply to a request for joinder under subsection (c).

(c) Joinder.—If the Director institutes an inter partes review, the Director, in his or her discretion, may join as a party to that inter partes review any person who properly files a petition under section 311 that the Director, after receiving a preliminary response under section 313 or the expiration of the time for filing such a response, determines warrants the institution of an inter partes review under section 314.

(d) Multiple Proceedings.—Notwithstanding sections 135(a), 251, and 252, and chapter 30, during the pendency of an inter partes review, if another proceeding or matter involving the patent is before the Office, the Director may determine the manner in which the inter partes review or other proceeding or matter may proceed, including providing for stay, transfer, consolidation, or termination of any such matter or proceeding.

(e) Estoppel.—

   (1) Proceedings Before the Office.—The petitioner in an inter partes review of a claim in a patent under this chapter that results in a final written decision under section 318(a), or the real party in interest or privy of the petitioner, may not request or maintain a proceeding before the Office with respect to that claim on any ground that the petitioner raised or reasonably could have raised during that inter partes review.

   (2) Civil Actions and Other Proceedings.—The petitioner in an inter partes review of a claim in a patent under this chapter that results in a final written decision under section 318(a), or the real party in interest or privy of the petitioner, may not assert either in a civil action arising in whole or in part under section 1338 of title 28 or in a proceeding before the International Trade Commission under section 337 of the Tariff Act of 1930 that the claim is invalid on any ground that the petitioner raised or reasonably could have raised during that inter partes review.

§ 316.   Conduct of Inter Partes Review

(a) Regulations.—The Director shall prescribe regulations—

   (1) providing that the file of any proceeding under this chapter shall be made available to the public, except that any petition or document filed with the intent that it be sealed shall, if accompanied by a motion to seal, be treated as sealed pending the outcome of the ruling on the motion;

   (2) setting forth the standards for the showing of sufficient grounds to institute a review under section 314(a);

   (3) establishing procedures for the submission of supplemental information after the petition is filed;

   (4) establishing and governing inter partes review under this chapter and the relationship of such review to other proceedings under this title;

   (5) setting forth standards and procedures for discovery of relevant evidence, including that such discovery shall be limited to—

      (A) the deposition of witnesses submitting affidavits or declarations; and

      (B) what is otherwise necessary in the interest of justice;

   (6) prescribing sanctions for abuse of discovery, abuse of process, or any other improper use of the proceeding, such as to harass or to cause unnecessary delay or an unnecessary increase in the cost of the proceeding;

   (7) providing for protective orders governing the exchange and submission of confidential information;

   (8) providing for the filing by the patent owner of a response to the petition under section 313 after an inter partes review has been instituted, and requiring that the patent owner file with such response, through affidavits or declarations, any additional factual evidence and expert opinions on which the patent owner relies in support of the response;

(9)   setting forth standards and procedures for allowing the patent owner to move to amend the patent under subsection (d) to cancel a challenged claim or propose a reasonable number of substitute claims, and ensuring that any information submitted by the patent owner in support of any amendment entered under subsection (d) is made available to the public as part of the prosecution history of the patent;

(10) providing either party with the right to an oral hearing as part of the proceeding;

(11) requiring that the final determination in an inter partes review be issued not later than 1 year after the date on which the Director notices the institution of a review under this chapter, except that the Director may, for good cause shown, extend the 1-year period by not more than 6 months, and may adjust the time periods in this paragraph in the case of joinder under section 315(c);

(12) setting a time period for requesting joinder under section 315(c); and

(13) providing the petitioner with at least 1 opportunity to file written comments within a time period established by the Director.

(b)   **Considerations.**—In prescribing regulations under this section, the Director shall consider the effect of any such regulation on the economy, the integrity of the patent system, the efficient administration of the Office, and the ability of the Office to timely complete proceedings instituted under this chapter.

(c)   **Patent Trial and Appeal Board.**—The Patent Trial and Appeal Board shall, in accordance with section 6, conduct each inter partes review instituted under this chapter.

(d)   **Amendment of the Patent.**—

(1)   **In General.**—During an inter partes review instituted under this chapter, the patent owner may file 1 motion to amend the patent in 1 or more of the following ways:

(A)   Cancel any challenged patent claim.

(B)   For each challenged claim, propose a reasonable number of substitute claims.

(2)   **Additional Motions.**—Additional motions to amend may be permitted upon the joint request of the petitioner and the patent owner to materially advance the settlement of a proceeding under section 317, or as permitted by regulations prescribed by the Director.

(3)   **Scope of Claims.**—An amendment under this subsection may not enlarge the scope of the claims of the patent or introduce new matter.

(e)   **Evidentiary Standards.**—In an inter partes review instituted under this chapter, the petitioner shall have the burden of proving a proposition of unpatentability by a preponderance of the evidence.

§ 317.   Settlement

(a)   **In General.**—An inter partes review instituted under this chapter shall be terminated with respect to any petitioner upon the joint request of the petitioner and the patent owner, unless the Office has decided the merits of the proceeding before the request for termination is filed. If the inter partes review is terminated with respect to a petitioner under this section, no estoppel under section 315(e) shall attach to the petitioner, or to the real party in interest or privy of the petitioner, on the basis of that petitioner's institution of that inter partes review. If no petitioner remains in the inter partes review, the Office may terminate the review or proceed to a final written decision under section 318(a).

(b)   **Agreements in Writing.**—Any agreement or understanding between the patent owner and a petitioner, including any collateral agreements referred to in such agreement or understanding, made in connection with, or in contemplation of, the termination of an inter partes review under this section shall be in writing and a true copy of such agreement or understanding shall be filed in the

Office before the termination of the inter partes review as between the parties. At the request of a party to the proceeding, the agreement or understanding shall be treated as business confidential information, shall be kept separate from the file of the involved patents, and shall be made available only to Federal Government agencies on written request, or to any person on a showing of good cause.

§ 318.   Decision of the Board

(a)   **Final Written Decision.**—If an inter partes review is instituted and not dismissed under this chapter, the Patent Trial and Appeal Board shall issue a final written decision with respect to the patentability of any patent claim challenged by the petitioner and any new claim added under section 316(d).

(b)   **Certificate.**—If the Patent Trial and Appeal Board issues a final written decision under subsection (a) and the time for appeal has expired or any appeal has terminated, the Director shall issue and publish a certificate canceling any claim of the patent finally determined to be unpatentable, confirming any claim of the patent determined to be patentable, and incorporating in the patent by operation of the certificate any new or amended claim determined to be patentable.

(c)   **Intervening Rights.**—Any proposed amended or new claim determined to be patentable and incorporated into a patent following an inter partes review under this chapter shall have the same effect as that specified in section 252 for reissued patents on the right of any person who made, purchased, or used within the United States, or imported into the United States, anything patented by such proposed amended or new claim, or who made substantial preparation therefor, before the issuance of a certificate under subsection (b).

(d)   **Data on Length of Review.**—The Office shall make available to the public data describing the length of time between the institution of, and the issuance of a final written decision under subsection (a) for, each inter partes review.

§ 319.   Appeal

A party dissatisfied with the final written decision of the Patent Trial and Appeal Board under section 318(a) may appeal the decision pursuant to sections 141 through 144. Any party to the inter partes review shall have the right to be a party to the appeal.

CHAPTER 32. POST-GRANT REVIEW

§ 321.   Post-grant Review

(a)   **In General.**—Subject to the provisions of this chapter, a person who is not the owner of a patent may file with the Office a petition to institute a post-grant review of the patent. The Director shall establish, by regulation, fees to be paid by the person requesting the review, in such amounts as the Director determines to be reasonable, considering the aggregate costs of the post-grant review.

(b) Scope.—A petitioner in a post-grant review may request to cancel as unpatentable 1 or more claims of a patent on any ground that could be raised under paragraph (2) or (3) of section 282(b) (relating to invalidity of the patent or any claim).

(c) Filing Deadline.—A petition for a post-grant review may only be filed not later than the date that is 9 months after the date of the grant of the patent or of the issuance of a reissue patent (as the case may be).

§ 322.　Petitions

(a) Requirements of Petition.—A petition filed under section 321 may be considered only if—

(1)　the petition is accompanied by payment of the fee established by the Director under section 321;

(2)　the petition identifies all real parties in interest;

(3)　the petition identifies, in writing and with particularity, each claim challenged, the grounds on which the challenge to each claim is based, and the evidence that supports the grounds for the challenge to each claim, including—

(A)　copies of patents and printed publications that the petitioner relies upon in support of the petition; and

(B)　affidavits or declarations of supporting evidence and opinions, if the petitioner relies on other factual evidence or on expert opinions;

(4)　the petition provides such other information as the Director may require by regulation; and

(5)　the petitioner provides copies of any of the documents required under paragraphs (2), (3), and (4) to the patent owner or, if applicable, the designated representative of the patent owner.

(b) Public Availability. As soon as practicable after the receipt of a petition under section 321, the Director shall make the petition available to the public.

§ 323.　Preliminary Response to Petition

If a post-grant review petition is filed under section 321, the patent owner shall have the right to file a preliminary response to the petition, within a time period set by the Director, that sets forth reasons why no post-grant review should be instituted based upon the failure of the petition to meet any requirement of this chapter.

§ 324.　Institution of Post-grant Review

(a) Threshold.—The Director may not authorize a post-grant review to be instituted unless the Director determines that the information presented in the petition filed under section 321, if such information is not rebutted, would demonstrate that it is more likely than not that at least 1 of the claims challenged in the petition is unpatentable.

(b) Additional Grounds.—The determination required under subsection (a) may also be satisfied by a showing that the petition raises a novel or unsettled legal question that is important to other patents or patent applications.

(c) Timing.—The Director shall determine whether to institute a post-grant review under this chapter pursuant to a petition filed under section 321 within 3 months after—

(1)　receiving a preliminary response to the petition under section 323; or

(2)　if no such preliminary response is filed, the last date on which such response may be filed.

(d) Notice.—The Director shall notify the petitioner and patent owner, in writing, of the Director's determination under subsection (a) or (b), and shall make such notice available to the public as soon as is practicable. Such notice shall include the date on which the review shall commence.

(e) No Appeal.—The determination by the Director whether to institute a post-grant review under this section shall be final and nonappealable.

§ 325. Relation to Other Proceedings or Actions

(a) Infringer's Civil Action.—

(1) Post-grant Review Barred by Civil Action.—A postgrant review may not be instituted under this chapter if, before the date on which the petition for such a review is filed, the petitioner or real party in interest filed a civil action challenging the validity of a claim of the patent.

(2) Stay of Civil Action.—If the petitioner or real party in interest files a civil action challenging the validity of a claim of the patent on or after the date on which the petitioner files a petition for post-grant review of the patent, that civil action shall be automatically stayed until either—

(A)   the patent owner moves the court to lift the stay;

(B)   the patent owner files a civil action or counterclaim alleging that the petitioner or real party in interest has infringed the patent; or

(C)   the petitioner or real party in interest moves the court to dismiss the civil action.

(3) Treatment of Counterclaim.—A counterclaim challenging the validity of a claim of a patent does not constitute a civil action challenging the validity of a claim of a patent for purposes of this subsection.

(b) Preliminary Injunctions.—If a civil action alleging infringement of a patent is filed within 3 months after the date on which the patent is granted, the court may not stay its consideration of the patent owner's motion for a preliminary injunction against infringement of the patent on the basis that a petition for post-grant review has been filed under this chapter or that such a post-grant review has been instituted under this chapter.

(c) Joinder.—If more than 1 petition for a post-grant review under this chapter is properly filed against the same patent and the Director determines that more than 1 of these petitions warrants the institution of a post-grant review under section 324, the Director may consolidate such reviews into a single post-grant review.

(d) Multiple Proceedings.—Notwithstanding sections 135(a), 251, and 252, and chapter 30, during the pendency of any post-grant review under this chapter, if another proceeding or matter involving the patent is before the Office, the Director may determine the manner in which the post-grant review or other proceeding or matter may proceed, including providing for the stay, transfer, consolidation, or termination of any such matter or proceeding. In determining whether to institute or order a proceeding under this chapter, chapter 30, or chapter 31, the Director may take into account whether, and reject the petition or request because, the same or substantially the same prior art or arguments previously were presented to the Office.

(e) Estoppel.—

(1) Proceedings Before the Office.—The petitioner in a post-grant review of a claim in a patent under this chapter that results in a final written decision under section 328(a), or the real party in interest or privy of the petitioner, may not request or maintain a proceeding before the Office with respect to that claim on any ground that the petitioner raised or reasonably could have raised during that post-grant review.

(2) **Civil Actions and Other Proceedings.**—The petitioner in a post-grant review of a claim in a patent under this chapter that results in a final written decision under section 328(a), or the real party in interest or privy of the petitioner, may not assert either in a civil action arising in whole or in part under section 1338 of title 28 or in a proceeding before the International Trade Commission under section 337 of the Tariff Act of 1930 that the claim is invalid on any ground that the petitioner raised or reasonably could have raised during that post-grant review.

(f) **Reissue Patents.**—A post-grant review may not be instituted under this chapter if the petition requests cancellation of a claim in a reissue patent that is identical to or narrower than a claim in the original patent from which the reissue patent was issued, and the time limitations in section 321(c) would bar filing a petition for a post-grant review for such original patent.

§ 326. Conduct of Post-grant Review

(a) **Regulations.**—The Director shall prescribe regulations—

(1) providing that the file of any proceeding under this chapter shall be made available to the public, except that any petition or document filed with the intent that it be sealed shall, if accompanied by a motion to seal, be treated as sealed pending the outcome of the ruling on the motion;

(2) setting forth the standards for the showing of sufficient grounds to institute a review under subsections (a) and (b) of section 324;

(3) establishing procedures for the submission of supplemental information after the petition is filed;

(4) establishing and governing a post-grant review under this chapter and the relationship of such review to other proceedings under this title;

(5) setting forth standards and procedures for discovery of relevant evidence, including that such discovery shall be limited to evidence directly related to factual assertions advanced by either party in the proceeding;

(6) prescribing sanctions for abuse of discovery, abuse of process, or any other improper use of the proceeding, such as to harass or to cause unnecessary delay or an unnecessary increase in the cost of the proceeding;

(7) providing for protective orders governing the exchange and submission of confidential information;

(8) providing for the filing by the patent owner of a response to the petition under section 323 after a post-grant review has been instituted, and requiring that the patent owner file with such response, through affidavits or declarations, any additional factual evidence and expert opinions on which the patent owner relies in support of the response;

(9) setting forth standards and procedures for allowing the patent owner to move to amend the patent under subsection (d) to cancel a challenged claim or propose a reasonable number of substitute claims, and ensuring that any information submitted by the patent owner in support of any amendment entered under subsection (d) is made available to the public as part of the prosecution history of the patent;

(10) providing either party with the right to an oral hearing as part of the proceeding;

(11) requiring that the final determination in any postgrant review be issued not later than 1 year after the date on which the Director notices the institution of a proceeding under this chapter, except that the Director may, for good cause shown, extend the 1-year period by not more than 6 months, and may adjust the time periods in this paragraph in the case of joinder under section 325(c); and

(12) providing the petitioner with at least 1 opportunity to file written comments within a time period established by the Director.

(b) Considerations.—In prescribing regulations under this section, the Director shall consider the effect of any such regulation on the economy, the integrity of the patent system, the efficient administration of the Office, and the ability of the Office to timely complete proceedings instituted under this chapter.

(c) Patent Trial and Appeal Board.—The Patent Trial and Appeal Board shall, in accordance with section 6, conduct each post-grant review instituted under this chapter.

(d) Amendment of the Patent.—

(1) In General.—During a post-grant review instituted under this chapter, the patent owner may file 1 motion to amend the patent in 1 or more of the following ways:

(A) Cancel any challenged patent claim.

(B) For each challenged claim, propose a reasonable number of substitute claims.

(2) Additional Motions.—Additional motions to amend may be permitted upon the joint request of the petitioner and the patent owner to materially advance the settlement of a proceeding under section 327, or upon the request of the patent owner for good cause shown.

(3) Scope of Claims.—An amendment under this subsection may not enlarge the scope of the claims of the patent or introduce new matter.

(e) Evidentiary Standards.—In a post-grant review instituted under this chapter, the petitioner shall have the burden of proving a proposition of unpatentability by a preponderance of the evidence.

§ 327. Settlement

(a) In General.—A post-grant review instituted under this chapter shall be terminated with respect to any petitioner upon the joint request of the petitioner and the patent owner, unless the Office has decided the merits of the proceeding before the request for termination is filed. If the post-grant review is terminated with respect to a petitioner under this section, no estoppel under section 325(e) shall attach to the petitioner, or to the real party in interest or privy of the petitioner, on the basis of that petitioner's institution of that post-grant review. If no petitioner remains in the post-grant review, the Office may terminate the post-grant review or proceed to a final written decision under section 328(a).

(b) Agreements in Writing.—Any agreement or understanding between the patent owner and a petitioner, including any collateral agreements referred to in such agreement or understanding, made in connection with, or in contemplation of, the termination of a post-grant review under this section shall be in writing, and a true copy of such agreement or understanding shall be filed in the Office before the termination of the post-grant review as between the parties. At the request of a party to the proceeding, the agreement or understanding shall be treated as business confidential information, shall be kept separate from the file of the involved patents, and shall be made available only to Federal Government agencies on written request, or to any person on a showing of good cause.

§ 328. Decision of the Board

(a) Final Written Decision.—If a post-grant review is instituted and not dismissed under this chapter, the Patent Trial and Appeal Board shall issue a final written decision with respect to the patentability of any patent claim challenged by the petitioner and any new claim added under section 326(d).

(b) Certificate.—If the Patent Trial and Appeal Board issues a final written decision under subsection (a) and the time for appeal has expired or any appeal has terminated, the Director shall issue and publish a certificate canceling any claim of the patent finally determined to be unpatentable, confirming any claim of the patent determined to be patentable, and incorporating in the patent by operation of the certificate any new or amended claim determined to be patentable.

    (c) Intervening Rights.—Any proposed amended or new claim determined to be patentable and incorporated into a patent following a post-grant review under this chapter shall have the same effect as that specified in section 252 of this title for reissued patents on the right of any person who made, purchased, or used within the United States, or imported into the United States, anything patented by such proposed amended or new claim, or who made substantial preparation therefor, before the issuance of a certificate under subsection (b).

    (d) Data on Length of Review.—The Office shall make available to the public data describing the length of time between the institution of, and the issuance of a final written decision under subsection (a) for, each post-grant review.

§ 329. Appeal

    A party dissatisfied with the final written decision of the Patent Trial and Appeal Board under section 328(a) may appeal the decision pursuant to sections 141 through 144. Any party to the post-grant review shall have the right to be a party to the appeal.

PART IV. PATENT COOPERATION TREATY

Chap.

CHAPTER 35. DEFINITIONS

Sec.

---

§ 351. Definitions

    When used in this part unless the context otherwise indicates—

    (a) The term "treaty" means the Patent Cooperation Treaty done at Washington, on June 19, 1970.

    (b) The term "Regulations", when capitalized, means the Regulations under the treaty, done at Washington on the same date as the treaty. The term "regulations", when not capitalized, means the regulations established by the Director under this title.

    (c) The term "international application" means an application filed under the treaty.

    (d) The term "international application originating in the United States" means an international application filed in the Patent and Trademark Office when it is acting as a Receiving Office under the treaty, irrespective of whether or not the United States has been designated in that international application.

    (e) The term "international application designating the United States" means an international application specifying the United States as a country in which a patent is sought, regardless where such international application is filed.

    (f) The term "Receiving Office" means a national patent office or intergovernmental organization which receives and processes international applications as prescribed by the treaty and the Regulations.

(g) The terms "International Searching Authority" and "International Preliminary Examining Authority" mean a national patent office or intergovernmental organization as appointed under the treaty which processes international applications as prescribed by the treaty and the Regulations.

(h) The term "International Bureau" means the international intergovernmental organization which is recognized as the coordinating body under the treaty and the Regulations.

(i) Terms and expressions not defined in this part are to be taken in the sense indicated by the treaty and the Regulations.

CHAPTER 36. INTERNATIONAL STAGE

§ 361. Receiving Office

(a) The Patent and Trademark Office shall act as a Receiving Office for international applications filed by nationals or residents of the United States. In accordance with any agreement made between the United States and another country, the Patent and Trademark Office may also act as a Receiving Office for international applications filed by residents or nationals of such country who are entitled to file international applications.

(b) The Patent and Trademark Office shall perform all acts connected with the discharge of duties required of a Receiving Office, including the collection of international fees and their transmittal to the International Bureau.

(c) International applications filed in the Patent and Trademark Office shall be filed in the English language, or an English translation shall be filed within such later time as may be fixed by the Director.

(d) The international fee, and the transmittal and search fees prescribed under section 376(a) of this part, shall either be paid on filing of an international application or within such later time as may be fixed by the Director.

§ 362. International Searching Authority and International Preliminary Examining Authority

(a) The Patent and Trademark Office may act as an International Searching Authority and International Preliminary Examining Authority with respect to international applications in accordance with the terms and conditions of an agreement which may be concluded with the International Bureau, and may discharge all duties required of such Authorities, including the collection of handling fees and their transmittal to the International Bureau.

(b) The handling fee, preliminary examination fee, and any additional fees due for international preliminary examination shall be paid within such time as may be fixed by the Director.

§ 363.   International Application Designating the United States: Effect

An international application designating the United States shall have the effect, from its international filing date under article 11 of the treaty, of a national application for patent regularly filed in the Patent and Trademark Office.

§ 364.   International Stage: Procedure

(a) International applications shall be processed by the Patent and Trademark Office when acting as a Receiving Office, International Searching Authority, or International Preliminary Examining Authority, in accordance with the applicable provisions of the treaty, the Regulations, and this title.

(b) An applicant's failure to act within the prescribed time limits in connection with requirements pertaining to an international application may be excused as provided in the treaty and the Regulations.

§ 365.   Right of Priority; Benefit of the Filing Date of a Prior Application

(a)   In accordance with the conditions and requirements of subsections (a) through (d) of section 119, a national application shall be entitled to the right of priority based on a prior filed international application which designated at least one country other than the United States.

(b)   In accordance with the conditions and requirements of section 119(a) and the treaty and the Regulations, an international application designating the United States shall be entitled to the right of priority based on a prior foreign application, or a prior international application designating at least one country other than the United States. The Director may establish procedures, including the requirement for payment of the fee specified in section 41(a)(7), to accept an unintentionally delayed claim for priority under the treaty and the Regulations, and to accept a priority claim that pertains to an application that was not filed within the priority period specified in the treaty and Regulations, but was filed within the additional 2-month period specified under section 119(a) or the treaty and Regulations.

(c)   In accordance with the conditions and requirements of section 120, an international application designating the United States shall be entitled to the benefit of the filing date of a prior national application, a prior international application designating the United States, or a prior international design application as defined section 381(a)(6) designating the United States, and a national application shall be entitled to the benefit of the filing date of a prior international application designating the United States. If any claim for the benefit of an earlier filing date is based on a prior international application which designated but did not originate in the United States or a prior international design application as defined in section 381(a)(6) which designated but did not originate in the United States, the Director may require the filing in the Patent and Trademark Office of a certified copy of such application together with a translation thereof into the English language, if it was filed in another language.

§ 366.   Withdrawn International Application

Subject to section 367 of this part, if an international application designating the United States is withdrawn or considered withdrawn, either generally or as to the United States, under the conditions of the treaty and the Regulations, before the applicant has complied with the applicable requirements prescribed by section 371(c) of this part, the designation of the United States shall have no effect after the date of withdrawal and shall be considered as not having been made, unless a claim for benefit of a prior filing date under section 365(c) of this section was made in a national application, or an international application designating the United States, or a claim for benefit under section 386(c) was made in an international design application designating the United States, filed before the date of such withdrawal. However, such withdrawn international application may serve as the basis for a claim of priority under section 365(a) and (b), or under section 386 (a) or (b), if it designated a country other than the United States.

§ 367.   Actions of Other Authorities: Review

(a)   Where a Receiving Office other than the Patent and Trademark Office has refused to accord an international filing date to an international application designating the United States or where it has held such application to be withdrawn either generally or as to the United States, the applicant may request review of the matter by the Director, on compliance with the requirements of and within the time limits specified by the treaty and the Regulations. Such review may result in a determination that such application be considered as pending in the national stage.

(b)   The review under subsection (a) of this section, subject to the same requirements and conditions, may also be requested in those instances where an international application designating the United States is considered withdrawn due to a finding by the International Bureau under article 12(3) of the treaty.

§ 368.   Secrecy of Certain Inventions; Filing International Applications in Foreign Countries

(a)   International applications filed in the Patent and Trademark Office shall be subject to the provisions of chapter 17.

(b)   In accordance with article 27(8) of the treaty, the filing of an international application in a country other than the United States on the invention made in this country shall be considered to constitute the filing of an application in a foreign country within the meaning of chapter 17, whether or not the United States is designated in that international application.

(c)   If a license to file in a foreign country is refused or if an international application is ordered to be kept secret and a permit refused, the Patent and Trademark Office when acting as a Receiving Office, International Searching Authority, or International Preliminary Examining Authority, may not disclose the contents of such application to anyone not authorized to receive such disclosure.

CHAPTER 37.   NATIONAL STAGE

§ 371.   National Stage: Commencement

(a)   Receipt from the International Bureau of copies of international applications with any amendments to the claims, international search reports, and international preliminary examination reports including any annexes thereto may be required in the case of international applications designating or electing the United States.

(b)   Subject to subsection (f) of this section, the national stage shall commence with the expiration of the applicable time limit under article 22(1) or (2), or under article 39(1)(a) of the treaty.

(c)   The applicant shall file in the Patent and Trademark Office—

(1)   the national fee provided in section 4(a);

(2)   a copy of the international application, unless not required under subsection (a) of this section or already communicated by the International Bureau, and a translation into the English language of the international application, if it was filed in another language;

(3)   amendments, if any, to the claims in the international application, made under article 19 of the treaty, unless such amendments have been communicated to the Patent and Trademark Office by the International Bureau, and a translation into the English language if such amendments were made in another language;

(4)   an oath or declaration of the inventor (or other person authorized under chapter 11) complying with the requirements of section 115 and with regulations prescribed for oaths or declarations of applicants;

(5)   a translation into the English language of any annexes to the international preliminary examination report, if such annexes were made in another language.

(d)   The requirements with respect to the national fee referred to in subsection (c)(1), the translation referred to in subsection (c)(2), and the oath or declaration referred to in subsection (c)(4) of this section shall be complied with by the date of the commencement of the national stage or by such later time as may be fixed by the Director. The copy of the international application referred to in subsection (c)(2) shall be submitted by the date of the commencement of the national stage. Failure to comply with these requirements shall be regarded as abandonment of the application by the parties thereof. The payment of a surcharge may be required as a condition of accepting the national fee referred to in subsection (c)(1) or the oath or declaration referred to in subsection (c)(4) of this section if these requirements are not met by the date of the commencement of the national stage. The requirements of subsection (c)(3) of this section shall be complied with by the date of the commencement of the national stage, and failure to do so shall be regarded as a cancellation of the amendments to the claims in the international application made under article 19 of the treaty. The requirement of subsection (c)(5) shall be complied with at such time as may be fixed by the Director and failure to do so shall be regarded as cancellation of the amendments made under article 34(2)(b) of the treaty.

(e)   After an international application has entered the national stage, no patent may be granted or refused thereon before the expiration of the applicable time limit under article 28 or article 41 of the treaty, except with the express consent of the applicant. The applicant may present amendments to the specification, claims and drawings of the application after the national stage has commenced.

(f)   At the express request of the applicant, the national stage of processing may be commenced at any time at which the application is in order for such purpose and the applicable requirements of subsection (c) of this section have been complied with.

§ 372.   National Stage: Requirements and Procedure

(a)   All questions of substance and, within the scope of the requirements of the treaty and Regulations, procedure in an international application designating the United States shall be determined as in the case of national applications regularly filed in the Patent and Trademark Office.

(b)   In case of international applications designating but not originating in, the United States—

(1)   the Director may cause to be reexamined questions relating to form and contents of the application in accordance with the requirements of the treaty and the Regulations;

(2)   the Director may cause the question of unity of invention to be reexamined under section 121, within the scope of the requirements of the treaty and the Regulations and;

(3)   the Director may require a verification of the translation of the international application or any other document pertaining to the application if the application or other document was filed in a language other than English.

§ 373.　**[Repealed]**

§ 374.　**Publication of International Application**

The publication under the treaty defined in section 351(a), of an international application designating the United States shall be deemed a publication under section 122(b), except as provided in section 154(d).

§ 375.　**Patent Issued on International Application: Effect**

(a)　A patent may be issued by the Director based on an international application designating the United States, in accordance with the provisions of this title. Such patent shall have the force and effect of a patent issued on a national application filed under the provisions of chapter 11.

(b)　Where due to an incorrect translation the scope of a patent granted on an international application designating the United States, which was not originally filed in the English language, exceeds the scope of the international application in its original language, a court of competent jurisdiction may retroactively limit the scope of the patent, by declaring it unenforceable to the extent that it exceeds the scope of the international application in its original language.

§ 376.　**Fees**

(a)　The required payment of the international fee and the handling fee, which amounts are specified in the Regulations, shall be paid in United States currency. The Patent and Trademark Office shall charge a national fee as provided in section 41(a), and may also charge the following fees:

(1)　A transmittal fee (see section 361(d)).

(2)　A search fee (see section 361(d)).

(3)　A supplemental search fee (to be paid when required).

(4)　A preliminary examination fee and any additional fees (see section 362(b)).

(5)　Such other fees as established by the Director.

(b)　The amounts of fees specified in subsection (a) of this section, except the international fee and the handling fee, shall be prescribed by the Director. He may refund any sum paid by mistake or in excess of the fees so specified, or if required under the treaty and the Regulations. The Director may also refund any part of the search fee, the national fee, the preliminary examination fee and any additional fees, where he determines such refund to be warranted.

PART V.　THE HAGUE AGREEMENT CONCERNING INTERNATIONAL REGISTRATION OF INDUSTRIAL DESIGNS

Chap.

CHAPTER 38.　INTERNATIONAL DESIGN APPLICATIONS

Sec.

---

§ 381. Definitions

(a) In General.—When used in this part, unless the context otherwise indicates—

(1) the term "treaty" means the Geneva Act of the Hague Agreement Concerning the International Registration of Industrial Designs adopted at Geneva on July 2, 1999;

(2) the term "regulations"—

(A) when capitalized, means the Common Regulations under the treaty; and

(B) when not capitalized, means the regulations established by the Director under this title;

(3) the terms "designation", "designating", and "designate" refer to a request that an international registration have effect in a Contracting Party to the treaty;

(4) the term "International Bureau" means the international intergovernmental organization that is recognized as the coordinating body under the treaty and the Regulations;

(5) the term "effective registration date" means the date of international registration determined by the International Bureau under the treaty;

(6) the term "international design application" means an application for international registration; and

(7) the term "international registration" means the international registration of an industrial design filed under the treaty.

(b) Rule of Construction.—Terms and expressions not defined in this part are to be taken in the sense indicated by the treaty and the Regulations.

§ 382. Filing International Design Applications

(a) In General.—Any person who is a national of the United States, or has a domicile, a habitual residence, or a real and effective industrial or commercial establishment in the United States, may file an international design application by submitting to the Patent and Trademark Office an application in such form, together with such fees, as may be prescribed by the Director.

(b) Required Action.—The Patent and Trademark Office shall perform all acts connected with the discharge of its duties under the treaty, including the collection of international fees and transmittal thereof to the International Bureau. Subject to chapter 17, international design applications shall be forwarded by the Patent and Trademark Office to the International Bureau, upon payment of a transmittal fee.

(c) Applicability of Chapter 16.—Except as otherwise provided in this chapter, the provisions of chapter 16 shall apply.

(d) Application Filed in Another Country.—An international design application on an industrial design made in this country shall be considered to constitute the filing of an application in a foreign country within the meaning of chapter 17 if the international design application is filed—

(1) in a country other than the United States;

(2) at the International Bureau; or

(3) with an intergovernmental organization.

§ 383.   International Design Application

In addition to any requirements pursuant to chapter 16, the international design application shall contain—

(1)   a request for international registration under the treaty;

(2)   an indication of the designated Contracting Parties;

(3)   data concerning the applicant as prescribed in the treaty and the Regulations;

(4)   copies of a reproduction or, at the choice of the applicant, of several different reproductions of the industrial design that is the subject of the international design application, presented in the number and manner prescribed in the treaty and the Regulations;

(5)   an indication of the product or products that constitute the industrial design or in relation to which the industrial design is to be used, as prescribed in the treaty and the Regulations;

(6)   the fees prescribed in the treaty and the Regulations; and

(7)   any other particulars prescribed in the Regulations.

§ 384.   Filing Date

(a)   In General.—Subject to subsection (b), the filing date of an international design application in the United States shall be the effective registration date. Notwithstanding the provisions of this part, any international design application designating the United States that otherwise meets the requirements of chapter 16 may be treated as a design application under chapter 16.

(b)   Review.—An applicant may request review by the Director of the filing date of the international design application in the United States. The Director may determine that the filing date of the international design application in the United States is a date other than the effective registration date. The Director may establish procedures, including the payment of a surcharge, to review the filing date under this section. Such review may result in a determination that the application has a filing date in the United States other than the effective registration date.

§ 385.   Effect of International Design Application

An international design application designating the United States shall have the effect, for all purposes, from its filing date determined in accordance with section 384, of an application for patent filed in the Patent and Trademark Office pursuant to chapter 16.

§ 386.   Right of Priority

(a)   National Application.—In accordance with the conditions and requirements of subsections (a) through (d) of section 119 and section 172, a national application shall be entitled to the right of priority based on a prior international design application that designated at least 1 country other than the United States.

(b)   Prior Foreign Application.—In accordance with the conditions and requirements of subsections (a) through (d) of section 119 and section 172 and the treaty and the Regulations, an international design application designating the United States shall be entitled to the right of priority based on a prior foreign application, a prior international application as defined in section 351(c) designating at least 1 country other than the United States, or a prior international design application designating at least 1 country other than the United States.

(c)   Prior National Application.—In accordance with the conditions and requirements of section 120, an international design application designating the United States shall be entitled to the benefit of the filing date of a prior national application, a prior international application as defined in section 351(c) designating the United States, or a prior international design application designating the United States, and a national application shall be entitled to the benefit of the filing date of a prior international design application designating the United States. If any claim for the benefit of an earlier filing date is based on a prior international application as defined in section 351(c) which designated but did not originate in the United States or a prior international design application which designated but did not originate in the United States, the Director may require the filing in the Patent and Trademark Office of a certified copy of such application together with a translation thereof into the English language, if it was filed in another language.

§ 387. Relief From Prescribed Time Limits

An applicant's failure to act within prescribed time limits in connection with requirements pertaining to an international design application may be excused as to the United States upon a showing satisfactory to the Director of unintentional delay and under such conditions, including a requirement for payment of the fee specified in section 41(a)(7), as may be prescribed by the Director.

§ 388. Withdrawn of Abandoned International Design Application

Subject to sections 384 and 387, if an international design application designating the United States is withdrawn, renounced or canceled or considered withdrawn or abandoned, either generally or as to the United States, under the conditions of the treaty and the Regulations, the designation of the United States shall have no effect after the date of withdrawal, renunciation, cancellation, or abandonment and shall be considered as not having been made, unless a claim for benefit of a prior filing date under section 386(c) was made in a national application, or an international design application designating the United States, or a claim for benefit under section 365(c) was made in an international application designating the United States, filed before the date of such withdrawal, renunciation, cancellation, or abandonment. However, such withdrawn, renounced, canceled, or abandoned international design application may serve as the basis for a claim of priority under subsections (a) and (b) of section 386, or under subsection (a) or (b) of section 365, if it designated a country other than the United States.

§ 389. Examination of International Design Application

(a) In General.—The Director shall cause an examination to be made pursuant to this title of an international design application designating the United States.

(b) Applicability of Chapter 16.—All questions of substance and, unless otherwise required by the treaty and Regulations, procedures regarding an international design application designating the United States shall be determined as in the case of applications filed under chapter 16.

(c) Fees.—The Director may prescribe fees for filing international design applications, for designating the United States, and for any other processing, services, or materials relating to international design applications, and may provide for later payment of such fees, including surcharges for later submission of fees.

(d) Issuance of Patent.—The Director may issue a patent based on an international design application designating the United States, in accordance with the provisions of this title. Such patent shall have the force and effect of a patent issued on an application filed under chapter 16.

§ 390. Publication of International Design Application

The publication under the treaty of an international design application designating the United States shall be deemed a publication under section 122(b).

B. ECONOMIC ESPIONAGE ACT OF 1996 AS AMENDED BY THE DEFEND TRADE SECRETS ACT OF 2016

18 U.S.C. §§ 1831–1839

Contents

CHAPTER 90—PROTECTION OF TRADE SECRETS

§ 1831.   Economic Espionage

(a)   In General.—Whoever, intending or knowing that the offense will benefit any foreign government, foreign instrumentality, or foreign agent, knowingly—

(1)   steals, or without authorization appropriates, takes, carries away, or conceals, or by fraud, artifice, or deception obtains a trade secret;

(2)   without authorization copies, duplicates, sketches, draws, photographs, downloads, uploads, alters, destroys, photocopies, replicates, transmits, delivers, sends, mails, communicates, or conveys a trade secret;

(3)   receives, buys, or possesses a trade secret, knowing the same to have been stolen or appropriated, obtained, or converted without authorization;

(4)   attempts to commit any offense described in any of paragraphs (1) through (3); or

(5)   conspires with one or more other persons to commit any offense described in any of paragraphs (1) through (3), and one or more of such persons do any act to effect the object of the conspiracy,

shall, except as provided in subsection (b), be fined not more than $5,000,000 or imprisoned not more than 15 years, or both.

(b)   Organizations.—Any organization that commits any offense described in subsection (a) shall be fined not more than the greater of $10,000,000 or 3 times the value of the stolen trade secret to the organization, including expenses for research and design and other costs of reproducing the trade secret that the organization has thereby avoided.

§ 1832.   Theft of Trade Secrets

(a)   Whoever, with intent to convert a trade secret, that is related to a product or service used in or intended for use in interstate or foreign commerce, to the economic benefit of anyone other than the owner thereof, and intending or knowing that the offense will, injure any owner of that trade secret, knowingly—

(1) steals, or without authorization appropriates, takes, carries away, or conceals, or by fraud, artifice, or deception obtains such information;

(2) without authorization copies, duplicates, sketches, draws, photographs, downloads, uploads, alters, destroys, photocopies, replicates, transmits, delivers, sends, mails, communicates, or conveys such information;

(3) receives, buys, or possesses such information, knowing the same to have been stolen or appropriated, obtained, or converted without authorization;

(4) attempts to commit any offense described in paragraphs (1) through (3); or

(5) conspires with one or more other persons to commit any offense described in paragraphs (1) through (3), and one or more of such persons do any act to effect the object of the conspiracy,

shall, except as provided in subsection (b), be fined under this title or imprisoned not more than 10 years, or both.

(b) Any organization that commits any offense described in subsection (a) shall be fined not more than the greater of $5,000,000 or 3 times the value of the stolen trade secret to the organization, including expenses for research and design and other costs of reproducing the trade secret that the organization has thereby avoided.

§ 1833. Exceptions to Prohibitions

(a) In General.—This chapter does not prohibit or create a private right of action for—

(1) any otherwise lawful activity conducted by a governmental entity of the United States, a State, or a political subdivision of a State; or

(2) the disclosure of a trade secret in accordance with subsection (b)

(b) Immunity From Liability for Confidential Disclosure of a Trade Secret to the Government or in a Court Filing.—

(1) Immunity.—An individual shall not be held criminally or civilly liable under any Federal or State trade secret law for the disclosure of a trade secret that—

(A) is made—

(i) in confidence to a Federal, State, or local government official, either directly or indirectly, or to an attorney; and

(ii) solely for the purpose of reporting or investigating a suspected violation of law; or

(B) is made in a complaint or other document filed in a lawsuit or other proceeding, if such filing is made under seal.

(2) Use of trade secret information in anti-retaliation lawsuit.—An individual who files a lawsuit for retaliation by an employer for reporting a suspected violation of law may disclose the trade secret to the attorney of the individual and use the trade secret information in the court proceeding, if the individual—

(A) files any document containing the trade secret under seal; and

(B) does not disclose the trade secret, except pursuant to court order

(3) Notice.—

(A) In general.—An employer shall provide notice of the immunity set forth in this subsection in any contract or agreement with an employee that governs the use of a trade secret or other confidential information.

(B) Policy document.—An employer shall be considered to be in compliance with the notice requirement in subparagraph (A) if the employer provides a cross-reference to a policy document provided to the employee that sets forth the employer's reporting policy for a suspected violation of law.

(C) Non-compliance.—If an employer does not comply with the notice requirement in subparagraph (A), the employer may not be awarded exemplary damages or attorney fees under subparagraph (C) or (D) of section 1836(b)(3) in an action against an employee to whom notice was not provided.

(D) Applicability.—This paragraph shall apply to contracts and agreements that are entered into or updated after the date of enactment of this subsection.

(4) Employee defined.—For purposes of this subsection, the term 'employee' includes any individual performing work as a contractor or consultant for an employer.

(5) Rule of construction.—Except as expressly provided for under this subsection, nothing in this subsection shall be construed to authorize, or limit liability for, an act that is otherwise prohibited by law, such as the unlawful access of material by unauthorized means.

§ 1834.   Criminal Forfeiture

Forfeiture, destruction, and restitution relating to this chapter shall be subject to section 2323, to the extent provided in that section, in addition to any other similar remedies provided by law.

§ 1835.   Orders to Preserve Confidentiality

(a) In General.—In any prosecution or other proceeding under this chapter, the court shall enter such orders and take such other action as may be necessary and appropriate to preserve the confidentiality of trade secrets, consistent with the requirements of the Federal Rules of Criminal and Civil Procedure, the Federal Rules of Evidence, and all other applicable laws. An interlocutory appeal by the United States shall lie from a decision or order of a district court authorizing or directing the disclosure of any trade secret.

(b) Rights Of Trade Secret Owners.—The court may not authorize or direct the disclosure of any information the owner asserts to be a trade secret unless the court allows the owner the opportunity to file a submission under seal that describes the interest of the owner in keeping the information confidential. No submission under seal made under this subsection may be used in a prosecution under this chapter for any purpose other than those set forth in this section, or otherwise required by law. The provision of information relating to a trade secret to the United States or the court in connection with a prosecution under this chapter shall not constitute a waiver of trade secret protection, and the disclosure of information relating to a trade secret in connection with a prosecution under this chapter shall not constitute a waiver of trade secret protection unless the trade secret owner expressly consents to such waiver.

§ 1836.   Civil Proceedings

(a) The Attorney General may, in a civil action, obtain appropriate injunctive relief against any violation of this chapter.

(b) Private Civil Actions.—

(1) In general.—An owner of a trade secret that is misappropriated may bring a civil action under this subsection if the trade secret is related to a product or service used in, or intended for use in, interstate or foreign commerce.

(2) Civil seizure.—

(A) In general.—

(i) Application.—Based on an affidavit or verified complaint satisfying the requirements of this paragraph, the court may upon ex parte application but only in extraordinary circumstances, issue an order providing for the seizure of property necessary to prevent the propagation or dissemination of the trade secret that is the subject of the action.

(ii) Requirements for issuing order.—The court may not grant an application under clause (i) unless the court finds that it clearly appears from specific facts that—

(I) an order issued pursuant to Rule 65 of the Federal Rules of Civil Procedure or another form of equitable relief would be inadequate to achieve the purpose of this paragraph because the party to which the order would be issued would evade, avoid, or otherwise not comply with such an order;

(II) an immediate and irreparable injury will occur if such seizure is not ordered;

(III) the harm to the applicant of denying the application outweighs the harm to the legitimate interests of the person against whom seizure would be ordered of granting the application and substantially outweighs the harm to any third parties who may be harmed by such seizure;

(IV) the applicant is likely to succeed in showing that—

(aa) the information is a trade secret; and

(bb) the person against whom seizure would be ordered—

(AA) misappropriated the trade secret of the applicant by improper means; or

(BB) conspired to use improper means to misappropriate the trade secret of the applicant;

(V) the person against whom seizure would be ordered has actual possession of—

(aa) the trade secret; and

(bb) any property to be seized;

(VI) the application describes with reasonable particularity the matter to be seized and, to the extent reasonable under the circumstances, identifies the location where the matter is to be seized;

(VII) the person against whom seizure would be ordered, or persons acting in concert with such person, would destroy, move, hide, or otherwise make such matter inaccessible to the court, if the applicant were to proceed on notice to such person; and

(VIII) the applicant has not publicized the requested seizure.

(B) Elements of order.—If an order is issued under subparagraph (A), it shall—

(i) set forth findings of fact and conclusions of law required for the order;

(ii) provide for the narrowest seizure of property necessary to achieve the purpose of this paragraph and direct that the seizure be conducted in a manner that minimizes any interruption of the business operations of third parties and, to the extent possible, does not interrupt the legitimate business operations of the person accused of misappropriating the trade secret;

(iii)

(I) be accompanied by an order protecting the seized property from disclosure by prohibiting access by the applicant or the person against whom the order is directed, and prohibiting any copies, in whole or in part, of the seized property, to prevent undue damage to the party against whom the order has issued or others, until such parties have an opportunity to be heard in court; and

(II) provide that if access is granted by the court to the applicant or the person against whom the order is directed, the access shall be consistent with subparagraph (D);

(iv) provide guidance to the law enforcement officials executing the seizure that clearly delineates the scope of the authority of the officials, including—

(I) the hours during which the seizure may be executed; and

(II) whether force may be used to access locked areas;

(v) set a date for a hearing described in subparagraph (F) at the earliest possible time, and not later than 7 days after the order has issued, unless the party against whom the order is directed and others harmed by the order consent to another date for the hearing, except that a party against whom the order has issued or any person harmed by the order may move the court at any time to dissolve or modify the order after giving notice to the applicant who obtained the order; and

(vi) require the person obtaining the order to provide the security determined adequate by the court for the payment of the damages that any person may be entitled to recover as a result of a wrongful or excessive seizure or wrongful or excessive attempted seizure under this paragraph.

(C) Protection from publicity.—The court shall take appropriate action to protect the person against whom an order under this paragraph is directed from publicity, by or at the behest of the person obtaining the order, about such order and any seizure under such order.

(D) Materials in custody of court.—

(i) In general.—Any materials seized under this paragraph shall be taken into the custody of the court. The court shall secure the seized material from physical and electronic access during the seizure and while in the custody of the court.

(ii) Storage medium.—If the seized material includes a storage medium, or if the seized material is stored on a storage medium, the court shall prohibit the medium from being connected to a network or the Internet without the consent of both parties, until the hearing required under subparagraph (B)(v) and described in subparagraph (F).

(iii) Protection of confidentiality.—The court shall take appropriate measures to protect the confidentiality of seized materials that are unrelated to the trade secret information ordered seized pursuant to this paragraph unless the person against whom the order is entered consents to disclosure of the material.

(iv) Appointment of special master.—The court may appoint a special master to locate and isolate all misappropriated trade secret information and to facilitate the return of unrelated property and data to the person from whom the property was seized. The special master appointed by the court shall agree to be bound by a non-disclosure agreement approved by the court.

(E) Service of order.—The court shall order that service of a copy of the order under this paragraph, and the submissions of the applicant to obtain the order, shall be made by a Federal law enforcement officer who, upon making service, shall carry out the seizure under the order. The court may allow State or local law enforcement officials to participate, but may not permit the applicant or any agent of the applicant to participate in the seizure. At the request of law enforcement officials, the court may allow a technical expert who is unaffiliated with the applicant and who is bound by a court-approved non-disclosure agreement to participate in the seizure if the court determines that the participation of the expert will aid the efficient execution of and minimize the burden of the seizure.

(F)　Seizure hearing.—

(i)　Date.—A court that issues a seizure order shall hold a hearing on the date set by the court under subparagraph (B)(v).

(ii)　Burden of proof.—At a hearing held under this subparagraph, the party who obtained the order under subparagraph (A) shall have the burden to prove the facts supporting the findings of fact and conclusions of law necessary to support the order. If the party fails to meet that burden, the seizure order shall be dissolved or modified appropriately.

(iii)　Dissolution or modification of order.—A party against whom the order has been issued or any person harmed by the order may move the court at any time to dissolve or modify the order after giving notice to the party who obtained the order.

(iv)　Discovery time limits.—The court may make such orders modifying the time limits for discovery under the Federal Rules of Civil Procedure as may be necessary to prevent the frustration of the purposes of a hearing under this subparagraph.

(G)　Action for damage caused by wrongful seizure.—A person who suffers damage by reason of a wrongful or excessive seizure under this paragraph has a cause of action against the applicant for the order under which such seizure was made, and shall be entitled to the same relief as is provided under section 34(d)(11) of the Trademark Act of 1946 (15 U.S.C. 1116(d)(11)). The security posted with the court under subparagraph (B)(vi) shall not limit the recovery of third parties for damages.

(H)　Motion for encryption.—A party or a person who claims to have an interest in the subject matter seized may make a motion at any time, which may be heard ex parte, to encrypt any material seized or to be seized under this paragraph that is stored on a storage medium. The motion shall include, when possible, the desired encryption method.

(3)　Remedies.—In a civil action brought under this subsection with respect to the misappropriation of a trade secret, a court may—

(A)　grant an injunction—

(i)　to prevent any actual or threatened misappropriation described in paragraph (1) on such terms as the court deems reasonable, provided the order does not—

(I)　prevent a person from entering into an employment relationship, and that conditions placed on such employment shall be based on evidence of threatened misappropriation and not merely on the information the person knows; or

(II)　otherwise conflict with an applicable State law prohibiting restraints on the practice of a lawful profession, trade, or business;

(ii)　if determined appropriate by the court, requiring affirmative actions to be taken to protect the trade secret; and

(iii)　in exceptional circumstances that render an injunction inequitable, that conditions future use of the trade secret upon payment of a reasonable royalty for no longer than the period of time for which such use could have been prohibited

(B)　award—

(i)

(I)　damages for actual loss caused by the misappropriation of the trade secret; and

(II) damages for any unjust enrichment caused by the misappropriation of the trade secret that is not addressed in computing damages for actual loss; or

(ii) in lieu of damages measured by any other methods, the damages caused by the misappropriation measured by imposition of liability for a reasonable royalty for the misappropriator's unauthorized disclosure or use of the trade secret;

(C) if the trade secret is willfully and maliciously misappropriated, award exemplary damages in an amount not more than 2 times the amount of the damages awarded under subparagraph (B); and

(D) if a claim of the misappropriation is made in bad faith, which may be established by circumstantial evidence, a motion to terminate an injunction is made or opposed in bad faith, or the trade secret was willfully and maliciously misappropriated, award reasonable attorney's fees to the prevailing party.

(c) Jurisdiction.—The district courts of the United States shall have original jurisdiction of civil actions brought under this section.

(d) Period of Limitations.—A civil action under subsection (b) may not be commenced later than 3 years after the date on which the misappropriation with respect to which the action would relate is discovered or by the exercise of reasonable diligence should have been discovered. For purposes of this subsection, a continuing misappropriation constitutes a single claim of misappropriation.

§ 1837. Applicability to Conduct Outside the United States

This chapter also applies to conduct occurring outside the United States if—

(1) the offender is a natural person who is a citizen or permanent resident alien of the United States, or an organization organized under the laws of the United States or a State or political subdivision thereof; or

(2) an act in furtherance of the offense was committed in the United States.

§ 1838. Construction With Other Laws

Except as provided in § 1833(b), this chapter shall not be construed to preempt or displace any other remedies, whether civil or criminal, provided by United States Federal, State, commonwealth, possession, or territory law for the misappropriation of a trade secret, or to affect the otherwise lawful disclosure of information by any Government employee under section 552 of title 5 (commonly known as the Freedom of Information Act).

§ 1839. Definitions

As used in this chapter—

(1) the term "foreign instrumentality" means any agency, bureau, ministry, component, institution, association, or any legal, commercial, or business organization, corporation, firm, or entity that is substantially owned, controlled, sponsored, commanded, managed, or dominated by a foreign government;

(2) the term "foreign agent" means any officer, employee, proxy, servant, delegate, or representative of a foreign government;

(3) the term "trade secret" means all forms and types of financial, business, scientific, technical, economic, or engineering information, including patterns, plans, compilations, procedures, programs, or codes, whether tangible or intangible, and whether or how stored, compiled, or memorialized physically, electronically, graphically, photographically, or in writing if—

(A) the owner thereof has taken reasonable measures to keep such information secret; and

(B) the information derives independent economic value, actual or potential, from not being generally known to, and not being readily ascertainable through proper means by, another person who can obtain economic value from the disclosure or use of the information;

(4) the term "owner", with respect to a trade secret, means the person or entity in whom or in which rightful legal or equitable title to, or license in, the trade secret is reposed;

(5) the term 'misappropriation' means—

(A) acquisition of a trade secret of another by a person who knows or has reason to know that the trade secret was acquired by improper means; or

(B) disclosure or use of a trade secret of another without express or implied consent by a person who—

(i) used improper means to acquire knowledge of the trade secret;

(ii) at the time of disclosure or use, knew or had reason to know that the knowledge of the trade secret was—

(I) derived from or through a person who had used improper means to acquire the trade secret;

(II) acquired under circumstances giving rise to a duty to maintain the secrecy of the trade secret or limit the use of the trade secret; or

(III) derived from or through a person who owed a duty to the person seeking relief to maintain the secrecy of the trade secret or limit the use of the trade secret; or

(iii) before a material change of the position of the person, knew or had reason to know that—

(I) the trade secret was a trade secret; and

(II) knowledge of the trade secret had been acquired by accident or mistake;

(6) the term 'improper means'—

(A) includes theft, bribery, misrepresentation, breach or inducement of a breach of a duty to maintain secrecy, or espionage through electronic or other means; and

(B) does not include reverse engineering, independent derivation, or any other lawful means of acquisition; and

(7) the term 'Trademark Act of 1946' means the Act entitled 'An Act to provide for the registration and protection of trademarks used in commerce, to carry out the provisions of certain international conventions, and for other purposes, approved July 5, 1946 (15 U.S.C. § 1051 et seq.) (commonly referred to as the 'Trademark Act of 1946' or the 'Lanham Act').

C. UNIFORM TRADE SECRETS ACT WITH 1985 AMENDMENTS

Contents

---

§ 1.   Definitions

As used in this [Act], unless the context requires otherwise:

(1)   "Improper means" includes theft, bribery, misrepresentation, breach or inducement of a breach of a duty to maintain secrecy, or espionage through electronic or other means;

(2)   "Misappropriation" means:

(i)   acquisition of a trade secret of another by a person who knows or has reason to know that the trade secret was acquired by improper means; or

(ii)   disclosure or use of a trade secret of another without express or implied consent by a person who

(A)   used improper means to acquire knowledge of the trade secret; or

(B)   at the time of disclosure or use, knew or had reason to know that his knowledge of the trade secret was

(I)   derived from or through a person who had utilized improper means to acquire it;

(II)   acquired under circumstances giving rise to a duty to maintain its secrecy or limit its use; or

(III) derived from or through a person who owed a duty to the person seeking relief to maintain its secrecy or limit its use; or

(C)   before a material change of his [or her] position, knew or had reason to know that it was a trade secret and that knowledge of it had been acquired by accident or mistake.

(3)   "Person" means a natural person, corporation, business trust, estate, trust, partnership, association, joint venture, government, governmental subdivision or agency, or any other legal or commercial entity.

(4)　"Trade secret" means information, including a formula, pattern, compilation, program, device, method, technique, or process, that:

(i)　derives independent economic value, actual or potential, from not being generally known to, and not being readily ascertainable by proper means by, other persons who can obtain economic value from its disclosure or use, and

(ii)　is the subject of efforts that are reasonable under the circumstances to maintain its secrecy.

§ 2.　Injunctive Relief

(a)　Actual or threatened misappropriation may be enjoined. Upon application to the court, an injunction shall be terminated when the trade secret has ceased to exist, but the injunction may be continued for an additional reasonable period of time in order to eliminate commercial advantage that otherwise would be derived from the misappropriation.

(b)　In exceptional circumstances, an injunction may condition future use upon payment of a reasonable royalty for no longer than the period of time for which use could have been prohibited. Exceptional circumstances include, but are not limited to, a material and prejudicial change of position prior to acquiring knowledge or reason to know of misappropriation that renders a prohibitive injunction inequitable.

(c)　In appropriate circumstances, affirmative acts to protect a trade secret may be compelled by court order.

§ 3.　Damages

(a)　Except to the extent that a material and prejudicial change of position prior to acquiring knowledge or reason to know of misappropriation renders a monetary recovery inequitable, a complainant is entitled to recover damages for misappropriation. Damages can include both the actual loss caused by misappropriation and the unjust enrichment caused by misappropriation that is not taken into account in computing actual loss. In lieu of damages measured by any other methods, the damages caused by misappropriation may be measured by imposition of liability for a reasonable royalty for a misappropriator's unauthorized disclosure or use of a trade secret.

(b)　If willful and malicious misappropriation exists, the court may award exemplary damages in an amount not exceeding twice any award made under subsection (a).

§ 4.　Attorney's Fees

If (i) a claim of misappropriation is made in bad faith, (ii) a motion to terminate an injunction is made or resisted in bad faith, or (iii) willful and malicious misappropriation exists, the court may award reasonable attorney's fees to the prevailing party.

§ 5.　Preservation of Secrecy

In an action under this [Act], a court shall preserve the secrecy of an alleged trade secret by reasonable means, which may include granting protective orders in connection with discovery proceedings, holding in-camera hearings, sealing the records of the action, and ordering any person involved in the litigation not to disclose an alleged trade secret without prior court approval.

§ 6.　Statute of Limitations

An action for misappropriation must be brought within 3 years after the misappropriation is discovered or by the exercise of reasonable diligence should have been discovered. For the purposes of this section, a continuing misappropriation constitutes a single claim.

§ 7. Effect on Other Law

(a) Except as provided in subsection (b), this [Act] displaces conflicting tort, restitutionary, and other law of this State providing civil remedies for misappropriation of a trade secret.

(b) This [Act] does not affect:

(1) contractual remedies, whether or not based upon misappropriation of a trade secret;

(2) other civil remedies that are not based upon misappropriation of a trade secret; or

(3) criminal remedies, whether or not based upon misappropriation of a trade secret.

§ 8. Uniformity of Application and Construction

This [Act] shall be applied and construed to effectuate its general purpose to make uniform the law with respect to the subject of this [Act] among states enacting it.

§ 9. Short Title

This [Act] may be cited as the Uniform Trade Secrets Act.

§ 10. Severability

If any provision of this [Act] or its application to any person or circumstances is held invalid, the invalidity does not affect other provisions or applications of the [Act] which can be given effect without the invalid provision or application, and to this end the provisions of this [Act] are severable.

§ 11. Time of Taking Effect

This [Act] takes effect on _____, and does not apply to misappropriation occurring prior to the effective date. With respect to a continuing misappropriation that began prior to the effective date, the [Act] also does not apply to the continuing misappropriation that occurs after the effective date.

§ 12. Repeal

The following Acts and parts of Acts are repealed:

(1)

(2)

(3)

D. PATENT COOPERATION TREATY OF JUNE 19, 1970

(Done at Washington on June 19, 1970, amended on September 28, 1979, modified on February 3, 1984, and October 3, 2001)

Contents[1]

Preamble

Introductory Provisions

---

[1]   This Table of Contents does not appear in the official text of the Treaty.

Chapter II.   International Preliminary Examination

Chapter III.   Common Provisions

Chapter IV.   Technical Services

[Chapter V, Articles 53–58, have been omitted].

Chapter VI.   Disputes

Chapter VII.   Revision and Amendment

[Chapter VIII, Articles 62–69, have been omitted].

Preamble

The Contracting States,

Desiring to make a contribution to the progress of science and technology,

Desiring to perfect the legal protection of inventions,

Desiring to simplify and render more economical the obtaining of protection for inventions where protection is sought in several countries,

Desiring to facilitate and accelerate access by the public to the technical information contained in documents describing new inventions,

Desiring to foster and accelerate the economic development of developing countries through the adoption of measures designed to increase the efficiency of their legal systems, whether national or regional, instituted for the protection of inventions by providing easily accessible information on the availability of technological solutions applicable to their special needs and by facilitating access to the ever expanding volume of modern technology,

Convinced that cooperation among nations will greatly facilitate the attainment of these aims,

Have concluded the present Treaty.

Introductory Provisions

Article 1

Establishment of a Union

1.   The States party to this Treaty (hereinafter called "the Contracting States") constitute a Union for cooperation in the filing, searching, and examination, of applications for the protection of inventions, and for rendering special technical services. The Union shall be known as the International Patent Cooperation Union.

2.   No provision of this Treaty shall be interpreted as diminishing the rights under the Paris Convention for the Protection of Industrial Property of any national or resident of any country party to that Convention.

Article 2

Definitions

For the purposes of this Treaty and the Regulations and unless expressly stated otherwise:

(i)   "application" means an application for the protection of an invention; references to an "application" shall be construed as references to applications for patents for inventions, inventors' certificates, utility certificates, utility models, patents or certificates of addition, inventors' certificates of addition, and utility certificates of addition;

(ii)   references to a "patent" shall be construed as references to patents for inventions, inventors' certificates, utility certificates, utility models, patents or certificates of addition, inventors' certificates of addition, and utility certificates of addition;

(iii)   "national patent" means a patent granted by a national authority;

(iv)   "regional patent" means a patent granted by a national or an intergovernmental authority having the power to grant patents effective in more than one State;

(v)   "regional application" means an application for a regional patent;

(vi)   references to a "national application" shall be construed as references to applications for national patents and regional patents, other than applications filed under this Treaty;

(vii) "international application" means an application filed under this Treaty;

(viii) references to an "application" shall be construed as references to international applications and national applications;

(ix)   references to a "patent" shall be construed as references to national patents and regional patents;

(x)   references to "national law" shall be construed as references to the national law of a Contracting State or, where a regional application or a regional patent is involved, to the treaty providing for the filing of regional applications or the granting of regional patents;

(xi) "priority date," for the purposes of computing time limits, means:

(a) where the international application contains a priority claim under Article 8, the filing date of the application whose priority is so claimed;

(b) where the international application contains several priority claims under Article 8, the filing date of the earliest application whose priority is so claimed;

(c) where the international application does not contain any priority claim under Article 8, the international filing date of such application;

(xii) "national Office" means the government authority of a Contracting State entrusted with the granting of patents; references to a "national Office" shall be construed as referring also to any intergovernmental authority which several States have entrusted with the task of granting regional patents, provided that at least one of those States is a Contracting State, and provided that the said States have authorized that authority to assume the obligations and exercise the powers which this Treaty and the Regulations provide for in respect of national Offices;

(xiii) "designated Office" means the national Office of or acting for the State designated by the applicant under Chapter I of this Treaty;

(xiv) "elected Office" means the national Office of or acting for the State elected by the applicant under Chapter II of this Treaty;

(xv) "receiving Office" means the national Office or the intergovernmental organization with which the international application has been filed;

(xvi) "Union" means the International Patent Cooperation Union;

(xvii) "Assembly" means the Assembly of the Union;

(xviii) "Organization" means the World Intellectual Property Organization;

(xix) "International Bureau" means the International Bureau of the Organization and, as long as it subsists, the United International Bureau for the Protection of Intellectual Property (BIRPI);

(xx) "Director General" means the Director General of the Organization and, as long as BIRPI subsists, the Director of BIRPI.

CHAPTER I. INTERNATIONAL APPLICATION AND INTERNATIONAL SEARCH

Article 3

The International Application

1.   Applications for the protection of inventions in any of the Contracting States may be filed as international applications under this Treaty.

2.   An international application shall contain, as specified in this Treaty and the Regulations, a request, a description, one or more claims, one or more drawings (where required), and an abstract.

3.   The abstract merely serves the purpose of technical information and cannot be taken into account for any other purpose, particularly not for the purpose of interpreting the scope of the protection sought.

4.   The international application shall:

(i)   be in a prescribed language;

(ii)   comply with the prescribed physical requirements;

(iii) comply with the prescribed requirement of unity of invention;

(iv) be subject to the payment of the prescribed fees.

Article 4

The Request

1.   The request shall contain:

(i)   a petition to the effect that the international application be processed according to this Treaty;

(ii)   the designation of the Contracting State or States in which protection for the invention is desired on the basis of the international application ("designated States"); if for any designated State a regional patent is available and the applicant wishes to obtain a regional patent rather than a national patent, the request shall so indicate; if, under a treaty concerning a regional patent, the applicant cannot limit his application to certain of the States party to that treaty, designation of one of those States and the indication of the wish to obtain the regional patent shall be treated as designation of all the States party to that treaty; if, under the national law of the designated State, the designation of that State has the effect of an application for a regional patent, the designation of the said State shall be treated as an indication of the wish to obtain the regional patent;

(iii)   the name of and other prescribed data concerning the applicant and the agent (if any);

(iv)   the title of the invention;

(v)   the name of and other prescribed data concerning the inventor where the national law of at least one of the designated States requires that these indications be furnished at the time of filing a national application. Otherwise, the said indications may be furnished either in the request or in separate notices addressed to each designated Office whose national law requires the furnishing of the said indications but allows that they be furnished at a time later than that of the filing of a national application.

2.   Every designation shall be subject to the payment of the prescribed fee within the prescribed time limit.

3.   Unless the applicant asks for any of the other kinds of protection referred to in Article 43, designation shall mean that the desired protection consists of the grant of a patent by or for the designated State. For the purposes of this paragraph, Article 2(ii) shall not apply.

4.   Failure to indicate in the request the name and other prescribed data concerning the inventor shall have no consequence in any designated State whose national law requires the furnishing of the said indications but allows that they be furnished at a time later than that of the filing of a national application. Failure to furnish the said indications in a separate notice shall have no consequence in any designated State whose national law does not require the furnishing of the said indications.

Article 5

The Description

The description shall disclose the invention in a manner sufficiently clear and complete for the invention to be carried out by a person skilled in the art.

Article 6

The Claims

The claim or claims shall define the matter for which protection is sought. Claims shall be clear and concise. They shall be fully supported by the description.

Article 7

The Drawings

1.   Subject to the provisions of paragraph (2)(ii), drawings shall be required when they are necessary for the understanding of the invention.

2.   Where, without being necessary for the understanding of the invention, the nature of the invention admits of illustration by drawings:

      (i)   the applicant may include such drawings in the international application when filed,

      (ii)   any designated Office may require that the applicant file such drawings with it within the prescribed time limit.

Article 8

Claiming Priority

1.   The international application may contain a declaration, as prescribed in the Regulations, claiming the priority of one or more earlier applications filed in or for any country party to the Paris Convention for the Protection of Industrial Property.

2.   (a) Subject to the provisions of sub-paragraph (b), the conditions for, and the effect of, any priority claim declared under paragraph (1) shall be as provided in Article 4 of the Stockholm Act of the Paris Convention for the Protection of Industrial Property.

    (b)   The international application for which the priority of one or more earlier applications filed in or for a Contracting State is claimed may contain the designation of that State. Where, in the international application, the priority of one or more national applications filed in or for a designated State is claimed, or where the priority of an international application having designated only one State is claimed, the conditions for, and the effect of, the priority claim in that State shall be governed by the national law of that State.

Article 9

The Applicant

1.   Any resident or national of a Contracting State may file an international application.

2.   The Assembly may decide to allow the residents and the nationals of any country party to the Paris Convention for the Protection of Industrial Property which is not party to this Treaty to file international applications.

3.   The concepts of residence and nationality, and the application of those concepts in cases where there are several applicants or where the applicants are not the same for all the designated States, are defined in the Regulations.

Article 10

The Receiving Office

The international application shall be filed with the prescribed receiving Office, which will check and process it as provided in this Treaty and the Regulations.

Article 11

Filing Date and Effects of the International Application

1.   The receiving Office shall accord as the international filing date the date of receipt of the international application, provided that the Office has found that, at the time of receipt:

(i)   the applicant does not obviously lack, for reasons of residence or nationality, the right to file an international application with the receiving Office,

(ii)   the international application is in the prescribed language,

(iii) the international application contains at least the following elements:

(a)   an indication that it is intended as an international application,

(b)   the designation of at least one Contracting State,

(c)   the name of the applicant, as prescribed,

(d)   a part which on the face of it appears to be a description,

(e)   a part which on the face of it appears to be a claim or claims.

2.   (a) If the receiving Office finds that the international application did not, at the time of receipt, fulfill the requirements listed in paragraph (1), it shall, as provided in the Regulations, invite the applicant to file the required correction.

(b)   If the applicant complies with the invitation, as provided in the Regulations, the receiving Office shall accord as the international filing date the date of receipt of the required correction.

3.   Subject to Article 64(4), any international application fulfilling the requirements listed in items (i) to (iii) of paragraph (1) and accorded an international filing date shall have the effect of a regular national application in each designated State as of the international filing date, which date shall be considered to be the actual filing date in each designated State.

4.   Any international application fulfilling the requirements listed in items (i) to (iii) of paragraph (1) shall be equivalent to a regular national filing within the meaning of the Paris Convention for the Protection of Industrial Property.

Article 12

Transmittal of the International Application to the International Bureau and the International Searching Authority

1.   One copy of the international application shall be kept by the receiving Office ("home copy"), one copy ("record copy") shall be transmitted to the International Bureau, and another copy ("search copy") shall be transmitted to the competent International Searching Authority referred to in Article 16, as provided in the Regulations.

2.   The record copy shall be considered the true copy of the international application.

3.   The international application shall be considered withdrawn if the record copy has not been received by the International Bureau within the prescribed time limit.

Article 13

Availability of Copy of the International Application to Designated Offices

1.   Any designated Office may ask the International Bureau to transmit to it a copy of the international application prior to the communication provided for in Article 20, and the International Bureau shall transmit such copy to the designated Office as soon as possible after the expiration of one year from the priority date.

2.   (a) The applicant may, at any time, transmit a copy of his international application to any designated Office.

(b)   The applicant may, at any time, ask the International Bureau to transmit a copy of his international application to any designated Office, and the International Bureau shall transmit such copy to the designated Office as soon as possible.

(c)   Any national Office may notify the International Bureau that it does not wish to receive copies as provided for in sub-paragraph (b), in which case that sub-paragraph shall not be applicable in respect of that Office.

Article 14

Certain Defects in the International Application

1.   (a) The receiving Office shall check whether the international application contains any of the following defects, that is to say:

(i)   it is not signed as provided in the Regulations;

(ii)   it does not contain the prescribed indications concerning the applicant;

(iii)   it does not contain a title;

(iv)   it does not contain an abstract;

(v)   it does not comply to the extent provided in the Regulations with the prescribed physical requirements.

(b)   If the receiving Office finds any of the said defects, it shall invite the applicant to correct the international application within the prescribed time limit, failing which that application shall be considered withdrawn and the receiving Office shall so declare.

2.   If the international application refers to drawings which, in fact, are not included in that application, the receiving Office shall notify the applicant accordingly and he may furnish them within the prescribed time limit and, if he does, the international filing date shall be the date on which the drawings are received by the receiving Office. Otherwise, any reference to the said drawings shall be considered non-existent.

3.   (a) If the receiving Office finds that, within the prescribed time limits, the fees prescribed under Article 3(4)(iv) have not been paid, or no fee prescribed under Article 4(2) has been paid in respect of any of the designated States, the international application shall be considered withdrawn and the receiving Office shall so declare.

(b)   If the receiving Office finds that the fee prescribed under Article 4(2) has been paid in respect of one or more (but less than all) designated States within the prescribed time limit, the designation of those States in respect of which it has not been paid within the prescribed time limit shall be considered withdrawn and the receiving Office shall so declare.

4.   If, after having accorded an international filing date to the international application, the receiving Office finds, within the prescribed time limit, that any of the requirements listed in items (i) to (iii) of Article 11(1) was not complied with at that date, the said application shall be considered withdrawn and the receiving Office shall so declare.

Article 15

The International Search

1.   Each international application shall be the subject of international search.

2.   The objective of the international search is to discover relevant prior art.

3.   International search shall be made on the basis of the claims, with due regard to the description and the drawings (if any).

4.   The International Searching Authority referred to in Article 16 shall endeavor to discover as much of the relevant prior art as its facilities permit, and shall, in any case, consult the documentation specified in the Regulations.

5.   (a) If the national law of the Contracting State so permits, the applicant who files a national application with the national Office of or acting for such State may, subject to the conditions provided for in such law, request that a search similar to an international search ("international-type search") be carried out on such application.

(b)   If the national law of the Contracting State so permits, the national Office of or acting for such State may subject any national application filed with it to an international-type search.

(c)   The international-type search shall be carried out by the International Searching Authority referred to in Article 16 which would be competent for an international search if the national application were an international application and were filed with the Office referred to in sub-paragraphs (a) and (b). If the national application is in a language which the International Searching Authority considers it is not equipped to handle, the international-type search shall be carried out on a translation prepared by the applicant in a language prescribed for international applications and which the International Searching Authority has undertaken to accept for international applications. The national application and the translation, when required, shall be presented in the form prescribed for international applications.

Article 16

The International Searching Authority

1.   International search shall be carried out by an International Searching Authority, which may be either a national Office or an intergovernmental organization, such as the International Patent Institute, whose tasks include the establishing of documentary search reports on prior art with respect to inventions which are the subject of applications.

2.   If, pending the establishment of a single International Searching Authority, there are several International Searching Authorities, each receiving Office shall, in accordance with the provisions of the applicable agreement referred to in paragraph (3)(b), specify the International Searching Authority or Authorities competent for the searching of international applications filed with such Office.

3.   (a) International Searching Authorities shall be appointed by the Assembly. Any national Office and any intergovernmental organization satisfying the requirements referred to in sub-paragraph (c) may be appointed as International Searching Authority.

(b)   Appointment shall be conditional on the consent of the national Office or intergovernmental organization to be appointed and the conclusion of an agreement, subject to approval by the Assembly, between such Office or organization and the International Bureau. The agreement shall specify the rights and obligations of the parties, in particular, the formal undertaking by the said Office or organization to apply and observe all the common rules of international search.

(c)   The Regulations prescribe the minimum requirements, particularly as to manpower and documentation, which any Office or organization must satisfy before it can be appointed and must continue to satisfy while it remains appointed.

(d)   Appointment shall be for a fixed period of time and may be extended for further periods.

(e)   Before the Assembly makes a decision on the appointment of any national Office or intergovernmental organization, or on the extension of its appointment, or before it allows any such appointment to lapse, the Assembly shall hear the interested Office or organization and seek the advice of the Committee for Technical Cooperation referred to in Article 56 once that Committee has been established.

Article 17

Procedure Before the International Searching Authority

1.   Procedure before the International Searching Authority shall be governed by the provisions of this Treaty, the Regulations, and the agreement which the International Bureau shall conclude, subject to this Treaty and the Regulations, with the said Authority.

2.   (a) If the International Searching Authority considers

(i)   that the international application relates to a subject matter which the International Searching Authority is not required, under the Regulations, to search, and in the particular case decides not to search, or

(ii)   that the description, the claims, or the drawings, fail to comply with the prescribed requirements to such an extent that a meaningful search could not be carried out,

the said Authority shall so declare and shall notify the applicant and the International Bureau that no international search report will be established.

(b)   If any of the situations referred to in sub-paragraph (a) is found to exist in connection with certain claims only, the international search report shall so indicate in respect of such claims, whereas, for the other claims, the said report shall be established as provided in Article 18.

3.   (a) If the International Searching Authority considers that the international application does not comply with the requirement of unity of invention as set forth in the Regulations, it shall invite the applicant to pay additional fees. The International Searching Authority shall establish the international search report on those parts of the international application which relate to the invention first mentioned in the claims ("main invention") and, provided the required additional fees have been paid within the prescribed time limit, on those parts of the international application which relate to inventions in respect of which the said fees were paid.

(b)   The national law of any designated State may provide that, where the national Office of that State finds the invitation, referred to in sub-paragraph (a), of the International Searching Authority justified and where the applicant has not paid all additional fees, those parts of the international application which consequently have not been searched shall, as far as effects in that State are concerned, be considered withdrawn unless a special fee is paid by the applicant to the national Office of that State.

Article 18

The International Search Report

1.   The international search report shall be established within the prescribed time limit and in the prescribed form.

2.   The international search report shall, as soon as it has been established, be transmitted by the International Searching Authority to the applicant and the International Bureau.

3.   The international search report or the declaration referred to in Article 17(2)(a) shall be translated as provided in the Regulations. The translations shall be prepared by or under the responsibility of the International Bureau.

Article 19

Amendment of the Claims Before the International Bureau

1.   The applicant shall, after having received the international search report, be entitled to one opportunity to amend the claims of the international application by filing amendments with the International Bureau within the prescribed time limit. He may, at the same time, file a brief statement, as provided in the Regulations, explaining the amendments and indicating any impact that such amendments might have on the description and the drawings.

2.   The amendments shall not go beyond the disclosure in the international application as filed.

3.   If the national law of any designated State permits amendments to go beyond the said disclosure, failure to comply with paragraph (2) shall have no consequence in that State.

Article 20

Communication to Designated Offices

1.   (a) The international application, together with the international search report (including any indication referred to in Article 17(2)(b)) or the declaration referred to in Article 17(2)(a), shall be communicated to each designated Office, as provided in the Regulations, unless the designated Office waives such requirement in its entirety or in part.

(b)   The communication shall include the translation (as prescribed) of the said report or declaration.

2.   If the claims have been amended by virtue of Article 19(1), the communication shall either contain the full text of the claims both as filed and as amended or shall contain the full text of the claims as filed and specify the amendments, and shall include the statement, if any, referred to in Article 19(1).

3.   At the request of the designated Office or the applicant, the International Searching Authority shall send to the said Office or the applicant, respectively, copies of the documents cited in the international search report, as provided in the Regulations.

Article 21

International Publication

1.   The International Bureau shall publish international applications.

2.   (a) Subject to the exceptions provided for in subparagraph (b) and in Article 64(3), the international publication of the international application shall be effected promptly after the expiration of 18 months from the priority date of that application.

(b)   The applicant may ask the International Bureau to publish his international application any time before the expiration of the time limit referred to in sub-paragraph (a). The International Bureau shall proceed accordingly, as provided in the Regulations.

3.   The international search report or the declaration referred to in Article 17(2)(a) shall be published as prescribed in the Regulations.

4.   The language and form of the international publication and other details are governed by the Regulations.

5.   There shall be no international publication if the international application is withdrawn or is considered withdrawn before the technical preparations for publication have been completed.

6.   If the international application contains expressions or drawings which, in the opinion of the International Bureau, are contrary to morality or public order, or if, in its opinion, the international application contains disparaging statements as defined in the Regulations, it may omit such expressions, drawings, and statements, from its publications, indicating the place and number of words or drawings omitted, and furnishing, upon request, individual copies of the passages omitted.

Article 22

Copy, Translation and Fee to Designated Offices

1.   The applicant shall furnish a copy of the international application (unless the communication provided for in Article 20 has already taken place) and a translation thereof (as prescribed), and pay the national fee (if any), to each designated Office not later than at the expiration of 30 months from the priority date. Where the national law of the designated State requires the indication of the name of and other prescribed data concerning the inventor but allows that these indications be furnished at a time later than that of the filing of a national application, the applicant shall, unless they were contained in the request, furnish the said indications to the national Office of or acting for the State not later than at the expiration of 30 months from the priority date.

2.   Where the International Searching Authority makes a declaration, under Article 17(2)(a), that no international search report will be established, the time limit for performing the acts referred to in paragraph (1) of this article shall be the same as that provided for in paragraph (1).

3.   Any national law may, for performing the acts referred to in paragraphs (1) or (2), fix time limits which expire later than the time limit provided for in those paragraphs.

Article 23

Delaying of National Procedure

1.   No designated Office shall process or examine the international application prior to the expiration of the applicable time limit under Article 22.

2.   Notwithstanding the provisions of paragraph (1), any designated Office may, on the express request of the applicant, process or examine the international application at any time.

Article 24

Possible Loss of Effect in Designated States

1.   Subject, in case (ii) below, to the provisions of Article 25, the effect of the international application provided for in Article 11(3) shall cease in any designated State with the same consequences as the withdrawal of any national application in that State:

(i)   if the applicant withdraws his international application or the designation of that State;

(ii) if the international application is considered withdrawn by virtue of Article 12(3), 14(1)(b), 14(3)(a), or 14(4), or if the designation of that State is considered withdrawn by virtue of Article 14(3)(b);

(iii) if the applicant fails to perform the acts referred to in Article 22 within the applicable time limit.

2.   Notwithstanding the provisions of paragraph (1), any designated Office may maintain the effect provided for in Article 11(3) even where such effect is not required to be maintained by virtue of Article 25(2).

Article 25

Review by Designated Offices

1.   (a) Where the receiving Office has refused to accord an international filing date or has declared that the international application is considered withdrawn, or where the International Bureau has made a finding under Article 12(3), the International Bureau shall promptly send, at the request of the applicant, copies of any document in the file to any of the designated Offices named by the applicant.

(b)   Where the receiving Office has declared that the designation of any given State is considered withdrawn, the International Bureau shall promptly send, at the request of the applicant, copies of any document in the file to the national Office of such State.

(c)   The request under sub-paragraphs (a) or (b) shall be presented within the prescribed time limit.

2.   (a) Subject to the provisions of sub-paragraph (b), each designated Office shall, provided that the national fee (if any) has been paid and the appropriate translation (as prescribed) has been furnished within the prescribed time limit, decide whether the refusal, declaration, or finding, referred to in paragraph (1) was justified under the provisions of this Treaty and the Regulations, and, if it finds that the refusal or declaration was the result of an error or omission on the part of the receiving Office or that the finding was the result of an error or omission on the part of the International Bureau, it shall, as far as effects in the State of the designated Office are concerned, treat the international application as if such error or omission had not occurred.

(b)   Where the record copy has reached the International Bureau after the expiration of the time limit prescribed under Article 12(3) on account of any error or omission on the part of the applicant, the provisions of sub-paragraph (a) shall apply only under the circumstances referred to in Article 48(2).

Article 26

Opportunity to Correct Before Designated Offices

No designated Office shall reject an international application on the grounds of non-compliance with the requirements of this Treaty and the Regulations without first giving the applicant the opportunity to correct the said application to the extent and according to the procedure provided by the national law for the same or comparable situations in respect of national applications.

Article 27

National Requirements

1.   No national law shall require compliance with requirements relating to the form or contents of the international application different from or additional to those which are provided for in this Treaty and the Regulations.

2.   The provisions of paragraph (1) neither affect the application of the provisions of Article 7(2) nor preclude any national law from requiring, once the processing of the international application has started in the designated Office, the furnishing:

(i)   when the applicant is a legal entity, of the name of an officer entitled to represent such legal entity,

(ii)   of documents not part of the international application but which constitute proof of allegations or statements made in that application, including the confirmation of the international application by the signature of the applicant when that application, as filed, was signed by his representative or agent.

3.   Where the applicant, for the purposes of any designated State, is not qualified according to the national law of that State to file a national application because he is not the inventor, the international application may be rejected by the designated Office.

4.   Where the national law provides, in respect of the form or contents of national applications, for requirements which, from the viewpoint of applicants, are more favorable than the requirements provided for by this Treaty and the Regulations in respect of international applications, the national Office, the courts and any other competent organs of or acting for the designated State may apply the former requirements, instead of the latter requirements, to international applications, except where the applicant insists that the requirements provided for by this Treaty and the Regulations be applied to his international application.

5.   Nothing in this Treaty and the Regulations is intended to be construed as prescribing anything that would limit the freedom of each Contracting State to prescribe such substantive conditions of patentability as it desires. In particular, any provision in this Treaty and the Regulations concerning the definition of prior art is exclusively for the purposes of the international procedure and, consequently, any Contracting State is free to apply, when determining the patentability of an invention claimed in an international application, the criteria of its national law in respect of prior art and other conditions of patentability not constituting requirements as to the form and contents of applications.

6.   The national law may require that the applicant furnish evidence in respect of any substantive condition of patentability prescribed by such law.

7.   Any receiving Office or, once the processing of the international application has started in the designated Office, that Office may apply the national law as far as it relates to any requirement that the applicant be represented by an agent having the right to represent applicants before the said Office and/or that the applicant have an address in the designated State for the purpose of receiving notifications.

8.   Nothing in the Treaty and the Regulations is intended to be construed as limiting the freedom of any Contracting State to apply measures deemed necessary for the preservation of its national security or to limit, for the protection of the general economic interests of that State, the right of its own residents or nationals to file international applications.

Article 28

Amendment of the Claims, the Description, and the Drawings, Before Designated Offices

1.   The applicant shall be given the opportunity to amend the claims, the description, and the drawings, before each designated Office within the prescribed time limit. No designated Office shall grant a patent, or refuse the grant of a patent, before such time has expired except with the express consent of the applicant.

2.   The amendments shall not go beyond the disclosure in the international application as filed unless the national law of the designated State permits them to go beyond the said disclosure.

3.   The amendments shall be in accordance with the national law of the designated State in all respects not provided for in this Treaty and the Regulations.

4.   Where the designated Office requires a translation of the international application, the amendments shall be in the language of the translation.

Article 29

Effects of the International Publication

1.   As far as the protection of any rights of the applicant in a designated State is concerned, the effects, in that State, of the international publication of an international application shall, subject to the provisions of paragraphs (2) to (4), be the same as those which the national law of the designated State provides for the compulsory national publication of unexamined national applications as such.

2.   If the language in which the international publication has been effected is different from the language in which publications under the national law are effected in the designated State, the said national law may provide that the effects provided for in paragraph (1) shall be applicable only from such time as:

(i)   a translation into the latter language has been published as provided by the national law, or

(ii)   a translation into the latter language has been made available to the public, by laying open for public inspection as provided by the national law, or

(iii)   a translation into the latter language has been transmitted by the applicant to the actual or prospective unauthorized user of the invention claimed in the international application, or

(iv)   both the acts described in (i) and (iii), or both the acts described in (ii) and (iii), have taken place.

3.   The national law of any designated State may provide that, where the international publication has been effected, on the request of the applicant, before the expiration of 18 months from the priority date, the effects provided for in paragraph (1) shall be applicable only from the expiration of 18 months from the priority date.

4.   The national law of any designated State may provide that the effects provided for in paragraph (1) shall be applicable only from the date on which a copy of the international application as published under Article 21 has been received in the national Office of or acting for such State. The said Office shall publish the date of receipt in its Official Gazette as soon as possible.

Article 30

Confidential Nature of the International Application

1.　(a) Subject to the provisions of sub-paragraph (b), the International Bureau and the International Searching Authorities shall not allow access by any person or authority to the international application before the international publication of that application, unless requested or authorized by the applicant.

(b)　The provisions of sub-paragraph (a) shall not apply to any transmittal to the competent International Searching Authority, to transmittals provided for under Article 13, and to communications provided for under Article 20.

2.　(a) No national Office shall allow access to the international application by third parties, unless requested or authorized by the applicant, before the earliest of the following dates:

    (i)　date of the international publication of the international application,

    (ii)　date of the receipt of the communication of the international application under Article 20,

    (iii)　date of the receipt of a copy of the international application under Article 22.

(b)　The provisions of sub-paragraph (a) shall not prevent any national Office from informing third parties that it has been designated, or from publishing that fact. Such information or publication may, however, contain only the following data: identification of the receiving Office, name of the applicant, international filing date, international application number, and title of the invention.

(c)　The provisions of sub-paragraph (a) shall not prevent any designated Office from allowing access to the international application for the purposes of the judicial authorities.

3.　The provisions of paragraph (2)(a) shall apply to any receiving Office except as far as transmittals provided for under Article 12(1) are concerned.

4.　For the purposes of this article, the term "access" covers any means by which third parties may acquire cognizance, including individual communication and general publication, provided, however, that no national Office shall generally publish an international application or its translation before the international publication or, if international publication has not taken place by the expiration of 20 months from the priority date, before the expiration of 20 months from the said priority date.

CHAPTER II.　INTERNATIONAL PRELIMINARY EXAMINATION

Article 31

Demand for International Preliminary Examination

1.　On the demand of the applicant, his international application shall be the subject of an international preliminary examination as provided in the following provisions and the Regulations.

2.　(a) Any applicant who is a resident or national, as defined in the Regulations, of a Contracting State bound by Chapter II, and whose international application has been filed with the receiving Office of or acting for such State, may make a demand for international preliminary examination.

(b)　The Assembly may decide to allow persons entitled to file international applications to make a demand for international preliminary examination even if they are residents or nationals of a State not party to this Treaty or not bound by Chapter II.

3.   The demand for international preliminary examination shall be made separately from the international application. The demand shall contain the prescribed particulars and shall be in the prescribed language and form.

4.   (a) The demand shall indicate the Contracting State or States in which the applicant intends to use the results of the international preliminary examination ("elected States"). Additional Contracting States may be elected later. Election may relate only to Contracting States already designated under Article 4.

(b)   Applicants referred to in paragraph (2)(a) may elect any Contracting State bound by Chapter II. Applicants referred to in paragraph (2)(b) may elect only such Contracting States bound by Chapter II as have declared that they are prepared to be elected by such applicants.

5.   The demand shall be subject to the payment of the prescribed fees within the prescribed time limit.

6.   (a) The demand shall be submitted to the competent International Preliminary Examining Authority referred to in Article 32.

(b)   Any later election shall be submitted to the International Bureau.

7.   Each elected Office shall be notified of its election.

Article 32

The International Preliminary Examining Authority

1.   International preliminary examination shall be carried out by the International Preliminary Examining Authority.

2.   In the case of demands referred to in Article 31(2)(a), the receiving Office, and, in the case of demands referred to in Article 31(2)(b), the Assembly, shall, in accordance with the applicable agreement between the interested International Preliminary Examining Authority or Authorities and the International Bureau, specify the International Preliminary Examining Authority or Authorities competent for the preliminary examination.

3.   The provisions of Article 16(3) shall apply, *mutatis mutandis,* in respect of International Preliminary Examining Authorities.

Article 33

The International Preliminary Examination

1.   The objective of the international preliminary examination is to formulate a preliminary and non-binding opinion on the questions whether the claimed invention appears to be novel, to involve an inventive step (to be non-obvious), and to be industrially applicable.

2.   For the purposes of the international preliminary examination, a claimed invention shall be considered novel if it is not anticipated by the prior art as defined in the Regulations.

3.   For the purposes of the international preliminary examination, a claimed invention shall be considered to involve an inventive step if, having regard to the prior art as defined in the Regulations, it is not, at the prescribed relevant date, obvious to a person skilled in the art.

4.   For the purposes of the international preliminary examination, a claimed invention shall be considered industrially applicable if, according to its nature, it can be made or used (in the technological sense) in any kind of industry. "Industry" shall be understood in its broadest sense, as in the Paris Convention for the Protection of Industrial Property.

5.   The criteria described above merely serve the purposes of international preliminary examination. Any Contracting State may apply additional or different criteria for the purpose of deciding whether, in that State, the claimed invention is patentable or not.

6.   The international preliminary examination shall take into consideration all the documents cited in the international search report. It may take into consideration any additional documents considered to be relevant in the particular case.

Article 34

Procedure Before the International Preliminary Examining Authority

1.   Procedure before the International Preliminary Examining Authority shall be governed by the provisions of this Treaty, the Regulations, and the agreement which the International Bureau shall conclude, subject to this Treaty and the Regulations, with the said Authority.

2.   (a) The applicant shall have a right to communicate orally and in writing with the International Preliminary Examining Authority.

(b)   The applicant shall have a right to amend the claims, the description, and the drawings, in the prescribed manner and within the prescribed time limit, before the international preliminary examination report is established. The amendment shall not go beyond the disclosure in the international application as filed.

(c)   The applicant shall receive at least one written opinion from the International Preliminary Examining Authority unless such Authority considers that all of the following conditions are fulfilled:

(i)   the invention satisfies the criteria set forth in Article 33(1),

(ii)   the international application complies with the requirements of this Treaty and the Regulations in so far as checked by that Authority,

(iii)   no observations are intended to be made under Article 35(2), last sentence.

(d)   The applicant may respond to the written opinion.

3.   (a) If the International Preliminary Examining Authority considers that the international application does not comply with the requirement of unity of invention as set forth in the Regulations, it may invite the applicant, at his option, to restrict the claims so as to comply with the requirement or to pay additional fees.

(b)   The national law of any elected State may provide that, where the applicant chooses to restrict the claims under sub-paragraph (a), those parts of the international application which, as a consequence of the restriction, are not to be the subject of international preliminary examination shall, as far as effects in that State are concerned, be considered withdrawn unless a special fee is paid by the applicant to the national Office of that State.

(c)   If the applicant does not comply with the invitation referred to in sub-paragraph (a) within the prescribed time limit, the International Preliminary Examining Authority shall establish an international preliminary examination report on those parts of the international application which relate to what appears to be the main invention and shall indicate the relevant facts in the said report. The national law of any elected State may provide that, where its national Office finds the invitation of the International Preliminary Examining Authority justified, those parts of the international application which do not relate to the main invention shall, as far as effects in that State are concerned, be considered withdrawn unless a special fee is paid by the applicant to that Office.

4.   (a) If the International Preliminary Examining Authority considers

(i)   that the international application relates to a subject matter on which the International Preliminary Examining Authority is not required, under the Regulations, to carry out an international preliminary examination, and in the particular case decided not to carry out such examination, or

(ii)   that the description, the claims, or the drawings, are so unclear, or the claims are so inadequately supported by the description, that no meaningful opinion can be formed on the novelty, inventive step (non-obviousness), or industrial applicability, of the claim invention,

the said Authority shall not go into the questions referred to in Article 33(1) and shall inform the applicant of this opinion and the reasons therefor.

(b)   If any of the situations referred to in sub-paragraph (a) is found to exist in, or in connection with, certain claims only, the provisions of that sub-paragraph shall apply only to the said claims.

Article 35

The International Preliminary Examination Report

1.   The international preliminary examination report shall be established within the prescribed time limit and in the prescribed form.

2.   The international preliminary examination report shall not contain any statement on the question whether the claimed invention is or seems to be patentable or unpatentable according to any national law. It shall state, subject to the provisions of paragraph (3), in relation to each claim, whether the claim appears to satisfy the criteria of novelty, inventive step (non-obviousness), and industrial applicability, as defined for the purposes of the international preliminary examination in Article 33(1) to (4). The statement shall be accompanied by the citation of the documents believed to support the stated conclusion with such explanations as the circumstances of the case may require. The statement shall also be accompanied by such other observations as the Regulations provide for.

3.   (a) If, at the time of establishing the international preliminary examination report, the International Preliminary Examining Authority considers that any of the situations referred to in Article 34(4)(a) exists, that report shall state this opinion and the reasons therefor. It shall not contain any statement as provided in paragraph (2).

(b)   If a situation under Article 34(4)(b) is found to exist, the international preliminary examination report shall, in relation to the claims in question, contain the statement as provided in sub-paragraph (a), whereas, in relation to the other claims, it shall contain the statement as provided in paragraph (2).

Article 36

Transmittal, Translation, and Communication, of the International Preliminary Examination Report

1.   The international preliminary examination report, together with the prescribed annexes, shall be transmitted to the applicant and to the International Bureau.

2.   (a) The international preliminary examination report and its annexes shall be translated into the prescribed languages.

(b)   Any translation of the said report shall be prepared by or under the responsibility of the International Bureau, whereas any translation of the said annexes shall be prepared by the applicant.

3. (a) The international preliminary examination report, together with its translation (as prescribed) and its annexes (in the original language), shall be communicated by the International Bureau to each elected Office.

(b) The prescribed translation of the annexes shall be transmitted within the prescribed time limit by the applicant to the elected Offices.

4. The provisions of Article 20(3) shall apply, *mutatis mutandis*, to copies of any document which is cited in the international preliminary examination report and which was not cited in the international search report.

Article 37

Withdrawal of Demand or Election

1. The applicant may withdraw any or all elections.

2. If the election of all elected States is withdrawn, the demand shall be considered withdrawn.

3. (a) Any withdrawal shall be notified to the International Bureau.

(b) The elected Offices concerned and the International Preliminary Examining Authority concerned shall be notified accordingly by the International Bureau.

4. (a) Subject to the provisions of sub-paragraph (b), withdrawal of the demand or of the election of a Contracting State shall, unless the national law of that State provides otherwise, be considered to be withdrawal of the international application as far as that State is concerned.

(b) Withdrawal of the demand or of the election shall not be considered to be withdrawal of the international application if such withdrawal is effected prior to the expiration of the applicable time limit under Article 22; however, any Contracting State may provide in its national law that the aforesaid shall apply only if its national Office has received, within the said time limit, a copy of the international application, together with a translation (as prescribed), and the national fee.

Article 38

Confidential Nature of the International
Preliminary Examination

1. Neither the International Bureau nor the International Preliminary Examining Authority shall, unless requested or authorized by the applicant, allow access within the meaning, and with the proviso, of Article 30(4) to the file of the international preliminary examination by any person or authority at any time, except by the elected Offices once the international preliminary examination report has been established.

2. Subject to the provisions of paragraph (1) and Articles 36(1) and (3) and 37(3)(b), neither the International Bureau nor the International Preliminary Examining Authority shall, unless requested or authorized by the applicant, give information on the issuance or nonissuance of an international preliminary examination report and on the withdrawal or non-withdrawal of the demand or of any election.

Article 39

Copy, Translation and Fee to Elected Offices

1. (a) If the election of any Contracting State has been effected prior to the expiration of the 19th month from the priority date, the provisions of Article 22 shall not apply to such State and the applicant shall furnish a copy of the international application (unless the communication under Article

20 has already taken place) and a translation thereof (as prescribed), and pay the national fee (if any), to each elected Office not later than at the expiration of 30 months from the priority date.

(b)   Any national law may, for performing the acts referred to in subparagraph (a), fix time limits which expire later than the time limit provided for in that sub-paragraph.

2.   The effect provided for in Article 11(3) shall cease in the elected State with the same consequences as the withdrawal of any national application in that State if the applicant fails to perform the acts referred to in paragraph (1)(a) within the time limit applicable under paragraph (1)(a) or (b).

3.   Any elected Office may maintain the effect provided for in Article 11(3) even where the applicant does not comply with the requirements provided for in paragraph (1)(a) or (b).

Article 40

Delaying of National Examination and Other Processing

1.   If the election of any Contracting State has been effected prior to the expiration of the 19th month from the priority date, the provisions of Article 23 shall not apply to such State and the national Office of or acting for that State shall not proceed, subject to the provisions of paragraph (2), to the examination and other processing of the international application prior to the expiration of the applicable time limit under Article 39.

2.   Notwithstanding the provisions of paragraph (1), any elected Office may, on the express request of the applicant, proceed to the examination and other processing of the international application at any time.

Article 41

Amendment of the Claims, the Description and the Drawings, Before Elected Offices

1.   The applicant shall be given the opportunity to amend the claims, the description, and the drawings before each elected Office within the prescribed time limit. No elected Office shall grant a patent, or refuse the grant of a patent, before such time limit has expired, except with the express consent of the applicant.

2.   The amendments shall not go beyond the disclosure in the international application as filed, unless the national law of the elected State permits them to go beyond the said disclosure.

3.   The amendments shall be in accordance with the national law of the elected State in all respects not provided for in this Treaty and the Regulations.

4.   Where an elected Office requires a translation of the international application, the amendments shall be in the language of the translation.

Article 42

Results of National Examination in Elected Offices

No elected Office receiving the international preliminary examination report may require that the applicant furnish copies, or information on the contents, of any papers connected with the examination relating to the same international application in any other elected Office.

CHAPTER III.   COMMON PROVISIONS

Article 43

Seeking Certain Kinds of Protection

In respect of any designated or elected State whose law provides for the grant of inventors' certificates, utility certificates, utility models, patents or certificates of addition, inventors' certificates of addition, or utility certificates of addition, the applicant may indicate, as prescribed in the Regulations, that his international application is for the grant, as far as that State is concerned, of an inventor's certificate, a utility certificate, or a utility model, rather than a patent, or that it is for the grant of a patent or certificate of addition, an inventor's certificate of addition, or a utility certificate of addition, and the ensuing effect shall be governed by the applicant's choice. For the purposes of this article and any Rule thereunder, Article 2(ii) shall not apply.

Article 44

Seeking Two Kinds of Protection

In respect of any designated or elected State whose law permits an application, while being for the grant of a patent or one of the other kinds of protection referred to in Article 43, to be also for the grant of another of the said kinds of protection, the applicant may indicate, as prescribed in the Regulations, the two kinds of protection he is seeking, and the ensuing effect shall be governed by the applicant's indications. For the purposes of this article, Article 2(ii) shall not apply.

Article 45

Regional Patent Treaties

1.   Any treaty providing for the grant of regional patents ("regional patent treaty"), and giving to all persons who, according to Article 9, are entitled to file international applications the right to file applications for such patents, may provide that international applications designating or electing a State party to both the regional patent treaty and the present Treaty may be filed as applications for such patents.

2.   The national law of the said designated or elected State may provide that any designation or election of such State in the international application shall have the effect of an indication of the wish to obtain a regional patent under the regional patent treaty.

Article 46

Incorrect Translation of the International Application

If, because of an incorrect translation of the international application, the scope of any patent granted on that application exceeds the scope of the international application in its original language, the competent authorities of the Contracting State concerned may accordingly and retroactively limit the scope of the patent, and declare it null and void to the extent that its scope has exceeded the scope of the international application in its original language.

Article 47

Time Limits

1.   The details for computing time limits referred to in this Treaty are governed by the Regulations.

2.   (a) All time limits fixed in Chapters I and II of this Treaty may, outside any revision under Article 60, be modified by a decision of the Contracting States.

(b)   Such decisions shall be made in the Assembly or through voting by correspondence and must be unanimous.

(c)   The details of the procedure are governed by the Regulations.

Article 48

Delay in Meeting Certain Time Limits

1.   Where any time limit fixed in this Treaty or the Regulations is not met because of interruption in the mail service or unavoidable loss or delay in the mail, the time limit shall be deemed to be met in the cases and subject to the proof and other conditions prescribed in the Regulations.

2.   (a) Any Contracting State shall, as far as that State is concerned, excuse for reasons admitted under its national law, any delay in meeting any time limit.

(b)   Any Contracting State may, as far as that State is concerned, excuse, for reasons other than those referred to in sub-paragraph (a), any delay in meeting any time limit.

Article 49

Right to Practice Before International Authorities

Any attorney, patent agent, or other person, having the right to practice before the national Office with which the international application was filed, shall be entitled to practice before the International Bureau and the competent International Searching Authority and competent International Preliminary Examining Authority in respect of that application.

CHAPTER IV.   TECHNICAL SERVICES

Article 50

Patent Information Services

1.   The International Bureau may furnish services by providing technical and any other pertinent information available to it on the basis of published documents, primarily patents and published applications (referred to in this article as "the information services").

2.   The International Bureau may provide these information services either directly or through one or more International Searching Authorities or other national or international specialized institutions, with which the International Bureau may reach agreement.

3.   The information services shall be operated in a way particularly facilitating the acquisition by Contracting States which are developing countries of technical knowledge and technology, including available published know-how.

4.   The information services shall be available to Governments of Contracting States and their nationals and residents. The Assembly may decide to make these services available also to others.

5.   (a) Any service to Governments of Contracting States shall be furnished at cost, provided that, when the Government is that of a Contracting State which is a developing country, the service shall be furnished below cost if the difference can be covered from profit made on services furnished to others than Governments of Contracting States or from the sources referred to in Article 51(4).

(b)   The cost referred to in sub-paragraph (a) is to be understood as cost over and above costs normally incident to the performance of the services of a national Office or the obligations of an International Searching Authority.

6.   The details concerning the implementation of the provisions of this article shall be governed by decisions of the Assembly and, within the limits to be fixed by the Assembly, such working groups as the Assembly may set up for that purpose.

7.   The Assembly shall, when it considers it necessary, recommend methods of providing financing supplementary to those referred to in paragraph (5).

Article 51

Technical Assistance

1.   The Assembly shall establish a Committee for Technical Assistance (referred to in this article as "the Committee").

2.   (a) The members of the Committee shall be elected among the Contracting States, with due regard to the representation of developing countries.

(b)   The Director General shall, on his own initiative or at the request of the Committee, invite representatives of intergovernmental organizations concerned with technical assistance to developing countries to participate in the work of the Committee.

3.   (a) The task of the Committee shall be to organize and supervise technical assistance for Contracting States which are developing countries in developing their patent systems individually or on a regional basis.

(b)   The technical assistance shall comprise, among other things, the training of specialists, the loaning of experts, and the supply of equipment both for demonstration and for operational purposes.

4.   The International Bureau shall seek to enter into agreements, on the one hand, with international financing organizations and intergovernmental organizations, particularly the United Nations, the agencies of the United Nations, and the Specialized Agencies connected with the United Nations concerned with technical assistance, and, on the other hand, with the Governments of the States receiving the technical assistance, for the financing of projects pursuant to this article.

5.   The details concerning the implementation of the provisions of this article shall be governed by decisions of the Assembly and, within the limits to be fixed by the Assembly, such working groups as the Assembly may set up for that purpose.

Article 52

Relations With Other Provisions of the Treaty

Nothing in this chapter shall affect the financial provisions contained in any other chapter of this Treaty. Such provisions are not applicable to the present chapter or to its implementation.

[CHAPTER V.   ARTICLES 53–58 HAVE BEEN OMITTED]

CHAPTER VI.   DISPUTES

Article 59

Disputes

Subject to Article 64(5), any dispute between two or more Contracting States concerning the interpretation or application of this Treaty or Regulations, not settled by negotiation, may, by any one of the States concerned, be brought before the International Court of Justice by application in conformity with the Statute of the Court, unless the States concerned agree on some other method of settlement. The Contracting State bringing the dispute before the Court shall inform the International Bureau; the International Bureau shall bring the matter to the attention of the other Contracting States.

CHAPTER VII.   REVISION AND AMENDMENT

Article 60

Revision of the Treaty

1.   This Treaty may be revised from time to time by a special conference of the Contracting States.

2.   The convocation of any revision conference shall be decided by the Assembly.

3.   Any intergovernmental organization appointed as International Searching or Preliminary Examining Authority shall be admitted as observer to any revision conference.

4.   Articles 53(5), (9) and (11), 54, 55(4) to (8), 56, and 57, may be amended either by a revision conference or according to the provisions of Article 61.

Article 61

Amendment of Certain Provisions of the Treaty

1.   (a) Proposals for the amendment of Articles 53(5), (9) and (11), 54, 55(4) to (8), 56, and 57, may be initiated by any State member of the Assembly, by the Executive Committee, or by the Director General.

(b)   Such proposals shall be communicated by the Director General to the Contracting States at least six months in advance of their consideration by the Assembly.

2.   (a) Amendments to the articles referred to in paragraph (1) shall be adopted by the Assembly.

(b)   Adoption shall require three-fourths of the votes cast.

[CHAPTER VIII.   ARTICLES 62–69
HAVE BEEN OMITTED]

E. HAGUE AGREEMENT ON THE INTERNATIONAL REGISTRATION OF INDUSTRIAL DESIGNS

Geneva Act of July 2, 1999

Table of Contents

INTRODUCTORY PROVISIONS

Article 1

Abbreviated Expressions

For the purposes of this Act:

(i) "the Hague Agreement" means the Hague Agreement Concerning the International Deposit of Industrial Designs, henceforth renamed the Hague Agreement Concerning the International Registration of Industrial Designs;

(ii) "this Act" means the Hague Agreement as established by the present Act;

(iii) "Regulations" means the Regulations under this Act;

(iv) "prescribed" means prescribed in the Regulations;

(v) "Paris Convention" means the Paris Convention for the Protection of Industrial Property, signed at Paris on March 20, 1883, as revised and amended;

(vi) "international registration" means the international registration of an industrial design effected according to this Act;

(vii) "international application" means an application for international registration;

(viii) "International Register" means the official collection of data concerning international registrations maintained by the International Bureau, which data this Act or the Regulations require or permit to be recorded, regardless of the medium in which such data are stored;

(ix) "person" means a natural person or a legal entity;

(x) "applicant" means the person in whose name an international application is filed

(xi) "holder" means the person in whose name an international registration is recorded in the International Register;

(xii) "intergovernmental organization" means an intergovernmental organization eligible to become party to this Act in accordance with Article 27(1)(ii);

(xiii) "Contracting Party" means any State or intergovernmental organization party to this Act;

(xiv) "applicant's Contracting Party" means the Contracting Party or one of the Contracting Parties from which the applicant derives its entitlement to file an international application by virtue of satisfying, in relation to that Contracting Party, at least one of the conditions specified in Article 3; where there are two or more Contracting Parties from which the applicant may, under Article 3, derive its entitlement to file an international application, "applicant's Contracting Party" means the one which, among those Contracting Parties, is indicated as such in the international application;

(xv) "territory of a Contracting Party" means, where the Contracting Party is a State, the territory of that State and, where the Contracting Party is an intergovernmental organization, the territory in which the constituent treaty of that intergovernmental organization applies;

(xvi) "Office" means the agency entrusted by a Contracting Party with the grant of protection for industrial designs with effect in the territory of that Contracting Party;

(xvii) "Examining Office" means an Office which *ex officio* examines applications filed with it for the protection of industrial designs at least to determine whether the industrial designs satisfy the condition of novelty;

(xviii) "designation" means a request that an international registration have effect in a Contracting Party; it also means the recording, in the International Register, of that request;

(xix) "designated Contracting Party" and "designated Office" means the Contracting Party and the Office of the Contracting Party, respectively, to which a designation applies;

(xx) "1934 Act" means the Act signed at London on June 2, 1934, of the Hague Agreement;

(xxi) "1960 Act" means the Act signed at The Hague on November 28, 1960, of the Hague Agreement;

(xxii) "1961 Additional Act" means the Act signed at Monaco on November 18, 1961, additional to the 1934 Act;

(xxiii) "Complementary Act of 1967" means the Complementary Act signed at Stockholm on July 14, 1967, as amended, of the Hague Agreement;

(xxiv) "Union" means the Hague Union established by the Hague Agreement of November 6, 1925, and maintained by the 1934 and 1960 Acts, the 1961 Additional Act, the Complementary Act of 1967 and this Act;

(xxv) "Assembly" means the Assembly referred to in Article 21(1)(a) or any body replacing that Assembly;

(xxvi) "Organization" means the World Intellectual Property Organization;

(xxvii) "Director General" means the Director General of the Organization;

(xxviii) "International Bureau" means the International Bureau of the Organization;

(xxix) "instrument of ratification" shall be construed as including instruments of acceptance or approval.

Article 2

Applicability of Other Protection Accorded by Laws of Contracting Parties and by Certain International Treaties

(1) [*Laws of Contracting Parties and Certain International Treaties*] The provisions of this Act shall not affect the application of any greater protection which may be accorded by the law of a Contracting Party, nor shall they affect in any way the protection accorded to works of art and works of applied art by international copyright treaties and conventions, or the protection accorded to industrial designs under the Agreement on Trade-Related Aspects of Intellectual Property Rights annexed to the Agreement Establishing the World Trade Organization.

(2) [*Obligation to Comply with the Paris Convention*] Each Contracting Party shall comply with the provisions of the Paris Convention which concern industrial designs.

CHAPTER I

INTERNATIONAL APPLICATION AND INTERNATIONAL REGISTRATION

Article 3

Entitlement to File an International Application

Any person that is a national of a State that is a Contracting Party or of a State member of an intergovernmental organization that is a Contracting Party, or that has a domicile, a habitual residence or a real and effective industrial or commercial establishment in the territory of a Contracting Party, shall be entitled to file an international application.

Article 4

Procedure for Filing the International Application

(1) [*Direct or Indirect Filing*] (a) The international application may be filed, at the option of the applicant, either directly with the International Bureau or through the Office of the applicant's Contracting Party.

(b) Notwithstanding subparagraph (a), any Contracting Party may, in a declaration, notify the Director General that international applications may not be filed through its Office.

(2) [*Transmittal Fee in Case of Indirect Filing*] The Office of any Contracting Party may require that the applicant pay a transmittal fee to it, for its own benefit, in respect of any international application filed through it.

Article 5

Contents of the International Application

(1) [*Mandatory Contents of the International Application*] The international application shall be in the prescribed language or one of the prescribed languages and shall contain or be accompanied by

(i)   a request for international registration under this Act;

(ii) the prescribed data concerning the applicant;

(iii) the prescribed number of copies of a reproduction or, at the choice of the applicant, of several different reproductions of the industrial design that is the subject of the international application, presented in the prescribed manner; however, where the industrial design is two-dimensional and a request for deferment of publication is made in accordance with paragraph (5), the international application may, instead of containing reproductions, be accompanied by the prescribed number of specimens of the industrial design;

(iv) an indication of the product or products which constitute the industrial design or in relation to which the industrial design is to be used, as prescribed;

(v)   an indication of the designated Contracting Parties;

(vi) the prescribed fees;

(vii) any other prescribed particulars.

(2) [*Additional Mandatory Contents of the International Application*] (a) Any Contracting Party whose Office is an Examining Office and whose law, at the time it becomes party to this Act, requires that an application for the grant of protection to an industrial design contain any of the elements specified in subparagraph (b) in order for that application to be accorded a filing date under that law may, in a declaration, notify the Director General of those elements.

(b) The elements that may be notified pursuant to subparagraph (a) are the following:

(i)   indications concerning the identity of the creator of the industrial design that is the subject of that application;

(ii) a brief description of the reproduction or of the characteristic features of the industrial design that is the subject of that application;

(iii) a claim.

(c) Where the international application contains the designation of a Contracting Party that has made a notification under subparagraph (a), it shall also contain, in the prescribed manner, any element that was the subject of that notification.

(3) [*Other Possible Contents of the International Application*] The international application may contain or be accompanied by such other elements as are specified in the Regulations.

(4) [*Several Industrial Designs in the Same International Application*] Subject to such conditions as may be prescribed, an international application may include two or more industrial designs.

(5) [*Request for Deferred Publication*] The international application may contain a request for deferment of publication.

Article 6

Priority

(1) [*Claiming of Priority*] (a) The international application may contain a declaration claiming, under Article 4 of the Paris Convention, the priority of one or more earlier applications filed in or for any country party to that Convention or any Member of the World Trade Organization.

(b) The Regulations may provide that the declaration referred to in subparagraph (a) may be made after the filing of the international application. In such case, the Regulations shall prescribe the latest time by which such declaration may be made.

(2) [*International Application Serving as a Basis for Claiming Priority*] The international application shall, as from its filing date and whatever may be its subsequent fate, be equivalent to a regular filing within the meaning of Article 4 of the Paris Convention.

Article 7

Designation Fees

(1) [*Prescribed Designation Fee*] The prescribed fees shall include, subject to paragraph (2), a designation fee for each designated Contracting Party.

(2)[1] [*Individual Designation Fee*] Any Contracting Party whose Office is an Examining Office and any Contracting Party that is an intergovernmental organization may, in a declaration, notify the Director General that, in connection with any international application in which it is designated, and in connection with the renewal of any international registration resulting from such an international application, the prescribed designation fee referred to in paragraph (1) shall be replaced by an individual designation fee, whose amount shall be indicated in the declaration and can be changed in further declarations. The said amount may be fixed by the said Contracting Party for the initial term of protection and for each term of renewal or for the maximum period of protection allowed by the Contracting Party concerned. However, it may not be higher than the equivalent of the amount which the Office of that Contracting Party would be entitled to receive from an applicant for a grant of protection for an equivalent period to the same number of industrial designs, that amount being diminished by the savings resulting from the international procedure.

---

[1]   [WIPO Note]: Recommendation adopted by the Assembly of the Hague Union:

   "Contracting Parties that make, or that have made, a declaration under Article 7(2) of the 1999 Act or under Rule 36(1) of the Common Regulations are encouraged to indicate, in that declaration or in a new declaration, that for international applications filed by applicants whose sole entitlement is a connection with a Least Developed Country, in accordance with the list established by the United Nations, or with an intergovernmental organization the majority of whose member States are Least Developed Countries, the individual fee payable with respect to their designation is reduced to 10% of the fixed amount (rounded, where appropriate, to the nearest full figure). Those Contracting Parties are further encouraged to indicate that the reduction also applies in respect of an international application filed by an applicant whose entitlement is not solely a connection with such an intergovernmental organization, provided that any other entitlement of the applicant is a connection with a Contracting Party which is a Least Developed Country or, if not a Least Developed Country, is a member State of that intergovernmental organization and the international application is governed exclusively by the 1999 Act."

(3) [*Transfer of Designation Fees*] The designation fees referred to in paragraphs (1) and (2) shall be transferred by the International Bureau to the Contracting Parties in respect of which those fees were paid.

Article 8

Correction of Irregularities

(1) [*Examination of the International Application*] If the International Bureau finds that the international application does not, at the time of its receipt by the International Bureau, fulfill the requirements of this Act and the Regulations, it shall invite the applicant to make the required corrections within the prescribed time limit.

(2) [*Irregularities Not Corrected*] (a) If the applicant does not comply with the invitation within the prescribed time limit, the international application shall, subject to subparagraph (b), be considered abandoned.

    (b) In the case of an irregularity which relates to Article 5(2) or to a special requirement notified to the Director General by a Contracting Party in accordance with the Regulations, if the applicant does not comply with the invitation within the prescribed time limit, the international application shall be deemed not to contain the designation of that Contracting Party.

Article 9

Filing Date of the International Application

(1) [*International Application Filed Directly*] Where the international application is filed directly with the International Bureau, the filing date shall, subject to paragraph (3), be the date on which the International Bureau receives the international application.

(2) [*International Application Filed Indirectly*] Where the international application is filed through the Office of the applicant's Contracting Party, the filing date shall be determined as prescribed.

(3) [*International Application with Certain Irregularities*] Where the international application has, on the date on which it is received by the International Bureau, an irregularity which is prescribed as an irregularity entailing a postponement of the filing date of the international application, the filing date shall be the date on which the correction of such irregularity is received by the International Bureau.

Article 10[2]

International Registration, Date of the International Registration, Publication and Confidential Copies of the International Registration

(1) [*International Registration*] The International Bureau shall register each industrial design that is the subject of an international application immediately upon receipt by it of the international application or, where corrections are invited under Article 8, immediately upon receipt of the required corrections. The registration shall be effected whether or not publication is deferred under Article 11.

(2) [*Date of the International Registration*] (a) Subject to subparagraph (b), the date of the international registration shall be the filing date of the international application.

---

   [2] When adopting Article 10, the Diplomatic Conference understood that nothing in this Article precludes access to the international application or the international registration by the applicant or the holder or a person having the consent of the applicant or the holder.

(b) Where the international application has, on the date on which it is received by the International Bureau, an irregularity which relates to Article 5(2), the date of the international registration shall be the date on which the correction of such irregularity is received by the International Bureau or the filing date of the international application, whichever is the later.

(3) [*Publication*] (a) The international registration shall be published by the International Bureau. Such publication shall be deemed in all Contracting Parties to be sufficient publicity, and no other publicity may be required of the holder.

(b) The International Bureau shall send a copy of the publication of the international registration to each designated Office.

(4) [*Maintenance of Confidentiality Before Publication*] Subject to paragraph (5) and Article 11(4)(b), the International Bureau shall keep in confidence each international application and each international registration until publication.

(5) [*Confidential Copies*] (a) The International Bureau shall, immediately after registration has been effected, send a copy of the international registration, along with any relevant statement, document or specimen accompanying the international application, to each Office that has notified the International Bureau that it wishes to receive such a copy and has been designated in the international application.

(b) The Office shall, until publication of the international registration by the International Bureau, keep in confidence each international registration of which a copy has been sent to it by the International Bureau and may use the said copy only for the purpose of the examination of the international registration and of applications for the protection of industrial designs filed in or for the Contracting Party for which the Office is competent. In particular, it may not divulge the contents of any such international registration to any person outside the Office other than the holder of that international registration, except for the purposes of an administrative or legal proceeding involving a conflict over entitlement to file the international application on which the international registration is based. In the case of such an administrative or legal proceeding, the contents of the international registration may only be disclosed in confidence to the parties involved in the proceeding who shall be bound to respect the confidentiality of the disclosure.

Article 11

Deferment of Publication

(1) [*Provisions of Laws of Contracting Parties Concerning Deferment of Publication*]

(a) Where the law of a Contracting Party provides for the deferment of the publication of an industrial design for a period which is less than the prescribed period, that Contracting Party shall, in a declaration, notify the Director General of the allowable period of deferment.

(b) Where the law of a Contracting Party does not provide for the deferment of the publication of an industrial design, the Contracting Party shall, in a declaration, notify the Director General of that fact.

(2) [*Deferment of Publication*] Where the international application contains a request for deferment of publication, the publication shall take place,

(i) where none of the Contracting Parties designated in the international application has made a declaration under paragraph (1), at the expiry of the prescribed period or,

(ii) where any of the Contracting Parties designated in the international application has made a declaration under paragraph (1)(a), at the expiry of the period notified in such declaration or, where there is more than one such designated Contracting Party, at the expiry of the shortest period notified in their declarations.

(3) [*Treatment of Requests for Deferment Where Deferment Is Not Possible Under Applicable Law*] Where deferment of publication has been requested and any of the Contracting Parties designated in the international application has made a declaration under paragraph (1)(b) that deferment of publication is not possible under its law,

    (i)   subject to item (ii), the International Bureau shall notify the applicant accordingly; if, within the prescribed period, the applicant does not, by notice in writing to the International Bureau, withdraw the designation of the said Contracting Party, the International Bureau shall disregard the request for deferment of publication;

    (ii)   where, instead of containing reproductions of the industrial design, the international application was accompanied by specimens of the industrial design, the International Bureau shall disregard the designation of the said Contracting Party and shall notify the applicant accordingly.

(4) [*Request for Earlier Publication or for Special Access to the International Registration*] (a) At any time during the period of deferment applicable under paragraph (2), the holder may request publication of any or all of the industrial designs that are the subject of the international registration, in which case the period of deferment in respect of such industrial design or designs shall be considered to have expired on the date of receipt of such request by the International Bureau.

    (b)   The holder may also, at any time during the period of deferment applicable under paragraph (2), request the International Bureau to provide a third party specified by the holder with an extract from, or to allow such a party access to, any or all of the industrial designs that are the subject of the international registration.

(5) [*Renunciation and Limitation*] (a) If, at any time during the period of deferment applicable under paragraph (2), the holder renounces the international registration in respect of all the designated Contracting Parties, the industrial design or designs that are the subject of the international registration shall not be published.

    (b)   If, at any time during the period of deferment applicable under paragraph (2), the holder limits the international registration, in respect of all of the designated Contracting Parties, to one or some of the industrial designs that are the subject of the international registration, the other industrial design or designs that are the subject of the international registration shall not be published.

(6) [*Publication and Furnishing of Reproductions*] (a) At the expiration of any period of deferment applicable under the provisions of this Article, the International Bureau shall, subject to the payment of the prescribed fees, publish the international registration. If such fees are not paid as prescribed, the international registration shall be canceled and publication shall not take place.

    (b)   Where the international application was accompanied by one or more specimens of the industrial design in accordance with Article 5(1)(iii), the holder shall submit the prescribed number of copies of a reproduction of each industrial design that is the subject of that application to the International Bureau within the prescribed time limit. To the extent that the holder does not do so, the international registration shall be canceled and publication shall not take place.

Article 12

Refusal

(1) [*Right to Refuse*] The Office of any designated Contracting Party may, where the conditions for the grant of protection under the law of that Contracting Party are not met in respect

of any or all of the industrial designs that are the subject of an international registration, refuse the effects, in part or in whole, of the international registration in the territory of the said Contracting Party, provided that no Office may refuse the effects, in part or in whole, of any international registration on the ground that requirements relating to the form or contents of the international application that are provided for in this Act or the Regulations or are additional to, or different from, those requirements have not been satisfied under the law of the Contracting Party concerned.

(2) [*Notification of Refusal*] (a) The refusal of the effects of an international registration shall be communicated by the Office to the International Bureau in a notification of refusal within the prescribed period.

(b) Any notification of refusal shall state all the grounds on which the refusal is based.

(3) [*Transmission of Notification of Refusal; Remedies*] (a) The International Bureau shall, without delay, transmit a copy of the notification of refusal to the holder.

(b) The holder shall enjoy the same remedies as if any industrial design that is the subject of the international registration had been the subject of an application for the grant of protection under the law applicable to the Office that communicated the refusal. Such remedies shall at least consist of the possibility of a re-examination or a review of the refusal or an appeal against the refusal.

(4)[3] [*Withdrawal of Refusal*] Any refusal may be withdrawn, in part or in whole, at any time by the Office that communicated it.

Article 13

Special Requirements Concerning Unity of Design

(1) [*Notification of Special Requirements*] Any Contracting Party whose law, at the time it becomes party to this Act, requires that designs that are the subject of the same application conform to a requirement of unity of design, unity of production or unity of use, or belong to the same set or composition of items, or that only one independent and distinct design may be claimed in a single application, may, in a declaration, notify the Director General accordingly. However, no such declaration shall affect the right of an applicant to include two or more industrial designs in an international application in accordance with Article 5(4), even if the application designates the Contracting Party that has made the declaration.

(2) [*Effect of Declaration*] Any such declaration shall enable the Office of the Contracting Party that has made it to refuse the effects of the international registration pursuant to Article 12(1) pending compliance with the requirement notified by that Contracting Party.

(3) [*Further Fees Payable on Division of Registration*] Where, following a notification of refusal in accordance with paragraph (2), an international registration is divided before the Office concerned in order to overcome a ground of refusal stated in the notification, that Office shall be entitled to charge a fee in respect of each additional international application that would have been necessary in order to avoid that ground of refusal.

---

[3] When adopting Article 12(4), Article 14(2)(b) and Rule 18(4), the Diplomatic Conference understood that a withdrawal of refusal by an Office that has communicated a notification of refusal may take the form of a statement to the effect that the Office concerned has decided to accept the effects of the international registration in respect of the industrial designs, or some of the industrial designs, to which the notification of refusal related. It was also understood that an Office may, within the period allowed for communicating a notification of refusal, send a statement to the effect that it has decided to accept the effects of the international registration even where it has not communicated such a notification of refusal.

Article 14

Effects of the International Registration

(1) [*Effect as Application Under Applicable Law*] The international registration shall, from the date of the international registration, have at least the same effect in each designated Contracting Party as a regularly-filed application for the grant of protection of the industrial design under the law of that Contracting Party.

(2) [*Effect as Grant of Protection Under Applicable Law*] (a) In each designated Contracting Party the Office of which has not communicated a refusal in accordance with Article 12, the international registration shall have the same effect as a grant of protection for the industrial design under the law of that Contracting Party at the latest from the date of expiration of the period allowed for it to communicate a refusal or, where a Contracting Party has made a corresponding declaration under the Regulations, at the latest at the time specified in that declaration.

(b)[4] Where the Office of a designated Contracting Party has communicated a refusal and has subsequently withdrawn, in part or in whole, that refusal, the international registration shall, to the extent that the refusal is withdrawn, have the same effect in that Contracting Party as a grant of protection for the industrial design under the law of the said Contracting Party at the latest from the date on which the refusal was withdrawn.

(c) The effect given to the international registration under this paragraph shall apply to the industrial design or designs that are the subject of that registration as received from the International Bureau by the designated Office or, where applicable, as amended in the procedure before that Office.

(3) [*Declaration Concerning Effect of Designation of Applicant's Contracting Party*] (a) Any Contracting Party whose Office is an Examining Office may, in a declaration, notify the Director General that, where it is the applicant's Contracting Party, the designation of that Contracting Party in an international registration shall have no effect.

(b) Where a Contracting Party having made the declaration referred to in subparagraph (a) is indicated in an international application both as the applicant's Contracting Party and as a designated Contracting Party, the International Bureau shall disregard the designation of that Contracting Party.

Article 15

Invalidation

(1) [*Requirement of Opportunity of Defense*] Invalidation, by the competent authorities of a designated Contracting Party, of the effects, in part or in whole, in the territory of that Contracting Party, of the international registration may not be pronounced without the holder having, in good time, been afforded the opportunity of defending his rights.

(2) [*Notification of Invalidation*] The Office of the Contracting Party in whose territory the effects of the international registration have been invalidated shall, where it is aware of the invalidation, notify it to the International Bureau.

Article 16

Recording of Changes and Other Matters Concerning International Registrations

(1) [*Recording of Changes and Other Matters*] The International Bureau shall, as prescribed, record in the International Register

---

[4] See footnote on page 20.

(i)   any change in ownership of the international registration, in respect of any or all of the designated Contracting Parties and in respect of any or all of the industrial designs that are the subject of the international registration, provided that the new owner is entitled to file an international application under Article 3,

(ii)   any change in the name or address of the holder,

(iii) the appointment of a representative of the applicant or holder and any other relevant fact concerning such representative,

(iv) any renunciation, by the holder, of the international registration, in respect of any or all of the designated Contracting Parties,

(v)   any limitation, by the holder, of the international registration, in respect of any or all of the designated Contracting Parties, to one or some of the industrial designs that are the subject of the international registration,

(vi) any invalidation, by the competent authorities of a designated Contracting Party, of the effects, in the territory of that Contracting Party, of the international registration in respect of any or all of the industrial designs that are the subject of the international registration,

(vii) any other relevant fact, identified in the Regulations, concerning the rights in any or all of the industrial designs that are the subject of the international registration.

(2) [*Effect of Recording in International Register*] Any recording referred to in items (i), (ii), (iv), (v), (vi) and (vii) of paragraph (1) shall have the same effect as if it had been made in the Register of the Office of each of the Contracting Parties concerned, except that a Contracting Party may, in a declaration, notify the Director General that a recording referred to in item (i) of paragraph (1) shall not have that effect in that Contracting Party until the Office of that Contracting Party has received the statements or documents specified in that declaration.

(3) [*Fees*] Any recording made under paragraph (1) may be subject to the payment of a fee.

(4) [*Publication*] The International Bureau shall publish a notice concerning any recording made under paragraph (1). It shall send a copy of the publication of the notice to the Office of each of the Contracting Parties concerned.

Article 17

*Initial Term and Renewal of the International
Registration and Duration of Protection*

(1) [*Initial Term of the International Registration*] The international registration shall be effected for an initial term of five years counted from the date of the international registration.

(2) [*Renewal of the International Registration*] The international registration may be renewed for additional terms of five years, in accordance with the prescribed procedure and subject to the payment of the prescribed fees.

(3) [*Duration of Protection in Designated Contracting Parties*] (a) Provided that the international registration is renewed, and subject to subparagraph (b), the duration of protection shall, in each of the designated Contracting Parties, be 15 years counted from the date of the international registration.

(b) Where the law of a designated Contracting Party provides for a duration of protection of more than 15 years for an industrial design for which protection has been granted under that law, the duration of protection shall, provided that the international registration is renewed, be the same as that provided for by the law of that Contracting Party.

(c)   Each Contracting Party shall, in a declaration, notify the Director General of the maximum duration of protection provided for by its law.

(4)   [*Possibility of Limited Renewal*]   The renewal of the international registration may be effected for any or all of the designated Contracting Parties and for any or all of the industrial designs that are the subject of the international registration.

(5)   [*Recording and Publication of Renewal*] The International Bureau shall record renewals in the International Register and publish a notice to that effect. It shall send a copy of the publication of the notice to the Office of each of the Contracting Parties concerned.

Article 18

Information Concerning Published International Registrations

(1)   [*Access to Information*] The International Bureau shall supply to any person applying therefor, upon the payment of the prescribed fee, extracts from the International Register, or information concerning the contents of the International Register, in respect of any published international registration.

(2)   [*Exemption from Legalization*] Extracts from the International Register supplied by the International Bureau shall be exempt from any requirement of legalization in each Contracting Party.

CHAPTER II

ADMINISTRATIVE PROVISIONS

Article 19

Common Office of Several States

(1)   [*Notification of Common Office*] If several States intending to become party to this Act have effected, or if several States party to this Act agree to effect, the unification of their domestic legislation on industrial designs, they may notify the Director General

     (i)   that a common Office shall be substituted for the national Office of each of them, and

     (ii)   that the whole of their respective territories to which the unified legislation applies shall be deemed to be a single Contracting Party for the purposes of the application of Articles 1, 3 to 18 and 31 of this Act.

(2)   [*Time at Which Notification Is to Be Made*] The notification referred to in paragraph (1) shall be made,

     (i)   in the case of States intending to become party to this Act, at the time of the deposit of the instruments referred to in Article 27(2);

     (ii)   in the case of States party to this Act, at any time after the unification of their domestic legislation has been effected.

(3)   [*Date of Entry into Effect of the Notification*] The notification referred to in paragraphs (1) and (2) shall take effect,

     (i)   in the case of States intending to become party to this Act, at the time such States become bound by this Act;

     (ii)   in the case of States party to this Act, three months after the date of the communication thereof by the Director General to the other Contracting Parties or at any later date indicated in the notification.

Article 20

Membership of the Hague Union

The Contracting Parties shall be members of the same Union as the States party to the 1934 Act or the 1960 Act.

Article 21

Assembly

(1)   *[Composition]* (a) The Contracting Parties shall be members of the same Assembly as the States bound by Article 2 of the Complementary Act of 1967.

(b)   Each member of the Assembly shall be represented in the Assembly by one delegate, who may be assisted by alternate delegates, advisors and experts, and each delegate may represent only one Contracting Party.

(c)   Members of the Union that are not members of the Assembly shall be admitted to the meetings of the Assembly as observers.

(2)   *[Tasks]* (a) The Assembly shall

(i)   deal with all matters concerning the maintenance and development of the Union and the implementation of this Act;

(ii)   exercise such rights and perform such tasks as are specifically conferred upon it or assigned to it under this Act or the Complementary Act of 1967;

(iii) give directions to the Director General concerning the preparations for conferences of revision and decide the convocation of any such conference;

(iv) amend the Regulations;

(v)   review and approve the reports and activities of the Director General concerning the Union, and give the Director General all necessary instructions concerning matters within the competence of the Union;

(vi) determine the program and adopt the biennial budget of the Union, and approve its final accounts;

(vii) adopt the financial regulations of the Union;

(viii) establish such committees and working groups as it deems appropriate to achieve the objectives of the Union;

(ix) subject to paragraph (1)(c), determine which States, intergovernmental organizations and non-governmental organizations shall be admitted to its meetings as observers;

(x)   take any other appropriate action to further the objectives of the Union and perform any other functions as are appropriate under this Act.

(b)   With respect to matters which are also of interest to other Unions administered by the Organization, the Assembly shall make its decisions after having heard the advice of the Coordination Committee of the Organization.

(3)   *[Quorum]* (a) One-half of the members of the Assembly which are States and have the right to vote on a given matter shall constitute a quorum for the purposes of the vote on that matter.

(b)   Notwithstanding the provisions of subparagraph (a), if, in any session, the number of the members of the Assembly which are States, have the right to vote on a given matter and are represented is less than one-half but equal to or more than one-third of the members of the Assembly which are States and have the right to vote on that matter, the Assembly may make decisions but, with the exception of decisions concerning its own procedure, all such decisions shall take effect only if the conditions set forth hereinafter are fulfilled. The International Bureau shall communicate the said decisions to the members of the Assembly which are States, have the right to vote on the said matter and were not represented and shall invite them to express in writing their vote or abstention within a period of three months from the date of the communication. If, at the expiration of this period, the number of such members having thus expressed their vote or abstention attains the number of the members which was lacking for attaining the quorum in the session itself, such decisions shall take effect provided that at the same time the required majority still obtains.

(4)   [*Taking Decisions in the Assembly*] (a) The Assembly shall endeavor to take its decisions by consensus.

(b)   Where a decision cannot be arrived at by consensus, the matter at issue shall be decided by voting. In such a case,

(i)   each Contracting Party that is a State shall have one vote and shall vote only in its own name, and

(ii)   any Contracting Party that is an intergovernmental organization may vote, in place of its Member States, with a number of votes equal to the number of its Member States which are party to this Act, and no such intergovernmental organization shall participate in the vote if any one of its Member States exercises its right to vote, and *vice versa*.

(c)   On matters concerning only States that are bound by Article 2 of the Complementary Act of 1967, Contracting Parties that are not bound by the said Article shall not have the right to vote, whereas, on matters concerning only Contracting Parties, only the latter shall have the right to vote.

(5)   [*Majorities*] (a) Subject to Articles 24(2) and 26(2), the decisions of the Assembly shall require two-thirds of the votes cast.

(b)   Abstentions shall not be considered as votes.

(6)   [*Sessions*] (a) The Assembly shall meet once in every second calendar year in ordinary session upon convocation by the Director General and, in the absence of exceptional circumstances, during the same period and at the same place as the General Assembly of the Organization.

(b)   The Assembly shall meet in extraordinary session upon convocation by the Director General, either at the request of one-fourth of the members of the Assembly or on the Director General's own initiative.

(c)   The agenda of each session shall be prepared by the Director General.

(7)   [*Rules of Procedure*] The Assembly shall adopt its own rules of procedure.

Article 22

International Bureau

(1)   [*Administrative Tasks*] (a) International registration and related duties, as well as all other administrative tasks concerning the Union, shall be performed by the International Bureau.

(b)   In particular, the International Bureau shall prepare the meetings and provide the secretariat of the Assembly and of such committees of experts and working groups as may be established by the Assembly.

(2) [*Director General*] The Director General shall be the chief executive of the Union and shall represent the Union.

(3) [*Meetings Other than Sessions of the Assembly*] The Director General shall convene any committee and working group established by the Assembly and all other meetings dealing with matters of concern to the Union.

(4) [*Role of the International Bureau in the Assembly and Other Meetings*] (a) The Director General and persons designated by the Director General shall participate, without the right to vote, in all meetings of the Assembly, the committees and working groups established by the Assembly, and any other meetings convened by the Director General under the aegis of the Union.

(b) The Director General or a staff member designated by the Director General shall be *ex officio* secretary of the Assembly, and of the committees, working groups and other meetings referred to in subparagraph (a).

(5) [*Conferences*] (a) The International Bureau shall, in accordance with the directions of the Assembly, make the preparations for any revision conferences.

(b) The International Bureau may consult with intergovernmental organizations and international and national non-governmental organizations concerning the said preparations.

(c) The Director General and persons designated by the Director General shall take part, without the right to vote, in the discussions at revision conferences.

(6) [*Other Tasks*] The International Bureau shall carry out any other tasks assigned to it in relation to this Act.

Article 23

Finances

(1) [*Budget*] (a) The Union shall have a budget.

(b) The budget of the Union shall include the income and expenses proper to the Union and its contribution to the budget of expenses common to the Unions administered by the Organization.

(c) Expenses not attributable exclusively to the Union but also to one or more other Unions administered by the Organization shall be considered to be expenses common to the Unions. The share of the Union in such common expenses shall be in proportion to the interest the Union has in them.

(2) [*Coordination with Budgets of Other Unions*] The budget of the Union shall be established with due regard to the requirements of coordination with the budgets of the other Unions administered by the Organization.

(3) [*Sources of Financing of the Budget*] The budget of the Union shall be financed from the following sources:

(i) fees relating to international registrations;

(ii) charges due for other services rendered by the International Bureau in relation to the Union;

(iii) sale of, or royalties on, the publications of the International Bureau concerning the Union;

(iv) gifts, bequests and subventions;

(v) rents, interests and other miscellaneous income.

(4) [*Fixing of Fees and Charges; Level of the Budget*] (a) The amounts of the fees referred to in paragraph (3)(i) shall be fixed by the Assembly on the proposal of the Director General. Charges referred to in paragraph 3(ii) shall be established by the Director General and shall be provisionally applied subject to approval by the Assembly at its next session.

(b) The amounts of the fees referred to in paragraph (3)(i) shall be so fixed that the revenues of the Union from fees and other sources shall be at least sufficient to cover all the expenses of the International Bureau concerning the Union.

(c) If the budget is not adopted before the beginning of a new financial period, it shall be at the same level as the budget of the previous year, as provided in the financial regulations.

(5) [*Working Capital Fund*] The Union shall have a working capital fund which shall be constituted by the excess receipts and, if such excess does not suffice, by a single payment made by each member of the Union. If the fund becomes insufficient, the Assembly shall decide to increase it. The proportion and the terms of payment shall be fixed by the Assembly on the proposal of the Director General.

(6) [*Advances by Host State*] (a) In the headquarters agreement concluded with the State on the territory of which the Organization has its headquarters, it shall be provided that, whenever the working capital fund is insufficient, such State shall grant advances. The amount of those advances and the conditions on which they are granted shall be the subject of separate agreements, in each case, between such State and the Organization.

(b) The State referred to in subparagraph (a) and the Organization shall each have the right to denounce the obligation to grant advances, by written notification. Denunciation shall take effect three years after the end of the year in which it has been notified.

(7) [*Auditing of Accounts*] The auditing of the accounts shall be effected by one or more of the States members of the Union or by external auditors, as provided in the financial regulations. They shall be designated, with their agreement, by the Assembly.

Article 24

Regulations

(1) [*Subject Matter*] The Regulations shall govern the details of the implementation of this Act. They shall, in particular, include provisions concerning

(i) matters which this Act expressly provides are to be prescribed;

(ii) further details concerning, or any details useful in the implementation of, the provisions of this Act;

(iii) any administrative requirements, matters or procedures.

(2) [*Amendment of Certain Provisions of the Regulations*] (a) The Regulations may specify that certain provisions of the Regulations may be amended only by unanimity or only by a four-fifths majority.

(b) In order for the requirement of unanimity or a four-fifths majority no longer to apply in the future to the amendment of a provision of the Regulations, unanimity shall be required.

(c) In order for the requirement of unanimity or a four-fifths majority to apply in the future to the amendment of a provision of the Regulations, a four-fifths majority shall be required.

(3) [*Conflict Between This Act and the Regulations*] In the case of conflict between the provisions of this Act and those of the Regulations, the former shall prevail.

CHAPTER III

REVISION AND AMENDMENT

Article 25

Revision of This Act

(1) [*Revision Conferences*] This Act may be revised by a conference of the Contracting Parties.

(2) [*Revision or Amendment of Certain Articles*] Articles 21, 22, 23 and 26 may be amended either by a revision conference or by the Assembly according to the provisions of Article 26.

Article 26

Amendment of Certain Articles by the Assembly

(1) [*Proposals for Amendment*] (a) Proposals for the amendment by the Assembly of Articles 21, 22, 23 and this Article may be initiated by any Contracting Party or by the Director General.

(b) Such proposals shall be communicated by the Director General to the Contracting Parties at least six months in advance of their consideration by the Assembly.

(2) [*Majorities*] Adoption of any amendment to the Articles referred to in paragraph (1) shall require a three-fourths majority, except that adoption of any amendment to Article 21 or to the present paragraph shall require a four-fifths majority.

(3) [*Entry into Force*] (a) Except where subparagraph (b) applies, any amendment to the Articles referred to in paragraph (1) shall enter into force one month after written notifications of acceptance, effected in accordance with their respective constitutional processes, have been received by the Director General from three-fourths of those Contracting Parties which, at the time the amendment was adopted, were members of the Assembly and had the right to vote on that amendment.

(b) Any amendment to Article 21(3) or (4) or to this subparagraph shall not enter into force if, within six months of its adoption by the Assembly, any Contracting Party notifies the Director General that it does not accept such amendment.

(c) Any amendment which enters into force in accordance with the provisions of this paragraph shall bind all the States and intergovernmental organizations which are Contracting Parties at the time the amendment enters into force, or which become Contracting Parties at a subsequent date.

CHAPTER IV

FINAL PROVISIONS

Article 27

Becoming Party to This Act

(1) [*Eligibility*] Subject to paragraphs (2) and (3) and Article 28,

(i)   any State member of the Organization may sign and become party to this Act;

(ii)   any intergovernmental organization which maintains an Office in which protection of industrial designs may be obtained with effect in the territory in which the constituting treaty of the intergovernmental organization applies may sign and become party to this Act, provided that at least one of the member States of the intergovernmental organization is a member of the Organization and provided that such Office is not the subject of a notification under Article 19.

(2) [*Ratification or Accession*] Any State or intergovernmental organization referred to in paragraph (1) may deposit

(i) an instrument of ratification if it has signed this Act, or

(ii) an instrument of accession if it has not signed this Act.

(3) [*Effective Date of Deposit*] (a) Subject to subparagraphs (b) to (d), the effective date of the deposit of an instrument of ratification or accession shall be the date on which that instrument is deposited.

(b) The effective date of the deposit of the instrument of ratification or accession of any State in respect of which protection of industrial designs may be obtained only through the Office maintained by an intergovernmental organization of which that State is a member shall be the date on which the instrument of that intergovernmental organization is deposited if that date is later than the date on which the instrument of the said State has been deposited.

(c) The effective date of the deposit of any instrument of ratification or accession containing or accompanied by the notification referred to in Article 19 shall be the date on which the last of the instruments of the States members of the group of States having made the said notification is deposited.

(d) Any instrument of ratification or accession of a State may contain or be accompanied by a declaration making it a condition to its being considered as deposited that the instrument of one other State or one intergovernmental organization, or the instruments of two other States, or the instruments of one other State and one intergovernmental organization, specified by name and eligible to become party to this Act, is or are also deposited. The instrument containing or accompanied by such a declaration shall be considered to have been deposited on the day on which the condition indicated in the declaration is fulfilled. However, when an instrument specified in the declaration itself contains, or is itself accompanied by, a declaration of the said kind, that instrument shall be considered as deposited on the day on which the condition specified in the latter declaration is fulfilled.

(e) Any declaration made under subparagraph (d) may be withdrawn, in its entirety or in part, at any time. Any such withdrawal shall become effective on the date on which the notification of withdrawal is received by the Director General.

Article 28

Effective Date of Ratifications and Accessions

(1) [*Instruments to Be Taken into Consideration*] For the purposes of this Article, only instruments of ratification or accession that are deposited by States or intergovernmental organizations referred to in Article 27(1) and that have an effective date according to Article 27(3) shall be taken into consideration.

(2) [*Entry into Force of This Act*] This Act shall enter into force three months after six States have deposited their instruments of ratification or accession, provided that, according to the most recent annual statistics collected by the International Bureau, at least three of those States fulfill at least one of the following conditions:

(i) at least 3,000 applications for the protection of industrial designs have been filed in or for the State concerned, or

(ii) at least 1,000 applications for the protection of industrial designs have been filed in or for the State concerned by residents of States other than that State.

(3) [*Entry into Force of Ratifications and Accessions*] (a) Any State or intergovernmental organization that has deposited its instrument of ratification or accession three months or more before the date of entry into force of this Act shall become bound by this Act on the date of entry into force of this Act.

(b) Any other State or intergovernmental organization shall become bound by this Act three months after the date on which it has deposited its instrument of ratification or accession or at any later date indicated in that instrument.

Article 29

Prohibition of Reservations

No reservations to this Act are permitted.

Article 30

Declarations Made by Contracting Parties

(1) [*Time at Which Declarations May Be Made*] Any declaration under Articles 4(1)(b), 5(2)(a), 7(2), 11(1), 13(1), 14(3), 16(2) or 17(3)(c) may be made

(i) at the time of the deposit of an instrument referred to in Article 27(2), in which case it shall become effective on the date on which the State or intergovernmental organization having made the declaration becomes bound by this Act, or

(ii) after the deposit of an instrument referred to in Article 27(2), in which case it shall become effective three months after the date of its receipt by the Director General or at any later date indicated in the declaration but shall apply only in respect of any international registration whose date of international registration is the same as, or is later than, the effective date of the declaration.

(2) [*Declarations by States Having a Common Office*] Notwithstanding paragraph (1), any declaration referred to in that paragraph that has been made by a State which has, with another State or other States, notified the Director General under Article 19(1) of the substitution of a common Office for their national Offices shall become effective only if that other State or those other States makes or make a corresponding declaration or corresponding declarations.

(3) [*Withdrawal of Declarations*] Any declaration referred to in paragraph (1) may be withdrawn at any time by notification addressed to the Director General. Such withdrawal shall take effect three months after the date on which the Director General has received the notification or at any later date indicated in the notification. In the case of a declaration made under Article 7(2), the withdrawal shall not affect international applications filed prior to the coming into effect of the said withdrawal.

Article 31

Applicability of the 1934 and 1960 Acts

(1) [*Relations Between States Party to Both This Act and the 1934 or 1960 Acts*] This Act alone shall be applicable as regards the mutual relations of States party to both this Act and the 1934 Act or the 1960 Act. However, such States shall, in their mutual relations, apply the 1934 Act or the 1960 Act, as the case may be, to industrial designs deposited at the International Bureau prior to the date on which this Act becomes applicable as regards their mutual relations.

(2) [*Relations Between States Party to Both This Act and the 1934 or 1960 Acts and States Party to the 1934 or 1960 Acts Without Being Party to This Act*] (a) Any State that is party to both

this Act and the 1934 Act shall continue to apply the 1934 Act in its relations with States that are party to the 1934 Act without being party to the 1960 Act or this Act.

(b)   Any State that is party to both this Act and the 1960 Act shall continue to apply the 1960 Act in its relations with States that are party to the 1960 Act without being party to this Act.

Article 32

Denunciation of This Act

(1)   [*Notification*] Any Contracting Party may denounce this Act by notification addressed to the Director General.

(2)   [*Effective Date*] Denunciation shall take effect one year after the date on which the Director General has received the notification or at any later date indicated in the notification.   It shall not affect the application of this Act to any international application pending and any international registration in force in respect of the denouncing Contracting Party at the time of the coming into effect of the denunciation.

Article 33

Languages of This Act; Signature

(1)   [*Original Texts; Official Texts*] (a) This Act shall be signed in a single original in the English, Arabic, Chinese, French, Russian and Spanish languages, all texts being equally authentic.

(b)   Official texts shall be established by the Director General, after consultation with the interested Governments, in such other languages as the Assembly may designate.

(2)   [*Time Limit for Signature*] This Act shall remain open for signature at the headquarters of the Organization for one year after its adoption.

Article 34

Depositary

The Director General shall be the depositary of this Act.

IV. UNFAIR COMPETITION MATERIALS

A. THE FEDERAL TRADE COMMISSION ACT

15 U.S.C.A. §§ 41–58

Contents

---

§ 41. Federal Trade Commission Established; Membership; Vacancies; Seal

A commission is created and established, to be known as the Federal Trade Commission (hereinafter referred to as the Commission), which shall be composed of five Commissioners, who shall be appointed by the President, by and with the advice and consent of the Senate. Not more than three of the Commissioners shall be members of the same political party. The first Commissioners appointed shall continue in office for terms of three, four, five, six, and seven years, respectively, from September 26, 1914, the term of each to be designated by the President, but their successors shall be appointed for terms of seven years, except that any person chosen to fill a vacancy shall be appointed only for the unexpired term of the Commissioner whom he shall succeed: Provided, however, That upon the expiration of his term of office a Commissioner shall continue to serve until his successor shall have been appointed and shall have qualified. The President shall choose a chairman from the Commission's membership. No Commissioner shall engage in any other business, vocation, or employment. Any Commissioner may be removed by the President for inefficiency, neglect of duty, or malfeasance in office. A vacancy in the Commission shall not impair the right of the remaining Commissioners to exercise all the powers of the Commission.

The Commission shall have an official seal, which shall be judicially noticed.

§ 42. Employees; Expenses

The Commission shall appoint a secretary, who shall receive a salary, payable in the same manner as the salaries of the judges of the courts of the United States, and it shall have authority to employ and fix the compensation of such attorneys, special experts, examiners, clerks, and other employees as it may from time to time find necessary for the proper performance of its duties and as may be from time to time appropriated for by Congress.

With the exception of the secretary, a clerk to each Commissioner, the attorneys, and such special experts and examiners as the Commission may from time to time find necessary for the conduct of its work, all employees of the Commission shall be a part of the classified civil service, and shall enter the service under such rules and regulations as may be prescribed by the Commission and by the Civil Service Commission.

All of the expenses of the Commission, including all necessary expenses for transportation incurred by the Commissioners or by their employees under their orders, in making any investigation, or upon official business in any other places than in the city of Washington, shall be allowed and paid on the presentation of itemized vouchers therefor approved by the Commission.

Until otherwise provided by law, the Commission may rent suitable offices for its use.

The General Accounting Office* shall receive and examine all accounts of expenditures of the Commission.

§ 43. Office and Place of Meeting

The principal office of the Commission shall be in the city of Washington, but it may meet and exercise all its powers at any other place. The Commission may, by one or more of its members, or by such examiners as it may designate, prosecute any inquiry necessary to its duties in any part of the United States.

§ 44. Definitions

The words defined in this section shall have the following meaning when found in this subchapter, to wit:

---

* Under § 8(b) of Pub.L. 108–271 all references to the General Accounting Office are considered to refer to the Government Accountability Office.—*Ed.*

"Commerce" means commerce among the several States or with foreign nations, or in any Territory of the United States or in the District of Columbia, or between any such Territory and another, or between any such Territory and any State or foreign nation, or between the District of Columbia and any State or Territory or foreign nation.

"Corporation" shall be deemed to include any company, trust, so-called Massachusetts trust, or association, incorporated or unincorporated, which is organized to carry on business for its own profit or that of its members, and has shares of capital or capital stock or certificates of interest, and any company, trust, so-called Massachusetts trust, or association, incorporated or unincorporated, without shares of capital or capital stock or certificates of interest, except partnerships, which is organized to carry on business for its own profit or that of its members.

"Documentary evidence" includes all documents, papers, correspondence, books of account, and financial and corporate records.

"Acts to regulate commerce" means subtitle IV of Title 49 and the Communications Act of 1934 [47 U.S.C.A. § 151 et seq.] and all Acts amendatory thereof and supplementary thereto.

"Antitrust Acts" means the Act entitled "An Act to protect trade and commerce against unlawful restraints and monopolies", approved July 2, 1890; also sections 73 to 76, of an Act entitled "An Act to reduce taxation, to provide revenue for the Government, and for other purposes", approved August 27, 1894; also the Act entitled "An Act to amend sections 73 and 76 of the Act of August 27, 1894, entitled 'An Act to reduce taxation, to provide revenue for the Government, and for other purposes' ", approved February 12, 1913; and also the Act entitled "An Act to supplement existing laws against unlawful restraints and monopolies, and for other purposes", approved October 15, 1914.

"Banks" means the types of banks and other financial institutions referred to in section 57a(f)(2) of this title.

"Foreign law enforcement agency" means—

(1)   any agency or judicial authority of a foreign government, including a foreign state, a political subdivision of a foreign state, or a multinational organization constituted by and comprised of foreign states, that is vested with law enforcement or investigative authority in civil, criminal, or administrative matters; and

(2)   any multinational organization, to the extent that it is acting on behalf of an entity described in paragraph (1).

§ 45.   Unfair Methods of Competition Unlawful; Prevention by Commission

(a)   Declaration of Unlawfulness; Power to Prohibit Unfair Practices; Inapplicability to Foreign Trade

(1)   Unfair methods of competition in or affecting commerce, and unfair or deceptive acts or practices in or affecting commerce, are declared unlawful.

(2)   The Commission is empowered and directed to prevent persons, partnerships, or corporations, except banks, savings and loan institutions described in section 57a(f)(3) of this title, Federal credit unions described in section 57a(f)(4) of this title, common carriers subject to the Acts to regulate commerce, air carriers and foreign air carriers subject to the Federal Aviation Act of 1958, and persons, partnerships, or corporations insofar as they are subject to the Packers and Stockyards Act, 1921, as amended [7 U.S.C.A. § 181 et seq.], except as provided in section 406(b) of said Act [7 U.S.C.A. § 227(a)], from using unfair methods of competition in or affecting commerce and unfair or deceptive acts or practices in or affecting commerce.

(3)   This subsection shall not apply to unfair methods of competition involving commerce with foreign nations (other than import commerce) unless—

(A)   such methods of competition have a direct, substantial, and reasonably foreseeable effect—

(i)   on commerce which is not commerce with foreign nations, or on import commerce with foreign nations; or

(ii)   on export commerce with foreign nations, of a person engaged in such commerce in the United States; and

(B)   such effect gives rise to a claim under the provisions of this subsection, other than this paragraph.

If this subsection applies to such methods of competition only because of the operation of subparagraph (A)(ii), this subsection shall apply to such conduct only for injury to export business in the United States.

(4)(A)   For purposes of subsection (a), the term 'unfair or deceptive acts or practices' includes such acts or practices involving foreign commerce that—

(i)   cause or are likely to cause reasonably foreseeable injury within the United States; or

(ii)   involve material conduct occurring within the United States.

(B)   All remedies available to the Commission with respect to unfair and deceptive acts or practices shall be available for acts and practices described in this paragraph, including restitution to domestic or foreign victims.

(b)   Proceeding by Commission; Modifying and Setting Aside Orders

Whenever the Commission shall have reason to believe that any such person, partnership, or corporation has been or is using any unfair method of competition or unfair or deceptive act or practice in or affecting commerce, and if it shall appear to the Commission that a proceeding by it in respect thereof would be to the interest of the public, it shall issue and serve upon such person, partnership, or corporation a complaint stating its charges in that respect and containing a notice of a hearing upon a day and at a place therein fixed at least thirty days after the service of said complaint. The person, partnership, or corporation so complained of shall have the right to appear at the place and time so fixed and show cause why an order should not be entered by the Commission requiring such person, partnership, or corporation to cease and desist from the violation of the law so charged in said complaint. Any person, partnership, or corporation may make application, and upon good cause shown may be allowed by the Commission to intervene and appear in said proceeding by counsel or in person. The testimony in any such proceeding shall be reduced to writing and filed in the office of the Commission. If upon such hearing the Commission shall be of the opinion that the method of competition or the act or practice in question is prohibited by this subchapter, it shall make a report in writing in which it shall state its findings as to the facts and shall issue and cause to be served on such person, partnership, or corporation an order requiring such person, partnership, or corporation to cease and desist from using such method of competition or such act or practice. Until the expiration of the time allowed for filing a petition for review, if no such petition has been duly filed within such time, or, if a petition for review has been filed within such time then until the record in the proceeding has been filed in a court of appeals of the United States, as hereinafter provided, the Commission may at any time, upon such notice and in such manner as it shall deem proper, modify or set aside, in whole or in part, any report or any order made or issued by it under this section. After the expiration of the time allowed for filing a petition for review, if no such petition has been duly filed within such time, the Commission may at any time, after notice and opportunity for hearing, reopen and alter, modify, or set aside, in whole or in part, any report or order made or issued by it under this section, whenever in the opinion of the Commission conditions of fact or of law have so changed as to require such action or if the public interest shall so require, except that (1) the said person, partnership, or corporation may, within sixty days after service upon him or it of said report or order entered after such a reopening, obtain a review thereof in the appropriate court of appeals of the United States, in the manner provided in subsection (c) of this section; and (2) in the case of an order, the Commission shall reopen any such order to consider whether such order (including any affirmative relief provision contained in such order) should be altered, modified, or set aside, in whole or in part, if the person, partnership, or corporation involved files a request with the Commission which makes a satisfactory showing that changed conditions of law or fact require such order to be altered, modified, or set aside, in whole or in part. The Commission shall determine whether to alter, modify, or set aside any order of the Commission in response to a request made by a person, partnership, or corporation under paragraph (2) not later than 120 days after the date of the filing of such request.

(c) Review of Order; Rehearing

Any person, partnership, or corporation required by an order of the Commission to cease and desist from using any method of competition or act or practice may obtain a review of such order in the court of appeals of the United States, within any circuit where the method of competition or the act or practice in question was used or where such person, partnership, or corporation resides or carries on business, by filing in the court, within sixty days from the date of the service of such order, a written petition praying that the order of the Commission be set aside. A copy of such petition shall be forthwith transmitted by the clerk of the court to the Commission, and thereupon the Commission shall file in the court the record in the proceeding, as provided in section 2112 of Title 28. Upon such filing of the petition the court shall have jurisdiction of the proceeding and of the question determined therein concurrently with the Commission until the filing of the record and shall have power to make and enter a decree affirming, modifying, or setting aside the order of the Commission, and enforcing the same to the extent that such order is affirmed and to issue such writs as are ancillary to its jurisdiction or are necessary in its judgment to prevent injury to the public or to competitors pendente lite. The findings of the Commission as to the facts, if supported by evidence, shall be conclusive. To the extent that the order of the Commission is affirmed, the court shall thereupon issue its own order commanding obedience to the terms of such order of the Commission. If either party shall apply to the court for leave to adduce additional evidence, and shall show to the satisfaction of the court that such additional evidence is material and that there were reasonable grounds for the failure to adduce such evidence in the proceeding before the Commission, the court may order such additional evidence to be taken before the Commission and to be adduced upon the hearing in such manner and upon such terms and conditions as to the court may seem proper. The Commission may modify its findings as to the facts, or make new findings, by reason of the additional evidence so taken, and it shall file such modified or new findings, which, if supported by evidence, shall be conclusive, and its recommendation, if any, for the modification or setting aside of its original order, with the return of such additional evidence. The judgment and decree of the court shall be final, except that the same shall be subject to review by the Supreme Court upon certiorari, as provided in section 347 of Title 28.

(d) Jurisdiction of Court

Upon the filing of the record with it the jurisdiction of the court of appeals of the United States to affirm, enforce, modify, or set aside orders of the Commission shall be exclusive.

(e) Exemption From Liability

No order of the Commission or judgment of court to enforce the same shall in anywise relieve or absolve any person, partnership, or corporation from any liability under the Antitrust Acts.

(f) Service of Complaints, Orders and Other Processes; Return

Complaints, orders, and other processes of the Commission under this section may be served by anyone duly authorized by the Commission, either (a) by delivering a copy thereof to the person to be served, or to a member of the partnership to be served, or the president, secretary, or other executive officer or a director of the corporation to be served; or (b) by leaving a copy thereof at the residence or the principal office or place of business of such person, partnership, or corporation; or (c) by mailing a copy thereof by registered mail or by certified mail addressed to such person, partnership, or corporation at his or its residence or principal office or place of business. The verified return by the person so serving said complaint, order, or other process setting forth the manner of said service shall be proof of the same, and the return post office receipt for said complaint, order, or other process mailed by registered mail or by certified mail as aforesaid shall be proof of the service of the same.

(g) Finality of Order

An order of the Commission to cease and desist shall become final—

(1)   Upon the expiration of the time allowed for filing a petition for review, if no such petition has been duly filed within such time; but the Commission may thereafter modify or set aside its order to the extent provided in the last sentence of subsection (b) of this section.

(2)   Except as to any order provision subject to paragraph (4), upon the sixtieth day after such order is served, if a petition for review has been duly filed; except that any such order may be stayed, in whole or in part and subject to such conditions as may be appropriate, by—

(A)   the Commission;

(B)   an appropriate court of appeals of the United States, if (i) a petition for review of such order is pending in such court, and (ii) an application for such a stay was previously submitted to the Commission and the Commission, within the 30-day period beginning on the date the application was received by the Commission, either denied the application or did not grant or deny the application; or

(C)   the Supreme Court, if an applicable petition for certiorari is pending.

(3)   For purposes of subsection (m)(1)(B) and of section 19(a)(2) [§ 57b(a)(2)], if a petition for review of the order of the Commission has been filed—

(A)   upon the expiration of the time allowed for filing a petition for certiorari, if the order of the Commission has been affirmed or the petition for review has been dismissed by the court of appeals and no petition for certiorari has been duly filed;

(B)   upon the denial of a petition for certiorari, if the order of the Commission has been affirmed or the petition for review has been dismissed by the court of appeals; or

(C)   upon the expiration of 30 days from the date of issuance of a mandate of the Supreme Court directing that the order of the Commission be affirmed or the petition for review be dismissed.

(4)   In the case of an order provision requiring a person, partnership, or corporation to divest itself of stock, other share capital, or assets, if a petition for review of such order of the Commission has been filed—

(A)   upon the expiration of the time allowed for filing a petition for certiorari, if the order of the Commission has been affirmed or the petition for review has been dismissed by the court of appeals and no petition for certiorari has been duly filed;

(B)   upon the denial of a petition for certiorari, if the order of the Commission has been affirmed or the petition for review has been dismissed by the court of appeals; or

(C)   upon the expiration of 30 days from the date of issuance of a mandate of the Supreme Court directing that the order of the Commission be affirmed or the petition for review be dismissed.

(h) Modification or Setting Aside of Order by Supreme Court

If the Supreme Court directs that the order of the Commission be modified or set aside, the order of the Commission rendered in accordance with the mandate of the Supreme Court shall become final upon the expiration of thirty days from the time it was rendered, unless within such thirty days either party has instituted proceedings to have such order corrected to accord with the mandate, in which event the order of the Commission shall become final when so corrected.

(i) Modification or Setting Aside of Order by Court of Appeals

If the order of the Commission is modified or set aside by the court of appeals, and if (1) the time allowed for filing a petition for certiorari has expired and no such petition has been duly filed, or (2) the petition for certiorari has been denied, or (3) the decision of the court has been affirmed by the Supreme Court, then the order of the Commission rendered in accordance with the mandate of the court of appeals shall become final on the expiration of thirty days from the time such order of the Commission was rendered, unless within such thirty days either party has instituted proceedings to have such order corrected so that it will accord with the mandate, in which event the order of the Commission shall become final when so corrected.

(j) Rehearing Upon Order or Remand

If the Supreme Court orders a rehearing; or if the case is remanded by the court of appeals to the Commission for a rehearing, and if (1) the time allowed for filing a petition for certiorari has expired, and no such petition has been duly filed, or (2) the petition for certiorari has been denied, or (3) the decision of the court has been affirmed by the Supreme Court, then the order of the Commission rendered upon such rehearing shall become final in the same manner as though no prior order of the Commission had been rendered.

(k) "Mandate" Defined

As used in this section the term "mandate", in case a mandate has been recalled prior to the expiration of thirty days from the date of issuance thereof, means the final mandate.

(*l*) Penalty for Violation of Order; Injunctions and Other Appropriate Equitable Relief

Any person, partnership, or corporation who violates an order of the Commission after it has become final, and while such order is in effect, shall forfeit and pay to the United States a civil penalty of not more than $10,000 for each violation, which shall accrue to the United States and may be recovered in a civil action brought by the Attorney General of the United States. Each separate violation of such an order shall be a separate offense, except that in the case of a violation through continuing failure to obey or neglect to obey a final order of the Commission, each day of continuance of such failure or neglect shall be deemed a separate offense. In such actions, the United States district courts are empowered to grant mandatory injunctions and such other and further equitable relief as they deem appropriate in the enforcement of such final orders of the Commission.

(m) Civil Actions for Recovery of Penalties for Knowing Violations of Rules and Cease and Desist Orders Respecting Unfair or Deceptive Acts or Practices; Jurisdiction; Maximum Amount of Penalties; Continuing Violations; De Novo Determinations; Compromise or Settlement Procedure

(1)(A)   The Commission may commence a civil action to recover a civil penalty in a district court of the United States against any person, partnership, or corporation which violates any rule under this chapter respecting unfair or deceptive acts or practices (other than an interpretive rule or a rule violation of which the Commission has provided is not an unfair or deceptive act or practice in violation of subsection (a)(1) of this section) with actual knowledge or knowledge fairly implied on the basis of objective circumstances that such act is unfair or deceptive and is prohibited by such rule. In such action, such person, partnership, or corporation shall be liable for a civil penalty of not more than $10,000 for each violation.

(B)   If the Commission determines in a proceeding under subsection (b) of this section that any act or practice is unfair or deceptive, and issues a final cease and desist order with respect to such act or practice, then the Commission may commence a civil action to obtain a civil penalty in a district court of the United States against any person, partnership, or corporation which engages in such act or practice—

(1)   after such cease and desist order becomes final (whether or not such person, partnership, or corporation was subject to such cease and desist order), and

(2)   with actual knowledge that such act or practice is unfair or deceptive and is unlawful under subsection (a)(1) of this section.

In such action, such person, partnership, or corporation shall be liable for a civil penalty of not more than $10,000 for each violation.

(C)   In the case of a violation through continuing failure to comply with a rule or with subsection (a)(1) of this section, each day of continuance of such failure shall be treated as a separate violation, for purposes of subparagraphs (A) and (B). In determining the amount of such a civil penalty, the court shall take into account the degree of culpability, any history of prior such conduct, ability to pay, effect on ability to continue to do business, and such other matters as justice may require.

(2)   If the cease and desist order establishing that the act or practice is unfair or deceptive was not issued against the defendant in a civil penalty action under paragraph (1)(B) the issues of fact in such action against such defendant shall be tried de novo.

(3)   The Commission may compromise or settle any action for a civil penalty if such compromise or settlement is accompanied by a public statement of its reasons and is approved by the court.

(n) Standard of Proof; Public Policy Considerations

The Commission shall have no authority under this section or section 18 to declare unlawful an act or practice on the grounds that such act or practice is unfair unless the act or practice causes or is likely to cause substantial injury to consumers which is not reasonably avoidable by consumers themselves and not outweighed by countervailing benefits to consumers or to competition. In determining whether an act or practice is unfair, the Commission may consider established public policies as evidence to be considered with all other evidence. Such public policy considerations may not serve as a primary basis for such determination.

§ 45a. Labels on Products

To the extent any person introduces, delivers for introduction, sells, advertises, or offers for sale in commerce a product with a "Made in the U.S.A." or "Made in America" label, or the equivalent thereof, in order to represent that such product was in whole or substantial part of domestic origin, such label shall be consistent with decisions and orders of the Federal Trade Commission issued pursuant to section 5 of the Federal Trade Commission Act [15 USCS § 45]. This section only applies to such labels. Nothing in this section shall preclude the application of other provisions of law relating to labeling. The Commission may periodically consider an appropriate percentage of imported components which may be included in the product and still be reasonably consistent with such decisions and orders. Nothing in this section shall preclude use of such labels for products that contain imported components under the label when the label also discloses such information in a clear and conspicuous manner. The Commission shall administer this section pursuant to section 5 of the Federal Trade Commission Act and may from time to time issue rules pursuant to section 553 of title 5, United States Code, for such purpose. If a rule is issued, such violation shall be treated by the Commission as a violation of a rule under section 18 of the Federal Trade Commission Act (15 U.S.C. § 57a) regarding unfair or deceptive acts or practices. This section shall be effective upon publication in the Federal Register of a notice of the provisions of this section. The Commission shall publish such notice within six months after the enactment of this section.

§ 45b. Consumer Review Protection

(a) Definitions

In this section:

(1)   Commission

The term "Commission" means the Federal Trade Commission.

(2)   Covered communication

The term "covered communication" means a written, oral, or pictorial review, performance assessment of, or other similar analysis of, including by electronic means, the goods, services, or conduct of a person by an individual who is party to a form contract with respect to which such person is also a party.

(3) Form contract

(A) In general

Except as provided in subparagraph (B), the term "form contract" means a contract with standardized terms—

(i) used by a person in the course of selling or leasing the person's goods or services; and

(ii) imposed on an individual without a meaningful opportunity for such individual to negotiate the standardized terms.

(B) Exception

The term "form contract" does not include an employer-employee or independent contractor contract.

(4) Pictorial

The term "pictorial" includes pictures, photographs, video, illustrations, and symbols.

(b) Invalidity of contracts that impede consumer reviews

(1) In general

Except as provided in paragraphs (2) and (3), a provision of a form contract is void from the inception of such contract if such provision—

(A) prohibits or restricts the ability of an individual who is a party to the form contract to engage in a covered communication;

(B) imposes a penalty or fee against an individual who is a party to the form contract for engaging in a covered communication; or

(C) transfers or requires an individual who is a party to the form contract to transfer to any person any intellectual property rights in review or feedback content, with the exception of a non-exclusive license to use the content, that the individual may have in any otherwise lawful covered communication about such person or the goods or services provided by such person.

(2) Rule of construction

Nothing in paragraph (1) shall be construed to affect—

(A) any duty of confidentiality imposed by law (including agency guidance);

(B) any civil cause of action for defamation, libel, or slander, or any similar cause of action;

(C) any party's right to remove or refuse to display publicly on an Internet website or webpage owned, operated, or otherwise controlled by such party any content of a covered communication that—

(i) contains the personal information or likeness of another person, or is libelous, harassing, abusive, obscene, vulgar, sexually explicit, or is inappropriate with respect to race, gender, sexuality, ethnicity, or other intrinsic characteristic;

(ii) is unrelated to the goods or services offered by or available at such party's Internet website or webpage; or

(iii) is clearly false or misleading; or

(D) a party's right to establish terms and conditions with respect to the creation of photographs or video of such party's property when those photographs or video are created by an employee or independent contractor of a commercial entity and solely intended for commercial purposes by that entity.

(3) Exceptions

Paragraph (1) shall not apply to the extent that a provision of a form contract prohibits disclosure or submission of, or reserves the right of a person or business that hosts online consumer reviews or comments to remove—

(A) trade secrets or commercial or financial information obtained from a person and considered privileged or confidential;

(B) personnel and medical files and similar information the disclosure of which would constitute a clearly unwarranted invasion of personal privacy;

(C) records or information compiled for law enforcement purposes, the disclosure of which would constitute a clearly unwarranted invasion of personal privacy;

(D) content that is unlawful or otherwise meets the requirements of paragraph (2)(C); or

(E) content that contains any computer viruses, worms, or other potentially damaging computer code, processes, programs, applications, or files.

(c) Prohibition

It shall be unlawful for a person to offer a form contract containing a provision described as void in subsection (b).

(d) Enforcement by Commission

(1) Unfair or deceptive acts or practices

A violation of subsection (c) by a person with respect to which the Commission is empowered under section 5(a)(2) of the Federal Trade Commission Act (15 U.S.C. 45(a)(2)) shall be treated as a violation of a rule defining an unfair or deceptive act or practice prescribed under section 18(a)(1)(B) of the Federal Trade Commission Act (15 U.S.C. 57a(a)(1)(B)).

(2) Powers of Commission

(A) In general

The Commission shall enforce this section in the same manner, by the same means, and with the same jurisdiction, powers, and duties as though all applicable terms and provisions of the Federal Trade Commission Act (15 U.S.C. 41 et seq.) were incorporated into and made a part of this Act.

(B) Privileges and immunities

Any person who violates this section shall be subject to the penalties and entitled to the privileges and immunities provided in the Federal Trade Commission Act (15 U.S.C. 41 et seq.).

(e) Enforcement by States

(1) Authorization

Subject to paragraph (2), in any case in which the attorney general of a State has reason to believe that an interest of the residents of the State has been or is threatened or adversely affected by the engagement of any person subject to subsection (c) in a practice that violates such subsection, the attorney general of the State may, as parens patriae, bring a civil action on behalf of the residents of the State in an appropriate district court of the United States to obtain appropriate relief.

 (2) Rights of Federal Trade Commission

  (A) Notice to Federal Trade Commission

   (i) In general

Except as provided in clause (iii), the attorney general of a State shall notify the Commission in writing that the attorney general intends to bring a civil action under paragraph (1) before initiating the civil action against a person described in subsection (d)(1).

   (ii) Contents

The notification required by clause (i) with respect to a civil action shall include a copy of the complaint to be filed to initiate the civil action.

   (iii) Exception

If it is not feasible for the attorney general of a State to provide the notification required by clause (i) before initiating a civil action under paragraph (1), the attorney general shall notify the Commission immediately upon instituting the civil action.

  (B) Intervention by Federal Trade Commission

The Commission may—

   (i) intervene in any civil action brought by the attorney general of a State under paragraph (1) against a person described in subsection (d)(1); and

   (ii) upon intervening—

    (I) be heard on all matters arising in the civil action; and

    (II) file petitions for appeal of a decision in the civil action.

 (3) Investigatory powers

Nothing in this subsection may be construed to prevent the attorney general of a State from exercising the powers conferred on the attorney general by the laws of the State to conduct investigations, to administer oaths or affirmations, or to compel the attendance of witnesses or the production of documentary or other evidence.

 (4) Preemptive action by Federal Trade Commission

If the Federal Trade Commission institutes a civil action or an administrative action with respect to a violation of subsection (c), the attorney general of a State may not, during the pendency of such action, bring a civil action under paragraph (1) against any defendant named in the complaint of the Commission for the violation with respect to which the Commission instituted such action.

 (5) Venue; service of process

  (A) Venue

Any action brought under paragraph (1) may be brought in—

   (i) the district court of the United States that meets applicable requirements relating to venue under section 1391 of Title 28; or

   (ii) another court of competent jurisdiction.

(B) Service of process

In an action brought under paragraph (1), process may be served in any district in which the defendant—

(i)   is an inhabitant; or

(ii) may be found.

(6) Actions by other State officials

(A) In general

In addition to civil actions brought by attorneys general under paragraph (1), any other consumer protection officer of a State who is authorized by the State to do so may bring a civil action under paragraph (1), subject to the same requirements and limitations that apply under this subsection to civil actions brought by attorneys general.

(B) Savings provision

Nothing in this subsection may be construed to prohibit an authorized official of a State from initiating or continuing any proceeding in a court of the State for a violation of any civil or criminal law of the State.

(f) Education and outreach for businesses

Not later than 60 days after December 14, 2016, the Commission shall commence conducting education and outreach that provides businesses with non-binding best practices for compliance with this Act.

(g) Relation to State causes of action

Nothing in this section shall be construed to affect any cause of action brought by a person that exists or may exist under State law.

(h) Savings provision

Nothing in this section shall be construed to limit, impair, or supersede the operation of the Federal Trade Commission Act or any other provision of Federal law.

(i) Effective dates

This section shall take effect on December 14, 2016, except that—

(1) subsections (b) and (c) shall apply with respect to contracts in effect on or after the date that is 90 days after December 14, 2016; and

(2) subsections (d) and (e) shall apply with respect to contracts in effect on or after the date that is 1 year after December 14, 2016.

§ 45c. Unfair and Deceptive Acts and Practices Relating to Circumvention of Ticket Access Control Measures

(a) Conduct prohibited

(1) In general

Except as provided in paragraph (2), it shall be unlawful for any person—

(A) to circumvent a security measure, access control system, or other technological control or measure on an Internet website or online service that is used by the ticket issuer to enforce posted event ticket purchasing limits or to maintain the integrity of posted online ticket purchasing order rules; or

(B) to sell or offer to sell any event ticket in interstate commerce obtained in violation of subparagraph (A) if the person selling or offering to sell the ticket either—

   (i) participated directly in or had the ability to control the conduct in violation of subparagraph (A); or

   (ii) knew or should have known that the event ticket was acquired in violation of subparagraph (A).

 (2) Exception

It shall not be unlawful under this section for a person to create or use any computer software or system—

  (A) to investigate, or further the enforcement or defense, of any alleged violation of this section or other statute or regulation; or

  (B) to engage in research necessary to identify and analyze flaws and vulnerabilities of measures, systems, or controls described in paragraph (1)(A), if these research activities are conducted to advance the state of knowledge in the field of computer system security or to assist in the development of computer security product.

(b) Enforcement by the Federal Trade Commission

 (1) Unfair or deceptive acts or practices

A violation of subsection (a) shall be treated as a violation of a rule defining an unfair or a deceptive act or practice under section 18(a)(1)(B) of the Federal Trade Commission Act (15 U.S.C. 57a(a)(1)(B)).

 (2) Powers of Commission

  (A) In general

The Commission shall enforce this section in the same manner, by the same means, and with the same jurisdiction, powers, and duties as though all applicable terms and provisions of the Federal Trade Commission Act (15 U.S.C. 41 et seq.) were incorporated into and made a part of this section.

  (B) Privileges and immunities

Any person who violates subsection (a) shall be subject to the penalties and entitled to the privileges and immunities provided in the Federal Trade Commission Act (15 U.S.C. 41 et seq.).

  (C) Authority preserved

Nothing in this section shall be construed to limit the authority of the Federal Trade Commission under any other provision of law.

(c) Enforcement by States

 (1) In general

In any case in which the attorney general of a State has reason to believe that an interest of the residents of the State has been or is threatened or adversely affected by the engagement of any person subject to subsection (a) in a practice that violates such subsection, the attorney general of the State may, as parens patriae, bring a civil action on behalf of the residents of the State in an appropriate district court of the United States—

  (A) to enjoin further violation of such subsection by such person;

  (B) to compel compliance with such subsection; and

  (C) to obtain damages, restitution, or other compensation on behalf of such residents.

 (2) Rights of Federal Trade Commission

  (A) Notice to Federal Trade Commission

(i)   In general

Except as provided in clause (iii), the attorney general of a State shall notify the Commission in writing that the attorney general intends to bring a civil action under paragraph (1) not later than 10 days before initiating the civil action.

(ii)   Contents

The notification required by clause (i) with respect to a civil action shall include a copy of the complaint to be filed to initiate the civil action.

(iii)   Exception

If it is not feasible for the attorney general of a State to provide the notification required by clause (i) before initiating a civil action under paragraph (1), the attorney general shall notify the Commission immediately upon instituting the civil action.

(B)   Intervention by Federal Trade Commission

The Commission may—

(i)   intervene in any civil action brought by the attorney general of a State under paragraph (1); and

(ii)   upon intervening—

(I)   be heard on all matters arising in the civil action; and

(II)   file petitions for appeal of a decision in the civil action.

(3)   Investigatory powers

Nothing in this subsection may be construed to prevent the attorney general of a State from exercising the powers conferred on the attorney general by the laws of the State to conduct investigations, to administer oaths or affirmations, or to compel the attendance of witnesses or the production of documentary or other evidence.

(4)   Preemptive action by Federal Trade Commission

If the Commission institutes a civil action or an administrative action with respect to a violation of subsection (a), the attorney general of a State may not, during the pendency of such action, bring a civil action under paragraph (1) against any defendant named in the complaint of the Commission for the violation with respect to which the Commission instituted such action.

(5)   Venue; service of process

(A)   Venue

Any action brought under paragraph (1) may be brought in—

(i)   the district court of the United States that meets applicable requirements relating to venue under section 1391 of Title 28; or

(ii)   another court of competent jurisdiction.

(B)   Service of process

In an action brought under paragraph (1), process may be served in any district in which the defendant—

(i)   is an inhabitant; or

(ii)   may be found.

(6)   Actions by other State officials

(A)   In general

In addition to civil actions brought by attorneys general under paragraph (1), any other consumer protection officer of a State who is authorized by the State to do so may bring a civil action under paragraph (1), subject to the same requirements and limitations that apply under this subsection to civil actions brought by attorneys general.

(B) Savings provision

Nothing in this subsection may be construed to prohibit an authorized official of a State from initiating or continuing any proceeding in a court of the State for a violation of any civil or criminal law of the State.

§ 45d. Unfair or Deceptive Acts or Practices with Respect to Substance Use Disorder Treatment Service and Products.

(a) Unlawful activity

It is unlawful to engage in an unfair or deceptive act or practice with respect to any substance use disorder treatment service or substance use disorder treatment product.

(b) Enforcement by the Federal Trade Commission

(1) Unfair or deceptive acts or practices

A violation of subsection (a) shall be treated as a violation of a rule under section 18 of the Federal Trade Commission Act (15 U.S.C. 57a) regarding unfair or deceptive acts or practices.

(2) Powers of the Federal Trade Commission

(A) In general

The Federal Trade Commission shall enforce this section in the same manner, by the same means, and with the same jurisdiction, powers, and duties as though all applicable terms and provisions of the Federal Trade Commission Act (15 U.S.C. 41 et seq.) were incorporated into and made a part of this section.

(B) Privileges and immunities

Any person who violates subsection (a) shall be subject to the penalties and entitled to the privileges and immunities provided in the Federal Trade Commission Act as though all applicable terms and provisions of the Federal Trade Commission Act (15 U.S.C. 41 et seq.) were incorporated and made part of this section.

(c) Authority preserved

Nothing in this subtitle shall be construed to limit the authority of the Federal Trade Commission or the Food and Drug Administration under any other provision of law.

§ 46. Additional Powers of Commission

The Commission shall also have power—

(a) Investigation of Persons, Partnerships, or Corporations

To gather and compile information concerning, and to investigate from time to time the organization, business, conduct, practices, and management of any person, partnership, or corporation engaged in or whose business affects commerce, excepting banks, savings and loan institutions described in section 57a(f)(3) of this title, Federal credit unions described in section 57a(f)(4) of this title, and common carriers subject to the Act to regulate commerce, and its relation to other persons, partnerships, and corporations.

(b) Reports of Persons, Partnerships, and Corporations

To require, by general or special orders, persons, partnerships, and corporations, engaged in or whose business affects commerce, excepting banks, savings and loan institutions described in section

57a(f)(3) of this title, Federal credit unions described in section 57a(f)(4) of this title, and common carriers subject to the Act to regulate commerce, or any class of them, or any of them, respectively, to file with the Commission in such form as the Commission may prescribe annual or special, or both annual and special, reports or answers in writing to specific questions, furnishing to the Commission such information as it may require as to the organization, business, conduct, practices, management, and relation to other corporations, partnerships, and individuals of the respective persons, partnerships, and corporations filing such reports or answers in writing. Such reports and answers shall be made under oath, or otherwise, as the Commission may prescribe, and shall be filed with the Commission within such reasonable period as the Commission may prescribe, unless additional time be granted in any case by the Commission.

(c) Investigation of Compliance With Antitrust Decrees

Whenever a final decree has been entered against any defendant corporation in any suit brought by the United States to prevent and restrain any violation of the antitrust Acts, to make investigation, upon its own initiative, of the manner in which the decree has been or is being carried out, and upon the application of the Attorney General it shall be its duty to make such investigation. It shall transmit to the Attorney General a report embodying its findings and recommendations as a result of any such investigation, and the report shall be made public in the discretion of the Commission.

(d) Investigations of Violations of Antitrust Statutes

Upon the direction of the President or either House of Congress to investigate and report the facts relating to any alleged violations of the antitrust Acts by any corporation.

(e) Readjustment of Business of Corporations Violating Antitrust Statutes

Upon the application of the Attorney General to investigate and make recommendations for the readjustment of the business of any corporation alleged to be violating the antitrust Acts in order that the corporation may thereafter maintain its organization, management, and conduct of business in accordance with law.

(f) Publication of Information; Reports

To make public from time to time such portions of the information obtained by it hereunder as are in the public interest; and to make annual and special reports to the Congress and to submit therewith recommendations for additional legislation; and to provide for the publication of its reports and decisions in such form and manner as may be best adapted for public information and use: *Provided,* That the Commission shall not have any authority to make public any trade secret or any commercial or financial information which is obtained from any person and which is privileged or confidential, except that the Commission may disclose such information (1) to officers and employees of appropriate Federal law enforcement agencies or to any officer or employee of any State law enforcement agency upon the prior certification of an officer of any such Federal or State law enforcement agency that such information will be maintained in confidence and will be used only for official law enforcement purposes, and (2) to any officer or employee of any foreign law enforcement agency under the same circumstances that making material available to foreign law enforcement agencies is permitted under section 57b–2(b) of this title.

(g) Classification of Corporations; Regulations

From time to time to classify corporations and (except as provided in section 57a(a)(2) of this title) to make rules and regulations for the purpose of carrying out the provisions of sections 41 to 46 and 47 to 58 of this title.

(h) Investigations of Foreign Trade Conditions; Reports

To investigate, from time to time, trade conditions in and with foreign countries where associations, combinations, or practices of manufacturers, merchants, or traders, or other conditions, may affect the foreign trade of the United States, and to report to Congress thereon, with such recommendations as it deems advisable.

(i) Investigations of Foreign Antitrust Laws Violations

With respect to the International Antitrust Enforcement Assistance Act of 1994 [15 U.S.C.A. § 6201 et seq.], to conduct investigations of possible violations of foreign antitrust laws (as defined in section 12 of such Act [15 U.S.C.A. § 6211]).

(j) Investigative Assistance for Foreign Law Enforcement Agencies

(1) In General.—Upon a written request from a foreign law enforcement agency to provide assistance in accordance with this subsection, if the requesting agency states that it is investigating, or engaging in enforcement proceedings against, possible violations of laws prohibiting fraudulent or deceptive commercial practices, or other practices substantially similar to practices prohibited by any provision of the laws administered by the Commission, other than Federal antitrust laws (as defined in section 6211(5) of this title), to provide the assistance described in paragraph (2) without requiring that the conduct identified in the request constitute a violation of the laws of the United States.

(2) Type of Assistance.—In providing assistance to a foreign law enforcement agency under this subsection, the Commission may—

(A) conduct such investigation as the Commission deems necessary to collect information and evidence pertinent to the request for assistance, using all investigative powers authorized by this Act; and

(B) when the request is from an agency acting to investigate or pursue the enforcement of civil laws, or when the Attorney General refers a request to the Commission from an agency acting to investigate or pursue the enforcement of criminal laws, seek and accept appointment by a United States district court of Commission attorneys to provide assistance to foreign and international tribunals and to litigants before such tribunals on behalf of a foreign law enforcement agency pursuant to section 1782 of title 28.

(3) Criteria for Determination.—In deciding whether to provide such assistance, the Commission shall consider all relevant factors, including—

(A) whether the requesting agency has agreed to provide or will provide reciprocal assistance to the Commission;

(B) whether compliance with the request would prejudice the public interest of the United States; and

(C) whether the requesting agency's investigation or enforcement proceeding concerns acts or practices that cause or are likely to cause injury to a significant number of persons.

(4) International Agreements.—If a foreign law enforcement agency has set forth a legal basis for requiring execution of an international agreement as a condition for reciprocal assistance, or as a condition for provision of materials or information to the Commission, the Commission, with prior approval and ongoing oversight of the Secretary of State, and with final approval of the agreement by the Secretary of State, may negotiate and conclude an international agreement, in the name of either the United States or the Commission, for the purpose of obtaining such assistance, materials, or information. The Commission may undertake in such an international agreement to—

(A) provide assistance using the powers set forth in this subsection;

(B) disclose materials and information in accordance with subsection (f) and section 57b–2(b) of this title; and

(C) engage in further cooperation, and protect materials and information received from disclosure, as authorized by this Act.

(5) Additional Authority.—The authority provided by this subsection is in addition to, and not in lieu of, any other authority vested in the Commission or any other officer of the United States.

(6) Limitation.—The authority granted by this subsection shall not authorize the Commission to take any action or exercise any power with respect to a bank, a savings and loan institution described in section 57a(f)(3) of this title, a Federal credit union described in section 57a(f)(4) of this title, or a common carrier subject to the Act to regulate commerce, except in accordance with the undesignated proviso following the last designated subsection of this section.

(7) Assistance to Certain Countries.—The Commission may not provide investigative assistance under this subsection to a foreign law enforcement agency from a foreign state that the Secretary of State has determined, in accordance with section 2405(j) of the Appendix to Title 50, has repeatedly provided support for acts of international terrorism, unless and until such determination is rescinded pursuant to section 2405(j)(4) of the Appendix to Title 50.

(k) Referral of Evidence for Criminal Proceedings

(1) In General.—Whenever the Commission obtains evidence that any person, partnership, or corporation, either domestic or foreign, has engaged in conduct that may constitute a violation of Federal criminal law, to transmit such evidence to the Attorney General, who may institute criminal proceedings under appropriate statutes. Nothing in this paragraph affects any other authority of the Commission to disclose information.

(2) International Information.—The Commission shall endeavor to ensure, with respect to memoranda of understanding and international agreements it may conclude, that material it has obtained from foreign law enforcement agencies acting to investigate or pursue the enforcement of foreign criminal laws may be used for the purpose of investigation, prosecution, or prevention of violations of United States criminal laws.

(*l*) Expenditures for Cooperative Arrangements

To expend appropriated funds for—

(1) operating expenses and other costs of bilateral and multilateral cooperative law enforcement groups conducting activities of interest to the Commission and in which the Commission participates; and

(2) expenses for consultations and meetings hosted by the Commission with foreign government agency officials, members of their delegations, appropriate representatives and staff to exchange views concerning developments relating to the Commission's mission, development and implementation of cooperation agreements, and provision of technical assistance for the development of foreign consumer protection or competition regimes, such expenses to include necessary administrative and logistic expenses and the expenses of Commission staff and foreign invitees in attendance at such consultations and meetings including—

    (A) such incidental expenses as meals taken in the course of such attendance;

    (B) any travel and transportation to or from such meetings; and

    (C) any other lodging or subsistence.

Provided, That the exception of "banks, savings and loan institutions described in section 57a(f)(3) of this title, Federal credit unions described in section 57a(f)(3) of this title, and common carriers subject to the Act to regulate commerce" from the Commission's powers defined in subsections (a), (b), and (j) of this section, shall not be construed to limit the Commission's authority to gather and compile information, to investigate, or to require reports or answers from, any person, partnership, or corporation to the extent that such action is necessary to the investigation of any person, partnership, or corporation, group of persons, partnerships, or corporations, or industry which is not engaged or is engaged only incidentally in banking, in business as a savings and loan institution, in business as a Federal credit union, or in business as a common carrier subject to the Act to regulate commerce.

The Commission shall establish a plan designed to substantially reduce burdens imposed upon small businesses as a result of requirements established by the Commission under clause (b) relating to the filing of quarterly financial reports. Such plan shall (1) be established after consultation with small businesses and persons who use the information contained in such quarterly financial reports; (2) provide for a reduction of the number of small businesses required to file such quarterly financial reports; and (3) make revisions in the forms used for such quarterly financial reports for the purpose of reducing the complexity of such forms. The Commission, not later than December 31, 1980, shall submit such plan to the Committee on Commerce, Science, and Transportation of the Senate and to the Committee on Energy and Commerce of the House of Representatives. Such plan shall take effect not later than October 31, 1981.

No officer or employee of the Commission or any Commissioner may publish or disclose information to the public, or to any Federal agency, whereby any line-of-business data furnished by a particular establishment or individual can be identified. No one other than designated sworn officers and employees of the Commission may examine the line-of-business reports from individual firms, and information provided in the line-of-business program administered by the Commission shall be used only for statistical purposes. Information for carrying out specific law enforcement responsibilities of the Commission shall be obtained under practices and procedures in effect on May 28, 1980, or as changed by law.

Nothing in this section (other than the provisions of clause (c) and clause (d)) shall apply to the business of insurance, except that the Commission shall have authority to conduct studies and prepare reports relating to the business of insurance. The Commission may exercise such authority only upon receiving a request which is agreed to by a majority of the members of the Committee on Commerce, Science, and Transportation of the Senate or the Committee on Energy and Commerce of the House of Representatives. The authority to conduct any such study shall expire at the end of the Congress during which the request for such study was made.

§ 46a. Concurrent Resolution Essential to Authorize Investigations

After June 16, 1933, no new investigations shall be initiated by the Commission as the result of a legislative resolution, except the same be a concurrent resolution of the two Houses of Congress.

§ 47. Reference of Suits Under Antitrust Statutes to Commission

In any suit in equity brought by or under the direction of the Attorney General as provided in the antitrust Acts, the court may, upon the conclusion of the testimony therein, if it shall be then of opinion that the complainant is entitled to relief, refer said suit to the Commission, as a master in chancery, to ascertain and report an appropriate form of decree therein. The Commission shall proceed upon such notice to the parties and under such rules of procedure as the court may prescribe, and upon the coming in of such report such exceptions may be filed and such proceedings had in relation thereto as upon the report of a master in other equity causes, but the court may adopt or reject such report, in whole or in part, and enter such decree as the nature of the case may in its judgment require.

§ 48. Information and Assistance From Departments

The several departments and bureaus of the Government when directed by the President shall furnish the Commission, upon its request, all records, papers, and information in their possession relating to any corporation subject to any of the provisions of sections 41 to 46 and 47 to 58 of this title, and shall detail from time to time such officials and employees to the Commission as he may direct.

§ 49. Documentary Evidence; Depositions; Witnesses

For the purposes of sections 41 to 46 and 47 to 58 of this title the Commission, or its duly authorized agent or agents, shall at all reasonable times have access to, for the purpose of examination, and the right to copy any documentary evidence of any person, partnership, or corporation being investigated or proceeded against; and the Commission shall have power to require by subpoena the attendance and testimony of witnesses and the production of all such documentary evidence relating to any matter under investigation. Any member of the Commission may sign subpoenas and members and examiners of the Commission may administer oaths and affirmations, examine witnesses, and receive evidence.

Such attendance of witnesses, and the production of such documentary evidence, may be required from any place in the United States, at any designated place of hearing. And in case of disobedience to a subpoena the Commission may invoke the aid of any court of the United States in requiring the attendance and testimony of witnesses and the production of documentary evidence.

Any of the district courts of the United States within the jurisdiction of which such inquiry is carried on may, in case of contumacy or refusal to obey a subpoena issued to any person, partnership, or corporation issue an order requiring such person, partnership, or corporation to appear before the Commission, or to produce documentary evidence if so ordered, or to give evidence touching the matter in question; and any failure to obey such order of the court may be punished by such court as a contempt thereof.

Upon the application of the Attorney General of the United States, at the request of the Commission, the district courts of the United States shall have jurisdiction to issue writs of mandamus commanding any person, partnership, or corporation to comply with the provisions of sections 41 to 46 and 47 to 58 of this title or any order of the Commission made in pursuance thereof.

The Commission may order testimony to be taken by deposition in any proceeding or investigation pending under said sections at any stage of such proceeding or investigation. Such depositions may be taken before any person designated by the Commission and having power to administer oaths. Such testimony shall be reduced to writing by the person taking the deposition, or under his direction, and shall then be subscribed by the deponent. Any person may be compelled to appear and depose and to produce documentary evidence in the same manner as witnesses may be compelled to appear and testify and produce documentary evidence before the Commission as hereinbefore provided.

Witnesses summoned before the Commission shall be paid the same fees and mileage that are paid witnesses in the courts of the United States, and witnesses whose depositions are taken and the persons taking the same shall severally be entitled to the same fees as are paid for like services in the courts of the United States.

§ 50.   Offenses and Penalties

Any person who shall neglect or refuse to attend and testify, or to answer any lawful inquiry or to produce any documentary evidence, if in his power to do so, in obedience to an order of a district court of the United States directing compliance with the subpoena or lawful requirement of the Commission, shall be guilty of an offense and upon conviction thereof by a court of competent jurisdiction shall be punished by a fine of not less than $1,000 nor more than $5,000, or by imprisonment for not more than one year, or by both such fine and imprisonment.

Any person who shall willfully make, or cause to be made, any false entry or statement of fact in any report required to be made under sections 41 to 46 and 47 to 58 of this title, or who shall willfully make, or cause to be made, any false entry in any account, record, or memorandum kept by any person, partnership, or corporation subject to said sections, or who shall willfully neglect or fail to make, or to cause to be made, full, true, and correct entries in such accounts, records, or memoranda of all facts and transactions appertaining to the business of such person, partnership, or corporation or who shall willfully remove out of the jurisdiction of the United States, or willfully mutilate, alter, or by any other means falsify any documentary evidence of such person, partnership, or corporation or who shall willfully refuse to submit to the Commission or to any of its authorized agents, for the purpose of inspection and taking copies, any documentary evidence of such person, partnership, or corporation in his possession or within his control, shall be deemed guilty of an offense against the United States, and shall be subject, upon conviction in any court of the United States of competent jurisdiction, to a fine of not less than $1,000 nor more than $5,000, or to imprisonment for a term of not more than three years, or to both such fine and imprisonment.

If any persons, partnership, or corporation required by sections 41 to 46 and 47 to 58 of this title to file any annual or special report shall fail so to do within the time fixed by the Commission for filing the same, and such failure shall continue for thirty days after notice of such default, the corporation shall forfeit to the United States the sum of $100 for each and every day of the continuance of such failure, which forfeiture shall be payable into the Treasury of the United States, and shall be recoverable in a civil suit in the name of the United States brought in the case of a corporation or partnership in the district where the corporation or partnership has its principal office or in any district in which it shall do business, and in the case of any person in the district where such person resides or has his principal place of business. It shall be the duty of the various United States attorneys, under the direction of the Attorney General of the United States, to prosecute for the recovery of forfeitures. The costs and expenses of such prosecution shall be paid out of the appropriation for the expenses of the courts of the United States.

Any officer or employee of the Commission who shall make public any information obtained by the Commission without its authority, unless directed by a court, shall be deemed guilty of a misdemeanor, and, upon conviction thereof, shall be punished by a fine not exceeding $5,000, or by imprisonment not exceeding one year, or by fine and imprisonment, in the discretion of the court.

§ 51. Effect on Other Statutory Provisions

Nothing contained in sections 41 to 46 and 47 to 58 of this title shall be construed to prevent or interfere with the enforcement of the provisions of the antitrust Acts or the Acts to regulate commerce, nor shall anything contained in said sections be construed to alter, modify, or repeal the said antitrust Acts or the Acts to regulate commerce or any part or parts thereof.

§ 52. Dissemination of False Advertisements

(a) Unlawfulness

It shall be unlawful for any person, partnership, or corporation to disseminate, or cause to be disseminated, any false advertisement—

(1) By United States mails, or in or having an effect upon commerce, by any means, for the purpose of inducing, or which is likely to induce, directly or indirectly the purchase of food, drugs, devices, services, or cosmetics; or

(2) By any means, for the purpose of inducing, or which is likely to induce, directly or indirectly, the purchase in or having an effect upon commerce of food, drugs, devices, services, or cosmetics.

(b) Unfair or Deceptive Act or Practice

The dissemination or the causing to be disseminated of any false advertisement within the provisions of subsection (a) of this section shall be an unfair or deceptive act or practice in or affecting commerce within the meaning of section 45 of this title.

§ 53. False Advertisements; Injunctions and Restraining Orders

(a) Power of Commission; Jurisdiction of Courts

Whenever the Commission has reason to believe—

(1) that any person, partnership, or corporation is engaged in, or is about to engage in, the dissemination or the causing of the dissemination of any advertisement in violation of section 52 of this title, and

(2)   that the enjoining thereof pending the issuance of a complaint by the Commission under section 45 of this title, and until such complaint is dismissed by the Commission or set aside by the court on review, or the order of the Commission to cease and desist made thereon has become final within the meaning of section 45 of this title, would be to the interest of the public,

the Commission by any of its attorneys designated by it for such purpose may bring suit in a district court of the United States or in the United States court of any Territory, to enjoin the dissemination or the causing of the dissemination of such advertisement. Upon proper showing a temporary injunction or restraining order shall be granted without bond. Any suit may be brought where such person, partnership, or corporation resides or transacts business, or wherever venue is proper under section 1391 of title 28, United States Code. In addition, the court may, if the court determines that the interests of justice require that any other person, partnership, or corporation should be a party in such suit, cause such other person, partnership, or corporation to be added as a party without regard to whether venue is otherwise proper in the district in which the suit is brought. In any suit under this section, process may be served on any person, partnership, or corporation wherever it may be found.

(b)   Temporary Restraining Orders; Preliminary Injunctions

Whenever the Commission has reason to believe—

(1)   that any person, partnership, or corporation is violating, or is about to violate, any provision of law enforced by the Federal Trade Commission, and

(2)   that the enjoining thereof pending the issuance of a complaint by the Commission and until such complaint is dismissed by the Commission or set aside by the court on review, or until the order of the Commission made thereon has become final, would be in the interest of the public—

the Commission by any of its attorneys designated by it for such purpose may bring suit in a district court of the United States to enjoin any such act or practice. Upon a proper showing that, weighing the equities and considering the Commission's likelihood of ultimate success, such action would be in the public interest, and after notice to the defendant, a temporary restraining order or a preliminary injunction may be granted without bond: *Provided, however,* That if a complaint is not filed within such period (not exceeding 20 days) as may be specified by the court after issuance of the temporary restraining order or preliminary injunction, the order or injunction shall be dissolved by the court and be of no further force and effect: *Provided further,* That in proper cases the Commission may seek, and after proper proof, the court may issue, a permanent injunction. Any suit may be brought where such person, partnership, or corporation resides or transacts business, or wherever venue is proper under section 1391 of title 28, United States Code. In addition, the court may, if the court determines that the interests of justice require that any other person, partnership, or corporation should be a party in such suit, cause such other person, partnership, or corporation to be added as a party without regard to whether venue is otherwise proper in the district in which the suit is brought. In any suit under this section, process may be served on any person, partnership, or corporation wherever it may be found.

(c)   Service of Process; Proof of Service

Any process of the Commission under this section may be served by any person duly authorized by the Commission—

(1)   by delivering a copy of such process to the person to be served, to a member of the partnership to be served, or to the president, secretary, or other executive officer or a director of the corporation to be served;

(2)   by leaving a copy of such process at the residence or the principal office or place of business of such person, partnership, or corporation; or

(3) by mailing a copy of such process by registered mail or certified mail addressed to such person, partnership, or corporation at his, or her, or its residence, principal office, or principal place or business.

The verified return by the person serving such process setting forth the manner of such service shall be proof of the same.

(d) Exception of Periodical Publications

Whenever it appears to the satisfaction of the court in the case of a newspaper, magazine, periodical, or other publication, published at regular intervals—

(1) that restraining the dissemination of a false advertisement in any particular issue of such publication would delay the delivery of such issue after the regular time therefor, and

(2) that such delay would be due to the method by which the manufacture and distribution of such publication is customarily conducted by the publisher in accordance with sound business practice, and not to any method or device adopted for the evasion of this section or to prevent or delay the issuance of an injunction or restraining order with respect to such false advertisement or any other advertisement,

the court shall exclude such issue from the operation of the restraining order or injunction.

§ 54. False Advertisements; Penalties

(a) Imposition of Penalties

Any person, partnership, or corporation who violates any provision of section 52(a) of this title shall, if the use of the commodity advertised may be injurious to health because of results from such use under the conditions prescribed in the advertisement thereof, or under such conditions as are customary or usual, or if such violation is with intent to defraud or mislead, be guilty of a misdemeanor, and upon conviction shall be punished by a fine of not more than $5,000 or by imprisonment for not more than six months, or by both such fine and imprisonment; except that if the conviction is for a violation committed after a first conviction of such person, partnership, or corporation, for any violation of such section, punishment shall be by a fine of not more than $10,000 or by imprisonment for not more than one year, or by both such fine and imprisonment: *Provided,* That for the purposes of this section meats and meat food products duly inspected, marked, and labeled in accordance with rules and regulations issued under the Meat Inspection Act, shall be conclusively presumed not injurious to health at the time the same leave official "establishments."

(b) Exception of Advertising Medium or Agency

No publisher, radio-broadcast licensee, or agency or medium for the dissemination of advertising, except the manufacturer, packer, distributor, or seller of the commodity to which the false advertisement relates, shall be liable under this section by reason of the dissemination by him of any false advertisement, unless he has refused, on the request of the Commission, to furnish the Commission the name and post-office address of the manufacturer, packer, distributor, seller, or advertising agency, residing in the United States, who caused him to disseminate such advertisement. No advertising agency shall be liable under this section by reason of the causing by it of the dissemination of any false advertisement, unless it has refused, on the request of the Commission, to furnish the Commission the name and post-office address of the manufacturer, packer, distributor, or seller, residing in the United States, who caused it to cause the dissemination of such advertisement.

§ 55. Additional Definitions

For the purposes of section 52 to 54 of this title—

(a) False Advertisement

(1) The term "false advertisement" means an advertisement, other than labeling, which is misleading in a material respect; and in determining whether any advertisement is misleading, there shall be taken into account (among other things) not only representations made or suggested by statement, word, design, device, sound, or any combination thereof, but also the extent to which the advertisement fails to reveal facts material in the light of such representations or material with respect to consequences which may result from the use of the commodity to which the advertisement relates under the conditions prescribed in said advertisement, or under such conditions as are customary or usual. No advertisement of a drug shall be deemed to be false if it is disseminated only to members of the medical profession, contains no false representation of a material fact, and includes, or is accompanied in each instance by truthful disclosure of, the formula showing quantitatively each ingredient of such drug.

(2) In the case of oleomargarine or margarine an advertisement shall be deemed misleading in a material respect if in such advertisement representations are made or suggested by statement, word, grade designation, design, device, symbol, sound, or any combination thereof, that such oleomargarine or margarine is a dairy product, except that nothing contained herein shall prevent a truthful, accurate, and full statement in any such advertisement of all the ingredients contained in such oleomargarine or margarine.

(b) Food

The term "food" means (1) articles used for food or drink for man or other animals, (2) chewing gum, and (3) articles used for components of any such article.

(c) Drug

The term "drug" means (1) articles recognized in the official United States Pharmacopoeia, official Homeopathic Pharmacopoeia of the United States, or official National Formulary, or any supplement to any of them; and (2) articles intended for use in the diagnosis, cure, mitigation, treatment, or prevention of disease in man or other animals; and (3) articles (other than food) intended to affect the structure or any function of the body of man or other animals; and (4) articles intended for use as a component of any article specified in clauses (1), (2), or (3); but does not include devices or their components, parts, or accessories.

(d) Device

The term "device" (except when used in subsection (a) of this section) means an instrument, apparatus, implement, machine, contrivance, implant, in vitro reagent, or other similar or related article, including any component, part, or accessory, which is—

(1) recognized in the official National Formulary, or the United States Pharmacopeia, or any supplement to them,

(2) intended for use in the diagnosis of disease or other conditions, or in the cure, mitigation, treatment, or prevention of disease, in man or other animals, or

(3) intended to affect the structure or any function of the body of man or other animals, and

which does not achieve any of its principal intended purposes through chemical action within or on the body of man or other animals and which is not depended upon being metabolized for the achievement of any of its principal intended purposes.

(e) Cosmetic

The term "cosmetic" means (1) articles to be rubbed, poured, sprinkled, or sprayed on, introduced into, or otherwise applied to the human body or any part thereof intended for cleansing, beautifying, promoting attractiveness, or altering the appearance, and (2) articles intended for use as a component of any such article; except that such term shall not include soap.

(f)   Oleomargarine or Margarine

For the purposes of this section and section 347 of Title 21, the term "oleomargarine" or "margarine" includes—

(1)   all substances, mixtures, and compounds known as oleomargarine or margarine;

(2)   all substances, mixtures, and compounds which have a consistence* similar to that of butter and which contain any edible oils or fats other than milk fat if made in imitation or semblance of butter.

§ 56.   Commencement, Defense, Intervention and Supervision of Litigation and Appeal by Commission or Attorney General

(a)(1)   Except as otherwise provided in paragraph (2) or (3), if—

(A)   before commencing, defending, or intervening in, any civil action involving sections 41 to 46 and 47 to 58 of this title (including an action to collect a civil penalty) which the Commission, or the Attorney General on behalf of the Commission, is authorized to commence, defend, or intervene in, the Commission gives written notification and undertakes to consult with the Attorney General with respect to such action; and

(B)   the Attorney General fails within 45 days after receipt of such notification to commence, defend, or intervene in, such action;

the Commission may commence, defend, or intervene in, and supervise the litigation of, such action and any appeal of such action in its own name by any of its attorneys designated by it for such purpose.

(2)   Except as otherwise provided in paragraph (3), in any civil action—

(A)   under section 53 of this title (relating to injunctive relief);

(B)   under section 57b of this title (relating to consumer redress);

(C)   to obtain judicial review of a rule prescribed by the Commission, or a cease and desist order issued under section 45 of this title;

(D)   under the second paragraph of section 49 of this title (relating to enforcement of a subpena) and under the fourth paragraph of such section (relating to compliance with section 46 of this title); or

(E)   under section 57b–2a of this title;

the Commission shall have exclusive authority to commence or defend, and supervise the litigation of, such action and any appeal of such action in its own name by any of its attorneys designated by it for such purpose, unless the Commission authorizes the Attorney General to do so. The Commission shall inform the Attorney General of the exercise of such authority and such exercise shall not preclude the Attorney General from intervening on behalf of the United States in such action and any appeal of such action as may be otherwise provided by law.

(3)(A)   If the Commission makes a written request to the Attorney General, within the 10-day period which begins on the date of the entry of the judgment in any civil action in which the Commission represented itself pursuant to paragraph (1) or (2), to represent itself through any of its attorneys designated by it for such purpose before the Supreme Court in such action, it may do so, if—

(i)   the Attorney General concurs with such request; or

(ii)   the Attorney General, within the 60-day period which begins on the date of the entry of such judgment—

---

*   So in original. Probably should read "consistency."—*Ed.*

(a) refuses to appeal or file a petition for writ of certiorari with respect to such civil action, in which case he shall give written notification to the Commission of the reasons for such refusal within such 60-day period; or

(b) the Attorney General fails to take any action with respect to the Commission's request.

(B) In any case where the Attorney General represents the Commission before the Supreme Court in any civil action in which the Commission represented itself pursuant to paragraph (1) or (2), the Attorney General may not agree to any settlement, compromise, or dismissal of such action, or confess error in the Supreme Court with respect to such action, unless the Commission concurs.

(C) For purposes of this paragraph (with respect to representation before the Supreme Court), the term "Attorney General" includes the Solicitor General.

(4) If, prior to the expiration of the 45-day period specified in paragraph (1) of this section or a 60-day period specified in paragraph (3), any right of the Commission to commence, defend, or intervene in, any such action or appeal may be extinguished due to any procedural requirement of any court with respect to the time in which any pleadings, notice of appeal, or other acts pertaining to such action or appeal may be taken, the Attorney General shall have one-half of the time required to comply with any such procedural requirement of the court (including any extension of such time granted by the court) for the purpose of commencing, defending, or intervening in the civil action pursuant to paragraph (1) or for the purpose of refusing to appeal or file a petition for writ of certiorari and the written notification or failing to take any action pursuant to paragraph 3(A)(ii).

(5) The provisions of this subsection shall apply notwithstanding chapter 31 of Title 28, or any other provision of law.

(b) Whenever the Commission has reason to believe that any person, partnership, or corporation is liable for a criminal penalty under sections 41 to 46 and 47 to 58 of this title, the Commission shall certify the facts to the Attorney General, whose duty it shall be to cause appropriate criminal proceedings to be brought.

(c) Foreign Litigation

(1) Commission Attorneys.—With the concurrence of the Attorney General, the Commission may designate Commission attorneys to assist the Attorney General in connection with litigation in foreign courts on particular matters in which the Commission has an interest.

(2) Reimbursement for Foreign Counsel.—The Commission is authorized to expend appropriated funds, upon agreement with the Attorney General, to reimburse the Attorney General for the retention of foreign counsel for litigation in foreign courts and for expenses related to litigation in foreign courts in which the Commission has an interest.

(3) Limitation on Use of Funds.—Nothing in this subsection authorizes the payment of claims or judgments from any source other than the permanent and indefinite appropriation authorized by section 1304 of title 31, United States Code.

(4) Other Authority.—The authority provided by this subsection is in addition to any other authority of the Commission or the Attorney General.

§ 57.   Separability Clause

If any provision of sections 41 to 46 and 47 to 58 of this title, or the application thereof to any person, partnership, corporation, or circumstance, is held invalid, the remainder of said sections, and the application of such provision to any other person, partnership, corporation, or circumstance, shall not be affected thereby.

§ 57a.   Unfair or Deceptive Acts or Practices Rulemaking Proceedings

(a) Authority of Commission to Prescribe Rules and General Statements of Policy

(1) Except as provided in subsection (h) of this section, the Commission may prescribe—

(A) interpretive rules and general statements of policy with respect to unfair or deceptive acts or practices in or affecting commerce (within the meaning of section 45(a)(1) of this title), and

(B) rules which define with specificity acts or practices which are unfair or deceptive acts or practices in or affecting commerce (within the meaning of section 45(a)(1) of this title), except that the Commission shall not develop or promulgate any trade rule or regulation with regard to the regulation of the development and utilization of the standards and certification activities pursuant to this section. Rules under this subparagraph may include requirements prescribed for the purpose of preventing such acts or practices.

(2) The Commission shall have no authority under sections 41 to 46 and 47 to 58 of this title, other than its authority under this section, to prescribe any rule with respect to unfair or deceptive acts or practices in or affecting commerce (within the meaning of section 45(a)(1) of this title). The preceding sentence shall not affect any authority of the Commission to prescribe rules (including interpretive rules), and general statements of policy, with respect to unfair methods of competition in or affecting commerce.

(b) Procedures Applicable

(1) When prescribing a rule under subsection (a)(1)(B) of this section, the Commission shall proceed in accordance with section 553 of Title 5 (without regard to any reference in such section to sections 556 and 557 of such title), and shall also (A) publish a notice of proposed rulemaking stating with particularity the text of the rule, including any alternatives, which the Commission proposes to promulgate, and the reason for the proposed rule; (B) allow interested persons to submit written data, views, and arguments, and make all such submissions publicly available; (C) provide an opportunity for an informal hearing in accordance with subsection (c) of this section; and (D) promulgate, if appropriate, a final rule based on the matter in the rulemaking record (as defined in subsection (e)(1)(B) of this section), together with a statement of basis and purpose.

(2)(A) Prior to the publication of any notice of proposed rulemaking pursuant to paragraph (1)(A), the Commission shall publish an advance notice of proposed rulemaking in the Federal Register. Such advance notice shall—

(i) contain a brief description of the area of inquiry under consideration, the objectives which the Commission seeks to achieve, and possible regulatory alternatives under consideration by the Commission; and

(ii) invite the response of interested parties with respect to such proposed rulemaking, including any suggestions or alternative methods for achieving such objectives.

(B) The Commission shall submit such advance notice of proposed rulemaking to the Committee on Commerce, Science, and Transportation of the Senate and to the Committee on Energy and Commerce of the House of Representatives. The Commission may use such additional mechanisms as the Commission considers useful to obtain suggestions regarding the content of the area of inquiry before the publication of a general notice of proposed rulemaking under paragraph (1)(A).

(C) The Commission shall, 30 days before the publication of a notice of proposed rulemaking pursuant to paragraph (1)(A), submit such notice to the Committee on Commerce, Science, and Transportation of the Senate and to the Committee on Energy and Commerce of the House of Representatives.

(3) The Commission shall issue a notice of proposed rulemaking pursuant to paragraph (1)(A) only where it has reason to believe that the unfair or deceptive acts or practices which are the subject of the proposed rulemaking are prevalent. The Commission shall make a determination that unfair or deceptive acts or practices are prevalent under this paragraph only if—

(A) it has issued cease and desist orders regarding such acts or practices, or

(B) any other information available to the Commission indicates a widespread pattern of unfair or deceptive acts or practices.

(c) Informal Hearing Procedure

The Commission shall conduct any informal hearings required by subsection (b)(1)(C) of this section in accordance with the following procedure:

(1)(A) The Commission shall provide for the conduct of proceedings under this subsection by hearing officers who shall perform their functions in accordance with the requirements of this subsection.

(B) The officer who presides over the rulemaking proceedings shall be responsible to a chief presiding officer who shall not be responsible to any other officer or employee of the Commission. The officer who presides over the rulemaking proceeding shall make a recommended decision based upon the findings and conclusions of such officer as to all relevant and material evidence, except that such recommended decision may be made by another officer if the officer who presided over the proceeding is no longer available to the Commission.

(C) Except as required for the disposition of ex parte matters as authorized by law, no presiding officer shall consult any person or party with respect to any fact in issue unless such officer gives notice and opportunity for all parties to participate.

(2) Subject to paragraph (3) of this subsection, an interested person is entitled—

(A) to present his position orally or by documentary submissions (or both), and

(B) if the Commission determines that there are disputed issues of material fact it is necessary to resolve, to present such rebuttal submissions and to conduct (or have conducted under paragraph (3)(B)) such cross-examination of persons as the Commission determines (i) to be appropriate, and (ii) to be required for a full and true disclosure with respect to such issues.

(3) The Commission may prescribe such rules and make such rulings concerning proceedings in such hearings as may tend to avoid unnecessary costs or delay. Such rules or rulings may include (A) imposition of reasonable time limits on each interested person's oral presentations, and (B) requirements that any cross-examination to which a person may be entitled under paragraph (2) be conducted by the Commission on behalf of that person in such manner as the Commission determines (i) to be appropriate, and (ii) to be required for a full and true disclosure with respect to disputed issues of material fact.

(4)(A) Except as provided in subparagraph (B), if a group of persons each of whom under paragraphs (2) and (3) would be entitled to conduct (or have conducted) cross-examination and who are determined by the Commission to have the same or similar interests in the proceeding cannot agree upon a single representative of such interests for purposes of cross-examination, the Commission may make rules and rulings (i) limiting the representation of such interest, for such purposes, and (ii) governing the manner in which such cross-examination shall be limited.

(B) When any person who is a member of a group with respect to which the Commission has made a determination under subparagraph (A) is unable to agree upon group representation with the other members of the group, then such person shall not be denied under the authority of subparagraph (A) the opportunity to conduct (or have conducted) cross-examination as to issues affecting his particular interests if (i) he satisfies the Commission that he has made a reasonable and good faith effort to reach agreement upon group representation with the other members of the group and (ii) the Commission determines that there are substantial and relevant issues which are not adequately presented by the group representative.

(5) A verbatim transcript shall be taken of any oral presentation, and cross-examination, in an informal hearing to which this subsection applies. Such transcript shall be available to the public.

(d) Statement of Basis and Purpose Accompanying Rule; "Commission" Defined; Judicial Review of Amendment or Repeal of Rule; Violation of Rule

(1)   The Commission's statement of basis and purpose to accompany a rule promulgated under subsection (a)(1)(B) of this section shall include (A) a statement as to the prevalence of the acts or practices treated by the rule; (B) a statement as to the manner and context in which such acts or practices are unfair or deceptive; and (C) a statement as to the economic effect of the rule, taking into account the effect on small business and consumers.

(2)(A)   The term "Commission" as used in this subsection and subsections (b) and (c) of this section includes any person authorized to act in behalf of the Commission in any part of the rulemaking proceeding.

(B)   A substantive amendment to, or repeal of, a rule promulgated under subsection (a)(1)(B) of this section shall be prescribed, and subject to judicial review, in the same manner as a rule prescribed under such subsection. An exemption under subsection (g) of this section shall not be treated as an amendment or repeal of a rule.

(3)   When any rule under subsection (a)(1)(B) of this section takes effect a subsequent violation thereof shall constitute an unfair or deceptive act or practice in violation of section 45(a)(1) of this title, unless the Commission otherwise expressly provides in such rule.

(e) Judicial Review; Petition; Jurisdiction and Venue; Rulemaking Record; Additional Submissions and Presentations; Scope of Review and Relief; Review by Supreme Court; Additional Remedies

(1)(A)   Not later than 60 days after a rule is promulgated under subsection (a)(1)(B) of this section by the Commission, any interested person (including a consumer or consumer organization) may file a petition, in the United States Court of Appeals for the District of Columbia circuit or for the circuit in which such person resides or has his principal place of business, for judicial review of such rule. Copies of the petition shall be forthwith transmitted by the clerk of the court to the Commission or other officer designated by it for that purpose. The provisions of section 2112 of Title 28 shall apply to the filing of the rulemaking record of proceedings on which the Commission based its rule and to the transfer of proceedings in the courts of appeals.

(B)   For purpose of this section, the term "rulemaking record" means the rule, its statement of basis and purpose, the transcript required by subsection (c)(5) of this section, any written submissions, and any other information which the Commission considers relevant to such rule.

(2)   If the petitioner or the Commission applies to the court for leave to make additional oral submissions or written presentations and shows to the satisfaction of the court that such submissions and presentations would be material and that there were reasonable grounds for the submissions and failure to make such submissions and presentations in the proceeding before the Commission, the court may order the Commission to provide additional opportunity to make such submissions and presentations. The Commission may modify or set aside its rule or make a new rule by reason of the additional submissions and presentations and shall file such modified or new rule, and the rule's statement of basis of purpose, with the return of such submissions and presentations. The court shall thereafter review such new or modified rule.

(3)   Upon the filing of the petition under paragraph (1) of this subsection, the court shall have jurisdiction to review the rule in accordance with chapter 7 of Title 5 and to grant appropriate relief, including interim relief, as provided in such chapter. The court shall hold unlawful and set aside the rule on any ground specified in subparagraphs (A), (B), (C), or (D) of section 706(2) of Title 5 (taking due account of the rule of prejudicial error), or if—

(A)   the court finds that the Commission's action is not supported by substantial evidence in the rulemaking record (as defined in paragraph (1)(B) of this subsection) taken as a whole, or

(B)   the court finds that—

(i)   a Commission determination under subsection (c) of this section that the petitioner is not entitled to conduct cross-examination or make rebuttal submissions, or

(ii) a Commission rule or ruling under subsection (c) of this section limiting the petitioner's cross-examination or rebuttal submissions,

has precluded disclosure of disputed material facts which was necessary for fair determination by the Commission of the rulemaking proceeding taken as a whole.

The term "evidence", as used in this paragraph, means any matter in the rulemaking record.

(4) The judgment of the court affirming or setting aside, in whole or in part, any such rule shall be final, subject to review by the Supreme Court of the United States upon certiorari or certification, as provided in section 1254 of Title 28.

(5)(A) Remedies under the preceding paragraphs of this subsection are in addition to and not in lieu of any other remedies provided by law.

(B) The United States Courts of Appeal shall have exclusive jurisdiction of any action to obtain judicial review (other than in an enforcement proceeding) of a rule prescribed under subsection (a)(1)(B) of this section, if any district court of the United States would have had jurisdiction of such action but for this subparagraph. Any such action shall be brought in the United States Court of Appeals for the District of Columbia circuit, or for any circuit which includes a judicial district in which the action could have been brought but for this subparagraph.

(C) A determination, rule, or ruling of the Commission described in paragraph (3)(B)(i) or (ii) may be reviewed only in a proceeding under this subsection and only in accordance with paragraph (3)(B). Section 706(2)(E) of Title 5 shall not apply to any rule promulgated under subsection (a)(1)(B) of this section. The contents and adequacy of any statement required by subsection (b)(1)(D) of this section shall not be subject to judicial review in any respect.

(f) Unfair or Deceptive Acts or Practices by Banks, Savings and Loan Institutions, or Federal Credit Unions; Promulgation of Regulations by Board of Governors of Federal Reserve System, Federal Home Loan Bank Board, and National Credit Union Administration Board; Agency Enforcement and Compliance Proceedings; Violations; Power of Other Federal Agencies Unaffected; Reporting Requirements

(1) In order to prevent unfair or deceptive acts or practices in or affecting commerce (including acts or practices which are unfair or deceptive to consumers) by banks or savings and loan institutions described in paragraph (3), each agency specified in paragraph (2) or (3) of this subsection shall establish a separate division of consumer affairs which shall receive and take appropriate action upon complaints with respect to such acts or practices by banks or savings and loan institutions described in paragraph (3) subject to its jurisdiction. The Board of Governors of the Federal Reserve System (with respect to banks) and the Federal Home Loan Bank Board (with respect to savings and loan institutions described in paragraph (3)) and the National Credit Union Administration Board (with respect to Federal credit unions described in paragraph (4)) shall prescribe regulations to carry out the purposes of this section, including regulations defining with specificity such unfair or deceptive acts or practices, and containing requirements prescribed for the purpose of preventing such acts or practices. Whenever the Commission prescribes a rule under subsection (a)(1)(B) of this section, then within 60 days after such rule takes effect each such Board shall promulgate substantially similar regulations prohibiting acts or practices of banks or savings and loan institutions described in paragraph (3), or Federal credit unions described in paragraph (4), as the case may be, which are substantially similar to those prohibited by rules of the Commission and which impose substantially similar requirements, unless (A) any such Board finds that such acts or practices of banks or savings and loan institutions described in paragraph (3), or Federal credit unions described in paragraph (4), as the case may be, are not unfair or deceptive, or (B) the Board of Governors of the Federal Reserve System finds that implementation of similar regulations with respect to banks, savings and loan institutions or Federal credit unions would seriously conflict with essential monetary and payments systems policies of such Board, and publishes any such finding, and the reasons therefor, in the Federal Register.

(2) Enforcement.—Compliance with regulations prescribed under this subsection shall be enforced under section 1818 of Title 12, in the case of—

(A) national banks and Federal branches and Federal agencies of foreign banks, by the division of consumer affairs established by the Office of the Comptroller of the Currency;

(B) member banks of the Federal Reserve System (other than national banks), branches and agencies of foreign banks (other than Federal branches, Federal agencies, and insured State branches of foreign banks), commercial lending companies owned or controlled by foreign banks, and organizations operating under section 25 or 25(a) of the Federal Reserve Act [12 U.S.C.A. §§ 601 et seq., 611 et seq.], by the division of consumer affairs established by the Board of Governors of the Federal Reserve System; and

(C) banks insured by the Federal Deposit Insurance Corporation (other banks* referred to in subparagraph (A) or (B)) and insured State branches of foreign banks, by the division of consumer affairs established by the Board of Directors of the Federal Deposit Insurance Corporation.

(3) Compliance with regulations prescribed under this subsection shall be enforced under section 1818 of Title 12 with respect to savings associations as defined in section 1813 of Title 12.

(4) Compliance with regulations prescribed under this subsection shall be enforced with respect to Federal credit unions under sections 120 and 206 of the Federal Credit Union Act (12 U.S.C. 1766 and 1786).

(5) For the purpose of the exercise by any agency referred to in paragraph (2) of its powers under any Act referred to in that paragraph, a violation of any regulation prescribed under this subsection shall be deemed to be a violation of a requirement imposed under that Act. In addition to its powers under any provision of law specifically referred to in paragraph (2), each of the agencies referred to in that paragraph may exercise, for the purpose of enforcing compliance with any regulation prescribed under this subsection, any other authority conferred on it by law.

(6) The authority of the Board of Governors of the Federal Reserve System to issue regulations under this subsection does not impair the authority of any other agency designated in this subsection to make rules respecting its own procedures in enforcing compliance with regulations prescribed under this subsection.

(7) Each agency exercising authority under this subsection shall transmit to the Congress each year a detailed report on its activities under this paragraph during the preceding calendar year.

The terms used in this paragraph that are not defined in this chapter or otherwise defined in section 1813(s) of Title 12 shall have the meaning given to them in section 3101 of Title 12.

(g) Exemptions and Stays From Application of Rules; Procedures

(1) Any person to whom a rule under subsection (a)(1)(B) of this section applies may petition the Commission for an exemption from such rule.

(2) If, on its own motion or on the basis of a petition under paragraph (1), the Commission finds that the application of a rule prescribed under subsection (a)(1)(B) of this section to any person or class or** persons is not necessary to prevent the unfair or deceptive act or practice to which the rule relates, the Commission may exempt such person or class from all or part of such rule. Section 553 of Title 5 shall apply to action under this paragraph.

(3) Neither the pendency of a proceeding under this subsection respecting an exemption from a rule, nor the pendency of judicial proceedings to review the Commission's action or failure to act under this subsection, shall stay the applicability of such rule under subsection (a)(1)(B) of this section.

---

* So in original. Probably should be "other than banks".—*Ed.*

** So in original. Probably should be "of".

(h) Restriction on Rulemaking Authority of Commission Respecting Children's Advertising Proceedings Pending on May 28, 1980

The Commission shall not have any authority to promulgate any rule in the children's advertising proceeding pending on May 28, 1980, or in any substantially similar proceeding on the basis of a determination by the Commission that such advertising constitutes an unfair act or practice in or affecting commerce.

(i) Meetings With Outside Parties

(1) For purposes of this subsection, the term "outside party" means any person other than (A) a Commissioner, (B) an officer or employee of the Commission; or (C) any person who has entered into a contract or any other agreement or arrangement with the Commission to provide any goods or services (including consulting services) to the Commission.

(2) Not later than 60 days after May 28, 1980, the Commission shall publish a proposed rule, and not later than 180 days after May 28, 1980, the Commission shall promulgate a final rule, which shall authorize the Commission or any Commissioner to meet with any outside party concerning any rulemaking proceeding of the Commission. Such rule shall provide that—

(A) notice of any such meeting shall be included in any weekly calendar prepared by the Commission; and

(B) a verbatim record or a summary of any such meeting, or of any communication relating to any such meeting, shall be kept, made available to the public, and included in the rulemaking record.

(j) Communications by Investigative Personnel With Staff of Commission Concerning Matters Outside Rulemaking Record Prohibited

Not later than 60 days after May 28, 1980, the Commission shall publish a proposed rule, and not later than 180 days after May 28, 1980, the Commission shall promulgate a final rule, which shall prohibit any officer, employee, or agent of the Commission with any investigative responsibility or other responsibility relating to any rulemaking proceeding within any operating bureau of the Commission, from communicating or causing to be communicated to any Commissioner or to the personal staff of any Commissioner any fact which is relevant to the merits of such proceeding and which is not on the rulemaking record of such proceeding, unless such communication is made available to the public and is included in the rulemaking record. The provisions of this subsection shall not apply to any communication to the extent such communication is required for the disposition of ex parte matters as authorized by law.

§ 57a–1. [Omitted]

§ 57b. Civil Actions for Violations of Rules and Cease and Desist Orders Respecting Unfair or Deceptive Acts or Practices

(a) Suits by Commission Against Persons, Partnerships, or Corporations; Jurisdiction; Relief for Dishonest or Fraudulent Acts

(1) If any person, partnership, or corporation violates any rule under this chapter respecting unfair or deceptive acts or practices (other than an interpretive rule, or a rule violation of which the Commission has provided is not an unfair or deceptive act or practice in violation of section 45(a) of this title), then the Commission may commence a civil action against such person, partnership, or corporation for relief under subsection (b) of this section in a United States district court or in any court of competent jurisdiction of a State.

(2) If any person, partnership, or corporation engages in any unfair or deceptive act or practice (within the meaning of section 45(a)(1) of this title) with respect to which the Commission has issued a final cease and desist order which is applicable to such person, partnership, or

corporation, then the Commission may commence a civil action against such person, partnership, or corporation in a United States district court or in any court of competent jurisdiction of a State. If the Commission satisfies the court that the act or practice to which the cease and desist order relates is one which a reasonable man would have known under the circumstances was dishonest or fraudulent, the court may grant relief under subsection (b) of this section.

(b) Nature of Relief Available

The court in an action under subsection (a) of this section shall have jurisdiction to grant such relief as the court finds necessary to redress injury to consumers or other persons, partnerships, and corporations resulting from the rule violation or the unfair or deceptive act or practice, as the case may be. Such relief may include, but shall not be limited to, rescission or reformation of contracts, the refund of money or return of property, the payment of damages, and public notification respecting the rule violation or the unfair or deceptive act or practice, as the case may be; except that nothing in this subsection is intended to authorize the imposition of any exemplary or punitive damages.

(c) Conclusiveness of Findings of Commission in Cease and Desist Proceedings; Notice of Judicial Proceedings to Injured Persons, etc.

(1) If (A) a cease and desist order issued under section 45(b) of this title has become final under section 45(g) of this title with respect to any person's, partnership's, or corporation's rule violation or unfair or deceptive act or practice, and (B) an action under this section is brought with respect to such person's, partnership's, or corporation's rule violation or act or practice, then the findings of the Commission as to the material facts in the proceeding under section 45(b) of this title with respect to such person's, partnership's, or corporation's rule violation or act or practice, shall be conclusive unless (i) the terms of such cease and desist order expressly provide that the Commission's findings shall not be conclusive, or (ii) the order became final by reason of section 45(g)(1) of this title, in which case such finding shall be conclusive if supported by evidence.

(2) The court shall cause notice of an action under this section to be given in a manner which is reasonably calculated, under all of the circumstances, to apprise the persons, partnerships, and corporations allegedly injured by the defendant's rule violation or act or practice of the pendency of such action. Such notice may, in the discretion of the court, be given by publication.

(d) Time for Bringing of Actions

No action may be brought by the Commission under this section more than 3 years after the rule violation to which an action under subsection (a)(1) of this section relates, or the unfair or deceptive act or practice to which an action under subsection (a)(2) of this section relates; except that if a cease and desist order with respect to any person's, partnership's, or corporation's rule violation or unfair or deceptive act or practice has become final and such order was issued in a proceeding under section 45(b) of this title which was commenced not later than 3 years after the rule violation or act or practice occurred, a civil action may be commenced under this section against such person, partnership, or corporation at any time before the expiration of one year after such order becomes final.

(e) Availability of Additional Federal or State Remedies; Other Authority of Commission Unaffected

Remedies provided in this section are in addition to, and not in lieu of, any other remedy or right of action provided by State or Federal law. Nothing in this section shall be construed to affect any authority of the Commission under any other provision of law.

§ 57b–1. Civil Investigative Demands

(a) Definitions

For purposes of this section:

(1)   The terms "civil investigative demand" and "demand" mean any demand issued by the Commission under subsection (c)(1) of this section.

(2)   The term "Commission investigation" means any inquiry conducted by a Commission investigator for the purpose of ascertaining whether any person is or has been engaged in any unfair or deceptive acts or practices in or affecting commerce (within the meaning of section 45(a)(1) of this title).

(3)   The term "Commission investigator" means any attorney or investigator employed by the Commission who is charged with the duty of enforcing or carrying into effect any provisions relating to unfair or deceptive acts or practices in or affecting commerce (within the meaning of section 45(a)(1) of this title).

(4)   The term "custodian" means the custodian or any deputy custodian designated under section 57b–2(b)(2)(A) of this title.

(5)   The term "documentary material" includes the original or any copy of any book, record, report, memorandum, paper, communication, tabulation, chart, or other document.

(6)   The term "person" means any natural person, partnership, corporation, association, or other legal entity, including any person acting under color or authority of State law.

(7)   The term "violation" means any act or omission constituting an unfair or deceptive act or practice in or affecting commerce (within the meaning of section 45(a)(1) of this title).

(8)   The term "antitrust violation" means—

(A)   any unfair method of competition (within the meaning of section 45(a)(1) of this title);

(B)   any violation of the Clayton Act or of any other Federal statute that prohibits, or makes available to the Commission a civil remedy with respect to, any restraint upon or monopolization of interstate or foreign trade or commerce;

(C)   with respect to the International Antitrust Enforcement Assistance Act of 1994 [15 U.S.C.A. § 6201 et seq.], any violation of any of the foreign antitrust laws (as defined in section 12 of such Act [15 U.S.C.A. § 6211]) with respect to which a request is made under section 3 of such Act [15 U.S.C.A. § 6202]; or

(D)   any activity in preparation for a merger, acquisition, joint venture, or similar transaction, which if consummated, may result in any such unfair method of competition or in any such violation.

(b) Actions Conducted by Commission Respecting Unfair or Deceptive Acts or Practices in or Affecting Commerce

For the purpose of investigations performed pursuant to this section with respect to unfair or deceptive acts or practices in or affecting commerce (within the meaning of section 45(a)(1) of this title), all actions of the Commission taken under section 46 and section 49 of this title shall be conducted pursuant to subsection (c) of this section.

(c) Issuance of Demand; Contents; Service; Verified Return; Sworn Certificates; Answers; Taking of Oral Testimony

(1)   Whenever the Commission has reason to believe that any person may be in possession, custody, or control of any documentary material, or may have any information, relevant to unfair or deceptive acts or practices in or affecting commerce (within the meaning of section 45(a)(1) of this title), the Commission may, before the institution of any proceedings under sections 41 to 46 and 47 to 58 of this title, issue in writing, and cause to be served upon such person, a civil investigative demand requiring such person to produce such documentary material for inspection and copying or reproduction, to file written reports or answers to questions, to give oral testimony

concerning documentary material or other information, or to furnish any combination of such material, answers, or testimony.

(2)   Each civil investigative demand shall state the nature of the conduct constituting the alleged violation which is under investigation and the provision of law applicable to such violation.

(3)   Each civil investigative demand for the production of documentary material shall—

(A)   describe each class of documentary material to be produced under the demand with such definiteness and certainty as to permit such material to be fairly identified;

(B)   prescribe a return date or dates which will provide a reasonable period of time within which the material so demanded may be assembled and made available for inspection and copying or reproduction; and

(C)   identify the custodian to whom such material shall be made available.

(4)   Each civil investigative demand for the submission of tangible things shall—

(A)   describe each class of tangible things to be submitted under the demand with such definiteness and certainty as to permit such things to be fairly identified;

(B)   prescribe a return date or dates which will provide a reasonable period of time within which the things so demanded may be assembled and submitted; and

(C)   identify the custodian to whom such things shall be submitted.

(5)   Each civil investigative demand for written reports or answers to questions shall—

(A)   propound with definiteness and certainty the reports to be produced or the questions to be answered;

(B)   prescribe a date or dates at which time written reports or answers to questions shall be submitted; and

(C)   identify the custodian to whom such reports or answers shall be submitted.

(6)   Each civil investigative demand for the giving of oral testimony shall—

(A)   prescribe a date, time, and place at which oral testimony shall be commenced; and

(B)   identify a Commission investigator who shall conduct the investigation and the custodian to whom the transcript of such investigation shall be submitted.

(7)(A)   Any civil investigative demand may be served by any Commission investigator at any place within the territorial jurisdiction of any court of the United States.

(B)   Any such demand or any enforcement petition filed under this section may be served upon any person who is not found within the territorial jurisdiction of any court of the United States, in such manner as the Federal Rules of Civil Procedure prescribe for service in a foreign nation.

(C)   To the extent that the courts of the United States have authority to assert jurisdiction over such person consistent with due process, the United States District Court for the District of Columbia shall have the same jurisdiction to take any action respecting compliance with this section by such person that such district court would have if such person were personally within the jurisdiction of such district court.

(8)   Service of any civil investigative demand or any enforcement petition filed under this section may be made upon a partnership, corporation, association, or other legal entity by—

(A)   delivering a duly executed copy of such demand or petition to any partner, executive officer, managing agent, or general agent of such partnership, corporation, association, or other legal entity, or to any agent of such partnership, corporation, association, or other legal entity authorized by appointment or by law to receive service of process on behalf of such partnership, corporation, association, or other legal entity;

(B) delivering a duly executed copy of such demand or petition to the principal office or place of business of the partnership, corporation, association, or other legal entity to be served; or

(C) depositing a duly executed copy in the United States mails, by registered or certified mail, return receipt requested, duly addressed to such partnership, corporation, association, or other legal entity at its principal office or place of business.

(9) Service of any civil investigative demand or of any enforcement petition filed under this section may be made upon any natural person by—

(A) delivering a duly executed copy of such demand or petition to the person to be served; or

(B) depositing a duly executed copy in the United States mails by registered or certified mail, return receipt requested, duly addressed to such person at his residence or principal office or place of business.

(10) A verified return by the individual serving any civil investigative demand or any enforcement petition filed under this section setting forth the manner of such service shall be proof of such service. In the case of service by registered or certified mail, such return shall be accompanied by the return post office receipt of delivery of such demand or enforcement petition.

(11) The production of documentary material in response to a civil investigative demand shall be made under a sworn certificate, in such form as the demand designates, by the person, if a natural person, to whom the demand is directed or, if not a natural person, by any person having knowledge of the facts and circumstances relating to such production, to the effect that all of the documentary material required by the demand and in the possession, custody, or control of the person to whom the demand is directed has been produced and made available to the custodian.

(12) The submission of tangible things in response to a civil investigative demand shall be made under a sworn certificate, in such form as the demand designates, by the person to whom the demand is directed or, if not a natural person, by any person having knowledge of the facts and circumstances relating to such production, to the effect that all of the tangible things required by the demand and in the possession, custody, or control of the person to whom the demand is directed have been submitted to the custodian.

(13) Each reporting requirement or question in a civil investigative demand shall be answered separately and fully in writing under oath, unless it is objected to, in which event the reasons for the objection shall be stated in lieu of an answer, and it shall be submitted under a sworn certificate, in such form as the demand designates, by the person, if a natural person, to whom the demand is directed or, if not a natural person, by any person responsible for answering each reporting requirement or question, to the effect that all information required by the demand and in the possession, custody, control, or knowledge of the person to whom the demand is directed has been submitted.

(14)(A) Any Commission investigator before whom oral testimony is to be taken shall put the witness on oath or affirmation and shall personally, or by any individual acting under his direction and in his presence, record the testimony of the witness. The testimony shall be taken stenographically and transcribed. After the testimony is fully transcribed, the Commission investigator before whom the testimony is taken shall promptly transmit a copy of the transcript of the testimony to the custodian.

(B) Any Commission investigator before whom oral testimony is to be taken shall exclude from the place where the testimony is to be taken all other persons except the person giving the testimony, his attorney, the officer before whom the testimony is to be taken, and any stenographer taking such testimony.

(C)   The oral testimony of any person taken pursuant to a civil investigative demand shall be taken in the judicial district of the United States in which such person resides, is found, or transacts business, or in such other place as may be agreed upon by the Commission investigator before whom the oral testimony of such person is to be taken and such person.

(D)(i)   Any person compelled to appear under a civil investigative demand for oral testimony pursuant to this section may be accompanied, represented, and advised by an attorney. The attorney may advise such person, in confidence, either upon the request of such person or upon the initiative of the attorney, with respect to any question asked of such person.

(ii)   Such person or attorney may object on the record to any question, in whole or in part, and shall briefly state for the record the reason for the objection. An objection may properly be made, received, and entered upon the record when it is claimed that such person is entitled to refuse to answer the question on grounds of any constitutional or other legal right or privilege, including the privilege against self-incrimination. Such person shall not otherwise object to or refuse to answer any question, and shall not himself or through his attorney otherwise interrupt the oral examination. If such person refuses to answer any question, the Commission may petition the district court of the United States pursuant to this section for an order compelling such person to answer such question.

(iii)   If such person refuses to answer any question on grounds of the privilege against self-incrimination, the testimony of such person may be compelled in accordance with the provisions of section 6004 of Title 18.

(E)(i)   After the testimony of any witness is fully transcribed, the Commission investigator shall afford the witness (who may be accompanied by an attorney) a reasonable opportunity to examine the transcript. The transcript shall be read to or by the witness, unless such examination and reading are waived by the witness. Any changes in form or substance which the witness desires to make shall be entered and identified upon the transcript by the Commission investigator with a statement of the reasons given by the witness for making such changes. The transcript shall then be signed by the witness, unless the witness in writing waives the signing, is ill, cannot be found, or refuses to sign.

(ii)   If the transcript is not signed by the witness during the 30-day period following the date upon which the witness is first afforded a reasonable opportunity to examine it, the Commission investigator shall sign the transcript and state on the record the fact of the waiver, illness, absence of the witness, or the refusal to sign, together with any reasons given for the failure to sign.

(F)   The Commission investigator shall certify on the transcript that the witness was duly sworn by him and that the transcript is a true record of the testimony given by the witness, and the Commission investigator shall promptly deliver the transcript or send it by registered or certified mail to the custodian.

(G)   The Commission investigator shall furnish a copy of the transcript (upon payment of reasonable charges for the transcript) to the witness only, except that the Commission may for good cause limit such witness to inspection of the official transcript of his testimony.

(H)   Any witness appearing for the taking of oral testimony pursuant to a civil investigative demand shall be entitled to the same fees and mileage which are paid to witnesses in the district courts of the United States.

(d)   Procedures for Demand Material

Materials received as a result of a civil investigative demand shall be subject to the procedures established in section 57b–2 of this title.

(e)   Petition for Enforcement

Whenever any person fails to comply with any civil investigative demand duly served upon him under this section, or whenever satisfactory copying or reproduction of material requested pursuant to the demand cannot be accomplished and such person refuses to surrender such material, the Commission, through such officers or attorneys as it may designate, may file, in the district court of the United States for any judicial district in which such person resides, is found, or transacts business, and serve upon such person, a petition for an order of such court for the enforcement of this section. All process of any court to which application may be made as provided in this subsection may be served in any judicial district.

(f)   Petition for Order Modifying or Setting Aside Demand

(1)   Not later than 20 days after the service of any civil investigative demand upon any person under subsection (c) of this section, or at any time before the return date specified in the demand, whichever period is shorter, or within such period exceeding 20 days after service or in excess of such return date as may be prescribed in writing, subsequent to service, by any Commission investigator named in the demand, such person may file with the Commission a petition for an order by the Commission modifying or setting aside the demand.

(2)   The time permitted for compliance with the demand in whole or in part, as deemed proper and ordered by the Commission, shall not run during the pendency of such petition at the Commission, except that such person shall comply with any portions of the demand not sought to be modified or set aside. Such petition shall specify each ground upon which the petitioner relies in seeking such relief, and may be based upon any failure of the demand to comply with the provisions of this section, or upon any constitutional or other legal right or privilege of such person.

(g)   Custodial Control of Documentary Material, Reports, etc.

At any time during which any custodian is in custody or control of any documentary material, reports, answers to questions, or transcripts of oral testimony given by any person in compliance with any civil investigative demand, such person may file, in the district court of the United States for the judicial district within which the office of such custodian is situated, and serve upon such custodian, a petition for an order of such court requiring the performance by such custodian of any duty imposed upon him by this section or section 57b–2 of this title.

(h)   Jurisdiction of Court

Whenever any petition is filed in any district court of the United States under this section, such court shall have jurisdiction to hear and determine the matter so presented, and to enter such order or orders as may be required to carry into effect the provisions of this section. Any final order so entered shall be subject to appeal pursuant to section 1291 of Title 28. Any disobedience of any final order entered under this section by any court shall be punished as a contempt of such court.

(i)   Commission Authority to Issue Subpoenas or Make Demand for Information

Notwithstanding any other provision of law, the Commission shall have no authority to issue a subpoena or make a demand for information, under authority of sections 41 to 46 and 47 to 58 of this title or any other provision of law, unless such subpoena or demand for information is signed by a Commissioner acting pursuant to a Commission resolution. The Commission shall not delegate the power conferred by this section to sign subpoenas or demands for information to any other person.

(j)   Applicability of This Section

The provisions of this section shall not—

(1)   apply to any proceeding under section 45(b) of this title, any proceeding under section 11(b) of the Clayton Act (15 U.S.C. 21(b)), or any adjudicative proceeding under any other provision of law; or

(2) apply to or affect the jurisdiction, duties, or powers of any agency of the Federal Government, other than the Commission, regardless of whether such jurisdiction, duties, or powers are derived in whole or in part, by reference to sections 41 to 46 and 47 to 58 of this title.

§ 57b–2. Confidentiality

(a) Definitions

For purposes of this section:

(1) The term "material" means documentary material, written reports or answers to questions, and transcripts of oral testimony.

(2) The term "Federal agency" has the meaning given it in section 552(e) of Title 5.

(b) Procedures Respecting Documents, Tangible Things or Transcripts of Oral Testimony Received Pursuant to Compulsory Process or Investigation

(1) With respect to any document, tangible thing or transcript of oral testimony received by the Commission pursuant to compulsory process in an investigation, a purpose of which is to determine whether any person may have violated any provision of the laws administered by the Commission, the procedures established in paragraph (2) through paragraph (7) shall apply.

(2)(A) The Commission shall designate a duly authorized agent to serve as custodian of documentary material, tangible things, or written reports or answers to questions, and transcripts of oral testimony, and such additional duly authorized agents as the Commission shall determine from time to time to be necessary to serve as deputies to the custodian.

(B) Any person upon whom any demand for the production of documentary material has been duly served shall make such material available for inspection and copying or reproduction to the custodian designated in such demand at the principal place of business of such person (or at such other place as such custodian and such person thereafter may agree and prescribe in writing or as the court may direct pursuant to section 57b–1(h) of this title) on the return date specified in such demand (or on such later date as such custodian may prescribe in writing). Such person may upon written agreement between such person and the custodian substitute copies for originals of all or any part of such material.

(3)(A) The custodian to whom any documentary material, tangible things, written reports or answers to questions, and transcripts of oral testimony are delivered shall take physical possession of such material, reports or answers, and transcripts, and shall be responsible for the use made of such material, reports or answers, and transcripts, and for the return of material, pursuant to the requirements of this section.

(B) The custodian may prepare such copies of the documentary material, written reports or answers to questions, and transcripts of oral testimony, and may make tangible things available, as may be required for official use by any duly authorized officer or employee of the Commission under regulations which shall be promulgated by the Commission. Notwithstanding subparagraph (C), such material, things, and transcripts may be used by any such officer or employee in connection with the taking of oral testimony under this section.

(C) Except as otherwise provided in this section, while in the possession of the custodian, no documentary material, tangible things, reports or answers to questions, and transcripts of oral testimony shall be available for examination by any individual other than a duly authorized officer or employee of the Commission without the consent of the person who produced the material, things, or transcripts. Nothing in this section is intended to prevent disclosure to either House of the Congress or to any committee or subcommittee of the Congress, except that the Commission immediately shall notify the owner or provider of any such information of a request for information designated as confidential by the owner or provider.

(D) While in the possession of the custodian and under such reasonable terms and conditions as the Commission shall prescribe—

(i) documentary material, tangible things, or written reports shall be available for examination by the person who produced the material, or by any duly authorized representative of such person; and

(ii) answers to questions in writing and transcripts of oral testimony shall be available for examination by the person who produced the testimony or by his attorney.

(4) Whenever the Commission has instituted a proceeding against a person, partnership, or corporation, the custodian may deliver to any officer or employee of the Commission documentary material, tangible things, written reports or answers to questions, and transcripts of oral testimony for official use in connection with such proceeding. Upon the completion of the proceeding, the officer or employee shall return to the custodian any such material so delivered which has not been received into the record of the proceeding.

(5) if any documentary material, tangible things, written reports or answers to questions, and transcripts of oral testimony have been produced in the course of any investigation by any person pursuant to compulsory process and—

(A) any proceeding arising out of the investigation has been completed; or

(B) no proceeding in which the material may be used has been commenced within a reasonable time after completion of the examination and analysis of all such material and other information assembled in the course of the investigation;

then the custodian shall, upon written request of the person who produced the material, return to the person any such material which has not been received into the record of any such proceeding (other than copies of such material made by the custodian pursuant to paragraph (3)(B)).

(6) The custodian of any documentary material, written reports or answers to questions, and transcripts of oral testimony may deliver to any officers or employees of appropriate Federal law enforcement agencies, in response to a written request, copies of such material for use in connection with an investigation or proceeding under the jurisdiction of any such agency. The custodian of any tangible things may make such things available for inspection to such persons on the same basis. Such materials shall not be made available to any such agency until the custodian receives certification of any officer of such agency that such information will be maintained in confidence and will be used only for official law enforcement purposes. Such documentary material, results of inspections of tangible things, written reports or answers to questions, and transcripts of oral testimony may be used by any officer or employee of such agency only in such manner and subject to such conditions as apply to the Commission under this section. The custodian may make such materials available to any State law enforcement agency upon the prior certification of any officer of such agency that such information will be maintained in confidence and will be used only for official law enforcement purposes. The custodian may make such material available to any foreign law enforcement agency upon the prior certification of an appropriate official of any such foreign law enforcement agency, either by a prior agreement or memorandum of understanding with the Commission or by other written certification, that such material will be maintained in confidence and will be used only for official law enforcement purposes, if—

(A) the foreign law enforcement agency has set forth a bona fide legal basis for its authority to maintain the material in confidence;

(B) the materials are to be used for purposes of investigating, or engaging in enforcement proceedings related to, possible violations of—

(i)   foreign laws prohibiting fraudulent or deceptive commercial practices, or other practices substantially similar to practices prohibited by any law administered by the Commission;

(ii)   a law administered by the Commission, if disclosure of the material would further a Commission investigation or enforcement proceeding; or

(iii)   with the approval of the Attorney General, other foreign criminal laws, if such foreign criminal laws are offenses defined in or covered by a criminal mutual legal assistance treaty in force between the government of the United States and the foreign law enforcement agency's government;

(C)   the appropriate Federal banking agency (as defined in section 1813(q) of Title 12) or, in the case of a Federal credit union, the National Credit Union Administration, has given its prior approval if the materials to be provided under subparagraph (B) are requested by the foreign law enforcement agency for the purpose of investigating, or engaging in enforcement proceedings based on, possible violations of law by a bank, a savings and loan institution described in section 57a(f)(3) of this title, or a Federal credit union described in section 57a(f)(4) of this title; and

(D)   the foreign law enforcement agency is not from a foreign state that the Secretary of State has determined, in accordance with section 2405(j) of the Appendix to Title 50, has repeatedly provided support for acts of international terrorism, unless and until such determination is rescinded pursuant to section 2405(j)(4) of the Appendix to Title 50.

Nothing in the preceding sentence authorizes the disclosure of material obtained in connection with the administration of the Federal antitrust laws or foreign antitrust laws (as defined in paragraphs (5) and (7), respectively, of section 6211 of this title to any officer or employee of a foreign law enforcement agency.

(7)   In the event of the death, disability, or separation from service in the Commission of the custodian of any documentary material, tangible things, written reports or answers to questions, and transcripts of oral testimony produced under any demand issued under sections 41 to 46 and 47 to 58 of this title, or the official relief of the custodian from responsibility for the custody and control of such material, the Commission promptly shall—

(A)   designate under paragraph (2)(A) another duly authorized agent to serve as custodian of such material; and

(B)   transmit in writing to the person who produced the material or testimony notice as to the identity and address of the successor so designated.

Any successor designated under paragraph (2)(A) as a result of the requirements of this paragraph shall have (with regard to the material involved) all duties and responsibilities imposed by this section upon his predecessor in office with regard to such material, except that he shall not be held responsible for any default or dereliction which occurred before his designation.

(c)   Information Considered Confidential

(1)   All information reported to or otherwise obtained by the Commission which is not subject to the requirements of subsection (b) of this section shall be considered confidential when so marked by the person supplying the information and shall not be disclosed, except in accordance with the procedures established in paragraph (2) and paragraph (3).

(2)   If the Commission determines that a document marked confidential by the person supplying it may be disclosed because it is not a trade secret or commercial or financial information which is obtained from any person and which is privileged or confidential, within the meaning of section 46(f) of this title, then the Commission shall notify such person in writing that

the Commission intends to disclose the document at a date not less than 10 days after the date of receipt of notification.

(3)   Any person receiving such notification may, if he believes disclosure of the document would cause disclosure of a trade secret, or commercial or financial information which is obtained from any person and which is privileged or confidential, within the meaning of section 46(f) of this title, before the date set for release of the document, bring an action in the district court of the United States for the district within which the documents are located or in the United States District Court for the District of Columbia to restrain disclosure of the document. Any person receiving such notification may file with the appropriate district court or court of appeals of the United States, as appropriate, an application for a stay of disclosure. The documents shall not be disclosed until the court has ruled on the application for a stay.

(d)   Particular Disclosures Allowed

(1)   The provisions of subsection (c) of this section shall not be construed to prohibit—

(A)   the disclosure of information to either House of the Congress or to any committee or subcommittee of the Congress, except that the Commission immediately shall notify the owner or provider of any such information of a request for information designated as confidential by the owner or provider;

(B)   the disclosure of the results of any investigation or study carried out or prepared by the Commission, except that no information shall be identified nor shall information be disclosed in such a manner as to disclose a trade secret of any person supplying the trade secret, or to disclose any commercial or financial information which is obtained from any person and which is privileged or confidential;

(C)   the disclosure of relevant and material information in Commission adjudicative proceedings or in judicial proceedings to which the Commission is a party; or

(D)   the disclosure to a Federal agency of disaggregated information obtained in accordance with section 3512 of Title 44, except that the recipient agency shall use such disaggregated information for economic, statistical, or policymaking purposes only, and shall not disclose such information in an individually identifiable form.

(2)   Any disclosure of relevant and material information in Commission adjudicative proceedings or in judicial proceedings to which the Commission is a party shall be governed by the rules of the Commission for adjudicative proceedings or by court rules or orders, except that the rules of the Commission shall not be amended in a manner inconsistent with the purposes of this section.

(e)   Effect on Other Statutory Provisions Limiting Disclosure

Nothing in this section shall supersede any statutory provision which expressly prohibits or limits particular disclosures by the Commission, or which authorizes disclosures to any other Federal agency.

(f)   Exemption From Public Disclosure

(1)   **In General.**—Any material which is received by the Commission in any investigation, a purpose of which is to determine whether any person may have violated any provision of the laws administered by the Commission, and which is provided pursuant to any compulsory process under this Act or which is provided voluntarily in place of such compulsory process shall not be required to be disclosed under section 552 of title 5, United States Code, or any other provision of law, except as provided in paragraph (2)(B) of this section.

(2)   **Material Obtained From a Foreign Source.—**

(A)   **In General.**—Except as provided in subparagraph (B) of this paragraph, the Commission shall not be required to disclose under section 552 of title 5, United States Code, or any other provision of law—

(i) any material obtained from a foreign law enforcement agency or other foreign government agency, if the foreign law enforcement agency or other foreign government agency has requested confidential treatment, or has precluded such disclosure under other use limitations, as a condition of providing the material;

(ii) any material reflecting a consumer complaint obtained from any other foreign source, if that foreign source supplying the material has requested confidential treatment as a condition of providing the material; or

(iii) any material reflecting a consumer complaint submitted to a Commission reporting mechanism sponsored in part by foreign law enforcement agencies or other foreign government agencies.

(B) Savings Provision.—Nothing in this subsection shall authorize the Commission to withhold information from the Congress or prevent the Commission from complying with an order of a court of the United States in an action commenced by the United States or the Commission.

§ 57b–2a. Confidentiality and Delayed Notice of Compulsory Process for Certain Third Parties

(a) Application with Other Laws

The Right to Financial Privacy Act (12 U.S.C. § 3401 et seq.) and chapter 121 of title 18, United States Code, shall apply with respect to the Commission, except as otherwise provided in this section.

(b) Procedures for Delay of Notification or Prohibition of Disclosure

The procedures for delay of notification or prohibition of disclosure under the Right to Financial Privacy Act (12 U.S.C. §§ 3401 et seq.) and chapter 121 of title 18, United States Code, including procedures for extensions of such delays or prohibitions, shall be available to the Commission, provided that, notwithstanding any provision therein—

(1) a court may issue an order delaying notification or prohibiting disclosure (including extending such an order) in accordance with the procedures of section 1109 of the Right to Financial Privacy Act (12 U.S.C. § 3409) (if notification would otherwise be required under that Act), or section 2705 of title 18, United States Code, (if notification would otherwise be required under chapter 121 of that title), if the presiding judge or magistrate judge finds that there is reason to believe that such notification or disclosure may cause an adverse result as defined in subsection (g) of this section; and

(2) if notification would otherwise be required under chapter 121 of title 18, United States Code, the Commission may delay notification (including extending such a delay) upon the execution of a written certification in accordance with the procedures of section 2705 of that title if the Commission finds that there is reason to believe that notification may cause an adverse result as defined in subsection (g) of this section.

(c) Ex Parte Application by Commission

(1) In General.—If neither notification nor delayed notification by the Commission is required under the Right to Financial Privacy Act (12 U.S.C. §§ 3401 et seq.) or chapter 121 of title 18, United States Code, the Commission may apply ex parte to a presiding judge or magistrate judge for an order prohibiting the recipient of compulsory process issued by the Commission from disclosing to any other person the existence of the process, notwithstanding any law or regulation of the United States, or under the constitution, or any law or regulation, of any State, political subdivision of a State, territory of the United States, or the District of Columbia. The presiding judge or magistrate judge may enter such an order granting the requested prohibition of disclosure for a period not to exceed 60 days if there is reason to believe that disclosure may cause an adverse result as defined in subsection (g). The presiding judge or magistrate judge may grant extensions of this order of up to 30 days each in accordance with this subsection, except that in no event shall the prohibition continue in force for more than a total of 9 months.

(2) Application.—This subsection shall apply only in connection with compulsory process issued by the Commission where the recipient of such process is not a subject of the investigation or proceeding at the time such process is issued.

(3) Limitation.—No order issued under this subsection shall prohibit any recipient from disclosing to a Federal agency that the recipient has received compulsory process from the Commission.

(d) No Liability for Failure to Notify

If neither notification nor delayed notification by the Commission is required under the Right to Financial Privacy Act (12 U.S.C. §§ 3401 et seq.) or chapter 121 of title 18, United States Code, the recipient of compulsory process issued by the Commission under this Act shall not be liable under any law or regulation of the United States, or under the constitution, or any law or regulation, of any State, political subdivision of a State, territory of the United States, or the District of Columbia, or under any contract or other legally enforceable agreement, for failure to provide notice to any person that such process has been issued or that the recipient has provided information in response to such process. The preceding sentence does not exempt any recipient from liability for—

(1) the underlying conduct reported;

(2) a failure to comply with the record retention requirements under section 1104(c) of the Right to Financial Privacy Act (12 U.S.C. § 3404), where applicable; or

(3) any failure to comply with any obligation the recipient may have to disclose to a Federal agency that the recipient has received compulsory process from the Commission or intends to provide or has provided information to the Commission in response to such process.

(e) Venue and Procedure

(1) In General.—All judicial proceedings initiated by the Commission under the Right to Financial Privacy Act (12 U.S.C. §§ 3401 et seq.), chapter 121 of title 18, United States Code, or this section may be brought in the United States District Court for the District of Columbia or any other appropriate United States District Court. All ex parte applications by the Commission under this section related to a single investigation may be brought in a single proceeding.

(2) In Camera Proceedings.—Upon application by the Commission, all judicial proceedings pursuant to this section shall be held in camera and the records thereof sealed until expiration of the period of delay or such other date as the presiding judge or magistrate judge may permit.

(f) Section not to Apply to Antitrust Investigations or Proceedings

This section shall not apply to an investigation or proceeding related to the administration of Federal antitrust laws or foreign antitrust laws (as defined in paragraphs (5) and (7), respectively, of section 6211 of this title).

(g) Adverse Result Defined

For purposes of this section the term 'adverse result' means—

(1) endangering the life or physical safety of an individual;

(2) flight from prosecution;

(3) the destruction of, or tampering with, evidence;

(4) the intimidation of potential witnesses; or

(5) otherwise seriously jeopardizing an investigation or proceeding related to fraudulent or deceptive commercial practices or persons involved in such practices, or unduly delaying a trial related to such practices or persons involved in such practices, including, but not limited to, by—

(A) the transfer outside the territorial limits of the United States of assets or records related to fraudulent or deceptive commercial practices or related to persons involved in such practices;

(B) impeding the ability of the Commission to identify persons involved in fraudulent or deceptive commercial practices, or to trace the source or disposition of funds related to such practices; or

(C) the dissipation, fraudulent transfer, or concealment of assets subject to recovery by the Commission.

§ 57b–2b. Protection for Voluntary Provision of Information

(a) In General

(1) **No Liability for Providing Certain Material.**—An entity described in paragraphs (2) or (3) of subsection (d) that voluntarily provides material to the Commission that such entity reasonably believes is relevant to—

(A) a possible unfair or deceptive act or practice, as defined in section 45(a) of this title; or

(B) assets subject to recovery by the Commission, including assets located in foreign jurisdictions;

shall not be liable to any person under any law or regulation of the United States, or under the constitution, or any law or regulation, of any State, political subdivision of a State, territory of the United States, or the District of Columbia, for such provision of material or for any failure to provide notice of such provision of material or of intention to so provide material.

(2) **Limitations.**—Nothing in this subsection shall be construed to exempt any such entity from liability—

(A) for the underlying conduct reported; or

(B) to any Federal agency for providing such material or for any failure to comply with any obligation the entity may have to notify a Federal agency prior to providing such material to the Commission.

(b) Certain Financial Institutions

An entity described in paragraph (1) of subsection (d) shall, in accordance with section 5318(g)(3) of title 31, United States Code, be exempt from liability for making a voluntary disclosure to the Commission of any possible violation of law or regulation, including—

(1) a disclosure regarding assets, including assets located in foreign jurisdictions—

(A) related to possibly fraudulent or deceptive commercial practices;

(B) related to persons involved in such practices; or

(C) otherwise subject to recovery by the Commission; or

(2) a disclosure regarding suspicious chargeback rates related to possibly fraudulent or deceptive commercial practices.

(c) Consumer Complaints

Any entity described in subsection (d) that voluntarily provides consumer complaints sent to it, or information contained therein, to the Commission shall not be liable to any person under any law or regulation of the United States, or under the constitution, or any law or regulation, of any State, political subdivision of a State, territory of the United States, or the District of Columbia, for such provision of material or for any failure to provide notice of such provision of material or of intention to so provide material. This subsection shall not provide any exemption from liability for the underlying conduct.

(d) Application

This section applies to the following entities, whether foreign or domestic:

(1) A financial institution as defined in section 5312 of title 31, United States Code.

(2) To the extent not included in paragraph (1), a bank or thrift institution, a commercial bank or trust company, an investment company, a credit card issuer, an operator of a credit card system, and an issuer, redeemer, or cashier of travelers' checks, money orders, or similar instruments.

(3) A courier service, a commercial mail receiving agency, an industry membership organization, a payment system provider, a consumer reporting agency, a domain name registrar or registry acting as such, and a provider of alternative dispute resolution services.

(4) An Internet service provider or provider of telephone services.

§ 57b–3. Rulemaking Process

(a) Definitions

For purposes of this section:

(1) The term "rule" means any rule promulgated by the Commission under section 46 or section 57a of this title, except that such term does not include interpretive rules, rules involving Commission management or personnel, general statements of policy, or rules relating to Commission organization, procedure, or practice. Such term does not include any amendment to a rule unless the Commission—

(A) estimates that such amendment will have an annual effect on the national economy of $100,000,000 or more;

(B) estimates that such amendment will cause a substantial change in the cost or price of goods or services which are used extensively by particular industries, which are supplied extensively in particular geographic regions, or which are acquired in significant quantities by the Federal Government, or by State or local governments; or

(C) otherwise determines that such amendment will have a significant impact upon persons subject to regulation under such amendment and upon consumers.

(2) The term "rulemaking" means any Commission process for formulating or amending a rule.

(b) Notice of Proposed Rulemaking; Regulatory Analysis; Contents; Issuance

(1) In any case in which the Commission publishes notice of a proposed rulemaking, the Commission shall issue a preliminary regulatory analysis relating to the proposed rule involved. Each preliminary regulatory analysis shall contain—

(A) a concise statement of the need for, and the objectives of, the proposed rule;

(B) a description of any reasonable alternatives to the proposed rule which may accomplish the stated objective of the rule in a manner consistent with applicable law; and

(C) for the proposed rule, and for each of the alternatives described in the analysis, a preliminary analysis of the projected benefits and any adverse economic effects and any other effects, and of the effectiveness of the proposed rule and each alternative in meeting the stated objectives of the proposed rule.

(2) In any case in which the Commission promulgates a final rule, the Commission shall issue a final regulatory analysis relating to the final rule. Each final regulatory analysis shall contain—

(A) a concise statement of the need for, and the objectives of, the final rule;

(B) a description of any alternatives to the final rule which were considered by the Commission;

(C) an analysis of the projected benefits and any adverse economic effects and any other effects of the final rule;

(D) an explanation of the reasons for the determination of the Commission that the final rule will attain its objectives in a manner consistent with applicable law and the reasons the particular alternative was chosen; and

(E) a summary of any significant issues raised by the comments submitted during the public comment period in response to the preliminary regulatory analysis, and a summary of the assessment by the Commission of such issues.

(3)(A) In order to avoid duplication or waste, the Commission is authorized to—

(i) consider a series of closely related rules as one rule for purposes of this subsection; and

(ii) whenever appropriate, incorporate any data or analysis contained in a regulatory analysis issued under this subsection in the statement of basis and purpose to accompany any rule promulgated under section 57a(a)(1)(B) of this title, and incorporate by reference in any preliminary or final regulatory analysis information contained in a notice of proposed rulemaking or a statement of basis and purpose.

(B) The Commission shall include, in each notice of proposed rulemaking and in each publication of a final rule, a statement of the manner in which the public may obtain copies of the preliminary and final regulatory analyses. The Commission may charge a reasonable fee for the copying and mailing of regulatory analyses. The regulatory analyses shall be furnished without charge or at a reduced charge if the Commission determines that waiver or reduction of the fee is in the public interests because furnishing the information primarily benefits the general public.

(4) The Commission is authorized to delay the completion of any of the requirements established in this subsection by publishing in the Federal Register, not later than the date of publication of the final rule involved, a finding that the final rule is being promulgated in response to an emergency which makes timely compliance with the provisions of this subsection impracticable. Such publication shall include a statement of the reasons for such finding.

(5) The requirements of this subsection shall not be construed to alter in any manner the substantive standards applicable to any action by the Commission, or the procedural standards otherwise applicable to such action.

(c) Judicial Review

(1) The contents and adequacy of any regulatory analysis prepared or issued by the Commission under this section, including the adequacy of any procedure involved in such preparation or issuance, shall not be subject to any judicial review in any court, except that a court, upon review of a rule pursuant to section 57a(e) of this title, may set aside such rule if the Commission has failed entirely to prepare a regulatory analysis.

(2) Except as specified in paragraph (1), no Commission action may be invalidated, remanded, or otherwise affected by any court on account of any failure to comply with the requirements of this section.

(3)   The provisions of this subsection do not alter the substantive or procedural standards otherwise applicable to judicial review of any action by the Commission.

(d) Regulatory Agenda; Contents; Publication Dates in Federal Register

(1)   The Commission shall publish at least semiannually a regulatory agenda. Each regulatory agenda shall contain a list of rules which the Commission intends to propose or promulgate during the 12-month period following the publication of the agenda. On the first Monday in October of each year, the Commission shall publish in the Federal Register a schedule showing the dates during the current fiscal year on which the semiannual regulatory agenda of the Commission will be published.

(2)   For each rule listed in a regulatory agenda, the Commission shall—

   (A)   describe the rule;

   (B)   state the objectives of and the legal basis for the rule; and

   (C)   specify any dates established or anticipated by the Commission for taking action, including dates for advance notice of proposed rulemaking, notices of proposed rulemaking, and final action by the Commission.

(3)   Each regulatory agenda shall state the name, office address, and office telephone number of the Commission officer or employee responsible for responding to any inquiry relating to each rule listed.

(4)   The Commission shall not propose or promulgate a rule which was not listed on a regulatory agenda unless the Commission publishes with the rule an explanation of the reasons the rule was omitted from such agenda.

§ 57b–4. Good Faith Reliance on Actions of Board of Governors

(a) Board of Governors Defined

For purposes of this section, the term "Board of Governors" means the Board of Governors of the Federal Reserve System.

(b) Use as Defense

Notwithstanding any other provision of law, if—

(1)   any person, partnership, or corporation engages in any conduct or practice which allegedly constitutes a violation of any Federal law with respect to which the Board of Governors of the Federal Reserve System has rulemaking authority; and

(2)   such person, partnership, or corporation engaged in such conduct or practice in good faith reliance upon, and in conformity with, any rule, regulation, statement of interpretation, or statement of approval prescribed or issued by the Board of Governors under such Federal law;

then such good faith reliance shall constitute a defense in any administrative or judicial proceeding commenced against such person, partnership, or corporation by the Commission under sections 41 to 46 and 47 to 58 of this title or in any administrative or judicial proceeding commenced against such person, partnership, or corporation by the Attorney General of the United States, upon request made by the Commission, under any provision of law.

(c) Applicability of Subsection (b)

The provisions of subsection (b) of this section shall apply regardless of whether any rule, regulation, statement of interpretation, or statement of approval prescribed or issued by the Board of Governors is amended, rescinded, or held to be invalid by judicial authority or any other authority after a person, partnership, or corporation has engaged in any conduct or practice in good faith reliance upon, and in conformity with, such rule, regulation, statement of interpretation, or statement of approval.

(d) Request for Issuance of Statement or Interpretation Concerning Conduct or Practice

If, in any case in which—

(1)   the Board of Governors has rulemaking authority with respect to any Federal law; and

(2)   the Commission is authorized to enforce the requirements of such Federal law;

any person, partnership, or corporation submits a request to the Board of Governors for the issuance of any statement of interpretation or statement of approval relating to any conduct or practice of such person, partnership, or corporation which may be subject to the requirements of such Federal law, then the Board of Governors shall dispose of such request as soon as practicable after the receipt of such request.

§ 57b–5. Agricultural Cooperatives

(a)   The Commission shall not have any authority to conduct any study, investigation, or prosecution of any agricultural cooperative for any conduct which, because of the provisions of sections 291 and 292 of Title 7, is not a violation of any of the antitrust Acts or this subchapter.

(b)   The Commission shall not have any authority to conduct any study or investigation of any agricultural marketing orders.

§ 57c.   [Omitted]

§ 57c–1. Staff Exchanges

(a) In General

(1)   retain or employ officers or employees of foreign government agencies on a temporary basis as employees of the Commission pursuant to section 42 of this title or section 3101 or section 3109 of title 5; and

(2)   detail officers or employees of the Commission to work on a temporary basis for appropriate foreign government agencies.

(b) Reciprocity and Reimbursement

The staff arrangements described in subsection (a) need not be reciprocal. The Commission may accept payment or reimbursement, in cash or in kind, from a foreign government agency to which this section is applicable, or payment or reimbursement made on behalf of such agency, for expenses incurred by the Commission, its members, and employees in carrying out such arrangements.

(c) Standards or Conduct

A person appointed under subsection (a)(1) shall be subject to the provisions of law relating to ethics, conflicts of interest, corruption, and any other criminal or civil statute or regulation governing the standards of conduct for Federal employees that are applicable to the type of appointment.

§ 57c–2. Reimbursement of Expenses

The Commission may accept payment or reimbursement, in cash or in kind, from a domestic or foreign law enforcement agency, or payment or reimbursement made on behalf of such agency, for expenses incurred by the Commission, its members, or employees in carrying out any activity pursuant to a statute administered by the Commission without regard to any other provision of law. Any such payments or reimbursements shall be considered a reimbursement to the appropriated funds of the Commission.

§ 58.   Short Title

This subchapter may be cited as the "Federal Trade Commission Act".

B. UNIFORM DECEPTIVE TRADE PRACTICES ACT

1966 Revision[*]

Contents

---

§ 1. Definitions

As used in this Act, unless the context otherwise requires:

(1) "article" means a product as distinguished from its trademark, label, or distinctive dress in packaging;

(2) "certification mark" means a mark used in connection with the goods or services of a person other than the certifier to indicate geographic origin, material, mode of manufacture, quality, accuracy, or other characteristics of the goods or services or to indicate that the work or labor on the goods or services was performed by members of a union or other organization;

(3) "collective mark" means a mark used by members of a cooperative, association, or other collective group or organization to identify goods or services and distinguish them from those of others, or to indicate membership in the collective group or organization;

(4) "mark" means a word, name, symbol, device, or any combination of the foregoing in any form or arrangement;

(5) "person" means an individual, corporation, government, or governmental subdivision or agency, business trust, estate, trust, partnership, unincorporated association, two or more of any of the foregoing having a joint or common interest, or any other legal or commercial entity;

(6) "service mark" means a mark used by a person to identify services and to distinguish them from the services of others;

(7) "trademark" means a mark used by a person to identify goods and to distinguish them from the goods of others;

(8) "trade name" means a word, name, symbol, device, or any combination of the foregoing in any form or arrangement used by a person to identify his business, vocation, or occupation and distinguish it from the business, vocation or occupation of others.

---

[*] A prior version of the Uniform Deceptive Trade Practice Act was promulgated in 1964. Some states have adopted each version of the uniform law. In 2000 the National Conference of Commissioners on Uniform State Laws withdrew the UDTPA as "obsolete." An excellent summary of the provisions of laws of this type in each of the 50 states can be found online at www.nclc.org/images/pdf/udap/report_50_states.pdf—*Ed*.

§ 2.   Deceptive Trade Practices

(a)   A person engages in a deceptive trade practice when, in the course of his business, vocation, or occupation, he:

(1)   passes off goods or services as those of another;

(2)   causes likelihood of confusion or of misunderstanding as to the source, sponsorship, approval, or certification of goods or services;

(3)   causes likelihood of confusion or of misunderstanding as to affiliation, connection, or association with, or certification by, another;

(4)   uses deceptive representations or designations of geographic origin in connection with goods or services;

(5)   represents that goods or services have sponsorship, approval, characteristics, ingredients, uses, benefits, or quantities that they do not have or that a person has a sponsorship, approval, status, affiliation, or connection that he does not have;

(6)   represents that goods are original or new if they are deteriorated, altered, reconditioned, reclaimed, used, or second-hand;

(7)   represents that goods or services are of a particular standard, quality, or grade, or that goods are of a particular style or model, if they are of another;

(8)   disparages the goods, services, or business of another by false or misleading representation of fact;

(9)   advertises goods or services with intent not to sell them as advertised;

(10) advertises goods or services with intent not to supply reasonably expectable public demand, unless the advertisement discloses a limitation of quantity;

(11) makes false or misleading statements of fact concerning the reasons for, existence of, or amounts of price reductions; or

(12) engages in any other conduct which similarly creates a likelihood of confusion or of misunderstanding.

(b)   In order to prevail in an action under this Act, a complainant need not prove competition between the parties or actual confusion or misunderstanding.

(c)   This section does not affect unfair trade practices otherwise actionable at common law or under other statutes of this state.

§ 3.   Remedies

(a)   A person likely to be damaged by a deceptive trade practice of another may be granted an injunction against it under the principles of equity and on terms that the court considers reasonable. Proof of monetary damage, loss of profits, or intent to deceive is not required. Relief granted for the copying of an article shall be limited to the prevention of confusion or misunderstanding as to source.

(b)   Costs shall be allowed to the prevailing party unless the court otherwise directs. The court [in its discretion] may award attorneys' fees to the prevailing party if (1) the party complaining of a deceptive trade practice has brought an action which he knew to be groundless or (2) the party charged with a deceptive trade practice has willfully engaged in the trade practice knowing it to be deceptive.

(c)   The relief provided in this section is in addition to remedies otherwise available against the same conduct under the common law or other statutes of this state.

§ 4. Application

(a)   This Act does not apply to:

(1)   conduct in compliance with the orders or rules of, or a statute administered by, a federal, state, or local governmental agency;

(2)   publishers, broadcasters, printers, or other persons engaged in the dissemination of information or reproduction of printed or pictorial matters who publish, broadcast, or reproduce material without knowledge of its deceptive character; or

(3)   actions or appeals pending on the effective date of this Act.

(b)   Subsections 2(a)(2) and 2(a)(3) do not apply to the use of a service mark, trademark, certification mark, collective mark, trade name, or other trade identification that was used and not abandoned before the effective date of this Act, if the use was in good faith and is otherwise lawful except for this Act.

§ 5. Uniformity of Interpretation

This Act shall be construed to effectuate its general purpose to make uniform the law of those states which enact it.

§ 6. Short Title

This Act may be cited as the Uniform Deceptive Trade Practices Act.

§ 7. Severability

If any provision of this Act or the application thereof to any person or circumstance is held invalid, the invalidity does not affect other provisions or applications of the Act which can be given effect without the invalid provision or application, and to this end the provisions of this Act are severable.

§ 8. Repeals

The following acts or parts of acts are repealed:

(1)

(2)

(3)

§ 9. Time of Taking Effect

This Act takes effect _____

C. THE RESTATEMENT OF UNFAIR COMPETITION THIRD*

CHAPTER ONE. THE FREEDOM TO COMPETE

§ 1. General Principles

One who causes harm to the commercial relations of another by engaging in a business or trade is not subject to liability to the other for such harm unless:

(a)   the harm results from acts or practices of the actor actionable by the other under the rules of this Restatement relating to:

(1)   deceptive marketing, as specified in Chapter Two;

(2)   infringement of trademarks and other indicia of identification, as specified in Chapter Three;

(3)   appropriation of intangible trade values including trade secrets and the right of publicity, as specified in Chapter Four;

or from other acts or practices of the actor determined to be actionable as an unfair method of competition, taking into account the nature of the conduct and its likely effect on both the person seeking relief and the public; or

(b)   the acts or practices of the actor are actionable by the other under federal or state statutes, international agreements, or general principles of common law apart from those considered in this Restatement.

CHAPTER TWO. DECEPTIVE MARKETING

---

§ 2.   Deceptive Marketing: General Principle

One who, in connection with the marketing of goods or services, makes a representation relating to the actor's own goods, services, or commercial activities that is likely to deceive or mislead prospective purchasers to the likely commercial detriment of another under the rule stated in § 3 is subject to liability to the other for the relief appropriate under the rules stated in §§ 35–37.

§ 3. Commercial Detriment of Another

A representation is to the likely commercial detriment of another if:

(a) the representation is material, in that it is likely to affect the conduct of prospective purchasers; and

(b) there is a reasonable basis for believing that the representation has caused or is likely to cause a diversion of trade from the other or harm to the other's reputation or good will.

§ 4. Misrepresentations Relating to Source: Passing Off

One is subject to liability to another under the rule stated in § 2 if, in connection with the marketing of goods or services, the actor makes a representation likely to deceive or mislead prospective purchasers by causing the mistaken belief that the actor's business is the business of the other, or that the actor is the agent, affiliate, or associate of the other, or that the goods or services that the actor markets are produced, sponsored, or approved by the other.

§ 5. Misrepresentations Relating to Source: Reverse Passing Off

One is subject to liability to another under the rule stated in § 2 if, in marketing goods or services manufactured, produced, or supplied by the other, the actor makes a representation likely to deceive or mislead prospective purchasers by causing the mistaken belief that the actor or a third person is the manufacturer, producer, or supplier of the goods or services if the representation is to the likely commercial detriment of the other under the rule stated in § 3.

§ 6. Misrepresentations in Marketing the Goods or Services of Another

One is subject to liability to another under the rule stated in § 2 if, in marketing goods or services of which the other is truthfully identified as the manufacturer, producer, or supplier, the actor makes a representation relating to those goods or services that is likely to deceive or mislead prospective purchasers to the likely commercial detriment of the other under the rule stated in § 3.

§ 7. Contributory Liability of Printers, Publishers, and Other Suppliers

(1) One who, by supplying materials or rendering services to a third person, directly and substantially assists the third person in making a representation that subjects the third person to liability to another for deceptive marketing under the rules stated in §§ 2–6 is subject to liability to that other for contributory deceptive marketing.

(2) If an actor subject to contributory liability under the rule stated in Subsection (1) acted without knowledge that the actor was assisting the third person in making a representation likely to deceive or mislead, the actor is subject only to appropriate injunctive relief.

§ 8. Contributory Liability of Manufacturers and Distributors

One who markets goods or services to a third person who further markets the goods or services in a manner that subjects the third person to liability to another for deceptive marketing under the rules stated in §§ 2–6 is subject to liability to that other for contributory deceptive marketing if:

(a) the actor intentionally induces the third person to engage in such conduct; or

(b) the actor fails to take reasonable precautions against the occurrence of the third person's conduct in circumstances in which that conduct can be reasonably anticipated.

RESTATEMENT OF UNFAIR COMPETITION
CHAPTER THREE.   THE LAW OF TRADEMARKS

TOPIC 1.   SUBJECT MATTER OF TRADEMARK LAW

TOPIC 2.   ACQUISITION AND PRIORITY OF RIGHTS

TOPIC 3.   INFRINGEMENT OF RIGHTS

TOPIC 4.   DEFENSES AND LIMITATIONS ON RELIEF

TOPIC 5.   LICENSING AND ASSIGNMENT OF RIGHTS

TOPIC 6.   REMEDIES

TOPIC 1.   SUBJECT MATTER OF TRADEMARK LAW

_____

§ 9. Definitions of Trademark and Service Mark

A trademark is a word, name, symbol, device, or other designation, or a combination of such designations, that is distinctive of a person's goods or services and that is used in a manner that identifies those goods or services and distinguishes them from the goods or services of others. A service mark is a trademark that is used in connection with services.

§ 10. Definition of Collective Mark

A collective mark is a word, name, symbol, device, or other designation, or a combination of such designations, that is distinctive of a cooperative, association, organization, or other collective group and that is used by members of the collective group in a manner that:

(a) identifies the goods or services of members and distinguishes them from the goods or services of nonmembers; or

(b) indicates membership in the collective group.

§ 11. Definition of Certification Mark

A certification mark is a word, name, symbol, device, or other designation, or a combination of such designations, that is distinctive of goods or services certified by a person but produced and marketed by others and that is used by the others in a manner that certifies regional origin, composition, quality, method of manufacture, or other characteristics of the goods or services.

§ 12. Definition of Trade Name

A trade name is a word, name, symbol, device, or other designation, or a combination of such designations, that is distinctive of a person's business or other enterprise and that is used in a manner that identifies that business or enterprise and distinguishes it from the businesses or enterprises of others.

§ 13. Distinctiveness; Secondary Meaning

A word, name, symbol, device, or other designation, or a combination of such designations, is "distinctive" under the rules stated in §§ 9–12 if:

(a) the designation is "inherently distinctive," in that, because of the nature of the designation and the context in which it is used, prospective purchasers are likely to perceive it as a designation that, in the case of a trademark, identifies goods or services produced or sponsored by a particular person, whether known or anonymous, or in the case of a trade name, identifies the business or other enterprise of a particular person, whether known or anonymous, or in the case of a collective mark, identifies members of the collective group or goods or services produced or sponsored by members, or in the case of a certification mark, identifies the certified goods or services; or

(b) the designation, although not "inherently distinctive," has become distinctive, in that, as a result of its use, prospective purchasers have come to perceive it as a designation that identifies goods, services, businesses, or members in the manner described in Subsection (a). Such acquired distinctiveness is commonly referred to as "secondary meaning."

§ 14. Descriptive, Geographic, and Personal Name Designations

A designation that is likely to be perceived by prospective purchasers as merely descriptive of the nature, qualities, or other characteristics of the goods, services, or business with which it is used, or as merely geographically descriptive of their origin or location, or as the personal name of a person connected with the goods, services, or business, is not inherently distinctive under the rule stated in § 13(a). Such a designation is distinctive only if it has acquired secondary meaning under the rule stated in § 13(b).

§ 15. Generic Designations

(1) A designation that is understood by prospective purchasers to denominate the general category, type, or class of the goods, services, or business with which it is used is a generic designation. A user cannot acquire rights in a generic designation as a trademark, trade name, collective mark, or certification mark.

(2) If prospective purchasers have come to perceive a trademark, trade name, collective mark, or certification mark primarily as a generic designation for the category, type, or class of the goods, services, or business with which it is used, the designation is no longer eligible for protection as a trademark, trade name, collective mark, or certification mark.

§ 16. Configurations of Packaging and Products: Trade Dress and Product Designs

The design of elements that constitute the appearance or image of goods or services as presented to prospective purchasers, including the design of packaging, labels, containers, displays, decor, or the design of a product, a product feature, or a combination of product features, is eligible for protection as a mark under the rules stated in this Chapter if:

(a) the design is distinctive under the rule stated in § 13; and

(b) the design is not functional under the rule stated in § 17.

§ 17. Functional Designs

A design is "functional" for purposes of the rule stated in § 16 if the design affords benefits in the manufacturing, marketing, or use of the goods or services with which the design is used, apart from any benefits attributable to the design's significance as an indication of source, that are important to effective competition by others and that are not practically available through the use of alternative designs.

TOPIC 2.   ACQUISITION AND PRIORITY OF RIGHTS

---

§ 18. Acquisition of Rights

Rights can be acquired in a designation only when the designation has been actually used as a trademark, trade name, collective mark, or certification mark as defined in §§ 9–12, or when an applicable statutory provision recognizes a protectable interest in the designation prior to actual use. A designation is "used" as a trademark, trade name, collective trademark, or certification mark when the designation is displayed or otherwise made known to prospective purchasers in the ordinary course of business in a manner that associates the designation with the goods, services, or business of the user or, in the case of a certification mark, with the certified goods or services. A designation is "used" as a collective membership mark when the designation is displayed or otherwise made known in a manner that signifies membership in the collective group.

§ 19. Priority of Rights

One who has used a designation as a trademark, trade name, collective mark, or certification mark under the rule stated in § 18 has priority in the use of the designation over another user:

> (a)   in any geographic area in which the actor has used the designation in good faith or in which the designation has become associated with the actor as a result of good faith use before the designation is used in good faith by, or becomes associated with, the other; and

> (b)   in any additional geographic area in which the actor has priority over the other under an applicable statutory provision.

TOPIC 3.   INFRINGEMENT OF RIGHTS

---

§ 20. Standard of Infringement

(1)   One is subject to liability for infringement of another's trademark, trade name, collective mark, or certification mark if the other's use has priority under the rules stated in § 19 and in identifying the actor's business or in marketing the actor's goods or services the actor uses a designation that causes a likelihood of confusion:

> (a)   that the actor's business is the business of the other or is associated or otherwise connected with the other; or

> (b)   that the goods or services marketed by the actor are produced, sponsored, certified, or approved by the other; or

> (c)   that the goods or services marketed by the other are produced, sponsored, certified, or approved by the actor.

(2)   One is also subject to liability for infringement of another's collective membership mark if the other's use has priority under the rules stated in § 19 and the actor uses a designation that causes a likelihood of confusion that the actor is a member of or otherwise associated with the collective group.

§ 21. Proof of Likelihood of Confusion: Market Factors

Whether an actor's use of a designation causes a likelihood of confusion with the use of a trademark, trade name, collective mark, or certification mark by another under the rule stated in § 20 is determined by a consideration of all the circumstances involved in the marketing of the respective goods or services or in the operation of the respective businesses. In making that determination the following market factors, among others, may be important:

(a)   the degree of similarity between the respective designations, including a comparison of

(i)   the overall impression created by the designations as they are used in marketing the respective goods or services or in identifying the respective businesses;

(ii)   the pronunciation of the designations;

(iii)   the translation of any foreign words contained in the designations;

(iv)   the verbal translation of any pictures, illustrations, or designs contained in the designations;

(v)   the suggestions, connotations, or meanings of the designations;

(b)   the degree of similarity in the marketing methods and channels of distribution used for the respective goods or services;

(c)   the characteristics of the prospective purchasers of the goods or services and the degree of care they are likely to exercise in making purchasing decisions;

(d)   the degree of distinctiveness of the other's designation;

(e)   when the goods, services, or business of the actor differ in kind from those of the other, the likelihood that the actor's prospective purchasers would expect a person in the position of the other to expand its marketing or sponsorship into the product, service, or business market of the actor;

(f)   when the actor and the other sell their goods or services or carry on their businesses in different geographic markets, the extent to which the other's designation is identified with the other in the geographic market of the actor.

§ 22. Proof of Likelihood of Confusion: Intent of the Actor

(1)   A likelihood of confusion may be inferred from proof that the actor used a designation resembling another's trademark, trade name, collective mark, or certification mark with the intent to cause confusion or to deceive.

(2)   A likelihood of confusion should not be inferred from proof that the actor intentionally copied the other's designation if the actor acted in good faith under circumstances that do not otherwise indicate an intent to cause confusion or to deceive.

§ 23. Proof of Likelihood of Confusion: Evidence of Actual Confusion

(1)   A likelihood of confusion may be inferred from proof of actual confusion.

(2)   An absence of likelihood of confusion may be inferred from the absence of proof of actual confusion if the actor and the other have made significant use of their respective designations in the same geographic market for a substantial period of time, and any resulting confusion would ordinarily be manifested by provable facts.

§ 24. Use of Another's Trademark on Genuine Goods

One is not subject to liability under the rule stated in § 20 for using another's trademark, trade name, collective mark, or certification mark in marketing genuine goods or services the source, sponsorship, or certification of which is accurately identified by the mark unless:

(a)   the other uses a different mark for different types or grades of goods or services and the actor markets one of the types or grades under a mark used for another type or grade; or

(b)   the actor markets under the mark genuine goods of the other that have been repaired, reconditioned, altered, or used, or genuine services that do not conform to the standards imposed by the other, and the actor's use of the mark causes a likelihood of confusion that the goods are new or unaltered or that the repair, reconditioning, or alteration was performed, authorized, or certified by the other, or that the services conform to the other's standards.

§ 25. Liability Without Proof of Confusion: Dilution and Tarnishment

(1) One may be subject to liability under the law of trademarks for the use of a designation that resembles the trademark, trade name, collective mark, or certification mark of another without proof of a likelihood of confusion only under an applicable antidilution statute. An actor is subject to liability under an antidilution statute if the actor uses such a designation in a manner that is likely to associate the other's mark with the goods, services, or business of the actor and:

(a) the other's mark is highly distinctive and the association of the mark with the actor's goods, services, or business is likely to cause a reduction in that distinctiveness; or

(b) the association of the other's mark with the actor's goods, services, or business, or the nature of the actor's use, is likely to disparage the other's goods, services, or business or tarnish the images associated with the other's mark.

(2) One who uses a designation that resembles the trademark, trade name, collective mark, or certification mark of another, not in a manner that is likely to associate the other's mark with the goods, services, or business of the actor, but rather to comment on, criticize, ridicule, parody, or disparage the other or the other's goods, services, business, or mark, is subject to liability without proof of a likelihood of confusion only if the actor's conduct meets the requirements of a cause of action for defamation, invasion of privacy, or injurious falsehood.

§ 26. Contributory Infringement by Printers, Publishers, and Other Suppliers

(1) One who, on behalf of a third person, reproduces or imitates the trademark, trade name, collective mark, or certification mark of another on goods, labels, packaging, advertisements, or other materials that are used by the third person in a manner that subjects the third person to liability to the other for infringement under the rule stated in § 20 is subject to liability to that other for contributory infringement.

(2) If an actor subject to contributory liability under the rule stated in Subsection (1) acted without knowledge that the reproduction or imitation was intended by the third person to confuse or deceive, the actor is subject only to appropriate injunctive relief.

§ 27. Contributory Infringement by Manufacturers and Distributors

One who markets goods or services to a third person who further markets the goods or services in a manner that subjects the third person to liability to another for infringement under the rule stated in § 20 is subject to liability to that other for contributory infringement if:

(a) the actor intentionally induces the third person to engage in the infringing conduct; or

(b) the actor fails to take reasonable precautions against the occurrence of the third person's infringing conduct in circumstances in which the infringing conduct can be reasonably anticipated.

TOPIC 4.   DEFENSES AND LIMITATIONS ON RELIEF

§ 28. Descriptive Use (Fair Use)

In an action for infringement of a trademark, trade name, collective mark, or certification mark, it is a defense that the term used by the actor is descriptive or geographically descriptive of the actor's goods, services, or business, or is the personal name of the actor or a person connected with the actor, and the actor has used the term fairly and in good faith solely to describe the actor's goods, services, or business or to indicate a connection with the named person.

§ 29. Consent

In an action for infringement of a trademark, trade name, collective mark, or certification mark, it is a defense that the actor's use is within the scope of the owner's consent as manifested by an agreement between the parties or by other conduct from which the owner's consent can reasonably be inferred.

§ 30. Abandonment

(1)   In an action for infringement of a trademark, trade name, collective mark, or certification mark, it is a defense that the designation was abandoned by the party asserting rights in the designation prior to the commencement of use by the actor.

(2)   A trademark, trade name, collective mark, or certification mark is abandoned if:

(a)   the party asserting rights in the designation has ceased to use the designation with an intent not to resume use; or

(b)   the designation has lost its significance as a trademark, trade name, collective mark, or certification mark as a result of a cessation of use or other acts or omissions by the party asserting rights in the designation.

§ 31. Unreasonable Delay (Laches)

If the owner of a trademark, trade name, collective mark, or certification mark unreasonably delays in commencing an action for infringement or otherwise asserting the owner's rights and thereby causes prejudice to another who may be subject to liability to the owner under the rules stated in this Chapter, the owner may be barred in whole or in part from the relief that would otherwise be available under §§ 35–37.

§ 32. Plaintiff's Misconduct (Unclean Hands)

If a designation used as a trademark, trade name, collective mark, or certification mark is deceptive, or if its use is otherwise in violation of public policy, or if the owner of the designation has engaged in other substantial misconduct directly related to the owner's assertion of rights in the trademark, trade name, collective mark, or certification mark, the owner may be barred in whole or in part from the relief that would otherwise be available under §§ 35–37.

TOPIC 5.   LICENSING AND ASSIGNMENT OF RIGHTS

Sec.
33.   Licensing of Trademarks.
34.   Assignment of Trademarks.

---

§ 33. Licensing of Trademarks

The owner of a trademark, trade name, collective mark, or certification mark may license another to use the designation. If the licensor exercises reasonable control over the nature and quality of the goods, services, or business on which the designation is used by the licensee, any rights in the designation arising from the licensee's use accrue to the benefit of the licensor. Failure of the licensor to exercise reasonable control over the use of the designation by the licensee can result in abandonment of the designation under the rule stated in § 30(2)(b).

§ 34. Assignment of Trademarks

The owner of a trademark, trade name, collective mark, or certification mark may transfer ownership of the designation to another through an assignment. An assignment of ownership transfers the assignor's priority in the use of the designation to the assignee only if the assignee also acquires the line of business that is associated with the designation or otherwise maintains continuity in the use of the designation by continuing the line of business without substantial change. An assignment of ownership that does not maintain continuity in the use of the designation can result in abandonment of the designation under the rule stated in § 30.

TOPIC 6.   REMEDIES

§ 35.   Injunctions: Trademark Infringement and Deceptive Marketing

(1)   Unless inappropriate under the rule stated in Subsection (2), injunctive relief will ordinarily be awarded against one who is liable to another for:

     (a)   deceptive marketing under the rules stated in §§ 2–8; or

     (b)   infringement of the other's trademark, trade name, collective mark, or certification mark under the rule stated in § 20; or

     (c)   dilution of the other's trademark, trade name, collective mark, or certification mark under the rule stated in § 25.

(2)   The appropriateness and scope of injunctive relief depend upon a comparative appraisal of all the factors of the case, including the following primary factors:

     (a)   the nature of the interest to be protected;

     (b)   the nature and extent of the wrongful conduct;

     (c)   the relative adequacy to the plaintiff of an injunction and of other remedies;

     (d)   the relative harm likely to result to the legitimate interests of the defendant if an injunction is granted and to the legitimate interests of the plaintiff if an injunction is denied;

     (e)   the interests of third persons and of the public;

     (f)   any unreasonable delay by the plaintiff in bringing suit or otherwise asserting its rights;

     (g)   any related misconduct on the part of the plaintiff; and

     (h)   the practicality of framing and enforcing the injunction.

§ 36.   Damages: Trademark Infringement and Deceptive Marketing

(1)   One who is liable to another for deceptive marketing under the rules stated in §§ 2–8 or for infringement of the other's trademark, trade name, collective mark, or certification mark under the rule stated in § 20 is liable for the pecuniary loss to the other caused by the deceptive marketing or

infringement, unless an award of damages for such pecuniary loss is prohibited by statute or is otherwise inappropriate under the rule stated in Subsection (3).

(2)   The pecuniary loss for which damages may be recovered under this Section includes:

(a)   loss resulting to the plaintiff from sales or other revenues lost because of the actor's conduct;

(b)   loss resulting from sales made by the plaintiff at prices that have been reasonably reduced because of the actor's conduct;

(c)   harm to the market reputation of the plaintiff's goods, services, business, or trademark; and

(d)   reasonable expenditures made by the plaintiff in order to prevent, correct, or mitigate the confusion or deception of prospective purchasers resulting from the actor's conduct.

(3)   Whether an award of damages for pecuniary loss is appropriate depends upon a comparative appraisal of all the factors of the case, including the following primary factors:

(a)   the degree of certainty with which the plaintiff has established the fact and extent of the pecuniary loss caused by the actor's conduct;

(b)   the relative adequacy to the plaintiff of other remedies, including an accounting of the actor's profits;

(c)   the intent of the actor and the extent to which the actor knew or should have known that the conduct was unlawful;

(d)   the role of the actor in bringing about the infringement or deceptive marketing;

(e)   any unreasonable delay by the plaintiff in bringing suit or otherwise asserting its rights; and

(f)   any related misconduct on the part of the plaintiff.

§ 37. Accounting of Defendant's Profits: Trademark Infringement and Deceptive Marketing

(1)   One who is liable to another for deceptive marketing under the rules stated in §§ 2–8 or for infringement of the other's trademark, trade name, collective mark, or certification mark under the rule stated in § 20 is liable for the net profits earned on profitable transactions resulting from the unlawful conduct, but only if:

(a)   the actor engaged in the conduct with the intention of causing confusion or deception; and

(b)   the award of profits is not prohibited by statute and is otherwise appropriate under the rule stated in Subsection (2).

(2)   Whether an award of profits is appropriate depends upon a comparative appraisal of all the factors of the case, including the following primary factors:

(a)   the degree of certainty that the actor benefitted from the unlawful conduct;

(b)   the relative adequacy to the plaintiff of other remedies, including an award of damages;

(c)   the interests of the public in depriving the actor of unjust gains and discouraging unlawful conduct;

(d)   the role of the actor in bringing about the infringement or deceptive marketing;

(e)   any unreasonable delay by the plaintiff in bringing suit or otherwise asserting its rights; and

(f)   any related misconduct on the part of the plaintiff.

CHAPTER FOUR.   APPROPRIATION OF TRADE VALUES

TOPIC 1.   MISAPPROPRIATION

TOPIC 2.   TRADE SECRETS

TOPIC 3.   RIGHT OF PUBLICITY

TOPIC 1.   MISAPPROPRIATION

---

§ 38.   Appropriation of Trade Values

One who causes harm to the commercial relations of another by appropriating the other's intangible trade values is subject to liability to the other for such harm only if:

(a)   the actor is subject to liability for an appropriation of the other's trade secret under the rules stated in §§ 39–45; or

(b)   the actor is subject to liability for an appropriation of the commercial value of the other's identity under the rules stated in §§ 46–49; or

(c)   the appropriation is actionable by the other under federal or state statutes or international agreements, or is actionable as a breach of contract, or as an infringement of common law copyright as preserved under federal copyright law.

TOPIC 2.   TRADE SECRETS

45.   Monetary Relief: Appropriation of Trade Secrets.

---

§ 39. Definition of Trade Secret

A trade secret is any information that can be used in the operation of a business or other enterprise and that is sufficiently valuable and secret to afford an actual or potential economic advantage over others.

§ 40. Appropriation of Trade Secrets

One is subject to liability for the appropriation of another's trade secret if:

(a)   the actor acquires by means that are improper under the rule stated in § 43 information that the actor knows or has reason to know is the other's trade secret; or

(b)   the actor uses or discloses the other's trade secret without the other's consent and, at the time of the use or disclosure,

(1)   the actor knows or has reason to know that the information is a trade secret that the actor acquired under circumstances creating a duty of confidence owed by the actor to the other under the rule stated in § 41; or

(2)   the actor knows or has reason to know that the information is a trade secret that the actor acquired by means that are improper under the rule stated in § 43; or

(3)   the actor knows or has reason to know that the information is a trade secret that the actor acquired from or through a person who acquired it by means that are improper under the rule stated in § 43 or whose disclosure of the trade secret constituted a breach of a duty of confidence owed to the other under the rule stated in § 41; or

(4)   the actor knows or has reason to know that the information is a trade secret that the actor acquired through an accident or mistake, unless the acquisition was the result of the other's failure to take reasonable precautions to maintain the secrecy of the information.

§ 41. Duty of Confidence

A person to whom a trade secret has been disclosed owes a duty of confidence to the owner of the trade secret for purposes of the rule stated in § 40 if:

(a)   the person made an express promise of confidentiality prior to the disclosure of the trade secret; or

(b)   the trade secret was disclosed to the person under circumstances in which the relationship between the parties to the disclosure or the other facts surrounding the disclosure justify the conclusions that, at the time of the disclosure,

(1)   the person knew or had reason to know that the disclosure was intended to be in confidence, and

(2)   the other party to the disclosure was reasonable in inferring that the person consented to an obligation of confidentiality.

§ 42. Breach of Confidence by Employees

An employee or former employee who uses or discloses a trade secret owned by the employer or former employer in breach of a duty of confidence is subject to liability for appropriation of the trade secret under the rule stated in § 40.

§ 43. Improper Acquisition of Trade Secrets

"Improper" means of acquiring another's trade secret under the rule stated in § 40 include theft, fraud, unauthorized interception of communications, inducement of or knowing participation in a breach of confidence, and other means either wrongful in themselves or wrongful under the circumstances of the case. Independent discovery and analysis of publicly available products or information are not improper means of acquisition.

§ 44. Injunctions: Appropriation of Trade Secrets

(1)   If appropriate under the rule stated in Subsection (2), injunctive relief may be awarded to prevent a continuing or threatened appropriation of another's trade secret by one who is subject to liability under the rule stated in § 40.

(2)   The appropriateness and scope of injunctive relief depend upon a comparative appraisal of all the factors of the case, including the following primary factors:

(a)   the nature of the interest to be protected;

(b)   the nature and extent of the appropriation;

(c)   the relative adequacy to the plaintiff of an injunction and of other remedies;

(d)   the relative harm likely to result to the legitimate interests of the defendant if an injunction is granted and to the legitimate interests of the plaintiff if an injunction is denied;

(e)   the interests of third persons and of the public;

(f)   any unreasonable delay by the plaintiff in bringing suit or otherwise asserting its rights;

(g)   any related misconduct on the part of the plaintiff; and

(h)   the practicality of framing and enforcing the injunction.

(3)   The duration of injunctive relief in trade secret actions should be limited to the time necessary to protect the plaintiff from any harm attributable to the appropriation and to deprive the defendant of any economic advantage attributable to the appropriation.

§ 45. Monetary Relief: Appropriation of Trade Secrets

(1)   One who is liable to another for an appropriation of the other's trade secret under the rule stated in § 40 is liable for the pecuniary loss to the other caused by the appropriation or for the actor's own pecuniary gain resulting from the appropriation, whichever is greater, unless such relief is inappropriate under the rule stated in Subsection (2).

(2)   Whether an award of monetary relief is appropriate and the appropriate method of measuring such relief depend upon a comparative appraisal of all the factors of the case, including the following primary factors:

(a)   the degree of certainty with which the plaintiff has established the fact and extent of the pecuniary loss or the actor's pecuniary gain resulting from the appropriation;

(b)   the nature and extent of the appropriation;

(c)   the relative adequacy to the plaintiff of other remedies;

(d)   the intent and knowledge of the actor and the nature and extent of any good faith reliance by the actor;

(e)   any unreasonable delay by the plaintiff in bringing suit or otherwise asserting its rights; and

(f)   any related misconduct on the part of the plaintiff.

TOPIC 3. RIGHT OF PUBLICITY

---

§ 46. Appropriation of the Commercial Value of a Person's Identity: The Right of Publicity

One who appropriates the commercial value of a person's identity by using without consent the person's name, likeness, or other indicia of identity for purposes of trade is subject to liability for the relief appropriate under the rules stated in §§ 48 and 49.

§ 47. Use for Purposes of Trade

The name, likeness, and other indicia of a person's identity are used "for purposes of trade" under the rule stated in § 46 if they are used in advertising the user's goods or services, or are placed on merchandise marketed by the user, or are used in connection with services rendered by the user. However, use "for purposes of trade" does not ordinarily include the use of a person's identity in news reporting, commentary, entertainment, works of fiction or nonfiction, or in advertising that is incidental to such uses.

§ 48. Injunctions: Appropriation of the Commercial Value of a Person's Identity

(1) If appropriate under the rule stated in Subsection (2), injunctive relief may be awarded to prevent a continuing or threatened appropriation of the commercial value of another's identity by one who is subject to liability under the rule stated in § 46.

(2) The appropriateness and scope of injunctive relief depend upon a comparative appraisal of all the factors of the case, including the following primary factors:

    (a) the nature of the interest to be protected;

    (b) the nature and extent of the appropriation;

    (c) the relative adequacy to the plaintiff of an injunction and of other remedies;

    (d) the relative harm likely to result to the legitimate interests of the defendant if an injunction is granted and to the legitimate interests of the plaintiff if an injunction is denied;

    (e) the interests of third persons and of the public;

    (f) any unreasonable delay by the plaintiff in bringing suit or otherwise asserting his or her rights;

    (g) any related misconduct on the part of the plaintiff; and

    (h) the practicality of framing and enforcing the injunction.

§ 49. Monetary Relief: Appropriation of the Commercial Value of a Person's Identity

(1) One who is liable for an appropriation of the commercial value of another's identity under the rule stated in § 46 is liable for the pecuniary loss to the other caused by the appropriation or for the actor's own pecuniary gain resulting from the appropriation, whichever is greater, unless such relief is precluded by an applicable statute or is otherwise inappropriate under the rule stated in Subsection (2).

(2)   Whether an award of monetary relief is appropriate and the appropriate method of measuring such relief depend upon a comparative appraisal of all the factors of the case, including the following primary factors:

(a)   the degree of certainty with which the plaintiff has established the fact and extent of the pecuniary loss or the actor's pecuniary gain resulting from the appropriation;

(b)   the nature and extent of the appropriation;

(c)   the relative adequacy to the plaintiff of other remedies;

(d)   the intent of the actor and whether the actor knew or should have known that the conduct was unlawful;

(e)   any unreasonable delay by the plaintiff in bringing suit or otherwise asserting his or her rights; and

(f)   any related misconduct on the part of the plaintiff.

V. GENERAL INTERNATIONAL INTELLECTUAL PROPERTY MATERIALS

A. COORDINATION AND STRATEGIC PLANNING PROVISIONS OF THE PRO-IP ACT OF 2008[*]

Contents

§ 8111. Intellectual Property Enforcement Coordinator

(a) **Intellectual Property Enforcement Coordinator.** The President shall appoint, by and with the advice and consent of the Senate, an Intellectual Property Enforcement Coordinator (in this subchapter referred to as the "IPEC") to serve within the Executive Office of the President. As an exercise of the rulemaking power of the Senate, any nomination of the IPEC submitted to the Senate for confirmation, and referred to a committee, shall be referred to the Committee on the Judiciary.

(b) **Duties of IPEC**

(1) In general. The IPEC shall—

(A) chair the interagency intellectual property enforcement advisory committee established under subsection (b)(3)(A);

(B) coordinate the development of the Joint Strategic Plan against counterfeiting and infringement by the advisory committee under section 8113 of this title;

(C) assist, at the request of the departments and agencies listed in subsection (b)(3)(A), in the implementation of the Joint Strategic Plan;

(D) facilitate the issuance of policy guidance to departments and agencies on basic issues of policy and interpretation, to the extent necessary to assure the coordination of intellectual property enforcement policy and consistency with other law;

(E) report to the President and report to Congress, to the extent consistent with law, regarding domestic and international intellectual property enforcement programs;

(F) report to Congress, as provided in section 8114 of this title, on the implementation of the Joint Strategic Plan, and make recommendations, if any and as appropriate, to Congress for improvements in Federal intellectual property laws and enforcement efforts; and

(G) carry out such other functions as the President may direct.

(2) Limitation on authority. The IPEC may not control or direct any law enforcement agency, including the Department of Justice, in the exercise of its investigative or prosecutorial authority.

---

[*] The provisions of this law are codified in Title 15 of the U.S. Code and the sections numbers above are the U.S. Code sections.—*Ed.*

(3)   Advisory committee

(A)   Establishment. There is established an interagency intellectual property enforcement advisory committee composed of the IPEC, who shall chair the committee, and the following members:

(i)   Senate-confirmed representatives of the following departments and agencies who are involved in intellectual property enforcement, and who are, or are appointed by, the respective heads of those departments and agencies:

(I)   The Office of Management and Budget.

(II)   Relevant units within the Department of Justice, including the Federal Bureau of Investigation and the Criminal Division.

(III) The United States Patent and Trademark Office and other relevant units of the Department of Commerce.

(IV) The Office of the United States Trade Representative.

(V)   The Department of State, the United States Agency for International Development, and the Bureau of International Narcotics Law Enforcement.

(VI) The Department of Homeland Security, United States Customs and Border Protection, and United States Immigration and Customs Enforcement.

(VII) The Food and Drug Administration of the Department of Health and Human Services.

(VIII) The Department of Agriculture.

(IX) Any such other agencies as the President determines to be substantially involved in the efforts of the Federal Government to combat counterfeiting and infringement.

(ii)   The Register of Copyrights, or a senior representative of the United States Copyright Office appointed by the Register of Copyrights.

(B)   Functions. The advisory committee established under subparagraph (A) shall develop the Joint Strategic Plan against counterfeiting and infringement under section 8113 of this title.

§ 8112.   Definition

For purposes of this subchapter, the term "intellectual property enforcement" means matters relating to the enforcement of laws protecting copyrights, patents, trademarks, other forms of intellectual property, and trade secrets, both in the United States and abroad, including in particular matters relating to combating counterfeit and infringing goods.

§ 8113.   Joint Strategic Plan

(a)   **Purpose.** The objectives of the Joint Strategic Plan against counterfeiting and infringement that is referred to in section 8111(b)(1)(B) of this title (in this section referred to as the "joint strategic plan") are the following:

(1)   Reducing counterfeit and infringing goods in the domestic and international supply chain.

(2)   Identifying and addressing structural weaknesses, systemic flaws, or other unjustified impediments to effective enforcement action against the financing, production, trafficking, or sale of counterfeit or infringing goods, including identifying duplicative efforts to enforce, investigate, and prosecute intellectual property crimes across the Federal agencies and Departments that comprise the Advisory Committee and recommending how such duplicative efforts may be

minimized. Such recommendations may include recommendations on how to reduce duplication in personnel, materials, technologies, and facilities utilized by the agencies and Departments responsible for the enforcement, investigation, or prosecution of intellectual property crimes.

(3) Ensuring that information is identified and shared among the relevant departments and agencies, to the extent permitted by law, including requirements relating to confidentiality and privacy, and to the extent that such sharing of information is consistent with Department of Justice and other law enforcement protocols for handling such information, to aid in the objective of arresting and prosecuting individuals and entities that are knowingly involved in the financing, production, trafficking, or sale of counterfeit or infringing goods.

(4) Disrupting and eliminating domestic and international counterfeiting and infringement networks.

(5) Strengthening the capacity of other countries to protect and enforce intellectual property rights, and reducing the number of countries that fail to enforce laws preventing the financing, production, trafficking, and sale of counterfeit and infringing goods.

(6) Working with other countries to establish international standards and policies for the effective protection and enforcement of intellectual property rights.

(7) Protecting intellectual property rights overseas by—

(A) working with other countries and exchanging information with appropriate law enforcement agencies in other countries relating to individuals and entities involved in the financing, production, trafficking, or sale of counterfeit and infringing goods;

(B) ensuring that the information referred to in subparagraph (A) is provided to appropriate United States law enforcement agencies in order to assist, as warranted, enforcement activities in cooperation with appropriate law enforcement agencies in other countries; and

(C) building a formal process for consulting with companies, industry associations, labor unions, and other interested groups in other countries with respect to intellectual property enforcement.

(b) **Timing.** Not later than 12 months after October 13, 2008, and not later than December 31 of every third year thereafter, the IPEC shall submit the joint strategic plan to the Committee on the Judiciary and the Committee on Appropriations of the Senate, and to the Committee on the Judiciary and the Committee on Appropriations of the House of Representatives.

(c) **Responsibility of the IPEC.** During the development of the joint strategic plan, the IPEC—

(1) shall provide assistance to, and coordinate the meetings and efforts of, the appropriate officers and employees of departments and agencies represented on the advisory committee appointed under section 8111(b)(3) of this title who are involved in intellectual property enforcement; and

(2) may consult with private sector experts in intellectual property enforcement in furtherance of providing assistance to the members of the advisory committee appointed under section 8111(b)(3) of this title.

(d) **Responsibilities of other departments and agencies.** In the development and implementation of the joint strategic plan, the heads of the departments and agencies identified under section 8111(b)(3) of this title shall—

(1) designate personnel with expertise and experience in intellectual property enforcement matters to work with the IPEC and other members of the advisory committee; and

(2) share relevant department or agency information with the IPEC and other members of the advisory committee, including statistical information on the enforcement activities of the

department or agency against counterfeiting or infringement, and plans for addressing the joint strategic plan, to the extent permitted by law, including requirements relating to confidentiality and privacy, and to the extent that such sharing of information is consistent with Department of Justice and other law enforcement protocols for handling such information.

(e) **Contents of the joint strategic plan.** Each joint strategic plan shall include the following:

(1) A description of the priorities identified for carrying out the objectives in the joint strategic plan, including activities of the Federal Government relating to intellectual property enforcement.

(2) A description of the means to be employed to achieve the priorities, including the means for improving the efficiency and effectiveness of the Federal Government's enforcement efforts against counterfeiting and infringement.

(3) Estimates of the resources necessary to fulfill the priorities identified under paragraph (1).

(4) The performance measures to be used to monitor results under the joint strategic plan during the following year.

(5) An analysis of the threat posed by violations of intellectual property rights, including the costs to the economy of the United States resulting from violations of intellectual property laws, and the threats to public health and safety created by counterfeiting and infringement.

(6) An identification of the departments and agencies that will be involved in implementing each priority under paragraph (1).

(7) A strategy for ensuring coordination among the departments and agencies identified under paragraph (6), which will facilitate oversight by the executive branch of, and accountability among, the departments and agencies responsible for carrying out the strategy.

(8) Such other information as is necessary to convey the costs imposed on the United States economy by, and the threats to public health and safety created by, counterfeiting and infringement, and those steps that the Federal Government intends to take over the period covered by the succeeding joint strategic plan to reduce those costs and counter those threats.

(f) **Enhancing enforcement efforts of foreign Governments.** The joint strategic plan shall include programs to provide training and technical assistance to foreign governments for the purpose of enhancing the efforts of such governments to enforce laws against counterfeiting and infringement. With respect to such programs, the joint strategic plan shall—

(1) seek to enhance the efficiency and consistency with which Federal resources are expended, and seek to minimize duplication, overlap, or inconsistency of efforts;

(2) identify and give priority to those countries where programs of training and technical assistance can be carried out most effectively and with the greatest benefit to reducing counterfeit and infringing products in the United States market, to protecting the intellectual property rights of United States persons and their licensees, and to protecting the interests of United States persons otherwise harmed by violations of intellectual property rights in those countries;

(3) in identifying the priorities under paragraph (2), be guided by the list of countries identified by the United States Trade Representative under section 2242(a) of Title 19; and

(4) develop metrics to measure the effectiveness of the Federal Government's efforts to improve the laws and enforcement practices of foreign governments against counterfeiting and infringement.

(g) **Dissemination of the joint strategic plan.** The joint strategic plan shall be posted for public access on the website of the White House, and shall be disseminated to the public through such other means as the IPEC may identify.

§ 8114. Reporting

(a) **Annual report.** Not later than December 31 of each calendar year beginning in 2009, the IPEC shall submit a report on the activities of the advisory committee during the preceding fiscal year. The annual report shall be submitted to Congress, and disseminated to the people of the United States, in the manner specified in subsections (b) and (g) of section 8113 of this title.

(b) **Contents.** The report required by this section shall include the following:

(1) The progress made on implementing the strategic plan and on the progress toward fulfillment of the priorities identified under section 8113(e)(1) of this title.

(2) The progress made in efforts to encourage Federal, State, and local government departments and agencies to accord higher priority to intellectual property enforcement.

(3) The progress made in working with foreign countries to investigate, arrest, and prosecute entities and individuals involved in the financing, production, trafficking, and sale of counterfeit and infringing goods.

(4) The manner in which the relevant departments and agencies are working together and sharing information to strengthen intellectual property enforcement.

(5) An assessment of the successes and shortcomings of the efforts of the Federal Government, including departments and agencies represented on the committee established under section 8111(b)(3) of this title.

(6) Recommendations, if any and as appropriate, for any changes in enforcement statutes, regulations, or funding levels that the advisory committee considers would significantly improve the effectiveness or efficiency of the effort of the Federal Government to combat counterfeiting and infringement and otherwise strengthen intellectual property enforcement, including through the elimination or consolidation of duplicative programs or initiatives.

(7) The progress made in strengthening the capacity of countries to protect and enforce intellectual property rights.

(8) The successes and challenges in sharing with other countries information relating to intellectual property enforcement.

(9) The progress made under trade agreements and treaties to protect intellectual property rights of United States persons and their licensees.

(10) The progress made in minimizing duplicative efforts, materials, facilities, and procedures of the Federal agencies and Departments responsible for the enforcement, investigation, or prosecution of intellectual property crimes.

(11) Recommendations, if any and as appropriate, on how to enhance the efficiency and consistency with which Federal funds and resources are expended to enforce, investigate, or prosecute intellectual property crimes, including the extent to which the agencies and Departments responsible for the enforcement, investigation, or prosecution of intellectual property crimes have utilized existing personnel, materials, technologies, and facilities.

§ 8115. Savings and Repeals

(a) **Transition from NIPLECC to IPEC**

(1) Omitted

(2) Continuity of performance of duties. Upon confirmation by the Senate, and notwithstanding paragraph (1), the IPEC may use the services and personnel of the National Intellectual Property Law Enforcement Coordination Council, for such time as is reasonable, to perform any functions or duties which in the discretion of the IPEC are necessary to facilitate the

orderly transition of any functions or duties transferred from the Council to the IPEC pursuant to any provision of this Act or any amendment made by this Act.

(b) **Current authorities not affected.** Except as provided in subsection (a), nothing in this subchapter shall alter the authority of any department or agency of the United States (including any independent agency) that relates to—

(1) the investigation and prosecution of violations of laws that protect intellectual property rights;

(2) the administrative enforcement, at the borders of the United States, of laws that protect intellectual property rights; or

(3) the United States trade agreements program or international trade.

(c) **Rules of construction.** Nothing in this subchapter—

(1) shall derogate from the powers, duties, and functions of any of the agencies, departments, or other entities listed or included under section 8111(b)(3)(A) of this title; and

(2) shall be construed to transfer authority regarding the control, use, or allocation of law enforcement resources, or the initiation or prosecution of individual cases or types of cases, from the responsible law enforcement department or agency.

B. PARIS CONVENTION FOR THE PROTECTION OF INDUSTRIAL PROPERTY

[Of March 20, 1883, as revised at Brussels on December 14, 1900,
at Washington on June 2, 1911, at The Hague on November 6, 1925,
at London on June 2, 1934, at Lisbon on October 31, 1958, and
at Stockholm on July 14, 1967, and amended on September 28, 1979]

Contents

Articles 13 through 30 [omitted].

Article 1

[Establishment of the Union; Scope of Industrial Property]*

1.   The countries to which this Convention applies constitute a Union for the protection of industrial property.

2.   The protection of industrial property has as its object patents, utility models, industrial designs, trademarks, service marks, trade names, indications of source or appellations of origin, and the repression of unfair competition.

3.   Industrial property shall be understood in the broadest sense and shall apply not only to industry and commerce proper, but likewise to agricultural and extractive industries and to all manufactured or natural products, for example, wines, grain, tobacco leaf, fruit, cattle, minerals, mineral waters, beer, flowers, and flour.

4.   Patents shall include the various kinds of industrial patents recognized by the laws of the countries of the Union, such as patents of importation, patents of improvement, patents and certificates of addition, etc.

Article 2

[National Treatment for Nationals of Countries of the Union]

1.   Nationals of any country of the Union shall, as regards the protection of industrial property, enjoy in all the other countries of the Union the advantages that their respective laws now grant, or may hereafter grant, to nationals; all without prejudice to the rights specially provided for by this Convention. Consequently, they shall have the same protection as the latter, and the same legal remedy against any infringement of their rights, provided that the conditions and formalities imposed upon nationals are complied with.

2.   However, no requirement as to domicile or establishment in the country where protection is claimed may be imposed upon nationals of countries of the Union for the enjoyment of any industrial property rights.

3.   The provisions of the laws of each of the countries of the Union relating to judicial and administrative procedure and to jurisdiction, and to the designation of an address for service or the appointment of an agent, which may be required by the laws on industrial property are expressly reserved.

Article 3

[Same Treatment for Certain Categories of Persons as for Nationals of Countries of the Union]

Nationals of countries outside the Union who are domiciled or who have real and effective industrial or commercial establishments in the territory of one of the countries of the Union shall be treated in the same manner as nationals of the countries of the Union.

---

*   Articles have been given titles to facilitate their identification. There are no titles in the signed (French) text.

Article 4

[A to I—Patents, Utility Models, Industrial Designs, Marks, Inventors' Certificates: Right of Priority

G—Patents: Division of the Application]

A.   1. Any person who has duly filed an application for a patent, or for the registration of a utility model, or of an industrial design, or of a trademark, in one of the countries of the Union, or his successor in title, shall enjoy, for the purpose of filing in the other countries, a right of priority during the periods hereinafter fixed.

2.   Any filing that is equivalent to a regular national filing under the domestic legislation of any country of the Union or under bilateral or multilateral treaties concluded between countries of the Union shall be recognized as giving rise to the right of priority.

3.   By a regular national filing is meant any filing that is adequate to establish the date on which the application was filed in the country concerned, whatever may be the subsequent fate of the application.

B.   Consequently, any subsequent filing in any of the other countries of the Union before the expiration of the periods referred to above shall not be invalidated by reason of any acts accomplished in the interval, in particular, another filing, the publication or exploitation of the invention, the putting on sale of copies of the design, or the use of the mark, and such acts cannot give rise to any third-party right or any right of personal possession. Rights acquired by third parties before the date of the first application that serves as the basis for the right of priority are reserved in accordance with the domestic legislation of each country of the Union.

C.   1. The periods of priority referred to above shall be twelve months for patents and utility models, and six months for industrial designs and trademarks.

2.   These periods shall start from the date of filing of the first application; the day of filing shall not be included in the period.

3.   If the last day of the period is an official holiday, or a day when the Office is not open for the filing of applications in the country where protection is claimed, the period shall be extended until the first following working day.

4.   A subsequent application concerning the same subject as a previous first application within the meaning of paragraph (2), above, filed in the same country of the Union, shall be considered as the first application, of which the filing date shall be the starting point of the period of priority, if, at the time of filing the subsequent application, the said previous application has been withdrawn, abandoned, or refused, without having been laid open to public inspection and without leaving any rights outstanding, and if it has not yet served as a basis for claiming a right of priority. The previous application may not thereafter serve as a basis for claiming a right of priority.

D.   1. Any person desiring to take advantage of the priority of a previous filing shall be required to make a declaration indicating the date of such filing and the country in which it was made. Each country shall determine the latest date on which such declaration must be made.

2.   These particulars shall be mentioned in the publications issued by the competent authority, and in particular in the patents and the specifications relating thereto.

3.   The countries of the Union may require any person making a declaration of priority to produce a copy of the application (description, drawings, etc.) previously filed. The copy, certified as correct by the authority which received such application, shall not require any authentication, and may in any case be filed, without fee, at any time within three months of the filing of the subsequent application. They may require it to be accompanied by a certificate from the same authority showing the date of filing, and by a translation.

4.   No other formalities may be required for the declaration of priority at the time of filing the application. Each country of the Union shall determine the consequences of failure to comply with the formalities prescribed by this article, but such consequences shall in no case go beyond the loss of the right of priority.

5.   Subsequently, further proof may be required.

Any person who avails himself of the priority of a previous application shall be required to specify the number of that application; this number shall be published as provided for by paragraph (2), above.

E.   1. Where an industrial design is filed in a country by virtue of a right of priority based on the filing of a utility model, the period of priority shall be the same as that fixed for industrial designs.

2.   Furthermore, it is permissible to file a utility model in a country by virtue of a right of priority based on the filing of a patent application, and vice versa.

F.   No country of the Union may refuse a priority or a patent application on the ground that the applicant claims multiple priorities, even if they originate in different countries, or on the ground that an application claiming one or more priorities contains one or more elements that were not included in the application or applications whose priority is claimed, provided that, in both cases, there is unity of invention within the meaning of the law of the country.

With respect to the elements not included in the application or applications whose priority is claimed, the filing of the subsequent application shall give rise to a right of priority under ordinary conditions.

G.   1. If the examination reveals that an application for a patent contains more than one invention, the applicant may divide the application into a certain number of divisional applications and preserve as the date of each the date of the initial application and the benefit of the right of priority, if any.

2.   The applicant may also, on his own initiative, divide a patent application and preserve as the date of each divisional application the date of the initial application and the benefit of the right of priority, if any. Each country of the Union shall have the right to determine the conditions under which such division shall be authorized.

H.   Priority may not be refused on the ground that certain elements of the invention for which priority is claimed do not appear among the claims formulated in the application in the country of origin, provided that the application documents as a whole specifically disclose such elements.

I.   1. Applications for inventors' certificates filed in a country in which applicants have the right to apply at their own option either for a patent or for an inventor's certificate shall give rise to the right of priority provided for by this article, under the same conditions and with the same effects as applications for patents.

2.   In a country in which applicants have the right to apply at their own option either for a patent or for an inventor's certificate, an applicant for an inventor's certificate shall, in accordance with the provisions of this article relating to patent applications, enjoy a right of priority based on an application for a patent, a utility model, or an inventor's certificate.

Article 4*bis*

[Patents: Independence of Patents Obtained for the Same Invention in Different Countries]

1.   Patents applied for in the various countries of the Union by nationals of countries of the Union shall be independent of patents obtained for the same invention in other countries, whether members of the Union or not.

2.   The foregoing provision is to be understood in an unrestricted sense, in particular, in the sense that patents applied for during the period of priority are independent, both as regards the grounds for nullity and forfeiture, and as regards their normal duration.

3.   The provision shall apply to all patents existing at the time when it comes into effect.

4.   Similarly, it shall apply, in the case of the accession of new countries, to patents in existence on either side at the time of accession.

5.   Patents obtained with the benefit of priority shall, in the various countries of the Union, have a duration equal to that which they would have, had they been applied for or granted without the benefit of priority.

Article 4*ter*

[Patents: Mention of the Inventor in the Patent]

The inventor shall have the right to be mentioned as such in the patent.

Article 4*quater*

[Patents: Patentability in Case of Restrictions of Sale by Law]

The grant of a patent shall not be refused and a patent shall not be invalidated on the ground that the sale of the patented product or of a product obtained by means of a patented process is subject to restrictions or limitations resulting from the domestic law.

Article 5

[A—Patents: Importation of Articles; Failure to Work or Insufficient Working; Compulsory Licenses

B—Industrial Designs: Failure to Work; Importation of Articles

C—Marks: Failure to Use; Different Forms; Use by Co-Proprietors

D—Patents, Utility Models, Marks, Industrial Designs: Marking]

A.   1. Importation by the patentee into the country where the patent has been granted of articles manufactured in any of the countries of the Union shall not entail forfeiture of the patent.

2.   Each country of the Union shall have the right to take legislative measures providing for the grant of compulsory licenses to prevent the abuses which might result from the exercise of the exclusive rights conferred by the patent, for example, failure to work.

3.   Forfeiture of the patent shall not be provided for except in cases where the grant of compulsory licenses would not have been sufficient to prevent the said abuses. No proceedings for the forfeiture or revocation of a patent may be instituted before the expiration of two years from the grant of the first compulsory license.

4.   A compulsory license may not be applied for on the ground of failure to work or insufficient working before the expiration of a period of four years from the date of filing of the patent application or three years from the date of the grant of the patent, whichever period expires last; it shall be refused if the patentee justifies his inaction by legitimate reasons. Such a compulsory license shall be non-exclusive and shall not be transferable, even in the form of the grant of a sub-license, except with that part of the enterprise or goodwill which exploits such license.

5.   The foregoing provisions shall be applicable, *mutatis mutandis,* to utility models.

B.   The protection of industrial designs shall not, under any circumstance, be subject to any forfeiture, either by reason of failure to work or by reason of the importation of articles corresponding to those which are protected.

C.   1. If, in any country, use of the registered mark is compulsory, the registration may be cancelled only after a reasonable period, and then only if the person concerned does not justify his inaction.

2.   Use of a trademark by the proprietor in a form differing in elements which do not alter the distinctive character of the mark in the form in which it was registered in one of the countries of the Union shall not entail invalidation of the registration and shall not diminish the protection granted to the mark.

3.   Concurrent use of the same mark on identical or similar goods by industrial or commercial establishments considered as co-proprietors of the mark according to the provisions of the domestic law of the country where protection is claimed shall not prevent registration or diminish in any way the protection granted to the said mark in any country of the Union, provided that such use does not result in misleading the public and is not contrary to the public interest.

D.   No indication or mention of the patent, of the utility model, of the registration of the trademark, or of the deposit of the industrial design, shall be required upon the goods as a condition of recognition of the right to protection.

Article 5*bis*

[All Industrial Property Rights: Period of Grace for the Payment of Fees for the Maintenance of Rights; Patents: Restoration]

1.   A period of grace of not less than six months shall be allowed for the payment of the fees prescribed for the maintenance of industrial property rights, subject, if the domestic legislation so provides, to the payment of a surcharge.

2.   The countries of the Union shall have the right to provide for the restoration of patents which have lapsed by reason of non-payment of fees.

Article 5*ter*

[Patents: Patented Devices Forming Part of Vessels, Aircraft, or Land Vehicles]

In any country of the Union the following shall not be considered as infringements of the rights of a patentee:

(1)   The use on board vessels of other countries of the Union of devices forming the subject of his patent in the body of the vessel, in the machinery, tackle, gear and other accessories, when such vessels temporarily or accidentally enter the waters of the said country, provided that such devices are used there exclusively for the needs of the vessel;

(2) The use of devices forming the subject of the patent in the construction or operation of aircraft or land vehicles of other countries of the Union, or if accessories of such aircraft or land vehicles, when those aircraft or land vehicles temporarily or accidentally enter the said country.

Article 5*quater*

[Patents: Importation of Products Manufactured by a Process Patented in the Importing Country]

When a product is imported into a country of the Union where there exists a patent protecting a process of manufacture of the said product, the patentee shall have all the rights, with regard to the imported product, that are accorded to him by the legislation of the country of importation, on the basis of the process patent, with respect to products manufactured in that country.

Article 5*quinquies*

[Industrial Designs]

Industrial designs shall be protected in all the countries of the Union.

Article 6

[Marks: Conditions of Registration; Independence of Protection of Same Mark in Different Countries]

1. The conditions for the filing and registration of trademarks shall be determined in each country of the Union by its domestic legislation.

2. However, an application for the registration of a mark filed by a national of a country of the Union in any country of the Union may not be refused, nor may a registration be invalidated, on the ground that filing, registration, or renewal, has not been affected in the country of origin.

3. A mark duly registered in a country of the Union shall be regarded as independent of marks registered in the other countries of the Union, including the country of origin.

Article 6*bis*

[Marks: Well-Known Marks]

1. The countries of the Union undertake, *ex officio* if their legislation so permits, or at the request of an interested party, to refuse or to cancel the registration, and to prohibit the use, of a trademark which constitutes a reproduction, an imitation, or a translation, liable to create confusion, of a mark considered by the competent authority of the country of registration or use to be well known in that country as being already the mark of a person entitled to the benefits of this Convention and used for identical or similar goods. These provisions shall also apply when the essential part of the mark constitutes a reproduction of any such well-known mark or an imitation liable to create confusion therewith.

2. A period of at least five years from the date of registration shall be allowed for requesting the cancellation of such a mark. The countries of the Union may provide for a period within which the prohibition of use must be requested.

3. No time limit shall be fixed for requesting the cancellation or the prohibition of the use of marks registered or used in bad faith.

Article 6*ter*

[Marks: Prohibitions Concerning State Emblems, Official Hallmarks, and Emblems of Intergovernmental Organizations]

1.   (a) The countries of the Union agree to refuse or to invalidate the registration, and to prohibit by appropriate measures the use, without authorization by the competent authorities, either as trademarks or as elements of trademarks, of armorial bearings, flags, and other State emblems, of the countries of the Union, official signs and hallmarks indicating control and warranty adopted by them, and any imitation from a heraldic point of view.

(b)   The provisions of sub-paragraph (a), above, shall apply equally to armorial bearings, flags, other emblems, abbreviations, and names, of international intergovernmental organizations of which one or more countries of the Union are members, with the exception of armorial bearings, flags, other emblems, abbreviations, and names, that are already the subject of international agreements in force, intended to ensure their protection.

(c)   No country of the Union shall be required to apply the provisions of sub-paragraph (b), above, to the prejudice of the owners of rights acquired in good faith before the entry into force, in that country, of this Convention. The countries of the Union shall not be required to apply the said provisions when the use or registration referred to in sub-paragraph (a), above, is not of such a nature as to suggest to the public that a connection exists between the organization concerned and the armorial bearings, flags, emblems, abbreviations, and names, or if such use or registration is probably not of such a nature as to mislead the public as to the existence of a connection between the user and the organization.

2.   Prohibition of the use of official signs and hallmarks indicating control and warranty shall apply solely in cases where the marks in which they are incorporated are intended to be used on goods of the same or a similar kind.

3.   (a) For the application of these provisions, the countries of the Union agree to communicate reciprocally, through the intermediary of the International Bureau, the list of State emblems, and official signs and hallmarks indicating control and warranty, which they desire, or may hereafter desire, to place wholly or within certain limits under the protection of this article, and all subsequent modifications of such list. Each country of the Union shall in due course make available to the public the lists so communicated.

Nevertheless such communication is not obligatory in respect of flags of States.

(b)   The provisions of sub-paragraph (b) of paragraph (1) of this article shall apply only to such armorial bearings, flags, other emblems, abbreviations, and names, of international intergovernmental organizations as the latter have communicated to the countries of the Union through the intermediary of the International Bureau.

4.   Any country of the Union may, within a period of twelve months from the receipt of the notification, transmit its objections, if any, through the intermediary of the International Bureau, to the country or intergovernmental organization concerned.

5.   In the case of State flags, the measures prescribed by paragraph (1), above, shall apply solely to marks registered after November 6, 1925.

6.   In the case of State emblems other than flags, and of official signs and hallmarks of the countries of the Union, and in the case of armorial bearings, flags, other emblems, abbreviations, and names, of international intergovernmental organizations, these provisions shall apply only to marks registered more than two months after receipt of the communication provided for in paragraph (3), above.

7.   In cases of bad faith, the countries shall have the right to cancel even those marks incorporating State emblems, signs, and hallmarks, which were registered before November 6, 1925.

8.   Nationals of any country who are authorized to make use of the State emblems, signs, and hallmarks, of their country may use them even if they are similar to those of another country.

9.   The countries of the Union undertake to prohibit the unauthorized use in trade of the State armorial bearings of the other countries of the Union, when the use is of such a nature as to be misleading as to the origin of the goods.

10.   The above provisions shall not prevent the countries from exercising the right given in paragraph (3) of Article 6 quinquies, Section B, to refuse or to invalidate the registration of marks incorporating, without authorization, armorial bearings, flags, other State emblems, or official signs and hallmarks adopted by a country of the Union, as well as the distinctive signs of international intergovernmental organizations referred to in paragraph (1), above.

Article 6*quater*

[Marks: Assignment of Marks]

1.   When, in accordance with the law of a country of the Union, the assignment of a mark is valid only if it takes place at the same time as the transfer of the business or goodwill to which the mark belongs, it shall suffice for the recognition of such validity that the portion of the business or goodwill located in that country be transferred to the assignee, together with the exclusive right to manufacture in the said country, or to sell therein, the goods bearing the mark assigned.

2.   The foregoing provision does not impose upon the countries of the Union any obligation to regard as valid the assignment of any mark the use of which by the assignee would, in fact, be of such a nature as to mislead the public, particularly as regards the origin, nature, or essential qualities, of the goods to which the mark is applied.

Article 6*quinquies*

[Marks: Protection of Marks Registered in One Country of the Union in the Other Countries of the Union]

A.   (1) Every trademark duly registered in the country of origin shall be accepted for filing and protected as is in the other countries of the Union, subject to the reservations indicated in this article. Such countries may, before proceeding to final registration, require the production of a certificate of registration in the country of origin, issued by the competent authority. No authentication shall be required for this certificate.

(2)   Shall be considered the country of origin the country of the Union where the applicant has a real and effective industrial or commercial establishment, or, if he has no such establishment within the Union, the country of the Union where he has his domicile, or, if he has no domicile within the Union but is a national of a country of the Union, the country of which he is a national.

B.   Trademarks covered by this article may be neither denied registration nor invalidated except in the following cases:

(1)   When they are of such a nature as to infringe rights acquired by third parties in the country where protection is claimed;

(2)   When they are devoid of any distinctive character, or consist exclusively of signs or indications which may serve, in trade, to designate the kind, quality, quantity, intended purpose, value, place of origin, of the goods, or the time of production, or have become customary in the

current language as in the bona fide and established practices of the trade of the country where protection is claimed;

(3)   When they are contrary to morality or public order and, in particular, of such a nature as to deceive the public. It is understood that a mark may not be considered contrary to public order for the sole reason that it does not conform to a provision of the legislation on marks, except if such provision itself relates to public order.

This provision is subject, however, to the application of Article 10bis.

C.   (1) In determining whether a mark is eligible for protection, all the factual circumstances must be taken into consideration, particularly the length of time the mark has been in use.

(2)   No trademark shall be refused in the other countries of the Union for the sole reason that it differs from the mark protected in the country of origin only in respect of elements that do not alter its distinctive character and do not affect its identity in the form in which it has been registered in the said country of origin.

D.   No person may benefit from the provisions of this article if the mark for which he claims protection is not registered in the country of origin.

E.   However, in no case shall the renewal of the registration of the mark in the country of origin involve an obligation to renew the registration in the other countries of the Union in which the mark has been registered.

F.   The benefit of priority shall remain unaffected for applications for the registration of marks filed within the period fixed by Article 4, even if registration in the country of origin is effected after the expiration of such period.

Article 6*sexies*

[Marks: Service Marks]

The countries of the Union undertake to protect service marks. They shall not be required to provide for the registration of such marks.

Article 6*septies*

[Marks: Registration in the Name of the Agent or Representative of the Proprietor Without the Latter's Authorization]

1.   If the agent or representative of the person who is the proprietor of a mark in one of the countries of the Union applies, without such proprietor's authorization, for the registration of the mark in his own name, in one or more countries of the Union, the proprietor shall be entitled to oppose the registration applied for or demand its cancellation or, if the law of the country so allows, the assignment in his favor of the said registration, unless such agent or representative justifies his action.

2.   The proprietor of the mark shall, subject to the provisions of paragraph (1), above, be entitled to oppose the use of his mark by his agent or representative if he has not authorized such use.

3.   Domestic legislation may provide an equitable time limit within which the proprietor or a mark must exercise the rights provided for in this article.

Article 7

[Marks: Nature of the Goods to Which the Mark Is Applied]

The nature of the goods to which a trademark is to be applied shall in no case form an obstacle to the registration of the mark.

Article 7bis

[Marks: Collective Marks]

1.   The countries of the Union undertake to accept for filing and to protect collective marks belonging to associations the existence of which is not contrary to the law of the country of origin, even if such associations do not possess an industrial or commercial establishment.

2.   Each country shall be the judge of the particular conditions under which a collective mark shall be protected and may refuse protection if the mark is contrary to the public interest.

3.   Nevertheless, the protection of these marks shall not be refused to any association, the existence of which is not contrary to the law of the country of origin, on the ground that such association is not established in the country where protection is sought or is not constituted according to the law of the latter country.

Article 8

[Trade Names]

A trade name shall be protected in all the countries of the Union without the obligation of filing or registration, whether or not it forms part of a trademark.

Article 9

[Marks, Trade Names: Seizure, on Importation, etc., of Goods Unlawfully Bearing a Mark or Trade Name]

1.   All goods unlawfully bearing a trademark or trade name shall be seized on importation into those countries of the Union where such mark or trade name is entitled to legal protection.

2.   Seizure shall likewise be effected in the country where the unlawful affixation occurred or in the country into which the goods were imported.

3.   Seizure shall take place at the request of the public prosecutor, or any other competent authority, or any interested party, whether a natural person or a legal entity, in conformity with the domestic legislation of each country.

4.   The authorities shall not be bound to effect seizure of goods in transit.

5.   If the legislation of a country does not permit seizure on importation, seizure shall be replaced by prohibition of importation or by seizure inside the country.

6.   If the legislation of a country permits neither seizure on importation nor prohibition of importation nor seizure inside the country, then, until such time as the legislation is modified accordingly, these measures shall be replaced by the actions and remedies available in such cases to nationals under the law of such country.

Article 10

[False Indications: Seizure, in Importation etc., of Goods Bearing False Indications as to Their Source or the Identity of the Producer]

1.   The provisions of the preceding article shall apply in cases of direct or indirect use of a false indication of the source of the goods or the identity of the producer, manufacturer, or merchant.

2.   Any producer, manufacturer, or merchant, whether a natural person or a legal entity, engaged in the production or manufacture of or trade in such goods and established either in the locality falsely indicated as the source, or in the region where such locality is situated, or in the country falsely indicated, or in the country where the false indication of source is used, shall in any case be deemed an interested party.

Article 10bis

[Unfair Competition]

1.   The countries of the Union are bound to assure to nationals of such countries effective protection against unfair competition.

2.   Any act of competition contrary to honest practices in industrial or commercial matters constitutes an act of unfair competition.

3.   The following in particular shall be prohibited:

(1)   all acts of such a nature as to create confusion by any means whatever with the establishment, the goods, or the industrial or commercial activities, of a competitor;

(2)   false allegations in the course of trade of such a nature as to discredit the establishment, the goods, or the industrial or commercial activities, of a competitor;

(3)   indications or allegations the use of which in the course of trade is liable to mislead the public as to the nature, the manufacturing process, the characteristics, the suitability for their purpose, or the quantity, of the goods.

Article 10ter

[Marks, Trade Names, False Indications, Unfair Competition: Remedies, Right to Sue]

1.   The countries of the Union undertake to assure to nationals of the other countries of the Union appropriate legal remedies effectively to repress all the acts referred to in Articles 9, 10, and 10bis.

2.   They undertake, further, to provide measures to permit federations and associations representing interested industrialists, producers, or merchants, provided that the existence of such federations and associations is not contrary to the laws of their countries, to take action in the courts or before the administrative authorities, with a view to the repression of the acts referred to in Articles 9, 10, and 10bis, insofar as the law of the country in which protection is claimed allows such action by federations and associations of that country.

Article 11

[Inventions, Utility Models, Industrial Designs, Marks: Temporary Protection at Certain International Exhibitions]

1.   The countries of the Union shall, in conformity with their domestic legislation, grant temporary protection to patentable inventions, utility models, industrial designs, and trademarks, in respect of goods exhibited at official or officially recognized international exhibitions held in the territory of any of them.

2.   Such temporary protection shall not extend the periods provided by Article 4. If, later, the right of priority is invoked, the authorities of any country may provide that the period shall start from the date of introduction of the goods into the exhibition.

3.   Each country may require, as proof of the identity of the article exhibited and of the date of its introduction, such documentary evidence as it considers necessary.

Article 12

[Special National Industrial Property Services]

1.   Each country of the Union undertakes to establish a special industrial property service and a central office for the communication to the public of patents, utility models, industrial designs, and trademarks.

2.   This service shall publish an official periodical journal. It shall publish regularly:

(a)   the names of the proprietors of patents granted, with a brief designation of the inventions patented;

(b)   the reproductions of registered trademarks.

[Articles 13 through 30 have been omitted]

C. CHAPTER 17 OF THE NORTH AMERICAN FREE TRADE AGREEMENT

NORTH AMERICAN FREE TRADE AGREEMENT BETWEEN THE GOVERNMENT OF THE UNITED STATES OF AMERICA, THE GOVERNMENT OF CANADA AND THE GOVERNMENT OF THE UNITED MEXICAN STATES

* * *

PART SIX. INTELLECTUAL PROPERTY CHAPTER SEVENTEEN: INTELLECTUAL PROPERTY

Article 1701

Nature and Scope of Obligations

1.   Each Party shall provide in its territory to the nationals of another Party adequate and effective protection and enforcement of intellectual property rights, while ensuring that measures to enforce intellectual property rights do not themselves become barriers to legitimate trade.

2.   To provide adequate and effective protection and enforcement of intellectual property rights, each Party shall, at a minimum, give effect to this Chapter and to the substantive provisions of:

(a)   the *Geneva Convention for the Protection of Producers of Phonograms Against Unauthorized Duplication of their Phonograms,* 1971 (Geneva Convention);

(b)   the *Berne Convention for the Protection of Literary and Artistic Works,* 1971 (Berne Convention);

(c)   the *Paris Convention for the Protection of Industrial Property,* 1967 (Paris Convention); and

(d)   the *International Convention for the Protection of New Varieties of Plants,* 1978 (UPOV Convention), or the *International Convention for the Protection of New Varieties of Plants,* 1991 (UPOV Convention).

If a Party has not acceded to the specified text of any such Conventions on or before the date of entry into force of this Agreement, it shall make every effort to accede.

3.   Annex 1701.3 applies to the Parties specified in that Annex.

Article 1702

More Extensive Protection

A Party may implement in its domestic law more extensive protection of intellectual property rights than is required under this Agreement, provided that such protection is not inconsistent with this Agreement.

Article 1703

National Treatment

1.   Each Party shall accord to nationals of another Party treatment no less favorable than that it accords to its own nationals with regard to the protection and enforcement of all intellectual property rights. In respect of sound recordings, each Party shall provide such treatment to producers and

performers of another Party, except that a Party may limit rights of performers of another Party in respect of secondary uses of sound recordings to those rights its nationals are accorded in the territory of such other Party.

2. No Party may, as a condition of according national treatment under this Article, require right holders to comply with any formalities or conditions in order to acquire rights in respect of copyright and related rights.

3. A Party may derogate from paragraph 1 in relation to its judicial and administrative procedures for the protection or enforcement of intellectual property rights, including any procedure requiring a national of another Party to designate for service of process an address in the Party's territory or to appoint an agent in the Party's territory, if the derogation is consistent with the relevant Convention listed in Article 1701(2), provided that such derogation:

(a) is necessary to secure compliance with measures that are not inconsistent with this Chapter; and

(b) is not applied in a manner that would constitute a disguised restriction on trade.

4. No Party shall have any obligation under this Article with respect to procedures provided in multilateral agreements concluded under the auspices of the World Intellectual Property Organization relating to the acquisition or maintenance of intellectual property rights.

Article 1704

Control of Abusive or Anticompetitive Practices or Conditions

Nothing in this Chapter shall prevent a Party from specifying in its domestic law licensing practices or conditions that may in particular cases constitute an abuse of intellectual property rights having an adverse effect on competition in the relevant market. A Party may adopt or maintain, consistent with the other provisions of this Agreement, appropriate measures to prevent or control such practices or conditions.

Article 1705

Copyright

1. Each Party shall protect the works covered by Article 2 of the Berne Convention, including any other works that embody original expression within the meaning of that Convention. In particular:

(a) all types of computer programs are literary works within the meaning of the Berne Convention and each Party shall protect them as such; and

(b) compilations of data or other material, whether in machine readable or other form, which by reason of the selection or arrangement of their contents constitute intellectual creations, shall be protected as such.

The protection a Party provides under subparagraph (b) shall not extend to the data or material itself, or prejudice any copyright subsisting in that data or material.

2. Each Party shall provide to authors and their successors in interest those rights enumerated in the Berne Convention in respect of works covered by paragraph 1, including the right to authorize or prohibit:

(a) the importation into the Party's territory of copies of the work made without the right holder's authorization;

    (b)   the first public distribution of the original and each copy of the work by sale, rental or otherwise;

    (c)   the communication of a work to the public; and

    (d)   the commercial rental of the original or a copy of a computer program.

Subparagraph (d) shall not apply where the copy of the computer program is not itself an essential object of the rental. Each Party shall provide that putting the original or a copy of a computer program on the market with the right holder's consent shall not exhaust the rental right.

3.   Each Party shall provide that for copyright and related rights:

    (a)   any person acquiring or holding economic rights may freely and separately transfer such rights by contract for purposes of their exploitation and enjoyment by the transferee; and

    (b)   any person acquiring or holding such economic rights by virtue of a contract, including contracts of employment underlying the creation of works and sound recordings, shall be able to exercise those rights in its own name and enjoy fully the benefits derived from those rights.

4.   Each Party shall provide that, where the term of protection of a work, other than a photographic work or a work of applied art, is to be calculated on a basis other than the life of a natural person, the term shall be not less than 50 years from the end of the calendar year of the first authorized publication of the work or, failing such authorized publication within 50 years from the making of the work, 50 years from the end of the calendar year of making.

5.   Each Party shall confine limitations or exceptions to the rights provided for in this Article to certain special cases that do not conflict with a normal exploitation of the work and do not unreasonably prejudice the legitimate interests of the right holder.

6.   No Party may grant translation and reproduction licenses permitted under the Appendix to the Berne Convention where legitimate needs in that Party's territory for copies or translations of the work could be met by the right holder's voluntary actions but for obstacles created by the Party's measures.

7.   Annex 1705.7 applies to the Parties specified in that Annex.

Article 1706

Sound Recordings

1.   Each Party shall provide to the producer of a sound recording the right to authorize or prohibit:

    (a)   the direct or indirect reproduction of the sound recording;

    (b)   the importation into the Party's territory of copies of the sound recording made without the producer's authorization;

    (c)   the first public distribution of the original and each copy of the sound recording by sale, rental or otherwise; and

    (d)   the commercial rental of the original or a copy of the sound recording, except where expressly otherwise provided in a contract between the producer of the sound recording and the authors of the works fixed therein.

Each Party shall provide that putting the original or a copy of a sound recording on the market with the right holder's consent shall not exhaust the rental right.

2.   Each Party shall provide a term of protection for sound recordings of at least 50 years from the end of the calendar year in which the fixation was made.

3.   Each Party shall confine limitations or exceptions to the rights provided for in this Article to certain special cases that do not conflict with a normal exploitation of the sound recording and do not unreasonably prejudice the legitimate interests of the right holder.

Article 1707

Protection of Encrypted Program-Carrying Satellite Signals

Within one year from the date of entry into force of this Agreement, each Party shall make it:

(a)   a criminal offense to manufacture, import, sell, lease or otherwise make available a device or system that is primarily of assistance in decoding an encrypted program-carrying satellite signal without the authorization of the lawful distributor of such signal; and

(b)   a civil offense to receive, in connection with commercial activities, or further distribute, an encrypted program-carrying satellite signal that has been decoded without the authorization of the lawful distributor of the signal or to engage in any activity prohibited under subparagraph (a).

Each Party shall provide that any civil offense established under subparagraph (b) shall be actionable by any person that holds an interest in the content of such signal.

Article 1708

Trademarks

1.   For purposes of this Agreement, a trademark consists of any sign, or any combination of signs, capable of distinguishing the goods or services of one person from those of another, including personal names, designs, letters, numerals, colors, figurative elements, or the shape of goods or of their packaging. Trademarks shall include service marks and collective marks, and may include certification marks. A Party may require, as a condition for registration, that a sign be visually perceptible.

2.   Each Party shall provide to the owner of a registered trademark the right to prevent all persons not having the owner's consent from using in commerce identical or similar signs for goods or services that are identical or similar to those goods or services in respect of which the owner's trademark is registered, where such use would result in a likelihood of confusion. In the case of the use of an identical sign for identical goods or services, a likelihood of confusion shall be presumed. The rights described above shall not prejudice any prior rights, nor shall they affect the possibility of a Party making rights available on the basis of use.

3.   A Party may make registrability depend on use. However, actual use of a trademark shall not be a condition for filing an application for registration. No Party may refuse an application solely on the ground that intended use has not taken place before the expiry of a period of three years from the date of application for registration.

4.   Each Party shall provide a system for the registration of trademarks, which shall include:

(a)   examination of applications;

(b)   notice to be given to an applicant of the reasons for the refusal to register a trademark;

(c)   a reasonable opportunity for the applicant to respond to the notice;

(d)   publication of each trademark either before or promptly after it is registered; and

(e)   a reasonable opportunity for interested persons to petition to cancel the registration of a trademark.

A Party may provide for a reasonable opportunity for interested persons to oppose the registration of a trademark.

5.   The nature of the goods or services to which a trademark is to be applied shall in no case form an obstacle to the registration of the trademark.

6.   Article 6bis of the Paris Convention shall apply, with such modifications as may be necessary, to services. In determining whether a trademark is well-known, account shall be taken of the knowledge of the trademark in the relevant sector of the public, including knowledge in the Party's territory obtained as a result of the promotion of the trademark. No Party may require that the reputation of the trademark extend beyond the sector of the public that normally deals with the relevant goods or services.

7.   Each Party shall provide that the initial registration of a trademark be for a term of at least 10 years and that the registration be indefinitely renewable for terms of not less than 10 years when conditions for renewal have been met.

8.   Each Party shall require the use of a trademark to maintain a registration. The registration may be canceled for the reason of non-use only after an uninterrupted period of at least two years of non-use, unless valid reasons based on the existence of obstacles to such use are shown by the trademark owner. Each Party shall recognize, as valid reasons for non-use, circumstances arising independently of the will of the trademark owner that constitute an obstacle to the use of the trademark, such as import restrictions on, or other government requirements for, goods or services identified by the trademark.

9.   Each Party shall recognize use of a trademark by a person other than the trademark owner, where such use is subject to the owner's control, as use of the trademark for purposes of maintaining the registration.

10.   No Party may encumber the use of a trademark in commerce by special requirements, such as a use that reduces the trademark's function as an indication of source or a use with another trademark.

11.   A Party may determine conditions on the licensing and assignment of trademarks, it being understood that the compulsory licensing of trademarks shall not be permitted and that the owner of a registered trademark shall have the right to assign its trademark with or without the transfer of the business to which the trademark belongs.

12.   A Party may provide limited exceptions to the rights conferred by a trademark, such as fair use of descriptive terms, provided that such exceptions take into account the legitimate interests of the trademark owner and of other persons.

13.   Each Party shall prohibit the registration as a trademark of words, at least in English, French or Spanish, that generically designate goods or services or types of goods or services to which the trademark applies.

14.   Each Party shall refuse to register trademarks that consist of or comprise immoral, deceptive or scandalous matter, or matter that may disparage or falsely suggest a connection with persons, living or dead, institutions, beliefs or any Party's national symbols, or bring them into contempt or disrepute.

Article 1709

Patents

1.   Subject to paragraphs 2 and 3, each Party shall make patents available for any inventions, whether products or processes, in all fields of technology, provided that such inventions are new, result from an inventive step and are capable of industrial application. For purposes of this Article, a Party may deem the terms "inventive step" and "capable of industrial application" to be synonymous with the terms "non-obvious" and "useful", respectively.

2.   A Party may exclude from patentability inventions if preventing in its territory the commercial exploitation of the inventions is necessary to protect *ordre public* or morality, including to protect human, animal or plant life or health or to avoid serious prejudice to nature or the environment, provided that the exclusion is not based solely on the ground that the Party prohibits commercial exploitation in its territory of the subject matter of the patent.

3.   A Party may also exclude from patentability:

(a)   diagnostic, therapeutic and surgical methods for the treatment of humans or animals;

(b)   plants and animals other than microorganisms; and

(c)   essentially biological processes for the production of plants or animals, other than non-biological and microbiological processes for such production.

Notwithstanding subparagraph (b), each Party shall provide for the protection of plant varieties through patents, an effective scheme of *sui generis* protection, or both.

4.   If a Party has not made available product patent protection for pharmaceutical or agricultural chemicals commensurate with paragraph 1:

(a)   as of January 1, 1992, for subject matter that relates to naturally occurring substances prepared or produced by, or significantly derived from, microbiological processes and intended for food or medicine, and

(b)   as of July 1, 1991, for any other subject matter,

that Party shall provide to the inventor of any such product or its assignee the means to obtain product patent protection for such product for the unexpired term of the patent for such product granted in another Party, as long as the product has not been marketed in the Party providing protection under this paragraph and the person seeking such protection makes a timely request.

5.   Each Party shall provide that:

(a)   where the subject matter of a patent is a product, the patent shall confer on the patent owner the right to prevent other persons from making, using or selling the subject matter of the patent, without the patent owner's consent; and

(b)   where the subject matter of a patent is a process, the patent shall confer on the patent owner the right to prevent other persons from using that process and from using, selling, or importing at least the product obtained directly by that process, without the patent owner's consent.

6.   A Party may provide limited exceptions to the exclusive rights conferred by a patent, provided that such exceptions do not unreasonably conflict with a normal exploitation of the patent and do not unreasonably prejudice the legitimate interests of the patent owner, taking into account the legitimate interests of other persons.

7.   Subject to paragraphs 2 and 3, patents shall be available and patent rights enjoyable without discrimination as to the field of technology, the territory of the Party where the invention was made and whether products are imported or locally produced.

8.   A Party may revoke a patent only when:

(a)   grounds exist that would have justified a refusal to grant the patent; or

(b)   the grant of a compulsory license has not remedied the lack of exploitation of the patent.

9.   Each Party shall permit patent owners to assign and transfer by succession their patents, and to conclude licensing contracts.

10.   Where the law of a Party allows for use of the subject matter of a patent, other than that use allowed under paragraph 6, without the authorization of the right holder, including use by the

government or other persons authorized by the government, the Party shall respect the following provisions:

(a)   authorization of such use shall be considered on its individual merits;

(b)   such use may only be permitted if, prior to such use, the proposed user has made efforts to obtain authorization from the right holder on reasonable commercial terms and conditions and such efforts have not been successful within a reasonable period of time. The requirement to make such efforts may be waived by a Party in the case of a national emergency or other circumstances of extreme urgency or in cases of public non-commercial use. In situations of national emergency or other circumstances of extreme urgency, the right holder shall, nevertheless, be notified as soon as reasonably practicable. In the case of public non-commercial use, where the government or contractor, without making a patent search, knows or has demonstrable grounds to know that a valid patent is or will be used by or for the government, the right holder shall be informed promptly;

(c)   the scope and duration of such use shall be limited to the purpose for which it was authorized;

(d)   such use shall be non-exclusive;

(e)   such use shall be non-assignable, except with that part of the enterprise or goodwill that enjoys such use;

(f)   any such use shall be authorized predominantly for the supply of the Party's domestic market;

(g)   authorization for such use shall be liable, subject to adequate protection of the legitimate interests of the persons so authorized, to be terminated if and when the circumstances that led to it cease to exist and are unlikely to recur. The competent authority shall have the authority to review, on motivated request, the continued existence of these circumstances;

(h)   the right holder shall be paid adequate remuneration in the circumstances of each case, taking into account the economic value of the authorization;

(i)   the legal validity of any decision relating to the authorization shall be subject to judicial or other independent review by a distinct higher authority;

(j)   any decision relating to the remuneration provided in respect of such use shall be subject to judicial or other independent review by a distinct higher authority;

(k)   the Party shall not be obliged to apply the conditions set out in subparagraphs (b) and (f) where such use is permitted to remedy a practice determined after judicial or administrative process to be anticompetitive. The need to correct anticompetitive practices may be taken into account in determining the amount of remuneration in such cases. Competent authorities shall have the authority to refuse termination of authorization if and when the conditions that led to such authorization are likely to recur;

(l)   the Party shall not authorize the use of the subject matter of a patent to permit the exploitation of another patent except as a remedy for an adjudicated violation of domestic laws regarding anticompetitive practices.

11.   Where the subject matter of a patent is a process for obtaining a product, each Party shall, in any infringement proceeding, place on the defendant the burden of establishing that the allegedly infringing product was made by a process other than the patented process in one of the following situations:

(a)   the product obtained by the patented process is new; or

(b)   a substantial likelihood exists that the allegedly infringing product was made by the process and the patent owner has been unable through reasonable efforts to determine the process actually used.

In the gathering and evaluation of evidence, the legitimate interests of the defendant in protecting its trade secrets shall be taken into account.

12.   Each Party shall provide a term of protection for patents of at least 20 years from the date of filing or 17 years from the date of grant. A Party may extend the term of patent protection, in appropriate cases, to compensate for delays caused by regulatory approval processes.

Article 1710

Layout Designs of Semiconductor Integrated Circuits

1.   Each Party shall protect layout designs (topographies) of integrated circuits ("layout designs") in accordance with Articles 2 through 7, 12 and 16(3), other than Article 6(3), of the *Treaty on Intellectual Property in Respect of Integrated Circuits* as opened for signature on 26 May 1989.

2.   Subject to paragraph 3, each Party shall make it unlawful for any person without the right holder's authorization to import, sell or otherwise distribute for commercial purposes any of the following:

(a)   a protected layout design;

(b)   an integrated circuit in which a protected layout design is incorporated; or

(c)   an article incorporating such an integrated circuit, only insofar as it continues to contain an unlawfully reproduced layout design.

3.   No Party may make unlawful any of the acts referred to in paragraph 2 performed in respect of an integrated circuit that incorporates an unlawfully reproduced layout design, or any article that incorporates such an integrated circuit, where the person performing those acts or ordering those acts to be done did not know and had no reasonable ground to know, when it acquired the integrated circuit or article incorporating such an integrated circuit, that it incorporated an unlawfully reproduced layout design.

4.   Each Party shall provide that, after the person referred to in paragraph 3 has received sufficient notice that the layout design was unlawfully reproduced, such person may perform any of the acts with respect to the stock on hand or ordered before such notice, but shall be liable to pay the right holder for doing so an amount equivalent to a reasonable royalty such as would be payable under a freely negotiated license in respect of such a layout design.

5.   No Party may permit the compulsory licensing of layout designs of integrated circuits.

6.   Any Party that requires registration as a condition for protection of a layout design shall provide that the term of protection shall not end before the expiration of a period of 10 years counted from the date of:

(a)   filing of the application for registration; or

(b)   the first commercial exploitation of the layout design, wherever in the world it occurs.

7.   Where a Party does not require registration as a condition for protection of a layout design, the Party shall provide a term of protection of not less than 10 years from the date of the first commercial exploitation of the layout design, wherever in the world it occurs.

8.   Notwithstanding paragraphs 6 and 7, a Party may provide that the protection shall lapse 15 years after the creation of the layout design.

9.   Annex 1710.9 applies to the Parties specified in that Annex.

Article 1711

Trade Secrets

1.   Each Party shall provide the legal means for any person to prevent trade secrets from being disclosed to, acquired by, or used by others without the consent of the person lawfully in control of the information in a manner contrary to honest commercial practices, in so far as:

(a)   the information is secret in the sense that it is not, as a body or in the precise configuration and assembly of its components, generally known among or readily accessible to persons that normally deal with the kind of information in question;

(b)   the information has actual or potential commercial value because it is secret; and

(c)   the person lawfully in control of the information has taken reasonable steps under the circumstances to keep it secret.

2.   A Party may require that to qualify for protection a trade secret must be evidenced in documents, electronic or magnetic means, optical discs, microfilms, films or other similar instruments.

3.   No Party may limit the duration of protection for trade secrets, so long as the conditions in paragraph 1 exist.

4.   No Party may discourage or impede the voluntary licensing of trade secrets by imposing excessive or discriminatory conditions on such licenses or conditions that dilute the value of the trade secrets.

5.   If a Party requires, as a condition for approving the marketing of pharmaceutical or agricultural chemical products that utilize new chemical entities, the submission of undisclosed test or other data necessary to determine whether the use of such products is safe and effective, the Party shall protect against disclosure of the data of persons making such submissions, where the origination of such data involves considerable effort, except where the disclosure is necessary to protect the public or unless steps are taken to ensure that the data is protected against unfair commercial use.

6.   Each Party shall provide that for data subject to paragraph 5 that are submitted to the Party after the date of entry into force of this Agreement, no person other than the person that submitted them may, without the latter's permission, rely on such data in support of an application for product approval during a reasonable period of time after their submission. For this purpose, a reasonable period shall normally mean not less than five years from the date on which the Party granted approval to the person that produced the data for approval to market its product, taking account of the nature of the data and the person's efforts and expenditures in producing them. Subject to this provision, there shall be no limitation on any Party to implement abbreviated approval procedures for such products on the basis of bioequivalence and bioavailability studies.

7.   Where a Party relies on a marketing approval granted by another Party, the reasonable period of exclusive use of the data submitted in connection with obtaining the approval relied on shall begin with the date of the first marketing approval relied upon.

Article 1712

Geographical Indications

1.   Each Party shall provide, in respect of geographical indications, the legal means for interested persons to prevent:

(a)   the use of any means in the designation or presentation of a good that indicates or suggests that the good in question originates in a territory, region or locality other than the true place of origin, in a manner that misleads the public as to the geographical origin of the good;

(b)   any use that constitutes an act of unfair competition within the meaning of Article 10bis of the Paris Convention.

2.   Each Party shall, on its own initiative if its domestic law so permits or at the request of an interested person, refuse to register, or invalidate the registration of, a trademark containing or consisting of a geographical indication with respect to goods that do not originate in the indicated territory, region or locality, if use of the indication in the trademark for such goods is of such a nature as to mislead the public as to the geographical origin of the good.

3.   Each Party shall also apply paragraphs 1 and 2 to a geographical indication that, although correctly indicating the territory, region or locality in which the goods originate, falsely represents to the public that the goods originate in another territory, region or locality.

4.   Nothing in this Article shall be construed to require a Party to prevent continued and similar use of a particular geographical indication of another Party in connection with goods or services by any of its nationals or domiciliaries who have used that geographical indication in a continuous manner with regard to the same or related goods or services in that Party's territory, either:

(a)   for at least 10 years, or

(b)   in good faith, before the date of signature of this Agreement.

5.   Where a trademark has been applied for or registered in good faith, or where rights to a trademark have been acquired through use in good faith, either:

(a)   before the date of application of these provisions in that Party, or

(b)   before the geographical indication is protected in its Party of origin,

no Party may adopt any measure to implement this Article that prejudices eligibility for, or the validity of, the registration of a trademark, or the right to use a trademark, on the basis that such a trademark is identical with, or similar to, a geographical indication.

6.   No Party shall be required to apply this Article to a geographical indication if it is identical to the customary term in common language in that Party's territory for the goods or services to which the indication applies.

7.   A Party may provide that any request made under this Article in connection with the use or registration of a trademark must be presented within five years after the adverse use of the protected indication has become generally known in that Party or after the date of registration of the trademark in that Party, provided that the trademark has been published by that date, if such date is earlier than the date on which the adverse use became generally known in that Party, provided that the geographical indication is not used or registered in bad faith.

8.   No Party shall adopt any measure implementing this Article that would prejudice any person's right to use, in the course of trade, its name or the name of its predecessor in business, except where such name forms all or part of a valid trademark in existence before the geographical indication became protected and with which there is a likelihood of confusion, or such name is used in such a manner as to mislead the public.

9.   Nothing in this Chapter shall be construed to require a Party to protect a geographical indication that is not protected, or has fallen into disuse, in the Party of origin.

Article 1713

Industrial Designs

1.   Each Party shall provide for the protection of independently created industrial designs that are new or original. A Party may provide that:

(a) designs are not new or original if they do not significantly differ from known designs or combinations of known design features; and

(b) such protection shall not extend to designs dictated essentially by technical or functional considerations.

2. Each Party shall ensure that the requirements for securing protection for textile designs, in particular in regard to any cost, examination or publication, do not unreasonably impair a person's opportunity to seek and obtain such protection. A Party may comply with this obligation through industrial design law or copyright law.

3. Each Party shall provide the owner of a protected industrial design the right to prevent other persons not having the owner's consent from making or selling articles bearing or embodying a design that is a copy, or substantially a copy, of the protected design, when such acts are undertaken for commercial purposes.

4. A Party may provide limited exceptions to the protection of industrial designs, provided that such exceptions do not unreasonably conflict with the normal exploitation of protected industrial designs and do not unreasonably prejudice the legitimate interests of the owner of the protected design, taking into account the legitimate interests of other persons.

5. Each Party shall provide a term of protection for industrial designs of at least 10 years.

Article 1714

Enforcement of Intellectual Property Rights: General Provisions

1. Each Party shall ensure that enforcement procedures, as specified in this Article and Articles 1715 through 1718, are available under its domestic law so as to permit effective action to be taken against any act of infringement of intellectual property rights covered by this Chapter, including expeditious remedies to prevent infringements and remedies to deter further infringements. Such enforcement procedures shall be applied so as to avoid the creation of barriers to legitimate trade and to provide for safeguards against abuse of the procedures.

2. Each Party shall ensure that its procedures for the enforcement of intellectual property rights are fair and equitable, are not unnecessarily complicated or costly, and do not entail unreasonable time-limits or unwarranted delays.

3. Each Party shall provide that decisions on the merits of a case in judicial and administrative enforcement proceedings shall:

(a) preferably be in writing and preferably state the reasons on which the decisions are based;

(b) be made available at least to the parties in a proceeding without undue delay; and

(c) be based only on evidence in respect of which such parties were offered the opportunity to be heard.

4. Each Party shall ensure that parties in a proceeding have an opportunity to have final administrative decisions reviewed by a judicial authority of that Party and, subject to jurisdictional provisions in its domestic laws concerning the importance of a case, to have reviewed at least the legal aspects of initial judicial decisions on the merits of a case. Notwithstanding the above, no Party shall be required to provide for judicial review of acquittals in criminal cases.

5. Nothing in this Article or Articles 1715 through 1718 shall be construed to require a Party to establish a judicial system for the enforcement of intellectual property rights distinct from that Party's system for the enforcement of laws in general.

6.　　For the purposes of Articles 1715 through 1718, the term "right holder" includes federations and associations having legal standing to assert such rights.

Article 1715

Specific Procedural and Remedial Aspects of Civil and Administrative Procedures

1.　　Each Party shall make available to right holders civil judicial procedures for the enforcement of any intellectual property right provided in this Chapter. Each Party shall provide that:

(a)　defendants have the right to written notice that is timely and contains sufficient detail, including the basis of the claims;

(b)　parties in a proceeding are allowed to be represented by independent legal counsel;

(c)　the procedures do not include imposition of overly burdensome requirements concerning mandatory personal appearances;

(d)　all parties in a proceeding are duly entitled to substantiate their claims and to present relevant evidence; and

(e)　the procedures include a means to identify and protect confidential information.

2.　　Each Party shall provide that its judicial authorities shall have the authority:

(a)　where a party in a proceeding has presented reasonably available evidence sufficient to support its claims and has specified evidence relevant to the substantiation of its claims that is within the control of the opposing party, to order the opposing party to produce such evidence, subject in appropriate cases to conditions that ensure the protection of confidential information;

(b)　where a party in a proceeding voluntarily and without good reason refuses access to, or otherwise does not provide relevant evidence under that party's control within a reasonable period, or significantly impedes a proceeding relating to an enforcement action, to make preliminary and final determinations, affirmative or negative, on the basis of the evidence presented, including the complaint or the allegation presented by the party adversely affected by the denial of access to evidence, subject to providing the parties an opportunity to be heard on the allegations or evidence;

(c)　to order a party in a proceeding to desist from an infringement, including to prevent the entry into the channels of commerce in their jurisdiction of imported goods that involve the infringement of an intellectual property right, which order shall be enforceable at least immediately after customs clearance of such goods;

(d)　to order the infringer of an intellectual property right to pay the right holder damages adequate to compensate for the injury the right holder has suffered because of the infringement where the infringer knew or had reasonable grounds to know that it was engaged in an infringing activity;

(e)　to order an infringer of an intellectual property right to pay the right holder's expenses, which may include appropriate attorney's fees; and

(f)　to order a party in a proceeding at whose request measures were taken and who has abused enforcement procedures to provide adequate compensation to any party wrongfully enjoined or restrained in the proceeding for the injury suffered because of such abuse and to pay that party's expenses, which may include appropriate attorney's fees.

3.　　With respect to the authority referred to in subparagraph 2(c), no Party shall be obliged to provide such authority in respect of protected subject matter that is acquired or ordered by a person before that person knew or had reasonable grounds to know that dealing in that subject matter would entail the infringement of an intellectual property right.

4.   With respect to the authority referred to in subparagraph 2(d), a Party may, at least with respect to copyrighted works and sound recordings, authorize the judicial authorities to order recovery of profits or payment of pre-established damages, or both, even where the infringer did not know or had no reasonable grounds to know that it was engaged in an infringing activity.

5.   Each Party shall provide that, in order to create an effective deterrent to infringement, its judicial authorities shall have the authority to order that:

     (a)   goods that they have found to be infringing be, without compensation of any sort, disposed of outside the channels of commerce in such a manner as to avoid any injury caused to the right holder or, unless this would be contrary to existing constitutional requirements, destroyed; and

     (b)   materials and implements the predominant use of which has been in the creation of the infringing goods be, without compensation of any sort, disposed of outside the channels of commerce in such a manner as to minimize the risks of further infringements.

In considering whether to issue such an order, judicial authorities shall take into account the need for proportionality between the seriousness of the infringement and the remedies ordered as well as the interests of other persons. In regard to counterfeit goods, the simple removal of the trademark unlawfully affixed shall not be sufficient, other than in exceptional cases, to permit release of the goods into the channels of commerce.

6.   In respect of the administration of any law pertaining to the protection or enforcement of intellectual property rights, each Party shall only exempt both public authorities and officials from liability to appropriate remedial measures where actions are taken or intended in good faith in the course of the administration of such laws.

7.   Notwithstanding the other provisions of Articles 1714 through 1718, where a Party is sued with respect to an infringement of an intellectual property right as a result of its use of that right or use on its behalf, that Party may limit the remedies available against it to the payment to the right holder of adequate remuneration in the circumstances of each case, taking into account the economic value of the use.

8.   Each Party shall provide that, where a civil remedy can be ordered as a result of administrative procedures on the merits of a case, such procedures shall conform to principles equivalent in substance to those set out in this Article.

Article 1716

Provisional Measures

1.   Each Party shall provide that its judicial authorities shall have the authority to order prompt and effective provisional measures:

     (a)   to prevent an infringement of any intellectual property right, and in particular to prevent the entry into the channels of commerce in their jurisdiction of allegedly infringing goods, including measures to prevent the entry of imported goods at least immediately after customs clearance; and

     (b)   to preserve relevant evidence in regard to the alleged infringement.

2.   Each Party shall provide that its judicial authorities shall have the authority to require any applicant for provisional measures to provide to the judicial authorities any evidence reasonably available to that applicant that the judicial authorities consider necessary to enable them to determine with a sufficient degree of certainty whether:

(a) the applicant is the right holder;

(b) the applicant's right is being infringed or such infringement is imminent; and

(c) any delay in the issuance of such measures is likely to cause irreparable harm to the right holder, or there is a demonstrable risk of evidence being destroyed.

Each Party shall provide that its judicial authorities shall have the authority to require the applicant to provide a security or equivalent assurance sufficient to protect the interests of the defendant and to prevent abuse.

3.   Each Party shall provide that its judicial authorities shall have the authority to require an applicant for provisional measures to provide other information necessary for the identification of the relevant goods by the authority that will execute the provisional measures.

4.   Each Party shall provide that its judicial authorities shall have the authority to order provisional measures on an *ex parte* basis, in particular where any delay is likely to cause irreparable harm to the right holder, or where there is a demonstrable risk of evidence being destroyed.

5.   Each Party shall provide that where provisional measures are adopted by that Party's judicial authorities on an *ex parte* basis:

(a) a person affected shall be given notice of those measures without delay but in any event no later than immediately after the execution of the measures;

(b) a defendant shall, on request, have those measures reviewed by that Party's judicial authorities for the purpose of deciding, within a reasonable period after notice of those measures is given, whether the measures shall be modified, revoked or confirmed, and shall be given an opportunity to be heard in the review proceedings.

6.   Without prejudice to paragraph 5, each Party shall provide that, on the request of the defendant, the Party's judicial authorities shall revoke or otherwise cease to apply the provisional measures taken on the basis of paragraphs 1 and 4 if proceedings leading to a decision on the merits are not initiated:

(a) within a reasonable period as determined by the judicial authority ordering the measures where the Party's domestic law so permits; or

(b) in the absence of such a determination, within a period of no more than 20 working days or 31 calendar days, whichever is longer.

7.   Each Party shall provide that, where the provisional measures are revoked or where they lapse due to any act or omission by the applicant, or where the judicial authorities subsequently find that there has been no infringement or threat of infringement of an intellectual property right, the judicial authorities shall have the authority to order the applicant, on request of the defendant, to provide the defendant appropriate compensation for any injury caused by these measures.

8.   Each Party shall provide that, where a provisional measure can be ordered as a result of administrative procedures, such procedures shall conform to principles equivalent in substance to those set out in this Article.

Article 1717

Criminal Procedures and Penalties

1.   Each Party shall provide criminal procedures and penalties to be applied at least in cases of willful trademark counterfeiting or copyright piracy on a commercial scale. Each Party shall provide that penalties available include imprisonment or monetary fines, or both, sufficient to provide a deterrent, consistent with the level of penalties applied for crimes of a corresponding gravity.

2.   Each Party shall provide that, in appropriate cases, its judicial authorities may order the seizure, forfeiture and destruction of infringing goods and of any materials and implements the predominant use of which has been in the commission of the offense.

3.   A Party may provide criminal procedures and penalties to be applied in cases of infringement of intellectual property rights, other than those in paragraph 1, where they are committed wilfully and on a commercial scale.

Article 1718

Enforcement of Intellectual Property Rights at the Border

1.   Each Party shall, in conformity with this Article, adopt procedures to enable a right holder, who has valid grounds for suspecting that the importation of counterfeit trademark goods or pirated copyright goods may take place, to lodge an application in writing with its competent authorities, whether administrative or judicial, for the suspension by the customs administration of the release of such goods into free circulation. No Party shall be obligated to apply such procedures to goods in transit. A Party may permit such an application to be made in respect of goods that involve other infringements of intellectual property rights, provided that the requirements of this Article are met. A Party may also provide for corresponding procedures concerning the suspension by the customs administration of the release of infringing goods destined for exportation from its territory.

2.   Each Party shall require any applicant who initiates procedures under paragraph 1 to provide adequate evidence:

(a)   to satisfy that Party's competent authorities that, under the domestic laws of the country of importation, there is *prima facie* an infringement of its intellectual property right; and

(b)   to supply a sufficiently detailed description of the goods to make them readily recognizable by the customs administration.

The competent authorities shall inform the applicant within a reasonable period whether they have accepted the application and, if so, the period for which the customs administration will take action.

3.   Each Party shall provide that its competent authorities shall have the authority to require an applicant under paragraph 1 to provide a security or equivalent assurance sufficient to protect the defendant and the competent authorities, and to prevent abuse. Such security or equivalent assurance shall not unreasonably deter recourse to these procedures.

4.   Each Party shall provide that, where pursuant to an application under procedures adopted pursuant to this Article, its customs administration suspends the release of goods involving industrial designs, patents, integrated circuits or trade secrets into free circulation on the basis of a decision other than by a judicial or other independent authority, and the period provided for in paragraphs 6 through 8 has expired without the granting of provisional relief by the duly empowered authority, and provided that all other conditions for importation have been complied with, the owner, importer or consignee of such goods shall be entitled to their release on the posting of a security in an amount sufficient to protect the right holder against any infringement. Payment of such security shall not prejudice any other remedy available to the right holder, it being understood that the security shall be released if the right holder fails to pursue its right of action within a reasonable period of time.

5.   Each Party shall provide that its customs administration shall promptly notify the importer and the applicant when the customs administration suspends the release of goods pursuant to paragraph 1.

6.   Each Party shall provide that its customs administration shall release goods from suspension if within a period not exceeding 10 working days after the applicant under paragraph 1 has been served notice of the suspension, the customs administration has not been informed that:

    (a)   a party other than the defendant has initiated proceedings leading to a decision on the merits of the case, or

    (b)   a competent authority has taken provisional measures prolonging the suspension,

provided that all other conditions for importation or exportation have been met. Each Party shall provide that, in appropriate cases, the customs administration may extend the suspension by another 10 working days.

7.   Each Party shall provide that if proceedings leading to a decision on the merits of the case have been initiated, a review, including a right to be heard, shall take place on request of the defendant with a view to deciding, within a reasonable period, whether these measures shall be modified, revoked or confirmed.

8.   Notwithstanding paragraphs 6 and 7, where the suspension of the release of goods is carried out or continued in accordance with a provisional judicial measure, Article 1716(6) shall apply.

9.   Each Party shall provide that its competent authorities shall have the authority to order the applicant under paragraph 1 to pay the importer, the consignee and the owner of the goods appropriate compensation for any injury caused to them through the wrongful detention of goods or through the detention of goods released pursuant to paragraph 6.

10.   Without prejudice to the protection of confidential information, each Party shall provide that its competent authorities shall have the authority to give the right holder sufficient opportunity to have any goods detained by the customs administration inspected in order to substantiate the right holder's claims. Each Party shall also provide that its competent authorities have the authority to give the importer an equivalent opportunity to have any such goods inspected. Where the competent authorities have made a positive determination on the merits of a case, a Party may provide the competent authorities the authority to inform the right holder of the names and addresses of the consignor, the importer and the consignee, and of the quantity of the goods in question.

11.   Where a Party requires its competent authorities to act on their own initiative and to suspend the release of goods in respect of which they have acquired prima facie evidence that an intellectual property right is being infringed:

    (a)   the competent authorities may at any time seek from the right holder any information that may assist them to exercise these powers;

    (b)   the importer and the right holder shall be promptly notified of the suspension by the Party's competent authorities, and where the importer lodges an appeal against the suspension with competent authorities, the suspension shall be subject to the conditions, with such modifications as may be necessary, set out in paragraphs 6 through 8; and

    (c)   the Party shall only exempt both public authorities and officials from liability to appropriate remedial measures where actions are taken or intended in good faith.

12.   Without prejudice to other rights of action open to the right holder and subject to the defendant's right to seek judicial review, each Party shall provide that its competent authorities shall have the authority to order the destruction or disposal of infringing goods in accordance with the principles set out in Article 1715(5). In regard to counterfeit goods, the authorities shall not allow the re-exportation of the infringing goods in an unaltered state or subject them to a different customs procedure, other than in exceptional circumstances.

13.   A Party may exclude from the application of paragraphs 1 through 12 small quantities of goods of a non-commercial nature contained in travellers' personal luggage or sent in small consignments that are not repetitive.

14.   Annex 1718.14 applies to the Parties specified in that Annex.

Article 1719

Cooperation and Technical Assistance

1.   The Parties shall provide each other on mutually agreed terms with technical assistance and shall promote cooperation between their competent authorities. Such cooperation shall include the training of personnel.

2.   The Parties shall cooperate with a view to eliminating trade in goods that infringe intellectual property rights. For this purpose, each Party shall establish and notify the other Parties by January 1, 1994 of contact points in its federal government and shall exchange information concerning trade in infringing goods.

Article 1720

Protection of Existing Subject Matter

1.   Except as required under Article 1705(7), this Agreement does not give rise to obligations in respect of acts that occurred before the date of application of the relevant provisions of this Agreement for the Party in question.

2.   Except as otherwise provided for in this Agreement, each Party shall apply this Agreement to all subject matter existing on the date of application of the relevant provisions of this Agreement for the Party in question and that is protected in a Party on such date, or that meets or subsequently meets the criteria for protection under the terms of this Chapter. In respect of this paragraph and paragraphs 3 and 4, a Party's obligations with respect to existing works shall be solely determined under Article 18 of the Berne Convention and with respect to the rights of producers of sound recordings in existing sound recordings shall be determined solely under Article 18 of that Convention, as made applicable under this Agreement.

3.   Except as required under Article 1705(7), and notwithstanding the first sentence of paragraph 2, no Party may be required to restore protection to subject matter that, on the date of application of the relevant provisions of this Agreement for the Party in question, has fallen into the public domain in its territory.

4.   In respect of any acts relating to specific objects embodying protected subject matter that become infringing under the terms of laws in conformity with this Agreement, and that were begun or in respect of which a significant investment was made, before the date of entry into force of this Agreement for that Party, any Party may provide for a limitation of the remedies available to the right holder as to the continued performance of such acts after the date of application of this Agreement for that Party. In such cases, the Party shall, however, at least provide for payment of equitable remuneration.

5.   No Party shall be obliged to apply Article 1705(2)(d) or 1706(1)(d) with respect to originals or copies purchased prior to the date of application of the relevant provisions of this Agreement for that Party.

6.   No Party shall be required to apply Article 1709(10), or the requirement in Article 1709(7) that patent rights shall be enjoyable without discrimination as to the field of technology, to use without the authorization of the right holder where authorization for such use was granted by the government before the text of the Draft Final Act Embodying the Results of the Uruguay Round of Multilateral Trade Negotiations became known.

7.   In the case of intellectual property rights for which protection is conditional on registration, applications for protection that are pending on the date of application of the relevant provisions of this Agreement for the Party in question shall be permitted to be amended to claim any enhanced protection provided under this Agreement. Such amendments shall not include new matter.

Article 1721

Definitions

1.   For purposes of this Chapter:

confidential information includes trade secrets, privileged information and other materials exempted from disclosure under the Party's domestic law.

2.   For purposes of this Agreement:

encrypted program-carrying satellite signal means a program-carrying satellite signal that is transmitted in a form whereby the aural or visual characteristics, or both, are modified or altered for the purpose of preventing the unauthorized reception, by persons without the authorized equipment that is designed to eliminate the effects of such modification or alteration, of a program carried in that signal;

geographical indication means any indication that identifies a good as originating in the territory of a Party, or a region or locality in that territory, where a particular quality, reputation or other characteristic of the good is essentially attributable to its geographical origin;

in a manner contrary to honest commercial practices means at least practices such as breach of contract, breach of confidence and inducement to breach, and includes the acquisition of undisclosed information by other persons who knew, or were grossly negligent in failing to know, that such practices were involved in the acquisition;

intellectual property rights refers to copyright and related rights, trademark rights, patent rights, rights in layout designs of semiconductor integrated circuits, trade secret rights, plant breeders' rights, rights in geographical indications and industrial design rights;

nationals of another Party means, in respect of the relevant intellectual property right, persons who would meet the criteria for eligibility for protection provided for in the *Paris Convention* (1967), the *Berne Convention* (1971), the *Geneva Convention* (1971), the *International Convention for the Protection of Performers, Producers of Phonograms and Broadcasting Organizations* (1961), the *UPOV Convention* (1978), the *UPOV Convention* (1991) or the *Treaty on Intellectual Property in Respect of Integrated Circuits,* as if each Party were a party to those Conventions, and with respect to intellectual property rights that are not the subject of these Conventions, "nationals of another Party" shall be understood to be at least individuals who are citizens or permanent residents of that Party and also includes any other natural person referred to in Annex 201.1;

public includes, with respect to rights of communication and performance of works provided for under Articles 11, 11*bis* (1) and 14(1)(ii) of the *Berne Convention,* with respect to dramatic, dramatico-musical, musical and cinematographic works, at least, any aggregation of individuals intended to be the object of, and capable of perceiving, communications or performances of works, regardless of whether they can do so at the same or different times or in the same or different places, provided that such an aggregation is larger than a family and its immediate circle of acquaintances or is not a group comprising a limited number of individuals having similarly close ties that has not been formed for the principal purpose of receiving such performances and communications of works; and

secondary uses of sound recordings means the use directly for broadcasting or for any other public communication of a sound recording.

CHAPTER 17 OF NAFTA

Annex 1701.3

Intellectual Property Conventions

1.   Mexico shall:

(a)   make every effort to comply with the substantive provisions of the 1978 or 1991 *UPOV Convention* as soon as possible and shall do so no later than two years after the date of signature of this Agreement; and

(b)   accept from the date of entry into force of this Agreement applications from plant breeders for varieties in all plant genera and species and grant protection, in accordance with such substantive provisions, promptly after complying with subparagraph (a).

2.   Notwithstanding Article 1701(2)(b), this Agreement confers no rights and imposes no obligations on the United States with respect to Article 6bis of the Berne Convention, or the rights derived from that Article.

Annex 1705.7

Copyright

The United States shall provide protection to motion pictures produced in another Party's territory that have been declared to be in the public domain pursuant to 17 U.S.C. section 405. This obligation shall apply to the extent that it is consistent with the Constitution of the United States, and is subject to budgetary considerations.

Annex 1710.9

Layout Designs

Mexico shall make every effort to implement the requirements of Article 1710 as soon as possible, and shall do so no later than four years after the date of entry into force of this Agreement.

Annex 1718.14

Enforcement of Intellectual Property Rights

Mexico shall make every effort to comply with the requirements of Article 1718 as soon as possible and shall do so no later than three years after the date of signature of this Agreement.

D. INTELLECTUAL PROPERTY PROVISION OF THE UNITED STATES, MEXICO, CANADA TRADE AGREEMENT (USMCA)*

Table of Contents

---

*   This treaty was signed by the heads of state of the three contracting parties on November 30, 2018, but at the time this edition went to press none of the three had ratified the treaty.—*Ed.*

CHAPTER 20 INTELLECTUAL PROPERTY RIGHTS

Section A: General Provisions

Article 20.1:   Definitions

1.   For the purposes of this Chapter:

Berne Convention means the *Berne Convention for the Protection of Literary and Artistic Works*, done at Berne on September 9, 1886, as revised at Paris on July 24, 1971;

Brussels Convention means the *Convention Relating to the Distribution of Programme-Carrying Signals Transmitted by Satellite*, done at Brussels on May 21, 1974;

Budapest Treaty means the *Budapest Treaty on the International Recognition of the Deposit of Microorganisms for the Purposes of Patent Procedure* (1977), done at Budapest on April 28, 1977, as amended on September 26, 1980;

Declaration on TRIPS and Public Health means the *Declaration on the TRIPS Agreement and Public Health* (WT/MIN(01)/DEC/2), adopted on November 14, 2001;

geographical indication means an indication that identifies a good as originating in the territory of a Party, or a region or locality in that territory, where a given quality, reputation, or other characteristic of the good is essentially attributable to its geographical origin;

Hague Agreement means the *Geneva Act of the Hague Agreement Concerning the International Registration of Industrial Designs*, done at Geneva on July 2, 1999;

intellectual property refers to all categories of intellectual property that are the subject of Sections 1 through 7 of Part II of the TRIPS Agreement;

Madrid Protocol means the *Protocol Relating to the Madrid Agreement Concerning the International Registration of Marks*, done at Madrid on June 27, 1989;

Paris Convention means the *Paris Convention for the Protection of Industrial Property,* done at Paris on March 20, 1883 as revised at Stockholm on July 14, 1967;

performance means a performance fixed in a phonogram, unless otherwise specified;

with respect to copyright and related rights, **right to authorize or prohibit** refers to exclusive rights;

PLT means the *Patent Law Treaty* adopted by the WIPO Diplomatic Conference done at Geneva on June 1, 2000;

Singapore Treaty means the *Singapore Treaty on the Law of Trademarks*, done at Singapore on March 27, 2006;

UPOV 1991 means the *International Convention for the Protection of New Varieties of Plants*, done at Paris on December 2, 1961, as revised at Geneva on March 19, 1991;

WCT means the *WIPO Copyright Treaty*, done at Geneva on December 20, 1996;

WIPO means the World Intellectual Property Organization;

for greater certainty, **work** includes a cinematographic work, photographic work, and computer program; and

WPPT means the *WIPO Performances and Phonograms Treaty*, done at Geneva on December 20, 1996.

2.   For the purposes of Article 20.8 (National Treatment), Article 20.30 (Administrative Procedures for the Protection or Recognition of Geographical Indications), and Article 20.62 (Related Rights):

a **national** means, in respect of the relevant right, a person of a Party that would meet the criteria for eligibility for protection provided for in the agreements listed in Article 20.7 (International Agreements) or the TRIPS Agreement.

Article 20.2:   Objectives

The protection and enforcement of intellectual property rights should contribute to the promotion of technological innovation and to the transfer and dissemination of technology, to the mutual advantage of producers and users of technological knowledge and in a manner conducive to social and economic welfare, and to a balance of rights and obligations.

Article 20.3:   Principles

1.   A Party may, in formulating or amending its laws and regulations, adopt measures necessary to protect public health and nutrition, and to promote the public interest in sectors of vital importance to their socio-economic and technological development, provided that those measures are consistent with the provisions of this Chapter.

2.   Appropriate measures, provided that they are consistent with the provisions of this Chapter, may be needed to prevent the abuse of intellectual property rights by right holders or the resort to practices which unreasonably restrain trade or adversely affect the international transfer of technology.

Article 20.4:   Understandings in Respect of this Chapter

Having regard to the underlying public policy objectives of national systems, the Parties recognize the need to:

(a)   promote innovation and creativity;

(b)   facilitate the diffusion of information, knowledge, technology, culture, and the arts; and

(c)   foster competition and open and efficient markets;

through their respective intellectual property systems, while respecting the principles of transparency and due process, and taking into account the interests of relevant stakeholders, including right holders, service providers, users, and the public.

Article 20.5:   Nature and Scope of Obligations

1.   Each Party shall provide in its territory to the nationals of another Party adequate and effective protection and enforcement of intellectual property rights, while ensuring that measures to enforce intellectual property rights do not themselves become barriers to legitimate trade.

2.   A Party may, but shall not be obliged to, provide more extensive protection for, or enforcement of, intellectual property rights under its law than is required by this Chapter, provided that such protection or enforcement does not contravene this Chapter. Each Party shall be free to determine the appropriate method of implementing the provisions of this Chapter within its own legal system and practice.

Article 20.6:   Understandings Regarding Certain Public Health Measures

The Parties affirm their commitment to the Declaration on TRIPS and Public Health. In particular, the Parties have reached the following understandings regarding this Chapter:

(a)   The obligations of this Chapter do not and should not prevent a Party from taking measures to protect public health. Accordingly, while reiterating their commitment to this Chapter, the Parties affirm that this Chapter can and should be interpreted and implemented in a manner supportive of each Party's right to protect public health and, in particular, to promote access to medicines for all. Each Party has the right to determine what constitutes a national emergency or other circumstances of extreme urgency, it being understood that public health crises, including those relating to HIV/AIDS, tuberculosis, malaria, and other epidemics, can represent a national emergency or other circumstances of extreme urgency.

(b)   In recognition of the commitment to access to medicines that are supplied in accordance with the Decision of the WTO General Council of August 30, 2003 on the *Implementation of Paragraph Six of the Doha Declaration on the TRIPS Agreement and Public Health* (WT/L/540) and the WTO General Council Chairman's Statement Accompanying the Decision (JOB(03)/177, WT/GC/M/82), as well as the Decision of the WTO General Council of December 6, 2005 on the *Amendment of the TRIPS Agreement*, (WT/L/641) and the WTO General Council Chairperson's Statement Accompanying the Decision (JOB(05)/319 and Corr. 1,WT/GC/M/100) (collectively, the "TRIPS/health solution"), this Chapter does not and should not prevent the effective utilization of the TRIPS/health solution.

(c)   With respect to the aforementioned matters, if any waiver of a provision of the TRIPS Agreement, or any amendment of the TRIPS Agreement, enters into force with respect to the Parties, and a Party's application of a measure in conformity with that waiver or amendment is contrary to the obligations of this Chapter, the Parties shall immediately consult in order to adapt this Chapter as appropriate in the light of the waiver or amendment.

Article 20.7:   International Agreements

1.   Each Party affirms that it has ratified or acceded to the following agreements:

(a)   *Patent Cooperation Treaty,* as amended on September 28, 1979, and modified on February 3, 1984;

(b)   Paris Convention;

    (c)   Berne Convention;

    (d)   WCT; and

    (e)   WPPT.

2.   Each Party shall ratify or accede to each of the following agreements, if it is not already a party to that agreement, by the date of entry into force of this Agreement:

    (a)   Madrid Protocol;

    (b)   Budapest Treaty;

    (c)   Singapore Treaty;[1]

    (d)   UPOV 1991;

    (e)   Hague Agreement; and

    (f)   Brussels Convention.

3.   Each Party shall give due consideration to ratifying or acceding to the PLT, or, in the alternative, shall adopt or maintain procedural standards consistent with the objective of the PLT.

Article 20.8:   National Treatment

1.   In respect of all categories of intellectual property covered in this Chapter, each Party shall accord to nationals of another Party treatment no less favorable than it accords to its own nationals with regard to the protection[2] of intellectual property rights.

2.   A Party may derogate from paragraph 1 in relation to its judicial and administrative procedures, including requiring a national of another Party to designate an address for service of process in its territory, or to appoint an agent in its territory, provided that this derogation is:

    (a)   necessary to secure compliance with laws or regulations that are not inconsistent with this Chapter; and

    (b)   not applied in a manner that would constitute a disguised restriction on trade.

3.   Paragraph 1 does not apply to procedures provided in multilateral agreements concluded under the auspices of WIPO relating to the acquisition or maintenance of intellectual property rights.

Article 20.9:   Transparency

1.   Further to Article 20.81 (Enforcement Practices with Respect to Intellectual Property Rights), each Party shall endeavor to publish online its laws, regulations, procedures, and administrative rulings of general application concerning the protection and enforcement of intellectual property rights.

---

   [1] A Party may satisfy the obligations in paragraphs 2(a) and 2(c) by ratifying or acceding to either the Madrid Protocol or the Singapore Treaty.

   [2] For the purposes of this paragraph, "protection" shall include matters affecting the availability, acquisition, scope, maintenance and enforcement of intellectual property rights as well as matters affecting the use of intellectual property rights specifically covered by this Chapter. Further, for the purposes of this paragraph, "protection" also includes the prohibition on the circumvention of effective technological measures set out in Article 20.67 (Technological Protection Measures) and the provisions concerning rights management information set out in Article 20.68 (Rights Management Information). For greater certainty, "matters affecting the use of intellectual property rights specifically covered by this Chapter" in respect of works, performances, and phonograms, include any form of payment, such as licensing fees, royalties, equitable remuneration, or levies, in respect of uses that fall under the copyright and related rights in this Chapter. The preceding sentence is without prejudice to a Party's interpretation of "matters affecting the use of intellectual property rights" in footnote 3 of the TRIPS Agreement.

2.   Each Party shall, subject to its law, endeavor to publish online information that it makes public concerning applications for trademarks, geographical indications, designs, patents, and plant variety rights.[3,4]

3.   Each Party shall, subject to its law, publish online information that it makes public concerning registered or granted trademarks, geographical indications, designs, patents, and plant variety rights, sufficient to enable the public to become acquainted with those registered or granted rights.[5]

Article 20.10:   Application of Chapter to Existing Subject Matter and Prior Acts

1.   Unless otherwise provided in this Chapter, including in Article 20.64 (Application of Article 18 of the Berne Convention and Article 14.6 of the TRIPS Agreement), this Chapter gives rise to obligations in respect of all subject matter existing at the date of entry into force of this Agreement and that is protected on that date in the territory of a Party where protection is claimed, or that meets or comes subsequently to meet the criteria for protection under this Chapter.

2.   Unless provided in Article 20.64 (Application of Article 18 of the Berne Convention and Article 14.6 of the TRIPS Agreement), a Party shall not be required to restore protection to subject matter that on the date of entry into force of this Agreement has fallen into the public domain in its territory.

3.   This Chapter does not give rise to obligations in respect of acts that occurred before the date of entry into force of this Agreement.

Article 20.11:   Exhaustion of Intellectual Property Rights

Nothing in this Agreement prevents a Party from determining whether or under what conditions the exhaustion of intellectual property rights applies under its legal system.[6]

Section B: Cooperation

Article 20.12:   Contact Points for Cooperation

Each Party may designate and notify the other Parties of one or more contact points for the purpose of cooperation under this Section.

Article 20.13:   Cooperation

The Parties shall endeavor to cooperate on the subject matter covered by this Chapter, such as through appropriate coordination and exchange of information between their respective intellectual property offices, or other agencies or institutions, as determined by each Party.

Article 20.14:   Committee on Intellectual Property Rights

1.   The Parties hereby establish a Committee on Intellectual Property Rights (IPR Committee), composed of government representatives of each Party.

2.   The IPR Committee shall:

---

[3]   For greater certainty, paragraphs 2 and 3 are without prejudice to a Party's obligations under Article 20.23 (Electronic Trademarks System).

[4]   For greater certainty, paragraph 2 does not require a Party to publish online the entire dossier for the relevant application.

[5]   For greater certainty, paragraph 3 does not require a Party to publish online the entire dossier for the relevant registered or granted intellectual property right.

[6]   For greater certainty, this Article is without prejudice to any provisions addressing the exhaustion of intellectual property rights in international agreements to which a Party is a party.

(a) exchange information, pertaining to intellectual property rights matters, including how intellectual property protection contributes to innovation, creativity, economic growth, and employment, such as:

   (i) developments in domestic and international intellectual property law and policy,

   (ii) economic benefits related to trade and other analysis of the contributions arising from the protection and enforcement of intellectual property rights,

   (iii) intellectual property issues particularly relevant to small and medium-sized enterprises; science, technology, and innovation activities; and to the generation, transfer, and dissemination of technology,

   (iv) approaches for reducing the infringement of intellectual property rights, as well as effective strategies for removing the underlying incentives for infringement,

   (v) programs on education and awareness related to intellectual property and building capacity regarding intellectual property rights matters, and

   (vi) implementation of multilateral intellectual property agreements, such as those concluded or administered under the auspices of WIPO;

(b) work towards strengthening border enforcement of intellectual property rights through the promotion of collaborative operations in customs and exchange of best practices;

(c) exchange information regarding trade secret-related matters, including the value of trade secrets and the economic loss associated with trade secret misappropriation;

(d) discuss proposals to enhance procedural fairness in patent litigation, including with respect to choice of venue; and

(e) upon request of a Party and in the interest of advancing transparency, endeavor to reach a mutually agreeable solution before taking measures in connection with future requests of recognition or protection of a geographical indication from any other country through a trade agreement.

3.   The Parties shall endeavor to cooperate on providing technical assistance regarding trade secret protection to the relevant authorities of non-Parties and identify appropriate opportunities to increase cooperation between the Parties on trade-related intellectual property rights protection and enforcement.

4.   The IPR Committee shall meet within one year after the date of entry into force of this Agreement and thereafter as necessary.

Article 20.15: Patent Cooperation and Work Sharing

1.   The Parties recognize the importance of improving the quality and efficiency of their respective patent registration systems as well as simplifying and streamlining the procedures and processes of their respective patent offices to the benefit of all users of the patent system and the public as a whole.

2.   Further to paragraph 1, the Parties shall endeavor to cooperate among their respective patent offices to facilitate the sharing and use of search and examination work of the Parties. This may include:

(a) making search and examination results available to the patent offices of the other Parties;[7] and

---

[7]   The Parties recognize the importance of multilateral efforts to promote the sharing and use of search and examination results with a view to improving the quality of search and examination processes and to reducing the costs for both applicants and patent offices.

(b)   exchanging information on quality assurance systems and quality standards relating to patent examination.

3.   In order to reduce the complexity and cost of obtaining the grant of a patent, the Parties shall endeavor to cooperate to reduce differences in the procedures and processes of their respective patent offices.

Article 20.16: Cooperation on Request

Cooperation activities undertaken under this Chapter are subject to the availability of resources, and on request, and on terms and conditions mutually decided upon between the Parties involved. The Parties affirm that cooperation under this Section is additional to and without prejudice to other past, ongoing, and future cooperation activities, both bilateral and multilateral, between the Parties, including between their respective intellectual property offices.

Section C: Trademarks

Article 20.17: Types of Signs Registrable as Trademarks

No Party shall require, as a condition of registration, that a sign be visually perceptible, nor shall a Party deny registration of a trademark only on the ground that the sign of which it is composed is a sound. Additionally, each Party shall make best efforts to register scent marks. A Party may require a concise and accurate description, or graphical representation, or both, as applicable, of the trademark.

Article 20.18: Collective and Certification Marks

Each Party shall provide that trademarks include collective marks and certification marks. A Party is not required to treat certification marks as a separate category in its law, provided that those marks are protected. Each Party shall also provide that signs that may serve as geographical indications are capable of protection under its trademark system.[8]

Article 20.19: Use of Identical or Similar Signs

Each Party shall provide that the owner of a registered trademark has the exclusive right to prevent third parties that do not have the owner's consent from using in the course of trade identical or similar signs, including subsequent geographical indications[9] for goods or services that are related to those goods or services in respect of which the owner's trademark is registered, if that use would result in a likelihood of confusion. In the case of the use of an identical sign for identical goods or services, a likelihood of confusion shall be presumed.

Article 20.20: Exceptions

A Party may provide limited exceptions to the rights conferred by a trademark, such as fair use of descriptive terms, provided that those exceptions take account of the legitimate interests of the owner of the trademark and of third parties.

Article 20.21: Well-Known Trademarks

1.   No Party shall require as a condition for determining that a trademark is well-known that the trademark has been registered in the Party or in another jurisdiction, included on a list of well-known trademarks, or given prior recognition as a well-known trademark.

---

[8]   Consistent with the definition of a geographical indication in Article 20.1 (Definitions), any sign, or combination of signs, shall be eligible for protection under one or more of the legal means for protecting geographical indications, or a combination of those means.

[9]   For greater certainty, the Parties understand that this Article should not be interpreted to affect their rights and obligations under Articles 22 and 23 of the TRIPS Agreement.

2.   Article 6*bis* of the Paris Convention shall apply, *mutatis mutandis*, to goods or services that are not identical or similar to those identified by a well-known trademark,[10] whether registered or not, provided that use of that trademark in relation to those goods or services would indicate a connection between those goods or services and the owner of the trademark, and provided that the interests of the owner of the trademark are likely to be damaged by that use.

3.   The Parties recognize the importance of the *Joint Recommendation Concerning Provisions on the Protection of Well-Known Marks* as adopted by the Assembly of the Paris Union for the Protection of Industrial Property and the General Assembly of WIPO at the Thirty-Fourth Series of Meetings of the Assemblies of the Member States of WIPO September 20 to 29, 1999.

4.   Each Party shall provide for appropriate measures to refuse the application or cancel the registration and prohibit the use of a trademark that is identical or similar to a well-known trademark,[11] for identical or similar goods or services, if the use of that trademark is likely to cause confusion with the prior well-known trademark. A Party may also provide those measures including in cases in which the subsequent trademark is likely to deceive.

Article 20.22:   Procedural Aspects of Examination, Opposition, and Cancellation

Each Party shall provide a system for the examination and registration of trademarks that includes among other things:

(a) communicating to the applicant in writing, which may be by electronic means, the reasons for any refusal to register a trademark;

(b) providing the applicant with an opportunity to respond to communications from the competent authorities, to contest any initial refusal, and to make a judicial appeal of any final refusal to register a trademark;

(c) providing an opportunity to oppose the registration of a trademark and an opportunity to seek cancellation[12] of a trademark through, at a minimum, administrative procedures; and

(d) requiring administrative decisions in opposition and cancellation proceedings to be reasoned and in writing, which may be provided by electronic means.

Article 20.23:   Electronic Trademarks System

Further to Article 20.9.3 (Transparency), each Party shall provide a:

(a) system for the electronic application for, and maintenance of, trademarks; and

(b) publicly available electronic information system, including an online database, of trademark applications and of registered trademarks.

Article 20.24:   Classification of Goods and Services

Each Party shall adopt or maintain a trademark classification system that is consistent with the *Nice Agreement Concerning the International Classification of Goods and Services for the Purposes of the Registration of Marks,* done at Nice, June 15, 1957, as revised and amended (Nice Classification). Each Party shall provide that:

---

[10] In determining whether a trademark is well-known in a Party, that Party need not require that the reputation of the trademark extend beyond the sector of the public that normally deals with the relevant goods or services.

[11] The Parties understand that a well-known trademark is one that was already well-known before, as determined by a Party, the application for, registration of, or use of the first-mentioned trademark.

[12] For greater certainty, cancellation for the purposes of this Section may be implemented through a nullification or revocation proceeding.

(a) registrations and the publications of applications indicate the goods and services by their names, grouped according to the classes established by the Nice Classification;[13] and

(b) goods or services may not be considered as being similar to each other on the ground that, in any registration or publication, they are classified in the same class of the Nice Classification. Conversely, each Party shall provide that goods or services may not be considered as being dissimilar from each other on the ground that, in any registration or publication, they are classified in different classes of the Nice Classification.

Article 20.25: Term of Protection for Trademarks

Each Party shall provide that initial registration and each renewal of registration of a trademark is for a term of no less than 10 years.

Article 20.26: Non-Recordal of a License

No Party shall require recordal of trademark licenses:

(a) to establish the validity of the licenses; or

(b) as a condition for use of a trademark by a licensee to be deemed to constitute use by the holder in a proceeding that relates to the acquisition, maintenance, or enforcement of trademarks.

Article 20.27: Domain Names

1. In connection with each Party's system for the management of its country-code top-level domain (ccTLD) domain names, the following shall be available:

(a) an appropriate procedure for the settlement of disputes that, based on, or modelled along the same lines as, the principles established in the *Uniform Domain-Name Dispute-Resolution Policy*, or that:

    (i) is designed to resolve disputes expeditiously and at low cost,

    (ii) is fair and equitable,

    (iii) is not overly burdensome, and

    (iv) does not preclude resort to judicial proceedings; and

(b) online public access to a reliable and accurate database of contact information concerning domain name registrants,

in accordance with each Party's law and, if applicable, relevant administrator policies regarding protection of privacy and personal data.

2. In connection with each Party's system for the management of ccTLD domain names, appropriate remedies[14] shall be available at least in cases in which a person registers or holds, with a bad faith intent to profit, a domain name that is identical or confusingly similar to a trademark.

---

[13] A Party that relies on translations of the Nice Classification shall follow updated versions of the Nice Classification to the extent that official translations have been issued and published.

[14] The Parties understand that those remedies may, but need not, include revocation, cancellation, transfer, damages, or injunctive relief.

Section D: Country Names

Article 20.28:   Country Names

Each Party shall provide the legal means for interested persons to prevent commercial use of the country name of a Party in relation to a good in a manner that misleads consumers as to the origin of that good.

Section E: Geographical Indications

Article 20.29:   Recognition of Geographical Indications

The Parties recognize that geographical indications may be protected through a trademark or a *sui generis* system or other legal means.

Article 20.30: Administrative Procedures for the Protection or Recognition of Geographical Indications

If a Party provides administrative procedures for the protection or recognition of geographical indications, whether through a trademark or a *sui generis* system, with respect to applications for that protection or petitions for that recognition, that Party shall:

(a)   accept those applications or petitions without requiring intercession by a Party on behalf of its nationals;[15]

(b)   process those applications or petitions without imposing overly burdensome formalities;

(c)   ensure that its laws and regulations governing the filing of those applications or petitions are readily available to the public and clearly set out the procedures for these actions;

(d)   make available information sufficient to allow the general public to obtain guidance concerning the procedures for filing applications or petitions and the processing of those applications or petitions in general; and allow an applicant, a petitioner, or their representative to ascertain the status of specific applications and petitions;

(e)   require that applications or petitions may specify particular translation or transliteration for which protection is being sought;

(f)   examine applications or petitions;

(g)   ensure that those applications or petitions are published for opposition and provide procedures for opposing geographical indications that are the subject of applications or petitions;

(h)   provide a reasonable period of time during which an interested person may oppose the application or petition;

(i)   require that administrative decisions in opposition proceedings be reasoned and in writing, which may be provided by electronic means;

(j)   require that administrative decisions in cancellation proceedings be reasoned and in writing, which may be provided by electronic means; and

(k)   provide for cancellation[16] of the protection or recognition afforded to a geographical indication.

---

[15]   This subparagraph also applies to judicial procedures that protect or recognize a geographical indication.

[16]   For greater certainty, for the purposes of this Section, cancellation may be implemented through nullification or revocation proceedings.

Article 20.31: Grounds of Denial, Opposition, and Cancellation[17]

1.   If a Party protects or recognizes a geographical indication through the procedures referred to in Article 20.30 (Administrative Procedures for the Protection or Recognition of Geographical Indications), that Party shall provide procedures that allow interested persons to object to the protection or recognition of a geographical indication, and that allow for that protection or recognition to be refused or otherwise not afforded, at least, on the grounds that the geographical indication is:

(a)   likely to cause confusion with a trademark that is the subject of a pre-existing good faith pending application or registration in the territory of the Party;

(b)   likely to cause confusion with a pre-existing trademark, the rights to which have been acquired in accordance with the Party's law; and

(c)   a term customary in common language as the common name[18],[19],[20] for the relevant good in the territory of the Party.

2.   If a Party has protected or recognized a geographical indication through the procedures referred to in Article 20.30 (Administrative Procedures for the Protection or Recognition of Geographical Indications), that Party shall provide procedures that allow for interested persons to seek the cancellation of a geographical indication, and that allow for the protection or recognition to be cancelled, at least, on the grounds listed in paragraph 1. A Party may provide that the grounds listed in paragraph 1 apply as of the time of filing the request for protection or recognition of a geographical indication in the territory of the Party.[21]

3.   No Party shall preclude the possibility that the protection or recognition of a geographical indication may be cancelled, or otherwise cease, on the basis that the protected or recognized term has ceased meeting the conditions upon which the protection or recognition was originally granted in that Party.

4.   If a Party has in place a *sui generis* system for protecting unregistered geographical indications by means of judicial procedures, that Party shall provide that its judicial authorities have the authority to deny the protection or recognition of a geographical indication if any circumstance identified in paragraph 1 has been established.[22] That Party shall also provide a process that allows interested persons to commence a proceeding on the grounds identified in paragraph 1.

5.   If a Party provides protection or recognition of a geographical indication through the procedures referred to in Article 20.30 (Administrative Procedures for the Protection or Recognition of Geographical Indications) to the translation or transliteration of that geographical indication, that

---

[17]   A Party is not required to apply this Article to geographical indications for wines and spirits or to applications or petitions for those geographical indications.

[18]   If a Party refuses to protect or recognize a compound geographical indication on the grounds that an individual term of that geographical indication is the common name for the relevant good in the territory of a Party, the Party may withdraw its refusal of protection or recognition if the applicant or registrant agrees to disclaim any claim of exclusive rights to the particular individual term that was the basis for the refusal.

[19]   For greater certainty, if a Party provides for the procedures in Article 20.30 (Administrative Procedures for the Protection or Recognition of Geographical Indications) and this Article to be applied to geographical indications for wines and spirits or applications or petitions for those geographical indications, that Party is not required to protect or recognize a geographical indication of any other Party with respect to products of the vine for which the relevant indication is identical with the customary name of a grape variety existing in the territory of that Party.

[20]   For greater certainty, a term customary in common language as the common name may refer to a single-component term or individual components of a multi-component term.

[21]   For greater certainty, if the grounds listed in paragraph 1 did not exist in a Party's law as of the time of filing of the request for protection or recognition of a geographical indication under Article 20.30 (Administrative Procedures for the Protection or Recognition of Geographical Indications), that Party is not required to apply those grounds for the purposes of paragraphs 2 or 4 of this Article in relation to that geographical indication.

[22]   As an alternative to this paragraph, if a Party has in place a *sui generis* system of the type referred to in this paragraph as of the applicable date under Article 20.35.6 (International Agreements), that Party shall at least provide that its judicial authorities have the authority to deny the protection or recognition of a geographical indication if the circumstances identified in paragraph 1(c) have been established.

Party shall make available procedures that are equivalent to, and grounds that are the same as, those referred to in paragraphs 1 and 2 with respect to that translation or transliteration.

Article 20.32: Guidelines for Determining Whether a Term is the Term Customary in the Common Language

With respect to the procedures in Article 20.30 (Administrative Procedures for the Protection or Recognition of Geographical Indications) and Article 20.31 (Grounds of Denial, Opposition, and Cancellation), in determining whether a term is the term customary in common language as the common name for the relevant good in the territory of a Party, that Party's authorities shall have the authority to take into account how consumers understand the term in the territory of that Party. Factors relevant to that consumer understanding may include:

(a)   whether the term is used to refer to the type of good in question, as indicated by competent sources such as dictionaries, newspapers, and relevant websites;

(b)   how the good referenced by the term is marketed and used in trade in the territory of that Party;

(c)   whether the term is used, as appropriate, in relevant international standards recognized by the Parties to refer to a type or class of good in the territory of the Party, such as pursuant to a standard promulgated by the Codex Alimentarius; and

(d)   whether the good in question is imported into the Party's territory, in significant quantities,[23] from a place other than the territory identified in the application or petition, and whether those imported goods are named by the term.

Article 20.33: Multi-Component Terms

With respect to the procedures in Article 20.30 (Administrative Procedures for the Protection or Recognition of Geographical Indications) and Article 20.31 (Grounds of Denial, Opposition, and Cancellation), an individual component of a multi-component term that is protected as a geographical indication in the territory of a Party shall not be protected in that Party if that individual component is a term customary in the common language as the common name for the associated good.

Article 20.34: Date of Protection of a Geographical Indication

If a Party grants protection or recognition to a geographical indication through the procedures referred to in Article 20.30 (Administrative Procedures for the Protection or Recognition of Geographical Indications), that protection or recognition shall commence no earlier than the filing date[24] in the Party or the registration date in the Party, as applicable.

Article 20.35: International Agreements

1.   If a Party protects or recognizes a geographical indication pursuant to an international agreement, as of the applicable date under paragraph 6, involving a Party or a non-Party and that geographical indication is not protected through the procedures referred to in Article 20.30 (Administrative Procedures for the Protection or Recognition of Geographical Indications)[25] or Article 20.31 (Grounds of Denial, Opposition, and Cancellation), that Party at least shall apply procedures and grounds that are equivalent to those in Article 20.30(f), (g), (h), and (i) (Administrative Procedures

---

[23] In determining whether the good in question is imported in significant quantities, a Party may consider the amount of importation at the time of the application or petition.

[24] For greater certainty, the filing date referred to in this paragraph includes, as applicable, the priority filing date under the Paris Convention. No Party shall use the date of protection in a country of origin of a geographical indication to establish a priority date in the territory of the Party, unless filed within the Paris Convention priority period.

[25] Each Party shall apply Article 20.32 (Guidelines for Determining Whether a Term is the Term Customary in the Common Language) and Article 20.33 (Multi-Component Terms) in determining whether to grant protection or recognition of a geographical indication pursuant to this paragraph.

for the Protection or Recognition of Geographical Indications) and Article 20.31.1 (Grounds of Denial, Opposition, and Cancellation), as well as:

(a)   make available information sufficient to allow the general public to obtain guidance concerning the procedures for protecting or recognizing the geographical indication and allow interested persons to ascertain the status of requests for protection or recognition;

(b)   to publish online details regarding the terms that the Party is considering protecting or recognizing through an international agreement involving a Party or a non-Party, including specifying whether the protection or recognition is being considered for any translations or transliterations of those terms, and with respect to multi-component terms, specifying the components, if any, for which protection or recognition is being considered, or the components that are disclaimed;

(c)   in respect of opposition procedures, provide a reasonable period of time for interested persons to oppose the protection or recognition of the terms referred to in subparagraph (b). That period shall allow for a meaningful opportunity for any interested person to participate in an opposition process; and

(d)   inform the other Parties of the opportunity to oppose, no later than the commencement of the opposition period.

2.   In respect of international agreements referred to in paragraph 6 that permit the protection or recognition of a new geographical indication, a Party shall:[26],[27]

(a)   apply paragraph 1(b) and apply at least procedures and grounds that are equivalent to those in Article 20.30(f), (g), (h), and (i) (Administrative Procedures for the Protection or Recognition of Geographical Indications) and Article 20.31.1 (Grounds of Denial, Opposition, and Cancellation);

(b)   provide an opportunity for interested persons to comment regarding the protection or recognition of the new geographical indication for a reasonable period of time before that term is protected or recognized; and

(c)   inform the other Parties of the opportunity to comment, no later than the commencement of the period for comment.

3.   For the purposes of this Article, a Party shall not preclude the possibility that the protection or recognition of a geographical indication could cease.

4.   For the purposes of this Article, a Party is not required to apply Article 20.31 (Grounds of Denial, Opposition, and Cancellation), or obligations equivalent to Article 20.31, to geographical indications for wines and spirits or applications for those geographical indications.

5.   The protection or recognition that each Party provides pursuant to paragraph 1 shall commence no earlier than the date on which that agreement enters into force or, if that Party grants that protection or recognition on a date after the entry into force of that agreement, on that later date.

6.   No Party shall be required to apply this Article to geographical indications that have been specifically identified in, and that are protected or recognized pursuant to, an international agreement involving a Party or a non-Party, provided that the agreement:

---

[26]   In respect of an international agreement referred to in paragraph 6 that has geographical indications that have been identified, but have not yet received protection or recognition in the territory of the Party that is a party to that agreement, that Party may fulfil the obligations of paragraph 2 by complying with the obligations of paragraph 1.

[27]   A Party may comply with this Article by applying Article 20.30 (Administrative Procedures for the Protection or Recognition of Geographical Indications) and Article 20.31 (Grounds of Denial, Opposition, and Cancellation).

(a)   was concluded, or agreed in principle,[28] prior to the date of conclusion, or agreement in principle, of this Agreement;

(b)   was ratified by a Party prior to the date of ratification of this Agreement by that Party; or

(c)   entered into force for a Party prior to the date of entry into force of this Agreement.

Section F: Patents and Undisclosed Test or Other Data

Subsection A: General Patents

Article 20.36: Patentable Subject Matter

1.   Subject to paragraphs 3 and 4, each Party shall make patents available for any invention, whether a product or process, in all fields of technology, provided that the invention is new, involves an inventive step, and is capable of industrial application.[29]

2.   Subject to paragraphs 3 and 4 and consistent with paragraph 1, each Party confirms that patents are available for inventions claimed as at least one of the following: new uses of a known product, new methods of using a known product, or new processes of using a known product.

3.   A Party may exclude from patentability inventions, the prevention within their territory of the commercial exploitation of which is necessary to protect *ordre public* or morality, including to protect human, animal, or plant life or health or to avoid serious prejudice to nature or the environment, provided that such exclusion is not made merely because the exploitation is prohibited by its law. A Party may also exclude from patentability:

(a)   diagnostic, therapeutic, and surgical methods for the treatment of humans or animals;

(b)   animals other than microorganisms, and essentially biological processes for the production of plants or animals, other than non-biological and microbiological processes.

4.   A Party may also exclude from patentability plants other than microorganisms. However, consistent with paragraph 1 and subject to paragraph 3, each Party confirms that patents are available at least for inventions that are derived from plants.

Article 20.37: Grace Period

Each Party shall disregard at least information contained in public disclosures used to determine if an invention is novel or has an inventive step, if the public disclosure:[30]

(a)   was made by the patent applicant or by a person that obtained the information directly or indirectly from the patent applicant; and

(b)   occurred within twelve months prior to the filing date in the territory of the Party.

Article 20.38: Patent Revocation

1.   Each Party shall provide that a patent may be cancelled, revoked, or nullified only on grounds that would have justified a refusal to grant the patent. A Party may also provide that fraud,

---

[28] For the purpose of this Article, an agreement "agreed in principle" means an agreement involving another government, government entity, or international organization in respect of which a political understanding has been reached and the negotiated outcomes of the agreement have been publically announced.

[29] For the purposes of this Section, a Party may deem the terms "inventive step" and "capable of industrial application" to be synonymous with the terms "non-obvious" and "useful", respectively. In determinations regarding inventive step, or non-obviousness, each Party shall consider whether the claimed invention would have been obvious to a person skilled in the art, or having ordinary skill in the art, having regard to the prior art.

[30] For greater certainty, a Party may limit the application of this Article to disclosures made by, or obtained directly or indirectly from, the inventor or joint inventor. For greater certainty, a Party may provide that, for the purposes of this Article, information obtained directly or indirectly from the patent applicant may be information contained in the public disclosure that was authorized by, or derived from, the patent applicant.

misrepresentation, or inequitable conduct may be the basis for cancelling, revoking, or nullifying a patent or holding a patent unenforceable.

2.   Notwithstanding paragraph 1, a Party may provide that a patent may be revoked, provided it is done in a manner consistent with Article 5A of the Paris Convention and the TRIPS Agreement.

Article 20.39: Exceptions

A Party may provide limited exceptions to the exclusive rights conferred by a patent, provided that those exceptions do not unreasonably conflict with a normal exploitation of the patent and do not unreasonably prejudice the legitimate interests of the patent owner, taking account of the legitimate interests of third parties.

Article 20.40: Other Use Without Authorization of the Right Holder

The Parties understand that nothing in this Chapter limits a Party's rights and obligations under Article 31 of the TRIPS Agreement, and any waiver of or amendment to that Article that the Parties accept.

Article 20.41: Amendments, Corrections, and Observations

Each Party shall provide a patent applicant with at least one opportunity to make amendments, corrections, and observations in connection with its application.[31]

Article 20.42: Publication of Patent Applications

1.   Recognizing the benefits of transparency in the patent system, each Party shall endeavor to publish unpublished pending patent applications promptly after the expiration of 18 months from the filing date or, if priority is claimed, from the earliest priority date.

2.   If a pending application is not published promptly in accordance with paragraph 1, a Party shall publish that application or the corresponding patent, as soon as practicable.

3.   Each Party shall provide that an applicant may request the early publication of an application prior to the expiration of the period referred to in paragraph 1.

Article 20.43: Information Relating to Published Patent Applications and Granted Patents

For published patent applications and granted patents, and in accordance with the Party's requirements for prosecution of those applications and patents, each Party shall make available to the public at least the following information, to the extent that this information is in the possession of the competent authorities and is generated on, or after, the date of the entry into force of this Agreement:

(a)   search and examination results, including details of, or information related to, relevant prior art searches;

(b)   as appropriate, non-confidential communications from applicants; and

(c)   patent and non-patent related literature citations submitted by applicants and relevant third parties.

Article 20.44: Patent Term Adjustment for Unreasonable Granting Authority Delays

1.   Each Party shall make best efforts to process patent applications in an efficient and timely manner, with a view to avoiding unreasonable or unnecessary delays.

---

[31] A Party may provide that those amendments or corrections must not exceed the scope of the disclosure of the invention, as of the filing date.

2.   A Party may provide procedures for a patent applicant to request to expedite the examination of its patent application.

3.   If there are unreasonable delays in a Party's issuance of a patent, that Party shall provide the means to, and at the request of the patent owner shall, adjust the term of the patent to compensate for those delays.

4.   For the purposes of this Article, an unreasonable delay at least shall include a delay in the issuance of a patent of more than five years from the date of filing of the application in the territory of the Party, or three years after a request for examination of the application has been made, whichever is later. A Party may exclude, from the determination of those delays, periods of time that do not occur during the processing[32] of, or the examination of, the patent application by the granting authority; periods of time that are not directly attributable[33] to the granting authority; as well as periods of time that are attributable to the patent applicant.[34]

Subsection B: Measures Relating to Agricultural Chemical Products

Article 20.45: Protection of Undisclosed Test or Other Data for Agricultural Chemical Products

1.   If a Party requires, as a condition for granting marketing approval[35] for a new agricultural chemical product, the submission of undisclosed test or other data concerning the safety and efficacy of the product,[36] that Party shall not permit third persons, without the consent of the person that previously submitted that information, to market the same or a similar[37] product on the basis of that information or the marketing approval granted to the person that submitted that test or other data for at least 10 years[38] from the date of marketing approval of the new agricultural chemical product in the territory of the Party.

2.   If a Party permits, as a condition of granting marketing approval for a new agricultural chemical product, the submission of evidence of a prior marketing approval of the product in another territory, that Party shall not permit third persons, without the consent of the person that previously submitted undisclosed test or other data concerning the safety and efficacy of the product in support of that prior marketing approval, to market the same or a similar product based on that undisclosed test or other data, or other evidence of the prior marketing approval in the other territory, for at least 10 years from the date of marketing approval of the new agricultural chemical product in the territory of the Party.

3.   For the purposes of this Article, a new agricultural chemical product is one that contains a chemical entity that has not been previously approved in the territory of the Party for use in an agricultural chemical product.

---

[32] For the purposes of this paragraph, a Party may interpret processing to mean initial administrative processing and administrative processing at the time of grant.

[33] A Party may treat delays "that are not directly attributable to the granting authority" as delays that are outside the direction or control of the granting authority.

[34] Notwithstanding Article 20.10 (Application of Chapter to Existing Subject Matter and Prior Acts), this Article shall apply to all patent applications filed after the date of entry into force of this Agreement, or the date two years after the signing of this Agreement, whichever is later.

[35] For the purposes of this Chapter, the term "marketing approval" is synonymous with "sanitary approval" under a Party's law.

[36] Each Party confirms that the obligations of this Article apply to cases in which the Party requires the submission of undisclosed test or other data concerning: (a) only the safety of the product, (b) only the efficacy of the product, or (c) both.

[37] For greater certainty, for the purposes of this Section, an agricultural chemical product is "similar" to a previously approved agricultural chemical product if the marketing approval, or, in the alternative, the applicant's request for that approval, of that similar agricultural chemical product is based upon the undisclosed test or other data concerning the safety and efficacy of the previously approved agricultural chemical product, or the prior approval of that previously approved product.

[38] For greater certainty, a Party may limit the period of protection under this Article to 10 years.

Subsection C: Measures Relating to Pharmaceutical Products

Article 20.46: Patent Term Adjustment for Unreasonable Curtailment

1.   Each Party shall make best efforts to process applications for marketing approval of pharmaceutical products in an efficient and timely manner, with a view to avoiding unreasonable or unnecessary delays.

2.   With respect to a pharmaceutical product that is subject to a patent, each Party shall make available an adjustment[39] of the patent term to compensate the patent owner for unreasonable curtailment of the effective patent term as a result of the marketing approval process.

3.   For greater certainty, in implementing the obligations of this Article, each Party may provide for conditions and limitations, provided that the Party continues to give effect to this Article.

4.   With the objective of avoiding unreasonable curtailment of the effective patent term, a Party may adopt or maintain procedures that expedite the processing of marketing approval applications.

Article 20.47: Regulatory Review Exception

Without prejudice to the scope of, and consistent with, Article 20.39 (Exceptions), each Party shall adopt or maintain a regulatory review exception for pharmaceutical products.

Article 20.48: Protection of Undisclosed Test or Other Data

1.   (a)   If a Party requires, as a condition for granting marketing approval for a new pharmaceutical product, the submission of undisclosed test or other data concerning the safety and efficacy of the product,[40] that Party shall not permit third persons, without the consent of the person that previously submitted that information, to market the same or a similar[41] product on the basis of:

(i)   that information, or

(ii)   the marketing approval granted to the person that submitted that information, for at least five years[42] from the date of marketing approval of the new pharmaceutical product in the territory of the Party;

(b)   If a Party permits, as a condition of granting marketing approval for a new pharmaceutical product, the submission of evidence of prior marketing approval of the product in another territory, that Party shall not permit third persons, without the consent of a person that previously submitted the information concerning the safety and efficacy of the product, to market a same or a similar product based on evidence relating to prior marketing approval in the other territory for at least five years from the date of marketing approval of the new pharmaceutical product in the territory of that Party.

---

[39] For greater certainty, a Party may alternatively make available a period of additional *sui generis* protection to compensate for unreasonable curtailment of the effective patent term as a result of the marketing approval process. The *sui generis* protection must confer the rights conferred by the patent, subject to any conditions and limitations pursuant to paragraph 3.

[40] Each Party confirms that the obligations of this Article and Article 20.49 (Biologics) apply to cases in which the Party requires the submission of undisclosed test or other data concerning: (i) only the safety of the product, (ii) only the efficacy of the product, or (iii) both.

[41] For greater certainty, for the purposes of this Section, a pharmaceutical product is "similar" to a previously approved pharmaceutical product if the marketing approval, or, in the alternative, the applicant's request for that approval, of that similar pharmaceutical product is based upon the undisclosed test or other data concerning the safety and efficacy of the previously approved pharmaceutical product, or the prior approval of that previously approved product.

[42] For greater certainty, a Party may limit the period of protection under paragraph 1 to five years, and the period of protection under Article 20.49.1 (Biologics) to 10 years.

2.   Each Party shall:[43]

(a)   apply paragraph 1, *mutatis mutandis*, for a period of at least three years with respect to new clinical information submitted as required in support of a marketing approval of a previously approved pharmaceutical product covering a new indication, new formulation, or new method of administration; or, alternatively,

(b)   apply paragraph 1, *mutatis mutandis*, for a period of at least five years to new pharmaceutical products that contain a chemical entity that has not been previously approved in that Party.[44]

3.   Notwithstanding paragraphs 1 and 2 and Article 20.49 (Biologics), a Party may take measures to protect public health in accordance with:

(a)   the Declaration on TRIPS and Public Health;

(b)   any waiver of a provision of the TRIPS Agreement granted by WTO Members in accordance with the WTO Agreement to implement the Declaration on TRIPS and Public Health and that is in force between the Parties; or

(c)   any amendment of the TRIPS Agreement to implement the Declaration on TRIPS and Public Health that enters into force with respect to the Parties.

Article 20.49: Biologics

1.   With regard to protecting new biologics, a Party shall, with respect to the first marketing approval in a Party of a new pharmaceutical product that is, or contains, a biologic,[45],[46] provide effective market protection through the implementation of Article 20.48.1 (Protection of Undisclosed Test or Other Data) and Article 20.48.3 (Protection of Undisclosed Test or Other Data), *mutatis mutandis*, for a period of at least ten years from the date of first marketing approval of that product in that Party.

2.   Each Party shall apply this Article to, at a minimum,[47] a product that is produced using biotechnology processes and that is, or contains, a virus, therapeutic serum, toxin, antitoxin, vaccine, blood, blood component or derivative, allergenic product, protein, or analogous product, for use in human beings for the prevention, treatment, or cure of a disease or condition.

Article 20.50: Definition of New Pharmaceutical Product

For the purposes of Article 20.48.1 (Protection of Undisclosed Test or Other Data), a **new pharmaceutical product** means a pharmaceutical product that does not contain a chemical entity that has been previously approved in that Party.

---

[43] A Party that provides a period of at least eight years of protection under paragraph 1 is not required to apply paragraph 2.

[44] For the purposes of Article 20.48.2(b) (Protection of Undisclosed Test or Other Data), a Party may choose to protect only the undisclosed test or other data concerning the safety and efficacy relating to the chemical entity that has not been previously approved.

[45] Nothing requires a Party to extend the protection of this paragraph to:

(a)   any second or subsequent marketing approval of such a pharmaceutical product; or

(b)   a pharmaceutical product that is, or contains, a previously approved biologic.

[46] Each Party may provide that an applicant may request approval of a pharmaceutical product that is, or contains, a biologic under the procedures set forth in Article 20.48.1(a) (Protection of Undisclosed Test or Other Data) and Article 20.48.1(b) (Protection of Undisclosed Test or Other Data) on or before March 23, 2020, provided that other pharmaceutical products in the same class of products have been approved by that Party under the procedures set forth in in Article 20.48.1(a) (Protection of Undisclosed Test or Other Data) and Article 20.48.1(b) (Protection of Undisclosed Test or Other Data) before the date of entry into force of this Agreement.

[47] For greater certainty, for the purposes of this Article, the Parties understand that "at a minimum" means that a Party may limit the application to the scope specified in this paragraph.

Article 20.51: Measures Relating to the Marketing of Certain Pharmaceutical Products

1. If a Party permits, as a condition of approving the marketing of a pharmaceutical product, persons, other than the person originally submitting the safety and efficacy information, to rely on evidence or information concerning the safety and efficacy of a product that was previously approved, such as evidence of prior marketing approval by the Party or in another territory, that Party shall provide:

(a) a system to provide notice to a patent holder[48] or to allow for a patent holder to be notified prior to the marketing of such a pharmaceutical product, that such other person is seeking to market that product during the term of an applicable patent claiming the approved product or its approved method of use;

(b) adequate time and sufficient opportunity for such a patent holder to seek, prior to the marketing of an allegedly infringing product, available remedies in subparagraph (c); and

(c) procedures, such as judicial or administrative proceedings, and expeditious remedies, such as preliminary injunctions or equivalent effective provisional measures, for the timely resolution of disputes concerning the validity or infringement of an applicable patent claiming an approved pharmaceutical product or its approved method of use.

2. As an alternative to paragraph 1, a Party shall instead adopt or maintain a system other than judicial proceedings that precludes, based upon patent-related information submitted to the marketing approval authority by a patent holder or the applicant for marketing approval, or based on direct coordination between the marketing approval authority and the patent office, the issuance of marketing approval to any third person seeking to market a pharmaceutical product subject to a patent claiming that product, unless by consent or acquiescence of the patent holder.

Article 20.52: Alteration of Period of Protection

Subject to Article 20.48.3 (Protection of Undisclosed Test or Other Data), if a product is subject to a system of marketing approval in the territory of a Party pursuant to Article 20.45 (Protection of Undisclosed Test or Other Data for Agricultural Chemical Products), Article 20.48, or Article 20.49 (Biologics) and is also covered by a patent in the territory of that Party, that Party shall not alter the period of protection that it provides pursuant to Article 20.45, Article 20.48, or Article 20.49 in the event that the patent protection terminates on a date earlier than the end of the period of protection specified in Article 20.45, Article 20.48, or Article 20.49.

Section G: Industrial Designs

Article 20.53: Protection

1. Each Party shall ensure adequate and effective protection of industrial designs consistent with Articles 25 and 26 of the TRIPS Agreement.

2. Consistent with paragraph 1, each Party confirms that protection is available for designs embodied in a part of an article.

Article 20.54: Non-Prejudicial Disclosures/Grace Period[49]

Each Party shall disregard at least information contained in public disclosures used to determine if an industrial design is new, original, or, where applicable, non-obvious, if the public disclosure:[50]

---

[48] For greater certainty, for the purposes of this Article, a Party may provide that a "patent holder" includes a patent licensee or the authorized holder of marketing approval.

[49] Articles 20.54 (Non-Prejudicial Disclosures/Grace Period) and 20.55 (Electronic Industrial Design System) apply with respect to industrial design patent systems or industrial design registration systems.

[50] For greater certainty, a Party may limit the application of this Article to disclosures made by, or obtained directly or indirectly from, the creator or co-creator and provide that, for the purposes of this Article, information obtained directly

   (a)   was made by the design applicant or by a person that obtained the information directly or indirectly from the design applicant; and

   (b)   occurred within 12 months prior to the filing date in the territory of the Party.

Article 20.55: Electronic Industrial Design System

Each Party shall provide a:

   (a)   system for the electronic application for industrial design rights; and

   (b)   publicly available electronic information system, which must include an online database of protected industrial designs.

Article 20.56: Term of Protection

Each Party shall provide a term of protection for industrial designs of at least 15 years from either: (a) the date of filing, or (b) the date of grant or registration.

Section H: Copyright and Related Rights

Article 20.57: Definitions

For the purposes of Article 20.58 (Right of Reproduction) and Article 20.60 (Right of Distribution) through Article 20.69 (Collective Management), the following definitions apply with respect to performers and producers of phonograms:

broadcasting means the transmission by wireless means for public reception of sounds or of images and sounds or of the representations thereof; such transmission by satellite is also "broadcasting"; transmission of encrypted signals is "broadcasting" if the means for decrypting are provided to the public by the broadcasting organization or with its consent; "broadcasting" does not include transmission over computer networks or any transmissions where the time and place of reception may be individually chosen by members of the public;

communication to the public of a performance or a phonogram means the transmission to the public by any medium, other than by broadcasting, of sounds of a performance or the sounds or the representations of sounds fixed in a phonogram;

fixation means the embodiment of sounds, or of the representations thereof, from which they can be perceived, reproduced, or communicated through a device;

performers means actors, singers, musicians, dancers, and other persons who act, sing, deliver, declaim, play in, interpret, or otherwise perform literary or artistic works or expressions of folklore;

phonogram means the fixation of the sounds of a performance or of other sounds, or of a representation of sounds, other than in the form of a fixation incorporated in a cinematographic or other audio-visual work;

producer of a phonogram means a person that takes the initiative and has the responsibility for the first fixation of the sounds of a performance or other sounds, or the representations of sounds; and

publication of a performance or phonogram means the offering of copies of the performance or the phonogram to the public, with the consent of the right holder, and provided that copies are offered to the public in reasonable quantity.

---

or indirectly from the design applicant may be information contained in the public disclosure that was authorized by, or derived from, the design applicant.

Article 20.58: Right of Reproduction

Each Party shall provide[51] to authors, performers, and producers of phonograms[52] the exclusive right to authorize or prohibit all reproduction of their works, performances, or phonograms in any manner or form, including in electronic form.

Article 20.59: Right of Communication to the Public

Without prejudice to Article 11(1)(ii), Article 11*bis*(1)(i) and (ii), Article 11*ter*(1)(ii), Article 14(1)(ii), and Article 14*bis*(1) of the Berne Convention, each Party shall provide to authors the exclusive right to authorize or prohibit the communication to the public of their works, by wire or wireless means, including the making available to the public of their works in such a way that members of the public may access these works from a place and at a time individually chosen by them.[53]

Article 20.60: Right of Distribution

Each Party shall provide to authors, performers, and producers of phonograms the exclusive right to authorize or prohibit the making available to the public of the original and copies[54] of their works, performances, and phonograms through sale or other transfer of ownership.

Article 20.61: No Hierarchy

Each Party shall provide that, in cases in which authorization is needed from both the author of a work embodied in a phonogram and a performer or producer that owns rights in the phonogram, the need for the authorization of the:

(a) author does not cease to exist because the authorization of the performer or producer is also required; and

(b) performer or producer does not cease to exist because the authorization of the author is also required.

Article 20.62: Related Rights

1. Further to the protection afforded to performers and producers of phonograms as "nationals" under Article 20.8 (National Treatment), each Party shall accord the rights provided for in this Chapter to performances and phonograms first published or first fixed[55] in the territory of another Party.[56] A performance or phonogram is considered first published in the territory of a Party if it is published in the territory of that Party within 30 days of its original publication.

2. Each Party shall provide to performers the exclusive right to authorize or prohibit:

---

[51] For greater certainty, the Parties understand that it is a matter for each Party's law to prescribe that works, performances, or phonograms in general or any specified categories of works, performances and phonograms are not protected by copyright or related rights unless the work, performance, or phonogram has been fixed in some material form.

[52] References to "authors, performers, and producers of phonograms" refer also to any of their successors in interest.

[53] The Parties understand that the mere provision of physical facilities for enabling or making a communication does not in itself amount to communication within the meaning of this Chapter or the Berne Convention. The Parties further understand that nothing in this Article precludes a Party from applying Article 11*bis*(2) of the Berne Convention.

[54] The expressions "copies" and "original and copies", that are subject to the right of distribution in this Article, refer exclusively to fixed copies that can be put into circulation as tangible objects.

[55] For the purposes of this Article, fixation means the finalization of the master tape or its equivalent.

[56] For greater certainty, consistent with Article 20.8 (National Treatment), each Party shall accord to performances and phonograms first published or first fixed in the territory of another Party treatment no less favorable than it accords to performances or phonograms first published or first fixed in its own territory.

    (a)   the broadcasting and communication to the public of their unfixed performances, unless the performance is already a broadcast performance; and

    (b)   the fixation of their unfixed performances.

3.   (a)   Each Party shall provide to performers and producers of phonograms the exclusive right to authorize or prohibit the broadcasting or any communication to the public of their performances or phonograms, by wire or wireless means[57] and the making available to the public of those performances or phonograms in such a way that members of the public may access them from a place and at a time individually chosen by them.

   (b)   Notwithstanding subparagraph (a) and Article 20.65 (Limitations and Exceptions), the application of the right referred to in subparagraph (a) to analog transmissions and non-interactive free over-the-air broadcasts, and exceptions or limitations to this right for those activities, is a matter of each Party's law.[58]

   (c)   Each Party may adopt limitations to this right in respect of other non-interactive transmissions in accordance with Article 20.65.1 (Limitations and Exceptions), provided that the limitations do not prejudice the right of the performer or producer of phonograms to obtain equitable remuneration.

Article 20.63: Term of Protection for Copyright and Related Rights

Each Party shall provide that in cases in which the term of protection of a work, performance, or phonogram is to be calculated:

    (a)   on the basis of the life of a natural person, the term shall be not less than the life of the author and 70 years after the author's death;[59] and

    (b)   on a basis other than the life of a natural person, the term shall be:

       (i)   not less than 75 years from the end of the calendar year of the first authorized publication[60] of the work, performance, or phonogram, or

      (ii)   failing such authorized publication within 25 years from the creation of the work, performance, or phonogram, not less than 70 years from the end of the calendar year of the creation of the work, performance, or phonogram.

Article 20.64: Application of Article 18 of the Berne Convention and Article 14.6 of the TRIPS Agreement

Each Party shall apply Article 18 of the Berne Convention and Article 14.6 of the TRIPS Agreement, *mutatis mutandis*, to works, performances, and phonograms, and the rights in and protections afforded to that subject matter as required by this Section.

---

[57] For greater certainty, the obligation under this paragraph does not include broadcasting or communication to the public, by wire or wireless means, of the sounds or representations of sounds fixed in a phonogram that are incorporated in a cinematographic or other audio-visual work.

[58] For the purposes of this subparagraph the Parties understand that a Party may provide for the retransmission of non-interactive, free over-the-air broadcasts, provided that these retransmissions are lawfully permitted by that Party's government communications authority; any entity engaging in these retransmissions complies with the relevant rules, orders, or regulations of that authority; and these retransmissions do not include those delivered and accessed over the Internet. For greater certainty this footnote does not limit a Party's ability to avail itself of this subparagraph.

[59] The Parties understand that if a Party provides its nationals a term of copyright protection that exceeds life of the author plus 70 years, nothing in this Article or Article 20.8 (National Treatment) precludes that Party from applying Article 7(8) of the Berne Convention with respect to the term in excess of the term provided in this subparagraph of protection for works of another Party.

[60] For greater certainty, for the purposes of subparagraph (b), if a Party's law provides for the calculation of term from fixation rather than from the first authorized publication that Party may continue to calculate the term from fixation.

Article 20.65: Limitations and Exceptions

1.   With respect to this Section, each Party shall confine limitations or exceptions to exclusive rights to certain special cases that do not conflict with a normal exploitation of the work, performance, or phonogram, and do not unreasonably prejudice the legitimate interests of the right holder.

2.   This Article does not reduce or extend the scope of applicability of the limitations and exceptions permitted by the TRIPS Agreement, the Berne Convention, the WCT, or the WPPT.

Article 20.66: Contractual Transfers

Each Party shall provide that for copyright and related rights, any person acquiring or holding an economic right[61] in a work, performance, or phonogram:

(a)   may freely and separately transfer that right by contract; and

(b)   by virtue of contract, including contracts of employment underlying the creation of works, performances, or phonograms, must be able to exercise that right in that person's own name and enjoy fully the benefits derived from that right.[62]

Article 20.67: Technological Protection Measures[63]

1.   In order to provide adequate legal protection and effective legal remedies against the circumvention of effective technological measures that authors, performers, and producers of phonograms use in connection with the exercise of their rights and that restrict unauthorized acts in respect of their works, performances, and phonograms, each Party shall provide[64] that a person who:

(a)   knowingly, or having reasonable grounds to know,[65] circumvents without authority an effective technological measure that controls access to a protected work, performance, or phonogram;[66] or

(b)   manufactures, imports, distributes, offers for sale or rental to the public, or otherwise provides devices, products, or components, or offers to the public or provides services, that:

(i)   are promoted, advertised, or otherwise marketed by that person for the purpose of circumventing any effective technological measure,

(ii)   have only a limited commercially significant purpose or use other than to circumvent any effective technological measure, or

(iii)   are primarily designed, produced, or performed for the purpose of circumventing any effective technological measure,

---

[61]   For greater certainty, this Article does not affect the exercise of moral rights.

[62]   Nothing in this Article affects a Party's ability to establish: (i) which specific contracts underlying the creation of works, performances, or phonograms shall, in the absence of a written agreement, result in a transfer of economic rights by operation of law; and (ii) reasonable limits to protect the interests of the original right holders, taking into account the legitimate interests of the transferees.

[63]   Nothing in this Agreement requires a Party to restrict the importation or domestic sale of a device that does not render effective a technological measure the only purpose of which is to control market segmentation for legitimate physical copies of a cinematographic film, and is not otherwise a violation of its law.

[64]   A Party that, prior to the date of entry into force of this Agreement, maintains legal protections for technological protection measures consistent with Article 20.67.1 (Technological Protection Measures), may maintain its current scope of limitations, exceptions, and regulations regarding circumvention.

[65]   For greater certainty, for the purposes of this subparagraph, a Party may provide that reasonable grounds to know may be demonstrated through reasonable evidence, taking into account the facts and circumstances surrounding the alleged illegal act.

[66]   For greater certainty, no Party is required to impose civil or criminal liability under this subparagraph for a person that circumvents any effective technological measure that protects any of the exclusive rights of copyright or related rights in a protected work, performance, or phonogram, but does not control access to that work, performance, or phonogram.

is liable and subject to the remedies provided for in Article 20.82.18 (Civil and Administrative Procedures and Remedies).[67]

Each Party shall provide for criminal procedures and penalties to be applied when a person, other than a non-profit library, archive,[68] educational institution, or public non-commercial broadcasting entity, is found to have engaged willfully and for the purposes of commercial advantage or financial gain in any of the foregoing activities.

Criminal procedures and penalties listed in subparagraphs (a), (c), and (f) of Article 20.85.6 (Criminal Procedures and Penalties) shall apply, as applicable to infringements *mutatis mutandis*, to the activities described in subparagraphs (a) and (b) of this paragraph.

2.   In implementing paragraph 1, no Party shall be obligated to require that the design of, or the design and selection of parts and components for, a consumer electronics, telecommunications, or computing product provide for a response to any particular technological measure, so long as the product does not otherwise violate any measure implementing paragraph 1.

3.   Each Party shall provide that a violation of a measure implementing this Article is a separate cause of action, independent of any infringement that might occur under the Party's law on copyright and related rights.

4.   Each Party shall confine exceptions and limitations to measures implementing paragraph 1 to the following activities, which shall be applied to relevant measures in accordance with paragraph 5:[69]

(a)   non-infringing reverse engineering activities with regard to a lawfully obtained copy of a computer program, carried out in good faith with respect to particular elements of that computer program that have not been readily available to the person engaged in those activities, for the sole purpose of achieving interoperability of an independently created computer program with other programs;

(b)   non-infringing good faith activities, carried out by an appropriately qualified researcher who has lawfully obtained a copy, unfixed performance, or display of a work, performance, or phonogram and who has made a good faith effort to obtain authorization for those activities, to the extent necessary for the sole purpose of research consisting of identifying and analyzing flaws and vulnerabilities of technologies for scrambling and descrambling of information;

(c)   the inclusion of a component or part for the sole purpose of preventing the access of minors to inappropriate online content in a technology, product, service, or device that itself is not prohibited under the measures implementing paragraph (1)(b);

(d)   non-infringing good faith activities that are authorized by the owner of a computer, computer system, or computer network for the sole purpose of testing, investigating, or correcting the security of that computer, computer system, or computer network;

(e)   non-infringing activities for the sole purpose of identifying and disabling a capability to carry out undisclosed collection or dissemination of personally identifying information reflecting the online activities of a natural person in a way that has no other effect on the ability of any person to gain access to any work;

(f)   lawfully authorized activities carried out by government employees, agents, or contractors for the purpose of law enforcement, intelligence, essential security, or similar governmental purposes;

---

[67]   For greater certainty, no Party is required to impose liability under this Article and Article 20.68 (Rights Management Information) for actions taken by that Party or a third person acting with authorization or consent of the Party.

[68]   For greater certainty, a Party may treat a non-profit museum as a non-profit archive.

[69]   A Party may request consultations with the other Parties to consider how to address, under paragraph 4, activities of a similar nature that a Party identifies after the date this Agreement enters into force.

(g)   access by a nonprofit library, archive, or educational institution to a work, performance, or phonogram not otherwise available to it, for the sole purpose of making acquisition decisions; and

(h)   in addition, a Party may provide additional exceptions or limitations for non-infringing uses of a particular class of works, performances, or phonograms, when an actual or likely adverse impact on those non-infringing uses is demonstrated by substantial evidence in a legislative, regulatory, or administrative proceeding in accordance with the Party's law.

5.   The exceptions and limitations to measures implementing paragraph 1 for the activities set forth in paragraph 4 may only be applied as follows, and only to the extent that they do not impair the adequacy of legal protection or the effectiveness of legal remedies against the circumvention of effective technological measures under the Party's legal system:

(a)   measures implementing paragraph (1)(a) may be subject to exceptions and limitations with respect to each activity set forth in paragraph (4);

(b)   measures implementing paragraph (1)(b), as they apply to effective technological measures that control access to a work, performance, or phonogram, may be subject to exceptions and limitations with respect to activities set forth in paragraphs (4)(a), (b), (c), (d), and (f); and

(c)   measures implementing paragraph (1)(b), as they apply to effective technological measures that protect any copyright or any rights related to copyright, may be subject to exceptions and limitations with respect to activities set forth in paragraphs (4)(a) and (f).

6.   **Effective technological measure** means a technology, device, or component that, in the normal course of its operation, controls access to a protected work, performance, or phonogram, or protects copyright or rights related to copyright.[70]

Article 20.68:   Rights Management Information[71]

1.   In order to provide adequate and effective legal remedies to protect rights management information (RMI), each Party shall provide that any person that, without authority, and knowing, or having reasonable grounds to know, that it would induce, enable, facilitate, or conceal an infringement of the copyright or related right of authors, performers, or producers of phonograms, knowingly:[72]

(a)   removes or alters any RMI;

(b)   distributes or imports for distribution RMI knowing that the RMI has been altered without authority;[73] or

(c)   distributes, imports for distribution, broadcasts, communicates, or makes available to the public copies of works, performances, or phonograms, knowing that RMI has been removed or altered without authority, is liable and subject to the remedies set out in Article 20.82 (Civil and Administrative Procedures and Remedies).

2.   Each Party shall provide for criminal procedures and penalties to be applied if a person is found to have engaged willfully and for purposes of commercial advantage or financial gain in any of the activities referred to in paragraph 1.

---

[70]   For greater certainty, a technological measure that can, in a usual case, be circumvented accidentally is not an "effective" technological measure.

[71]   A Party may comply with the obligations in this Article by providing legal protection only to electronic rights management information.

[72]   For greater certainty, a Party may extend the protection afforded by this paragraph to circumstances in which a person engages without knowledge in the acts in subparagraphs (a), (b), and (c), and to other related right holders.

[73]   A Party may meet its obligation under this subparagraph if it provides effective protection for original compilations, provided that the acts described in this subparagraph are treated as infringements of copyright in those original compilations.

3.   A Party may provide that the criminal procedures and penalties do not apply to a non-profit library, museum, archive, educational institution or public non-commercial broadcasting entity.[74]

4.   For greater certainty, nothing prevents a Party from excluding from a measure that implements paragraphs 1 through 3 a lawfully authorized activity that is carried out for the purpose of law enforcement, essential security interests, or other related governmental purposes, such as the performance of a statutory function.

5.   For greater certainty, nothing in this Article obligates a Party to require a right holder in a work, performance, or phonogram to attach RMI to copies of the work, performance, or phonogram, or to cause RMI to appear in connection with a communication of the work, performance, or phonogram to the public.

6.   **RMI** means:

   (a)   information that identifies a work, performance, or phonogram, the author of the work, the performer of the performance, or the producer of the phonogram; or the owner of a right in the work, performance, or phonogram;

   (b)   information about the terms and conditions of the use of the work, performance, or phonogram; or

   (c)   any numbers or codes that represent the information referred to in subparagraphs (a) and (b),

if any of these items is attached to a copy of the work, performance, or phonogram or appears in connection with the communication or making available of a work, performance, or phonogram to the public.

Article 20.69:   Collective Management

The Parties recognize the important role of collective management societies for copyright and related rights in collecting and distributing royalties[75] based on practices that are fair, efficient, transparent, and accountable, which may include appropriate record keeping and reporting mechanisms.

Section I: Trade Secrets[76,77]

Article 20.70:   Protection of Trade Secrets

In the course of ensuring effective protection against unfair competition as provided in Article 10bis of the Paris Convention, each Party shall ensure that persons have the legal means to prevent trade secrets lawfully in their control from being disclosed to, acquired by, or used by others (including state-owned enterprises) without their consent in a manner contrary to honest commercial practices.

Article 20.71:   Civil Protection and Enforcement

In fulfilling its obligation under paragraphs 1 and 2 of Article 39 of the TRIPS Agreement, each Party shall:

---

[74]   For greater certainty, a Party may treat a broadcasting entity established without a profit-making purpose under its law as a public non-commercial broadcasting entity.

[75]   For greater certainty, royalties may include equitable remuneration.

[76]   For greater certainty, the enforcement obligations and principles set forth in Section J also apply to the obligations in this section, as relevant.

[77]   For greater certainty, this Section is without prejudice to a Party's measures protecting good faith lawful disclosures to provide evidence of a violation of that Party's law.

(a)   provide civil judicial procedures[78] for any person lawfully in control of a trade secret to prevent, and obtain redress for, the misappropriation of the trade secret by any other person; and

(b)   not limit the duration of protection for a trade secret, so long as the conditions in Article 20.73 (Definitions) exist.

Article 20.72: Criminal Enforcement

1.   Subject to paragraph 2, each Party shall provide for criminal procedures and penalties for the unauthorized and willful misappropriation[79] of a trade secret.

2.   With respect to the acts referred to in paragraph 1, a Party may, as appropriate, limit the availability of its procedures, or limit the level of penalties available, to one or more of the following cases in which the act is:

(a)   for the purposes of commercial advantage or financial gain;

(b)   related to a product or service in national or international commerce; or

(c)   intended to injure the owner of that trade secret.

Article 20.73: Definitions

For the purposes of this Section:

trade secret means information that:

(a)   is secret in the sense that it is not, as a body or in the precise configuration and assembly of its components, generally known among or readily accessible to persons within the circles that normally deal with the kind of information in question;

(b)   has actual or potential commercial value because it is secret; and

(c)   has been subject to reasonable steps under the circumstances, by the person lawfully in control of the information, to keep it secret;

misappropriation means the acquisition, use, or disclosure of a trade secret in a manner contrary to honest commercial practices, including the acquisition, use, or disclosure of a trade secret by a third party that knew, or had reason to know, that the trade secret was acquired in a manner contrary to honest commercial practices.[80] Misappropriation does not include situations in which a person:

(a)   reverse engineered an item lawfully obtained;

(b)   independently discovered information claimed as a trade secret; or

(c)   acquired the subject information from another person in a legitimate manner without an obligation of confidentiality or knowledge that the information was a trade secret; and

manner contrary to honest commercial practices means at least practices such as breach of contract, breach of confidence, and inducement to breach, and includes the acquisition of undisclosed information by third parties that knew, or were grossly negligent in failing to know, that those practices were involved in the acquisition.

---

[78] For greater certainty, civil judicial procedures do not have to be federal provided that those procedures are available.

[79] For the purposes of this Article, "willful misappropriation" requires a person to have known that the trade secret was acquired in a manner contrary to honest commercial practices.

[80] For greater certainty, "misappropriation" as defined in this paragraph includes cases in which the acquisition, use, or disclosure involves a computer system.

Article 20.74: Provisional Measures

In the civil judicial proceedings described in Article 20.71 (Civil Protection and Enforcement), each Party shall provide that its judicial authorities have the authority to order prompt and effective provisional measures, such as orders to prevent the misappropriation of the trade secret and to preserve relevant evidence.

Article 20.75: Confidentiality

In connection with the civil judicial proceedings described in Article 20.71 (Civil Protection and Enforcement), each Party shall provide that its civil judicial authorities have the authority to:

(a) order specific procedures to protect the confidentiality of any trade secret, alleged trade secret, or any other information asserted by an interested party to be confidential; and

(b) impose sanctions on parties, counsel, expert, or other person subject to those proceedings, related to violation of orders concerning the protection of a trade secret or alleged trade secret produced or exchanged in that proceeding, as well as other information asserted by an interested party to be confidential.

Each Party shall further provide in its law that, in cases in which an interested party asserts information to be a trade secret, its judicial authorities shall not disclose that information without first providing that person with an opportunity to make a submission under seal that describes the interest of that person in keeping the information confidential.

Article 20.76: Civil Remedies

In connection with the civil judicial proceedings described in Article 20.71 (Civil Protection and Enforcement), each Party shall provide that its judicial authorities have the authority at least to order:

(a) injunctive relief that conforms to Article 44 of the TRIPS Agreement against a person that misappropriated a trade secret; and

(b) a person that misappropriated a trade secret to pay damages adequate to compensate the person lawfully in control of the trade secret for the injury suffered because of the misappropriation of the trade secret[81] and, if appropriate, because of the proceedings to enforce the trade secret.

Article 20.77: Licensing and Transfer of Trade Secrets

No Party shall discourage or impede the voluntary licensing of trade secrets by imposing excessive or discriminatory conditions on those licenses or conditions that dilute the value of the trade secrets.

Article 20.78: Prohibition of Unauthorized Disclosure or Use of a Trade Secret by Government Officials Outside the Scope of Their Official Duties

1. In civil, criminal, and regulatory proceedings in which trade secrets may be submitted to a court or government entity, each Party shall prohibit the unauthorized disclosure of a trade secret by a government official at the central level of government outside the scope of that person's official duties.

2. Each Party shall provide for in its law deterrent level penalties, including monetary fines, suspension or termination of employment, and imprisonment, to guard against the unauthorized disclosure of a trade secret described in paragraph 1.

---

[81] For greater certainty, a Party may provide that the determination of damages is carried out after the determination of misappropriation.

Section J: Enforcement

Article 20.79: General Obligations

1.   Each Party shall ensure that enforcement procedures as specified in this Section are available under its law so as to permit effective action against an act of infringement of intellectual property rights covered by this Chapter, including expeditious remedies to prevent infringements and remedies that constitute a deterrent to future infringements.[82] These procedures shall be applied in such a manner as to avoid the creation of barriers to legitimate trade and to provide for safeguards against their abuse.

2.   Each Party confirms that the enforcement procedures set forth in Article 20.82 (Civil and Administrative Procedures and Remedies), Article 20.83 (Provisional Measures), and Article

20.85 (Criminal Procedures and Penalties) shall be available to the same extent with respect to acts of trademark infringement, as well as copyright or related rights infringement, in the digital environment.

3.   Each Party shall ensure that its procedures concerning the enforcement of intellectual property rights are fair and equitable. These procedures shall not be unnecessarily complicated or costly, or entail unreasonable time-limits or unwarranted delays.

4.   This Section does not create any obligation:

   (a)   to put in place a judicial system for the enforcement of intellectual property rights distinct from that for the enforcement of law in general, nor does it affect the capacity of each Party to enforce its law in general; or

   (b)   with respect to the distribution of resources as between the enforcement of intellectual property rights and the enforcement of law in general.

5.   In implementing this Section in its intellectual property system, each Party shall take into account the need for proportionality between the seriousness of the infringement of the intellectual property right and the applicable remedies and penalties, as well as the interests of third parties.

Article 20.80: Presumptions

1.   In civil, criminal, and, if applicable, administrative proceedings involving copyright or related rights, each Party shall provide for a presumption[83] that, in the absence of proof to the contrary:

   (a)   the person whose name is indicated in the usual manner[84] as the author, performer, or producer of the work, performance, or phonogram, or if applicable the publisher, is the designated right holder in that work, performance, or phonogram; and

   (b)   the copyright or related right subsists in that subject matter.

2.   In connection with the commencement of a civil, administrative, or criminal enforcement proceeding involving a registered trademark that has been substantively examined by its competent authority, each Party shall provide that the trademark be considered *prima facie* valid.

3.   In connection with the commencement of a civil or administrative enforcement proceeding involving a patent that has been substantively examined and granted by the competent authority of a

---

[82]   For greater certainty, and subject to Article 44 of the TRIPS Agreement and this Agreement, each Party confirms that it makes those remedies available with respect to enterprises, regardless of whether the enterprises are private or state-owned.

[83]   For greater certainty, a Party may implement this Article on the basis of sworn statements or documents having evidentiary value, such as statutory declarations. A Party may also provide that these presumptions are rebuttable presumptions that may be rebutted by evidence to the contrary.

[84]   For greater certainty, a Party may establish the means by which it shall determine what constitutes the "usual manner" for a particular physical support.

Party, that Party shall provide that each claim in the patent be considered *prima facie* to satisfy the applicable criteria of patentability in its territory.[85, 86]

Article 20.81: Enforcement Practices with Respect to Intellectual Property Rights

1.   Each Party shall provide that final judicial decisions and administrative rulings of general application pertaining to the enforcement of intellectual property rights:

   (a)   are in writing and preferably state any relevant findings of fact and the reasoning or the legal basis on which the decisions and rulings are based; and

   (b)   are published[87] or, if publication is not practicable, otherwise made available to the public in a national language in such a manner as to enable interested persons and Parties to become acquainted with them.

2.   Each Party recognizes the importance of collecting and analyzing statistical data and other relevant information concerning infringements of intellectual property rights as well as collecting information on best practices to prevent and combat infringements.

3.   Each Party shall publish or otherwise make available to the public information on its efforts to provide effective enforcement of intellectual property rights in its civil, administrative, and criminal systems, such as statistical information that the Party may collect for those purposes.

Article 20.82: Civil and Administrative Procedures and Remedies

1.   Each Party shall make available to right holders civil judicial procedures concerning the enforcement of any intellectual property right covered in this Chapter.[88]

2.   Each Party shall provide that its judicial authorities have the authority to order injunctive relief that conforms to Article 44 of the TRIPS Agreement, including to prevent goods that involve the infringement of an intellectual property right under the law of the Party providing that relief from entering into the channels of commerce.

3.   Each Party shall provide[89] that, in civil judicial proceedings, its judicial authorities have the authority at least to order the infringer to pay the right holder damages adequate to compensate for the injury the right holder has suffered because of an infringement of that person's intellectual property right by an infringer who knowingly, or with reasonable grounds to know, engaged in infringing activity.

4.   In determining the amount of damages under paragraph 3, each Party's judicial authorities shall have the authority to consider, among other things, any legitimate measure of value the right holder

---

[85]   For greater certainty, if a Party provides its administrative authorities with the exclusive authority to determine the validity of a registered trademark or patent, nothing in paragraphs 2 and 3 shall prevent that Party's competent authority from suspending enforcement procedures until the validity of the registered trademark or patent is determined by the administrative authority. In those validity procedures, the party challenging the validity of the registered trademark or patent shall be required to prove that the registered trademark or patent is not valid. Notwithstanding this requirement, a Party may require the trademark holder to provide evidence of first use.

[86]   A Party may provide that this paragraph applies only to those patents that have been applied for, examined, and granted after the entry into force of this Agreement.

[87]   For greater certainty, a Party may satisfy the requirement for publication by making the decision or ruling available to the public online.

[88]   For the purposes of this Article, the term "right holders" includes those authorized licensees, federations, and associations that have the legal standing and authority to assert those rights. The term "authorized licensee" includes the exclusive licensee of any one or more of the exclusive intellectual property rights encompassed in a given intellectual property.

[89]   A Party may also provide that the right holder may not be entitled to any of the remedies set out in paragraphs 3, 5, and 7 if there is a finding of non-use of a trademark. For greater certainty, there is no obligation for a Party to provide for the possibility of any of the remedies in paragraphs 3, 5, 6, and 7 to be ordered in parallel.

submits, which may include lost profits, the value of the infringed goods or services measured by the market price, or the suggested retail price.

5.   At least in cases of copyright or related rights infringement and trademark counterfeiting, each Party shall provide that, in civil judicial proceedings, its judicial authorities have the authority to order the infringer, at least in cases described in paragraph 3, to pay the right holder the infringer's profits that are attributable to the infringement.[90]

6.   In civil judicial proceedings with respect to the infringement of copyright or related rights protecting works, phonograms, or performances, each Party shall establish or maintain a system that provides for one or more of the following:

(a)   pre-established damages, which shall be available on the election of the right holder; or

(b)   additional damages.[91]

7.   In civil judicial proceedings with respect to trademark counterfeiting, each Party shall also establish or maintain a system that provides for one or more of the following:

(a)   pre-established damages, which shall be available on the election of the right holder; or

(b)   additional damages.[92]

8.   Pre-established damages referred to in paragraphs 6 and 7 shall be in an amount sufficient to constitute a deterrent to future infringements and to compensate fully the right holder for the harm caused by the infringement.

9.   In awarding additional damages referred to in paragraphs 6 and 7, judicial authorities shall have the authority to award those additional damages as they consider appropriate, having regard to all relevant matters, including the nature of the infringing conduct and the need to deter similar infringements in the future.

10.   Each Party shall provide that its judicial authorities, if appropriate, have the authority to order, at the conclusion of civil judicial proceedings concerning infringement of at least copyright or related rights, patents, and trademarks, that the prevailing party be awarded payment by the losing party of court costs or fees and appropriate attorney's fees, or any other expenses as provided for under the Party's law.

11.   If a Party's judicial or other authorities appoint a technical or other expert in a civil proceeding concerning the enforcement of an intellectual property right and require that the parties in the proceeding pay the costs of that expert, that Party should seek to ensure that those costs are reasonable and related appropriately, among other things, to the quantity and nature of work to be performed and do not unreasonably deter recourse to those proceedings.

12.   Each Party shall provide that in civil judicial proceedings:

(a)   at least with respect to pirated copyright goods and counterfeit trademark goods, its judicial authorities have the authority, at the right holder's request, to order that the infringing goods be destroyed, except in exceptional circumstances, without compensation of any sort;

(b)   its judicial authorities have the authority to order that materials and implements that have been used in the manufacture or creation of the infringing goods be, without compensation of any sort, promptly destroyed or, in exceptional circumstances, without compensation of any sort, disposed of outside the channels of commerce in such a manner as to minimize the risk of further infringement; and

---

[90] A Party may comply with this paragraph by presuming those profits to be the damages referred to in paragraph 3.

[91] For greater certainty, additional damages may include exemplary or punitive damages.

[92] For greater certainty, additional damages may include exemplary or punitive damages.

(c)   in regard to counterfeit trademark goods, the simple removal of the trademark unlawfully affixed is not sufficient, other than in exceptional circumstances, to permit the release of goods into the channels of commerce.

13.   Without prejudice to its law governing privilege, the protection of confidentiality of information sources, or the processing of personal data, each Party shall provide that, in civil judicial proceedings concerning the enforcement of an intellectual property right, its judicial authorities have the authority, on a justified request of the right holder, to order the infringer or the alleged infringer, as applicable, to provide to the right holder or to the judicial authorities, at least for the purpose of collecting evidence, relevant information as provided for in its applicable laws and regulations that the infringer or alleged infringer possesses or controls. This information may include information regarding any person involved in any aspect of the infringement or alleged infringement and the means of production or the channels of distribution of the infringing or allegedly infringing goods or services, including the identification of third persons alleged to be involved in the production and distribution of the goods or services and of their channels of distribution.

14.   In cases in which a party in a proceeding voluntarily and without good reason refuses access to, or otherwise does not provide relevant evidence under its control within a reasonable period, or significantly impedes a proceeding relating to an enforcement action, each Party shall provide that its judicial authorities shall have the authority to make preliminary and final determinations, affirmative or negative, on the basis of the evidence presented, including the complaint or the allegation presented by the party adversely affected by the denial of access to evidence, subject to providing the parties an opportunity to be heard on the allegations or evidence.

15.   Each Party shall ensure that its judicial authorities have the authority to order a party at whose request measures were taken and that has abused enforcement procedures to provide to a party wrongfully enjoined or restrained adequate compensation for the injury suffered because of that abuse. The judicial authorities shall also have the authority to order the applicant to pay the defendant expenses, which may include appropriate attorney's fees.

16.   Each Party shall provide that in relation to a civil judicial proceeding concerning the enforcement of an intellectual property right, its judicial or other authorities have the authority to impose sanctions on a party, counsel, expert, or other person subject to the court's jurisdiction for violation of judicial orders concerning the protection of confidential information produced or exchanged in that proceeding.

17.   To the extent that a civil remedy can be ordered as a result of administrative procedures on the merits of a case, each Party shall provide that those procedures conform to principles equivalent in substance to those set out in this Article.

18.   In civil judicial proceedings concerning the acts described in Article 20.67 (Technological Protection Measures) and Article 20.68 (Rights Management Information):

(a)   each Party shall provide that its judicial authorities have the authority at least to:[93]

   (i)   impose provisional measures, including seizure or other taking into custody of devices and products suspected of being involved in the prohibited activity,

   (ii)   order the type of damages available for copyright infringement, as provided under its law in accordance with this Article,

   (iii)   order court costs, fees or expenses as provided for under paragraph 10, and

   (iv)   order the destruction of devices and products found to be involved in the prohibited activity; and

(b)   a Party may provid4e that damages are not available against a non-profit library, museum, archive, educational institution, or public non-commercial broadcasting entity, if it sustains

---

[93]   For greater certainty, a Party may, but is not required to, put in place separate remedies in respect of Article 20.67 (Technological Protection Measures) and 20.68 (Rights Management Information), if those remedies are available under its copyright law.

the burden of proving that it was not aware or had no reason to believe that its acts constituted a prohibited activity.

Article 20.83:   Provisional Measures

1.   Each Party's authorities shall act on a request for relief in respect of an intellectual property right *inaudita altera parte* expeditiously in accordance with that Party's judicial rules.

2.   Each Party shall provide that its judicial authorities have the authority to require the applicant for a provisional measure in respect of an intellectual property right to provide any reasonably available evidence in order to satisfy the judicial authority, with a sufficient degree of certainty, that the applicant's right is being infringed or that the infringement is imminent, and to order the applicant to provide security or equivalent assurance set at a level sufficient to protect the defendant and to prevent abuse. That security or equivalent assurance shall not unreasonably deter recourse to those procedures.

3.   In civil judicial proceedings concerning copyright or related rights infringement and trademark counterfeiting, each Party shall provide that its judicial authorities have the authority to order the seizure or other taking into custody of suspected infringing goods, materials, and implements relevant to the infringement, and, at least for trademark counterfeiting, documentary evidence relevant to the infringement.

Article 20.84:   Special Requirements Related to Border Measures

1.   Each Party shall provide for applications to suspend the release of, or to detain, suspected counterfeit or confusingly similar trademark or pirated copyright goods that are imported into the territory of the Party.[94]

2.   Each Party shall provide that a right holder, submitting an application referred to in paragraph 1, to initiate procedures for the Party's competent authorities[95] to suspend release into free circulation of, or to detain, suspected counterfeit or confusingly similar trademark or pirated copyright goods, is required to:

  (a)   provide adequate evidence to satisfy the competent authorities that, under the law of the Party providing the procedures, there is *prima facie* an infringement of the right holder's intellectual property right; and

  (b)   supply sufficient information that may reasonably be expected to be within the right holder's knowledge to make the suspect goods reasonably recognizable by its competent authorities.

The requirement to provide that information shall not unreasonably deter recourse to these procedures.

3.   Each Party shall provide that its competent authorities have the authority to require a right holder submitting an application referred to in paragraph 1 to provide a reasonable security or equivalent assurance sufficient to protect the defendant and the competent authorities, and to prevent abuse. Each Party shall provide that such security or equivalent assurance does not unreasonably deter recourse to these procedures. A Party may provide that the security may be in the form of a bond

---

[94] For the purposes of this Article:

(a)   "counterfeit trademark goods" means goods, including packaging, bearing without authorization a trademark that is identical to the trademark validly registered in respect of those goods, or that cannot be distinguished in its essential aspects from such a trademark, and that thereby infringes the rights of the owner of the trademark in question under the law of the Party providing the procedures under this Section; and

(b)   "pirated copyright goods" means goods that are copies made without the consent of the right holder or person duly authorized by the right holder in the country of production and that are made directly or indirectly from an article when the making of that copy would have constituted an infringement of a copyright or a related right under the law of the Party providing the procedures under this Section.

[95] For the purposes of this Article, unless otherwise specified, competent authorities may include the appropriate judicial, administrative, or law enforcement authorities under a Party's law.

conditioned to hold the defendant harmless from any loss or damage resulting from any suspension of the release of goods in the event the competent authorities determine that the article is not an infringing good.

4.   Without prejudice to a Party's law pertaining to privacy or the confidentiality of information:

(a)   if a Party's competent authorities have detained or suspended the release of goods that are suspected of being counterfeit trademark or pirated copyright goods, that Party may provide that its competent authorities have the authority to inform the right holder without undue delay of the names and addresses of the consignor, exporter, consignee, or importer; a description of the goods; the quantity of the goods; and, if known, the country of origin of the goods;[96] or

(b)   if a Party does not provide its competent authority with the authority referred to in subparagraph (a) when suspect goods are detained or suspended from release, it shall provide, at least in cases of imported goods, its competent authorities with the authority to provide the information specified in subparagraph (a) to the right holder normally within 30 working days of the seizure or determination that the goods are counterfeit trademark goods or pirated copyright goods.

5.   Each Party shall provide that its competent authorities may initiate border measures *ex officio* against suspected counterfeit trademark goods or pirated copyright goods under customs control[97] that are:

(a)   imported;

(b)   destined for export;

(c)   in transit;[98] and

(d)   admitted into or exiting from a free trade zone or a bonded warehouse.

6.   Nothing in this Article precludes a Party from exchanging, if appropriate and with a view to eliminating international trade in counterfeit trademarked goods or pirated copyrighted goods, available information to another Party in respect of goods that it has examined without a local consignee and that are transshipped through its territory and are destined for the territory of the other Party, to inform that other Party's efforts to identify suspect goods upon arrival in its territory.

7.   Each Party shall adopt or maintain a procedure by which its competent authorities may determine within a reasonable period of time after the initiation of the procedures described in paragraphs 1 and 5, whether the suspect goods infringe an intellectual property right. If a Party provides administrative procedures for the determination of an infringement, it may also provide its authorities with the authority to impose administrative penalties or sanctions, which may include fines or the seizure of the infringing goods following a determination that the goods are infringing.

8.   Each Party shall provide that its competent authorities have the authority to order the destruction of goods following a determination that the goods are infringing. In cases in which the goods are not destroyed, each Party shall ensure that, except in exceptional circumstances, the goods are disposed of outside the channels of commerce in such a manner as to avoid harm to the right holder. In regard to counterfeit trademark goods, the simple removal of the trademark unlawfully affixed shall not be sufficient, other than in exceptional cases, to permit the release of the goods into the channels of commerce.

---

[96]   For greater certainty, a Party may establish reasonable procedures to receive or access that information.

[97]   For the purposes of this Article, "goods under customs control" means goods that are subject to a Party's customs procedures.

[98]   For the purposes of this Article, an "in-transit" good means a good that is under "Customs transit" or "transshipped," as defined in the *International Convention on the Simplification and Harmonization of Customs Procedures* (as amended), done at Kyoto on May 18, 1973, as amended at Brussels on June 26, 1999.

9.   If a Party establishes or assesses, in connection with the procedures described in this Article, an application fee, storage fee, or destruction fee, that Party shall not set the fee at an amount that unreasonably deters recourse to these procedures.

10.   This Article applies to goods of a commercial nature sent in small consignments. A Party may exclude from the application of this Article small quantities of goods of a non-commercial nature contained in travelers' personal luggage.[99]

Article 20.85:   Criminal Procedures and Penalties

1.   Each Party shall provide for criminal procedures and penalties to be applied at least in cases of willful trademark counterfeiting or copyright or related rights piracy on a commercial scale. In respect of willful copyright or related rights piracy, "on a commercial scale" includes:

   (a)   acts carried out for commercial advantage or financial gain; and

   (b)   significant acts, not carried out for commercial advantage or financial gain, that have a substantial prejudicial impact on the interests of the copyright or related rights holder in relation to the marketplace.[100],[101]

2.   Each Party shall treat willful importation or exportation of counterfeit trademark goods or pirated copyright goods on a commercial scale as unlawful activities subject to criminal penalties.[102]

3.   Each Party shall provide for criminal procedures and penalties to be applied in cases of willful importation[103] and domestic use, in the course of trade and on a commercial scale, of a label or packaging:

   (a)   to which a trademark has been applied without authorization that is identical to, or cannot be distinguished from, a trademark registered in its territory; and

   (b)   that is intended to be used in the course of trade on goods or in relation to services that are identical to goods or services for which that trademark is registered.

4.   Each Party shall provide for criminal procedures to be applied against a person who, willfully and without the authorization of the holder[104] of copyright or related rights in a cinematographic work, knowingly uses or attempts to use an audiovisual recording device to transmit or make a copy of the cinematographic work or any part thereof, from a performance of the motion picture or other audiovisual work in a movie theater or other venue that is being used primarily for the exhibition of a copyrighted motion picture. In addition to the criminal procedures, a Party may provide for administrative enforcement procedures.

---

[99] For greater certainty, a Party may also exclude from the application of this Article small quantities of goods of a non-commercial nature sent in small consignments.

[100] The Parties understand that a Party may comply with subparagraph (b) by addressing those significant acts under its criminal procedures and penalties for non-authorized uses of protected works, performances and phonograms in its law.

[101] A Party may provide that the volume and value of any infringing items may be taken into account in determining whether the act has a substantial prejudicial impact on the interests of the copyright or related rights holder in relation to the marketplace.

[102] The Parties understand that a Party may comply with its obligation under this paragraph by providing that distribution or sale of counterfeit trademark goods or pirated copyright goods on a commercial scale is an unlawful activity subject to criminal penalties. The Parties understand that criminal procedures and penalties as specified in paragraphs 1, 2, and 3 are applicable in any free trade zones in a Party.

[103] A Party may comply with its obligation relating to importation of labels or packaging through its measures concerning distribution.

[104] For greater certainty, the theater or venue owner or operator shall be entitled to contact the criminal law enforcement authorities with respect to the suspected commission of the acts referred to in this provision. For greater certainty, nothing in this paragraph expands or diminishes the existing rights and obligations of a theater or venue owner or operator with respect to the cinematographic work.

5.   With respect to the offenses for which this Article requires a Party to provide for criminal procedures and penalties, each Party shall ensure that criminal liability for aiding and abetting is available under its law.

6.   With respect to the offenses described in paragraphs 1 through 5, each Party shall provide:

(a)   penalties that include sentences of imprisonment as well as monetary fines sufficiently high to provide a deterrent to future acts of infringement, consistent with the level of penalties applied for crimes of a corresponding gravity;[105]

(b)   that its judicial authorities have the authority, in determining penalties, to account for the seriousness of the circumstances, which may include circumstances that involve threats to, or effects on, health or safety;[106]

(c)   that its judicial or other competent authorities have the authority to order the seizure of suspected counterfeit trademark goods or pirated copyright goods, any related materials and implements used in the commission of the alleged offense, documentary evidence relevant to the alleged offense, and assets derived from, or obtained through the alleged infringing activity. If a Party requires identification of items subject to seizure as a prerequisite for issuing a judicial order referred to in this subparagraph, that Party shall not require the items to be described in greater detail than necessary to identify them for the purpose of seizure;

(d)   that its judicial authorities have the authority to order the forfeiture, at least for serious offenses, of any assets derived from or obtained through the infringing activity;

(e)   that its judicial authorities have the authority to order the forfeiture or destruction of:

(i)   all counterfeit trademark goods or pirated copyright goods,

(ii)   materials and implements that have been predominantly used in the creation of pirated copyright goods or counterfeit trademark goods, and

(iii)   any other labels or packaging to which a counterfeit trademark has been applied and that have been used in the commission of the offense,

In cases in which counterfeit trademark goods and pirated copyright goods are not destroyed, the judicial or other competent authorities shall ensure that, except in exceptional circumstances, those goods are disposed of outside the channels of commerce in such a manner as to avoid causing any harm to the right holder. Each Party shall further provide that forfeiture or destruction under this subparagraph and subparagraph (d) occur without compensation of any kind to the defendant;

(f)   that its judicial or other competent authorities have the authority to release or, in the alternative, provide access to, goods, material, implements, and other evidence held by the relevant authority to a right holder for civil[107] infringement proceedings; and

(g)   that its competent authorities may act upon their own initiative to initiate legal action without the need for a formal complaint by a third person or right holder.

7.   With respect to the offenses described in paragraphs 1 through 5, a Party may provide that its judicial authorities have the authority to order the seizure or forfeiture of assets, or alternatively, a fine, the value of which corresponds to the assets derived from, or obtained directly or indirectly through, the infringing activity.

---

[105] The Parties understand that there is no obligation for a Party to provide for the possibility of imprisonment and monetary fines to be imposed in parallel.

[106] A Party may also account for those circumstances through a separate criminal offense.

[107] A Party may also provide this authority in connection with administrative infringement proceedings.

Article 20.86: Protection of Encrypted Program-Carrying Satellite and Cable Signals

1.   Each Party shall make it a criminal offense to:

  (a) manufacture, assemble,[108] modify, import, export,[109] sell, or otherwise distribute a tangible or intangible device or system knowing or having reason to know[110] that the device or system meets at least one of the following conditions:

    (i)   it is intended to be used to assist, or

    (ii) it is primarily of assistance,

  in decoding an encrypted program-carrying satellite signal without the authorization of the lawful distributor[111] of that signal;[112] and

  (b) with respect to an encrypted program-carrying satellite signal, willfully:

    (i)   receive[113] that signal, or

    (ii) further distribute[114] that signal,

  knowing that it has been decoded without the authorization of the lawful distributor of the signal.

2.   Each Party shall provide for civil remedies for a person that holds an interest in an encrypted program-carrying satellite signal or its content and that is injured by an activity described in paragraph 1.

3.   Each Party shall provide for criminal penalties and civil[115] remedies for willfully:

  (a) manufacturing or distributing equipment knowing that the equipment is intended to be used in the unauthorized reception of any encrypted program-carrying cable signal; and

  (b) receiving, or assisting another to receive,[116] an encrypted program-carrying cable signal without authorization of the lawful distributor of the signal.

Article 20.87: Government Use of Software

1.   Each Party recognizes the importance of promoting the adoption of measures to enhance government awareness of respect for intellectual property rights and of the detrimental effects of the infringement of intellectual property rights.

---

[108] For greater certainty, a Party may treat "assemble" as incorporated in "manufacture."

[109] The obligation regarding export may be met by making it a criminal offense to possess and distribute a device or system described in this paragraph.

[110] For the purposes of this paragraph, a Party may provide that "having a reason to know" may be demonstrated through reasonable evidence, taking into account the facts and circumstances surrounding the alleged illegal act, as part of the Party's "knowledge" requirements. A Party may treat "having reason to know" as meaning "willful negligence".

[111] With regard to the criminal offenses and penalties in paragraphs 1 and 3, a Party may require a demonstration of intent to avoid payment to the lawful distributor, or a demonstration of intent to otherwise secure a pecuniary benefit to which the recipient is not entitled.

[112] For the purposes of this Article, a Party may provide that a "lawful distributor" means a person that has the lawful right in that Party's territory to distribute the encrypted program carrying signal and authorize its decoding.

[113] For greater certainty and for the purposes of paragraphs 1(b) and 3(b), a Party may provide that willful receipt of an encrypted program carrying satellite or cable signal means receipt and use of the signal, or means receipt and decoding of the signal.

[114] For greater certainty, a Party may interpret "further distribute" as "retransmit to the public".

[115] In providing for civil remedies, a Party may require a demonstration of injury.

[116] A Party may comply with its obligation in respect of "assisting another to receive" by providing for criminal penalties to be available against a person willfully publishing any information in order to enable or assist another person to receive a signal without authorization of the lawful distributor of the signal.

2.   Each Party shall adopt or maintain appropriate laws, regulations, policies, orders, government-issued guidelines, or administrative or executive decrees that provide that its central government agencies use only non-infringing computer software protected by copyright and related rights, and, if applicable, only use that computer software in a manner authorized by the relevant license. These measures apply to the acquisition and management of the software for government use.

Article 20.88:   Internet Service Providers

1.   For the purpose of Article 20.89 (Legal Remedies and Safe Harbors), an Internet Service Provider is:

    (a)   a provider of services for the transmission, routing, or providing of connections for digital online communications without modification of their content, between or among points specified by a user, of material of the user's choosing, undertaking the function in Article 20.89.2(a) (Legal Remedies and Safe Harbors); or

    (b)   a provider of online services undertaking the functions in Article 20.89.2(b), Article 20.89.2(c), or Article 20.89.2(d) (Legal Remedies and Safe Harbors).

2.   For the purposes of Article 20.89 (Legal Remedies and Safe Harbors), "copyright" includes related rights.

Article 20.89:   Legal Remedies and Safe Harbors[117]

1.   The Parties recognize the importance of facilitating the continued development of legitimate online services operating as intermediaries and, in a manner consistent with Article 41 of the TRIPS Agreement, providing enforcement procedures that permit effective and expeditious action by right holders against copyright infringement covered under this Chapter that occurs in the online environment. Accordingly, each Party shall ensure that legal remedies are available for right holders to address that copyright infringement and shall establish or maintain appropriate safe harbors in respect of online services that are Internet Service Providers. This framework of legal remedies and safe harbors shall include:

    (a)   legal incentives for Internet Service Providers to cooperate with copyright owners to deter the unauthorized storage and transmission of copyrighted materials or, in the alternative, to take other action to deter the unauthorized storage and transmission of copyrighted materials; and

    (b)   limitations in its law that have the effect of precluding monetary relief against Internet Service Providers for copyright infringements that they do not control, initiate or direct, and that take place through systems or networks controlled or operated by them or on their behalf.

2.   The limitations described in paragraph 1(b) shall include limitations in respect of the following functions:

    (a)   transmitting, routing, or providing connections for material without modification of its content or the intermediate and transient storage of that material done automatically in the course of such a technical process;[118]

    (b)   caching carried out through an automated process;

    (c)   storage, at the direction of a user, of material residing on a system or network controlled or operated by or for the Internet Service Provider; and

---

[117] Annex 20-A (Annex to Section J) applies to Articles 20.89.3, 20.89.4, and 20.89.6.

[118] The Parties understand that these limitations shall apply only where the Internet Service Provider does not initiate the chain of transmission of the materials, and does not select the material or its recipients.

    (d)   referring or linking users to an online location by using information location tools, including hyperlinks and directories.

3.   To facilitate effective action to address infringement, each Party shall prescribe in its law conditions for Internet Service Providers to qualify for the limitations described in paragraph 1(b), or, alternatively, shall provide for circumstances under which Internet Service Providers do not qualify for the limitations described in paragraph 1(b):[119]

    (a)   With respect to the functions referred to in paragraphs 2(c) and 2(d), these conditions shall include a requirement for Internet Service Providers to expeditiously remove or disable access to material residing on their networks or systems upon obtaining actual knowledge of the copyright infringement or becoming aware of facts or circumstances from which the infringement is apparent, such as through receiving a notice[120] of alleged infringement from the right holder or a person authorized to act on its behalf.

    (b)   An Internet Service Provider that removes or disables access to material in good faith under subparagraph (a) shall be exempt from any liability for having done so, provided that it takes reasonable steps in advance or promptly after to notify the person whose material is removed or disabled.[121]

4.   For the purposes of the functions referred to in paragraphs 2(c) and 2(d), each Party shall establish appropriate procedures in its laws or regulations for effective notices of claimed infringement, and effective counter-notices by those whose material is removed or disabled through mistake or misidentification. If material has been removed or access has been disabled in accordance with paragraph 3, that Party shall require that the Internet Service Provider restores the material that is the subject of a counter-notice, unless the person giving the original notice seeks relief through civil judicial proceedings within a reasonable period of time as set forth in that Party's laws or regulations.

5.   Each Party shall ensure that monetary remedies are available in its legal system against a person that makes a knowing material misrepresentation in a notice or counter-notice that causes injury to any interested party[122] as a result of an Internet Service Provider relying on the misrepresentation.

6.   Eligibility for the limitations in paragraph 1 shall be conditioned on the Internet Service Provider:

    (a)   adopting and reasonably implementing a policy that provides for termination in appropriate circumstances of the accounts of repeat infringers;

    (b)   accommodating and not interfering with standard technical measures accepted in the Party's territory that protect and identify copyrighted material, that are developed through an open, voluntary process by a broad consensus of copyright owners and service providers, that are available on reasonable and nondiscriminatory terms, and that do not impose

---

[119] The Parties understand that a Party that has yet to implement the obligations in paragraphs 3 and 4 will do so in a manner that is both effective and consistent with that Party's existing constitutional provisions. To that end, a Party may establish an appropriate role for the government that does not impair the timeliness of the process provided in paragraphs 3 and 4, and does not entail advance government review of each individual notice.

[120] For greater certainty, a notice of alleged infringement, as may be set out under a Party's law, must contain information that:

(a) is reasonably sufficient to enable the Internet Service Provider to identify the work, performance or phonogram claimed to be infringed, the alleged infringing material, and the online location of the alleged infringement; and

(b) has a sufficient indicia of reliability with respect to the authority of the person sending the notice.

[121] With respect to the function in paragraph 2(b), a Party may limit the requirements of paragraph 3 related to an Internet Service Provider removing or disabling access to material to circumstances in which the Internet Service Provider becomes aware or receives notification that the cached material has been removed or access to it has been disabled at the originating site.

[122] For greater certainty, the Parties understand that, "any interested party" may be limited to those with a legal interest recognized under that Party's law.

substantial costs on service providers or substantial burdens on their systems or networks; and

(c)   with respect to the functions identified in paragraphs 2(c) and 2(d), not receiving a financial benefit directly attributable to the infringing activity, in circumstances where it has the right and ability to control such activity.

7.   Eligibility for the limitations identified in paragraph 1 shall not be conditioned on the Internet Service Provider monitoring its service or affirmatively seeking facts indicating infringing activity, except to the extent consistent with the technical measures identified in paragraph 6(b).

8.   Each Party shall provide procedures, whether judicial or administrative, in accordance with its legal system, and consistent with principles of due process and privacy, that enable a copyright owner that has made a legally sufficient claim of copyright infringement to obtain expeditiously from an Internet Service Provider information in the provider's possession identifying the alleged infringer, in cases in which that information is sought for the purpose of protecting or enforcing that copyright.

9.   The Parties understand that the failure of an Internet Service Provider to qualify for the limitations in paragraph 1(b) does not itself result in liability. Further, this Article is without prejudice to the availability of other limitations and exceptions to copyright, or any other defenses under a Party's legal system.

10.   The Parties recognize the importance, in implementing their obligations under this Article, of taking into account the impact on the right holders and Internet Service Providers.

Section K: Final Provisions

Article 20.90: Final Provisions

1.   Except as otherwise provided in Article 20.10 (Application of Chapter to Existing Subject Matter and Prior Acts) and paragraphs 2 and 3, each Party shall implement the provisions of this Chapter on the date of entry into force of this Agreement.

2.   During the relevant periods set out below, a Party shall not amend an existing measure or adopt a new measure that is less consistent with its obligations under the Articles referred to below for that Party than relevant measures that are in effect on the date of signature of this Agreement.

3.   With regard to obligations subject to a transition period, Mexico shall fully implement its obligations under the provisions of this Chapter no later than the expiration of the relevant time period specified below, which begins on the date of entry into force of this Agreement:

(a)   Article 20.7 (International Agreements), UPOV 1991, four years;

(b)   Article 20.45 (Protection of Undisclosed Test or Other Data for Agricultural Chemical Products), five years;

(c)   Article 20.46 (Patent Term Adjustment for Unreasonable Curtailment), 4.5 years;

(d)   Article 20.48 (Protection of Undisclosed Test or Other Data), five years;

(e)   Article 20.49 (Biologics), five years;

(f)   Article 20.71 (Civil Protection and Enforcement), Article 20.74 (Provisional Measures) and Article 20.76 (Civil Remedies), five years; and

(g)   Articles 20.88 (Internet Service Providers) and 20.89 (Legal Remedies and Safe Harbors), three years.

4.   With regard to obligations subject to a transition period, Canada shall fully implement its obligations under the provisions of this Chapter no later than the expiration of the relevant time period specified below, which begins on the date of entry into force of this Agreement.

(a)   Article 20.7.2(f) (International Agreements), four years;

(b)   Article 20.44 (Patent Term Adjustment for Unreasonable Granting Authority Delays), 4.5 years;

(c)   Article 20.49 (Biologics), five years; and

(d)   Article 20.63(a) (Term of Protection for Copyright and Related Rights), 2.5 years.

ANNEX 20-A

ANNEX TO SECTION J

1.   In order to facilitate the enforcement of copyright online and to avoid unwarranted market disruption in the online environment, Articles 20.89.3, 20.89.4, and 20.89.6 (Legal Remedies and Safe Harbors) shall not apply to a Party provided that, as from the date of agreement in principle of this Agreement, the Party continues to:

(a)   prescribe in its law circumstances under which Internet Service Providers do not qualify for the limitations described in Article 20.89.1(b) (Legal Remedies and Safe Harbors);

(b)   provide statutory secondary liability for copyright infringement in cases in which a person, by means of the Internet or another digital network, provides a service primarily for the purpose of enabling acts of copyright infringement, in relation to factors set out in its law, such as:

   (i)   whether the person marketed or promoted the service as one that could be used to enable acts of copyright infringement;

   (ii)   whether the person had knowledge that the service was used to enable a significant number of acts of copyright infringement;

   (iii)   whether the service has significant uses other than to enable acts of copyright infringement;

   (iv)   the person's ability, as part of providing the service, to limit acts of copyright infringement, and any action taken by the person to do so;

   (v)   any benefits the person received as a result of enabling the acts of copyright infringement; and

   (vi)   the economic viability of the service if it were not used to enable acts of copyright infringement;

(c)   require Internet Service Providers carrying out the functions referred to in Article 20.89.2(a) and (c) (Legal Remedies and Safe Harbors) to participate in a system for forwarding notices of alleged infringement, including if material is made available online, and if the Internet Service Provider fails to do so, subjecting that provider to pre-established monetary damages for that failure;

(d)   induce Internet Service Providers offering information location tools to remove within a specified period of time any reproductions of material that they make, and communicate to the public, as part of offering the information location tool upon receiving a notice of alleged infringement and after the original material has been removed from the electronic location set out in the notice; and

(e)   induce Internet Service Providers carrying out the function referred to in Article 20.89.2(c) (Legal Remedies and Safe Harbors) to remove or disable access to material upon becoming aware of a decision of a court of that Party to the effect that the person storing the material infringes copyright in the material.

2.   For a Party to which Articles 20.89.3, 20.89.4, and 20.89.6 (Legal Remedies and Safe Harbors) do not apply pursuant to paragraph 1, and in light of, among other things, paragraph 1(b), for the

purposes of Article 20.89.1(a), legal incentives shall not mean the conditions for Internet Service Providers to qualify for the limitations provided for in Article 20.89.1(b), as set out in Article 20.89.3.

3.   Pursuant to paragraph 1, for a Party to which Articles 20.89.3, 20.89.4, and 20.89.6 (Legal Remedies and Safe Harbors) do not apply:

(a)   the term "modification" in paragraphs 20.88.1(a) and 20.89.2(a) does not include modifications made for solely technical reasons such as division into packets; and

(b)   with regard to paragraph 20.89.7, "except to the extent consistent with the technical measures identified in paragraph 6(b)" does not apply.

E. AGREEMENT ON TRADE-RELATED ASPECTS OF INTELLECTUAL PROPERTY RIGHTS, INCLUDING TRADE IN COUNTERFEIT GOODS (TRIPS)

Table of Contents

AGREEMENT ON TRADE-RELATED ASPECTS OF INTELLECTUAL PROPERTY RIGHTS, INCLUDING TRADE IN COUNTERFEIT GOODS

Members,

Desiring to reduce distortions and impediments to international trade, and taking into account the need to promote effective and adequate protection of intellectual property rights, and to ensure that measures and procedures to enforce intellectual property rights do not themselves become barriers to legitimate trade;

Recognizing, to this end, the need for new rules and disciplines concerning:

   (a)   the applicability of the basic principles of the GATT 1994 and of relevant international intellectual property agreements or conventions;

   (b)   the provision of adequate standards and principles concerning the availability, scope and use of trade-related intellectual property rights;

   (c)   the provision of effective and appropriate means for the enforcement of trade-related intellectual property rights, taking into account differences in national legal systems;

   (d)   the provision of effective and expeditious procedures for the multilateral prevention and settlement of disputes between governments; and

   (e)   transitional arrangements aiming at the fullest participation in the results of the negotiations;

Recognizing the need for a multilateral framework of principles, rules and disciplines dealing with international trade in counterfeit goods;

Recognizing that intellectual property rights are private rights;

Recognizing the underlying public policy objectives of national systems for the protection of intellectual property, including developmental and technological objectives;

Recognizing also the special needs of the least-developed country Members in respect of maximum flexibility in the domestic implementation of laws and regulations in order to enable them to create a sound and viable technological base;

Emphasizing the importance of reducing tensions by reaching strengthened commitments to resolve disputes on trade-related intellectual property issues through multilateral procedures;

Desiring to establish a mutually supportive relationship between the WTO and the World Intellectual Property Organization (referred to in this Agreement as "WIPO") as well as other relevant international organizations;

Hereby agree as follows:

PART I.   GENERAL PROVISIONS AND BASIC PRINCIPLES

Article 1

Nature and Scope of Obligations

1.   Members shall give effect to the provisions of this Agreement. Members may, but shall not be obliged to, implement in their law more extensive protection than is required by this Agreement, provided that such protection does not contravene the provisions of this Agreement. Members shall be free to determine the appropriate method of implementing the provisions of this Agreement within their own legal system and practice.

2.   For the purposes of this Agreement, the term "intellectual property" refers to all categories of intellectual property that are the subject of Sections 1 to 7 of Part II.

3.   Members shall accord the treatment provided for in this Agreement to the nationals of other Members.[1] In respect of the relevant intellectual property right, the nationals of other Members shall be understood as those natural or legal persons that would meet the criteria for eligibility for protection provided for in the Paris Convention (1967), the Berne Convention (1971), the Rome Convention and the Treaty on Intellectual Property in Respect of Integrated Circuits, were all Members of the WTO members of those Conventions.[2] Any Member availing itself of the possibilities provided in paragraph 3 of Article 5 or paragraph 2 of Article 6 of the Rome Convention shall make a notification as foreseen in those provisions to the Council for Trade-Related Aspects of Intellectual Property Rights (the "Council for TRIPS").

---

[1]   When "nationals" are referred to in this Agreement, they shall be deemed, in the case of a separate customs territory Member of the WTO, to mean persons, natural or legal, who are domiciled or who have a real and effective industrial or commercial establishment in that customs territory.

[2]   In this Agreement, "Paris Convention" refers to the Paris Convention for the Protection of Industrial Property: "Paris Convention (1967)" refers to the Stockholm Act of this Convention of 14 July 1967. "Berne Convention" refers to the Berne Convention for the Protection of Literary and Artistic Works: "Berne Convention (1971)" refers to the Paris Act of this Convention of 24 July 1971. "Rome Convention" refers to the International Convention for the Protection of Performers, Producers of Phonograms and Broadcasting Organisations, adopted at Rome on 26 October 1961. "Treaty on Intellectual Property in Respect of Integrated Circuits" (IPIC Treaty) refers to the Treaty on Intellectual Property in Respect of Integrated Circuits, adopted at Washington on 26 May 1989. "WTO Agreement" refers to Agreement Establishing the WTO.

Article 2

Intellectual Property Conventions

1.   In respect of Parts II, III and IV of this Agreement, Members shall comply with Articles 1 through 12 and 19, of the Paris Convention (1967).

2.   Nothing in Parts I to IV of this Agreement shall derogate from existing obligations that Members may have to each other under the Paris Convention, the Berne Convention, the Rome Convention and the Treaty on Intellectual Property in Respect of Integrated Circuits.

Article 3

National Treatment

1.   Each Member shall accord to the nationals of other Members treatment no less favourable than that it accords to its own nationals with regard to the protection[3] of intellectual property, subject to the exceptions already provided in, respectively, the Paris Convention (1967), the Berne Convention (1971), the Rome Convention or the Treaty on Intellectual Property in Respect of Integrated Circuits. In respect of performers, producers of phonograms and broadcasting organizations, this obligation only applies in respect of the rights provided under this Agreement. Any Member availing itself of the possibilities provided in Article 6 of the Berne Convention (1971) or paragraph 1(b) of Article 16 of the Rome Convention shall make a notification as foreseen in those provisions to the Council for TRIPS.

2.   Members may avail themselves of the exceptions permitted under paragraph 1 in relation to judicial and administrative procedures, including the designation of an address for service or the appointment of an agent within the jurisdiction of a Member, only where such exceptions are necessary to secure compliance with laws and regulations which are not inconsistent with the provisions of this Agreement and where such practices are not applied in a manner which would constitute a disguised restriction on trade.

Article 4

Most-Favoured-Nation Treatment

With regard to the protection of intellectual property, any advantage, favour, privilege or immunity granted by a Member to the nationals of any other country shall be accorded immediately and unconditionally to the nationals of all other Members. Exempted from this obligation are any advantage, favour, privilege or immunity accorded by a Member:

(a)   deriving from international agreements on judicial assistance or law enforcement of a general nature and not particularly confined to the protection of intellectual property;

(b)   granted in accordance with the provisions of the Berne Convention (1971) or the Rome Convention authorizing that the treatment accorded be a function not of national treatment but of the treatment accorded in another country;

(c)   in respect of the rights of performers, producers of phonograms and broadcasting organizations not provided under this Agreement;

(d)   deriving from international agreements related to the protection of intellectual property which entered into force prior to the entry into force of the WTO Agreement, provided

---

[3]   For the purposes of Articles 3 and 4, "protection" shall include matters affecting the availability, acquisition, scope, maintenance and enforcement of intellectual property rights as well as those matters affecting the use of intellectual property rights specifically addressed in this Agreement.

that such agreements are notified to the Council for TRIPS and do not constitute an arbitrary or unjustifiable discrimination against nationals of other Members.

Article 5

Multilateral Agreements on Acquisition or Maintenance of Protection

The obligations under Articles 3 and 4 above do not apply to procedures provided in multilateral agreements concluded under the auspices of WIPO relating to the acquisition or maintenance of intellectual property rights.

Article 6

Exhaustion

For the purposes of dispute settlement under this Agreement, subject to the provisions of Articles 3 and 4 above nothing in this Agreement shall be used to address the issue of the exhaustion of intellectual property rights.

Article 7

Objectives

The protection and enforcement of intellectual property rights should contribute to the promotion of technological innovation and to the transfer and dissemination of technology, to the mutual advantage of producers and users of technological knowledge and in a manner conducive to social and economic welfare, and to a balance of rights and obligations.

Article 8

Principles

1.   Members may, in formulating or amending their laws and regulations, adopt measures necessary to protect public health and nutrition, and to promote the public interest in sectors of vital importance to their socio-economic and technological development, provided that such measures are consistent with the provisions of this Agreement.

2.   Appropriate measures, provided that they are consistent with the provisions of this Agreement, may be needed to prevent the abuse of intellectual property rights by right holders or the resort to practices which unreasonably restrain trade or adversely affect the international transfer of technology.

PART II.   STANDARDS CONCERNING THE AVAILABILITY, SCOPE AND USE OF INTELLECTUAL PROPERTY RIGHTS

SECTION 1: COPYRIGHT AND RELATED RIGHTS

Article 9

Relation to Berne Convention

1.   Members shall comply with Articles 1 through 21 of the Berne Convention (1971) and the Appendix thereto. However, Members shall not have rights or obligations under this Agreement in respect of the rights conferred under Article 6bis of that Convention or of the rights derived therefrom.

2.   Copyright protection shall extend to expressions and not to ideas, procedures, methods of operation or mathematical concepts as such.

Article 10

Computer Programs and Compilations of Data

1.   Computer programs, whether in source or object code, shall be protected as literary works under the Berne Convention (1971).

2.   Compilations of data or other material, whether in machine readable or other form, which by reason of the selection or arrangement of their contents constitute intellectual creations shall be protected as such. Such protection, which shall not extend to the data or material itself, shall be without prejudice to any copyright subsisting in the data or material itself.

Article 11

Rental Rights

In respect of at least computer programs and cinematographic works, a Member shall provide authors and their successors in title the right to authorize or to prohibit the commercial rental to the public of originals or copies of their copyright works. A Member shall be excepted from this obligation in respect of cinematographic works unless such rental has led to widespread copying of such works which is materially impairing the exclusive right of reproduction conferred in that Member on authors and their successors in title. In respect of computer programs, this obligation does not apply to rentals where the program itself is not the essential object of the rental.

Article 12

Term of Protection

Whenever the term of protection of a work, other than a photographic work or a work of applied art, is calculated on a basis other than the life of a natural person, such term shall be no less than 50 years from the end of the calendar year of authorized publication, or, failing such authorized publication within 50 years from the making of the work, 50 years from the end of the calendar year of making.

Article 13

Limitations and Exceptions

Members shall confine limitations or exceptions to exclusive rights to certain special cases which do not conflict with a normal exploitation of the work and do not unreasonably prejudice the legitimate interests of the right holder.

Article 14

Protection of Performers, Producers of Phonograms (Sound Recordings) and Broadcasting Organizations

1. In respect of a fixation of their performance on a phonogram, performers shall have the possibility of preventing the following acts when undertaken without their authorization: the fixation of their unfixed performance and the reproduction of such fixation. Performers shall also have the possibility of preventing the following acts when undertaken without their authorization: the broadcasting by wireless means and the communication to the public of their live performance.

2. Producers of phonograms shall enjoy the right to authorize or prohibit the direct or indirect reproduction of their phonograms.

3. Broadcasting organizations shall have the right to prohibit the following acts when undertaken without their authorization: the fixation, the reproduction of fixations, and the rebroadcasting by wireless means of broadcasts, as well as the communication to the public of television broadcasts of the same. Where Members do not grant such rights to broadcasting organizations, they shall provide owners of copyright in the subject matter of broadcasts with the possibility of preventing the above acts, subject to the provisions of the Berne Convention (1971).

4. The provisions of Article 11 in respect of computer programs shall apply *mutatis mutandis* to producers of phonograms and any other right holders in phonograms as determined in a Member's law. If, on 15 April 1994, a Member has in force a system of equitable remuneration of right holders in respect of the rental of phonograms, it may maintain such system provided that the commercial rental of phonograms is not giving rise to the material impairment of the exclusive rights of reproduction of right holders.

5. The term of the protection available under this Agreement to performers and producers of phonograms shall last at least until the end of a period of 50 years computed from the end of the calendar year in which the fixation was made or the performance took place. The term of protection granted pursuant to paragraph 3 shall last for at least 20 years from the end of the calendar year in which the broadcast took place.

6. Any Member may, in relation to the rights conferred under paragraphs 1, 2 and 3, provide for conditions, limitations, exceptions and reservations to the extent permitted by the Rome Convention. However, the provisions of Article 18 of the Berne Convention (1971) shall also apply, *mutatis mutandis*, to the rights of performers and producers of phonograms in phonograms.

SECTION 2. TRADEMARKS

Article 15

Protectable Subject Matter

1. Any sign, or any combination of signs, capable of distinguishing the goods or services of one undertaking from those of other undertakings, shall be capable of constituting a trademark. Such signs, in particular words including personal names, letters, numerals, figurative elements and combinations of colours as well as any combination of such signs, shall be eligible for registration as

trademarks. Where signs are not inherently capable of distinguishing the relevant goods or services, Members may make registrability depend on distinctiveness acquired through use. Members may require, as a condition of registration, that signs be visually perceptible.

2.   Paragraph 1 shall not be understood to prevent a Member from denying registration of a trademark on other grounds, provided that they do not derogate from the provisions of the Paris Convention (1967).

3.   Members may make registrability depend on use. However, actual use of a trademark shall not be a condition for filing an application for registration. An application shall not be refused solely on the ground that intended use has not taken place before the expiry of a period of three years from the date of application.

4.   The nature of the goods or services to which a trademark is to be applied shall in no case form an obstacle to registration of the trademark.

5.   Members shall publish each trademark either before it is registered or promptly after it is registered and shall afford a reasonable opportunity for petitions to cancel the registration. In addition, Members may afford an opportunity for the registration of a trademark to be opposed.

Article 16

Rights Conferred

1.   The owner of a registered trademark shall have the exclusive right to prevent all third parties not having the owner's consent from using in the course of trade identical or similar signs for goods or services which are identical or similar to those in respect of which the trademark is registered where such use would result in a likelihood of confusion. In case of the use of an identical sign for identical goods or services, a likelihood of confusion shall be presumed. The rights described above shall not prejudice any existing prior rights, nor shall they affect the possibility of Members making rights available on the basis of use.

2.   Article 6*bis* of the Paris Convention (1967) shall apply, *mutatis mutandis,* to services. In determining whether a trademark is well known, Members shall take account of the knowledge of the trademark in the relevant sector of the public, including knowledge in that Member concerned which has been obtained as a result of the promotion of the trademark.

3.   Article 6*bis* of the Paris Convention (1967) shall apply, *mutatis mutandis,* to goods or services which are not similar to those in respect of which a trademark is registered, provided that use of that trademark in relation to those goods or services would indicate a connection between those goods or services and the owner of the registered trademark and provided that the interests of the owner of the registered trademark are likely to be damaged by such use.

Article 17

Exceptions

Members may provide limited exceptions to the rights conferred by a trademark, such as fair use of descriptive terms, provided that such exceptions take account of the legitimate interests of the owner of the trademark and of third parties.

Article 18

Term of Protection

Initial registration, and each renewal of registration, of a trademark shall be for a term of no less than seven years. The registration of a trademark shall be renewable indefinitely.

Article 19

Requirement of Use

1.   If use is required to maintain a registration, the registration may be cancelled only after an uninterrupted period of at least three years of non-use, unless valid reasons based on the existence of obstacles to such use are shown by the trademark owner. Circumstances arising independently of the will of the owner of the trademark which constitute an obstacle to the use of the trademark, such as import restrictions on or other government requirements for goods or services protected by the trademark, shall be recognized as valid reasons for non-use.

2.   When subject to the control of its owner, use of a trademark by another person shall be recognized as use of the trademark for the purpose of maintaining the registration.

Article 20

Other Requirements

The use of a trademark in the course of trade shall not be unjustifiably encumbered by special requirements, such as use with another trademark, use in a special form or use in a manner detrimental to its capability to distinguish the goods or services of one undertaking from those of other undertakings. This will not preclude a requirement prescribing the use of the trademark identifying the undertaking producing the goods or services along with, but without linking it to, the trademark distinguishing the specific goods or services in question of that undertaking.

Article 21

Licensing and Assignment

Members may determine conditions on the licensing and assignment of trademarks, it being understood that the compulsory licensing of trademarks shall not be permitted and that the owner of a registered trademark shall have the right to assign the trademark with or without the transfer of the business to which the trademark belongs.

SECTION 3: GEOGRAPHICAL INDICATIONS

Article 22

Protection of Geographical Indications

1.   Geographical indications are, for the purposes of this Agreement, indications which identify a good as originating in the territory of a Member, or a region or locality in that territory, where a given quality, reputation or other characteristic of the good is essentially attributable to its geographical origin.

2.   In respect of geographical indications, Members shall provide the legal means for interested parties to prevent:

(a)   the use of any means in the designation or presentation of a good that indicates or suggests that the good in question originates in a geographical area other than the true place of origin in a manner which misleads the public as to the geographical origin of the good;

(b)   any use which constitutes an act of unfair competition within the meaning of Article 10*bis* of the Paris Convention (1967).

3.   A Member shall, *ex officio* if its legislation so permits or at the request of an interested party, refuse or invalidate the registration of a trademark which contains or consists of a geographical

indication with respect to goods not originating in the territory indicated, if use of the indication in the trademark for such goods in that Member is of such a nature as to mislead the public as to the true place of origin.

4. The protection under paragraphs 1, 2 and 3 shall be applicable against a geographical indication which, although literally true as to the territory, region or locality in which the goods originate, falsely represents to the public that the goods originate in another territory.

Article 23

Additional Protection for Geographical Indications for Wines and Spirits

1. Each Member shall provide the legal means for interested parties to prevent use of a geographical indication identifying wines for wines not originating in the place indicated by the geographical indication in question or identifying spirits for spirits not originating in the place indicated by the geographical indication in question, even where the true origin of the goods is indicated or the geographical indication is used in translation or accompanied by expressions such as "kind", "type", "style", "imitation" or the like.[4]

2. The registration of a trademark for wines which contains or consists of a geographical indication identifying wines or for spirits which contains or consists of a geographical indication identifying spirits shall be refused or invalidated, *ex officio* if a Member's legislation so permits or at the request of an interested party, with respect to such wines or spirits not having this origin.

3. In the case of homonymous geographical indications for wines, protection shall be accorded to each indication, subject to the provisions of paragraph 4 of Article 22. Each Member shall determine the practical conditions under which the homonymous indications in question will be differentiated from each other, taking into account the need to ensure equitable treatment of the producers concerned and that consumers are not misled.

4. In order to facilitate the protection of geographical indications for wines, negotiations shall be undertaken in the Council for TRIPS concerning the establishment of a multilateral system of notification and registration of geographical indications for wines eligible for protection in those Members participating in the system.

Article 24

International Negotiations; Exceptions

1. Members agree to enter into negotiations aimed at increasing the protection of individual geographical indications under Article 23. The provisions of paragraphs 4 through 8 below shall not be used by a Member to refuse to conduct negotiations or to conclude bilateral or multilateral agreements. In the context of such negotiations, Members shall be willing to consider the continued applicability of these provisions to individual geographical indications whose use was the subject of such negotiations.

2. The Council for TRIPS shall keep under review the application of the provisions of this Section; the first such review shall take place within two years of the entry into force of the WTO Agreement. Any matter affecting the compliance with the obligations under these provisions may be drawn to the attention of the Council, which, at the request of a Member, shall consult with any Member or Members in respect of such matter in respect of which it has not been possible to find a satisfactory solution through bilateral or plurilateral consultations between the Members concerned.

---

[4] Notwithstanding the first sentence of Article 42, Members may, with respect to these obligations, instead provide for enforcement by administrative action.

The Council shall take such action as may be agreed to facilitate the operation and further the objectives of this Section.

3.   In implementing this Section, a Member shall not diminish the protection of geographical indications that existed in that Member immediately prior to the date of entry into force of the WTO Agreement.

4.   Nothing in this Section shall require a Member to prevent continued and similar use of a particular geographical indication of another Member identifying wines or spirits in connection with goods or services by any of its nationals or domiciliaries who have used that geographical indication in a continuous manner with regard to the same or related goods or services in the territory of that Member either *(a)* for at least 10 years preceding 15 April 1994 or *(b)* in good faith preceding that date.

5.   Where a trademark has been applied for or registered in good faith, or where rights to a trademark have been acquired through use in good faith either:

(a)   before the date of application of these provisions in that Member as defined in Part VI; or

(b)   before the geographical indication is protected in its country of origin;

measures adopted to implement this Section shall not prejudice eligibility for or the validity of the registration of a trademark, or the right to use a trademark, on the basis that such a trademark is identical with, or similar to, a geographical indication.

6.   Nothing in this Section shall require a Member to apply its provisions in respect of a geographical indication of any other Member with respect to goods or services for which the relevant indication is identical with the term customary in common language as the common name for such goods or services in the territory of that Member. Nothing in this Section shall require a Member to apply its provisions in respect of a geographical indication of any other Member with respect to products of the vine for which the relevant indication is identical with the customary name of a grape variety existing in the territory of that Member as of the date of entry into force of the WTO Agreement.

7.   A Member may provide that any request made under this Section in connection with the use or registration of a trademark must be presented within five years after the adverse use of the protected indication has become generally known in that Member or after the date of registration of the trademark in that Member provided that the trademark has been published by that date, if such date is earlier than the date on which the adverse use became generally known in that Member, provided that the geographical indication is not used or registered in bad faith.

8.   The provisions of this Section shall in no way prejudice the right of any person to use, in the course of trade, that person's name or the name of that person's predecessor in business, except where such name is used in such a manner as to mislead the public.

9.   There shall be no obligation under this Agreement to protect geographical indications which are not or cease to be protected in their country of origin, or which have fallen into disuse in that country.

SECTION 4: INDUSTRIAL DESIGNS

Article 25

Requirements for Protection

1.   Members shall provide for the protection of independently created industrial designs that are new or original. Members may provide that designs are not new or original if they do not significantly differ from known designs or combinations of known design features. Members may provide that such protection shall not extend to designs dictated essentially by technical or functional considerations.

2.   Each Member shall ensure that requirements for securing protection for textile designs, in particular in regard to any cost, examination or publication, do not unreasonably impair the opportunity to seek and obtain such protection. Members shall be free to meet this obligation through industrial design law or through copyright law.

Article 26

Protection

1.   The owner of a protected industrial design shall have the right to prevent third parties not having the owner's consent from making, selling or importing articles bearing or embodying a design which is a copy, or substantially a copy, of the protected design, when such acts are undertaken for commercial purposes.

2.   Members may provide limited exceptions to the protection of industrial designs, provided that such exceptions do not unreasonably conflict with the normal exploitation of protected industrial designs and do not unreasonably prejudice the legitimate interests of the owner of the protected design, taking account of the legitimate interests of third parties.

3.   The duration of protection available shall amount to at least 10 years.

SECTION 5: PATENTS

Article 27

Patentable Subject Matter

1.   Subject to the provisions of paragraphs 2 and 3, patents shall be available for any inventions, whether products or processes, in all fields of technology, provided that they are new, involve an inventive step and are capable of industrial application.[5] Subject to paragraph 4 of Article 65, paragraph 8 of Article 70 and paragraph 3 of this Article, patents shall be available and patent rights enjoyable without discrimination as to the place of invention, the field of technology and whether products are imported or locally produced.

2.   Members may exclude from patentability inventions, the prevention within their territory of the commercial exploitation of which is necessary to protect *ordre public* or morality, including to protect human, animal or plant life or health or to avoid serious prejudice to the environment, provided that such exclusion is not made merely because the exploitation is prohibited by their law.

3.   Members may also exclude from patentability:

(a)   diagnostic, therapeutic and surgical methods for the treatment of humans or animals;

(b)   plants and animals other than micro-organisms, and essentially biological processes for the production of plants or animals other than non-biological and microbiological processes. However, Members shall provide for the protection of plant varieties either by patents or by an effective *sui generis* system or by any combination thereof. The provisions of this subparagraph shall be reviewed four years after the date of entry into force of the WTO Agreement.

---

[5]   For the purposes of this Article, the terms "inventive step" and "capable of industrial application" may be deemed by a Member to be synonymous with the terms "non-obvious" and "useful" respectively.

Article 28

Rights Conferred

1.　A patent shall confer on its owner the following exclusive rights:

(a)　where the subject matter of a patent is a product, to prevent third parties not having the owner's consent from the acts of: making, using, offering for sale, selling, or importing[6] for these purposes that product;

(b)　where the subject matter of a patent is a process, to prevent third parties not having the owner's consent from the act of using the process, and from the acts of: using, offering for sale, selling, or importing for these purposes at least the product obtained directly by that process.

2.　Patent owners shall also have the right to assign, or transfer by succession, the patent and to conclude licensing contracts.

Article 29

Conditions on Patent Applicants

1.　Members shall require that an applicant for a patent shall disclose the invention in a manner sufficiently clear and complete for the invention to be carried out by a person skilled in the art and may require the applicant to indicate the best mode for carrying out the invention known to the inventor at the filing date or, where priority is claimed, at the priority date of the application.

2.　Members may require an applicant for a patent to provide information concerning the applicant's corresponding foreign applications and grants.

Article 30

Exceptions to Rights Conferred

Members may provide limited exceptions to the exclusive rights conferred by a patent, provided that such exceptions do not unreasonably conflict with a normal exploitation of the patent and do not unreasonably prejudice the legitimate interests of the patent owner, taking account of the legitimate interests of third parties.

Article 31

Other Use Without Authorization of the Right Holder

Where the law of a Member allows for other use[7] of the subject matter of a patent without the authorization of the right holder, including use by the government or third parties authorized by the government, the following provisions shall be respected:

(a)　authorization of such use shall be considered on its individual merits;

(b)　such use may only be permitted if, prior to such use, the proposed user has made efforts to obtain authorization from the right holder on reasonable commercial terms and conditions and that such efforts have not been successful within a reasonable period of time. This requirement may be waived by a Member in the case of a national emergency or other circumstances of extreme urgency or in cases of public non-commercial use. In situations of national emergency or other

---

[6]　This right, like all other rights conferred under this Agreement in respect of the use, sale, importation or other distribution of goods, is subject to the provisions of Article 6.

[7]　"Other use" refers to use other than that allowed under Article 30.

circumstances of extreme urgency, the right holder shall, nevertheless, be notified as soon as reasonably practicable. In the case of public non-commercial use, where the government or contractor, without making a patent search, knows or has demonstrable grounds to know that a valid patent is or will be used by or for the government, the right holder shall be informed promptly;

(c)   the scope and duration of such use shall be limited to the purpose for which it was authorized, and in the case of semi-conductor technology shall only be for public non-commercial use or to remedy a practice determined after judicial or administrative process to be anti-competitive.

(d)   such use shall be non-exclusive;

(e)   such use shall be non-assignable, except with that part of the enterprise or goodwill which enjoys such use;

(f)   any such use shall be authorized predominantly for the supply of the domestic market of the Member authorizing such use;

(g)   authorization for such use shall be liable, subject to adequate protection of the legitimate interests of the persons so authorized, to be terminated if and when the circumstances which led to it cease to exist and are unlikely to recur. The competent authority shall have the authority to review, upon motivated request, the continued existence of these circumstances;

(h)   the right holder shall be paid adequate remuneration in the circumstances of each case, taking into account the economic value of the authorization;

(i)   the legal validity of any decision relating to the authorization of such use shall be subject to judicial review or other independent review by a distinct higher authority in that Member;

(j)   any decision relating to the remuneration provided in respect of such use shall be subject to judicial review or other independent review by a distinct higher authority in that Member;

(k)   Members are not obliged to apply the conditions set forth in sub-paragraphs (b) and (f) where such use is permitted to remedy a practice determined after judicial or administrative process to be anti-competitive. The need to correct anti-competitive practices may be taken into account in determining the amount of remuneration in such cases. Competent authorities shall have the authority to refuse termination of authorization if and when the conditions which led to such authorization are likely to recur;

(l)   where such use is authorized to permit the exploitation of a patent ("the second patent") which cannot be exploited without infringing another patent ("the first patent"), the following additional conditions shall apply:

(i)   the invention claimed in the second patent shall involve an important technical advance of considerable economic significance in relation to the invention claimed in the first patent;

(ii)   the owner of the first patent shall be entitled to a cross-licence on reasonable terms to use the invention claimed in the second patent; and

(iii)   the use authorized in respect of the first patent shall be non-assignable except with the assignment of the second patent.

[Proposed]   Article 31*bis**

1.   The obligations of an exporting Member under Article 31(f) shall not apply with respect to the grant by it of a compulsory licence to the extent necessary for the purposes of production of a pharmaceutical product(s) and its export to an eligible importing Member(s) in accordance with the terms set out in paragraph 2 of the Annex to this Agreement.

2.   Where a compulsory licence is granted by an exporting Member under the system set out in this Article and the Annex to this Agreement, adequate remuneration pursuant to Article 31(h) shall be paid in that Member taking into account the economic value to the importing Member of the use that has been authorized in the exporting Member. Where a compulsory licence is granted for the same products in the eligible importing Member, the obligation of that Member under Article 31(h) shall not apply in respect of those products for which remuneration in accordance with the first sentence of this paragraph is paid in the exporting Member.

3.   With a view to harnessing economies of scale for the purposes of enhancing purchasing power for, and facilitating the local production of, pharmaceutical products: where a developing or least-developed country WTO Member is a party to a regional trade agreement within the meaning of Article XXIV of the GATT 1994 and the Decision of 28 November 1979 on Differential and More Favourable Treatment Reciprocity and Fuller Participation of Developing Countries (L/4903), at least half of the current membership of which is made up of countries presently on the United Nations list of least-developed countries, the obligation of that Member under Article 31(f) shall not apply to the extent necessary to enable a pharmaceutical product produced or imported under a compulsory licence in that Member to be exported to the markets of those other developing or least-developed country parties to the regional trade agreement that share the health problem in question. It is understood that this will not prejudice the territorial nature of the patent rights in question.

4.   Members shall not challenge any measures taken in conformity with the provisions of this Article and the Annex to this Agreement under subparagraphs 1(b) and 1(c) of Article XXIII of GATT 1994.

5.   This Article and the Annex to this Agreement are without prejudice to the rights, obligations and flexibilities that Members have under the provisions of this Agreement other than paragraphs (f) and (h) of Article 31, including those reaffirmed by the Declaration on the TRIPS Agreement and Public Health (WT/MIN(01)/DEC/2), and to their interpretation. They are also without prejudice to the extent to which pharmaceutical products produced under a compulsory licence can be exported under the provisions of Article 31(f).

Article 32

Revocation/Forfeiture

An opportunity for judicial review of any decision to revoke or forfeit a patent shall be available.

---

*   On December 6, 2005, the General Council of the WTO adopted a Protocol proposing an amendment to the TRIPS agreement which would result in the inclusion of new Article 31*bis* reproduced above, and the inclusion of a new Annex to the TRIPS agreement following Article 73. The Protocol is open for acceptance by members of the World Trade Organization and will take effect if ratified by two-thirds of those members. The period for acceptance of this protocol has been extended by the Council of the World Trade Organization until December 31, 2011.—*Ed.*

Article 33

Term of Protection

The term of protection available shall not end before the expiration of a period of twenty years counted from the filing date.[8]

Article 34

Process Patents: Burden of Proof

1.   For the purposes of civil proceedings in respect of the infringement of the rights of the owner referred to in paragraph 1(b) of Article 28, if the subject matter of a patent is a process for obtaining a product, the judicial authorities shall have the authority to order the defendant to prove that the process to obtain an identical product is different from the patented process. Therefore, Members shall provide, in at least one of the following circumstances, that any identical product when produced without the consent of the patent owner shall, in the absence of proof to the contrary, be deemed to have been obtained by the patented process:

(a)   if the product obtained by the patented process is new;

(b)   if there is a substantial likelihood that the identical product was made by the process and the owner of the patent has been unable through reasonable efforts to determine the process actually used.

2.   Any Member shall be free to provide that the burden of proof indicated in paragraph 1 shall be on the alleged infringer only if the condition referred to in subparagraph (a) is fulfilled or only if the condition referred to in subparagraph (b) is fulfilled.

3.   In the adduction of proof to the contrary, the legitimate interests of defendants in protecting their manufacturing and business secrets shall be taken into account.

SECTION 6: LAYOUT-DESIGNS (TOPOGRAPHIES) OF INTEGRATED CIRCUITS

Article 35

Relation to IPIC Treaty

Members agree to provide protection to the layout-designs (topographies) of integrated circuits (referred to in this Agreements "layout-designs") in accordance with Articles 2 through 7 (other than paragraph 3 of Article 6), Article 12 and paragraph 3 of Article 16 of the Treaty on Intellectual Property in Respect of Integrated Circuits and, in addition, to comply with the following provisions.

Article 36

Scope of the Protection

Subject to the provisions of paragraph 1 of Article 37, Members shall consider unlawful the following acts if performed without the authorization of the right holder:[9] importing, selling, or otherwise distributing for commercial purposes a protected layout-design, an integrated circuit in

---

[8]   It is understood that those Members which do not have a system of original grant may provide that the term of protection shall be computed from the filing date in the system of original grant.

[9]   The term "right holder" in this Section shall be understood as having the same meaning as the term "holder of the right" in the IPIC Treaty.

which a protected layout-design is incorporated, or an article incorporating such an integrated circuit only in so far as it continues to contain an unlawfully reproduced layout-design.

Article 37

Acts not Requiring the Authorization of the Right Holder

1.   Notwithstanding Article 36, no Member shall consider unlawful the performance of any of the acts referred to in that Article in respect of an integrated circuit incorporating an unlawfully reproduced layout-design or any article incorporating such an integrated circuit where the person performing or ordering such acts did not know and had no reasonable ground to know, when acquiring the integrated circuit or article incorporating such an integrated circuit, that it incorporated an unlawfully reproduced layout-design. Members shall provide that, after the time that such person has received sufficient notice that the layout-design was unlawfully reproduced, that person may perform any of the acts with respect to the stock on hand or ordered before such time, but shall be liable to pay to the right holder a sum equivalent to a reasonable royalty such as would be payable under a freely negotiated licence in respect of such a layout-design.

2.   The conditions set out in subparagraphs (a) through (k) of Article 31 shall apply *mutatis mutandis* in the event of any non-voluntary licensing of a layout-design or of its use by or for the government without the authorization of the right holder.

Article 38

Term of Protection

1.   In Members requiring registration as a condition of protection, the term of protection of layout-designs shall not end before the expiration of a period of 10 years counted from the date of filing an application for registration or from the first commercial exploitation wherever in the world it occurs.

2.   In Members not requiring registration as a condition for protection, layout-designs shall be protected for a term of no less than 10 years from the date of the first commercial exploitation wherever in the world it occurs.

3.   Notwithstanding paragraphs 1 and 2, a Member may provide that protection shall lapse 15 years after the creation of the layout-design.

SECTION 7: PROTECTION OF UNDISCLOSED INFORMATION

Article 39

1.   In the course of ensuring effective protection against unfair competition as provided in Article 10*bis* of the Paris Convention (1967), Members shall protect undisclosed information in accordance with paragraph 2 and data submitted to governments or governmental agencies in accordance with paragraph 3.

2.   Natural and legal persons shall have the possibility of preventing information lawfully within their control from being disclosed to, acquired by, or used by others without their consent in a manner contrary to honest commercial practices[10] so long as such information:

---

[10] For the purpose of this provision, "a manner contrary to honest commercial practices" shall mean at least practices such as breach of contract, breach of confidence and inducement to breach, and includes the acquisition of undisclosed information by third parties who knew, or were grossly negligent in failing to know, that such practices were involved in the acquisition.

(a)   is secret in the sense that it is not, as a body or in the precise configuration and assembly of its components, generally known among or readily accessible to persons within the circles that normally deal with the kind of information in question;

(b)   has commercial value because it is secret; and

(c)   has been subject to reasonable steps under the circumstances, by the person lawfully in control of the information, to keep it secret.

3.   Members, when requiring, as a condition of approving the marketing of pharmaceutical or of agricultural chemical products which utilize new chemical entities, the submission of undisclosed test or other data, the origination of which involves a considerable effort, shall protect such data against unfair commercial use. In addition, Members shall protect such data against disclosure, except where necessary to protect the public, or unless steps are taken to ensure that the data are protected against unfair commercial use.

SECTION 8: CONTROL OF ANTI-COMPETITIVE PRACTICES IN CONTRACTUAL LICENCES

Article 40

1.   Members agree that some licensing practices or conditions pertaining to intellectual property rights which restrain competition may have adverse effects on trade and may impede the transfer and dissemination of technology.

2.   Nothing in this Agreement shall prevent Members from specifying in their legislation licensing practices or conditions that may in particular cases constitute an abuse of intellectual property rights having an adverse effect on competition in the relevant market. As provided above, a Member may adopt, consistently with the other provisions of this Agreement, appropriate measures to prevent or control such practices, which may include for example exclusive grantback conditions, conditions preventing challenges to validity and coercive package licensing, in the light of the relevant laws and regulations of that Member.

3.   Each Member shall enter, upon request, into consultations with any other Member which has cause to believe that an intellectual property right owner that is a national or domiciliary of the Member to which the request for consultations has been addressed is undertaking practices in violation of the requesting Member's laws and regulations on the subject matter of this Section, and which wishes to secure compliance with such legislation, without prejudice to any action under the law and to the full freedom of an ultimate decision of either Member. The Member addressed shall accord full and sympathetic consideration to, and shall afford adequate opportunity for, consultations with the requesting Member, and shall cooperate through supply of publicly available non-confidential information of relevance to the matter in question and of other information available to the Member, subject to domestic law and to the conclusion of mutually satisfactory agreements concerning the safeguarding of its confidentiality by the requesting Member.

4.   A Member whose nationals or domiciliaries are subject to proceedings in another Member concerning alleged violation of that other Member's laws and regulations on the subject matter of this Section shall, upon request, be granted an opportunity for consultations by the other Member under the same conditions as those foreseen in paragraph 3.

PART III. ENFORCEMENT OF INTELLECTUAL PROPERTY RIGHTS

SECTION 1: GENERAL OBLIGATIONS

Article 41

1.   Members shall ensure that enforcement procedures as specified in this Part are available under their law so as to permit effective action against any act of infringement of intellectual property rights covered by this Agreement, including expeditious remedies to prevent infringements and remedies which constitute a deterrent to further infringements. These procedures shall be applied in such a manner as to avoid the creation of barriers to legitimate trade and to provide for safeguards against their abuse.

2.   Procedures concerning the enforcement of intellectual property rights shall be fair and equitable. They shall not be unnecessarily complicated or costly, or entail unreasonable time-limits or unwarranted delays.

3.   Decisions on the merits of a case shall preferably be in writing and reasoned. They shall be made available at least to the parties to the proceeding without undue delay. Decisions on the merits of a case shall be based only on evidence in respect of which parties were offered the opportunity to be heard.

4.   Parties to a proceeding shall have an opportunity for review by a judicial authority of final administrative decisions and, subject to jurisdictional provisions in a Member's laws concerning the importance of a case, of at least the legal aspects of initial judicial decisions on the merits of a case. However, there shall be no obligation to provide an opportunity for review of acquittals in criminal cases.

5.   It is understood that this Part does not create any obligation to put in place a judicial system for the enforcement of intellectual property rights distinct from that for the enforcement of laws in general, nor does it affect the capacity of Members to enforce their law in general. Nothing in this Part creates any obligation with respect to the distribution of resources as between enforcement of intellectual property rights and the enforcement of law in general.

SECTION 2: CIVIL AND ADMINISTRATIVE PROCEDURES AND REMEDIES

Article 42

Fair and Equitable Procedures

Members shall make available to right holders[11] civil judicial procedures concerning the enforcement of any intellectual property right covered by this Agreement. Defendants shall have the right to written notice which is timely and contains sufficient detail, including the basis of the claims. Parties shall be allowed to be represented by independent legal counsel, and procedures shall not impose overly burdensome requirements concerning mandatory personal appearances. All parties to such procedures shall be duly entitled to substantiate their claims and to present all relevant evidence. The procedure shall provide a means to identify and protect confidential information, unless this would be contrary to existing constitutional requirements.

---

[11] For the purpose of this Part, the term "right holder" includes federations and associations having legal standing to assert such rights.

Article 43

Evidence

1.   The judicial authorities shall have the authority, where a party has presented reasonably available evidence sufficient to support its claims and has specified evidence relevant to substantiation of its claims which lies in the control of the opposing party, to order that this evidence be produced by the opposing party, subject in appropriate cases to conditions which ensure the protection of confidential information.

2.   In cases in which a party to a proceeding voluntarily and without good reason refuses access to, or otherwise does not provide necessary information within a reasonable period, or significantly impedes a procedure relating to an enforcement action, a Member may accord judicial authorities the authority to make preliminary and final determinations, affirmative or negative, on the basis of the information presented to them, including the complaint or the allegation presented by the party adversely affected by the denial of access to information, subject to providing the parties an opportunity to be heard on the allegations or evidence.

Article 44

Injunctions

1.   The judicial authorities shall have the authority to order a party to desist from an infringement, *inter alia* to prevent the entry into the channels of commerce in their jurisdiction of imported goods that involve the infringement of an intellectual property right, immediately after customs clearance of such goods. Members are not obligated to accord such authority in respect of protected subject matter acquired or ordered by a person prior to knowing or having reasonable grounds to know that dealing in such subject matter would entail the infringement of an intellectual property right.

2.   Notwithstanding the other provisions of this Part and provided that the provisions of Part II specifically addressing use by governments, or by third parties authorized by a government, without the authorization of the right holder are complied with, Members may limit the remedies available against such use to payment of remuneration in accordance with subparagraph (h) of Article 31 above. In other cases, the remedies under this Part shall apply or, where these remedies are inconsistent with a Member's law, declaratory judgments and adequate compensation shall be available.

Article 45

Damages

1.   The judicial authorities shall have the authority to order the infringer to pay the right holder damages adequate to compensate for the injury the right holder has suffered because of an infringement of that person's intellectual property right by an infringer who knowingly, or with reasonable grounds to know, engaged in infringing activity.

2.   The judicial authorities shall also have the authority to order the infringer to pay the right holder expenses, which may include appropriate attorney's fees. In appropriate cases, Members may authorize the judicial authorities to order recovery of profits and/or payment of pre-established damages even where the infringer did not knowingly, or with reasonable grounds to know, engage in infringing activity.

Article 46

Other Remedies

In order to create an effective deterrent to infringement, the judicial authorities shall have the authority to order that goods that they have found to be infringing be, without compensation of any sort, disposed of outside the channels of commerce in such a manner as to avoid any harm caused to the right holder, or, unless this would be contrary to existing constitutional requirements, destroyed. The judicial authorities shall also have the authority to order that materials and implements the predominant use of which has been in the creation of the infringing goods be, without compensation of any sort, disposed of outside the channels of commerce in such a manner as to minimize the risks of further infringements. In considering such requests, the need for proportionality between the seriousness of the infringement and the remedies ordered as well as the interests of third parties shall be taken into account. In regard to counterfeit trademark goods, the simple removal of the trademark unlawfully affixed shall not be sufficient, other than in exceptional cases, to permit release of the goods into the channels of commerce.

Article 47

Right of Information

Members may provide that the judicial authorities shall have the authority, unless this would be out of proportion to the seriousness of the infringement, to order the infringer to inform the right holder of the identity of third persons involved in the production and distribution of the infringing goods or services and of their channels of distribution.

Article 48

Indemnification of the Defendant

1.   The judicial authorities shall have the authority to order a party at whose request measures were taken and who has abused enforcement procedures to provide to a party wrongfully enjoined or restrained adequate compensation for the injury suffered because of such abuse. The judicial authorities shall also have the authority to order the applicant to pay the defendant expenses, which may include appropriate attorney's fees.

2.   In respect of the administration of any law pertaining to the protection or enforcement of intellectual property rights, Members shall only exempt both public authorities and officials from liability to appropriate remedial measures where actions are taken or intended in good faith in the course of the administration of such laws.

Article 49

Administrative Procedures

To the extent that any civil remedy can be ordered as a result of administrative procedures on the merits of a case, such procedures shall conform to principles equivalent in substance to those set forth in this Section.

SECTION 3: PROVISIONAL MEASURES

Article 50

1.   The judicial authorities shall have the authority to order prompt and effective provisional measures:

    (a)   to prevent an infringement of any intellectual property right from occurring, and in particular to prevent the entry into the channels of commerce in their jurisdiction of goods, including imported goods immediately after customs clearance;

    (b)   to preserve relevant evidence in regard to the alleged infringement.

2.   The judicial authorities shall have the authority to adopt provisional measures *inaudita altera parte* where appropriate, in particular where any delay is likely to cause irreparable harm to the right holder, or where there is a demonstrable risk of evidence being destroyed.

3.   The judicial authorities shall have the authority to require the applicant to provide any reasonably available evidence in order to satisfy themselves with a sufficient degree of certainty that the applicant is the right holder and that the applicant's right is being infringed or that such infringement is imminent, and to order the applicant to provide a security or equivalent assurance sufficient to protect the defendant and to prevent abuse.

4.   Where provisional measures have been adopted *inaudita altera parte,* the parties affected shall be given notice, without delay after the execution of the measures at the latest. A review, including a right to be heard, shall take place upon request of the defendant with a view to deciding, within a reasonable period after the notification of the measures, whether these measures shall be modified, revoked or confirmed.

5.   The applicant may be required to supply other information necessary for the identification of the goods concerned by the authority that will execute the provisional measures.

6.   Without prejudice to paragraph 4, provisional measures taken on the basis of paragraphs 1 and 2 shall, upon request by the defendant, be revoked or otherwise cease to have effect, if proceedings leading to a decision on the merits of the case are not initiated within a reasonable period, to be determined by the judicial authority ordering the measures where a Member's law so permits or, in the absence of such a determination, not to exceed 20 working days or 31 calendar days, whichever is the longer.

7.   Where the provisional measures are revoked or where they lapse due to any act or omission by the applicant, or where it is subsequently found that there has been no infringement or threat of infringement of an intellectual property right, the judicial authorities shall have the authority to order the applicant, upon request of the defendant, to provide the defendant appropriate compensation for any injury caused by these measures.

8.   To the extent that any provisional measure can be ordered as a result of administrative procedures, such procedures shall conform to principles equivalent in substance to those set forth in this Section.

SECTION 4. SPECIAL REQUIREMENTS RELATED TO BORDER MEASURES[12]

Article 51

Suspension of Release by Customs Authorities

Members shall, in conformity with the provisions set out below, adopt procedures[13] to enable a right holder, who has valid grounds for suspecting that the importation of counterfeit trademark or pirated copyright goods[14] may take place, to lodge an application in writing with competent

---

[12] Where a Member has dismantled substantially all controls over movement of goods across its border with another Member with which it forms part of a customs union, it shall not be required to apply the provisions of this Section at that border.

[13] It is understood that there shall be no obligation to apply such procedures to imports of goods put on the market in another country by or with the consent of the right holder, or to goods in transit.

[14] For the purposes of this Agreement:

authorities, administrative or judicial, for the suspension by the customs authorities of the release into free circulation of such goods. Members may enable such an application to be made in respect of goods which involve other infringements of intellectual property rights, provided that the requirements of this Section are met. Members may also provide for corresponding procedures concerning the suspension by the customs authorities of the release of infringing goods destined for exportation from their territories.

Article 52

Application

Any right holder initiating the procedures under Article 51 shall be required to provide adequate evidence to satisfy the competent authorities that, under the laws of the country of importation, there is *prima facie* an infringement of the right holder's intellectual property right and to supply a sufficiently detailed description of the goods to make them readily recognizable by the customs authorities. The competent authorities shall inform the applicant within a reasonable period whether they have accepted the application and, where determined by the competent authorities, the period for which the customs authorities will take action.

Article 53

Security or Equivalent Assurance

1.   The competent authorities shall have the authority to require an applicant to provide a security or equivalent assurance sufficient to protect the defendant and the competent authorities and to prevent abuse. Such security or equivalent assurance shall not unreasonably deter recourse to these procedures.

2.   Where pursuant to an application under this Section the release of goods involving industrial designs, patents, layout-designs or undisclosed information into free circulation has been suspended by customs authorities on the basis of a decision other than by a judicial or other independent authority, and the period provided for in Article 55 has expired without the granting of provisional relief by the duly empowered authority, and provided that all other conditions for importation have been complied with, the owner, importer, or consignee of such goods shall be entitled to their release on the posting of a security in an amount sufficient to protect the right holder for any infringement. Payment of such security shall not prejudice any other remedy available to the right holder, it being understood that the security shall be released if the right holder fails to pursue his right of action within a reasonable period of time.

Article 54

Notice of Suspension

The importer and the applicant shall be promptly notified of the suspension of the release of goods according to Article 51.

(a) "counterfeit trademark goods" shall mean any goods, including packaging, bearing without authorization a trademark which is identical to the trademark validly registered in respect of such goods, or which cannot be distinguished in its essential aspects from such a trademark, and which thereby infringes the rights of the owner of the trademark in question under the law of the country of importation;

(b) "pirated copyright goods" shall mean any goods which are copies made without the consent of the right holder or person duly authorized by the right holder in the country of production and which are made directly or indirectly from an article where the making of that copy would have constituted an infringement of a copyright or a related right under the law of the country of importation.

Article 55

Duration of Suspension

If, within a period not exceeding 10 working days after the applicant has been served notice of the suspension, the customs authorities have not been informed that proceedings leading to a decision on the merits of the case have been initiated by a party other than the defendant, or that the duly empowered authority has taken provisional measures prolonging the suspension of the release of the goods, the goods shall be released, provided that all other conditions for importation or exportation have been complied with: in appropriate cases, this time-limit may be extended by another 10 working days. If proceedings leading to a decision on the merits of the case have been initiated, a review, including a right to be heard, shall take place upon request of the defendant with a view to deciding, within a reasonable period, whether these measures shall be modified, revoked or confirmed. Notwithstanding the above, where the suspension of the release of goods is carried out or continued in accordance with a provisional judicial measure, the provisions of paragraph 6 of Article 50 shall apply.

Article 56

Indemnification of the Importer and of the Owner of the Goods

Relevant authorities shall have the authority to order the applicant to pay the importer, the consignee and the owner of the goods appropriate compensation for any injury caused to them through the wrongful detention of goods or through the detention of goods released pursuant to Article 55.

Article 57

Right of Inspection and Information

Without prejudice to the protection of confidential information, Members shall provide the competent authorities the authority to give the right holder sufficient opportunity to have any goods detained by the customs authorities inspected in order to substantiate the rights holder's claims. The competent authorities shall also have authority to give the importer an equivalent opportunity to have any such product inspected. Where a positive determination has been made on the merits of a case, Members may provide the competent authorities the authority to inform the right holder of the names and addresses of the consignor, the importer and the consignee and of the quantity of the goods in question.

Article 58

Ex Officio Action

Where Members require competent authorities to act upon their own initiative and to suspend the release of goods in respect of which they have acquired *prima facie* evidence that an intellectual property right is being infringed:

    (a)   the competent authorities may at any time seek from the right holder any information that may assist them to exercise these powers;

    (b)   the importer and the right holder shall be promptly notified of the suspension. Where the importer has lodged an appeal against the suspension with the competent authorities, the suspension shall be subject to the conditions, *mutatis mutandis,* set out at Article 55;

    (c)   Members shall only exempt both public authorities and officials from liability to appropriate remedial measures where actions are taken or intended in good faith.

Article 59

Remedies

Without prejudice to other rights of action open to the right holder and subject to the right of the defendant to seek review by a judicial authority, competent authorities shall have the authority to order the destruction or disposal of infringing goods in accordance with the principles set out in Article 46. In regard to counterfeit trademark goods, the authorities shall not allow the re-exportation of the infringing goods in an unaltered state or subject them to a different customs procedure, other than in exceptional circumstances.

Article 60

De Minimis Imports

Members may exclude from the application of the above provisions small quantities of goods of a non-commercial nature contained in travellers' personal luggage or sent in small consignments.

SECTION 5: CRIMINAL PROCEDURES

Article 61

Members shall provide for criminal procedures and penalties to be applied at least in cases of wilful trademark counterfeiting or copyright piracy on a commercial scale. Remedies available shall include imprisonment and/or monetary fines sufficient to provide a deterrent, consistently with the level of penalties applied for crimes of a corresponding gravity. In appropriate cases, remedies available shall also include the seizure, forfeiture and destruction of the infringing goods and of any materials and implements the predominant use of which has been in the commission of the offence. Members may provide for criminal procedures and penalties to be applied in other cases of infringement of intellectual property rights, in particular where they are committed wilfully and on a commercial scale.

PART IV.   ACQUISITION AND MAINTENANCE OF INTELLECTUAL PROPERTY RIGHTS AND RELATED *INTER-PARTES* PROCEDURES

Article 62

1.   Members may require, as a condition of the acquisition or maintenance of the intellectual property rights provided for under Sections 2 through 6 of Part II, compliance with reasonable procedures and formalities. Such procedures and formalities shall be consistent with the provisions of this Agreement.

2.   Where the acquisition of an intellectual property right is subject to the right being granted or registered, Members shall ensure that the procedures for grant or registration, subject to compliance with the substantive conditions for acquisition of the right, permit the granting or registration of the right within a reasonable period of time so as to avoid unwarranted curtailment of the period of protection.

3.   Article 4 of the Paris Convention (1967) shall apply *mutatis mutandis* to service marks.

4.   Procedures concerning the acquisition or maintenance of intellectual property rights and, where a Member's law provides for such procedures, administrative revocation and *inter partes* procedures such as opposition, revocation and cancellation, shall be governed by the general principles set out in paragraphs 2 and 3 of Article 41.

5.   Final administrative decisions in any of the procedures referred to under paragraph 4 shall be subject to review by a judicial or quasi-judicial authority. However, there shall be no obligation to provide an opportunity for such review of decisions in cases of unsuccessful opposition or administrative revocation, provided that the grounds for such procedures can be the subject of invalidation procedures.

PART V.   DISPUTE PREVENTION AND SETTLEMENT

Article 63

Transparency

1.   Laws and regulations, and final judicial decisions and administrative rulings of general application, made effective by a Member pertaining to the subject matter of this Agreement (the availability, scope, acquisition, enforcement and prevention of the abuse of intellectual property rights) shall be published, or where such publication is not practicable made publicly available, in a national language, in such a manner as to enable governments and right holders to become acquainted with them. Agreements concerning the subject matter of this Agreement which are in force between the government or a governmental agency of a Member and the government or a governmental agency of another Member shall also be published.

2.   Members shall notify the laws and regulations referred to in paragraph 1 to the Council for TRIPS in order to assist that Council in its review of the operation of this Agreement. The Council shall attempt to minimize the burden on Members in carrying out this obligation and may decide to waive the obligation to notify such laws and regulations directly to the Council if consultations with WIPO on the establishment of a common register containing these laws and regulations are successful. The Council shall also consider in this connection any action required regarding notifications pursuant to the obligations under this Agreement stemming from the provisions of Article 6*ter* of the Paris Convention (1967).

3.   Each Member shall be prepared to supply, in response to a written request from another Member, information of the sort referred to in paragraph 1. A Member, having reason to believe that a specific judicial decision or administrative ruling or bilateral agreement in the area of intellectual property rights affects its rights under this Agreement, may also request in writing to be given access to or be informed in sufficient detail of such specific judicial decisions or administrative rulings or bilateral agreements.

4.   Nothing in paragraphs 1, 2 and 3 shall require Members to disclose confidential information which would impede law enforcement or otherwise be contrary to the public interest or would prejudice the legitimate commercial interests of particular enterprises, public or private.

Article 64

Dispute Settlement

1.   The provisions of Articles XXII and XXIII of GATT 1994 as elaborated and applied by the Dispute Settlement Understanding shall apply to consultations and the settlement of disputes under this Agreement except as otherwise specifically provided herein.

2.   Subparagraphs 1(b) and 1(c) of GATT 1994 shall not apply to the settlement of disputes under this Agreement for a period of five years from the date of entry into force of the WTO Agreement.

3.   During the time period referred to in paragraph 2, the Council for TRIPS shall examine the scope and modalities for complaints of the type provided for under subparagraphs 1(b) and 1(c) of Article XXIII of GATT 1994 made pursuant to this Agreement, and submit its recommendations to the Ministerial Conference for approval. Any decision of the Ministerial Conference to approve such

recommendations or to extend the period in paragraph 2 shall be made only by consensus, and approved recommendations shall be effective for all Members without further formal acceptance process.

PART VI.   TRANSITIONAL ARRANGEMENTS

Article 65

Transitional Arrangements

1.   Subject to the provisions of paragraphs 2, 3 and 4, no Member shall be obliged to apply the provisions of this Agreement before the expiry of a general period of one year following the date of entry into force of the WTO Agreement.

2.   Any developing country Member is entitled to delay for a further period of four years the date of application, as defined in paragraph 1, of the provisions of this Agreement other than Articles 3, 4 and 5.

3.   Any other Member which is in the process of transformation from a centrally-planned into a market, free-enterprise economy and which is undertaking structural reform of its intellectual property system and facing special problems in the preparation and implementation of intellectual property laws and regulations, may also benefit from a period of delay as foreseen in paragraph 2.

4.   To the extent that a developing country Member is obliged by this Agreement to extend product patent protection to areas of technology not so protectable in its territory on the general date of application of this Agreement for that Member, as defined in paragraph 2, it may delay the application of the provisions on product patents of Section 5 of Part II to such areas of technology for an additional period of five years.

5.   Any Member availing itself of a transitional period under paragraphs 1, 2, 3 or 4 shall ensure that any changes in its laws, regulations and practice made during that period do not result in a lesser degree of consistency with the provisions of this Agreement.

Article 66

Least-Developed Country Members

1.   In view of their special needs and requirements of least-developed country Members, their economic, financial and administrative constraints, and their need for flexibility to create a viable technological base, such Members shall not be required to apply the provisions of this Agreement, other than Articles 3, 4 and 5, for a period of 10 years from the date of application as defined under paragraph 1 of Article 65. The Council for TRIPS shall, upon duly motivated request by a least-developed country Member, accord extensions of this period.

2.   Developed country Members shall provide incentives to enterprises and institutions in their territories for the purpose of promoting and encouraging technology transfer to least-developed country Members in order to enable them to create a sound and viable technological base.

Article 67

Technical Cooperation

In order to facilitate the implementation of this Agreement, developed country Members shall provide, on request and on mutually agreed terms and conditions, technical and financial cooperation in favour of developing and least-developed country Members. Such cooperation shall include assistance in the preparation of laws and regulations on the protection and enforcement of intellectual property rights as well as on the prevention of their abuse, and shall include support regarding the establishment or reinforcement of domestic offices and agencies relevant to these matters, including the training of personnel.

PART VII.   INSTITUTIONAL ARRANGEMENTS: FINAL PROVISIONS

Article 68

Council for Trade-Related Aspects of Intellectual Property Rights

The Council for TRIPS shall monitor the operation of this Agreement and, in particular, Members' compliance with their obligations hereunder, and shall afford Members the opportunity of consulting on matters relating to the trade-related aspects of intellectual property rights. It shall carry out such other responsibilities as assigned to it by the Members, and it shall, in particular, provide any assistance requested by them in the context of dispute settlement procedures. In carrying out its functions, the Council for TRIPS may consult with and seek information from any source it deems appropriate. In consultation with WIPO, the Council shall seek to establish, within one year of its first meeting, appropriate arrangements for cooperation with bodies of that Organization.

Article 69

International Cooperation

Members agree to cooperate with each other with a view to eliminating international trade in goods infringing intellectual property rights. For this purpose, they shall establish and notify contact points in their administrations and be ready to exchange information on trade in infringing goods. They shall, in particular, promote the exchange of information and cooperation between customs authorities with regard to trade in counterfeit trademark goods and pirated copyright goods.

Article 70

Protection of Existing Subject Matter

1.   This Agreement does not give rise to obligations in respect of acts which occurred before the date of application of the Agreement for the Member in question.

2.   Except as otherwise provided for in this Agreement, this Agreement gives rise to obligations in respect of all subject matter existing at the date of application of this Agreement for the Member in question, and which is protected in that Member on the said date, or which meets or comes subsequently to meet the criteria for protection under the terms of this Agreement. In respect of this paragraph and paragraphs 3 and 4, copyright obligations with respect to existing works shall be solely determined under Article 18 of the Berne Convention (1971), and obligations with respect to the rights of producers of phonograms and performers in existing phonograms shall be determined solely under Article 18 of the Berne Convention (1971) as made applicable under paragraph 6 of Article 14 of this Agreement.

3.   There shall be no obligation to restore protection to subject matter which on the date of application of this Agreement for the Member in question has fallen into the public domain.

4.   In respect of any acts in respect of specific objects embodying protected subject matter which become infringing under the terms of legislation in conformity with this Agreement, and which were commenced, or in respect of which a significant investment was made, before the date of acceptance of the WTO Agreement by that Member, any Member may provide for a limitation of the remedies

available to the right holder as to the continued performance of such acts after the date of application of the Agreement for that Member. In such cases the Member shall, however, at least provide for the payment of equitable remuneration.

5.   A Member is not obliged to apply the provisions of Article 11 and of paragraph 4 of Article 14 with respect to originals or copies purchased prior to the date of application of this Agreement for that Member.

6.   Members shall not be required to apply Article 31, or the requirement in paragraph 1 of Article 27 that patent rights shall be enjoyable without discrimination as to the field of technology, to use without the authorization of the right holder where authorization for such use was granted by the government before the date this Agreement became known.

7.   In the case of intellectual property rights for which protection is conditional upon registration, applications for protection which are pending on the date of application of this Agreement for the Member in question shall be permitted to be amended to claim any enhanced protection provided under the provisions of this Agreement. Such amendments shall not include new matter.

8.   Where a Member does not make available as of the date of entry into force of the WTO Agreement patent protection for pharmaceutical and agricultural chemical products commensurate with its obligations under Article 27, that Member shall:

     (a)   notwithstanding the provisions of Part VI, provide as from the date of entry into force of the WTO Agreement a means by which applications for patents for such inventions can be filed;

     (b)   apply to these applications, as of the date of application of this Agreement, the criteria for patentability as laid down in this Agreement as if those criteria were being applied on the date of filing in that Member or, where priority is available and claimed, the priority date of the application; and

     (c)   provide patent protection in accordance with this Agreement as from the grant of the patent and for the remainder of the patent term, counted from the filing date in accordance with Article 33 of this Agreement, for those of these applications that meet the criteria for protection referred to in subparagraph (b).

9.   Where a product is the subject of a patent application in a Member in accordance with paragraph 8(a), exclusive marketing rights shall be granted, notwithstanding the provisions of Part VI, for a period of five years after obtaining market approval in that Member or until a product patent is granted or rejected in that Member, whichever period is shorter, provided that, subsequent to the entry into force of the WTO Agreement, a patent application has been filed and a patent granted for that product in another Member and marketing approval obtained in such other Member.

Article 71

Review and Amendment

1.   The Council for TRIPS shall review the implementation of this Agreement after the expiration of the transitional period referred to in paragraph 2 of Article 65. The Council shall, having regard to the experience gained in its implementation, review it two years after that date, and at identical intervals thereafter. The Council may also undertake reviews in the light of any relevant new developments which might warrant modification or amendment of this Agreement.

2.   Amendments merely serving the purpose of adjusting to higher levels of protection of intellectual property rights achieved, and in force, in other multilateral agreements and accepted under those agreements by all Members of the WTO may be referred to the Ministerial Conference for action in accordance with paragraph 6 of Article X, of the WTO Agreement on the basis of a consensus proposal from the Council for TRIPS.

Article 72

Reservations

Reservations may not be entered in respect of any of the provisions of this Agreement without the consent of the other Members.

Article 73

Security Exceptions

Nothing in this Agreement shall be construed:

(a)   to require a Member to furnish any information the disclosure of which it considers contrary to its essential security interests; or

(b)   to prevent a Member from taking any action which it considers necessary for the protection of its essential security interests;

   (i)   relating to fissionable materials or the materials from which they are derived;

   (ii)   relating to the traffic in arms, ammunition and implements of war and to such traffic in other goods and materials as is carried on directly or indirectly for the purpose of supplying a military establishment;

   (iii)   taken in time of war or other emergency in international relations; or

(c)   to prevent a Member from taking any action in pursuance of its obligations under the United Nations Charter for the maintenance of international peace and security.

[PROPOSED] ANNEX TO THE TRIPS AGREEMENT*

1.   For the purposes of Article 31*bis* and this Annex:

(a)   "pharmaceutical product" means any patented product, or product manufactured through a patented process, of the pharmaceutical sector needed to address the public health problems as recognized in paragraph 1 of the Declaration on the TRIPS Agreement and Public Health (WT/MIN(01)/DEC/2). It is understood that active ingredients necessary for its manufacture and diagnostic kits needed for its use would be included[1];

(b)   "eligible importing Member" means any least-developed country Member, and any other Member that has made a notification[2] to the Council for TRIPS of its intention to use the system set out in Article 31*bis* and this Annex ("system") as an importer, it being understood that a Member may notify at any time that it will use the system in whole or in a limited way, for example only in the case of a national emergency or other circumstances of extreme urgency or in cases of public non-commercial use. It is noted that some Members will not use the system as importing Members[3] and that some other Members have stated that, if they use the system, it would be in no more than situations of national emergency or other circumstances of extreme urgency;

---

*   On December 6, 2005, the General Council of the WTO adopted a Protocol proposing an amendment to the TRIPS agreement which would result in the inclusion of new Article 31*bis*, and the inclusion of a new Annex to the TRIPS agreement following Article 73, reproduced above The Protocol is open for acceptance by members of the World Trade Organization and will take effect if ratified by two-thirds of those members. The period of acceptance of this protocol has been extended by the Council of the World Trade Organization until December 31, 2011.—*Ed.*

[1]   This subparagraph is without prejudice to subparagraph 1(b).

[2]   It is understood that this notification does not need to be approved by a WTO body in order to use the system.

[3]   Australia, Canada, the European Communities with, for the purposes of Article 31*bis* and this Annex, its member States, Iceland, Japan, New Zealand, Norway, Switzerland, and the United States.

(c) "exporting Member" means a Member using the system to produce pharmaceutical products for, and export them to, an eligible importing Member.

2.   The terms referred to in paragraph 1 of Article 31*bis* are that:

(a)   the eligible importing Member(s)[4] has made a notification[2] to the Council for TRIPS, that:

(i)   specifies the names and expected quantities of the product(s) needed[5];

(ii)   confirms that the eligible importing Member in question, other than a least-developed country Member, has established that it has insufficient or no manufacturing capacities in the pharmaceutical sector for the product(s) in question in one of the ways set out in the Appendix to this Annex; and

(iii) confirms that, where a pharmaceutical product is patented in its territory, it has granted or intends to grant a compulsory licence in accordance with Articles 31 and 31*bis* of this Agreement and the provisions of this Annex[6];

(b)   the compulsory licence issued by the exporting Member under the system shall contain the following conditions:

(i)   only the amount necessary to meet the needs of the eligible importing Member(s) may be manufactured under the licence and the entirety of this production shall be exported to the Member(s) which has notified its needs to the Council for TRIPS;

(ii)   products produced under the licence shall be clearly identified as being produced under the system through specific labelling or marking. Suppliers should distinguish such products through special packaging and/or special colouring/shaping of the products themselves, provided that such distinction is feasible and does not have a significant impact on price; and

(iii) before shipment begins, the licensee shall post on a website[7] the following information:

—the quantities being supplied to each destination as referred to in indent (i) above; and

—the distinguishing features of the product(s) referred to in indent (ii) above;

(c)   the exporting Member shall notify[8] the Council for TRIPS of the grant of the licence, including the conditions attached to it.[9] The information provided shall include the name and address of the licensee, the product(s) for which the licence has been granted, the quantity(ies) for which it has been granted, the country(ies) to which the product(s) is (are) to be supplied and the duration of the licence. The notification shall also indicate the address of the website referred to in subparagraph (b)(iii) above.

3.   In order to ensure that the products imported under the system are used for the public health purposes underlying their importation, eligible importing Members shall take reasonable measures within their means, proportionate to their administrative capacities and to the risk of trade diversion

---

[4]   Joint notifications providing the information required under this subparagraph may be made by the regional organizations referred to in paragraph 3 of Article 31*bis* on behalf of eligible importing Members using the system that are parties to them, with the agreement of those parties.

[5]   The notification will be made available publicly by the WTO Secretariat through a page on the WTO website dedicated to the system.

[6]   This subparagraph is without prejudice to Article 66.1 of this Agreement.

[7]   The licensee may use for this purpose its own website or, with the assistance of the WTO Secretariat, the page on the WTO website dedicated to the system.

[8]   It is understood that this notification does not need to be approved by a WTO body in order to use the system.

[9]   The notification will be made available publicly by the WTO Secretariat through a page on the WTO website dedicated to the system.

to prevent re-exportation of the products that have actually been imported into their territories under the system. In the event that an eligible importing Member that is a developing country Member or a least-developed country Member experiences difficulty in implementing this provision, developed country Members shall provide, on request and on mutually agreed terms and conditions, technical and financial cooperation in order to facilitate its implementation.

4.   Members shall ensure the availability of effective legal means to prevent the importation into, and sale in, their territories of products produced under the system and diverted to their markets inconsistently with its provisions, using the means already required to be available under this Agreement. If any Member considers that such measures are proving insufficient for this purpose, the matter may be reviewed in the Council for TRIPS at the request of that Member.

5.   With a view to harnessing economies of scale for the purposes of enhancing purchasing power for, and facilitating the local production of, pharmaceutical products, it is recognized that the development of systems providing for the grant of regional patents to be applicable in the Members described in paragraph 3 of Article 31*bis* should be promoted. To this end, developed country Members undertake to provide technical cooperation in accordance with Article 67 of this Agreement, including in conjunction with other relevant intergovernmental organizations.

6.   Members recognize the desirability of promoting the transfer of technology and capacity building in the pharmaceutical sector in order to overcome the problem faced by Members with insufficient or no manufacturing capacities in the pharmaceutical sector. To this end, eligible importing Members and exporting Members are encouraged to use the system in a way which would promote this objective. Members undertake to cooperate in paying special attention to the transfer of technology and capacity building in the pharmaceutical sector in the work to be undertaken pursuant to Article 66.2 of this Agreement, paragraph 7 of the Declaration on the TRIPS Agreement and Public Health and any other relevant work of the Council for TRIPS.

7.   The Council for TRIPS shall review annually the functioning of the system with a view to ensuring its effective operation and shall annually report on its operation to the General Council.

APPENDIX TO THE ANNEX TO THE TRIPS AGREEMENT

Assessment of Manufacturing Capacities in the Pharmaceutical Sector

Least-developed country Members are deemed to have insufficient or no manufacturing capacities in the pharmaceutical sector.

For other eligible importing Members insufficient or no manufacturing capacities for the product(s) in question may be established in either of the following ways:

(i)   the Member in question has established that it has no manufacturing capacity in the pharmaceutical sector; or

(ii)   where the Member has some manufacturing capacity in this sector, it has examined this capacity and found that, excluding any capacity owned or controlled by the patent owner, it is currently insufficient for the purposes of meeting its needs. When it is established that such capacity has become sufficient to meet the Member's needs, the system shall no longer apply.